THIS AGE
OF CONFLICT

REVISED EDITION

A CONTEMPORARY WORLD HISTORY

1914 to the Present

FRANK P. CHAMBERS LONDON SCHOOL OF ECONOMICS

CHRISTINA PHELPS HARRIS THE HOOVER INSTITUTE AND LIBRARY, STANFORD UNIVERSITY

CHARLES C. BAYLEY McGILL UNIVERSITY

Maps by John Woodcock

NEW YORK HARCOURT, BRACE AND COMPANY

140288

PRINTED IN THE UNITED STATES OF AMERICA

A WONDERFUL STORY *is unfolding before our eyes. How it will end we are not allowed to know. . . . We are sure that the character of human society will be shaped by the resolves we take and the deeds we do.*

We need not bewail the fact that we have been called upon to face such solemn responsibilities. We may be proud and even rejoice amid our tribulations that we have been born at this cardinal time for so great an age, so splendid an opportunity of service here below. . . .

WINSTON CHURCHILL
on the occasion of his receiving an honorary degree by
proxy from the University of Rochester, June 16, 1941.

PREFACE

Two World Wars and their intervening wars, revolutions, and crises are now generally recognized to be episodes in a single Age of Conflict which began in 1914 and has not yet run its course. It is an age that has brought the world more change and tragedy than any other equal span in recorded time. Yet, whatever may be its ultimate meaning and consequence, we can already think of it — and write of it — as a historic whole. As such it is the subject of the present book.

The authors have undertaken an entire revision and rewriting of the earlier edition of the same title. They have again adopted the conventional form of a survey of international relations. They have set out their material in the main upon a nation-by-nation basis, and they have paid little attention to the domestic affairs of any nation except where those domestic affairs seemed to them to contribute to its international position and policy. In short, their theme has been war and peace in our world today.

The rate of obsolescence, so to speak, of a book of this sort must always be extraordinarily high. The facts that we know do not change, but emphasis and significance do. Often the most interesting events are those where our records are least definitive. Even while the book was in proof items of information were coming out which it was impossible to ignore. The authors have carried their narrative down to within a few months of publication, but they can only beg for the readers' indulgence for the very provisional character of the later chapters.

The manuscript was circulated among specialists before going to press, and parts of it were read and checked in considerable detail. The authors, of course, remain responsible for their book, but they are very conscious of the advice and assistance they have had, and, in particular, they make grateful acknowledgment to the following: Dr. Gordon A. Craig of Princeton University, Dr. Carleton J. H. Hayes of Columbia University, Dr. Gordon Wright of the University of Oregon, Dr. Howard McGaw Smyth of Washington, D.C., Dr. Paul E. Eckel of the University of Pennsylvania, Dr. Forrest C. Pogue of Washington, D.C., Dr. Eric Goldman of Princeton University, Dr. Geroid T. Robinson of the Russian Institute, Columbia University, the late Dr. W. B. Thorson of Washington State College, Dr. Dwight E. Lee of Clark University, and Professor Harry H. Kimber of Michigan State College, Mr. Leslie R. Aldous, Miss Violet Conolly, Dr. Michael Florinsky, Mr. G. L. Goodwin, Prof. C. A. W. Manning, Mr. T. E. M. McKitterick, Mr. G. H. McLean, Mr. Walter Mitham, Mr. G. Richards, Mr. G. L. Robinson, Mr. S. Rose, Mr. Brian Tunstall, Mr. Sydney Walton, Miss Elizabeth

Wiskemann, and Miss Dorothy Woodman. Special thanks are due to Dr. David Harris for his constant interest in the book, for his many helpful comments and suggestions, and for his contribution to Chapter 51; to Mrs. F. P. Chambers for her very careful reading and editing of the proofs; and to Mr. A. W. Butler for permission to use a paper of his on the British Commonwealth which appears, almost without alteration, in Chapter 50. Special thanks are also due to members of the library staff and information department of the Royal Institute of International Affairs for the many facilities which they so courteously provided at Chatham House. Research assistance and typing were done by four indefatigable aides, Miss Daphne Werner, Miss Joan Hills, Miss Joyce Pulman, and Mrs. M. MacGibbon. The present edition still bears the stamp of the work which that very good friend, Dr. Veit Valentin, did on the first edition just before his sudden and greatly regretted death.

NOTE ON ARRANGEMENT

The book is divided into five parts. The assignment of Part One to the First World War, Part Four to the Second World War, and Part Five to the post-1945 period explains itself. The division of the intervening Parts Two and Three is not so obvious, and probably no ideal arrangement of so complex a period is possible.

In the first edition, the interwar years from 1919 to 1939 were divided into a Part Two, entitled "The Period of Settlement," and a Part Three, entitled "The Period of Crisis." Such an arrangement, it is still the view of the authors, does reflect the actual course of events and is generally retained in the present edition. The entire theme of the interwar years is interpretable first as the apparent success, and then the failure, of the Peace of 1919. But the chapters of Part Two are not now rounded off simultaneously at any arbitrary date, namely at the crash of 1929 and the Depression that followed; chronological neatness is not attempted; and, though 1929 does in fact remain the flash point of the crisis throughout the world, each chapter is worked out independently to some logical conclusion, appropriate to itself, which may or may not coincide therewith. Germany in Part Two is therefore carried to the death of Stresemann in 1929, Poland to the death of Pilsudski in 1935, Turkey to the death of Kemal in 1938, and so forth. Thus we have:

PART ONE, THE FIRST WORLD WAR, Chapters 1–7:

Chapter 1 is in the nature of a general introduction to the entire book.

PART TWO, THE PERIOD OF SETTLEMENT, Chapters 8–24:

Chapters 8–16 describe "the Versailles system," i.e., the Peace Conference of Paris and the peace treaties, the League of Nations and its ancillary organs, the search for security, and the individual histories of the several nations which were changed, created, or otherwise immediately affected by the settlement, i.e., Germany, Austria, Hungary, Czechoslovakia, Poland, the Balkans, and the Near East.

Chapters 17–19 describe Soviet Russia and Fascist Italy, the two great political experiments of the interwar years.

Chapters 20–23 describe the nations which were the main victors of the First World War and the Big Three of the Peace Conference — France, Britain, and the United States, the nations, namely, which preserved their pre-1914 form and character intact and which afterward became the bulwarks of the settlement against revolutionary and totalitarian aggression. There is a separate chapter on India (22), and another (24) of general summary and retrospect.

PART THREE, THE PERIOD OF CRISIS, Chapters 25–39:

Chapters 25–33 describe the "crisis" itself, i.e., the Depression, the Far East, Nazi Germany, the immediate reactions to Nazism in Europe and the Balkans, and the wars in Ethiopia and Spain.

Chapters 34–38 describe those nations which played a passive or defensive role in the crisis, the Soviet Union, France, Britain, and the United States. There is finally a chapter (39) on the Approach of War.

PART FOUR, THE SECOND WORLD WAR, Chapters 40–46

PART FIVE, THE POST-1945 PERIOD, Chapters 47–54

NOTE ON SPELLING

The spelling of names and place names is always one of the minor difficulties of a project of this sort. Webster and the United States National Geographic Board have been the main guides. Beneš appears with his š; Pashich without his š. First names have been anglicized; Stepan becomes Stephen, Grigorii becomes Gregory, and so forth.

Of place names the most familiar version has been used — Teschen, for example, not Těšin or Cieszyn. Many place names have changed during the years covered by this book. Lwów, Istanbul, Cóbh, Oslo, Peiping, and many others were unknown a generation ago. Generally, where it seemed important, the names used are those of their respective times. Thus St. Petersburg, Petrograd, Leningrad change with their chronological context. In the same way, ranks and titles of persons, where mentioned, are also those of their respective times.

In the case of Arabic names and place names, the various currently accepted systems of transliteration are too involved for the general reader. At the risk of inconsistency, therefore, Arabic names follow the spelling of the National Geographic Board, in so far as they appear there, and the spelling of the others follows a simplified system adopted from the Arabic Department of the British Museum.

CONTENTS

THE LIST OF MAPS

THIS AGE OF CONFLICT

PART ONE

THE FIRST WORLD WAR

1 THE OUTBREAK OF THE WAR

THE WORLD OF 1914

From time to time in the course of history human affairs reach an equilibrium, an equilibrium so stable as almost to give its contemporaries the
illusion of permanence. The ages come to their sum and apex. Institutions,
manners, conventions, the entire sociocultural complex seem fixed and final.
Yet, in fact, behind the façade the structure may be already creaking to its
collapse, and whatever survives or is rebuilt from the ruin is very different
from what has gone before.

Such was 1914. Here too was an unquestioned, an almost unconsciously
accepted stability; here was confidence and boundless optimism; here did
man think of change only in terms of perpetual progress. Yet here too the
structure crashed, and the design of what is to come, different though we
know it will be, is not yet clear to us.

By any standard the century that stretched from 1815 to 1914 was among
the most expansive, teeming, and varied of any equal period of time. Man,
it seemed, was coming to control his own fate. Science promised new material conquests and the answer to nature's riddles. Mechanized industry
poured out its products in rising volume and at falling cost. New modes of
transport and communication made all men neighbors. Exploration opened
up the last unknown tracts and corners of the globe. Medicine and public
health increased the length and enjoyment of life. Education brought literacy and widened interests to multitudes. Women were emancipated from
age-old restrictions. Missions, social services, insurance, and laws for the
protection of children and animals bore witness to a new humanitarianism.
Slavery and the slave trade were generally abolished. Penal codes were
constantly revised in the direction of understanding and leniency. The
world's rulers, it seemed, were learning at last that politics is the science of
welfare. Recreational facilities for people of all classes were available as
never before. Culturally, the century was extraordinarily rich. There were
brilliant minds at work in every art and discipline – in poetry, fiction,
drama, music, history, and philosophy. Printing was cheap, and books had
never been so plentiful. Historians have hardly yet appreciated the sheer
efflorescence of creative genius in these years.

But there was another side to the picture. Even in the eyes of its most conservative contemporaries, the world of 1914 was still far from the earthly paradise. With all its technological advances, poverty and social injustice were still the lot of the many. The century's triumphs had been won partly as the result of, and partly in spite of, an economic system that often made the individual little better than a commodity. Only perpetual expansion had disguised the defects and deficiencies of the system — but expansion had its physical limits, and the limits might soon be reached. Science had brought new things into the world, new powers and new luxuries, but old habits sometimes failed to respond to the many changes. Large-scale industry had upset the balance of town and country, and the land was losing its population to sprawling, urban growths which demanded novel and difficult social readjustments. The phenomenon of mass politics and mass demagogy was appearing. Meanwhile, among those who held the purse strings, the struggle for markets and for overseas possessions continued. Capitalism was fast reaching its saturation point. Especially since 1900 several of the more "advanced" nations, having industrialized themselves, were competing to their mutual exasperation in fields which till then had been the preserve and monopoly of England. Most political leaders and many economists in Europe had lost faith in the classic virtues of free competition and had turned to the cartel and the combine as the proper policy for their respective countries. Yet there were very few who conceived of a state of affairs radically different from the existing. Marx, Nietzsche, and their prophetic brethren may have a little pricked the conscience of the world but hardly moved its deep complacency. Genuine reform, it was believed, was still achievable by peaceful means within the established order; revolution could still take place without subversion.

Europe then dominated the world. During the century from 1815 to 1914 her population increased from 200,000,000 to 450,000,000, and Europeans outside Europe increased from 20,000,000, to 200,000,000. Europe was the fertile mother of an irrepressible migration. Every one of the four other continents was brought under the influence or actual control of Europeans or of men of recent European origin. The plains of North America and Siberia and the larger islands of Australasia were colonized; Africa was partitioned; India passed under British rule. Even lands nominally independent, like Turkey or Persia, China or Japan, felt the impact of Western ways of life and Western acquisitiveness. A major event in Europe had repercussions far outside its native borders.

That peculiarly European institution, the nation, impressed itself on all peoples. The nation everywhere was the geographic and economic unit and the unit of political sovereignty. Nationalism, which had taken such aggressive forms during the Napoleonic Wars, became a passion that ruled men's lives, gave them a new egotism, glorified their history, and rationalized their conflicts. Even trade followed its respective flag. "Submerged" nationalities grew conscious of themselves and began to demand their independence as a right. In the course of the century, and especially at the end of it, there were frequent nationalist revolts. In 1914 it was estimated that, of Europe's total population, one man in four lived under a hated and alien domination.

Outside Europe the same story of rising nationalist fervor was being re-peated. The Arab lands, India, Latin America, even the distant Philippines — often as a result of European tutelage — all had their versions of the na-tionality problem.

In the contemporary attitude toward war two contradictory ideologies were at work. On the one hand, war was still regarded as a legitimate in-strument of policy and, popularly, was still invested with a good deal of romance and glamour. In a world which only recently had rung with the names of Napoleon, Nelson, Wellington, and Blücher, the soldier and sailor were still the national heroes. In the course of the century from 1815 to 1914, wars had been common enough. There were national wars, civil wars, wars of liberation, colonial wars. The new Germany and Italy, the United States, and Japan had all been born or matured in war. In Germany, par-ticularly after 1871, war was almost a philosophy of life. War was the test of national virtue, ardently and romantically wished for; it was history's forge and workshop, and the evidence of history — as witness Germany's own history — was the proof thereof. The current economic doctrine of compe-tition and the current biological doctrine of the survival of the fittest seemed to support the view that war was a necessary, natural, and beneficial form of human behavior.

On the other hand, though its wars were common, the century was ac-tually one of the least belligerent in history. Its wars happened to be local-ized, of short duration, and of declining incidence. None disturbed the overriding stability and permanence of the time. Except in the actual path of a campaign, war meant no more than a rise in prices, a change of dynasty or government, a cession of territory, a limited impoverishment or gain — results which were often admittedly desirable. In those days no one spoke of the crisis of civilization or the annihilation of man. It is with some justice therefore that the period from the Congress of Berlin in 1878 to the out-break of the First World War in 1914 has been called the Great Peace, the *Pax Europeana*. By 1914 the great majority of mankind no longer remem-bered what war was.

The situation gave hope that internationalism might gain on nationalism, that nationalist passions, like religious sectarianism formerly, might learn to exist without intolerance, and that the romanticism of war, wherever that romanticism was cultivated, might remain at a harmless, imaginary level. There were, for instance, those oft-cited minor triumphs of interna-tional co-operation — patents, copyright, the postal service, and the Red Cross. Latterly a number of international disputes had been successfully arbitrated. The Powers had partitioned Africa without recourse to war among themselves. Science and scientific research had developed a great international freemasonry. Music and the arts were cosmopolitan and be-longed to all peoples. Interesting peace movements and institutions, such as the Carnegie Endowment and the Nobel Prize, had been founded. So-cialism in all countries was internationalist and pacifist. High finance was a mysterious, invisible, but generally pacifist force; for high finance, though it had been known to support a small war and certainly supported armaments, was averse to risking any irrevocable subversion of the system of which it was so integral a part. Conceivably then, as the years went by, war might become less and less appropriate to a matured and progressive civilization. Diplomacy, that delicate art practiced by a small aristocracy of careerists skillful in adjusting a difference or redressing an incident, might be relied on more and more to keep the peace.

More sinister than the possible direct "causes" of war were the increasing elaboration and enlargement of modern life. The world of 1914 was like a cosmic system, an expanding universe, outwardly fixed, but inwardly able to maintain itself only in perpetual and accelerating motion. If it slowed down, or if its finely balanced interplay of forces was tampered with, the whole might break up altogether. Cities were bigger; governments were assuming greater responsibilities; industries were more monopolistic; national budgets were higher; armaments were increasing fantastically; for everyone the business of living was becoming more complicated and expensive. Peoples were more closely knit than ever before; distances were shrinking; "One World" was almost a practical conception. But peoples could no longer live to themselves. A famine in India, a flood in China, a financial panic in the United States, an assassination in the Balkans, left a circle of widening repercussions. Here indeed was an additional argument for peace. But if war on an extended scale should ever come, then, quite apart from its technological frightfulness, it would involve human life and wealth in ways unimagined hitherto. Not only would it mean unprecedented financial loss — financial collapse was the favorite "expert" prophecy before 1914 — but it would be a peoples' war, fought with an almost religious fanaticism, absorbing every man and woman and all the resources of a nation. German military theorists had already coined the term "absolute war" or "total war," but the coming war was to have a "totality" which even they, these professional philosophers of war, had not conceived.

Such was the world of 1914. It is an academic question to ask whether, by any chance, it could have continued to exist, whether the particular turn of events which brought it down could have been prevented. The deeper inwardness of the great collapse is still largely hidden from us. Yet this world of 1914, a world seemingly so progressive and secure, so rich in accomplishment, so full of hope and promise, was about to enter upon one of those intervals of general war which have sometimes marked the close of an old historical phase and the beginning of a new. Mankind was in the presence of events which for significance and magnitude can only be compared with such transitional epochs as the Fall of Rome, the Reformation, or the French Revolution. The Great Peace dissolved in an Age of Conflict, whose course, it seems likely, is not yet fully run.

THE LAST YEARS OF PEACE

The century from 1815 to 1914 had seen the arrival of four new states to the front rank of importance — two in Europe, one in the Far East, and one in the Western Hemisphere. At the beginning of the century Germany and Italy were geographical expressions, Japan was an unknown fastness, and the United States was a fringe of coastal settlements. At the end of the century the four states were Great Powers. At the same time four other states were gradually falling into decay and anachronism — Imperial Austria, Tsarist Russia, Ottoman Turkey, and Manchu China. Usually history's troubles come singly. But it was now one of her major misfortunes that these eight states should all represent "problems" simultaneously crying out for a solution.

Certainly, of the eight problems, the German was the most clamant. Modern Germany, the so-called Second Reich, had been formed under the leadership of her "Iron Chancellor," Bismarck, after a decade of aggressive wars culminating in the victory over France in 1870–71. Her unification had been provocatively proclaimed in the presence of the King of Prussia, "German Kaiser," in the Hall of Mirrors of the Palace of Versailles. But thereafter Bismarck had made a sudden turnabout, and it had seemed as if he would go down in history as one of Europe's most cautious and pacific statesmen. Germany in 1871, he said, was "saturated" and wanted nothing so much as to be confirmed and strengthened in the position which his recent policies had won for her. She was now a Great Power, and would indeed be greater, but she would never be impregnable; and Bismarck devoted the remainder of his official life to giving his country a well-deserved rest and an opportunity for natural economic growth. He built up his diplomatic defenses against the two foreseeable sources of disturbance — against an attempt by France to avenge her defeat at his hands and to recover the provinces of Alsace-Lorraine that she had lost at that time, and against the involvement of Germany in a possible Austro-Russian conflict in the Balkans.

As "the honest broker," Bismarck sponsored the Congress of Berlin in 1878, a gathering of the Powers for the general settlement of Europe. The measure of success of the Congress — with all its admitted imperfections — was the Great Peace that followed. Except in the Balkans — notably in Bulgaria — and in Scandinavia, Europe suffered no further changes of frontier till the First World War. In 1878 the eight states which we have mentioned had taken the shape and character they were to have when the First World War broke out. Germany had become a united Reich, governed by a chancellor and a Kaiser. Italy was a united kingdom. Imperial Austria, Tsarist Russia, and Ottoman Turkey were enjoying a largely fictitious prolongation of their power. In the Far East, China was opened to foreign "penetration," and internally was fast sinking into revolution and anarchy. Japan was refashioning herself on Western lines and was about to go to war with China for Korea. In the Western Hemisphere the young United States was vigorously developing its continental hinterland.

One area in Europe with which the Congress of Berlin had been directly concerned was the "turbulent Balkans." Here, in 1878, lived a cluster of peoples half subject to, half freed from, Turkish rule. Here crossed and clashed the interests of several European Powers. Here eventually was to arise the immediate cause of the First World War. Since the seventeenth century, Ottoman Turkey had been receding from her conquests in the Middle Danube; and Austria, once Europe's defender against the Turk, had fallen heir to the evacuated territories and to the medley of nationalities that inhabited them. In theory, Turkish recession and Austrian advance might have gone on indefinitely. But south of the Danube, in the Balkans, in the line of Austria's advance, lay an area of some wealth and of the greatest strategic importance. Some of the Balkan peoples were Slav, notably the Serbs and Bulgars; Constantinople was both the Rome of Russian Orthodoxy and Russia's hoped-for outlet to the sea. Russia therefore also considered herself a claimant to the residual Ottoman estate. For over a century the decline of Turkey had posed the question whether Russia and Austria could collaborate in driving back the Turk or whether they would fall out over the intended spoils. Austria, having been excluded from the new German Empire, returned to an expansionist Balkan policy at the very moment when Russia's political activities and Pan-Slav aspirations were leading that Power in the same direction. Furthermore, two other Powers, France and Britain, themselves strongly entrenched in the Near East, had always striven to keep the Ottoman Empire alive, not out of love for the Turk as such, but to prevent further Russian encroachment. The Crimean War of 1854–56 was evidence of the lengths to which France and Britain were prepared to go to keep Russia at a safe distance from their preserves.

The Congress of Berlin had thought to stabilize this complex of contending forces, the "Eastern Question" as it was called. But for Bismarck, professedly disinterested in the area, Balkan pacification was only incidental to a larger policy. Bismarck's real interests had lain elsewhere. In 1879, in response to Russia's exasperation at Germany's role at the Congress, he drew Germany and Austria-Hungary into a Dual Alliance. But in 1881 he was able to restore friendly contacts between Austria-Hungary and Russia which had also been damaged by the Congress, and he fortified Germany's relations with both Powers by concluding a new League of the Three Emperors — that is, the German Kaiser, Austrian Emperor, and Russian Tsar. In 1882 he further amplified his system of treaty guarantees and drew Germany, Austria-Hungary, and Italy into a Triple Alliance. In 1887, when once more the line between Berlin and St. Petersburg broke down, he entered into a "reinsurance treaty" with Russia. Meanwhile he was careful to keep on good terms with Britain. Nowhere and at no time did German and British policy then come into conflict. Thanks to Bismarck, a decade after the Congress of Berlin Germany was hedged about with friends and allies, and France was Europe's diplomatic outcast. With herself the strongest Power in Europe, her most likely enemy in isolation, and the Balkans quiescent, Germany's barometer of state should have set fair for years to come.

But a decade after the Congress of Berlin, in 1888, William II became German Kaiser. Under the German imperial constitution of the day he held all but absolute power, and every major act of German policy was executed in his name and on his responsibility. Yet the Kaiser, whatever else his faults, was not the ogre of iniquity he was once made out to be. No one man could have loosed on the world all the ills of 1914. He is more to be condemned for what he represented than for what he was himself; for there is a curious way in which a monarch's qualities often reveal those of his people. He was born and bred to military heroics. He adored the pomp and plumage of the parade ground. Of his many titles, that of Supreme War Lord always pleased him the most. Photographs of himself with bristling mustaches, belligerently postured, in full military regalia, were to be seen in every shop and home of his Reich. Brilliant he was, gifted and versatile, but boisterous, touchy, and irresponsible. Impulsive arrogance and timid withdrawals always marked his participation in affairs. His public speeches — and he spoke on every possible occasion — were awaited with anxiety throughout Europe. And all this, as the world was soon to learn, was very, very German.

In 1890 the Kaiser, chafing under Bismarck's domination, dismissed him from the chancellorship. Almost at once the Bismarckian alliance system went to pieces. France came out of her isolation to enter into an "entente" with Russia, to be followed in 1894 by a precise military convention. And then, slowly but surely, Britain fell into line with France and Russia — Britain who till then had been well disposed to Germany, who in blood and language was partly descended from Germany, whose royal family was of German origin, who admired German culture and scholarship, who had lately encouraged German colonial enterprise, and who had even made offers of a German alliance.

With the fall of Bismarck went also his cautious and pacific policy. Germany, he had said, was a "saturated" Power averse to further foreign adventures. But it is a fact that German colonial expansion had been taking place during his later years in office and, in 1890, when he fell from grace, the bulk of the German Empire overseas was already acquired. Various patriotic associations came into existence in Germany to articulate the heightened national feeling and to conduct special propaganda campaigns, such as the Colonial League, the Pan-German League, and the Navy League, and their efforts were often financially supported by German industrial magnates and armament manufacturers. The old Hanseatic cities, Lübeck, Hamburg, and Bremen, were reviving their tradition of commercial and overseas enterprise. The Pan-German argument was very simple: other European Powers had colonies; Germany was a Power; *ergo,* Germany must have colonies. But Bismarck, much as he may have sympathized with Germany's "forward" *Weltpolitik,* had never permitted it to jeopardize his European settlement. German expansionism was confined to those areas in Africa and the Pacific unhampered by possible diplomatic complications. Under Bismarck it had been Germany's remarkable achievement to have seized a round million square miles of overseas territory without exciting British suspicion.

By the international standards of the day, Germany's expansionism was perfectly correct and meritorious. But even if it had continued to be conducted with Bismarckian caution, it would probably have reached a stage where, sooner or later, it must have encountered the hostility of Britain and, to a less extent, of France and Russia. It was now to be conducted with the gratuitous addition of that tactlessness and intimidation which, since Bismarck, has come to be associated with German foreign politics, and the Kaiser and his post-Bismarckian advisers reveled in a colonial diplomacy that succeeded in alarming and antagonizing their European neighbors. For instance, in 1894 Germany dispatched a warship to Delagoa Bay at the moment when Britain was trying to obtain Portuguese consent to the use of the port for the disembarkation of British troops. In 1896, over the signature of the Kaiser, Germany sent Kruger, the Boer President, a telegram congratulating him on the repulse of the Jameson Raid. In 1897 she made use of the murder of two German missionaries in China to seize Tsingtao, to the extreme annoyance of Russia, who had promised that territory to herself. Meanwhile she was busy in Turkey, building the last stretches of the Berlin to Baghdad railroad, acquiring an influence in the country which was virtually converting it into a German economic dependency, and realizing in a new direction the *Drang nach Osten* which was always supposed to have inspired the Germanic conqueror. In 1898 the Kaiser, on a visit to Palestine, only two years after the Armenian massacres, offered his protection to the Ottoman Sultan "Abdul the Damned" and to the thirty million Moslems scattered all over the Near East. During the Boer War the German Government's attitude was officially very circumspect, but no attempt was made to soften the fact that public opinion in Germany was vehemently pro-Boer.

In 1898 came the first of Germany's navy bills. Here again, by the international standards of the time, Germany's action was perfectly correct, but the action was performed in a manner to alarm and antagonize. Germany now had extensive overseas possessions and maritime trade to protect, and she was manifestly entitled to build as many cruisers and dreadnoughts as she pleased. But the action, justified in itself, took on a very different meaning when, in successive navy bills, it became evident that of set purpose Germany was challenging the supremacy at sea which Britain had enjoyed since the Battle of Trafalgar; when Germany was ignoring or rebuffing every successive British effort to appease her ambitions; and when finally the Kaiser himself was consistently preferring the advice of his belligerent Admiral von Tirpitz over that of his civilian chancellors and was obviously regarding his High Seas Fleet as his special toy. By the turn of the century the great Anglo-German naval race was on.

The growing coolness between Britain and Germany left Britain with an uncomfortable sense of friendlessness, and she discovered with some surprise the unpopularity she had earned herself in Europe from years of successful and prosperous imperialism all over the world. Traditionally Britain had been anti-Russian and anti-French. Her interests conflicted with those of Russia not only in the Near East but in Persia, Afghanistan, and the Far East, and they had lately conflicted with those of France in North Africa. She had had a long history of French wars, interrupted only once, by the Franco-British alliance in the Crimean War. In 1902, as a counterweight to Russian influence in the Far East, she concluded an alliance with Japan and thereby undoubtedly helped to precipitate the Russo-Japanese War of two years later. Yet at this juncture, in belated realization of the German peril, she revised her entire foreign policy and hastily patched up her former differences with Russia and France. The Triple Entente of Britain, Russia, and France, as it was eventually formed, was a far looser association than the Triple Alliance — the newspapers of the day used to talk of the "Entente Cordiale" — but it was the foundation of a progressively closer diplomatic collaboration. By 1907 it may be said that the Triple Entente of Britain, Russia, and France stood in potential hostility to the Triple Alliance of Germany, Austria-Hungary, and Italy. The Powers of Europe were marshaled into two great camps, and both were piling up armaments. Military expenditures were more than doubled between 1900 and 1914. European general staffs were known to be perfecting detailed plans for war. In 1912, Britain went so far as to engage in military and naval talks with France and to conclude with her a secret naval agreement. Germany complained of "encirclement"; Britain, she declared, "was pursuing her ancient policy of opposing whatever Continental Power happened momentarily to be the strongest."

Yet even then, to the average European *Homo sapiens* a general war seemed a remote and altogether theoretical possibility. Diplomacy, it seemed, was still an unreal game played by specialists behind closed doors, with no effect upon the normal life of the nations at large. Even the much-advertised armaments race was little more than a budgetary annoyance. The illusion of peace was deepened by the successful circumvention of the three penultimate minor crises and the three penultimate minor wars which preceded the final catastrophe — namely, the Morocco crisis of 1905, the Bosnian crisis of 1908, the Agadir crisis of 1911, the Tripolitan War of 1911, the First Balkan War of 1912, and the Second Balkan War of 1913.

In 1905 came the Morocco crisis. France regarded herself as having prior claims in Morocco. The territory adjoined her Algerian colony, and she contemplated its eventual annexation. But German commercial interests had also gained a foothold there. At the height of the crisis the Kaiser, with his unfailing instinct for provocative situations, visited Tangier in state and offered the Sultan of Morocco his championship and protection. Britain took the part of her new ally, France, and would certainly have gone to her aid in the event of war. A conference of the Powers was called together at Algeciras; Morocco was confirmed in nominal independence; and the scare of war in Europe passed.

In 1908 came the Bosnian crisis, and with it the entire Eastern Question, dormant since the Congress of Berlin, reawakened in an urgent, menacing form. In that summer a revolution occurred in Turkey, the government of "Abdul the Damned" was overthrown, and a new political party, the "Young Turks," with a zealous program of reforms, seized control. Bulgaria made use of the occasion to revolt from Turkish rule and proclaim her independence. Austria, fearing changes in the Balkan map that might aggrandize Serbia and thereby encourage unrest among her own Slavic subjects at home, proceeded formally to annex the Turkish provinces of Bosnia and Herzogovina, of which, since 1878, she had been in military occupation. The provinces were largely inhabited by Serbs, and Russia, interested in the Balkans and protectively inclined toward the Serbs, made as if she might intervene in force. But Russia, just recovering from the recent Russo-Japanese War, was in no fit state for new adventures. Germany gave notice that she would support Austria in all eventualities. Once more the scare of war passed; Austria kept her provinces; Russia swallowed a severe diplomatic defeat; Germany had the satisfaction of standing "in shining armor" beside her Austrian ally; Serbs in Bosnia and Herzegovina stored up their hatred and frustration for a future day.

In 1911 came the Agadir crisis. France and Germany again clashed over their interests in Morocco. The French marched into the Sultan's capital at Fez. Germany protested that the Algeciras agreement had been broken. A German gunboat, the *Panther,* appeared off Agadir, ostensibly to protect German nationals in Morocco. Britain again took the part of France. In a famous speech which was all the more significant because of his pacifist reputation at that time, Lloyd George warned Germany that Britain would not buy peace at the price of humiliation. Once more the scare of war passed. Germany recognized France's right to a protectorate over Morocco and received in compensation a strip of the French Congo.

In 1911, Italy, jealously eying the recent British and French colonial successes in North Africa and considering that she too deserved a share of the receding Ottoman Empire, declared war on Turkey and seized the Turkish dependency of Tripoli in North Africa and the Dodecanese Islands in the Mediterranean. She had long since secured British and French consent to the acquisition, and her own allies, Germany and Austria, could hardly say her nay. Tripoli was surrendered to her after an unexpected and embarrassing resistance. She undertook to withdraw from the Dodecanese Islands, but in 1915, when she entered the First World War, she was still in occupation.

The Young Turk revolution, the Bulgar revolt, and Italy's Tripolitan War were a tempting revelation of the weakness of the Ottoman Empire. In 1912, Serbia, Montenegro, Greece, and Bulgaria banded together as the Balkan League of Christian States, resolved to complete the expulsion of the Turk from Europe and to free the remainder of their respective countrymen from the Turkish yoke, declared war on Turkey, and in a short triumphant campaign drove the Turks back onto their capital, Constantinople. The European Powers, now profoundly concerned over the deterioration of the Balkans after years of quiescence, called a conference in London. It was a very pallid re-edition of the Congress of Berlin. Austria, seeking as always to curb the vaulting ambition of the Serbs, recognized the insurgent Albanians, sponsored an entirely new state of Albania under a German prince, and thereby blocked the Serbs from access to the Adriatic Sea. Otherwise Serbia, Montenegro, Greece, and Bulgaria benefited by various appropriate extensions of their territories. Turkey lost all her remaining Balkan possessions except the small strip of Thrace which covered Constantinople and the Dardanelles.

In 1913 the four victors of the Balkan League fell to quarreling over the division of the spoils. The London agreement was ignored. War broke out between Bulgaria on the one side and Serbia, Montenegro, Greece, and Rumania on the other. Turkey returned to the charge, herself declared war on

Bulgaria, and recaptured Adrianople. Bulgaria, overwhelmed by so strong a coalition, made peace at the cost of heavy concessions.

The total result of the Tripolitan and the two Balkan wars was a further stage in Turkey's perpetual recession. Serbia, even without a coveted outlet on the Adriatic, emerged as a state of some importance, whetted ambitions, and problematic future. Turkey and Bulgaria were left aggrieved and revengeful. Italy had tasted the sweets of an easy conquest in North Africa. But the general European peace had still been preserved.

THE WAR BEGINS

The brief review in the last few pages is an inadequate tribute to the vast literature which has grown up about the pre-history of the First World War. But the many incidents of the "international anarchy" up to 1914 were of small importance in themselves. They were like the sharp, painful twinges, ignored as soon as gone, which a man feels who has enjoyed a normal and scarcely conscious habit of good health, but which are in fact the warnings of a mortal sickness. There was no theoretical reason why the crisis of 1914 should have led to war any more than the crisis of 1905 or 1908 or of any other intervening year. But each successive crisis wore away a little more of the patient's margin of resistance, and the time would have to come when the hidden consumption suddenly took full possession of his members.

The Bosnian crisis of 1908 left the Serbs in a state of the greatest excitement. The Serbian Government had assured the Austro-Hungarian Government that extreme irredentist agitation in Serbia would be prohibited. But Austria's subsequent repressive policy in the newly annexed provinces of Bosnia and Herzegovina, and the creation of the new state of Albania in 1912, dealt nascent Serbian nationalism a blow to which the Serbian patriot could give only one answer. Serbs in Serbia and their brothers under Austrian rule were soon in full conspiracy for their national unification and independence. They agitated, intrigued, and terrorized. They aided and abetted the general nationalist unrest throughout Austria-Hungary. Their secret societies had access to Serbian arms and to the services of the Serbian military intelligence, and were covertly encouraged by Russia. Meanwhile there were patent Austrian military preparations against Serbia, though they did not amount even to partial mobilization. In the eighteen months preceding the actual outbreak of war in 1914, Conrad von Hötzendorf, the Austrian Chief of Staff, urged war against Serbia on twenty-five different occasions. A serious situation had been long in preparation, therefore, when on June 28, 1914, during a ceremonial visit to the Bosnian capital of Sarajevo, the Archduke Francis Ferdinand, heir to the thrones of Austria-Hungary, and his wife were assassinated by a young Bosnian student.

The Serbian Government's complicity in the crime was not immediately proved, but no one at that time, on either side, was in a mood to consider too judicially where the real guilt lay. The crime was barbarous enough, and at first it lost the Serbs much of the sympathy that sections of opinion in Aus-

tria and abroad had begun to give them on the merits of their case. In Sarajevo itself, a few hours after the assassination, exited crowds paraded the
streets, singing Austrian patriotic songs, shouting "Down with Serbia!" and
raiding Serbian shops and hotels. Anti-Serbian demonstrations broke out
through the length and breadth of Austria-Hungary. Even onetime preach-
ers of racial conciliation in Austria-Hungary realized that firm repressive
measures must be taken against the treacherous "Greater Serbia" agitation
and punitive action be meted out to Serbia herself, if the Monarchy's security and good name were to be preserved.

Meanwhile, the Serbian attitude had aggravated the situation. The crime
had been committed on a Serbian national holiday, the anniversary of the
famous Battle of Kossovo against the Turks,[1] and the coincidence was too
much for a people of primitive temper, not given to hiding their feelings.
The Serbian Prince Regent addressed his formal condolences to the Austrian Emperor, and the holiday celebrations were officially canceled. But in
the streets of Belgrade men had been seen to cry for joy and to embrace
each other. Serbian newspapers pictured the assassin of Sarajevo as the
martyr of Austrian tyranny. Irritation fed on irritation, and the people of
both countries were almost surprised that war had not immediately broken
out between them.

However, the Austro-Hungarian Government seemed in no hurry to act,
and the rest of Europe was deceived by the evident relaxing of a crisis which
at first had looked hardly more serious than other international crises of the
past few years. The European press was content to condemn this new Balkan
atrocity and to trust that, as seemed already likely, time would heal the injury. The Balkans would always be the "turbulent" Balkans, liable to recurrent "imbroglios." For the average citizen of 1914 peace was a habit of
mind, and summer was the holiday season. The day of Bismarck, when a
war could be wantonly engineered, was only remembered in schoolboy textbooks. Surely the most lurid prophets of doom in their wildest fantasies
could not have foretold that a sordid political killing in a remote Balkan
town was to let loose upon the world such wars and revolutions as it had
never known before, or conceived a fraction of all the woes and agonies that
were now to be crowded into the experience of a single generation.

In all the controversy that has raged around the events of that fatal July
and August in 1914, certain facts are salient.

One is that neither Germany nor France exerted a sufficient deterrent
action on their respective allies, Austria-Hungary and Russia. Thus Austria-
Hungary could not have acted as she did without prior assurances of Germany's support, even in the event of her provoking an offensive war in
Serbia, nor could Russia have acted as she did without similar assurances
of France's support. Another fact is that the Russian General Staff had no
plan for partial mobilization against Austria-Hungary and that the general
Russian mobilization, which was eventually ordered, at once appeared to
threaten Germany. Another is that, as the crisis rapidly developed, the initiative passed more and more out of the hands of the political leaders every-

where into those of the military, notably the German General Staff, and that
thereafter war was automatic and unpreventable.

On July 5, 1914, at Potsdam, the Kaiser gave definite assurances to the
Austro-Hungarian ambassador in Germany that Austria-Hungary could
count on Germany's support "in this case also," especially in the event of
Russia's bestirring herself on Serbia's behalf, and he sent instructions to
much the same effect to the German ambassador in Vienna. He repeated
his assurances later on July 14 in an autograph letter to the Austrian Emperor, Francis Joseph. The German Government — that is to say the Chancellor, Bethmann-Hollweg, and his civilian colleagues in the Wilhelmstrasse
— at this time tended to regard the crisis as Austria's private business, and
hoped and expected that it would be "localized."

The impression therefore prevailed in Vienna that the German Government would endorse strong action — even war — on the part of Austria-Hungary against Serbia. Count Berchtold, the Austro-Hungarian Foreign Minister, considered the way open and his conscience clear "to make Serbia
permanently innocuous by a display of force," and he resolved to present her
with an ultimatum that would give her the alternatives of destruction or
vassalage and forever remove the menace of Slav nationalism from the Balkans. Count Tisza, the Hungarian Premier, alone offered Berchtold any responsible opposition. But even Count Tisza withdrew his objections when
convinced of Germany's attitude. Berchtold's ultimatum, after calculated
delays, was delivered to the Serbian Government in Belgrade on July 23.
It demanded the suppression of all subversive nationalist propaganda and
of conspirative societies in Serbia, the dismissal of officials in the Serbian
Government who were suspected of connivance in the assassination at Sarajevo and whom the Austro-Hungarian Government would afterward name,
and the collaboration of Austrian representatives in investigations to be
conducted by the Serbian police. A time limit of forty-eight hours was given
for the unconditional acceptance of the terms.

The German Government had known the tenor of the ultimatum for
some days and saw its actual text twenty-four hours before it was delivered.
On July 24 the German Government addressed notes to Russia, France, and
Britain asserting that Austria-Hungary demanded no more than was "equitable and just" and urging a localization of the crisis. Grey, the British
Foreign Secretary, speaking of the ultimatum, avowed that he "had never
seen one state address to another independent state a document of so formidable a character." He appealed urgently for a conference of mediation
between the Powers not directly involved, namely Germany, France, Italy,
and Britain. His proposal was accepted by France and Italy, but declined
by Germany on the plea that she could not be expected "to drag Austria
before a European tribunal." Then, at one moment, Berchtold seemed to
be on the point of entering into direct negotiations with Sazonov, the Russian Foreign Minister. But it was becoming evident that Russia would not
stand by while Austria-Hungary subjugated Serbia, a kindred Slavic state,
and played havoc with Russian interests in the Balkans. If Russia fought,
Austria's ally Germany would fight; if Germany fought, Russia's ally France

would fight. Berchtold, it seemed, had unstopped the European dike. His punitive expedition against Serbia already bade fair to become a general European war.

The reply of the Serbian Government to Berchtold's ultimatum was in the hands of the Austro-Hungarian minister in Belgrade on July 25, within a few minutes of the time limit; but nevertheless that gentleman is said to have broken off relations there and then and hurried home to Vienna. Except for one or two details, the reply had made a general capitulation. The Kaiser, hearing the news, jotted the note, "A great moral victory for Vienna. . . . Every reason for war has disappeared." Berchtold and his Austrian aides, on the contrary, affected to believe that the capitulation was neither sufficient nor sincere, and certainly the Serbian mobilization on July 25 had not looked like the act of a penitent asking for clemency. On July 26 the Austro-Hungarian Government ordered partial mobilization, and on July 28 declared war on Serbia. On July 29 Austrian artillery bombarded Belgrade.

But the center of gravity of the crisis had already shifted from the chancelleries to the general staffs, and it was now a race between the high army commands to press forward their mobilizations, if war there was to be, and to secure the advantages of the initiative in the field. The time of year was favorable to military operations; the harvests in most European countries had been gathered in; vast plans were ready to go into effect; the maneuvering of armies of millions of men could not wait for politics. Probably Sazonov would have preferred Russia to mobilize in the south only, thus threatening Austria and perhaps inducing Berchtold to come to terms. But the Russian General Staff, as we have said, had no plan ready for partial mobilization. For Russia, it was general mobilization or none. The Tsar, fighting weakly for peace, bewildered by events, and perhaps deliberately misled by his advisers, signed two alternative orders, one for partial and one for general mobilization. But under strong pressure from the Russian Ministry of War, the Tsar consented to issue the order for general mobilization on July 30. The prior mobilization of Russia was always cited thereafter by German propaganda to charge her with the principal guilt of the war. The Kaiser replied by proclaiming "a state of danger of war." Ever since July 23, Berlin had been full of rumors and reports of Russian "preliminary military measures." At midnight on July 31, Germany sent an ultimatum to Russia demanding the cessation of warlike preparations within twelve hours. On August 1 the German Government ordered general mobilization and declared war on Russia.

President Poincaré of France returned to Paris on July 29 from a state visit to St. Petersburg, the Russian capital, whither he had gone for a ceremonial confirmation of the Franco-Russian alliance. On July 31 a German ultimatum to France demanded to know the French attitude in the event of hostilities between Germany and Russia, but the most the German ambassador in Paris could elicit was the short answer that France "would act as her interests required." If France on this occasion had offered to remain neutral, the German ambassador had been instructed to make the impossible demand that she surrender the fortresses of Toul and Verdun as a "pledge." But on August 1 the French Government ordered general mobilization — actually a few hours before the German general mobilization on the same day. On August 3 Germany declared war on France.

In 1914, Belgium and Luxembourg, precariously wedged between France and Germany, were states whose perpetual neutrality and inviolability the Powers — Germany among them — had solemnly guaranteed.[2] But on August 2, in accordance with long-elaborated plans, German troops invaded Luxembourg. The same day Germany sent the Belgian Government a twelve-hour ultimatum demanding a free passage for the German Army across Belgium to the French frontier. She offered to reward Belgium's compliance with a pledge of independence and integrity, but would treat her resistance as an act of war. The Belgian Government refused the German demand, and appealed to Britain for aid. On August 4, German troops invaded Belgium.

All through these strenuous days opinion in Britain had been vacillating and divided. The average Briton had little interest in war or international politics. Few had heard of the Entente or of the British naval commitments to France until that moment, and fewer knew of the existing guarantees of the neutrality of Belgium and Luxembourg. There was an important isolationist element in the British Cabinet. But the German ultimatum of August 2 to Belgium, no less than the peremptory tone in which it was couched, decided the swing of public opinion, and on the morning of August 4 the British Government, with the full backing of Parliament, dispatched an ultimatum to Germany demanding to know by midnight whether Germany would respect her treaty guarantees to Belgium. The German Chancellor, on receipt of the ultimatum, asked bitterly if Britain, "just for a word 'neutrality,' . . . just for a scrap of paper, was going to make war on a kindred nation who desired nothing better than to be friends with her," thus uttering what must surely be one of the most famous and revealing lapses of the tongue in history. At midnight on August 4, Britain was at war with Germany.

Of the Great Powers of Europe, Italy alone stood aloof. Deeming that her German and Austrian allies had provoked an aggressive war without consulting her, in violation of the precise terms of the Triple Alliance, Italy declared her neutrality on August 3.

The British Dominions and India responded to the crisis spontaneously and ardently and made ready to give the mother country every support in their power. The little Balkan state of Montenegro made common cause with Serbia. Portugal proclaimed her fidelity to an old alliance with England. Finally, on August 23, England's ally in the Far East, Japan, declared war on Germany. In Europe, Asia, Australasia, and Africa, populations aggregating nearly 1,000,000,000 were at war.

Yet we should commit a grave error if we believed that the immediate causes of the First World War had been all a matter of diplomatic notes and conferences, and that a few gold-braided, bemedaled gentlemen seated round half a dozen tables in half a dozen chancelleries ordered 1,000,000,000 human beings to kill or be killed. The popular excitement in that July and August was less palpable than the minutes and documents which historians have since pored over so diligently, but that excitement was nonetheless a historical fact, a fact deserving of more emphasis than it has sometimes been given. Deep as the Great Peace had been, the First World War, at the moment of its outbreak, was undeniably a popular war. There were few men with imagination enough to know what modern fighting would mean. In no nation affected was there an important antiwar party. Pacifism and socialism either played the apostate, or were driven from the field in confusion. The International Socialist Bureau, meeting at Brussels at the end of July, was entirely ineffective in the face of the crisis. Political parties of every belligerent country, in the midst of domestic strife, declared their *Burgfriede* or their *Union Sacrée*. The British House of Commons on August 3, the German Reichstag on August 4, the French Chamber on August 4, the Russian Duma on August 8, expressed their respective wills with all but complete unanimity. For the men and the women who lived through the first week of August 1914, the outstanding impression was of the cheering, singing, marching masses. It was the same before the Winter Palace in St. Petersburg, on the Unter den Linden in Berlin, on the Champs Elysées in Paris, in Trafalgar Square or the Mall in London.

It was as if the expanding wealth and multiplying populations, as if the unconscious boredom of peace over so many unbroken years had stored up in the nations a terrific potential, which only waited for an accident to touch it off. Far from being innocents led to the slaughter, the peoples of Europe led their leaders. Ministers of Tsar, Kaiser, King, and President watched the press and the streets during these demented days and fell victim to the hysteria as helplessly as any of the nameless multitudes about them. It was as if some historic fatality, expressing itself in a sort of elemental mass passion, for a moment had suspended all the normal processes of reason and humanity.

2 THE OPENING CAMPAIGNS

THE CAMPAIGNS OF 1914 ON LAND

It was part of the professional duty of every European general staff to prepare its plans for that hypothetical day when its army and country might be
involved in war. The plans made allowances for such ponderables as rates
of mobilizations, strengths of reserves, and possible combinations of enemies
and fighting fronts. They were revised to meet new developments, new
alliances, new weapons and tactics. They were rehearsed in part at annual
maneuvers. In the first week of August 1914, four great general staffs, by the
dispatch of a few sheaves of telegrams, set in motion colossal dispositions
long prepared and practiced in the minutest detail. The common belief at
the time was that the war would be a short, orgiastic interlude. At the signal,
armies of millions rushed into their schedules and spent their manpower and
material in a huge gamble for lightning Napoleonic victories. Europe, which
had not seen a major battle since 1877,[1] was led by officers for whom war
was largely a matter of staff-college manuals into massacres that are only
comparable with the Mongol ravages of the fourteenth century.

Ever since the conclusion of the Franco-Russian Entente (see p. 7),
Germany had been haunted by the fear of simultaneous war on two fronts
against numerically stronger enemies. In 1914 it was probable that France
and Russia could put armies into the field numbering 4,000,000 and 5,000,-
000, as against Austria-Hungary's and Germany's 3,000,000 and 4,000,000.
In this critical situation the German General Staff determined to use a plan
originally drawn up by Count von Schlieffen, its Chief of Staff from 1891 to
1907, a plan devised to take advantage of the slow Russian mobilization to
defeat France and Russia in two short successive campaigns. The General
Staff also determined to gain a temporary preponderance of numbers by its
own rapid mobilization, by efficient railroad transit, and particularly by
throwing its entire forces, first-line troops and reservists, into the initial offensives. It would outflank the great French fortification system between
Verdun and Belfort and invade France by way of the comparatively open
northeastern frontier, thus involving Belgium and Luxembourg, of whose
neutrality Germany was herself a guarantor.[2] The operation would take the
form of a huge encirclement, hinging on Verdun, up the Belgian Meuse and
across the Champagne, and would end in a decisive battle against the reversed French lines in the western foothills of the Vosges. Once France had
been eliminated, the victorious German Army would then turn at its leisure
against the now gathering Russian hordes on the East Prussian frontier.
Schlieffen, it is said, bequeathed his plan to his successors with the words,
"The fight must come. Only make the right wing strong!" In the first week
of August 1914 the plan went into operation. Five German armies crossed

the frontiers of Belgium and Luxembourg. Seventeen-inch Krupp howitzers began pounding the Belgian fortress of Liége.[3]

The first part of the plan went like clockwork. Five hundred German troop trains a day ran up to the Belgian frontier. The Belgian defense was stubborn and must have been very disconcerting to the "paper strategists" in the German High Command [4] but, contrary to accounts put out at the time, it did not seriously delay the invasion timetable. Some of the forts at Liége held for two weeks, long after they had been by-passed by the main German forces. General Joffre, the French commander, in accordance with his own plan, Plan 17, had meanwhile attempted the invasion and recon-quest of the lost provinces of Alsace-Lorraine, an entirely political move which was defeated with heavy losses and had not the least effect on the Germans making their sweeping progress into northern France. The British Expeditionary Force, successfully shipped across the Channel, fought its first action at Mons against divisions of the German extreme right wing.

We know now that the Schlieffen Plan failed because it was too unwieldy. It attempted too much, and too quickly. The maneuvering of the huge armies of modern times is an elaborate science. Even in the Second World War, with all the motorized forces, air reconnaissance, and radio then avail-able, two hundred miles was the farthest an army could advance without pausing to re-form. Yet Schlieffen expected his famous right wing to cover four hundred. In 1914 a million Germans poured into France, sometimes marching twenty miles a day on foot, and a campaign which had been per-fectly prepared and perfectly begun was soon a swarming, headlong, tired mass of men which any setback would throw into complete disorder. In those days communications were kept by cavalry or motor cyclists, many of whom now lost their way in the pace and confusion of the advance. The German cavalry in France, with misguided zeal, indiscriminately destroyed telegraph lines and stations. By the last week in August, German divisional commanders were often out of touch with their headquarters and with one another. Several divisions had outmarched their artillery, their supplies, and even their field kitchens. Unbelievable as it may seem, Moltke, the German commander, hardly knew for several days at a time where his armies were.

Moltke moreover made the serious error of detaching eleven divisions from his right wing for the reduction of Antwerp and other isolated centers of resistance in Belgium. British marines and cavalry were operating along the coast; there were strange and persistent rumors of a Russian landing in Flanders and, in German eyes, the Russians were always invested with un-namable terrors; and all these called for Moltke's precautionary diversions. But Moltke weakened the main German deployment at the very point which Schlieffen, in his dying words, had warned his heirs to load most heavily; and, as if the plan had not been misread enough, Moltke afterward trans-ferred four of the eleven divisions to East Prussia in answer to an urgent summons for reinforcements from that front.

In the first week of September 1914 the Germans had reached the river Marne, and then the French and British armies counterattacked. They at-tacked the depleted German right wing, and they attacked an enemy who had already lost his original cohesion and momentum. Both Joffre and the

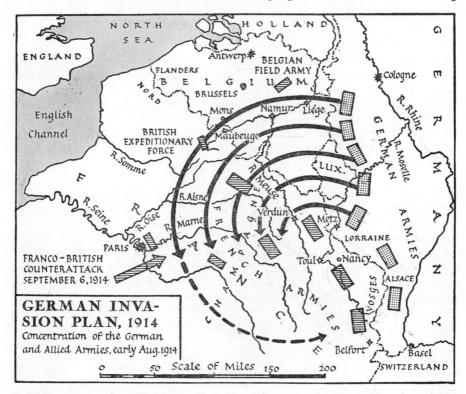

British commander, Field Marshal Sir John French, are believed to have been opposed to the action at first but, when they struck at last, they struck for a decision. The First Battle of the Marne occupied five days, from September 6 to 10, 1914. It was one of the great deliverances of history. Every available man was thrown in. The Paris garrison was rushed up to the line in taxis and busses off the Paris streets. At the height of the action, Moltke sent his special aide, Colonel Hentsch, to visit in turn the five German armies west of Verdun and gave him instructions to co-ordinate a general retirement "should it have already been initiated." The Colonel motored from the headquarters of one army to the next through confused, congested country, meeting everywhere an unaccountable sense of depression. The Franco-British Allies had already won the "psychological" victory. The bewildered Germans, who for four weeks had tumbled irresistibly through Belgium and northern France, halted and drew back, hardly understanding what had beaten them or whether indeed they had been beaten.

The success of the attack persuaded Joffre to repeat it, and the opposing armies now entered upon a competition in flanking and counterflanking ever more westward and ever more northward, a competition which developed into what has since been called the "Race to the Sea." Joffre sent General Foch to co-ordinate the heterogeneous group of French, British, and Belgian divisions which now assembled in the Nord. By mid-October the combatants stretched from the coast of Flanders to the frontier of Switz erland, locked in that curious tactical immobility in which for the next four years they were fated to remain.

On September 14, 1914, General von Falkenhayn had succeeded Moltke in the supreme command of the German Army. Moltke retired quietly from a post which he should never have held and which, to do him justice, he had originally tried to refuse. The new commander paid a last despairing homage to Schlieffen and, during October and November, he delivered against the British forces in Flanders a series of attacks which have become known to us as the First Battle of Ypres and which were intended to turn the British flank and seize the Channel ports. The British line held, and the last chances of an early German decision in the West irrevocably faded away.

Meanwhile operations had been proceeding along the Russian front. On August 3, 1914 the Tsar had appointed his uncle, the Grand Duke Nicholas, Commander in Chief of the Russian Army. The Grand Duke had recently administered the St. Petersburg Military District and had devoted himself in particular to the tactical training of the troops under his command. But he had taken no part in the discussions of the Russian General Staff. Russia's plan for war against Germany and Austria-Hungary was drawn up by Sukhomlinov, the Russian Minister of War, and his associates. The Grand Duke, on assuming his new duties, found himself committed to agreements concluded without his co-operation, or even without his knowledge, and to an understanding made secretly with France. On no other basis can we explain the precipitate offensives which he launched on all sectors of the Russian front. Rennenkampf, commanding the Russian First Army, crossed the frontier of East Prussia toward Königsberg; Samsonov, commanding the Russian Second Army farther to the south, crossed the frontier toward Danzig. Four Russian armies on the southwest were almost immediately at grips with opposing Austro-Hungarian forces.

The Schlieffen Plan had provided for the German defense of East Prussia by a single army, which should fight a delaying action toward the Vistula while the main German forces were still engaged in the West. But the success of the plan had depended upon the great distances and poor communications of Russia, and upon the consequent slowness of the Russian mobilization. The early delivery and power of the Grand Duke's invasion of East Prussia came as a most unpleasant surprise to the German High Command. Moltke, as we have seen, had already detached eleven divisions from his right wing in Belgium, four of which he sent to East Prussia. He also dismissed the commander of the German army in East Prussia. In his stead he appointed Hindenburg, a retired general, one of stolid nerve and credited with special knowledge of the East Prussian terrain, and as Chief of Staff gave him Ludendorff, a major general who had distinguished himself in the recent fighting at Liége.

The result was the Battle of Tannenberg, one of those Hannibalic setpieces which are the joy of military historians and the grave of nations. While Samsonov's and Rennenkampf's infantry trudged painfully under a sweltering August sun across the sandy East Prussian soil, the Germans used their excellent railroad system to concentrate their lesser forces against each of the Russian generals in turn. The Battle of Tannenberg was fought between August 23 and 31, 1914, and ended in the annihilation of Samsonov's army and the slaughter or capture of 100,000 of his men. A week later the busy railroads carried the German forces northward to their second triumph, the Battle of the Masurian Lakes, over Rennenkampf.[5]

Yet while Russia suffered this frightful double disaster on her northwestern front, her four armies on the southwest were winning victories. Conrad von Hötzendorf, the Austrian Chief of Staff, had advanced through Galicia into Russian Poland with admirable precipitancy, had fought a series of battles of a strategic ambition far beyond his real resources, and was at last borne down by the greater Russian numbers. Conrad had neither the men nor the railroads of Hindenburg, and the Russian armies were shortly driving him back deep into Austrian territory. In the course of eight weeks of continuous fighting, Conrad lost Galicia, one of the most fertile agricultural provinces of Austria-Hungary, and 350,000 men.

In Germany, Hindenburg and to a less extent Ludendorff, the two victors of East Prussia, became the objects of a hero worship that non-German people can hardly understand. But it is to be remembered that to the German mind the battles in East Prussia represented the veritable exorcism of an all-pervading terror. The Empire of the Tsar, mysteriously remote, incalculably powerful, a hinterland of barbarism, and the matrix throughout history of devastating migrations — this was Germany's popular enemy. The German High Command disputed — and until 1917 continued to dispute — the respective claims of "Western" and "Eastern" strategy, but the common people of Germany always believed that the war would be won in the East. The check at the Marne seemed a small thing in comparison with the laying of the Russian specter. Tannenberg created the mythic warrior, Hindenburg, into whose hands it was inevitable that, sooner or later, the German Fatherland should come to entrust its fate.

While these tremendous events were going forward on the German fronts, the Balkans, which had been their indirect cause, had become a minor theater of the war. The Austrian High Command had long been prepared for simultaneous operations against Serbia and Russia, but its original plan was modified, even as the Schlieffen Plan was modified, to meet the unforeseen rapidity of the Russian concentration. The consequent dispatch of heavy reinforcements to the Russian front left the two Austrian armies in the south with a total strength only slightly superior to that of their Serbian enemy. Yet with his depleted effectives, Potiorek, the Austrian commander on that front, still resolved to attack. European war or no European war, the original "punitive expedition" against Serbia was not to be forgotten.

The Serbian commander disposed of three armies, consisting largely of veterans of the Balkan Wars, every one of them born to the fiercest hatred of Austrian tyranny. The war had not yet developed that competition in "material" which came to neutralize the crude advantages of numbers and, man for man, the Serb was the equal of any Austrian soldier in the field.

Potiorek fought two campaigns against Serbia in 1914, both ending in inglorious failures. His first advance, in August, across the Danube was repulsed in exactly three days. The terrain was difficult, and whole divisions — many of them Slavs — proved none too loyal. In November, Austrians and Serbs joined battle for the second time. On December 2, Potiorek was able to send the aged Austrian Emperor, on his eighty-fourth birthday, the news of the capture of Belgrade. But the Serbs counterattacked, and once more the luckless Potiorek was repulsed. By Christmas 1914, Serbian soil was freed of its invaders. "The hated pig-farmers of Serbia," writes Churchill, "for the sake of whose punishment almost the whole world had been plunged in war, had added to the Austrian annals this most ignominious, rankling and derisory defeat. . . . The prodigy of the Serbian resistance was hardly comprehended by the busy world at war; but those who were best informed were the most astonished." [6]

A considerable number of scattered "colonial" actions meanwhile had been fought in outlying parts of the globe. German possessions overseas began to fall, one by one, to British and French expeditions. In August and September 1914, Samoa fell to New Zealand, and New Guinea and the Bismarck Archipelago to Australia. Togoland was occupied by Anglo-French forces. Germans and Portuguese were fighting in Angola. On September 2 the Japanese landed in Shantung, and in a hard-fought campaign of two months they took the German port of Tsingtao. During November they occupied the German islands in the North Pacific, including the island of Yap.

By the end of 1914 only the American hemisphere had escaped the omnipresence of military operations.

THE ENTRY OF TURKEY INTO THE WAR

A private quarrel between Austria-Hungary and Serbia had been the occasion of the present European conflict, but the respective sympathies and alignments of the other Balkan States were not predictable. The Balkan wars of 1912–13 had weakened them, but left them with unsatisfied antagonisms, and perhaps disposed them to new adventures (see pp. 9–11). Their friendships had been much sought after by the European Powers and were already mortgaged under loans and military missions. Their active alliances might now be purchasable with promises of territory. Meanwhile they watched the opening battles of 1914 on the Meuse, the Vistula, and the Danube, and wondered whom among the giants it might soon be most expedient to support.

It was not surprising that Turkey should have been first to forsake the straight and narrow way of neutrality. For many years past she had been subject to the attentions of Germany. Her loans had been floated in Berlin; her new railroads had been built by German engineers; her army had been remodeled by a German military mission. The Young Turk "Triumvirate," Talaat Pasha, Enver Pasha, and Jemal Pasha, who shared the chief offices in the Ottoman Government, were ambitious place seekers and probable Germanophiles if the right kind of persuasion were applied.

Two German warships, the *Goeben* and the *Breslau,* finally tipped the

Turkish scales in favor of Germany. The outbreak of war found the ships cruising the Mediterranean, and early in August they appeared at the mouth of the Dardanelles. By the Treaty of London of 1871 that waterway was closed to battleships in time of war. But Enver Pasha, without consulting his cabinet, acceded to the pressure of his German advisers and ordered the forts along the Dardanelles to allow the *Goeben* and the *Breslau* an unchallenged passage.

The *Goeben* and the *Breslau* at once gave Turkey the control of the Black Sea — the Russian fleet had no ships of like armament — and they could even terrorize Constantinople in case of need. The Allied ambassadors protested and threatened. But the Turkish Government went through the form of purchasing the ships for its own navy, the German sailors on board were served out with fezzes, and the ships remained. Events now moved quickly. At the end of August 1914 the Turkish Government ordered general mobilization. On October 29 an engagement between the Russian and Turkish fleets took place in the Black Sea; the *Goeben* and the *Breslau* participated, and the Russian port of Odessa was bombarded. During early November, Russia, Britain, and France formally declared war on Turkey. An Allied squadron bombarded the outer forts of the Dardanelles. A British-Indian force landed in Mesopotamia. Britain declared a protectorate over Egypt. The "Anzacs," the Australian–New Zealand Army Corps,[7] began to arrive in the Suez area for the defense of the Canal.

In mid-November 1914 the Sultan solemnly proclaimed a Holy War. He rehearsed at length the iniquities of Russian, British, and French imperialism in the Near East and called upon the faithful to rise up against their infidel oppressors. There were some processions in Constantinople, but it was known that the noisiest demonstrators were in government pay. The riffraff of the city improved the occasion by attacking alien residents and Armenians. But the Oriental is old in political cynicism, and the Holy War was not very convincing. The Moslems of Persia, Afghanistan, India, and the French and Italian colonies in North Africa remained quiet. The Arabs nursed anti-Turkish grievances of their own. The Sherif of Mecca had already made friendly contacts with the British High Commissioner in Cairo (see p. 66).

Militarily, Turkey plunged headlong into the offensive with entirely inadequate resources. The Young Turk leaders, Enver and Jemal, left for their respective fronts and conducted two campaigns both apparently under the stimulus of their personal rivalry and of their common hatred of England. Enver's offensive into Russian Armenia, which he intended to be the first step toward an Alexandrian advance on India, bogged down in winter snows, high altitudes, and typhus. Jemal's offensive against the Suez Canal was more cautiously planned and ably executed. In January 1915 his forces actually crossed the Sinai Desert — no mean feat — and fought a sharp engagement with British defenders on the very banks of the Canal. But there was no real power behind the offensive, and Jemal retired. He had the satisfaction, however, of celebrating his "victory" in Constantinople with gun salutes and fireworks. Only a few adventurous Turkish patrols ever again succeeded in reaching the Canal.

THE BEGINNINGS OF THE ALLIED NAVAL BLOCKADE

Naval strength was preponderantly on the side of the Allies. As a convenient index, Britain in 1914 had fifty-five battleships in commission, France twenty-one, Germany thirty-three, and Austria-Hungary thirteen, and the preponderance was even more pronounced in other categories of ships. From the start Britain was resolved that her advantage would be used to the fullest effect. In July 1914 the British Navy was already mobilized for the Royal Naval Review at Portland. On July 26 the British Admiralty countermanded the order to disperse. On August 4 the Grand Fleet, under the command of Admiral Sir John Jellicoe, was at its war stations.

The naval warfare of the autumn months of 1914 was largely cruiser warfare. One by one, German warships at sea were sunk or chased to home or neutral ports. The German battle cruiser *Goeben* and the light cruiser *Breslau* made good their escape into the Dardanelles. The German cruiser *Emden,* after three destructive months as a commerce raider in the Indian Ocean, was wrecked in an action with the Australian cruiser *Sydney.* Count von Spee's squadron in the Pacific, containing the new armored cruisers *Scharnhorst* and *Gneisenau,* destroyed Admiral Craddock's squadron at Coronel off the coast of Chile at the end of October, and was itself trapped and destroyed by Admiral Sturdee's battle cruisers off the Falkland Islands on December 8. At the end of the year 1914 the light cruiser *Dresden* was the last German surface ship at sea, and she was sunk in March 1915.

Yet the actions, dates, and names of warships, such as we have mentioned, give a limited idea of the real war at sea. The "mopping-up" operations — for they were little else — conducted by the British and Allied navies in the first months of the war were part of a larger strategy best expressed by the word "siege." By the end of August 1914, German merchantmen had been swept from the seas. The Battle of the Falkland Islands was the finale of German cruiser warfare. Except for sporadic cruiser raids across the North Sea and except for the Battle of Jutland in 1916, the German Navy made no attempt to break the cover of its home bases and mine fields. Gradually the Allies deployed their immense naval superiority and established against the Central Empires that impenetrable wall of blockade which, more than any other factor, contributed most decisively to the outcome of the war.

The blockade was a long-range blockade unlike any other in naval history. It was conducted from northern waters, mainly from the British bases at Rosyth and Scapa Flow, and from the Strait of Dover. British ships made no attempt to attack or patrol German ports direct, as the German Admiral Staff had originally expected. The North Sea, in effect, was sealed off and became a sort of no man's land, a free battleground for the naval forces of both sides. The British cruiser sweep into the Helgoland Bight at the end of August 1914 — which cost the Germans three cruisers — was the only surface action in German home waters which the British Navy attempted in the course of the war. German merchant coastal shipping with Holland and the Scandinavian countries continued with little interruption. Meanwhile, British east-coast seaside towns were left relatively naked of naval protection, and from time to time some of them suffered from raids by German ships, doubtless made in the hope of drawing British naval forces into piecemeal actions and into a consequent disruption of their basic strategy.

The blockade soon spread beyond its immediate naval and economic objects and became a ramifying political struggle which involved belligerents and neutrals alike. For as soon as her own ports were rendered idle, Germany had recourse to those of her neutral neighbors. Norway, Sweden, Denmark, Holland, Switzerland, the Balkans — and Italy till her entry into the war — became back-door entrances for a suddenly expanded transit trade with the Reich. Christiania, Copenhagen, Rotterdam, and Genoa took the place of Hamburg, Bremen, Antwerp, and Trieste. The Allied blockade, already successful in the stoppage of German commerce, developed perforce into the stoppage of abnormal neutral commerce as well.

The step thence into the erudite complexities of international law was a short one. Today, perhaps, a cynical world can almost marvel at the reams of paper that were once so closely written and closely argued upon the interminable topics of visit and search, continuous voyage, and contraband. The existing international law was based upon the old conceptions of direct blockade and had to be adapted to the new long-range blockade. Suffice it to say that Britain and France, supposedly in the interests of safety, established the practice of diverting neutral merchant ships to their own ports for purposes of search, and they proceeded to seize any goods whose "destination, ownership, or origin were presumed to be hostile." They continually added to their lists of contraband, till there was hardly an importable commodity which, if found on a neutral ship near German waters, was exempt from seizure. Foodstuffs as well as the more obvious materials and munitions of war were made subject to the most rigorous control. By 1916 and 1917, Britain and France were even "rationing" neutrals and seizing any goods which appeared to be entering neutral ports contiguous to Germany in excess of former peacetime quantities.

The blockade tactics of Britain and France were highhanded in the extreme, but it was never easy to establish against either Power literal or explicit breaches of international law. In particular the United States — a neutral till 1917 — whose trade with European neutrals was thus arbitrarily intercepted, protested with the greatest vigor and, but for Germany's more criminal and spectacular malpractices at sea, Britain's and France's conduct might not have escaped so lightly. We have only to read the diplomatic correspondence between Britain and the United States in 1915 and 1916 to realize how fine was the edge of friendship and rupture between the two Atlantic nations.

3 THE EXTENSION OF THE WAR

THE GERMAN SUBMARINE CAMPAIGN

In 1915 the war was spreading like an infection. The Ottoman Empire had already become involved in November 1914; Italy became involved in May 1915, and Bulgaria in October 1915. The Allies attempted to force the passage of the Dardanelles. But, even more than this, the Allied naval blockade, as we described it in the previous chapter, had brought home the presence of war to nations far outside the immediate arena of hostilities. No part of a world that lived by trade and industry could now remain an indifferent spectator or maintain other than a technical neutrality. The war was approaching the proportions of a global war. In 1915, Germany threw her own maritime weapon, the submarine, into the scales and thereby directly challenged the United States.

On February 4, 1915, in a note to the United States, the German Government announced that, in retaliation for the Allied blockade, Allied merchantmen in a "war zone" comprising the coasts of Britain and northern France would be destroyed without warning and without consideration for the lives of crews and passengers. Neutral ships in the same area would also be exposed to danger so long as the ruse which allowed a belligerent to fly a neutral flag made it impossible to identify a ship's nationality.

Britain may sometimes have sailed very close to the legal wind at sea, but here in the German note were crimes in contemplation which no law or necessity could admit. President Wilson replied to the note in terms about as severe as the diplomacy of those days allowed one friendly Power to address to another and gave clear warning that the United States Government would hold the German Government "to a strict accountability" for such acts as resulted in the loss of American vessels or American lives on the high seas.

President Wilson followed up his reply with identical notes to Britain and Germany, urging the one to exempt foodstuffs from blockade and the other to forego submarine attacks on merchantmen. It seemed to him that a compromise might be reached between the essential "wrongs" of the blockade and the submarine. The German Government pleaded with great adroitness that it must find some defense against the increasing traffic in American munitions to the Allies. But the actual sinkings at sea left President Wilson with no choice but to take further and further refuge in the absolute legalities and to lose sight of those extralegal merits which, on calmer reflection, might have been conceded to the German case. One American life was lost on the British liner *Falaba*, torpedoed on March 28, 1915. Three American lives were lost on the American oil tanker *Gulflight*, torpedoed on May 1. The Cunard liner *Lusitania* was torpedoed off the southern coast of Ireland on May 7. She sank in eighteen minutes. Of her 1,959 passengers and crew, 1,198 were lost; of 159 Americans, 128 were lost; of 129 children, 94 were lost.

Mere description, mere quotation, can give no idea of the reaction in America and in the non-German world to this supreme outrage. "Condemnation of the act," said the *Literary Digest,* "seems only to be limited by the restrictions of the English language." For once in the history of journalism the glamorous strivings of the headline artist were neither exaggerated nor insincere. Gerard, the American ambassador in Berlin, Page, the American ambassador in London, and Colonel House, then in London, all counseled and expected war. Meanwhile the pacifists and isolationists at home struck an attitude of "I told you so!" But President Wilson remained cool and collected. Never did his much-abused aloofness stand him in such good stead. Congress was not then in session, or its floods of oratory might even then have swept him into war. On May 10, 1915, at Philadelphia, he delivered himself in these words: "The example of America must be a special example. The example of America must be the example not merely of peace because it will not fight, but of peace because peace is the healing and elevating influence of the world, and strife is not. There is such a thing as a man being too proud to fight. There is such a thing as a nation being so right that it does not need to convince others by force that it is right."

The abuse and ridicule with which this speech was received by large sections of the American press may have persuaded the President to bend a little to the popular storm, and his note to Germany on May 13 no more than avoided the finality of an ultimatum: "[The United States Government] confidently expects that the Imperial German Government will disavow the acts of which [it] complains, that they will make reparation so far as reparation is possible for injuries which are without measure, and that they will take immediate steps to prevent the recurrence of anything so obviously subversive of the principles of warfare. . . ."

Throughout the year 1915, American wrath rose and subsided in response to the storms and lulls at sea. The harassed German ambassador in Washington, Count von Bernstorff, tried to make his government aware of the intensity of feeling the submarine war had excited and sadly likened himself to "another Sisyphus" who had hardly composed one German outrage before another was committed. However, he was able to satisfy Lansing, the American Secretary of State, that submarine attacks on "liners" would not be made, and the actual decrease in the number of sinkings in the late summer and autumn certainly pointed to a turn for the better. The most serious incident in the latter part of the year was the torpedoing of the *Ancona* in the Mediterranean in November, not by a German but by an Austro-Hungarian submarine.

Plots and sabotage, evidently engineered by German agents in American munition plants, which were now beginning to supply the Allies, provided meanwhile a lesser but cumulative irritation. American freighters went to sea carrying infernal machines which exploded mysteriously in mid-ocean.

There were reports of bridges and canals being blown up in Canada. The German military and naval attachés, Captain von Papen and Captain Boy-Ed, were sent home for espionage. President Wilson rounded off the events of the year with his famous "Preparedness" speech to Congress in December. But it was still to be eighteen months before the United States was to declare war against the disturber of its security and peace.

THE ENTRY OF ITALY INTO THE WAR

In 1914, Germany, Austria-Hungary, and Italy were members of the Triple Alliance (see p. 6). But the alliance was specifically defensive and involved the members in no commitments in the event of one of them provoking an offensive war. The alliance was also a guarantee of the *status quo* in the Near East, and it was understood not to be directed against England. The Austrian ultimatum to Serbia in July 1914, however, presumed an offensive war; it bore all the traces of having been hatched by Austria-Hungary and Germany in secret without consultation with their Italian ally; it patently disturbed the *status quo* in the Near East; and it led indirectly to the involvement of England. Every obligation that had bound Italy to the Triple Alliance had been incontinently broken, and on August 3, 1914 she declared her neutrality.

Thereafter, till her entry into the war in May 1915, Italy played a tantalizing diplomatic game. "Compensations" from either belligerent group to entice the reluctant nation into the fray became larger and more pressing with repetition. The Kaiser sent his former chancellor and onetime German ambassador in Italy, Prince von Bülow, to Rome, with tempting offers of a new "morsel." Count Burian had now succeeded the ill-starred Berchtold as Austro-Hungarian Foreign Minister, and his emperor and government authorized him to offer the Italian-speaking Tirol. He might have been induced to offer more. Sonnino, the Italian Foreign Minister, bargained with skill, but it was abundantly clear, as time went on, that Italy had ambitions far beyond what Austria-Hungary would ever be willing, or even able, to satisfy. Italy wanted the liberation of those of her nationals who were still subject to Austrian domination, but she also wanted a general extension of her interests and influence in the Adriatic, Balkans, and Near East, and only the Allies, Britain and France, if victorious, would be in a position to meet her full demands.

In the course of March and April 1915, largely through the efforts of Grey, the British Foreign Secretary, Italy's terms were reduced to precise diplomatic form, and on April 26, 1915, Britain, France, Russia, and Italy signed the secret Treaty of London. Italy engaged herself to enter the war jointly with the Allies "against all their enemies." Her acquisitions would include the Trentino and Tirol up to the Brenner Pass, Trieste, Istria, Dalmatia, and the Dodecanese. She would have a share in the partition of Anatolia and compensation in Africa in the event of France and Britain increasing, at Germany's expense, their colonial territories there. Fiume, it is interesting to note in view of its later importance, and certain other Adriatic ports were to be assigned to "Croatia, Serbia, and Montenegro" (see pp. 119 and 294).

To many an observer, Italian affairs in 1914 and early 1915 were moving not to war but to revolution. The condition in which the country found itself was not unlike the condition in which the country was again to find itself in 1922, just before the Fascist seizure of control. Yet in the end the transition to active belligerency was achieved with something of the zest of the other nations in the war. On May 4, 1915 the Italian Government denounced the Triple Alliance. On May 20 the Italian Premier, Salandra, asked the Chamber for extraordinary powers. Four hundred and eighty-one Deputies were present at the session, the only notable absentee being the noninterventionist, Giolitti. Salandra's bill was adopted by an overwhelming vote. The Deputies rose to their feet, cheering and singing wildly. "Moments like these," wrote Salandra afterward, "go far to compensate for the long weariness of living."

On May 23, 1915, Italy declared war on Austria-Hungary. Two days later the King left for the front, taking General Cadorna with him as his Chief of Staff. But, though Italy had engaged herself to enter the war on the side of the Allies "against *all* their enemies," she showed a remarkable reluctance to break with her former German ally, and she seemed to be trying to fight a lesser war of limited liability within the greater one. She did not formally declare war on Germany till August 1916.

THE CAMPAIGNS OF 1915 ON LAND

The respite of winter had been used by the belligerents for their future preparations. The failure of the Schlieffen Plan in 1914 had dashed Germany's hopes of a lightning victory, and she found herself committed to a war whose length and character none could yet gauge. But the German High Command still held the initiative on land, it operated on "interior lines," and it was free to choose the place and time of its next strategic moves. Its choice was hard, a choice between "Western" and "Eastern" doctrines which was now to haunt the higher direction of the war on both the German and the Allied sides. But the successes of Hindenburg and Ludendorff in 1914 resulted in Falkenhayn's deciding to fight his main offensive operation of 1915 on the Eastern front and there develop a vast action which might reduce Russia to defeat and force her out of the war. The Western, Serbian, and Italian fronts meanwhile he would hold defensively with minimum effectives.

A somewhat similar dilemma embarrassed the Allied commands. Thanks to the British Navy, the Allies held the initiative at sea, and they could make a strategic descent wherever the sea gave access. In particular Britain could be expected to adapt herself quickly and naturally to a war of a kind she had fought through the centuries, a war in which her Continental allies bore the main burden of operations on land, while she herself engaged in amphibious diversions along the periphery. Generally it was the civilians, such as Churchill and Lloyd George, who argued for diversions, and the professional soldiers and sailors, such as Kitchener, Fisher, and Jellicoe, who pleaded for the restriction of strategy. In the upshot the Allied commands in 1915 made concessions to both Westerners and Easterners. French and British armies fought major offensives against Falkenhayn's defensive system on the Western front and at the same time were active in the Near East. The participation of Turkey and Italy and the projected Austro-German offensive against Russia presented commitments and opportunities which the most doctrinaire of Westerners could not ignore. In 1915 the Allies made their great assault upon the Dardanelles.

All these considerations were aggravated by an unexpected military impasse. The First World War was a war of mass armies and new tactical sciences, the implications of which were at first beyond the conservative imagination of the time. Waterloo had been fought by 170,000 men; Sedan by 300,000; the First Battle of the Marne by over a million. And the expansion was not only quantitative. Yet Moltke and Falkenhayn, no less than Joffre, still clung to the old chessboard concepts. War was a matter of fronts, communications, deployments, envelopments. Even Kitchener in Britain, who had the exceptional imagination to foresee a four-year conflict and to demand a British army of the unprecedented size of 70 divisions and 3,000,-000 men, could not appreciate the technical foundations on which these quantities needed to be built. It was left to a few civilians of genius, like Rathenau in Germany and Lloyd George in Britain, to rise to a full understanding of the situation.

On the actual field of battle a new kind of fighting was in full development. The rapid-firing rifle and the machine gun were the "dominant" weapons, and their "fire power," when both sides possessed them, all but reduced the combatant to immobility. On the Western front, from the end of 1914, 5,000,000 infantrymen crouched in earthen ditches from which they could emerge only at the cost of prohibitive casualties and then after intensive "artillery prepartion." Two lines of trenches meandered from the borders of Switzerland to the North Sea, and between them lay the ragged, shell-pocked, wire-entangled isthmus of "no man's land," sometimes widening to several hundred yards, sometimes approaching to points less than fifty feet apart. Behind the lines, concentrations of artillery sought to compensate for the excessive fire power of the infantry. Cavalry, the old mobile arm, was completely useless, although optimistic generals of the older school held cavalry divisions in reserve against the happy day when an infantry "break-through" might once again allow them to revert to more traditional types of maneuver warfare.

The soldier living under such conditions suffered appalling hardship, especially in low-lying country in bad weather when his trenches were waterlogged. Only the most efficient medical services saved him from being swept away by sickness. But this was the pattern of warfare on the Western front, and the situation was soon analogous even in different geographies and terrains like Gallipoli or the Italian Alps. Deadlock supervened on any front wherever arms and man power on either side bore any reasonable equivalence. An inventive age, which gave so much of its best intelligence to military science, might have been expected to discover a solution. In 1915 the

Germans, for example, tried the flame thrower. They tried poison gas, a weapon depending on the surprise of its first employment, after which its effectiveness was largely lost to appropriate defenses and to retaliation. The hand grenade, trench mortar, and steel helmet were added to the equipment of the infantryman. In 1917 the British in Flanders dug tunnels under the German positions which they then mined.

But generally the professional soldiers, German, French, and British, came to rely more and more on their artillery. The enemy's barbed wire and trenches, rifles and machine guns were to be battered into total demolition. *"L'artillérie conquiert, l'infantérie occupe,"* as the French put it. Tactical discussions then raged around the weight and duration of the bombardment. Even in 1915, 250,000 shells could be fired in a single offensive and, as if to make a virtue of necessity, it was already a normal thing to talk eruditely about "attrition," *"la bataille d'usure."* But the time was to come when the British, for example at the Somme in 1916, used one gun for every twenty yards on a fourteen-mile front and 1,500,000 shells; at Vimy in April 1917, one gun for every nine yards on an eleven-mile front and 2,600,000 shells; and at Messines in June 1917, one gun for every seven yards on a six-mile front and 3,000,000 shells. These bombardments often lasted a week or more. In April 1917, during Nivelle's offensive in the Champagne, on a twenty-five mile front, the French Fifth and Sixth Armies fired 6,000,000 shells. And these figures were surpassed in 1918. Yet, despite all the metal thus squandered, the losses in men ran into thousands and the gains in ground were strategically negligible. The Germans used to refer to the "field of corpses" left in front of their trenches after an Allied offensive.

Though the tank — the armored car borne on caterpillar tractors, the ultimate solution of the trench deadlock — existed in embryo in 1914, it was built in parsimonious quantity in 1916, and went into action for the first time in September of that year. The first major tank action was the Battle of Cambrai in November 1917.

But we anticipate. On the Western front in 1915, we have said, the Germans stood on the defensive, and the Allies delivered through the year a series of offensives against their trench positions — the British at Neuve Chapelle and Loos, the French in the Champagne, costing them respectively, in killed and wounded, 13,000 and 40,000 and 150,000 men. These were famous battles in their time but, as we look back on them from today, what stands out most strikingly is the stubborn confidence of the Allied commanders, French and Joffre, a confidence not shaken by the repeated failure of their methods, that they could pierce the enemy's trench system and expel him from France. General Sir Douglas Haig succeeded French shortly after the failure at Loos, and he remained commander of the British forces on the Western front to the end of the war. But the substitution introduced no change; Haig clung with even greater tenacity to the exorbitant tactics of his predecessor.

The Allied campaign in the Dardanelles began as a purely naval action. It was reputedly conceived by Churchill, then First Lord of the Admiralty, on the advice of his naval commanders in the Mediterranean. Its objectives were sufficiently tempting. If successful, it would open a highway to beleaguered Russia, recover the grain and coal trade of the Black Sea, probably force Turkey to sue for peace, and read a stern lesson to pro-German or other wavering elements throughout the Balkans and Near East. It might have prevented the Russian Revolution and shortened the war by a full two years. Moreover, the original plan of attack called only for the use of ships which for fleet operations were obsolete and for minimum land forces, sufficient for subsequent occupation and policing. The French Government promised supporting naval units.

On February 19, 1915 the combined British and French fleets began the bombardment of the outer forts of the Dardanelles. The entire action was then hopefully expected to take a month. The political effects were immediate and encouraging. The Balkan countries were in the wildest excitement. The Greek Premier, Venizelos, pro-Ally in his sympathies, urged his country's instant declaration of war on Turkey, and offered the Allies an army corps of three divisions. But then the difficulties began. General Liman von Sanders, head of the German military mission in Turkey, assumed command of the Turkish defenses. Elaborate entrenchments crisscrossed every vulnerable point on the Gallipoli Peninsula. On March 18 the Allied fleets, beginning the second phase of their bombardment, lost four of their heaviest ships.

The attack was evidently developing a magnitude and a hazard beyond all expectation. It could still have been broken off without reproach. But with perverse, if admirable, magnanimity Kitchener at the War Office in London now declared that the fighting must go on. General Sir Ian Hamilton was sent out to lead a military landing in the Dardanelles and reported that he must undertake a considerable campaign, requiring new bases, unstinted shipping, and all the detail of large operations. Kitchener gave him two British divisions and the Australian–New Zealand Army Corps (Anzac) in Egypt (see p. 23). The French sent a division. At daybreak on April 25, 1915 the first landings were carried out, the British on the Gallipoli Peninsula and the French on the Asiatic mainland. Two hundred ships, men-of-war and transports, participated in the operation, and there began a campaign of eight and a half months, which ultimately brought together on these rugged tongues of rock and scrub 500,000 fighting men.

The Dardanelles was Britain's greatest failure of the war, and its consequences were in evidence in the course of the year. Turkey's closure of the great waterway had severed what might have been the main communication between Russia and her Western allies. Russia, though so huge a country with so long a coastline, was virtually cut off by sea, and her beleaguerment throughout the First World War was as complete as that of blockaded Germany. A corrupt government and undeveloped industries found her unprepared for a modern war, and essential materials, which allies or neutrals might have supplied, could reach her fighting front only in the smallest quantities after interminable and expensive railroad transit from distant ports like Archangel and Vladivostok.

Meanwhile, on May 1, 1915, between Gorlice and Tarnow, Falkenhayn

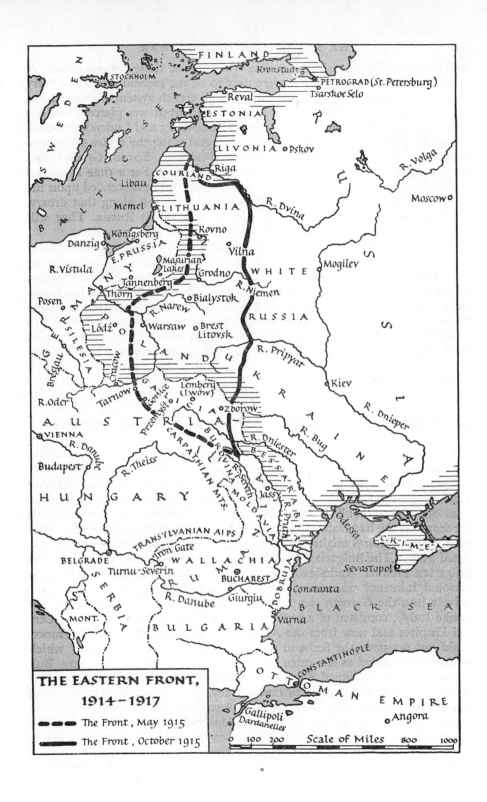

THE EASTERN FRONT,
1914–1917

▪▪▪ The Front, May 1915

▬▬ The Front, October 1915

0   100   200   Scale of Miles   800   1000

had launched his offensive in Russia with one of those concentrations of artillery which, as we have said, were now to be the tactical feature in every theater. But here, in Russia, was no bristling trench system with machine-gun nests at every hundred yards. The Russian front was pierced, and the great Russian retirement began. In July, Hindenburg and Ludendorff struck across the river Narew. Fighting became general along the entire eight hundred miles of the Eastern front. Warsaw, Bialystok, Kovno, Grodno, and Brest Litovsk fell in August. Vilna fell in September. For a time it seemed that Petrograd was in danger. Winter in its rigors at last descended upon the front, and the exhausted Russian armies came to a rest along that dreary, indefinite morass that lies between Poland and White Russia. They still held Riga in the north and the Austrian Bukovina in the south.

The Russian retirement of 1915 resembled the campaign of 1812 — and the campaign of 1941 of more recent memory. But in 1915 there was no Russian recovery. The retirement cost Russia 15 per cent of her territories, 10 per cent of her railroads, and 30 per cent of her industries. Of her population, 20 per cent were dispersed or passed under Austro-German rule. "Scorched earth," in these days, was not the thorough operation it was to become in the Second World War, but the retirement nevertheless was marked everywhere by extensive and deliberate devastation. The Russian Army's casualties are said to have amounted to 2,500,000 in killed, wounded, and prisoners.

THE ENTRY OF BULGARIA INTO THE WAR AND THE FALL OF SERBIA

The deterioration of the Allied position in the Near East tempted wavering Balkan governments to consult their interests and lean toward the more successful power. In particular Bulgaria, lying astride the road between Turkey and the Central Empires, was in a most delicate position. She had come out of the Second Balkan War of 1913 defeated and revengeful. On all her frontiers she had claims to make and wrongs to right, and it seemed that the Central Empires might be more able to give her satisfaction at the disputed points. The Bulgarian Tsar, Ferdinand, was a German prince, and the Bulgarian Premier, Radoslavov, was a prominent Germanophile, and their personal influence was strong enough at last to swing their country decisively into the German camp. Bulgaria's diplomatic history in 1915, not unlike Italy's, consisted of a repetition of inducements, now from the Central Empires and now from the Allies. But the Allies, Britain and France, could not persuade the Serbs to cede the portions of their territory which Bulgaria demanded as her price for joining them. In September 1915, Bulgaria and Turkey signed a convention which granted Bulgaria a minor "rectification" of her frontier toward Turkey. In the same month she signed a secret agreement with Germany and Austria-Hungary to make war on Serbia in return for Serbian territory in Macedonia and along the Morava.

Venizelos, the Greek Premier, would have used the Bulgarian crisis to bring his country into the war on the Allied side. Greece and Serbia, by a treaty of 1913, were bound to each other's defense against the aggression of "a third Power" — that is to say, Bulgaria — and Serbia had agreed to contribute to the common struggle a force of 150,000 men. But it was obvious that Serbia was too preoccupied with Austria-Hungary and with the prospective attack from Bulgaria to be able to muster so large a force for the co-operative defense of Greece. Venizelos sought an audience with the Greek King, Constantine, and, in the course of what must have been a long and grilling interview, obtained the royal consent to secure the missing 150,000 men from the Allies. Probably, in the heat of the moment, neither Venizelos nor the King realized the real consequences of their decision. But France and Britain took Venizelos at his word, and on October 2, 1915, the French minister at Athens formally announced the arrival at Salonika of the first detachments of the Allied forces. During the next few days the entire Salonika area came under Allied occupation. The French General Sarrail was put in command. Venizelos, now protesting lamely and too late against "this unqualified violation of our soil," was given orders to resign. A new government was formed in Athens which declared itself to be neutral. Greece thereafter remained an inactive but uncomfortable spectator of the fall of Serbia.

That fall came quickly. On October 6, 1915 a joint German, Austro-Hungarian, and Bulgarian army converged upon the little country. In 1914 the Serbs had beaten off two Austrian offensives. But they were now assailed by odds which even Serbian bravery could not be expected to withstand. They put up a gallant fight, and they fought alone. The townspeople of Nish, the temporary headquarters of the Serbian Government, hung out their decorations in hourly expectation of their French and British allies from Salonika, who never came. At the end of October the Serbian Army was in full retreat across the Kossovo and up the defiles of the Albanian mountains amid the rain and snow and mud of autumn. Less than 100,000 survivors reached points along the Adriatic coast, whence they were rescued by Allied ships. The aged King Peter of Serbia accompanied the retirement to its bitter end, carried on a stretcher. It has been estimated that Serbia lost one-sixth of her population by enemy action, flight, epidemics, and famine. The Allied forces under General Sarrail, ignored and undisturbed by the victorious German, Austro-Hungarian, and Bulgarian army in Serbia, remained in occupation — for the time being in useless occupation — of Salonika.

The fall of Serbia ended the isolation of Turkey from her European allies. The four Powers, Germany, Austria-Hungary, Bulgaria, and Turkey, now constituted a single Quadruple Alliance, rounded out by the recent advances in Russia, all conveniently operating on "interior lines." An immediate consequence, so far as Britain and France were concerned, was to be their abandonment of the Dardanelles. If the Anglo-French forces could not defeat Turkey when Turkey fought alone, they could hardly expect to defeat her now that German and Austrian units and munitions were available to stiffen the Turkish defenses. The Allies were consoled perhaps by the skill and cheapness of the eventual withdrawal. There was no "Coruña" as had been dreaded.[1] But it was a sad and mortifying end to a great enterprise. In the first week of January 1916, 135,000 men were re-embarked from the Dardanelles with hardly a casualty.

4 THE HOME FRONT

FRANCE

The First World War was a war of peoples, and its real history is often to be found less in its Marnes and Tannenbergs than in the grinding, universal struggle on its home fronts. To us today the implications of total war have become a part of our national experience and are almost regarded as "normal." But in 1914 they were new, seldom foreseen, and improperly understood. The great emergencies, as they crowded in upon governments and peoples — the mobilization of resources, the shortages of supplies and munitions, the efficient allocation of man power, the vagaries of morale, the development of new administrative techniques — all these things had to be matters of improvisation, experiment, and often excusable failure.

For France at home, the first event of the war was the political unification of the country under the famous watchword *"L'Union Sacrée."* A truce hushed the antagonisms of parties; fears of social upheavals vanished. Political enemies of long standing hurried to embrace one another and to swear undying devotion to France. On August 26, 1914, Viviani, the French Premier,[1] in recognition of the *Union Sacrée,* reconstituted his cabinet and included even Socialists and Marxists among his chosen colleagues. Almost unnoticed meanwhile, the government established a state of siege, imposed a censorship of the press, and put the police under military control. The High Command made all the major decisions of policy,[2] and President Poincaré ruled by decree.

The people lived momentarily in that rarefied ecstasy which everywhere seemed to belong to the early days of the war. They expected the fighting to be a short and vivid episode. The first communiqués reported the glorious advance into the lost provinces of Alsace-Lorraine. The faithful ally Russia had put her irresistible millions into motion. The British Expeditionary Force had debarked on French soil. In this state of mind the government stood above error and criticism. The people of France surrendered their lives and liberties to their elected leaders and waited in suspense for news of victory.

But by the end of the first month of war the mood had changed. The advance into Alsace-Lorraine had been repulsed with heavy losses, and the German vanguard had passed Mons (see p. 18). Refugees began to trail into Paris from the northeast with stories of the stupendous German invasion and of the systematic terrorism of the German troops. On August 31 the French Government left for Bordeaux.

In September 1914, after the Battle of the Marne, France began to encounter in all their force the great "economic" problems of the war. The

French Army was suffering appalling losses. General Joffre, the Commander in Chief, persisted in the belief that the war would be of short duration and maintained all along the fighting front a prodigal expenditure of material and human life. During October the so-called war of position which had now developed on the Aisne and in Picardy involved a "wastage" of 150,000 men, of whom a third were killed or taken prisoner. Millerand, the Minister of War, felt obliged at last to remind the Commander in Chief that the present rate of sacrifice of the nation's effectives could not go on forever.

The expenditure of munitions surpassed all calculations. History could offer no precedent, and the mind could hardly conceive, of a battle extending along three hundred miles of front and lasting for days, weeks, and even months. During August 1914 the general economic confusion had retarded — it had been expected to retard — the output of the national arsenals. But on the resumption of work, the production of shells corresponded to the expenditure of a single army corps. In mid-September scarcely a month's reserve of shells was left. The enemy's occupation of the northeast departments had robbed the country of 40 per cent of its coal deposits and 90 per cent of its iron ores. Of 125 blast furnaces in France, 95 lay in areas affected by the war. Mobilization had withdrawn thousands of skilled workers from industry and was withdrawing more with every month. The personnel at the great armament plant of Le Creusot, for instance, was nearly halved. Millerand, with the help of leading manufacturers, threshed out schemes for stepping up the supply of munitions. In May 1915, Albert Thomas the Socialist, a man with wide experience of labor conditions and an engineer's knowledge of technical processes, was made Under Secretary of State for Artillery and Munitions and given "the most minute control over all branches of the manufacture of artillery material." Several classes of skilled workers were exempted from military service and returned to their workshops. In 1915, France felt the first sharp pinch of a labor shortage.

In the week before Christmas 1914 the French Government returned from Bordeaux to Paris, and the chambers once more reassembled for their normal sessions. The stabilization of the front induced a feeling of security, of which political factions took advantage to reopen their old antagonisms. The loss of life and the shortage of munitions provided material enough, if material were wanted, for criticism. The parliamentary committees began to make the most persistent investigations into the government's conduct of the war.[3] They toured the front and inspected the factories; they even sent petitions and deputations to President Poincaré. At last, in October 1915, after having weathered months of stormy interpellations, Viviani went the way of so many premiers of the Third Republic and resigned from office. Perhaps it was a healthy sign that her normal parliamentary activities should be resumed, but France also resumed her habit of too constantly changing her ministers and ministries. The *Union Sacrée* was a little less united than a year before.

Aristide Briand succeeded Viviani, and his first wartime ministry lasted from October 1915 to December 1916. His choice of cabinet colleagues was broad and varied, and conformed to the spirit of the *Union Sacrée*. Thomas remained Under Secretary for Artillery and Munitions. But it was soon evident that the change of Premier had not satisfied the malcontents in the Chamber, and Briand was soon being subjected to the same sort of persecution that had driven Viviani from office. Clemenceau was now president of the Parliamentary Committees of Foreign Affairs and the Army, and he directed his critical assaults in particular against the High Command. The offensive in the Champagne in September 1915, an offensive which Joffre had promised "would compel the Germans to retire to the Meuse and possibly end the war," had resulted, like all the other offensives, in a bloody repulse, and there seemed to be no limit to the fiendish liberality with which the army commanders squandered human life.

France, in fact, had come face to face with an acute form of the problem which, sooner or later, every belligerent encountered, namely, the old persistent feud between military and civilian authorities. It was inevitable that, in time of war, increased powers should be allocated to the military authorities. While the French Government had been at Bordeaux, President Poincaré had ruled by decree under the avowed guidance of the High Command. But on the government's return to Paris the chambers had begun to carp and challenge, and the old liberties of free speech were not to be denied them. The High Command, however, was by now more difficult to dislodge; it had almost become a "little government" in itself. Briand, supported by all the talent and pertinacity of the parliamentary committees, could not break its powers; only the disastrous campaign at Verdun in 1916 could discredit it enough to enable the prerogatives of the country's political leadership to be re-established.

BRITAIN

Britain in August 1914, like France, had successfully established a political truce at home. The German invasion of Belgium had rallied the lagging conscience and convictions of the entire British people. Irish Home Rule, women's suffrage, trade-union unrest, all the strikes and factions of the previous months, somehow lost their relevance and rationale. On August 5, 1914, Lord Kitchener was appointed Secretary of State for War, and probably no other man in England so enjoyed the confidence and the hero worship of the people at large. In October, Lord Fisher, a vehement old sailor and one of the creators of Britain's dreadnought navy, became First Sea Lord, and made an appropriate colleague for Winston Churchill, then First Lord of the Admiralty (see Glossary). Under the Defense of the Realm Act (DORA) the government obtained the passage of emergency measures which were tantamount to martial law. In November 1914, Asquith, the Prime Minister, created a War Council, chiefly of Cabinet ministers, to be a sort of political general staff for the conduct of the war.

Leadership and authority were thus secured. But long-term policies were harder to come by. The nation, and all but a few of its leaders, had no comprehension of the real nature of the struggle to which they were now committed. For the average Briton, war had always been the business of a small professional army, interfering only indirectly with his normal life. Kitchener's "Call to Arms" in August 1914 and the opening of a nation-wide recruiting campaign were things new to his historical experience. In November 1914, Asquith gave out in the House of Commons that the British regular army then numbered over 1,000,000 men and that 700,000 recruits had joined since the outbreak of war, not including 200,000 Territorials. But a problem newer and more obstinate than man power, the supply of this huge force with the arms and equipment of modern continental warfare, was now to engage the government and the country.

Military conservatism recoiled from the unprecedented. The higher army officers, with excusable pride, expected to repeat their old colonial triumphs in France and Belgium. Kitchener's own experience had been in fields where mobility counted for more than munitions, and the commanders of the British Expeditionary Force in France, such as French and Haig, had all made their names as cavalry generals on the South African veld. The needs of the new war of position were entirely lost on military opinion in London — and, in particular, on Kitchener. Toward the end of 1914, Field Marshal French from his headquarters in Flanders was sending almost daily telegrams to the War Office pleading for more shells, and yet more shells. Asquith resorted to the usual tactics of government leaders in a quandary and turned over his problem to a committee. Between October 1914 and April 1915 he successively created a Cabinet Committee on Munitions, an Armaments Output Committee, and a Munitions War Committee. Not without reason were these early days of the war called "the golden age of committeedom."

The press became restless, and in May 1915 Lord Northcliffe, through the columns of his *Daily Mail,* began to attack Kitchener in person. Copies of the offending newspaper were ceremoniously burned on the London Stock Exchange, but knowledge of the "shell crisis" was now public property. Tongues and pens were loosed; old fears and discretions went by the board. Lurid stories appeared of batteries at the front which had existed for months on two rounds per gun per day. British artillery was outclassed by the German in caliber and range; British machine guns, trench mortars, hand grenades, all the paraphernalia of the new war of position, were disastrously insufficient and inefficient. At Neuve Chapelle, it was said, British infantry had "gone over the top" behind a scant one-hour or two-hour artillery preparation and had been slaughtered by the thousand.

Meanwhile the Dardanelles had become an additional anxiety. Lord Fisher resigned from the Admiralty in May 1915, after a somewhat petulant quarrel with Churchill. Asquith was persuaded at last to reconstruct his government. On May 25 he announced a coalition to include all parties, and appointed his former Chancellor of the Exchequer, Lloyd George, to a newly created department, the Ministry of Munitions.

Asquith's Coalition resembled its earlier analogy in France. At a moment of national emergency it was natural to wish to invite the counsel of all the nation's acknowledged leaders irrespective of party. Churchill, paying the price for the ill success of the Dardanelles campaign, of which, reputedly, he had been the principal inspirer, was the most notable absentee in the new combination. Grey remained Foreign Secretary, and Kitchener remained Secretary for War. Curzon, Lansdowne, Balfour, Bonar Law, Austen Chamberlain (Conservatives), Simon (Liberal), and Henderson (Labor) received posts. The War Council, Asquith's creation of November 1914, continued to meet under the name of the Dardanelles Committee, a name which gives an indication of its main interest at the time.

The Coalition signaled the real emergence of Britain's great wartime leader, David Lloyd George. He was now fifty-two years of age and at the height of his powers. He had followed a varied political career of pronouncedly radical leanings. He had risen from poor beginnings, through an apprenticeship in law, to represent his native Welsh constituency in the House of Commons. For two decades there was not an important political fight in which he did not figure and in which he did not take sides against established wealth and privilege. He was an unconventional but magnificent orator, deadly in repartee, and a born master of mass emotions. In 1908, Asquith had made him Chancellor of the Exchequer, a post which was no more than his evident abilities deserved, but he was a mercurial, troublesome colleague and already too much of "a mirror to public applause." He is said to have at first opposed Britain's entry into the war, but after the German invasion of Belgium he inevitably felt the compulsion of crowd magnetism and threw himself into the crusade against Germany with the same ardor with which he had formerly thrown himself into crusades against the social evils of his day. His irrepressible energies craved to be occupied, and he was soon putting a busy, probing finger into every administrative problem which the Asquith government appeared to be meeting with insufficient determination. In May 1915 he became Minister of Munitions and faced a work as huge and as anxious as his heart could desire.

Lloyd George, against all precedent, appointed several businessmen and professional experts as his ministerial colleagues. He had surveys made of the industrial potentialities of Britain — and of America — and laid his plans to equip a British army of seventy divisions for a prolonged campaign in the trench network of France. He toured the manufacturing centers in England and Wales. He met representatives of owners, trade-unions, and workers. He secured the passage of a Ministry of Munitions Act which gave him a virtual dictatorship over British industry.

Statistics sometimes give a good idea of the facts. During the war British factories produced, in round numbers, 4,000,000 rifles, 240,000 machine guns, between 200,000,000 and 250,000,000 shells, and over 40,000 planes,[4] and it fell to Lloyd George to be the director of this huge productivity at that most difficult stage when it was being organized and developed. In June 1916 he left the Ministry of Munitions to succeed Kitchener at the War Office. The great "shell crisis" was a thing of the past. In July 1916 the British Army fought the Battle of the Somme, that first of the great "battles of material," as the Germans called them, and inflicted the first lasting wounds on the body and soul of military Germany.

In 1915 and 1916 there began to appear in Britain that concomitant of total war, a labor shortage. The pace of recruiting and the production of materials and munitions approached the point beyond which further augmentation seemed to be physically impossible. Enlistment in 1915 had been particularly heavy in the big industrial districts, and the more intelligent and skilled workers had always been the first to answer the "Call to Arms." Kitchener objected to restrictions upon recruiting and objected even more to returning a man to civil life once he had joined the colors. Attempts to transfer workers from one occupation to another, or from one locality to another, were regarded by the workers with suspicion, and generally failed. The "dilution" of skilled workers with unskilled or semiskilled workers seemed to offer one solution of the labor shortage, but a special agreement had to be made with the trade-unions to lay their traditional fears of scab labor. The workers found themselves, for the first time in their history, in a strong bargaining position, and both government and employers were afraid of incurring disputes with them in the midst of a national emergency. In July 1915, 200,000 coal miners in South Wales went on strike and incidentally demonstrated how thin was the happy truce under which all the pre-1914 discontents were supposed to have been so safely buried.

In July 1915, Parliament passed a National Registration Act, providing for a thoroughgoing census of the population for military and industrial purposes, and it is again a reflection on the novelty of the situation that the bill was stubbornly contested in all its stages. In August 1915, Asquith appointed a Cabinet committee to investigate the nation's resources of man power. At that time 3,000,000 men had offered themselves for military service, and casualties in killed and wounded had already exceeded a tenth of the number. At the end of the year, Lord Derby was directing an intensified recruiting campaign, the "Derby Scheme," as it was popularly called, which was in effect a last despairing effort on behalf of voluntary service.

In January 1916, Asquith introduced conscription for single men and childless widowers. In May 1916, under the Universal Military Service Act, he introduced conscription for all men, married and unmarried, between the ages of eighteen and forty-one. Ireland was excluded from the act, and special tribunals were set up to grant or withhold the exemption of "conscientious objectors." Labor and the trade-unions made some show of resistance, but Asquith succeeded in obtaining that "progressive general consent" he had hoped for, and the British people, in a spirit of grim acquiescence, bowed to the new discipline and to the absolute reversal of every tradition and principle for which they had stood in the past.

From 1915 onward, women were progressively employed, not only in munition factories, but in all branches of the war effort — as agricultural workers in the Land Army and Timber Corps, as drivers and conductors in the transport services, and in the police — to say nothing of the nursing and ambulance services. By mid-1916 nearly 350,000 women and girls were thus employed, and by the end of the war their number was well over 800,000. Women's auxiliary services were attached to the armed forces. They provided cooks, canteen workers, secretaries, telephonists, interpreters. In 1917 the Women's Army Auxiliary Corps (WAAC) and the Women's Royal

Naval Service (WRNS) were formed and, in 1918, the Women's Royal Air Force (WRAF) — with a total enrollment of over 90,000. We have somewhat forgotten today what an extraordinary novelty a woman in overalls or uniform used once to be. Certainly the First World War, on the home fronts of all the belligerents, was the great emancipator of women. The Representation of the People Act, passed by Parliament early in 1918, adopting women's suffrage, was an inevitable recognition of devoted service.

IRELAND

At this point we must speak, somewhat parenthetically, of one incident that occurred in 1916, the Irish Easter Rebellion.

In recent times Ireland had become a laboratory of usual twentieth-century problems — religious, agrarian, and industrial problems, overlaid upon the typical striving of an "oppressed minority" for political independence. Southern Ireland, or "Nationalist" Ireland, was Catholic, and her culture and traditions were Celtic. Northern Ireland, or Ulster, was Protestant, and her culture and traditions were Scotch-English. Between the two, and between Southern Ireland and England, stood centuries of misunderstanding and conflict. The Irish people, by temperament, were mercurial and quarrelsome, and their memories were very long and unforgiving.

In 1914, Ireland's status was still governed by the Act of Union of 1800, when the local Irish parliament at Dublin, after a short, experimental career, had been merged into the British Parliament at Westminster. Irish affairs were administered through a Chief Secretary, of Cabinet rank, in London and a Lord Lieutenant, representing the King, in Dublin. The country's politics in the years since 1800 had centered round the agitation in Southern Ireland for Home Rule. Northern Ireland desired to preserve the British connection or, in the event of Home Rule, to secure the complete separation of Southern Ireland from herself. The situation was always complicated, first, by the existence of a strong body of Conservative landed proprietors in Southern Ireland, who were often of British origin or of British sympathy; and second, by the persisting fears of the British Government that an independent Ireland, in a war involving a European Power, might be used as a hostile strategic base.

In July and August 1914, Ireland had been in the midst of a serious crisis. Asquith's Home Rule Act had just been passed — the royal assent was given after the actual outbreak of the war — and then another bill was hurriedly passed suspending the act "for the duration." But the act had not mollified the traditional hatreds of the Irish parties. In Northern Ireland the Ulster leaders, Sir Edward Carson and F. E. Smith,[5] had for some time been busy building up bodies of volunteers of a type we have since come to recognize in the Fascist squads and the German Free Corps of a later day; while in Southern Ireland other volunteers in turn were recruiting, drilling, gunrunning, and generally aping the inflammatory tactics of their northern antagonists. It needed the greater war in Europe to distract the Irish people from their littler war in Ireland and to induce them to share in the same kind of political truce that England had herself established. John Redmond, the Nationalist leader in Southern Ireland, was not much mistaken when, in the House of Commons on August 3, 1914, he had declared the loyalty of his countrymen and had assured the British Government that it could safely withdraw its troops from Irish soil.

In 1914, Ireland, especially rural Ireland, was markedly prosperous. Thanks to good legislation and to intelligent co-operation on the part of the farmer, Irish agriculture was in a better condition than at any time in living memory. The war proceeded to drive up the prices of all agricultural produce, and Ireland seemed almost like a favored neutral growing rich upon the necessities of a warring neighbor.

The Easter Rebellion of 1916 therefore could hardly have arisen from those economic aggravations to which so many of the country's ancient troubles have so often been charged. Nor, in view of the apparent popularity of the war, could the Rebellion be said to have claimed the sympathies of any large section of the Irish people. During the war upward of 250,000 Irishmen served in the British forces by voluntary enlistment, and 40,000 were killed or died of wounds.[6] But Asquith had been most unwise in some of his official appointments. In August 1914, for instance, he had made F. E. Smith, hotfoot from his Ulster seditions, press censor in England. In May 1915, with the formation of the Coalition, Carson appeared as Attorney General, to be followed in October 1915 by F. E. Smith. Then during 1915 and 1916 there was a constantly recurring fear that the British Government meant to extend some form of military conscription to Ireland. The recalcitrant minority in Ireland had, or thought it had, good reasons for renewed recalcitrance, and perhaps, in addition, it was not wholly innocent of secret German aid. At all events, Sinn Fein, the Irish Volunteers, and the Citizen Army in Southern Ireland planned open rebellion.[7]

The British Government meanwhile had allowed the agitation by these groups to grow without serious interference. The agitation may have represented a very small numerical strength, but it was well organized and endowed with all the desperate power of corporate fanaticism. Redmond and the Chief Secretary refused to take alarm. Police warnings were not regarded very seriously. The outbreak, when it came, therefore came as a surprise. It bore all the signs of being another of those flank attacks upon the tyrant England of which the past history of Ireland records several examples. England's misfortune once more, it seemed, was to be Ireland's opportunity.

The Irish Easter Rebellion of 1916 was well planned but unlucky. A German freighter, the *Aud,* was to land munitions near Queenstown; Sir Roger Casement, late of the British consular service, and recently engaged in Germany in trying to seduce the loyalty of Irish prisoners of war, was to be put ashore from a German U-boat; Irish Volunteers and the Citizen Army were to seize strategic points in Dublin and in various parts of the country. But the *Aud* was intercepted by British destroyers and scuttled by her crew; Casement was duly put ashore on a lonely stretch of the Kerry coast, but lost his way and was arrested. Nevertheless, on Easter Monday, April 24, 1916, the Rebellion began. The Sinn Feiners issued a call to the Irish people to support their "Provisional Government." The British Government rushed reinforcements to Ireland and proclaimed martial law. In a week the Rebellion had been suppressed, and its leaders put under lock and key.

It is far from easy to estimate the seriousness of the Irish Easter Rebellion of 1916. About a thousand of the "Irish Republican Army" are said to have been engaged, and the loss of life among British troops, mostly half-trained youngsters, amounted to nearly a hundred. The figures are not very considerable. But the British Government took a grave view. Fifteen rebel leaders were executed. Casement was taken to London, tried for treason, and hanged. Eamon de Valera and William Cosgrave were among those whose sentences were commuted to penal servitude. Arthur Griffith and Michael Collins were "deported" to jails in England. There were debates in the Commons and the Lords, and negotiations with Nationalist and Ulster leaders. But no settlement was reached. On the contrary, the situation, whether or not it had been serious in April, certainly was serious now. The execution of the rebel leaders, though perfectly in accordance with the law, revolted many Irishmen otherwise loyal to Britain and, by a masterpiece of British callousness and ineptitude, F. E. Smith had been the prosecutor at Casement's trial — "a shocking conjunction," as one historian has described it. The old Nationalists as a party, from this time onward, began to lose their hold, and Sinn Fein was well launched upon its career to ultimate power in Southern Ireland.

RUSSIA

In Russia four authorities participated in the government of the country and thence in the conduct of the war — the bureaucracy, the High Command, the Duma, and the Tsar — and it was in their complex interplay and counterplay that the inner political history of Russia during these years may be said to have lain.

The bureaucracy, in a sense, was the ruling class of old Russia. Peter the Great, at the end of the seventeenth century, had taken over, and largely re-created, the bureaucracy as he found it. Bent on centralizing all authority in himself, but mistrusting the existing lordlings of his realm, who were either too independent or too provincial for his purpose, he had no choice but to pick his own officials and work out his own official system. The great hierarchy which he then bequeathed to his successors was subjected from time to time to reforms of detail, but never lost the character he had given it. In 1914 it was made up of a vast corps of "professional administrators," including the Council of the Empire, the Council of Ministers, the ministries, the judges and the courts of justice, the police, the provincial governors and governments — all controlled from a single center and responsible to a single autocrat. Its ranks, to a considerable extent, were recruited from the universities, and no doubt it contained men of culture and ability. But it suffered from all the vices of long-entrenched privilege. It was rigid and cumbrous, indolent and corrupt. In that fateful year 1914 it was suddenly confronted by an emergency which proved to be too great for it.

Nor had many weeks passed before disagreements arose between the bureaucracy and the Russian parliament, the Duma. The want of confidence of the two institutions in one another was of long standing and indeed dated from their earliest association. Neither had any conception of that responsibility of government to legislature which parliamentary systems of the West take for granted. The Duma of 1905 had been a half-hearted concession to popular pressure. The Tsar admitted that he had been forced to create it "in a moment of fever." He feared and detested it, and he was soon glad enough of a chance to retract its more radical powers. In the years that followed, drastic curtailment of the electoral laws had left the Duma a very parody of what a legislative assembly should have been. On the outbreak of the war the Duma assembled for a short session of one day, August 8, 1914, and the Deputies, forgetting their grievances, surrendered to the passion of the moment and pledged themselves body and soul to the support of their Tsar. Thus for a time Russia too achieved her *Union Sacrée*. Only a small, despised group of Deputies on the extreme Left had dared to vote in opposition.

The Duma then adjourned for six months, the Tsar's ministers addressed themselves to their several labors, and the Duma, supposedly paralyzed by reaction and war, was expected to lapse into desuetude. But as 1914 passed and 1915 wore on, and as the disasters at the front flowed back upon the dismayed country, the Duma and the people it represented began to form working organizations of their own to try to make up for the patent inefficiencies of bureaucratic government. The chief of these organizations grew out of the Union of Zemstvos and Towns,[8] managing a vast array of hospitals and relief works, and it was the Duma and the Duma's Deputies in particular that provided the main driving force of its labors. Certainly a country had come to a strange pass when the work of whole government departments had to be done by popular, improvised, and largely volunteer enterprises outside the regular circles of officialdom.

Tsar Nicholas II was the inadequate figurehead of the Russian system. He had been bred in the school of his redoubtable sire, Alexander III. He believed with all the fervor of his pious nature that autocracy and orthodoxy were the twin pillars of the Russian fabric, and that their preservation was his God-appointed task. He was Autocrat of all the Russias, absolute ruler of 175,000,000 human souls and of one-sixth of the earth's surface, "Supreme Defender and Preserver" of the Orthodox Faith, Commander in Chief of the Army and Navy, and head of the most complicated bureaucracy in the world. He would have made an ideal country gentleman, devoting his life to his wife and children, his farms and his sport, but he had not one qualification for the glittering office he was actually called to occupy.

The Tsarina Alexandra was formerly Princess Alix of Hesse-Darmstadt, a granddaughter of Queen Victoria of England. She was German by birth and English by upbringing, and never overcame, or even seemed to try to overcome, the strangeness of her surroundings in Russia. Naturally she became unpopular and, mistaking the cause, she withdrew more and more into an impenetrable domestic isolation. Gradually shunned, yet blaming others, impassive, haughty, and cold, she seemed almost to defy the approaches of other human beings, and the imperial family virtually imprisoned itself in the Palace of Tsarskoe Selo, twenty miles from St. Petersburg, away from friends, from advice, and even from current information. There, during her many hours of solitude, she gave herself up to a sort of pietism, not always of the healthiest. Latterly she was nervous, hysterical, and sometimes very ill. Her son, the Tsarevitch Alexis, her fifth child, was a hemophiliac, and it did not help her mental condition to have to realize that she herself had been the transmitter of his ailment. She befriended a stupid, characterless woman, Madame Vyrubova, as self-persecuted as herself, who assisted at her religious exercises, and she fell under the spell of the debauched monkish charlatan, Gregory Rasputin, whose hypnotic gifts had purportedly been able to relieve the hemorrhages of the suffering little Tsarevitch.

In this strange household reposed the ultimate fate of a vast and populous empire. Perhaps it is not necessary for us to build up any further a picture so fraught with the possibilities of revolution. But we may venture the remark that what is most striking about the Russian situation in the years 1914–17 is the incredible patience of the human species, which can bear so much abuse and tyranny before it breaks down under the strain.

Both France and Britain, as we have seen, passed through their munitions shortages, but in Russia the shortage was far more serious and incurable. The Russian Army was larger; the background of industries, supplies, and communications was smaller; the bureaucratic machinery was less adaptable to the crisis; and, finally, General Sukhomlinov, the Russian Minister of War, if not actually corrupt, was about as negligent an officer as was ever inflicted upon a department of state. The shortage was already apparent in September 1914, and seriously handicapped the Russian drive into Galicia against the Austrians. At the end of 1914, Russian factories were producing only a third of the shells required at the front. In several sectors, infantry attacked only at night, with the bayonet, because the men had no artillery support and no rifle ammunition. In true Russian manner, the officials responsible were playing hide-and-seek with one another and, in elaborate apologies, were shifting the blame wherever they could.

The Duma had been called together in February 1915 to pass the budget, and opened that campaign of criticism which it hoped might harry the government into some sort of action. Rodzianko, the President of the Duma, persuaded the Tsar at last to set up a Special Council, much on the lines of the contemporary Ministry of Munitions in Britain. Rodzianko urged particularly the dismissal of Sukhomlinov, the Minister of War. Meanwhile conferences were going on throughout Russia. Societies and institutions of every kind, official and unofficial, had broken into an uproar of protest and would not be silenced. Liberal Deputies in the Duma formed themselves into a Progressive Bloc demanding "the creation of a government enjoying the confidence of the country." The Union of Zemstvos and Towns was in continuous session. A group of industrial leaders organized itself into a War Industries Committee.

The bureaucracy was far from pleased with the growing revolt against its authority, and reactionary ministers tried to frighten the Tsar with reminders of the subversive violences of 1905. But in June 1915, nonetheless, the first of the Special Councils was set up, and it included members of the bureaucracy, the Duma, the Zemstvos, and the War Industries Committee. At the same time several culpable officials were dismissed, including Sukhomlinov. General Polivanov, an officer popular with the Duma, was appointed Minister of War.

Then suddenly the whole beneficial effect of these reforms was ruined. In August 1915, apparently under the influence of that evil genius, Rasputin, the Tsar dismissed the Grand Duke Nicholas from the command of the army and announced to his astonished ministers that he would assume the post himself. In his curious, half-mystical way he seemed to think that his own self-sacrifice could restore the situation at the front. "Perhaps a sin offering is needed to save Russia," he said. "I shall be the victim. God's will be done!" It was announced simultaneously that General Alekseev, recently commanding an army on the southwestern front, would be the Tsar's Chief of Staff.

The Tsar's decision was catastrophic. In effect, it left the Tsarina — and of course Rasputin — with a sort of regency in all ministerial affairs in Petrograd, while the deluded Tsar ensconced himself quite uselessly at Headquarters. It made the worst possible impression on the country and the army. Corruption and defeat were producing their results, of which desertions at the front, strikes at home, and continued ministerial changes were the eloquent evidence. In September 1915 the Tsar ordered the suspension of the Duma.

Polivanov at the Ministry of War, and the new Special Councils — there were ultimately four of them — exerted themselves against crushing discouragement, and did indeed effect some heartening, but transient, improvements. The "Polivanov drafts" at the front were noted for their good morale. Munitions were relatively more plentiful and, in the course of 1916, the Russian Army was even able to take the offensive and to fight that unexpected action in the southwest, under General Brusilov, the last and most spectacular military effort of Imperial Russia (see p. 60) .

But the Tsarina now held the reins. Daily she plied the Tsar at Headquarters with those strange, passionate, half-literate letters of hers, referring constantly to the two main prepossessions of her mind, the sickly little Tsarevitch and "Our Friend," the Man of God, and recommending this or that ministerial change, which the Tsar, that docile autocrat, invariably ordered to be made forthwith. Thus in February 1916, Goremykin, the octogenarian President of the Council of Ministers, resigned and was followed by a succession of the Tsarina's nominees, one of whom, Boris Stürmer, was probably pro-German. In March 1916, Polivanov was dismissed. In the weeks preceding the Revolution, the Tsarina's favorite political mentor seems to have been Protopopov, Minister of the Interior, at one time a safe and well-respected administrator, but latterly a protégé of Rasputin and probably afflicted with a serious mental derangement.

Meanwhile the economic war had not abated its rigors. In 1916 Russia experienced acute food, fuel, and transport crises and, finally and unbelievably, an acute labor crisis. At the end of 1916, the army alone had mobilized 14,500,000 men. It required 300,000 men a month to replace its "wast-age." In round numbers it lost 1,000,000 men in killed and wounded, and 500,000 prisoners, every six months.[9] Even a population of 175,000,000 could not for long endure the loss of its best and bravest at such a rate. At the same time the farms were being depleted, and the Special Councils could not find the labor for their new industrial programs. General Gurko might well write in his report to the Special Council for Defense at the end of 1916 that not only the army, but industry in the rear, "the entire mechanism of the state and the life of the country at large are suffering from a shortage of men." The "Russian steam roller," so belauded in the British and French press, was gradually running down for want of its human fuel.

GERMANY

In August 1914 Germany established her *Burgfriede* — "the peace of the city" — as she called it, using the name which was given to the civil truces of the Middle Ages. In his speech from the throne on August 4 in the Royal Palace in Berlin, the Kaiser uttered the famous words: "I recognize parties no more. I recognize only Germans!" That same day, in special session, the Reichstag by unanimous vote granted the Chancellor's request for war credits. It seemed that Social Democracy and Junkerdom had brought to an end two decades of strife and were joined together in the common defense of Germany. For every class and creed the decision of war had almost the conviction of a religious experience. To have stood aside, to have sown discord, to have remembered old grievances at this grand, historic moment would have been blasphemy against the manifest destiny of the Fatherland.

Germany absorbed with ease the first economic shocks of the war. A mild food panic in August 1914 subsided as quickly as it had begun. There was no run on the banks; there was no general moratorium. The mobilization of the army, the advance on Paris, the repulse of the Russians in East Prussia diverted the public from its immediate fears at home. None of the expected terrors and privations materialized. The people even felt a certain exhilaration at finding how little difference the state of war made to their habits of life. Hotels and restaurants served their usual fare, and shops displayed their usual plenty. The sums spent by the government on requisitions found their way into general circulation, and there was even a minor boom in business. Everyone expected the war would be a "brisk and merry war," a *frischfröhlicher Krieg*, of sudden and tremendous victories.

But farseeing Germans, and one farseeing German in particular, were not easy in mind in regard to the future. The Allied blockade quickly destroyed the greater part of Germany's overseas commerce, and she was now alone, terribly alone, in an encirclement of hostile forces. Though better prepared in a military sense than any other belligerent, Germany had never yet considered the husbanding of her raw materials and food or the efficient regrouping of her noncombatant man power. There were many materials essential to civilized life, and to war, which could not be won from the soil of the Fatherland. The supply of coal and iron was assured, but copper, nickel, tin, mercury, manganese, bauxite, saltpeter and other nitrates, sulphur, asbestos, mineral oils, gasoline, lubricants, and all such tropical or subtropical materials as rubber, cotton, jute, hemp, and silk were no longer obtainable. Other essential materials, for instance phosphates, skins and hides, wool, timber of all kinds, could be produced at home only in small quantities, and normally the nation's requirements had been generously supplemented with foreign imports. Agriculture, prosperous though it seemed, depended on fertilizers and fodder from abroad. Yet the German Army went off gaily to battle in 1914 all oblivious of the huge exertions it was so soon to call upon the home front to make in its behalf, and all ignorant of the certain famine of those material resources without which it could not have held the field for a day.

It was Walther Rathenau, more than any other man, who organized Germany to resist the stringencies which he saw a long war would entail. In 1914 he was one of Germany's leading industrial magnates. He was director of the A.E.G. (*Allgemeine Elektrizitäts-Gesellschaft*), the largest combine in Europe, and of some eighty other companies. His was a mind of infinite interests, equally at home with principles and with detail, and curiously uniting the qualities of poet, philosopher, and man of affairs. He was of Jewish stock, loyal to his race and to his country. Undeniably he emerges after all these years as one of the "great men" of the war.

On August 9, 1914, Rathenau and General von Falkenhayn met and discussed the formation of a new department of state which should have power to control the entire material resources of the Reich. The War Raw Materials Department, the K.R.A. (*Kriegsrohstoffabteilung*), came into being by decree, and Rathenau took up his headquarters as its director in the Prussian Ministry of War. In course of time Rathenau created a number of sub-departments which were organized on the lines of stock companies and were run by businessmen. They bore some analogy to the big combines which distinguished German business; but they worked under government supervision, issued no shares, and made no profits. Their function was to sequestrate the raw materials and transfer them to the manufacturer at such times, at such prices, and in such quantities as would enable him to fulfill his contracts with the government. Almost every week saw the birth of such companies. First came the War Metal Company, then the War Chemicals Company, and then the companies controlling jute, wool, worsted, rubber, cotton, leather, hides, flax, linen, horsehair, and so forth. On April 1, 1915, Rathenau handed over his creation to the Prussian Ministry of War, declaring confidently that Germany's supplies were secure, that the Allied blockade had been defeated, and that a scarcity of essential materials no longer threatened the outcome of the war.

Food supplies proved to be more difficult to maintain than raw materials, if for no other reason than the existence of an absolute shortage which no organizing could resolve and which sooner or later must make itself felt. The government began by issuing simple decrees. The first decree, for instance, on September 1, 1914, prohibited the slaughter of calves. On September 28 came regulations prescribing the degrees of fineness for the milling of flour. "K-bread" made its appearance, a name conveniently ambiguous, as it could signify either "war bread" or "potato bread" (*Kriegsbrot* or *Kartoffelbrot*). In January 1915 the government introduced the rationing of flour and bread and issued its first flour and bread cards. But all these measures proved insufficient and unrelated, and in June 1915 the government at last set up an Imperial Grain Office, somewhat on the lines of Rathenau's companies.

The Imperial Grain Office worked very well. That wretched hydra of war-time scarcity, the bread line, was kept within manageable bounds. Every citizen — man, woman, and child — was assured a daily ration at reasonable prices. Before the war, protectionist policy had made Germany the home of the highest grain prices in the world but, thanks to the new office, German bakers were now selling bread at prices below those obtaining in most of the belligerent and neutral countries. The Imperial Grain Office became a pattern for other food offices. Grain happens to be an easy commodity to administer. It is durable, it can be stored and distributed in any bulk, and it is classifiable under simple types. Complex and perishable foods, such as fruit, vegetables, meat, fish, and dairy produce, present far greater difficulties. But the government was compelled to extend its controls. Shortages here and there were threatened, or some particular depredation of the profiteer was discovered, and one by one almost every type of food was brought under the surveillance of an appropriate authority.

Outside government controls lay the numerous substitutes (ersatz materials) which now appeared on the market. The days before the war had already known such preparations as margarine, artificial honey, artificial coffee, gravy tablets, dried soups, and puddings, which were made from substances far different from what they represented. But preparation which had once been made for cheapness were made now because no better could be bought at any price. In course of time, substitutes multiplied and took a recognized place in the nation's diet. The chef and the housewife learned a new domestic lore and cooked attractive dishes out of materials that once would hardly have been given to cattle.

The shortage of fodder was hardly less serious, and not less difficult to meet, than that of food. It affected all beasts of burden; it affected dairy produce, animal fats, manure, and leather. In normal times Germany imported the larger part of her fodder, bran, oats, oil cake, and meal of various kinds, and she was now obliged to supplement her restricted supplies with makeshifts and substitutes. In 1914 the authorities opened a drive against waste; garbage was saved; potato peels, fruit parings, and food refuse were put aside. New drying processes converted potatoes, potato plants, turnip tops, and chopped straw into "stretching" material to mix with more acceptable forms of cattle feed.

Meanwhile German science and invention had undertaken a colossal program. Processes hitherto uneconomic were developed into important industries. Human ingenuity was never so taxed nor yet so resourceful. Aluminum was extracted from native clays and largely took the place of copper in munitions and electric fittings. Calcium carbide provided illuminants and replaced certain hardening metals required in the manufacture of steel.

Wood-pulp products saved the textile industry from a complete breakdown and were used for packing materials, artificial silk and paper, yarns, and army sandbags. Glycerine was produced from sugar, and oil from seeds, animal tissues, and shale. There were processes for regenerating rubber, and toward the end of the war small quantities of synthetic rubber were produced. Altogether some 200 to 300 patents were taken out on artificial rubbers and substitutes for rubber. Perhaps the greatest single achievement of German science was the manufacture of nitrates from the air. Huge state factories were built in 1915, sufficient to produce all the nitrates necessary for explosives and in part also for artificial fertilizers.

Germany entirely overhauled such of her trade with neutrals as still survived, or remained independent of, the all-pervasive Allied blockade. In 1914 purchasing missions of all kinds, German and Austrian, industrial, military, and civil, had scrambled in the same neutral markets, and their senseless competition had driven up prices and depressed the rates of exchange. The situation was intolerable and could not be allowed to continue. Helfferich at the Imperial Treasury gradually developed a system of co-operative purchase, and at last succeeded in forming a Central Purchasing Company — once more a company after Rathenau's prototype — the Z.E.G. (*Zentral Einkaufs-Gesellschaft*), which would have the monopoly of all German purchases abroad. Similar companies were formed in Austria and Hungary.

The Z.E.G. fought as difficult and as complicated a battle as any on the home front. In 1916 its personnel numbered more than 4,000, and its turnover reached billions. It was the greatest trading organization in the world. And for a time it seemed to have reasserted the purchasing power of Germany in neutral countries. Statistics show that Germany competed successfully with Britain, for instance, in Holland and Denmark, and indeed diverted to herself a goodly proportion of the dairy produce which Britain normally imported from those countries. Germany's exports to neutrals in the course of the war could not always be prevented from declining, but the flow of imports from neutrals was tolerably well maintained. It is certain that without the Z.E.G. what was left of Germany's foreign trade would have been swallowed up by the neutral speculator and profiteer.

Rathenau's K.R.A., Helfferich's Z.E.G., the Imperial Grain Office, the nitrate factories, and all their several subsidiaries and auxiliaries throughout the Reich made up a vast interrelated system for the prosecution of total war. German officialdom accomplished a heroic undertaking with its customary efficiency and without favors or corruption. But by 1916 the system was already beginning to fail. Clothing and clothing materials, leather, and thread were already growing scarce. Cotton was not to be had, and wool was a luxury. The better stocks of leather went to the army, and the civilian had to be content with what was left. Substitute leathers appeared on the market, and the poorer people were clattering about the streets ingeniously shod with wood. In February 1916 available stocks of clothing were sequestrated, and thenceforth an Imperial Clothing Office rationed all supplies for home consumption.

In May 1916 the government appointed Batocki director of a new War Food Office. The food situation was now giving cause for extreme anxiety,

and there had been considerable agitation in the press for a "Food Dictator." Batocki had recently carried out the reconstruction of the areas in East
Prussia which had been ravaged during the campaign of 1914, and he now
came to Berlin with a record of unusual capacity and the reputation of a
strong man. But the situation was stronger than Batocki. He could only see
justice done, and if he could not create plenty from shortage, he could at
least bring the cold comfort of an equal misery for everyone.

In the beginning, privations had accumulated so slowly that their first ill
effects had passed unnoticed. There was then a joy in asceticism and a com-
panionship in the common discomfort. But the very monotony of hunger
can wear away a man's resistance. Food becomes an obsession; evading the
regulations is the serious business of life; old disciplines lose their force; and
any chaos seems sweeter in the prospect than this ordered and unending
want. Patience is on edge, some stupid, worried official loses his head, and
a dangerous riot breaks out. The whole people seems to suffer from a sort
of mass claustrophobia, and the tangents of its moods or of its weariness may
take any unforeseen direction. The year 1916 closed with the supreme horrors of the "turnip winter." Premature frosts spoiled the potato harvest, now
the basis of so many substitute foods, and the humble turnip became the
staple diet of the German people. The soldier home on leave from the front
found his wife and children not only undernourished, stretching their rations with substitutes, short of fuel, needing almost all the things that make
life tolerable, but looking drab and shoddy, their clothes two, three, and
four years old and many times made over. When a state like this is reached,
pride of race, self-respect, dignity, morale are wearing thin, and a helpless,
consuming poverty is laying its hold upon the nation.

But of all the economic weaknesses to which Germany must attribute her
defeat in the First World War, the greatest, most fundamental, and most
incurable was the shortage of labor. The outbreak of war in 1914 had resulted in an unemployment crisis. Hundreds of businesses had closed, thousands of men had been thrown out of work, and neither the mobilization
nor the new war industries had immediately rectified the situation. In 1915
and 1916 unemployment was transformed into a severe scarcity of labor. The
labor market in the autumn of 1916 was such that two men applied for
every three vacancies. Women and children, prisoners of war, and forced
labor from Belgium and France were put to work. But the shortage gathered
momentum, and a labor shortage, as the nation was soon to learn, becomes
a vicious circle growing ever wider and more ruinous as it persists. Coal
seams, however rich, are of small value when there are not miners enough
to mine them. Railroads, however efficient, will wear out if there are not
men enough in the yards and on the road bed. Coal, railroads, and industry
are interlocked; the deterioration of any one of them will react upon the
other two. Agriculture will suffer not only from a loss of fertilizers, but from
the loss of able-bodied hands. While millions are fighting at the front and
millions are drudging in munitions factories, a nation's economy will break
down for the mere want of workers to keep it going.

The great "battle of material" on the Somme in 1916 (see p. 61) first convinced the German High Command that a more intensified production of munitions was necessary, and Germany was faced at last with that crisis which, in one form or another, her enemies had already encountered and which, thanks to her preparedness, she herself had so far escaped — namely, a munitions crisis. In August 1916, Hindenburg and Ludendorff replaced Falkenhayn in the High Command (see p. 62). The two soldiers were economists enough to realize that the crisis was at bottom a labor crisis, and they were quite prepared, with that drastic largeness of new men in a new office, to demand a labor levy tantamount to a conscription of the entire civil population of the Reich. They were impervious to the fears of Bethmann-Hollweg, the Chancellor, and of Helfferich, lately appointed Vice-Chancellor and Home Secretary, neither of whom could reconcile himself to the social and political implications of the proposed levy.

On November 1, 1916, by order of the Kaiser, a Kriegsamt (War Office), came into existence under the directorship of General Groener. The new office was attached to the Prussian Ministry of War and was endowed with wide powers, especially in respect to industry and labor. In December 1916, after considerable and often heated debate in the Reichstag, an Auxiliary Service Law was promulgated providing for the compulsory employment of every male German citizen between the ages of seventeen and sixty who was not already in the combatant forces. At the same time, industries were ruthlessly "silenced" which could not be considered as "important for war purposes." Transport was reorganized, and traffic by rail was controlled by rigid "urgency lists." All these measures were collectively called the "Hindenburg Program." As a result, in May 1917 the Kriegsamt could report a substantial increase in German iron and steel production. Munitions generally had reached a figure three times that of the corresponding period preceding.

But Bethmann-Hollweg and Helfferich were not so wrong in the end. The Auxiliary Service Law entailed a serious social upheaval. The Social Democrats and the trade-unions had both agreed to support the law, but they did not hide their aversion to it. The High Command had expected the Hindenburg Program to go into force behind a great patriotic outburst, but it had not the skill or the psychological astuteness with which the Nazis afterward conducted these things, and its expectations misfired lamentably. The dedication of the entire wealth of a nation to unproductive ends could lead only to impoverishment and ultimate collapse. The winter of 1916–17 was the "turnip winter." Frosts were continuous. The canals, which in Germany furnish so important a means of transport, were frozen for weeks, and the railroads carried a volume of traffic beyond their limit of safety. For the first time during the war, coal was short, and the High Command was faced with the alternative of reducing the munitions program or releasing more miners from service in the army. A special coal commissioner was attached to the Kriegsamt with independent and absolute authority over the nation's coal supplies, but the problem was already beyond a solution. The High Command had laid a burden upon the devoted country which was more than it could bear.

BELGIUM

In 1914, a century after the Battle of Waterloo, Belgium once again be·
came the battleground of Western Europe. The German High Command
demanded of her an open passage for the right wing of its invasion of
France; the German Government offered her the rough alternative of moral
or political surrender; she made her choice without hesitation. During August 1914 the German Army swept across her territory. Brussels fell on
August 20, and Antwerp on October 10. The Belgian Government escaped
to Le Havre in France. King Albert established his headquarters at La
Panne, in the little strip of Belgian territory behind Ypres which still remained free of the enemy.

Plunder, fire, murder, rape have always accompanied military invasion.
But the German outrages in Belgium and France were not merely acts of
individual soldiers following their own brutish devices. They were part of a
policy of calculated terrorism. The Schlieffen Plan required the annihilation
of all effective resistance in Belgium in three weeks, and the German, High
Command was in no mood to permit irregular fighting by bands of sharp-
shooters or *franc-tireurs* such as had harassed the Prussians in 1870–71.
Whole towns and villages were given over to fire and destruction as reprisal
for the merest suspicion of civilian resistance. "Military necessity" covered a
multitude of the most hideous atrocities. The university, the library, the
Church of St. Pierre, and masses of houses at Louvain were razed to the
ground. Various degrees of devastation befell Aerschot, Malines, Termonde,
Alost, Dinant, and other places. Refugees to the extent perhaps of a sixth of
the Belgian population fled before the invaders.

The Germans set up a virtual military government at Brussels under their
Governor General, General von Bissing.[10] Belgian police and civil servants
who were willing were retained in office. Belgium was quickly subjected to
the status of a conquered country. National flags and emblems were proscribed. Railroads, canals, postal services, and telegraphs were put under
rigid control. Schools and textbooks were rigorously inspected. There were
fines and terms of imprisonment for "Germanophobes," and there were rewards for informers. All men of military age were kept under strict surveillance, and those who tried to escape abroad were punished by imprisonment or deportation and sometimes with confiscation of property. A
crude propaganda constantly reminded the people of their lot; placards
announced the names of those condemned to death for espionage and of
those killed by Allied air raids over Belgian cities. Meanwhile the country
suffered from absolute isolation, both from Allies and neutrals. Electrified
wiring guarded the Belgo-Dutch frontier. Belgian papers which refused to
submit to control were suspended, and German-sponsored papers took their
place. Loyal Belgians depended on smuggled literature for their news, or on
secretly printed native papers, like *La Libre Belgique*.

The German military authorities requisitioned where and as they pleased,
and either never paid for what they seized or gave receipts of doubtful value.
The War Raw Materials Department (see p. 49) at Berlin extended its

operations into all occupied territories, and Belgium became an economic annex of the Prussian Ministry of War. The German Z.E.G. (see p. 51) regulated Belgian exports and imports. War contributions were levied both from the country as a whole and from individual cities. Many factories which had been forced to close down were dismantled, and their machinery was shipped to munition centers in Germany. Private houses were stripped of metallic movables, ornaments, and kitchen utensils. In justice to General von Bissing, it must be said that he was often opposed to edicts to which he signed his name and was forced to act upon instructions from the High Command. But, notwithstanding her miseries, Belgium showed a marvellous moral tenacity, and never in the four years of the occupation did she despair of her ultimate deliverance. Her leaders, men like Cardinal Mercier, Archbishop of Malines, and Adolphe Max, Burgomaster of Brussels, made a heroic fight for common justice and common humanity, and if their efforts brought small material relief, their example was infinitely heartening to the oppressed people.

A serious economic crisis had already begun to develop in Belgium in 1914. The invasion had left a trail of chaos in its wake; buildings and factories had been demolished; the retiring Belgian Army had destroyed bridges and railroads, and opened low-lying land to inundation. The chief industrial centers, Liége, Charleroi, and Mons, lay on the main line of the German advance, and they had suffered accordingly. The requisitions and contributions were ruinous. The Belgian people, as a whole, showed little disposition to serve their new masters, and numbers of industries lay idle because both employers and employees refused to go to work. In addition, Belgian was cut off from most of her former markets by the Allied blockade, and for Belgium, an industrial country "like an England on a smaller scale," blockade was the supreme calamity. By 1915 the urban centers were already suffering from a food shortage. Philanthropic organizations, such as the Commission for Relief in Belgium, directed from London by the American engineer and businessman, Herbert C. Hoover, could only afford a very partial remedy.

Moreover the urban centers were suffering from unemployment. Many men were refusing to work, but there was little work for them to do in any event. The Germans made every effort to promote employment, especially in the heavy industries which were useful to them. They opened a recruiting campaign for Belgian workers to volunteer for employment in Germany. The Governor General issued decrees imposing fines and imprisonment for refusal to work. Meanwhile, Germany herself had approached that crisis in her own man power which we described above (see p. 52). It seemed to her an intolerable anomaly that she should be suffering from an acute shortage of labor while, across her frontier in Belgium, there existed a huge human reservoir going to waste. Germany's Auxiliary Service Law demanded the total levy of her own working population, and its promoters were soon casting hungry eyes upon Belgium's idle millions. In September 1916 the German Government resolved on the mass deportation of all unemployed Belgians.

Under existing circumstances, the deportations were defensible — economically; but they contravened any normal interpretation of international law, and they were carried out with extreme brutality. The Belgian authorities, with natural pride, refused to furnish the data upon which the smooth functioning of so drastic a measure depended, whereupon the Germans rounded up and carried off any able-bodied Belgian who, upon a cursory examination, seemed eligible for work. The Allied press received the news of this latest of German atrocities with horror. Protests by local groups and personalities and diplomatic representations by neutral Powers were all unavailing. The German High Command was not disposed to spare a conquered country from a conscription which it had already planned to impose upon its own Fatherland. Nevertheless, the deportations fell very short of calculation. The High Command had counted on 400,000 workers; it obtained 120,000, only half of whom were actually employed in Germany — hardly an adequate compensation for the misery and loathing that were left behind.[11]

Meanwhile the Germans attempted the political division of Belgium. They exploited the nascent nationalism of the Flemish element of the Belgian population against the Walloon, French-speaking element. They affected to regard the Flemings as candidates for absorption into a Greater Germany. They Flemicized the University of Ghent and ordered all teaching there to be conducted in the Flemish tongue. In March 1917, Bissing decreed the administrative separation of Flanders and Wallonia and set up two rival capitals at Brussels and Namur respectively. Pro-German Flemish "Activists" formed themselves into a "Council of Flanders," which became a sort of government of collaboration and a center of separatist propaganda. The German policy in Belgium at this time was a forecast in miniature of the wholesale reconstruction of Europe under the Nazi occupation twenty-five years afterward.

POLAND AND THE BALTIC

The twists and turns of German occupation policy as between the two World Wars are interesting. Toward Belgium, in the First World War, the Germans behaved with the extreme brutalities we have just described; in the Second World War, their occupation at least started off with studied correctness. Toward Poland, in the First World War, the Germans acted almost as professed allies; in the Second, they aimed at the total national extinction of the Polish people. The Baltic area, in both wars, was regarded as a special German preserve. By 1914 the Baltic ports, Libau, Riga, and Reval, had long been virtually German cities — their inhabitants and their businesses were largely German — and throughout the Baltic hinterland were prosperous landed communities of Baltic "Barons" of German extraction. Conservative and military opinion in Germany regarded the Baltic, as it regarded Flemish Belgium, as an area ripe for annexation to the Reich.

In 1914, Poland was a memory and a name. The Poles were one of those unhappy European peoples whose loyalties the war tore asunder. Polish conscripts fought in three separate armies, often against one another and on Polish soil. In 1914, Pilsudski, one Polish patriot leader, at the head of his "Polish Legion," went off to fight on the Austro-German side, and another, Dmowski, at the head of a similar "Polish Legion," to fight on the Russian side. In the course of 1915, as a result of the Russian retirement, the whole of Poland and the greater part of the Baltic fell under Austro-German occu- pation. The Germans set up their administration in Warsaw; the Austrians at Lublin. The "Polish Question" and the "Baltic Question" for the polit- ical disposal of the occupied territories became major political issues at the courts and chancelleries of the Central Empires.

Germany, of course, intended to keep her hold upon the Polish territories which, since the Partitions of the eighteenth century, were already hers. She might also demand strategic rectifications of frontier to fill up the weak Posen "armpit" with a stronger Prussian "biceps." Similarly Austria would keep her hold upon Galicia. The Polish Question therefore concerned the disposal of whatever might be left of the former Russian Poland. At first both the German and Austro-Hungarian Governments favored a solution which would have made the territory a German dependency but with an Austrian archduke for its puppet king. Many leading Poles at the time — Pilsudski among them — accepted this prospect of German dominance with good grace. It was, in their view, preferable to Russian dominance.

In 1916 occupied Poland felt the repercussions of Germany's man-power crisis, which we described above (see p. 52). The German High Command did not ask for deportations, as it did in the case of Belgium but, more subtly, it tried to exploit the anti-Russian sentiment in Poland to recruit a Polish army for service against Russia. In November 1916, in order to win the gratitude and co-operation of the Poles toward the High Command's military program, the Central Empires solemnly proclaimed the independ- ence of Poland and set about organizing a "Polish Government." Pilsudski became the Minister of War in the new regime. But then the trouble started. Pilsudski's Legion, while eager enough to shed its blood for the Polish father- land, refused to take an oath of "fraternity of arms" with Germany and Austria-Hungary. Pilsudski was arrested by his German sponsors and im- prisoned in the fortress of Magdeburg. The Polish army in the end proved to be, in Ludendorff's phrase, a plowing of the sands.

However, the Central Empires continued to develop their plans in Poland. In September 1917 they created a Council of Regency in Warsaw, composed of three Poles, to exercise supreme power in the country until such time as a "hereditary, constitutional king" might be chosen, and pledged them- selves to promote the election of a new Council of State by popular fran- chise. But these measures were entirely theatrical. The real power remained with the German High Command. The members of the Council of Regency were virtually its nominees. The Council of State was duly elected, but it only assembled for about five weeks in the summer of 1918. The new King of Poland remained a pious and ineffectual hope.

The Germans made every effort to cajole the peoples of the Baltic into some sort of political union with themselves, though their long-term objec- tives did not prevent them from levying the usual requisitions of an occupy-

ing power. Extensive German colonization in the area was mooted. The so-
called Baltic Barons, that caste of landowning gentry of German origin in
the area, were of course much to the fore throughout the attendant discussions. German plans in the Baltic included the formation of a Duchy of
Courland and a Duchy of Estonia and Livonia in personal union with
Prussia; and early in 1918 the Kaiser graciously accepted the grand-ducal
crowns of both territories at the hands of representatives of the Baltic
Barons. An independent Lithuania was to be formed in "alliance" with Germany under a princeling of the House of Württemberg, allegedly descended
from ancient Lithuanian royalty. But all these fine plans were brought to an
abrupt end by the Armistice of November 1918.

5 THE DOGFALL[1]

VERDUN, THE BRUSILOV OFFENSIVE, AND THE SOMME

The campaigns of 1915 raised the Central Empires to the zenith of their military fortunes. The Tsar's armies were rolled back into the depths of Russia. Poland went the way of Belgium. Serbia was conquered and trodden down. French and British offensives in the West were everywhere repulsed. Italy four times attacked the Austrian front on the Isonzo with insignificant results. The Allied expedition to the Dardanelles failed and withdrew. Only at sea did the Allies remain unbeaten.

But for all their victories the Central Empires had nowhere won a "political" decision. The year 1916 promised them a continuance of their military superiority in the field, but it is always of the essence of military superiority that the enemy sooner or later shall show a disposition toward peace. That disposition was not yet demonstrable even in Russia. The German High Command was faced with a fundamental dilemma: whether to push the advance in the East and perhaps complete the subjugation of Russia, or to attempt a decisive action elsewhere. France, Flanders, and Italy offered tempting alternatives. Further lengthy campaigning in the East would doubtless result in Germany's absorption of more of the Russian hinterland — at least of the Ukraine and the Black Sea — while these areas were still unexhausted by war; it might eventually force the British to evacuate Mesopotamia and the Persian Gulf; and it would provide the material resources with which to resist the naval beleaguerment for years. But a campaign in the West, for instance in France, while calling for a greater immediate effort and sacrifice, always offered the chance of final victory and peace within a measurable space of time. If the German High Command still hoped for the shortest possible war — and thereto the grand strategy of Germany had always been dedicated — it were better to leave its task in the East unfinished and strike a major blow on the Western front.

The upshot was the Battle of Verdun. Falkenhayn, the German commander, desired not so much to capture the fortress as to inflict on France, at a vital point, a wound which would not be allowed to heal. Weeks of continuous shelling and limited advances by infantry would conform more nearly to the spirit of such a campaign than a great Sedanesque victory on the upper reaches of the Meuse. Verdun was easy to attack and hard to defend. It lay less than ten miles distant from the nearest German railhead and, thanks to the salient of St. Mihiel, which had remained in German hands since 1914, it was connected with its own bases in France only by a single road and rail line. The terrain was dry and elevated, and unaffected by vicissitudes of weather. Verdun would make an ideal laboratory for a supreme experiment in the tactics of attrition.

The Austrian High Command prepared a complementary operation against Italy. Conrad, the Austrian Chief of Staff, was consumed with a hatred of "this most traitorous of Austria's enemies," and now that Russia and Serbia had both fallen, he conceived of an Italian campaign as the most proper task for the Austro-Hungarian Army. Falkenhayn discouraged the project and preferred Conrad to maintain the Eastern front against a possible revival of Russia. He refused Conrad's request for nine German divisions which, according to Conrad, would have made Galicia invulnerable. Nevertheless, Conrad persisted in his obsession and laid his plans for a great offensive in the Trentino for the late spring.

The German assault on Verdun began on February 21, 1916. News of the first French retirements appeared in the French press three days later. The French people, army, and government were aware that one of the decisive engagements of the war had been thrust upon them. Paris experienced a sudden surge of pessimism. All the panic of the early days of the war returned, and the public seemed to live in hourly suspense from one communiqué to the next. The French people had become so acclimatized to the war of position that they magnified the smallest retirements into disasters. In 1914 they had accepted the loss of thirty miles of Picardy with greater calmness than they now accepted the loss of a single strong point. As Falkenhayn had well calculated, the moral effect of a French defeat at Verdun, even if it had meant only a slight territorial change, would be terrible. Yet, as the fighting continued, reports began to come in of the incredible heroism of the defense. The force of will seemed to transcend physical danger and strategic disadvantage. "They shall not pass" became all at once a sort of sacred incantation with which, by the mere repetition, a man could cast out fear and horror. The Battle of Verdun still remains in point of duration and casualties the greatest battle of all time. It lasted seven months and cost France and Germany nearly a million men.[2]

Joffre gave the command of Verdun to General Pétain and, under Pétain's leadership, the French defense stood. Falkenhayn had chosen his weapons and his ground and was soon more deeply and inextricably engaged than perhaps he desired. Conrad's offensive against Italy was duly delivered in May 1916 and was repulsed with heavy losses. And then, all of a sudden, the Russian front flared up into activity. Early in March 1916 the Russians had made an attack in the sector near Vilna. The attack had broken down, and its easy defeat had reassured the German and Austrian High Commands in their belief that no serious offensive warfare on the part of Russia was again to be expected. But the reorganization of the Russian rearward services under Polivanov and the Special Councils (see p. 47) persuaded the Russian High Command that Russia might yet fight again, and France and Italy, hard pressed at Verdun and the Trentino, had appealed to their ally for some kind of diversion.

On June 4, 1916, General Brusilov, commanding the Russian armies on the southwestern front, began that celebrated action always called after him the Brusilov Offensive. It was intended at first to be no more than a feint. But the Austro-Hungarian Army in Galicia, weakened by withdrawals of its reserves to the Trentino, deceived by the long inaction of winter and spring,

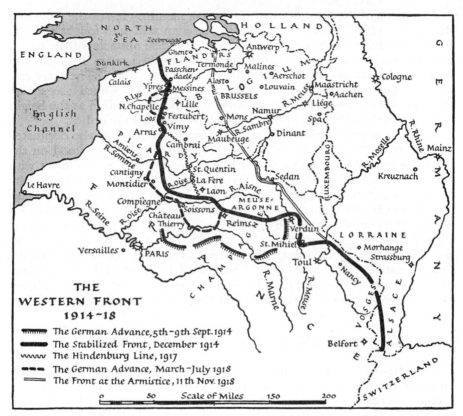

THE
WESTERN FRONT
1914~18

~~~~~~~~ The German Advance, 5th~9th Sept. 1914
████████ The Stabilized Front, December 1914
wwww The Hindenburg Line, 1917
▬▬▬ The German Advance, March~July 1918
═══ The Front at the Armistice, 11th Nov. 1918

0   50   Scale of Miles   150   200

and itself beginning to show signs of internal decay, "broke like a piecrust"
on a front of two hundred miles. The Russian High Command ordered
Brusilov to throw every force he could muster into his developing advance,
and he pursued the five Austro-Hungarian armies before him into Bukovina
and once more across the old Galician battlefields. Conscripts of Slavic blood
in the five armies "surrendered" by the regiment.

The Battle of the Somme had originally been intended to be part of a
great Franco-British offensive, planned by the Allied commands for the year
1916. The German attack on Verdun had anticipated the French part in the
action and left the British forces to fight their battle as best they might.
Haig, the British commander, disposed of twenty-four divisions of Kitchener's "New Army" —"every man a volunteer" — and the fruits of Lloyd
George's munitions campaign. He entertained the most vivid expectations of
the offensive he was about to launch, a grand break-through at last, of the
type of which the Allies had dreamed since 1914, and he held three cavalry
divisions in reserve to exploit his success. On the main frontage of his attack
he concentrated over 1,500 guns, one gun to every twenty yards, and he
opened his offensive at the end of June 1916 with a bombardment of the
German lines of eight days' duration. In the early morning of July 1 the
British infantry went "over the top."

The Battle of the Somme lasted nearly five months. "It was the glory and the graveyard of Kitchener's Army," as one man said who fought through it. Despite Haig's hopes and calculations, the tactical obstacles of the trench were not overcome, and the battle degenerated into a series of sanguinary partial actions to be justified, after the event, as "attrition." The three cavalry divisions were never used. In the end the British gained 120 square miles for the loss of 400,000 men.[3] Only an army and a nation at the height of their moral and material power could have survived the ordeal.

But if the Somme decimated the New Army of England, it also decimated the enemy. For the first time in the war the German soldier stood on the defensive against a foe who opposed him with equal weapons — if not with equal skill — and with fiercer resolution. The Somme finally broke Falkenhayn's reputation. In August 1916, Hindenburg and Ludendorff jointly succeeded him in the German High Command, and the two new leaders set about the reorganization of the munitions industries on the German home front which we described in the last chapter (see p. 53). German military literature in later years constantly referred to the devastating effect of the British bombardments in 1916 and harked back to the great defensive action of the German soldier in "the battle of material" on the Somme with the almost nostalgic remark: "He never fought so well again!"

THE ENTRY OF RUMANIA INTO THE WAR

Since the outbreak of the war Rumania, like her Balkan fellows, had been an uncertain and hesitating neutral. But as time went on, Rumanian public opinion veered more and more toward the Allied cause, and Rumania almost followed Italy into the war in 1915. Bratianu, the Rumanian Premier, however, had continued to resist the pressing courtships of the two belligerent groups, and certainly while the armies of the Central Empires were winning victories in Russia and Serbia no other policy seemed possible. Rumania had immense natural resources, especially in grain and oil, and none too efficient an army with which to defend them, and her position was most delicate.

But in May 1916, Conrad, the Austrian Chief of Staff, had so denuded his Carpathian and Transylvanian frontiers for his foolhardy operation in the Trentino as positively to invite "a Rumanian military promenade," and in June and July the Brusilov Offensive galvanized all Southeastern Europe with expectations of a certain Austrian collapse. Bratianu began to bethink himself that he had held off Rumania's suitors too long, and she had better yield now or lose her chance forever.

On August 17, 1916, Rumania concluded an alliance with the Allied Powers and undertook to attack Austria-Hungary with all her available forces not later than the twenty-eighth of that month. For her aid Rumania would receive territories including Bukovina, Transylvania, and the Banat, a preposterous promise, for the half of which at least there could be no justification, ethnic or strategic. A military convention accompanied the alliance, according to which Rumania's intervention would be assisted by a Franco-British offensive from Salonika, a Russian offensive "along the entire Austrian front," and the arrival in Rumania of a Russian reinforcement of three divisions for joint action against Bulgaria. On August 27, 1916, Rumania was at war.

But the Rumanian Government and army command had miscalculated terribly. The Rumanian plan of campaign had assumed Germany to be fully engaged at Verdun and on the Somme. Nevertheless Germany found herself able to detach a couple of divisions from the Western front for service against Rumania. The promised Franco-British operation at Salonika hardly deserved the name of an offensive. Brusilov's victorious advance against the Austrians in Galicia exhausted itself at the point where it promised to achieve a major decision. Instead of the three Russian divisions stipulated in the Allied military convention, only 20,000 Russians were sent to the new Rumanian front. Finally Rumanian sentiment clamored for an advance into Transylvania, an operation which had as much permanent military value as the French invasion of Alsace-Lorraine in 1914.

The Austro-German "punitive expedition" under the command of Falkenhayn descended on Rumania with humiliating speed. The Rumanians advanced into Transylvania, leaving an open and unprotected rear. On September 10 the Bulgarians invaded the Dobruja and at once upset the balance of the Rumanian strategy. The Rumanian columns in Transylvania lost their momentum, hesitated, and began to fall back. The Austro-German forces swung across the Transylvanian Alps into the Wallachian lowland and, on December 6, 1916, entered Bucharest. Immense stores of grain were burned by the retreating Rumanians, and a British technical mission wrought such systematic havoc in the Rumanian oil fields as to make them unworkable for months. The gold reserves and the archives were sent for greater safety to Moscow and were eventually sequestered by the Bolsheviks.

On December 12, 1916 the Central Empires celebrated their Rumanian victory by issuing a general offer of peace in the form of a note to the Allies, a rather vague but strident protestation of innocence and disclaimer of all further responsibility for the continuance of the great struggle. But they made no mention of the specific objects — Belgium, Alsace-Lorraine, and Serbia — for which the Allies were fighting. Allied statesmen rejected the offer out of hand. Meanwhile, during January 1917 the Rumanian front became stabilized along the Sereth (Siret), and the Rumanian Government established itself at Jassy. The German commanders were content for the moment to rest on their laurels. Their forces were better reserved for use elsewhere than for pursuing the Rumanian rout to the limit of annihilation.

THE ENTRY OF GREECE INTO THE WAR

The Dardanelles in 1915 had been an essentially British enterprise. Salonika was an essentially French one (see p. 35). France dominated Allied diplomacy in Greece, and her commitments there soon involved her inextricably in Greek domestic affairs. The French Foreign Ministry doubtless tried to follow a moderate, politic course; it tried to collaborate sincerely with

Britain, Russia, and Italy; and it tried to respect the Greek people's own desire for an honorable neutrality. But the French Foreign Ministry had counted without the complexities of the problem in the Balkans and without the ignorance and self-seeking of French representatives on the spot. In the end Greece was forced, a none too willing victim, into the war, and her king was driven into exile. The story is not an edifying one.

In the highest command at Salonika was General Sarrail, who had owed his appointment to political intrigue in France; who, by his own confession, had no previous knowledge of Greece or of the Greeks; and who, being an extreme anticlerical and republican, was not likely to sympathize with a people of deeply religious and monarchical instincts. The force at his disposal at Salonika was too weak for the task assigned to it, and all its "offensives" into Macedonia ended in inglorious retirements. His own temper was masterful and captious, and the other Allied staffs at Salonika spent months urging their governments to secure his recall. Several of the French subordinate officers and officials at Salonika had been improper and even dangerous selections, and the French Intelligence in Greece acted more like a "fifth column," as we would call it today, than as the branch of a reputable government service.

The Greek King Constantine had married the Kaiser's sister, and he must have had temptations and opportunities in plenty for casting his lot with Germany. But he was honest and sincere, desiring the best for his country, though not a brilliant man, sometimes egoistical and often very credulous. Several times, it seemed, he might well have sided with the Allies could they have offered him a reasonable military risk. Yet whatever his innermost sympathies may have been, he never deserved the studied vilification of his character which was heaped upon him in the Allied press. His partner in statesmanship, Eleutherios Venizelos, Greek Premier at various times, a tempestuous, headstrong patriot, was an unhesitating supporter of the Allies, and dreamed dreams of a Greater Greece, a Hellenized Constantinople, and vast Greek acquisitions in Asia Minor. Meanwhile the distracted common people of Greece were divided between the Royalist and the Venizelist parties.

Throughout 1916 a state of uneasy tension continued in Greece and "incidents" were frequent. And then the Rumanian entry into the war created a new situation. "I believed," said Venizelos, "that considerations were now removed which had hitherto kept me from undertaking the fight against autocracy." On August 27 he addressed a huge crowd from the balcony of his house in Athens and urged that a deputation of citizens be sent to the King to beseech him to follow the manifest wishes of the Greek people. The deputation went, but the King refused to receive it. A few days later, at Salonika, a band of patriots, discreetly supported by Sarrail, raised the standard of revolt against the Royalist regime. They were eventually joined by Venizelos and converted into a Provisional Government with full diplomatic recognition by the Allies. Constantine meanwhile tried to govern the parts of Greece which had remained loyal to him with a succession of nonpolitical premiers.

Finally, early in 1917 the Russian Revolution removed the restraining jealousies of the old Tsarist Foreign Ministry toward Allied ambitions in the Near East, and America's entry into the war silenced possible strictures from across the Atlantic. In June 1917 the French sent a commissioner to Athens, forced Constantine to abdicate in favor of his second son, Alexander, and installed Venizelos as Premier of the new King. Venizelos obediently declared that the era of unconstitutional rule was at an end, and broke off relations with the Central Empires. Greece was at last at war.

TURKEY AND THE ARAB REVOLT

Turkey emerged from her great military trial at the Dardanelles with a deserved, if temporary, accession of morale. The Germans had evidently succeeded in infusing into the Ottoman Army a strength and a confidence that it had not known for a century, and now, with a clear victory to its credit, its commanders turned their attention to other pressing fronts.

In 1914, after the entry of Turkey into the war, a British Indian force had occupied Basra at the head of the Persian Gulf, aiming in part to protect the near-by oil fields of British ownership and in part to defend the approaches to India and the Indian Ocean. The success with which the force repulsed the first Turkish attempts to dislodge it persuaded the British command to press farther into the interior of Mesopotamia, and in 1915 a division under General Townshend advanced up the Tigris past Kut el-Amara to within a few miles of Baghdad. It was against this division that the Turks now directed their efforts. Townshend was defeated at Ctesiphon, and he retired to Kut el-Amara, where he was surrounded and eventually, in April 1916, was forced to capitulate.

But at Kut el-Amara apparently the Turkish fortunes reached their zenith. The Russians on the long-dormant Caucasian front, now under the command of the Grand Duke Nicholas (see p. 47), opened strong attacks against the Turkish defenses in Armenia. They captured Erzerum in February 1916 and Trebizond in April. General Maude reorganized the British army in Mesopotamia and, by "imperceptible" stages, resumed offensive operations in that theater. Kut el-Amara was recaptured in February 1917, and the British entered Baghdad in March. Meanwhile the British forces based on Egypt and the Suez Canal began their slow, plodding "exodus" across the Sinai Desert, building their railroad as they advanced. In March 1917 they reached Gaza, where they encountered reinforced Turkish defenses and were forced to halt for the time being.

The sudden turn of weakness of the Turkish armies in 1916 and 1917 after so promising a revival was doubtless due to political and economic deterioration on the home front. In 1915 Armenians in the border districts along the Caucasian front had been behaving very suspiciously. Some of them had deserted to the Russians, and some had treacherously attacked local Moslem villagers. For their crimes, potential and actual, the Ottoman Government had decreed the wholesale deportation of its Armenian subjects to less strategic areas, and the order was carried out with extreme cruelty. At the same time the food situation, especially in Constantinople, had been growing critical, and it was a situation with which an inefficient government, ridden with corruption, was not exactly fitted to deal. Centers of population were swollen with refugees; there had been a serious locust plague in parts of the country; mobilizations and wars since 1911 had drained the land of its able-bodied cultivators. The Allied naval blockade was the least of Turkey's economic burdens.

But the most significant political event in the Ottoman Empire in 1916 and 1917 was the revolt of the Arabs of the Hejaz, the "Revolt in the Desert." In 1914, a couple of months before the outbreak of war, the Emir Abdullah, second son of Sherif Hussein of Mecca, had already sought an interview with Kitchener, then in Cairo, for the purpose of ascertaining whether Britain, in the event of war, could be persuaded to support the Arabs in a revolt against the Ottoman Sultan. Hussein had first ignored and then denounced the Sultan's call to a Holy War (see p. 23). Subsequently Cairo made discreet contacts with him, and in October 1915 Sir Henry McMahon, the British High Commissioner in Cairo, gave him a definite pledge — the McMahon Pledge, as it was afterward called — that the British Government would support and recognize Arab independence, within certain limits and with certain express reservations, in return for his open rupture with the Ottoman Empire. The Arab Revolt accordingly began in June 1916.

Faced with the dissolution of the Ottoman Empire, Britain could find her only safeguard — both in respect of her imperial communications and her Near Eastern oil supplies — in a friendly Arab world. Strategic considerations required her co-operation with the rival rulers of northern Arabia: Hussein, Sherif of Mecca and guardian of the Holy Cities of the Hejaz, who controlled the Arabian coast of the Red Sea, and Ibn Saud, Sultan of the Nejd, who controlled the Arabian coast of the Persian Gulf. Consequently, even before negotiations had been completed between McMahon and Hussein, the Government of India succeeded in establishing formal treaty relations with Ibn Saud. There was no inherent incompatibility in these concurrent negotiations. The active alliance of Hussein and the benevolent neutrality of Ibn Saud were both secured without prejudice to the rights of either. Palestine was not mentioned in any negotiation. (See Appendix E.)

Meanwhile the Allies had been discussing among themselves the future partition of the Ottoman Empire. During 1915, Britain, France, and Italy had agreed to Russia's possession of Constantinople and the Dardanelles. The Treaty of London, in April 1915, recognized Italy's demands in the Dodecanese and pledged her a share in the eventual disposal of Anatolia (see p. 28). From time to time attempts were made to bribe Greece into the war with offers of Smyrna. France was interested in Syria. In 1916 it fell to Mark Sykes and Georges Picot [4] to reduce this welter of imperialism to some sort of precision, and the Ottoman Empire was so parceled out among the prospective victors that the Turkish core would have been reduced to a small territory falling within a 200- to 250-mile radius of Angora (Ankara). In particular, the Sykes-Picot Agreement provided for an independent Arab state or confederation of states, for wide British and French spheres of influence, and also for the placing of Palestine and the Holy Places under a special international regime. Finally, in November 1917, Balfour made his famous declaration: "His Majesty's Government view with favour the establishment in Palestine of a national home for the Jewish people." (See Appendix D.)

From the moment of the Arab Revolt, the British Government supplied Hussein with what has been alliteratively called a constant stream of corn, cash, and cartridges. T. E. Lawrence, formerly a roving Oxford archaeologist in the Near East and at that time a second lieutenant, made his first unobtrusive visit to the Hejaz in October 1916, after the revolt had broken out. His business in the Hejaz was military, not political; and contrary to popular belief, he had nothing to do with any "promises" made to the Arabs. But he had everything to do with the desert campaign that followed. With Feisal, the third of Hussein's sons, he directed the Arabs' raids on the Turkish railroad connecting Medina and Damascus. With Feisal he rode at their head, and he shared their trials and their triumphs. He was one of the great "resistance" leaders of all time and well deserved his name of "Lawrence of Arabia."

General Allenby took over command of the British forces in Palestine shortly after the setback they had suffered at Gaza, and under him their advance was resumed. He entered Jerusalem in December 1917. Throughout the advance Lawrence, on his desert flank, co-operated closely with every move he made.

THE WAR AT SEA

On February 21, 1916 the German Government declared its intention to open "intensified" submarine war.[5] The declaration was an answer to the arming of merchantmen, which was now the regular practice of the British Admiralty, and affirmed that "enemy merchantmen armed with guns no longer have the right to be considered as peaceable vessels of commerce." Unfortunately, from the German point of view, intensified submarine war had all the diplomatic disadvantages and none of the military advantages of "unrestricted" submarine war, which was ultimately declared a year later.

On March 24, 1916 the French Channel packet *Sussex*, an unarmed ship, was torpedoed without warning. Her bows were blown off, but she remained afloat. About 80 passengers were killed or injured by the explosion, and several of those injured were American citizens. The American Government at first reacted slowly and cautiously. The exact circumstances were uncertain. For a time it was thought that the ship had not been torpedoed but mined, and in any case an unarmed ship was hardly a test case for "intensified" submarine war. With proper — and honest — handling, the sinking of the *Sussex* might have been relegated to the lengthening list of unsettled and defunct incidents. Admiral von Tirpitz had only just recently resigned from the German Marine Office, where he had been a baleful influence for so long, and there seemed good reason to hope that moderate counsels were gaining ground in Germany. But the German Foreign Office handed Gerard, the American ambassador in Berlin, a note which explained that after an examination of the logs of all submarines known to be operating on the date and in the area in question, no evidence could be found of a ship resembling the *Sussex* having been attacked. This "most unfortunate document that ever passed from Berlin to Washington" lost much of its force when fragments of a German torpedo were found embedded in the hull of the stricken ship. President Wilson thought he detected a falsehood, and at last lost patience. The new American note to Germany on April 18, 1916 was tantamount to an ultimatum; it insisted that " unless the Imperial German Government should now immediately declare and effect an abandonment of its present methods of submarine warfare against passenger and freight-carrying vessels, the Government of the United States can have no other choice but to sever diplomatic relations with the German Empire altogether." Wilson gave unmistakable importance to the occasion by laying the note personally before a special session of Congress.

The *Sussex* note, like the *Lusitania* note of the previous year, was another milestone in the long American-German debate over the war at sea (see p. 27). Once more Colonel House expected war, and once more Bernstorff begged his government for a gesture with which he could placate American opinion. On May 4 the German Government formally disavowed and abandoned its "intensified" submarine campaign, and the scare of war for the moment was laid to rest.

The naval warfare of 1914 and 1915 had been a cruiser warfare, and to date no action between the British and German battle fleets had yet taken place. For their part, Admiral Jellicoe and the British naval leaders had rightly resolved to preserve their existing favorable balance rather than risk a fight for the mere sake of fighting. They maintained their long-range blockade, they renounced some cherished traditions of their service, but they kept their command of the sea. As Churchill once put it: "The standpoint of the Commander-in-Chief of the British Grand Fleet was unique. His responsibilities were on a different scale from all others. It might fall to him as to no other man — Sovereign, Statesman, Admiral or General — to issue orders which in the space of *two or three* hours might nakedly decide who won the war. The destruction of the British Battle Fleet was final. Jellicoe was the only man on either side who could lose the war in an afternoon." [6]

But in January 1916, Admiral Scheer, Tirpitz's protégé, was appointed commander of the German High Seas Fleet, and he entered upon his duties determined, if he could, to bring the heavy forces of his superior adversary to battle piecemeal. The "intensified" submarine war just mentioned was all of a part with the new aggressiveness at sea now to be essayed by the German Navy. Falkenhayn, from his headquarters in France, was appealing for a naval diversion which might embarrass the British Army, then known to be preparing its Somme offensive on the Western front. Scheer's plans, however, were continually hindered by bad weather, and not till the end of May did he venture upon the maneuver that resulted in the one great naval engagement of the war.

Early on the morning of May 31, 1916, Scheer, having sent out his scouting force of cruisers and battle cruisers under Hipper to cruise demonstratively off the southern tip of Norway, followed with the German High Seas Fleet fifty miles astern. Flotillas of U-boats were already in positions off the Scottish coast. The British Admiralty, intercepting the German wireless, ordered Jellicoe, who was at Scapa Flow with the Grand Fleet, to put to sea. Admiral Beatty with the Battle Cruiser Squadron simultaneously sailed from Rosyth with the deliberate object of offering himself and his squadron as a bait to draw the High Seas Fleet into battle with the Grand Fleet. Beatty encountered Hipper off Jutland in the late afternoon of the 31st, and in the subsequent brush his flagship was disabled and two of his other ships were sunk. The German gunnery was excellent, and the British ships were discovered to have a serious defect of magazine design. Hipper emerged from the action without a major casualty. The British Grand Fleet and the German High Seas Fleet sighted one another shortly after 6 P.M., and again after 7 P.M. There was a partial action on each occasion, but the fighting was hampered by mists and defective signaling. By sundown the German High Seas Fleet had escaped. Desultory cruiser and destroyer action continued during the night. But the final tally rested with the Germans. In twenty-four hours the British had lost roughly double the tonnage of their enemy and more than double the life.

It was a gloomy Britain which read the news of the Battle of Jutland. On June 2 the Admiralty bluntly announced the facts, and with sailorly candor mentioned only those German losses which it had definitely ascertained. It did not mention — it could not then have known — the severe damage, amounting to disablement, which many of the surviving German ships had suffered. On June 5, while the country was still in suspense, there came the further news of the loss at sea of Lord Kitchener while proceeding on a mission to Russia. The double blow was very hard. In Germany, of course, the Skagerrak, as the Germans called the battle, was celebrated as a victory, the veritable dusk of the Nelsonian legend. It was only as the weeks went by that the true strategic balance sheet of Jutland could be drawn up. Neither side, in fact, had gained its objective. The British had failed in their objective — to bring the German High Seas Fleet to battle and to destruction. The Germans had failed in their objective — to reduce the overwhelming British preponderance and disconcert the blockade. Jutland was the first and last of Scheer's piecemeal actions. The German Navy retired to the refuge of its mine fields and harbors never again to challenge the might of Britain on the open sea. In October 1918 its final "death cruise" was frustrated by mutiny and revolution.

6 "THE YEAR OF AGONY," 1917

THE UNRESTRICTED SUBMARINE CAMPAIGN

The year 1917 was one of suffering and demoralization for every people in the war. For Russia the year brought revolution, for Britain the submarine terror, for France mutiny and defeatism, for Germany increasing shortage and political crisis, for Austria near famine and racial disintegration, for Italy a crushing defeat in the field. It was, as might be expected, a year of peace intrigues and peace rumors. It was a year of the weighing of many imponderables, and its military events, as we read them today, are best appreciated not so much as "battles," but as extensions of an ever widening, all consuming siege of peoples in which fighting fronts and home fronts were merged in a single, indivisible ordeal. Its only independent event, so to speak, still prompted by free will and not by necessity, and ultimately its outstanding and decisive event, was America's declaration of war on Germany.

Germany entered 1917 already badly shaken by reverses and upheavals. Verdun, the Brusilov Offensive, and the Somme had been serious in themselves. The Rumanian war which had followed (see p. 63), though a lesser episode, had been even more disturbing to self-confidence. All Germany's former victories on the Eastern front had not deterred a little Balkan state, of the least military importance, from joining the enemy.

Hindenburg and Ludendorff were now in supreme command. The partnership which had begun so triumphantly at Tannenberg in 1914 had assumed the virtual dictatorship of the Reich. The first fruits of the new leadership had been the reorganization of the home front (see p. 53). On the fighting front the two soldiers elected to stand on the defensive. Early in 1917 a great arc of territory from Arras to the river Aisne was laid waste and evacuated, and the German forces were voluntarily withdrawn to a new fortified position, the Siegfried Line — or as it was called more familiarly, the Hindenburg Line. The retirement was courageous, and the devastation the Germans left behind them was carried out with extreme ruthlessness. For if the British were to resume their offensive on the Somme, Hindenburg and Ludendorff preferred to meet it on a "shortened" front and, as we shall see, their military judgment on this point was not in error.

Hindenburg and Ludendorff resolved that their main offensive stroke of the year should be made — not on their own element, the dry land — but at sea. They argued strongly for the opening of unrestricted submarine warfare. The Western front, it seemed, had degenerated into a complete tactical stalemate. Military action on land, in the present condition of military science, could never bring the war to a conclusion. But the Allied blockade remained. Economic pressure behind the German lines was increasing from day to day. Time would tell against the Central Empires, even as it always told against beleaguered forces. But the resources of the Allies were coextensive with the outer world and would never be exhausted. Clearly, unrestricted submarine war would provide the way of escape. It would be directed particularly against England, the spine of the Allied coalition and the mainspring of its economic and moral strength. It would employ that arm of the fighting services, the German Navy, which — with the exception of the Skagerrak — had hardly had the chance to show its mettle (see p. 69) .

Into these considerations international law and humanitarian principles did not enter. Indeed there was a certain grim justice in hoisting upon England the cruelties of her own hunger blockade. It only remained to make allowances for the reaction of neutrals. The fate of Serbia and Rumania should act as a sufficient deterrent to Holland and Denmark. And as for the Americas, plainly they were averse to war. The United States had tried to avoid a war even with Mexico. The United States was more concerned with Japan than with Germany. But even if the United States, under President Wilson's prompting, should take the unexpected course and enter the war against Germany, the power of England would certainly be broken before American aid became effective. And finally, in view of the existing flow of American munitions to the Allies, the United States at war could hardly be more dangerous than the United States at peace.

So argued Germany's military leaders, and a specious and encouraging argument it was. There was little that the Chancellor and his civilian colleagues, for all their private fears and doubts, could offer in reply. The final decision was taken by the Kaiser on January 9, 1917, and unrestricted submarine war opened on February 1.

THE ENTRY OF THE UNITED STATES INTO THE WAR

Unrestricted submarine war brings us directly to the United States, of whose entry into the war it was the immediate occasion. Thus far, mention of American affairs has only been incidental. But perhaps we should now examine, if briefly, the entire American attitude toward the war and President Wilson's statesmanship during the first three years of it. We interrupt our chronology and return for a moment to 1914.

At the start of the war, President Wilson had at once taken a correct and rigid neutral attitude. In his message to the American people in August 1914, he urged them to avoid impulsive prejudices and excitements: "I venture to speak a solemn word of warning to you against that deepest, most subtle, most essential breach of neutrality which may spring out of partisanship, out of passionately taking sides. The United States must be neutral in fact as well as in name during these days that are to try men's souls." But the American people did take sides, and they took sides passionately. For nearly three years of technical neutrality, American public opinion, like a great tree with its roots deeply sunk in tradition, was violently buffeted by the

winds of circumstance, and at last wrenched bodily into the universal storm.
Strong isolationist sentiment going back to the eighteenth century, a hostility to the old tyrant England, a profound contempt for the European
order — as well as the active counterpressure of Americans of German origin
and the American press of German-American editorship — all this seemed
to do battle against the shock and horror of Germany's conduct of the war,
her invasion of Belgium, her submarine campaign, her use of poison gas,
her bombing of open cities, and the crowning folly of her note to Mexico
(see p. 74). Finally there was an influential group which feared that Germany's victory in Europe would have to be met by the permanent militarization of the Western Hemisphere and that the heavy consequent financial
and political burden would have to be borne by a hitherto pacifist American
people.

At the same time, the British waged a war of propaganda of great psychological skill. The British press service in the United States was well organized. The transatlantic cables were under British control, and their use
was supervised by British censors. American correspondents were not allowed at the front, and American papers could only reproduce communiqués
and the comments of British writers. British diplomacy was in the cautious,
competent hands of Sir Edward Grey, the British Foreign Secretary, a great
Liberal and a great admirer of American democracy — and, it must be admitted, in the hands also of that complete Anglophile, Grey's personal
friend, the American ambassador in London, Walter Hines Page. Never
once did Grey allow British blockade tactics to exasperate American pride
and patience beyond their limit, and Page manfully came to his aid whenever the extreme of discretion seemed sometimes to have been overpassed.
Grey steered his diplomatic ship, in his own words, "through uncharted seas,
perilous with shoals and rocks and treacherous currents." But he kept his
course, and he brought his ship to port.

Finally there came the influence of the American financial and industrial
commitments in the Allied cause. It is a fact that Germany was the first
belligerent to borrow in the United States in 1914. But thereafter all but a
very small fraction of American funds went to the Allies. Bryan, then Secretary of State and a leading isolationist, succeeded in imposing a "moral embargo" on loans to belligerents, but the embargo was quashed by President
Wilson in October 1914. Natural sympathy, the passionate taking of sides,
may have largely determined the direction of "this vile traffic," as Bryan and
his fellow isolationists called it, but Allied blockade effectively discouraged
any attempt to divert any part of it to Germany. As the German note of
April 1915 so bitterly complained: "The United States is delivering goods
only to the enemies of Germany. The theoretical willingness to supply Germany also, if shipments thither were possible, does not alter the case." Isolationist sentiment in 1914–17 was a powerful force in American affairs, and
the American people were never unanimously pro-Ally at any time during
the First World War. Indeed, when they did enter that war, they did so
pointedly, not as an "Ally," but as an "Associated Power." Yet it is undeniable that a certain moral predisposition existed in favor of the Western
democracies, Britain and France, and it is also undeniable that increasing

and one-sided financial involvement of the United States was a substantial propellent in the same direction.

Throughout America's neutral period President Wilson was constantly exercised in mind over the problems and prospects of peace. His ambition to be the impartial mediator between the belligerents at some greater Portsmouth Conference of the future amounted to an obsession in which it is sometimes difficult to say whether humanitarianism or vanity was the real motivating force. He offered to mediate in August 1914, and again in September 1914. In January 1915 he sent his friend and adviser, Colonel House, to Europe to visit the belligerent capitals and sound out the belligerent statesmen as to their views on war and peace. Colonel House's discussions ranged over the blockade and freedom of the seas, international arbitration and collective security. He made valuable contacts and friendships, and he gathered information which was afterward useful to his President. But it was a forlorn quest. The *Lusitania* in May 1915 brought his efforts to an abrupt end.

In January and February 1916, House went on the second of his pacific itineraries, with much the same results. German militarism, at the time, seemed more intractable and oppressive than ever. The Kaiser was in one of his lofty moods and spoke as if the great dynasts of Europe, "I and my cousins, George and Nicholas," would confer the boon of peace as soon as it suited them to do so. In France the situation was as difficult, if for quite other reasons. Nor even in England did the Colonel find statesmen or people too eagerly disposed toward his ideas of a "reasonable" peace. He planned with Grey a great conference to put an end to the war, and considered that the United States would "probably" enter the war against Germany if Germany refused an invitation to be represented at it. But, once he had returned to the United States, little more was ever heard of his ambitious scheme. At the moment the Battle of Verdun was infinitely more important to the warring world than the peace plans of Colonel House.

President Wilson considered that his success in the presidential election of 1916 represented a sufficient vote of confidence in his foreign policy to justify him in one more effort for peace, and on December 18, 1916 he sent an identical note to all the belligerent governments inviting them to state their war aims. "An interchange of views would clear the way at least for a conference," ran the note, "and make the permanent concord of the nations a hope for the immediate future, a concert of nations immediately practicable." But President Wilson had been rudely anticipated a few days earlier by the publication of a peace offer which the Central Empires had issued just after their triumphal entry into Bucharest (see p. 63). In the highly wrought psychology of the time the two peace notes, appearing thus simultaneously, merely nullified each other. Britain, France, and Russia reacted angrily toward what appeared to them to be an untimely attempt of the American President to "inject himself" into the peace intrigue of their enemies. Nevertheless, on January 22, 1917, in a message to the Senate, the sanguine President reviewed the replies of varying degrees of militancy or evasiveness which he had received from the belligerents and declared his belief that "we are that much nearer a definite discussion of the peace which shall end the present war."

A week later Germany launched her unrestricted submarine campaign, and ten weeks later the United States itself was in the war.

On the afternoon of January 31, 1917, at Washington, Bernstorff, the German ambassador, handed Lansing, the American Secretary of State, the note of the German Government announcing its intention to wage unrestricted submarine war. The note referred to the Allies' "brutal methods of war" and then proceeded: "Germany will meet the illegal measures of her enemies by forcibly preventing after February 1, 1917, in a zone around Great Britain, France, Italy, and in the eastern Mediterranean, all navigation, that of neutrals included, from and to England, from and to France, etc. All ships met within the zone will be sunk."

The United States had no alternative but to break off diplomatic relations with Germany. On February 3, Bernstorff was given his passports, and Gerard, the American ambassador, was recalled from Berlin. The same day President Wilson addressed Congress. Deeply moved as he was, he still hoped that the German announcement might prove to be no worse than a threat intended for diplomatic effect, and he was resolved to postpone a declaration of war until some "actual overt acts" had been committed by German submarines at sea.

But on March 1, Germany's note to Mexico, the notorious Zimmermann telegram, appeared in the press. It had been picked up by the British Naval Intelligence and handed over to the American Government. It proposed a German-Mexican alliance and Germany's diplomatic support for Mexico's reconquest of "her lost territory in Texas, New Mexico, and Arizona." Upon its publication, Zimmermann, at that time German Foreign Secretary, far from seeking to disown it, put the question of its authenticity beyond all doubt by acknowledging his responsibility and by attempting to justify himself in the Reichstag. The whole incident, in letter and spirit, shocked American susceptibilities where they were most sensitive. All the evils of old European statecraft in their most disingenuous form were thrust upon the American system. Monroe had come face to face with Machiavelli.

By mid-March the submarine sinkings had begun, and the overt acts for which President Wilson had waited were committed beyond question. Then the first news of the Russian Revolution arrived. On March 19, Wilson held one of his semiweekly cabinet meetings, and it was as clear to him as to his colleagues that war could not be avoided. On March 20 the United States recognized the Russian Provisional Government. Even Russia was now a land of free men battling the autocracies of Central Europe.

Congress was convened for an extraordinary session on April 2. President Wilson read his "War Message" to the assembled legislators. "The world must be made safe for democracy," he said. "Its peace must be planted upon the tested foundations of political liberty. We have no selfish ends to serve. We desire no conquest, no dominion. We seek no indemnities for ourselves, no material compensation for the sacrifices we shall freely make. We are but one of the champions of the rights of mankind. We shall be satisfied when those rights have been made as secure as the faith and the freedom of nations can make them." On April 4 and 6, 1917 the Senate and the House passed a joint resolution declaring a state of war between the United States and the Imperial German Government. The presidential proclamation followed on the same day.[1]

POLITICAL CRISIS IN BRITAIN

Britain entered 1917 with a new government. Asquith and his Coalition had been forced out of office by the growing public criticism of his evident want of drive and energy. "Wait and see" indeed had been poor comfort to a nation that had just been through the Battle of the Somme and was shortly to meet the shocks and trials of unrestricted submarine war. Britain, in effect, at the end of 1916 made much the same change in her leadership as she made in the Second World War when Chamberlain gave place to Churchill.

This time the hero of the occasion was Lloyd George, former Minister of Munitions and successor to Kitchener as Secretary of State for War. He came to office in December 1916 with a second Coalition, mainly of Conservatives. At the head of his government was a War Cabinet of four members: Lords Curzon and Milner (Conservatives), Henderson (Labor), and himself. He also repeated his earlier experiment at the Ministry of Munitions and appointed businessmen to new ministerial departments. Sir Maurice Hankey was "Secretary" to the Cabinet — another innovation.

By the end of 1916, Britain had completed her transition to a war basis. She had built up a great army and she had solved the twin problems of munitions and man power. But she was plainly beginning to feel the first pinch of privation and the first dull ache of war weariness, and her merchant ships were suffering very considerable losses from the German submarine. The Board of Trade and the Admiralty could no longer hide from public knowledge their grave anxieties over the war at sea. Admiral Jellicoe had been transferred from the Grand Fleet to become First Sea Lord (see Glossary), and his views were believed to be pessimistic in the extreme.

The situation which Lloyd George's government inherited was therefore already formidable enough when it was greatly aggravated by Germany's declaration of unrestricted submarine war on February 1, 1917. Losses to British merchant shipping in 1914 "from acts of war" had amounted, on an average, to 51,000 tons a month; in 1915 to 74,000 tons a month; and in 1916 to 103,000 tons a month. The losses for the first three months of unrestricted submarine war are shown in the accompanying table.

ALLIED SHIPPING LOSSES IN 1917

	British	British, Allied, and Neutral
February 1917	310,868 tons	532,000 tons
March	352,344	599,000
April	526,447	869,000

Orthodox methods of naval defense proved to be nothing better, in the Admiralty's phrase, than "palliation." Merchantmen had already been armed, but the bigger submarines now carried a heavier surface armament or resorted to torpedo attack. Camouflage, "dazzle-painting" as it was then called, was an interesting experiment, but more interesting than effective. Mine fields were laid down, in the Helgoland Bight, for instance, but they were difficult to maintain, and they made heavy calls on munition factories which were already working at top pressure. Decoy ships, heavily armed and disguised as tramps, hunted up and down the sea but, for all their tedious work, their ingenuity and valor, it is doubtful if they accounted for more than a dozen of the enemy's undersea fleet. Meanwhile Maclay, the former Glasgow shipowner, Lloyd George's Shipping Controller at his new Ministry of Shipping, was squeezing every ton of usefulness out of the country's diminishing resources. The strictest priorities were enforced; all unessential imports were prohibited; heavy purchases of shipping were made abroad; an ambitious shipbuilding program of over 1,000,000 tons per annum was laid down. Finally, the government approached Japan for a destroyer flotilla, especially for operations in the Mediterranean. Japan complied and was compensated by a secret treaty, by which Britain and the Allies engaged themselves to support Japan's claims to the former German territories in the Pacific north of the equator — a treaty which, as shall be related in another place, was to have some unfortunate consequences (see pp. 109 and 120).

A screen of destroyers as protection to a battle fleet had long been a commonplace of naval warfare. The principle was as old as classical antiquity. But there seemed at first good reasons against a thoroughgoing organization of the Allied seaways commerce into convoy units. Admiral Jellicoe, in particular, argued that the number of escorting craft available for merchant convoys — namely, destroyers and armed trawlers — was far from sufficient, and he would never permit the Grand Fleet to be denuded of its destroyers. Jellicoe only began to moderate his objections when the American entry into the war provided him with a powerful reinforcement of the type of escorting craft he wanted. Further, the convoy, if it was to become a workable, efficient weapon, called for weeks of patient, expensive, and often dangerous experiment. The task of forming the convoy at the port of departure would be slow and difficult; the delays involved by ships waiting for the convoy to assemble would entail serious economic loss; the speed of the convoy would be governed by the slowest ship; the shipmasters, having no experience in sailing or maneuvering in company could not be trusted to "keep station"; the convoy would be dispersed by fog or storm; the convoy would offer an enlarged target to the submarine; the convoy, especially in the North Sea, might be raided by units of the German Fleet in strength; the final arrival of the convoy at the home port would result in undue congestion; and so on.

But good reasons must give place to better. The opponents of the convoy system had gone sadly astray in their estimate of the number of ships requiring escort. Perhaps 140 merchantmen arrived at British ports per week, perhaps 20 per day, and the tactical and administrative task of convoy therefore lay within manageable proportions. The Ministry of Shipping was in possession of daily, almost hourly, information regarding the positions of ships in every part of the world and could quickly organize the assembling of convoys at convenient points. Direct routing compensated for slow speeds; individual ships lost more time warily zigzagging across the sea than did the convoy sailing at the pace of one sluggish tramp. The merchant skipper was no mean seaman and had skill enough — and more — to keep his station. Furthermore, the convoy gave its members a sense of security, and the moral effect of the group was profound. If a ship was hit, rescue was assured. The masters consigned their worries to their escort and devoted themselves, with benefit to all concerned, to their proper task of navigation. Far from being a larger target, the convoy escaped the notice which the old "protected approach areas" invariably attracted. The secrecy of routes and destinations could be far better kept than when individual ships wirelessed for instructions and instantly betrayed their whereabouts. Finally, the convoy constituted a strong combatant force. Surface attack was impossible, and torpedo attack exposed the submarine to the deadly retaliation of the depth charge.

Admiral Beatty, who had succeeded Jellicoe in the command of the Grand Fleet, was himself inclined to join the proponents of the convoy. Admiral Sims, commanding American naval forces in European waters, who had visited England shortly after the American entry into the war, was convinced of the good points of the convoy and reported favorably to the American Government. Lloyd George, Maclay, the Shipping Controller, and that unfailing adviser of the British Government in difficult moments, Sir Maurice Hankey, were supporting the convoy with increasing force and impatience.[2] Meanwhile the "controlled sailings" of colliers between England and France had been proving very successful, and in April experimental convoys on the same lines were tried with happy results between Norway and the Humber. Early in May 1917, if we are to believe Lloyd George's account of the controversy, the government virtually ordered the Admiralty to initiate convoys from Gibraltar. In mid-May the Admiralty set up a Committee on Convoys. By June and July the system was in full and regular operation on routes from America, Gibraltar, and Dakar, and in the North Sea. It was extended and developed in every direction. It was instituted for outgoing as well as incoming voyages. It ensured an ever increasing immunity from submarine attack. Between midsummer 1917 and November 1918, 16,657 ships were convoyed to or from British ports with a loss of only 0.71 per cent.

The food crisis of 1917 in Britain was the obverse of the submarine war, and its main battles were fought out at the time of the convoy controversy. The crisis had been long developing. Sugar had been made a government monopoly as early as October 1914, but no other controls were established for another two years. While the dragon of want was already consuming Central Europe, a British government department in September 1916 could still report that "there is less total distress in the country than in an ordinary year of peace." But by the fall and winter of that year the bread line was beginning to infest several Midland towns and cities, and certain of the more critically disposed Members of the House of Commons, such as Lloyd George and Churchill, were beginning to take an anxious interest in food problems. In December 1916, Lloyd George created a Ministry of Food which gradually extended its huge network of Food Commissioners and Committees throughout the country. The annual turnover of the Ministry's purchasing operations ran to £900,000,000, and ultimately 94 per cent of everything eaten and drunk in Great Britain was made subject to its controls. By April 1918 a complete rationing system of all foods, except milk, fish, and fresh vegetables, was in force and running smoothly.

The British people little knew and, once their daily portion had been assured, little cared about these huge transactions and the exact manner of their working. They bore their restrictions with their traditional blend of grumbling and patience, but the margin of their safety was sometimes very narrow. In the end they survived the war the best fed of all the European belligerents.

VIMY RIDGE AND THE NIVELLE OFFENSIVE; MESSINES, PASSCHENDAELE, AND CAMBRAI

Unlike their enemy, the Allies on the Western front had not forsworn offensive fighting for the year 1917. Joffre, bearing the blame for the complacent unpreparedness at Verdun, had now retired to a decorative post in Paris with the rank of Marshal of France. His place in the French High Command was taken by General Nivelle, a relatively young officer with a spectacular promotion behind him. Nivelle had recently conducted some daring and brilliantly successful "raids" at Verdun. He had come to his new duties with inspiring theories regarding the "general offensive" and had been confidently hailed by the British and French press as the military genius who held the secret that had eluded nearly three years of sterile Allied generalship. Lloyd George, for one, was completely overwhelmed by the Nivellesque optimism. Somewhere, it seemed, in the rolling fields and hills of northern France, the new French Commander in Chief would deal the enemy a blow which would out-Somme the Somme and out-Marne the Marne.

Plans were made for the coming offensive at Allied conferences in February 1917. Haig, the British commander, undertook "to conform to the orders of Nivelle." But Haig, that dour Scot, was never the man to conform to anyone's orders, let alone those of a somewhat ebullient and didactic Gaul, and from the start this first experiment in unified Allied command was not too happy. Then General Lyautey, at that time French Minister of War, one of the few who had never had much faith in Nivelle, quarreled with the French Chamber and resigned. There were incidental breaches of security, and complete battle orders fell into the hands of the German Intelligence. Finally, the German forces on the Somme made their retreat to the Hindenburg Line and evacuated the very area which Nivelle had marked out as the British objective. Ludendorff could hardly have executed an operation better calculated to upset the Franco-British plans.

Nonetheless, the British Third Army under Allenby and the Canadian Corps under Byng made their prescribed attack in the Arras theater — at the northern tip of the new Hindenburg Line. Three weeks of wire cutting, followed by five days' bombardment by nearly 3,000 guns — one gun to every nine yards — preceded the infantry assault of April 9. Sixty tanks went into the action. The first day's advance was very encouraging; the Canadians took the stubborn bastion of Vimy Ridge, and performed perhaps as brilliant a feat of arms as the four years of trench warfare in France ever witnessed. But thereafter the German resistance stiffened, and the advance bogged down. In the end, a fortnight's fighting gained some seventy-five square miles at the cost of 30,000 killed and 75,000 wounded.

The French part of the Nivelle Offensive in the Champagne, east and west of Reims, launched on April 16, met one of the bloodiest repulses of the war. But Nivelle pressed the attack with crass obstinacy. Immediate conferences of Allied statesmen and soldiers advised that, for reasons of prestige, the offensive must continue, even if only with "limited" objectives. The French Government appointed Pétain Chief of the General Staff, and Pétain, on the whole, acted as a restraining influence on the infatuated Commander in Chief.

The French Army itself revolted at last against the whole madcap massacre. At the end of April there were reports of insubordination in the French Sixth Army; but Nivelle's mind seemed sealed against any information unwelcome to his overmastering ambition. A mild riot in one of the Negro colonial divisions was suppressed without much difficulty. But the trouble spread, and toward the middle of May mutinies broke out in the Fourth, Fifth, Sixth, and Tenth Armies — the armies in the offensive sectors. The worst case occurred at Soissons, where a couple of regiments declared their intention of marching on Paris, and for a few days, between Soissons and Paris, only two divisions could be relied on as "safe." It is remarkable that the enemy, though so well informed regarding the original offensive, appeared to know nothing of its later repercussions behind the lines and took no advantage of the situation.

On May 15, Pétain replaced Nivelle as Commander in Chief. Foch became his Chief of Staff. The two new leaders at once addressed themselves to a thorough disciplinary and psychological recuperation of the French Army. Some 150 death sentences were passed, but only 23 were actually carried out. Pétain toured the front lines and interested himself personally in the comforts of the common soldier. He ordered rations and billets to be improved and leaves to be regularized. He stopped the abuse of fatigues. Everywhere his evident simplicity and good faith made a healing impression. Gradually the old equilibrium was recovered. Yet not only had France and her army been terribly shaken, but her allies also. The French mutinies of 1917 explain the extreme hesitation both of Haig and later of Pershing in 1918 in accepting a French officer for the unified command of the Allied armies on the Western front.

The French mutinies left the British Army to bear the brunt of the remaining campaigning months of 1917. For some weeks Haig maintained the pressure round Arras, hoping to give relief to the French front. Then on June 7 the British Second Army under Plumer began the Battle of Messines, and executed a model set piece of siege warfare. Nineteen mines, involving the tunneling of 8,000 yards of underground galleries, were exploded under the German trenches, and the infantry assault was supported by 2,300 guns — one gun to every seven yards. The operation was pressed no farther than the limit of its impetus, and at the end of seven days it was brought voluntarily to a halt.

We know now that Haig should have been satisfied with what he had won. But it soon appeared that Messines was to be only the first stage of a great offensive in Flanders on which the British commander had set his heart. He believed that Germany was approaching the end of her man power; he believed he could take the Belgian coast; he almost believed he could defeat the German Army and bring the war to an end. In the light of our after-knowledge, Haig's delusions are astonishing. But the result was the Battle of Passchendaele, the most melancholy action in British military history. The Fifth Army led off the new attack with a ten-day bombardment by 3,000 guns — one gun to every six yards — and an expenditure of 4,250,000 shells. The infantry assault began on July 31; the fighting continued for more than three months. The British gained fifty square miles at the cost of 340,000 men, a number equal to those rescued at Dunkirk in 1940. Passchendaele, the immediate objective, by then an unrecognizable heap of mud and rubble, was announced as captured by the Canadian forces on November 6.

The Battle of Cambrai in November 1917 was a slight consolation for the anguish of Passchendaele. The battle is of the greatest tactical interest, as it was at Cambrai that the tank was first used as a major weapon. There was no artillery bombardment to advertise the coming offensive. In the half-light of dawn on November 20, 380 British tanks, lightly followed by infantry, crashed over the German trenches before Cambrai and took the defenders completely by surprise. The battle should have been a raid, as indeed it was originally intended to be. But the British commanders, as surprised at their success as their German enemies, now pressed forward the attack and tried to hold the ground the tanks had gained. The Germans counterattacked in force, and a battle which was almost a victory came very near to being a defeat. In the end the lines were re-established little changed from their original position. But the tank had received its baptism of fire; professionalism was at last convinced of its immense possibilities; modern mechanized warfare had made a most spectacular beginning.

POLITICAL CRISIS IN FRANCE

The French mutinies of 1917 may not have been directly attributable to subversive political organizations, but they were an undeniable sign of declining morale in the army and country at large. France had traveled a long way from the inspired unanimity of 1914. Impatience over the conduct of the war had gradually degenerated into a very serious discontent with the war itself. A dangerous weariness began to express itself in popular watchwords: "Let's have done with it" — *"Il faut en finir, il faut en finir!"* In particular the Socialists and the trade-unions were withdrawing from their former support of the government. Briand's first ministry, formed in October 1915, had survived Verdun, but only at the cost of a severe dunning by the parliamentary committees and of turbulent secret sessions of the Chamber. In December 1916, at the time Lloyd George had formed the second Coalition in England, Briand reorganized his Cabinet and made General Lyautey of Morocco his Minister of War. But General Lyautey's soldierly brusqueness somewhat riled the Chamber, and he resigned with some disgust in March 1917, just before the Nivelle Offensive, bringing down with him the entire Briand government.

Between that date and November 1917, Ribot and Painlevé were successively premiers of governments, both distinguished for their weakness. There was an outcrop of typically French political scandals during the summer months of 1917, some of them treasonable in character. Malvy, the Minister of the Interior, though apparently not implicated, was nevertheless accused of negligent supervision of foreign suspects and was forced to resign. A certain Paul Bolo was arrested for spreading defeatist propaganda. The financier Caillaux, that *enfant terrible* of French politics, was said to be pecuniarily interested in the *Bonnet Rouge,* a paper whose directors had been receiving funds from an enemy source. Even Briand, the former Premier — though his own action in the matter was entirely proper — was involved in a peace intrigue with Belgian intermediaries. The France of 1917, in more than one way, resembled the France of 1940.

The situation was saved by Clemenceau. On November 15, 1917, President Poincaré called him to the premiership. He succeeded in infusing more than a little of the old *Union Sacrée* into his new government and, like Lloyd George in Britain, he was soon symbolizing in his own person the very spirit of victory. He remained Premier of France during the last phases of the war, the Armistice, and the Peace Conference.

POLITICAL CRISIS IN GERMANY

Under the Bismarckian system in Germany, the Chancellor bore no responsibility to the Reichstag such as a democratic premier normally bears to a popular assembly. The Chancellor found it convenient in practice to have the support of the Reichstag, but he was the appointee of the Kaiser and responsible to the Kaiser alone. The Chancellor's secretaries were not Deputies of the Reichstag, bound to him by ties of policy or party, but professional civil servants and heads of bureaucratic departments. Germany herself was a federation of states, each state having its own Diet, and each Diet sometimes being elected in accordance with suffrage laws which supported the landed and vested interests. Political agitation in Germany before 1914 had aimed at securing parliamentary responsibility for the Chancellor and ministerial appointments for Reichstag Deputies.[3] Political agitation in the states, especially in Prussia, had aimed at securing reforms of the suffrage laws.

That agitation had been stilled by the *Burgfriede* of 1914 (see p. 48), and Germany had gone to war a united nation. But in 1916 there were signs that the truce was breaking down and that the old political issues were being revived. By 1917 the controversy over the "democratization" of the government had grown as loud and clamorous as it had ever been. The Social Democrats in increasing numbers were voting against the budget and against the supplementary credits, and were forming themselves into what in democratic countries would be called a parliamentary Opposition. In particular, party lines were now being aggravated by the question of war aims. The Right and the Conservatives subscribed to vast programs of conquests and annexations; the Left and the Social Democrats subscribed to a peace of reconciliation and a peace of the *status quo*.

The Chancellor, Bethmann-Hollweg, was persuaded that the Kaiser must make a voluntary gesture and promise the common soldiers of the army increased rights in the state they had victoriously defended. On March 14, 1917, in a memorable speech in the Prussian Landtag, the Chancellor broadly hinted at "the transformation of our political life which must result from the experiences of the war," and he referred in particular to reforms of the Prussian suffrage system. By one of those accidents of history which seem almost preordained, the first news of the Russian Revolution arrived in Berlin an hour or two after the Chancellor's speech. Then, on April 6, the United States declared war. The impact of the two events on Germany was tremendous.

On April 8 came the Kaiser's much-heralded gesture in the form of an "Easter Message" guardedly promising "the extension of our political, economic, and social life" after the war. Three months later, on July 12, he officially pledged new suffrage laws in Prussia "before the next elections." But these successive and patronizing concessions encouraged rather than quieted the growing unrest. The Reichstag appointed a Constitution Committee which began somewhat tactlessly to investigate the entire question of ministerial responsibility. Erzberger, a Deputy of the Center, opened a controversial debate on the unrestricted submarine campaign, of whose ill success uncomfortable rumors were now circulating. Finally several of the Deputies of the Reichstag resolved themselves into a committee to draft a formal Peace Resolution.

The Kaiser and the Chancellor and the Conservatives were now thoroughly alarmed. Peace talk would dangerously intensify the reviving party cleavages. Hindenburg and Ludendorff telegraphed from the front threatening their resignations if the impending Peace Resolution were not stopped. But instead Bethmann-Hollweg resigned, and the Kaiser, on the recommendation of Ludendorff, appointed Michaelis, a Prussian food official of no great distinction, to the chancellorship.

The Peace Resolution was brought before the Reichstag, and on July 19, 1917 it was passed by that assembly by 212 votes to 126 (see Appendix A). Michaelis, the new Chancellor, in his maiden speech agreed to support the Peace Resolution, "as I interpret it" — a lame reservation indeed, whose evasiveness and prevarication the Reichstag was not slow to detect. However, Michaelis made some gesture toward the "democratization" of the government, and appointed one or two Reichstag Deputies to minor ministerial posts. For the first time in history Germany came before the world with the makings of a cabinet.

So ended the July Crisis, as it was called. The Kaiser had made his promises, the Reichstag had passed a Peace Resolution, Michaelis had accepted Deputies as administrative colleagues. The Peace Resolution was followed by no appropriate action; the government made no attempt to translate it into a peace offer to the enemy; the Reichstag Deputies, having won their point by securing its passage, lost further interest in it. The country's attention was soon diverted by a new trouble — this time in the navy. The lower naval ratings had been much affected by recent events, notably by the Russian Revolution, and it also appears that they had been subject to revolutionary propaganda on the part of certain Reichstag Deputies of the Left. The enforced idleness of the German Navy — with the exception of the Skagerrak — had been very damaging to discipline. There had been hunger strikes, and the men had been deserting their ships as a protest against the stoppage of leave. In the end the naval authorities opened an investigation, several sailors were condemned to death, and two were actually shot. The affair should have stopped there and then. But Michaelis, in the heat of a debate in the Reichstag during October, suddenly blurted out charges against Social Democrat Deputies, mentioning them by name, and though he had no proper proofs, he virtually accused them of stirring up mutiny in the navy.

Michaelis confessed later that he had made a "tactical error." It was folly for him to remain longer in office. Yet there was more in Michaelis' "naval incident" than the maladroitness of a harassed chancellor. Germany and her leaders were not a happy company in 1917. Nerves were tense, tempers were short — and stomachs were empty — and it is not difficult to read into the Reichstag debates of that summer evidences of a very serious political demoralization. Michaelis was dismissed by the Kaiser on November 1, 1917 and was succeeded the same day by Count Hertling.

POLITICAL CRISIS IN AUSTRIA–HUNGARY

If strong and vigorous nations like France and Germany had relapsed into their characteristic peacetime divisions, it was hardly to be expected that Austria-Hungary, whose constitution in 1914 had not been too robust, should have borne more steadfastly the stresses and strains of the great conflict. Yet Austria-Hungary had gone to war in 1914 with a semblance of the unanimity of other belligerents. For two years she passed through a sort of historyless phase in which her population accepted the state of war with an almost deceptive resignation. While the tide of fighting ebbed and flowed about her frontiers, she patiently suffered the depletion of her farms and industries, the loss of her overseas commerce, the controls and the profiteering and shortages in all the necessaries of life.

But by the fall of 1916 patience and resignation were exhausted. The Battle of Luck, as the Brusilov Offensive was called in Austria, was a terrible military and political disaster. Austria and Hungary, the two components of the Monarchy, were themselves at odds. Austria, containing the major industrial areas, and Hungary, containing the greater agricultural areas, were waging a minor economic war and were each trying to blackmail the other with embargoes on their mutual exports. Count Tisza, the Hungarian Premier, had even established a "customs barrier" along the Austro-Hungarian frontier. On October 21, 1916, Stürgkh, the Austrian Premier, was assassinated in a Vienna café by Friedrich Adler, son of Viktor Adler, the well-known Austrian Social Democrat. It was one of those symbolic assassinations which come at critical moments in history to release over-charged and pent-up popular passions. On November 21 the aged Emperor Francis Joseph died, and the last restraint on the nation's traditional loyalty and discipline seemed to have been removed.

The new Emperor Charles, who succeeded, was young, warmhearted, com-panionable, and personally well liked. Given even normally favorable odds, he would have brought his people a well-deserving and a prosperous reign. But Charles had now come into a debtor's inheritance, and the troubles which beset him would have broken stronger men. He tried reforms in the food supplies. He appointed new aides and court officials. He dismissed Austria's redoubtable strategist and Chief of Staff, Field Marshal Conrad von Hötzendorf, who had led the Austrian armies with such uninterrupted ill success since 1914. But Austria and Hungary kept up their private eco-nomic feud, and Tisza, the Hungarian Premier, remained in a mood of typically Hungarian egoism and obstinacy. The Monarchy was forced into sharing the risks and the stigma of Germany's unrestricted submarine war. Finally, the old, old nationality question reappeared. All the subject races of the Monarchy, Czechs, Yugoslavs, Rumanians, and Poles, in so far as they could be articulate, resumed their former agitation for their independ-ent national rights.

Count Ottokar Czernin, the Austro-Hungarian Foreign Minister, seems to have been Charles's principal political mentor at this time. Early in April 1917, Czernin set down his views of the general situation, as he saw it, in a confidential memorandum, the so-called April Memorandum. He pointed frankly to the approaching end of the Monarchy's military endurance, the shortages of raw materials and munitions, the exhaustion of human effec-tives, the suffering and despair of the people at home. The army and the country, he argued, could not support another winter of war; revolution stalked through Europe, five monarchs already had been dethroned, and an empire united only by a dynastic principle must stand in special danger. "If the monarchs of the Central Powers cannot make peace in the coming months," he wrote, "it will be made for them by their peoples." It was not too late to propose peace to an enemy which had not yet suspected the Monarchy's weakness.

Czernin also advised that the Reichsrat, the Austrian parliament, sus-pended since early in 1914, should be reconvened, and that some constitu-tional concessions be made. The renewed nationalist agitation, he felt, could no longer be safely repressed, though it is doubtful if he expected the crisis he now invited. The Reichsrat met in Vienna in May 1917. Several of its Deputies were in jail on charges of sedition, or had fled the country into exile. Those who remained immediately used the Reichsrat sessions to deliver revolutionary manifestoes. The Czech and Yugoslav Deputies demanded the separation of their respective states into autonomous democratic units. In July, Charles tried the conciliatory effects of a general amnesty, and several political prisoners were released. But clemency of this kind could avail little now. There were waves of "desertions" at the front, and Czech regiments in particular could no longer be considered safe. In Budapest meanwhile, the Hungarian Diet was in its own toils. Here the agitation was taking the usual form of demands from the non-Magyar parties for electoral reforms. Tisza had resigned at the end of May and gone off to the front "to seek a hero's death," and the administration fell to a succession of Magyar oligarchs of the same breed as Tisza, who either would not, or could not, realize the seriousness of the popular revolt.

Abroad, groups of nationalist "emigrants" from Austria-Hungary forgathered in neutral and Allied countries, formed themselves into centers of propaganda, presumed an authority over their brethren at home, recruited contingents to serve in the Allied armies, and demanded the diplomatic recognition of the Allied Powers. The Czechs and the Yugoslavs established national councils in Paris, the nuclei of future national governments. In Russia the revolutionary Provisional Government in 1917 formed a Polish Corps and a Czech Legion out of Polish and Czech prisoners of war. At the end of 1917, Polish and Czech units were organized in France for service on the Western front. A Yugoslav division fought with the Allies at Salonika.

CAPORETTO

Unlike her allies and her foes, Italy had originally gone to war bearing the burden of an antiwar party. In 1915 she had been even less united than Austria. Both extreme Conservatives and Official Socialists were pacifist — though for different reasons — and the Clericals were pro-Austrian. The Vatican was officially neutral, but was suspected of being pro-Austrian. Then the fact that Italy had declared war on Austria-Hungary in May 1915 but had not declared war on Germany till August 1916 — at the time Rumania entered the war — had created for months an anomalous and psychologically disturbing situation.

In June 1916, Boselli had formed a coalition government of all but the noninterventionist parties, and he had even given a Clerical a minor cabinet post. Sonnino was his Foreign Minister, and Orlando his Minister of the Interior. The Italian armies were still hammering at the mountainous borders of Austria, and during 1916 they had fought the Fifth, Sixth, Seventh, Eighth, and Ninth Battles of the Isonzo. As on the Western front, small territorial gains had borne no reasonable proportion to the enormous loss of life.

By 1917, Italy was suffering from all the usual hardships of the war. Perhaps the lack of coal was the most serious. There had also been a partial failure of the previous year's harvest, and supplies in some of the larger cities were often at the point of exhaustion. Price fixing and rationing had not entirely eliminated the bread line and the bread riot. And, like every belligerent, Italy experienced all the stringencies of an acute labor shortage.

In August 1917 there were strikes at Turin. Numbers of strikers were rounded up and sent to the front, where presumably they would be under military discipline. "Penal" contingents were put into the line at Monte Nero, near Caporetto, then a relatively quiet sector. There had been rumors of an Austro-German offensive to take place in the autumn, and more than one commander felt anxious about "unreliable" elements which were said to be infecting the good spirit of the army. Catholic chaplains were regarded as sources of sympathy with Austria, and they were doubly suspect after the Vatican's peace note of August 1917 (see p. 92). There had been epidemics of fraternization with enemy outposts during lulls in the fighting. Continual, and seemingly organized, desertions of "nationalist" soldiers from the Austrian Army had had profoundly unsettling effects. General Cadorna, the Italian Chief of Staff, had been a successful leader, however, and patriotic opinion could hardly believe that a terrain which had proved almost impassable to the gallant armies of Italy should suddenly become an open highway for an Austro-German invasion. The Italian High Command refused to credit stories of disaffection in the trenches, and Cadorna even dismissed officers who brought him alarmist reports. The Tenth and Eleventh Battles of the Isonzo in May and in August showed no apparent diminution of the Italian offensive spirit. On October 24, General Giardino, newly appointed Minister of War, made his maiden speech in the Chamber in Rome and, amid ringing applause, declared that the army was sound to the core and would continue to be the bulwark of Italy. That very day the Austro-German forces broke through the Italian lines at Caporetto.

The Twelfth Battle of the Isonzo, as Caporetto was called in Italy, was the only considerable offensive operation essayed by the Central Powers in 1917. It was planned in complete secrecy. It began in the morning of October 24, and by evening the entire Italian position on the Isonzo was broken. The Italian Second Army was turned into a "fugitive rabble." Cadorna tried to make a stand on the Tagliamento, and finally on the Piave, where at last during mid-November the lines were once more stabilized. Italy lost 6,000 square miles of territory and 600,000 men, and for a few chaotic weeks it seemed as if she had gone down to final defeat.

But the very completeness of the disaster provided its own salvation. Italy was tested as she had never been tested before. It was not only that Venetia and Lombardy might once more become Austrian provinces, or that all the labor and sacrifice of 1860, 1866, and 1870 might be undone. It was rather that the very nationhood of Italy was under challenge in the eyes of the world. Caporetto stung the pride of a people but recently restored to political self-respect, reminiscent of a former servitude, and fiercely sensitive of their reputed want of martial qualities.

The military crisis was complicated by a ministerial crisis which broke simultaneously with, and indeed independently of, the first news of the great Austro-German offensive. General Giardino had enjoyed his moment of triumph, and the Boselli government suddenly fell. Bread riots had broken out again, and the Opposition was able to muster a heavy vote against the government's alleged mismanagement of food supplies. The King took counsel with Boselli and, on his advice, invited Orlando to form a cabinet. The shock of Caporetto had already chastened the Chamber, and Orlando found all the principal parties united in his support. Giolitti, the noninterventionist, after months of unsympathetic silence appeared dramatically in the Chamber and gave one of the bravest speeches of his long political career. Cadorna was replaced by General Diaz, "Italy's Pétain," as he was called.

Meanwhile French and British divisions had been hurried to the Italian front. American and British relief organizations went to work among the refugees who had fled before the Austro-German advance, and did much to counteract the panic of the civil population. On November 4, 1917, Allied premiers and military chiefs met in conference at Rapallo and discussed not only the reorganization of the Italian command but the entire question of military co-operation between the Allies. Under the driving initiative of Lloyd George, the conference finally drew up an agreement to establish a Supreme War Council at Versailles. Caporetto was an expensive lesson, but it purified Italy like a fire, and it was the precursor of unified command on the Western front (see pp. 97 and 98).

THE RUSSIAN REVOLUTION

By the end of 1916, Russia was at the point of collapse. Corruption and incompetence at home, defeat and demoralization at the front, had done their work. "Revolution was in the air," wrote Buchanan, the British ambassador in Petrograd, "and the only moot point was whether it would come from above or below." Petrograd throbbed with rumors. The Tsar's dethronement by force was the topic of conversation everywhere. General Alekseev and the High Command were said to be meditating a military dictatorship. On the night of December 29, Rasputin was assassinated.

The first stages of the Russian Revolution developed, without plan, aim, or leadership, from the strikes and street demonstrations which were taking place in Petrograd in the early days of March 1917. There were some clashes, but the bloodshed was small compared with many another less momentous disturbance in Russian history. The fearsome Cossacks fraternized with the crowd; army officers and police fled; the Petrograd garrison "demobilized itself." The Revolution, as one observer put it, "just walked into empty trenches." In the course of a week, the other cities of Russia revolted with as little effort, and as few excesses, as the capital.

The Tsar was at Headquarters at Mogilev when the news of the outbreaks in Petrograd arrived. A battalion was dispatched to the city to restore order, but the men deserted en route. The Tsar tried to dissolve the Duma, but it disobeyed his decree and continued its sessions. The Tsar then set out for Tsarskoe Selo himself, where the Tsarina and the imperial family were in residence, but soldiers and workers along the railroad diverted his train to Pskov, and he was there placed under virtual arrest. The Duma, however, was entirely unprepared for the Revolution. It eventually elected a Temporary Committee, which found itself obliged to act as a Provisional Government under the premiership of Prince Lvov, former director of the Zemstvo relief organizations (see p. 45). The first care of the new government was to send a deputation of two of its ministers to the Tsar at Pskov, and at Pskov on March 15, 1917, under their urgent advice, undramatically and unprotestingly, the Tsar signed his abdication.

Meanwhile the soldiers, sailors, and workers had been erecting their own impromptu hierarchy and building up their system of committees — or soviets — which, more than anything else, was to give the Russian Revolution its peculiar character. The Petrograd Soviet of some 2,500 soldiers and workers represented the regiments and factories in the capital but, being too unwieldy and unorganized for practical business, it elected a Soviet Executive Committee, which was soon holding a key position in the developing revolution. The Soviet Executive Committee welcomed the formation of the Provisional Government and agreed to — and to some extent dictated — its program. At the end of March the body politic of Russia presented a curious dualism. On the one hand stood the Provisional Government, an inheritance from the old Duma, and on the other stood the Soviet Executive Committee, an independent creation of the Petrograd soldiers and workers.

Abroad, the democratic world hailed the Russian Revolution fervently. Britain, France, and Italy — and the United States, which was then about to enter the war — at once recognized the Provisional Government, believing that the overthrow of the old autocracy would release the suppressed patriotic passions of the Russian people and inspire them to greater efforts in the war. But, as was too soon to appear, the Provisional Government was woefully weak. True, it had broken with the old autocracy, but it had achieved only the sufferance of the workers. The middle-class interests, which really composed it, represented no real power at all. A long tradition of criticism and opposition in the Duma had not fitted it for constructive politics. The police had vanished; the army was still an unknown quantity; the instruments of authority in the state were uncertain or nonexistent. Prince Lvov himself was a kindly Tolstoyan type, who believed in "nonresistance to evil" and "bloodless revolutions." In the circumstances, fundamental reforms were not in prospect. The workers wanted the factories, the peasants wanted the land, the soldiers wanted peace; but the Provisional Government tended to defer these matters to a future Constituent Assembly. Fortunately winter, both in the trenches and at home, imposed its own armistice. The German and Austrian High Commands preserved a quiet front — we are told they were chiefly interested at this time in preventing fraternization between the opposing troops — and the peasants were hardly able to seize land that was still under several feet of snow.

Hence the Provisional Government declared an amnesty for all political and religious offenses; freedom of speech, of the press, and of assembly; removal of all caste, religious, and racial distinctions; replacement of the police by a people's militia; and abolition of all restrictions on the enjoyment of civil rights by soldiers. It consented to factory reforms which it could not prevent, the eight-hour day for instance. But the real questions of the moment, peace and land, it was afraid to touch. It made little effort to parcel out the large estates, and it enunciated no agrarian policy. It sought to hold the army together and to prosecute the war in accordance with the commitments to the Allies made by the Tsarist regime. On April 10 it issued a manifesto on war aims declaring that "the aim of free Russia is not domination over other peoples, deprivation of their national possessions, violent acquisitions of alien territory, but the establishment of a stable peace on the basis of self-determination." Nevertheless "the Russian people will not permit their motherland to come out of the great struggle humiliated and crippled in its vital forces." On May 1, Prince Lvov's Foreign Minister, Miliukov, communicated the manifesto to the Allies. In an accompanying note, he emphasized further that Russia was determined to prosecute the war and to observe all her former obligations, and asserted that the Revolution had only strengthened the determination of the Russian people to bring the war to a victorious conclusion.

May 1, 1917 was Revolutionary Russia's first Labor Day, and it was celebrated in every part of the country. But the publication of Miliukov's note to the Allies came as a bitter anticlimax. The Soviets denounced "this imperialistic war." Antigovernment riots broke out in Petrograd. Prince Lvov was forced to replace his pro-Ally ministers by men who were supposed to be more interested in the cause of peace. Kerensky, formerly leader of the Labor group in the Duma, became Minister of War and the leading power in the new combination. Brusilov, who of all the Russian generals had taken most kindly to the Revolution, was appointed Chief of Staff in the High Command.

However, Kerensky, for all his former pacifism, was now as bellicose as any Tsarist minister. He toured the front and made a series of flaming speeches to restore the morale and discipline of the army. French and British Socialist leaders, then visiting Russia in the interests of Allied solidarity, sent home the most enthusiastic reports about him. On July 1 the Russian southwestern armies actually launched an offensive in Galicia, the theater of Brusilov's triumphs in 1916, but after some initial successes against Austrian troops as demoralized as themselves, they encountered German reserves and retired in disorder. A brigade of the Czech Legion covered itself with useless glory on the famous field of Zborow. Brusilov, sadly discredited, relinquished his command to General Kornilov. On September 2 the Germans captured Riga.

Profiting by the Provisional Government's amnesty, exiled Bolshevik leaders had been returning home. Stalin arrived in March. Lenin left Zürich, passing through Germany in a sealed car under the special protection of the German High Command, anxious to introduce this likely troublemaker into the rear of Germany's enemy; traveling by way of Sweden, he arrived safely in Petrograd on April 16. Trotsky arrived in May. At this time, the Bolshevik following in the Soviets had not been considerable. But Lenin was quick to realize that the Soviets were the only organizations with the promise of a future in the new Russia, and under his famous watchword "All Power to the Soviets" he began to foment the revolutionary force latent in them and to convert it to his own purposes. In June the Soviet Executive

Committee in Petrograd called together the First All-Russian Congress of Soviets, but at this Congress the Bolsheviks were still only a minority delegation.

The rioting which broke out in Petrograd in July, at the time of Kerensky's offensive, found the Bolsheviks unprepared and took them by surprise. The "July Days," as they were called, looked like a proletarian demonstration in favor of a Soviet regime; but the Soviet was not to be stampeded into responsibilities which it was not yet ready to bear. Four hundred lost their lives in the rioting; Trotsky and Kamenev were arrested; Lenin went into hiding; *Pravda* and the other Bolshevik papers were suppressed; and for the moment the Bolsheviks seemed to have disappeared from the face of Russia as completely as they had disappeared in 1914. Encouraged by the easy collapse of what he had believed to be a dangerous conspiracy against the government, Kerensky felt that he could further consolidate his position. He assumed the premiership and declared Russia a republic. During August, at Moscow, he organized a monster State Conference, representing all classes and communities, and tried strenuously to round out his authority with the moral sanction of a spectacular political fete in Russia's ancient capital.

But the Bolsheviks had now not long to wait. The State Conference was Kerensky's apogee. He was already at odds with Kornilov, who was determined to follow his own methods for restoring army discipline. By late summer of 1917 there were no longer two, but three authorities competing for political power in Russia — the Provisional Government, the Soviets, and the High Command. The Provisional Government and the High Command might have profitably combined against the Soviets, but negotiations between them were mishandled by a dishonest intermediary. In September, Kerensky at last dismissed Kornilov from his command, and Kornilov attempted to save himself by setting up a military dictatorship. The coup failed, and Kornilov finally surrendered himself to arrest.

Kerensky seemed to have won out; but it was a hollow victory. An unpleasant feeling got abroad that Kerensky was no better than many a lesser place seeker in the revolutionary hustings at Petrograd. In an effort to gain flagging popular support, Kerensky made a number of concessions, notably the release of the Bolshevik leaders arrested after the July riots. The Revolution, which till now had been remarkably free from terrorism, took on an uglier aspect. The workers went on strike and sacked the food shops and bakeries; the peasants plundered the land, burned the manors, and murdered the landlords; there were sudden massacres of officers in the army and navy; the army itself resorted to mass desertion, and the High Command expected it to withdraw from the field of its own volition; the non-Russian nationalities manifested a tendency to secede and form themselves into independent republics — notably Finland. The Soviet Executive Committee set up a Military Revolutionary Committee, ostensibly for the defense of the capital.

The Bolsheviks took quick advantage of their restored freedom. Bolshevik newspapers reappeared. The Petrograd Soviet elected Trotsky to its presidency. It was rapidly turning violent in its views, and Trotsky had little difficulty in promoting its happy conversion to Bolshevism. The Second All-Russian Congress of Soviets was planned to take place in Petrograd in November, and it was evident that the Bolsheviks, this time, not only expected to have a commanding majority at its meetings but also to gain control over the all-important Military Revolutionary Committee and to use the occasion to proclaim a new government.

Kerensky only slowly realized the danger in which he stood. He spent the first week of November vainly hunting for a body of troops to defend his regime. On November 7 he left for the front, where prospects of finding reliable men were still said to be good. Almost at that hour, the Military Revolutionary Committee issued a manifesto, "To the Citizens of Russia," written by Lenin, announcing the overthrow of the Provisional Government and its own assumption of power. Late in the evening of the same day, at the Smolny Institute in Petrograd, the Second All-Russian Congress of Soviets opened its sessions. During the night, after a short and almost bloodless bombardment, the Bolsheviks occupied the Winter Palace and arrested some of the ministers of the Provisional Government who were sheltering there. The Winter Palace was the Bastille of the Russian Revolution.

Lenin addressed the Congress of Soviets at its session on the evening of November 8. He read a "Decree of Peace," addressed to "the peoples and governments of the belligerent countries" and proposing "a just, democratic peace without annexations or indemnities." He read a "Decree on Land," abolishing landlord property without compensation and transferring its ownership "to the whole people." The Congress then appointed a Council of People's Commissars as the new organ of government in Russia, "pending the convocation of a Constituent Assembly," with Lenin as President, Trotsky as Commissar for Foreign Affairs, Rykov as Commissar of Internal Affairs, and Stalin as Commissar for Nationalities.

The Bolshevik triumph was complete. Menshevik and Social-Revolutionary opposition at the Congress had been conspicuously disunited and ineffectual. All the members of the new Council of People's Commissars were Bolsheviks. The single act of open insurrection by young army cadets in Moscow was suppressed. In December, Lenin created Cheka, "the Extraordinary Commission for Combatting Counterrevolution."

Trotsky opened the Russian peace offensive on November 22 with a note to all Allied ambassadors in Petrograd proposing "an immediate armistice on all fronts and the immediate initiation of peace negotiations." The Western Allies made a last attempt to foil the Bolshevik plans and tried to enlist the support of the old Russian High Command. But the Bolsheviks replied by making one of their party, an ensign named Krylenko, Commander in Chief of the Russian Army, and the High Command was virtually dissolved.

On November 27 three Russian envoys under the white flag crossed the German lines. Arrangements were made through them for a Russian delegation — including Joffe, Kamenev, Sokolnikov, Madame Bitzenko, together with a common soldier, a sailor, a peasant, and a worker — to be received at the German headquarters at Brest Litovsk, and at Brest Litovsk on December 5, 1917 an armistice was duly signed by this strangely assorted party of plenipotentiaries.

PEACE OFFERS AND PEACE INTRIGUES

The war weariness, of which these many political crises of 1917 in France, Germany, Austria-Hungary, and Russia were evidence, also showed itself in various peace offers and peace intrigues in the course of the year. The Austro-German peace offer of December 1916 was a maneuver dictated more by military than pacific considerations (see p. 63), but the German Reichstag's Peace Resolution of July 1917 was perhaps of a different character; it was a desperate popular agitation momentarily breaking through the restraints of patriotism and political expedience.

The Austrian Emperor Charles, in March 1917, established secret contacts with the French Government, using the Bourbon princes, Sixte and Xavier, as intermediaries. Poincaré was the chief negotiator in France, and Lloyd George was afterward an enthusiastic participant in the intrigue. Czernin, the Austro-Hungarian Foreign Minister, established his own contacts with the French High Command, using intermediaries in Switzerland. In the summer months of 1917, Baron von der Lancken, formerly Counselor of the German Embassy in Paris and during the war attached to the staff of the German Governor General in Belgium, made contacts with Briand in France by means of Belgian intermediaries. But these efforts led to no other result than unpleasant "revelations" afterward. International Socialist peace conferences had already been held in Switzerland, at Zimmerwald in 1915 and at Kiental in 1916, the latter remarkable for the presence of Lenin. In June and July 1917, at Stockholm, Socialist leaders of Holland and Sweden organized a third International Socialist peace conference, which was attended by a smattering of unofficial delegates from various parts of belligerent and neutral Europe. Needless to say, none of these Socialist conferences had the least effect on the belligerent governments.

It was hoped at one time that more substantial success might have resulted from the intercession of the Vatican. Pope Benedict XV's political antecedents well qualified him for the role of mediator, and he had in Pacelli, the nuncio at Munich, a diplomat of infinite tact and experience. But the Vatican's position was never a strong one; the war cut across religious allegiances of every kind; Catholics in their thousands fought on either side. The Vatican's every move was open to misconstruction. Even in 1917, when hopes of peace beat faster and more insistently, the Pope's efforts led to failure.

"In the presence of anguish and peril" — so ran the papal peace note to the belligerents on August 1, 1917 — "we, who have no special political aim, who heed neither the suggestions nor the interests of either belligerent party, but are impelled solely by the consciousness of our supreme duty as the common father of the peoples, by the prayers of our children who implore us to intervene and give peace, by the very voice of humanity and of reason, we raise again a cry for peace and renew a pressing appeal to those in whose hands lie the destinies of nations." The note then referred to the problems of disarmament, of an international court of arbitration, and of the freedom of the seas. "As to the reparation of damage and to the costs of war, we see no way to solve the question save by laying down the general principle of the complete restitution of occupied territories," in particular the evacuation of Belgium and northern France by Germany, and of the German colonies by the Allies. The note begged for a spirit of conciliation and equity in the matter of territorial questions between Italy and Austria, between Germany and France, in Armenia, in the Balkans, and in Poland. "As for us, closely united in prayer and penitence with all faithful souls who sigh for peace, we pray that the Divine Spirit grant you light and counsel."

Official replies from the belligerents to the papal note were polite and evasive. The British Government was disposed to make use of it to extract from Germany a definite statement of her war aims, especially in regard to Belgium, but no such statement was forthcoming from Berlin, and the German Chancellor, Michaelis, appears to have taken it upon himself to notify by letter the papal nuncio, Pacelli, that "conditions" did not make it possible for him "to issue a decisive declaration of policy." Whether or not the papal peace note could ever have induced the belligerents to come to terms seems doubtful, but Michaelis' obtuse diplomacy was certainly one concrete contribution to its failure to do so.

The winter months of 1917–18 were used by the statesmen of the belligerent nations for a new kind of diplomacy of "long-distance debate" by speech and press. The feeling that the war was now rushing to a decision perhaps induced a certain mood for apologetics. At least the great climactic effort on the Western front could not be made without due clarification of objectives. Lord Lansdowne may be said to have opened the debate in his letter to the *Daily Telegraph* on November 29, 1917, appealing for a negotiated peace. President Wilson, Lloyd George, Balfour, Hertling, Czernin, and Sonnino made their several statements on their national war aims. Finally, President Wilson, in his address to the joint session of Congress on January 8, 1918, enunciated his Fourteen Points and imparted a definitive literary form to all the searching, groping ideologies of the Allied cause.

The Fourteen Points, in Wilson's words, were "the program of the world's peace." (See Appendix B.) They were "essential rectifications of wrong and assertions of right." They were couched in the form of categorical demands: Point 1, for "open covenants of peace" and for the abolition of "private international understandings" and of secret diplomacy in general; Point 2, for the freedom of the seas; Point 3, for "the removal of all economic barriers and the establishment of an equality of trade conditions"; Point 4, for the reduction of armaments "to the lowest point consistent with domestic safety"; Point 5, for "the impartial adjustment of all colonial claims"; Point 6, for "the evacuation [by the Central Powers] of all Russian territory" and the settlement of Russian questions in a spirit of "intelligent and unselfish sympathy"; Point 7, for the evacuation and restoration of Belgium; Point 8, for the freeing of invaded French territory and the retrocession to France of Alsace-Lorraine; Point 9, for "a readjustment of the frontiers of Italy . . .

along clearly recognizable lines of nationality"; Point 10, for "the freest opportunity of autonomous development" for the peoples of Austria-Hungary; Point 11, for the evacuation and restoration of Rumania, Serbia, and Montenegro; Point 12, for the separation of non-Turkish nationalities from Ottoman rule and for the establishment of the Dardanelles as a free international waterway; Point 13, for the creation of "an independent Polish state . . . which should include the territories inhabited by indisputably Polish populations, which should be assured a free and secure access to the sea"; and Point 14, for "a general association of nations . . . for the purpose of affording mutual guarantees of political independence and territorial integrity." As addenda and amplification of these Fourteen Points, President Wilson, in the course of 1918, further enunciated Four Principles, Four Ends, and Five Particulars (see Appendix B). The whole constitutes what we shall call in later chapters the Wilsonian code, the formal basis of the eventual peace treaties of 1919–20.

BREST LITOVSK AND BUCHAREST

Early in 1918, Germany was able to terminate hostilities on the Eastern front and turn to concentrate her forces for a final campaign in the West. On December 5, 1917 the Russians, and on December 9 the Rumanians, signed armistices which were tantamount to military surrender. Negotiations for a peace treaty between the Central Empires and the Russian Soviet Government opened at Brest Litovsk on December 22 and were concluded there on March 3, 1918. A Rumanian peace treaty was signed at Bucharest on May 7, 1918.

A recent writer has referred to Brest Litovsk as the "Forgotten Peace," [4] and he might have described Bucharest in the same words. Both treaties were renounced by Germany after her defeat and, except among historians whose business it is to remember these things, they have become truly forgotten peaces. Both treaties were cynical to a degree and were an undisguised fulfillment of Teutonic annexationism in the Baltic, the Ukraine, and the Balkans. They foreshadowed the acquisitions which Germany once more tried to make in 1941–45.

The negotiations at Brest Litovsk brought together an interesting galaxy of conflicting personalities — Kühlmann, the German Foreign Secretary, who so earnestly hoped to draft a model peace; General Hoffmann, the special representative of the German High Command and former staff officer of Ludendorff at the Battle of Tannenburg, who steadily refused to renounce one kilometer of the conquests of the German Army; Czernin, the Austro-Hungarian Foreign Minister, who wanted nothing so much as the wheat of the Ukraine for his starving Vienna; and Trotsky, the Soviet Foreign Commissar, who tried to play off one party against the other and save what he could from the wreck of his defeated homeland. But military power won, and not all Trotsky's sharpened wit and dialectical skill could secure him from the stolid dictation of the representative of the German High Command. Probably Trotsky would have preferred a last-ditch resistance with what Russian forces still held the field. But Lenin advised peace, even a German peace. In the end the Soviet Government, under the terms of the Treaty of Brest Litovsk, ceded the territories of Lithuania, Courland, and Poland, and agreed to evacuate Livonia, Estonia, Finland, and the Ukraine. An Austro-Hungarian commission was dispatched to Kiev for the purchase of wheat. Turkey received Kars, Ardahan, and Batum.

The Treaty of Bucharest gave legal form to the German conquest and occupation of Rumania. It granted the Central Empires a monopoly of Rumanian agricultural produce for nine years and of Rumanian oil for a period of thirty years — with the option of two further periods of thirty years each. Hungary acquired a frontier along the Carpathians which would secure her from a future Rumanian attack. The ports of Constanta, Giurgiu, and Turnu-Severin were leased to Germany and Austria-Hungary. The Dobruja, though claimed by Bulgaria, was allotted to the joint administration of the four "Allied Powers": Germany, Austria-Hungary, Bulgaria, and Turkey. Bessarabia was permitted to join herself to the Rumanian territories.

WORLD WAR

Several Latin-American republics followed the lead of the United States into the war, some in a spirit of "continental solidarity" with her, some in protest against specific outrages by German submarines upon their shipping. Between April 1917 and midsummer 1918, Panama, Cuba, Guatemala, Brazil, Nicaragua, Costa Rica, Haiti, and Honduras declared war on Germany. Bolivia, Peru, Uruguay, Ecuador, and the Dominican Republic severed relations. Argentina gave the German envoy his passports, but did not proceed to a complete rupture.

Thirty sovereign states were ultimately involved in the war. China severed relations with Germany in March 1917, partly as the result of Anglo-Japanese pressure and partly as the result of her own expressed indignation at the German submarine campaign, and in August of the same year the Peking Government, on behalf of all China, declared war on Germany and Austria-Hungary. In July 1917, Siam (Thailand) declared war on Germany and Austria-Hungary and seized German shipping in her ports. In August 1917 the African republic of Liberia declared war on Germany.

Twenty-four states — Serbia, Russia, France, Luxembourg, Belgium, the British Empire, Montenegro, Portugal, Japan, Italy, Rumania, Greece, the United States, Panama, Cuba, Guatemala, Siam, China, Liberia, Brazil, Nicaragua, Costa Rica, Haiti, and Honduras — thus came to be ranged against four: Austria-Hungary, Germany, Turkey, and Bulgaria — and we may add Albania and Persia, which were variously engaged. Russia and Rumania made peace, as has just been described, early in 1918. In the end, out of a world population of 1,600,000,000, it may be said that 1,400,000,000 were involved in the First World War.

7 THE CLOSING CAMPAIGNS: 1918

THE GERMAN OFFENSIVE IN THE WEST

In 1918, Germany staked her all on a final decision on the Western front. Thanks to the Russian collapse in 1917 and the treaties of peace at Brest Litovsk and Bucharest, the military situation had turned momentarily to her advantage, and for the first time since 1914 the German High Command could concentrate a superiority, or at least a favorable equivalence of numbers, in France and Belgium. The unrestricted submarine campaign still continued, though it had long since fallen short of the rosy prophecies of the German Admiral Staff, and the transportation of American troops across the Atlantic had proceeded without the loss of a ship.[1] If then an offensive there was to be, it was imperative to launch it before the new American formations compensated for the elimination of Russia. The German Army on the whole was still sound, though malingering was on the increase and disturbing "incidents" had been reported. Some of the new drafts had been of poor quality, and men repatriated from Russian prisoner-of-war camps had arrived in a wretched physical and mental condition. It was to be hoped, however, that the transition from the defensive to the offensive in the West would give its own encouragement to morale.

Germany's allies were fast approaching, if indeed they had not already reached, the point of exhaustion, and their continued loyalty would seem to depend more and more upon her gaining a reassuring victory in France. The Austro-Hungarian Army, it was painfully evident, no longer possessed its old fighting value. The Emperor Charles prayed insistently for an end to the war. Bulgaria was in a parlous state. Her old enemies, Serbia and Rumania, were beaten, and she wanted peace. The Bulgarian Government and people had always taken a parochial view of the war and could not understand the reason for prolonging it now that their main objects were, or seemed likely to be, attained. Turkey was fighting losing engagements in Palestine and Mesopotamia, and her Arab subjects were in revolt. "The state of our allies, of ourselves, and of the army," writes Ludendorff, "all called for an attack that would bring about an early decision. This could only be accomplished on the Western front. Everything that had gone before was a means to the one end of creating a military situation that would make it possible. Until now the situation had not arisen." [2]

In January 1918 preparations for the coming offensive were going forward. The German High Command combed the expanse of the Reich for effectives and supplies. A corps of "storm troops" was specially trained in "shock tactics" and "infiltration." By mid-March, three German armies, totaling 62 divisions, were ready poised on a 45-mile front below Arras. The prospect of defeat Ludendorff appears not to have considered. Supposedly the German Army could at any time break off the offensive, resume the defensive, and hold the enemy as firmly as it had done before. If the new offensive failed, the only deduction would be that, under tactical conditions in the West, the offensive was still not a practicable operation. The German Army would then have merely repeated its old campaign before Verdun and confirmed the experience of the French and British armies in every attack they had essayed from 1915 to 1917. Yet Ludendorff had not deeply realized how far German morale — both at the front and at home — was now nourished on the hope of the decision he had promised. In a war of nations there is no middle term between victory and defeat, and Germany could not now survive another military disappointment. She was to learn, too late, the error of allowing her fate to have fallen into the hands of one man of limited abilities, even in his own profession as a soldier, and of incredible political naïveté. As the event proved, the alternative to the offensive this time was not the resumption of position warfare, but utter and irretrievable ruin.

The situation on the Allied side was difficult. The French Army was still shaken from the mutinies of 1917. The British Army had been sadly depleted by the obstinate massacre of Passchendaele, and there was not a division in it but needed rest, refitting, and training. In January 1918 the British Army took over twenty-five miles of the French front. Administrative friction in England, evidenced by sudden and mystifying changes in the higher offices and commands, and even by scandalous "revelations" in the press, did not help the situation. American troops were just beginning to arrive in strength, but American divisions to date were being assigned only to quiet sectors of the line. Actually American divisions were sustaining major actions from May 1918 onward, and during the summer of the year American arrivals in France rose to the rate of 10,000 men a day. But so stupendous an achievement of training and logistics had been beyond all expectation at the time the German offensive commenced.[3]

Yet there was one bright side to the picture. The political and economic organization of the Allies, since the American entry into the war, had reached a point of high efficiency. Meetings of the Imperial War Cabinet in London in 1917 and the establishment of permanent Inter-Allied Councils for the allocation of raw materials and shipping had integrated the entire Allied war effort. Propaganda against the enemy, especially against Austria-Hungary, was being well co-ordinated and was becoming effective. All the peoples of Central Europe had heard of President Wilson's Fourteen Points. The unification of command on the Western front had been partially achieved by the Supreme War Council at Versailles.

The German offensive opened at dawn on March 21, 1918 with Ludendorff's massed barrage. Churchill, who then happened to be visiting a divisional headquarters of the British Fifth Army, has described it as "the most tremendous cannonade I shall ever hear." Legends have grown up around the offensive, even as they have grown up around the First Battle of the Marne. It was said that the British Fifth Army was badly led and practically annihilated, or that Haig, at the height of the action, gave orders to evacuate

Amiens and retire to the Channel, or that the field was only saved in the nick of time by a hastily collected force of 3,000 engineers and railroad men. Official accounts from both sides have given us somewhat less dramatic views, as official accounts invariably do, but they have not detracted from the gravity and anguish of the great battle. In round numbers, between March 21 and April 5 the Germans gained 1,500 square miles between St. Quentin and Amiens on the British front, inflicted 160,000 casualties, and themselves lost as heavily. The brunt of the attack was borne by the British Fifth Army, occupying the twenty-five miles recently taken over from the French and so thinly deployed there as to be outnumbered by five to one.

Yet if those March days now lie before us as a simple story, for their protagonists behind the lines they were days of chaos and indecision. British Headquarters at first was slow to take alarm, and Pétain at the French High Command at first tried to believe the whole attack to be a feint to induce him to divert his own reserves. The Cabinet and the War Office in London appear to have been far more sensitive to the seriousness of the early incoming news — or lack of news — than the generals on the spot. Conference followed conference in an atmosphere of increasing gloom. Pétain was frankly defeatist. Even Clemenceau was at a loss.

But it was the moment that Foch had been waiting for. He rose to the occasion like a man called to his destiny. When generals and statesmen who had grown old in the hard school of leadership were all faltering, his was the one driving, chiding voice among them. "M. Clemenceau has accepted Pétain's point of view, but I take no responsibility for that," he said. "I have sent M. Clemenceau a note explaining my opinion. Common sense demands that when the enemy makes a breach, you do not widen it. You close it or try to close it. You have only to try and to will, and the rest is easy. You stick to your ground and defend it foot by foot. We did that at Ypres, and we did it at Verdun."

At an Allied conference at the little Picard town of Doullens on March 26, Foch was appointed to "co-ordinate the action of the Allied armies on the Western front." No American officer attended the conference, but General Pershing wrote to Foch afterward in cordial terms, accepting the agreement in its entirety. Finally, on April 14, Foch was invested with the formal title of Commander in Chief of the Allied Armies in France. The decision completed the last link in the Allied organization, and France, Britain, and the United States thereafter met the hazards of the great military crisis in complete unity.

Ludendorff had called the German Army's task "the greatest in military history." But the task proved far too great. He had tried to destroy the British Army in France, and he drove it back some thirty miles on a section of its front. But his effort in March was still his most successful, and in four more offensives in as many months he did not approach even these imperfect results. In April he attacked the British on the Lys in Flanders; in May, the French on the Chemin-des-Dames; in June, the French around Compiègne; in July, the French around Reims. "If my attack at Reims succeeds now," he said on the first day of the last offensive, "we have won the war." "If the

German attack at Reims succeeds," Foch is reported to have said on the same day, "we have lost the war." The attack did not succeed. Ludendorff had exhausted his reserves — what was worse, he had exhausted his army's morale — but at no point had he stretched the Allied line beyond its limit of resistance.

That Ludendorff had not been entirely satisfied with the progress of his army was shown by "the diplomatic feelers" permitted by the German High Command and Government — and by Ludendorff — during the midsummer of 1918. The maneuver was clumsily managed and is mainly interesting to-day as revealing the German Government's total incomprehension of the psychology both of the German home front and of the Allies. Kühlmann, the German Foreign Secretary, raised the question in a speech in the Reichstag toward the end of June. "In view of the magnitude of this coalition war, in view of the numbers of Powers engaged, here and overseas," he said, "an absolute end to the war, by military decisions alone, without an exchange of ideas and without diplomacy, is not to be expected." Germany in that summer was drunk with victory and was entirely unprepared for so sobering a shock as this. Kühlmann, even though he had spoken with the entire approval of his Chancellor and in honest interpretation of the views of the High Command, was now dismissed in disgrace. The Kaiser appointed in his place a somewhat picturesque newcomer to politics, a certain Admiral von Hintze.

THE ALLIED COUNTEROFFENSIVE

Ludendorff's Reims offensive in July had been intended to deepen the gains he had made against the French in May, but he only developed a vulnerable and inviting salient on the Marne. The French High Command had expected the operation and received its first onset with their new "elastic" defense.[4] On July 18, Foch delivered a sudden tank attack from the Forest of Compiègne against the flank of the new salient and compelled the Germans to retire.

Ludendorff at first had not regarded Foch's counteroffensive as more than a local effort. Nonetheless it had been a painful surprise to him. After four months of continuous initiative, he could hardly credit his foe with offensive powers. But the Second Battle of the Marne, as we call it now, was in fact the turning point of the campaign of 1918 and the beginning of the end of the war. Further painful surprises were now in store. On the morning of August 8 the British attacked the German lines before Amiens. Canadian and Anzac divisions, supported by a fleet of 450 tanks, formed the main weight of the assault. The German positions on the Somme were overwhelmed; German divisional staffs were captured unawares at breakfast at their headquarters. In a day's fighting the attacking forces made a drive of from seven to eight miles and took 16,000 prisoners. On August 9 the French struck at Montdidier and joined the advance on the right of their allies.

Measured by the standards of the German offensives of March, April, May, and June, the gains in ground and prisoners in the Second Battle of the

Marne and the Battle of Amiens were not considerable. But they established the tank as the real offensive weapon in trench warfare — the weapon, more-over, which the Germans had neglected to adopt. During the fighting whole bodies of Germans had surrendered, sometimes to single infantrymen. Re-tiring German troops, meeting fresh units going into the line, had greeted them with shouts of "Strikebreakers!" and "War-prolongers!" Well might Ludendorff call August 8 "the black day of the German Army."

The Kaiser held a Crown Council on August 14 at the headquarters of the German High Command, then at the Belgian watering place of Spa, to dis-cuss the military situation. Hintze, the new Foreign Secretary, talked of further "diplomatic feelers" and seemed to have fully acquiesced in the view that " the objective of our strategy must now be to exhaust the enemy by defensive tactics." Ludendorff was confident that his front would hold fast and considered that, if the peace initiative did not come from the enemy, Germany could afford to wait for "the psychological moment" — that is, for the next success in the West — before taking the necessary steps herself. The Austrian Emperor Charles, who had come to Spa and was afterward present at some of the discussions, pressed urgently for an immediate appeal for peace. He was accompanied by Count Burian, recently reappointed Austro-Hungarian Foreign Minister, who was of the same mind as himself. Austrian offensives on the Asiago and Piave, designed to complement Ludendorff's operations in France, had been dismal failures. Subversive nationalist agita-tion in both Austria and Hungary was rising to new heights of audacity. There were constant ministerial changes in the Austrian and Hungarian governments.

But in August 1918 the inwardness of the great conflict in all its gauntness rises to the surface, and the war becomes nakedly a war of morale. The Allied tank, formidable though it was, would never have so easily overrun the German positions if their living defenders had had any heart left in them. The Allied peoples in their homes were too wrapped up in their own tribulations to give a thought to those of their enemies, and after four years of deadlock they had hardly the mental resilience to comprehend that the German Army was at last in the midst of a general strategic retirement. But the Allied leaders saw more clearly and were now calculating the chances of a psychological collapse in Central Europe. They imagined perhaps a wave of strikes and mutinies, or at least a new crisis in the Reichstag on a par with that of July 1917. The English and French press gave an exuberant publicity to talk of party strife in Berlin, to every new evidence of privation or depression behind the German lines, to every captured German army order against desertion or overstaying of leave.

The rot in the German Army quickened as August passed. Certain Ger-man divisions "obviously showed a disinclination to attack." The dressing stations were filled with men who hurried out of the trenches without orders. Offenses were committed "to escape duty by undergoing punishment." There was a good deal of disease, especially influenza and dysentery, both exceptionally weakening to the patient and hard to throw off without those dietary comforts which could no longer be obtained. Numbers of men from the last comb-out in Germany had come from the industrial districts; they were not untouched by revolutionary socialism, and they resented the change from high wages in the factory to the danger and dirt of the trenches. Then the old officer corps, once the backbone of the army's spirit and discipline, had long been decimated and the new officer types had neither the same training nor authority. "We had reached such a point," writes Ludendorff, "that before an action units used to detail a reserve of officers, who did not take part in the fighting, in order that there might be someone left in command at the end of it." [5]

THE COLLAPSE OF BULGARIA

Bulgaria was the first Power to forsake the Central Empires. The absence of recent military activity upon her front had perhaps caused both friends and enemies to underestimate the seriousness of her condition. Her army — after six years of wars [6] — was demoralized; the men were streaming back to their villages, and those who still stood in the trenches above Salonika could have offered little resistance to a major attack. The German "stiffening" had been taken away to reinforce Ludendorff's offensives in the West. The Bulgarian Government and the country's conservative interests remembered with rankling humiliation the scant sympathy their German allies had given their demands at the recent peace conference at Bucharest. In June 1918, Radoslavov, Bulgarian Premier for five years and the chief representative of Germanophilism in Sofia, resigned and was replaced by Malinov, a statesman of liberal sympathies, well disposed toward the Allies.

The Bulgarian press at once began to discuss the prospects of a separate peace. The American chargé d'affaires traveled freely about the country and, according to the common belief, did not disdain to advance subversive propaganda with American gold.[7] The Bulgarian Tsar Ferdinand, ostensibly in poor health but really in fear of a peasant uprising, left for medical treatment in Austria. He begged in vain for German reinforcements. Suddenly in mid-September General Franchet d'Esperey, commanding the Allied forces in Salonika, attacked and broke the Bulgarian lines, and in four days was advancing into the heart of Serbia. Bulgaria had no choice but to sue for an armistice. Salonika, that "unwanted" front, once so hotly debated in the military councils of the Allies, had at last been justified.

On September 29, 1918 the Bulgarian Armistice Commission was received at Franchet d'Esperey's headquarters and signed the terms he offered. On October 3, Tsar Ferdinand abdicated in favor of his son Boris. Bulgaria was out of the war.

THE GERMAN APPEAL TO PRESIDENT WILSON

Meanwhile the German position on the Western front had steadily deteriorated. Since August 8 fighting had developed all along the line. Foch had struck where and as he pleased. The British had advanced over the old Somme battlefields and were astride the Hindenburg Line. The French were advancing relentlessly in the Champagne. The Americans, now established under General Pershing in their own sector of the line on either side of Verdun, won their first action as a united army against the Germans in the old salient at St. Mihiel and, on September 26, began their great seven-week engagement in the Meuse-Argonne. Since the opening of the offensive in March the Germans had lost 1,000,000 men, and their casualties were now fast gaining on replacements. The German divisions were at half strength, and some had been continuously in action for weeks. The depots and railroad stations swarmed with deserters. At the same time the Americans were landing at the rate of 250,000 men a month, and to date there were 3,000,000 in France, a number equivalent to the then total strength of the German forces on all fronts. In 1919 an American army of 5,000,000 might be expected, trained, fresh, and equipped with all the wealth of the Western Hemisphere.

Events at the front were reflected in the unrest in Berlin. The Social Democrats especially had begun to raise their voices again on behalf of a "peace of understanding" and to revive all the old cries for electoral reform in Prussia and for cabinet responsibility in Germany. Every German knew, by now, the text and import of the Fourteen Points. All the Wilsonian propaganda, with relentless repetition, had made it plain that even a peace of understanding would not be obtainable to Germany until she had transformed herself into a genuine parliamentary state. Nor indeed was it to be expected that the present German Government could rally the German people to further sacrifices and privations without giving them something more than glib verbal assurances in regard to those democratic measures they had so long and earnestly desired. Thus argued Social Democrats like Ebert and Scheidemann, who were now coming to the forefront of German politics. As need hardly be said, Hertling, the Chancellor, an amiable old gentleman, was totally out of sympathy, even as he was totally out of touch, with the rising agitation.

On September 28, 1918 the decision to sue for peace "without delay" had already been taken by the German High Command. Both Ludendorff and Hindenburg — Hindenburg, the great figurehead, who had always been content to accept the initiative of his junior partner but, in the crisis, had now to take the supreme responsibility — had independently come to the same conclusion. In view of the controversy that afterward grew up around the precise events of the collapse of Germany, it is important to note that this decision was taken by the High Command irrespective of the political developments in Berlin, concerning which the army commanders at Spa were profoundly unaware and profoundly uninterested. At conferences at Spa on September 29, Hindenburg demanded an immediate armistice and an appeal to President Wilson, who seemed likely to be the most lenient arbiter of the fate of Central Europe. Hertling arrived at Spa on the same day, only to hand in his resignation.

The Kaiser at once issued a proclamation: "I desire that men who are supported by the confidence of the people shall share in wide measure in the rights and duties of government." Evidently the masters of Germany, as Hintze put it, were bent on introducing a "revolution from above." Hintze returned to Berlin and busied himself with preparations for the forthcoming parliamentary reformation in Germany. On October 2 the Kaiser appointed Prince Max of Baden the new Chancellor, and Prince Max under panic pressure from the High Command immediately dispatched a note to President Wilson requesting an armistice and peace negotiations "on the basis of his message to Congress on January 8, 1918 [on the Fourteen Points], and of his subsequent pronouncements. . . ."

On October 4, Burian, on behalf of the Austro-Hungarian Government, addressed an appeal to Wilson couched in similar terms.

Of all the events of this time none is quite so extraordinary, or so revealing of the situation in Germany in 1918, as the way in which the German people were apprised of the impending collapse. There had been agitation in Berlin, as we have seen; there had been natural concern and anxiety; there had been much physical suffering; but nothing was further from the mind of the average German citizen than the sudden announcement of catastrophe he was now to receive. Within an hour the German High Command was to reverse four years of victory propaganda in the roughest, most thoughtless, offhand, and contemptuous manner.

After the conferences at Spa on September 29, Hintze had returned to Berlin taking with him Baron von dem Bussche, a staff major under special instructions to inform the Reichstag party leaders of the military situation. On October 2, Bussche duly met the leaders and read them a prepared statement, previously approved by Ludendorff, to the effect that "the High Command has come to the extremely painful conclusion that, according to all human calculation, there no longer exists any possibility of forcing the enemy to make peace. . . . The enemy's tanks have been unexpectedly numerous. . . . Our reserves are coming to an end. . . . The General Field-Marshal [Hindenburg] and General Ludendorff have decided to propose to His Majesty [the Kaiser] that an attempt be made to break off the struggle. . . . No time must be lost. Every twenty-four hours can impair the situation and give the enemy an opportunity to discover our present weakness. . . ." At this announcement, "Ebert went as pale as death," runs one account; "Stresemann looked as if he had been struck; the Prussian Minister Waldow left the room with the words, 'There is nothing to do now but put a bullet through one's head!'" Probably no single incident contributed so much to the German Revolution as this gauchely conducted interview. The same afternoon the news was all over Germany. There was no preparatory press campaign; there was no softening of the blow. "Up to this moment, the home front had stood unbroken," writes Prince Max. "Now the spark leaped across to the people at large."

THE COLLAPSE OF TURKEY

Turkey was now at the point of collapse. Since the fall of Jerusalem, British forces under General Allenby had advanced deep into Palestine, and at the Battle of Megiddo they had decisively defeated the Turkish Syrian Army. Simultaneously the British forces in Mesopotamia had almost reached Mosul.

An Allied force from Salonika was threatening Constantinople. As a result of Bulgaria's capitulation, Turkey was left isolated in the midst of advancing enemies. Her army everywhere was falling back in disorder. Deserters are said to have amounted to more than 500,000, swarms of whom terrorized the country and levied blackmail on the helpless villagers. During the first week of October, Talaat Pasha's old cabinet at last resigned. On October 30, 1918, at Mudros in Lemnos in the Aegean, delegates of a new Turkish government of nonpartisan views accepted armistice terms from Admiral Calthorpe, commanding the British Mediterranean Fleet.

THE COLLAPSE OF AUSTRIA–HUNGARY

October found the Dual Monarchy in dissolution, and its nationalities in full revolt. National assemblies were springing up and arrogating the real authority to themselves. On October 3 the German-Austrian Social Democrats declared their desire for a German-Austrian state which would control "its relations with the other Austrian nationalities and with the German Reich, according to its own needs." On October 6 representatives of the Serbs, Croats, and Slovenes met in Agram and declared their right to regulate the affairs of Yugoslavs in Austria-Hungary. On October 7 the Polish Council of Regency at Warsaw proclaimed its independence.

The Emperor Charles, trying to save a little from the ruin, stooped to long and futile audiences with nationalist and party leaders. At the eleventh hour he also introduced his "revolution from above" and proclaimed the division of the Monarchy into four autonomous nationalist subkingdoms; but the nationalities, it was clear, no longer recognized his competence. Even Hungary was now cutting loose. On October 16, in the Hungarian Diet, Count Michael Karolyi, leader of a pacifist and secessionist group, was boldly demanding the recall of "our Hungarian Army" from the front and the dissolution of the alliance with Germany. With amazing blindness, patriot Hungarians believed they could now break with Germany, and with Austria no less, and still preserve their domain intact — indeed, that defeat in war entitled them to the same free voice in their national destiny as victory would have given them. But the Diet's optimism was short-lived. "I must acknowledge Count Karolyi is right," said Tisza, speaking the following day. "I must acknowledge we have lost the war!" President Wilson's reply to Burian's peace appeal was to make it plain that Hungary, like Austria, would be shorn of her ethnic appendages.

On October 18, over the signature of Secretary of State Lansing, the President of the United States deemed it his duty to say that "certain events of the utmost importance" had occurred since his address of January 8 [on the Fourteen Points], namely that the United States had recognized the Czechoslovak National Council in Paris as a belligerent government and had also recognized the nationalistic aspirations of the Yugoslavs. "The President is, therefore, no longer at liberty to accept a mere 'autonomy' of these peoples as a basis of peace, but is obliged to insist that they, and not he, shall be the judges of what action on the part of the Austro-Hungarian Government will satisfy their aspirations and their conception of their rights and destiny as members of the family of nations."

Allied forces from Salonika under Franchet d'Esperey were now advancing through Serbia; the Rumanians were back on the Danube. On October 24 the Italians opened their offensive on the Piave, and at the Battle of Vittorio Veneto broke up the last resistance of the Austro-Hungarian Army. An Austro-Hungarian Armistice Commission accepted the terms of the Italian Supreme Command at Padua on November 3. Franchet d'Esperey reached Belgrade on November 6 and there concluded a separate armistice, on behalf of Hungary, with Count Karolyi.

On November 11, Charles renounced his sovereign rights. On the following day the German Austrians proclaimed a republic, and on November 16, Karolyi proclaimed a republic in Hungary.

THE COLLAPSE OF GERMANY

Prince Max, the German Chancellor, was a cousin of the Kaiser and heir to the grand-ducal throne of Baden. He had the reputation of a liberal and pacifist statesman, and his war service with the Red Cross had been unexceptionable. To both friends and enemies he seemed an appropriate leader of the new "democratized" German Government and collaborator in a peace of the Fourteen Points. He included a wide selection of Reichstag Deputies in his cabinet, and the Reichstag at his behest rushed through a series of enactments designed to invest the country with the forms of a responsible, popular constitution. Between October 3 and November 5 the German Government sent four notes to President Wilson and received as many replies. All four notes pressed for an armistice, and sought to give convincing answers to the great transatlantic democrat of the far-reaching changes being carried out in Germany's political life. But, in the midst of the exchange, the *Leinster,* a steamship plying between England and Ireland, was torpedoed with the loss of hundreds of American and British lives. The sinking, whether accidental or deliberate, inevitably stiffened President Wilson's attitude. Even in the moment of defeat and retribution, it seemed, Germany had not the wit to forswear her inhumanities on the high seas. The President therefore made it very clear, in his reply of October 14, that the armistice conditions were matters "which must be left to the judgment and advice of the military advisers" of the American and Allied governments and "that no arrangement can be accepted . . . which does not provide absolutely satisfactory safeguards and guarantees of the maintenance of the present military supremacy of the armies of the United States and of the Allies in the field."

Further, in his reply of October 23 the President insisted "that the nations of the world do not and can not trust the word of those who have hitherto been the masters of German policy. . . . In concluding peace and attempting to undo the infinite injuries and injustices of this war the Government of the United States can not deal with any but veritable representatives of the German people. . . . If it must deal with the military masters and the monarchical autocrats of Germany now . . . or later . . . it must demand not peace negotiations but surrender."

On October 26, Ludendorff, the first of those military masters, resigned. Hindenburg was left, and was associated in his command with General Groener, Ludendorff's official successor and former director of the Kriegsamt. But the chief of the monarchical autocrats still remained. The Kaiser seemed, of all men, to embody in himself the arrogance and domination of Prussian Germany, and the final act of the war revolves largely about the question of his abdication. Doubtless he would have earned the gratitude of his people and the respect of his enemies if he had voluntarily renounced the throne. Even Tsar Ferdinand of Bulgaria, not usually an example to monarchs, had lately gone with dignity. But the Kaiser was now stricken with an obstinacy which neither reason, nor appeals, nor entreaties, nor threats would shake, and in the end his throne was taken from him by what looked very like a trick.

Toward the end of October even Conservatives were advising an abdication; the Social Democrats were categorically demanding it. Prince Max was sick with influenza and for some days was quite incapable of attending to business. On October 29 the Kaiser left Berlin for High Command Headquarters, then at Spa, where he basked in the reverence of Hindenburg and dreamed dreams of riding home at the head of loyal troops to suppress the coming German Revolution.

But on that day the first phase of that revolution had already broken out. The Admiral Staff, without consulting the Chancellor, had issued orders for the fleet to put to sea. For the crews the operation could only be a "death cruise," a gesture of despair on the part of a vanquished navy seeking to evade surrender, and they mutinied. Dock laborers and garrisons ashore made common cause with them. On November 4 the port of Kiel was in revolt. The government sent Gustav Noske, the Social Democrat, to treat with the mutineers. He reached Kiel on the evening of November 4, opened negotiations with the sailors' representatives, and promised an amnesty for their comrades under arrest. He was proclaimed Governor of Kiel and in twenty-four hours reduced the insurgent seaport to some semblance of order.

But the dam could hold no longer. Noske might well patch up one crack; the torrent broke through at another. On November 5, Lübeck was in revolt; on the 6th, Hamburg, Cuxhaven, and Bremen. On the 7th, the Socialist Kurt Eisner, at the head of a mass of workers and soldiers, proclaimed the Republic of Bavaria. By November 8 the revolution had swept the entire Rhineland and had reached the very outposts of Spa. The King of Bavaria, the Duke of Brunswick, and other gilded potentates were abdicating or in flight.

On November 9 at Spa, with heavy heart, Hindenburg at last decided to inform His Majesty that his power was at an end, his people in revolt, and his army no longer fit to fight. For a moment the Kaiser, scenting a means of escape, believed that he could abdicate as "German Kaiser," and retain the title of King of Prussia, and this preposterous compromise was actually telegraphed to Berlin. In the end the Chancellor acted on his own responsibility and issued the announcement that "the Kaiser and King has decided to renounce the throne." At daybreak on November 10 the Kaiser crossed the Dutch frontier into exile. Yet years afterward he still protested that his Chancellor, without consulting him, had announced an abdication which had never taken place! [8]

Allied discussions on the German armistice terms began informally at Paris at the end of October and were continued thereafter at the Supreme War Council at Versailles. Colonel House, President Wilson's aide and companion, arrived in Paris on October 26 to persuade the somewhat fractious and doubting Allied premiers to accede to the Fourteen Points, even as the German Government had done. With his last note to Germany on November 5 the President forwarded a "Memorandum of Observations," by which the Allied governments accepted the Fourteen Points — but with a reservation on Point 2 concerning the freedom of the seas and with a demand that Germany make reparation "for all damage done to the civilian population of the Allies and their property." (See Appendix C.)

The German Armistice Commission, headed by Erzberger, was received by Foch on November 8 in a carriage of his special train on a siding near Rethondes in the Forest of Compiègne, and early on the morning of November 11, after two days' negotiations, the terms were signed. Hindenburg and the High Command approved the signing.

Germany agreed to the evacuation of all territories invaded by her, and of Alsace-Lorraine; the evacuation of the left bank of the Rhine and of the three bridgeheads at Mainz, Coblenz, and Cologne; the Allied occupation of this area and the support of the Allied Army of Occupation; the establishment of a neutral, demilitarized zone ten kilometers wide along the right bank of the Rhine; the surrender of 5,000 guns, 25,000 machine guns, 3,000 motors, and 1,700 airplanes, of 5,000 locomotives, 150,000 railroad cars, and 5,000 trucks, of all submarines, 6 battle cruisers, 10 battleships, 8 light cruisers, and 50 destroyers; the restitution of all gold deposits removed from Belgium, Russia, and Rumania; the repatriation of all inhabitants from the evacuated territories; the repatriation of all prisoners of war without reciprocity; and the annulment of the treaties of Brest Litovsk and Bucharest. At the same time, the existing blockade conditions would remain unchanged, but the Allies would consider the provisioning of Germany during the Armistice as should be found necessary.

Sporadic fighting still continued in Russia, in the Ukraine and Galicia, and in parts of the Near East. But the First World War may be said to have closed with the German Armistice on November 11, 1918. It had lasted four years and three months, involved thirty sovereign states, overthrown four empires, given birth to seven new nations, taken 10,000,000 lives on the field of battle and perhaps an equal number of noncombatant lives by privation, disease, and revolution, and wasted incalculable wealth.[9] The civilized world might well believe that it deserved a new era and a millennial peace.

PART TWO

THE PERIOD OF SETTLEMENT

8 THE PEACE CONFERENCE OF PARIS

AND THE PEACE TREATIES

PREPARATIONS AND PRELIMINARIES

The end of the war found the victors unprepared for a rapid and legal transition to peace. During the conflict there had been public pronouncements on war aims by representative statesmen. But war aims belonged rather to the category of morale and propaganda. They were not precise agenda for a peace conference, and they were no more than the most general guide to all the detail of frontiers, armaments, reparations, and debts which had now to be devised. Certainly so long as the war lasted the discussion, say in the press, of concrete peace terms would have been entirely unreal, a foolish tempting of providence, and dangerous to fighting morale. The all-absorbing military issues had left little room for questions of a still hypothetical future.

Certain of the Allied governments had bound themselves with secret treaties. The participation of Italy and Rumania in the war had been purchased at a price, and the payment, no one doubted, would be demanded in full (see pp. 28 and 62). There was a secret agreement over the partition of the Ottoman Empire (see p. 66), there were pledges to the Arabs (see p. 66), and there was an agreement with Japan over the disposal of German territories in the North Pacific (see p. 76). Latterly the League of Nations had been a topic of serious official consideration, especially in the United States, Britain, and France. But in general, Allied governments in their wartime dealings with one another had fought shy of questions of peace and had avoided risking their hard-won military and economic unity in irrelevant conversations which could so easily have led to disagreements among themselves. Moreover, it is to be remembered always that the collapse of Germany at the end of 1918 had surpassed the most sanguine expectations. Allied commands at the time, far from preparing themselves for a peace conference, were laying their plans for the big offensive of 1919.

Among the Allied statements of war aims, however, the addresses of President Wilson of the United States had come to occupy an exceptional and predominant place. Germany had originally requested an armistice and peace on the basis of the Fourteen Points and of the President's "subsequent pronouncements" — a series of declarations which we have collectively described as the Wilsonian code (see p. 103). The pre-Armistice exchange of notes had implied that the object of the ensuing peace conference "would be only to agree upon the practical details of their application." The European Allies, in their Memorandum of Observations forwarded to Germany with the American note of November 5, 1918, had made important reservations in regard to the freedom of the seas and reparations (see p. 107). In the end, all five armistices had been signed without actual reference to the Fourteen Points or to any of the "subsequent pronouncements"; but only a perverse legal casuistry would now attempt to argue away the fact that, in November 1918, Allied and Central Powers had generally accepted the Wilsonian code as binding upon them and indeed as taking precedence over whatever prior commitments there might otherwise have been. Even so, the Wilsonian code and the Memorandum of Observations were a long way from being the text of a peace treaty, and the practical details of their application allowed of many interpretations. (See Appendixes B and C.)

Governmental and other official bodies had also busied themselves with collecting considerable files of information. Thus in the fall of 1917, President Wilson had established under Colonel House a group of research workers who came to be known as "the House Inquiry," and later the American delegation in Paris was remarkable for the teams of experts accompanying it. In the same way the British Foreign Office published a series of Peace Handbooks, each written by an acknowledged specialist. Various other nations, groups, and interests produced their appropriate statistical apologias. All this work was highly competent and thorough, and most assuredly it could have been dignified with the name of "preparation" for the coming conference, but one of the minor tragedies of the Peace Conference was that it was never properly used. The delegates at Paris in 1919 worked under appalling pressure, and they could hardly have been expected to digest a whole library of textbooks on the history, economics, and ethnography of Europe, however excellently done and however necessary to their labors. The sad fact remains — sadder because it is still hard to say what else could have been done under the circumstances — that the victors of the First World War were "surprised into peace" and met to decide the fate of their world with little to guide them beyond a tangle of secret treaties, a mass of unread literature, and the lofty but vague pronouncements of the American President.

ORGANIZATION AND PROCEDURE

There was never much doubt that Paris would be the place of the Peace Conference. The choice was a compliment to France, but there were also good practical reasons for it. The pre-Armistice negotiations of the Allies had taken place in Paris. Subordinate offices of the Supreme War Council, many of the American organizations, as well as the "governments" of the new states, Czechoslovakia, Yugoslavia, and Poland, were congregated there.

Yet there were many, then and afterward, who criticized the selection of Paris. Neutral cities, such as Geneva or The Hague, held out much the same practical advantages and avoided the overpowering psychology of a belligerent capital. The eventual peace, it was devoutly to be wished, would be a peace of justice. Hatred and revenge were useless if Germany had really learned the lesson of her defeat, if her recent republicanism really signified a change of heart, and if she were really willing to be reclaimed into the comity of civilized nations; and Paris was the very symbol of hatred and revenge. *A fortiori*, if Paris was a mistake, the final signing of the German treaty at Versailles was a brutal and miserable blunder.

The organization and procedure of the Conference were not expected to be difficult. The Allies had been holding conferences for four years and should by now have become adept at the technique of negotiation. In the event, it happened that the first peace meeting of the Allies in Paris on January 12, 1919, was a continuation of the Supreme War Council, and the so-called Council of Ten, which assumed the initiative and direction of the Conference during its early stages, developed naturally from that body. This arrangement, as was perhaps to be expected, put the main control into the hands of the five "Principal Allied and Associated Powers" — Britain, France, Italy, Japan, and the United States. The smaller Powers afterward complained that they were excluded from important deliberations, that they were often asked to subscribe to decisions concerning their vital interests to which they contributed nothing. The Peace Conference, they argued, should have signalized the triumph of the smaller Powers; the war itself had been their war of liberation. Certainly there was justice in these complaints; but in the Paris of 1919 there were sometimes other things more urgent than justice. As Clemenceau remarked, the five principal Powers at the time of the Armistice had 12,000,000 men under arms — and, he added laconically, *"C'est un titre."* There would be occasion enough for disagreement without throwing open the Conference to the politics and propaganda of every minor pleader that came to it.

One prickly question of procedure was publicity. President Wilson had called for "open covenants of peace, openly arrived at." Certainly the old aristocratic secrecy of the Congress of Vienna did not have to be repeated. The diplomatic methods known to Metternich and Talleyrand, it was hoped, belonged to an age that the war had brought to a deserved end. But neither did anyone expect the Conference to be turned into a Senate investigating committee with a mob of pressmen and photographers in attendance. Private meetings there had to be; censorships there had to be. In the end, the press was admitted only to the six plenary sessions of the Conference, which were entirely formal affairs, and in the intervals was left to satisfy itself, as best it might, with "revelations" and "leakages." The arrangement was not altogether happy.

But the most important question of procedure to be left unsettled — inexcusably and incredibly unsettled — was the question whether the peace should be preliminary or final. Many of the delegates, notably Marshal Foch, had favored a preliminary peace and indeed had come to the Conference with that end in view. Such a peace would have been a frank, dictated peace, containing military, territorial, and reparations clauses alone; a second peace, quietly and honorably negotiated between victors and vanquished, would then have worked out the larger problems of economic reconstruction, disarmament, and the League. The new world order was not to be built in a moment of heat, and the interval between the preliminary and the final treaties might have allowed the most extreme passions of the war to cool.

But public opinion was impatient and imperative. It would never have borne so protracted a business as a double peace conference with each of the defeated Powers. The principal delegates at the Conference were politicians, for whom a long absence from their homes and constituencies might have been very irksome. Colonel House believed "that it was more important to bring about peace quickly than it was to haggle over details," and he "would rather see an immediate peace and the world brought to order . . . than a better peace and delay." President Wilson himself at first had been in favor of "a preliminary military convention," but in the end it was probably he as much as anyone who was determined that there should be one peace and one peace only with each of the defeated Powers, with his own historic creation, the League of Nations, as its cornerstone.

Yet we know that, for weeks after the Conference had met, many of the delegates had not entirely freed themselves from the idea of a preliminary peace. Clauses in the treaty were sometimes hastily adopted, or sometimes adopted for no better reason than to maintain unity among the Allies, but adopted with the tacit reservation that they could be revised at a future date. And there was always Article 19 of the League Covenant to fall back on, expressly providing for "the reconsideration of treaties which had become inapplicable." The peacemakers of Paris, certainly the Britons among them, in their moments of discouragement — and there must have been many such moments — always took refuge in the thought that their labors made no claim to finality, and they were afterward appalled to discover that clauses they had recommended in the Commissions were intended not merely to implement an armistice, but to be written into a permanent and definitive settlement.

Manifestly a conference of such size and importance needed time. It needed time to assemble and time to deliberate. Peace conferences of the past had sometimes lasted years. The mere geographical difficulties of assembling a great number of men, some of them from countries as far away as America and Japan, and of accommodating them in quarters in Paris in those circumstances of comfort and dignity which statesmanship regards as its due, all called for weeks of careful staff work. Some delegates wished to consult public opinion before leaving home. Lloyd George went to the length of a general election. President Wilson felt obliged to give his annual message to Congress. Delegates also had to come from the new nations, nations in many cases hardly yet delivered from the matrix of revolution, and their dates of arrival were not always matters of easy calculation in advance. The work of the Conference could not but be delayed by the unstable condition of Europe. Though the war was over in the West, other little wars were in progress or impending in Central Europe, in Poland, and in Russia. The new nations were not a happy family. Peoples suddenly liberated from centuries of subjection seemed more anxious to try to recapture the glories of some mythic national existence of the past than to submit gratefully and peacefully to their status in the present. Wherever and whenever they could do so, they tried to anticipate the decisions of the Conference by seizing debatable territories on their own account. Even when it had at last assembled, the Conference found its authority far more often and far more dangerously defied by the new smaller Powers than by all the sullen, growling arrogance of defeated Germany herself.

So many things conspired to delay and obstruct. Yet never did a conference work under such enormous pressure. The impatience of public opinion has already been hinted at. A war-torn world was trying to repair its social and economic life; twenty-seven nations were waiting almost hourly for the official proclamation of peace. Demobilization could not be safely completed, nor the naval blockade be raised. Indeed the demobilization of the British and American forces proceeded at such a rate that the French High Command feared the Allied military predominance over Germany was being seriously jeopardized. And every day the prevailing unsettlement was allowed to continue, Bolshevism, that creeping paralysis, would spread into Europe. Hungary succumbed to it in March 1919, Austria and Germany were gravely menaced, and only a quick liquidation of the war and a safe return to the stabilities of peace could halt its advance. Civil war was raging in Russia. To the victors of Paris, as they surveyed their tasks in the early months of 1919, it seemed as if the forces of peace and the forces of anarchy were engaged in a desperate race for the possession of Europe.

Yet, for all the "dawdling" of which it was accused, the Conference's timetable in the end was not discreditable. The first plenary session was held only nine to ten weeks after the Armistice of November 1918, and less than four months later the text of the German treaty was ready. When we consider the intricate problems that had to be resolved and the precarious state of Europe in 1919, we cannot but regard these dates as representing a Herculean achievement.

STATES OF MIND

If the Peace Conference thus met in a chaos of unpreparedness, it also met in a chaos of states of mind. For all the Fourteen Points and for all the pre-Armistice agreements, there was not one delegate who came to Paris in 1919 without mental reservations of one kind or another. And wonderful were the rationalizings by which the reservations were sometimes defended. The Italians, for example, demanded the cession to them of territory inhabited by several thousand German-speaking Tirolese. Their demand contradicted the principle of nationality in Point 9 of the Fourteen Points. But, in the view of the Italians, a single exception made in their favor — and a minor one at that — could hardly be said to vitiate the general settlement.

What mattered the bartering about of a few thousand Tirolese who happened to live on the wrong side of the Brenner Pass? Should a few thousand Tirolese stand in the way of a "strategic rectification of frontiers" essential to the security of 40,000,000 Italians? Every delegate, it was said, wanted to apply the Fourteen Points to every other country but his own. The United States was zealous to condemn "special covenants" and "regional agreements," so long as no aspersions were cast upon the Monroe Doctrine. Britain and the British Dominions were glad to see fair play in the redistribution of the German and Ottoman possessions, so long as none of those possessions they had themselves occupied in the course of the war were involved in the transaction. Lloyd George was always accused of being statesmanlike at others' expense. General Smuts planned the most ambitious Utopias, but always excluded German Southwest Africa therefrom. Hughes, the Australian Prime Minister, bluntly defied President Wilson to apply his principles to the Australian-occupied islands in the Pacific.[1] Well might the President complain of "the negation of detail" so prevalent in Paris.

Then behind each delegate at Paris was a nation. The Peace Conference was a democratic conference, the first of its kind in history, and however well or ill intentioned the individual delegates may have been, they were still "delegates." They were answerable to governments and to peoples at home, and they were sensitive — extremely sensitive — to their national presses. Democracy, in 1919, was in a strange, abnormal mood. Propaganda, which had once done excellent service for wartime morale, could not suddenly be switched back to the service of peace. The Frankenstein monsters of hatred and terror which the war had raised up could not be expected to die just because the angels of love and brotherhood had suddenly been invited to take over the guidance of human affairs. Throughout the Conference the delegates were dunned by their respective national presses at home to show no "weakness" either to defeated enemies or jealous allies. "It must be admitted," writes Nicolson, "that after a war in which seventy million young men had been mobilised, in which ten million had been killed, in which thirty million had been wounded, it would be unreasonable to suppose that any democracy could regard with unclouded nerves the spectacle of four gentlemen sitting in a guarded room together, discussing the result. Nor would it be sensible to expect a population which had been appalled by naval and military defeat, terrified by aerial bombardment, anguished by the dread of starvation, to behave in a moment of unimagined victory with the feudal chivalry of the Black Prince." [2]

The realist and idealist states of mind at the Conference — as they might be called — were embodied in two of its leading personalities, Clemenceau and Wilson, the principal delegates of France and the United States. Clemenceau came to the Conference with the disillusioned wisdom of an old man who has seen all the evil of the world. He regarded war as the eternal pattern of human society — certainly of European society. Peace, he said, "is the continuation of war by other means" or at best "an equilibrium of forces." The French and German peoples had always contended for supremacy, and their long histories had swung back and forth between their successes and failures. In 1918, France was the victor — temporarily perhaps — in a war, the greatest war, in a perpetual series. It would be criminal folly for her not to use the opportunity she now enjoyed to extend for as long as possible the period of her advantage. Fourteen Points or no Fourteen Points, the Conference in her eyes would be a miserable betrayal if its eventual terms did not ensure the military disablement of Germany, the imposition of punitive and crippling indemnities, the permanent occupation of the Rhineland, even the dismemberment of the Reich into its components of 1815, and the creation of a ring of strong new border states in vigilant alliance.

President Wilson's character is still difficult to analyze. He came to Europe bearing the gravest responsibility, to face the greatest opportunity, that ever befell a man. Here, for the first time in history, was the philosopher-king with a Maxima Carta in his hand and the military power to enforce it. The common people of Europe were prepared to worship the very ground he trod. The victors hoped for his justice, the vanquished for his mercy, and all for his peace. "He was received in Paris on his first appearance," writes Lloyd George, "with an organized adulation of applause in the streets and in the press which was intoxicating. . . . Streets were named after him, Senate and Chamber of Deputies gave him an official welcome, a palace was placed at his disposal, the picked regiments of France provided his escort, and their best bands played him through the most impressive avenues of the city." [3] In like manner, he visited Rome and London. There was not an honor, not a mark of trust and devotion, which was not laid at his feet.

But Wilson had his weaknesses and contradictions. Like so many introverts he was complex and elusive in the extreme, withdrawn, solitary, and apt to be misunderstood. Great natural endowments, literary power, a burning moral fervor, deep religious convictions, even a touch of the visionary were combined with unreal, academic habits of mind and a sensitive, humorless vanity. He believed in his political philosophy with all the inflexibility of his Presbyterian upbringing; he believed no less in himself as its chosen mouthpiece on earth. But he never seemed to understand how other men could be so ungrateful or so unregenerate and obtuse as not to believe in it also. Latterly he had grown difficult to advise, unapproachable and suspicious in his dealings with his colleagues, and preferred to overwork himself to the point of collapse rather than delegate his business to aides and subordinates. In the end he became estranged even from his old friend, Colonel House.

For Wilson the League of Nations, his League of Nations, was to be the supreme product of the Peace Conference. The Covenant embodied all his idealism and took precedence over all his other pledges and pronouncements. It was, as Lloyd George put it, "if not a whole Treaty, at least the only part of the Treaty in which he was interested." The Treaty, in short, might have its faults — the Treaty could not be expected to be perfect — but the Covenant would compensate for everything. The Covenant would be the nucleus of a new corpus of legislation, a veritable constitution of mankind. Just as a new age had dated from the Fathers of 1787, Wilson doubtless pictured a new and greater age dating from himself.

To this end, against the advice of many of his colleagues, had Wilson really come to Paris. In the first place, it was then a breach of precedent for a President of the United States to travel abroad during his term of office. In the second place, the President's high status at Washington, above the battle, three thousand miles away, would have put him out of the reach of the local antagonisms of Europe. If he spoke for a superhuman cause, he could not help prejudicing his position by consorting with lesser breeds of men at a cosmopolitan conference. The American delegates at Paris could have referred back their difficulties to Washington, as occasion required, and called in the distant oracle to strengthen their hands. But Wilson was determined that the Covenant should be drafted under no other direction than his own. He may have been unaware of his inexperience in diplomacy, as diplomacy was understood in Europe. He might encounter sharper wits and keener intellects. But he believed in his Covenant; he would wear it like an invincible armor; perhaps he imagined himself in the role of a Parsifal, whose very unwisdom would discomfit the wickedness of Europe.

However, apart from all this, an immediate and probably the most important tactical cause of Wilson's failure was his own false position in Paris. He, the great democrat, did not really represent his people. The Congressional elections of November 1918 had resulted in Republican majorities in the Senate and the House. To make matters worse, he took only one Republican representative with him to Paris. He seemed oblivious of his weakness, or he may have thought that Congress, like Europe, would not dare to oppose his righteousness. But, as time was to show, Congress did dare, and we may hazard the guess that Clemenceau, for instance, would not have treated Wilson so cavalierly, nor would Lloyd George have been quite so smug, had they felt that Wilson could have claimed undisputed support at home. It is not enough to regard Wilson at Paris as the bigoted Covenanter led to the slaughter by gloating European executioners. He would never have been so led but for the fact that he had committed democracy's unpardonable sin — he had no majority.

THE FIRST PERIOD OF THE CONFERENCE

Twenty-seven Powers were represented at Paris, and they took seats at the plenary session of the Conference in rough accordance with their military strength — seventy seats in all. Clemenceau and Pichon were the delegates of France, Lloyd George and Balfour of Britain, Orlando and Sonnino of Italy, Wilson and Lansing of the United States, and Saionji and Makino of Japan.[4] These delegates used to meet as a so-called Council of Ten, which bore the main responsibilities of the Conference during its first period. Colonel House, in his curiously anomalous, unofficial position, was President Wilson's constant adviser. Sir Maurice Hankey, that obscure but competent, ubiquitous figure, formerly secretary of Lloyd George's cabinet, acted as secretary to the Ten and probably exerted an immense influence in questions of procedure. There were also various experts, permanent officials, interpreters, clerks, and typists attached to each delegation to the number of several hundreds. It was remarked that the professional diplomat was conspicuously absent. Some of the most distinguished and picturesque personalities were found among the smaller Powers: Dmowski and Paderewski of Poland, Kramář and Beneš of Czechoslovakia, Pashich and Trumbich of Yugoslavia, Bratianu of Rumania, Venizelos of Greece, the Emir Feisal of the Hejaz, and Wellington Koo of China. And to these we may add Borden of Canada, Hughes of Australia, and Botha and Smuts of South Africa.

A host of more or less unofficial and unrecognized delegates came streaming to Paris — Finns, Balts, Ukrainians, Ruthenes, Georgians, Armenians, Kurds, Lebanese, Syrians, Persians, Egyptians, Koreans, Albanians, Sinn Feiners, Zionists, counterrevolutionary and White Russians. All the world brought its troubles to Paris and to President Wilson, the prophet and intercessor of the new order. Many of these delegates did indeed get hearings, some were admitted to the regular meetings or commissions, but most of them went away afterward with heavy hearts and empty hands.

Delegates of enemy Powers were not admitted to the Conference. The Allies were resolved that there was going to be no German Talleyrand at Paris to sow dissension among them. Enemy delegates were invited merely to receive, and to limit themselves to written "observations" on, the treaty texts.

The representation of Russia was a problem which consumed a great deal of the time and patience of the Conference and especially of the Council of Ten. Russia was in the throes of civil war. White Russian armies were fighting with the aid of Allied munitions. Allied forces were occupying various outposts in Russia. The Powers at the Conference could not agree on a united Russian policy. The French officially abhorred Bolshevism and all its works. British and American abhorrence was tempered with curiosity and, it must be admitted, with a secret admiration for revolutions as such. Yet no one denied that events taking place in Russia were of prodigious importance to the world, and a peace conference without Russia must somehow be unreal and ineffective. Under the tactful prompting of President Wilson and Lloyd George, proposals were made to invite all Russian parties, Bolsheviks and anti-Bolsheviks alike, to a meeting with the Allies at some place in the Near East sufficiently convenient of access and yet sufficiently isolated to prevent the spread of any undesirable political contagion, and the Island of Prinkipo in the Sea of Marmora was selected to be the site of this somewhat fantastic annex of the Peace Conference of Paris.

But it was like inviting heretics to an ecumenical council. No party would trust the others. Paris was already a refuge of White Russian émigrés, who intrigued incessantly against the proposal. Chicherin, the Soviet Foreign Commissar, had his own good reasons for being cautious. In the end, no Russian of any color or complexion met the Allies in conference either at Prinkipo or at Paris.

The Peace Conference formally opened with its first plenary session on January 18, 1919, in the Salon de Paix at the Quai d'Orsay. Its history thereafter falls into two periods. Its first period was mainly taken up with the appointment of various Commissions for the study of specific problems — a Commission on the League of Nations, a Commission on Responsibility for

War and Guarantees, a Commission on Reparation for Damage, a Commission on International Labor Legislation, a Commission on Minorities, and so forth. There were Commissions to draft the military, territorial, and financial terms of the future treaties. The Commissions were set up on different dates, as they seemed to be wanted, their terms of reference were not always precise, and there was little co-ordination between them. But most of the detailed and technical work of the Conference was in fact done by them. By the time the German treaty was completed, there were over fifty Commissions of various kinds in existence. A Supreme Economic Council provided for relief and reconstruction in the devastated areas of Europe.

Fourteen nations were represented in the Commission on the League of Nations, and it held ten sittings under the chairmanship of President Wilson.[5] The first period of the Conference ended with the third plenary session on February 14, when the draft Covenant of the League was discussed. The next day President Wilson left for the United States, where Republican opposition to his policies was already becoming too serious to be ignored.

THE SECOND PERIOD OF THE CONFERENCE

The Council of Ten had dominated the first period of the Conference, but the more abbreviated and informal Council of Four dominated the second. The change from one to the other was not entirely deliberate. At the end of February 1919, Lloyd George and Orlando, like Wilson, had been absent from Paris. The Japanese delegates were following a policy of noninterference in European discussions and, though they remained in Paris, they had been keeping away from meetings. Then, on February 19, Clemenceau was shot by a half-witted youth of anarchist leanings. He was not seriously wounded, but he was confined to his apartment for some days. Colonel House, Balfour, and Sonnino visited him there, and the prototype of the Council of Four thus came almost by accident.

The new arrangement immensely speeded the dispatch of business. And it seemed that there were going to be good reasons for more speed. The press, especially in Britain and France, had again started a campaign against the "dawdlers of Paris." The "leakage" of secrets was not contributing to amity and good temper. Certainly it must be admitted that the published and publishable results of the Conference to date had not been very impressive. President Wilson returned to Paris on March 14, and he, Clemenceau, Lloyd George, and Orlando at once constituted themselves the "Big Four" for their future conversations. Hankey was their secretary and constant attendant. During the ensuing two months, the main decisions of the Conference were reached, the Commissions submitted their reports, the main terms of the five treaties were agreed, and the text of the German treaty was drafted in detail. But it was during these two months that the bigger crises of the Conference occurred, among them three in particular, the crisis over the Rhineland, the crisis over Fiume, and the crisis over Shantung.

France's rights to a Rhine frontier on grounds of security were not to be denied. A demilitarized Rhenish buffer state, controlled by French troops, would have solved her strategic problems. The project had been canvassed at Allied conferences during the war, Marshal Foch had been its consistent advocate, and Marshal Foch exerted enormous influence. But no logic could have reconciled a French Rhineland with the Wilsonian code. Lloyd George showed every sympathy for France's temporary occupation of the Rhineland and of the Saar, but he stoutly opposed the creation of another Alsace-Lorraine in Europe. Clemenceau fought with every weapon he had. An open breach between him and President Wilson and a disruption of the whole Conference seemed unavoidable. The French press attacked President Wilson viciously. President Wilson threatened to leave Paris. Clemenceau eventually gave way, but he obtained from the President and from Lloyd George a pledge of American and British aid against Germany in the event of a future aggression, a pledge which was afterward written into formal treaties of assistance and signed concurrently with the Treaty of Versailles. On the whole, French opinion was satisfied with the compromise, but it was a compromise which was fated never to become effective (see p. 136).

The crisis over Fiume arose out of the secret Treaty of London of 1915, under whose terms Italy had entered the war (see p. 28). Orlando put forward the argument that if Dalmatia, which that treaty had assigned to Italy, were now to be incorporated in the new state of Yugoslavia, Italy deserved a "compensation" in the shape of the Adriatic port of Fiume. The British had little patience with the Italian viewpoint. They had always disdained a Power whose alliance they had had to "buy" and whose military performance had hardly justified the price. The Americans left no doubt of their repugnance for the Treaty of London, as for all the secret treaties, from the very moment they had got wind of its terms. The Yugoslavs, for their part, insisted that Fiume was their only practicable harbor and that the possession of it was vital to the economy of their new state. In an attempt to break the deadlock, President Wilson took the extreme step of appealing to the Italian people in a public statement over the heads of the Italian delegates at Paris. Orlando in high dudgeon left Paris, and the public statement, far from appeasing the Italian people, roused them to a fury which must have given the President a most painful surprise.

In the absence of Orlando, the Four became Three, and the conversations continued. In fact, the Three rather gained than lost by the withdrawal of Italian obstructionism. A new clause was inserted in the text of the German treaty to the effect that ratification by the three principal Powers should be sufficient to bring it into force. On April 28, at the fifth plenary session, the Covenant of the League of Nations was adopted, and its text published to the world. The next day the German delegates arrived at Versailles. The Italians put on the best face they could and hurried back to Paris in time to show a "united Allied front" at the sixth plenary session on May 6, when the German treaty was approved. But the question of Fiume was left in abeyance.

President Wilson had bested Clemenceau and Orlando, but he did not best the Japanese delegates. Shantung was his most serious defeat at the Conference. It was a personal defeat and a defeat of principle. Japan had come to Paris to secure three things: first, the cession to her of the former German islands in the North Pacific; second, the cession to her of the rights formerly exercised by Germany in Tsingtao and Shantung; and third, the inclusion of an article or clause in the Covenant of the League of Nations recognizing "the equality of races." Japan had continued to occupy the islands in question, Tsingtao, and a considerable part of Shantung since her seizures of them in 1914. She now claimed the territories *in perpetuo* under her agreement with Britain in 1917 (see p. 76). The islands were eventually ceded to her as Class C mandates. But Tsingtao and Shantung were undisputably Chinese and, by any interpretation of the Wilsonian code, should revert to China — to China, moreover, who was an Allied Power in the war and at the Peace Conference. In regard to the article on the equality of races, the American and British delegates were sympathetic. For the Japanese, the article was a matter of prestige; they had set their hearts on it; its inclusion in the League Covenant could have done no harm — and much good. But Australia, in the person of her Prime Minister Hughes, vehemently objected, fearing presumably that any such recognition of the equality of races might afterward be used to dictate to her in regard to her "white" immigration policy. Consequently none of the equality resolutions put up by the Japanese in the Commission on the League of Nations were adopted. Japan, in fact, faced defeat in all three of her cherished objectives at the Peace Conference.

The Japanese delegates threatened to leave the Conference and to decline membership in the League of Nations if their claims were not met. The Chinese delegates were as importunate in the opposite direction. The Rhineland crisis had only just been settled; the Fiume crisis was at its height; and President Wilson, exhausted by two heavy disputes, agreed to compromise. Where indeed would the peace treaty and the League have been if both Italy and Japan had withdrawn from them? Japan was therefore confirmed in "temporary" possession of Tsingtao and Shantung; but she made a declaration that it was her "policy" to hand back the territory to China at a date not specified, "retaining only the economic privileges [hitherto] granted to Germany." The compromise cost President Wilson the friendship of China, and Chinese delegates did not sign the Treaty of Versailles.[6]

THE TREATY OF VERSAILLES

Count von Brockdorff-Rantzau, then the German Foreign Minister, headed the German delegation. He was received at Versailles on April 30, 1919, with proper, if frigid, courtesy; he was given facilities for communicating directly with Germany; but he was under strict guard against meeting or speaking with visitors, journalists, or members of other delegations. On May 7, in the Trianon Palace Hotel at Versailles, in the presence of Allied representatives, he received the text of the treaty from the hands of Clemenceau. He was notified that fifteen days would be given him for written observations, but that no oral discussions would be allowed. The ceremony did not pass off without its incident. The Count was quick to react to the prevailing temper around him and, disdaining to rise from his seat, he gave in a biting, truculent speech what was presumably still the official view in Germany of Germany's war guilt.

"We have no illusions as to the extent of our defeat and the measure of · our impotence," he said. "We know that the power of German arms is broken, and we are aware of the fury of the hatred which greets us. We are asked to assume the sole guilt of the war. Such a confession from my lips would be a lie. We have no intention of absolving Germany from all responsibility for the war. . . . But we expressly contend that Germany, whose people was convinced that it was fighting a defensive war, should not be saddled with the whole responsibility. None of us will argue that the mischief began with the murder of the Archduke. In the last fifty years Imperialism has poisoned the international position of all European states. The policy of revenge, the policy of expansion, and the flouting of the rights of self-determination have contributed to the crisis. The Russian mobilization gave the decision to the military authorities.

"Public opinion among our foes dilates on the crimes committed by Germany during the conflict. We are not here to deny the responsibility of the men who directed the war, or the violations of international law. We repeat the declaration that wrong was done to Belgium, and we are ready to make it good. But in the waging of the war Germany was not the only offender. . . . Crimes in times of war may be unpardonable, but they are committed in the heat of the contest. The hundreds and thousands of noncombatants who have died of the blockade since 11th November were killed in cold blood after the victory had been won. Think of that when you speak of crime and punishment." [7] (See p. 149.)

The German written observations on the treaty were made as directed. The Allies conceded a few minor points. Lloyd George is said to have been in favor of drastic eleventh-hour revisions in the direction of leniency. But the text was left substantially intact. It was returned to the Germans with the threat that war would be resumed if it was not accepted within five days. The publication of the terms led to a crisis in Germany. Brockdorff-Rantzau resigned, and a new government was formed in Berlin which sent to Versailles Hermann Müller and Johannes Bell, its Foreign and Colonial Ministers. The significance of one being "Colonial Minister" did not pass unnoticed. On June 21, as a prelude to the ignominy of the peace to be, the German Navy, interned at Scapa Flow under the terms of the Armistice, was scuttled by its crews. The signing of the treaty took place on June 28, 1919, the fifth anniversary of Sarajevo, in the Hall of Mirrors of the Palace of Versailles, where forty-eight years before, in its moment of triumph, the German Empire had been proclaimed.

The Treaty of Versailles was a formidable document of 15 parts and 440 clauses. Part I was the Covenant of the League of Nations. It was an essential component of the treaty as drafted. Several clauses named the League as the executant of their provisions. Questions still unsettled were referable to it; certain plebiscites were to be conducted by it; the new administrations of

Danzig and the Saar were vested in it; the new mandatories were answerable to it; minorities could plead their grievances before it. The remaining parts of the treaty concerned Germany's frontiers in Europe, her territories and rights abroad, the disbandment of her armed forces, penalties for her transgressions, reparations for damage, and guarantees for the future. There were parts on the internationalization of certain rivers, on labor legislation, and on other miscellaneous matters.

To read the "retributive" clauses is almost to read the history of imperial Germany. Not a crime of the past was left unmentioned or unredressed. The spoliation of Denmark in 1864, of France in 1871, of Belgium in 1914, of Russia in 1917 — and even of the old Kingdom of Poland in the Partitions of the eighteen century — were put to rights. Trophies and works of art captured by the Prussian Army in 1870–71 were to be restored to France. Books were to be furnished to the University of Louvain to compensate for the sack of 1914. Allied tribunals would try the Kaiser "for a supreme offence against international morality and the sanctity of treaties" and other German nationals for "acts in violation of the laws and customs of war."

Under the political clauses, Germany ceded to Belgium the areas round Eupen and Malmédy. She returned to France the "lost provinces" of Alsace-Lorraine and agreed to the liquidation of all German property therein. She undertook not to build fortifications or assemble armed forces on the left bank of the Rhine or within fifty kilometers of the right bank. She ceded to France the coal mines of the Saar for a period of fifteen years "in full and absolute possession . . . as compensation for the destruction of the coal mines in the north of France." During the fifteen years the Saar would be administered by the League of Nations "in the capacity of trustee," and at the end of the fifteen years a plebiscite of the inhabitants would decide the future status of the territory. Germany recognized the independence of the Austrian Republic, and agreed that "this independence shall be inalienable, except with the consent of the Council of the League of Nations." She ceded to Czechoslovakia a small district near Troppau. She ceded to Poland the so-called Corridor, comprising the greater part of Posen (Poznań) and West Prussia. Plebiscites were to be held in East Prussia and Upper Silesia. Danzig was created a free city to be administered by the League of Nations and was to serve as Poland's access to the sea. Memel was placed at the disposal of the Allies, eventually to serve as Lithuania's access to the sea. Plebiscites were to be held in Schleswig to determine the new frontier with Denmark. The naval base at Helgoland was to be demolished. Germany recognized the independence of all the former Russian territories and confirmed her abrogation of the Treaty of Brest Litovsk. She renounced "all her rights and titles over her overseas possessions," now to be incorporated into the new mandates under the League of Nations, and thus dissolved a colonial empire of over a million square miles.

Under the military clauses Germany was to reduce her army to 100,000 men, recruited by voluntary enlistment and serving for twelve years. After the defeat at Jena in 1806, the Prussians had evaded Napoleon's terms of demobilization and had maintained a large army by putting successive batches of men through short periods of intensive training. The twelve-year

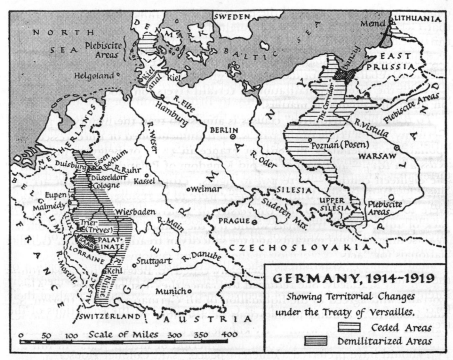

GERMANY, 1914-1919

Showing Territorial Changes under the Treaty of Versailles.

Ceded Areas
Demilitarized Areas

stipulation was intended by the Allies to prevent a repetition of any such subterfuge. Officers would serve for twenty-five years. Military equipment and the manufacture of munitions would be proportionate to the size of the new army. The General Staff was to be dissolved. Germany was not to maintain a navy in excess of six battleships of 10,000 tons, six light cruisers, twelve destroyers, and twelve torpedo boats. Germany was neither to manufacture nor to possess submarines, military aircraft, heavy artillery, tanks, and poison gas. The Supreme Council decided at a later date that, in compensation for the ships scuttled at Scapa Flow in the week before the treaty was signed, Germany was to surrender certain ships, floating docks, tugs, and dredges. The military clauses were to be carried out under the supervision of an Allied Commission of Control.

Under the reparations clauses, "the Allied and Associated Governments affirm and Germany accepts the responsibility of Germany and her allies for causing all the loss and damage to which the Allies and Associated Governments and their nationals have been subjected as a consequence of the war imposed upon them by the aggression of Germany and her allies." The Allies recognized that the resources of Germany were not adequate to make complete reparation. But they required of Germany every reparation within her capacity, in money and in kind, for damage to civilians, and they included in this category "all pensions to military and naval victims of war . . . and allowances to families and dependents of mobilized persons." The Allies also required of Germany the reimbursement of all sums which they had loaned Belgium during the war. A Reparation Commission was to be appointed to determine the amounts of all these sums and to arrange for their transfer, so that Germany's entire obligation might be discharged "within a period of thirty years." "In order to enable the Allied and Associated Powers to proceed at once to the restoration of their industrial and economic life," Germany was to pay the equivalent of 20,000,000,000 gold marks by May 1, 1921. She was to deliver coal and timber to France and livestock to Belgium. She was to deliver ships, principally to Britain, "ton for ton and class for class," to compensate for the havoc of the submarine war (see p. 160).

Under the financial and economic clauses, Germany agreed to make reparations a first charge upon her national revenues, to bear the costs of Allied armies of occupation, to acknowledge her prewar debts, not to increase her tariffs above their prewar levels, and not to discriminate against Allied trade. She undertook to internationalize the four rivers serving states beyond her frontiers and passing through or by her territory: the Elbe, the Oder, the Niemen, and the Danube, and she undertook to maintain the Kiel Canal "free and open to the vessels of all nations at peace with Germany on terms of entire equality."

Finally, under "Guarantees," the Allies declared that their occupation of the Rhineland would be continued for fifteen years, but they affirmed their intention to reduce the area of occupation by successive withdrawals of their forces every five years, according as Germany fulfilled the conditions of the treaty.

"I should have preferred a different peace," said Colonel House.

"I think it will be found that the compromises, which were accepted as inevitable, nowhere cut at the heart of any principle; the work of the Conference squares, as a whole, with the principles agreed upon as the basis of peace as well as with the practical possibilities," said President Wilson.

"It is a stern but just treaty," said Lloyd George.

"The day has come when might and right — terribly divorced hitherto — have united to give peace to the peoples in travail," said Clemenceau.

"This is not peace; it is an armistice for twenty years," said Foch.

"The promise of the new life, the victory of the great human ideals are not written in this treaty. . . . The real peace of the peoples ought to follow, complete, and amend the peace of the statesmen," said General Smuts.

"What hand would not wither that signed such a peace?" said Scheidemann.

"Do not expect us to be our own executioners," said Erzberger.

THE TREATY OF ST. GERMAIN

The signing of the Treaty of Versailles concluded the main work of the Conference. The Council of Four ceased to be the organ of Allied discussions, and the treaties with Austria, Bulgaria, and Hungary were framed by the Supreme Council, the name under which the old Supreme War Council still continued in existence at Versailles. Questions arising out of the execution of the Treaty of Versailles were afterward referred to a Conference of

Ambassadors sitting at Paris, and consisting of the American, British, Italian, and Japanese ambassadors in France and a French representative. The treaty with Turkey was drawn up in London in 1920 and signed at Sèvres on August 20, 1920 (see p. 226).

The Austrian delegates, headed by the Austrian Chancellor, Dr. Renner, arrived at St. Germain-en-Laye on May 14, 1919, where they were lodged under the same conditions of restraint as the Germans at Versailles. There was some difficulty over their credentials. The Supreme Council would not admit their claim to represent "German Austria," a state distinct from the old Austria of Austria-Hungary, and made it clear that they dealt with "Austria" and "Austria" only. There was also some delay while the final act at Versailles was played out, and the patient delegates at St. Germain were suffered to wait ignominiously for almost three weeks before their own treaty was handed to them.

The first draft of the Austrian treaty contained a number of omissions and even serious errors, and three more months were needed to bring it to a final form. Renner and his aides were indefatigable with "observations" and protests, and important concessions were allowed them. But the Supreme Council admitted no commutation of the bigger issue. Austria was not, as Renner argued, a new nation, as truly new as any "succession state," and therefore deserving of friendly treatment. Austria was still Austria, the old Austria, with whom the Allies had gone to war in 1914, and now come to St. Germain, as Germany to Versailles, to hear sentence. And on this basis, at St. Germain on September 10, 1919, the treaty with Austria was signed.

The Treaty of St. Germain was modeled on Versailles. Whole clauses were reincorporated into it without the change of a word. Part I was the Covenant of the League. Under the territorial clauses, Austria ceded to Italy Trieste, Istria, and the Tirol up to the strategic Brenner Pass; to Czechoslovakia she ceded Bohemia, Moravia, Austrian Silesia, and parts of Lower Austria; to Rumania she ceded Bucovina; to Yugoslavia she ceded Bosnia, Hercegovina, and Dalmatia. Only from Hungary did she receive a small strip of territory, which came to be known at this time as the Burgenland. A plebiscite was to decide the future Austrian or Yugoslav allegiance of Klagenfurt. Union (*Anschluss*) with Germany was prohibited in a clause stating that "the independence of Austria is inalienable otherwise than with the consent of the Council of the League of Nations . . . and Austria undertakes to abstain from any act which might directly or indirectly or by any means whatever compromise her independence, particularly . . . by participation in the affairs of another Power." Austria was to reduce her army to 30,000 long-term volunteers, and to limit her navy to three police boats on the Danube. The penalty, reparations, and financial clauses of the treaty were similar to those of Versailles.

In sum, Austria survived as a relic of her former self, shorn of her empire and shorn of her minorities. Her prewar area (excluding Hungary) was reduced from 115,000 square miles to 32,000, and her prewar population (again excluding Hungary) from 30,000,000 to 6,000,000. The old historic

frontiers of Bohemia, including their 3,000,000 Germans, would be the frontiers of the new Czech state.

THE TREATY OF NEUILLY

The Bulgarian delegates arrived in Paris in July 1919, but the presentation of the Allied terms was again delayed, and the delegates waited nearly
two months for their treaty. They affected to be surprised that they should
be treated as enemies and argued, much as Renner had argued, that the Bulgaria they represented was a new Bulgaria, a regenerated democracy, deserving of a temperate peace. But the Supreme Council gave them small consolation. In October, Stambulisky became Bulgarian Premier, and at once gave
out that "he had no illusions" and "would sign even a bad peace." The treaty
with Bulgaria was duly signed by him at Neuilly-sur-Seine on November 27,
1919.

The Treaty of Neuilly was again modeled on Versailles. Territorially Bulgaria survived with much the same frontiers as she had had in 1914. Her one
big cession was that of Western Thrace to Greece. Her forces were reduced
to an army of 20,000 and gendarmerie and frontier corps of 13,000, all long-
term volunteers.

THE TREATY OF TRIANON

The Allies had intended to conclude a treaty with Hungary simultaneously with Austria. But Béla Kun's Communist revolution broke out in
Budapest in March 1919, and no agreement could be reached with him. The
Supreme Council accordingly drew up the frontiers to be assigned to Czechoslovakia, Yugoslavia, and Rumania, and duly notified Béla Kun of their
decisions. Hungarian forces were eventually ejected from the territories by
force. When Count Apponyi arrived in December 1919, representing a Hungarian government which the Allies felt they could recognize, important and
irrevocable commitments regarding the future frontiers of Hungary had already been made. The treaty was signed, after the usual protests, at the
Grand Trianon at Versailles on June 4, 1920.

The Treaty of Trianon was again modeled on Versailles. Territorially it
was the harshest of the postwar treaties. To Rumania alone Hungary ceded
an area larger than the total territory left to her. Her prewar area was reduced from 125,000 square miles to 36,000, and her population from 21,000,-
000 to 8,000,000. Three million Magyars passed under alien rule. The Hungarian Army was reduced to 35,000 long-term volunteers.

9 THE ORGANIZATION OF PEACE

THE ORIGINS OF THE LEAGUE OF NATIONS

The League of Nations was no new idea in the world. Rather it was the synthesis and climax of a long historical development. Perpetual peace was a theme that had been pondered by churchmen and philosophers of all ages. International law in the modern sense, theories of mediation and arbitration between states, theories of inquiry and delay in international disputes, theories of safeguards and sanctions had all been familiar since the seventeenth century. The Holy Alliance and the subsequent Concert of Powers, meeting in periodic consultation, had both been leagues of a kind. The conferences at The Hague in 1899 and 1907 had borne fruit in the Hague Court of Arbitration. Peace movements and institutions — such as the Carnegie Endowment and the Nobel Peace Prize — indicated the trend of "enlightened" public opinion and philanthropy. Prewar socialism in all countries had a pacifist and internationalist tradition. All this was a body of precedent which gave the framers of the Covenant of 1919 inspiration and authority for their handiwork.

The idea of a league had been canvassed during the war. President Wilson, in his note of December 1916, had suggested "a concert of nations" (see p. 73). Pope Benedict XV, in his peace note of August 1917, had pleaded for a court of arbitration (see p. 93). As the war approached its end, several Allied statesmen were giving earnest thought to a peacetime league. The French Chamber debated a league in 1917, and the British Imperial War Cabinet discussed it at the same time. Lord Robert Cecil, then British Under Secretary for Foreign Affairs, and General Smuts, then South African Minister of Defense, were busy with tentative constitutions and memoranda. On January 8, 1918, as Point 14 of his Fourteen Points, President Wilson declared that "a general association of nations must be formed under specific covenants for the purpose of affording mutual guarantees of political independence with territorial integrity to great and small states alike," and from that moment President Wilson became, in the eyes of all the world, the great apostle of the idea.

When the Commission on the League of Nations at the Peace Conference began its meetings, it was therefore in possession of several tentative leagues (see p. 109). As was so often said, the League was the only problem of the peace on which, before the Armistice, any real forethought had been expended. The draft of the Covenant was adopted at the fifth plenary session of the Peace Conference on April 28, 1919. Its main composers were the American David Hunter Miller and the Englishman Sir Cecil Hurst. Generally the American experts contributed the principles and the British the legal framework.

THE CONSTITUTION AND WORKING OF THE LEAGUE

(In the words of the Preamble of the Covenant, the League was created "in order to promote international co-operation and to achieve international peace and security — by the acceptance of obligations not to resort to war; by the prescription of open, just, and honorable relations between nations; by the firm establishment of the understandings of international law as the actual rule of conduct among Governments; and by the maintenance of justice and a scrupulous respect for all treaty obligations in the dealings of organized peoples with one another.")

Constitutionally the League functioned through an Assembly, a Council, and a Secretariat. The Assembly consisted of representatives of all the member nations, and acted as the League's parliament. The Council consisted of the representatives of the "Principal Allied and Associated Powers" — of which, of course, the United States was originally intended to be one — each with a "permanent seat," and in addition the representatives of lesser Powers to "be selected by the Assembly from time to time in its discretion." The Council has been described as the League's cabinet; it was more of an executive committee, an inner circle of Powers and, in many ways, it was reminiscent of the Council of Ten of the Peace Conference (see p. 111). The Secretariat was a permanent body, consisting of a Secretary General and staff, and acted as the League's civil service. The seat of the League was Geneva, and there in due course the magnificent Palace of Nations was erected to house it. The League also created, or associated itself with, a number of organs, such as the Mandates Commission, the Committee on Intellectual Co-operation, the International Labor Organization, and the World Court.

The League held its first meeting in 1920, shortly after the exchange of ratifications of the Treaty of Versailles. There were forty-three original members; thirty were Allied signatories of the Treaty of Versailles, and thirteen were "neutrals," "invited to accede." China had refused to sign the Treaty of Versailles (see p. 120), but joined the League in July 1920 upon the ratification of the Treaty of St. Germain and counted among the "originals." The United States and the Hejaz, both signatories of Versailles, failed to ratify and never subsequently became members (see p. 131). Germany became a member in 1926, and the Soviet Union in 1934. Up to 1936, nineteen additional states had become members, and six — including Japan, Germany, and Italy — had seceded. The Soviet Union was expelled in 1940, the only member ever to be so treated (see p. 650). The Twenty-first (and last) Assembly of the League was held in April 1946.

The Covenant of the League of Nations is printed in part at the end of this volume (see Appendix F). The articles concerning the terms of membership in the League, the powers and functions of the Assembly and the Council and the convening of their meetings, and the League's costs of administration are all plain and straightforward. They were never the occasions of serious dispute, and they do not need to be explained in detail. But the articles on the reduction of armaments, the arbitration of disputes, the imposition of sanctions against an aggressor state, the registration and revision of treaties, and the validity of regional understandings were full of contentious material, and in them resided the strength and the weakness of the League and the potentialities of its success and failure.

Thus Article 8 placed on the League Council the obligation to "formulate plans" for the reduction of armaments "for the consideration and action of the several Governments." From this auspicious and plausible text arose the melancholy tale of the World Disarmament Conference. Article 10 was a mutual guarantee of territorial integrity and political independence, and it was the cornerstone of the entire security edifice. Articles 11 to 17 concerned the direct prevention of war. These articles seem somehow wanting in forcible phrasing. But they were the synthesis of several contributions, and they represented a compromise, the best compromise which then seemed possible, between collective action among nations and noninterference in the sovereignty of any one of them. Articles 11 to 17 made much of the principles of investigation and publicity, which by themselves were held often to be enough to discourage an international dispute in its early stages. The procedure to be followed somewhat naïvely presupposed the good faith of the parties in the dispute and of the guarantors of the system and, as experience was to show, the League could seldom rely on that virtue being present, especially at those moments when — and in those governments where — it was most wanted. Under Article 15, recommendations for the settlement of a dispute could be adopted only on the basis of unanimity: "If the Council fails to reach a report which is unanimously agreed to by the members thereof, other than the representative of one or more parties to the dispute, the Members of the League reserve to themselves the right to take such action as they shall consider necessary for the maintenance of right and justice." Article 16 laid down the sanctions to be applied by members of the League against one of their number resorting to war "in disregard of its Covenants" under the foregoing articles and the mutual support which the members would then render one another. It is interesting that Article 16 was to be entirely automatic in operation and presumably would not wait on decisions of the Council or Assembly.

Article 18 provided for the registration and publication of all treaties and international engagements entered into by member states. "No such treaty or international engagement shall be binding until so registered." The article embodied Point 1 of President Wilson's Fourteen Points, demanding "open covenants of peace." It would throw a revealing light of preventive publicity onto any dark or doubtful international transaction and forever abolish the old secret diplomacy which could commit the fate of whole nations to pacts and alliances known only to a small circle of statesmen.

Article 19 provided for "the reconsideration of treaties which have become inapplicable, and the consideration of international conditions whose continuance might endanger the peace of the world." The framers of the Covenant were well aware that their institution might become the refuge of conservatism and that every *status quo,* as soon as it has become a *status quo,* tends also to become a *status sacrosanctus.* The British delegates at the Peace Conference, in particular, regarded Article 19 as an escape clause under which the wrongs of Versailles might be gradually and peaceably redressed. But unhappily the British delegates had counted without the unanimity clause. States were notoriously stubborn about considering changes in an existing international situation which appeared to be to their advantage, even when the continuance of that situation was clearly a threat to peace. Any member state of the League could block the unanimity necessary for making revisions and, as so often happened, the legal "right" lay in the hands of those most interested in evading the revisions.

It was also hoped by the framers of the Covenant that the League might supersede all the ententes and alliances of the old diplomacy which they considered had been so fertile of wars. But Article 21, inserted at the behest of the American delegates, made an exception in the case of "regional understandings like the Monroe Doctrine, for securing the maintenance of peace," and it was not long after the signing of Versailles that the nations of Europe were once more as busy with their regional understandings as ever they had been in the past, all of which they too asserted were for securing the maintenance of peace. Far from being a superalliance, an alliance which obviated the need of all others, the League was soon to be strenuously buttressed about with alliances and treaties, pacts and protocols, such as made the ensuing twenty years the most active and complicated in the history of professional diplomacy.

Perhaps it was in France that criticisms of the "weakness" of the League were most persistent. The French, with their essentially military conception of international relations, had always wanted a military league, and they would have been satisfied with nothing less than a universal general staff and a universal army. It seemed to them that the League as constituted was only a sort of secular papacy without the temporal force to sustain it. Léon Bourgeois, for example, the French delegate on the League of Nations Commission of the Peace Conference, pleaded interminably for the inclusion in the Covenant of definite military clauses, or at least for the proper international "surveillance" and "verification" of armaments and effectives. But no other Power, certainly not the United States or Britain or Japan, would have been willing to commit itself in advance to the responsibilities and controls which such a League would have entailed, and it would have been hard to imagine France and Italy — with perhaps Germany and Russia — combining together as a military Concert of Powers.

The French were soon justified in their forebodings when it appeared that certain member states of the League were beginning to chafe even under the vague and equivocal obligations of the existing Covenant. From the very first League Assembly in 1920, amendments were being proposed, notably in regard to Article 16, the Sanctions Article. At the Fourth Assembly in 1923, at the instance of the Canadian delegate, an interpretative resolution was brought forward in respect of Article 10 to the effect that every government should itself be the judge of the extent of its military commitments. The resolution failed of adoption, but it was significant nonetheless.

The inescapable fact is that no nation entered the League, just as no nation had originally come to the Peace Conference at Paris, without mental reservations of one sort or another. Local needs, local prejudices, local habits of thought contributed variously to the way each, of the nations interpreted its rights and duties under the Covenant. When all is said and done, France measured the usefulness of the League to herself in proportion as it could be turned into an instrument for the suppression of Germany. Fascist Italy regarded the League as a standing obstacle to her expansionism. Republican Germany looked to the League as an aid to her liberation from Versailles, but at the same time she could never reconcile herself to the fact that the Covenant had been written into the text of the treaty, and that her great hope and her great humiliation were most diabolically intermixed. America's reservation was her old abhorrence of European entanglements. We shall describe elsewhere President Wilson's breach with the Republican party chiefs and Congress's consequent rejection of the Treaty of Versailles, the League, and the World Court (see pp. 362–63 and 373). But it is appropriate to note here that America's reservation was, of all the reservations, the one that mattered most. The absence of the Great Power which had done so much to create the League became a fatal limitation of its prestige and usefulness.

Yet for all these criticisms and for all the League's notorious failures in the major crises of the Period of Crisis to come, it is unfair and unhistorical to forget the several concrete achievements of the League in its best days. Up to the Manchurian crisis in 1931, the League dealt with twenty-seven political disputes between states, and between 1931 and 1939 with fifteen; and, of this total of forty-three disputes, twelve were successfully settled by the League, twelve unsuccessfully, and the remaining nineteen were afterward withdrawn, directly negotiated between the disputants, often with the participation or advice of the League Council, or else referred to the World Court. Many of the successful settlements were models of their kind, examples of the function that a world organization like the League was eminently fitted to perform. The total record is no mean one. Moreover, the League administered the Saar and Danzig under the terms of the Treaty of Versailles; it assisted the financial reconstruction of certain states, notably Austria; it supervised plebiscites; and it engaged in humanitarian, health, and educational work, notably in regard to the drug traffic, slavery, and refugees. Some of these matters will be considered along with their contexts in other parts of this book. The League's activities in regard to mandates and minorities, humanitarian work and intellectual co-operation, the International Labor Organization, and the World Court deserve to be specially noticed at this point.

THE MANDATES

Article 22 of the League Covenant, the Mandates Article, provided for the disposal and distribution of the foreign and overseas territories of Germany and the Ottoman Empire under a system of mandates. The territories were forfeited by Germany and the Ottoman Empire by reason of their deplorable record as rulers of subject races. Open annexation of the territories by the victor Allies would have contravened the high purposes of the Wilsonian code. Yet the territories, inhabited as they were "by peoples not yet able to stand by themselves under the strenuous conditions of the modern world," could not be expected to exist without the tutelage of "advanced nations." Under the mandates system, the territories would be granted to colonial Powers — or rather, those Allied Powers which had occupied the territories in the course of the war would now be confirmed in possession — but the territories would be held in trust on behalf of the League, and the worst abuses of the old imperialism, it was hoped, would be avoided. The Mandatory Powers, according to the "character of the mandate" and "the stage of the development of the people," would then be obligated to respect freedom of religion, to prohibit the slave trade, to prevent the building of fortifications and the military training of the natives, and finally to "render to the Council [of the League] an annual report" upon their stewardship. A Mandates Commission was created to sit at Geneva, to receive the annual reports of the Mandatory Powers, to submit its own observations to the League Council, and generally to supervise the mandates system.

There were three classes of mandates, A, B, and C, differing roughly in accordance with the political development of the people in question. To Class A belonged the former possessions of the Ottoman Empire, inhabited by newly liberated peoples who were expected eventually to become independent. Of these possessions, Mesopotamia and Palestine were allotted to Britain as the Mandatory Power, and Syria and Lebanon to France. To Class B belonged the former Central and East African possessions of Germany, inhabited by people who were not expected to become independent. Of these possessions, the greater part of Tanganyika was allotted to Britain, the remainder to Belgium, and Togoland and the Cameroons were divided between Britain and France. Finally, to Class C belonged former German possessions which passed wholly "under the laws of the Mandatory as integral portions of its territory." Thus the former German Southwest Africa was allotted to the Union of South Africa, the former German islands in the Pacific north of the equator were allotted to Japan, and those south of the equator to Australia and New Zealand.

The allotment of these mandates was made at Allied conferences, notably at the Peace Conference in 1919 and at the San Remo Conference in 1920 (see pp. 224 and 240). In general it may be said that the mandates system worked very well. The mandates in Syria and Palestine proved most troublesome and threw unexpectedly heavy burdens on the respective Mandatories, France and Britain; and these were the areas where the Mandates Commission used its powers to make observations on the mandatory administrations. Japan abused her undertakings in respect of her mandate over the former German islands in the North Pacific in erecting fortifications and refusing to permit League inspection. In 1932, Iraq (Mesopotamia) was the first state to be emancipated from its mandatory status to become an independent kingdom and a member of the League of Nations.

THE MINORITIES

The peace treaties of 1919–20, as Birdsall has said, represented "the closest approximation to an ethnographic map of Europe that has ever been achieved." [1] The variegated peoples of that restless, fluctuating continent, it seemed, had really found at last an appropriate political geography. Nationality and self-determination, twin ideals, were largely coincident and mutually satisfied. Yet, in places, there were still "minorities" on the wrong side of a frontier. It was estimated that 30,000,000 of Europe's population would still be compelled to live under alien rule. Austria-Hungary and the Ottoman Empire had both been reduced to their national elements, and the new states arising out of them could not always be homogeneous. The new governments were inexperienced; sentiments everywhere were inflamed by war and by long, embittered historical memories; it was impossible to expect that several nationalities, once repressed and now dominant and revengeful, would not wreak their hatred on "islands" of their former overlords which the peace treaties would leave within their borders. Other communities, notably the Jews, created special problems.

There is no mention of minorities in the League Covenant, for the Covenant was drawn up and published before the minority problem had begun seriously to disturb the Peace Conference at Paris. But the five minorities treaties of 1919 and 1920 all subsequently cited the League as the trustee and court of appeal of the populations whose rights they sought to protect. The treaties were largely the work of the Minorities Commission of the Peace Conference. The smaller Powers, on whom the necessary legislation was to be imposed, naturally enough, were not slow to protest against the implied derogation of their sovereignty, and it needed all the tact and authority of President Wilson and Clemenceau to smooth their ruffled pride..

The Polish Minorities Treaty was the first to be drawn up. For obvious reasons it had to be ready at the same time as the Treaty of Versailles. It took the form of a treaty between the five Principal Allied and Associated Powers and Poland. Poland obligated herself to give her citizens "full and complete protection of life and liberty . . . without distinction of birth, nationality, language, race, or religion," to permit them "the free exercise, whether public or private, of any creed, religion, or belief," and to provide "in the public educational system in towns and districts, in which a considerable proportion of Polish nationals of other than Polish speech are residents, adequate facilities in primary schools . . . for instruction to be given to the children through the medium of their own language." All these clauses constituted "obligations of international concern and shall be placed under the guarantee of the League of Nations." Any member of the League Council might bring to the attention of the Council "any infraction, or any danger of infraction, of any of these obligations." The Polish Minorities Treaty was signed concurrently with the Treaty of Versailles on June 28, 1919.

Similar treaties were signed during 1919 and 1920 with Yugoslavia, Czechoslovakia, Rumania, and Greece. Special minority clauses were inserted in the peace treaties with Austria, Hungary, Bulgaria, and Turkey. Albania and the new Baltic States made declarations recognizing their obligations to their minorities. But it cannot be said that all these treaties and declarations were conspicuously successful. Complicated, ancient hatreds were not to be written off just with the stroke of a pen. Later, as the League system weakened, so also its more precarious elements weakened, and in the era of the dictatorships, so soon to arrive, the minorities became convenient pawns to be sacrificed in the game of power politics.

THE HUMANITARIAN AND INTELLECTUAL WORK OF THE LEAGUE

Various ancillary organs and committees of the League accomplished an immense amount of work in regard to international health, the traffic in drugs, the traffic in women, slavery, obscene publications, the repatriation of prisoners of war, and the relief of refugees and of communities stricken by epidemics, floods, and earthquakes.

In 1921 the Second Assembly created a Committee on Intellectual Co-operation "to secure for intellectual work the place which befits it and to assist in the freer and more rapid circulation of the great intellectual currents of the world." The Committee included such names as Albert Einstein, Henri Bergson, Gilbert Murray, Robert Andrews Millikan, and Madame Curie.

THE INTERNATIONAL LABOR ORGANIZATION

The International Labor Organization, the I.L.O., was brought into existence at the Peace Conference under the kindly direction of the Commission on International Labor Legislation. Its purpose and constitution were set out in the peace treaties and in Article 23 of the Covenant of the League. It recognized the world-wide interest in social and labor problems which the war and the postwar revolutionary movements had stirred up. It would help, it was sincerely hoped, to remove the "injustice, hardship, and privation" which had involved such large numbers of people and had imperiled "the peace and harmony of the world." It would be "established at the seat of the League of Nations as a part of the organization of the League," and it would endeavor "to secure and maintain fair and humane conditions of labor for men, women, and children, both in their own countries and in all countries to which their commercial and industrial relations extend." By its agency, the peace treaties would not only create in the world a better political order, but a better social order as well.

The I.L.O. consisted of a General Conference, a Governing Body, and an Office, departments which corresponded analogously with the Assembly, Council, and Secretariat of the League itself. All member states of the League were members of it. Brazil and Japan, on withdrawing from the League, retained their membership, and the United States became a member in 1934. Its first Director was Albert Thomas of France.

The first General Conference was held in Washington in 1919. From 1921 to 1939 it met regularly in Geneva. During the Second World War, in 1940, the Office moved to Montreal and occupied modest premises in McGill University. A conference was held in New York in 1941, and the regular sessions of the General Conference were resumed in 1944. Up to 1939, the Conference had adopted 73 recommendations and 67 conventions, dealing with working hours, night work, woman and child labor, the weekly day of rest, workmen's compensation, sickness benefit, occupational diseases, minimum wages, unemployment, and so forth. Over 900 ratifications had been received from more than 60 states. In addition, the I.L.O. had appointed various committees on such subjects as industrial hygiene, the prevention of accidents, and native labor. Lloyd George might well say, "there is no section of the Treaty which so far has brought such unmixed blessings to untold millions of the humblest workers in many lands."

The Office, meanwhile, besides performing the regular secretarial work of the I.L.O., became a central clearinghouse of a vast mass of information on economic and social matters. It collected statistics, prepared reports, and published several periodicals. Its personnel of about four hundred men and women was drawn from some forty nationalities. It maintained branch offices in many parts of the world.

THE WORLD COURT

The Permanent Court of International Justice, or the World Court as it came to be known, was not an immediate product of the Peace Conference. The framers of the League Covenant at first expected that arbitral tribunals created *ad hoc,* or else the former Hague Court of Arbitration, would deal with future international disputes. Article 14 of the Covenant, which became the basis of the Court's existence, was a highly technical and controversial issue, and in the form in which it was inserted in the Covenant it left room for future discussion and development.

Some time elapsed before the Court could be created. Its constitution and particularly the rules for appointing its judges were full of difficulties. But the delay was not a disadvantage. The Court was not wanted at once, it did not need to be tied to the peace treaties, as was the League Covenant, and every detail of its constitution could be studied meanwhile with meticulous care. A committee of eight eminent jurists, among whom were Elihu Root and Lord Phillimore, was set up at the second meeting of the League Council in February 1920. The committee sat at The Hague for two months and eventually drew up a draft statute which was duly referred back to the League Council. After exhaustive examination, the statute was approved in December 1920 by the First Assembly of the League. The Permanent Court of International Justice, or World Court, was formally opened on February 15, 1922.

The establishment of the World Court at The Hague instead of at Geneva was a tribute partly to the long tradition of international jurisprudence in Holland and partly to the American donors of the Peace Palace. The Court was not intended to supersede the Hague Court of Arbitration, which actually continued in independent existence. It was, as its name implied, a permanent court, holding annual sessions and convenable for extraordinary sessions at short notice. Normally disputes could be referred to it only by states signatory to its Statute, and the disputes had to be of specifically "legal" character, for instance, those arising out of an interpretation of international law or an alleged breach of treaty. The Court therefore was in no way a duplicate or supersession of the League or of the League's functions in regard to political disputes under Articles 12, 13, 15, and 16 of the Covenant. The Court had no power to require a state to appear before it, nor to enforce its verdict afterward. An "Optional Clause" was inserted in its Statute, to which states were invited to adhere, thereby bringing themselves into a system for the compulsory settlement of legal disputes. The World Court was undeniably one of the greater creations of the peace settlement, but it suffered from the weakness of all "League Institutions." In the last analysis, it relied wholly upon the tenuous constraints of good will and good faith.

The World Court began with thirty-four participating states. It eventually had fifty. By a resolution of the League Council, eleven states, though not members of the League, were entitled to appear before it. In course of time, forty states subscribed to the Optional Clause.[2] More than four hundred international treaties and conventions of various kinds contained clauses providing for the reference of disputes to the Court. The United States, after a long controversy, declined to become a member (see p. 373).

THE SECURITY OF FRANCE

The great, central problem of peace in post-Versailles Europe was France's fear for her own security. We shall refer in later chapters to France's domestic politics, which were the background to the problem, and also to other cognate events in Europe, such as the German-Soviet Treaty of Rapallo, the French occupation of the Ruhr, the formation of the Little Entente in the Middle Danube, and the attempted settlement of German reparations under the Dawes Plan, all of which bore upon the selfsame problem. But it would be suitable at this point to complete what we have said about the League of Nations with some discussion of those further general transactions whereby an anxious France — and Europe — sought to infuse a bit more reality into the organization of peace.

During the Peace Conference at Paris, as we have observed, Clemenceau had fought doggedly for France's claim to a frontier on the Rhine, but he had been forced to accept in its stead treaties of assistance on the part of the United States and Britain against future German aggression (see p. 119). The treaties had been signed concurrently with the Treaty of Versailles, but the United States afterward failed to ratify the Treaty of Versailles, and the entire arrangement had lapsed (see p. 362). France consequently found herself on the morrow of the peace without her Rhine frontier, without her treaties of assistance, and with only a League of Nations, ethically imposing but militarily powerless, to fill the strategic vacuum. She saw upon her eastern frontier a great warlike nation with a still growing population, half again as great as hers, with industrial resources that had survived the war intact, a nation which, though momentarily reduced in armaments, was doubtless full of ideas of sweet revenge as soon as the opportunity should beckon.

There were two courses of action open to France — courses of action which were at once complementary and contradictory. She could either construct across Europe a system of alliances to the complete diplomatic isolation and encirclement of Germany; or else she could make the most of such powers as the League of Nations already represented and perhaps develop out of them a security system which, in her view, might be more sufficient and dependable. The first course was perhaps better suited to the French historical tradition, and it resulted in a series of bilateral treaties with Belgium, Poland, the states of the Little Entente, and finally with the Soviet Union (see pp. 321, 489, and 492). The second course resulted in a series of general pacts, in which France was one of several signatories.

During 1922 the French and British Governments each approached the other with proposals of treaties. In particular the British Government was anxious to make amends for the failure of the treaty of assistance of 1919. The discussions were shortly involving not only France and Britain but all the members of the League. Thus a Draft Treaty of Mutual Assistance was debated at the League's Fourth Assembly in 1923. A Protocol for the Pacific Settlement of International Disputes — the Geneva Protocol, as it came to be called — was drawn up at the League's Fifth Assembly in 1924. Each of these documents denoted a step forward; each lay within the framework of the League. But each failed of acceptance over the precise nature of the assistance that Britain should be called upon to give. It was easy enough to name the arbitrator in an international dispute; the arbitrator would be the League Council or such other body as the League Council might appoint. It was easy enough to name the aggressor; the aggressor would then be the party which refused arbitration. All this was good diplomatic logic. But only those states which patently expected to want assistance were prepared to define their military commitments in advance.

Britain was traditionally averse to underwriting sweeping guarantees which should be automatically binding in every unpredictable circumstance, and the British Dominions expressed themselves courteously but frankly as uninterested in any instrument which in practice could never be much more than a European regional pact. As the Canadian delegate at Geneva once said, "In this association of mutual assistance against fire, the risks assumed by the different states are not equal. We [in Canada] live in a fire-proof house, far from inflammable materials." In 1925, Austen Chamberlain, then British Foreign Secretary, made a statement before the League Council intimating his government's "insuperable objections to signing and ratifying the [Geneva] Protocol in its present shape."

LOCARNO

Thrice had Britain thus declined responsibilities on the Continent of Europe. The treaty of assistance of 1919, the Draft Treaty, and the Geneva Protocol had largely failed because of her attitude. Hers was a world-wide commonwealth, and she regarded herself as already sufficiently committed to maintaining the universal *status quo* without new and sometimes indefinite guarantees on paper. There was not a breath of unrest in the five continents or on the seven seas which did not inevitably touch her interests or prestige. There was not a war which might break out on man's earth but she might be forced to participate. British opinion was exasperated again and again by the naïve assumption of oppressed and threatened peoples everywhere that they had only to call out and Britain would rush chivalrously to their rescue. Britain moreover had domestic and imperial troubles of her own, in Ireland, Egypt, India, in lands outside the ken of Continental Europe, where she needs must fight alone and where no foreign Power ever gave her anything but criticism. Her homeland was sunk in its interwar economic and moral lethargy and wanted not an increase, but a relaxation, of international responsibility. To give a blank guarantee to the Polish Corridor or Danzig, for example, or to the new frontiers of Bohemia or Rumania or Silesia, or to any of the dozen "danger spots" of Europe — for all that Britain was signatory of the treaties which had created them and must continue indirectly to be concerned in their preservation — was more than the British Parliament and public, with the best will in the world, could afford to do.

Nevertheless, the British Government felt it incumbent to make some gesture to compensate for the three nugatory pacts. In particular it was anxious to evolve an instrument which did not look, as the French-sponsored schemes had always looked, like an alliance of the Versailles Powers for the perpetual subjugation of Germany. In the end, curiously enough, the solution was found in a return to the idea of a Rhineland treaty of assistance, and the initial proposals came from Germany herself.

The time was hardly propitious. At the end of 1922, Germany had defaulted on her reparations payments; French troops had occupied her industrial Ruhr area as a measure of enforcing payment; Germany and France had thence lapsed into a state of passive war, the upshot of which had been the collapse of the German currency. In 1923 a new political figure had appeared in Germany in the person of Gustav Stresemann, and his efforts to restore his country's finances and make peace with France had come to fruition in 1924 in the Dawes Plan (see p. 166). Then, early in 1925, the first stages of the Allied evacuation of the Rhineland, occupied under the terms of the Treaty of Versailles, should have begun. But the Allied Control Commission had reported unfavorably on the progress of German disarmament, and accordingly the evacuation was not to take place. The German press reverted to its old tone of aggrievement and defiance, and the French to their interminable thesis of a Rhine frontier. All these events we shall elaborate in later chapters. Yet in February 1925, with bland indifference to the situation as it appeared to be, Stresemann in Germany transmitted to Herriot, the French Premier at the time, proposals for a regional pact of nonaggression and arbitration to include France, Britain, Italy, and Germany and, if possible, to find a general solution of current international disagreements in Western Europe.

Complicated negotiations followed. Britain relented to the extent of accepting commitments for the Rhineland, but she was still averse to guaranteeing the whole mixed ragbag of Central and Eastern Europe. In April 1925 the Herriot government fell in France, but Painlevé succeeded, with the moderate Briand as Foreign Minister, and the continuity of the negotiations was not interrupted. In October the Powers — France, Britain, Italy, Germany, Belgium, Poland, and Czechoslovakia — met in the Swiss town of Locarno on Lake Maggiore. Austen Chamberlain, the British Foreign Secretary, represented Britain; Briand represented France; Hans Luther, the German Chancellor, and Stresemann, the German Foreign Minister, represented Germany. Mussolini, the Italian dictator, was present during the concluding stages of the conference. The pact was initialed at Locarno on October 16 and signed in London on December 1, 1925.

The Locarno Pact comprised a whole series of interlocking treaties. In an introductory Protocol the Powers declared their intention to "seek by common agreement means for preserving their respective nations from the scourge of war, and for providing for the peaceful settlement of disputes," and pledged themselves to co-operate sincerely in the League's endeavors toward disarmament. The first of the treaties was a Treaty of Mutual Guarantee, the Rhineland Pact, as it was popularly known, under which Britain, France, Belgium, Italy, and Germany, collectively and severally, guaranteed the western frontiers of Germany and the demilitarization of the Rhineland. France, Belgium, and Germany agreed "in no case to attack or to invade each other or to resort to war against each other," except in a flagrant breach of the Protocol, or in fulfillment of League action against an aggressor state. The responsibility for determining the flagrant breach devolved upon the League Council.

There then followed four arbitration treaties between Germany on the one side and France, Belgium, Poland, and Czechoslovakia severally on the other, providing for their disputes to be submitted to a Conciliation Commission and thence, if need be, to the World Court or the League Council; and two treaties of guarantee, virtually defensive alliances, between France and Poland, and France and Czechoslovakia.

Locarno made a tremendous impression at the time. The whole setting of the conference had been skillfully stage-managed to banish the psychology of Versailles. The delegates met informally at country inns and on boating excursions on Lake Maggiore. The very words "ally" and "enemy" were ruled out of their vocabulary. Photographs of Chamberlain, Briand, and Stresemann, in smiling, intimate conversation amid the calm and beauty of an Alpine autumn, were distributed to the press throughout the world. On his return to England, Chamberlain declared the Locarno Pact marked "the real dividing line between the years of war and the years of peace," and a grateful King created him Knight of the Garter. Briand, in the eloquent French of which he was so great a master, apostrophized the new era of "conciliation, arbitration, and peace!" Even Stresemann found it in his heart to say: "We are citizens each of his own country . . . but we are also citizens of Europe and are joined together by a great conception of civilization. We have the right to speak of a European idea."

A first result of Locarno was the admission of Germany to the League of Nations and to a permanent seat on the League Council. But unhappily that symbolic welcome to the family of nations was marred and nearly ruined by a serious incident. The League Council at the time consisted of four permanent members — Britain, France, Italy, and Japan — and six members elected for annual periods. The prospective appointment of Germany to an additional permanent seat on the Council encouraged a number of the lesser Powers — Poland, Spain, Brazil, and China — also to aspire to the supreme distinction themselves. France, naturally enough, supported the candidature of her ally, Poland. An undignified altercation followed. Germany, who had never looked too kindly upon the League in any case, might well seem confirmed in her mistrust of it. She showed her disgust and resentment, as she was to do on her other occasions of difficulty with the Western Powers, by turning toward Russia, and on April 24, 1926, at Berlin, she entered into a treaty of friendship and neutrality with the Soviet Union. The new treaty was not much publicized at the time; both signatories claimed that they were merely extending the benefits of the Locarno system to Eastern Europe. But it was not the first or last time that Germany and Russia sprang an unpleasant diplomatic surprise on the rest of the world. The storm at Geneva, however, eventually subsided. On September 8, 1926, at the Seventh League Assembly, Germany was formally elected to membership and to a permanent seat on the League Council, and all was well again.

Criticism today has stripped Locarno of its former glamour and has represented it as a surrender to typical German chicanery. Certainly Germany undertook nothing which she had not undertaken already; a Rhineland Pact, overlaid upon the Rhineland demilitarization clauses of the Treaty of Versailles, was a work of supererogation and, as the world was so soon to learn, the mere multiplication of pacts did not enhance their sanctity. Certainly too, Locarno had its reverse side. The progress of German disarmament to date left much to be desired. We know now that, in 1925, huge stocks of munitions remained undestroyed in Germany, that the German armaments industry was being intensively rationalized for future expansion, that illicit military organizations were flourishing, that no one outside the Reichswehr Ministry in Berlin knew the real strength of the German Army, and that, in short, the military stipulations of Versailles were very far from being observed.

Yet Stresemann was not slow to draw from Locarno the conclusions which best suited him. If the new peace was really a peace, then the Rhineland must be evacuated and the Allied Control Commission must go home. In the prevailing "Locarno atmosphere" Germany must not be denied an appropriate alleviation of her burdens. In return for her signature, in return for giving the world a momentary glow of hope, Germany was to gain for herself very concrete advantages. Consequently the evacuation of the Rhineland by the Allied occupation forces was begun in December 1925, the day the Locarno Pact was signed; the Control Commission was withdrawn in January 1927. But in 1928 the postscript to Locarno was already being written in the sudden spurt of Germany's military budget.

In 1928 was signed that greater Locarno, the Pact of Paris. This time, the United States was also drawn into the vortex of peace.

THE PACT OF PARIS

The Pact of Paris, though conformable with League ideology, had in fact no connection with the League and could therefore attract signatories who were currently not members of the League. It was born of American initiative and French courtesy. As far as the United States was concerned, it was originally intended to compensate for the slow progress of disarmament since the war and, in particular, of naval disarmament, in which the United States had so strong an interest (see pp. 363–66 and 369–71). As far as France was concerned — and, in particular, as far as Briand, the French Foreign Minister, was concerned — it was originally intended to be no more than a gesture. On April 6, 1927, in a statement to the press, Briand proposed that France and the United States should celebrate the tenth anniversary of the entry of the United States into the World War in 1917 by subscribing to an engagement outlawing war between themselves. Briand doubtless expected that the entire affair would begin and end with an exchange of courtesies of the type he and his countrymen knew so well how to make. A couple of speeches, a couple of signatures cost nothing, and it was all very pleasant mummery among friends.

The reaction in the United States was slow in coming, but it gradually gathered force, and before many weeks had passed the "outlawry of war" had become a national movement of extraordinary power. In December 1927, having waited more than six months while the tide of popular pacifism swirled around his Department, Secretary of State Kellogg replied to Briand's proposal by suggesting a world-wide multilateral pact binding all nations "to renounce war as an instrument of national policy."

This was far more than Briand had bargained for. The French Government at once took the line that so universal an engagement might conflict with France's own postwar treaty system in Europe. But in April 1928, Kellogg circulated among the British, German, Italian, and Japanese governments the draft of a pact which, in his view, met the needs of the case. The German Government was the first to accept the draft, and it accepted it with alacrity. The Italian and Japanese governments also accepted. The British Government appeared to hesitate — like France, it also had prior commitments to consider, and perhaps it was a little cynically inclined toward what it felt to be a piece of American naïveté and exuberance — but it was soon forced to fall into line by demonstrations of popular enthusiasm in Britain as impressive as any in the United States. Some time was consumed nevertheless while official French and British "reservations" were reconciled with the Kellogg formula, and by the end of June 1928 a more acceptable draft had been sent, for final consideration and comment, to the governments of all the Locarno Powers.

On August 27, 1928 the plenipotentiaries of fifteen Powers [3] met in Paris to conclude a General Treaty for the Renunciation of War, the Pact of Paris, or the Kellogg-Briand Pact, as it was familiarly called. Among them were Briand, Kellogg, and Stresemann. It was the first time since 1870 that a German Foreign Minister had been officially received on French soil. The ceremony was staged in the Quai d'Orsay. All the little properties of the occasion were chosen with tact and taste. The plenipotentiaries signed with a gold pen presented to Kellogg by the city of Le Havre and bearing the inscription: "*Si vis pacem para pacem* (If you desire peace, prepare for peace)." The inkstand was the inkstand used in the signing of the treaty of 1778. "In the face of the whole world," said Briand, "by means of a solemn covenant, involving the honor of great nations that have behind them a past heavy with political conflicts, war is unreservedly renounced as an instrument of national policy, that is to say, war in its most specific and dreaded form, egoistic and willful war."

In this festival of nations the most important absentee had been the Soviet Union. Chicherin, the Soviet Commissar for Foreign Affairs, naturally regarded as suspect a pact to which all the world was party but his own country, and pronounced it a typical capitalist intrigue. He recalled with some asperity that the Soviet Union had also been absent from Locarno. Nor could he refrain from questioning the value of pacts, however high their apparent idealism, so totally wanting in coercive machinery. Nevertheless, with the good offices of the French Government, one of the only two governments which signed the Pact of Paris then having relations with Moscow, the adhesion of the Soviet Union to the pact — with certain reservations, notably in regard to disarmament — was secured within a couple of days of the main event in Paris.

The Soviet Union, in fact, went further. Having at first condemned the Pact of Paris, the Soviet Union was shortly constructing a pact of its own. Litvinov, Chicherin's successor, proposed that the Soviet Union, Poland, and Lithuania should recognize the Pact of Paris as binding on themselves. Eventually, on February 9, 1929, the Litvinov Protocol, as it was called, was signed in Moscow and was afterward ratified by the Soviet Union and eight other states around its littoral.[4] The whole world, it seemed, was being bound, pact by pact, to peace.

DISARMAMENT

We have described in this chapter the origins and constitution of the League of Nations, its supervision of the mandates and minorities, its humanitarian, intellectual, and juridical activities; and we have described the pacts of Locarno and Paris. Peace was an ever growing structure; every year added some new buttress or ornament to it. The League Assembly of 1928 had laid before it nine "model treaties" of conciliation, arbitration, and mutual assistance which it then proceeded to combine into a General Act for the Pacific Settlement of International Disputes containing detailed provisions for well-nigh every possible contingency and crisis. The League Assembly of 1929 began to consider possible amendments to the Covenant so as to incorporate the more universal prescriptions of the Pact of Paris. And so it went on, always rising, always broadening — "the tower to de-Babelize the scattered children of men."

Today, as we survey the wreck of the structure, we find it hard to recapture the vast hopes it once stood for. Whatever of political wisdom and good will that then existed seemed to have gone into it. "[We] believed . . . that we were headed toward a new and better world," wrote an American statesman of that time. "We were confident that the errors of the past were to be valiantly corrected; that human wrong would all be righted; that the self-determination of peoples would end oppression; that human freedom and individual security would become realities; that war, in this new dawn breaking over the earth, was now a nightmare of the past." [5] Yet there was already at hand the acid test of the new pacifism. The nations had still to make the one demonstration of their good faith that would give their rhetoric meaning and reality. They had still to disarm. And on this supremely critical theme we may perhaps suitably close our chapter.

Disarmament had been the frequent theme of peace proposals during the First World War. It was given definitive canonical form in Point 4 of Wilson's Fourteen Points. Article 8 of the Covenant of the League of Nations enjoined "the reduction of national armaments to the lowest point consistent with national safety," and relegated to the Council of the League the eventual formulation of "plans for such reduction." The Treaty of Versailles imposed unilateral disarmament on Germany "in order to render possible the initiation of a general limitation of the armaments of all nations," and the Allied treaties with Austria, Hungary, and Bulgaria contained similarly worded clauses. In reply to one of the German "observations" at Versailles, the Allies declared further that "their requirements were not made solely with the object of rendering it impossible [for Germany] to resume her policy of military aggression. They are also the first step towards the reduction and limitation of armaments which they seek to bring about as one of the most fruitful preventives of war, and which it will be one of the first duties of the League of Nations to promote."

Yet, while the arguments might be incontestable, "the practical details of their application" were not so easy. For fifteen years, from 1919 to 1933, the best minds in the world were trying to devise the ways and means of disarmament. Never did intelligent men seem so much in love with peace, never should they have been so ready to take concerted action against war. None of them believed any more in the vicious old maxim, *Si vis pacem para bellum*.[6] Yet in these years the limitation of armaments was found to be a problem only very partially soluble, and then only for a short time.

Today science is again changing the face of warfare and politics, and the old arguments, though they may remain in their fundamentals, are changing with it. During the interwar period, the real problem of disarmament, in the practical, technical sense, was its extreme complexity. Louis XIV in his day stopped dueling only by forbidding the carrying of swords. But the nations of this Age of Conflict carried more than swords in their belts. Their armaments varied so greatly in type and function as to defy comparison and to defy reduction to workable legal formulas. The real military power and potential of nations depended on complicated conditions, on their geography and way of life, on their isolation and vulnerability, on their raw materials and industries — on their geopolitics, as we should say today — as well as on less ponderable factors, the intelligence and literacy of their peoples, their birth rate, their national pride and prestige, their ideology, even their religion. It was difficult to find a common denominator, a "yardstick," by which to assess the various kinds of a nation's effectives. Armies could not be measured by divisions, nor navies by tonnage, nor air forces by the simple computation of the number of planes. It was difficult to assess the respective requirements of a naval Power like Britain, with scattered possessions and widely flung trade routes, and a naval Power like the United States, with a concentration of interests in two oceans. It was difficult to assess the requirements of an inland state like Hungary, crowded about with potentially hostile neighbors, and of a state in a strategic lee like Canada, with one neighbor and that a friendly one. It was difficult to assess the real strength of a state like the Soviet Union, supported mainly by an agrarian economy, and a state like Britain, supported mainly by an industrial economy, and states like France or Germany, supported by a combination of both. It was difficult to assess the real meaning of budgetary expenditures on armaments of a state like Japan, with a low standard of living, and a state like the United States, with a high standard of living. It was difficult to assess the budgetary expenditures on armaments of states having different systems of taxation or accounting. It was difficult to assess the effectiveness of secret armaments or of newly invented and untried weapons. It was difficult to assess different methods of training, speed of mobilization, and organization of reserves. It was difficult to assess the military value of an industrial plant, say a dye factory, convertible at short notice to the manufacture of poison gas, or of a fleet of commercial aircraft convertible at short notice into a bombing squadron, or of a luxury liner convertible at short notice into an auxiliary cruiser or an aircraft carrier. It was difficult to assess the degree of "offensiveness" or "defensiveness" of a particular weapon; one Power might regard the submarine as offensive and therefore propose its abolition, whereas another Power might regard it as defensive and therefore propose its retention; one Power might regard the tank as offensive, whereas another Power might regard only heavy tanks above 70 tons as offensive. The private manufacture of arms and the international traffic in arms, the neutralization of certain ports and waterways, the demilitarization of certain frontiers — all these bristled with problems and perplexities.

Many of these things are now forgotten. We already have new terrors to contend with. But such was the problem of disarmament as it appeared in the still aspiring twenties, a supremely difficult but worthy goal for a world to strive for, to its greater glory and happiness.

In the actual history of disarmament in the interwar period, naval disarmament did achieve temporarily a certain measure of success. The success was mainly attributable to the fact that, of the three principal naval Powers of the day, two were willing to compound their already similar strategic requirements at the expense of the third Power. The history of naval disarmament begins with the Washington Conference of 1921 and continues through the conferences at Geneva and London in 1927 and 1930. As American initiative and influence were here so strong, we leave the discussion of these conferences to our chapters on the United States (see pp. 363–66 and 369–71). Land disarmament makes a more confused and melancholy story.

In 1920, in accordance with Article 8 of the Covenant, the League Council appointed a Permanent Advisory Committee on Armaments, alongside of which were successively added the Temporary Mixed Commission and then, in 1926, the Preparatory Commission for the Disarmament Conference. Meanwhile a further conference had been convened at Geneva to examine that vexatious and delicate problem, the private traffic in arms, and it eventually drew up a convention establishing a system of supervision and publicity in the private traffic in certain types of arms. It also drew up the so-called Gas Protocol condemning the use of chemical and bacteriological warfare. At the end of 1925, twenty nations had adhered to the Gas Protocol, including Italy, who was to repudiate it so incontinently ten years afterward.

The Preparatory Commission began its sessions in Geneva in May 1926 and confined itself at first to questions of procedure, terms of reference, and the collection of evidence. Discussions and hearings continued at a second session in September 1926. The German delegate, who now attended for the first time, recalled to the attention of the Commission the Allied pledge at Versailles to initiate "a general limitation of the armaments of all nations," and asked his fellow delegates to consider, as their "final objective," the removal of "the existing disproportion between the armaments of the League's members," thereby raising an issue which, with increasing emphasis, was to haunt the disarmament conversations at Geneva till their final breakdown seven years later.

Third and fourth sessions of the Preparatory Commission were held in 1927. The Soviet Union sent a delegate for the first time to the fourth session, in the person of Litvinov,[7] who enlivened the proceedings with attacks on the "capitalist" Powers and then proposed a sweeping and immediate disbandment of all armies, navies, and air forces, the destruction of all war materials and manufactures, and the abolition of all war ministries, general staffs, and military colleges. The Preparatory Commission, it may be said, did not take Litvinov's thunderings very seriously. It prepared a Draft Convention in the form of the text of a treaty between the Powers, but left blank spaces in regard to the actual effectives and matériel. A World Disarmament Conference was then to be called, with the Draft Convention as the basis of its discussions, to fill in the blank spaces with exact figures. The history of that Conference we defer to a later page (see pp. 472–74).

GERMANY: REVOLUTION AND REPUBLIC

THE GERMAN REVOLUTION

There were three main party groupings in the prewar German Reichstag: the Right, a middle group, and the Left. The Right comprised the Conservatives and the Reich party (Junkers, court society, and landowners); the middle group comprised the National Liberals (big business) and the Center party (Roman Catholics); the Left comprised the Progressives (intelligentsia and certain radical banking and commercial circles) and the Social Democrats (labor and trade-unions). In general terms, the Right supported the monarchy as it existed, the army, and the policy of imperial expansion; the Center largely represented local and provincial interests; the Left inclined to a limited "democratized" monarchy, to antimilitarism, and to anti-imperialism. In August 1914, at a meeting of their party caucus, a small dissident faction of Social Democrats had hesitated and havered, but they had afterward fallen into line, and all parties of the Reichstag had then unanimously voted for the government's war policy.

As the war continued, the party truce, or *Burgfriede* (see p. 48) began to break down, and the old prewar party strifes were gradually resumed. The dissident faction of the Social Democrats seceded from its fellows and formed the Independent Socialists, in opposition to the government. The loyal remnant of the Social Democrats continued to support the government and took the name of the Majority Social Democrats. In 1916 a small "International group," popularly called the Spartacists, under the leadership of Rosa Luxemburg and Karl Liebknecht, moved still further leftward and openly agitated for revolution and peace. In 1917 the Center itself split on the war issue and precipitated the July Crisis of that year (see p. 82). Thereafter the retreat from Right to Left, from war to peace, from loyalty to revolution was a steadily quickening process, which reached its conclusion at last in the Revolution of November 1918.

The Revolution as such was the work of the Left, and it installed the Left in power. On November 9, 1918, when Prince Max announced the abdication of the Kaiser and himself resigned the chancellorship, his natural successor was Friedrich Ebert, the leader of the Majority Social Democrats, a workingman and a saddler by trade. But the shape which the new revolutionary Germany was to take was not immediately apparent. For himself, Ebert would have been content with a limited monarchy, such as his party had always stood for. He hated social revolution, as he once admitted — "I hate it like sin." But Workers' and Soldiers' Councils were starting up spontaneously throughout the country and at the front, much like the Soviets in the Russian Revolution, and it looked for a moment as if Germany might turn Communist. In the end, Philipp Scheidemann, a Majority Social Democrat, perhaps alarmed at rumors that Liebknecht was preparing a Communist coup, took it upon himself, on his own initiative and without prior consultation with his colleagues, to proclaim Germany a republic.

Ebert set about ruling the country with a provisional cabinet or council of six "commissars," three being Majority Social Democrats and three Independent Socialists, and found himself receiving general support. Even the Workers' and Soldiers' Councils at a mass meeting in Berlin voted overwhelmingly in his favor. He also secured — though this was not known at the time — the recognition of General Groener, Ludendorff's successor in the High Command and, through Groener, the "fidelity" of the army; and he pledged Groener in return that the process of "democratization" — at least in the army — would not be pressed too far. Almost his first duty in office was to agree to the Allied armistice terms and to authorize Erzberger to sign. He then proceeded to organize elections for a National Assembly which would draw up the constitution of the new German Republic.

Such were the main events of the German Revolution. Looking back upon it, from this distance, we are constantly struck by its almost anticlimactic mildness. The crowds that surged through the streets of Berlin on November 9 seemed to be entirely without organization or purpose. It would have been hard to call them a revolutionary "mob." If anything, they resembled the Armistice crowds of two days later in the Champs Elysées, or Trafalgar Square, or Fifth Avenue. Some shooting occurred. Army officers who chanced to be in the streets were sometimes assaulted and their decorations and epaulets torn off. There was some looting of government property. The Red flag was hoisted on public buildings, and hawkers appeared miraculously from nowhere selling red rosettes, red ribbons, and red tags of all descriptions. But, in general, the people had not forgotten their characteristic German discipline, and after four years of war they were in no condition for new excitements. Except for an occasional incident, the subsequent history of the German Revolution followed the orderly pattern of its first few days. One such incident was Spartacus Week.

The Spartacists had not been represented in Ebert's Council of Commissars. Liebknecht, the Spartacist leader, had declined an invitation to be one of the elect. He preferred to tour Berlin on his own account, haranguing his followers, and to keep his hands free for future revolutionary action. Liebknecht and his colleague, Rosa Luxemburg, advocated a sort of Leninist program: all power to the Workers' and Soldiers' Councils, the abolition of the bourgeois government, a Red militia in place of the army, and extensive expropriations. The Spartacists might have been more dangerous if they had been more united. But they were incurably addicted to that type of dialectical quarreling which was so often the mark of extreme Left movements in Continental Europe, and the open relations of many of them with Joffe, the "ambassador" whom Soviet Russia now sent to Berlin, a notorious distributor of "subscriptions," was repellent to any German still preserving a little probity or patriotism.

Early in 1919, Liebknecht believed his historic moment had come. The so-called People's Naval Division had been giving trouble. It was a pretty draggletailed gang of impromptu mercenaries, mainly made up of naval deserters. It had hailed from Kiel in November, it claimed to have brought the Revolution to Berlin, and it expected privileged treatment. It had occupied the Royal Palace in Berlin and demanded arrears of pay. All efforts to disband or eject it from the Palace had proved futile. Ebert at last appealed to General Groener for loyal troops to maintain order. The Independent Socialists at once denounced him as a lackey of the High Command and resigned from the Council of Commissars. Ebert appointed two Majority Social Democrats in their place, one being Gustav Noske, who had been Governor of Kiel during the November naval mutiny (see p. 106). Ebert, probably under pressure from the High Command, improved the occasion by dismissing a number of Independent Socialist sympathizers in the government offices and police. Liebknecht thereupon threw in his lot with the Independent Socialists, formed a Revolutionary Committee, called on the workers for a general strike, and proclaimed the overthrow of the government. If violent revolution was ever to succeed in Germany it must be now.

In the emergency, Ebert turned to Noske, the queller of mutinies, and Noske turned to those irregular bodies of troops, the Free Corps, the flotsam and jetsam of the demobilizing army which still retained their weapons and something of their corporate spirit. The Free Corps asked for nothing better. Most of them, in the nature of things, were reactionary and not averse to a bit of bloodshed. From January 6 to 15, 1919 — Spartacus Week as it came to be called — Noske's irregulars and the Spartacists were fighting it out in the streets of Berlin. Liebknecht and Rosa Luxemburg were captured and shot "while trying to escape." Casualties were said to have exceeded a thousand. Spartacus Week was the whiff of grapeshot which destroyed the extreme Left in Berlin.

Meanwhile, in Bavaria, a complementary series of events was in train. Bavaria, the second largest of the Federal States that composed the German Reich, had always had strong particularist traditions. On November 7, 1918, in the Bavarian capital Munich, Kurt Eisner, with the support of the local Workers', Soldiers', and Peasants' Councils, had proclaimed an independent "Bavarian Republic." Eisner was a Socialist and a Jew, perhaps the one man produced by the German Revolution who bears comparison with the great Russian revolutionaries. In January 1919, while Spartacus Week was raging in Berlin, Bavaria elected a new Diet. Eisner formed a coalition government of the Left parties and at once began to make his mark as a practical and forceful administrator. But on February 21 he was assassinated by a counterrevolutionary student.

At this moment the National Assembly, as we shall shortly relate, was meeting in Weimar and debating the new liberal constitution for all Germany. The country as a whole, after its experiment with Workers' Councils and Commissars' Councils, was feeling its way back to normal bourgeois respectability. Bavaria alone grew more and more revolutionary and more and more separatist, and characteristically resented Berlin's centralizing

tendencies. Bolshevik rule was set up in Hungary in March, and it looked as
if "permanent revolution" might soon sweep through Europe. At the end
of April, Munich was staging its own version of Spartacus Week; political
adventurers and visionaries, many of them pathological types, were pushing
themselves forward, claiming to be People's Commissars; the Munich district
was virtually an independent soviet state.

Noske in Berlin was determined that Bavaria should be saved from chaos
and secession. His force of Free Corps, assisted by Bavarian volunteers, descended upon Munich. Anything that smacked of sovietism in the city was
crushed without mercy. There were the usual cases of execution "by mistake." An unexceptionable democratic government was reinstated in Munich when the bloody work was done.

The continuation of the Allied blockade after the Armistice led to a good
deal of embittered propaganda in Germany at the time and to much mysti-
fied comment in Allied countries. The Armistice had clearly stated that
blockade conditions would remain in force, but that the Allies would consider the provisioning of Germany during the armistice period "as shall be
found necessary." It is said that Churchill, on the morrow of the Armistice,
wanted to send food ships to Germany, but was overruled by French objections. The whole question was formally raised in January 1919, at Trier,
when Allies and Germans met for the first of their periodic renewals of the
Armistice. The Allies made the very reasonable proposal that the German
Government should employ its own ships, long lying idle during the war
years, to obtain the required foodstuffs and should pay for the foodstuffs out
of the very considerable surviving German gold reserves. But this the German Government refused to do. Presumably the German High Command
regarded the nation's ships and gold as war potential, or as a bargaining
point of possible usefulness at the Peace Conference, not to be released for
a mere commercial transaction.

Meanwhile the German people suffered all the privations of the winter of
1918–19. Field Marshal Plumer, commanding the British forces in the Rhineland, warned the War Office in London that he could not prevent his men
from sharing their rations with the German children. Brockdorff-Rantzau
at Versailles berated the inhumanity of the Allies (see p. 121). In March
1919 the German Government at last acceded to the Allied proposal, and
foodstuffs, carried in German ships and paid for in German gold, began to
arrive at German ports. But, even then, the German High Command induced the German Government not to distribute the imported fats till after
June, when the Treaty of Versailles was signed and all chance of using existing war potential as a diplomatic argument had disappeared.[1]

Surface events, however, only partly describe the condition and mood of
Germany at this stage. The most important factors were not political, but
economic and moral. The war was lost; the people were bewildered and
broken-spirited. With or without the continuance of the blockade, shortage
and privation were worse in the winter of 1918–19, far worse, than at any

time during the war. And ever in the background was the gnawing apprehension of the fate the peacemakers in Paris might be devising for the hapless country.

The defeat of a proud nation is a terrible thing and produces its own peculiar pathology. Germany's casualties in the First World War had been 1,800,000 dead and 4,300,000 wounded. Shortage of labor and four years of blockade had exhausted the people and their economy. The cash costs of the conflict were put at $30,000,000,000. Wastage and wear and tear of the necessities and amenities of life were beyond calculation. Wartime "silencing" had decimated the consumer industries. Home-grown cereal crops between 1914 and 1918 were nearly halved, and the supply of meat and fats had fallen even more steeply. The population as a whole was 20 per cent underweight. The moral disintegration was complete. All the more unlovely features of the German character seemed to be on exhibition. Visitors to Berlin and other German cities at this time came back with gruesome tales of the license and perversion they saw there, the spate of pornographic literature, the vicious night life, and the gross productions on the stage. The Teutonic fury, balked of its victory, seemed to have sublimated itself into still uglier forms.

THE WEIMAR CONSTITUTION

On January 19, 1919, a few days after Spartacus Week, elections were held throughout the Reich for a National Assembly. With the exception of the Spartacists, all parties put forward candidates. The parties were the old parties of the Reichstag, now emerging from the bewilderment of the Revolution and preparing to resume their place in the political life of the nation. But some of them, to avoid the stigma of the prerevolutionary past, took different names. The Conservatives and Reich party thus appeared as the Nationalists, and the right wing of the National Liberals as the People's party. The Catholic Center appeared as the Christian People's party, but later reverted to its old name. The left-wing National Liberals and Progressives appeared as the Democrats. The Social Democrats dropped the wartime label, "Majority." The seats in the National Assembly were distributed by proportional representation. Eighty-five per cent of the electorate voted, a figure significant of the returning political vigor of the country. The results were overwhelmingly in favor of the moderate Left. Thirty-six of the elected Deputies were women.

The National Assembly was summoned to the old Thuringian city of Weimar, partly to escape the disturbances of Berlin and partly to advertise to the world the attachment of the new Republic to the memory of more peaceful heroes, Goethe and Schiller, and the Grand Duke Charles August, sponsor of one of the first liberal constitutions in Germany. The meetings were held in the Weimar National Theater. Ebert was elected "Provisional" President of the Republic.[2] Scheidemann headed the first government. Noske was Defense Minister; Bauer (Social Democrat) was Labor Minister; Erzberger (Center), Minister without portfolio; Preuss (Democrat), Minister of the Interior; Count von Brockdorff-Rantzau (no party), Foreign Minister.

The National Assembly's first business was to draw up a constitution for the German Republic. The chief author of it was Preuss, Minister of the Interior, a professor of constitutional law. The crisis over the Treaty of Versailles delayed its smooth passage, and it was not finally approved by the National Assembly till July 31, 1919.

The Weimar Constitution, though republican and democratic in its principles, made discreet allowances for the mixed composition of the National Assembly and embodied many compromises. The question of state rights in a country of federal structure was basic and had to be adjusted with the greatest delicacy and skill. Preuss himself would have liked the constitution to be an instrument for the complete unification of Germany, and his first draft went a long way to creating a "unitary" state. Whatever the result of the war and revolution might be, Germany would not be permitted to revert to her pre-Bismarckian particularism. Representatives of the Federal States, sitting in committee, however, tended to argue for a certain degree of federal decentralization. In the end, the central government in Berlin was vested with considerable powers; it had the right of veto over state legislation affecting the national interest; it could alter state frontiers and even create a new state; it had the right to levy direct taxes. But the Federal States, the *Länder,* as they were now called, were left in the enjoyment of autonomous functions not very explicitly defined.

In the words of Article 1 of the Constitution, "The German Reich is a Republic. Constitutional power proceeds from the people." Every German citizen was secured his "fundamental rights" — liberty of person, liberty of speech and of assembly, and inviolability of private property. The Reichstag was the lower chamber of the parliament, and its Deputies were to be elected for a term of four years by the universal, equal, direct, and secret suffrage of all men and women over twenty years of age, on the principle of proportional representation. The Reichsrat was a sort of upper chamber and represented the Federal States and the Prussian provinces; its delegates were to be members of the state governments, and would vote in the Reichsrat in rough proportion to the population of their states. The President of the Reich was to be elected for a term of seven years, again on the basis of universal suffrage, and must obtain a clear majority. The President appointed and dismissed the Chancellor, and the Chancellor required the confidence of the Reichstag for the exercise of his office. In certain circumstances the President could call for a national plebiscite, and in grave emergencies he could suspend the Constitution. In the words of Article 48, later to be so famous: "Should public order and safety be seriously disturbed or threatened, the President may take the necessary measures to restore public order and safety; in case of need he may use armed force, . . . and he may, for the time being, declare the fundamental rights of the citizen wholly or partly in abeyance."

In January and February 1919, shortly after the elections for the National Assembly, parallel elections were held in the Federal States, again generally resulting in victories of the Left, and each state duly drew up a democratic constitution of its own. Prussia, that onetime bastille of reaction, it is interesting to note, was governed by a Social Democrat ministry from this moment till the final collapse of the German Republic in 1933.

THE ACCEPTANCE OF VERSAILLES

Count von Brockdorff-Rantzau, the Reich Foreign Minister, headed the German delegation to Versailles, and he received the text of the treaty there on May 7, 1919 (see p. 120). The terms had been expected to be harsh, and circumstantial rumors regarding detailed decisions of the Peace Conference had begun to circulate in Germany soon after President Wilson's return to Paris in March 1919. But the reality surpassed the gloomiest expectations. The German people were sick and weary, yet they found energy in their tired spirits for something very like defiance. The National Assembly at Weimar went into continuous session; its debates were long, anxious, and bitter; the struggle for rejection or acceptance cut across all party lines. Brockdorff-Rantzau from Versailles counseled rejection. Erzberger argued acceptance, and seemed to become spokesman for all those of like mind with himself. Rejection, he contended, would only bring the Allies to Berlin to enforce the terms at the point of the bayonet and bring about the complete dissolution of Germany as a nation. Patriotism, like misery, makes strange bedfellows, and Erzberger's arguments found support in an unexpected quarter — the High Command. But Scheidemann could not stomach the treaty, and he and his government resigned. Bauer became Chancellor of a new government pledged to acceptance. Erzberger was the new Finance Minister and doubtless exerted an important influence. Hermann Müller and Johannes Bell, the Foreign and Colonial Ministers respectively, were sent to Versailles, and they signed the treaty on June 28, 1919 (see p. 121).

The execution of the terms occupied the German Government for many months to come. Members of the Allied Control Commission arrived on German soil, and went about their business as unobtrusively as they could. At Paris the Allies appointed a Conference of Ambassadors to receive the reports of the Control Commission and generally to act as executors of the treaty (see p. 122). Posen and the Polish Corridor were transferred to their new owners. The new League administrators of the Saar and of Danzig entered upon their duties. The plebiscites were duly held in Schleswig and resulted, as was expected, in the northern part of Schleswig being assigned to Denmark, and the middle and southern parts to Germany. The plebiscites were duly held in East Prussia, and both sections of the territory in question voted overwhelmingly for adhesion to Germany.

The settlement in Upper Silesia was deferred till 1921. The plebiscites, eventually held there in March of that year, showed German majorities in the north and west, Polish majorities in the south and east, and a center inextricably mixed. Both Germans and Poles, of course, contended that the Silesian coal fields made a single economic unit which it would be ruination to divide. Both carried on a furious propaganda and did not hesitate to reinforce more peaceful methods of persuasion with terrorism. The French members of the Allied Boundary Commission sent to Silesia were not the most impartial of judges and tended to give their Polish friends the benefit of the doubt in all the disputed communes. The Boundary Commission, in the end, failed to reach a decision and referred the whole case to the League of Nations. In October 1921 the League Council announced an award apportioning the area between the claimants, an award perhaps as fair and neutral as any that could have been devised in the circumstances. The Germans, who traditionally despised the Poles and regarded the League as the perpetuation of Versailles, were hardly placated, and they agreed to the award with every show of ill grace. A convention between Germany and Poland, regulating their Silesian affairs, was signed at Geneva in May 1922.

The penalty clauses of the Treaty of Versailles were the most passionately resented by the German people, and were, in fact, clauses which remained almost wholly inoperative. The former Kaiser was not brought to trial before an Allied tribunal. The Netherlands Government, which had given him sanctuary, refused to allow him to be extradited, and the Allies were probably much relieved to acquiesce in its decision. In February 1920 the French Premier, Millerand, presented the German Government with a portentous list of the other "war criminals," a list which included Hindenburg, Ludendorff, Tirpitz, Bethmann-Hollweg, several princes of the blood, and 900 officers and soldiers. The German people to a man rose against this colossal indictment; a government which attempted to arrest and hand over the nation's heroes to the judgment of its enemies would not have lasted a day; and clearly the Allies were averse to enforcing their claims if it meant a renewal of hostilities. The list was gradually cut and cut, till a mere twelve cases were left, mostly submarine officers and prison commandants. The twelve were eventually tried in May and June 1921 before the Reich Supreme Court at Leipzig and either acquitted or let off with farcically light sentences.

The execution of the military and reparations clauses of the treaty is discussed in later sections of this and the next chapters.

THE FREE CORPS

The Free Corps, which have already been mentioned, were irregular bodies of men, demobilized soldiers who had found no proper civilian employment and who were usually organized in the support of some political clique or faction. It was perhaps to be expected that they would exist and flourish at a lawless time, especially in a country long accustomed to militarism and now under sentence of disarmament. Some of them owed the government a provisional allegiance, notably the Free Corps used in more than one punitive foray by Noske. But generally the government was powerless to deal with them, and the Allied Control Commission in Germany fared no better than the government. The Reichswehr, as the German Army was now to be called, cast a somewhat indulgent eye upon them, and frankly regarded them as recruiting and training agencies, a convenient circumvention of Versailles.

Thus, in 1919 and thereafter, Germany became enmeshed in a network of illicit military and paramilitary gangs, the convenient fomenters of putsches and the rallying points of disaffected conservative or monarchist elements and of young hotheads denied a legitimate military career. The raising of Free Corps became the regular pastime of far too many of the older ranking officers of counterrevolutionary ambitions, and was financed by sympathetic industrialists. Hitler's National Socialists in Munich were at first just such an organization.

The Free Corps were ruinous to the spirit of the Weimar Republic. The courts of justice quite openly and shamelessly protected the Free Corps in all such cases as came to their notice. The judge was a rare man who preferred the evidence of a mere Socialist or civilian before an expert witness from the Reichswehr Ministry, and any action which questioned the legality of the Free Corps could always be quashed. The attendant secrecy, spying, graft, terrorism, and universal suspicion made the culture out of which such ills as Nazism were eventually bred.

THE KAPP PUTSCH

The Kapp Putsch was the Conservative counterpart of Spartacus Week and was the most considerable upheaval of the Right during the early years of the Weimar Republic. It was also a fair demonstration of Free Corps tactics. Dr. Wolfgang Kapp, an agricultural finance official from East Prussia, had been the cofounder of the propagandist Fatherland party, originally formed in 1917 to combat the subversive effects of the July Crisis of that year (see p. 82). General von Lüttwitz, Commander in Chief of the Berlin district, was the military organizer of the putsch, and Ludendorff may also have been more or less directly implicated. The main force employed was Ehrhardt's Free Corps, remnants of the German occupying forces in the Baltic which had refused to disband and still retained their identity.

Kapp and his fellow conspirators evidently hoped to exploit the unpopularity of the Bauer government and of its most influential minister, Erzberger, an unpopularity which had been growing steadily ever since the Treaty of Versailles had been signed. Their aims included the repudiation of Versailles, the end of disarmament, and the establishment of an authoritarian state. They meditated putting the Crown Prince into the presidency. On March 10, 1920, Lüttwitz called on Ebert and delivered him a virtual ultimatum demanding a new Reichstag election, a new presidential election, the formation of a government of "experts," and a halt in the demobilization of the old army. The Russo-Polish War had just broken out and was causing some apprehension in East Prussia, the home of reaction, the home of Kapp, and the home of Ehrhardt's Free Corps. Ebert, an old hand at negotiation, put Lüttwitz off without a direct answer, but he was determined to fight for his government if need be. He relied heavily on

Noske, already a veteran of many Free Corps imbroglios and, on Noske's advice, he peremptorily ordered the dismissal of Lüttwitz from his command. This precipitated the crisis. On March 13, 1920, Ehrhardt's Free Corps marched into Berlin and seized key positions in the city, everywhere flaunting its badge, the swastika — the first apparition of that strange device. Ebert, Bauer, Noske, and the government fled to Stuttgart. Erzberger resigned. Kapp formed a "government" of his own in Berlin. But, within a couple of days, it was clear that he had none of the essentials of power. He might be a competent putschist, but he was no revolutionary. He had little popular support. The ordinary people of Berlin, so far as could be observed, were either frightened or frankly bored; the workers everywhere were hostile. The central bureaucracy refused to obey Kapp's orders; the Reichsbank officials would not honor his drafts. Far more serious than this, Kapp failed to enlist the support of the Reichswehr. Many Reichswehr officers were of the same mind as himself but considered his action hotheaded and untimely, and could do little but wait and see how the putsch fared before they committed themselves. General von Seeckt, the Reichswehr commander, had no wish to get his forces mixed up in an affair which was almost sure to provoke Allied intervention. However, the Reichswehr at least did not oppose the putsch. It was not to be expected that soldiers of the Reichswehr would ever be called on to "suppress" their comrades of the Free Corps.

From Stuttgart the government proclaimed a general strike. The workers responded with something like 100 per cent unanimity and gave the world a classic illustration of "direct action," that dream of Socialists, perhaps only this once ever carried to complete effect.[3] For Kapp it was the last straw. His "government" was paralyzed. Berlin was without public services; water, electricity, streetcars, newspapers, even the transport of foodstuffs stopped dead. The Free Corps took its revenge in desultory shooting. On March 17, Kapp and Lüttwitz were in flight, and the Free Corps evacuated the city. A detachment of the Free Corps, retiring by way of the Brandenburger Tor, fired point-blank into the jeering crowds which had collected there to speed its departure. It was significant of the state of Germany that Ehrhardt's Free Corps was not disbanded, and none of the participants in the putsch was ever punished.

THE REICHSWEHR

Under the military clauses of the Treaty of Versailles, the German Army was to be reduced to 100,000 long-term volunteers, without tanks, planes, or heavy artillery. Conscription was abolished, and the General Staff was dissolved. A single National Defense Force, or Reichswehr, took the place of the Prussian, Bavarian, Saxon, and Württemberger contingents of the old army. But it was impossible for the Allied Control Commission to verify the actual numbers of men under arms in Germany and, despite all German asseverations to the contrary, the limit of 100,000 must have been considerably exceeded. The Free Corps were beyond supervision and gloried in all the tricks of cunning and concealment at which they had now become so adept. The destruction of fortifications and of heavy arms and the inspection of armament works were easier matters, and the members of the Allied Control Commission soon learned the technique of surprise visits. But there must have been hundreds of secret hoards, especially of rifles and machine guns, which no skillful probing and no surprise visits could ever have unearthed. After 1925 a "Black Reichswehr" for short-service military training was secretly maintained by the Reichswehr Ministry as an adjunct of the regular Reichswehr. General Hans von Seeckt, Commander in Chief of the Reichswehr, carried on a long and weary battle of wits with the Allied Control Commission, but the atmosphere of subterfuge was ruinous to dignity and to decent relations.

The conception of an "army" as a political force in a nation's affairs is foreign to the Anglo-Saxon mind. The Praetorian Guard of the Roman Caesars is the classic example, and once only, in the time of Cromwell, has the phenomenon appeared in an English-speaking country. But the army as such was common enough in modern times in countries of standing conscript armies, even if it was sometimes difficult to define or identify its controlling personalities. Thus the army won itself an unpleasant notoriety in France during the Dreyfus scandal; it was all important in Prussian Germany; it wielded considerable, if obscure, power in interwar Turkey, Poland, Italy, Spain, Japan, Latin America — and republican Germany. The army occupied a unique position in Germany from the very moment of the Revolution. Far from being destroyed by the Revolution, it was the only military defense the Revolution ever had. President Ebert, as we have seen, had entered into a bargain with General Groener in November 1918 to secure its loyalty, a bargain which, from that moment, made it the spoiled child of the Republic. Thus the army gave rather more than its moral support toward the suppression of the Spartacists in Berlin and Munich. Its benevolent inactivity sealed the fate of the Kapp Putsch.

The real creator of the Reichswehr was General von Seeckt, "the sphinx with the monocle," one of the ablest technicians and organizers in the General Staff. He was assisted by the compliant Gessler, who became Reichswehr Minister in 1920 and held that office till 1928 through six changes of government. In the teeth of the prevailing confusion and the crippling restrictions of Versailles, Seeckt wrought his *Führerheer*, his "army of leaders," specially trained in the arts of mechanization, in which he already foresaw the pattern of future warfare. He imbued it with the spirit of the old army, he geared it for future expansion, and he won for it the respect of his own and other countries. Qualitatively, it was the finest army in the world, "a real jewel" as a perspicacious Frenchman once described it. But Seeckt recruited it almost entirely from reactionary, and even monarchical, elements. Social Democracy, traditionally antimilitarist, would have nothing to do with it, and the Weimar Republic, to its eternal loss, never produced a workers' army. The Reichswehr became the asylum of demobilized "front fighters," while many of its younger officers were drawn from those Junker families who still regarded military service as the one and only profession for a man. It cultivated all the exclusive Prussian traditions. In its midst were the Roehms and the Schleichers, reactionaries every one of them, political soldiers of a type unknown to the German Army of an earlier and better day, men for whom there was no dividing line between military service and political conspiracy. The General Staff, far from being dissolved, surreptitiously kept itself alive, first as a rather obscure department of the Reichswehr Ministry, and later as a "Military Science Co." As Gessler once remarked, "There is no clause in the treaty which stops us from reconstituting the General Staff as a limited liability company." Meanwhile the government was not ungenerous in its military appropriations, appropriations which continued to rise steadily throughout the Weimar period.

The Social Democrats acquiesced in the political character of the new army. Yet when, in 1926, Seeckt allowed a son of the former Crown Prince to take part in summer maneuvers, he was dismissed. In 1928 Gessler was replaced by Groener. But, by then, the Reichswehr had achieved a form which only foreign war or civil war would ever again have altered. For better or for worse, it had become a "state within the state," a stronghold of all that was least republican in the Republic.

Nor was this all. The restrictions of Versailles indirectly projected the Reichswehr into foreign politics. The young German officer had to go abroad for his education in the weapons which he was not allowed to handle at home, and the only countries open to him were the potential enemies of the Versailles Powers. "Attachés" therefore went to Russia to study military aviation and to see tanks and heavy guns in action. Armament plants were secretly reserved in Russia, and to some extent in Sweden and Spain, for the manufacture of those weapons against the day when Versailles might be relaxed. The Treaty of Rapallo in 1922, between Germany and Russia, and to a less extent, the Treaty of Berlin in 1926, it is often believed, represented in part the collusion between Seeckt and the Red Army generals (see pp. 162 and 541). Russia politically may have been anathema to German governments of every age, but in the interwar years Russia militarily was the only important friend that Germany had, and the diplomatic flirting of Berlin and Moscow in those years was probably inspired far more by the Reichswehr than by the Reich Foreign Ministry.

PROGRESS TOWARD REACTION

The Kapp Putsch in 1920 had left a wake of disturbances behind it. In Bavaria a group of army officers forced the local government to resign — the government, namely, which had succeeded the soviet experiment there — and installed as commissioner a certain Gustav von Kahr, a civil servant and an extreme conservative. There was a "Red" scare in the Ruhr, much exaggerated by the German press. Units of the Reichswehr marched into the Ruhr, in violation of Versailles, ostensibly to restore order. The French replied by temporarily occupying Frankfurt.

These events unsettled the central government. Bauer resigned the chan-

STRENGTHS OF THE PARTIES IN THE REICHSTAG — 1919–1939 [4]

Elections	Jan. 1919	June 1920	May 1924	Dec. 1924	May 1928	Sept. 1930	July 1932	Nov. 1932	Mar. 1933
Total Members	422	466	472	493	490	577	608	584	566
Nationalists (Deutsche-Nationale Partei)	42	66	106	111	78	41	40	54	53
People's party (Deutsche Volkspartei)	22	62	44	51	45	30	7	16	2
Center (Zentrum)	} 90 {	69	65	69	61	68	75	70	73
Bavarian People's party (Bayerische Volkspartei)		20	16	19	17	19	22	20	19
Democrats (Deutsche Demokratische Partei)	75	45	28	32	25	14*	4*	2*	5*
Social Democrats (Sozial-Demokratische Partei)	164	113	100	131	152	143	133	121	120
Independent Social Democrats (Unabhängige Sozial-Demokratische Partei)	22	81	—	—	—	—	—	—	—
Communists (Kommunistische Partei Deutschlands)	—	2	62	45	54	77	89	100	81†
National Socialists (National-Sozialistische Deutsche Arbeiterpartei)	—	—	32	14	12	107	230	196	288
Minor parties	7	8	19	21	46	78	8	5	6

* Renamed Deutsche Staatspartei   † Did not sit

cellorship and was followed by Hermann Müller as the head of an interim government with Dr. Wirth of the Center as Finance Minister. Müller acknowledged the justice of at least one of the demands that Lüttwitz had made, and called for Reichstag elections. The National Assembly had completed the Constitution, its work was done, and the new Reichstag was due to be brought formally into existence. The elections were held during June 1920, and they were disastrous to the "Weimar parties." Ebert's handling of the Kapp crisis and the apparent success of the workers' general strike availed nothing. Fehrenbach of the Center party became Chancellor, with Wirth again as Finance Minister and Simons as Foreign Minister.

Fehrenbach's chancellorship was the beginning of that somewhat amorphous period in German interwar politics which was marked by a succession of middle-class governments and was consumed, almost to the exclusion of everything else, with the problem of reparations. It was also the beginning of the end of Weimar and of all that Weimar represented. The moderate Left, in particular the Social Democrats, who had largely inspired the National Assembly of 1919, were never again to recover their strength. The fault may not have been entirely theirs, and it will always remain one of the burning questions of history whether a different treaty of peace or greater support and sympathy from the democratic powers abroad could not have made the Weimar Republic a more convincing and lasting experiment. But Versailles, the cessions of territory, the trial of the war criminals — and subsequently the Ruhr crisis, the inflation, the interminable diplomatic persecution by France, which we have still to describe — all mounted up into a sad complex of humiliation and blighted hope, and the moderate Left had no answer to it. Democracy, the League of Nations, the peaceful concert of the world, which, for the Allies, were honorable ideals, came to be associated in the consciousness of the German people with their national degradation. It is important to remember that the elections to the original National Assembly and the shaping of the Constitution were accomplished in the first flush of the Revolution, before the Treaty of Versailles was signed. Reactionary propaganda in Germany afterward never found much difficulty in attributing the peace to the "November criminals," who had treacherously stabbed a loyal nation in the back. The German people, who in their moment of penitence many thought had made a safe conversion to democracy, from this time onward took the road that eventually led them to the counterrevolution of 1933.

Yet, as has been so often pointed out, Weimar had really changed very little. The old ornaments had been removed. The Kaiser and the German princelings had gone into exile. But there had been no dispossession of the former castes and classes. The great land estates were not parceled out; the Kaiser's own properties were not expropriated; the industrial cartels and monopolies were not broken up. Little new legislation was introduced, except in the field of labor relations and welfare. The bureaucracy, the judiciary, and the police remained intact. German officialdom, the pride of Bismarck's Reich, emerged afresh, rather strengthened by its feeling of indispensability to the new order than discredited by its connection with the old. The golden opportunity for effecting long-needed reforms in the universities was lost; the principle of academic freedom required that even the most antidemocratic and anti-Semitic faculties and fraternities should not be touched. Finally the Officers Corps continued to exist and to cultivate its inherited traditions; the new Reichswehr was the old army in miniature. In her own way, like so many other countries of the interwar era, Germany tried to return to the "normalcy" of 1914 and mentally to dismiss the war as an unfortunate but temporary breach in the accustomed order of things.

We are left with two views of Weimar. It was a promising project which failed for want of encouragement; or it was just a façade — and a fraudulent one at that — raised up by a defeated people at the dictation of their victors and in violation of their true national sentiments, a device which changed little, inspired no confidence, and only temporarily overlaid the deeper tensions of German political life. The truth perhaps lies somewhere in between. In either view, the story is not an encouraging one.

11 GERMANY: REPARATIONS AND RECOVERY

REPARATIONS

Prior to the Armistice, Allied policy in regard to German reparations had been vague in the extreme. It was assumed that Germany would be forced to pay for what she had destroyed, but the type and amount of compensation were not discussed in advance. The Allies had had no desire to introduce into their councils a problem which not only promised to be difficult in itself but which would have complicated their propaganda campaign against the enemy. President Wilson in his Fourteen Points had called for Belgium, northern France, Rumania, Serbia, and Montenegro to be "restored." The Allied Memorandum which had accompanied the American note to Germany on November 5, 1918 had stipulated that "compensation will be made by Germany for all damage done to the civilian population of the Allies and their property by the aggression of Germany by land, by sea, and from the air." (See p. 107.) Finally inserted in the armistice text was a somewhat obscure clause in regard to "reparation for damage done" and in regard to the restitution of all gold reserves and all documents taken in the invaded countries — "with the reservation that any subsequent concessions and claims by the Allies and the United States remain unaffected." These few utterances made up the total "legal" basis of the reparations clauses in the Treaty of Versailles, and the total anticipation and warning in regard to her obligations which, at the date of the Armistice, the Allies had vouchsafed to their defeated enemy.

Technically, the problem of reparations was of an unexpected novelty. The Allies always had before them the precedent of the French indemnity of 1871, and did not doubt that the German indemnity of 1919 would be as simple to impose and collect. They did not foresee the close relation of reparations with inter-Allied debts and with the general recovery of their own prosperous estate. Nor were they united in their essential objects. France regarded the entire Treaty of Versailles as an instrument for the permanent enfeeblement of her hereditary foe; Britain regarded it as a judgment and a penalty to be alleviated in proportion as the culprit gave evidence of self-improvement. France would have treated Germany as a bankrupt whose assets must henceforth be administered by and for her creditors; Britain, though glad enough to transfer to Germany as large a portion as possible of her own wartime indebtedness, was far more anxious to restore Germany to her prewar position of a good customer. The United States, meanwhile, more interested in Allied debts, considered reparations as a purely European problem.

The clauses in the treaty affirming Germany's responsibility and specifying the various categories of damage which she was to make good, including the much-controverted claim for military pensions, were described in Chapter 8 (see p. 123). It is only necessary to recall that, except for the deliveries in kind and the initial 20,000,000,000 gold marks ($4,750,000,000) payable by May 1, 1921, the treaty had mentioned no definite sums. Estimates bandied about in Paris in 1919 started as low as Keynes's "safe" $10,000,-000,000[1] and went up to more than ten times that figure. Between Germany's capacity to pay and the astronomic expectations of public opinion in Allied countries no discoverable mean seemed to exist. Clearly a proper and reliable assessment would have meant sending committees of investigation into the devastated areas and giving hearings to the thousands of claimants for damages, and the Peace Conference did not have the time for so protracted a proceeding.

In the end, the Peace Conference had taken refuge in a Reparation Commission, to be composed of Allied delegates, which would determine the exact amounts and methods of payment, report "voluntary defaults," and in general secure the discharge of "the entire obligation within a period of thirty years." But the Reparation Commission, from its first sessions, was in difficulties. It was no easy matter to equate British notions of "fairness," French implacability, and German aggrievement. Then, as the result of the nonratification of the Treaty of Versailles by the United States, the Commission met without the detached influence of its intended American chairman. The rights and wrongs and the pros and cons of reparations were soon being lost sight of in the ways and means thereof. The Germans never tired of raising their voices against the *"Diktat"* of Versailles, they always complained that they appeared before the Reparation Commission as before a court-martial, but they appealed more circumstantially to their favorite argument that the payment of reparations was impracticable.

Apparently the Germans made a good case. In the early interwar years, there was hardly an Allied conference at which the subject of reparations was not mentioned and at which the reparations figure was not scaled downward. Thus in July 1920, when Allies and Germans met in conference at Spa, the figure mentioned was 269,000,000,000 gold marks ($64,000,000,000) spread over forty-two years. This was the first time that Allies and Germans had sat at the same table, but it could not be described as a happy reunion. Hugo Stinnes, who accompanied the German delegation as the representative of the German coal owners, made a belligerent speech which began with the words "I rise to look my enemies in the eye . . ." Fehrenbach, the German Chancellor, was afterward at pains to explain that Stinnes did not express the views of his government. In January 1921 the Allies presented Germany with the so-called Paris Resolutions, which then fixed the reparations figure at 226,000,000,000 gold marks ($54,000,000,000). The German press raved and railed. In a speech Simons, the German Foreign Minister, was so impolitic as to repudiate Germany's war guilt. Later, in London, Simons was to make proposals which, in effect, would have reduced the reparations figure to 30,000,000,000 gold marks and which Lloyd George curtly characterized as "an offense and an exasperation." Meanwhile the Allies at their conference at Spa had reached an agreement among themselves for the division of reparations receipts, France being allotted 52 per cent, the British Empire 22, Italy 10, Belgium 8, and the other Allies lesser shares.

The crucial May 1, 1921 was now approaching when under the terms of the treaty the initial German payment of 20,000,000,000 gold marks was to be made. But the Reparation Commission, totting up the account, calculated that the receipts from Germany by that date had fallen short of the stipulated sum by more than half. The Commission then assessed the total reparations figure at 132,000,000,000 gold marks ($32,000,000,000), and this assessment was duly forwarded to Berlin. The Allied Supreme Council also improved the occasion by recapitulating various defalcations committed by Germany in respect of disarmament and the trial of the war criminals.

Fehrenbach thereupon resigned, and his successor, Dr. Wirth, formed a government. Wirth declared frankly that he advocated a policy of "fulfillment" in order to show that fulfillment was impossible. Germany at the time was fiercely agitated over the plebiscite in Upper Silesia and the trial of the war criminals at Leipzig. An outbreak of strikes was unpleasantly reminiscent of Spartacus Week. As a certain index of the parlous situation into which the country seemed to be drifting, the mark dropped to 100 to the American dollar. The first phase of the inflation had begun. On August 25, 1921 came one encouraging item of news — the formal conclusion of peace between Germany and the United States (see p. 363) — but the date was marred by the assassination of Erzberger, signatory of the Armistice and advocate for Versailles, at the hands of two Free Corps troopers.

GENOA AND RAPALLO

Lloyd George, the British Prime Minister, was then working on a scheme to be the cure of Germany's and Europe's contemporary ills. He envisaged a "European Consortium," a sort of economic League of Nations, which would undertake the reconstruction of Europe with the collaboration of Russia. It would be the crowning glory of his career. To this end he organized a monster international conference, only second in impressiveness to the Peace Conference of Paris itself, and it eventually assembled at Genoa in April 1922. Poincaré, the archfoeman of Germany, had just become Premier of France, and he sent Barthou to represent him; Russia sent Chicherin; Germany sent her Chancellor, Wirth, and her Foreign Minister, Rathenau.

But Genoa met in an atmosphere of unreality; it was one of the few conferences of these years at which reparations, for reasons of diplomacy, were debarred from the agenda. The delegates consumed their time discussing Russian debts and British oil concessions. Chicherin, far from showing gratitude for Soviet Russia's first postwar readmission to Europe's common councils, presented the Allies with a bill for 50,000,000,000 francs on account of damage done by the Allied intervention in the Russian Civil War. To cap the tragicomedy, Chicherin and Rathenau motored out to Rapallo on Easter Sunday, April 16, 1922 and there, over a quiet luncheon in that delectable Mediterranean spot, signed a consortium of their own.

On the surface the Treaty of Rapallo between Soviet Russia and Germany was innocent enough. It provided for the mutual resumption of diplomatic relations, the mutual renunciation of reparations, and the mutual facilitation of trade. But it was a sinister hark back to Bismarck, and it was undoubtedly a coup, not unlike other coups with which Russians and Germans would again startle the world. The two pariahs of Europe had come together. The bogy which France had always feared — a Russo-German *rapprochement* — this horrid, spectral shape had been conjured up under the very noses of the Genoa delegates. The Allies addressed some acrimonious notes to Germany, upbraiding her for her underhand behavior, and the German delegates thereupon withdrew from the conference. Lloyd George's great scheme for the recovery of Europe was dead.

Rathenau himself did not long survive his triumph. On June 24, 1922 he was shot dead as he was being driven in his car in Berlin. He had been a national figure in finance and industry, a man of many gifts and interests, a philosopher and connoisseur, and a liberal in politics. During the First World War he had directed Germany's War Raw Materials Department, which had made so great a contribution to her long resistance (see p. 49). Latterly he had been a consistent and respected advocate of a "reasonable" reparations settlement. His murder was in line with other recent political crimes, and it was almost beginning to look as if achievement in public life in republican Germany was tantamount to inviting murderous attentions on the part of some crazy young Free Corps trooper.[2]

For Poincaré and Barthou the Rapallo incident was proof positive, if proof they wanted, that France would get no satisfaction from Germany in the matter of reparations without recourse to force. Germany was incorrigible and showed no conviction of defeat. Barthou was now the French delegate on the Reparation Commission. In July 1922 the German Government requested the Reparation Commission for a moratorium on the next two years' reparations payments. The mark already stood at 500 to the dollar and was declining fast. Poincaré countered with talk of "productive pledges." If Germany could not pay in currency, she could pay in mines, forests, and chemicals; she could buy her moratorium with securities. In November 1922 the Wirth government resigned and was replaced by the so-called "business government" of Dr. Cuno, manager of the Hamburg-American Line. In December the Reparation Commission unanimously reported that Germany had defaulted in deliveries of timber to France. The British delegate on the Commission characterized the default as "almost microscopic," but it was enough for Poincaré and Barthou. Early in January 1923 came further reports of a default in deliveries of coal.

On January 10, 1923 the American Army of Occupation began its withdrawal from the Rhine. The next day French and Belgian troops, with a "token" contingent of Italians, marched into the Ruhr. The British took no part in the invasion.

THE OCCUPATION OF THE RUHR

The Ruhr district, which Poincaré had now seized in reprisal for Germany's reparations defaults, contained 10 per cent of Germany's population, 80 per cent of her coal, 80 per cent of her iron and steel industries, and the most intricate railroad system in the world. It was therefore a "productive pledge" of considerable value, and its occupation must soon have disabled the entire economy of the Reich. The legalities of Poincaré's action were never very clear; nor were his real and ultimate aims. He may have wanted to break the resistance of the big iron and steel magnates of the Ruhr, whom he believed to have been mainly responsible for obstructing the reparations settlement, and of whose interests and attitude Cuno, the new German Chancellor, was himself a representative. He may have wanted, as he said, to create such a state of suffering in Germany "that she will prefer the execution of the Treaty of Versailles to the conditions produced by the occupation." He may have wanted to set up an independent Rhenish state and so achieve the ambition which Clemenceau had been forced to relinquish at the Peace Conference (see p. 118). He may have wanted to build up a huge combine, consisting of Lorraine, the Saar, and the Ruhr, for the benefit of his industrialist supporters of the National Bloc in France (see p. 317). At all events he believed that compulsion was the only language which Germany understood, and he believed that he had adequate reasons for now resorting to it.

The German Government met the Franco-Belgian invasion with a policy of passive resistance. The German ambassador in Paris and the German minister in Brussels were recalled. All reparations payments and all deliveries in kind to France and Belgium were stopped. Railroad employees in the Ruhr refused to take orders from the French authorities. Postal and telegraph employees refused to transmit French and Belgian letters and telegrams. Local newspapers refused to publish French notices and ordinances. Officials of all ranks "affected to be unaware of the presence of the invaders."

Meanwhile the French and Belgian forces were soon in possession of the industrial and public services of the Ruhr. They established as their central agency in the district a *Mission Interallié de Contrôle des Usines et des Mines,* familiarly known as the MICUM. They retaliated against the passive resistance campaign. They seized the local customs. They confiscated anything from foodstuffs to cash deposits. They deported recalcitrant workers. They arrested leading industrialists and tried them before military courts. By the end of February, the directors of the Krupp works and the mayors of almost every town and city in the district had been imprisoned. Riots and shootings were of daily occurrence. French colonial Negro troops were said to have been the cause of troublemaking, though in the blare of propaganda it is difficult to discover the real facts regarding their alleged indiscipline.

The mark collapsed altogether. In January 1923 it had dropped to 20,000 to the dollar, in April to 100,000, in August to 5,000,000. The situation was fantastic. Wages and salaries had to be revised monthly, then weekly, and daily, and even then could not keep pace with rising prices. The German employee never knew how much his pay would buy. His wife went out to make her household purchases with a whole basketful of notes which might well fall further in value as she stood waiting in the shopping line. A tourist with a few francs or dollars lived like a prince. A postage stamp or glass of beer cost millions. Paper investments, bank balances, savings, mortgages, annuities vanished. Those classes of the German population suffered most whose stabilizing influence the country so desperately needed. The *rentier* and the pensioner were pauperized. In after years Germans used to speak of the inflation of 1923 as a more terrible experience than the war and the Revolution.

As in the case of other financial crises, no one at the moment seemed to know exactly what had gone wrong. Certainly the German Government had never shown the least "willingness" to fulfill the reparations clauses. The Treaty of Versailles had been an imposition which every good German believed himself morally entitled to sabotage. On this showing, the inflation might well be interpreted as a gigantic conspiracy of evasion. The more chaotic Germany's finances became, the better case for the nonpayment of reparations she could put forward. Thus the budget need not be balanced, public expenditures need not be cut, and deficits of revenue could be made up by working the printing presses overtime. Meanwhile the big magnates, the controllers of financial policy — like the fabulous Hugo Stinnes — indeed any possessors of goods or real property, could make fortunes. But the magnates did not count the costs of their operations to their less fortunate countrymen. A full, impartial account of this whole episode in Germany has still to be written.

The Cuno government resigned in August 1923. Gustav Stresemann, leader of the People's party, succeeded as Chancellor and Foreign Minister and resolved to give up the contest in the Ruhr as lost. On September 27, 1923, President Ebert signed a decree rescinding all ordinances passed in support of passive resistance. Poincaré had seemingly won all along the line.

The surrender in the Ruhr, however, was the signal for the outbreak of new disturbances elsewhere. Political crisis in Germany always gave opportunities to champions of centrifugalism. Groups of separatists in Düsseldorf and Aachen, with covert French support, tried to set up an independent "Rhineland Republic." The Palatinate was declared to be "autonomous." The legitimate burgomasters were forced to declare their allegiance to the new regimes. A Communist "government" with secessionist aims enjoyed a short life in Saxony and Thuringia.

The most spectacular of these disturbances occurred in the old storm center of Munich. For some time Gustav von Kahr, the reactionary Commissioner of Bavaria, had been making himself the focus of a complicated and ramifying movement whose object was said to be the restoration of the former Bavarian royal family. Kahr had for his chief aides General von Lossow, commander of the Reichswehr in Bavaria, and Colonel von Seisser, the Munich Chief of Police. He had secured the participation of Ludendorff, and he had arranged for a certain Adolf Hitler, a fanatic and leader of a new National Socialist Workers' party, to contribute a force of irregular troopers.

Kahr built up a formidable organization, and he was strong enough to go about his business without concealment and in defiance of all the threats that President Ebert and General von Seeckt hurled at him from Berlin. Kahr evidently had some putsch in preparation for early November 1923. But his plans were precipitated a couple of days too soon by this same Adolf Hitler.

On the evening of November 8, 1923, Kahr, Lossow, and Seisser were holding a mass meeting of their supporters at the Bürgerbräukeller, a beerhouse in East Munich, when Hitler's troopers began to invest the building. Hitler himself forced his way into the middle of the hall, fired his revolver dramatically at the ceiling, mounted the platform, quelled the meeting with the words, "The National Revolution has begun. . . . The Bavarian Government is deposed. . . . The Reich Government is deposed," and then summoned the astonished Kahr, Lossow, and Seisser to a rear room where, at the point of his revolver, he proceeded to appoint them to posts in his "government."

Seeckt in Berlin was holding detachments of the Reichswehr in readiness for emergencies. But the putsch in Munich collapsed the next day without his intervention. Kahr, Lossow, and Seisser, as soon as they were out of Hitler's reach, recovered their senses and announced in a public proclamation that "declarations extorted from them by force were null and void" and that they would now support constitutional law and order against the "deception and perfidy of ambitious comrades."

Hitler and his associates — among them Ludendorff — were thus left in the lurch. The next morning, November 9, they collected their troopers and began their march from the Bürgerbräukeller, across the river, and into the heart of Munich. They overcame some police cordons without bloodshed, but the inevitable shooting began when they reached the Feldherrnhalle, the Hall of the Generals, near the Royal Palace. In confused fighting, Ludendorff was taken prisoner unhurt; Hitler fled with a dislocated arm; fourteen of his troopers were killed. The putsch was over. Arrests, trials, and mild sentences of confinement followed, and it was some time before the world was again to hear of Adolf Hitler.

THE DAWES PLAN

In October 1923 the mark stood at 25,000,000,000 to the dollar.[3] All the German Government's efforts to open negotiations with France were unsuccessful. Poincaré rejected its most contrite overtures so long as the stoppage in reparations payments continued. The unhappy German people, it would seem, could look forward only to a future of perpetual and ravaging conflict with their Gallic taskmasters. Yet, when hope was darkest, there came the first glimmerings of a solution. The British Government had constantly exerted itself to bring the estranged parties in the Ruhr together and was able at last to persuade the United States to forsake its official aloofness to the extent of participating in a conference of "impartial" experts to investigate Germany's finances. For Poincaré the prospect of joint Anglo-American intervention was decisive. He could not afford diplomatic isolation, especially as returns were beginning to show that the entire Ruhr adventure was far less productive than he had promised, and his popularity in France was definitely on the wane. In November 1923 a new government was formed in Germany under Wilhelm Marx of the Center party, with Stresemann as Foreign Minister. It issued a Rentenmark as an emergency currency — one Rentenmark being equal to a trillion marks — guaranteed by a general mortgage on the country's real estate; it balanced the Reich budget by the imposition of new taxes and a drastic cutting of expenditures; apparently it succeeded in doing everything that had previously been declared to be impossible. At least Germany seemed now to want to show that she herself was leaving nothing undone to retrieve her financial stability and to deserve the "just" consideration of the impending "experts'" conference.

In December 1923 the Reparation Commission appointed two committees of investigation to meet in Paris, the first of which eventually drew up the Dawes Plan, so called after the committee's American chairman, General Charles G. Dawes.[4] Dr. Hjalmar Schacht, the new president of the Reichsbank and the future "wizard of German finance," made his first international appearance and acted throughout the discussions as the principal German representative. In May 1924, Poincaré and his government in France fell, and a more liberal French premier, Herriot, bent on conciliation, accepted the Dawes Plan in its entirety.

The Dawes Plan still left undetermined Germany's total reparations liability, but it fixed the annual payment at 1,000,000,000 gold marks ($238,-000,000) for the first year, rising to a "standard annuity" of 2,500,000,000 gold marks ($595,000,000) in the fifth year. The "standard annuity" could be reduced or increased in accordance with an "index of prosperity." Securities for these sums would be met in part in the first year by an international loan of 800,000,000 gold marks ($190,000,000), and subsequently by taxes and a mortgage on the German railroads. A Transfer Committee would be set up to supervise the conversion of the sums into foreign currencies. Finally, the Reichsbank would be reorganized as a central bank and empowered to issue an entirely new monetary unit, the Reichsmark, equivalent to 23.8 United States cents and bearing a stable relation to gold.

The Dawes Plan became effective on September 1, 1924, and the evacuation of the Ruhr began at once. The international loan of 800,000,000 gold marks was successfully subscribed, 55 per cent being raised in the United States.

THE STRESEMANN ERA

The Dawes settlement in May 1924 coincided with Reichstag elections in Germany which then happened to be taking place. It was hardly a time for cool decisions, and the elections were rowdy enough. The Social Democrats lost heavily; the reactionary parties gained; Hitler's National Socialists scored their first electoral success with thirty-two seats. The new Reichstag ultimately ratified the Dawes Plan by a margin of three votes. Fresh elections

in December 1924 rectified the extremism of the earlier election and succeeded in returning a Reichstag of more moderate, but still reactionary,
composition.

The general trend of public feeling in Germany soon had another opportunity to declare itself. On February 28, 1925 occurred the death of
Friedrich Ebert, President of the Reich.[5] There was at first no obvious successor. The first ballot of the new presidential elections was cast in March
1925 but failed to secure for any one of the seven candidates the clear majority which the constitution required. The second ballot might have been
as indecisive an affair as the first, had not the Nationalists sent a deputation
to Field Marshal von Hindenburg — the initiative was said to have come
from Admiral von Tirpitz — and persuaded him that it was his duty to step
into the breach. Hindenburg was now seventy-seven and since the war had
been living in retirement. He acceded to the new summons with genuine
reluctance. On April 25, 1925, he was elected President by a fair majority
over Marx, the former Chancellor. There is no reason for believing that he
entered upon his office with any other resolve than to serve his country and
obey its constitution as best he might. But he was a Prussian born and bred
and as good a representative of the old monarchy and the old military spirit
as could have been found, and his election was unmistakable evidence of
the growing conservative and nationalist humor in Germany.

It is not necessary to take the reader through the history of the subsequent
German chancellorships of the twenties. Luther, Marx, and Hermann Müller successively held office till March 1930. The real force in German politics
throughout these years was Gustav Stresemann. He had become Chancellor
and Foreign Minister in August 1923, and Foreign Minister he remained
until his death on October 3, 1929. For six years he was the protagonist of
every event and transaction of importance in his country. It was he more
than any other man who called off the campaign of passive resistance in the
Ruhr, advised the strongest measures against Hitler in Munich and against
the Communists in Saxony and Thuringia, introduced the Rentenmark, and
obtained the ratification of the Dawes Plan in the Reichstag. In 1925 he
went to Locarno to negotiate the series of treaties described in Chapter 9,
the so-called Locarno Pact, which was intended to be the definite settlement
and pacification of Europe (see p. 139). In 1926 he went to Geneva to assist
at Germany's admission to the League of Nations (see p. 140). In 1927 he
was awarded the Nobel Peace Prize. Surely his record was no mean one. He
found Germany in 1923 a pariah among nations; he left her in 1929 once
more a Power.

Yet never did Stresemann win unqualified gratitude and popularity at
home. The Left considered him reactionary; the Right mistrusted him for
his faithfulness to the Weimar Constitution; patriots of all classes chafed
at his policy of seeking the restoration of Germany by truckling to her enemies. He failed in his one major domestic design. He tried to create a permanent "grand coalition" of the middle group and Social Democrats and thus
to eliminate the endless shufflings and maneuverings of the German multi-
party system. But he was forced, as every German statesman before Hitler

was forced, to maintain himself by means of party blocs. Only in after years has it been possible to appraise the extraordinary singleness and pertinacity of his policy of "liberation."

The Stresemann era, as we might call it, gave Germany her one interval of stability during the interwar years. By 1926 most of Stresemann's work in the international field was completed and, strange as it may have seemed, foreign politics ceased for a time to dominate national policy in Germany.[6] Currency was stable; unemployment was falling; foreign trade was growing; new buildings were going up in every street. The German people were surprised, almost alarmed, at the seeming ease with which they had at last recovered from the desperate days of the Revolution and the Ruhr. And no one was so ungenerous as to cast a doubt upon a prosperity founded, in the last analysis, on the shifting sands of foreign loans.

For non-Germans the great problem of the Stresemann era must always be the character and sincerity of the man, Stresemann himself. Certainly he was a patriot and a romantic. But it is useful sometimes to remember that, in the First World War, Stresemann had been one of the annexationists, he had supported unrestricted submarine warfare, and he had earned for himself the nickname of "Ludendorff's young man." In the Weimar National Assembly he had voted for the rejection of the Treaty of Versailles. He was leader of the People's party, the party of big business and therefore of the armament manufacturers, the inheritor of the old National Liberal economic expansionism. He continued to correspond dutifully with the former Crown Prince. These were unlikely antecedents for a man who was later to stand as the great exponent of reconciliation with France and of the League of Nations. It is also certain that Germany waited only for the withdrawal of the Allied Control Commission in 1927 to begin the serious business of rearmament. But it was then too late for protest. After Locarno, diplomatic courtesy required that German good faith should be accepted at its face value, that the policy of "fulfillment" should not be impugned. Perhaps Stresemann justified that state of affairs to his German conscience, but he made good capital nonetheless out of Allied wishful thinking and disunity. A few weeks after Locarno he is reported to have said, apropos of that pact, "No worse nonsense has been talked lately than about secret diplomacy. But every man had his own secret diplomacy." The fact that Hitler afterward used to refer reverentially to his memory is of some significance.

12 POLAND AND THE BALTIC:
DEMOCRATIC EXPERIMENT AND DICTATORSHIP

THE POLISH REVOLUTION

On October 6, 1918, the Council of Regency threw off the pretense of submission to Germany and declared "a free and united Poland." (See pp. 57 and 104.) On November 10, Pilsudski, the Polish national hero, released from his confinement in Germany, returned to his homeland in triumph. He accepted the resignation of the Council of Regency and assumed the title of Chief of State. He was vested by the army with the supreme rank of First Marshal. He entrusted Moraczewski, a Socialist, with the formation of a provisional government. Moraczewski announced a democratic franchise and called for general elections for a Polish parliament, the Sejm.

But the Polish Revolution of October and November 1918, however decisive, complete, and satisfying it might seem, was only the first and easiest chapter in the history of the Poland that was now to be. The country was in a parlous physical condition. The Austro-German campaign and the Russian retirement of 1915 had wasted wide tracts of land. Farms had been destroyed, livestock slaughtered, forests burned, and factories dismantled. Whole towns were deserted of their inhabitants. The German occupation thereafter had been milder in Poland than in Belgium or northern France, but the requisitions of the occupying armies had been heavy nonetheless, and toward the end of the war, in 1918, there had been widespread epidemics and famine. Without the simultaneous collapse of its three former overlords, Russia, Austria, and Germany, an independent Poland could never have arisen, but that collapse — miraculous historical coincidence though it was — now left the country suspended, so to speak, in an amorphous sea of dissolution. The all-important access to the outer world of the Allies was blocked by the hostile ports of Danzig and Memel.

The country's former partition [1] between alien Powers had prevented the growth of a native governing or official class, and only in Galicia could it be said that a Polish bureaucracy had ever existed at all: The departure of the Austro-German armies afforded a grateful relief, but it turned over a Poland, formerly accustomed to three separate administrations and three systems of law, to the tender mercies of wholly new and hastily constituted authorities for whom political responsibility was a novel experience. The Council of Regency had proclaimed "a free and united Poland," but freedom and unity did not result automatically just because hated foreign oppressions had been removed, and freedom and unity were soon proving to be, in practice, not easily reconcilable principles. It would be ungenerous to say that a people as ancient, as gifted, and as potentially great as the Poles were not yet ready for political independence, but their release from oppression was also a release from discipline, a release for which they were quite unprepared. Three-quarters of the population in 1919 were still illiterate, serfdom had been abolished only half a century before, and there was without question, from the first days of the Revolution, an instability of character in evidence among the Poles which did not bode too well for the future. Irish, Hungarians, Spaniards are examples perhaps of "difficult" peoples, but the modern Poles were soon to prove themselves their peers in difficulty. The Polish temper in 1919, as we shall see, was such as to make the national liberation an adventure almost foredoomed to disaster.

There were three main party divisions in the new Poland. On the Left stood the Polish Socialist party. It had had a revolutionary and terroristic tradition in the former Russian areas of Poland, where it had produced leaders like Pilsudski, and it had a parliamentary tradition in the former Austrian areas of Poland, where it had produced leaders like Daszyński. Generally it was nationalist and anti-Russian. On the Right stood the National Democratic party, called the "Endeks," reactionary, nationalist, Catholic, anti-Semitic, supported by the propertied classes and the universities. It was led by Roman Dmowski. In the thirties, its extreme wing became hardly distinguishable from Fascism. In the Center was a group of peasant parties — remarkably small considering the importance of the Polish peasantry — led by men like Witos. In addition there were the Christian Democrats, inclining to the Right, resembling the Christian Socialists in Austria (see p. 191). There were some "Independents," Communists, Jews, and national minorities. The whole formed a variegated and unpromising texture out of which to design a responsible democracy.

The conflict of Left and Right was personified in the rivalry of the two men most prominent in Poland's postwar politics. Joseph Pilsudski was of aristocratic Lithuanian stock, originally trained in medicine at the University of Kharkov; but he had spent his early life in Socialist agitation against Tsarist Russia. He had played his part in revolutionary conspiracy, and he had suffered imprisonment in Warsaw and Siberia. Love of Poland and hatred of Russia were complementary strands in a rugged, pugnacious, and powerful character. Roman Dmowski was of artisan stock, originally trained in natural science at the University of Warsaw. He had represented Warsaw in the second and third Dumas in St. Petersburg. He looked for some sort of compromise with the Russian Government of that day, he believed perhaps in an autonomous Poland under the suzerainty of the Tsar and, though never a lover of Russia, he always regarded Germany as the real foeman of his homeland. He was opportunist, inclined to intrigue, reactionary to the core.

The antagonism formed thus early between the two men had continued into the First World War. In 1914, Pilsudski led his famous Polish Legion into action against the Russians in the van of the Austrian Army. In 1914, Dmowski founded a Polish National Committee in Warsaw which collaborated with the Russian Government, and he raised another Polish Legion to fight beside the Russians against the Austro-German invaders. In 1916,

Pilsudski was given an important role in the Poland of the Central Empires but, as we said above, he afterward atoned for his rash faith in the Kaiser's friendship in the prison of the fortress of Magdeburg (see p. 57). Dmowski continued to work for Russia and the Allies. He eventually became a principal figure in a Polish National Committee in Paris and one of the organizers of a Polish force on the Western front. In 1919 when the Allies assembled for the Peace Conference in Paris, they had long been accustomed to Dmowski's expositions of Polish affairs and regarded him as the official spokesman of resurgent Poland, and they were disinclined to "recognize" Pilsudski, the elected Polish Chief of State.

In January 1919, Paderewski, the great pianist, arrived in Warsaw on a mission of reconciliation, bearing the good wishes of the Allies and of Dmowski. He was invited by Pilsudski to become Premier of a new government, and he then returned to Paris, where he and Dmowski represented Poland at the Peace Conference. The general elections, promised by Moraczewski, took place according to plan and passed off without disorder, and Pilsudski opened the first session of the Sejm in February 1919. But Paderewski's truce lasted hardly a month. Questions of foreign policy and agrarian reform and, in particular, the constitution, which it was to be the duty of the Sejm to draft, all sundered the young assembly. Paderewski returned to Warsaw from Paris more than once during 1919 to exercise his gifts as a conciliator but, in December, he was at last forced to resign. The kindest and blindest could not pretend that the new Poland had started off too well. Observers at the time cynically remarked that the Republic was already displaying the qualities which had destroyed the old Kingdom a century and a half before.

Abroad the Poles have always been regarded as men of piquant and exotic culture, often wearing the cosmopolitan charm, and speaking the language, of Paris, and their history was written in terms of their national heroes, artists, and scientists — Kosciuszko, Sienkiewicz, Chopin, Rubinstein, Paderewski, Madame Curie, and many other names as glittering. But the Poles of popular story were not the only Poles of Poland. At home the central, elemental fact of Polish life was the peasantry, the predominant mass of the population, living in small primitive hamlets, cultivating "dwarfish holdings," illiterate and burdened down with debt. Parts of the country, Poznań, the former German Posen, for instance, were tolerably fertile and flourishing; but Volhynia or the northeastern provinces at the opposite end of the scale belonged to the worst of Europe's "poverty corners." Moreover, the Polish birth rate was the highest in Europe, and the pressure on the land increased alarmingly year by year.

Over and above this dead level of destitution and misery existed a "gentry," the descendants of the petty nobility before the Partitions,[1] and the repository still of Polish historic tradition, and in them, perhaps 5 per cent of the entire population and the core of the Rightist parties, was concentrated the agrarian wealth of the country and all its most ultraconservative forces. Nowhere, except in Hungary, was the squirearchical system so strongly entrenched as in the new Polish Republic. It was as if, through the nineteenth century, Poland had stood still while the world with all its material and so-

POLAND AND THE BALTIC, 1920~39

cial changes had passed by her prison, and when, in 1918, she was free again, she had resumed her old life and become the same old feudal state that she had been more than a hundred years before.

THE BATTLE OF THE FRONTIERS

While Dmowski and the Allies at the Peace Conference of Paris were deliberating the future frontiers of Poland, Marshal Pilsudski at home was already consulting more direct ways of securing and extending them. As soon as he had arrived in Warsaw he had set about recruiting an army. The remnants of his Polish Legion and the Poles who were demobilized from the former Austrian, German, and Russian armies were drafted into it. In March 1919 the Sejm passed a universal service law. In April 1919 the Polish force from the Western front was repatriated mainly by train across Germany, under protest from the German Government. Within a few months the strength of the Polish forces under arms reached the handsome figure of 600,000, a motley, polyglot host, but full of a militant energy which it was to take four years of fighting to satisfy.

Most of the new nations in 1919 were engaged in frontier fighting of one kind or another. There were old enemies to be expelled; there were the awards of the Peace Conference to be anticipated; there were the general interests of future security to be considered. But sometimes the fighting was of a more grandiose order. All the oppressed peoples of "Intermediate Europe" (see p. 384) looked back to a golden age, and the postwar revolutions seemed to offer them a chance to realize visions of a former greatness, visions on which, during the darker years, their hope and courage, their entire ideology of independence had been fed. They had "historic rights"; they had "cultural missions"; they were the defenders of their particular civilizations against "hereditary enemies." Liberty in Europe in 1919 was a heady wine, made headier by the long starvation of so many of its drinkers.

In December 1918 the new Polish armies were already in Galicia. In January and February 1919 a stubborn battle was fought for the capture of Teschen from the Czechs (see p. 196). In April, Vilna and Grodno were wrested from the Bolsheviks. Pilsudski, it was evident, was forcing a long-term policy of expansion and seeking to reconquer the area of the former Kingdom of Poland. Indeed he could make historic claims of some sort to all the lands from the Oder to the Dniester. He seemed ready to pick a quarrel anywhere with anybody, and in the end there was not one of Poland's six near neighbors, except Rumania, whom he had not attacked or was not attacking. Clemenceau in Paris gave a tacit encouragement to a series of campaigns which were aggrandizing a prospective ally of France and forming a strong resistive block against a possible renascence of Germany or a possible westward penetration on the part of Bolshevik Russia. As Pichon put it, France wanted a Poland *"grande et forte, très forte."* President Wilson and Lloyd George, appalled at these indiscriminate hostilities so soon after the Armistice, were soon threatening Pilsudski with blockades and embargoes.

Early in 1920, in accordance with the Treaty of Versailles, the Free City of Danzig came into being (see p. 122). The Poles took over their new territories in the so-called Corridor. The settlement, of course, caused extreme bitterness in Germany. Danzig was a German city, an ancient Hanseatic port, and its relegation to the convenience of a despised Slavic race and the resulting separation of East Prussia from the German Fatherland — for all that the Fourteen Points had promised Poland "a free and secure access to the sea" — these were sacrifices not to be endured. While the Free City of Danzig and the Corridor existed, the peace of Germany and Poland could never be more than formal. Moreover, repeated attempts in Paris to ease the tension between Poles and Czechs over the vexed question of Teschen by means of negotiation between the interested parties had all failed. Neither Poles nor Czechs would renounce their rights to the disputed area and its wealth of coal mines. In July 1920 the Conference of Ambassadors in Paris at last made an award dividing Teschen between the two disputants — and satisfying neither (see p. 196). But at that date Pilsudski had reached the climax of his expansionist policy and was in the midst of a major war with Soviet Russia.

The Peace Conference of 1919 had left undefined the future frontiers of Russia and the new Polish state. Nor had Russia been represented at Paris. Meanwhile the Russian Civil War had broken out, and the government of Lenin and Trotsky was fighting for its life against a ring of counterrevolutionary uprisings. In an attempt at least to clarify the situation as far as Poland was concerned, the Allied Supreme Council, in December 1919, had laid down as the eastern frontier of Poland a tentative line, corresponding roughly to the ethnical division, a line which later came to be known as the Curzon Line after the British Foreign Secretary at the time. But it was soon evident that neither the Poles nor their French friends had the least intention of recognizing so limited an interpretation of Poland's aspirations toward the East.

Pilsudski's ultimate ambition, it is believed, was the federation of all the liberated states of "Intermediate Europe," including Lithuania and the Ukraine, under Polish hegemony, and in the furtherance of that ambition, he must have been tempted more than once to join forces with the White counterrevolutionary armies already fighting in Russia. But it was not till April 1920 that he entered into agreements with Petlyura, leader of the Ukrainian nationalists, and with General Wrangel, leader of the White Russians in the Crimea and, under the evident patronage of France, a plan for a concerted war against Russia by Ukrainians, Whites, and Poles began to take shape.

The course of the Russo-Polish War of 1920 and its extraordinary reversals of fortune are best described in the context of the Russian Civil War in Chapter 17 (see pp. 267–68). It was in July 1920, at the moment that the Poles were in headlong rout, that Grabski, then Polish Premier, hurried to Spa, where the Allies were holding a conference on reparations, to appeal for help. He was received "very coldly" and was told to accept the Curzon Line. The Poles were then in a mood to accept any frontier. The Russians were driving the last remnants of Polish resistance before them, and it seemed as if the whole of Eastern and Central Europe, if not the entire Versailles settlement, would be swallowed up in Bolshevism. The summer of that year, 1920, was as cruel and anxious a time as any that this generation of many crises was to endure. General Weygand arrived in Poland at the head of a French military mission and organized the defense of Warsaw. The British Government threatened naval action against the Russians in the Baltic. Pilsudski issued an impassioned appeal to the Polish people. The crisis passed; Warsaw was held; the Polish forces began a triumphant counteradvance. The Russo-Polish War was eventually terminated by the Treaty of Riga in March 1921, by which Poland received a frontier a generous 150 miles east of the Curzon Line, a frontier which she was to keep till 1939. Meanwhile the Vilna incident occurred.

Vilna was Lithuania's ancient capital and the symbol of Lithuania's culture and independence, albeit more than half the city's population was solidly Polish. After the Russian defeat and retirement in 1920, Vilna was expected to revert to Lithuania, and in October 1920 the League Council induced the Poles and the Lithuanians to sign an agreement at Suwalki to that effect. But in October 1920, General Zeligowski, himself a Lithuanian Pole, suddenly marched into Vilna at the head of a Polish force and set himself up as "Chief of a Central Lithuanian State." The Polish Government officially disavowed the contumacious General, but it was more than probable that he had Pilsudski's sympathy and support, and in Poland at large his coup was hailed with evident delight. Lithuania appealed to the League, and the League arranged for Polish and Lithuanian delegates to meet in conference at Brussels. But Zeligowski was still in Vilna, and in this, as in many another matter of international concern, possession was nine points of the law. Vilna was eventually incorporated into Poland and, in April 1922, Marshal Pilsudski, accompanied by a retinue of civil and religious dignitaries, made his ceremonial entry into the city. In March 1923 the Conference of Ambassadors (see p. 124) reluctantly recognized the situation and drafted a frontier which assigned the whole of the city and territory to Poland.

Poland emerged from all these events a victorious Power, almost a Great Power, and one to be respected and courted by the nations of Europe, and she was quick to confirm her new position by alliances with France and Rumania. A Franco-Polish alliance was signed in February 1921 at the time of Marshal Pilsudski's state visit to Paris. A treaty with Rumania followed a few weeks later. Poland's many triumphs, if not her exhaustion, might now perhaps have given pause to her belligerent energies. But her frontiers continued to sound with alarms and excursions. In March 1921 the Upper Silesian plebiscite was held, with results that have been mentioned elsewhere (see p. 152). The final settlement of that territory was not completed till May 1922, and until then both sides remained in a state of the utmost possible tension. At times only the thin khaki line of British troops, sent to organize the plebiscite, stood between Upper Silesia and civil war.

From the end of 1918 to 1923, Poland had been engaged in more than four years' continuous fighting. The Battle of the Frontiers, as her campaigns have been called, gave her an area of 150,000 square miles, about four-fifths the area of republican Germany, of which only 90,000 square miles could be described as "indisputably Polish," and a population of nearly 30,000,000, of whom only 20,000,000 could be described as indisputably Poles. Of her final frontiers, in the words of one Polish statesman, "75 per cent were permanently menaced, 20 per cent were insecure, and only 5 per cent really safe."

THE POLISH MINORITIES

Poland, like Belgium or the Middle Danube, had always been the crossroads of cultures and invasions, all of which had left their "minorities" behind them. The Battle of the Frontiers had greatly intensified a problem which would have existed in any event. In 1923, as we have said, a third of the population of the new Poland was non-Polish — mainly White Russians, Ukranians, Germans, and Jews. After Czechoslovakia, no other nation in the new Europe contained so large an alien percentage in its midst.

The Polish Minorities Treaty, signed at Versailles in 1919 (see p. 133), had guaranteed to the minorities in question the usual rights, such as protection of life and liberty, facilities for vernacular education, freedom of worship, and so forth. Poland, always very sensitive of her national pride, had resented the implied reflection upon her sovereignty, but she ratified the "Little Versailles," as the treaty was called, and its terms were written into the Polish constitution of 1921.

The White Russians,[2] numbering some 900,000, inhabited the "poverty areas" in the east bordering Soviet White Russia. Their lands had been overrun in the World War and in the Russo-Polish War, as they had been overrun before whenever Russia had fought with Western states. Theirs was a problem not of politics, but of the most elemental economics, and any sense of nationality in them must have long since been extinguished. As a minority, the White Russians never became a question of great importance or difficulty.

It was otherwise with the Ukrainians, a people that were gifted and vigorous, a people with a language, culture, history, and national consciousness of their own. Like the Poles themselves, they had suffered partition between adjacent Powers, and they were the one important European folk group that the First World War had not liberated. Their aspirations were supported and publicized by the very numerous Ukrainian immigrants in the United States and Canada. Thus the 4,250,000 Ukrainians in Poland regarded themselves as the brothers of the 40,000,000 Ukrainians inhabiting the southern Russian plains, and as belonging to a single "Ukraine" from the Carpathians to the Don, a land of great wealth, and likely to achieve political importance of the first order. Ukrainians and Poles had clashed in 1919 when Pilsudski had first occupied East Galicia. Pilsudski's further plans in the Ukraine had collapsed ingloriously in the Russo-Polish War in 1920, but East Galicia and its Ukrainians remained a part of the new Poland. The Polish Government, in violation of the Minorities Treaty and of pledges of local autonomy, thenceforth engaged in a policy of systematic Polonization. But the Ukrainians were well organized. They had their own co-operatives and political parties, and their own national Uniat Church.[3] The struggle which the Polish landowners launched against them was likely to be long and stubborn, and by 1931 the Ukrainian question had developed into a minor civil war.

The Jews in Poland had enjoyed a long historic tradition. Time was when the country was the refuge of European Jewry and when four-fifths of all the Jews in the world were to be found within its borders. In the new Poland the Jews numbered over 2,500,000, living mostly in the big cities, Warsaw, Łódź, Cracow, and Lwów. The Partitions had destroyed many of their ancient privileges, and Poland had since become what apparently she had never been before, an anti-Semitic country. Nevertheless, the Jews still monopolized much of the commerce and banking, and provided Poland with the only middle class she ever really had. Since 1914 the feeling against the Jews had certainly grown much stronger, and the National Democratic party, the most conservative and "patriotic" of the Polish political parties, was tacitly identified with anti-Semitism. The Polish Government made no provision for Jewish minority schools, and Yiddish, of course, was never officially recognized as a minority language. There were many glaring "injustices" committed against the Jews in the new Poland and, were all the information available, the story would not be a very edifying one.

POLISH DOMESTIC POLITICS

The military achievements of Pilsudski might have been more impressive had they been built upon a foundation of real strength at home. But beneath them lay the extreme poverties and the cleavages of class and nationality which we have described. They had been won in defiance of neighbors momentarily weak — notably Russia and Germany — and the balance of forces they had created was, in the nature of the case, unstable in the extreme. There was always something fictitious in the restless, quenchless vitality of the new Poland.

On the home front an infallible index of the realities of the situation was the country's finance. During 1920 the Polish mark dropped from 120 to 150 to the dollar. During 1921, despite a virtual capital levy, it dropped to 3,000. In 1923 it finally responded to the total collapse of the German currency. Another infallible index was the perpetual parliamentary discord. Paderewski himself had been unable to control or quiet the Sejm. Cabinets rose and fell in a way that is reminiscent of France or Czechoslovakia, except that Poland never possessed the sound bureaucratic substructure which gave the real toughness and continuity to the politics of those countries. Between the resignation of Paderewski in 1919 and Pilsudski's coup in 1926, thirteen premiers held office, the longest term being that of Grabski and his "business cabinet" from December 1923 to November 1925.

The three main domestic questions before the Sejm were labor, agrarian reform, and the constitution. Polish labor laws were among the most advanced in Europe. Freedom of assembly, recognition of trade-unions, humane working hours were all enacted in 1919. Poland co-operated with enthusiasm in the work of the International Labor Organization and ratified most of its conventions. Unfortunately the legislation, good as it looked on paper, was constantly evaded. The Polish workingman had neither the education nor tradition of organization to stand up for his own rights, and the history of labor in the new Poland reads like nothing so much as the early history of the Industrial Revolution in England. Sweated labor, accidents and disease, squalid housing, the whole gamut of industrial tragedy was there.

The first agrarian reform bill came before the Sejm in July 1919 and was passed by a majority of one during the following year. It limited the land owned by any one person to 150–250 acres; the lands thus made available were to be expropriated and turned over to indigent peasants. Again the legislation looked good on paper. But the act remained largely inoperative during the Russo-Polish War and the inflation, and it then lapsed altogether. A further bill was passed in December 1925, but it was loaded with obstructive amendments, and the great historic estates were left untouched. In extenuation it was argued by economic experts that even if the act had been implemented in practice, the natural increase of population would have outdated every reparcelation of land as soon as it had been effected, and that furthermore the ignorance and backwardness of the peasants were such that they could never have cut themselves free of the tutelage of their landlords. In 1931 three-quarters of the agricultural holdings in Poland were still less than the subsistence minimum of twelve acres.

The constitution was delayed by the Russo-Polish War. It was finally passed by the Sejm after considerable debate but by a large majority on March 17, 1921, a few days before the signing of the Treaty of Riga. It contained provisions for universal suffrage and a bicameral legislature, a Sejm and a Senate, all of the usual democratic form. It somewhat resembled the French constitution, especially in its one exceptional provision, the deliberate limitation of the presidential prerogatives. Out of fear and hatred of Pilsudski, who the Right fully expected would be the first President of the Republic, the President's office was reduced to a ceremonial title. He had no right of veto; worst of all, he was to be deprived of command of the army in time of war. Naturally enough, in December 1922, when the presidential elections were held, Pilsudski refused to accept candidature, though eventually his friend the former Socialist, Wojciechowski, was elected.

The final passage and enactment of the constitution therefore was interpretable as a victory of the Right and a personal defeat for Pilsudski. Six years of political turmoil followed, of which Pilsudski was of course the butt and center. Polish foreign relations were in good order. It was the heyday of the Franco-Polish alliance. France won her Battle of the Ruhr, even as Poland had won her Battle of the Frontiers, and mutual congratulations were in order. French statesmen and soldiers, including Marshal Foch, made ceremonial visits to Warsaw. In 1925, Poland shared the benefits and felicities of Locarno. But the political and financial situation in Warsaw did not improve. At the end of 1923, Grabski and his "business cabinet" put into force financial reforms, reminiscent of those of Stresemann in Germany at the time, and introduced a new monetary unit, the zloty, equal to the gold franc, the Polish mark then being 1,800,000 to the zloty. A loan was obtained from France. Grabski called his government "nonparty" — actually it was a foretaste of dictatorship.

PILSUDSKI'S COUP AND DICTATORSHIP

There were many signs that the inevitable explosion would occur in 1926. Poland was not unlike the Italy of 1922. Both countries had reached a pass where they were wearied beyond endurance with the impotence, futility, and corruption of the democratic system as that system appeared to them. The mounting charge was touched off by a deterioration in Poland's foreign relations. Germany, early in 1926, had just imposed heavy restrictions on the import of Polish goods, and a veritable German-Polish tariff war was in progress. Germany was also to be admitted to the League of Nations, and she was expected to take a permanent seat in the League Council, but the latter privilege, it was soon clear, was not to be extended to Poland. Then in April 1926, Germany and the Soviet Union signed a treaty in circumstances that recalled the Rapallo coup of 1922 (see pp. 140 and 541). It was ostensibly a treaty of "friendship and neutrality," but the Poles could never regard any Russo-German *rapprochement* as anything but sinister and suspect. As usual the situation was reflected in finance. The new zloty was evidently sliding toward "the second inflation."

Early in May 1926, Witos, the Peasant leader, succeeded in forming a coalition government with the extreme Right and, in effect, mobilized all the anti-Pilsudskian parties. Then, as if in deliberate provocation, he appointed an anti-Pilsudskian general as Minister of War. Pilsudski, who latterly had been living in a sort of watchful political retirement, considered that Witos was trying to deprive him of his control over the army and decided to act. He raised his standard and, after the style of the Fascist revolt in 1922, began a march on Warsaw. He was reinforced by a contingent from Vilna under his old comrade in arms, General Śmigly-Rydz. After three days of fighting, Witos and President Wojciechowski resigned. Warsaw surrendered unconditionally.

Pilsudski still declined to accept the presidency, though the Sejm and the Senate went through the form of electing him to that supreme honor. On June 1, 1926, Moscicki, a chemist and university professor and a personal friend, was elected President of Poland. Pilsudski himself was less interested in offices than in reforms of the constitution which would restore some of the presidential prerogatives and rid the legislature of the "eternal quarrels and eternal discords" of the parties. Amendments to the constitution, which were accordingly passed in August 1926, gave the President power to dissolve the Sejm and the Senate, to enforce the passage of the budget and, in emergencies, to issue decrees having the force of law. In October, Pilsudski became Premier and Minister of War.

Pilsudski himself must have deplored as keenly as any of his opponents the violent revolution which had put him into power in 1926. Yet, by his action, order had given place to chaos, the old haunting fear of Polish disunity — the disunity which, as the Marshal believed, had been the cause of Poland's self-destruction in the eighteenth century — was momentarily overcome, and the country found itself able to participate in the general economic betterment in Europe in the Locarno era. It cannot be said that the fundamental questions of the Polish body politic were any nearer a solution. Peasants and workers remained destitute, and minorities oppressed. But, for the next few years, the budget showed a surplus, trade showed a favorable balance, the zloty was stable, and these were joys and triumphs exhilaratingly new in the experience of the young republic. The new port of Gdynia, the pride of the nation, recently constructed as a political gesture wholly upon Polish soil and therefore free from the restrictive complications of Danzig, was handling increasing shipments of goods. First-class Atlantic liners were being added to the Polish merchant fleet. A great development was being planned in the Central Industrial Region, "Poland's TVA," as it was once called.

Pilsudski was determined that the old constitution which had collapsed so dramatically in 1926 must be revised or scrapped altogether. The government, at his instance, organized a "Nonparty Bloc of Co-operation with the Government," or as it was popularly called, the "Sanitation party," whose moving spirits were "Colonels" of the old romantic days of the Polish Legion in the First World War. It had little program beyond an almost mystical idolatry of the all-puissant Marshal. Elections were held in March 1928, but the Bloc did not gain the two-thirds majority which would have entitled it to introduce constitutional changes. The new Sejm, in fact, indicated its temper by electing Daszyński, a Socialist and a prominent anti-Pilsudskian, as its "Marshal" or presiding officer. Pilsudski resigned the premiership and relieved his feelings toward the Sejm in angry and abusive interviews to the press. Pilsudski's own character, it was noticed at this time, was changing. He was prone to recall his noble pedigree; he sometimes forsook his old Socialist comrades and made friendly gestures toward the industrial magnates; he liked to accept invitations to the houses and castles of the great landed aristocrats.

Jan Pilsudski, Marshal Pilsudski's brother, undertook to draw up a new constitution which would legitimatize the Pilsudskian autocracy. It was submitted to the Sejm in February 1929, but the Sejm showed not the slightest inclination to adopt it. During 1930, Marshal Pilsudski called for new general elections and issued a list of government candidates headed by himself. He arrested and imprisoned a number of the more recalcitrant Opposition leaders, including Witos. Public parades and demonstrations were prohibited, and the press was put under strict control. The actual election day was like a Nazi plebiscite. But there were still over thirty political parties in the field, five of them from the Center and Left now forming a bloc of their own. From the government's point of view, the election results were only partially "satisfactory." Only in the Senate was there the two-thirds majority required for constitutional changes. Pilsudski left for Madeira "for a rest cure."

Public indignation at the alleged ill-treatment of the imprisoned Opposition leaders forced the government to release them on bail. They were eventually brought to trial in November 1931 for conspiring "to eliminate by violence the members of the government." The court held over fifty sittings and examined over two hundred witnesses. Like so many of the "treason trials" of this enlightened time, the actual culpability of the prisoners was obscured in a fog of propaganda. The prisoners made long harangues against Pilsudski, full reports of which were allowed to appear in the press. In the end, prison sentences were passed ranging from eighteen months to three years, but the condemned men remained at liberty while they appealed their cases, and most of them, including Witos, used the interval to flee the country.

It is not necessary to carry this story much further. The world-wide economic depression began to exert its baleful force in 1931, and Poland's unemployed in that year numbered 350,000. Marshal Pilsudski, however, persevered with his new constitution and eventually secured its acceptance by the Sejm in January 1934. The document was signed by him on April 23, 1935 at the Presidential Residence in the presence of state dignitaries and to the accompaniment of a salute of a hundred and one guns.

A few days later, on May 12, 1935, Marshal Pilsudski died.

The story of Poland is one of the most turbulent and unsatisfactory of postwar Europe. The country suffered from the severest disabilities of history, economics, and geography, and its human material was both heterogeneous and backward. The agrarian problem was basic, and was never solved. There were many outside Poland who expected better things of the newly born state, and perhaps in a less troubled world their hopes might not have been so disappointed. Yet it is impossible to escape the feeling that the Poles were their own worst enemies, and that they condemned themselves in advance to certain destruction. Marshal Joseph Pilsudski was the hero of the Polish Revolution and the father of his country, a dictator who tried to observe the democratic forms of government and who, like Caesar, again and again declined a more majestic title. Yet his own tempestuous character somehow epitomized that of his country. Real peace and democracy were values which the Poland of the twenties and thirties was unable to give the world.

THE NEW BALTIC STATES: ESTONIA, LATVIA, AND LITHUANIA

On the east side of the Baltic Sea is a low-lying, once marshy and deeply forested land, since brought under partial cultivation by a peasant people of somewhat mixed origins. Through the centuries the land was successively ruled by the Teutonic Knights and by the kingdoms of Poland and Sweden. From the time of Peter the Great, it fell under the sway of Russia, and Russian it remained till the end of the First World War. Its population consisted in part of the indigenous peasantry, still tenants of landowners of German extraction — the so-called Baltic Barons, descended from the original Teutonic Knights (see p. 56) — and in part of the more recent industrial and dock workers. Its chief ports, Reval (Tallinn), Riga, Libau, and Memel, were largely German. Its more recent history had been marked by the rise of a national consciousness and by consequent revolts and repressions such as were then common to all the lesser peoples of Europe. Its workers shared in the contemporary revolutionary movements. There were workers' risings in Reval and Riga in 1905 and again in 1917. From 1915 to 1918 the land as far north as the Dvina had come under German military occupation. At the end of 1918 the autochthonous racial elements re-emerged in a sharp distinction as the three new national republics of Estonia, Latvia, and Lithuania.

For a time German Free Corps and Bolsheviks disputed the land anew. Allied military missions and Allied naval squadrons exerted themselves in the interests of the new republics. Yudenich, the Russian counterrevolutionary commander, used Estonia as his base during the Russian Civil War. Peace and independence were not established till 1920. Estonia and Russia signed a treaty of peace at Dorpat (Tartu) in February 1920, the first treaty of peace to be signed by Russia with a border state. Similar treaties followed between Russia and Lithuania at Moscow in July 1920, and between Russia and Latvia at Riga in August 1920. All three states were admitted to the membership of the League of Nations in September 1921.

Of the internal condition of Estonia and Latvia it is enough to say that both states had the usual minority problems, and both introduced far-reaching agrarian reforms which, in practice, meant the dispossession of the old landowning classes, notably the Baltic Barons, for the benefit of the landless peasantry. Both set up democratic constitutions which, for one reason or another, did not function very smoothly. The all too common faults and failings of young republics in these interwar years, inexperience and egoism, the multiplication of parties and the frequency of cabinet changes, and the inevitable experimentation in government by blocs — all this was sadly manifest in the two countries. When we read that, from 1920 to 1934, Estonia had eighteen cabinets and some dozen distinct political parties, and Latvia had sixteen cabinets and between twenty and thirty distinct political parties — and this in populations of only 1,100,000 and 1,800,000 respectively — we might well despair of democracy in the Baltic. Eventually both Estonia and Latvia produced their brands of Fascism and, in 1934, both established dictatorships, or at least governments with strong executive powers. Meanwhile the mass of the workers in the Baltic republics, notably in the seaports, clung to their revolutionary tradition and made ready for their future absorption into the Soviet Union.

Yet, all in all, the interwar careers of Estonia and Latvia were relatively quiet and exemplary. With Lithuania it was otherwise. Lithuania was the *enfant terrible* of the Baltic. She was one of those liberated states that remembered too well a once great and glorious past. In contemporary Europe her population exceeded only that of Albania and her two neighbors, Estonia and Latvia. Yet she arrogated to herself the ambitions of a Power. In the first decade of her existence she antagonized Russia, Poland, and Germany, defied the Conference of Ambassadors in Paris and, though a Catholic country, broke off relations with the Vatican. Fortunately she lay outside the main danger zones of the time. A state of the same pretensions in the Middle Danube or the Balkans would not have survived the adventure of independent nationhood a single year.

With Russia, Lithuania's relations would have been delicate in any event. The propertied classes of the country regarded Bolshevism with abhorrence, an abhorrence which was all the fiercer for their actual experience of it in 1919 and 1920 and for their continued proximity to it thereafter. But so long as Poland held Vilna, there would be a solid protective corridor between Lithuanian and Russian territory. Whatever else might be said of the "tragedy of Vilna," it at least gave the Lithuanians one less neighbor to quarrel with and, for that reason perhaps, Lithuania eventually resigned herself to a state of peace with Russia. She responded to the blandishments of that persistent architect of peace pacts, Litvinov, and signed a treaty of nonaggression with the Soviet Union in September 1926.

With Poland, Lithuania's relations were obstructed by the stumbling block of Vilna, her ancient capital. The seizure of the city by the Polish General Zeligowski has already been described (see p. 176). A "state of war" between Lithuania and Poland continued thereafter, the frontier remained closed, and all economic intercourse was halted. In 1925, Poland signed a concordat with the Vatican which "recognized" Vilna as a Polish diocese, and Lithuania immediately retorted by breaking off relations with the Vatican.

With Germany, Lithuania's relations were obstructed by that other Baltic stumbling block of Memel. Like Danzig, Memel was an essentially German city on the littoral of a non-German hinterland, and the people made no secret of their desire to return to the Reich. Under the Treaty of Versailles, Germany had renounced her rights in the territory, and French troops were sent to garrison it. Though Lithuanian jurisdiction was clearly intended, a settlement was postponed until the general situation in the Baltic had stabilized. But the Lithuanians were not a people to acquiesce in delays. They had before them the example of D'Annunzio in Fiume and of Zeligowski in Vilna. In January 1923, at the time of the Ruhr crisis, when both France and Germany were otherwise preoccupied, Lithuanian troops invaded and took possession of Memel by force. The Allies, faced with a *fait accompli,* could only withdraw the French garrison and make the best possible terms with the Lithuanian Government. In May 1924 at Paris, a convention regulating the status of Memel was signed by Lithuania and the Allies. For Germany the settlement was a bitter, unforgivable blow. But so long as Versailles was Versailles she had no legal grounds for protest. The day of restitution would come anon.

Like Estonia and Latvia, Lithuania began her independent career as a republic. From 1918 to May 1926 her domestic affairs were dominated by a bloc of moderately democratic and Catholic parties. But popular indignation had been roused over Poland's concordat with the Vatican in 1925 which, as we have said, had assigned Vilna to a Polish diocese, and in the elections in May 1926 this bloc suffered a heavy defeat. A new bloc, rather less clerical and rather more Socialist in persuasion, then held office for about six months. But in December 1926, Lithuania's experiment in republicanism came to a sudden and violent end.

The year 1926 was the year of Pilsudski's coup in Warsaw, and though the Lithuanians lost no love for the Poles, it was not in the nature of things that they should remain indifferent to so important an event in a neighboring state. In December 1926 a group of landowners, industrialists, and army officers, not unlike Pilsudski's "Colonels," led by Smetona and Voldemaras, both old fighters for Lithuanian independence, seized control. Smetona, formerly a lawyer, was elected President; Voldemaras, formerly a professor of social science and history at the University of Lithuania, and the real brains of the adventure, became Premier and virtual dictator of the state. There were the usual arrests of Opposition leaders; martial law and a press censorship were established; a squadrist troop, which went by the name of the Iron Wolf, was organized. In short, Lithuania assumed the familiar guise of an authoritarian state.

Unhappily Pilsudski's coup and Voldemaras's coup, however similar, did not help the relations of Poland and Lithuania. Both dictators were adepts in belligerent Mussolinian oratory, and both were adepts at magnifying into "incidents" all those irritations which Polish and Lithuanian governments would have been better advised to ignore. Both states were soon persecuting each other's minorities, both were soon rumored to be concentrating troops, and by the latter part of 1927 it was a matter of some surprise that open hostilities had not broken out.

In December 1927 the League Council intervened at last. Voldemaras and Pilsudski were induced to meet at Geneva — an unforgettable occasion. A resolution was accepted by them recommending direct negotiations between Poland and Lithuania in the interests of "the good understanding between nations upon which peace depends." Poland and Lithuania formally terminated the "state of war" which had existed for the past seven years. But Voldemaras continued to delay and obstruct, and rejected every proposal to implement the new "state of peace." He professed himself uninterested in a Polish offer of nonaggression. In May 1928, in a speech in celebration of the tenth anniversary of Lithuania's independence, he proclaimed a new clause in the Lithuanian constitution, recognizing Vilna as the capital of the state.

Yet not all of Voldemaras's colleagues approved of his fire-breathing politics, and he was not so successful as were some other dictators in liquidating his opponents. He was foolish enough to quarrel with President Smetona, who now proved himself the stronger and more popular leader. In September 1929, Voldemaras resigned. In July 1930 he was banished to the country, and in August 1930 the Iron Wolf was dissolved. In September 1929 a new government was formed by Tubelis, Smetona's brother-in-law. Some effort was made to follow a milder policy toward Poland. By the early thirties the situation was much improved. But at that time it was not Vilna and Poland but Memel and Germany which absorbed the foremost attention of the Lithuanian Government.

FINLAND

The Finns inhabit a northern country of lakes and forests resembling a greater Minnesota. They are a people of many accomplishments, especially in music, architecture, and physical culture. Their land is poor, but they have great hardihood and enterprise. Like the Swiss, Czechs, Serbs, and Irish, they nourish a long tradition of revolt. In December 1917 they threw off fifty years of subservience to Russia, and the Finnish Diet proclaimed the independence of the country.

But the type and style of government in Finland were not decided without bloodshed. The Russian Soviet recognized the independence of Finland with apparent alacrity, but it was soon supporting a Finnish Socialist Workers' Republic which seized power in Helsinki at the end of January 1918. General von Mannerheim, a Swedo-Finn, formerly of the Russian Imperial Army, organized a White Guard and, with the help of a German contingent, drove the Soviet forces out of Finland.

These four months of fighting in the early part of 1918 were afterward called the Finnish War of Independence. But they cost the Finns 24,000 lives and left a trail of embitterment and class hostility behind them. A subsequent "White Terror" is said to have claimed 10,000 victims. German intervention was symbolized by the election of Prince Frederick Charles of Hesse as King of Finland and, but for the Armistice of November 1918, the country must soon have been reduced to a military and economic outpost of the Reich.

In December 1918 the German forces were withdrawn, and General von Mannerheim temporarily assumed the regency. Finland thence entered upon a phase of constitution building and of acute party strife, but she eventually appeared in formal democratic guise and, in July 1919, was declared a republic. The Treaty of Dorpat (Tartu) in October 1920 defined her Russian frontier. She renounced her claims to Eastern Karelia; the Soviet renounced its claim to Petsamo, which became Finland's ice-free port on the Arctic Sea. The long quarrel with Sweden over the Aland Islands was referred to the League of Nations, and in June 1921 the League Council awarded the islands to Finland, but later added the important stipulation that they should not be fortified.

For the remainder of the twenties, the main problems of the young republic were domestic and, in many ways, they were not unlike those of other succession states in Europe. The Swedo-Finns presented the inevitable minorities and language problems. Legislation passed in 1927 marked the beginning of a comprehensive agrarian reform and, by the late thirties, it was estimated that one family out of every three owned the land it tilled. An experiment in prohibition followed much the same course as that in the United States. On the whole, the interwar years were promising and prosperous, the people were at peace with themselves and with their neighbors, and the world had good reason to expect well of Finland — until, once more, she became a frontier outpost in a new conflict of European power politics.

13 THE MIDDLE DANUBE: THE NEW AUSTRIA, CZECHOSLOVAKIA, AND HUNGARY

THE MIDDLE DANUBE

In 1914 Austria connoted an aggregation of nationally diverse territories grouped round a German core, including Czech Bohemia and Moravia, Polish Galicia, and Italian and Slavic regions to the south. She was one of two autonomous halves of the Dual Monarchy, jointly ruled by Francis Joseph I of Hapsburg-Lorraine, Emperor of Austria and Apostolic King of Hungary. Even at that time it had become customary to speak of the "ramshackle Hapsburg Empire." Emperor, aristocracy, bureaucracy, army, and Catholic Church made a five-pillared structure, once beautifully interbalanced like a system of Gothic arches, but since crumbling with time. Francis Joseph, in 1914, was old and about to lay down a life which had been a succession of misfortunes. The German bureaucracy of Austria, tolerably efficient and incorruptible, had been extended in recent years to meet the innovations of a progressive century, and it was now not only overstaffed but staffed to an increasing degree with non-German personnel. In the country at large, non-German languages had been legalized. Experiments in parliamentarianism had adulterated the exclusiveness and the authority of the old order. The subject nationalities recked nothing of German organization, Austrian benevolence, or Hapsburg romanticism. They would rather govern themselves than be governed well. Half a dozen Irelands were in revolt against a Power which had nursed them for generations. New political parties, the Christian Socialists and the Social Democrats, made fresh fissures in the already complex strata of the state. In 1918 this conglomerate and divided realm at last broke into its elements. The new Republic of Austria emerged, with a quarter of Imperial Austria's population and with rather less than a quarter of her territory.

In 1914 the second half of the Monarchy, the proud and ancient Kingdom of Hungary, occupied the great plains in the very heart and center of the Middle Danube. Her frontiers had existed, with only minor variations, for nine hundred years. As a self-conscious unitary state she was older even than England or France. But here too the ethnic pattern was not simple, and it is doubtful whether at any time the great plains had been inhabited by a single Magyar folk. The Turks had retired, leaving waste spaces which were often replenished by non-Magyar colonies. In 1914 the "ruling" race of Hungary, the Magyars, amounted to only half the population then included in the Hungarian frontiers and, not only round the periphery of the Kingdom, but deeply penetrated into the great plains, were numerous outcroppings of Germans, Slovaks, Rumanians, Croats, Serbs, and Ruthenes.

The Magyars themselves were a people whom it has been the custom to vilify. In 1914 their hitherto romantic land of horsemen and gypsies, of fine wines and rhapsodies, had come to be portrayed abroad as one of the most ruthless nationalist tyrannies in Europe, a country where a caste of landowners lorded its power over lesser breeds of men, where a "superiority complex" was a national affliction, and where there flourished a chauvinism that had to be seen and, even then, could hardly be believed. The view was doubtless exaggerated. But it is a fact that, in the Hungary of 1914, one-third of the land was owned by less than a hundred great families, that the Hungarian Diet in Budapest was elected almost exclusively from the Magyar squirearchy, and that a policy of "Magyarization" was being pressed with increasing harshness upon the non-Magyar minorities in the country. It is also a fact that the Magyar national character was singularly egoistic, insular, and unyielding. In 1918, Hungary shared the collapse of the Central Empires, a short-lived republic was set up in Budapest, and nearly three-quarters of her lands were wrested from her. Of all the defeated belligerents of the First World War, the proud and ancient kingdom suffered the most humiliating loss.

THE NEW AUSTRIA

At the end of the war, in November 1918, the Austrian people hoped to begin their political life afresh, freed of the burden of the past and freed of all legal connection with the Hapsburg Empire that had been dissolved. They represented themselves to be as truly new as any of the "succession states." Republicanism was in the air, and the Social Democrat elements in Austria strongly desired to be united with the new republican Germany. On November 12, 1918, the Provisional National Assembly in Vienna, consisting largely of Austrian Social Democrats of the former Austrian Reichsrat, issued a declaration to the effect that "German Austria is a component part of the German Republic." The Allied Supreme Council in Paris categorically quashed these optimistic pretensions and insisted that it was dealing with a defeated belligerent and a relic of the former Austro-Hungarian Empire. Democratic Austria was born into the interwar world with an unwanted birthright and in an environment of guilt and intimidation.

Elections for a Constituent Assembly took place throughout Austria early in 1919 and resulted in the return of a small Social Democrat majority. The Communists, contrary to expectation, made no showing at all. In March 1919, Dr. Karl Renner, a Social Democrat, became Chancellor. He represented his country at St. Germain-en-Laye and put his signature to the treaty of peace (see p. 125). A democratic constitution for the new state was completed and promulgated during 1920. Austria took the form of a federal republic of nine provinces, each with its local Diet. The federal legislature at Vienna was a bicameral body, with a president, chancellor, and ministry in accordance with the usual democratic pattern of the day. In December 1920, Austria was the first of the nonoriginal states to be admitted to the League of Nations.

But no formal description of the constitution, elections, and governmental changes can give the real story of the Austrian Republic. That story is rather one of hunger, humiliation, and hopelessness. The German remnant of a once extensive empire was reduced to a demoralized capital city and a truncated, inadequate hinterland. The residue of ancient charm and culture, arts and music — "the wistful romance and nostalgic legend" — this heritage of great days was a sorry husk in a life that had become weary and futureless. The Treaty of St. Germain wrote the inexorable finis, not only to imperial glory but even to an economically wholesome existence, and its ratification crushed the spirits of those Austrians who, in the revolutionary excitement of November 1918, had persuaded themselves that some kind of national reconstruction and recovery was still possible.

Since the Peace Conference of Paris, a great deal has been written on the subject of the "viability," the *Lebensfähigkeit*, of states. Many factors can bring a state into being and make it "viable" — for instance, a dynasty, a military campaign, an economic need, a popular revolution, even an idea. But Austria's whole rationale seemed to have disappeared with the fall of the Hapsburg Monarchy. Political union (*Anschluss*) with Germany was forbidden her. A Middle Danubian customs union was never made possible. For the new Austria there was nothing left but an all-pervading negation of purpose. If she was now to continue to exist at all, she was to do so at the behest and in the interest of a group of Powers who refused to let her die.

Descending from these generalities to the specific facts, we find an Austria in 1919 and 1920 in the extremity of social and economic hardship. The repeated army requisitions of the war had impoverished the land; conscription had depleted the resources of labor. Public utilities, roads, railroads, electricity, and water supplies were suffering from four years of progressive disrepair. Fuel was scarce, whether for commercial or for domestic uses. Industries which were dependent on coal were at a standstill. The return of the defeated armies from the front took place in the midst of the political disorganization. For weeks, in 1919, the country swarmed with soldiers of many nationalities demobilizing themselves, and with prisoners of war releasing themselves, all ransacking the shops and farms, trying to find their way back to their homes on congested roads or on broken-down railroads. Impromptu levies of troops, especially in the rural areas, claiming authority to maintain law and order, often enough were fighting among themselves. While the city of Vienna tried to feed and house its thousands of refugees, its own citizens were scouring the countryside hawking any portable article they could lay their hands on for a loaf of bread or a pint of milk. Outside Austria lay the ring of the new succession states, already reinforcing their frontiers with prohibitive tariffs, and beyond them again lay the ring of the victorious Allies maintaining, with occasional grudging charities, the rigors of the wartime blockade.

The financial situation was fantastic. The shadow of debts and reparations hung over everything. The government in Vienna continually exerted itself to relieve unemployment by spending money it did not possess. During the first three years of the Austrian Republic, the state revenues were less than half its expenditure, and the expenditure could not have been described as lavish. A few people with the right kind of property or the right kind of wits speculated feverishly, especially in foreign exchange. The total result was inflation, and then more inflation. The huge middle class of Vienna — the official, the *rentier,* the professor, the urbanized absentee land-lord, the artist, the writer — was reduced to pauperism. What cultured life survived — and it is surprising how much survived — did so by the mere force of tradition.

In 1914 the Middle Danube had had a single currency and a single customs union. Industrial Austria in many ways had complemented agricultural Hungary. The Dual Monarchy, with all its faults, did constitute a logical economic unit. Now the Middle Danube was divided into a number of "succession states," each one of which seemed to be motivated by a long-repressed hatred of "Austrianism." In the pride of their new-won independence these states adopted a policy of economic self-sufficiency, or autarchy as it was sometimes called. States which were preponderantly agricultural built up industries at uneconomic cost; states which had been developing industries were forced to revert in part to agriculture; and in either case they protected themselves by mutually ruinous tariffs. New fears and hatreds distorted even those problems to which an elementary common interest should have pointed obvious solutions, and every fresh mistake or provocation, instead of being a lesson, only aggravated the difficulties that had caused it. Restrictions on foreign trade in the Middle Danube, and even on foreign travel, at times, could not even be excused as protective, and looked more like punitive measures, reciprocally increasing.

To be sure, Austria retained within her reduced frontiers a good deal of valuable industrial equipment, not to speak of the acquired skill of her workers. She still had extensive resources, such as iron ore, salt, timber, sugar, and wheat. But extensive as these were, they competed at a hopeless disadvantage in an environment whose chief economic principles were egoism and vindictiveness. She had to import the fuels with which to reduce her ore; her agriculture produced only 40 per cent of her food requirements. Within the city of Vienna itself were crowded 2,000,000 citizens, a third of the population of the Austrian Republic. Services, industries, and a complex bureaucratic apparatus, once designed for an empire, were now an expensive liability. Vienna was like a staff without an army, a board of directors without a company, a head without a body. In their determination to show their independence of the city which had once held them in thrall, the succession states had withdrawn their banks and their places of business. Czechoslovakia, for example, made it illegal for a Czech firm to maintain a head office in Vienna. The old Austro-Hungarian Bank was slowly and painfully liquidated.

A distressing feature of postwar Austria was the division that arose between the city and the country, between the "Reds" and the "Blacks," as the parlance of the time described it. For not only did the succession states put themselves in irreconcilable antagonism toward Vienna, but so also did the very provinces of Austria. At the end of 1918 many of the provinces had set up their own administrations. The municipality of Vienna at the time was only one of several provincial Diets. The federal constitution of 1920, mentioned above, recognized the situation and in some ways legalized it. And the party system in Austria reflected it. There were two main parties, the Social Democratic party which, as elsewhere, was essentially the party of the urban workingman, and the Christian Socialist party [1] which, despite its misleading name, was the "Conservative" party, the party of the peasants — and of the Catholic Church.

But this division had further implications. The Austrian Social Democratic party derived a good deal of support from the Jews, notably the Jews of Vienna; many of the party's leaders were Jews; and the Jews constituted a "problem" in Vienna and Austria, a problem which, in less concentrated form, appeared in other Central European countries. They numbered a fifth of the total population of Vienna, and they were in virtual control of its commerce, law, education, medicine, journalism, literature, fine arts — and, of course, its Social Democracy. With curious inconsistency, one class of Jews seemed to embody the very spirit of capitalism, and another class seemed to embody the very spirit of socialism and revolution. In old Austria, a proverbially polyglot land, the Jews might have been counted as just one of many minority groups, except that they had so deeply penetrated the urban life of the state and were even less assimilable than other nationalities. To the Social Democratic party they gave that doctrinaire intellectualism and anticlericalism so characteristic of the Socialist parties of Continental Europe. By contrast, the Christian Socialist party was deeply Catholic, anti-Semitic, and afterward inclined to Fascism. The antagonism between these two parties, and between all they stood for, was the theme that was to run through the whole of Austria's interwar political history.

THE AUSTRIAN *ANSCHLUSS* MOVEMENT

Union (*Anschluss*) with Germany might have been one solution of Austria's "viability." But it is difficult to estimate the strength of the *Anschluss* movement. Such as it was, it always lay under an interdict, and it was never tested by a free vote. On the whole, the Social Democrats favored the *Anschluss*. They at first regarded it as Austria's natural and inevitable course, so long as the Germany with which they desired to be united was herself socialist and democratic, and they believed that the new principle of self-determination in Europe should assure it to them. The Christian Socialists, who had inherited all the old Austrian distaste for Prussian Germany, were indifferent or adverse.

At all events, any hint of an *Anschluss* was always frowned upon by the Allies, especially by France, ever watchful of any accession of strength to their defeated enemies. In a clause in the Treaty of Versailles, Germany acknowledged the independence of Austria as "inalienable, except with the consent of the Council of the League of Nations." The Treaty of St. Germain prescribed complementary conditions. The succession states, Czechoslovakia, Yugoslavia, and Rumania, which were afterward allied in the Little Entente, would have regarded the *Anschluss* almost as a *casus belli*. Italy was always fearful of it. Popular agitation in Austria in favor of the *Anschluss* continued in spite of these summary prohibitions, though the agitation usually took innocent "cultural" forms. Successive governments in Vienna did what they could to suppress any too inconvenient outbursts of self-determination. Later Allied loans to Austria were always coupled with some sort of anti-*Anschluss* proviso which threatened the direst consequences if the movement were not kept under control.

THE LEAGUE LOANS

Chancellor after chancellor in Austria struggled with the financial situation. They seemed always to be begging from one European capital to the next for loans and commercial treaties. In 1921, Britain, France, and Italy agreed to suspend their claims on Austrian reparations. But conditions did not improve. In May 1922, Ignaz Seipel became Austrian Chancellor. He was one of the most remarkable men of the interwar era in Central Europe. He was a Catholic priest, a man of unworldly learning and ascetic life. He cut a strange, detached figure in the seething modern world of politicians, diplomats, and bankers. Yet he was just as shrewd in temporal affairs as they. He entered public life through the Christian Socialist party, and gradually became its recognized leader. His appointment as Chancellor signified the eclipse of Social Democracy and the beginning of the conversion of the Austrian Republic to a clericalized authoritarianism.

For the next seven years the political history of Austria, in great part, is the history of Seipel's financial program. In 1922 he appealed to the Allies, then holding a reparations conference in London, and the Allies finally referred the whole case of Austria's finances to the League of Nations. Between the London meeting and the League's meeting, Seipel visited Prague, Berlin, and Verona. At Verona he went so far as to propose a currency and customs union with Italy, offering to accept the "protection" of Italy in return. Beneš of Czechoslovakia, unwilling to tolerate any such newfangled Italian *Anschluss* or the further penetration of Italy into the Middle Danube — of an Italy, moreover, just then going over to Fascism — at once came out strongly for a League loan to Austria. Seipel's maneuvering had not been without astuteness.

At a later date the League organized financial help to other states, but in 1922 the appeal to the League on Austria's behalf was an original, unexpected move. No one till then had ever considered the League's possible usefulness in the field of international finance. The League Council set up an Austrian Committee at Geneva, and in October 1924 the Geneva Protocols were signed, under which Austria was granted a loan of 650,000,000 gold crowns (nearly $130,000,000), guaranteed in the main by Britain, France, Italy, and Czechoslovakia. A Committee of Control was set up in Geneva, and a Commissioner General was sent to Vienna to supervise the disbursement of the sum on the spot. Austria undertook drastic retrenchments, established a virtual financial dictatorship, and of course once more pledged herself "not to alienate her independence . . . and to abstain from any negotiation or from any economic or financial engagement calculated directly or indirectly to compromise this independence."

The Geneva Protocols gave a quietus to the *Anschluss* movement for a time. Germany for her part had other pressing concerns, and the movement received little encouragement from her side. But the Protocols did improve the condition of Austria. The necessary retrenchments were put in hand. A legion of supernumerary state employees, to the number of 80,000, many still uselessly surviving from the old imperial bureaucracy, were pensioned off or dismissed. A new bank of issue, the Austrian National Bank, was set up. Exchange was stabilized, and foreign capital began to be attracted to Vienna. The Social Democrats abused Seipel for selling his country to the Allies. They pointed to the fact that unemployment showed little diminution, and that strikes were as frequent as before. But elections in October 1923 resulted in no big changes in party strength and were considered to have confirmed Seipel's policies. In 1924 the budget was balanced for the first time, the feeling of stability returned, and in 1926 the recovery of Austria seemed to be so far advanced that the League control was withdrawn.

Seipel, in or out of office, continued to be the moving spirit in all these events. His career corresponds in some ways with that of Stresemann. At the end of 1924 a serious injury, caused by an attempt to assassinate him, forced him to retire from active politics for a time, but his work was carried on by a faithful disciple, Dr. Ramek. Seipel was reappointed Chancellor in November 1926, and held office till April 1929. He died in August 1932.

Yet Austria's recovery was more apparent than real. The exchange and the budget may have looked well on paper, but they did not mend the fundamental weaknesses of the new state. Vienna was still the overgrown city, parasitic on a reduced and hostile countryside. The conflict of worker and peasant still kept breaking out. The old practice of raising private levies of troops, a practice which we have noticed in the rural areas just after the Armistice, became a matter of very serious concern during the second Seipel administration, especially as it was evident that urban and rural forces tended to coalesce into two main opposing camps. In the later twenties, an urban Social Democratic Schutzbund and a rural Christian Socialist Heimwehr, both well armed, well officered, and well trained, were engaging in bloody forays. As we shall see in another chapter, the government, far from suppressing them, seemed to provoke the one and encourage the other by leaning more and more on the Heimwehr.

But the further conflict of these groups, and of both with Nazism, and the final engulfment of Austria in an *Anschluss* she did not bargain for must be left for future chapters.

CZECHOSLOVAKIA

The name "Czechoslovakia" had none of the euphony and romance of "Bohemia," yet this graceless hyphenation represented for many brave and promising years one of the more successful creations of the Peace Conference. The Czechs were the dominating group in the new partnership. Their history had been cast in heroic mold, and their future bade fair to be as glorious as their past. They were an energetic, virile people, trained in the hard school of national revolt, and worthy, if any people were worthy, of the supreme reward of freedom. Their new state concentrated within its borders diverse and abundant resources. Its soil and industries, its mines and forests yielded a wealth above average. Its affairs were in the hands of men of force and distinction who enjoyed unbounded respect abroad. Czechoslovakia was fortune's favorite in the Middle Danube.

The new state was forged amid the usual difficulties of its time. It was first proclaimed in Paris on October 18, 1918 and established by a bloodless uprising in Prague on October 28. The two then existing Czechoslovak "governments" — that of the Czechoslovak National Council in Paris under Masaryk, Beneš, and Stefanik, and that of the patriot leaders at home under Kramář — were merged without friction. Masaryk became the first President, Kramář Premier, and Beneš Foreign Minister of a Provisional National Government at Prague.

Unsettled conditions prevented the early framing of a constitution, and not till February 1920 was the constitution finally enacted. The National Assembly was to consist of a Senate and a Chamber, elected by universal suffrage. The President of the Republic was to be elected by the Assembly for a term of seven years. There was a marked resemblance to the Constitution of the United States. Meanwhile the state finances were put in order. Native Czech banks and businesses came out of the war in a surprisingly sound condition. Czech financial leadership was courageous, and the population showed its spirit by its willingness, even eagerness, to accept risks and sacrifices. Czechoslovakia cut loose from the old Austrian currency, and from 1919 she adopted a monetary unit of her own, the Czech crown.

From the first, political parties were numerous, as might be expected in a country of diverse elements — thirty to forty distinct parties made their appearance in the four elections between 1920 and 1935. There were crises, many crises — religious crises, agrarian crises, tariff crises, exchange crises, minority crises — which gave point to the party tangle. Nevertheless Czechoslovakia showed a more hopeful "viability" and a more stable equilibrium than many a state of older and simpler composition. One steadying factor was doubtless the old Bohemian official class, which had survived from prewar days and which now became the cadre of a new civil service. A second steadying factor was the tendency of successive coalition governments to swing more and more toward conservatism. A third steadying factor was that the country possessed for so long one president and one foreign minister. Masaryk, President in 1918, was re-elected in 1920, 1927, and 1934. He resigned in December 1935, and died in September 1937. Beneš, Foreign Minister in 1918, was reappointed through fourteen changes of government, till December 1935, when he succeeded Masaryk as President. A fourth steadying factor was the pronouncedly democratic outlook of the nation as a whole, irrespective of party.

The new republic's fundamental economic problem, like Austria's, was the development of industry within a circle of hostile nationalisms. Czechoslovak agriculture was not contemptible; the state was nearly self-sufficient in basic foodstuffs; Moravia, Slovakia, and Ruthenia were almost wholly agricultural provinces. But the wealth of the country, by international standards, lay in industry. If Czechoslovakia was now to prosper, as her leaders and her people were determined she should prosper, she would have to become a manufacturing country. Her economy would depend on the import of raw materials and the export of finished goods. In a wisely ordered world, Czechoslovakia would have been a little England and the exemplar par excellence of free trade. In the world as she found it, Czechoslovakia became another bastion of tariffs and quotas.

But Czechoslovakia showed great energy and enterprise, and between 1920 and 1930 she probably signed more commercial treaties with foreign states than did any other country. In particular she made the most of her popularity with her former Allies; she developed a decided "Western orientation," ignoring by comparison the now unstable markets of the Middle Danube, and she sold the best and the most of her textiles, glass, and shoes to Britain, France, Italy, the Americas — and Germany.

In interwar Europe a primary domestic problem was agrarian reform, especially in those new revolutionary states where a radical regime had supervened upon an older aristocracy. The peace, it was ardently hoped, would be a peace of many emancipations and would be a glorious opportunity to redress the centuries-old history of peasant oppression in Central and Eastern Europe. In Czechoslovakia, agrarian reform was an integral part — Masaryk himself used to consider it the greatest achievement — of the Czech revolution. The new Czechoslovak Government indeed had hardly been six months in existence when, in April 1919, it passed a law for the expropriation of the big landed estates. Former crown lands were to be expropriated without compensation; other lands were to be expropriated with compensation, but the compensation was to be paid in the new Czech crowns at the prices obtaining in 1914. The land so acquired would then be sold on easy terms to hitherto landless peasants and exservicemen.

The anti-Catholic reaction of the early interwar years had no direct connection with the agrarian reform, but it was unfortunate that the two should have had to come at the same time. Anticlericalism in itself was no novelty in Czechoslovakia, or at least in Bohemia, albeit the majority of Czechs were good Catholics. Yet the memory of the reformer, John Huss, was traditional to Czech nationalism. In the old imperial days Czechs had always considered that there had been too many German bishops in Bohemia, and in Czech eyes the evident alliance of Pope and Hapsburg had never reflected on the good name of either. Now in 1919 the ecclesiastical estates at long last were to fall to the ax of the law, and the Church was to be treated like any other overswollen landowner.

In 1920 a "National" Czech Church seceded from the Roman Catholic Church and put forward, among its articles of belief, the abolition of the celibacy of priests, the celebration of the mass in Czech, and civil marriage and divorce. There were attempts to secularize education, and in 1924 members of the government participated in the anniversary celebration of Huss's martyrdom. The Vatican took affront, as indeed it was meant to do, and severed diplomatic relations. A compromise was reached in 1928, and Vatican-Czech relations were resumed. The old diocesan boundaries were redrawn to coincide with the new political frontiers, and it was agreed that, in future, only Czechoslovak citizens should be nominated to Czechoslovak bishoprics. The religious controversy blew over, but not until considerable harm had been done, especially — as shall be explained — in regard to Czech and Slovak good-fellowship.

THE CZECHOSLOVAK MINORITIES

Czechoslovakia, the model republic, democracy's stronghold, labored under the same burden of divided nationality that lay so heavily upon the entire Middle Danube. In 1921 a population of 13,600,000 consisted of 6,570,-000 Czechs, 2,190,000 Slovaks, 3,123,000 Germans, 747,000 Magyars, 459,000 Ruthenes, 76,000 Poles, 180,000 Jews, and 255,000 others defying ethnical definition.

Czechoslovakia's minority legislation was liberal, well intentioned, and a good deal gentler in operation than that of other succession states. On the whole it conformed with the letter and the spirit of the Czechoslovak Minorities Treaty of 1919 (see p. 133). By law all nationalities had the right to use their language for official and legal business in the areas where they predominated, and they had the right to their own schools. But in practice there was discrimination, especially against the Magyars, the most hated of the minorities. Military action in 1919 had been necessary to expel the Magyars from Slovakia, and the campaign had done much to set the tone of Czech and Magyar relations thereafter.

The Ruthenes of "Sub-Carpathian Ruthenia" were related to the Ukrainians — "Ruthene" was a corruption of "Russian." They were mountaineers, living in a remote corner, a hardy folk not greatly endowed with the blessings of civilization. Up to 1914 they were the obedient clients of Hungary. During the First World War they were almost forgotten, though the Tsar at one time had some notion of annexing their territory to the Ukraine. At the Peace Conference no one took much interest in them, and they were finally joined with the Slovaks in the new state of Czechoslovakia. They were promised "the widest autonomy," but never achieved it. On the whole they seem to have accepted without protest the arrangements made for them. They were always quite untroublesome.

Between Poles and Czechs the main bone of contention was Teschen (see p. 174). The original proposal at Paris in 1919 that this much-disputed territory should be divided between its claimants by means of a plebiscite was allowed to lapse, and the final disposition of it was drawn up in 1920 by the Conference of Ambassadors. Most of the old town and the industrial equipment went to Poland, and most of the mines to Czechoslovakia. Neither side was satisfied. The Poles thereafter nursed a grievance and argued that the settlement had been extorted from them while they had been otherwise distracted by the Russo-Polish War. Altogether a minority of 76,000 Poles were incorporated into the new Czechoslovakia round about Teschen and along the Czechoslovak-Polish borders.[2]

The Germans in Czechoslovakia, especially the Sudeten Germans, so called after the Sudeten Mountains along the German-Bohemian frontier where numbers of them lived, were treated by the Czech Government with almost calculating favor. Never was a minorities treaty so scrupulously observed as in their case. But the hatred of Germans and Czechs was one of the oldest nationalist hatreds in Europe, long predating the nationalist movements of the nineteenth century, and it would have been surprising if, in their everyday unofficial relationships, friction between the two populations had not occurred. The Germans objected particularly to the constitution of 1920, which they claimed had relegated them to a minority status, and they objected to the Czech Government's foreign policy in the matter of the alignment with France and the formation of the Little Entente. Finally, if these questions were not enough, there was always a source of trouble in the schools.

But in these early years no minority raised such serious difficulties as did that other component people of the republic, the Czech's own blood brothers and copartners, the Slovaks. Though so much alike in race and language, Czechs and Slovaks seemed to be at odds in almost every other attribute which makes for national unity. Their past histories had been separate, and with the best will in the world they could not suddenly be brought together. The Czechs had formerly lived under the relatively enlightened Austrian rule; they were men of the modern era; they needed no instruction in the liberal way of life; they assumed at once the rank of democratic people and an international Power. But the Slovaks had lived under the harsher Hungarian rule, they had become a backward and docile peasantry, and they now emerged for the first time from generations of servitude. The visions of the peacemakers and state-makers of 1919 must have been sadly disappointed when it was discovered that there was not a sufficient number of educated Slovaks to staff a local civil service or officer a Slovak army contingent. Masaryk had Slovak interests much at heart — he himself was a Slovak from Moravia. But generally, in the prewar years, the few Slovaks of education and progressive spirit belonged to that very class which had been most readily Magyarized, and these Slovaks now, instead of wanting to collaborate in the work of a united Czechoslovak state, were clamoring for a return to the old Hungarian allegiance. Their natural economic link was with the Hungarian plain, and formerly had always been so. Finally the Czechs were Catholics, but with a strong trait of anticlericalism and free thought; the Slovaks were Catholics of simple, unquestioning, medieval faithfulness. The religious and agrarian controversy, just mentioned, had profoundly revolted Slovak sentiment. Father Hlinka, leader of the Slovak People's party, at one time agitated for complete severance from Czech rule.

Masaryk and the Czech leaders, there is every good reason for believing, were genuinely grieved and embarrassed to have gone back on promises of regional autonomy which had been made to the Slovaks during the war. The French furthermore used their influence against the decentralization — and the consequent weakening — of a state which was to become an important ally in Central Europe. The central Czech Government in Prague, for several reasons therefore, found itself compelled increasingly to assume responsibility for local Slovak affairs and to send into Slovakia a veritable army of Czech officials, Czech police, Czech teachers, and Czech businessmen. In 1914 there were said to be 7,500 Czechs in Slovakia; in 1921 there were ten times that number. The Slovaks watched the Czech "invasion" with growing resentment and, by the end of the twenties, felt they had become subjects of a nationalist persecution as oppressive as any they had endured in the old Magyar era.

THE NEW HUNGARY

Of all the postwar revolutionary regimes, Karolyi's in Hungary must surely have been the most pitiable. Count Michael Karolyi himself was an aristocrat of advanced socialist views. He was a mixture of naïve, humanitarian optimism and consuming personal ambition. During the latter part of the war, he had founded a party advocating severance from Austria, collaboration with the Allies, and acceptance of a Wilsonian peace. Traditionally in Hungary, none but the titled could aspire to political eminence, and the new party was doubtless glad enough to find a ready-made count willing to assume its leadership. Thus in November 1918, Karolyi became the nominal Premier of a Hungarian People's Republic, with a cabinet composed of Socialists and members of his own party. His War Minister was Béla Linder, the man to whom has been attributed the famous pacifist remark, "I want to see no more soldiers!"

Karolyi's troubles began when he discovered that his good will was lost on the subject nationalities of Hungary. Czechs, Yugoslavs, and Rumanians wanted their freedom and were resolved to take it, and without them Karolyi's Hungary would be a rump of its former territorial limits. He discovered too that his peaceful professions had not gained him the favor of the Allies. He had rejected the Austro-Hungarian armistice of Padua because of the severity of its terms, believing he could negotiate better with General Franchet d'Esperey, commander of Allied forces in Salonika, who had now established himself at Belgrade (see p. 105). The General is said to have greeted Karolyi's delegation with the remark, "I did not believe a man could sink so low!" and then had imposed on him terms far worse than those of Padua. The new armistice had not even delimited the areas of occupation by foreign troops, and Czechs, Yugoslavs, and Rumanians were soon taking advantage of the elasticity thus afforded them to push their own prospective frontiers even more deeply into the rich lands of Hungary.

In January 1919, Karolyi formally assumed the presidency of the Hungarian Republic. He promised elections to a constituent assembly, but the promise could not be fulfilled. The assembly could have been representative only of the shrinking territory he now administered and, by inference, it would have "recognized" that territory's extent as a final settlement. Ka-

rolyi also promised sweeping agrarian reforms and made a start by distributing his own private estates of 50,000 acres among his tenants, but it was as
far as he was able to go. In fact, in the four months that Karolyi held office,
no single item of his once ambitious program was translated into practice.
The real power of the moment passed more and more into the hands of the
Bolshevik Workers' and Soldiers' Councils which were then growing up in
Budapest. On March 19, 1919, by order of the Allied commander at Belgrade, Karolyi was instructed to allow the occupation of the whole of Transylvania by Rumanian forces. This was the end of Karolyi. He resigned the
next day, and soon afterward disappeared into exile.

On Karolyi's departure the Workers' and Soldiers' Councils took control
and, with their support, Béla Kun set up a Soviet Republic in Budapest.
Béla Kun was a middle-class Jew, successively a reporter, a secretary of a
workers' benefit society, a soldier, a prisoner of war in Russia, a friend of
Kerensky and of Lenin. He had returned from Russia at the end of November 1918, a trained professional revolutionary, deputed by the Third
International to foment Bolshevism in Hungary. Normally he should have
found the stoniest soil for his seed, and it is doubtful if even in the Hungary
of 1919 his ultimate influence spread much beyond the streets of Budapest.
The peasantry, for all their grievances, were never very deeply touched by
"these scoundrels from the city."

Béla Kun followed the usual Communist program — control of the press,
nationalization of banks and industries, expropriation of the land, and secularization of education. But, for all his terrorism and revolutionary zeal, he
could not conjure away the dread economic and military realities. Budapest
was nearly starving, and the armed forces of the Allies and of the succession
states still laid siege to the country's frontiers. In April 1919 the Allied Supreme Council sent General Smuts to treat with Béla Kun — a strange conjunction of personalities — and, not surprisingly, General Smuts returned to
Paris to advise the Supreme Council to wash its hands of Hungary for the
time being.

But a counterrevolutionary movement was already organizing. The old
Magyar lords of Hungary, bewildered and scattered by the collapse of 1918,
were slowly recovering their self-possession. In May 1919, Count Julius Karolyi (a distant cousin of the luckless Count Michael), Count Bethlen, Admiral Nicholas Horthy, and others of their ilk raised their standard at
Szeged in the French occupied zone, formed a national government, and
began to recruit a national army.

In July 1919, Béla Kun sent his "Red Army" against the Rumanians in
Transylvania. Perhaps he was currying popularity in Budapest by thus attacking the most despised and hated of Hungary's enemies; perhaps, like
other dictators, he sought to use a foreign war to forestall domestic crisis.
But the "Red Army" was signally defeated, and the Rumanians began to
counteradvance into the heart of Hungary. Within a month Béla Kun was in
flight, and King Ferdinand of Rumania was making his triumphal entry
into Budapest. Rumanian troops "confiscated" Hungarian property, grain,
fodder, rolling stock, and agricultural machinery, protesting that they were

recouping themselves for the similar spoliation of their own country by the Austro-Hungarian and German invaders of 1916. They advanced as far as Lake Balaton, while trainloads of their booty streamed back to Rumania. It was not till November that the Allied Supreme Council at last induced them to withdraw to the line they had occupied before Béla Kun's foolhardy and provocative attack.

On November 16, 1919, Admiral Horthy reached Budapest at the head of the new national army. He was received with hysterical rejoicings and, what was of more immediate importance, he was received with something like "recognition" by the Allies in Paris. Even so, peace was not restored at once. A disorderly White Terror beset the country, far worse than the worst terrorism it had experienced under Béla Kun. Patriotic gangs, such as the "Awakening Magyars," tortured and murdered at will. Some 300 to 400 adherents of the former regime, mostly Jews, were "executed." Hungary had the melancholy distinction of having created the prototype of Fascist and Nazi squadrism.

Yet, after all the blood and tears of the past months, Hungary — and Europe no less — must have sighed with heartfelt relief to see installed a stable government in Budapest, albeit it was the rule of the old Magyar magnates in its most conservative form. The Allied Supreme Council intimated that it would accept the credentials of the new government, and early in 1920 a Hungarian delegation was sent to receive the Allied peace terms. Elections were held in Hungary for a National Assembly, and large reactionary majorities were returned. The government proclaimed that Hungary would remain a kingdom, though without a king, and on March 1, 1920 the new Assembly elected Admiral Horthy "Regent."

The signing of the Treaty of Trianon has been described elsewhere (see p. 126). It was ratified in Budapest, in an atmosphere of protest and crisis, in December 1920. In respect of its territorial terms, it was the severest of the European peace treaties, and the Hungarian people were never reconciled to it. Hungarian "revisionism" became a popular cause more insistently pleaded and more empoisoning to international relations in Europe than even the revisionism of the Treaty of Versailles itself. "No, no, never! (*Nem, nem, soha!*)" was a rallying cry overriding all the lesser causes of party, class, and creed.

At the end of March 1921, Charles, King of Hungary and former Emperor of Austria, left his exile in Switzerland, crossed the Hungarian border, and eventually reached Budapest by automobile, accompanied by a few supporters. His arrival there was entirely unplanned and unannounced. He had acted perhaps from misinformation and flattery, and had counted too much on the loyalty of monarchist elements in the Horthy regime. Horthy, good monarchist though he was himself, was placed in a most painful dilemma. He could only refuse to hand over the government to its new claimant without the consent of the National Assembly. Fortunately there was no popular outburst to complicate the situation. France, Italy, and Britain, in a joint note, protested that a Hapsburg restoration contravened the solemn assurances of the Hungarian Government and must jeopardize the very basis of peace. Hungary's neighbors, Czechoslovakia, Yugoslavia, and Rumania, threatened a military demonstration. Charles returned once more to Switzerland.

It is characteristic of dispossessed royalty to cling to lost causes. Far from taking his rebuff to heart, Charles redoubled his efforts at restoration, and a considerable monarchist movement was soon afoot in Hungary. In October 1921, Charles made a second attempt, this time with better preparation and this time in the company of his consort Zita, who was probably the real inspirer of the adventure. He reached Budaors, a few miles from Budapest, where he encountered some government troops under a Major Gömbös sent to oppose his progress.

Czechoslovakia, Yugoslavia, and Rumania again threatened a military demonstration. It was obvious that if Charles persisted in his course he would precipitate a general intervention of foreign Powers in the affairs of Hungary, perhaps with the accompaniment of civil war. He could only beat another retreat. But he refused to sign his name to a legal abdication, and he determined to remain a king, even a king in exile. Nor would Switzerland now give refuge to the royal truant. On November 1, 1921, Charles and Zita left Hungary aboard a gunboat of the British Danube Flotilla. Under diplomatic duress the Hungarian National Assembly passed a law permanently excluding the Hapsburg succession in Hungary. The monarchical form of the state was maintained, the Regent was still Regent, but "the election to the throne was adjourned." Charles was eventually taken to Madeira, where five months later he died. Zita continued to live abroad, but neither she nor her sons ever renounced the hope of an eventual Hapsburg restoration.

Count Bethlen became Hungarian Premier in April 1921, shortly after Charles's first attempt to regain the throne, and he remained in office for ten years. His administration was thoroughly reactionary. He was induced only with the greatest difficulty to recognize the trade-unions and grant freedom of speech, of the press, and of public assembly. Proposals for agrarian reform were whittled down almost to nothing. A new electoral law, depending upon intricate restrictions as to residence and education, eliminated all voters but the acceptable members of the squirearchy; the abolition of the secret ballot in the rural districts had the effect of disfranchising the peasant masses. In 1926 the National Assembly created a second chamber which virtually resurrected the Table of Magnates, the upper house of the old Magyar nobles in the days before the revolution of 1918. All in all, Hungary passed through a decade of historical stagnation. Magyar feudalism, in its fundamentals, remained unchanged. Such revolutionary activity as there was took Fascist forms. The "Awakening Magyars" or the "Defenders of the Race," led by men like Major Gömbös, had much in common with concurrent political developments in Italy. Bethlen sufficiently indicated his own views by appointing Gömbös Minister of War in 1929 and promoting him to the rank of general.

In his foreign policy Bethlen sought manfully to assuage the unrelenting suspicion of his country's neighbors. The Burgenland was a bone of conten-

tion with Austria (see p. 125); the Hapsburg question, so dramatically revived by Charles's own restorationist activities, was the bone of contention
with the lesser succession states. The formation of the Little Entente between
Czechoslovakia, Yugoslavia, and Rumania blocked all hopes of peaceful
treaty revision and seemed to condemn the country to perpetual diplomatic
isolation. Only in Fascist Italy could Bethlen find any signs of friendship,
for Mussolini had his own good reasons for disliking the Little Entente. In
1927, Hungary and Italy entered into a treaty of amity and arbitration.

THE LITTLE ENTENTE

The foreign policy of Czechoslovakia, as of all the succession states, reduced itself to the preservation of the peace settlement which had called her
into existence. From Austria, Czechoslovakia had little to fear so long as the
Anschluss remained a moribund issue. Austria was as weak and ineffectual a
unit as the map of the Middle Danube could show, and French and Italian
vigilance could be depended on to keep her in that condition. But the proud,
tyrannous, monarchical Magyar, who forgot nothing and learned nothing,
presented a more serious problem, and Czechoslovakia was shortly concerting with Yugoslavia and Rumania for a very explicit alliance against Hungary and for the uncompromising maintenance of the Treaty of Trianon.
Conversations between Czechoslovakia, Yugoslavia, and Rumania — even
then under the driving initiative of Beneš — were already taking place at the
end of 1918, and continued thereafter during the Peace Conference at Paris.
The first convention between Yugoslavia and Czechoslovakia was signed at
Belgrade in August 1920, the Treaty of Trianon being at that time hardly
two months old. Further conversations between the three states might well
have been dilatory had they not been jolted into urgent activity by Charles's
attempts to regain the Hungarian throne. The diplomatic repercussions now
were emphatic and precise. A convention between Rumania and Czechoslovakia was signed at Bucharest in April 1921, and a convention between
Yugoslavia and Rumania was signed in Belgrade in June 1921. All three
conventions were alliances of mutual assistance, similarly worded, to go into
effect in the event of an unprovoked attack upon a signatory on the part of
Hungary.[3]
Czechoslovakia's relations with the greater Powers are discussed in other
chapters. But we may remark in passing the essential inclination of Czech
policy at all times toward France. America, for all her whilom patronage
of Masaryk, had retired from her European entanglements; Britain, though
to a lesser extent, had done likewise. France remained to the young republic
the main author and guarantor of its existence. France, anxious to multiply
her outposts about Germany, had always reciprocated Czech advances; she
had stood encouragingly in the background while the links in the Little
Entente had been forged; and she had then entered separately into agreements with each of the three states in the system. In January 1924 she concluded an alliance with Czechoslovakia, in June 1926, with Rumania, and
in November 1927, with Yugoslavia.

14 THE BALKANS: "BALKANIZATION"

AND UNION

THE BALKAN PENINSULA AND ITS PEOPLES

The Balkan Peninsula derives its name from the formidable chain of mountains which stretches across its eastern part. It is the termination of Southeastern Europe, and it extends to, and includes, Peloponnesian Greece. To the south and west, the Balkan barrier is reinforced by the Rhodope and Shar mountains and the Dinaric Alps. Through these clusters and chains of mountains a few rocky passes and river valleys lead down to Greece and to the sea. The rivers for the most part are not navigable, but the valleys of the Maritsa, the Struma, and the Vardar give greatly prized highways to the Aegean Sea; the Drin and one or two lesser rivers have outlets on the Adriatic Sea; and farther south still, Greece and its equally precipitous mountains are divided in two by the beautiful Gulf of Corinth. The landward boundary of the Balkan Peninsula is commonly equated with the great river route of the Danube and Sava, but Rumania north of the Danube is regarded as a Balkan state. An interesting and historically significant fact is that the Danube is not a natural frontier. It invites rather than repels invasion. To make matters worse, mountains on the Balkan side of the Danube slope gently northward, whereas to the south they fall away steeply, and they therefore make a far more effective military barrier against an army of conquest coming up from the Aegean Sea than down from Central Europe or from the Middle Danube. The proverbial separatism of the Balkan countries, as well as the relative isolation of the various communities within those countries, has been fostered by the fact that they are all more readily accessible from the Danube or the sea than they are accessible to each other.

At once a barrier and a corridor, the Balkan Peninsula for centuries has been the crossroads of two continents and the great land route from Central Europe to the Near East. Not without good reason was it called the "turbulent Balkans." Anciently it was absorbed into the Roman Empire, and then into the Byzantine Empire. The southern branch of the Slavs (South Slavs) filtered into it at the beginning of the sixth century A.D., to be followed a hundred years later by the Bulgars. The Slavs were Indo-Europeans, and the Bulgars were Mongols; but the Bulgars settled long enough to become Slavicized, unlike their brother birds of passage, the Huns and Avars, who re-emigrated and disappeared. During the early Middle Ages, the South Slavs filled the Balkan Peninsula to overflowing, except for the Hellenized coasts and cities, which they left to their Greek inhabitants. The peoples into whose midst they injected themselves either became Slavicized, which was the fate of the Dacians, who mingled with the Carpathian Slavs and the Hungarians and then emerged as the Rumanians; or they were crowded up into the rugged and infertile highlands, as was the fate of the Illyrians, who survived as the Albanians. Gradually four distinct groups of South Slavs were formed. The Bulgars were the most easterly of the four. The Serbs held all the central living space north of Greece, and they established the states which survived until the First World War under the names of Serbia, Bosnia, and Montenegro. The Croats occupied the west, and the Slovenes the extreme northwest.

In the fourteenth century the Ottoman Turks, a Central Asiatic horde, converts to Islam and the last of the historic Oriental empire builders, began the conquest of the Balkans. In 1389 they destroyed a great Slav army under Serbian leadership at the famous Battle of Kossovo (see p. 12). Ultimately they took Constantinople, which they made their capital, and laid siege to Vienna. The whole of Southeastern Europe bore their yoke until their gradual recession between the seventeenth and twentieth centuries. As we approach our own time, the Balkans become a theater of conflicting interests between three great Powers — namely, the still declining Ottoman Empire and the two rivals for its vacated possessions, Austria-Hungary and Russia. In that theater was played the prologue to the First World War.

All this was deeply written into the ethos of the South Slavs. Their history and strategic position cleft them between the forces of East and West. Those of them, like the Serbs and Bulgars, that had been longest subservient to the successive Byzantine and Ottoman empires and had inherited thence a Greek Orthodox or Moslem tradition were intrinsically Balkan. Those, like the Croats, that had been converted to Roman Catholicism and were culturally linked with Italy, Austria, and the Middle Danube, were intrinsically non-Balkan. Some, like the Bosnians and Albanians, were inextricably divided. Thus the Bosnian landowning nobility was converted to Islam; the Bosnian peasantry was Greek Orthodox in the east and in Hercegovina, and Roman Catholic in the west. Minority clusters in the Albanian highlands were Moslem and indelibly Orientalized.

The boundaries of these Slavic nations, before and after the Ottoman period, and even during it, never ceased to fluctuate, and in recent times confusion was worse confounded by the wholesale "bartering" of territories at the behest of the greater European Powers. The former Bulgarian and Serbian empires waxed and waned, and their frontier populations almost made a habit of changing their political allegiances. Bosnia, whose princes or kings remained independent throughout the Byzantine period, alternately shrank or expanded to the east or the west in compensation for territorial losses to Serbia or to Hungary. Slices of Croatia were occasionally incorporated in Bosnia. The outstanding example of changing status was that of Macedonia, the trapezoid area of land in the core of the Balkan Peninsula upon which Bulgaria, Serbia, and Greece converged. In the tenth and again in the thirteenth century, Macedonia was a part of the First and then of the Second Bulgarian Empire; in the fourteenth century, it belonged to the Serbian Empire of Tsar Stephen Dushan; in the intervals, it was parceled out between both nations. By the nineteenth century, when nationalism became the cult of Europe, the Slavicized Macedonians hardly knew to what national group they rightfully belonged.

The modern problem of Macedonia dates from 1870, when the Macedonians began to be subjected to intensive Bulgarian propaganda. The revived Bulgar (Orthodox) Church at the time was trying to emancipate itself from the Greek Patriarch. Not to be outdone, the Serbs and the Greeks thereupon loosed rival propaganda campaigns in the districts of Macedonia contiguous to themselves and, in each case, religious propaganda automatically became part of political irredentist activities. From then onward, the Macedonian problem became increasingly acute, and a politically nonexistent "Macedonia," which was still under Ottoman rule, was the chronic objective of three competitive nationalisms. In 1893 the Internal Macedonian Revolutionary Organization, known as the IMRO, was founded by Macedonian patriots for the purpose of liberating Macedonia from the Ottoman Turks. It was an extra-legal organization of armed desperadoes, and it survived into modern times as little more than a quasi-professional band of terrorists, but at first it was honestly fired by nationalist loyalty. By 1903 Macedonia had become so engulfed in anarchy that the Ottoman Sultan was forced to agree to its international policing. The whole story of Macedonia is not untypical of this restless corner of the world.[1]

In 1878 the Congress of Berlin had sought to finalize Balkania's fluctuating geography (see p. 5). It effected another "bartering" of peoples and territories — Russia took the rich province of southern Bessarabia from Rumania, and Rumania was compensated for the loss by the acquisition of the southern Dobruja, which in turn was taken from Bulgaria; and the Bulgarians were put under three different administrations. At the same time, the Congress recognized the complete independence of Rumania, Serbia, and Montenegro. The Greek people had won their independence, with the help of the Great Powers, earlier in the nineteenth century and had become established as a kingdom.

From time to time, especially in the eighties, the "stability" created by the Congress was rudely shaken, but frontiers stood fixed for thirty years, a period remarkably long by Balkan standards. After 1908 the borderline Balkan territories began again changing and rechanging hands. Croatia, Bosnia, Macedonia, Bessarabia, the Dobruja — to say nothing of Thrace, Istria and Dalmatia, Transylvania, and the Banat, with their respective disputatious histories — were all variously carved and chopped up by the revolutions, wars, and settlements of 1908, 1912–13, 1914–18, and 1939–45. Bulgaria achieved her independence in 1908, and Albania in 1913.

DEMOCRACY, FASCISM, AND ECONOMICS IN THE BALKANS

In the interwar years from 1919 to 1939, the Balkans, like the Middle Danube, became for a time a laboratory of self-determination. The treaties of St. Germain, Neuilly, and Trianon in 1919 and 1920 hopefully drew up a new and "definitive" Balkan map. The frontiers followed the contours of language and nationality fairly accurately on the whole, though some

areas were too far gone in complication for even the most disinterested dis-
entanglement, and some unhappy minorities had inevitably to be stranded
on alien soils. Bulgaria, the twice-defeated member of the Balkan confra-
ternity, felt herself to have been deliberately penalized by the treaties and
was left to nourish her revisionist grievances in bitterness and isolation.

Quasi-democratic governments with a full panoply of parliamentary forms
functioned during the twenties in all Balkan countries. But democracy in
the Balkans was at best an experiment. No general democratic tradition, no
sufficient education, no adequate middle class — except perhaps in Greece —
existed. The historical background, whether before, during, or after the
Ottoman period, had been habitually autocratic. Each of the Balkan governments soon found ways of acquiring a majority of seats with a minority
of votes, and sooner or later all relapsed into some form of dictatorship.
Kings and courts and armies of somewhat Ruritanian luster came into their
own again, often with popular acclamation. Thus dictatorships were set up
in Yugoslavia in 1929–31, in Bulgaria in 1935, in Greece in 1936, and in
Rumania in 1938. Albania, whose short-lived republic had been converted
into a "limited" monarchy, would no doubt have followed suit if Italy's conquest of her in 1939 had not settled the outcome in advance.

One modern ideology was conspicuously absent in the Balkan countries.
Fascism was alien to them all. Even afterward, the Nazi tyranny sat unnaturally upon them. Balkan kings and generals found no place for Fascism in
their lands, and there was no strong, class-conscious bourgeoisie, with or
without economic grievances, to support such a movement. There was only
narrow bureaucracy above and widespread poverty beneath. The great peasant majorities that formed 75 per cent of the Balkan population were indifferent, individualistic, or communal in a primitively family sense. They
were determined to hold what little of personal freedom they had always
known and cultivate their meager acres in peace. Like all peasants their
views were grimly practical, and they were more interested in crops and
taxes than in doctrines.

As in Poland and the Middle Danube, the agrarian problem was acute.
The Balkan countries were all overpopulated. Even where the large estates
were broken up and parceled out, as in Rumania and Bulgaria, there was
never land enough for the increasing masses of impoverished and landless
people. The average agricultural holding was between seven and ten acres.
The demographic situation, combined with the depredations of terrorist
groups, the intense political animosities, and party jobbery infinitely aggravated the task of politicians who were still inexpert in the arts of democratic
rule. Inevitably the doors of any Balkan government were open to the
"strong man" and aspirant dictator.

All the agricultural countries of Southeastern Europe suffered from the
discrepancy between agricultural and industrial prices. The stark poverty
of the peasant population always contrasted with the garish, vicious luxury
of the capital cities. Foreign credit was scarce and costly, and the purchasing
power of the currencies was generally low. The lack of political security
frightened off potential investors from abroad. Yet there was also much foreign exploitation, chiefly by Germany who, even before 1914, regarded the

Balkans as part of her economic sphere of influence and a requisite corollary to her *Drang nach Osten*. The balance was redressed with protection and "fighting tariffs," or with import quotas. Yet two of the Balkan countries were potentially rich. Yugoslavia had a wealth of mineral resources, largely untapped; Rumania was the granary of the Middle Danube and produced more oil than the rest of non-Russian Europe.[2]

In this connection, one chronic Balkan problem should be mentioned. Under the Treaty of Versailles certain European waterways were internationalized (see p. 124). The European Commission of the Danube, originally set up in 1856 for the administration of the Danube Delta, was reinstated, all enemy Powers were expelled therefrom, and a new International Commission was created. The Delta was administered as formerly by the European Commission, and the river above the Delta was administered by the new International Commission. Through this dual medium the riverain states represented on the two commissions were to provide uniform civil, commercial, sanitary, and veterinary regulations for the navigation of the Danube from Ulm to the Black Sea. Certain portions of the river's tributaries were internationalized. Lastly, by the Definitive Statute of the Danube of June 30, 1922, navigation on the Danube system was declared to be "unrestricted and open to all flags, on a footing of complete equality."

YUGOSLAVIA

In June 1917, during the First World War, representatives of Serbia, Montenegro, and the South Slav provinces of Austria-Hungary signed the Pact of Corfu, declaring their intention, upon the coming of peace, to erect a single, democratic nation under the Karageorgevich dynasty of Serbia. In October 1918 a Yugo-Slav (South Slav) National Council was established at Zagreb. In November the National Assembly of Montenegro deposed the Montenegrin King Nicholas and proclaimed the union of Montenegro with Serbia. Prince Alexander of Serbia accepted the regency of the new state. By the constitution of 1921 the Kingdom of the Serbs, Croats, and Slovenes, later to be known as Yugoslavia, became a unitary, constitutional monarchy, with a unicameral parliament based on manhood suffrage.

This composite kingdom included the former Serbia and Montenegro, and the former Austro-Hungarian provinces of Croatia-Slavonia, Dalmatia, and Bosnia-Herzegovina, together with a part of the Banat of Temesvar, the Voivodina, and a part of Bulgarian Macedonia. As we said above, the main rift was between the forces of East and West. Almost half the population were Orthodox Serbs, and rather more than a third were Catholic Croats and Slovenes. Orthodox and Catholic had followed separate histories and were as temperamentally dissimilar as Northern and Southern Irishmen. They spoke much the same language, but typically the Serbs used the Cyrillic alphabet, and Croats and Slovenes used the Roman. Yet all three nationalities were of the same blood, they were born and bred in hardy, mountainous country and, though so often subject to conquest and despotism, they remained fiercely independent and intractable. Illiteracy was their most serious handicap, and their meager political education made them an easy prey to corruption and crooked electioneering.

The new kingdom suffered under one grave geographical disability. It had no good outlet to the sea. The creation of Albania in 1913 had denied to Serbia a coastline on the Adriatic, and Albania had thereafter fallen under strong Italian influence. An essential part of the port of Fiume was ceded to Italy, under circumstances which are described elsewhere, and the subsequent Italo-Yugoslav agreement of 1924 had confirmed the arrangement (see pp. 294–95 and 296). Zara was Italian. Salonika, Yukoslavia's "natural" commercial and strategic outlet to the Aegean Sea, was Greek. Between 1923 and 1925, the Greeks provided Yugoslavia with a "free zone" in Salonika, but there were persistent disputes over dock dues and railroad facilities. In 1924 Yugoslavia caused a minor crisis by denouncing the old Greco-Serbian alliance, which Greece herself had formerly failed to uphold (see p. 34). It was not until 1929 that the issues were ironed out. But Yugoslavia continued to be a relatively landlocked state.

Domestically, the foremost problem of the new Yugoslavia was the reconciliation of her diverse racial elements. It is sufficiently indicative of the situation to say that Yugoslav cabinets averaged three a year; in the ten years after the constitution of 1921, only two cabinets remained in office as long as eleven months. The Croats always complained that they had failed to secure in the new state even that degree of autonomy they had enjoyed under Hapsburg rule. During the early twenties, Nicholas Pashich and Stephen Radich represented the two sides of the basic Serbo-Croat division. Pashich was a Serb imperialist who envisaged Yugoslavia as a Greater Serbia with a central capital at Belgrade. Radich was leader of the Croat Peasant party and advocated a loose federation with a separate Croat capital at Zagreb. For some years, Radich boycotted the parliament and refused to participate in the nation's political life. But in 1925, Radich accepted the significant post of Minister of Education, and a temporary *rapprochement* between the two contestants was achieved. Then in 1926, Pashich died. In June 1928, Radich was shot during a debate in the Skupshtina (the Yugoslav national assembly), and the Croat Deputies, withdrawing in a body, set up their separatist "parliament" at Zagreb.

The defection of the Croats and the breakdown of parliamentary government led not unnaturally to a royal dictatorship. King Alexander progressively centralized the power in himself, and his rule was legalized by the new constitution of 1931. A single party, the Government party, was imposed upon the country. A new bicameral national assembly was set up. But nearly half the Senators of the upper house were royal appointees. The lower house was elected by direct manhood suffrage, though by open ballot. And, if this was not enough, a final safeguard lay in the provision that the constitution could be suspended "whenever the public interest is generally menaced." The Serbo-Croat division for the time being lay under royal interdict.

King Alexander is one of those men whose stature increases with the passage of time. He was the second son of King Peter of Serbia. He was educated in Russia at the court of the Tsar and served in the Serbian Army in the wars of 1912, 1913, and 1914. He was heir apparent to the Serbian crown when he became Regent, and then King, of Yugoslavia. He was a scholar by inclination and, differently born, would doubtless have followed an academic career. Happier circumstances might have made him a model constitutional monarch, rare in his or in any royal Balkan family. He devoted his life quietly and unobtrusively to smoothing party and factional friction. He was himself responsible for the personal reconciliation of Pashich and Stephen Radich in 1925. In his good hands Yugoslavia might have become unified and have gone forward to a great future. But in October 1934 he was assassinated by Croat terrorist exiles at Marseille, while on his way to Paris. The story of the consequences of this tragedy, however, we shall defer to a later page (see pp. 488 and 533).

ALBANIA

Yugoslavia's closest neighbor on the Adriatic was Albania. As a modern state, Albania dated from 1913, after the conclusion of the Balkan wars. Its population included Orthodox Christians, Roman Catholics, and Moslems. During the First World War, it escaped partition by a hairsbreadth. In June 1917, Italy declared a protectorate over it. During Italy's weak pre-Fascist phase in 1920, the protectorate was withdrawn, but Italy never abandoned her semi-imperialist, semipaternal interest in the country.

The interwar history of Albania centers round the figure of Ahmed Bey Zogu, a national hero of the First World War and founder of a revolutionary dictatorship in the first years of peace. In 1924 he was driven into exile, but returned to mount the rungs of power — Commander in Chief, Premier, and President. On September 1, 1928 he assumed the title of Zog I, King of the Albanians. In his time, Zog introduced a Westernizing program — roads, bridges, public works, public health, schools, legal codes. But the financial backing throughout was Italian. In November 1927 a twenty-year defensive alliance between Albania and Italy was signed at the Albanian capital, Tirana. The Albanian Army was Italian trained. By the thirties Albania, to all intents and purposes, was again becoming an Italian protectorate.

GREECE

Greece would have started the first interwar decade in a much stronger position had she not become involved at such serious cost in the Turkish War of Independence, the fuller story of which we had best relegate to our chapter on Turkey (see p. 224). We have already described the establishment of Venizelos's revolutionary pro-Ally government in 1917 and the deposition of King Constantine in favor of his second son, Alexander (see p. 65). Three years later, in October 1920, Alexander died as the result of blood poisoning from a monkey's bite, and his death was the signal for a popular revulsion against Venizelos's pro-Allied policies. Venizelos was defeated at the polls, and King Constantine — the allegedly pro-German Constantine of the First World War — returned from exile in triumph. France and Britain had supported Greece as long as Venizelos, their special protégé, had been in power; but they were now glad enough to wash their hands of a people so troublesome and inconstant. The Greeks were then in the midst of their war with the Nationalist Turks. So successful had they been in their opening campaigns in Turkey that they had overreached themselves. Initial victories had inspired them to push far into the interior of Anatolia. But they were stopped just short of Angora and then suffered one heavy reverse after another, culminating in their defeat at Smyrna and expulsion from Anatolia (see p. 226).

King Constantine abdicated for a second time, and the army took control in the name of his eldest son, George. Five of Constantine's ministers expiated with death the disaster at Smyrna. On May 1, 1924, Greece was proclaimed a republic. Paul Kondouriotis, veteran Venizelist, became Provisional President. The work of drafting a new constitution was interrupted by a one-day dictatorship of General Pangalos, and the constitution was not promulgated till September 1926. Venizelos eventually became Premier, and he held office through Greece's Locarno era, from 1928 to 1932. In 1935, King George returned. Greece was then in the doldrums of the Depression, and she slipped by inevitable stages into the dictatorship of General Metaxas.

One unusual problem in Greece during the early twenties was the "return" of over a million Greek refugees from Asia Minor, after the Turkish war, under the Greco-Turkish compulsory exchange-of-population agreement of 1923. Simultaneously some 100,000 Greek refugees arrived from Bulgaria and Soviet Russia. These refugees raised the total population of Greece to 6,000,000. It was feared, at first, that they would prove a serious political and psychological liability. But financial assistance was forthcoming from the League of Nations and from private donors in America, and the transplanted peoples were not only absorbed into their new homeland but added considerably to its demographic and economic strength. They brought new industries — for example, the Anatolian carpet industry — and they brought new blood and energy. One curious result of the compulsory exchange of population was that Greece was unique among the new European nations in having virtually no minority problem.

BULGARIA

Bulgaria faced the interwar world with handicaps that were shared by no other Balkan Power. She had been defeated in the Second Balkan War of 1913. She had been defeated in the First World War and was saddled with the Treaty of Neuilly, with all its losses of territory and demands for reparations. Unredeemed Bulgarian populations were left subject to Rumania in the Dobruja and to Greece and Yugoslavia in Western Thrace and Macedonia.

Bulgaria had a further grievance, namely the loss of access to the Aegean Sea. A free port was offered her at Dedeagach (Alexandroupolis), comparable to the Yugoslav Free Zone at Salonika. But the offer was rejected by her on the ground that such a port would be useless to her unless the surrounding territory were effectively neutralized. In other words, Bulgaria requested a right of way which should be under international administration, but that right of way would then have had to be carved out of the Greek territory of Western Thrace, and there seemed to be no way of compensating Greece for the resultant loss. Except for outlets on the Black Sea, Bulgaria remained a landlocked state.

Bulgaria, thus contemned and crippled, suffered a psychological and political revolution. The pro-German interventionists of 1915 were discredited, and Stambulisky, "the peasant dictator," was carried to a domestic victory on the shoulders of his Agrarian party. As Premier he initiated many radical reforms. His consuming interest was the land, and he envisaged a sort of South Slav federation ruled by democratic, peasant governments (see p. 213). He gave high-ranking appointments in his administration to men of peasant origin, and naturally he antagonized the nonagricultural 20 per cent of the Bulgarian population.

In the end, Stambulisky's conciliatory foreign policy cost him his life. He tried to collaborate with his country's old foeman, Yugoslavia. The Macedonian Revolutionary Organization, the IMRO, joined forces with the professional classes and the army in a general revolt against him and his Agrarian party. He was assassinated in a *coup d'état* in June 1923, and a violent anti-Agrarian, anti-Communist campaign broke out. The IMRO virtually dominated Sofia, and for some years Liapchev, himself a Macedonian, was Premier. Officially the pacific foreign policy of the previous Agrarian government was continued, but the activities of the IMRO, both inside and outside Bulgaria, were so scandalous that peaceful relations with Yugoslavia and Greece were continually threatened.

Boris III succeeded his exiled father, the Tsar Ferdinand, in October 1918, after the First World War. He tried to rule constitutionally according to his lights. But even in Stambulisky's time there was little of the democratic spirit in his realm. After Liapchev, a series of reactionary governments ended, as usual, in 1935 with a royal dictatorship.

RUMANIA

Rumania had entered the First World War in 1916 on the Allied side under pledges of extensive acquisitions in the event of victory (see p. 62). The pledges were duly honored, and Rumania emerged from the peace settlement more than doubled in area. From the former Austria she received Bucovina; from the former Hungary she received territories including Transylvania and half the Banat of Temesvar; from the former Russia she received Bessarabia. Her frontier with Bulgaria reverted to its position in 1914 — which, in Bulgarian eyes, had the effect of giving her a part of the Bulgarian Dobruja. No other belligerent of the First World War had been so proportionately enriched. But the new territories brought her the enmity of the dispossessed nations, they brought her more than the usual quota of minority problems, and they brought her economic readjustments resulting from the territories' new Rumanian orientation. There was considerable friction between the "new province" Rumanians in these territories, and the "old kingdom" Rumanians.

However, throughout the twenties, the enlarged kingdom followed an interesting, progressive history. For the first few years, Rumania's internal politics were dominated by the famous Transylvanian agrarian leader, Julius Maniu, and his Peasant party. Agrarian laws from 1917 to 1921 broke up the old landed estates and distributed them among the peasants. The Conservative party, already discredited because of its pro-German affiliations, represented the landowning class, and it was further disintegrated by the execution of the agrarian laws. The Liberal party, representing business and banking interests, was in the saddle from 1922 to 1928, under the three Bratianu brothers, with a policy of centralization, national self-sufficiency, and the nationalization of forests and mines. The Liberals were partly responsible for Prince Carol's renunciation of his rights to the throne in December 1925 — for the sake of his mistress, Madame Lupescu. The Peasant party under Maniu succeeded the Liberals from 1928 to 1930. But Carol returned, the early promise of Rumania's interwar history was not maintained, and eventually, in February 1938, a royal dictatorship was proclaimed.

Both Peasant and Liberal parties were Francophile, and through the twenties Rumania followed a foreign policy of friendship with France and of strong adherence to the Little Entente (see p. 202). Like Poland she was ringed with potential enemies and occupied an international status far beyond her real strength. Significantly she was linked with Poland by a treaty signed in 1921 (see p. 176).

FOREIGN POLICY AND BALKAN UNION

The Balkans used to be an example of all that was most disruptive in modern nationalism, and "Balkanization" was a word to be applied derogatively to any situation where racial and sectarian divisions played havoc with economic expediency and political common sense. Yet Balkania often owed her divisions as much to the interference of rival Powers from outside as to her own inherent heterogeneity. In one sense, she had always felt a tendency toward union, once her nationalities were actively recalled to an awareness of their individual identities. The very political framework of the Ottoman Empire, in which these nationalities had once been severally submerged, gave them a superficial unity and, as soon as they began to thrust through the brittle Ottoman shell, their weakness — and their Christianity, various though its expression was — drew them inevitably together. Sporadically, through alliances and military treaties, they had looked to each other as well as to interested Powers for help against their common oppressor, the Turk.

One obstacle to Balkan union was Bulgaria. She had emerged from the Balkan War of 1913 and from the First World War a defeated, dissatisfied Power. She was the Hungary of the Balkans, an outcast and "have-not," penalized by treaties to which she could never become reconciled, surrounded by states themselves leagued together to prevent a peaceful revision of her grievances. The results of the Treaty of Neuilly in 1919 have been previously explained (see p. 126). We have also explained how Czechoslovakia, Yugoslavia, and Rumania had entered into a series of interlocking treaties, the Little Entente, for upholding the peace settlement in the Middle Danube, treaties which Bulgaria could only regard as an encircling chain to be endured under protest and under duress (see p. 202). It is to be remembered that, in this series, Yugoslavia and Rumania were also linked together against unprovoked aggression against them by Bulgaria. Bulgaria's alienation from wider Balkan interests and her intransigence, when Balkan union first came up as a matter of practical politics, were therefore not surprising, and her eventual *rapprochement* with her neighbor states during the early thirties was all the more remarkable.

Another obstacle to Balkan union might have been Turkey herself. But after the First World War, Turkey's position entirely changed. From being omnipresent in the domestic affairs of the Balkan nations and the enemy of their nationalist aspirations, Kemalist Turkey withdrew from every part of the Balkan national stage. With the dissolution of the Ottoman Empire, Turkey's role turned from that of oppressor to that of friend and collaborator. In 1930 she even became reconciled to Greece and thereafter was eager to respond to Balkan overtures and plans for economic and political co-operation, and to count herself a "Balkan State."

An active ideological force pressing for Balkan union was the movement for the unification of all the South Slavs. This movement was a somewhat incoherent and localized offshoot of the older Pan-Slav movement, and was often confused with it. Actually, two separate streams diverged from the common source of Pan-Slavism. The Russian Slavs cultivated an imperialist Pan-Slavism and would have subordinated South Slav interests to their own, whereas the Pan-Slavism of the Austrian and Balkan Slavs had in it the germ of confederation. It was among the Balkan Slavs that practical plans first emerged for the organizing of co-operation across national frontiers.

The more concrete forces making for Balkan union generally took three forms. The first was the growth of peasant parties and agricultural co-operatives; the second was the movement among the professional and industrial classes for inter-Balkan economic collaboration and, eventually, for political confederation; the third was the desire of the Balkan governments themselves for some sort of diplomatic instrument in the interests of stabilization and regional security.

In the days before the First World War, a Federation of Soil-Tillers had been organized in Bulgaria by Alexander Stambulisky, the Bulgarian "peasant dictator," whom we have already mentioned. Meanwhile two brothers, Ante and Stephen Radich, one a peasant writer and the other a brilliant orator, had founded the Croat Peasant party. Both organizations were built solidly, with an eye to future opportunities, in a spirit of quiet, determined optimism. Immediately after the First World War, Rumania followed suit; village schoolteachers and priests joined with a few intellectual idealists from the towns to found the Rumanian Peasant party, whose great leader, Julius Maniu, we have also already mentioned. Stambulisky thought the time ripe for a horizontal, Balkan-wide movement for peasant co-operation.

In 1920 he initiated an evanescent "Green International," which was to be neither capitalist nor Marxist, and tried to bring together all the South-eastern European peasant parties. Even the violent deaths of Stambulisky in 1923 and Stephen Radich in 1928 did not seriously interrupt the work to which they had given their lives; and after 1930 the peasant co-operative movement became imperceptibly a part of the larger movement for Balkan union.

Considering that about 75 per cent of the population of the Balkan Peninsula was agricultural, and that a large proportion of that population was likely to remain so indefinitely, no other type or form of "co-operation" could be more fitting. And when we note that this co-operation was not limited to mutual agricultural benefits, but extended deeply into the educational and cultural spheres, the movement bade fair to prove one of the most hopeful and constructive developments of the interwar period. Stambulisky clearly aimed at an agrarian democracy, based on a landowning peasantry, on free speech, free ballot, and as much equality of wealth as practicable, and his peasant-citizens would then be the common instruments for uniting the divided states of Southeastern Europe. A network of agricultural co-operatives would offer the advantages of large-scale enterprise, and yet would function through the individual peasant's holdings. For only a landowner, argued Stambulisky, could be really free. There would be no place for the middleman or trader, and the state would assume the control and ownership of essential public services only. Labor would be collectivized, but not property. The whole idea was congenial to the Balkan peasant, because in his memory lingered the tradition of the zadruga — a form of communal family life, depending on collective work, shared ownership, and mutual aid, and still surviving in remoter, more inaccessible regions of the Peninsula. The contrast to the Soviet collective farm is evident. The Balkan peasantry, for the most part, were always hostile to the Third International and its influence.

The initiative toward Balkan union, politically, was taken by Greece, ably seconded by Turkey. During the twenties every Balkan state signed a commercial treaty with its respective neighbors — with the single exception of Bulgaria — and most of the treaties contained clauses providing for neutrality and arbitration. Generally speaking, the twenties were remarkable for the progress of Balkan conciliation — always, again, with the exception of Bulgaria. Even Turkey and Greece signed a treaty of conciliation in 1930.

Geneva, by precept and example, contributed not a little to the growth of the fraternal spirit in the Balkans. The Locarno Pact, the Pact of Paris, and the Litvinov Protocol had their effect. The Little Entente was a model, very close to home, of co-operation between small states for objectives which any Balkan country could well appreciate. All this was duly read, marked, learned, and inwardly digested by a group of thoughtful Greeks, and in October 1929, at Athens, at a session of the Universal Congress of Peace, the Greek delegation proposed a permanent Balkan Entente. The guiding spirit behind the proposal was Alexander Papanastasiou, president of the Congress and a former premier of Greece. The First Balkan Conference, including Turkey and all the Balkan States — including even Bulgaria — was held in October 1930 in the Greek Chamber of Deputies in Athens. There was some derision from extreme Greek rightists and some denunciation from Communists. The two "unsatisfied" Balkan nations, Bulgaria and Albania, raised a procedural difficulty; they tried to insist upon a full discussion of the thorny problem of minorities; but they were outvoted by Greece, Turkey, Rumania, and Yugoslavia, acting on the advice of Venizelos, who suggested that the Conference should create a favorable atmosphere in the beginning by tackling first of all questions "on which agreement is easier to arrive at." Eventually machinery was set up for convoking annual Balkan Conferences, with a Permanent Council, Assembly, Secretariat, and six commissions for the study of special mutual problems. In fact, the Balkans was to have its own miniature League of Nations.

Four Balkan Conferences were held between 1930 and 1934 — successively in Athens, Istanbul, Bucharest, and Salonika. Conferences and membership were strictly unofficial and private; leading political personalities did attend, but governments as such did not participate, and no one was under obligation to ratify or implement a resolution. The educational and pacificatory value of the Conferences, however, was considerable, especially in a corner of the world notorious for its animosities. There were created a Balkan Chamber of Commerce and Industry, a Maritime Office, a Chamber of Agriculture, a Tourist Federation, a Commission of Jurists, a Medical Federation, and so forth, and as in the case of the League of Nations it was the ancillary organs which were often more productive in practice than the master body. The Third Balkan Conference of 1932 framed a "Draft Balkan Pact" of nonaggression and friendship, with detailed provisions for the pacific settlement of disputes and the protection of minorities. But the Balkan governments could not be persuaded to adopt this Draft Pact. In 1934, as we shall tell elsewhere, a Balkan Pact was signed, but the motivating purpose in the mid-thirties — in the Period of Crisis — was then very different (see pp. 528–31).

Political thinkers and statesmen have often pondered the problem of putting some sort of order into the crazy patchwork that is Europe. Some of their mooted schemes clearly served narrow, egoistic interests, some were as wide as humankind; some were regional, some embraced the Continent. Naumann's *Mitteleuropa*,[3] Pilsudski's Intermediate European Federation, Coudenhove-Kalergi's Pan-Europa, Briand's United States of Europe, Tardieu's Danubia, Hitler's New Order, and the recent Western European Union — to say nothing of analogies in other parts of the world, the British Commonwealth, the Soviet Union, the Arab League, the Pan-American movement, Japan's Co-prosperity Sphere — all have illustrated this deeply experienced need, so recurrent in our day, for larger political combinations. Whatever success Balkan union could ever have been expected to have, it represented at least a brave, constructive effort toward one such combination. In the words of Mustapha Kemal (Ataturk), at the notably successful Second Balkan Conference held in Istanbul, Balkan union must be thought of as "a natural consequence of the historical and national evolution of the Balkan peoples."

15 THE NEAR EAST: THE INDEPENDENT STATES

THE ISLAMIC WORLD AND THE OTTOMAN EMPIRE

The continents of Europe, Asia, and Africa meet and coalesce in the Near East,[1] a region lying between the Mediterranean, Red Sea, Persian Gulf, Caspian, and Black Sea, and therefore sometimes called the Land of the Five Seas. In ancient times it was the seat of great empires. Egyptians, Hittites, Assyrians, Persians, Greeks, Romans, Parthians, Byzantines, Arabs, and Turks ruled over it. It was probably more fertile once than now. It supported historic cultures and teeming populations. Four living religions originated there, the Jewish, the Zoroastrian, the Christian, and the Moslem. Mesopotamia and Egypt produced two of the oldest civilizations of which we have any knowledge; the Greek and Hellenistic world was the nursery of ideas that are alive today.

The Near East was traversed by important commercial and strategic communications, notably the ancient caravan routes, the Straits — the Bosporus and the Dardanelles — and the narrow neck of Suez. The sieges and captures of Constantinople, founded by the Romans on the ancient Greek site of Byzantium, have been key dates of history. The Suez Canal was projected by Egyptians and Romans, and by Napoleon, before it was successfully executed in our own scientific and engineering age. And caravan routes have crossed the Syrian Desert since man first domesticated the camel.

In character, the Near East and its inhabitants changed little through the centuries, and then only very slowly — till recent times. Men lived and labored, tilled their fields or watched their flocks, built their cities or pitched their tents, followed the same caravan routes, and fought the same battles for soil, water, and pasture, much as they had done since the days of Abraham. But by 1914 new wine was being poured into these very old bottles. Cities, often built on old historic sites, were showing modern European influence — Cairo, Alexandria, Beirut, Basra. Railroads were laid, or were being laid, from Belgrade to Baghdad, Aleppo to Medina, Cairo to the Cape. The trade of all the East flowed through the Suez Canal. Oil was discovered in Mesopotamia (Iraq), Persia (Iran) and, eventually in 1931, in Arabia. Since 1918 the Near East has become a network of motor roads, air routes, and pipe lines. And, even more important and disruptive, Western ideas, Western education, and Western concepts of nationalism have been seeping into the Near Eastern consciousness.

Perhaps the easiest, though not the safest, generalization to make about the changing Near East of our time would be to compare it with the breakup of the medieval system in the West and with the resulting emergence of nation-states — states which were dependent for their survival upon financial sophistication and an educated middle class. A process of economic and cultural interaction between the East and the West which had begun with the Crusades was now bearing fruit. The Near East, which until the twentieth century had remained essentially unchanged — a medieval economy with all that it implies — was being reopened to contact with the West. And the West which came once more to the East for cultural enrichment and economic gain was a social order that had itself been transformed. During the intervening centuries, the West (but not the East) had undergone fundamental social and economic changes in a series of commercial, industrial, and agrarian revolutions. How, then, could the modern phase of the impact of the West upon the East be unaccompanied by pain and by a kind of restless antagonism?

The Moslem religion dominated the Near East of our time. It was founded in the seventh century A.D. by the Arab Prophet, Mohammed. It was called Islam, meaning "resignation to the will of God." Its sacred book was the Koran, a series of texts originally enunciated by Mohammed while under an inspired trance and believed by Moslems to be the very living word of Allah dictated to His Prophet. Its Holy Cities were Mecca and Medina, where Mohammed lived, taught, and fought. It enjoined on the true believer five specific duties: bearing witness to the unity of the one God, Allah; reciting daily the prescribed prayers at the prescribed hours; giving legal alms; observing Ramadan, the annual month of fasting; and making the Pilgrimage, or Hajj, to Mecca once in a lifetime. During and after the seventh century, and after the total conversion of Arabia, the religion spread, mainly by conquest, westward along the Mediterranean littoral to Morocco — and, for a time, to Spain — southward into Central Africa, northward into Syria, Anatolia, and parts of the Balkans, and eastward into Mesopotamia, Persia, Central Asia, India, China, Malaya, and several islands of the East Indies.

In the later seventh century the Islamic world was split in two by a great political schism, the revolt of the Shi'a against the Sunni. The Shi'a (literally "the followers" of Ali, son-in-law of Mohammed, and thence also known as the Alids) repudiated the Sunni, who were the "orthodox" adherents of the first four caliphs or elected "successors" of Mohammed. In the ensuing civil war, Ali and his two sons were killed, and the Shi'a were defeated and became a heretic group. It was the great body of the "orthodox" or Sunni Moslems which established the historic caliphates, the temporal and spiritual empires of the Umayyad and Abbasid caliphs, with their capitals successively at Damascus and Baghdad, from the later seventh century to the mid-thirteenth. The schism between the Shi'a and Sunni was never healed, and a breach that had at first been purely political came to have religious connotations. To this day the Shi'a and Sunni are irreconcilable, and both groups furthermore are subdivided into numerous religious sects. Shi'a groups remained as islands in a Sunni sea in the North African or western parts of the Caliphate and in Syria; they also survived in Arabia, notably in the Yemen and in the Persian Gulf; but their great concentration of strength was in southern Iraq, and modern Persians are all officially Shi'a.

Clusters of the older Jewish and Christian communities in the Near East survived and were all given a special position in Islam, under Koranic law, as the "Protected Peoples," but they were little more than enclaves in the larger Moslem-dominated whole. The Maronites of the Lebanon, the Copts of Egypt, the Assyrians of Mesopotamia (Iraq), and the Armenians of Anatolia and the Levant were Christian minorities, each with a social and ecclesiastical organization of its own. The Jews — of several denominations — were to be found mostly in Syria, Palestine, Mesopotamia, Egypt, the Yemen, and Tunisia and, from the beginning of the sixteenth century, at Salonika and in eastern Anatolia. Jerusalem became a city sacred to Jews, Christians, and Moslems alike.

The Moslems themselves belonged either to the so-called Islamic "core" or to the "fringe." The "core" included Turkey, Syria, Palestine, Egypt, Arabia, Mesopotamia — namely, the territories within the former Ottoman Empire — and Persia. The "fringe" included the Moslems of Central Africa, Central Asia, the Soviet Union, India, China, and the East Indies. The Moslems of Libya, Tunisia, Algeria, and Morocco belonged successively both to the "core" and to the "fringe."

The Moslems of the "core" had always had a kind of historic unity. They had been fellow members of overlapping or successive empires, and they shared a common cultural inheritance. At one time or another — though not necessarily at the same time — they had known the same political superstructures, the same religious concepts, and many of the same linguistic influences. They had all been pagans, and they had all become monotheists. They were all at home in arid or in semiarid surroundings, and they enjoyed for the most part a common climate and the same types of flora and fauna. If there was one social distinction that could be made, it was between the nomad of the desert on the one hand, and the peasant and the town dweller on the other. The inhabitants of the desert were active, restless, chronically poor, but courageous and often aggressive. The inhabitants of the "sown," or settled lands, had some degree of sophistication and the beginnings of Western education. But all alike, whether Moslems of the desert or Moslems of the "sown," regardless of their varying levels of economic and political development, had had at some time similar habits and customs. They wore — until recently — similar clothes, and they possessed a comparable attitude to life and to work. The last is rather an elusive psychological point, but demonstrable nonetheless. A well-known British administrator, after a lifetime of experience in the East, once remarked that there was one sort of a brain under a hat, and quite another sort of a brain under a tarbush — and, he might have added, under a keffiya, the Beduin headgear.

The Ottoman Empire was the last of the great empires of the Near East. The original Ottoman Turks, so called after their first "national" chieftain, Osman, were a Central Asiatic horde who anchored themselves in Anatolia at the end of the thirteenth century. They subjugated the remains of the Byzantine Empire and made Constantinople their imperial capital. They conquered the Christian Balkans up to the "bend" of the Danube, including the trans-Danubian territories that were later to re-emerge as Hungary and

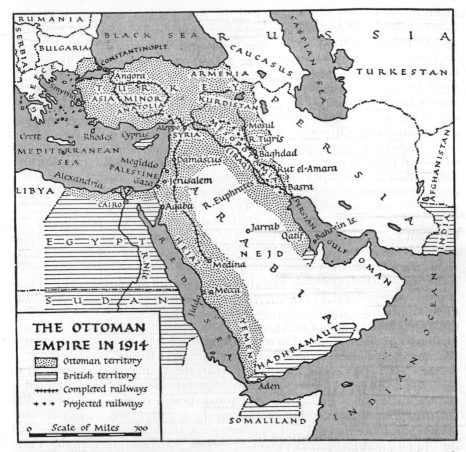

THE OTTOMAN
EMPIRE IN 1914

- Ottoman territory
- British territory
- ┼┼┼┼ Completed railways
- ◆ ◆ ◆ Projected railways

0   Scale of Miles   700

Rumania. They were themselves converted to Islam, and eastward their lands
were eventually coterminous with the great Moslem caliphates of the past.
After conquering Egypt, they claimed to be the protectors of the Holy Cities
of Arabia. In the sixteenth century, their Sultan assumed the title of Caliph,
"Successor" of the Prophet.[2]

At the end of the nineteenth century, the Ottoman Empire still lay across
the Land of the Five Seas — a great, sprawling giant whom many wishful
thinkers of the time called the Sick Man of Europe. A very sick man he was,
but one nevertheless who was unconscionably long a-dying and was still
capable of sudden revivifications. One such revivification was the revolt in
1908 of the so-called Young Turks of the Committee of Union and Progress.
The despot who then ruled Turkey, Abdul Hamid II, "Abdul the Damned,"
the last great Sultan of the Ottoman Empire, was overthrown, and the Turks
entered upon a course of political and social education along Western lines.
The revolt represented a general, if belated, renaissance of the Turkish
spirit, it paralleled the contemporary cultural movements then stirring
among the Arab subjects of the Ottoman Empire, and it was in many ways a
delayed reverberation of Europe's great age of enlightenment and of the

ideals of the French Revolution. But the Young Turk victory at home was soon overshadowed by military defeat, first at the hands of Italy, to whom, in the Tripolitan War of 1911, Turkey lost her North African province of Tripoli, and then at the hands of the Balkan peoples, to whom, in the Balkan wars of 1912–13, she lost almost all of her Balkan territory except a last small corner covering Constantinople, its immediate hinterland, and the Straits. But, even more fatal for the Ottoman Government, the domestic policies of the Young Turks lost them the allegiance of the Arabs, who were in a majority in the Ottoman Empire. The Arabs resisted all Young Turk efforts to assimilate them, and they repudiated the policy of Ottomanization contained in the new Pan-Turanian ideology, which sought to give Turkish nationalism a philosophy of racial flavor.[3] Repressive measures, naturally enough, only intensified Arab separatism and, as we have seen in 1914–18 (see p. 65), were to cost the Young Turks very dearly.

At the same time, Western capital and industry were penetrating the Ottoman Empire. Much of the enterprise was British and French; but it was also German and was inspired by the German ideology of the day — the *Drang nach Osten*, the German Drive to the East. Turkish loans were floated in Berlin; Turkish railroads were built by German engineers; the Turkish Army was remodeled by a German military mission. It was not surprising therefore in 1914, shortly after the outbreak of the First World War, that the Young Turks should make common cause with Germany. The Sultan, in alliance with the Young Turks, proclaimed a Jehad, or Holy War, against the encircling imperialism of Britain, France, and Russia (see p. 22).

During the years of the First World War, the Young Turks continued to press forward their domestic programs. Several reforms were introduced — the beginnings of civil and criminal codes, prison reform, and the partial emancipation of women. But the Young Turk regime was quite incapable of meeting the industrial and administrative challenge of "total war." All the old Oriental inefficiencies and corruptions flourished. In 1918 the Turkish armies were defeated, a humiliating armistice was signed at Mudros, and the discredited Young Turk leaders fled the country (see p. 104). The Ottoman Empire was dismembered. The first few years of a tortured peace were spent in bitter quarrels between the Sick Man's heirs apparent and other would-be inheritors. Yet a new Turkey, the only surviving blood relation of the many members of the departed empire, emerged at last, a nation as vigorous and progressive as its parent had been ailing and reactionary, a nation as compact and homogeneous as its progenitor had been unwieldy and composite — an alluring subject for the thoughtful historian, crowded as it is with suggestive contrasts.

ISLAMIC AND ARAB NATIONALISM

Islamic nationalism took a variety of forms and was crossed by several influences. Pan-Islamism and Pan-Arabism, for instance, which were so often confused, were entirely separate movements; and the former underwent a radical transformation after the abolition of the Caliphate in 1924. Before the Young Turk revolution of 1908, Pan-Islamism was preached by Moslem reformers of the time and was utilized by Abdul Hamid II for a double purpose: on the one hand, to unify the Ottoman Empire against the Great Powers; and on the other, to restrain the forces of liberalism and the nationalist aspirations of his own non-Turkish subjects. As long as Pan-Islamism was identified with Turkish rule, it was looked upon by the Arabs as a weapon for their exploitation. After the defeat of Turkey in the First World War, Arab nationalists were reluctant to organize a Pan-Islamic movement of their own because of its divisive potentialities; they were anxious to retain the support of the Christian Arabs, who had shared equally in the Arab national movement, and who insisted that politics could and should be divorced from religion. Furthermore, upon the advent of Mustapha Kemal (see p. 224), Turkey soon provided a noteworthy example of secular rule, and also demonstrated the fact that modernization was compatible with independence from foreign economic, as well as political, control.

Modernization, an ancillary objective of Arab nationalism, was an aspect of the intricate problem of Westernization. The Near Easterners' reaction against their indigenous medievalism was as inevitable as their resentment against Western intrusion was logical. But not all reform, or modernization, was Westernization; and not all Westernization took the form of *foreign* exploitation. Furthermore, reaction against the West was so often tied up with resurgent nationalism, or at the very least intensified by nationalist aspirations, that the two have frequently been mistaken for each other. Modernization, often justifiably synonymous with Westernization, entailed a difficult social adjustment; and changes, especially accelerated economic changes, brought relatively great hardships in their train. When the natural process of growth and change were interwoven with nationalist ambitions, intruders from the West became logical, not to say convenient, scapegoats for the inescapable concomitant suffering. And so it happened that xenophobia often resulted from a situation of this kind as much as from the thwarting, by a foreign Power or Powers, of some nationalist political objective.

Since the late nineteenth century, there had been two main categories of Islamic nationalism, which had advanced, or become fused, into still a third category. The first, to borrow a happy analogy of Toynbee's, was comparable to the ultraconservative Zealots of the first century A.D.; and the second to their contemporaries, the ultraprogressive Herodians. The Zealots so feared the contact of an alien and a stronger civilization that they took aggressive refuge in everything in their own tradition that was reactionary, or "antithetical to the intrusive force." The Herodians so admired the alien civilization, and were so convinced of its superiority, that they were impelled to imitation. There were accordingly the nationalists, like the Wahhabi warriors of Ibn Saud, who lived by the sword and the Book, and who wrapped the cloak of Islam tightly round them; and there were the nationalists, like Kemal of Turkey or Feisal of Iraq, who put their trust in Western education and Western skills. Then there came a time when the Zealot type of nationalists began to adopt Western ways in order to fight the West with its own weapons, and when the Herodian type of nationalists began to feel that, if ever national states were to be established on the Western pattern, the ascendancy of the West would first have to be destroyed.

It was during this later evolutionary stage that these two categories of nationalism took on some of each other's attributes, with a resulting partial coalescence and confusion of identity. This stage of evolution roughly corresponded with the end of the First World War. It was marked by military revolts and demonstrations against the West throughout the Islamic world, beginning among the Moslems of the "core." In 1919 and 1920 the Turks rose against the Greeks and repudiated the peace terms of the Allied Powers; the Egyptians and Iraqis rose against the British; the Syrians defied the French. Between 1921 and 1925 there was sporadic guerrilla warfare, or desert raiding, on the part of the Saudi Arabs against the British mandates of Iraq and Trans-Jordan. There were inevitable repercussions among the Moslems of the "fringe," sensitive as always to the aspirations and activities of the "core." There was Moslem agitation in India. Amanullah, the reforming Emir of Afghanistan, engaged British and Indian forces in the most formidable of frontier wars in British-Indian history. In Morocco in 1921, Abd el-Krim, the Riff chieftain, defeated the best armies that Spain could send against him and only capitulated to combined Spanish and French forces in 1926. There was almost continuous warfare on the part of the Beduin of Libya against the Italians.

By the middle thirties, almost all the Moslems of the "core" — apart from those in Palestine — had come to terms with the West. With the illustrious exception of the Turks, their resistance had generally failed. But, more important, public opinion in the West, in Britain and France, was developing an anti-imperialist ideology and exerted a delayed reaction on governmental policies in the East. For example, the defeated Afghans were given their political freedom and an extension of territory. The uprisings in Egypt, Iraq, and Syria were put down by Britain and France, but thereafter the inhabitants of these countries each received successive, though not identical, concessions, toward self-government.

The nature of Pan-Arabism may perhaps be inferred from the foregoing. Pan-Arabism was only a single facet of Pan-Islamism. It was an attempt on the part of the Arab members of the Islamic world to organize themselves and co-ordinate their efforts toward the achieving of total independence. Pan-Arabism passed through many phases and, at the time of the Second World War, was far from 100 per cent Islamic. The earliest Pan-Arab movement in modern times took place in the heart of the late Ottoman Empire. Early in the nineteenth century, even before the Turks became "Turanian"-conscious,[3] a cultural and linguistic Arab renaissance was initiated in Syria. This supplemented, or was parallel to — but it was not a part of — the earlier religious resurgence in Arabia, associated with the fundamentalist fanaticism of Mohammed ibn Abd el-Wahhab and the Wahhabi followers of the founder of the Saudi dynasty (see p. 232). The second stage of the Arab renaissance found its outlet in the beginnings of political agitation. Arab members of the earlier Syrian "scientific societies" and philosophical-literary groups, Christian Arabs as well as Moslem Arabs, began to found secret societies, first in Syria and later in Iraq. Their distinctive, and only reasonably safe, political weapon was the publicizing of Arab propaganda by means of anonymous anti-Turk placards which they secretly posted in public places. The ensuing persecution by Abdul Hamid II drove the Arab agitators underground; but they did not abandon their secret societies, which eventually became potent organizations for revolution. In 1908 the Young Turks momentarily gave them hope and encouragement but, as late as 1914, nothing practical had come of repeated negotiations between the Arab and Turk politicians. During the First World War, a few Arabs from Syria and Iraq and the Hejaz finally banded together and worked out a common platform for joint action — not only against the Turks, but specifically for their mutual national independence. The next step after reaching an understanding among themselves was to bargain with the British for aid; and this was done through the medium of their common spokesman, Hussein, Sherif of Mecca (see p. 66). When, after the war, only some of their hopes were fulfilled and only a portion of their program was implemented, the Arab movement of the Ottoman era became metamorphosed into the modern movement for Arab unity. Pan-Arabism might be likened to an irredentist movement, having for its ultimate objective the re-establishment, in national units, of all the Arab lands once included in the great caliphates of the seventh, eighth, and ninth centuries. A first step toward the possible future confederation of all these Arab national units was taken by the founding of the Arab League (see p. 869).

THE SUCCESSION STATES OF THE OTTOMAN EMPIRE

The forms of the succession states of the Ottoman Empire were decided at the Peace Conference of Paris, largely in accordance with agreements and secret treaties made by the Allies in the course of the First World War (see p. 66). The attempt to partition Turkey herself, under the abortive Treaty of Sèvres, will shortly be described. Nevertheless, an effort was made to discover the political preferences of some of the peoples of these late Ottoman lands. On November 7, 1918 a joint Anglo-French Declaration explicitly assured the peoples of Syria, Palestine, and Mesopotamia that they were to have a voice in the eventual establishment of national governments (see concluding paragraphs of Appendix E). During 1919, at the instigation of President Wilson, an American commission of inquiry, the King-Crane Commission, toured Syria and Palestine — or Northern and Southern Syria as they were then called. It visited thirty-six towns, received delegations from over fifteen hundred villages, and studied more than eighteen hundred petitions. Its findings clearly indicated that the Syrians were wholly averse to French control and, to the extent that they wanted "technical and economic assistance" over a transitional period, they preferred to look for that assistance first to the United States and second to Britain. The Commission also recommended that Northern and Southern Syria (including the Lebanon and Palestine) should become a single political and administrative unit under a single mandate; and it gave warning that the feeling against Zionism was "not confined to Palestine, but was shared very generally by the people throughout Syria." It added, however, that there was "no reason why Palestine could not be included in a united Syrian State, just as other portions of the country, the holy places being cared for by an international and inter-religious commission" — provided that only a "greatly reduced Zionist programme" were attempted. It further recommended that no economic barriers be erected between Syria and Iraq.

It is common knowledge that the findings of the King-Crane Commission were completely disregarded. Its report, in point of fact, was not made public until it was too late for appropriate action. President Wilson meanwhile had fallen ill and did not press the issue; the United States was averse to taking any mandatory responsibility in the Near East; and there was danger that the precarious "unity" of the Allies at the Peace Conference might be imperiled by the injection of a fresh problem into their midst. The British did what they could to champion the cause of Arab independence, and to honor the McMahon Pledge. But, wherever the ultimate blame may lie, it is certain that French pressure was partly responsible for the shelving of a report which was outspokenly adverse to their interests.

At the fateful San Remo Conference in April 1920, the Allies made the final territorial division among themselves (see p. 132). Syria was partitioned. The mandate for Syria-Lebanon was assigned to France; the mandate for Palestine, the Jordan Valley, and Trans-Jordan, and the mandate for Iraq were assigned to Britain. The Palestine mandate explicitly carried with it an obligation to apply the Balfour Declaration (see Appendix D).

The interwar status of the "core" certainly lived up to Islam's predilection for variety. Turkey was a republic. Saudi Arabia was an absolute monarchy, supported by a quasi-nomadic tribal system. Persia (Iran) was a military dictatorship based on a crumbling feudal system. Egypt was a monarchy on the Buckingham Palace model, with all the trappings of parliamentarianism. Syria, Palestine, and Iraq were mandates, Iraq subsequently becoming a limited, independent monarchy. Trans-Jordan was a tribal emirate, comparable to Arabia, with the added consolation and complication of British "protection."

THE TURKISH WAR OF INDEPENDENCE AND THE TREATY OF LAUSANNE

The Turkish Revolutionary Reformation, or *Devrim*, the great creative movement that made modern Turkey, was a second renaissance, different from the Young Turk movement described above. It grew directly out of the Allies' attempt in 1919 to partition the country. It was organized and led by "The First among Turks," Mustapha Kemal Pasha, later named "Ataturk" by a grateful National Assembly. The *Devrim* succeeded because it was a veritable cleansing from within and entailed the abolition of every hampering custom and obsolete law. It resulted in the complete secularization of Turkish life, and the reorientation of Turkish economics and society along Western lines.

Mustapha Kemal Ataturk was born in Salonika, in 1881, the son of parents who were Turks of Albania and Macedonia, and it was not without significance for the achievements of the later Turkish Republic that he was a native of European, rather than of Asiatic, Turkey. He was trained in the military academies of Salonika and Monastir, where he earned the name of Kemal for his excellence in mathematics. He early joined the Young Turk party and took part in the revolt of 1908. At the outbreak of the First World War he was an isolationist and, though he afterward put aside his scruples and distinguished himself in the fighting in Gallipoli in 1915, he never wholeheartedly reconciled himself to the Young Turk "Triumvirate" who conducted the war, or to the German-Turkish alliance.

After the signing of the Mudros armistice, the Sultan's government attempted to negotiate with the Allies without any reference to the nationalist views and feelings that might still survive in Turkey. The Young Turk party had collapsed and had been replaced by a Liberal Entente party which avowed no faith in Turkey's national future. Neither the Sultan nor the new party therefore made any effort to prevent the proposed Allied partition of Turkey, and in the early months of 1919, French, British, and Italian forces were taking over their prospective territories in Anatolia, Syria, and Iraq. In May 1919 the Greeks invaded the western key district of Smyrna (Izmir), a district at that time largely populated by Greeks. All this military occupation was legal in the sense that it was covered by the terms of the Mudros armistice. But the Greek policing of Smyrna soon degenerated into marauding and aggression, and atrocities against Turks were undeniably committed.

Had it not been for the fact and the manner of the Greek invasion, the Turkish people might have entirely surrendered their national existence at this time. In October 1920 the Greek King Alexander died, Constantine of pro-German repute was recalled to the Greek throne in circumstances described elsewhere (see p. 209), and the Allies withdrew the support that Greece till then had been receiving from them. In May 1919, when the Greeks first landed at Smyrna, the Sultan, knowing Mustapha Kemal's sympathies and his popularity, removed him from Constantinople by appointing him Inspector General of the Third Army, then stationed in the interior. It was like Kemal to turn an apparent setback to his own advantage. He proceeded at once to consolidate the nationalist forces in the interior in defiance both of the Sultan and the Allied governments. In the summer of 1919 he called congresses at Erzerum and Sivas, which drafted a program for a new and independent National Turkey. On January 28, 1920, in answer to the Sultan's alleged agreement to a British protectorate, the "National Pact," virtually a Turkish Declaration of Independence, was enacted at Angora (Ankara). It abolished — indirectly — the Capitulations,[4] asserted the inviolability of Constantinople, guaranteed the rights of minorities, emancipated all Arab territories, and pledged free plebiscites to determine the destinies of all the parts of the late Ottoman Empire then in Allied occupation. The Sultan's government made a feeble and unsuccessful attempt to conciliate the Nationalists. The Allies occupied Constantinople. The rupture between the old Turkey and the new was complete.

In April 1920 a "Grand National Assembly" was convened at Angora to govern National Turkey, and Kemal was elected its president — though not, as yet, President of Turkey. The Sultan's government in Constantinople outlawed the Nationalists and condemned Kemal (*in absentia*) to death. It then proceeded to accept an Allied ultimatum presented to the Sultan in the shape of the Treaty of Sèvres. The treaty was signed by the Sultan's delegates on August 10, 1920, and amounted to an acquiescence in the partition of the country. The Greeks were confirmed in the possession of Smyrna; tracts of territory in Anatolia were to be assigned to Britain, France, and Italy; an independent Armenia was to be carved out of the eastern vilaycts; the Straits were to be internationalized. The treaty would have left Turkey a mere rump of land around Angora.

The psychological effect in Angora was instant. Kemal repudiated the treaty, gathered his forces, and gave battle to the Greek invaders. After initial defeats and successive Greek offensives, the Nationalists halted the Greeks just short of Angora. The victories of Ismet Pasha at Inonu, in January and April 1921, and Kemal's subsequent campaign, culminating in the Battle of the Sakkaria in the late summer of the same year, convinced an astonished world that the new Turkey was capable of asserting and defending its national existence.

Kemal's first reward was diplomatic recognition. In March 1921 the Italian Government agreed to evacuate its prospective territory in Anatolia in return for extensive economic concessions. Soviet Russia recognized the Angora government. The Treaty of Moscow of March 1921 fixed the eastern boundaries of Turkey, confirmed the Turks in their occupation of Kars and Ardahan, and retroceded Batum to Russia (see p. 95). Later a French mission negotiated a Franco-Turkish Accord, whereby the French Government agreed to evacuate its prospective territory in Anatolia and to establish a special regime in the Alexandretta zone (see p. 537). Meanwhile the Greek retirement had become a rout, and in September 1922 the Nationalist forces recaptured Smyrna. Atrocities were afterward charged against each other by Greeks and Turks. No hands were wholly clean at this time, and even recent allies, Britain and France, were respectively backing the Greeks and the Turks in their efforts. Smyrna was sacked and left on fire, and a stream of destitute Greek refugees made their escape, as best they could, across the Aegean to Greece.

In October 1922, at Mudania, Britain, France, and Italy agreed to an armistice with the Turkish Nationalists — just in time to prevent a clash between the advancing Turks and the British force then occupying the Dardanelles zone at Chanaq which had been demilitarized under the terms of the Mudros armistice (see p. 339). On July 24, 1923 the Allies and Nationalist Turkey signed the Treaty of Lausanne. Sèvres was superseded and forgotten. Mustapha Kemal, in short, had capped his military victory with one, no less signal, in the field of diplomacy. He had convincingly demonstrated the unexpected strength of the Turkish Nationalists, and he had perhaps taken the measure of the preoccupation of the Allies with their other postwar problems. In any event, the Treaty of Sèvres would have been costly for the Allies to enforce and would have further embittered their own none too cordial relations.

By the Treaty of Lausanne, Turkey cheerfully renounced every claim to rule over Arabs and other non-Turkish peoples. She recovered Eastern Thrace to the Maritsa River. Italy retained the Dodecanese Islands, including Rhodes, and Britain retained Cyprus. The Dardanelles was to remain demilitarized, open in peace and war to the ships of all nations, except only if Turkey herself was at war. Turkey accepted treaties for the protection of minorities, and she signed an agreement with Greece for the compulsory exchange of populations. Most important of all from the point of view of the new state, Turkey was to pay no reparations, and the Capitulations were definitively abolished.[4]

THE KEMALIST REFORMATION IN TURKEY

Once the Treaty of Lausanne was signed, the Allies evacuated Constantinople, and Angora was made the capital of Turkey. On October 29, 1923 the Turkish Republic was formally proclaimed. Mustapha Kemal was elected President of Turkey by the Grand National Assembly, and Ismet Pasha became Premier. The wars were over, the imperialist Powers had withdrawn, and Kemal could now turn his energies to the rebuilding of the nation he had saved. The domestic program of the new republic, the complex of policies and enactments known as Kemalism, became identified with the one man whose strength and vision had proved adequate for the national emergency of 1919.

The first problem was the abolition of the Caliphate.[2] Three weeks after the Mudania armistice the National Assembly decreed the abolition of the Sultanate only, in spite of the fact that the Sultanate-Caliphate had become, historically speaking, an indivisible office. The Sultan, Mohammed VI, left his palace secretly and fled Constantinople aboard a British warship. He was a kindly, elderly gentleman, and evidently glad enough to quit the scene where latterly he had been little more than the puppet of circumstances. The Assembly "elected" as Caliph, in his place, his cousin Abdul Mejid.

At this stage, Kemal and the Nationalists compromised. They did not repudiate the Caliphate for another year and a half, until, in fact, it seemed clear to them that the reconstruction of Turkey could not be accomplished otherwise. They attempted to separate the temporal and spiritual powers in accordance with Western concepts. But the abolition of the Sultanate — with the resulting division of a theoretically indivisible authority — involved them in still further complications. Eventually the Nationalists embarked upon a policy of complete secularization and of divorcement from Islam, a policy to which they found themselves becoming more and more committed. In the end, on March 3, 1924, the Assembly enacted the abolition of the Caliphate.

The Assembly next proceeded to adopt a constitution. It adopted, in fact, a development of the "Fundamental" or "Organic" Law, which it had passed earlier in 1921, and this constitution was afterward further amplified and amended in later statutes, between 1924 and 1935. Among its basic articles was the declaration that "sovereignty belongs unconditionally to the nation" and that the Grand National Assembly of Turkey was "the sole lawful representative of the nation." It adopted the usual democratic forms. The President of the Republic, who was likewise President of the Assembly, was elected by the Assembly and was responsible to it. He appointed a premier, who governed through a cabinet of ministers, chosen from among the Deputies of the Assembly. The Deputies, after an amendment in 1934, were Turkish men and women, elected quadrennially — and indirectly — by the universal suffrage of Turkish men and women over twenty-one years of age. One section of the constitution was a comprehensive declaration of individual rights, namely, freedom of conscience, of travel and contract, of labor, of private property, of assembly and association, of speech and press; equality of all Turks before the law, the inviolability of life, property, and the home; and the abolition of "all privileges of whatever description," whether of groups, families, classes, or individuals. Some legal "limitations," however, were put upon certain of these theoretical freedoms. Primary education was made both free and obligatory. The constitution also created secular courts and judges, though Islam was, until 1928, the state religion.

The work of internal reconstruction was interrupted early in 1925 by a serious Kurdish revolt in the southeastern provinces. The Kurds were bitterly opposed to the secularization policy of the government, and they desired the restoration of the Sultanate-Caliphate. Moreover, they had been encouraged to hope for autonomy by the abortive Treaty of Sèvres and resented their eventual incorporation into the Turkish Republic. After several months the revolt was put down, at considerable cost to both Turks and Kurds; but the net result of it was to accelerate the Turkish program of secularization. All religious orders were suppressed by decree, including even the intractable Dervishes.[5] The unification of the state-supported school system progressed rapidly. Various changes in social customs were introduced in sympathy with Westernizing trends, and to emphasize the establishment of new mental and social habits. It became illegal, for example, for any man to wear a tarbush or fez. Women were still allowed to wear veils, but their use was increasingly discouraged. Even marriage customs were radically revised. Polygamy became illegal, divorce was introduced, and civil marriage was made compulsory.

The year 1926 became famous as the year of new codes. Long study by special Turkish commissions resulted in the replacement of the Koranic Shari'at [6] by new civil, criminal, and commercial codes. The new codes were based respectively upon the Swiss, Italian, and German legal systems. Economic isolationism was deliberately fostered. Foreign investments were consistently rejected, foreign concessions were gradually bought out, and protective tariffs were set up. In 1928 the use of the Latin alphabet was inaugurated, and the intricate Turkish script supplanted in newspapers and books. Arabic and Persian words were weeded out of the Turkish language. At length, in 1930, etymological reform was carried to the point of changing place names. Constantinople became Istanbul, Angora Ankara, Smyrna Izmir, and Adrianople Edirne. In less than a decade, Turkey shed the Oriental backwardness of centuries and assumed the vesture of a modern state.

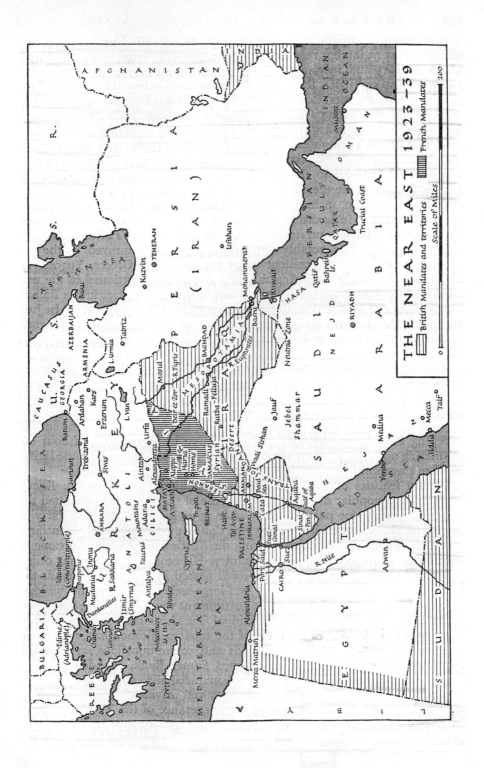

THE NEAR EAST 1923–39

British Mandates and territories
French Mandates

Scale of Miles
0 — 200

AFGHANISTAN

PERSIA (IRAN)

SAUDI ARABIA

NEJD

HASA

HEJAZ

NEUTRAL ZONE

ARABIA

OMAN

INDIAN OCEAN

PERSIAN GULF

Trucial Coast

QATAR

Bahrein Is.

Qatif

Kuwait

Mohammerah

Basra

Baghdad

MESOPOTAMIA (IRAQ)

Mosul

R.Tigris

R.Euphrates

Deir-ez-Zor

Ramadi

Rutba

Fellujah

Syrian Desert

Wadi Sirhan

Jebel Shammar

Jauf

RIYADH

Medina

Mecca

Jidda

Yenbo

Taif

RED SEA

EGYPT

SUDAN

LIBYA

R.Nile

Aswan

CAIRO

Suez

Port Said

Suez Canal

Mersa Matruh

Alexandria

CYPRUS

MEDITERRANEAN SEA

PALESTINE

TRANSJORDAN

JERUSALEM

AMMAN

Gaza

Dead Sea

Aqaba

Gulf of Aqaba

Sinai Pen.

Tel Aviv

Haifa

LEBANON

BEIRUT

Tripoli

DAMASCUS

Homs

Hama

Aleppo

HATAY

Antioch

Alexandretta

Adana

Aintab

Urfa

L.Van

Kars

Erzurum

Sivas

CILICIA

Taurus Mountains

ANATOLIA

TURKEY

ANKARA

Istanbul (Constantinople)

Bosporus

Mudania

Inonu

R.Sakkaria

Antalya

Izmir (Smyrna)

Is.(It.)

Rhodes

Crete

Dodecanese

Dardanelles

Chanak

Gallipoli

GREECE

BULGARIA

Edirne (Adrianople)

BLACK SEA

Samsun

Trebizond

Batum

Ardahan

GEORGIA

ARMENIA

AZERBAIJAN

Baku

CAUCASUS

U.S.S.R.

CASPIAN SEA

Tabriz

L.Urmia

Teheran

Kazvin

Isfahan

R.

S.

Domestic preoccupations did not prevent the republic from taking a constructive part in foreign relations. Two treaties were signed with the Soviet Union in 1925 and 1929, establishing political and economic relations between the two countries. But it is noteworthy that, before the signing of the second of these treaties, Communist propaganda was officially suppressed in Turkey. Nonaggression pacts were signed with Italy and with Persia in 1928, and a treaty was signed with Bulgaria in 1929. The only incident that seriously threatened Turkey's external relations during this period was a dispute with Britain about the possession of the city and oil fields of Mosul. The case was finally submitted to the League of Nations for arbitration, and the League Council made the Mosul Award late in 1925, assigning most of the territory in question, including the oil fields, to Iraq. A treaty with Britain the following year, in accordance with the League's decision, was a deserving triumph for the pacific and statesmanlike spirit of the new Turkey. Relations with Balkan neighbors, notably with Greece, gradually improved. By the end of 1930, Turkey was in excellent treaty relations with Greece, Yugoslavia, Rumania, and Bulgaria. During the early thirties, as mentioned in the previous chapter (see p. 213), Turkey participated to good effect in the Balkan Conferences and took to describing herself as "also a Balkan Power." In July 1937, the Saadabad or Middle Eastern Pact of Nonaggression was signed between Turkey, Iraq, Persia (Iran), and Afghanistan (see pp. 236 and 536).

The question is often raised as to whether the Turkish Republic was a dictatorship *de facto*. It was a young state in process of eradicating the inherited evils of centuries of despotic misrule. It was a state in revolution and fully conscious of the fact, and revolutions at one stage or other of their development are notoriously authoritarian. Nor was it to be expected that the sweeping Kemalist reforms should everywhere be introduced without encountering opposition. Their secularist spirit must often have wounded strict Moslem susceptibilities.

Certain features of the regime looked familiarly authoritarian. Kemal himself was a popular dictator in every sense of the word. He permitted the existence of only one political party after 1930, his own "People's Party of the Republic," with which Assembly and Cabinet were completely identified. In course of time and especially during the thirties, his government came to control the whole economy of the country. His economic policy was called "etatism," a sort of state socialism, which placed in government hands the total regulation of Turkish industry and large-scale enterprise. The apology, of course, was the usual one that the government was more competent financially and technically than any individual Turkish citizen could be. Thus the government held the monopoly of the tobacco, alcohol, salt, match, explosive, and sugar industries, railroads and communications, and all the municipal public services. A state-owned Sumer Bank, founded in 1933, owned and operated cotton, linen, wool, artificial silk, paper, and cellulose factories. At the same time private property and private enterprise were specifically guaranteed; and, in view of the importance of the Turkish peasant in the national economy, a most significant provision was made for safeguarding and extending peasant proprietorship — each Turkish farmer was to become a landowner. Some of the smaller factories were left in private hands, and concessions were occasionally granted to foreign firms. In the later thirties, "Five-Year Plans" were inaugurated. The Labor Code of 1937 provided for the compulsory settlement of disputes and prohibited strikes and lockouts. Simultaneously the government interested itself in the welfare of the employee, in social insurance, in maternity clinics, day nurseries, public health services, agriculture co-operatives, trade schools, and community cultural centers (the famous *Halkevis*) for the development of art and adult education and physical education. Every department of life and work was gradually covered.

Whether all these measures added up to totalitarianism or not, they were at least benevolent and pacific. Kemal himself — though here again he resembled many another contemporary dictator — tried genuinely and sincerely to act the democrat; and, though literally the ruler of Turkey, he was re-elected President every four years. He regarded authoritarian rule as a transitional expedient, during which the Turkish people might be trained to think and act democratically, vote intelligently, and participate fully in public life. Certainly there was no terrorism in Turkey and no institution comparable to the Cheka or Gestapo. There were only two "purges," and they cost a total of sixty lives. After the Amnesty Law of 1938, Turkey had neither political prisoners nor exiles.

In 1934 a law was passed requiring the adoption of family names. Mustapha Kemal himself was given the name of Ataturk, "the Father of the Turks," by vote of the Grand National Assembly. Ismet Pasha was given the name of Inonu in commemoration of his victories in the Turkish War of Independence. Kemal died on November 10, 1938, full of honors, mourned by a loyal and grateful people, and was succeeded in the presidency by this same Inonu, his close friend and coadjutor.

ARABIA

Across the Red Sea from Egypt lies Arabia, the primary source of Arab culture, the last stronghold of the Arabs of the Desert. From the days of Suleiman the Magnificent, Arabia had been theoretically included within the Ottoman Empire, but over the people of its interior wastes and highlands the Ottoman Sultans had rarely been able to establish more than a shadowy sovereignty. The clans of Arabia, from time immemorial, were in a chronic state of flux, constantly regrouping themselves around first one able tribal sheikh and then another. Consequently the history of Arabia, as of any other tribally organized country, seems complex and without any international significance, except on the rare occasions when one or more commanding personalities emerge. Such a personality was the Prophet Mohammed; and such a one, in our time, was Abd el-Aziz II ibn Saud, for whom almost the whole of Arabia eventually came to be named. Before the First World War, however, Ibn Saud's reputation was still in the making, and most eyes that looked toward Arabia were likely to rest expectantly upon the dignified figure of his ambitious rival, Sherif Hussein of the Hejaz, Protector of the Holy Cities of Mecca and Medina, and a member of the House of Hashim in Mohammed's own tribe of the Quraish.

Ibn Saud started life as a landless exile in the principality of Kuwait on the Persian Gulf. At the beginning of the twentieth century he began to reconstruct the state of his ancestors in the Nejd in central Arabia. But he was no mere desert conqueror, typical of so many others in the Arabian scene. He was a statesman and the leader of a religious movement. He married a descendant of el-Wahhab, founder of the fundamentalist Wahhabi sect of Islam, a branch of the Sunni (see p. 217); and he was himself a descendant of the original Abd el-Aziz ibn Saud, who had joined with el-Wahhab to establish the short-lived Wahhabi Empire of the eighteenth century. Once established in the Nejd, Ibn Saud conceived the idea of building a second Wahhabi Empire, fired with the same faith. He maintained a disciplined standing army, the nucleus of a hardy and self-sufficient national community, anchored to the soil of Arabia and organized in groups of "militant salvationist agricultural colonies." The colonists were designated Ikhwan or "Brethren," and he founded the first such group at the desert wells of Artawiya in 1912. During the twenties, some 70 colonies were in existence with a total population of over 100,000 and a standing army of nearly 50,000 men.

Ibn Saud made use of the First World War to further his career of expansion. At the time, there were three other important rulers in Arabia—the Imam Yahya of the Yemen, Ibn Rashid of Jebel Shammar, and Sherif Hussein, just mentioned, of the Hejaz. During the First World War, Ibn Rashid of Jebel Shammar was actively loyal to the Turks, as well as being in German pay; the Imam Yahya of the Yemen was passively loyal to the Turks; Sherif Hussein of the Hejaz became the ally of Britain and, with his son Feisal, the leader of the Arab Revolt. Ibn Saud was technically neutral but entered into treaty relations with Britain, and indeed received a subsidy from the British Government; but he fought out his own private feud with the pro-German Ibn Rashid and defeated him in 1915 at the Battle of Jarrab.

The results of the First World War in Arabia were twofold. The Turks withdrew permanently from every part of it, and the British sphere of influence was extended over the whole peninsula. Hussein, now King of the Hejaz, and Ibn Saud continued to receive their wartime subsidies from the British Government. British de facto protectorates were confirmed over the territories of all the Gulf Chiefs—in Kuwait, Bahrein, Qatar, the Trucial Coast, and in the Sultanate of Muscat and Oman. Nevertheless, Ibn Saud was recognized as ruler of the Hasa, Qatif, and Jubail, with their ports on the Persian Gulf, as well as ruler of the Nejd. Britain also eventually established a protectorate in the Hadhramaut—an extension of the Pax Britannica that was of real and enduring benefit to the quarrelsome Hadhramauti tribesmen. Ibn Rashid and the Imam of the Yemen were in no way penalized for their loyalty to the Turks, but they remained isolated and outside the nexus of Anglo-Arabian relationships. In fact, so independent was the Imam Yahya that he was temporarily left in occupation of that part of the Aden Protectorate which he had seized during the war. But, when he continued to remain impervious to all British remonstrances, his forces were bombed by the Royal Air Force — though not until 1928 — and compelled to withdraw to the Anglo-Turkish frontier that had been established between Aden and the Yemen in 1904–05.[7] In 1930 the Asir, the turbulent buffer state between the Yemen and the Hejaz, was taken under Ibn Saud's protection and became known as the Idrisi Province after its ruling house.

Meanwhile Ibn Saud girded himself to resume his expansion in Arabia and, in particular, to meet in a decisive trial of strength his great rival, Hussein of the Hejaz. He sent Wahhabi missionaries to proselytize among the Hejazi frontier tribes, and in 1919, when Hussein provoked him to active hostility by attacking the Wahhabitized Khurma Oasis, he gave instant battle and defeated Hussein's son, Abdullah, at Turaba. He did not immediately follow up his advantage but turned to complete his subjugation of the Rashid. The ruling Rashid was assassinated by a member of his own family, and his territories, sunk in a minor civil war, were an easy conquest. By the end of 1921, Ibn Saud had possessed himself of the whole of Jebel Shammar and, before another year was out, he had also added the strategic Jauf-Sakaka oases to the Sultanate of the Nejd, thus gaining unimpeded access to the Syrian Desert.

When in March 1924 Kemal Ataturk abolished the Caliphate, Hussein, at the instigation of his son, the Emir Abdullah of Trans-Jordan, took it upon himself to assume the vacant title. The dream of Arab federation under the Hashemite dynasty and a restoration of the Caliphate in his own person had never quite faded from the old man's mind. But it cannot be said that Hussein had shown a deep sense of his religious responsibilities in the Hejaz, and he had lately alienated Moslem respect by his evident tolerance of the financial exploitation of the pilgrims to the Holy Cities and by his indifference to their health and safety. For Ibn Saud, Hussein's assumption of the Caliphate was a sufficient *casus belli*. At the head of an army of his Wahhabi warriors, he invaded the Hejaz and captured the key town of Taif. Hussein abdicated in favor of his eldest son, Ali, and escaped to Cyprus on a British ship. Ali finally capitulated after Ibn Saud's protracted siege of Jidda.

On January 8, 1926, in the Great Mosque of Mecca, Ibn Saud was proclaimed King of the Hejaz. A year later, at the request of its tribesmen, he likewise became King of Nejd. In May 1927 the Anglo-Saudi Treaty of Jidda established more formal and stable relations with Britain and recognized the "complete" and "absolute" independence of the King of the Hejaz and of Nejd and its Dependencies.[8] Thenceforth Ibn Saud united his two kingdoms in a personal theocratic union.

In June 1926, in order to conciliate adverse sectarian opinion and legitimize his position in Islam, Ibn Saud, as King of the Hejaz, summoned an Islamic Congress at Mecca, eventually attended by over sixty delegates and four official national delegations. He gave assurances to the Congress for the future welfare and honest treatment of the pilgrims to the Holy Cities. Even before the convening of this Congress, Ibn Saud had established effective public security in the Hejaz.

The vigor of Ibn Saud's realm lay partly in its military strength — topographical and otherwise; partly in its medial position in the Arab world, forming as it did a natural geographic nucleus for any projected Arab entente or union; partly in its great historic prestige as the Islamic cradle of the Arab peoples; and partly, and not least, in Ibn Saud himself. On September 22, 1932 his territories, the Kingdom of the Hejaz and the Kingdom of Nejd and its Dependencies, were jointly renamed Saudi Arabia. There seemed to be no limits to the influence he might hope to acquire in the Arab world.

Perhaps his strongest, certainly his unique, claim to distinction in Arabia was his good-neighbor policy. After finally making himself the undisputed master in his own house, and after twenty years of aggression in the Arabian peninsula, Ibn Saud became unreservedly a man of peace. In 1934 he won a seven weeks' war against the last of his rivals, the Imam Yahya of the Yemen; but he crowned his victory with a settlement that left the Imam completely independent, despite the fact that the Imam had been the aggressor in the war. He entered into treaties with Trans-Jordan and Iraq, both of them ruled by sons of Hussein, his one-time adversary, and the second of these treaties was the famous Treaty of Arab Brotherhood and Alliance of 1936, to which the Yemen adhered twelve months later. Ibn Saud even succeeded in negotiating a treaty with the King of Egypt.

Arabia, alone of all the countries we are describing in this group of chapters, had so far no problem of Western commercial exploitation. Her deserts, in that regard, were not inviting — until 1932, when vast reserves of oil were discovered in eastern Arabia. But, in 1933 and again in 1939, Ibn Saud granted important concessions to an American oil company, "Aramco" (Arabian-American Oil Company),[9] and it may be said that the United States thereby entered upon the slippery path of commercial imperialism in the Middle East, with all its interesting potentialities for the future.

PERSIA (IRAN)

Most remote and oriental of the Near Eastern peoples were the Persians, highlanders of the great Iranian plateau that marched with the Mesopotamian plain. The country — more recently known as Iran — was rather smaller than Mexico. Much of it was desert or semiarid land, and its climate varied from subarctic to tropical. Ancient Persia was famous for her warriors and kings, for her three great successive empires, and for her philosophy, poetry, art, and architecture. Her history, like her exquisite language and her domed and minaretted cities, was full of glint and color. Her people were successively influenced by heterogeneous cultures but remained intrinsically and triumphantly Persian. Islam, carried thither by the seventh-century Arabs, became distinctively organized in the Shi'a tradition.

Modern Persia, in a materialistic age, was best known as one of the world's greatest sources of oil. Her other commercial products were opium, dried and fresh fruits, tobacco, rice, cotton, wool, gums, silk, and skins; her rugs and carpets were prized the world over. She first entered upon the stage of recent history in the early twentieth century, a decaying Oriental despotism, under the shahs of the semi-Turkish Qajar dynasty, reluctantly but impotently exposed to the usual Westernizing influences and to the keen economic rivalry of Britain and Russia. In 1907 an Anglo-Russian treaty divided her into British and Russian "spheres of influence," with a neutral buffer zone between. The southern British sphere became the special preserve of the Anglo-Persian Oil Company.

During the First World War, despite her declaration of neutrality, Persia was invaded by all three belligerents adjacent to her frontiers — Turks, Russians, and British. German agents under the able direction of Wassmuss, "the German Lawrence," tried to organize a rising of Persian tribesmen against the British, and established contacts with Afghanistan. By the end of the war, Persia was in a state of anarchy; British forces were fighting Turks in northern Persia and supporting Russian counterrevolutionaries against the Bolsheviks. In 1919 an Anglo-Persian agreement was signed providing for the rehabilitation of the country and the restoration of order with British supervision and British finance. But the agreement was never ratified, albeit British financial support had preserved the Persian Government during the war, and British political and military support had saved Persia from partial dismemberment at the hands of the Bolsheviks during the years 1918–21. Bolshevik pressure, however, reinforced by a new nationalist impulse in Persia, began to displace British influence. And then Persia staged her version of a Kemalist revolution.

Riza Khan Sartip was the scion of a landowning family of the Caspian province of Mazanderan, a patriot and a military adventurer. In February 1921, at the head of a band of 3,000 Cossacks, he seized control in Teheran and appointed himself Commander in Chief and Minister of War in a government of his own creation. He rejected the still-pending British agreement and concluded an alliance with the Soviet Union, under which all Russian forces eventually evacuated Persia and all Russian debts, concessions, and extraterritorial privileges (dating from 1828) were canceled.[10] British financial advisers were later replaced by American experts; foreign officers in the Persian Army were dismissed.

Riza Khan had fully intended to be the first president of a Persian republic. There was a repetition of the earlier events in Turkey. The Shah, like the Sultan, left his country, after having been forced to give up his throne. But the Shi'a theologians in Persia were too strong for a parallel program of secularization to be effected, and they persuaded the new dictator that anything other than the traditional monarchy in Persia would be "contrary to religion." On December 12, 1925, accordingly, Riza Khan became Riza Shah Pahlavi. The Persian crown was transferred from the Qajars to the Pahlavi dynasty and entailed upon descendants of the founder born of Persian mothers.

The remainder of the program generally followed the Kemalist precedent, especially in respect of modernization. With advancing security the new Shah's rule became more, rather than less, autocratic. The Majlis, the Persian National Assembly, degenerated into a body of puppets, whose acquiescence was rewarded by opportunities for private graft. The Shah's rule was always aggressively nationalist. In 1932 even the Anglo-Persian Oil Company's concession was canceled, and a new and much reduced concession was negotiated much to Persia's advantage. Capitulations were abolished.[4] The name of Persia was changed to Iran, in indication of her cultural and spiritual leadership of all the peoples of the Iranian plateau. The Shah's rule also became more etatist. Private enterprise was not outlawed, but trade and industry were increasingly controlled. Oil and opium were made government monopolies. Meanwhile the army was reorganized. Education spread apace. Roads and railroads were built; aviation was encouraged. The Trans-Iranian Railway from the Caspian Sea to the Persian Gulf, built by foreign engineers but financed entirely with Iranian capital, was opened just before the Second World War. And with her international neighbors in these years Iran lived in peace and amity. The Middle Eastern Pact of Nonaggression between Turkey, Iraq, Iran, and Afghanistan was signed in the Shah's palace at Saadabad in July 1937 (see p. 536). But Riza Khan had not the ability of Kemal; and Iran had neither sufficient homogeneity nor the requisite national unity to enable the country to be "reformed" and modernized as basically as was Kemalist Turkey.

EGYPT

Egypt, in the early interwar years, was a problem as baffling as that of any of the mandates. No state was ever in a more anomalous position. Until 1914 the Khedive, the independent ruler of Egypt, was theoretically a vassal of the Ottoman Sultan and paid him an annual tribute. But the Khedive's authority in fact was limited by Britain, the official "protecting Power." Since 1882 Britain had been in military occupation of the country, and in 1904 her "special position" had been recognized by the Great Powers. An efficient financial administration was set up; Egypt was given the best of Britain's administrators, Cromer and Kitchener; and she became a model of all that was expert, stable, and incorruptible in the British imperial tradition. In December 1914, shortly after Turkey's entry into the First World War, Britain established over Egypt a formal protectorate.

The Sudan, geographically and historically, except in ancient times, had lain apart from Egypt until its conquest under Mohammed Ali in the early nineteenth century. In 1898, Kitchener defeated the successor of the fanatical "Mahdi," who, in the eighties, had led a revolt against Egypt, and reconquered the country in the name of Britain and Egypt, with the help of a small number of Egyptian troops. Sudanese affairs thereafter were regulated by the Anglo-Egyptian Condominium, which established joint Anglo-Egyptian sovereignty and administration *de jure*, but which, in effect, placed the real control in British hands. The country was rich, mainly in cotton, but its inhabitants — largely Arab Moslem in the northern Sudan and Negroid in the southern Sudan — were woefully poor and superstitious; their contacts with the outer world hitherto had been through the slave trader, and they were in need of the most elementary gifts of civilization.

These gifts they now received to some extent, and the Sudan became a model of British imperial administration.

Sincere but unsuccessful efforts were made after 1907 to transfer the administrative responsibility in Egypt to Egyptian officials, and education along Western lines was greatly extended. Kitchener eventually sponsored a legislative assembly, though with purely consultative functions. The First World War interrupted these laudable experiments, but they had given Egyptian nationalism the encouragement it needed. President Wilson's Fourteen Points and the joint Anglo-French Declaration of 1918 (see Appendix E), emancipating Arab lands from the Turks, read like concessions in the same direction, and by the end of the war Egyptian nationalism, under the vigorous cultivation of Saad Pasha Zaghlul, had become a hardy, spreading plant. In 1919, when Zaghlul and other overactive Nationalists were deported to Malta, anti-British feeling in Egypt reached the proportions of a general rising.

At the end of 1919 a mission to find a working compromise was dispatched to Egypt under Lord Milner, the Conservative statesman, at that time Colonial Secretary. Such was then the strength of the Egyptian Nationalist sentiment in favor of complete independence that the Milner Mission recommended that Anglo-Egyptian relations should be regulated upon a treaty basis. But Zaghlul scorned even this concession, believing that the projected treaty would merely amount to a "veiled protectorate." He called into question Britain's right to the joint administration of the Sudan. Further negotiations ended in a stalemate, and the British Government, strongly counseled by Lord Allenby, then High Commissioner in Egypt, determined to put an end to the protectorate by unilateral declaration. On February 28, 1922, Egypt was proclaimed an independent and sovereign state. But Egyptian independence was made subject to four "points" which were "absolutely reserved" to the discretion of the British Government, pending "free and friendly accommodation on both sides"; namely, the security of the Suez Canal and other imperial communications; the defense of Egypt herself against foreign aggression or interference; the protection of foreign interests and minorities; and the dependent status of the Sudan. Fuad, hitherto Sultan, took the title of King. The Nationalists refused to recognize the declaration. For the next fourteen years, the history of Anglo-Egyptian relations hinged upon repeated efforts to negotiate a bilateral treaty acceptable alike to British and Egyptian opinion, and the treaty in its turn hinged upon the four "reserved points" of Allenby's declaration.

The Wafd, literally "delegation," had originally been constituted by the Egyptian Nationalists to lay their case before the Peace Conference. It had been refused permission to leave Egypt — though Zaghlul himself had gone "officially" to Paris — but its name had afterward been adopted by the Egyptian Nationalist party. In the elections of January 1924 it returned 188 supporters, as against only 27 of other parties, and King Fuad invited its leader, Zaghlul, to form a government. From that time forth the Wafd changed from a people's party to a dictatorship — a political organization that did not scruple to employ secret agents and terrorist methods. From time to time it included 80 or even 90 per cent of the population of Egypt, but the majority of its members were politically ignorant fellaheen or half-educated effendis.[11]

The Wafd's one insistent demand was for irresponsible independence and the sabotage of all persons and parties unsympathetic to its program. Its governments were apt to be antagonistic to the monarchy, and apparently disliked King Fuad as much as they did the British High Commissioner. Its aversion, it may be said, was heartily reciprocated by King Fuad. The Wafd moreover shared a most regrettable peculiarity with other violently nationalist groups in the Near East. It was entirely self-absorbed and intolerant of other nationalisms. Its attitude to the Sudanese was on a par with that of the Turks and Iraqis to the Kurds. As an example of its political immaturity it is enough to mention the extraordinary methods that had to be resorted to, during Zaghlul's administration in 1924, in order to get any business transacted in the Egyptian Parliament. Three different kinds of bells were first used by the president to warn Members against shouting each other down and to force them to listen to each other's speeches — all to no effect — and he had finally to install, for the purpose, a powerful electric fire-alarm buzzer. It is also recorded that in 1936, on a typical occasion, the Egyptian Government intervened to request the lowering of university grades, so that a sufficient number of students who had spent their time in political riots and strikes should be enabled to pass their examinations.

In September 1924, Zaghlul went to London to confer with the Prime Minister, then Ramsay MacDonald. Presumably he hoped that British Labor would make concessions. But, as he was prepared to concede nothing himself and as MacDonald took his stand on the Suez and Sudan reservations of 1922, the discussions failed. The breakdown had immediate and unfortunate repercussions in Egypt. An epidemic of political crime broke out, and serious disturbances were caused by detachments of the Egyptian Army in the Sudan. Sir Lee Stack, who was both Governor General of the Sudan and Sirdar, or Commander in Chief, of the Egyptian Army, was murdered in the streets of Cairo. Lord Allenby thereupon, in the name of the British Government, confronted the Egyptian Government with an ultimatum, demanding the punishment of the criminals, an apology, an indemnity of £500,000, and the withdrawal of Egyptian troops from the Sudan. The ultimatum had to be reinforced by the occupation of the Alexandria customs office by British troops. Zaghlul was forced to resign, and seven Egyptians were subsequently executed for Sir Lee Stack's murder. In 1927, Zaghlul died and was succeeded in the leadership of the Wafd by Mustapha Nahas Pasha.

After the fall of the Wafd government, moderate policies predominated, and a succession of temperate governments carried on — with chronic opposition from the Wafd — until 1929. The temporary restoration of the Wafd, at the end of that year, led to its final repudiation by King Fuad and the establishment of a dictatorship supported by the throne. There was also a change of high commissioners. Allenby was replaced by Sir George Lloyd, better known as Lord Lloyd, an exponent of "strong" administration in the best Cromerian tradition.

Negotiations for the bilateral treaty were unsuccessfully resumed in 1928 and again in 1930. But by 1930, in spite of the general stalemate, certain important questions were settled, notably the question of the maintenance of British troops on Egyptian soil. The vital economic issue of the utilization of the Nile waters was settled definitively by an exchange of notes. The only important matter then left outstanding was the Sudan. The catalyst which induced Anglo-Egyptian *rapprochement* undoubtedly was the Italo-Ethiopian War of 1935–36. For once a defensive alliance seemed equally in the interest of Britain and Egypt, and a party coalition, the "United Front," took the decision to make some concessions for the sake of British "protection." The death of King Fuad in April 1936 and the setting up of a regency council to govern for the boy King Farouk may have retarded the renewed discussions. The Wafd, in imitation of the Fascists and Nazis, had now adopted a "blue shirt" — together with the street tactics, parades, and demonstrations associated therewith. But, internal unrest notwithstanding, an Anglo-Egyptian Treaty was finally signed in August 1936.

Under the treaty Egypt received her unqualified independence. The four reservations of 1922 were disposed of as follows: the defense of the Suez Canal and of Egypt was secured by what amounted to a defensive alliance — with a stipulated time limit of twenty years; an "invisible" British occupation was to be temporarily substituted for the "visible" British occupation so irksome to Egyptian Nationalists. At the end of twenty years — or ten years if both parties agreed — the situation was to be reviewed. British forces were to be confined (in peacetime) to the Suez Canal zone. The British Navy was to have the use of the harbor of Alexandria for eight years — presumably until such time as Egypt's own communications had improved to the point of adequacy. Egyptian aid, in the event of war, was specifically limited to the loan of airports, anchorages, and transport facilities for instant use in case of emergency, and the free use of all Egyptian territory, territorial waters, and air by the British armed forces. All these provisions were in force at the outbreak of the Second World War in 1939. The protection of foreign interests and minorities was left for future consideration by the interested Powers; but, within a year, at a conference at Montreux, it was decided to abolish the Capitulations [4] and the mixed courts which operated under them — after a twelve-year period of transition. The juridical status of the Sudan remained substantially unchanged, though the *status quo ante* 1924 was virtually restored, and administration reforms were introduced. Egyptian personnel were made eligible to higher Sudanese appointments, discriminatory restrictions on Egyptian immigration and property-holding in the Sudan were abolished, and Egyptian troops, on an equal basis with British troops, were to be at the disposal of the Governor General of the Sudan.

In May 1937, Egypt became a member of the League of Nations. She was an independent state, in name and fact, for the first time in twenty-two hundred years.

16 THE NEAR EAST: THE MANDATES

SYRIA

Until 1920, Syria-Lebanon and Palestine were not separated. In Ottoman times they were spoken of as Northern and Southern Syria, but technically "Syria" was then a single area including the entire eastern littoral of the Mediterranean rectangle, the hinterland beyond the Jordan, and the western part of the Palmyrene steppe. After the First World War the country was "temporarily" divided into three Allied military administrations — along lines reminiscent of the Sykes-Picot Agreement of 1916 (see p. 66). The north went to France, and the south to Britain; the hinterland went to an "interior" Arab National State, originally intended to stretch from Aleppo to Ma'an, and the Emir Feisal ibn Hussein, leader of the Arab Revolt, was installed at Damascus as its ruler. Feisal, however, was responsible to Field Marshal Allenby, who was then in supreme command of all three administrations.

As mentioned in the previous chapter (see p. 223), a joint Anglo-French Declaration of November 1918 had explicitly assured the peoples of Syria, Palestine, and Mesopotamia that they should have a voice in the eventual establishment of their national governments. The King-Crane Commission (see p. 223), which toured Syria in 1919, strongly urged that the old territorial unity should be preserved, notwithstanding existing military divisions and notwithstanding previous wartime commitments between the Allies, and it emphasized in particular the popular aversion among Syrians toward the prospective French mandate. But both the Anglo-French Declaration and the King-Crane Commission were wholly disregarded. In March 1920 a Congress of Syrian Notables, at Damascus, attempted to influence the decisions of the Peace Conference. Feisal was offered by the Congress, and accepted, the crown of Syria and Palestine. The Allies forthwith repudiated the Congress, convened the fateful San Remo Conference, and there assigned the mandate for Syria-Lebanon to France and the mandate for Palestine, the Jordan Valley, and Trans-Jordan to Britain (see p. 132).

At this point the history of Syria-Lebanon becomes formally separated from that of Palestine and Trans-Jordan and, until the outbreak of the Second World War, the histories of these adjoining mandates can best be recounted independently. We should, however, never forget that the peoples of each mandate always remained peculiarly sensitive to the happenings in the other's territory.

But, though thus united for so long, Syria has always had her natural and racial components. Her geography offers every imaginable contrast of highland and lowland, of color and of soil. The towering mountains of the Lebanon coastal range, some of whose peaks are nine and ten thousand feet high, look eastward and downward upon the bleakly arid escarpments of the Anti-Lebanon. The level verdure of the Bekaa (or Biqa') Plain insinuates itself between these two jagged mountain ranges. From the further slopes of the Anti-Lebanon, semiarid steppeland stretches eastward to the Euphrates. Along the western margin of this vast tawny plateau, some two thousand feet in altitude, flourish the beautiful oasis of Damascus and its neighboring quasi-caravan cities of Homs, Hama, and Aleppo. Despite the inaccessibility of most of its mountain country, the valleys, which run roughly north and south, and the desert fringes of the steppeland have been immemorial highways between the East and the West. For some four thousand years Syria, at the crossroads of three continents, has lain at the mercy of successive invaders, and still retains, today, the imprint of them all. For the past four centuries, she had been an integral part of the Ottoman Empire.

In our time, the combined Syrian and Lebanese population of only 3,900,-000 was divided between eighteen distinct religious creeds, more or less mutually antagonistic. There was, nevertheless, a very large Moslem majority in Syria. Lebanon, on the other hand, with less than half the population of Syria, had until 1939 a Christian majority — by 1948, the Christian-Moslem ratio had become approximately even. The Lebanese Christian community of some 600,000 was subdivided into such sects as the Maronites (half the community), Greek and Syrian Catholics, Armenians, Chaldean and other Uniats, for the most part derived from heresies of the early Christian era, and finally Greek Orthodox. Each one of these sects had its independent ecclesiastical organization. There were some Protestants, a few Quakers, and a few Roman Catholics.[1] The Moslems of Syria and Lebanon were mainly of the orthodox Sunni sect; but there were several other Moslem and heterodox-Moslem communities, notably the Druze hillmen of the Jebel Druze and southern Lebanon, and the Alawi of the Latakia district, both of whom were offshoots of Shi'a Isma'ilian sects.

General Gouraud, the first French Commander in Chief and High Commissioner for Syria-Lebanon, was distrusted and obstructed at every turn in the territories under his command. To counter desultory Arab attacks on French units, a French army of about 90,000 men was concentrated in the districts west of Damascus, Homs, Hama, and Aleppo. Serious disorders followed in Syria, particularly in Damascus, where Feisal was compelled to use his own Sherifian troops for the purpose of restoring order. General Gouraud then forced upon Feisal an ultimatum that exacted, among other humiliating conditions, full recognition by the Arab Government of the French mandate and the French occupation of Aleppo. This, like the house that Jack built, resulted in further disorders, and the French determined to extend their military rule throughout the whole mandate. In July 1920, French forces marched into the interior, took Damascus, and expelled Feisal from his kingdom. The British, to whom Feisal would have turned in his hour of need, were bound by the decisions of the San Remo Conference and were unable to help.

For the next six years France governed Syria-Lebanon through what amounted to a military dictatorship. Generals Gouraud, Weygand, and Sarrail succeeded each other as high commissioners, and throughout the period France meted out different treatment to the Lebanon and to Syria. France, it seemed to many close observers, was bent on encouraging the idea that the Lebanon was, and should remain, politically separate from the rest of Syria. She recognized the economic ties which bound the Lebanon to its Syrian hinterland but insisted on the individual character of its political interests.

Thus Gouraud's first act, after the expulsion of Feisal, was to subdivide Syria into four smaller states and to create a "Greater Lebanon" state. The Lebanon, it is true, had had special administrative treatment even under Ottoman rule. In the sixties of the last century, a Maronite feudal revolt had indirectly resulted in widespread religious disturbances and the massacre of several thousand Christians, and the French Government had sent an expeditionary force to Beirut to protect the remaining Christians of the Lebanon. Eventually the Sultan had been forced to grant semiautonomy to the Lebanon and to put the territory under a Christian governor. The intervention of France on this occasion had given her a traditional prestige in the minds and imaginations of the Lebanese people. But the enlarging of the Lebanon in 1920, far from having the desired effect of increasing France's authority in her mandate, revived the political inequalities of Ottoman times in an even more racially provocative form. The Greater Lebanon was less loyal to France than its smaller, more homogeneous nucleus had been. It was about twice the size of its Ottoman predecessor. It included the great inland plain of the Bekaa, on the eastern slopes of the Lebanon Mountains, and the coastal cities of Tripoli, Beirut, Sidon, and Tyre; many Sunni Moslems were thereby added to the predominantly Christian population. Needless to say, the resulting internal dissensions in the Greater Lebanon state found alarming echoes in the Syrian states that had thus been deprived of fertile valleys and strategic ports.

THE DRUZE REBELLION

There were good reasons therefore for political unrest in Syria-Lebanon. In the first place, the French Mandatory Government had got away to a bad start, and in the second, it had made difficult matters worse by an administrative reorganization which had accentuated the communal particularism native to the country. General Weygand, however, did much during the period of his high-commissionership to overcome these initial errors, and personally he was relatively popular and well respected. His successor, Sarrail, precipitated a very serious insurrection.

General Sarrail had commanded an army at the Battle of the Marne in 1914, and he had commanded the Allied expeditionary force in Salonika in 1915 (see p. 64). Doubtless he was a distinguished soldier, but his political capacity had sometimes been in question, and he was well known for a masterful and captious temper. He arrived in Syria-Lebanon early in 1925, for a stormy tenure of just nine months. An embittered anticlerical, he was soon at odds with the religious communities — a strange role to play for the representative of a Power which traditionally claimed to be the "protector" of the Latin churches in Syria. First he tried to introduce anticlerical legislation into the Lebanon and to change the indirect electoral system of the Lebanese Council, a system customarily based upon the allocation of seats to the several religious communities in fixed proportions. He then antagonized the proud and sensitive chieftains of the Jebel Druze.

Trouble had been brewing in the Jebel ("the Mountain") ever since a certain Captain Carbillet, the French Resident Adviser, had been entrusted with the acting governorship of that feudally organized district. Carbillet was an efficient, conscientious, and disinterested official, but he had conceived it to be his duty to modernize the Jebel, to build roads, and to collect taxes for the Druze Treasury. The Druze chieftains of the great Atrash family, irritated by his program no less than by his rigorous, disciplinary methods of executing it, appealed over his head to the High Commissioner and cited a recent Franco-Druze Agreement of 1921 which had promised them a native governor and autonomy within a federation of Syrian states — an "independence" which had been officially proclaimed by the French on April 5, 1922. Sarrail replied by repudiating the agreement and arresting some members of the Atrash family whom he had treacherously invited to a conference.

Inevitably an insurrection broke out. The nationalists in Syria were unprepared for concerted action, and time was needed before they could organize a nationalist rebellion throughout Syria. In October, Druze and nationalist forces reached Damascus and, by orders of Sarrail and without declaration of martial law, French artillery bombarded the open, unfortified city for three days. The death roll was never correctly estimated, but foreign observers put it at 1,200. Many of the Syrian Christians, as well as Armenians, Circassians, and even Maronite peasants in the Lebanon were given arms by the French to "protect" themselves against the Druzes — thus reviving the ancient pattern of religious internecine warfare. To the credit of the Moslem nationalists be it said, no one of their groups countenanced or encouraged the promotion of Moslem-Christian strife.

General Sarrail was recalled to France in October 1925, immediately after the shelling of Damascus, and civil high commissioners inherited the invidious task of correcting his mistakes. In 1926 the Mandates Commission of the League of Nations administered a pointed rebuke to the French Government for having disregarded the "gathering discontent" and for pursuing a too "active and dominating" policy in Syria.[2] By the summer of 1927 the Druze Rebellion had petered out. The principal result of the two years of civil war was the irrevocable unification of the Syrian nationalists.

Happily the later twenties ended on a friendlier note, and good relations were progressively established through the middle thirties. Great Lebanon was officially proclaimed a republic in May 1926, while the Druze Rebellion was still in progress; the four Syrian states were likewise proclaimed a republic in May 1930. Syrian affairs were now falling into the hands of a new Syrian Nationalist Bloc, resulting from an alliance between the educated urban *bourgeoisie* and the young intelligentsia, *la jeunesse instruite*. Theirs was a new and implacable spirit, imbued with French liberal ideas, of a higher political caliber than the negative, feudal clannishness of the Druzes, and wholly converted to the ideals of the Arab renaissance. The Syrian Nationalist Bloc was the inspirer and organizer of a most effective fifty-day strike early in 1936, and a new government in France, the Popular Front, assuming office at the psychological moment, seemed well disposed toward making them the inevitable concessions. Franco-Syrian and Franco-Lebanese treaties of alliance were signed in September and November 1936, somewhat on the lines of the Anglo-Iraqi treaty of 1930. More willing recognition of French military interests was given by the Lebanese than by the Syrians, however, as the Lebanese counted upon more support from France in the future. Both treaties provided for the inclusion of Syria and Lebanon in the League of Nations three years after ratification. But the French Government had failed to ratify either of the treaties prior to the outbreak of the Second World War.

PALESTINE: THE BRITISH WARTIME COMMITMENTS

In all the vexed history of the Palestine mandate, a few salient points have too seldom been sufficiently emphasized. Two races inhabited modern Palestine, the Arab and the Jewish, both of which were there by right and not on sufferance. Both were legally entitled to hope for natural expansion and for social and economic betterment; and both had cultural and spiritual affinities with the land they shared in common. These races were not naturally incompatible or antagonistic, except in so far as their respective ambitions had made them so, but both had become intensely nationalistic and aspired to political ascendancy. The fact that the administrative scales were held temporarily — and only temporarily, according to the terms of the mandate — by a third and impartial Power meant that both races would continue to hope for a consummation of their nationalist ambitions, and this dual hope kept them from accepting any working compromise under the Mandatory Government.

The rights claimed by the Arabs in Palestine were threefold. First, they were in actual possession of Palestine before the First World War. Southern Syria had been Arab since the seventh century A.D., and its population was 90 per cent Arab in 1914. Second, Arab nationalists had earned their independence as allies of the victors of the war. The Palestinian Arabs had never risen in a body against the Turks, as had their brothers to the south of them; but it is still true to say that all Syrian and Iraqi Arabs of the Ottoman Empire had participated, directly or indirectly, in the Arab Revolt. Third, a pledge of independence to the Arabs of the Hejaz and of parts of Syria and Mesopotamia had been made in October 1915, on behalf of the British Government, by Sir Henry McMahon, then British High Commissioner in Cairo, in letters written by him to Sherif Hussein of the Hejaz, who proclaimed the revolt (see p. 66). The spirit of the McMahon Pledge, as it has been called, had been confirmed by the Anglo-French Declaration in November 1918 and extended to include all the Arabs of the Fertile Crescent

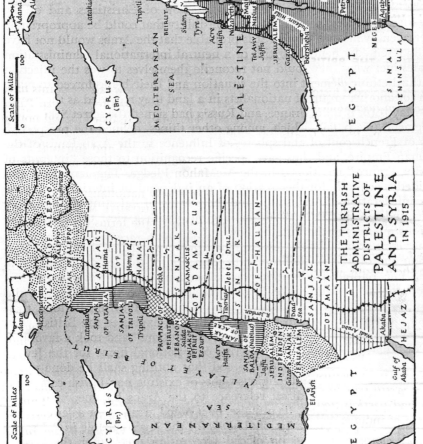

The map on the left is reproduced from *Correspondence between Sir Henry McMahon and the Sherif Hussein of Mecca, July 1915–March 1916*, Cmd. 5957, H. M. Stationery Office, London, 1939.

(Syria, Palestine, and Mesopotamia). Sherif Hussein, for his part, had been delegated by the Syrian secret societies to represent the Arabs of Syria as well as of the Hejaz and to base his demands on a secret document, formulated by them in May 1915 and known as the "Damascus Protocol." [3]

The McMahon Pledge made the important reservation that British promises referred only to those regions "wherein Great Britain is free to act without detriment to the interests of her ally, France." And it never specifically mentioned Jerusalem or Palestine. Presumably, as in other wartime measures, controversial issues were deliberately evaded. Sherif Hussein, having lived for many years in Constantinople, was not an unsophisticated desert Arab, and he was not unaccustomed to the usages of Western diplomacy. He must have known that Britain was in no position to promise him Jerusalem or Palestine, which were equally sacred to three world faiths, and he must have known that the protection of Christians and of the Holy Places in Palestine was not a responsibility that could be appropriately undertaken by his own people. It is probable that the Arabs would not have unduly resented a neutral British or a neutral international administration in Palestine; what they could not reconcile themselves to was the injection of a third ethnic element into the situation and their being forced to make room for another group of nationalists in a land they regarded as their own.

In May 1916, Britain, France, and Russia had signed the secret Sykes-Picot Agreement (see p. 66), which, among other things, defined the prospective areas of French control and spheres of influence in the Arab lands of the Ottoman Empire, and thus gave specific recognition to those "interests of her ally, France," mentioned in the McMahon Pledge. The agreement also provided specifically for the creation of an independent interior Arab state or a confederation of Arab states, and the placing of Palestine and the Holy Places under a special international regime, "with a view to securing the religious interests of the Entente Powers."

The rights claimed by the Jews in Palestine were based on the Balfour Declaration and on the whole historical connection of the Jews with the Holy Land. The Balfour Declaration was subsequent in date both to the McMahon Pledge and the Sykes-Picot Agreement. Like the promise to the Arabs, it took the form of a letter, in November 1917, from Balfour, then British Foreign Secretary, to Lord Rothschild. It expressed the British Government's sympathy "with Jewish Zionist aspirations" and took a favorable view of "the establishment in Palestine of a national home for the Jewish people, . . . it being clearly understood that nothing shall be done which may prejudice the civil and religious rights of existing non-Jewish communities in Palestine." Its indirect reference to the Arabs became, in itself, a source of future bitterness. Its promise, be it noted, was not for a Jewish state of Palestine, but only for a national *home* for the Jewish people *in* Palestine. Political Zionism received no official recognition until after the Second World War (see Appendix D).

The Balfour Declaration was as much a war measure as the McMahon Pledge and avoided possible controversial issues. But it was intended to be a definite contract with world Jewry. It was made with the full cognizance and approval of the Allies, including the United States, in an effort to transfer the influence and financial weight of world Jewry from the Central Powers to the Entente. It took a long view of British imperial interests — the establishment of a friendly outpost and strategic base on the highroad to India, adjoining the Suez Canal. It was lastly the result of unremitting labor on the part of Dr. Chaim Weizmann, president of the World Zionist Organization, among the British statesmen who were sympathetic to Zionist aspirations. We should note, however, that it was issued in spite of the practical objections raised by many anti-Zionist Jews in Britain and elsewhere.

Jewish communities had continued to live in Palestine since Bible days. Zionist immigration had begun in the latter part of the nineteenth century. Jews of the Diaspora [4] were "returning" to Palestine as early as 1860, and Jewish settlements, notably the seven pioneer "colonies," initiated by Baron Edmond de Rothschild between 1883 and 1900, had flourished under Ottoman rule. From Theodor Herzl to Chaim Weizmann, from the founding of the Zionist Organization in 1897 to the First World War, there had been a rising tide of Zionist irredentism. The breakup of the Ottoman Empire seemed suddenly to offer a larger fulfillment of these promising beginnings.

PALESTINE: ACHIEVEMENT AND PROSPERITY

In the transactions which we have been describing, the British Government did not stand convicted of bad faith so much as of over-optimism. The war had ended in victory; peace meant confidence. The British — perhaps typically — believed that economic advantage would overcome racial prejudice and would in the end win over the Arabs to Zionism. The Emir Feisal and Dr. Weizmann both attended the Peace Conference, the first as official delegate of the Arabs and the second as a representative of the Zionist Jews, and they had shown there a commendable willingness to co-operate. But Feisal had made his co-operation conditional upon the creation of a single Arab state in the interior. He said that, if the Arabs ruled a state stretching from Aleppo to Mecca, they could afford to allow Balfour's "small Palestinian notch" to be occupied by Jews, and he added the significant words, "The Jews are very close to the Arabs in blood, and there is no conflict of character between the two races. . . . Nevertheless, the Arabs cannot risk assuming the responsibility of holding level the scales in the clash of races and religions that have, in this one province, so often involved the world in difficulties. They would wish for the effective superposition of a great trustee, so long as a representative local administration commended itself by actively promoting the material prosperity of the country." [5] As we know, Feisal's single Arab state was overthrown by the French under Gouraud in 1920, and the southern part of his intended patrimony consequently became the autonomous Emirate of Trans-Jordan within the British Mandate for Palestine.

During the first decade of the mandate, however, it seemed that the Mandatory Government's optimism had been legitimate and would, in fact, be justified. In 1920, no individual and no government could have foreseen the nature or the extent of the dilemma of Continental Jewry after Hitler's advent to power in 1933. The enforced emigration of Jewish multitudes from Europe resulted in a pressure upon the Jewish National Home that completely unbalanced the intended policy in Palestine. Desperate exiles from Nazi-dominated countries turned a potential home into a unique refuge, and there resulted inevitably a dangerously unwise increase in the tempo of immigration into Palestine — dangerous because only so long as the Jews showed no signs of outgrowing their minority status could a reconciliation of the two nationalist groups remain in the realm of possibility.

The Arabs, it is true, from the beginning, refused to co-operate with the Mandatory Government, even at its pressing invitation. They might have participated in a legislative council or set up an Arab agency — as a companion piece to the Jewish Agency — but their action would then have been construed as a precedent or a *de facto* acceptance of the Jewish National Home. Arab and Jewish relations during this first decade were relatively good, however, and promised to be better. Rioting in Jaffa in 1921 was the only serious incident, prior to the disorders of 1929. British high commissioners, notably Sir Herbert Samuel and Lord Plumer, and Sir Ronald Storrs, nine years Governor of Jerusalem, were able men of traditional distinterestedness and integrity, and their terms of office passed with grateful smoothness. In 1926 the growing harmony was reflected in the almost complete demilitarization of Palestine. The British armed forces were reduced to a single Royal Air Force squadron and two companies of armored cars; and even the police were reorganized and reduced.

But subsequent events showed that latent antagonisms had not really been resolved. Contrary to the British hope, economic advantage had not overcome racial prejudice. The increasing prosperity of Palestine under Jewish enterprise, the very fact that the Zionists were hard-working, that they had brought with them advanced technical skills, that they were making an obvious and successful effort to reclaim the land and develop its resources, all this of itself gave rise to fears and forebodings. The Arabs came to fear, increasingly, the relentless advance and expansion of a relatively Westernized people, with foreign wealth and influence at its behest far beyond anything that they could themselves set up in competition. Even if they were not gradually and inexorably driven out of Palestine desertward, they feared that the Jews would soon outgrow their minority status and upset the equilibrium of populations in the country. They could not see them as co-workers, content to share the country and its fruits, but as "a menace to their livelihood and a possible overlord of the future."

The Mandatory Government might protest and reassure. Winston Churchill, in his oft-quoted Memorandum of 1922, made clear that British policy did not contemplate the subordination, still less the disappearance, of the Arab population, language, or culture, and did not intend the creation of "a wholly Jewish Palestine." And in this same statement of policy, the proposed extent of Jewish immigration in any given year was defined and limited to "the economic absorptive capacity of the country" in that year. But the bare facts of Jewish immigration soon gave substance to Arab fears — for what did the Arab peasants know of "economic absorptive capacity" or of any other legal slogan officially invented to justify the annual increases in immigration quotas? The Jews moreover often spoiled their case and lent countenance to the Arab attitude by their own hasty ways of going about their business. They invariably discriminated against Arab labor on land which had been bought and developed by the Jewish National Fund. Perhaps it was too much to expect of any people, at the moment of deliverance, the great moment longed for after centuries of homelessness and repression, to behave with the tact and moderation of seasoned statesmen. But Zionism came to Palestine in the twenties, not as a mature and graduated movement, but with all the shock of an organized invasion.

The Mandatory Government's problem was a triangular one. It was directly responsible, as trustee, to the League of Nations for the administration of the mandate, and it was indirectly responsible to Jews and Arabs outside Palestine, both of whom had powerful, but unequally effective, means of propaganda and political pressure at their command. It was faced with the task of balancing the scales between the expanding national programs of two strongly nationalistic groups within the limits of one small country — no larger than Wales or New Hampshire. And, as though that task was not enough, the two nationalistic groups were subdivided within themselves. The three Arab classes — the desert-bred Arabs, the fellaheen or peasantry, and the urban-bred all differed from each other. The first two were still tribal or semitribal in their concepts. But, in comparison with the Jewish immigrants, all three were lacking in sophistication, in education (of the Western variety), and in political cohesion. Among the Jews were various Zionist groups, moderate or otherwise, but all with political ambitions in Palestine. These were either Jews from Eastern Europe or else Occidental Jews from Western Europe and the United States. A small minority of intellectuals gravitated round the new Hebrew University in Jerusalem and concentrated upon cultural and economic rather than political interests. Then there were the strictly orthodox, or religious, nonpolitical Jews — probably less than 20 per cent of the Jewish population of Palestine. Many of these were Sephardic or Oriental Jews, who themselves were often resentful of the Zionist influx and Zionist objectives, and who alone were genuinely compatible with their cousin Arabs.

PALESTINE: THE COMMISSIONS AND WHITE PAPERS

For a decade, Palestine was never so prosperous. Thanks to devoted Jewish husbandry, its dry-baked and stony plains, long wasted under Turkish rule, sprouted and bloomed. The land flowed, if not with milk and honey, with wheat, citrus fruits, and tobacco. The Palestinian budget was always balanced, without the aid of foreign loans; and there was, quite logically, no unemployment problem.[6] Land was reclaimed, and irrigation works were built. The Jordan was harnessed for power; rich supplies of potash and bromides for the world market were extracted from the Dead Sea. Collective farms and co-operative societies for banking, insurance, transport, marketing, irrigation, and land-purchasing were organized and were, incidentally, most interesting experiments and object lessons, to Jews and Arabs alike, in community planning. There were match factories, cement factories, and vegetable-oil refineries. Tel Aviv, the only purely Jewish city in the world, multiplied its inhabitants tenfold between 1922 and 1936.

But all these good omens were later to be falsified. On September 24, 1928, in Jerusalem, during the service for the Jewish Day of Atonement, an incident occurred at the Wailing Wall, a lofty mass of masonry, once restored by Herod and some of it allegedly dating from Solomon, sacred to the Jews as the only relic of their ancient Temple. On the platform, bounded on one side by the Wailing Wall, stand two mosques, the Dome of the Rock and El-Aqsa, of which the latter ranks, after the mosques of Mecca and Medina as the third most holy mosque in Islam. During Ottoman times the Jews had enjoyed the right of access to the narrow pavement below the Wall — that is, the right of way and of station, in order to pray there; but the right carried with it the condition that no seats, screens, or other furniture should be erected. On the occasion of which we speak, the Jews did introduce a screen to divide the men from the women, and eventually the screen had to be forcibly removed by the police.

The incident was unpleasant, but small enough in itself. Nothing further untoward happened at the time. But for the next eleven months the Wall became a focus of propaganda and agitation by both Zionist and Moslem Arab groups. On August 15, 1929 the Jews marched in procession to the Wall; on the next day, the Arabs marched by the Wall to the mosque platform. A week later, Arabs were attacking Jews in different parts of Palestine, wrecking and burning. Six Jewish colonies were wiped out. The final death roll was more than a hundred on either side. It was as if an overburdened atmosphere had suddenly been discharged. The history of Palestine for the next decade, up to the Second World War, is that of successive commissions sent out by the British Government to find some working solution for a complex of circumstances that grew steadily more insoluble, and to counteract the rising tide of Arab Nationalist resistance to the inexorable expansion of the Jewish National Home.

The report of the second of these commissions, the Hope Simpson Report, was published in October 1930, and it was accompanied by a *Government Statement of Policy*, the white paper of Lord Passfield, then Colonial Secretary.[7] Inasmuch as the Passfield White Paper suggested restrictions on Jewish immigration quotas and on land sales to Jews, it seemed to the Jews to indicate a "reversal of policy" toward the Arab view. It was immediately repudiated by the Zionists, and Weizmann resigned as president of the Zionist Organization. The net result of the ensuing protests and conferences was the so-called "recantation" by the British Government — an explanatory letter written in February 1931 by Ramsay MacDonald, then Prime Minister, to Weizmann. This unhappy missive, known to the Arabs as the "Black Letter," gave the authoritative British "interpretation" of the Passfield White Paper. The only real difference between the letter and the white paper was one of tone and phraseology. The "Black Letter" did, in fact, succeed in reassuring the Zionists but, per contra, it destroyed the Arab hope of any limitation, territorial or demographic, of the Jewish National Home.

Both the white paper and the "Black Letter," however, stressed the fact that any future policy in Palestine, to be successful, would have to depend upon the initiation of "an understanding" between Jews and Arabs and upon their "willing co-operation." As the beginning of that co-operation, mixed municipal governments were inaugurated in Haifa and Tiberias and later, under an Arab mayor, in Jerusalem. Also, by 1935 a few Jews and Arabs were co-operating harmoniously in railroad and postal work and on a variety of economic committees. The process, in fact, was a good example of that "functional" approach, so much discussed at the present time, toward the solution of international discords.

Jewish immigration quotas in the early thirties, accordingly, took a sharply rising curve. It was calculated that if the immigration were to continue at the rate reached in 1935 the Jewish and Arab populations would have been equal in twelve years. During the four years 1929–32, 23,821 Jews were authorized to enter Palestine; during the three years 1933–35, 134,540 were authorized. At the same time, illicit Jewish immigration was on the increase. In 1930 and 1931, Arab bands committed several terrorist murders of Jews and destroyed Jewish farms and properties. Later, in 1933, the Arab Executive organized strikes and protested against government policies that favored any increase in Jewish immigration or Jewish purchase of land — the first time indeed that Arabs had come out formally and publicly against the Mandatory Government. There was some highly emotional controversy over alleged land purchase of plots of land, sometimes from absentee landlords, over the heads of tenants and cultivators, whose families had "possessed" those plots for generations, and heart-rending accounts were drawn of ignorant Arabs ejected and turned adrift by process of law, finance, and politics they did not understand. Official inquiry afterward showed the extent and the hardship of these dispossession cases to have been much exaggerated, but the attendant dispute did untold harm. A total of 3,000–4,000 Arabs had become landless by 1935 owing to Jewish purchases of their land, and most of them had drifted into the towns at a time of general world depression and of acute Arab unemployment.

In 1936 the prevailing unrest was aggravated by a number of external events. The Italo-Ethiopian War had its reactions in Palestine. In Egypt renewed negotiations for an Anglo-Egyptian treaty were in train to the accompaniment of student rioting. In Syria an effective nationalist strike forced the hand of the French Government into similar negotiations and into a similar, though not definitive, outcome. Successful appeals to force in neighboring countries thus served as object lessons to Arabs in Palestine, constantly humiliated by the sight of other Arab states coming of age politically and gaining their independence. In November 1935 all but one of the Arab parties in Palestine had united to draw up a memorandum which they presented to the Mandatory Government and, in terms which amounted to an ultimatum, demanded a democratic government, the prohibition of further transfer of

Arab lands to Jews, and the revision of the immigration system. A new re-formed constitution, which included a legislative council, was prepared by the Mandatory Government and offered to the Jewish and Arab leaders for their consideration. But it was unanimously rejected by the Jews, who were in the minority, as being "too representative"; and, as it was not considered democratic enough by the Arabs, it was accepted only by the moderates among them. The proposed reforms were deadlocked.

In April 1936 the Arabs declared a "National Political Strike." It was a spontaneous mass rising under Arab leaders who had temporarily sunk their chronic differences to combine in open revolt against the mandate. Organized terrorism was let loose upon the countryside. There were strikes in the towns, guerrilla warfare in the highlands, looting and armed robbery and sabotage throughout Palestine. An Arab Higher Committee, as it was sub-sequently called, consisting of leaders of all parties, plus two Christian Arabs and the Mufti of Jerusalem, the well-known Hajj Amin Effendi el-Husseini,[8] directed the campaign and co-ordinated locally-formed strike committees. A Syrian soldier of fortune, el-Kawakji, eventually became "Generalissimo" of the rebel forces; but the leadership of the strike remained in the hands of the Arab Higher Committee and took its inspiration from the Mufti. The strike lasted six months in all and caused about 400 Jewish casualties, less than one-quarter of which were fatal. About 800 Arabs lost their lives, but not at Zion-ist hands. The Jewish population behaved with extraordinary self-restraint, and there were scarcely any Jewish reprisals against the Arabs. The social and political maturity of the Jewish National Home and its high degree of group discipline were never so convincingly demonstrated – in striking contrast to the later period of Jewish terrorism in 1944–48.

Eventually, in October, in a joint note, the rulers of Iraq, Saudi Arabia, Trans-Jordan, and the Yemen appealed to the Arabs of Palestine "to resolve for peace" and, yielding to this unprecedented and most desirable expression of Arab solidarity, with its implications for future support from the Arab world at large, the Arab Higher Committee at last abandoned a struggle that was becoming more and more unequal.

As soon as the Arab National Strike ended, the Peel Commission was sent out to Palestine to investigate the "underlying causes" of the disturbances and, in July 1937, after eight months of intensive work, it published its report, a definitive document, fair and sympathetic to both sides, and a mine of source material on the country and its peoples.[9] It found the underlying causes of the disturbances of 1936 to be "the same" as those of the disturbances of 1921, 1929, and 1933, "namely, the desire of the Arabs for national independ-ence and their hatred and fear of the Jewish National Home." It suggested various palliatives: adequate representation for the Arabs; restriction and safeguarding of the sale of Arab lands; restriction of Jewish immigration in accordance with a new principle, "a political high level," as well as the eco-nomic absorptive capacity of the country; censorship of Jewish and Arab newspapers, improvement of Arab education, the formation of Arab co-oper-ative societies, and so forth. Its one revolutionary proposal was partition, the formation of "two sovereign independent states," Jewish and Arab, plus a mandated area or enclave which should contain Jerusalem and Bethlehem.

The Mandatory Power, in addition, was to administer a Nazareth enclave, to maintain the peace in Haifa, Acre, Safed, and Tiberias, and keep open an Arab corridor to the Mediterranean between Jerusalem and Jaffa. As a possible alternative to partition, it also suggested cantonization, namely, that the various existing communities of Jews and Arabs should be formed into cantons, or partially self-governing units, under a central or federal government. The Arabs uncompromisingly, and the Jews by a large majority, rejected these proposals. As Sir Herbert Samuel put it, partition would create "a Saar, a Polish Corridor, and half a dozen Danzigs and Memels in a country the size of Wales." As for the cantons, they would be both less decisive and less thorough than partition, they would contain minorities of the racially unwanted, they could not be efficiently insulated from each other and, most important, they would not wholly fulfill either Arab or Jewish aspirations.

The publication of the Peel Report was the signal for renewed violence, and the second phase of Arab insurrection was launched. The Arab Higher Committee petitioned the Mandates Commission of the League of Nations for an end of the Jewish National Home and for "an immediate cessation of immigration and of land purchases" until such time as the mandate should be replaced by an Anglo-Palestinian treaty, similar to the Anglo-Iraqi and Anglo-Egyptian treaties of 1930 and 1936. In September 1937 an Arab National Conference, meeting at Bludan in Syria, confirmed the demands of the Palestinian Arabs. In the same month, the Acting District Commissioner of Galilee was murdered. The British at once took drastic action. The Arab Higher Committee was dissolved; the Mufti of Jerusalem was deprived of his high offices, and he left the country secretly for the Lebanon. Military courts were set up, and a state of semimartial law was introduced. In November the Jews were stirred to reprisals for the first time. The Mandatory Government was unable to control the situation, and ubiquitous terrorism finally developed, in the spring of 1938, into open rebellion. By late autumn of 1938 there were between 18,000 and 20,000 British troops in Palestine. The Arab quarter of Jerusalem was occupied. The European situation, meanwhile, and the Nazi persecutions of the Jews were extra complications and distractions. Germany, following Italy's lead in 1936, spurred Arab rebels to extreme courses by unscrupulous propaganda and by concrete assistance in the shape of money and weapons. The Mufti, from his refuge in the Lebanon, continued to inspire the revolt. The extent of the Arab Rebellion may be gauged from the fact that casualties in 1938 amounted to 3,717 killed, nearly half being Arabs. The rebellion continued until May 1939.

In this atmosphere the British Government sent out to Palestine a new commission, the Woodhead Commission, to work out the geographic details of partition. The Commission's report, in October 1938, recommended against partition and put forward a fresh scheme, this time for "economic federalism," a modification of partition that would provide for the setting up of a customs union between Arab and Jewish "states" and several mandated areas. Simultaneously, a British white paper rejected the plan of partition. The political and financial difficulties of partition were considered insuperable. No frontiers could be drawn that would not leave many thousands of Arabs in the Jewish state; no Arab state could be set up that would be self-supporting or financially self-sufficient; no Jewish state could be devised that would not contain the bulk of the Arab-owned citrus areas; and no Jewish state would be adequately defensible or possessed of "natural frontiers."

Early in 1939 a Round Table Conference met in London. Delegates were chosen with some difficulty, but eventually they represented all shades of opinions, Jewish and Arab. Delegates also came from Saudi Arabia, Iraq, and Egypt. But the Palestinian Arabs — not, be it noted, the delegates of the Arab states — refused to sit with the Jews or to discuss their mutual problems with them face to face. Arabs and Jews were therefore interviewed separately by representatives of the British Government, and the Conference became in effect two parallel conferences. When British proposals for an agreed settlement were rejected in turn by both parties — even after revision — the conferences came to an untimely end. Mediation was subsequently attempted by the Arab states and the Moslems of India, who met the Palestinian Arabs at a further conference in Cairo, but without success.

In May 1939 the British Government issued a further white paper, its last word (up to the Second World War) on all the negotiations, investigations, conferences, and stalemates of the previous three years.[10] In a lengthy preamble, in answer to the various claims and counterclaims, and in order to avoid all further misunderstandings, the British Government announced its adherence to the view that "the whole of Palestine west of Jordan was excluded from Sir Henry McMahon's pledge." The fullest details and figures were given to illustrate the growth and development of the Jewish National Home. At the same time, despite its explicit recognition of Zionist achievement, the British Government declared "unequivocally" that Palestine should not become a Jewish state, since "His Majesty's Government believe that the framers of the Mandate in which the Balfour Declaration was embodied could not have intended that Palestine should be converted into a Jewish State against the will of the Arab population of the country."

On the positive side, the White Paper of 1939 envisioned "the establishment within ten years of an independent Palestine State," in treaty relationship with Britain. "The essential interests" of the Jews and Arabs were to be effectively safeguarded, and both peoples were to share in the government of their common state; but the exact form or nature of the proposed independent Palestine state was "in no way prejudged." The ten years would be a transitional period for the development of a sense of joint responsibility and education through participation in the machinery of government. But if, at the end of ten years, the British Government should conclude that the establishment of the independent state ought to be postponed, it agreed to submit the problem to "representatives of the people of Palestine, the Council of the League of Nations, and the neighboring Arab States," and seek their co-operation in achieving "the desired objective." During the transitional period, land sales were to be restricted, and their transfer regulated by the High Commissioner. Some 50,000 Jewish immigrants would be authorized in the next five years (a quota of 10,000 a year) together with an additional 25,000 refugees "as a contribution towards the solution of the Jewish refugee problem" — a total of 75,000. Thereafter Jewish immigration was to cease, "unless the Arabs of Palestine are prepared to acquiesce in it." Representatives of the people of Palestine and of the British Government were to meet together, five years after the restoration of peace and order, to work out a constitution for the proposed independent state. "His Majesty's Government cannot hope to satisfy the partisans of one party or the other in such controversy as the Mandate has aroused. Their purpose is to be just as between the two peoples in Palestine whose destinies in that country have been affected by the great events of recent years, and who, since they live side by side, must learn to practise mutual tolerance, goodwill, and co-operation."

TRANS–JORDAN

In British eyes "Transjordania," the land beyond the river Jordan, fell within the area pledged to Arab independence, and in October 1918 it became a part of the Arab National State that was organized under the Emir Feisal ibn Hussein, with its capital at Damascus. And so it remained until the French forces under General Gouraud annexed its northern, or Syrian, section in July 1920. The British felt it incumbent upon them to rescue the remnant of Feisal's "interior" Arab state which had been thus left derelict. Accordingly, in September 1922, the League Council approved the creation of a separate state, which should be exempt from the terms of the Jewish National Home. The new state was named Trans-Jordan and given an autonomous and subsidized government. A ruler was found for it in the person of Abdullah ibn Hussein, elder brother of the Emir Feisal.

This was the same Abdullah, son of the Sherif Hussein of the Hejaz, who had approached the British in Cairo in 1914 with regard to Arab independence (see p. 66). He now came from the Hejaz at the head of a desert force with the avowed intention of attacking the French in Syria and avenging their treatment of his brother Feisal. But he allowed himself to be diverted from that rash purpose and was grateful to be installed, instead, as Emir of Trans-Jordan. His government was proclaimed in May 1923. He agreed to accept British advisers on foreign relations, finance, and jurisdiction over foreigners, and arrangements to that end were afterward confirmed in the basic Anglo–Trans-Jordan Treaty of 1928. The British Resident at Amman, the Trans-Jordanian capital, was responsible to the High Commissioner of Palestine; but otherwise Trans-Jordan and Palestine were administratively insulated from each other. Throughout the period of the mandate, Jews were refused the right to settle or to acquire land across the Jordan.

The history of the country was uneventful, except for tribal raids by the Wahhabi warriors of the Nejd. In 1924 it seemed possible that the southern part of Trans-Jordan might fall into the compass of Ibn Saud's conquests; but subsequent agreements between the British and Ibn Saud, on the eve of the Saudi conquest of the Hejaz, defined its frontiers with the Nejd.[11] Trans-Jordan remained at peace, one of the chain of Arab states, but technically a part of the British Mandate for Palestine.

IRAQ

The easternmost of the mandates, Iraq, completes the number of Arab territories over which the League of Nations assumed indirect control in 1920. During the First World War, Britain had made it plain, both to the Arabs and to the French, that the southern part of Mesopotamia — the Ottoman vilayets of Baghdad and Basra — was a special object of her concern. She was interested in Mesopotamian and Persian oil. But, more than this, the Persian Gulf had virtually become a British-Indian lake, important to British strategy in the Near East. The treaty which Britain signed in 1899 with Sheikh Mubarak of Kuwait was the last link in a chain of veiled protectorates which she had established, one by one, by means of special treaties with the Arab rulers of the Gulf principalities. In 1914, when Turkey joined the Central Powers, Turkish intervention in the area would have been a continuing threat to British security in India, and a potential Turko-Arab coalition against Britain had to be forestalled. The result was the British-Indian campaign in Mesopotamia in 1914–18 (see pp. 23 and 65). In 1917 the Indian Government announced the annexation of Basra and Baghdad.

After the war the British introduced a civil administration into Iraq, and a new Iraqi judicial code and civil police, all modeled on British-Indian lines. Sir Percy Cox, as Chief Political Officer, also adopted the system so successfully used in Baluchistan by Sir Robert Sandeman. He rebuilt and strenghtened the tribal organization which had been shattered or dangerously weakened by the Young Turks before the war. Competent sheikhs, under British "advisers," were held responsible for peace and order in their respective tribes; and their loyalty was secured by subsidies and by the immunity of their tribes from taxation. But the system, effective enough and even necessary in an early period of rehabilitation, was really a restoration of the old feudalism and out of keeping with the political evolution which, in fact, the entire Near Eastern world was undergoing. Nor did it touch the Arabs of the towns, who, in the nature of things, had already broken with the tribal way of life.

Into this situation was injected the Arab nationalist movement. The Iraqis, after their glowing anticipation based on the Anglo-French Declaration of November 1918 (see p. 223), found that they were to be denied the same independence as was given to the Hejaz or even the limited independence accorded to the Arab National State in Syria, and in June 1920, a few days after the official proclamation of the mandate, a serious insurrection broke out. Several British officers were murdered, including the famous Colonel G. E. Leachman,[12] and the half year of disturbance eventually cost 10,000 British and Arab casualties, killed and wounded.

Independence, albeit partial, was the only proper answer to the insurrection, and in the autumn of 1920, once order had been restored, Sir Percy Cox, now High Commissioner, addressed himself to the task of creating an Iraqi national government. He formed a Council of State of eight Arab ministers, and he succeeded in persuading the venerable religious dignitary, Abdur Rahman el-Gailani, the Naqib of Baghdad, to accept its presidency. That remarkable woman, Orientalist and traveler, Gertrude Bell, as Sir

Percy's Oriental Secretary, assisted him in the work of tribal pacification which had to be undertaken anew, and it was due in great part to her efforts that the Emir Feisal was subsequently chosen King of Iraq by 96 per cent of the Iraqi people.

The problem of Iraq's ruler was not a simple one. It is true that only very few Iraqis were inclined to a republic and that most of them wanted a king; but there was no agreement, at first, as to who that king should be. Iraq had its own local candidates, more popular than Feisal. Some factions thought him too pro-British; but most of those who opposed his candidacy did so because he was an Arab of western Arabia and a son of the Sherif Hussein and, for all his distinguished leadership of the Arab Revolt and for all his stature and dignity, they did not want one of his family, the Hashimi, ruling in Iraq. Then also Ibn Saud, in the center of the Arabian peninsula, might conceivably object to the elevation of a hereditary rival on his northeastern flank. The British themselves favored a pro-British ruler and one, in particular, who by the wholeheartedness of his co-operation would enable them to reduce the already heavy cost, financial and political, of administering the mandate.

Abdullah had been elected King of Iraq in March 1920 by the same Congress of Notables that had elected his brother Feisal King of Syria. As we have already recounted, Feisal was subsequently ejected from his kingdom by the French. Abdullah was persuaded by more peaceful means to relinquish his title to Iraq — a delicate mission accomplished by Colonel T. E. Lawrence — and, as we described above, to accept in its place the new territory of Trans-Jordan. Feisal went to Iraq and was duly "elected" to its vacant throne. On the whole he was very well received, both by his new subjects and by the Arab world as a whole. Britain entered into relations with Iraq in the Anglo-Iraqi Treaty of October 1922, under whose terms the High Commissioner became "Adviser" to the King, supervised the country's military development, and controlled its finances. The treaty embodied for the most part the specific obligations originally assumed by Britain in the mandatory document. There was a special Judicial Agreement; and provision was made for the employment of British officials. An Organic Law, subsequently adopted, gave Iraq a constitutional, hereditary monarchy, a bicameral parliament, Moslem religious courts (Sunni as well as Shi'a), civil courts, and "Spiritual Councils" for the Christian and Jewish communities. The greatest defect of the administrative system thus inaugurated was the duality of responsibility implicit in the maintenance of two cadres of Iraqi and British officials.

Thereafter the kingdom made rapid strides toward independent status. A second treaty in 1927 relaxed the military and financial controls, and a third treaty in 1930 finally confirmed its complete independence and sovereignty. In 1932, Iraq became a member state of the League of Nations. Despite early prognoses to the contrary, this was a consummation achieved in record time.

Meanwhile Iraq gradually underwent a process of Westernization. In the early thirties it was practicable for local administration to be transferred progressively from British to Iraqi hands. These were the constructive years.

Agriculture was intensively developed, notably cotton and winter wheat. Oil remained, however, the country's greatest economic asset. The great trans-desert oil pipe lines from Mosul to Haifa and Tripoli were completed in 1935.

One problem that remained in Iraq was that of her non-Arab minorities, a full quarter of her population. Between 1922 and 1924 there had been an insurrection on the part of the Kurds living in the mountainous Iraqi-Turkish and Iraqi-Persian borderlands, a tribal, Sunni Moslem people with evident nationalist aspirations of their own. In 1928 there was trouble with the Baha'is, members of a modern religious community of Persian origin, whom the Iraqi Supreme Court, yielding to fanatical Shi'a pressure, had lately deprived of its properties in Baghdad. There was also in Iraq a curious "minority problem in reverse." The majority of the Arab-Moslem population belonged to the Shi'a sect but was traditionally ruled by the Sunni Moslem minority, and Iraq therefore was always peculiarly liable to feel the tensions of Shi'a and Sunni antagonism.

At the same time some Assyrians, recently driven out of Turkey, had settled among the Kurds and Arabs of northern Iraq. They were a Christian community, believed to be descended from the Nestorians of the Early Christian era, now destitute and wholly dependent on the hospitality of their Iraqi hosts — despite which they aspired to an autonomy of their own. From time to time, whenever they had gotten into difficulties with Kurds or Arabs, or with both, they had formed the habit of appealing over the heads of the Iraqi authorities to British army officers or inspectors or to the High Commissioner in person. Iraq's emancipation rendered such appeals illegal as well as tactless, and the situation became unbearable to both sides. Iraqi opinion hardened and turned militant, and the separatist demands of the Assyrians were persistently refused. In 1933 some of the Assyrians tried to emigrate from Iraq into Syria; the Syrians had minority problems of their own and were none too cordial. The Assyrians returned to Iraq and forthwith clashed with units of the Iraqi Army sent north to receive them back. The Assyrians were armed and fought with spirit and, for their temerity, the Iraqis indulged in a retaliatory massacre of about 600 of them who had been induced to surrender their arms in return for promises of safe conduct. This barbarous episode, occurring so soon after Iraq's attainment of her independence, was much publicized, greatly to the detriment of her prestige abroad. The League of Nations intervened to find a home for such of the Assyrians as had no declared intention of settling co-operatively in Iraq.

King Feisal died in 1933 in the middle of the Assyrian furor. His son became King Ghazi and ruled till he was killed in an automobile accident in 1939. Feisal latterly had tended to centralize more and more power in himself and was unobtrusively moving toward a royal dictatorship, a process which, under the younger, weaker, and more inexperienced Ghazi, degenerated into irresponsible authoritarianism. There were plots and counterplots, mostly by army officers. General Bakr Sidqi achieved his *coup d'état* in 1936 and installed a Pan-Arab cabinet. When four-year-old Feisal II came to the throne in 1939, Iraqi policies were in a serious way.

ARAB UNION

Since Napoleon's invasion of Egypt and Southern Syria, the Arab world had been rousing itself from its long torpor under Turkish rule to a recollection of its former greatness and to an anticipation of a greater future. The early renaissance of the nineteenth century was primarily cultural; the twentieth-century movement was primarily political. A national movement was born and developed, inspired by the desire for Arab unity, and having as its ultimate objective the complete emancipation of all lands which had once been united within the great Abbasid Caliphate of the ninth century, during the golden age of Arab political and cultural supremacy. In this book we have recounted the later phases of the Arab awakening, the "Revolt in the Desert" of 1916–18, the founding and dissolution of the Syrian Arab National State in 1918–20, and the subsequent emergence of the Arab lands, after their liberation from the Turks, in a bloc of mandates and monarchic states.

In 1916, and again in 1918, the Arabs had been given to expect their freedom or, at the very least, autonomy. But expectations had not been fulfilled. Northern Syria and the Lebanon had become a French mandate. Southern Syria (Palestine) and Trans-Jordan, together with Iraq, had become British mandates. Egypt had been metamorphosed into a kingdom, but remained under British control. Sherif Hussein's bid, in the First World War, for Arab hegemony and, in 1924, for the Caliphate ended in defeat at the hands of his Arabian rival, Ibn Saud of the Nejd, and in his resultant exile from the Hejaz. His ambitions, much reduced, survived him in his sons — Abdullah, who became Emir of Trans-Jordan, and Feisal, the original leader of the Revolt in the Desert, who became King of Iraq. Simultaneously, in the heart of Arabia, arose a new power in the person of Ibn Saud, who founded the theocratic Kingdom of Saudi Arabia after conquering Hussein's Kingdom of the Hejaz.

But the last chapter in the Arab story was far from told. Egypt and the mandated areas received a great impetus toward Westernization; they achieved stability and relative prosperity under ordered government. The spread of modern education, modern transport and communications, even to some extent modern capital and industry, were all strands in their developing nationalistic nexus. And eventually the modernization of Arab lands in close touch with the West produced repercussions in the remoter Arab countries. For these and other reasons, the ideal of Arab unity survived the partition of the Arab lands, and the Arab "nation" — by which is meant all the peoples of the Arab area — surmounted the barriers raised by the peace settlement of 1920. After 1930, in modern diplomatic form, Arabs increasingly gave expression to their desire for greater solidarity in conferences and congresses and pacts. An Islamic Congress, convened in Jerusalem in 1931, inspired the organization of a separate Arab Congress and resulted in the holding of later congresses, in which Christian Arab as well as Moslem Arab delegates participated. In the Pan-Arab Congress which met at Bludan, Syria, in September 1937, representatives from Palestine and six Arab countries took a strong position against the first official proposal that was made to partition Palestine. At the government level, there was also an increasing *rapprochement* between the Arab states. In 1936, Saudi Arabia and Egypt entered into diplomatic relations and, in that same year, Ibn Saud and the son of his old rival, Feisal of Iraq, signed a comprehensive Treaty of Arab Brotherhood and Alliance. In 1937 the distant Yemen adhered to the Saudi-Iraqi Pact — a pact whose participants invited the adherence of other independent Arab states.

The further progress of Arab union during the Second World War and the founding of the Arab League we defer to a later chapter (see p. 869).

17 RUSSIA: COUNTERREVOLUTION AND THE ESTABLISHMENT OF THE SOVIET REPUBLIC

COUNTERREVOLUTION AND THE CIVIL WAR

For Russia the First World War ended with the Treaty of Brest Litovsk in March 1918. She ceded territories in the Ukraine, the Don, the Baltic, and Finland which German and Austrian forces proceeded to plunder and forage (see p. 94). Lenin had been prepared to cut his losses, vast and humiliating though they were, to win a "breathing space" for his revolution in Great Russia.[1] Domestic questions were then more pressing than the renewal of war. And it almost seemed as if Lenin would succeed in his object. Up to that moment the Russian Revolution had shed little blood. As in Germany at the corresponding stage of the German Revolution, the people seemed too exhausted and dazed for violence. Organized counterrevolutionary opposition was slow in developing, and the Bolshevik triumph in Russia had therefore a deceptive air of effortlessness and decisiveness about it. An unprejudiced observer, in the early spring of 1918, could have scanned the wide expanse of Great Russia and seen scarcely a sign or signal of the civil war which was so soon to carry devastation into almost every one of the Russian provinces. In May 1918, to mark the consolidation of its position and demonstrate its break with the Tsarist past, the Bolshevik Government transferred itself from Petrograd to Moscow.

Already in March 1918, however, British naval units had been landed at the Arctic port of Murmansk, presumably to prevent its becoming a German submarine base and to repossess the military stores which the British Government had originally shipped there for the use of the Tsarist armies — and perhaps to encourage the overthrow of the Bolsheviks and the reopening of the Eastern front against Germany. Similarly, in April, Japanese naval units landed at Vladivostok, presumably to protect Japanese persons and property in the extreme east of Siberia. In May further British forces landed at Murmansk, and in August, at Archangel. In the same August, British and American forces landed at Vladivostok, presumably to keep a watchful eye upon the Japanese, who were already there. British forces advancing north from Mesopotamia occupied the oil fields at Baku and the Black Sea port of Batum. Early in 1919 a mixed force of French, Polish, Greek, and Rumanian troops, under French command, occupied Odessa. Meanwhile the Allied navies established a close blockade of all accessible Russian waters.

Counterrevolutionary and separatist movements would doubtless have developed in Russia in any event, but this widening Allied intervention gave them the material support and recognition which otherwise they would never have had. Here and there the Allies sponsored White "governments" favorable to themselves. The Japanese supported an anti-Bolshevik Cossack leader, Semënov by name, at Chita near Lake Baikal. The British supported a "Republican Government of the North" at Archangel and kept in touch with the picturesque Social Revolutionary and terrorist, Savinkov, who enjoyed a meteoric moment of power at Yaroslavl. Even the Germans, before the armistice of November 1918 compelled them to withdraw, had their favorite in the person of Skoropadsky, their puppet in the Ukraine, and in the Cossack General Krasnov in the Don. In Finland, German troops were assisting the Finnish Whites under General von Mannerheim in crushing the Finnish Reds. From the summer of 1918 onward, anti-Bolshevik uprisings of one sort or another were breaking out all over Russia. There were counterrevolutionary committees and constituent assemblies in Siberia and the Middle Volga. A "Volunteer Army" gathered north of the Caucasus under a staff of refugee Tsarist generals, such as Alekseev, Kornilov, and Denikin, and was shortly receiving French and British military supplies. Various nationalist groups, the Georgians, the Kalmyks, and others, tried to set up autonomous states. The Austro-German withdrawal from the Ukraine left that region in chaos. Ukrainian Nationalists under Petlyura ejected the pro-German Skoropadsky and set up an independent republic only to fall in turn before a strong force of Bolshevik troops. Roving guerrilla chieftains, like Grigoriev and Makhno, plundered the land at will. Savage Jewish pogroms took place in Kiev and Odessa. German Free Corps were operating in the Baltic States and, it was creditably rumored, were receiving aid from British warships, which had now entered the Baltic Sea. Lenin's "breathing space," so dearly bought at Brest Litovsk, had been a mockery of hardly two months' duration.

The most extraordinary of all the counterrevolutionary uprisings was that of the Czech Legion. The origin of this famous body of men has already been mentioned (see p. 85). Throughout 1917 it had fought on the Eastern front with distinction. Brest Litovsk had left it without aim or object, and Masaryk, the Czech leader, who was then visiting Russia, conceived the idea of transporting it round the world to the Western front in France by way of the Trans-Siberian Railway. Masaryk had preceded the Legion to Vladivostok and sailed thence to the United States with every expectation that it would shortly follow him.

Czechs and Bolsheviks in these early days had shown no special antipathy for one another. In March 1918, at Penza, Czech and Bolshevik representatives signed an agreement permitting the Czech Legion to retain a certain quota of its arms and arranging for its safe and expeditious passage over the Trans-Siberian Railway. Yet there must have been suspicion and friction between the two parties, despite their agreement and despite their common Slavic brotherhood; and the best-intentioned plans in a country in the midst of revolution may sometimes go awry. A decision on the part of the Soviet authorities to transport a contingent of the Czechs via Archangel may have given the impression that an effort was being made to divide the Legion and rescind the Penza agreement. Then, at Chelyabinsk in the Urals, a brawl is alleged to have broken out between some Czechs and Hungarian prisoners of war who, in this Asiatic fastness two thousand miles from their homes, had still not forgotten their racial animosities. At all events Trotsky began sending out panicky orders for the disarming of the Czechs, orders which the Czechs naturally resisted. The Czechs, now straddled out over the length of the Trans-Siberian Railway, were making their gradual progress eastward, and they proceeded forcibly to "occupy" important junctions along the line. During May and June 1918 the Czech Legion thus possessed itself of most of the Trans-Siberian Railway from Chelyabinsk to Vladivostok.

The disposition and timing of the Czech revolt, accidental though they were, happened to be of the first importance to the entire counterrevolutionary movement. The Czechs, who had no real interest in the domestic affairs of Russia and no real wishes other than to complete their roundabout itinerary to Europe, now found themselves by this strangest of fatalities forming a liaison force and linking together all the aimless, planless anti-Bolshevik groups throughout eastern Russia and Siberia. They were hailed as heroes by the Allied press, and their exploits lauded to the skies. Certainly their coup assisted the Allied recognition of the new Czechoslovakia in no small degree.

Whites and counterrevolutionaries from the Don to Vladivostok for the first time were suddenly in possession of a strategy and an objective. In September 1918 a State Conference of the anti-Bolshevik groups was held in Ufa in Bashkiria on the western edge of the Ural forests, and thither repaired a strange assortment of "governments" bent on forming a united front. The conference elected a Directory, which afterward maintained itself precariously at Omsk and came under the effective control of a nominee of the Allies, Kolchak, a former Tsarist admiral.

In the heart of Bolshevik Russia these uprisings had their repercussions in a number of political murders all too reminiscent of the shootings and bombing of Tsarist days. In July 1918 the German ambassador, Count Mirbach, who had come to Moscow after Brest Litovsk, and the general commanding the German occupation army in the Ukraine were both assassinated. At the end of August, Uritsky, head of the Cheka (the Bolshevik secret police) in Petrograd, was shot, and Lenin himself narrowly escaped death at the hands of a couple of women anarchists.

The end of the Tsar and the imperial family was another aspect of the same sanguinary picture. In April 1918 the Tsar and the imperial family and a few faithful servants had been removed from their confinement at Tobolsk to Ekaterinburg (Sverdlovsk) and were lodged there in pretty rough quarters at the direction of the local soviet. But fearing the outbreak of counterrevolution and the approach of one of the many White armies now operating in Siberia, the local soviet gave orders that they should be executed. On the night of July 16, 1918, in the cellar of their house, the deed was carried out. The bodies were afterward carted away to a small mining village some miles from Ekaterinburg and, in order that no relics should fall into friendly hands, were destroyed with sulphuric acid and benzine. Some charred scraps of jewelry were all that were afterward picked up.

Whether or not counterrevolution would have succeeded in Russia has long since ceased to be even an academic question. The eventual Bolshevik success bears the stamp of inevitability, as do all great historical events — after they have happened. Certainly Allied intervention was not energetic, nor was it well co-ordinated, and the Allied troops that were used were war weary and liable to catch the indiscipline of the revolutionary environment into which they were thrown. Official Britain and France detested a revolutionary government which had caused Russia to desert the war, betrayed the secrets of their diplomacy, appealed to their working-class population to revolt, and confiscated their Russian properties and investments. The Allied press generally devoted itself to essays of indiscriminate anti-Bolshevik vituperation. But Allied diplomatic and military activities were vacillating in the extreme. Britain and France, just after Brest Litovsk, had been inclined to carve Russia into "spheres of influence," as if she had been some decaying Oriental empire ready for colonial exploitation.[2] Lloyd George, from the Peace Conference at Paris, at one moment would be appealing to the Russian factions to sink their differences and discuss a settlement, and at another would be ordering the shipment of British munitions to the counterrevolutionary armies, while Russian *émigrés*, of course, sedulously propagated the view that Bolshevism was a passing phase, waiting to be overthrown (see p. 117). Allied agents in Russia, notably the British Bruce Lockhart and the American Colonel Robins, in closer touch with the situation, dared to recommend that Bolshevism was worthy of recognition and sympathy.[3] In March 1919, Bullitt, a member of the American peace delegation in Paris, was sent to Moscow and succeeded in obtaining definite concessions from the Soviet Government, only to be "disowned" on his return. Herbert Hoover and Fridtjof Nansen were then proposing to send food supplies to Russia "on condition that the Bolsheviks cease their military operations." The whole, as we look back on it now, was not a very creditable episode of blunder, misinformation, and prejudice.

KOLCHAK, DENIKIN, YUDENICH

Three White Russian commanders contended against the Soviet during 1919. The first was Admiral Kolchak, operating from Omsk in liaison with the Czech Legion in Siberia; the second was Denikin, now in command of the "Volunteer Army" occupying the Kuban and the Don; and the third, a comparative newcomer in the field, was Yudenich in Estonia. All three commanders obtained from Britain and France the munitions and supplies with which to conduct their campaigns. The histories of their three campaigns were very similar. They opened with sudden sorties from their base of operations, they gained rapid, initial successes, they seemed for a time to be on the high road to a decisive victory, but they gradually encountered difficulties, and they ended at last in humiliating retirement and "liquidation." In March 1919, Kolchak reached Ufa; in August and September, Denikin took Odessa, Kiev, and Orel; in October, Yudenich was in the very suburbs of Petrograd. The tides of White invasion into Red territory were deep and sweeping, yet they broke, one and all, and ebbed back again to their point of origin.

All three commanders had adopted a safe, democratic ideology. Their armies contained a goodly proportion of Tsarist officers, but any suspicion of monarchism was suppressed. No one attempted or suggested the restoration of the Tsar. Kolchak, Denikin, and Yudenich each bore before him a standard declaring that he would re-create "a great, united, undivided Russia" on democratic lines, and that his first action after victory would be to convene an all-Russian constituent assembly. Yet, in the main, the final repulse of the three commanders seems to have been attributable to their failure, first, to co-ordinate their own military efforts, and second, to enlist popular sympathy and support in the territories they occupied. Despite their professions, they introduced regimes which were essentially military and dictatorial, and they brought in their train the hated features of the old prerevolutionary order. Under their protection the exiled landlords returned to their estates, officials to their offices, capitalists to their factories, and these, like all repatriated *émigrés,* had learned nothing and forgotten nothing. White grain requisitions were as ruinous as the Red; the executions without trial were as arbitrary and as numerous; the White soldiery behaved as brutally and vilely. There were sanguinary peasant revolts and uprisings along the tenuous lines of communication, and the Red Army began its education in those guerrilla tactics which it was to use with such effect in the Second World War.

THE DEFEAT OF COUNTERREVOLUTION

The Soviet heart of Russia during the latter half of 1918 had fallen into such a state of atrophy and prostration that one is almost at a loss to explain how it ever survived. Factories were at a standstill; industrial output had declined to the vanishing point; the bigger urban centers, once busy and prosperous, were being virtually depopulated by an exodus of starving workers into the country. Railroads had deteriorated beyond pretense of usefulness, and the few trains that ran were seized by mobs of demobilized soldiers trying to get to their homes. Brest Litovsk had taken away the Ukrainian grain lands, 70 per cent of the former Russian iron and steel works, and 90 per cent of the former Russian sugar industries; and the Austro-German evacuation after the armistice of November 1918, far from restoring these resources, left them in an advanced stage of devastation and decay.

It was in accordance with Marxian principles that the old order should be destroyed before the new should be created. Thus the old bureaucracy, the police, the law courts, the banks had all been done away. Russia had lost the most elementary organs of civilized life. Class hatred, deliberately stirred up, assisted the process of destruction. Landowners, kulaks,[4] employers of labor, professional men, officials were "liquidated" as a class. Inflation enabled the government to command the resources it needed by the repeated issues of new paper money, and it seemed also designed to destroy everything which, under the former capitalist system, could be regarded as a saving or investment. There was very little in the way of urban-manufactured consumer goods for which the peasant might be induced to exchange his produce, and forcible methods of collecting grain had shortly to be used. During the summer of 1918, as the conditions in the cities declined to famine levels, the Food Commissar organized "Committees of the Poor," "unions of the hungry against the well fed," which were little better than foraging parties of the poorest peasants, whose function it was to "requisition" any hidden stores the kulaks and the "middle" peasants had laid by, and whose services were paid for with a rake-off of the takings. Such drastic methods did perhaps secure some foodstuffs for urban consumption, but they introduced the worst features of class warfare into the country districts. Then, in the autumn of 1918, exasperated by the Social Revolutionary conspiracies, by the assassination of Uritsky and the attempted assassination of Lenin, the Cheka, the dread Bolshevik secret police, inaugurated the "Red Terror" and, at a conjecture, accounted for 50,000 lives in the course of the Civil War.[5]

And to all this was superadded the counterrevolutionary assault, the nationalist secessions, and the Allied intervention. At the height of the Kolchak-Denikin-Yudenich episode, when the White encirclement reached its narrowest circumference, the area which still paid allegiance to Bolshevism barely amounted to the provinces round Petrograd and Moscow, an area, as has been pointed out, about equal to the Muscovite principality of the fifteenth century. Well might Lenin predict that the defeat of Germany would result in "an offensive of world capital against us."

But revolutionary fanaticism is irrepressible and admits not defeat. Perhaps the Soviets had better tactical leadership than their adversaries; perhaps the Communist party leavened the lump and gave the Soviets a more resilient organization than any the White forces ever possessed; perhaps that convenient and irrefutable phantasm we call "historic necessity" moved in its mysterious ways its wonders to perform and granted ultimate victory to the seemingly weakest side in the conflict. For, between 1918 and 1920, Soviet Russia, a country exhausted by war and revolution, threatened within by anarchy and economic collapse, threatened without by an advancing array of enemies, unrecognized and vilified by every other nation, not only survived but established itself as one of the Powers of the world. Even the most violent detractors of Bolshevism cannot deny the facts of its triumph, or withhold some tribute of admiration for its amazing struggle for existence.

Leon Trotsky was the man of the moment. His extreme political theories had not always found favor among his colleagues, his workmanship at Brest Litovsk was much criticized, his Semitic origin never helped him to real popularity; yet he was a military organizer of undeniable genius. In June 1918 he had set about conscripting a new army, the Red Army, disciplined by political commissars and largely commanded by former Tsarist officers. By the end of 1918 he is said to have had 500,000 men, tolerably well armed and trained. He had begun to dream of the reconquest of Finland, Poland, and the Baltic, and of forging links with the future Soviets of Germany and the Middle Danube.

Trotsky's forces were supported and supplied by an economic system known as War Communism. It was the final *reductio* of Marxian theory, "the expropriation of the expropriators," the concentration of all the means of production and distribution in the hands of the new Soviet bureaucracy, the militarization even of labor. From the founding of the Supreme Economic Council in December 1917 to the NEP in 1921, to be described later, the state "nationalized" the larger mines and industries — ultimately it took over all enterprises using mechanical equipment which employed more than five workers, and handicraft enterprises which employed more than ten workers; it staffed these enterprises, when necessary, with its own managers and made every worker therein a state employee. It seized, as and when it desired, houses, libraries, gold, jewelry, and movable private property of any kind; it even broke open the deposit boxes in the banks. Gradually it abolished the little that was left of private trade and assumed a monopoly of the exchange of goods. It eliminated money as a medium for transactions between state undertakings; it increasingly substituted wage payments in kind for wage payments in the ever depreciating paper ruble. Later it instituted forced labor in the form of "labor armies," especially for mining, forestry, road making, and repair work on the railroads. Finally, in so far as food was concerned, it supported itself by means of grain requisitions and distributed manufactured goods therefor through village co-operatives, but the process often enough degenerated into arbitrary raids on the peasants' stocks. Under such a regime lived Moscow, Petrograd, and their districts in 1919, and the regime gradually absorbed all Russia with the ebb of counterrevolution and civil war in 1920.

THE RUSSO–POLISH WAR

We have already mentioned the Russo-Polish War of 1920 in a previous chapter (see pp. 175–76). The Peace Conference had left undefined the future frontiers of Poland toward Russia, and no relations of any kind had been established between the governments of Moscow and Warsaw. We also mentioned that, in December 1919, the Allied Supreme Council had laid down the so-called Curzon Line, a tentative frontier corresponding roughly to the ethnical division (see p. 175). But many Poles, now that they had recovered their ancient liberties, were far from satisfied with so limited an interpretation of their aspirations, and were branching out to recover the ancient possessions of their fathers in the heyday of the former Polish Kingdom. Various schemes were mooted for a federation of the Russian border states, Estonia, Latvia, Lithuania, the Ukraine, and even the Don — all, of course, under Polish hegemony. Hereditary Russo-Polish antagonism and the squirearchical character of the new Poland supported these ambitions. France, who regarded Poland as her particular protégé and future ally, and also as a sturdy link in the *cordon sanitaire* which her Premier, Clemenceau, hoped to construct against Bolshevism, was glad of any expansionism that would increase Poland's strength. There were secret parleys between Russian and Polish agents during 1919, but they led to no result. Poland was evidently temporizing. Early in 1920 she was making preparations for war.

In April 1920, Denikin, the White Russian commander, resigned his command in southern Russia to General Wrangel, a man favorably disposed toward Polish ambitions, and under the evident patronage of France a joint invasion of Russia was launched by Wrangel, the Poles, and Petlyura, leader of the Ukrainian Nationalists. In a couple of weeks Wrangel was advancing strongly up the Dnieper; the Poles had captured Kiev; Petlyura ranged and ravaged like a nomad khan throughout the Ukraine.

Like every one of the counterrevolutionary campaigns, this one also opened with surprising initial successes and then developed into a halt and eventual retirement. The Polish onslaught roused Russian fervor and indignation more deeply than all the rapacities of Kolchak and Denikin. Racked and bled though she was, Russia experienced in herself a tremendous upsurge of patriotism. A number of Tsarist generals offered their services to the Red Army, and an advisory staff was organized under the direction of Brusilov, the hero of the Russian offensive of 1916 (see p. 60). By mid-June of 1920, the Red Army had retaken Kiev, and that hapless "Mother of Russian Cities," fought over by Germans, Austrians, Bolsheviks, Ukrainian Nationalists, Whites, guerrillas, and Poles, now changed hands again for the ninth time in three years of warfare. The Poles were in headlong rout. The Russians crossed the Berezina and took Vilna, Kovno, and Brest Litovsk. A Polish Soviet government was set up at Bialystok. Danzig longshoremen struck and refused to unload Allied munitions for Poland.

The Poles appealed to the Allies. In July, Grabski, the Polish Premier, went to Spa, where an Allied conference on reparations was being held, and he was bluntly advised to sue for an armistice on the terms of the Curzon Line. The French fully expected the collapse of all their policies in Eastern and Central Europe. General Weygand, Foch's former Chief of Staff, at the head of a French military mission, was sent to organize the defense of Warsaw and was generously provided with French munitions. Lloyd George in Britain, though harried and hectored by Labor opposition against new interventionist schemes in Russia, was constrained nevertheless to threaten naval action in the Baltic if the Red Army's progress was not brought to a halt. And then occurred the "Miracle of the Vistula." On August 15, 1920 the Poles counterattacked, and the Red Army retreated as precipitately as it had advanced.

Military experts have compared this strange, kaleidoscopic campaign with almost every famous battle from Marathon to the Marne. The Polish recovery on the Vistula has been variously attributed to the grim resolution of the Polish Marshal Pilsudski, to Weygand and French munitions, to the errors of Soviet cavalry tactics, and even to the unpredictable vagaries of the Russian temperament. It was now the Soviet which sued for an armistice. A preliminary peace was signed at Riga in October 1920. Poland secured an eastern frontier which put some 4,000,000 Russians under her rule, a frontier she held till 1939. The peace was confirmed in a definitive treaty at Riga on March 18, 1921.

The finale of the Russian Civil War was enacted in the picturesque peninsula of the Crimea, once the happy pleasance of grand dukes and tsars.

Here, at the end of 1920, Wrangel was penned up with 30,000 men and with them a motley host of fugitive nobles, governors, generals, bishops, and other ex-Tsarist officials, many with their wives and families. Only France still gave him aid. Britain, now winding up her Russian adventure, shunned him; British troops had evacuated Murmansk and Archangel; Krassin had been in London talking peace. In the end, White troops and refugees were evacuated from the Crimea in French warships, but thousands were left behind to be mercilessly massacred by the Red Army.

THE GREAT FAMINE AND THE NEP

Once again, as after Brest Litovsk, the Soviet Government addressed itself to the work of reconstruction. The successful termination of the Civil War gave it at last that "breathing space" it had wanted so desperately in 1918. The country, as Lenin well knew, had borne the cruel yoke of War Communism only so long as the immediate military necessities demanded, but the people's murmurings would soon be audible if the rigors of that regime were not lifted and the demobilization of the Red Army were not now accompanied by the promise of a brighter future. As a general index, industrial production in 1920 had declined to 13 per cent of its volume in 1913. Peasant land seizures and grain requisitions had reduced the area under cultivation by a third. In February 1921 the naval garrison at Kronstadt, once the stalwart supporters of the Bolshevik Revolution, mutinied, and almost simultaneously a peasant uprising occurred in Tambov, one of the central provinces, south of Moscow. For a moment it seemed as if the removal of the White peril was to be the signal for a general revolt of the impoverished, overburdened masses.

But still one more calamity was to visit Russia. Prolonged drought in 1920 caused a complete crop failure throughout the "black-earth" districts of the Volga, the Don, and over large parts of the Ukraine. War Communism, the requisitions, and the Allied blockade had exhausted the usual food reserves — even seed for sowing had been consumed — and the country's transportation system, wherewith other supplies might have been brought up, was in a ruinous state. By the summer of 1921 famine gripped a population of 20,000,000 to 30,000,000, a fifth of European Russian. In the most stricken areas the inhabitants were in flight or were being systematically evacuated by the government. Roughly 750,000 persons are said to have left their homes to be resettled, temporarily or permanently, elsewhere. Cholera and typhus ravaged the depleted towns and villages and were accompanied by those mental and moral phenomena of famine, the panics and suicides, the cannibalism and that terrible onset of apathy and resignation which was perhaps the most obstinate and incurable of the effects of the whole weary tragedy.

The Soviet Government was in no position to provide immediate relief on so huge a scale. Illustrated papers in Western countries published gruesome photographs of the cracked and barren Volga earth and the wretched, sunken-eyed, potbellied semiskeletons which then peopled it. Food and medicines were sent from abroad by charitable organizations in America, Britain,

France, and Germany. The American Relief Administration under Herbert Hoover sent in all $62,000,000 worth of commodities and at one time was feeding 10,000,000 persons daily. "White" influences tried to play politics and divert the relief into partisan channels.

Lenin already had a partial answer to Russia's economic situation. "We are in a condition of such poverty, ruin, and exhaustion of the productive powers of the workers and peasants," he said in his speech at the Tenth Communist Congress in March 1921, "that everything must be set aside to increase production," and he introduced a decree establishing a grain tax in the place of the former grain requisitions.[6] The NEP, the New Economic Policy, as it was called, took its rise from this famous decree. In effect, a free market was opened to the peasant for his produce, and "normal" and uncontrolled trade between town and country was again encouraged. A new ruble was put into circulation. The individual tenure and exploitation of land was permitted. A state bank was founded.

Many Bolshevik theorists, notably Trotsky, opposed the NEP on grounds of principle. War Communism, even with its compulsory features, they believed represented the true Marxism in practice and was a system to be kept in perpetuity, whether for war or for peace. Trotsky declared that all his hard-won victories over the enemies of revolution would be betrayed if Soviet Russia was now to truck with capitalism and to reintroduce, even as a temporary measure, the old abuses of money, profits, and private enterprise. But the problem now was not one of preserving Marxian purism for its own sake, but of producing consumers' goods. Lenin realized that the economic deterioration of Russia could go no further, and he decided "to beat a retreat." Lenin's grain decree of March 1921 was an outstanding example of his realism and of his courageous disregard, when necessary, of Communist shibboleths.

Even if the NEP once more encouraged the kulak to hoard grain, even if in time it bred its own peculiar progeny, the new bourgeois or "Nepmen," as they were called, it was not too high a price to pay if the proletariat could once more get food to eat and clothes to wear. Furthermore, the NEP relieved the appalling bureaucratic congestion at Moscow, it brought about a welcome "decentralization" of the greater part of the monopolies vested in such bodies as the Supreme Economic Council, it repaired a little of the fierce antagonism between town and country which the grain requisitions had inevitably engendered, it created a new system of "trusts" for the management of denationalized industries under private individuals, and it restored to the provincial soviets many of the functions which the stress of the Civil War had taken away from them. Above all, it abolished the forced labor which had been the most hateful and tyrannous feature of War Communism. The beneficial effects of the NEP were evident within the first year of its operation. Here again, as we so often see in this Age of Conflict, economic recovery, given conditions of peace, even after appalling devastation, can be extraordinarily rapid.

SOVIET FOREIGN RELATIONS AFTER THE CIVIL WAR

The defeat of their counterrevolutionary efforts forced the Allies to revise their Russian policy. Revolutions, it has been said, have a way of thriving on the resistance they offer to foreign intervention, and Bolshevism was no exception. During 1919 influential circles in Britain were already beginning to wonder whether the "Russian adventure" was not having the reverse of the intended effect. The British Labor party had always been opposed to intervention; Lloyd George had only been persuaded to give it a trial so long as it promised success; Lord Curzon's interest in Russia — he was then British Foreign Secretary — had been confined mainly to the Caucasian oil fields and to his fears of Russian aggression against his beloved India. Only Churchill and a few extreme Tories persisted in their implacable Russophobia and demanded that something should be retrieved from the £100,000,000 of munitions which the British Government had thrown into Murmansk and the Don. Psychologically Britain was then entering upon her postwar retreat to isolationism and pacificism, and was looking to trade rather than to warfare as the norm of her future relations with Europe. In December 1919, Litvinov had already opened parleys in Copenhagen with British agents for the exchange of prisoners of war. In January 1920, as a first indication of changed Anglo-Russian relations, the British Government raised the naval blockade. Between April and July 1920, British forces were withdrawn from northern Russia and Siberia. British forces were also withdrawn from the Caucasus, and British concession hunters tacitly renounced their quest for oil in the area. Soviet forces occupied Batum. Azerbaijan, Armenia, and later Georgia were organized as Soviet republics.

Krassin, the Soviet envoy, in the character of a "sober man of business," came to London to meet Lloyd George in May 1920 and, for the first time since the Bolshevik Revolution, ranking Western and Russian statesmen sat at the same conference table. Russia was "in the market" for trade agreements and diplomatic recognition, and it behooved Britain to make her bids while the bidding was good. But the conversations were anything but cordial. The press in both countries engaged in a malicious sniping campaign; the Russo-Polish War was raging simultaneously. Lloyd George, anxious though he was for Russian trade, was still determined to quarantine Russia spiritually and to put a stop to Russian propaganda, especially in the East. After interminable conversations, breakdowns, and resumptions, an Anglo-Russian trade agreement was signed on March 6, 1921, two days before the Soviet-Polish Treaty of Riga. Nevertheless, Britain's full recognition of the Soviet Union waited until the MacDonald cabinet in 1924 (see pp. 326 and 328).

By 1920–21, Russia was busy making peace with all her neighbors. She had signed treaties with Estonia in February 1920, with Lithuania in July 1920, with Latvia in August 1920, and with Finland in October 1920. She signed treaties with Persia and with Afghanistan in February 1921, and she signed a treaty with Turkey in March 1921.

France faced the inevitable with far greater reluctance. During 1920 she had still put her trust in Wrangel and had hoped that the Poles might triumph where Kolchak and Denikin had failed. French right-wing interests never recovered completely from their anti-Bolshevik complex; they never renounced their claims on the huge prewar indebtedness of Russia to France; they never gave the quietus to their fears of an eventual Russo-German *rapprochement*. France only re-established relations with the Soviet Union at the time of the Herriot ministry in October 1924 (see p. 318).

The United States, meanwhile, had withdrawn its forces from Siberia during 1920 but, despite this pacific gesture, it had continued in an attitude of official hostility toward the Soviet Government. It agreed, in Secretary of State Colby's note of August 10, 1920, that the boundaries of the new Russia "should properly include the whole of the former Russian Empire," with the exception of Finland, "ethnic Poland," and the "Armenian State," but it refused formal recognition of a government "whose conceptions of international relations are so entirely alien to its own, so utterly repugnant to its moral sense." The United States did not recognize the Soviet Union till 1933 (see pp. 596–97).

Japanese troops remained in Siberia during 1921, and the Japanese Government supported an anti-Bolshevik regime in Vladivostok. The troops were not withdrawn till November 1922, after considerable pressure from the United States, but a small Japanese force continued to occupy the northern part of Sakhalin. The Soviet Union thus completed its reoccupation of Siberia. A Soviet-Japanese settlement was made in a treaty signed in January 1925. Japan recognized the Soviet Union and agreed to evacuate the northern part of Sakhalin in return for certain oil and fishing concessions there.

During 1922, Lloyd George sought to secure Russian participation in his grandiose scheme for an economic "European Consortium." The NEP seemed to indicate a reformed attitude on the part of the Soviet Government, and reports then being received of the effects of the recent Volga famine were enough to convince any man with a drop of humanitarianism in his blood that, whatever the politics of Russia's leaders, her people were in the direst need of help and understanding. We have elsewhere discussd the conference at Genoa in April 1922, convened to give effect to this "Consortium" (see p. 162). Poincaré from Paris was unhelpful, and the Russian delegates used the conference as a political platform and then signed the Treaty of Rapallo with the German delegates. The "Consortium" was never heard of again. But, despite its disappointments, Genoa did signify Soviet Russia's graduation into the councils of European diplomacy.

THE SOVIET SYSTEM

The word *soviet* means "council" or "committee." In the revolts of 1905 the Russian soviets had been committees of workers improvised for the occasion, and the Revolution of 1917 created them afresh. Each factory, each battalion, each village was soon electing its soviet of workers, soldiers, or peasants as the case might be. As such there was nothing very novel, extraordinary, or erudite in the idea. In moments of grave emergency, when civilized life breaks down, men will always form themselves into bands of one sort or another. We recall the well-known chapter on "Clubbism" in Carlyle's *French Revolution:* "Are not such Societies [he might almost have said soviets] an incipient New Order of Society itself? The Aggregative Principle anew at work in a Society grown obsolete, cracked asunder, dissolving into rubbish and primary atoms?" But what was novel and extraordinary in the soviets of 1917 was their being employed, not only as "organs of rebellion," but also as the nuclei of a complete and permanent political system.

In the days before the First World War, in their party program of 1903, the Bolsheviks had demanded of their coming revolution nothing more than "a legislative assembly of the people's representatives," elected upon time-honored democratic lines. Nor apparently did Lenin himself, even after the Revolution of March 1917, entertain other views regarding the form of the future Russian state. But in the ensuing months Lenin began to sense the importance of the soviets and to envision them as the possible fabric of his new order. By November 1917 the idea of a legislative assembly had gone into the discard, and the Bolsheviks seized control under their strange device, "All Power to the Soviets." When the long-promised Constituent Assembly met in Petrograd in January 1918, it was dissolved by decree of the Soviet Executive Committee, and the non-Bolshevik deputies were ejected by force.

"The Soviets are become the apparatus of government" — we paraphrase Lenin's words in October 1917. "They are a connection with the masses that is so intimate, so indissoluble, so readily verifiable and renewable, so informal and democratic, that nothing like it has ever been approached before. They exist without bureaucratic formalities and represent the most diverse occupations. They are the vanguard and the school of the whole gigantic mass of the oppressed classes which till now have stood outside all political life and all history. Compared with bourgeois parliamentarianism they are a development of democracy which is of world significance."

The system pyramided upward from a broad base of many thousands of nuclei soviets. Thus the village *(selo)* soviets elected the territorial *(krai)* soviets; these elected the provincial *(oblast)* soviets; these elected the soviets of the constituent republics, and these finally elected the Congress of Soviets. The franchise at the base was of the greatest latitude. Every man and woman above the age of eighteen was qualified to vote and to be elected to any office. Only those employing labor for hire, those living on unearned incomes, and those mentally deranged or convicted of crimes, as well as monks, priests, and members and officials of the former ruling dynasty, were "deprived." Voting took place at public meetings by a show of hands.

The soviet system was regularized in a "constitution or fundamental law," adopted by the Fifth Congress of Soviets in July 1918, and at the same time the state was formally established under the title of the Russian Socialist Federated Soviet Republic, the R.S.F.S.R. The First All-Union Congress of Soviets, in December 1922, established the Soviet Union or Union of Soviet Socialist Republics, the U.S.S.R., of which the R.S.F.S.R. was henceforth to be only one of a group of constituent republics. A new constitution was adopted by the Second All-Union Congress of Soviets in January 1924 to regularize this augmented state. The constituent republics were then seven in number: the R.S.F.S.R., the Ukraine, White Russia, the Transcaucasian

Federation (itself a federation of three republics: Azerbaijan, Armenia, and Georgia), Turkmen, Uzbek, and Tajik.

In constitutional theory, the All-Union Congress of Soviets of some 2,000 Deputies or more, meeting once every two years, was the supreme repository of power. Each Deputy, in the roundabout way we have described, represented 25,000 town or city electors or 125,000 peasants, a disproportion greatly to the advantage of the urban proletariat, whose Communism was supposed to be more reliable and preponderant. But in practice the Congress of Soviets proved too unwieldy and intermittent for regular business. It became little more than a picturesque "biennial picnic" for distant provincial Deputies visiting the capital for the first time. It therefore elected, and delegated its authority to, the more permanent Central Executive Committee (TSIK), a bicameral body, which consisted of a Soviet of the Union of some 400 Deputies, representing the total population, and a Soviet of Nationalities of some 150 Deputies, representing the national subdivisions of the Soviet Union. The Presidium of the Central Executive Committee consisted of nine Deputies from the Soviet of the Union, nine from the Soviet of Nationalities, and nine elected by a joint session of those two bodies. The Presidium was a "collective presidency" of the Soviet Union, and it fulfilled the somewhat ceremonial and confirmatory functions exercised by the president or constitutional monarch of a democratic state. The greater part of the top-level executive work of the Soviet Government was formally entrusted by the Central Executive Committee to a Council of People's Commissars (*Sovnarkom*), which corresponded to the cabinet of ordinary democratic usages. At the time of which we are writing, Lenin was President of the Council of People's Commissars, and Trotsky was Commissar for War. Stalin, then not a widely known figure, was Commissar for Nationalities. The President of the Central Executive Committee and "President of the Soviet Union" was the former metalworker and Bolshevik, Kalinin.

A second constitution, the so-called Stalin Constitution, to be mentioned later, was adopted in 1936 (see pp. 290–91).

COMMUNIST THEORY AND THE COMMUNIST PARTY

The Russian state — the Communist, Bolshevik, Soviet State — sprang from a man and a doctrine. The man, it is true, was afterward glorified beyond his deserts, and the doctrine was corrupted by the inevitable pragmatism of living politics. But they inspired the pristine fervors of the Revolution, and the Russia of our era is not to be understood without them.

Karl Marx in the last century was the father of modern Communism. He was born in 1818 at Trier in Germany of a family of Christianized middle-class Jews. Extreme radicalism debarred him from what might have been a brilliant academic career, and he lived in exile, supporting himself as best he might by journalism, but keeping in active touch with revolutionary movements around him. He spent the latter part of his life in London, where he wrote his great treatise on *Capital,* and where, in 1883, he died.

Like all social reformers Marx was obsessed by the sufferings and the inequality of man. For him the whole theme of history was the struggle between strong and weak, oppressor and oppressed, rich and poor, master and slave, capitalist and worker — between the class that controlled the means of production and the class that was thereby controlled. Under modern capitalism, Marx argued, by an inexorable logic, the rich became richer and the poor became poorer; wealth accumulated at one end of the scale and poverty at the other. The upper strata of society continually narrowed into luxurious isolation; the lower strata of society continually broadened into indigent proletarianism. Competition between capitalists was swallowed up in mergers and monopolies, and in the process capitalism lost its competitiveness, its only virtue and recommendation. Imperialistic wars and recurrent economic crises of increasing frequency and severity revealed the self-contradictory and self-destructive elements inherent in the system.

Capitalism, Marx argued further, found it necessary to set up a coercive machinery for the advantage and preservation of its beneficiaries. The State, with its law, police, and army, was that machinery. The State was not so much a device for maintaining peace and order as a product of the class struggle, and it exacerbated the class struggle. And the struggle would only be brought to an end when the proletariat revolted, set up its own dictatorship, and created a free and equal classless society. The expropriators would then be expropriated; the State as such would no longer serve any political purpose.[7]

Marx regarded his revolution as something necessary and inevitable like a law of nature. He believed that his theories had given him the secret for understanding the movement of history and the development of human society. Yet, doctrinaire though he was, he had a remarkable insight into political tactics, and he was not above changing his tactics to suit the needs of the moment. His experience of the abortive revolution of 1848 convinced him that revolution in practice must be a complicated undertaking, an almost military campaign, needing a trained cadre of men to work for it and direct it. It cannot rely on mass forces to arise automatically. Especially does it need a trained cadre *after* it has succeeded.

We have become all too familiar today with the ways of revolutionary "parties." We have seen Fascists and Nazis at work. But time was when the Communist party was a unique organization, and when revolutionary apostleship was a mystery into whose powers and practices the world at large had still to be initiated. Perhaps it is best paralleled in historical experience with the preaching friars, Jesuits, Puritans, Jacobins, and other *corps d'élite* which from time to time have energized great human movements and which, for good or ill, have given a new direction to the normally inert masses of mankind.

It may be said that the major difference between Communism and democratic socialism was that the former vested its strength in the Party and the latter in the People. Communism was the politics of the professional revolutionary, who belonged to a small conspirative clique of men of hard training, fanatic courage, and iron discipline. Democratic socialism was the politics of the ballot box in which the people as a whole freely participated. Communism might intend the dictatorship of the proletariat, but the Communist party itself was almost a reversion to the aristocratic idea.

The professional revolutionary was peculiarly the product of Tsarist Russia. The mass of the old Russian peasantry was backward, ignorant, and stupidly reactionary. Certainly it was poor material for a revolution. It might contribute much — as indeed it had done in times past, and did again in 1917 — to the destructive side of a popular mass revolt, but little constructively to the permanent political form of a new state. Urban industrial labor was not to be despised, but it was relatively unorganized in Russia, lacked leadership and, up to 1917, it had never been the political force in the Russian population that it was in other industrialized countries. The old Russian middle class was numerically unimportant and without aggressive self-consciousness. If, then, revolution there was to be in Russia, it would have to be the work of that curious, declassed, self-alienated, self-disinherited group of men, the so-called intelligentsia. In the West the intelligentsia as such was unknown. The Western intellectual belonged to a certain level of education and spent his life in creative work in literature, art, or science. He might be of independent character, but he was not necessarily revolutionary nor even necessarily interested in politics. He bore no resemblance to the hero of a Dostoevsky novel. Yet there grew up in pre-1914 Russia a sectarian, terroristic, fanatical type — he might be peasant, bourgeois, or even a "repentant" nobleman, and he was often quite uneducated — but he was the stuff out of which the professional revolutionary, and thence the Party, was made.[8]

The Russian Social Democratic Workers' party was founded at Minsk in 1898. It already acknowledged the leadership of Vladimir Ilich Ulianov, otherwise known as Lenin. It was burned and sharpened in the fires of the time, as Lenin forged out of it the hard metal he needed. At a congress held in London in 1903, the more radical Bolsheviks (literally "the majority") under Lenin severed themselves from the more moderate Mensheviks (literally "the minority"). The issues were sharp and fundamental. Generally it may be said that the Bolsheviks represented the strict Party faction and the Mensheviks represented the parliamentary, democratic faction. In February 1917 the Bolsheviks are said to have numbered 30,000, dispersed throughout the Tsarist empire. During the eight months of the Provisional Government in 1917, they grew to 200,000. In 1918, shortly after the conclusion of the Treaty of Brest Litovsk, they took the name of "the Russian Communist Party (Bolsheviks)." In 1929, they numbered over 1,000,000; in 1939, they numbered over 1,500,000 and they boasted in addition some 5,000,000 young people under twenty-three years, known as Komsomols, Pioneers, and Octobrists. Never at any time before 1941, however, does it appear that the adult membership of the Party was much more than one per cent of the total population of the Soviet Union.

The Party was hardly a political party in the Western sense. It has been described as an oligarchy, a leadership corps, a blood brotherhood, "a machine for generating power," even a religious order. Certainly no religious order demanded more of its votaries. Admission was granted on the severest terms, and the credentials of every applicant were checked and cross-checked by competent investigators. A man or woman, once enrolled for membership, belonged body and soul to the Kremlin, subscribed to an absolute belief in the Marxian faith as interpreted by Lenin, and later by Stalin, and rendered a blind and unquestioning obedience to his or her particular superior in the hierarchy. "The Party," wrote Stalin, "is the vanguard of the working class . . . the organized detachment of the working class . . . the highest form of class-organization of the proletariat . . . the instrument of the dictatorship of the proletariat . . . the embodiment of unity of will, incompatible with the existence of factions. . . . It is strengthened by purging itself of opportunist elements." [9]

In organization, the Party pyramided upward like the soviets. Any three or more members, wherever they were gathered together, instituted a "cell" or primary party organ. Cell members, in duty bound, assumed the leadership, whether in farm or factory or office or regiment, presented themselves as candidates for election to the local soviet, assisted at local meetings with advice and inspiration, showed themselves tireless, zealous, and productive workers, acted as transmitting agents of the orders and decisions of the higher powers. To them inevitably fell the greater part of the farm and factory managerships and the posts in the new bureaucracy. Above the cells, in due succession, in exact analogy to the soviet system, rose the "conferences," the urban, provincial, and republican conferences, and topping the pile was the Party Congress of some 3,000 delegates meeting in Moscow every three or four years.

The core of the Party Congress appears to have been the All-Union Party Conference, meeting prior to the Congress itself, drawing up agenda and devising future policy which the Congress would then be asked to ratify. The core within the core was the Central Committee, and within the Central Committee again was the permanent Politburo, generally regarded as the most powerful body in the Soviet Union. The Secretary General of the Party since 1922 was Joseph Stalin. In a book of limited space we cannot begin to explain the various functions of these bodies, functions and bodies moreover which had a way of changing from time to time. Yet it should be clear enough that this huge, devious pseudo bureaucracy stretched downward from a central authority, highly and mysteriously pedestaled in Moscow, and reaching ultimately into every remote part of the Russian land and people.

Human nature is weak, and missionary ardor is apt to cool, and in the multitude of its members the Party was bound to contain a residue of "deviators," peculators, malingerers, and other undesirables. There were also the place seekers and climbers, as well as sincere renegades from orthodoxy. From time to time the Central Executive Committee therefore appointed control or cleansing commissions as the chief inquisitors of Communist zeal and orthodoxy. Besides individual tests, reprimands, and expulsions, there were wholesale "purges" of the Party. In 1921 one-third of the numbers were purged; in 1929, one-tenth; in 1933, one-eighth.

Yet to the outside observer of Russian affairs, far more sinister than these occasional political delinquencies and their periodic correction was the subtle social transformation of the Party's upper ranks. The higher Communist bureaucracy, by sure but imperceptible stages, took to itself all the trappings of a caste. Power, wealth, and precedence became concentrated in the hands of a few thousand men. Democratic countries, with instinctive wisdom, protect themselves from their bureaucracies by underpaying them, but in the Soviet Union bureaucracy and Party enjoyed the highest prizes in the state. Doubtless there was still room in the Party for convinced fanaticism and intense activity in behalf of the old revolutionary cause. But even admirers of the Soviet system could not fail to see, about the time of the early thirties onward, Party wives behaving like "socialites" and Party children acquiring the snobbery of the sons of millionaires. Even if salaries were officially and formally restricted, other privileges such as expensive living conditions, food, clothes, housing, and automobiles were being reserved to the fortunate few. Elegant prostitution was reminiscent of the gilded decadence of St. Petersburg in 1914. The classless utopia in less than a generation of its existence had come to be governed and exploited by class. The State, which in Communist prediction was "to wither away," was reborn in an infinitely more oppressive and vulgar form.

It is impossible to think of the Communist party, or indeed of the Soviet Government, without its secret police. "The Extraordinary Commission for Combating Counterrevolution and Speculation," the Cheka, had been originally founded by order of Lenin in December 1917. In those early genial days of the Russian Revolution, the Bolsheviks were theoretically opposed to the death penalty, and the Cheka was not a very powerful or sanguinary organization. But after the political assassinations of the summer of 1918, which, as we have said earlier, included Uritsky, the head of the Cheka, and nearly included Lenin himself, it was given a new head in the person of Felix Dzerzhinsky, and it entered upon its first campaign of terrorism. In February 1922, about the time that Russia was attempting to reconcile herself with foreign Powers, the Cheka changed its name to the United State Political Administration, the Ogpu; but apparently it changed neither its character nor much of its personnel. The old methods remained with it, the spying and delation, the secret arrests and interrogations, the tortures, the exiles, the forced labor camps, and "liquidations."

But in the eyes of the Bolsheviks such procedure was justified. The proletarian revolution was to be no shoddy palimpsest, but a clean new page in the history of the world, and certainly the Bolsheviks' own sufferings in the counterrevolution and the Civil War had not been such as to dispose them toward charitable policies. Trotsky, who must bear much of the responsibility for the Cheka's work, in neither his writings nor his speeches shows the slightest compunction or misgiving, and Lenin, in a characteristic passage, asked if "our war" of the exploited against the exploiters, which cost half a million or a million lives, was less justified than the war of "international imperialism," which cost ten million, "to decide whether British or German robbers should rule the whole world." [10]

Soviet Russia, it is impossible to deny, became a regular police state. Communism took the road to autocracy as once Tsardom had done. It has often been said that there was little difference between the ultimate development of Lenin's revolution and that of Peter the Great a century and a half before. Both initially were Western importations, both were violent ruptures with the native past, both introduced economic etatism, both created a privileged bureaucracy, both were highly militarized, both became disproportionately interested in the preservation of power, both exalted a supreme despot, both were permeated by terror.

THE THIRD INTERNATIONAL (COMINTERN)

In Communist theory, the proletarian revolution must be international. The worker knows no country. The world must be made safe for Communism. Marx himself founded the First International, or International Workingmen's Association, in 1864. It was a sort of cosmopolitan revolutionary congress and met annually. The Paris Commune of 1871 and the secession of the Anarchists under Bakunin brought its troubled history to an end. The Second (Social Democratic) International was founded in 1889. It belonged to the era of parliamentary participation, and its chief ornaments were the parliamentary Socialists of the day, Jaurès, Bebel, Ebert, MacDonald, and the rest. It met for the last time in Brussels in July 1914, though the international Socialist-pacifist conferences at Zimmerwald in 1915, at Kiental in 1916, and at Stockholm in 1917 might be regarded as its successors and rivals (see p. 92). The Third (Communist) International, or Comintern, was founded in Moscow in March 1919, by Lenin under the presidency of Zinoviev.

The Bolsheviks had once hopefully expected that their world revolution would follow automatically upon the end of the war in 1918 but, by the time the Peace Conference had assembled in Paris, it was slowly borne in upon them that the victor bourgeois-democratic Powers held the initiative in peacemaking and, if world revolution was now to succeed, a special agency must be established for its promotion. That agency, in Lenin's view, was not to be a loose congress meeting intermittently, like the First and Second Internationals, but a permanent headquarters with a staff of professional revolutionaries and with expertly organized espionage and propaganda ramifying through the length and breadth of the inhabited world. The conception was bold and novel, and it was carried into effect with Bolshevism's usual ruthlessness and revolutionary zeal.

The Third International, or Comintern, therefore, was the agency for world revolution. Its tactical method was to gain control, by propaganda and subsidies, over Communist parties in different countries, to plant "cells" in trade-unions and workers' co-operatives, and thus to build up, openly or surreptitiously, a "united proletarian front." The central organ, or bureau, of the Comintern, "temporarily" established in Moscow, was in close contact with the Soviet Government — both indeed were dominated by the Party — but it was always careful to distinguish itself therefrom and to represent itself to be an independent, supranational, supragovernmental body. It could therefore pursue its distinctively hostile campaign in foreign countries without compromising the Soviet Government and, contrariwise, at a later date Germany and Japan could form an Anti-Comintern Pact without affecting their normal diplomatic relations with that government.

THE DEATH AND GLORIFICATION OF LENIN

Early in 1922, it was plain that Lenin's health was failing. Unremitting study and hard work had gradually undermined a constitution which must once have been extraordinarily powerful. In May of that year, he suffered a paralytic stroke and for a time lost the faculty of speech. He recovered health enough to take an advisory part in affairs, but he was never as strong again. He died on January 21, 1924.

Lenin was that rare combination, a theorist and a man of action. He gave his life to a doctrine and to its fulfillment. Fanatic though he was, he could unhesitatingly withdraw from a strict theoretical position if, in practice, it was proving unworkable. He bowed to circumstances he could not alter. Thus he accepted Brest Litovsk; he adopted the soviets; he introduced the NEP; he abandoned — perhaps temporarily — the ideal of world revolution. His instinct for men and situations — at least for men and situations in his native Russia — amounted to prophecy. He knew when to strike and when to retreat with an almost military genius. He had no revolutionary romanticism, and almost no emotionalism. He avoided cruelty if he could, but never hesitated to be cruel if he thought it necessary. He had the defect of so many modern dictators and leaders of the people in that he was essentially cultureless. He had no deep sense of history or tradition. He only read for controversial purposes and for "technical" information. He had no spiritual talent whatever.

In appearance he was short, stocky, and unprepossessing. He was of pure Russian blood [11] — unlike so many key figures in Russian history. He was simple, averse to theatricality, direct in all his dealings. He submitted to correction at the hands of his colleagues without a trace of false pride. He lived austerely and, even in his days of power, he kept his old unaffected, familiar habits. He never wore a military uniform or decoration. Among European dictators, he must have been the least egotistic, the least histrionic, and the most normal. He was not ambitious for himself. He seized supreme power, but did not use it, or enjoy it, for its own sake. His obsession was his revolution. He was the protagonist of a colossal social upheaval. He brought a people of many millions through revolution, civil war, famine, and economic collapse, and he founded a state whose influence the world will feel for all time. Whatever may be our judgment of his political philosophy, he was, by any standard of measurement, one of the mightiest figures of his generation.

The "Lenin Legend," as it developed after his death, was not untainted with propaganda and even with the grossest fetishism. His body was embalmed and laid in a glass-topped coffin in a mausoleum beneath the Kremlin walls, where it was visited by continuous lines of devotees. Every device was used to invest his written works with an aura of canonicity. Streets, factories, clubs, stadiums, towns, and cities were named after him. Petrograd became Leningrad. His portraits in photographs, in statuettes, medals, stamped on handkerchiefs, on ash trays, on cigarette cases, were treated almost like icons. Bolshevism, which had forsworn cults, adopted all the trappings of a cult of its own.

THE RISE OF STALIN

Lenin's illness and death posed the dreaded question of his successor. Formerly his name had been linked with Trotsky's, so much so that, in Russia and abroad, the Lenin-Trotsky partnership had been looked upon as an indissoluble duumvirate. Lenin himself always had spoken as if Trotsky would succeed him as a matter of course. But it was soon to be seen that Trotsky had little strength alone. Despite Trotsky's services to the cause, despite his brilliance as organizer, executive, orator, and negotiator, he was not a real Party man — he had not even been a Party member before his return to Russia in 1917, nor would he ever stoop to those "political" practices imperative in a Party-ridden country. His highhanded dealing with his colleagues, especially during the Civil War — Stalin being one of them — and his many disagreements on policy with Lenin himself, notably over Brest Litovsk and the NEP, could all be remembered to his discredit when the time was ripe.

The Russian people after years of war, revolution, famine, and terror were physically and morally exhausted, and Trotsky's rhetorical, dynamic personality little matched their mood of prostration. The theory of permanent revolution which he preached and the exultant visions of a communized world which he was always seeing were jaded things to people who had almost forgotten what it was to be at peace. The harried and devastated Russian homeland was tired of mirages which in the realization turned out to be yet more massacre and starvation. The Russian Revolution had passed beyond the stage of terrorism and was ready to weariness for the stabilization of an autocratic leader.

The struggle between Trotsky and Stalin for Lenin's vacant office is a long and complex story, and many of its details are not yet clear. But the struggle was virtually decided at the time of the NEP, a measure which, as we have said, Trotsky had strongly and unsuccessfully opposed. Then the failure of Bolshevism in Hungary, Germany, and China signaled the end of Trotsky's permanent revolution and encouraged that retreat to "Socialism in one country" which Stalin made it his business to support. At the time of Lenin's death in 1924, Trotsky was in disgrace, and he actually received a telegram with news of the tragedy while he was standing on the station platform at Tiflis on his way to his first exile in the Caucasian Riviera. He might have staged a comeback at that moment. But he even failed to attend Lenin's funeral. Perhaps it is a point in his favor that Trotsky was always curiously unresponsive to the demagogic opportunity.

At the Eleventh Party Congress in 1922, Stalin succeeded Molotov as

Secretary General, and between then and the Twelfth Party Congress in 1924 he contrived to concentrate the real Party power in his own hands. His co-adjutors in the process were Zinoviev and Kamenev, and their main strategy appears to have been to disperse possible rivals by appointing them to posts in remote districts. In 1925, with the support of new lieutenants, Rykov and Bukharin, Stalin ousted Zinoviev and Kamenev, and then, in 1929, he ousted Rykov and Bukharin. In the end, Stalin was the last survivor of the "Old Bolsheviks." Trotsky from his various places of exile aided and abetted the successive malcontents, till his intriguing was "not to be distinguished from the activities of the White Guards," and in 1929 he was finally deported from Russia. He lived for a time in Turkey, in France, and in Mexico, nursing his wrath and writing his classic versions of the Russian Revolution.

The loss of Trotsky to Russia was also a heavy moral loss. He was at least an idealist, and ideals, even wrong ones, have an element of value. Stalin was never overmuch possessed of the milk of human conscience, and with him Russia reverted to "realism" in politics and diplomacy carefully rationalized by the familiar appeal to Communist doctrine. Yet the famous Stalin-Trotsky feud had something more fundamental in it than the antagonism of two men and two moralities. In the last analysis, the feud harked back to the old, old antithesis between East and West which has so often cleft the Russian character. Stalin, the provincial, the untraveled, the uncultured, represented the East; Trotsky, the international Jew, the master of foreign languages, acquainted with foreign countries, represented the West. There could be no mean between types so diverse, and all Russia was the theater of their conflict.

Joseph Vissarionovich Dzhugashvily was born in Gori, near Tiflis, in Georgia, in 1879 of peasant extraction. Intended for the priesthood, he was expelled from his seminary, and at the age of seventeen joined a local Social Democrat group. His career was then patterned after that of hundreds of other professional revolutionaries — agitation, intrigue, journalism, imprisonment, exile, escape. His physical constitution was above ordinary, and had need to be, for the life he led was never meant for weaklings. He changed his name several times, finally adopting the not unsuitable one of Stalin, from *stal* or "steel." He came to be recognized as a useful revolutionary handy man, an agent of commissions where action and nerve were wanted. Lenin described him as "too cruel" and "too brutal," but used him often enough. He saw service in the Civil War; he fought against Kolchak, Yudenich, and Pilsudski; his exploits at Tsaritsyn caused that city to be renamed for him, Stalingrad.

Clearly Stalin had none of the intellectual finesse of men like Lenin or Trotsky, though, as his numerous writings show, incondite and repetitive as they are, he was a plodding student and had all the true Communist's respect for theory. Trotsky indeed described him as "the outstanding mediocrity of the Party." Devoid of histrionic gifts, he early found his forte in the political machine, where he seemed content to remain a "practitioner," an executant of the ideas of others without interest in original or creative thinking of his own. "Never a tribune, never a strategist or leader of rebellion, he has ever been only a bureaucrat of revolution." He had courage and tenacity, an Asiatic patience, an infinite capacity for complicated intrigue, and a long vindictive memory, but these very characteristics flourished best in concealment and obscurity. He spoke in public and in committee on rare occasions; otherwise he was of legendary reticence and, though living in a country of the most accomplished talkers in the world and at a time when talking was the highway to political advancement, he was always as blunt and as sparing of mere words as it was possible to be.

After 1922, and especially after 1924, he began to amass enormous personal power, but he still preferred the background, and public acclamation for him — though he came to receive a surfeit of it — seemed much more the part of a deliberate policy than a reward desired and striven for. By 1936 he had become the supreme autocrat. He spoke in public more often and gave frequent interviews to foreign visitors, but somehow contrived each time to convey the impression of a man emerging into unaccustomed publicity to give an ex-cathedra pronouncement on policy. Even now it is hard to say that Stalin was ever one *known* to his contemporaries, or to see in his early obscurity the qualities which afterward made him the taskmaster of the Five-Year Plans and Marshal of the Second World War.

THE FIVE–YEAR PLANS

Stalin's "Socialism in one country" took shape in the Five-Year Plans. It was not all innovation. Historians have been at pains to point out that Peter the Great once projected a five-year plan. A recent book ably argued that Russia was already in process of accomplishing in 1914 all that Communism has since claimed to have done for her.[1] Under the later Tsars the canals, many of the railroads, the telegraphs, and certain banks were already state enterprises bureaucratically managed. The state also owned great tracts of land, and vodka was a government monopoly. The winter of 1917–18 witnessed that hazardous experiment, the workers' control of the factories, an experiment which even its most ardent advocates were forced to regard as a failure. In December 1917, to reduce the chaos in factories by means of drastic centralization, Lenin decreed the setting up of a Supreme Economic Council, the body which eventually organized the War Communism of 1918–20. Then in 1920, in the midst of the Russo-Polish War, a special commission drew up plans for the electrification of the country, a vast scheme dear to the heart of Lenin himself. The Communist literature of this time was already coming to be interlarded with those astronomical "control figures" (co-ordinated output targets) which were to become so familiar with the passing years of hope and trial. Finally, in February 1921, the State Planning Commission (Gosplan) came into existence. The first of the Five-Year Plans, which was to make Communism an economic reality, to enact the final liquidation of the capitalist system and establish a unified, prosperous, classless society of workers and peasants, was being publicly discussed in 1926 and was officially inaugurated on October 1, 1928.

The years from 1921 to 1928 had seen the inception and progress of the

NEP (see p. 270). But many orthodox Communists had never taken kindly to that famous concession to necessity, albeit Lenin himself had been the author of it. At best it was a temporary measure, and its continuance was not to be thought of. The arrogance of the Nepmen whom it had bred had grown in proportion to their prosperity, private enterprise was once more beginning to dominate Russia's economy, and all the work of the Revolution was being undone.

Communist doctrine had always dilated upon the supersession of capitalism's "anarchy of production" and the inequalities of wealth that went therewith — the unpredictable business cycles, the recurrent and increasingly disastrous slumps, and all the standing evils of unemployment and poverty — and upon the need of devising some long-term plan sufficient to secure to all the deserving inhabitants of the state the wherewithal of their physical and cultural sustenance. In broad terms, Soviet economic planning may be said to have had for its object, first, to transform a predominantly agrarian country into one of a greatly improved standard of living, possessing its own industries and capable of producing its own finished commodities from its own raw materials; second, to reorganize agriculture on the basis of the collective farm and thus to double or treble the productive capacity of the land; third, to reorganize the distributive system of the country, to encourage the co-operatives as distributing agents, and to eliminate the middleman; fourth, to reorganize the transportation system; fifth, to create within the Soviet Union the technical and economic resources for its defense against foreign aggression; sixth, to promote literacy and education.

Soviet economic planning represented a direct application of theory, a reversion to strict Communist orthodoxy after the heretical liberties of the NEP. It seemed to despise the type of day-to-day opportunism which afterward characterized the Nazi autarchy or the American New Deal, and almost to take delight in running counter to natural human inclination and the natural trend of events. It is not easy to imagine the conviction and will of a small number of men who set themselves to remold the way of life of a population of 175,000,000 existing at a relatively primitive stage and wasted by war, revolution, and famine, and to try to outpace within ten to fifteen years the century-old economic development of Britain, Germany, and the United States. With all the cruelties and miscalculations, the three Five-Year Plans must remain for all time an example of human energy and vision.

The first Five-Year Plan for the Development of National Economy, to give its full name, inaugurated in October 1928, was declared to have been completed under the time limit in December 1932. The second Five-Year Plan occupied the years from 1933 to 1937. The first was originally published in a three-volume text totaling some 1,600 pages, and the second in a two-volume text totaling over 1,300 pages. The volumes contained tables and statistics covering the development of the national economy: machine-building, electric power, fuel, mining, timber, chemistry, consumer's goods, food industries, and co-operatives; agriculture, transportation, postal service, telegraph and telephone; labor, wages, standards of living, distribution and consumption; schools, literature, newspapers, housing, public health, and social insurance; and finance. Throughout, the emphasis was laid on the

"modes of production," in Marxian parlance, and on the creation at last
of a classless, Communist society. The text of the third Five-Year Plan was
still in preparation when the Second World War broke out, though the
Plan itself was officially inaugurated in 1938.

This huge enterprise was directed, as we have said, by the State Planning
Commission (Gosplan), a committee of the Council of Commissars, of
which its chairman was a member. It superseded the Supreme Economic
Council, though that body continued to exercise a restricted function till
its abolition in 1932. It comprised a bureaucracy of experts, statisticians,
and other numerous officials, with subsidiary branches in every territorial
division of the Union. Its personnel and driving force were drawn largely
from the regular Party members, but also from those vigorous, completely
ruthless, but infinitely optimistic young Communists, the Komsomols — and,
of course, from the Ogpu.

The Soviet Union was 6,000 miles wide, east to west, at its greatest extent,
and averaged 2,000 miles north to south. Its total area was 8,500,000 square
miles, about the same area as the North American continent above Panama.
Its mineral geology was illimitably rich and advantageously distributed.
Upon so ample a foundation, Soviet economic planning could erect industries which by the late thirties were producing annually 133,000,000 tons of
coal, 29,000,000 tons of oil, 15,000,000 tons of pig iron, 18,000,000 tons of
steel, 200,000 tractors, and 20,000 automobiles.[2] New industrial cities were
being laid out and built in virgin territory on a scale dwarfing even those of
the boom days of the American West. The coal mines at Kuznetsk, the oil
wells and refineries of the Caucasus and the Urals, the hydroelectric station
of Dnepropetrovsk, the steel works at Magnitogorsk, the tractor factories at
Chelyabinsk and Stalingrad, the airplane factories at Moscow, the Volga-
Don and White Sea canals, the double-tracking of the Trans-Siberian Railway — all these, by any standard, represented stupendous achievements.
It is not to be forgotten that this was not all planning for peace. We have
said that one of the broad objectives of the Five-Year Plans was to create the
resources for defense, and the Red Army therefore was always a prior bene-
ficiary of the country's productiveness. In 1935, when the European world
was taking a renewed interest in armaments, foreign military experts were
already speaking of the Red Army's 10,000 tanks, 150,000 tractors, 100,000
other transport vehicles, and probably 10,000 first-line planes. Attachés who
attended the Red Army's maneuvers came away with a healthy respect for
its technical equipment and its technical personnel. In 1935, the standing
army of the Soviet Union numbered 1,300,000 men; by 1939, trained reserves probably numbered 12,500,000. These figures represented a force
which was shortly to make itself felt in the world's affairs.

THE SABOTAGE TRIALS

But the attractions of the Soviet economic landscape were not to be judged
by its peaks alone. Deep valleys in perpetual shadow lay between. Too many

writers have described the extreme shortages of the barest necessities of life, even in the allegedly productive years — the midwinter food lines, the overcrowded, underheated, and dilapidated apartments, the patched and ragged clothes of all but the upper Party members — for us to believe that the course of the Five-Year Plans was one smooth triumph. We have also the curious episode of the sabotage trials.

The incidental failures of the Plans could be charged to some extent to bureaucratic congestion and to lack of training and skill on the part of the Soviet worker. All this was occasionally admitted and publicly discussed. But the Kremlin dared not admit too much. If the target figures were not reached, if the machines were misused or overstrained, then the fault belonged to "wreckers" or enemy agents who must be uncovered and haled before the Soviet courts. We shall have something to say on a later page regarding the pathological fears and obsessions under which the Soviet Union worked in these years (pp. 539–40). Let it be enough to note here that the memory of foreign intervention and counterrevolution died hard. Thus it seemed that a series of deliberately staged sabotage trials was a necessary accompaniment of the Five-Year Plans. Foreign observers, bewildered and aghast, offered various explanations of these extraordinary performances. "The trials are really morality plays," wrote Eugene Lyons. "The forces of Evil, represented by the political villains of the moment, are confronted by the powers of Good, the state and the party, and duly conquered in mock combat. . . . The lines of the play are prescribed in advance . . . the guilt of the victims is taken for granted. The purpose is to 'demonstrate' that guilt, to dramatize it, rather than to prove it." [3]

As early as 1928, some fifty engineers were accused of sabotage in one of the Donets coal mines, allegedly at the instigation of the former owners, then refugees in Paris and Warsaw. Most of the defendants confessed, and confessed enthusiastically. "They confessed with a masochistic relish. They admitted sins of which they were not even accused and shouldered responsibility for crimes with which they could not possibly have had any connexion. The coal industry had, in fact, worked extremely badly — the trial was intended to illustrate why. It was a show to dramatize the claim that the country was honey-combed with internal enemies who must be crushed mercilessly." [4] In 1930 came the trial of another group of engineers, a certain Professor Ramsin and his associates, who again confessed to all the charges brought against them and incidentally implicated President Poincaré of France and Sir Henri Deterding, the oil magnate, in a nefarious plot to undermine the economic structure of the Soviet Union and overthrow its government.

The so-called Moscow Trials, measured by their international repercussions, were the most serious of these affairs. In 1933 the Ogpu arrested forty-one engineers working for the Metropolitan-Vickers Company in Moscow, six of them being British subjects. Allan Monkhouse, one of the six, writing of his experiences afterward, declared that he suffered no torture, but endured hours of cross-examination on two successive days, during which every effort was made to extort from him a written statement incriminating himself, his colleagues, and the company which employed him. He was accused of being an agent of the British Secret Service, a military spy, a saboteur, and a receiver of bribes, all of which, of course, he strenuously denied. But, he adds, "after having experienced that mental exhaustion, I understand and realize how it is that victims can be induced to make all manner of confessions, even without resort to the practices — hypnotism, drugs, and physical torture — which the Ogpu were accredited with employing." The judge at the trial was far from impartial, and the defending counsel, chosen from a panel, certainly placed no obstacles in the way of the prosecution. The Russians accused made stereotyped confessions. "One after another," writes Monkhouse, "they proceeded to the microphone and enumerated their wrecking activities with astonishing readiness." [4]

The final sentences in the Moscow Trials amounted to imprisonment for Soviet nationals and deportations for foreigners, sentences lenient by Soviet standards. There were several acquittals. But the trials meanwhile had raised a tremendous furor abroad. The British Government suspended negotiations then in train for a new Soviet trade treaty, recalled the British ambassador in Moscow for consultation, and embargoed about 80 per cent of Soviet imports. Litvinov, the Soviet Foreign Commissar, visiting London later in 1933 to attend the World Economic Conference, was able to pour a little oil on troubled waters. But feeling in Britain had run high, and the Soviet system, which the democratic world in 1933 was beginning to accept and acknowledge in tentative sympathy, suffered serious discredit.

But, as we shall see, these sabotage trials were only a curtain raiser for yet more extraordinary treason trials to come (see pp. 543-47).

COLLECTIVIZATION

Collectivization was the agricultural counterpart of the industrialism we have just been describing. The one supported the other. In Tsarist Russia the average area of cultivated land per head of the agricultural population had amounted to three acres, often fragmented in the course of generations into multiple strips. The most primitive methods were still very general — plowing with the wooden plow, sowing by hand, reaping with the sickle, and threshing with the flail. The total crop yield was one-quarter of that of England and one-half of that of France. Only in a few provinces had the custom grown for a periodic redistribution of peasant lands by the "village meeting," an old institution of Russian peasant life known as the *Mir;* but the communal tradition which that institution represented was likely to predispose the peasant toward the new Soviet collectivization policy.

The Soviet Government encouraged joint farming enterprises (*artels*) from the first and provided, when it was able, the necessary land and farm machinery. It also organized several state farms (*sovkhoz*). It looked askance at the kulak,[5] the richer independent peasant, especially if his status could in any way be described as that of a capitalist and employer of labor. Certainly the amalgamation of the scattered, fragmented peasant holdings into large collective farms (*kolkhoz*), each with a democratic management and each with the most up-to-date technical and mechanical assistance, had both ideological and practical attractiveness. To make the peasant a sharecropper in a system of mass farming seemed to be the very quintessence of Communism. Moreover the peasant was a notoriously stubborn, intractable type, given to moods of passive resistance — as even earlier regimes in Russia had discovered. Collectivization would bring him under government controls and enable a proper supervision both of himself and his produce to be carried out, and this would be no small advantage in a bureaucratically run economy.

The Fifteenth Party Congress, in December 1927, adopted a resolution for collectivizing peasant farms, but on a voluntary basis. The crisis which occurred in Soviet agriculture shortly afterward was precipitated, according to some accounts, by the kulaks.[5] The kulaks, like the Nepmen of the NEP, had grown independent with prosperity, and — crime of crimes — they had begun to show a class consciousness of their own. In 1928, over large areas they were evidently hoarding grain, though it is doubtful whether their operations amounted to an organized and deliberate "wheat strike." At all events the first Five-Year Plan, just about to be started, was deemed to be endangered, and Stalin virtually declared war upon individualist peasant economy throughout the Soviet Union. Collectivization was to be enforced.

Collectivization was not only enforced; it was pushed forward with exaggerated haste. Voroshilov, Commissar for War, is reported to have refused the support of the Red Army to quell possible peasant revolts. As in industry, the driving force in the campaign came from the Party and particularly from the young Komsomols. But we have throughout the impression of a welter of bureaucratic confusion. For instance, in many districts draft animals were slaughtered wholesale because it was expected that the new tractors would take their place, but the tractors often enough did not come up to expectation either in quantity or in quality. Travelers in the Soviet Union came back with stories of huge "cemeteries" of damaged, overworked, or otherwise defective machines. The Moscow planners seemed to regard the human being as so much economic material. The death rate was part of the incidental and unregretted cost of a program that must not be allowed to fail. The kulaks were chief sufferers. They had originally been obstacles to collectivization; they were liquidated as a class, and their lands turned over to the nearest collective farm. By the outbreak of the Second World War, agriculture in the Soviet Union was 80 per cent collectivized, 15 per cent was operated in the form of state farms (sovkhoz), and perhaps a last 5 per cent remained as individual peasant holdings.

It is difficult to arrive at a balance sheet of the collective farm movement in the Soviet Union. On the debit side, at a conservative estimate, we have three to four million deaths, and this does not include the forcible deportations to Siberia. On the credit side we have a mass of statistics which conceal the geographical variety of Soviet agriculture and the stubbornly surviving social differentiation of the Russian peasant. Arguably the peasant's lot under collectivization did not progress much beyond his condition in 1914, nor could the local Party manager always be regarded as an improvement on the old Tsarist landlord. Considerable scientific progress was still needed to overcome the basic, relative aridity of the Russian climate. The Soviet

Government itself was forced to admit that the harvests of the early thirties were subnormal. The standard of life in most parts of the rural Soviet Union was still a long way from the average in rural Western Europe or the rural United States.

THE STALIN CONSTITUTION

The constitution of 1936 indicated a conscious need on the part of the Soviet periodically to define itself and take stock of its own dynamic, developing condition. It was promulgated at a time inauspicious for new constitutions. A new wave of purges and trials was in progress throughout the Soviet Union (see pp. 543–47), the Italo-Ethiopian War had just come to an end, Hitler was German Chancellor and churning Europe into a turmoil — and the constitution may have been intended not only for domestic solidification but as a gesture toward the democratic West whose friendship, in the newly breaking era of aggression, had become so suddenly and surprisingly desirable.

In 1935 the Seventh All-Union Congress of Soviets had moved to revise the existing constitution (see pp. 273–74), and a Constitutional Commission was appointed under the chairmanship of Stalin. The Commission's draft was published in midsummer of 1936 and thrown open to public discussion, and we are given the impression that the Soviet Union for several months converted itself into a gigantic debating society upon the intricacies of the new *Lex Communista*. The 154,000 amendments voted and forwarded to Moscow by hundreds of local soviets do not appear to have exerted much influence on the Constitutional Commission, but there can be no question of the vitality of the discussions or of the education in political consciousness which they provided. The Eighth All-Union Congress of Soviets met in December 1936, amid the greatest enthusiasm, to vote with routine unanimity each of the 146 articles of the "Stalin Constitution."

The text of the constitution must rank high in the political literature and philosophy of our time. But in the practical working of it we fail to discover that the essentials of Soviet rule were greatly changed. The personal directorship of Stalin remained; the omnipresence and the omnipotence of the Communist party and the Ogpu remained. The subsequent elections in 1937 and 1938 yielded results conformable to the wishes of the Kremlin.

The constitution described the Soviet Union, the Union of Soviet Socialist Republics (the U.S.S.R.), as "a Socialist state of workers and peasants," and invested the wealth of the land in the people. It named eleven constituent republics, the R.S.F.S.R., the Ukraine, White Russia (Byelorussia), Azerbaijan, Georgia, Armenia, Turkmen, Uzbek, Tajik, Kazak, and Kirghiz, all enjoying "equality of rights," even to the right of secession. The former Central Executive Committee now appeared as the Supreme Soviet, "the highest organ of state power," but composed as before of two chambers, the Soviet of the Union and the Soviet of Nationalities. The Soviet of the Union was to be elected directly on the basis of one Deputy for every 300,000 of the population, and the former cumbersome system of pyramidal election was abolished (see pp. 273–74). The franchise was widened to include every citizen who had reached the age of eighteen, irrespective of sex, race, nationality, religion, education, residence, social origin, property status, or "past activity." Elections were to be effected by secret ballot. The Presidium, a collective presidency of the Union, and the Council of People's Commissars remained much as before. The Communist party was mentioned by name and given formal constitutional recognition for the first time.

RELIGION [6]

One factor in the life of the Soviet Union most difficult to appraise is religion. In the welter of their temporal politics and wars, we sometimes forget that the Russians at heart are a religious people and that, as Spengler insisted, their creative period in religion may only be beginning. The Orthodox Church in Russia in prerevolutionary times was always subordinated to the state, and the upper ecclesiastical hierarchy identified itself with the Tsarist system. Though the traditional pieties were very much alive in Russia, the old Church was undeniably corrupt and venal, obsequious to authority, and long overdue for a thorough cleansing. It tried to take advantage of the Revolution of March 1917 to shake itself free from its political disabilities. The Church Sobor or Council, meeting in 1917 for the first time in two centuries, elected Tikhon, then Metropolitan of Moscow, as Patriarch and created a Supreme Church Council and Synod for the Church's future governance. In the second phase of the Revolution, the Church was uncompromisingly and militantly anti-Bolshevik. Tikhon's "Message to the Church," in January 1918, threatened "the monsters of the human race" with hell-fire and excommunication. The Bolshevik Government replied with the famous decree "on freedom of conscience and religious societies" which, while permitting public worship, disestablished the Church, secularized all education, and confiscated ecclesiastical property.

The incidents of January 1918 set the tone for the relations of Church and state thereafter. The Church continued to be anti-Communist, and the state to be antireligious. The Soviet constitution of July 1918, for instance, deprived priests of the franchise. Religious instruction in schools was stopped by the simple device of stopping teachers' pay. Meanwhile the peasants seized a good deal of ecclesiastical land on their own account. In 1921 the Church even used the famine to mobilize opposition to the government. The government decreed the seizure of Church gold and treasures for the famine fund, a decree which the Patriarch Tikhon at once characterized as sacrilegious and uncanonical. Trials and executions of priests followed. Some priests broke away from the Patriarchate and attempted to come to terms with the government on their own account. Tikhon retired to a monastery on the outskirts of Moscow where he was kept under arrest and where, in 1925, he died. The press abroad played up the "persecution" of the Church in once Holy Russia in the usual lurid journalese of the time.

In 1929, just after the inauguration of the first Five-Year Plan, a time of tightening of principles, the government promulgated a sort of consolidated law on religion which acknowledged "freedom of religious worship and of antireligious propaganda." The Church was thus permitted the performance of its rites and no more. That is to say, it was not permitted to maintain religious associations and charities or to conduct the education of minors. Evidently the Church was to have no part in the new Soviet economy and social welfare. As the slogan of the day had it, "A church in a collective farm is a joke." At this time there was very little direct religious persecution, but so many church buildings had been destroyed or expropriated and converted into clubs, schools, museums, and the like that the main obstacle to public worship was the sheer shortage of physical space in which it might be carried on. The constitution of 1936 re-enfranchised priests, but otherwise it confirmed the law of 1929. The Church remained separate from the state, free to conduct worship only, and the schools remained separate from the Church. In this the Orthodox Church and all the other faiths and denominations in the Soviet Union were treated exactly alike.

But, on the whole, it appears that the Soviet Government was very cautious in its dealings with the Church. Lenin and the Patriarch were like Mussolini and the Pope. The dictator, much as he professed to despise the ecclesiastical authority, could not afford to antagonize it beyond all hope of eventual accommodation. Persecution of the Church, of priests and monks undoubtedly occurred, but it was probably intermittent both in extent and severity. Its worst waves naturally coincided with the periodic Party purges or with major changes of policy, as in 1929. The official Communist ideology was always implacably and aggressively atheistic and regarded religion as "an opiate of the people" and the Church as an anachronism once used by the exploiting class to keep the masses in ignorance and subjection. The Militant Atheists League, under the auspices of the Communist party, carried on an antireligious propaganda by means of periodicals, lectures, posters, and exhibitions. It delighted in exposing fraudulent relics and making mock of religious festivals. Yet, despite persecution and propaganda, despite confiscation and restrictions, we still have the impression that the Church in Revolutionary Russia enjoyed a continuous history, summoned its sobors and synods, inducted its patriarchs and metropolitans, held its usual controversies over its own internal schisms, kept alive a great number of its monastic institutions, celebrated its picturesque services and festivals, and generally ministered to the millions that still resorted to it.

A new spirit was manifested in the Second World War. The Church, from the moment of the invasion in 1941, threw its weight into the struggle against the "Fascist robbers." Nor did it take advantage of the situation to obtain secular privileges or in any way to seek to change its existing constitutional status. Doubtless the Church will have been much strengthened by the experience of the war. Its future is full of interest.[6]

19 ITALY: THE RISE AND ESTABLISHMENT

OF FASCISM

THE POSTWAR MOOD

The postwar nervous reaction affected Italy in a particularly virulent form. The Italian government under Salandra in 1915 had originally brought the country into the war, not so much out of necessity, but after protracted negotiations with both sides and despite considerable popular and parliamentary feeling averse to intervention. Throughout the war, the supporters of the government's war policy had had to contend with powerful groups who had not wanted war and did not believe in it. The Italian people were volatile by temperament and easily disheartened. To keep up their fighting spirit, therefore, and especially the fighting spirit of the forces at the front, the politicians had been almost driven to make overlavish promises and, with characteristic Italian exuberance, they had imagined triumphs which no mortal victory could ever have realized. The returned soldier, having made his sacrifice, felt cheated of his deserts and, as if insult had to be added to injury, he became the butt of a despicable campaign at the hands of the stay-at-home Socialist on the general theme of "I told you so!" Instead of the prodigal banquet of peace and glory which he had been led to expect a grateful homeland would spread out before him, he found an ashen feast of riots, strikes, lockouts, unemployment, and general social and economic disorder.

The internal politics of the country were in a sorry state. Italy had never made a complete conversion to democracy. By 1919, it must always be remembered, she had had only two generations of free institutions, and behind those generations her history stretched back through centuries of servitude and factional strife. Manhood suffrage had been granted only in 1912, and the election of 1913 was the first in which it had been exercised. The poverty of the average Italian worker left him with little time or inclination for interests outside the harsh necessities of his day-to-day existence, and what politics he had were sharply attached to local jealousies. Meanwhile the parliament at Rome had long since become the forcing ground of corruption "where a few hundred professional politicians occupied themselves with recurrent crises and ignored the real crises which they had been called together to resolve." The multi-party system, as it had grown up in the sixties and seventies, in direct reflection of the fierce parochialism of the country, had lent itself, as multi-party systems so often do, to intrigue and trickery, and Italian politics had become tied to party machines under a series of party "bosses," manipulating short-lived coalition blocs. In the early months of

Italy's participation in the war, it was hoped that the enthusiasm for the cause might have inaugurated a better era. But not only did the old habits return, but with the election of November 1919, the second election with manhood suffrage, a new complication arose, namely, the sharp rise of the two new popular parties, the Catholic party (*Popolari*), and the Socialists, both outside the old party machines. It was the fear of these parties, representing the enfranchised masses, that turned large numbers of the propertied classes against the democratic institutions. Much to the astonishment of foreigners, who usually thought of Italy in terms of the liberal tradition of Cavour, the extension of the vote was in part responsible, if indirectly, for ultimate parliamentary breakdown.

The state of foreign politics was not much better. Even Italians of insufficient education to appreciate the intricacies of world affairs had sensed the seeming anti-Italian bias of the Peace Conference at Paris, and they had been quick to take affront at the national humiliation which President Wilson appeared to be preparing there. The war was not the first war in which modern Italy had poured out her blood and treasure, only to be contemptuously thrust aside by her allies when it was all over. President Wilson had made his state visit to Rome early in January 1919; he had been extravagantly entertained; he had spoken in the Italian Chamber; he had been received by the King and the Pope; and then, in return for all the homage and panegyric, he had addressed his famous appeal from Paris to the Italian people and had presumed to lecture them upon the wickedness of their dearest aspirations (see p. 119). The Peace Conference, instead of giving peace to Italy, only roused her to a frenzy of frustration and injured pride.

Modern Italy had never won a war except by the aid of more powerful allies, and she deeply resented the fact. In 1859 she was embittered against Napoleon III because he did not gain Venetia for her in addition to Lombardy. In 1866 she was embittered against Bismarck because he refused to claim for her no more than Venetia. In 1919, Italian nationalists, instead of showing gratitude toward a coalition which had permitted them further acquisitions and had secured the complete destruction of their hereditary Hapsburg enemy, insisted on raising the old cry that they had been cheated. All in all, the anticlimax of the army's homecoming, the parliamentary turmoil, the reactionism of the propertied classes, and now the supreme mortification at Paris combined to produce in Italy a very dangerous situation.

FIUME AND THE ADRIATIC QUESTION

The question of Fiume and the Adriatic at the Peace Conference has been mentioned elsewhere (see p. 119). Fiume in fact became, in Italian eyes, a test case and symbol of the entire peace settlement. Since November 1918 a temporary joint Allied administration had been set up in the town, and a small Allied force was quartered there. In July 1919 the crisis over its affairs at the Peace Conference resulted in rioting in the town between bands of young Italian *Fiumiani* and local Croat inhabitants. Croat property was wrecked, and some French and Italian soldiers of the Allied force were killed. August was a calmer month. But on September 12, 1919, the Italian poet and aviator, Gabriele D'Annunzio, at the head of a corps of volunteers, marched into Fiume and claimed possession of it in the name of Italy. The Allied force retired without fighting and attempted to form a cordon round the district.

D'Annunzio set up his own government in Fiume. He adopted the motto "*Me ne frego* (I don't give a damn)." He was joined by many hundreds of sympathizers. He had some twenty planes and a number of ships, and on one occasion he captured an Italian destroyer. He was offered allegiance by the city of Zara. He sent a "delegate" to the Peace Conference, a gentleman who also opened a "legation" in Paris. Later he introduced a corporative constitution. There were daily parades and trooping of banners, edicts and ultimatums, and torrents of impassioned oratory. It was all a crazy, unreal sort of Ruritanian comic opera.

The Italian Government, of course, disavowed the coup, but took no immediate action. The Italian press was in ectasies. Certainly the coup was audacious and spectacular, and there was about it just enough of sporting defiance of authority, just enough of dangerous living, to appeal to popular sentiment. Various solutions and compromises were proposed in Paris, only to be rejected by one or other of the parties concerned, and a settlement was not reached till November 1920, when the Treaty of Rapallo was negotiated between the Italian and Yugoslav Governments. Even then D'Annunzio clung desperately to his conquest, and regular Italian troops had to be sent to eject him. In all, the poet maintained himself and his legionaries in Fiume for fifteen months.

THE DECLINE OF ITALIAN DEMOCRACY

Orlando, Italian Premier since the time of the Battle of Caporetto, had resigned in June 1919, shortly after his withdrawal from the Peace Conference (see p.119), and was followed by Francesco Nitti, a man of liberal pacifist views at the head of a moderate rightist coalition. Perhaps it was not to be expected that Nitti's term of office would be very fortunate. He represented the mixture of lassitude and disillusion that now characterized his country. His so-called Amnesty for Deserters in September 1919 was perhaps typical. Like every other "defeated" army at the end of the war, the Italian Army had been infected with the disease of large-scale desertion. One estimate had it that over 500,000 men were in hiding, especially in southern Italy and Sicily. The amnesty was no real amnesty, but only a measure for reducing to a practicable figure the number of trials and imprisonments for desertion. But it seemed to condone a dishonorable crime, it gave offense to loyal soldiers, and it certainly contributed to the general demoralization everywhere.

Meanwhile the workers were agitating for the syndical control of industry and making demands for a direct share of the management and profits. In May 1919 the metalworkers in a factory at Dalmine near Bergamo had hit upon the idea of "camping" in the factory. The idea seemed good, and it

spread like wildfire. Sometimes the former clerks and foremen, who were indispensable to the running of the plant, were compelled to remain at work
in the service of their new Socialist masters. Inevitably the disturbances
began to spill over into the open streets. Strikes led to rioting, looting, and
bloodshed. There were several fatal bomb-throwing incidents. In the country the peasants attempted to seize the big private estates, killed or drove
off the livestock, and set fire to the crops. Magistrates were afraid to give
sentences for "political" crimes. Bands of young men in colored shirts — blue
shirts and gray shirts and red shirts, each color representing some ardent
political faction, but among whom the blackshirted Fascisti seemed to be
the best organized and most determined — terrorized the populace and
wreaked vengeance on each other.

The government in Rome continued to decline in popular respect. Cabinets existed on a heterogeneity of supporters drawn from as many parties as
possible. "Scenes" in the Chamber were frequent and exhausting. In June
1919, Giolitti, the old political manipulator, was prevailed upon to form a
cabinet and, by dint of using all the methods which had already brought so
much discredit on the Italian parliamentary system, he maintained himself
in office for a full year. It was Giolitti who decided not to interfere in the
factories, but instead to leave the "campers" in possession so that they might
discover their own incompetence and exhaust themselves in sheer boredom
— a successful strategy, as it often proved, but characteristically Giolittian
and profoundly harmful to law and order. It was Giolitti also who decided
to make no further resistance to the irregular warfare which had broken out
in Italy's "Protectorate" across the Adriatic in Albania,[1] to withdraw all
Italian garrisons, and thereby to abdicate Italian influence in the Balkans.
And it was Giolitti too whose Foreign Minister, Count Sforza, signed the
"disgraceful" Treaty of Rapallo with Yugoslavia in November 1920, recognizing "the full liberty and independence" of the Free State of Fiume and
surrendering to Yugoslavia the whole of the Dalmatian coast. The affairs of
Italy, in the eyes of all patriotic Italians, could hardly have sunk lower.

Elections were held in May 1921, actually without much excitement, but
they resulted in a landslide gain of 35 seats for the new Fascist movement.
Giolitti resigned, but was shortly followed by Facta, a gentle, well-esteemed,
but quite incapable old parliamentarian of the Giolittian school. In October
1922 the government was overthrown by Fascism.

THE RISE AND ESTABLISHMENT OF FASCISM

The Fascists, who now claimed to bring order to Italy, in their own early
days had not been easily distinguishable from the revolutionaries they so
despised, and Mussolini and his squadrists had reveled in the melee of 1919
and 1920 as merrily as any wild extremist in it. In his tempestuous youth,
before the First World War, the future Duce of Fascism had himself been an
adherent of violent revolution and, though no serious political crimes were
ever brought home to him, his first flights in journalism had all been most
laudatory of the anarchist bombings and assassinations of that time. After

the war in 1919, his own paper, *Il Popolo d'Italia*, had always supported the strikes and seizures of the factories. Yet he marched to power in 1922 to a great extent by exploiting the antirevolutionary and anti-Bolshevik phobia that was then gripping all conservative Italians.

Mussolini's first *Fascio di Combattimento* was founded on March 23, 1919, at Milan, a brave nucleus of pioneers and missionaries, perhaps some hundred strong, mostly intellectuals and former soldiers. Its name was taken from the old fasces of the ancient Roman lictors, the symbol of unity and authority.[2] Similar Fasci were soon being formed in cities all over Italy. In every case their organization and doctrine were confused and frankly opportunist. They scorned rules and principles. They were antimonarchist, anticlerical, mainly antisocialist, and of course, vehemently anti-Communist. But they stood for certain tenets of socialist flavor such as proportional representation and a capital levy, and they adopted some syndicalist theories. They asserted that aggressive nationalism which D'Annunzio had lately illustrated so sensationally at Fiume. Finally, at a time when the wartime noninterventionists were in power, when criticism of Italy's war effort was widespread, they preached that the recent war had been a good thing, that it had shown the nobility of the Italian soul, and that the country must return to the spirit inspired by it. Mussolini's eloquent glorification of war, addressed to a people humiliated by "defeat" — like Hitler's after him — was not the least of the causes of his rapid rise to popularity.

Fascism put forward two candidates at the elections in November 1919, Mussolini being one, but neither was successful. It put forward candidates at the elections in May 1921, Mussolini again being one, and 35 were successful. In those eighteen months the movement had waxed and thrived, it had grown into a national force of the first importance, but it had gradually lost its pristine pure character. In May 1921 it probably counted 250,000 members, recruited largely from the "white youth" as they were called. Like Nazism after it, it was primarily a lower middle-class phenomenon. It incorporated D'Annunzio's legionaries. It also incorporated various nationalists, liberals, conservatives, property owners, landlords, manufacturers; all of them, out of their genuine patriotism or for the better security of their worldly goods, put their high hopes in the movement. Its squadrists, garbed always in their black shirts, armed with cudgels and sometimes with more dangerous weapons, held their daily processions and fought their daily battles with the "Reds." They administered generous doses of castor oil. In their more outraged and primitive moods, they did not shrink from arson and murder. The record of Fascism in the early days of its growth is stained by theatricalism and crime, but it had its moments of devotion and courage. For good or ill, the future of Italy for many years to come belonged to it. In November 1921, at its National Congress in Rome, it reconstituted itself as a regular political party, the *Partito Nazionale Fascista*.

Fascism became more and more rightist in complexion, and it certainly derived the major part of its funds at this time from rightist sources. The idealistic, stoical, impecunious "Fascists of the first hour" evolved by sure, if imperceptible, stages into an army of fanatical squirearchs. It was indeed an odd concatenation of circumstances, material and moral, that converted that rabid Socialist, the Benito Mussolini of 1914 and 1919, into the antisocialist, antidemocratic Duce of 1922.

The last year before the assumption of power was a period of veritable civil war. Encouraged by their growing popularity and flushed with the assurrance of triumph, the Black Shirts paraded and fought and murdered at will. They answered provocation with provocation; they visited reprisals with reprisals; they wrecked workingmen's clubs and co-operatives; they raided houses in working-class districts; they purged town offices of their Socialist mayors and Socialist officials. The general strike of August 1922, organized by the so-called Alliance of Labor, was the last serious challenge offered them. They were now an army of 300,000 men. They seized newspaper offices and strikers' headquarters; they broke up strikers' processsions and meetings; for some days they ran the public services. The general strike collapsed miserably.

In September and October 1922, it was an open secret that Fascism was planning a supreme coup. Mussolini prepared the way by reconciling himself to the monarchy and the Church. He declared Fascism's unswerving loyalty to King Victor Emmanuel, and he assured the Vatican that, in the event of violence, Fascism would respect churches and church property everywhere. He relied on the regular army to preserve a benevolent neutrality. The police and the *Guardia Regia*,[3] he knew, would take the same attitude as the regular army. He held a meeting at Naples on October 24 to discuss a final plan of action. To direct the execution of the plan, he appointed a military "Quadrumvirate" composed of four prominent comrades in the cause — Bianchi, Fascist Secretary; Balbo, commander of the Black Shirts; Count De Vecchi, leader of the Fascist group in the Chamber; and General De Bono. He appointed Grandi, then best known as the Fascist labor expert, as political chief of staff to the enterprise.

On October 27, 1922 the order for the mobilization of the Black Shirts went out, and the March on Rome began. Facta, the Premier, "still cherished the hope" that he could "compromise." Facta would probably have proclaimed martial law, but the King hesitated to sign the order. Mussolini himself did not lead, nor even accompany, the great March; he repaired rather unheroically to Milan — evidently to watch developments from a safer distance whence, in the event of ill success, he could perhaps take flight to neutral Switzerland. Grandi and De Vecchi acted for him in Rome, in the capacity of a diplomatic mission, and persuaded the King to make him Premier. October 30 was a day of wild celebration in Rome. Fifty thousand Black Shirts demonstrated for hours. Mussolini arrived to receive his appointment at the hands of the King. "I bring Your Majesty," he said, "the Italy of Vittorio Veneto reconstructed by a new victory." He then addressed his Black Shirts from the Tomb of the Unknown Soldier in the National Monument, lauded their revolution, and pledged himself to a strong government at home and a strong foreign policy abroad.

Mussolini's first act in power was to dismiss his Black Shirts to their homes. It was a statesmanlike move; it prevented the demonstrations from degenerating into uncontrolled and needless violence; and it was an effective test of that discipline on which Mussolini had always insisted. Rome was evacuated by her invaders within twenty-four hours, and all over Italy Fascist concentrations were demobilized. The final Fascist triumph, in the end, was orderly, bloodless, and decisive.

Mussolini did not at once disdain to use the usual machinery of parliamentary government. On the contrary, he now formed a "Ministry of Collaboration," composed, surprisingly, of only three Fascists and of nine members of other parties. In addition to the premiership, he himself took the portfolios of foreign and home affairs. On November 16 he addressed the Chamber — a Chamber in which only 6 per cent were Fascist Deputies. "To the melancholy zealots of superconstitutionalism," he said, "I leave the task of making their more or less pitiful lamentations on recent events. I maintain that revolution has its rights. I add, in order that all may know it, that I am here to defend and enforce in the highest degree the revolution of the Black Shirts, injecting them intimately into the history of the nation as a force of development, progress, and equilibrium. I refused to overdo the victory, though I could have done so. . . . With 300,000 youths, fully armed, fully determined, and almost mystically ready to act at my command, I could have chastised all those who have defamed and tried to injure Fascism. I could have made of this sordid, gray assembly hall a bivouac for *Squadristi*, I could have kicked out parliament and constructed a government exclusively of *Fascisti*. I could have done so, but I did not want to, at least not for the present."

On the next day, Mussolini laid the same arguments before the Senate, though this time in more respectful language. Eight days later the Chamber meekly voted a measure conferring upon him "full powers" for a year.

FASCIST FOREIGN POLITICS

Mussolini had not long to wait to give the world an example of a "strong" foreign policy. On August 27, 1923 an Italian general and some aides who were engaged as representatives of the Conference of Ambassadors in demarcating the Greco-Albanian frontier were murdered near Ioannina on Greek soil. Mussolini at once instructed his minister at Athens to deliver to the Greek Government a note demanding an apology for the crime, a solemn funeral with military honors for the victims, an inquiry "with the assistance of the Italian military attaché," death sentences for the culprits, and an indemnity of 50,000,000 lire. The Greek Government agreed to the apology, the funeral, and the military honors, but rejected the other terms as "violating the sovereignty of the state." Thereupon an Italian naval squadron appeared off the Greek island of Corfu, bombarded its unarmed and obsolete citadel, and killed fifteen Greek and Armenian refugees who had been quartered there.

The Greek Government appealed to the League of Nations, and at the same time declared its willingness to abide by any decision that might be reached in the matter by the Conference of Ambassadors. Public opinion throughout the world, especially in the smaller nations of the League, was deeply outraged by the brutal and cowardly action of the Italian Navy, and it was clear that the League was face to face with a test case which it could not afford to handle weakly. The Fourth Assembly of the League met two days after the incident and at once became a forum of bitter denunciation of Italy. The Italian member on the League Council, who happened to be Salandra, the former Premier, in prophetic anticipation of Italy's attitude in another and greater crisis twelve years afterward (see p. 505), maintained throughout the discussions that the League was not competent to deal with the case.

The League Council drew up a plan of settlement which it forwarded to the Conference of Ambassadors, and on that plan the dispute was eventually settled. Italy was awarded the total 50,000,000 lire she had originally demanded. The smoke of wrath and rancor died away, but it was difficult to establish whether the League had won its first unqualified success or whether the Italian upstart had suffered his first decisive defeat. The Corfu incident served to awaken the postwar world to the presence of a new aggression in its midst and was an unhappy evidence of the fact that the spirit which had dictated the ultimatum to Serbia in 1914 was not yet destroyed.

FASCIST DOMESTIC POLITICS

At home, Mussolini's first objects were to consolidate his power and to justify his many promises to the Italian people. He purged the public departments and offices, the police, the prefectures, and the municipalities of their surviving Socialist and Communist members, and substituted personnel of proven Fascist virtue. Stringent press regulations gave his government the right to suppress without appeal any extremist or anti-Fascist literature. A Fascist Militia was formed, in part for the purpose of reorganizing the old squads of Black Shirts, many of whom, in their original hasty and provisional recruitment, contained "unreliable elements," and in part in order that future squadrist activities might be carried out under the cloak of legality.

Mussolini made a vigorous attack on the economic distresses of the country. He had an able Finance Minister in Alberto de Stefani. Expenditures in the public departments and the railroads were cut; hundreds of officials were dismissed; war pensions were revised; all kinds of bonuses, free passes on the railroads, and similar perquisites were abolished; the income tax was levied on much wider income groups. At the same time legacy duties, certain taxes on real estate, and a number of taxes on wines and luxuries, which had been burdensome and unpopular, were reduced. Several state concerns, such as the telephones, were turned over to private companies, partly to save the endless government subsidies, partly in the hope that they might be more efficiently managed. Above all, social disturbances, strikes, and lockouts, which had been so constant a drain in the old days, were suppressed without mercy. It may have been the success of these drastic measures, or it may have been that Fascism's early years of power coincided with the general trade recovery of Mediterranean countries; but Italian finances incontestably improved. The budget of 1921–22 showed a deficit of 17,000,000,000 lire; the budget of 1924–25 showed a surplus of 200,000,000 lire.

Mussolini's parliamentary record was not so successful. Despite his undisguised contempt for the Chamber, he did at first make a sincere effort to work with and through it. But the Chamber, like the proverbial leopard, could not change its spots. The parties of the Ministry of Collaboration were anything but collaborative. Mussolini clearly was in no position to proceed with his program for the rejuvenation of Italy while a spiteful Opposition obstructed his every move. During 1923 a new electoral bill was introduced proposing that whatever party secured the plurality of votes in any election should automatically receive two-thirds of the seats in the Chamber. The old Chamber, Mussolini declared in so many words, was a nuisance and an anachronism, and he demanded, in effect, that it dissolve itself. And dissolve itself, after long and arduous debate, it did. The new electoral law was passed in July 1923.

Elections under the new law were held in April 1924. Mussolini was determined that Fascism should win a decisive victory. It is perhaps proof of the bankruptcy of the parliamentary system in Italy that, at this supremely critical moment, over twenty different parties appeared in various degrees of opposition to Fascism and to one another. Mussolini's "national list" won handsomely with 4,700,000 votes to the Opposition parties' 2,250,000. It would probably have won handsomely, even without the corruption and intimidation that were afterward alleged. But this rebuff still did not silence the Opposition. In the new Chamber the two Socialists, Amendola and Matteotti, were particularly fractious, and remained quite unconvinced when Mussolini patiently, but sternly, explained to them the true functions of a Fascist parliament. Then on the afternoon of June 10, 1924, Matteotti was kidnapped and killed.

Matteotti's was not the first of Fascism's murders. But he was an important Opposition leader, well respected and beloved, and usually Fascism had spilled the blood of lesser men. It was not then known, of course, to what extent the crime was "authorized," but Fascism was almost driven from its newly won power by the outburst of indignation which swept the country. Revelations made since 1943 have clearly implicated Mussolini himself. As it was, at the time, he had to face the full force of public suspicion. He stood contritely in the Chamber and swore to punish the guilty persons whoever they might be. "Only some enemy of mine," he said, "lying awake at night plotting something devilish against me, could have thought out this crime." In later years he took the view that the case was "a practical joke which degenerated into a horrible tragedy against the will of its authors." He reformed his cabinet, and he dismissed General De Bono, who since the March on Rome had been Chief of Police. But he refused to touch his Fascist Militia or to call for new elections. Several members of the Opposition, after the manner of the ancient Roman plebs, withdrew in protest to the Aventine,[4] where, under the unofficial leadership of Amendola, they established headquarters and waged a bitter, wordy campaign against the Fascist government.

As seems always to happen in the history of revolutions, a reign of terror succeeded to an earlier reign of moderation. It was evident that many of the Aventine Opposition were motivated less by a genuine horror of the Matteotti crime than by a desire to make political capital out of it and, as soon as their diatribes showed signs of weakening, Mussolini decided on final repressive measures. He appointed to the post of Secretary of the Fascist party Farinacci, an uncompromising veteran of the movement, and the old campaign of bludgeon and castor oil was resumed with a new ferocity. A mass of legislation was passed during 1925 in general furtherance of the program, "all in the State, nothing outside the State, nothing against the State." Non-Fascist members of the Cabinet were dismissed. The old political parties were disbanded. The bureaucracy and local government throughout the country were "Fascistized," local elections were suspended, and some seven thousand communes were relegated to mayors directly appointed by, and directly responsible to, the Ministry of the Interior. The censorship of the press was tightened, and only those journalists were allowed to exercise their profession who belonged to an authorized register. A thoroughgoing reform of the penal code was put in hand. In 1926, under a Defense of the State Act, a special tribunal was set up which was a sort of court-martial, operating by means of secret denunciation, arrest, and custody without hearing, and a more or less secret trial; and appropriately enough the tribunal's magistrates were not necessarily trained in law, but were high officers of the army or the Fascist Militia, often directly appointed by the Duce himself. Finally there was organized that necessary appanage of all dictatorships, a secret police, the OVRA (*Organizazione Vigilanza Reati Anti-Fascisti*).

Italy took on the aspect of a one-party totalitarian state. The Chamber became a mere rostrum for Fascist rhetoric, and its business was reduced more and more to the acclamatory approval of Fascist bills. In the words of Mussolini, the Chamber was at last a legislative assembly which really "functioned." In January 1926, when a few straggling survivors from the Aventine Opposition tried to resume their seats in the Chamber, they were forcibly refused admittance. The Senate, be it said in parenthesis, behaved throughout the reformatory process in a most exemplary manner. It voted overwhelmingly Fascist on all occasions and basked happily and securely in the favors of the Duce. The King became a Merovingian cipher.

In March 1926 the Matteotti trial was held at last in the remote township of Chieti. Of those originally accused of the crime a number had escaped or were absolved, and only five remained to face a reduced charge of manslaughter. Two of the five were found not guilty; three were condemned to imprisonment, but were released after two months under an amnesty conveniently granted by the King in celebration of the twenty-fifth anniversary of his reign. Farinacci himself, the Party Secretary, acted as advocate for the principal defendant. In Italy at large the trial and sentences raised no vocal comment.

Amendola, Matteotti's colleague, himself repeatedly injured in squadrist affrays, died a few days after the trial.

MUSSOLINI AND THE FASCIST PARTY

Mussolini's personality was a microcosm of Fascism. His combativeness, his opportunism, his showmanship, his vindictiveness — to say nothing of his physical appearance, the jerky, aggressive gait, the black, flashing eyes, and the jutting jaw — typified his cause and his party. "Not for nothing have I chosen for my motto in life 'Live dangerously,' " he declared, "and I say to you, like the old warrior, 'If I advance, follow me; if I retreat, kill me; if I die, avenge me!' " "Better a day like a lion than a hundred years like a sheep." "I am a cynic," he said again, "insensible to everything except adventure — mad adventure." These were characteristic utterances.

The facts of Mussolini's career are well known and quickly told. He was born in 1883. As a boy he suffered all the slings and arrows of the underprivileged. His father was a blacksmith and a Socialist in a Romagnese village where dreary, unrelieved want was the rule of life. He was cuffed and bullied and beaten. He got into barroom brawls and back-street stabbings. Only the greatest courage, perseverance, and hard work — and perhaps the influence of a devoted mother — could have raised him out of his environment and earned him his first success, a teacher's diploma.

He fled to Switzerland to escape military service which, as an antimilitarist, he abhorred. He supported himself, when he could, as a stonemason and a teacher. He attended lectures at the universities of Lausanne and Geneva. He was very much the center of that restaurant socialism which flourished in the Swiss border towns at the turn of the century. But his views were violent and subversive, and he was expelled from one canton after another. Once he was jailed for vagabondage.

In 1905 he returned to Italy and to his military service. He already had some following as an agitator, a journalist, and a fomenter of strikes. In 1912 he became editor of the Socialist paper *Avanti!* In August 1914 he was still violently pacifist. But in September 1914 he experienced "a miracle of conversion" — or perhaps, as has been creditably hinted, he was bought by French funds; — he acquired his own newspaper, *Il Popolo d'Italia*, and became violently pro-Ally and interventionist.

In September 1915 he was called to the colors and saw some weeks of active service in the trenches, though he appears never to have been through a major engagement. In February 1917, while at a training camp, he was wounded by the bursting of a mortar. He was invalided out of the army and went back to his *Popolo d'Italia*. Thence followed the turbulent years, the years of mad adventure, the strikes and lockouts, the seizures of the factories, the founding of the first Fascio, the party squabbles, the squadrism, the civil war of 1921–22, and the final meteoric rise to power.

Mussolini the Duce was perhaps not very different from Mussolini the journalist, the soldier, and the Black Shirt. But responsibility made room for the display of his more substantial capacities. The first impression he always gave was one of overpowering vitality. His normal working day was sixteen hours. He is said to have given eight thousand audiences in a single year. At one time he held the portfolios of eight state departments. Yet his many administrative duties never seemed to reduce the frequency of his public appearances, his speechmaking, or his attendance at meetings of Grand Council, Cabinet, or Chamber. His intellectual interests were wide and varied. He kept himself well informed and read voraciously. As one writer put it, no statesman since Gladstone was so concentratedly studious. His habits were frugal and abstemious. He made a cult of athletics. He had rare personal fascination, an intuitive judgment of men, and a demagogic genius of the first order. And yet, for all his many qualities, it is hard to think of another man of his time who before his career was run succeeded in making himself so utterly contemptible.

The Fascist party in 1922 was said to have numbered 300,000, and in 1934 over 1,500,000. It was organized into some 9,500 local Fasci which then pyramided upward, through the provincial federations, to a National Party Directorate, administered by that exalted official — after the Duce perhaps the most powerful man in Fascist Italy — the Secretary of the Party. The Fascist Grand Council of some twenty members, the Duce's own privy council, crowned the edifice, and was to all intents and purposes the real governing body of Italy.

The Fascist Militia or, to give it its full name, the Voluntary Militia for National Security, was the legalized form which the more reliable elements of the old squadrists were given in 1923. Its members used to regard themselves as the elite of the party, but in course of time they lost a good deal of their original function and importance. Like the SA in Nazi Germany, they were the front fighters in the early days of the movement, but it was afterward hard to find other than a ceremonial use for them, and their internal struggles are often reminiscent of the struggles of Rochm with the Nazi party and the Reichswehr. But they were privileged to count as an army reserve, they were subject to the army's code of discipline, and they were always regarded as standing ready for immediate mobilization in moments of national emergency.

The training of the country's youth was always an essential part of the Fascist program. There were organizations for boys, progressively graded according to age group, the *Balilla,* the *Avanguardia,* and the *Giovani Fascisti.* In 1934 their members numbered over 3,000,000. They were devoted to Fascist "education," to sports and ceremonies, and, in the uppermost age group, to military exercises. In 1927 the ranks of the Fascist party were closed except to those who had "graduated" from them. There were corresponding organizations for girls, the *Piccole Italiane* and the *Giovane Italiane.*

THE CORPORATIVE STATE

There have always been occupational associations. They existed in ancient Rome in the form of *collegia,* in the Middle Ages as guilds, and in modern times as trade-unions. Syndicalism, as first developed in France in the late nineteenth century, was the extension of the trade-union movement and regarded occupational associations as organs of direct political power. Government by such associations, that is, government by "groups of producers," so argued the syndicalists, was far more appropriate for an economic age than the old method of government by parties.

Syndicalism was strong in Italy in the eighties and nineties. The Church recognized the movement and encouraged the formation of Catholic associations. Leo XIII's famous encyclical in 1891, *Rerum Novarum*, gave the movement a doctrinal sanction. Syndicalism figured in early Fascist ideology. Syndicalism as such doubtless seemed conformable to the type of collective, highly organized state order which the Fascists were hoping to build. The Fascists made one innovation. They extended their syndicates to include all trades and professions, employers and employees alike.

Fascist syndicates were reduced to a constitutional system, notably by the Labor Charter of 1927. Thirteen confederations — later nine — of syndicates of employers, employees, and intellectual workers were defined. The syndicates were entitled to enter into "collective contracts" regulating wages, social insurance, holidays, and so forth. Labor disputes were referable to the confederation concerned, then, if no settlement was reached, to the Ministry of Corporations, and finally to one of several labor courts. Strikes and lockouts were declared illegal. Outside the system, but co-operating with it, were the "After Work" organizations ("*Dopolavoro*"), providing recreational and cultural facilities for workers and their families.

The next step was to bring syndicalism wholly into the Fascist system of government. In 1928, accordingly, a new electoral law empowered the confederations to propose 800 candidates for election to the Chamber of Deputies, and other associations to propose 200 more. From these names the Fascist Grand Council selected 400, which were then submitted, as a ballot, to the vote of the electorate. In 1934 a law was passed more precisely establishing and defining the functions of the corporations. The final form was reached in 1939 when Mussolini instituted the Chamber of the Fasci and Corporations to supersede the former Chamber of Deputies. In total result Italy was to be governed by a body whose members did not represent parties and constituencies, as in the usual democracy, but represented trades and professions. Throughout all these changes and developments, it is to be noted, the former Senate remained the upper legislative chamber with its powers and dignities theoretically unaltered.

The Corporative State was an ingenious, high-sounding compromise which gave the state wide powers of control over industry, respected vested interests while yet allowing Fascism to describe itself as a benevolent, "classless" economic system and, by implication, cast a contemptuous slur on Western democracy. Mussolini regarded it as Fascism's greatest contribution to political science.

FASCIST IDEOLOGY

On the superficial view, Fascism was indebted to certain literary and intellectual sources. Its leaders, like the leaders of the American and French revo-

lutions, were strongly and consciously influenced by the political speculation of their day. The Duce, once a schoolmaster, had belonged to the
intelligentsia and, especially during his Swiss period, he had lived on the
fringes of the academic world. In an arduous self-education such authors as
Machiavelli, Nietzsche, Sorel, Pareto and, to a less extent, Schopenhauer,
Hegel, Blanqui, William James, Bergson, Péguy, Marinetti, and even
Karl Marx made traceable contributions to that scholastic complex that
was Mussolini's mind. The Fascist movement subsequently produced its
own Haushofers and Rosenbergs, men like Giovanni Gentile, Alfredo
Rocco, and many others, who compiled their evangels and drew upon
political prophets from Plato onward to authenticate and dignify their faith.
On the superficial view, therefore, there was a side to Fascism that had a
decidedly intellectual and doctrinaire flavor.

At the same time Fascism was indebted less consciously to various contemporary influences. Its founder might indeed pick and choose the articles of
his creed as best suited him, but he was also guided in his choice, involun-
tarily guided, by an environment which was none of his devising. His own
lack of principles made him the more susceptible to the ideas which he
found around him and which constantly adulterated the almost irreducible
atavism that his thinking sometimes approached. Fascism, in fact, was a mass
of "historical residues." It existed in an age of progress in science and material welfare, of romanticism in art and literature, of pragmatism in philosophy, of nationalism in politics, of doubt and indifference in religion, and
every one of those things was observable in it. Its materialism, its emotionalism, its antirationalism, its realism, its pseudo mysticism are plain and
evident to any student of the history of recent "isms."

For example, a favorite Fascist "myth" was Imperial Rome. It had the
greatest theatrical and propagandist possibilities. It had a grand emblem-
atic heraldry, easy to revive; it had at hand all the ancient classic monuments, themselves relics of an architecture not altogether alien to the Fascist
spirit; it provided the Head of the State with the dignity of Caesar himself,
the most coveted dignity in the history of Europe. Imperial Rome as such
was in some ways a *reductio ad absurdum* of nationalism, and it was also in
some ways an extension of the rather more novel doctrine of the totalitarian
state. It was grand and lavish and very obvious, and it appealed to the fes-
tive, carnival gifts which the Italian people had always possessed so abundantly. "Rome is our point of departure and of reference; it is our symbol
. . . our myth," said Mussolini on one occasion. "We dream of a Roman
Italy, that is to say wise and strong, disciplined and imperial. Much of that
which was the immortal spirit of Rome resurges in Fascism; Roman are the
Lictor's Rods, Rome our fighting organization, Rome our pride and our
courage: *Civis romanus sum*." [5]

Modern nationalism was a part of the much wider Romantic Movement
which, since the late eighteenth and early nineteenth centuries, had so
strongly influenced the whole of European civilization. There is not the
room, nor is this the place, to describe that movement, but the reader can at
least be asked to recognize the peculiar type of romantic emotionalism in
modern nationalist, and therefore Fascist, doctrine. The Italian, by common

repute, was always more excitable in speech and manner than the northern European. But it remains an open question whether that excitability had become a part of the Italian national character before the *Risorgimento* in the nineteenth century. Machiavelli *and* Mazzini, it is well to remember, were both Italians typical of their day. But Mussolini, in the Indian summer of the European Romantic Movement, inherited the tone and style of the *Risorgimento* and made of Fascism an intensely emotional nationalism. It is not enough to say that the language of Mussolini, or D'Annunzio for instance, is spoiled in translation. It is not enough to say that verbatim reports of Mussolini's speeches in the foreign press always made the best of all anti-Fascist propaganda. Even in the original Italian there was always something in the sustained histrionism of the Duce's declamations which bordered on the absurd. He never put his tongue to a word or his hand to a gesture that was not pure theater. He was a consummate actor and an inexhaustible showman. Fascist parades and festivals perhaps were never dedicated to the sheerly colossal, as were the Nazi and the Soviet, but they surpassed them both in noise and color and intoxication of spirits.

So many of the more serious and "profounder" features of Fascism were pure emotional romance, and little else. The constant borrowing from the language of mysticism, the constant religiosity which, like a repressed dream, kept thrusting itself to the surface of the Fascist consciousness — these were romantic, romantic in the nineteenth-century sense. We cannot but feel that a great deal of the asceticism, the contempt of physical comfort, the emphasis on courage and hardihood, appealed not in themselves, but because of the stirring, pseudomystical verbiage in which they could be presented.

Yet, on the less superficial view, this analyzing of possible intellectual and historical sources always seems to miss the real rationale of the Fascist movement. As students of history we are often deceived perhaps by a too documentary approach to our problems, and we fail to recognize the inner nature of a movement which, in all essentials, was not reducible to texts and footnotes. Fascism, if anything, invested itself with literary dignity after, and not before, it had become a driving force in the world. It created its own dynamic first, and then borrowed its scholastic plumes as expediency seemed to direct. It borrowed not to enrich a creed or system, but to mobilize practical support for practical needs.

Fascism adopted its ideas, whether out of Plato or Machiavelli, Sorel or Pareto, or out of any other favorite authority in its patristic hodgepodge, not to point a moral, but to provide the springs of action. Its mood and temper, which we have just tried to interpret in terms of romanticism, were cultivated, perhaps to disguise an intellectual crudity and barrenness, but far more to inspire physical energy and power. To look therefore for a doctrinal basis in Fascism or to expect a well-rounded logical consistency in Fascism is to misunderstand it entirely. Fascism was more technique than doctrine. Such programs and slogans and constitutional enactments as it put forward from time to time were always makeshift and strategic, and were part and parcel of the technique. The Fascists themselves always harped on their "realism." They disdained abstractions and utopias. They expressed the faith that was in them by works. "I never think," exclaimed the young Fascist; "therefore I am!"

As he avowed, when he founded his first Fascio in 1919, Mussolini had "no specific doctrinal plan." He was always an extemporizer. "He had none of the scruples of those who, being convinced of an idea, fear to be false to it. He passed from theory to theory, from position to position, rapidly and inconsistently, without remorse or regret." He always had the advantage of other political leaders who had to be coherent and keep to a stated policy. In his rise to power he offered every party what it wanted and convinced each of his sincerity. Worker and magnate, peasant and landowner, layman and priest, commoner and king, at one time or another were all cajoled by his promises.

But a philosophy consistent only in inconsistency is no philosophy. A principle held only so long as it is convenient, only so long as it "works" or "produces results," is no principle. In the final analysis, the real fallacy of Fascism proceeded from an implicit spiritual negativity. It created an ethos without values. It expended a terrific energy, but expended it to no recognizable end. On such showing, the texts and doctrines, the sources and authorities, begin to fall away to reveal a Fascist ideology in all its nihilist nakedness.

We may say that there are three main streams whose confluence has given us the broad river of Western civilization: the law and universal peace of Rome; the love and salvation of Christianity; and the humanism and science of the Renaissance. All three streams found their historic source to an extraordinary degree in the Italian peninsula. But all three Fascism denied. Fascism was lawless, peaceless, and antidemocratic; it neither knew love on earth nor asked for salvation in heaven; it made use of the techniques of humanism and science with a total misunderstanding of their spirit.

Communism and Fascism, it has often been argued, had many things in common. Both were "latter-day" phenomena; both were party-inspired mass movements; both lent themselves to totalitarian dictatorships. But they had one essential difference. Communism has often been interpreted as our Western civilization's last and most uncompromising attempt to build the earthly paradise. On such showing, Communism was at least a positive doctrine. But Fascism was all negation. Fascism denied even the earthly paradise. As Mussolini put it, "We do not believe in the materialistic concept of an economic happiness." Fascism was not just a parochial Italian aberration, induced by a passing war weariness and an impatience with parliamentary discipline. It was the total renunciation of values. It was an example and a warning of the fate that could overtake any people, even a highly gifted and mature people, and a people of the richest cultural heritage, who likewise renounced their values. The question it posed for the generation whose history we are writing was how far other such peoples would renounce their values also. The question was how far the broad river of Western civilization would continue to run to waste in the deserts of modern nihilism or how far it could be used to fertilize the earth — or even how far a fresh new season of history might be made to grow and fructify upon its banks.

For man without values degenerates into the state of savagery and tribalism whence he first rose. He lives in perpetual warfare with his environment. The be-all and end-all of his existence is physical survival. His highest joys and rewards are the physical conquest of his enemies and the physical aggrandizement of himself. The very race or tribe or nation to which he belongs becomes an organism, like some lean beast of prey, whose muscles are toughened, whose claws are sharpened, and whose every nerve is co-ordinated to the task of eternal battle.

Fascism gloried therefore in all the warlike virtues — in power, ruthlessness, cruelty, efficiency, and egoism. Fascist rhetoric was interlarded with such words as "audacity," "will," "conflict," "decision," "conquest," "victory," "sacrifice," "discipline," and so forth, and an abundant rhetoric it was. Fascist squads bore characteristic names, the "Savages," the "Damned," the "Desperadoes." "Fascism," wrote Mussolini, "desires man to be active and engaged in action with all his energies: it wants him to be virilely conscious of existing difficulties and ready to meet them. It considers life a struggle, thinking that it is man's task to conquer for himself that which is really worthy of him." "Above all, Fascism . . . believes neither in the possibility nor the utility of perpetual peace. It thus repudiates the doctrine of Pacifism — born of a renunciation of the struggle and an act of cowardice in the face of sacrifice. War alone brings up to its highest tension all human energy and puts the stamp of nobility upon the people who have the courage to meet it." [6] Sometimes Mussolini played with the notion of a special caste of warriors, a heroic breed, after the manner of the Nazi master race, who would forever do battle for the glory of Italy. "To be sure this is a lofty dream," he said; "but I see it being realized little by little. . . . The goal is always — Empire! To build a city, to found a colony, to establish an empire, these are the prodigies of the human spirit. An empire is not merely territorial; it may be political, economic, spiritual. . . . Toward this must we move. And therefore we must resolutely abandon the whole liberal phraseology and way of thinking. The word of command can be none but this: Discipline. Discipline at home, in order that abroad we may present the granite block of a single national will." [7]

Time was when Mussolini's militarism used to be misunderstood. His vaunting, boastful tone was looked upon as mere Italian flamboyance and dismissed perhaps as the "defense mechanism" of a man who was too painfully aware of the absence of those virtues he lauded so much in the modern Italian people. To Anglo-Saxons especially, who wanted nothing so much as peace, it was sheer nausea to see this idolatry of war in a nation whose military exploits had not always been too glittering. Yet Mussolini's militarism was no mere pathology or megalomania. Fascism might contain no other logic or doctrine, but this at least proceeded logically, all too logically, from Fascist premises. Fascism, in short, was the creed of a race of men who preferred the morals of the tribe to the morals of civilization. Its categorical imperative left Italian people, for all their unmilitary temperament, with no alternative but to become a military, militant state.

Fascist government therefore was a military government. Fascist organizations were military organizations. The Fascist hierarchy was an officer corps. The Fascist party was an army cadre. The Fascist economy was autarchic, totalitarian, and ordered for war. The resources of the country, human and material, were trained and dedicated to the supreme inevitability. "The plan of control for Italian economic policy in the coming Fascist era," said Mussolini, "is determined by a single consideration: that our nation will be called to war. When? How? Nobody can say. But the wheel of fate is turning fast."

Granted the military state, therefore, tyranny and intolerance were reasonable and necessary. Mussolini demanded discipline of his party and his people as the commander demands discipline of his army. In a democratic state, where peace is regarded as a normal and perpetual condition, broken only by unnatural lapses into war, freedom of speech, freedom of conscience, political opposition, parliamentary debate, liberal individualism in general are permissible luxuries. But in a military state, where war is regarded as the normal and perpetual condition, broken only by unnatural lapses into peace, these things are tantamount to insubordination. Political opposition and parliamentary debate are no better than the discussion of orders; freedom of speech and freedom of conscience are destructive of the fighting morale and efficiency of the nation. Mussolini boasted of trampling upon "the more or less decomposed body of the Goddess of Liberty." "There is no longer any room for many things which were excellent in other times," he wrote. "Today, among the things for which there is no room, must be included the Opposition." "All parties must end, must fall. I want to see a panorama of ruins about me, the ruins of the other political forces, so that Fascism may stand alone, gigantic and dominant."

As the soldier becomes one with an army, so a citizen becomes one with a state. The individual is nothing, the state is everything. The individual serves most perfectly when he forgets himself and lives only to glorify and magnify the state. The fasces, the symbol of Fascism, signified the many bound together as the haft of an ax in a single powerful obedience. Fascist rhetoric was never so ecstatic, never so full of transcendent Hegelian universals, as when it described the secular Church, the State, to whose body individual man was so mystically united. "The Fascist State," wrote Mussolini, "the highest and most potent form of the personality, is a force, but spiritual. [That] force includes all the forms of the moral and intellectual life of man. It cannot therefore be limited to simple functions of order and supervision, as Liberalism proposed. It is not a simple mechanism which limits the sphere of presumed individual liberties. It is an interior form and norm, and disciplines the whole person; and penetrates the will no less than the intelligence. Its principle, the central inspiration of the human personality living in the civil community, descends into the deeps and makes its home in the heart of the man of action as of the thinker, of the artist as of the scientist: the very soul of the soul." [6]

THE VATICAN

In 1870 the Italian troops of Victor Emmanuel II had occupied the city of Rome, and the papal capital had been proclaimed the capital of united Italy. The Pope denounced the "usurping Power" and retired into voluntary imprisonment in the Vatican. He refused to recognize the Law of Papal Guarantees of 1871, by which the Italian Government tried to heal the estrangement. The Roman Question, as it was called, continued from that day to vex the conscience and ingenuity of Italian statesmanship, and ironic was the fate that decreed that the Fascist Government, the most secular of all Italian governments, should at long last be the one to find a solution of it.

Italy has had her skeptics and her anticlericals, and the Vatican was traditionally opposed to Italian unity. But the Italian people, as a whole, especially in the rural districts, were a Catholic people, loyal and faithful as the people of Poland, Mexico, or Quebec. Mussolini himself had once been anticlerical, even as he had been antimonarchical, and in all fundamentals Fascism stood in opposition to the Catholic Church. But in 1922, before the March on Rome, Mussolini had made his peace with the Church and the monarchy. Like Napoleon perhaps, he found it politic to be on good diplomatic terms with the Vatican. During his first years in power, he made valiant efforts not to injure Catholic sensibilities. He was careful never to seem to interfere with religious instruction in the schools. Some of his more anticlerical Fascists even found they could stomach Catholicism more easily by regarding it as a "national" religion! His suppression of Freemasonry and secret societies in Italy was evidently intended to approve himself in the eyes of the Church as a deserving friend and ally. The Corporative State was supposed to be consonant with Catholic social doctrine. Even so, there were occasional "incidents," and the Vatican had sometimes to deplore Fascist acts of violence against Catholic persons and property. In January 1927, Mussolini had the great temerity to disband the Catholic youth organization, the *Esploratori Cattolici,* which he felt to be a rival of his own *Balilla.*

However, despite the incidents, Mussolini's negotiations with the Vatican upon the Roman Question began quietly and informally in 1926 and lasted a difficult three years. Both sides clearly desired a final settlement. On February 11, 1929, at the Lateran Palace, Cardinal Gasparri, the Papal Secretary of State, and Mussolini signed a series of agreements.

The Lateran agreements comprised a treaty, a concordat, and a financial convention. Under the treaty, Italy recognized the sovereignty of the Holy See over "Vatican City," a neutral, inviolable territory — actually of less than a square mile in area with about 400 permanent inhabitants. Italy also granted extraterritorial rights to certain churches and other ecclesiastical property outside the Vatican. She accredited an ambassador to the Holy See and accepted an apostolic nuncio to herself. Under the concordat, she recognized Catholicism as the state religion, secured to the Church the performance of its rites and sacraments, bound herself to enforce canon law in regard to marriage, recognized the validity of ecclesiastical marriage without the necessity of a subsequent civil ceremony, and permitted compulsory religious instruction in both elementary and secondary schools. Under the financial convention, she paid the Vatican 1,750,000,000 lire (about $90,000,000) in cash and bonds "as a definite settlement of all its financial relations with Italy in consequence of the fall of the temporal power." Finally, the Holy See declared the Roman Question to be ended and eliminated, and recognized the Kingdom of Italy under the House of Savoy, with Rome as the capital of the Italian state. The ratifications were exchanged on June 7, 1929.

The Roman Catholic Church, in an age of spiritual agony, had become a powerful and growing influence. The extreme anticlericalism that had flourished in the nineteenth century had conspicuously declined. The twentieth century had no counterpart to Zola and Anatole France. Republican Spain and Nazi Germany were among exceptions to the rule but, generally speaking, at the time of which we are writing, the Church was treated with little hatred and considerable respect even by those who were furthest from it in their sympathies. Derogatory references to Catholics and their institutions were scrupulously avoided in the press, stage, and film in all democratic countries.

The Church enjoyed increasing international recognition. One country after another appreciated the importance of establishing diplomatic relations with it, and the Vatican became a unique cosmopolitan center, a "listening post" sensitive to every breath and breeze of political activity throughout the world. At Benedict XV's accession in 1914, fourteen states were represented at the Vatican; at his death in 1922, the number was twenty-five. In 1939 the number was thirty-seven. Myron Taylor went on his mission as President Roosevelt's "personal representative" to the Pope in 1940. During the interwar period, the Vatican renewed its practice of negotiating concordats with foreign Powers. In 1914 there were very few concordats in existence, and Pius X, in his pontificate from 1903 to 1914, negotiated only one, a concordat with Serbia which, because of the outbreak of the First World War, was never ratified. Pius XI negotiated concordats with all the leading governments of Europe except Britain and the Soviet Union. Furthermore, the Church showed its realization of its international responsibilities in its extended missionary activity and in its encouragement of new monastic and university foundations abroad. Of eighteen encyclicals issued between 1920 and 1939, eight concerned current international and economic questions. Pope Pius XII created twenty-six non-Italian cardinals at a single consistory in 1946, including a Chinese, an Armenian, a Persian, an Australian, a Canadian, three Americans, and five Latin Americans.

Both recent popes were international figures of international experience. Achille Ratti was papal nuncio at Warsaw during the Russo-Polish War and Archbishop of Milan during the early years of the Fascist struggle for power. He succeeded Benedict XV as Pius XI in 1922, and his pontificate almost exactly coincided with the interwar period. Eugenio Pacelli, a master of eight languages, was papal nuncio at Munich and Berlin, and then papal Secretary of State. He knew Brazil, the United States, England, and most European countries. He succeeded Pius XI as Pius XII in 1939.

FRANCE: FINANCE, PARTY POLITICS,

AND SECURITY

THE POSTWAR MOOD

It has often been pointed out that the game of politics counted for less in France than in many another country, that the continued ministerial changes were of no great moment, that the main strength of the country was not to be judged by the irresponsible behavior of its parliamentary assemblies. Even so, the political failure of France in modern times has appalled and surprised her many friends the more because it has seemed so utterly at variance with her rich intellectual gifts and with her superlative contributions to all the other arts of civilization. By 1914 the government of the Third Republic — perhaps not unlike the governments of some other modern democracies — had been gradually falling into the hands of a class of professional politicians. The best brains in France were not being drawn to public life. Little social kudos attached to membership in the Senate, and less to membership in the Chamber. A man had to be of tough fiber who was willing to submit to the vulgarity and coarseness of French electioneering. For those in power, patronage and jobbery were part of the normal way of things. Periodic financial scandals, relished by a scurrilous and sensational press, were evidence of the deep corruption everywhere. The electorate, grown old in cynicism, accepted the situation as a matter of course though, now and again, insulted and goaded beyond endurance, it would resort to acts of violence discreditable to itself and unhelpful to its real cause.

The Third Republic's party system, reflecting a curious social structure, had always been multiple and unstable. Modern France had begun with the Revolution of 1789. But the Revolution was not the wholesale upheaval that it is sometimes represented to have been. Catastrophic though it was, it was not the final liquidation of the older order. Powerful conservative elements survived, and the subsequent history of France from 1815 to 1940 is interpretable as the constant re-enactment of the selfsame revolutionary conflict. The Third Republic itself had come into being in the face of strong opposition — the adoption of the republican form of government by the Chamber of Deputies in 1875 had been carried by a majority of only one vote. Thiers had said at the time, "The Republic divided us least," and had thereby revealed the negative, compromising character of the new regime's ideology.

The parties of the Third Republic comprised two broad groups, the Right and the Left. On the Right was the old authoritarian France, pillared upon the myth of the *ancien régime*, monarchy, army, Church — and finance. On the Left was democratic France, pillared upon the myth of the Revolution, supporting and supported by "the small man," the worker and the peasant. The two groups of parties, implacably opposed, were often of equivalent voting strength. Hence arose the constant jockeying for position, the blocs and coalitions, the cabinet reshufflings, and all the changeableness and indiscipline of the Republic's parliamentary life. Between 1875 and 1920 there were fifty-nine different ministries, and in the interwar period, from 1920 to 1939, there were forty-one. Occasionally a minister survived through several changes, but few were long enough in office to carry out a consistent, long-term policy.

Then came the question of money. French politics were overshadowed by it. There was always something of the peasant in the French character, and the preoccupation with money was a national trait. In the eyes of foreign observers the perpetual financial tangle — the unbalanced budgets, evasion of taxes, mounting national debt and, after 1919, reparations and the fluctuation of exchange — was as typical of modern France as the perpetual parliamentary tangle.

France had a tradition in unbalanced budgets going back for centuries. Colbert, the patron saint of French ministers of finance, balanced only eight of his twenty-four budgets, and the eight in that respect were entirely exceptional. There was a short interim of surpluses during the French Revolution and another for a few years just before 1914. But generally the old tradition was resumed throughout the post-Revolutionary era. Not only were budgets unbalanced, but they were often passed months in arrears, and the sums were sometimes increased by various euphemistic "special" and "extraordinary" accounts. The system of taxation was complicated, by 1914 it was hopelessly out of date, and the evasion of taxes was a national scandal. But none of the political parties — the Socialists perhaps excepted — wanted to incur the odium of introducing reforms. It was a familiar saying that the average Frenchman would more gladly die for France than pay her a franc of his savings. In any event, the reactionary "two hundred families," who were alleged to control the country's financial houses and the Senate, always formed an insuperable obstacle to progressive legislation. Between 1907 and 1914, Caillaux had tried to introduce an income tax, and an emasculated income-tax bill did in fact become law in 1914, a few days before the outbreak of the First World War; but its operation was postponed till 1917, and it was not expected to yield a substantial return for some years.

During the First World War, France had spent money with little thought for the morrow. She had "muddled through" for so long, and wartime was no time to change the hallowed system. Victory could not be too dearly or too recklessly bought, and victory might pay for itself in the shape of German reparations. Except for an Excess War Profits Tax, which did not bring in a yield till 1918, and a luxury tax, no new taxes were imposed. Revenue on paper remained throughout the war about the same; but, whereas revenue in 1914 met 40 per cent of the total state expenditure, in 1918 it met only 12 per cent. Meanwhile "invisible" sources of income, notably interest on foreign investments which had formerly compensated for some of the deficit, disappeared. In 1914 these investments had reached the huge total of 45,000,000,000 francs ($9,000,000,000). But political motives had largely dictated French investment policy abroad, and the chief debtors of France were countries like Russia and Rumania, whose paying capacities the First World War had most disastrously interrupted.

A fiscal policy such as has been described could be carried on only by borrowing. In 1914 the French national debt was estimated at 34,000,000,000 francs ($6,600,000,000), a figure only slightly less than the national income at the time, and the service of the debt absorbed a third of the revenue. In 1918 the debt was over 150,000,000,000 francs, and in 1924 it was probably over 300,000,000,000 francs; in that year the service of the debt, plus war pensions of various kinds, absorbed over three-quarters of the revenue. The result, of course, was inflation. From 1914 to 1924 the gold reserve declined only slightly, but the note issue multiplied six times, and the percentage of gold to notes dropped from 70 to 10. In 1924, after the Ruhr episode, the value of the franc broke altogether.

Finance, therefore, in one way or another, was bound to be a major concern of interwar France, and no other country of the same size and potential wealth was so completely dominated by it. Throughout the twenties, France's affairs, domestic and foreign, revolved around the everlasting franc. Ministries, Right and Left, rose and fell in the ceaseless Battle of the Budget. France's insistence on German reparations was no wanton revengefulness or political cunning, but absolute necessity.[1] Traditional indebtedness, complex and outmoded taxation, the loss of foreign investments, four years of unparalleled economic effort, the material and human devastations of the war, the substantial failure of reparations — all these made an accumulation of burdens which the exhausted country could no longer support.

France was suffering from a deep sociocultural malaise. It is hard to discuss imponderables, particularly in the case of France, and particularly when her condition was the result of so many general and special causes which we still do not fully understand. France, for centuries the premier civilizing power in Europe, doubtless reacted more sensitively to, and herself anticipated, the wider European malaise of the twentieth century. But she had also very concrete reasons for showing an extreme exhaustion at this time. She had been steadily losing her man power in foreign wars since Louis XIV, and now, as the woeful climax of centuries of wastage, she had borne the brunt of the First World War. It was commonly said that, of every three Germans killed between 1914 and 1918, two had died by the hand of a French soldier.[2] Her own casualties had been 1,400,000 killed, or 10 per cent of her active male population — the heaviest percentage of any major belligerent — and 1,500,000 mutilated, or 11 per cent, again the heaviest of any major belligerent; and, in view of her declining birth rate, the loss was not likely to be made good. The German invasion and occupation had devastated ten of her departments, and they were the ten which contained her most populous and most highly industrialized districts. In this area 2,500,-000 of the inhabitants had been displaced, either by flight in 1914 or by forcible deportation afterward. Houses, farms, railroads, bridges, canals had been destroyed, and most of the coal mines flooded. Manufacturing equipment and removable resources had been systematically "skinned." The industrial crisis in France in the twenties was basically a production crisis resulting from her wartime losses and devastations.

Then, finally, came the successive disappointments and disillusionments of the interwar years. With whatever feelings of triumph France may have ended the war in 1918, she was soon slipping into a mood of defeatism of which the tragedy of 1940 was no more than the inevitable confirmation.

DOMESTIC POLITICS

The most moderate party of the Left, and usually the largest of all the political parties of the Third Republic was the Radical Socialist party (*le parti radical socialiste*). It was the heir of the French Revolution, much in the same way as the Republican party in the United States was the heir of the Civil War. It was the "normal" party, holding power in "normal" times, the party of the *petit bourgeois* and of all the innumerable individualities which had made the strength of the post-Revolutionary France. Its creed was liberty, equality, fraternity — private enterprise and private property, patriotism in foreign affairs, yet pacific at heart, the quintessence of French insularity. Compared with it, in their various degrees, the other parties were parties of protest or of special interests.

Further to the Left were the Socialists and Communists, the parties of the more extreme and doctrinaire urban and rural workers. Theoretically their aims were identical — the establishment of a socialist state. Liberty, equality, fraternity indeed seemed no longer adequate for the economic and spiritual needs of the new industrialized masses. But the Socialist party shaded off into Radicalism. It favored a gradual nonviolent program of reforms, respected majority decisions, and was willing to use legal and constitutional means to gain its ends. The Communists believed in the class struggle and the seizure of power by violence and, in the interwar years, they were in close liaison with the Comintern in Moscow. The domestic history of these two parties always centered around the burning question of collaboration with bourgeois governments.

Many of the parties of the Right, out of respect for the Revolutionary tradition, adopted safe democratic labels, such as the Republican Democratic Union or the Democratic Alliance. It is difficult — and not necessary for our purpose here — to specify all their exact shades of doctrine. Generally they were reactionary and represented big business and high finance; they were usually — but not always — staunchly Catholic; and latterly — though again not always — they were antidemocratic and inclined to Fascism. But there were also strong rightist parties which, like the Royalist *Action Française*, were antidemocratic, declined to be represented in the Chamber, and operated from "outside." [3] They were often served by brilliant writers and exerted a considerable literary influence.

During 1919 the attention of France — and of the world — was centered on the Peace Conference of Paris. The French people were understandably gratified that their capital should have been chosen for this historic congress of nations. The occasion was no more than a just tribute to their sacrifices and their contribution to the great victory. But the disappointments and disillusionments were to begin in the first year of peace. Klotz, then Minister of Finance, introduced his budget at the end of May 1919, and it was plain that all the regular indexes were already unfavorable. The treaty of peace with Germany was signed at Versailles in modest pomp on June 28, 1919, and after acrimonious debates was ratified by the Chambers between July and October. Evidently Clemenceau, despite his tigerish implacability, had been cajoled into too lenient measures against the enemy, and the Rhine frontier had not been secured (see p. 119). His defeat a year later in elections to the presidency of the Republic was due in part to old personal animosities and in part to the fear that he would not be content with a merely formal and decorative presidency, but the defeat also doubtless represented a national vote of censure on his work at the Conference. Clemenceau was like many another protagonist of the war years who suffered a revulsion of popularity at the coming of peace. He retired from public life. He was now eighty-one years of age, and perhaps he had some claim to spend "the evening of his thought" in leisure and quiet.

The first postwar phase was a rightist phase. Elections in November 1919, in many ways, resembled Lloyd George's "Khaki Election" in England (see p. 325). The "victors" of the war were returned in triumph — in this case, a coalition of rightist parties under Millerand which was to go by the name of the National Bloc. If there is a single word to epitomize the new government's state of mind, that word would be "anti-Sovietism." France in the early twenties went through the worst agonies of her Bolshevik phobia. She supported the White and Polish armies in the Russian Civil War. She also reopened all those doctrinal disputes which traditionally characterized the Right, notably the clerical question, and the Chamber approved the establishment of formal relations with the Vatican for the first time since 1870. Millerand was elected President of the Republic in September 1920. He immediately set out to prove himself a strong executive, and proposed reforms in the presidential prerogatives, proposals which, mild though they were, his political opponents at once represented as the foretaste of a rightist dictatorship in France.[4] In short — what with the Soviet question, the clerical question, and the presidential question — enough material was being collected to make the French parliament a very combustible institution.

The National Bloc, however, was not as popular as it seemed. Accidents in the electoral system had added misleadingly to its numbers in the Chamber. What was more important, the wave of wartime enthusiasm which had originally carried it to power subsided gradually in proportion as the nation became conscious of its real weariness. Briand was Premier in 1921 and was followed by Poincaré in January 1922. Poincaré, largely responsible for the French occupation of the Ruhr in 1923, began to lose support when it became apparent that the occupation was not yielding its expected results (see p. 167). But, as was always the way in France, it was finance which completed the overthrow of the National Bloc. Early in 1924, at the time of the Dawes reparations conference, the franc dropped to 130 to the pound and to nearly 30 to the dollar. Elections in May 1924 returned to power a coalition of leftist parties, Radical Socialist and Socialists, under the Radical Socialist Herriot, which took the name of the *Cartel des Gauches.*

The victory of the Cartel was as decisive as the former victory of the National Bloc. Herriot was now in control much as Millerand had once been, and he proceeded to reverse all the National Bloc's policies. For a start, he challenged Millerand's conception of the presidential prerogatives and demanded Millerand's resignation from the presidency. And resign Millerand did. Gaston Doumergue, a mild partisan of Millerand and at that time president of the Senate, was elected President. Herriot then took up the old clerical question. He played it for what it was worth, for anticlericalism was the single common denominator in all the variegated affinities of the parties of the Cartel, and he prepared to break off the newly restored relations with the Vatican. He tried to secularize the schools in Alsace, which had always been faithfully Catholic. Herriot's anticlericalism was symptomatic of the still unhealed revolutionary schisms in French society, and it stirred up an unfortunate "separatism" in Alsace, a province newly returned to French allegiance, where throughout all the years of the former German rule the Catholic Church had been the symbol of French nationality. Finally he revised the National Bloc's aggressive foreign policy. With Ramsay MacDonald, then Prime Minister in Britain, he liquidated the Ruhr invasion and agreed to the Dawes Plan (see p. 167). In October 1924, France formally recognized the Soviet Union.

As usual it was the wicked old serpent of finance which brought about the fall of the leftist paradise. Herriot, very much at home with doctrinal politics, was not the man to deal with so drab and sordid a thing as money. The Socialist party was unwise enough to raise the cry of a capital levy and, though he personally showed no sympathy, the party could hardly have picked an issue better calculated to split the frail ranks of the Cartel. In April 1925, Herriot and his ministry fell. The franc immediately weakened. Six short-lived ministries in a year wrestled with the financial problem. Even Caillaux, lately condemned for treasonable correspondence with the enemy during the First World War (see p. 81), was called out of his rustication for a few months to become Minister of Finance. In Paris, they called him the "Wizard," but he was a desperate and humiliating choice for the savior of financial France. A Herriot ministry enjoyed a single day of office during July 1926. The franc then stood at over 50 to the dollar, and France, like her franc, was said to be hovering on the brink of disaster. The press predicted national bankruptcy on a par with Germany's in 1923. The Paris mob, which always appeared at times like these, was already demonstrating noisily in the streets. Meanwhile it was creditably rumored that the Bank of France and the "two hundred families" had deliberately engineered the whole debacle to throw discredit onto the Socialist Left. The *crise du franc* had become a *crise de régime.*

On July 23, 1926, after the demise of Herriot's one-day ministry, Poincaré formed a ministry of all parties except the Socialists and Communists, and as a measure of the seriousness of the situation, the ministry included, besides himself, five past premiers, among whom was Herriot. Poincaré was his own Finance Minister. The Chamber, now thoroughly alarmed, would have done the bidding even of a Caillaux. It worked for Poincaré with unprecedented dispatch, and in a month it had voted that marvel of marvels in France, a balanced budget, this time moreover not in arrears, but actually in advance of the regular financial year. Yet all Poincaré's measures were perfectly orthodox. He increased taxation, tightened up the methods of collection, made drastic cuts in administrative expenses, and sheared off the French budget its all too numerous "special" and "extraordinary" appendages. The medicine was bitter, but it was effective. At the end of 1926 the franc stood at 25 to the dollar and was pegged at that level. In June 1928, France restored the gold standard.

Poincaré remained in office from July 1926 to July 1929. His three years coincided with the Locarno era, and they were years during which the whole of Europe was returning to something like prosperity. They were the most stable years, politically and financially, which France enjoyed in the interwar period. They showed, as had been shown already in other countries, how quickly a "technical" national bankruptcy could be relieved. But, by now, it seemed that at least some of the more superficial scars of war had been effaced. The building, automobile, silk, and luxury trades were almost flourishing. Paris was once more the leader of women's fashions. Every historic city and holiday resort in France was full of tourists.

Poincaré resigned at length, partly on grounds of ill-health, and was followed by a short-lived ministry under Briand and then by a ministry under his "political heir," André Tardieu. The ministries were reminiscent of the National Bloc and of the rightist tendencies of the early twenties. But the withdrawal of Poincaré's strong hand brought back all the old instability. Sessions in the Chamber were uniformly stormy, and the harassed Tardieu had sometimes to put the question of confidence three times a day. The Young Plan for the final settlement of Germany's reparations, signed in January 1930 (see pp. 401–402), was not popular in France. Then, in November 1930, occurred the Oustric bank failure, the first of a new round of financial scandals in France.

FOREIGN POLITICS

Three times in a century and twice in living memory had France been invaded, always by the same enemy, and always from the same direction. In 1918 she was bled, she was ravaged, she was utterly spent, but she was at last victorious. She had one policy for the future — she could have had no other: the permanent enfeeblement of her hereditary enemy and the permanent security of her sacred, thrice-violated soil.

She had no illusions. She did not believe, as Britain then did, that Germany had learned the lesson of defeat, and she did not believe, as Britain then did, that Germany was militarily and psychologically broken. She regarded the modern Germans as direct blood descendants of the barbarian tribes which had already extinguished one historic civilization. She knew the powers of recuperation of defeated nations, and she knew the all-compelling, all-possessing lure of a war of revenge. She beheld with fear in her heart a Germany with a population, a birth rate, and industrial resources which far overtopped her own. She doubted whether the fortunate concatenation of alliances in 1914–18 which had put Russia, Britain, and the United States on her side would always be repeated on future occasions. Consequently at the Peace Conference of Paris she demanded the disarmament of Germany, the imposition of crippling indemnities, and a strategic frontier on the Rhine.

In her own view, France did not obtain at the Peace Conference even the minimum requirements of her future security. She was, of course, confirmed in the repossession of Alsace-Lorraine. She obtained the coal mines of the Saar for a period of fifteen years as compensation for German damage to her own coal mines. But she did not secure the Rhine frontier. Clemenceau was persuaded to abandon his claims thereto for treaties of assistance by which the United States and Britain pledged immediate aid to France in the event of another German aggression, and the treaties were signed in June 1919 at the same time as Versailles (see p. 119). But the United States subsequently failed to ratify her part of the undertaking, and the treaties of assistance lapsed. The United States retired into isolation, and there were moments when Britain, reverting to her old policy of the balance of power, seemed almost to be supporting Germany against her onetime ally, France.

Nor had frustration ended there. France had persuaded herself that she could recoup her huge material losses in the war from German reparations; but German reparations became a sorry comedy. Then it was soon clear that Germany was evading the disarmament clauses of the Treaty of Versailles. Certainly Germany's moral disarmament was far from being effective; she could still show herself as perverse and truculent as in the heyday of her military greatness.

In the circumstances, two courses were available to French statesmanship: the first, to use sincerely and confidently the new organization of peace, represented by the League of Nations; and the second, to build up a strong alliance system in Europe. The two courses were at once complementary and contradictory and, in trying to follow both, France laid herself open to "the vacillations, inconsistencies, and even the hypocrisy" of which her interwar foreign policy was so often accused. At bottom, she disbelieved in the League, militarily ineffective as it was. Her efforts to bolster the League with over-all agreements like the Geneva Protocol and the Locarno Pact have been described elsewhere (see pp. 137–140).

Contemporary commentators spoke of the twenties as the period of French hegemony in Europe. With characteristic self-conscious historicity, the French saw themselves harking back to Napoleon, Louis XIV, and even to Charlemagne, when once before their land had been the premier civilizing power of the West and they had borne the standard of Latin culture for all the world.

Militarily speaking, Belgium in 1919 was already a part of France, and that condition was expected to continue indefinitely. Since 1914 the ghost of Schlieffen had been added to the other fearful preoccupations of France, and only a clear military understanding with her northern neighbor could ever protect her should that menace ever arise again. During 1920, therefore, Marshal Foch and the Belgian General Staff concluded a defensive convention against Germany. The new Poland, from the day of her foundation, became a client state of France. It was recalled that Poland and France had historic links going back to Henry III. A French mission under Weygand materially assisted the Poles in the campaign for the defense of Warsaw in 1920 (see p. 176), and a French mission was entrusted with the reorganization of the Polish Army. In February 1921, a Franco-Polish treaty was signed in Paris, concerting the foreign policies of the two countries "in conformity with the Covenant of the League of Nations," and binding them to a common defense against unprovoked aggression. A commercial treaty and French loans to Poland followed. An additional Franco-Polish treaty of guarantee was part of the Locarno Pact in 1925.

The Little Entente between Czechoslovakia, Yugoslavia, and Rumania, if not actually wrought under French encouragement and initiative, was in perfect harmony with French ambitions. In January 1924, France and Czechoslovakia entered into a treaty of alliance and friendship, and undertook "to act together in respect of all external questions calculated to endanger their security, or to disturb the order of things established by the peace treaties to which both have set their hand." An additional Franco-Czechoslovak treaty of guarantee was a part of the Locarno Pact. Finally France entered into treaties of "friendly understanding" with Rumania in June 1926, and with Yugoslavia in November 1927. The several agreements were further cemented from time to time by French loans to the three states. The Franco-Polish and the Franco–Little Entente systems were unhappily prevented from achieving a further unity by the rift between Poland and Czechoslovakia, but they were linked to some extent by the treaty between Poland and Rumania in March 1921 (see pp. 176 and 202).

From 1925 up to a couple of months before his death in March 1932, Briand remained firmly entrenched in the Foreign Ministry. His postwar political longevity compares with that of Stresemann, and like Stresemann, his name became indissolubly linked with the Locarno Pact and with the many treaties of conciliation and peace which were drawn up in the later twenties.

His character is an elusive one to draw. He was a brilliant orator and a shrewd parliamentary tactician. He was eleven times Premier. He was awarded the Nobel Peace Prize in 1926. But it is sometimes to be wondered if he was not a political Jekyll and Hyde — again perhaps like Stresemann; whether he did not combine in himself the character of the earnest, cosmopolitan, and somewhat amiable ambassador of peace which he displayed to the world, and the egotistic, astute French patriot which he reserved for his own colleagues.

He was the French Foreign Minister at Locarno in October 1925; and at

London in December 1925 he was one of the signatories of the Locarno Pact. In October 1926, he and Stresemann met over an informal lunch in the village of Thoiry, on the French side of the Franco-Swiss border and, among matters of general interest to their two countries, discussed in particular the speeding-up of the evacuation of the Rhine — and even of the Saar. It was a sort of miniature Locarno, and in after years journalists still referred to it as the "idyll of Thoiry." Perhaps it was a case of Greek meeting Greek. At all events, nothing resulted from it. Early in 1927, Briand made the proposal which eventually led to the Pact of Paris of 1928 (p. 141), but it is doubtful if he had ever intended that proposal to be much more than a graceful Gallic *geste*. In September 1929 he opened his famous discussions in Geneva on the United States of Europe. The scheme was afterward much publicized. But in all the fine phraseology — and Briand was a master of fine phraseology — the anxious lover of peace and justice among nations could look in vain for anything beyond rhetorical disguise of the Versailles *status quo*. At least there was a certain negative consistency in Briand's foreign policy.

In May 1931, Gaston Doumergue's term as President of the Republic drew to its appointed end. Briand, believing that he deserved well of France, stood for election. All his friends expected him to win, but the National Assembly elected not Briand, but Paul Doumer, then president of the Senate. Briand swallowed his defeat, a defeat more to his vanity than to his real ambition, and returned to his congenial duties at the Foreign Ministry.

One other matter should be mentioned in this chapter — the fortification of the northeastern frontier of France. The so-called Maginot Line was not the first fortification of that frontier, nor was it necessarily a sign of special doubts and anxieties. Every shift of frontier in the past had always entailed an appropriate revision of the defensive system. Earlier military engineers, Vauban under Louis XIV, and Sère de Rivière after 1871, had built fortifications in their day, and their work had not been regarded as inconsistent with a courageous military spirit or with the simultaneous formation of alliances with foreign Powers. During the early twenties a Commission of Frontier Defense prepared the blueprint of a new "Wall of France," and Painlevé, as Minister of War, approved it in 1927. André Maginot was Minister of War under Tardieu in 1929, and to him fell the task of securing the necessary credits, and of carrying out the first stages of the plan. "The Line" thereafter was always associated with his name. In the course of the next ten years, Alsace-Lorraine became a huge concrete molehill, studded with gun-turrets, tank traps, dragons' teeth, and all the paraphernalia of defensive warfare as then understood. The gun emplacements often weighed more than 120 tons apiece; 26,000,000 cubic feet of cement were used, and more armor plates than would have built a battle fleet. The cost was over $500,000,000.

The Maginot Line was not without its critics, even in 1929. One school of thought, albeit a one-man school, was represented by a young staff colonel, Charles de Gaulle, evidently a man of large and supple imagination, whose book, *Vers L'Armée de Métier*, published in 1934, pleaded for a highly trained, highly specialized, professional, long-service, mechanized army of six divisions — 100,000 men in all — an army "moving entirely on caterpillar tractors," an army of great mobility and striking power, attacking by surprise with echelons of tanks under a curtain of aircraft, operating independently of any base, hauling its own artillery and supplies, penetrating deep into hostile territory, rupturing the enemy's vital communications. De Gaulle, in a word, predicted with astonishing accuracy the blitzkrieg of the Second World War. Both his tactics and his state of mind were diametrically opposed to the Maginot "complex."

But the full story of the Maginot Line was not so simple. The fault, as we know now, was twofold. First, the Maginot Line was not intended to be more than a partial defense; but second, public opinion in France was lulled into thinking, on the contrary, that it was an absolute and total defense. The flat Franco-Belgian frontier was not suited to heavy fortification, and the main mass of the Maginot Line therefore came to an end at Sedan. The French High Command, at all events after 1927 when Pétain was Commander in Chief, conceived of the Belgian defensive system, anchored on Liége, Eben Emael, and the Albert Canal, as the proper extension of the Maginot Line, and planned to reinforce the Belgian Army with four French armies. Unfortunately, when the time came, Belgium had reverted to "neutrality" (see p. 497) , and the entire political premises of the French plan were falsified. The French High Command also committed errors of detail, the most serious being its assumption that the hilly and forested Ardennes would be impassable terrain for mechanized forces. But, far worse than all this was the belief, a belief widespread not only in France but among France's allies, that the Maginot Line stretched north of Sedan to the coast of Flanders and was, in fact, impregnable along its entire length of four hundred miles. Here, in concrete and steel, so French public opinion was confidently given to think, had modern military science at last discovered the means to dam the fatal gap which, since the days of the Huns, had opened the fair country to more than thirty invasions. This vicious confusion of politics and psychology, as we shall tell anon, issued in the tragedy of 1940.

21 BRITAIN AND THE BRITISH COMMONWEALTH:

LABOR, TRADE, AND IMPERIALISM

THE POSTWAR MOOD

The First World War had raised the British people to one of the high pinnacles, perhaps the highest, of their history. Once more, at the head of a Grand Alliance, they had fought and defeated a military despotism which, but for them, might have dominated the world. Hohenzollern Germany had gone the way of the French Empire, the French monarchy, and Spain. But never in all their former wars had the British people been called on to expend the same physical and moral energy, nor had they greeted the return of peace in so exhausted a condition. Nor, like the defeated belligerents, did they renew themselves by revolution. They failed to recognize that the old order of 1914 had passed away never to return. Blinded by tradition and prestige, they strained themselves even further in efforts to resume their former accustomed ways and habits. All their interwar policies pursued the mirage of Victorian and Edwardian ascendancy. Again and again after 1919, seemingly out of sheer inflexibility and false pride, Britain intensified her weariness, delayed and misdirected her possible recovery, and brought herself by sure, inevitable steps to the unhappy era of repudiation and broken hopes.

Britain had not suffered actually or relatively the losses of France. She had no devastated areas, and damage by air raid had been negligible. Her casualty list in the four years of the war amounted to 702,000 killed and 1,660,000 wounded. But her losses were more serious than the mere numbers signified. It is sometimes forgotten how terribly the voluntary service army, the Kitchener Army of 1914–16, superb achievement though it was, had creamed off the best of the race. Whereas other nations, which had had conscript armies from the beginning of the war, lost a general cross section of their male populations, Britain squandered the very flower of her manhood. She faced the problems of peace and reconstruction, therefore, fatally depleted in the most irreplaceable classes of men of education and responsibility.

Political Britain wakened from the delirium of Armistice Day to find herself preparing for a general election. Lloyd George, Prime Minister since December 1916 and the great architect of her war effort, had resolved to ask for a new mandate for his wartime Coalition government with which to face the Peace Conference at Paris. On constitutional grounds his attitude was entirely correct. The old Parliament, originally elected for five years, had lasted eight. Under the Representation of the People Act of 1918, millions

of new voters, including women for the first time, had been added to the
electorate. But the "Khaki Election," as it was called, unleashed the hurt
and hate of the past four years, and the British people, who had borne the
great struggle with such unexampled fortitude, allowed themselves perhaps
the most deplorable lapse of mass passion in their history. Lloyd George
himself was never party to the extremes in which even cabinet ministers indulged, but the voters went to the polls nevertheless whipped to frenzy with
the raucous electioneering slogans of "Hang the Kaiser!" and "Squeeze the
German orange till the pips squeak!"

The result of the election was a foregone conclusion. Lloyd George's Coalition parties swept the board. The independent Liberals, still under Asquith's
leadership, returned only 26 Members. Irish Sinn Fein returned 73 members, all of whom declined to take their seats. Lloyd George did indeed go to
Paris with his mandate, but the hectoring, chauvinistic House he left behind was a sore embarrassment to him.

A special Ministry of Reconstruction had been prospectively created in
1917 to tide over the transition from war to peace, and the government at
that time, apprehensive of the upheaval that must result from the sudden
influx of millions of workers into the labor market, had drafted a plan for
the gradual demobilization of the fighting forces and munition workers. But
when peace did come at last, nothing so leisurely would have satisfied the
popular mood. Soldiers and workers wanted only to get home, and the
quicker the better. At several camps in the winter of 1918–19, in both
England and France, British troops were mutinying because they considered
that their exodus from military life was not being made expeditious enough.
Where the government erred was in not foreseeing the boom which followed
the Armistice. The country in 1919, instead of being forced to retrench and
reorganize, found itself enjoying an artificial flurry of high prices. The
government hurried to drop the various controls it had so rigidly maintained during the war. Mines, railroads, agriculture, indeed all industry,
were allowed to lapse back to "normal" at the earliest possible moment. The
psychological release from war encouraged spending; peace brought demands
for luxuries long denied; war savings and gratuities were flung on the
market. Soldiers and workers were not only welcomed home, but the very
condition of the country seemed to encourage their return, and 4,000,000
were absorbed into civilian industry in the course of the first postwar year.

The bubble burst in 1920. All the measures which a wary government had
prepared and found unwanted had now to be put hurriedly into operation.
The old workers' insurance of 1911 was converted into an Unemployment
Insurance Act so as to provide a "dole" — in the unfortunate and misleading
slang of the time — available to a much wider category of workers. A Relief
Act was passed to empower government departments and local authorities to
carry out public works, roads, and housing. But at the end of 1920 nearly
700,000 were registered as unemployed, the number doubled in the early
weeks of 1921, and by March 1921, just before the great miners' strike, it
stood over 2,000,000.

For weeks on end, Parliament seemed to be debating nothing else than unemployment. The air was thick with schemes for housing, schemes for imperial preference, schemes for emigration. Two concrete measures resulted. First, an agreement was signed with the Soviet Government in March 1921 re-establishing commercial relations, and second a Safeguarding of Industries Act was passed in June to prevent foreign dumping and to protect, in particular, certain key industries essential to the country in time of war. The first was a clear departure from the anti-Soviet policy Britain had pursued in 1919, and the second was a clear departure from the old free-trade principles. But the British Government was desperate enough to revise policies and principles, however hallowed, if it could relieve in any possible way the country's sudden economic distress.

Naturally enough these early postwar years were full of labor unrest. Socialist ideas had penetrated Britain even as they had penetrated every part of the world. The war had postponed, and while postponing had aggravated, the old social and economic problems. Recent accessions of high wages and of bargaining power put organized labor in a recalcitrant mood, and there was a widespread — and not unjustified — belief that the employers had made huge profits out of the war. During 1919 and 1920 hardly a month passed but some strike or threat of strike, some lockout or threat of lockout, some acrimonious meeting of employers, workers, and government representatives did not occur in some part of industrial Britain. In August 1919 there was even a strike of London's policemen. From time to time trade-union extremists talked dangerously of a general strike of all their members, "direct action" as they called it.

The most serious and persistent unrest was among the miners. The coal-mining industry was in a parlous state. It was technically conservative and inefficient, and it needed thorough rationalization. New fuels, notably oil, competed in the old markets, and German reparation deliveries of coal also restricted the usual British sales abroad. Several coal mines which had operated under wartime prices could not be maintained at economic levels now that peace was restored, and it seemed that without continued government subsidies large coal fields would shortly be forced to go derelict. Meanwhile the squalid conditions under which the average miner was expected to live were a slur upon any self-respecting civilized state. Coal somehow symbolized the old prosperity of England, and the grave difficulties confronting the industry were in the nature of a test for the whole working-class movement.

As for the government, it made valiant efforts to bring employer and employee together in joint committees or before boards of arbitration, and in these postwar years we have the significant and often entertaining spectacle of mineowners, perhaps titled millionaires, seated at the same conference table with, and being cross-examined by, miners' delegates who kept themselves and their families on wages of 30 shillings a week. Early in 1919 the government set up a royal commission under the chairmanship of Sir John Sankey, which duly reported, condemning the existing system of mineownership and recommending some kind of amalgamation and public management. The government rejected the report.

The first of the miners' strikes lasted some three weeks, during October and November 1920, and was followed by a second much more serious stoppage between March and May 1921, involving nearly 1,000,000 miners. Even the pumpmen, who kept the pits free from flooding, were withdrawn. The government proclaimed an "emergency." Tin-hatted troops occupied the supply depots, and armored cars patrolled the streets in all strike areas. The miners appealed for "direct action" from their fellow workers in the railroad and transport trade-unions, and a general strike was within an ace of being declared. In the end the miners were forced to accept wage agreements on the mineowners' terms.

CONSERVATIVE — LABOR — CONSERVATIVE — LABOR

The Treaty of Versailles was received in Britain with mixed feelings. Some people were grimly satisfied, a few shocked and alarmed, the majority uninterested. But there was something in the nature of a guilt complex over the treaty, especially later, when British public opinion began to go through its anti-French phase. Then followed the fiasco of Genoa (see p. 162), and the unpleasant scare over Chanaq (see p. 339) — to say nothing of Ireland, Egypt, and India — and all this was a poor return for the hysterical anticipations of November 1918. Rightly or wrongly the blame was loaded onto Lloyd George and his Coalition. The British people as a whole were suffering from a mass reaction from the war and wanted a regime which approximated more nearly to the peacetime politics they had once known. In many ways the decline of the Coalition in England resembled the defeat of President Wilson in the United States or the defeat of the National Bloc in France. Lloyd George resigned in October 1922, and the country reverted with evident relief to the old party system and the old party struggles.

Conservative, Labor, Conservative, Labor followed one another during the remaining years of the decade. Unemployment and trade continued to be the main domestic problems, and each party, of course, regarded its particular doctrine as the sovereign panacea for the country's ills. The Conservatives argued for protection, the Liberals for free trade, and Labor for a capital levy and for the nationalization of key industries. Bonar Law succeeded Lloyd George as Prime Minister of an all-Conservative government for six months, with Lord Curzon as Foreign Secretary and Stanley Baldwin, a comparative newcomer, as Chancellor of the Exchequer. The French invasion of the Ruhr began in January 1923, an incident which disturbed British public opinion surprisingly little, except in so far as it added one more exasperation to the increasing suspicion and impatience toward France. In the same month, Baldwin crossed to the United States and opened negotiations for settling the Anglo-American war debt (see p. 367). The settlement, eventually agreed upon in June, had a stabilizing effect politically, but it gave no economic relief. In May 1923, Bonar Law retired from the prime ministership on grounds of ill-health, to be succeeded, not by Lord Curzon, whose seniority gave him some title to the office, but by Baldwin, and Baldwin decided he must ask for a dissolution of Parliament and a general election on the issue of protection.

The general election of November–December 1923 accordingly was a veritable battle of protection. The Liberals reunited their divided ranks under the old free-trade watchwords. In the end both Liberals and Labor made gains at Conservative expense. But no party now had a majority over the other two. Baldwin, though leader of the largest party, interpreted the election as a defeat and was disinclined to form a new government. It seemed that Labor might be able to govern, if it could obtain sufficient Liberal support. At all events, Labor was willing to try, and in January 1924, Ramsay MacDonald, then leader of the Labor party in Parliament, became Prime Minister and Foreign Secretary of Britain's first Labor cabinet. With him came an array of party colleagues, including Philip Snowden as Chancellor of the Exchequer and Arthur Henderson as Home Secretary.

The necessity of holding Liberal support put a decisive brake on Labor initiative and, for all Labor's electioneering manifestoes, MacDonald's government had now to make a very harmless and pallid display of Liberalism. Snowden, himself a zealous free trader, introduced a budget which, in all essentials, was a Liberal budget. He even abolished the Safeguarding of Industries Act of 1921. MacDonald regarded international affairs as his own proper province. He had been Britain's great wartime pacifist and martyr, and he now took to the Foreign Office as to a mission called. To heal the scars of war and of a peace that was no peace was surely a task worthy of a socialist and a man. By a happy conjunction Herriot, a believer in the same philosophy, was then Premier in France. The Dawes Plan and the Geneva Protocol, characteristic monuments, were built from their collaboration. Then, as a gesture to Japan, MacDonald suspended the work just then beginning on the new British naval base at Singapore. On February 1, 1924, MacDonald telegraphed Moscow an unconditional recognition of the Soviet Union and invited Soviet representatives to London "to draw up the preliminary basis of a complete treaty to settle all questions outstanding between the two countries."

The Labor government's foreign policy appeared to be uniformly successful. The British people had demanded a pacifist program, and MacDonald was more than ready to give it to them. But his Soviet policy perhaps overstepped the bounds of prudence. Not that his recognition of the Soviet Union was in itself ill-advised, for a new understanding with the Soviet was certainly due. But Russophobia was still a potent force in Britain, and it was the "unconditional" aspect of MacDonald's recognition which seemed more than a little precipitate. When therefore MacDonald signed a new treaty with Soviet representatives which promised a British loan to the Soviet Union for the purchase of British goods, he brought the Conservative Opposition down upon his head. In Tory eyes the granting of a loan to a revolutionary government which regarded repudiation as an article of faith was indefensible, even if it was hedged about with "conditions" and "guarantees," and even if it was to be spent in the encouragement of British exports to the Soviet Union. A Soviet commercial treaty was actually signed in August 1924, but MacDonald resigned shortly afterward. In October new elections were called.

The election was the second within a year. It was fought in a nervous, excitable mood, in the midst of a scandal such as not often ruffles the usual calm of British politics. A strange document, afterward popularly called the "Red Letter," had fallen into the possession of the Foreign Office in October, just before MacDonald's resignation. It purported to be addressed by the Comintern to the British Communist party urging violent revolution in Britain. It made some references to "agitation propaganda" in the British Army and Navy. It is now known to have been a forgery, but the Foreign Office, at the time apparently satisfied as to its authenticity, published it. MacDonald himself would neither acknowledge nor deny its authenticity. But an unscrupulous Tory press played it for all it was worth as proof positive that Labor had been suborned by Moscow, and thousands of laggard voters, who normally showed no more than a conventional interest in high politics, now surged to the polls with but one idea, that MacDonald and his traitorous cabal must go. The Conservatives won the election with a handsome majority over both Labor and Liberals. Baldwin resumed the prime ministership, with Churchill as Chancellor of the Exchequer and Austen Chamberlain [1] as Foreign Secretary. Britain entered upon five years of Conservative rule.

Except toward the Soviet Union, the new government carried on the conciliatory foreign policy of its predecessor. The Locarno Pact of 1925, Austen Chamberlain's crowning achievement, appeared at last to give Europe a fair and stable peace (pp. 138–39). At home the government followed traditional Conservative policies. All Churchill's budgets were reactionary and protectionist in spirit. In May 1925, Britain returned to the gold standard.

But depression and unrest continued. The "Red Letter," authentic or not, had dropped a little too conveniently out of the blue on the eve of a general election. Labor leaders felt they had been the butt of a sordid swindle and, in an angry mood, they began to gird themselves to renew the unfinished battles of 1920–21. The coal miners were again discussing "direct action." Baldwin resorted to Lloyd George's former tactics and threw the entire question of the coal industry afresh into the lap of a royal commission under Sir Herbert Samuel. The commission reported early in 1926, and though its recommendations were not so sweeping as those of the Sankey Commission in 1919, it did propose the nationalization of royalties and the amalgamation of certain pits. It also proposed drastic wage reductions. The miners replied with their slogan, "Not a penny off the pay, not a minute on the day," and after some weeks of futile negotiation, in which all sides showed all the obstinacy and blindness of their respective classes, the dispute reached a complete deadlock.

On May 4, 1926 the General Strike began. Miners, railroadmen, transport workers, iron and steel workers, builders, and printers — laboring men, to the number of 2,500,000 — quit work. The nation's industries were at a standstill. The government in reply declared a virtual state of siege. Sir John Simon in the House of Commons pronounced the strike "illegal." Troops guarded the depots and docks. Naval ratings occupied and operated the power stations and reservoirs. Hundreds of strikers were jailed. Supply organizations were quickly improvised throughout the country and staffed with volunteers. Army trucks, rusting in their dumps since 1919, were brought out, furbished up, and put to use. A huge "milk pool" was stationed in Hyde Park in London. Young men of college type drove the busses, the streetcars, the subways, and even the railroad trains, or patrolled the streets as special constables, hugely enjoying the excitement and novelty of the situation, and on the whole doing their jobs not too badly. Meanwhile, as the printers had gone on strike, the nation was without newspapers, and the government issued its own propaganda sheet, the *British Gazette*, reputedly under the editorship of Winston Churchill.

The strikers had expected the government to collapse like the walls of Jericho. When the government did not collapse, they were in a serious quandary. There were no Lenins among them, and they prepared no revolutionary organs for the seizure of control. The country as a whole, while sympathizing with the miners, would not brook "rebellion" on the part of the trade-unions as a class. It is to the credit of the Trades-Union General Council that they called off the General Strike as soon as they saw it had no chance of success and prevented it from degenerating into useless chaos and bloodshed. On May 12, 1926 the General Strike ended. But the miners, "betrayed" by their fellow workers, continued their struggle independently and did not return to work for another six months. In the end they accepted terms worse than those of 1921.

The General Strike resulted in an overwhelming defeat of the trade-union movement as a whole. The chance was lost to rationalize the coal-mining industry and to amalgamate some of the 1,400 independent pits into which it was divided. As if to add insult to injury, the government, early in 1927, passed a Trades Disputes Act which declared to be illegal all "sympathetic" strikes or any strikes calculated to coerce the government and intimidate the community.

Whether or not it was the exhaustion of the General Strike or the good effects of the lately signed Locarno Pact, Britain at all events now went through an interval of comparative calm. Baldwin, at the head of a safe Conservative government, seemed to be following a policy of calculated inertia. Unemployment remained at just over the million mark, but the government was sinking into an attitude of *laissez faire* and arguing that better conditions were not to be expected in an age of wars and strikes. One lively incident, in May 1927, was the police raid on Soviet House, the London offices of the Soviet Trade Agency and of Arcos Ltd.[2] These twin organizations had continued to exist and do business despite the virtual lapsing of Lloyd George's Russian treaty of 1921 and of MacDonald's more recent treaty of 1924, and had become the particular bugaboo of the Home Secretary, Joynson-Hicks. Whether or not Soviet House was ever a center of Soviet propaganda and military espionage was never definitely proved. But the police searched the premises from cellar to roof, and the Soviet agents were sent packing. The Labor party, with that geniality which is British politics, entertained the indignant agents at lunch in the House of Commons before their departure.

In February 1928, Asquith, the old Liberal leader, died, and it almost seemed as if an age had died with him. He had resigned from the Liberal party and from public life in 1926. Lloyd George remained leader of his own faction of the Liberal party. But Liberalism as a whole, divided and discredited despite the high caliber of many of its supporters, was never again a real parliamentary force in Britain.

The life of Parliament came to its statutory end, and general elections were held in May 1929. Baldwin and the Conservative party went to the country with the characteristic slogan "Safety First," a tame acquiescence, the Opposition said, in all the evils from which the country was acknowledged to be suffering. The election resulted in a general Conservative defeat. Ramsay MacDonald was called upon to form his second Labor government.

IRELAND

Since the Irish Easter Rebellion of 1916, Sinn Fein had become the most important party in Southern Ireland (pp. 43–44). In the general election of December 1918, it had returned 73 members out of a total Irish representation — including Northern Ireland, or Ulster — of 106. But the 73 declined to go to Westminster. They preferred instead to set up an independent parliament of their own, the Dail Eireann, and they held their first session in the Dublin Mansion House on January 21, 1919. The proceedings were prefaced by the reading of an Irish "Declaration of Independence." On his return to Ireland, after his escape from an English jail, Eamon de Valera, hero of the Easter Rebellion, was elected "President of the Irish Republic." The Dail, legally, was a rebel body, but the British authorities took no immediate steps to suppress it, or to suppress the outburst of Sinn Fein propaganda in the country which synchronized with its sessions. Rebel organizations were molested only when their activities appeared to be causing breaches of the peace, and the murders of two policemen, the first on the day of the first session of the Dail, brought no countermeasures beyond local proclamations under the wartime Defense of the Realm Act. The British Government evidently was reverting to its age-old Irish policy of blind leniency to be followed by equally blind violence.

Dan Breen, as is usually supposed, initiated the campaign of assassinating policemen, a campaign which, in the course of 1919, developed into the Irish Civil War. The Royal Irish Constabulary in the old days had always been a popular and highly respected force, recruited entirely from Irishmen, but its members now became the victims of systematic murder at the hands of their own countrymen. The crimes were normally credited to the self-styled Irish Republican Army, the I.R.A. They were carefully and skillfully planned; and were committed with virtual impunity, as no witness could be found who wished, or dared, to give evidence against an arrested suspect, and no jury could be empaneled which wished, or dared, to convict. If, as indeed did happen sometimes, a conviction was obtained, the prisoner went on a hunger strike and shortly had to be released.

The campaign soon turned against the military garrisons. Soldiers, as well as police, went in fear of their lives. They were fired on by passing cars, ambushed in the streets and country lanes, even shot down at the doors of their own homes by apparently innocent callers; and these activities were varied on occasion by raids on their barracks for the capture of arms. Soldiers and police, finding to their cost that the ordinary usages of the law were powerless to protect them, resorted to reprisals on their own account, and shot, wrecked, and burned with all the license of their assailants. Parish priests and bishops denounced the campaign from their pulpits, but with little effect. The majority of the Irish people seemed to have little sympathy with it, though there were many who could not but admire the courage and sheer persistence of the outrages. De Valera at the moment was in America enlisting sympathy and raising funds.

A curfew and other repressive measures went into force in September 1919. The Dail was proclaimed a dangerous association and forbidden to meet, and several Sinn Fein leaders were arrested. Search parties were sent out after hidden arms. Armored cars and cavalry swept the country. Dublin Castle looked like a besieged fortress. The British Government announced that hunger strikers would not be released. Terence MacSwiney, Mayor of Cork, died in Brixton Gaol on the seventy-fourth day of his hunger strike.

The "war" raged all through 1920. The British courts in several parts of Ireland ceased to function, and the Irish set up courts of their own. During the year strong reinforcements of troops arrived from England. An auxiliary police was formed of former army officers who, because there were insufficient police uniforms available, wore dark Glengarry caps and khaki, and came to be known as the "Black and Tans." On New Year's Day, 1921, "authorized reprisals" went into force. Districts where outrages had occurred were held collectively responsible on the general ground that the outrages could only have been possible with the assistance or connivance of the inhabitants — as indeed was usually the case — and they were collectively punished by burnings and demolitions. It could not be said that Southern Ireland was pacified by these measures. Murder and arson, countermurder and counterarson continued to run their ruinous course. Probably the Irish Republican Army had many more native sympathizers in 1921 than it had in 1919. But the measures did prove that the British Government possessed the means, whenever it had the will, to crush the Sinn Fein movement utterly.

Early in 1920 a new Government of Ireland Bill, to replace the long-since inoperative Home Rule Act of 1914, was being debated in the House of Commons in London and was eventually passed at the end of the year. The new act provided for two legislatures, one for Northern Ireland and one for Southern Ireland, and also for a joint Council of Ireland, where the discussion of matters common to both might take place. The British Government reserved to itself substantial control over the armed forces and over foreign relations. Ulster (Northern Ireland) accepted the Act without enthusiasm but proceeded to set up its separate legislature. In June 1921 the Northern Parliament accordingly assembled in Belfast; King George V attended the inauguration ceremonies in person and in his speech appealed to all Irishmen to bring their unhappy fratricidal feud to an end; Sir James Craig, leader of the old Ulster Unionists, became Prime Minister of the first Ulster Government. The Southern Parliament was declared open in Dublin later in the same month; but, out of 128 possible members, only four put in an appearance. The Southern Parliament did not meet again. So ended the century-old status of Ireland, as originally established under the Act of Union of 1800.

Throughout 1921, Ireland continued to be the first preoccupation of the British Government. The attitude of Lloyd George, then Prime Minister, was clear and logical. With one hand he offered peace within the Empire, and with the other he offered war to the finish. Ireland could have either. He and Churchill, who had just been made chairman of a Cabinet Committee on Irish Affairs, tried again and again to bring the protagonists in the struggle together in the quiet and dispassionate atmosphere of a round-table conference. De Valera had now returned from America and was living the life of a hunted outlaw with a price on his head. In July 1921, after many mysterious and secret exchanges, Lloyd George prevailed upon him to come to London, and for the moment a truce was proclaimed in Ireland.

Lloyd George received De Valera at No. 10 Downing Street on July 14, 1921. It was a moment of high drama. The head of a great, victorious empire confronted a man, technically a rebel, who determinedly posed throughout the meeting as the envoy of an independent state. Lloyd George, rising, as he always did, to an artistic opportunity, greeted his visitor as a brother Celt and replied to De Valera's opening speech in Irish with one in Welsh. Agreement, as was soon obvious, was going to be impossible, yet both sides were averse to allowing the parleys to break down. In October, in London, Lloyd George again met Sinn Fein delegates, this time headed by Arthur Griffith and Michael Collins. But two months of futile discussion exhausted what little was left of humor and patience. De Valera from his stronghold in Dublin kept issuing inflammatory proclamations on the general theme of "No Surrender." At last, on December 5, Lloyd George made his final offer of peace or war. He may have been bluffing, but apparently he convinced the Sinn Fein delegates that he was prepared, if need be, to go the lengths of a military reconquest of Ireland. On December 6, 1921, Arthur Griffith and Michael Collins capitulated and signed a treaty for the establishment of an Irish Free State.

The news of this wholly unexpected agreement raised a violent outcry, alike from English Conservatives, Ulster Unionists, and extreme Sinn Feiners. Each party, for its own good reasons, declared itself basely betrayed. Lloyd George and his colleague, Churchill, were the most reviled men in Britain. Griffith and Collins returned to Ireland to face an angry De Valera, who would not move an inch from his demands for the complete independence of a united Ireland. But on January 7, 1922, after three weeks' bitter debate, the Dail accepted the treaty by 64 votes to 57. De Valera promptly resigned his Presidency, and Griffith was elected in his place. A Provisional Irish Government was set up under Collins, and a committee appointed to draft a Southern Irish constitution. A subsequent general election in Ireland in June 1922 more than upheld the decision of the Dail.

The treaty gave the Irish Free State the status of a British Dominion. The members of its Parliament would be required to take an oath of "true faith and allegiance" to its constitution and of faithfulness to the King. The office of Lord Lieutenant was abolished, and a new representative of the Crown would be appointed by the British Government and entitled Governor General. The Free State would assume a share of the British national debt. It would maintain its own forces, but it would depend on the British Navy for the defense of its seas, and it would also concede certain naval and harbor facilities, notably at Berehaven and Queenstown, to the British Admiralty. These defensive provisions were held to be enough to allay the strategic fears which always lay at the bottom of England's attitude to Ireland.

The treaty also provided that Ulster (Northern Ireland) could elect either to come into the Free State or to retain her independence and separation. Northern Ireland preferred the latter option, and her Parliament and government, as already set up under the act of 1920, continued to operate. A commission was appointed to determine the boundary between Northern and Southern Ireland.

But whatever England does in Ireland is always wrong. If, now that the treaty had been signed, British troops had not left the country, the sincerity of the British Government would have been in serious question. So the British troops did leave the country. Barracks and armories were evacuated; Dublin Castle was "surrendered"; hundreds of Irish prisoners were released from jail. Perhaps the British Government found an ironic satisfaction in transferring the burden of law and order to the Irish themselves. Actually they transferred Ireland to the mercies of the Irish Republican Army. Irishmen who had been loyal to the Crown, especially farming landowners, found themselves without protection. Even Communism enjoyed a short, mad frolic. "Soviets" sprang up and landless laborers sought to solve the "agrarian question" on Russian lines by seizing farmers' property. In April 1922, Rory O'Connor, at the head of a band of Republican "irregulars," occupied the Four Courts in Dublin and proclaimed himself head of a Republican Government of all Ireland, and he was only ejected two months later with the loan of two British field guns. There were border affrays in Armagh and Tyrone, the disputed counties between Northern and Southern Ireland, and there were anti-Catholic riots in Belfast. Without any doubt the year 1922 was the wickedest and most squalid of the entire Irish Civil War.

Michael Collins was determined to exterminate lawlessness in Ireland. Unlike the old "Black and Tans," he knew his men and their tactics. But on August 12, 1922, Griffith died suddenly of heart disease, and two days later Collins himself was shot down in an ambush. The Irish Free State was left to begin its uncertain career under William Cosgrave.

The inevitable reaction set in. No people — not even the Irish — could have lived at this crisis tension indefinitely. By contrast with what had gone before, Cosgrave's era was almost pedestrian. He made an able President. He was committed to the treaty of 1921 and determined to see it carried out. A Tripartite Pact, in December 1925, at last settled the vexed boundary question between Northern and Southern Ireland, though the settlement was fiercely contested by De Valera's party. Ireland as a whole entered the later twenties in more peaceful circumstances than she had known for years. Many a wishful observer at the time believed that the Irish Question had been solved.

It was not solved. It was only in abeyance till the Depression which struck the economic world at the beginning of the thirties, and in Ireland, as elsewhere, the Depression was the great tester of solutions. De Valera meanwhile had continued his unfinished battle, often from "underground" as we would say today. He broke with Sinn Fein and founded a new party, the Fianna Fail, the "Soldiers of Destiny." There were still some murders but, though he and his party denied all implication in them, the public revulsion fastened itself upon the type of political tactics he represented. He remained ten years "in the wilderness of public obloquy," but it was probably an exile which deepened and dignified his character. Then, in the elections of February 1932, he won his first majority, became President, and put in hand a typical, if not unexpected, program of reforms.

He rescinded the ban which had stopped the Irish Republican Army from holding parades and released such of its members as were then in jail. He imposed tariffs on a wide range of manufactured goods from Britain. He withheld the land annuities paid by Irish tenant farmers to the British Government as interest on bonds formerly issued to help them purchase their land.[3] He replaced James McNeill, then Governor General, who had been complaining of discourtesies shown him by the Free State ministers, by one Donal Buckley, a Republican of pointed personal mediocrity, who took up his residence, not at the Viceregal Lodge, but in a house in a Dublin suburb. He finally abolished the oath of allegiance. One by one the clauses of the hated treaty of 1921 were repudiated. Britain did nothing to interfere beyond raising tariffs against Ireland sufficient to reimburse the British Treasury for the loss of the land annuities.

De Valera, a rebel and an idealist, was perhaps not too well versed in the niceties of constitutional and international law, and his actual aims at this time were far from clear. In fact, it was often said of the Irish that they were "strong in emotion but weak in precision." De Valera appeared to want an independent Irish Republic, yet he hesitated to burn his boats and to make a final irrevocable break with the British Commonwealth. He spoke of "external association" with the British Commonwealth, yet he could hardly have done more to impair, and even to insult, that association. Thus a Free State delegation attended the Imperial Ottawa Conference in 1932, but in December 1936, the Dail used the crisis over the abdication of Edward VIII to abolish the office of Governor General altogether, and the accession of George VI was not proclaimed in the Free State. At the same time, however, the Dail passed an External Relations Act, by which the King would act on behalf of the Free State "for the purposes of the appointment of diplomatic and consular representatives and the conclusion of international agreements." The act was the last remaining link with the British Crown and Commonwealth.

In May 1937, De Valera introduced the text of a new constitution and secured its approval in the Dail on June 14. The constitution ignored, and by inference replaced, the treaty of 1921. It provided for a President, with powers somewhat analogous to those of the President of the United States, and a Dail and a Senate of decidedly corporative flavor. It restored for Ireland the Gaelic name of "Eire." It mentioned neither King nor Commonwealth.

A year later, after extended negotiations, a financial agreement was signed in London ending the dispute over the land annuities. The British Government accepted £10,000,000 in satisfaction of its claims and handed over to Eire the port and harbor facilities which had been reserved for it under the treaty of 1921 — notably in Cóbh (Queenstown), Berehaven, and Lough Swilly. A trade agreement abolished the punitive tariffs between the two countries. Douglas Hyde, founder of the Gaelic League, a well-known scholar and a Protestant, was elected the first President of Eire in June 1938.

Meanwhile, it is to be noted parenthetically, Northern Ireland continued overwhelmingly in its British allegiance. In the Northern Ireland elections of November 1933, for example, Lord Craigavon's [4] Unionist party won 36 seats, an absolute majority of 20 over all other parties combined. De Valera, whom one constituency elected as its Member in that election, thus became the one man in Ireland with the right to sit in both parliaments. But he did not take his seat in Belfast.

THE NEW IMPERIALISM

The British Empire in 1914 was a vast, widely dispersed aggregation of territory covering 13,000,000 square miles, one-quarter of the earth's land surface, and inhabited by a population of 450,000,000, one-quarter of the human race. Its white population was about 70,000,000, mainly Anglo-Saxon, but also in part French, Dutch, and Spanish. The political structure of the Empire was complex in the extreme, and the particular status or administration of the different parts of it was perhaps explainable only in terms of their histories. Its main constituents were the United Kingdom of Great Britain (England, Scotland, and Wales) and Ireland; the Dominions of Canada, Newfoundland, Australia, New Zealand, and the Union of South Africa; the Indian Empire and the Crown Colonies and Protectorates. The Dominions were self-governing, and their political heads were responsible to popularly elected legislatures; but their laws were theoretically subject to the assent of a Governor General or Governor, representing the King. The Indian Empire was ultimately administered from the India Office in London. The Crown Colonies and Protectorates were administered in whole or in part from the Colonial Office in London. There was also a class of territory ruled by native chiefs with the assistance of British "residents"; and there were certain "spheres of influence," defined by international treaties. There was also the special position of Egypt, nominally independent but under British military occupation. To this aggregation the peace settlement of 1919–20 added 1,000,000 square miles of territory and native populations of 7,000,000 governable under the new mandates system.

The heterogeneity of the Empire was bewildering even to the best-informed of Britons. Nothing in French precision, German system, or American legal literalness could have conceived so unique an organism. The Empire had originally grown by no law but its own vitality; its ultimate governance was a code of conventions rather than a constitution. Time was when it represented no more than the military and economic ambition of a small class in Great Britain; but it had since become the repository of great political power, the field of a migration of peoples, and a vehicle of culture; and, like Rome itself, its culture was likely to survive, and to justify it in history, in long centuries after its power had gone and its people had lost their identity.

The British Empire began as one of the maritime and colonial enterprises of the seventeenth century. It expanded under eighteenth-century capitalism and the Industrial Revolution. It produced two classes of territory: first, the purely European settlements such as the original thirteen American States or the eventual Dominions; and second, the trading and bureaucratic dependencies such as India or the Crown Colonies. The first was the territory of permanent white immigrants, who regarded themselves as citizens of a new country; the second was the territory of impermanent white traders, soldiers, and officials, who went there for a "career" and then retired to England to live on their investments or their pensions. But, whatever form it took, the Empire was imbued with distinctive British ideas of government and bureaucratic integrity. Its white subjects enjoyed their degrees of democracy and representative institutions; its "dependent" subjects enjoyed the protection of a scrupulously administered law and medical, educational, and other paternalistic services, and they were invariably secured in their local creeds and customs. Nor was the Empire monopolistically British; it granted — at least in the nineteenth century — the same commercial opportunities to all nationalities, often including the native races themselves, as were enjoyed by the subjects of the Paramount Power.

Certainly the British Empire had sometimes exhibited the unpleasant aspects of all empires. In its time it had reared its freebooters, its slavers, and its nabobs. If it was a "white man's burden," it was a lucrative one. But freedom grew beside force, and trusteeship beside exploitation. Peace and law were established over areas of the world where they had been unknown before. The Empire's statesmen looked forward to the eventual independence of all its peoples. The truth is that British imperial ideology was always a changing, growing thing. Each crisis of imperial history taught an appropriate lesson, learned and not forgotten. It might be said that, in the past four centuries, the British had had four empires. The first began with Cromwell, the second with the American Revolution, the third with the Indian Mutiny, and the fourth with the First World War. It is the third, the later Victorian Empire, which it is now the fashion to decry so much, the so-called Jingo Empire of Kipling's verses and the Diamond Jubilee. Yet that Empire had its greatness. It was served by the best and finest Britain could give, men of the type of Grey, Dilke, Ripon, Lytton, Lansdowne, Cromer, Milner, Sandeman, Morley, Minto, Crewe, Lugard, Zetland, Curzon, and any number of others, products usually of the public schools and older universities, patricians every one of them. Their names conjure up proud historical recollections. But by 1919 even those of them who still lived were already figures of the past, fit to spend their latter days in retirement, perhaps writing memoirs of exquisite classical polish about the good old days when the word of a British official from the Nile to the Yangtze was absolute and undisputed law. Lord Lloyd, the last of the line, was dismissed from his post by Arthur Henderson, Foreign Secretary of the Labor government of 1929.

The fourth Empire was the Empire of the Fourteen Points, of self-determination and the sovereignty of small states. Its main contribution to the theory of imperialism was the mandate. The ideology that made the new Europe also unmade the old Victorian Empire. The history of Ireland, Egypt, or India during the twenties should have been well understood by the statesmen who contrived the revolts in Arabia or in the Middle Danube. The same ideology had already made new nations of the self-governing Dominions. In 1914 those Dominions had all entered the war of their own free will; in 1917 their representatives had met together as coequals of British statesmen at the Imperial War Conference in London; in 1919 their delegates had separately attended the Peace Conference in Paris and separately signed the Treaty of Versailles; they had become separate member states of the League of Nations. The very name, "British Empire," at this time was being superseded by the more liberal and sonorous "British Commonwealth of Nations."

It was a thousand pities that the fourth Empire should have coincided with a period of grave national lassitude in Britain and a correspondingly weak foreign policy. The period may be said to have begun in October 1919, when Lord Curzon became Foreign Secretary, and it was a period of one bitter defeat after the other. The British people after the war had no heart for the old idols, and were content to suffer disastrous losses of prestige in the interest of "peace." The strength of the Navy was allowed to fall below the relative level of security. At home the decline of the birth rate gradually dried up the principal tributary of Empire emigration. Curious and extraordinary must it have seemed nevertheless that a nation whose armies had just fought at Baghdad, Megiddo, and Salonika should now suddenly be accepting such deep and repeated humiliation at the hands of men like Zaghlul, Amanullah, Riza Khan, and Mustapha Kemal. And curious too and tragic that it should have been Curzon who had to initiate this period, Curzon with all his associations with the East, a former Viceroy of India, a very incarnation of the imperialism that had gone. Some of this story is told in these pages. But the general result was that transactions of policy, even though they were perfectly in line with the spirit of the times, instead of appearing to have been granted by a Power in the full consciousness of its strength and rightness, appeared rather to have been extorted from a sort of moral impotence. Yet never was there a time in history when the guidance and stability of this great Empire with all its massive traditions were more urgently needed.

One matter that deserves more than a passing mention is the Statute of Westminster of 1931. The British people might be satisfied with the heterogeneity of their Empire, but one or two events since the First World War had called attention to the desirability of a greater legal precision, especially in the relations between Britain and the self-governing Dominions. In 1922, for instance, occurred the Chanaq crisis, one of the now forgotten crises, but one which at its time seemed serious enough. Mustapha Kemal was then marching to victory over the Greeks in the Turkish War of Independence, and he narrowly avoided a clash with a small British force occupying the demilitarized zone of the Dardanelles at Chanaq (see p. 226). For a few anxious days, Britain was almost on the point of war with the new Nationalist Turkey. The British Government was in immediate consultation with the Dominions in regard to their attitude in the event of such a war breaking out. Australia and New Zealand, both interested in Mediterranean communications and both participants in the Dardanelles campaign of 1915, at once "associated" themselves with Britain and promised, if necessary, to send contingents of troops. South Africa's decision was delayed — General Smuts, then Prime Minister, was absent on a hunting expedition and could not be reached — and when her reply was ready, the crisis had already passed. Canada temporized and avoided making any commitment. But Mackenzie King, the Canadian Prime Minister, subsequently stated his position on the occasion of the Treaty of Lausanne with Turkey in 1923. While he could not take exception to any course the British Government deemed it advisable to take, he said, he could not regard Canada as being bound by any obligations beyond those which the Canadian Parliament of its own volition decided to recognize.

Through the early twenties the Dominions were all displaying considerable diplomatic independence. From the first sessions of the League Assembly, the Canadian delegate constantly struck out on a line of his own. In 1923, Canada created a precedent by signing a fisheries treaty with the United States, the first international treaty to be signed by a Dominion without the participation of a British representative. In 1925 a clause in the Locarno Pact specifically exempted the Dominions and India from any of its obligations unless and until they voluntarily adhered. In 1927, Canada took a seat on the Council of the League of Nations. It must be allowed that British foreign policy in the interwar years, weak as it sometimes was, was still weaker and more indecisive because of the necessity of consultation with the Dominions, none of whom felt much inclination to support far-flung commitments, often of no immediate concern to themselves, which might easily lead to their own involvement.

Imperial Conferences had been held in London more or less quadrennially since the Colonial Conference in the year of Queen Victoria's Jubilee, and it fell to the Imperial Conference of 1926 to try to regulate what could be regulated in the legalistic chaos of interimperial relations. A Committee on Interimperial Relations at that Conference, under the chairmanship of Balfour, reported that "the Empire, considered as a whole, defies classification and bears no real resemblance to any other political organization which now exists or has yet been tried," and then promulgated a definition which, as one historian put it, read like a clause from the Athanasian Creed: "[Great Britain and the Dominions] are autonomous communities within the British Empire, equal in status, in no way subordinate one to another in any aspect of their domestic or external affairs, though united by a common allegiance to the Crown, and freely associated as members of the British Commonwealth of Nations."

The discussions were resumed at the Imperial Conference of 1930, and in

December 1931 the British Parliament passed the Statute of Westminster, which in the words of the King's speech of that year was intended "to make clear the powers of Dominion parliaments." Under that statute, no law made by a Dominion parliament should be void or inoperative on the ground that it was repugnant to the law of England, and no act passed by the British Parliament should extend to a Dominion otherwise than at the request, and with the consent, of that Dominion. Even so, the statute was not yet a complete clarification of interimperial relations, and anyone acquainted with the intricate discussions which had contributed to it might have expected a great deal more. The real question of political autonomy, the right of neutrality in time of war, even the right of secession, were not specifically touched. Yet the *fact* was plain enough, whatever the *law* might say or signify. The self-governing Dominions of the British Commonwealth in future would bear themselves before the world as sovereign states.

CANADA

Though this book is interested mainly in international relations, the authors have felt bound to give a good deal of space in the course of it to the domestic politics of different states. A peculiarity of Europe, especially, has always been the constant interplay of foreign and home affairs, and the one can hardly be described without the other. But, with the exception perhaps of South Africa and India — and of course Ireland — the British Commonwealth was rather differently placed. It cannot be said that the larger questions of war and peace in the world were much affected by the domestic politics of Canada, Australia, or New Zealand, interesting though those party politics often were. We shall include in this chapter, therefore, a section on South Africa and a section only on such racial or population problems in Canada as may fairly be said to have an international bearing. India will be separately considered in the next chapter, and the special problems of Australia and New Zealand and the Pacific in Chapter 37.

Canada was settled by European colonists about the same time and in much the same way as the United States. But whereas the United States came to form a single English-speaking amalgam, Canada remained divided between her two main French-speaking and English-speaking groups. The French originally possessed themselves of the St. Lawrence region or "Lower Canada," now coterminous with the Province of Quebec. French Canadians later migrated in considerable numbers into the Maritime Provinces and Ontario. The English originally possessed themselves of Acadia (Nova Scotia). At the time of the American Revolution the United Empire Loyalists founded the English-speaking provinces of Ontario and New Brunswick. In 1763, Canada passed under British rule, and further immigration from France almost wholly ceased. The British and European immigrations of the later nineteenth century were accompanied, as they were in the United States, by the opening of the West and the building of great railroads. In

1921 the population of Canada was just under 10,000,000, of whom 30 per cent were French-speaking.[5]

In their Province of Quebec the French Canadians built up a civilization unique in the Western Hemisphere. Their language was French, but a French surviving from the eighteenth century; even their arts and architecture retained an eighteenth-century flavor. Their economy was almost entirely that of the small farmer, the habitant as he was called. Their religion was Roman Catholic. They were a people of great charm, and of great physical and moral hardihood; but they were a people also of quite extraordinary exclusiveness. The habitant never entirely lost a nostalgia — like the peasants of Spain, for instance — for the paternalist Catholic monarchy which had once ruled over him and, though he respected the British, and though he appreciated the equal status he was given, the British Empire as such lay outside his normal intellectual vision. In all the politics of Canada, domestic and foreign, therefore, the Canadian Government had always to recognize the existence of a group, numbering one-third of the electorate, which could be depended upon to take an isolationist attitude toward every problem that arose. And in Canada, as sometimes happens in democratic countries, it was the organized, politically conscious minority that so often gave direction to national policies as a whole.

National feeling in Canada was a question of some complexity. From time to time vague threats of secession, away from the Empire and away from each other, characterized both English- and French-speaking sections of the country. A nationalist movement latterly developed among French Canadians and became crystallized during the thirties in a new provincial political party, the *Union Nationale*. The party agitated for local social reforms, and against English-speaking and American ownership of Quebec's industries and resources, but it did not otherwise develop much of a program. Just before the Second World War, more extreme nationalism in French Canada was taking almost a Fascist and corporative form. Nationalism — or rather isolationism — of a sort was also common among Canadians of Irish origin. Britain and the United States each exerted its characteristic influence upon English-speaking Canadians; so much so that two types of English-speaking Canadians, the Anglophile and the Americophile, were always recognizable. All these are matters to be remembered in unraveling the mysteries of Canada's attitude toward the British Empire, toward the United States, toward the League of Nations, toward collective security, and toward the two World Wars.[6]

SOUTH AFRICA

The Union of South Africa covered rather less than 500,000 square miles at the southern extremity of the African continent. It was a rough, elevated land, the larger part a broad treeless veld, with warm temperatures and spasmodic rains, and an atmosphere as clear and as sunny as a mild summer's day in Canada. The southwestern part of Cape Colony enjoyed

"Mediterranean" conditions, grew fruits, and made wines; but the Union's main agricultural wealth was pastoral, and its chief agricultural exports were wool and hides. There were rich gold fields around Johannesburg, producing nearly half the world's gold supply, and rich diamond fields around Kimberley.

The Dutch East India Company ruled and developed the original Cape Colony from 1652 to 1795. It drew its settlers largely from the Netherlands and to a lesser extent from Rhineland Germany and Huguenot France. The three national strains gradually fused into a single Boer, or Afrikander, people speaking their distinctive Afrikaans language. The British occupied the territory in 1795, at first in order to deny it to the French, with whom they were at war; but from 1820 onward, British settlers began to make their way especially into the so-called Eastern Province. A considerable infiltration of Jews from the Baltic countries took place in the nineties, and latterly Jews amounted to about 5 per cent of the white population. East Indians, mainly low-caste Hindus originally imported as coolie labor, were found in parts of Natal and the Transvaal. The native races of South Africa consisted of the primitive Bushmen, the less primitive Hottentots, and the incomparably finer and more warlike Bantu. In addition there should be mentioned the very numerous poor whites and half-castes, perhaps the most difficult of the difficult problems in the Union. All told, at the time which we are considering, the total population consisted of 2,000,000 whites and 8,000,000 others. It used to be said that South Africa combined in a small compass the problems of Canada, India, Palestine, and the Southern United States.

The recent political history of the country centered around reconciliation of Boer and British rights, and of both with those of the domiciled native and East Indian populations. The Boer was independent, intolerant of strangers, religious in his way, wedded to his land and to his herds, a mixture — if we may stretch our imagination so far — of Magyar and Mormon. The British were enterprising and aggressive; they prospected and explored; their native policy was usually more liberal than that of the Boer; and ultimately the great mineral wealth of the country passed into their hands. Confederation of Boer and Briton along Canadian lines had been tried without success in 1877, and then South Africa had become involved in the general imperialist scramble for African territory which characterized the eighties and nineties. Out of that scramble emerged German Southwest Africa, the British Protectorate of Bechuanaland, and the British colonies of Southern and Northern Rhodesia, named after the great imperial pioneer and their virtual founder, Cecil Rhodes. The opening of the diamond fields and the gold fields and the building of the railroads created new rivalries. The entire accumulation of combustibles flared up at last in the Boer War of 1899–1902, a wasteful, senseless struggle which ended in the British annexation of the two Boer republics, the Transvaal and the Orange Free State.

The settlement in 1902 so far as it affected the Boer and the British was rapid and gratifying, and was doubtless due to the common good sense of the leadership on both sides. The liberal policies of men like Botha and Smuts, Boer generals in the recent war, prevailed over the narrow, embittered nationalism of men like Kruger. The Union of South Africa was founded in May 1910 with full Dominion status. Afrikaans and English were both made legal languages; each colony was allowed to keep its own franchise laws and native laws; and, by an ingenious compromise, Pretoria became the Union capital and the seat of the executive, Capetown the seat of Parliament, and Bloemfontein the seat of the Supreme Court.[7] Botha was Union Prime Minister from 1910 to his death in August 1919.

But the main problems, though quieted, were not wholly laid to rest. The problem of nonwhite labor, the problems of franchise and education, were always latent. The Union was the only one of the British Dominions in which secession was ever a serious practical issue. During the First World War, General Hertzog formed a Nationalist party with a frankly antiwar, anti-imperialist platform. A short-lived rebellion broke out in the former Boer republics. But Union troops, Boer and British fighting side by side, afterward conquered German Southwest Africa, and Union expeditionary forces were sent to German East Africa and to the Western front. Smuts attended the Imperial Conference in London in 1917, and Botha and he represented South Africa in Paris in 1919. Smuts emerged from his European sojourn as one of the architects of the League of Nations and a foremost international statesman of his day. Under the peace terms German Southwest Africa was assigned to the Union as a Class C mandate (see p. 132).

Smuts succeeded Botha as Prime Minister of the Union on Botha's death in 1919, but in 1924 his government was defeated in the face of a new upsurge of Boer nationalism and of Indian and labor unrest. Elections, fought with animus and violence, returned a big Nationalist majority, and General Hertzog became Prime Minister. During the remaining twenties, public controversy centered around legislation introduced by the new government — a bill to segregate Indian settlements, limit Indian landownership, and halt Indian immigration; a Color Bar Bill to legalize the color line, especially in the mines; a Flag and Nationality Bill for the design of a new flag for the Union expressing "our independent nationhood . . . and our accepted national status" — all of which sufficiently illustrated the direction of Boer sentiment. In 1930 a section of Hertzog's followers founded a Republican League, whose object was complete severance from Britain and the British Commonwealth. Hertzog himself denounced extremism of this sort, the Statute of Westminster in 1931 effected a certain mollification, and then South Africa passed into the new problems of the Depression.

At first South Africa had escaped the worst rigors of the Depression. As one of the premier gold producers of the world, she was in a fortunate position, and remained after 1931 a gold standard country. But the Depression overtook the Dominion's economy in the end. In March 1933, in order to meet the crisis, Hertzog and Smuts formed a coalition with Hertzog as Prime Minister and Smuts as Deputy Prime Minister, and their two parties were fused under the name of the United party. In the subsequent elections, the United party won an overwhelming success. Evidently economic adversity was having its effect and moderating the extremism of South African politics. Dr. Malan, a former supporter of Hertzog, broke away, however, and organized a new Nationalist party. The Hertzog-Smuts coalition was confirmed in elections in March 1938, "a decisive victory in the interest of national unity," although it was reported that there was considerable personal friction between the two leaders themselves. The proximity of war in Europe found Hertzog on the side of "neutrality," as he had been in 1914, and Smuts on the side of automatic loyalty to Britain.

22 INDIA: EMPIRE AND DOMINION

THE LAND AND ITS PEOPLES

India is a vast stump of territory which the continent of Asia thrusts into the tropics. It is 1,600,000 square miles in area, about the size of Europe without Russia, or two-thirds the United States, or twenty times Great Britain. Through the ages it has been subject to a succession of conquerors, coming mostly by way of the mountain passes in the northwest, and its population, as one wave of invaders overlaid the last, still gives a curious impression of stratification. The Aryan Hindus arrived supposedly between 2000 and 1000 B.C., and the Moslems from 1001 A.D. onward. According to the census of 1941, India had nearly 388,000,000 inhabitants, a fifth of the human race, speaking over two hundred languages and professing eight religions.[1]

European penetration of India came by sea and began in 1498, when the Portuguese explorer Vasco da Gama cast anchor off the Malabar Coast. Portuguese, Dutch, French, and British disputed the trade of the country till, by the middle of the eighteenth century, the British had firmly established themselves, not only in the "factories" of Bombay, Madras, and Calcutta, but in considerable areas of the hinterland. Wars, annexations, and treaties extended their sway, and they eventually ruled rather more than half of India, and exercised an indirect, but effective, "suzerainty" over the native Indian States in the remainder. The British Indian Empire was as crazed and patched as a map of medieval Germany, with a central all-inclusive monarchy ringing an agglomeration of lesser principalities.

India is an object lesson to those anthropologists who say that character is a function of the physical environment. For no two communities could have been more different than the Hindu and the Moslem. Yet the land they lived in was the same land, burned by the same sun, watered by the same rains. The Hindus comprised about two-thirds of the population. Their religion was contained in no one doctrine and no one sacred text, and consisted rather of a multiplicity of rites and customs, often reaching back to a pagan antiquity, varying from locality to locality and, with easy tolerance, allowing the coexistence of the crudest idol worship, a luxuriant mythology, and a deep philosophical pantheism. Generally the Hindus cremated their dead and believed in the transmigration of souls and in the ultimate extinction of the individual self. Their religion was static, confined to India. They never proselytized and rarely admitted a convert.

The Hindu castes formed the most elaborate system of color lines in the world. The priestly Brahmans, the highest of the castes, were guardians of the shrines and temples, and teachers in the village schools; yet they did not eschew, under necessity, the humbler professions of modern civilization as lawyers, newspapermen, clerks — and cooks. Beneath them the castes descended through the gamut of the trades and industries, the warrior, the merchant, the peasant, the moneylender, the cobbler, the barber — amounting to some 2,300 different castes in all. A man was born into his caste and never married outside it; a father passed on his calling and his property to his sons. The higher castes were strictly vegetarian, and all Hinduism regarded the slaughter of a cow as almost a greater crime than homicide. For Hindu women, marriage and child bearing were the be-all and end-all of existence, and both often took place before maturity. At the bottom of the caste system came the outcastes or "untouchables" — the Depressed Classes or Scheduled Castes, as official euphemism preferred to call them — who were supposed to number 50,000,000; they followed menial or "unclean" occupations and lived on the edge of starvation, segregated in their villages, forbidden the temples and schools, forbidden water from the communal well, sometimes even forbidden the very roads and highways, and hopeless of improving their degraded state so long as they remained within the Hindu community. The whole caste system was crossed and recrossed by special sects and cults and also by more recent professional and political vocations derived from Europe. Yet, despite its rigidity and anachronism, the caste system did provide a stable way of life, a division of labor, and an apparatus, surpassed nowhere in the world, for social security.

The Moslems, or Mohammedans (see p. 217), comprised nearly a quarter of the population. They were most numerous in districts nearest the invasion passes, in the Punjab and Kashmir, but also in Bengal. A proportion was descended from the original Pathan and Mogul conquerors, but the great majority were native converts. In contrast to the Hindus, the Moslems professed a simple monotheistic faith, founded by one Prophet, Mohammed, expressed in one sacred text, the Koran. They abominated idolatry and were generally disinclined to philosophical speculation. They had no priesthood and no caste system, and they preached and practiced the equality of man before God. They ate meat, but abstained from alcohol and usury. They buried their dead and believed in the resurrection, the Last Judgment, paradise, and hell. They had a long history of proselytism and conquest. When roused — and it was never difficult to rouse them — they were capable of the most savage fanaticism. Their womenfolk lived in purdah,[2] saw no men and were seen by none outside their own households, and only went out veiled or in closed conveyances.

The Hindu and Moslem communities stood against one another in sporadic and incurable hostility.[3] They might live side by side in formal peace in the same town or village for years, and then some little provocation, when least expected — perhaps the killing of a cow by Moslems or the playing of a band by a Hindu marriage or funeral procession passing a mosque at prayer time — could start a riot. As a community the Moslems keenly felt their inferior numbers, but at the same time were conscious of belonging to a great international Moslem world outside India, a world which looked not to Delhi or Benares but to Mecca, a world which the more parochial Hindu could never know. The Moslems, with their conservative Koranic traditions, also keenly felt their failure to keep abreast of modern education, and they, once the rulers and lords of India and still the main strength of the Indian fighting forces, found themselves constantly ousted from the professions and from government service by the sharper-witted and more fluent-tongued Hindus.

The remaining communities of India were relatively small in numbers, but often strong in influence. The Sikhs numbered 6,000,000; they were a martial people who revolted from Hinduism in the sixteenth century and lived in the eastern Punjab. The Jains numbered 1,500,000; they were another Hindu offshoot, characterized by great wealth, gaudy temples, and an aversion to taking any form of life. The native Indian Christians numbered 7,000,000. Some 100,000 Parsis, originally Zoroastrian fugitives from Persia, "the Jews of the East," were found in and around Bombay. They were often wealthy, devoted to commerce and the "white-collar" professions, and perhaps the most highly Europeanized of all the Indian peoples. Buddhism and its derivatives had largely forsaken the land of its birth. It was found in Burma and Ceylon and was professed by 15,000,000. In addition there were in the "backward areas" of India 10,000,000 heathen animists, tribal groups still living at an aboriginal stage of development. Burma was a Province of British India at the time of which we are writing, but always lay somewhat isolated and apart. We have relegated a short discussion of Burmese affairs to a separate section at the end of this chapter. Outside India, on the north-eastern Himalayan frontier, in the independent Kingdom of Nepal, were the Gurkhas, members of a martial Hindu caste, providing the Indian Army with one of its finest native contingents.

Europeans in India in modern times numbered 135,000, the smallest fraction of the population. They formed a self-contained community, almost a separate caste, spoiled perhaps by habits of privilege and authority, yet wielding extraordinary power. Unlike other conquerors of India in the past, they did not settle and did not allow themselves to be absorbed into Indian life and nationality. The Indian Civil Service, the "steel frame" of British rule, numbered a mere 1,200, about a half (in 1939) being British whites, recruited by examination from British public schools and universities, and the rest, a growing proportion, being Indians. White British troops to the strength of 60,000 were quartered in the country, mostly within striking distance of the old invasion passes in the North-West Frontier Province.

GOVERNMENT AND ECONOMICS

Politically India wore two faces, British India and the Indian States. After the Mutiny of 1857 (see p. 351), Britain abandoned her former annexationist policy and froze the map of India in its configuration at that time. Thenceforward British India, rather more than half the area of the land, was ruled by her "colonially," and nearly six hundred native Indian States remained "independent." Some of these States were as large and populous as a European country, some only measured a few square miles. Some had already enjoyed independence for centuries; some were fragments of the

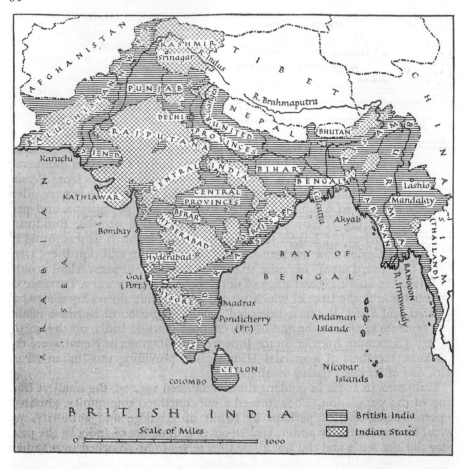

former Mogul Empire; some were puppet principalities created by the British Government. The States had no other rhyme or reason for their tangled frontiers than their accidental form in 1857; they cut across all racial and religious lines. But all were Oriental autocracies, ruled by a rajah, maharajah, or other potentate — the Princes, as they were collectively called — though in practice they respected the advice of British "Residents" accredited to them, and had no say in the foreign politics of the Indian Empire as a whole. Some States had advanced benevolent administrations; some even experimented with representative assemblies; some perhaps were "festering anachronisms of misrule." Each State had its separate treaty with the "Paramount Power."

Latterly British India was divided into seventeen Provinces, each with a provincial government, though the form of government varied in some detail with the Province's size, importance, and historical origin. All were administered by the Indian Civil Service. At the "Center" stood the Viceroy, appointed from London for five-year terms, governing with the assistance of an Executive Council, chosen by himself, and also, under the Council Act

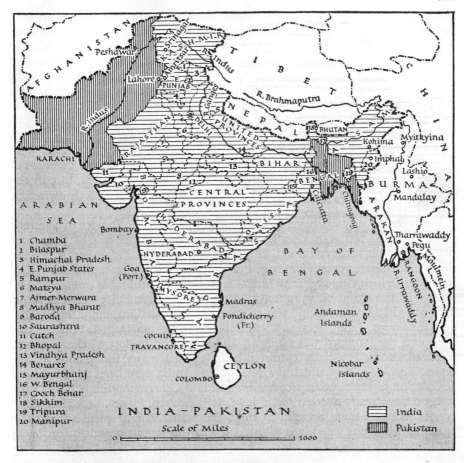

Map legend:
1 Chamba
2 Bilaspur
3 Himachal Pradesh
4 E. Punjab States
5 Rampur
6 Matsya
7 Ajmer-Merwara
8 Madhya Bharat
9 Baroda
10 Saurashtra
11 Cutch
12 Bhopal
13 Vindhya Pradesh
14 Benares
15 Mayurbhanj
16 W. Bengal
17 Cooch Behar
18 Sikkim
19 Tripura
20 Manipur

INDIA – PAKISTAN

Scale of Miles

India
Pakistan

of 1861, with the assistance of a Legislative Council, partly of nominated and partly of elected members. The ultimate responsibility for Indian affairs was borne by the Secretary of State for India, a Cabinet minister, and by the India Office in London, and the Secretary of State in turn was responsible to the British Parliament. After 1877 the British monarch bore the title of Emperor — or Empress — of India.

The Indian Empire was girded about with defensive outposts and "spheres of influence" in the Gulf of Aden and the Persian Gulf, in Afghanistan and Malaya, and in the numerous little islands in the Indian Ocean. It was linked with Britain by the Suez Canal and the naval stations of Malta and Gibraltar — and by the Cape of Good Hope. The whole constituted a vast interdependent organization, a supreme monument to the administrative, commercial, and military genius of the British people.

Divided though she was by race, religion, and governmental system, India had a remarkably uniform economy. Her life was the life of the peasant cultivator. Three-quarters of her population lived in 500,000 villages, often no more than a cluster of thatched, mud-walled huts, and cultivated lots, perhaps of five, sometimes even only of one, acre per family, lots often fragmented by generations of subdivision among heirs. The remaining quarter of her population was distributed among the trades, domestic service, and more recently the industries, the professions, and the army. Gradations of wealth and poverty varied from the landless cultivator and the urban coolie, supporting his emaciated body on a few annas a day, to the maharajah drawing private revenues of $50,000,000 a year.[4] The vast majority of the cultivators lived in perpetual debt to professional moneylenders, and their mean acres were mortgaged from generation to generation to pay for family weddings and funerals. Agricultural indebtedness was one of the most serious of India's domestic problems. Land tenure was of different kinds, but in the aggregate only a quarter of the cultivable land in India was directly owned by the cultivator who tilled it.

We have already discussed in another connection the impact of Western economics and technology on Eastern countries, and the case of India was not unlike that of Egypt, Syria, and Iraq (pp. 216–22). Whether or not the lot of the Indian peasant improved or deteriorated under capitalism — that is, under British rule and influence — is not a very profitable question. The factors in the situation were many, complex, and generally imponderable. The old village "feudalism" was replaced by landlordism, more impersonal and rapacious. Land became a commodity to be mortgaged, bought, and sold, and the landlord was often an absentee. The import of cheap manufactured goods, especially cotton fabrics, ruined many indigenous village crafts. The long peace which the British gave India permitted an increase of population of Malthusian progression and laid a correspondingly heavy pressure on the already overburdened land. It is probably true to say that whatever economic benefit accrued to India from British enterprise and British peace and law was steadily swallowed up in the fantastic multiplication of her hungry myriads.

Western capitalism also introduced railroads and factories, great ports and cities, banks and stock exchanges, and all the other paraphernalia of modern industrial life. The natural resources of India, considering her area, were not great, but in due course she had her coal mines, steel works, cotton mills, and hydroelectric power plants. British enterprise doubtless started the process, but it is to be remembered that most of the big industrial magnates of India were themselves Indians. Socially, India had to go through, in a far shorter time, all the toil and torment of nineteenth-century England. The tempo of industrialization was quickened by the two World Wars, and many Indians subsequently looked forward to "planned" national development on a grand scale. But the cleavage between the old and new in India was always present, between those who imagined the future of India on American or Soviet lines and those who, like Gandhi, symbolized her ideal state in the spinning wheel and harked back to the immemorial simplicities of village life.

THE GROWTH OF NATIONALISM

The Indian Mutiny of 1857 began with the revolt of the Bengal native army. It was the climax of a long unrest and was precipitated by the issue to the troops of cartridges allegedly greased with pig fat (unclean to Moslems) and cow fat (sacred to Hindus). It spread to several northern and north-western districts before being finally suppressed. It was a terrible event, and it left with the British a memory they never forgot of that sudden mass feroc-ity which it was normally so hard to credit to the native Indian character.

The political agitation, however, which grew up in British India in the last decade of the nineteenth century and the first decade of the twentieth was of a different order altogether. The malcontents now were not in the native army but in the native intelligentsia. In fact, they were mostly found among the least martial elements of the Indian people. They were young Hindus and Moslems of the "white-collar" class, products of British educa-tion in India. Some of them had attended schools and universities in Eng-land and the United States. Some of them were scholars, lawyers, doctors, and men of business; some of them became able servants of the government. But generally they had imbibed the doctrines of liberal democracy, and they found little in imperial India to satisfy a fiercely sensitive national pride. By 1910 there were already to be found in the British Provinces masses of trucu-lent young men with ambitions wider than their opportunities, adept at destructive criticism, eating out their hearts in hatred and bitterness. Ex-tremists among them turned to terrorism on the Russian anarchist model.

At no time, and certainly not after 1857, did the British regard their ad-ministration in India as a static and perfect instrument. Even Conservative Victorian statesmen believed in the eventual self-government of India and the eventual withdrawal of British power, though they might reserve their doubts as to when that self-government should be granted and as to whether that self-government should ever take the form of British parliamentary institutions. The Indian National Congress,[5] an unofficial association of Indians of all creeds and communities from all parts of British India, was founded in 1885 with the tacit approval and encouragement of the British Government of the time. Its resolutions at first were discreet and loyal, but it was soon regarding itself, if not as the germ of a native parliament, as least as a sort of durbar for the voicing of Indian aspirations. The All-Indian Moslem League, a similar association, but of exclusively Moslem member-ship, was founded in 1906. It must be emphasized that the nationalism which grew up in India was confined — at first — to British India. The Indian States, secure in their autocracy, would have none of it and made short shift of any "agitators" found within their borders. The Indian States remained somewhat aside and apart from the political development which we are now about to describe.

The Morley-Minto reforms, so called after Lord Morley, then Secretary of State for India, and Lord Minto, the Viceroy, were introduced in 1909, and — whatever their authors may have intended — they were regarded by In dians as a first cautious installment of ultimate responsible government in India. The Indian Army played a gallant part in the First World War. In the four years of 1914–18, India enrolled 877,000 combatants by voluntary enlistment, of whom 620,000 served overseas and 62,000 were killed. The Indian Princes were loyal and made lavish contributions to Britain's war effort. It was no more than a recognition of these many services to the imperial cause which, in 1917, prompted Montagu, then Secretary of State for India, to announce "the increasing association of Indians in every branch of the administration and the gradual development of self-governing institutions with a view to the progressive realization of responsible government in India as an integral part of the British Empire." At the end of 1917, Montagu visited India, and the results of his conferences with the Viceroy, Lord Chelmsford, were embodied in that "advanced and courageous" document, the Montagu-Chelmsford Report.

When all is said and done, Britain's war against Germany in 1914–18 never meant very much to Indians. But the revolt and emancipation represented by the Irish Easter Rebellion of 1916, the Russian Revolution of 1917, and the Wilsonian doctrine of self-determination meant a great deal. By the end of the war, in 1918, the National Congress and the Moslem League had outgrown their polite and deferential resolutions of former years, had become regular political parties, and were agitating openly and violently for *Swaraj*, or Home Rule. Hindus like Tilak, Moslems like the Ali brothers, and that unworldly wise but worldly unwise Englishwoman, Annie Besant, made a strange and ill-assorted coalition working for the expulsion of the British Raj. After the Armistice in 1918, the British Indian Government, alarmed over the situation, appointed a "Sedition Committee" under Sir Sidney Rowlatt and, upon the recommendations of that committee, passed the so-called Rowlatt Act providing for the summary trial in camera without jury and the deportation of seditious suspects. Moslems meanwhile were fearful that the Allies at the Peace Conference would dismember the Ottoman Empire and abolish the Caliphate. During the early months of 1919, there were riots and hartals,[6] particularly in the Punjab, and several districts were put under martial law. Gandhi, the Hindu leader, began the first of his non-co-operation movements. At Amritsar buildings were fired by the rioters, some Europeans were murdered, and an Englishwoman was said to have been assaulted. On April 13, 1919, in the Jalianwala Bagh, a public enclosure in Amritsar, General Dyer, firmly believing that only an "example" could now prevent widespread revolution in India, ordered his troops to fire without warning on a crowded political meeting. Nearly 400 persons were killed and 1,000 wounded, and the dead and wounded were callously left unattended where they lay. Meanwhile fighting had broken out with the Emir Amanullah of Afghanistan, and some 300,000 British and Indian troops were engaged in the most formidable of frontier wars in British-Indian history. Yet, undaunted and undeterred, the British Government at the end of 1919 gave effect to the Montagu-Chelmsford Report in a new India Act.

The act sought two things, first to introduce the elements of parliamentary democracy into India, and second to make an initial transfer of power into

Indian hands. It kept intact the main administrative division of British India into a Center and its retinue of Provinces. The Center, that is to say the Viceroy and his Executive Council, remained as before, except that the Indian membership in the Executive Council was increased. But the Legislative Council was now replaced by a bicameral parliamentary assembly of the Indian people, though, in view of the prevailing illiteracy and political inexperience, the electorate was drastically narrowed by means of a property qualification. The greatest difficulty of all was subdividing the electorate in such a way that every section of the multiracial composition of India should be represented. The electoral map of India, therefore, under the act, was a complicated patchwork of communal and minority constituencies. It was not a neat pattern and it gave endless opportunities for dispute, but it was a practical attempt to disentangle the basic problem of India.

In the Provinces a similar machinery was set up. It was here that the transfer of power — rather hesitatingly and experimentally — was put into effect. Certain fields of legislation were to be "transferred" to Indians, while other fields were to be "reserved" to the Crown. Thus local government, vernacular education, medical relief, sanitation, agriculture, and so forth were "transferred" and made over entirely to Indian jurisdiction; police, finance, famine relief, labor, and so forth were "reserved" and excluded from Indian jurisdiction. There was thus a division of responsibility — dyarchy, as it was called. It was intended that further subjects would be "transferred" from the "reserved" list according as the experiment justified itself, and each transference would then represent a fresh installment toward self-government. The act finally provided for a statutory commission to review the entire constitutional problem after the lapse of ten years.

Dyarchy had its faults. It was cumbersome, especially in finance, and its two lists of subjects were bound to conflict. Extremists in the National Congress received it ill. They wanted Swaraj — and at once. They were in no mood for steps and installments. The Treaty of Sèvres with Turkey, in August 1920 (see p. 226), confirmed the worst fears of Indian Moslems for the Caliphate at Constantinople. In November 1920 the Congress, now under the leadership of Gandhi, refused to take part in the elections under the new act, put forward no candidates, and recorded no votes.

That strange personage, Mohandas Karamchand Gandhi, from this moment plays an ever more prominent part in the Indian drama. He was born in 1869 of a shopkeeper family of hereditary officials in the Indian State of Kathiawar. His youth was without interest or distinction till he went to England to study law, a proceeding which in itself was unusual for an Indian at that time. He then returned to his native land and to the girl wife whom he had married before he left, and his life thereafter might have followed that of many another Hindu of Western education, an expatriate among his own people, who had risen above his caste but had no prospects of betterment elsewhere. Gandhi, according to the pattern of the modern demagogue, began as a frustrate and a misfit.

In 1893 he was glad enough to go to South Africa on a legal case, and there, in defense of the Indian coolie immigrants in that country, he found his true vocation (see p. 342). South Africa taught him all he could ever want to know of white man's tyranny, and he also learned the peculiar defense he could use against that tyranny, a defense which has been variously called non-co-operation, nonviolence, civil disobedience and "soul force." South Africa also developed his character. He lived as a strict vegetarian and a celibate. He was tried by much physical and moral suffering. He had his foibles and his ostentations. He would pray in public, observe fasts and silences, and affect a dress which became more and more abbreviated. Yet neither then nor afterward did he allow himself to be spoiled by mass adulation, and in these days of exaggerated demagogy it is still pleasant to make the acquaintance of an acknowledged national leader who never forgot his mother qualities of charm, kindliness, and good humor.

Gandhi was loyal to Britain in the Boer War, and he was loyal in 1914. On his return to India in 1914, he made trial of civil disobedience, at first over only minor issues. He interested himself in rural questions, the decline of peasant crafts, the prohibition of alcohol and opium, and untouchability. He began his famous "spinning-wheel" agitation for the exclusion of foreign manufactured fabrics. Only after the Rowlatt Act and Amritsar did he at last turn in uncompromising opposition to the British Government in India. In July 1920 he proclaimed general civil disobedience, a boycott of government offices, law courts, and schools, and a boycott of foreign goods. The great masses of Hindu India, "the dumb, toiling, semi-starved millions," already revered this quaint, toothless, shriveled, bespectacled little man in his homespun loincloth as a saint, and called him "Great Soul" or Mahatma.

In April 1921, Lord Chelmsford laid down his viceroyship and was succeeded by Rufus Isaacs, Lord Reading, Lord Chief Justice of England. Evidently the British Government felt the desirability of a legal mind in India to watch the working of the new India Act. Reading could hardly have begun his administration in too sanguine a frame of mind. During August 1921 the Moplah tribesmen of the Malabar Coast, a somewhat primitive Moslem community, rose in revolt and horribly maltreated many thousands of their unoffending Hindu neighbors. In November 1921, when the Prince of Wales landed in Bombay for his long-deferred visit to India, his arrival was greeted with hartals and riots, and he himself was protected only with difficulty from outright personal insult. In February 1922, at the village of Chauri Chaura in the United Provinces, a mob of Congress "volunteers" set upon twenty Indian policemen and hacked or burned them to death. Meanwhile communal [3] rioting between Hindus and Moslems in the five years of Reading's viceroyship cost several hundred lives and considerable loss of property. "Soul force" was evidently failing in everything but force, and Gandhi in a moment of deep remorse called off his civil-disobedience movement. Some days after the Chauri Chaura incident, he was arrested, tried for sedition, and jailed. He dropped political agitation for a time and resumed his campaign against untouchability, thereby alienating many of his Hindu friends. Early in 1924 he was taken ill with appendicitis, and he went so far in forsaking his strictures against Western science as to request that the operation be performed by a British surgeon.

The National Congress decided not to boycott the elections of 1923 as it had done the elections of 1920. It secured nearly half the seats in the central legislature, where it determined to pursue a policy of "uniform, continuous, and consistent obstruction." Yet the Moplah rising and the Chauri Chaura massacre had not been helpful to Congress politics and were proof enough that violence would benefit no one. Finally, as if to complete the cycle of events which at this moment was working to the discredit of extremism in India, Mustapha Kemal in Turkey abolished the Caliphate (see p. 227) and, at a stroke, the entire Moslem agitation in India on behalf of the Caliphate came tumbling to the ground. The Congress and the Moslem League in the late twenties were in a humbler mood; but the mood did not last long.

In 1926, Lord Irwin, later to become Lord Halifax, succeeded Reading as Viceroy.

REPORTS AND CONFERENCES

The India Act of 1919 provided for a statutory commission to review the constitutional problem in India after the lapse of ten years. But so serious had the situation become that the fulfillment of this provision was hastened, and the British Government announced the appointment of the commission in 1927. At its head was Sir John Simon, at that time no more than a successful parliamentarian and lawyer, and among its other members appeared the name of Attlee, who was just then on the threshold of his career in the Labor party. There was some justice therefore in the Congress's taunt that the government was fobbing off on India "a collection of nonentities." Worse still, from the Indian point of view, none of the members were Indians or had had any experience with Indian affairs. Indians of all parties were deeply offended. Not only extremists in the Congress, but moderates who had formerly co-operated with the government resolved to boycott the commission. Simon and his colleagues landed eventually and hopefully in Bombay in February 1928, to be met by mobs of demonstrators carrying funeral banners inscribed, "Simon, go back!" and, in a long itinerary through India, they found not one responsible Indian willing to give evidence before them.

The Viceroy, Lord Irwin, went home to England in the summer of 1929 to consult with the Cabinet, and on his return to India formally announced that "the national issue of India's constitutional progress is the attainment of Dominion status." He also announced that a round-table conference would be held in London at which Indians would deliberate the future of India with representatives of the Crown. Ramsay MacDonald's second Labor ministry had just been formed, and Indians always had the rosiest expectations of Labor. But the Congress was no longer satisfied with promises of Dominion status. It was now passing wholly under the control of men like Jawaharlal Nehru and Vallabhbhai Patel whose objective was absolute severance from the British connection. The Moslem League at this time still advocated Dominion status, but it too was passing under the control of Mohammed Ali Jinnah, who in his own way could be as intransigent as any

Nehru and who was shortly to make himself the spokesman for a separate Moslem state in India, Pakistan.

The Simon Commission paid a second visit to India in 1929 and met the same paralyzing boycott as before. The Commission's report was published, after calculated delays, in May 1930. On any unprejudiced view the report was a document of great breadth and thoroughness, and it remains still the classic account of the India of its day. But its whole aim and purpose were outdated by the time it appeared, and never perhaps has so considerable a state paper fallen so sterilely from the printing press.

By 1930 public unrest in India had entered upon a livelier phase. Civil disobedience was in full swing once more. Hartals, communal riots, murders of officials and police were of far too common occurrence. A new factor was the appearance of Indian Communists with evident affiliations with Moscow. Another new factor was the open participation of women in mass demonstrations. Favorite tactics were for men and women to sit or lie in the roads for hours obstructing the traffic. "Volunteers" picketed shops which sold British goods, especially cotton piece goods. There were "rent strikes" and "tax strikes." As in 1919 unrest in India was reflected on the borders. Afridi tribesmen raided Peshawar. An anti-British revolt flared up in the Tharrawaddy district in Burma. Meanwhile the Depression was beginning to make its characteristic contribution. The Indian budget for 1930 showed a big deficit.

During March and April 1930, Gandhi conducted his famous march to the sea, and at Dandi near Bombay made salt on the seashore, thereby committing a technical breach of the Government's salt monopoly.[7] In May he was arrested and, under an old regulation dating from 1827, he was held at Poona without trial "under restraint." By the end of 1930 some 23,000 offenders, including most of the Congress leaders, were being similarly held.

While results in the field of constitutional politics might be barren and disappointing, Indians were gaining the realities of independence in other ways. The Civil Service was being steadily Indianized. The army was appointing more Indian officers, and several units were being formed wholly officered by Indians. Indian tariff autonomy, tentatively recognized at the time of the India Act of 1919, was now an established right, and the Indian legislature could — and did — raise tariffs against any source of imports it wished, notably against Lancashire cotton. Indian businessmen more and more were buying out or otherwise replacing British firms. Whether India was fated to find a constitution or not, Indianization was becoming an automatic process leading of itself to the relinquishment of British power.

Lord Irwin had announced a Round-Table Conference in London. In the end, three conferences were held, of which the first opened in November 1930. The Congress resolved against participation, and in any case most of its leaders were now "under restraint." All other parties and the Indian States sent delegates. The King gave a speech of welcome; Ramsay MacDonald, the Prime Minister, took the chair. Lord Irwin afterward released Gandhi and his associates in order that the results of the Conference might be freely discussed in India. Lord Irwin also consented to personal conversations with Gandhi at Delhi. British die-hard imperialism might well be alarmed and nauseated, in the words of Winston Churchill, "to see Mr. Gandhi, a lawyer, who had become a seditious type of saint well known in the East, striding half-naked up the steps of the Viceregal Palace, while he was still organizing and conducting a defiant campaign of civil disobedience, to parley on equal terms with the representative of the King-Emperor." Certainly Gandhi's visits to Lord Irwin made a strange, if heroic, spectacle. In March 1931 they finally arrived at the so-called Delhi Pact, Gandhi called off his civil disobedience, and Irwin withdrew certain repressive ordinances.

The second Round-Table Conference was held in London in November 1931, and this time Gandhi attended as the sole delegate of the Congress. The date was not fortunate — Britain was in the midst of the Depression and had gone off the gold standard a few weeks before (see p. 408) — and the Conference consequently did not receive the attention from the British press which was its due. Perhaps for that reason, it accomplished a good deal of valuable legal spadework, undistracted by the usual demagogic excitement which normally would have been easy to arouse. Gandhi was not very helpful. He complained and criticized, he held obstructive "days of silence," he paid ostentatious visits to Oxford, Canterbury, Manchester, and the slums of London; but he never understood the technique of negotiation, and he was at a total loss without the accustomed publicity. All the delegates — except Gandhi — accepted the doctrine of Dominion status, and all — except Gandhi — assumed, almost as a matter of course, that the system of government would be modeled on the British parliamentary system. But the Conference, despite its near success, was adjourned at last over the old problem of communal and minority electorates, the problem that had bedeviled the former India Act of 1919 and was indeed the basic problem of India. The government intimated that it would be glad to accept a solution of the problem from the Indians themselves, but it would impose its own award if that solution were not forthcoming.

Lord Willingdon succeeded Lord Irwin as Viceroy in 1931, and the old battle was almost immediately rejoined. The Irwin-Gandhi Delhi Pact was already a dead letter. Gandhi made it known that he would signalize his return from London by reopening his civil-disobedience campaign, and shortly after landing in Bombay he was put under restraint again. But he was not to be repressed even in jail. He took up his former agitation against untouchability. Intellectually alien to the formal atmosphere of the Round-Table Conference, he could still wage the old, congenial war against a social or moral wrong. When the government at last made its award in the matter of minority electorates, and therein reserved separate electorates for untouchables, he replied in characteristic manner. He declared "a perpetual fast unto death from food of any kind save water." Separate electorates for untouchables, he argued, would only recognize and establish more firmly their exclusion from the Hindu community. Hindu leaders hastened to Gandhi's jail at Poona to reason with the intractable Mahatma. Even Rabindranath Tagore, the poet, came and knelt at Gandhi's cot beneath the mango tree. On the seventh day of his fast, Hindu leaders patched up the so-called Poona Pact, which was at once taken to represent India's own compromise on the question of separate electorates for untouchables. The government accepted the compromise "with great satisfaction," and Gandhi broke his fast.

The third Round-Table Conference assembled in London in November 1932, this time again without Gandhi and without a Congress delegate, and the final touches were put to India's new constitution. The Government of India Act was eventually passed by Parliament in 1935.

The new act was a formidable document of 451 clauses and 120,000 words. It provided for a federation of all the Provinces of British India and the Indian States, and in general the constitution resembled that of the Dominion of Canada, the Commonwealth of Australia, or the United States. The division of authority recalled the dyarchy of 1919. The paramount executive was the Viceroy, appointed by the Crown and responsible for defense, external affairs, currency, and so forth. He was assisted by a Council of Ministers, chosen by himself from the federal legislature. The federal legislature was bicameral and consisted of members partly elected in constituencies in British India, partly elected by the Provincial legislatures, and partly appointed by the Princes of the Indian States. The electoral distribution was a complicated compromise between general and communal electorates, on the lines of the Poona Pact, and it sometimes had a strikingly corporative flavor. In the Provinces a similar machinery was set up. The Princes were confirmed in their domestic autocracy. Burma was separated from India.

With all its compromises and anomalies the constitution of 1935 was statesmanship in the grand tradition. Unhappily it was never given a proper trial. A part of it went into force in the Provinces almost at once, but its full operation at the Center was delayed by last-minute procrastination on the part of the Princes, and the difficulties were still unsolved in 1939 when India was swept into the Second World War.

BURMA

Burma belonged naturally to the Indo-Chinese system rather than to India, to which, by the accident of British conquest, she was politically conjoined for half a century; and we are justified in treating her affairs very briefly as a sort of isolated addendum to this chapter. The French used to call her "L'Indo-Chine anglaise." Her people were of Mongolian extraction, migrating southward from China in remote times, and her languages were more akin to Chinese than to any of the Indian languages. The Burmans, who inhabited the river valleys and the delta region, were the most culturally advanced, a picturesque, leisurely, and unsophisticated people. They professed the Buddhist religion, and their monastic system was reminiscent of Tibet. Their ornate, spired, whitened pagodas were a feature of every village and hilltop in the country. The less advanced, half-pagan, but highly independent and often militant tribesmen, the Karens, Shans, Kachins, and Chins, occupied the country's mountainous periphery. Recent Indian immigrants provided most of the coolie labor, and a few Chinese, mainly in the

Rangoon area, were traders and craftsmen. Except for the oil wells near Rangoon, and forestry and mining, Burma was wholly agricultural, and her main products were rice, millet, and ground nuts.

Three Anglo-Burmese wars in the nineteenth century came to an end in 1866, when Thebaw, the last King of Burma, was deposed and the country passed wholly under British rule, thereafter to be governed as a Province of British India. An old Anglo-French rivalry in Burma persisted; some of the tribal areas were not pacified till the very turn of the century; but otherwise Burmese history till quite recent times was equable enough.

Burmese nationalism developed to some extent on the lines of the neighboring Indian nationalism, though the average Burman politician had little of the political acumen and sophistication of his Indian opposite. However, in 1923, Burma was included in the India Act of 1919 and was duly endowed with a British Governor and an enlarged Legislative Council, with "reserved" and "transferred" fields of legislation, on the contemporary Indian pattern. Meanwhile it was becoming normal for Burmans to be admitted to all branches of the administration. By the time of the Simon Commission, Burmese nationalism had fully adopted its twin objectives — responsible self-government and separation from India. Three native Burmans attended the first Round-Table Conference in London in 1930, and twenty-four attended a special Round-Table Conference for Burma, which met concurrently with the second. Under the India Act of 1935, Burma received a separate constitution whose main features were a British Governor of very wide powers and a bicameral legislature with a complicated electoral system designed to secure representation of all communities and interests in the country.

It was not really till after 1935 that a nationalism of revolutionary flavor appeared in Burma, partly in imitation of the Indian National Congress and partly in more sinister imitation of Nazism and Communism. The uprising in the Tharrawaddy district in 1930–31 had been largely an affair of local thuggery with no great political significance. Riots, strikes, boycotts, and student demonstrations had often taken an anti-British, anti-Indian, and even an anti-Chinese slant. But the intensely nationalist and revolutionary Thakins came forward as a distinctive political party in 1936, and thereafter there was a tendency for Burmese nationalism to evince pro-Japanese proclivities. Burmese parties, however, were fissile, unstable groupings. Most of their leaders were naïve to a degree, conventionally corrupt, characteristically touchy, and given to somewhat utopian election promises, but seemingly with little of the Indian nationalist's extreme personal embitterment. In March 1937, Dr. Ba Maw became Prime Minister with demands for greater independence and a Five-Year Plan of social reforms. He was arrested by the British authorities for sedition in 1940. U Saw, his great political rival, allegedly pro-Japanese in sympathy, became Prime Minister later in 1940 with what appeared to be a very similar program. U Saw happened to be visiting the United States when Pearl Harbor suddenly thrust his country into the front lines of the Second World War.

23 THE AMERICAS: ISOLATIONISM

AND PAN–AMERICANISM

THE FIRST WORLD WAR AND ITS AFTERMATH

News of an outbreak of war in Europe came to Americans like a thunder-clap in those brooding, faraway sultry days of August 1914. In domestic affairs, the press had been speculating uneasily on the causes of the current economic recession. On the more distant horizon, public interest had been caught and held by Francisco Villa, the picturesque Mexican bandit, whose massacre of United States citizens was to provoke the dispatch of a punitive expedition under General Pershing to Mexico in 1916. The murder of an Austrian archduke in the Balkans had been duly reported and dismissed as an incident not untypical of the politics of that perennially turbulent region. As the Great Powers, roped together by their entangling alliances like climbers on a dangerous glacier, fell one by one into the abyss of war, American opinion was compounded of fascinated amazement and of satis-faction at the happy remoteness of the American continent from the theater of hostilities.

President Wilson's appeal for neutrality "in fact as well as in name," though a counsel of perfection, was a shrewd appreciation of the coming cleavages in public opinion. The mass of the American people were, if not pro-Ally, at least anti-German. But seven million German-Americans — not to forget also four million Irish-Americans — constituted an intractable mass of Anglophobe sentiment. Fifteen hundred newspapers, sponsored by these and other immigrant groups, spoke with myriad tongues. At the other ex-treme, armchair strategists inclined to the argument that Britain was a fortified outpost of the American defensive sphere and, by the same reason-ing, might become an advanced striking base for an attack on American territory, if she ever fell into German hands. Some, including President Wil-son, believed that the United States would have to reply to a German victory by permanently militarizing itself and permanently supporting a crushing load of defensive armaments. But the old traditional isolationism and the old traditional mistrust of European politics were very powerful and a veri-table second Revolution had to take place before Americans could bring themselves to participate in a war of European origin — and not only to participate, but eventually to give an ideology to the entire Allied cause.

Gradually the American people accumulated a huge material stake in an Allied victory. The war boom raised the price of wheat to $2.20 a bushel and of cotton to 35 cents a pound. The great cities of the Eastern seaboard grew fat on Allied trade, and the "forgotten man" enjoyed a feast of heavy spending. The government, which had frowned on loans and credits to belligerents in August 1914, reversed its position in September 1915. By 1917 private banking interests had advanced $2,300,000,000 to the Allies — compared with $27,000,000 to Germany. In March of that year Walter Hines Page, the American ambassador in London, informed Washington confidentially that the British Government had exhausted its private American credits and that its purchases in the United States could no longer be continued on the same scale without credit facilities. Concurrently the German declaration of unrestricted submarine warfare outraged American patience to the breaking point. Atlantic ports became seriously congested when ships' captains refused to put out to sea unarmed. Losses of British merchant vessels began to assume catastrophic proportions.

The desire for an Allied victory, the financial stake therein, the loss of American lives by German submarine action, the conviction, strong after the publication of the German note to Mexico, that a triumphant Germany would meddle in the Western Hemisphere — all these were powerful incentives to belligerence (see p. 74). President Wilson could scarcely doubt that he had a substantially united nation behind him when on April 2, 1917, he requested Congress to accept the war which had been thrust on the United States. The taut conflict of wills between the United States and Germany, which had moved uneasily since 1914 on the plane of nonbelligerency, had at last flamed into actual hostilities. The causes of these hostilities, ideal and material, were perhaps best summed up in President Wilson's speech of February 26, 1917: "I have spoken of our commerce, and of the legitimate errands of our people on the seas but you must not be misled as to my main thoughts. . . . It is not of material interests merely that we are thinking. It is rather of fundamental human rights, chief of all the right to life itself."

The swing of American opinion away from the ardors of 1917–18 back to a high-walled isolationism was really the theme of American foreign policy during the twenties. Many factors contributed to the change. The Allies always used to contend that the United States had not been long enough in the war; that, despite the magnitude and decisiveness of its effort, the real iron of the great conflict had never entered its national soul; that the Meuse-Argonne, fantastic nightmare as it was, was a small thing beside the Marnes and the Passchendaeles which the French and the British had been fighting for four years; and that, in short, the Americans were better able psychologically to retire from the war than their fellow belligerents. Thus America's irruption into the war could be regarded as a momentary break, occasioned by the need of defending her rights as a neutral, in a continuous and well-established policy of isolationism. President Wilson's stimulating slogans — "the war to end war," "the war for democracy" — gave American intervention the air of a great crusade, and a crusade is a short-term enterprise. The recoil from high idealism supervened almost inevitably with the termination of hostilities. Thereafter the traditional, the well-tried watchword of American foreign policy — "no entangling alliances" — reasserted itself. The United States, like every other victor nation, hastened to restore as quickly as possible the "normal" conditions of 1914. It is perhaps significant that the big, all-absorbing popular issue in 1919 was not the question of war and peace, but the Eighteenth Amendment.

But it was probably President Wilson's injudicious revival of party differences which first set the antiwar temper in motion. Wilson's eloquent wartime pronouncements dropped to a sudden, chilly bathos when, in October 1918, he appealed for the return of a Democratic majority in the forthcoming Congressional elections and at a stroke injected party politics into the entire postwar settlement. In such an atmosphere the hardheaded matter-of-factness which always belonged to the American political character quickly leavened the old missionary zeal symbolized by the Fourteen Points. Unhappily the American people never realized how much the Fourteen Points had nourished stricken Europe's morale, or how deep was to be the feeling of disillusionment in Europe at the withdrawal of the United States from its position of ideological leadership in the world.

President Wilson by his own act therefore bound the peace settlement and the future League of Nations to the Democratic chariot. In the Congressional elections of 1918, fought largely on domestic issues, the electorate was so perverse as to vote in a Republican majority. Wilson consequently found himself, as he attended the Peace Conference in Paris, in the anomalous position of the leader of a party recently rejected at the polls by a majority of the American people (see p. 116). On his return to the United States, bearing with him the League Covenant for submission to Congress, he found a serried phalanx of Republican Senators, backed by a growingly uneasy popular opinion, prepared for battle. Senator Lodge's "Round Robin," which condemned the League in the form proposed by the President, obtained thirty-nine senatorial signatures — more than the one-third necessary to defeat ratification. Wilson defiantly expressed his intention of integrating the League Covenant with the treaty so closely that dissection would be impossible. But his caustic criticism of his old foes in the Senate did nothing to soothe the apprehensions of a large body of moderates who were particularly concerned over Article 10 of the League Covenant (see Appendix F).

It was highly significant that when, in July 1919, the President brought the completed treaty from Paris for ratification, Article 10 continued to be the focus of dispute. The opposition took the stand that acceptance of the principle of collective action against an aggressor would permanently embroil the United States in European conflicts, and would deprive Congress of its constitutional right to declare war. Yet, if that principle was inadmissible, "the League," as Wilson observed, "would be hardly more than an influential debating society." The incompatibility between untrammeled national sovereignty and an effective League was thus brought into sharp relief. In view of the exalted nationalism induced by the war, and the withering blight laid upon high idealism by party controversy, the Senate's failure, in March 1920, to ratify the Treaty of Versailles by the necessary two-thirds majority was not unexpected. To many Americans collective action against aggressors seemed to be a one-way street, down which American troops would march endlessly at the beck and call of the corrupt politicians of the Old World. Wilson, who had been struck down by illness at Pueblo, Colorado, as he made a speaking tour in a last desperate effort to save his handiwork, was helpless to stem the tide of party rancor which he had provoked. Throughout the long struggle in the Senate the sick man, perhaps too carefully insulated from the chilly blast of public opinion, resolutely refused to accept any of the fourteen "reservations" by which he might have bought the approval of the senatorial opposition. Clearly he hoped that, in the presidential election of 1920, the voice of the people would demand the League, and nothing but the League.

But the slide toward "one-hundred-per-cent Americanism" continued unchecked. Chauvinism turned inward against the enemy at home. The workman who struck for higher wages was branded a Bolshevik. In January 1920 a hunt for "Bolsheviks" ended with a mixed bag of 6,000 suspects being placed under lock and key. The Immigration Law of 1921 excluded Asiatics and severely restricted the influx of Latins and Slavs. By contrast, Wilson's pale elixir of internationalism lacked potency. The electorate, seeking a familiar refuge after the emotional storms of Wilsonism and after the disillusion and cynicism of Versailles, found it in the convivial Senator from Ohio, Warren G. Harding. During the election campaign of 1920, Harding straddled the fence on the issue of the League, performing prodigies of verbal acrobatics. But his formula, "Back to Normalcy," proved reassuring to an electorate suffering from "moral overstrain." The Republican triumph at the polls was taken to be a definite repudiation of hazardous experiments in international organization. A separate peace was concluded with the Central Powers in August 1921 (see p. 162), and the American people appeared thereafter to turn their backs on Europe. The quavering, almost inaudible voice of Wilson as he made an Armistice Day address to the nation through the novel medium of the radio already seemed a feeble echo from a dying past: "Armistice is a mere negation; it is a refraining from force. But peace is a very positive and constructive thing as the world stands nowadays, because it must be brought about by the systematic maintenance of common understanding and by co-operation — not by amiable phrases, but by active co-operation for justice."

THE WASHINGTON CONFERENCE

The recoil from Europe which characterized President Harding's administration could not be matched by an equally magnificent detachment from Pacific affairs. Time was when feudal Japan and ramshackle China had offered a minimum of obstruction to Western Powers, and the Pacific had inevitably become the scene of the United States's essay into commercial imperialism. But a modernized Japan had since developed a dynamic policy of her own, especially while the Great Powers had been absorbed in the First World War. Consequently when, in 1915, Japan attempted to establish a virtual protectorate over China by means of the celebrated Twenty-one Demands (see p. 423), Secretary of State Bryan hastened to refuse recognition in advance of any treaty affecting the integrity of China or infringing the principle of the "Open Door." [1] Japanese annoyance was extreme, especially since the United States was the only Power with its hands sufficiently free to block the enforcement of the Twenty-one Demands. The appropriation by Congress of $300,000,000 for naval construction in August 1916, though chiefly motivated by resentment against the rigor of the British blockade in the Atlantic, aroused uneasy speculations in the Japanese press.

American-Japanese relations deteriorated so seriously that President Wilson, three months after the entry of the United States into the war — and therefore three months after the two nations had become "associated" in hostilities against Germany — voiced his deep anxiety over possible Japanese designs on the Philippines. Japan however was not unimpressed by the unexpected tempo and magnitude of the American war effort, and construed it as an indirect warning gesture against further adventures in China. [2] An uneasy compromise was reached by the Lansing-Ishii Agreement of November 1917, which recognized Japan's "special" (not "paramount") interests in China by virtue of her geographical proximity. In return, the American principle of the "Open Door" was solemnly reaffirmed. A secret protocol bound each party to refrain from acts and policies in China likely to injure the rights of subjects of other friendly states.

Japan was far from mollified at the Peace Conference of Paris. She failed to secure the inclusion in the League Covenant of an article recognizing racial equality (see p. 120). The crisis over Shantung was solved only temporarily in her favor, and then only after it had engendered much ill feeling among all parties involved (see p. 120). The competitive occupation of eastern Siberia by American and Japanese forces in August 1918 seemed to be the prelude to a long campaign of check and countercheck on the Asiatic mainland.

The situation in the Pacific provided an apparent justification of the feverish naval construction by the United States, Britain, and Japan which continued after the Peace Conference. Each country had inherited vast programs of naval construction from the war period; each feared to stop while its competitors continued to build. The Anglo-Japanese Alliance of 1902 (see p. 8) was used vociferously by the "Big Navy" group in Congress to explain continued rearmament, although, in December 1920, Britain denied that the alliance was valid in the event of a war between the United States and Japan. Canada, as sensitive as the United States in the matter of Oriental immigration and all too aware of her six hundred miles of undefended Pacific seaboard, pressed hard at the Imperial Conference of 1921 for a termination of the alliance. Japan, feeling that both British and American guns were pointed in her direction, increased her naval expenditure from $85,000,000 in 1917 to $245,000,000 in 1921. Public opinion in the United States, puzzled and dismayed at the spectacle of extensive rearmament only three years after the "war to end wars," began to stir. In May and June 1921 an economy-minded Congress passed by large majorities Senator Borah's resolution in favor of restriction of naval expenditure. President Harding, perhaps not averse to demonstrating that the League of Nations was not the sole agency of peace on earth, hastened to seize the initiative by calling a conference on naval limitation, "in connection with which Pacific and Far

Eastern questions could also be discussed." The conference was to be held in Washington, and attended by the nine Powers — Soviet Russia alone excepted — which could be considered as having an interest in such questions: the United States, Britain, Japan, France, Italy, Belgium, the Netherlands. Portugal, and China.

Secretary of State Hughes, presiding over the opening session on November 12, 1921, proposed with impassive countenance the most sweeping and spectacular reductions, a ten-year naval holiday, and the all-round scrapping of nearly 2,000,000 tons of shipping. The Japanese delegates had come to Washington in a disgruntled and suspicious mood. They had expressed their willingness to consider naval reductions, and had probably even resigned themselves to the discontinuance of the Anglo-Japanese Alliance. But they were resolved, should the Anglo-American combination at the Conference compel them to pare their claws and to modify their recent aggressiveness in East Asia, to exact the maximum price for their complaisance. Even so, unless they confessed unfriendly designs, they could hardly do otherwise than accede to the general spirit of Hughes's policy. The eventual bargaining was keen, but the substantial success of the Conference was never in doubt. In February 1922 the United States, Britain, Japan, France, and Italy put their signatures to a Five-Power Treaty establishing the ratio of 5:5:3:1:1.67:1.67 respectively for the replacement tonnage of their capital ships. Roughly 40 per cent of the capital ships of the signatories, in commission or under construction, were to be scrapped; no new capital ship was to be constructed for another ten years; none might be replaced till twenty years old; capital ships constructed after the ten-year holiday were to be limited to

NAVAL TONNAGES SANCTIONED BY THE WASHINGTON CONFERENCE, 1921–22

	United States	Britain	Japan	France	Italy
Capital ships	525,000	525,000	315,000	175,000	175,000
Aircraft carriers	135,000	135,000	81,000	60,000	60,000

35,000 tons and 16-inch guns, and aircraft carriers to 27,000 tons. The United States, Britain, and Japan agreed to maintain the *status quo* with regard to their Pacific fortifications, with the exception of Hawaii and Singapore. The treaty was to remain in force till December 31, 1936, and a signatory was to give two years' notice before the date of its intention to terminate the agreement.

In addition, the nine Powers at the conference signed a Nine-Power Treaty reaffirming the "Open Door" in China (see p. 415). The United States, Britain, Japan, and France signed a Four-Power Treaty by which they agreed to respect one another's rights relating to their "insular possessions and insular Dominions in the Pacific Ocean" and to adjust any future differences there by mutual consultation. The last treaty was considered to have superseded and abrogated the old Anglo-Japanese Alliance. But it provided no machinery by which its provisions could be enforced, and the protection which it afforded to the Philippines, for example, was entirely conditional upon the good faith of Japan. The United States and Japan signed a treaty regarding the island of Yap in the midst of the Japanese mandated area, under the terms of which the United States was given access to that speck of territory and to the cable and radio installations upon it. Japan, after industrious American mediation, agreed to restore the province of Shantung to China (see p. 415). The Conference also passed resolutions prohibiting the use of poison gas and restricting the use of submarines to the rules of international law.

France played a characteristic role in this first of international conferences on the limitation of armaments. She had originally been willing to support the United States in return for a revival of the abortive Franco-American treaty of assistance against Germany signed at Versailles in 1919 (pp. 118–19). She doubtless feared that a successful limitation of naval armaments at Washington would pave the way for future discussions on the limitation of land armaments, a limitation which, without some compensatory diplomatic concession, she was not in any mood to accept. Secretary Hughes showed no inclination to bargain with the French delegates, who then took up an attitude of obstruction toward the entire Conference, and he was compelled to cable a direct appeal to the French Premier, Briand, before they would fall in with the allotted ratio in capital ships. But even the incisive diplomacy of Hughes could not bring the French to agree to any limitation on cruisers, destroyers, and submarines.

In the aggregate, however, the agreements reached at Washington appeared to be positive and encouraging. It was only gradually, in retrospect, that their weaknesses were perceived. The Nine-Power Treaty depended entirely on the good will and restraint of the signatories, since none of them was committed to defend the "Open Door" by force of arms. Japan's pledge to maintain the *status quo* with regard to her Pacific fortifications, that is to say, to maintain the demilitarized status of her new mandated islands north of the equator, again depended on good will and restraint (see p. 424). The limitation in capital-ship construction was a notable gain, but the Conference had not succeeded in extending a similar limitation to lesser naval craft. Britain was chagrined by the failure, largely on account of French obstructionism, to abolish the submarine. Finally, the bonds between Japan and her European ally, Britain, had been severed. When Japan emerged once more from her uncomfortable isolation, it was to associate herself with the forces of aggression in Europe. The statesmen at Washington, however, could not be expected to anticipate all these long-range consequences of their policies. Furthermore, they worked in the shadow cast by the American taxpayer, who, in 1922, was "more afraid of the tax collector than of any more distant foe."

RESTRICTIONS ON IMMIGRATION

Of recent years certain sections of American opinion had become greatly disturbed at the increased rate of immigration into the United States from southern and eastern Europe and at the threat of Anglo-Saxon Americanism which that immigration implied. An Immigration Act in 1917 established a literacy test for prospective immigrants, but it had failed to stop the human influx from the undesired areas. Immigration figures climbed steeply in the early postwar years, and labor, temporarily hit by the depression of 1921, began to demand new restrictions. Patriotic groups, regarding dubiously the turmoil in Europe, feared contamination of the body politic by the possibly subversive doctrines of the newcomers.

The Emergency Quota Act of 1921 abandoned the literacy test and imposed definite immigration maxima for each nationality. A bill in 1924 retained the same principle, but considerably narrowed the quotas. Each foreign nation henceforth would be permitted to send annually a maximum of 2 per cent of its nationals resident in the United States in 1890, a date when the Anglo-Saxon proportion of the population was high and the southern and eastern European proportion was low. In addition, aliens ineligible for citizenship would be completely excluded. Since this category included all Orientals, the "Gentleman's Agreement" of 1907–08 with Japan was automatically abrogated (see p. 426).

The new bill gave the deepest insult to a Japan already much injured by the recent Washington Conference. The Japanese ambassador in Washington delivered a note referring to the "grave consequences" which would ensue, whereupon Congress, construing the note as a threat, immediately voted the bill by imposing majorities. President Coolidge, though he approved of the bill in general and of Japanese exclusion in particular, condemned the needlessly brusque tactics of Congress. The recriminations of the Japanese press and an act of hara-kiri by a humiliated Japanese in front of the American Embassy in Tokyo left Congress unmoved and unrepentant. From 1924 onward, the doors of the land of opportunity were to be opened only to those who could be easily absorbed into Americanism.

WAR DEBTS AND REPARATIONS

A precarious return to "normalcy" in the Pacific had been attained at the Washington Conference. Simultaneously, the race in naval armaments which had threatened to consume the depleted financial resources of the European Powers had been temporarily stayed. The next step in the American program was clearly the liquidation of the Allied war debts, amounting to $10,350,000,000. Andrew Mellon, when he became Secretary of the Treasury in March 1921, would have preferred his Department to have plenary powers to deal with the entire problem. But Congress decided to set up a World War Foreign Debt Commission, responsible to itself. The new body began its meetings in April 1922 and eventually negotiated all the most important American funding agreements. The first such agreement was concluded with Finland in May 1923. Britain, formerly hopeful of joint Anglo-French action on the matter of war debts, dropped her policy of co-operation with France at the time of the Ruhr crisis (pp.164–65). In June 1923 she agreed to discharge her obligations over a period of 62 years at an interest rate of 3.3 per cent. Finland and Czechoslovakia agreed to pay the same rate of interest, which was adjusted in proportion to their presumed paying capacity. Italy and France proved recalcitrant until the State Department adopted a policy of discouraging private loans to these evasive debtors. . Italy came to terms in 1925, paying an exiguous interest rate of 0.4 per cent, and France came to terms in 1926, paying a more substantial 1.6 per cent. The reduction of the rates was an important relief, since the accumulated interest constituted a very high proportion of the debts. The reduction therefore contributed to the cancellation of 30 per cent of the British debt, 80 per cent of the Italian, and 60 per cent of the French. The total funded debt would have more than doubled the original loans.

The agreements at the time were regarded as ordinary commercial transactions, and years were to pass before American public opinion realized fully the complexity of the problems involved in repayment. We know now that full and punctual liquidation was a receding possibility from the first. The debtor nations, with the possible exception of France, had not enough gold available for any substantial and direct reduction of the principal. Repayment in the main could only take the form of goods and services, and these at once competed in the domestic and world market with American products. The American domestic market was stringently protected in 1922 by the Fordney-McCumber Tariff Act, largely devised to guard it against any Allied debtor who resorted to dumping to liquidate his obligations.

These basic difficulties were long obscured from the public by the cloud of arguments put out by all parties. The Balfour note of August 1922, which suggested a blanket cancellation of all inter-Allied and Allied-American indebtedness, was far from acceptable to American opinion. Cancellation would have meant converting more than $10,000,000,000 in domestic bonds. When the Allies pointed to their own vast expenditure of blood and treasure before the American entry into the war, the Americans could retort that the war was originally a European war, for which the Allies' own political and military systems were in great part responsible. But the economic dilemma remained obstinately unsolved. The debtor nations, faced by a frowning tariff wall and by keen American competition in world markets, were crippled in their capacity to pay.

The difficulties were further obscured by the persistent delusion that sufficient reparations could be exacted from Germany to meet the payments on the debts to the United States. Even though the official view in Washington had always refused to link reparations with debts, yet it could not be denied that reparations, for good or ill, had become an irrevocable part of the interwar economic nexus in Europe. American anxiety over the state of Germany was therefore very much a matter of enlightened self-interest. A few days before the French occupation of the Ruhr, Secretary of State Hughes bluntly observed: "The economic condition of Europe gives us the greatest concern. . . . It is idle to say that we are not interested in these problems, for we are deeply interested from an economic standpoint, as our credit and markets are involved, and also from a humanitarian standpoint." His accompanying proposal that Germany's capacity to pay reparations should be studied unofficially by a group of financial experts, though ignored by France at the time, bore fruit at length in the Dawes Plan of

1924 (see pp. 166–67). American interests subsequently contributed 55 per cent ($105,000,000) of the Dawes international loan.

But the Dawes Plan, as it proved, was only an apparent and temporary settlement. The increasing annuities which Germany was to pay assumed a definite world recovery, and until the late twenties the necessary conditions seemed to exist. The American private investor was therefore encouraged to buy German securities to the tune of $1,210,000,000, between 1924 and 1929, which returned an average interest of 7 per cent, as compared with a mere 3 per cent on domestic investments. Other advances to European countries, beginning with loans to Austria and Hungary in 1923, raised the grand total of American loans to Europe to over $3,500,000,000. The tremendous economic strength of the United States, by an inexorable chain of causation, was becoming enmeshed willy-nilly in the warp and woof of world politics.

THE THREE–POWER NAVAL CONFERENCE AT GENEVA

The attempts of the United States during the twenties to make Europe in general and Germany in particular economically "going concerns" were based in part on humanitarianism and in part on a realistic appreciation of American interests. But the recovery of Europe was not merely a problem of credits, production, and markets. The continuing war psychology and the resultant burden of armaments delayed recovery and imposed a severe strain on the finances of America's European debtors. The United States was in no position to influence land armaments in Europe, where a temporarily dominant France watched with grim foreboding the renovation of German industry and war potential under the stimulus of foreign loans. But it seemed that the United States was especially well fitted, both by precept and persuasion, to influence naval armaments in Europe.

The Washington Conference of 1921–22, ostensibly called to consider the limitation of all types of naval armament, had confined itself in the end to reducing the tonnages of capital ships and aircraft carriers. But from time to time American diplomats and publicists had returned to the charge in the hope that the reductions might be extended to cruisers, destroyers, and submarines, and that thereby the "gap" in the Washington agreements might be filled. Meanwhile the United States had not only failed to build up to the battleship strength allotted under the agreements, but was being outstripped by Britain and Japan in cruiser construction. The protests of the Navy Department were answered by the stock formulas of an economy-minded administration and Congress.

The happier middle twenties seemed to offer a new opportunity for concerted naval limitation. Locarno in 1925, though a European pact, had created a propitious atmosphere throughout the world. The British Admiralty was known to be working on a disarmament plan of its own. Calvin Coolidge, former Vice-President, had succeeded to the presidency on Harding's death in August 1923; he had been elected to a second term in 1924 and had appointed Frank B. Kellogg his Secretary of State. Both he and Kellogg were anxious to resume the good work begun at the Washington Conference, and invitations to the Powers for a new naval disarmament conference were duly issued early in 1927.

Unhappily, sanguine expectations were disappointed at the outset. France and Italy, whose rivalry, since the accession of Mussolini, was becoming one of the factors of the international complex, were scowling at one another across the placid expanses of the Mediterranean. Both declined President Coolidge's invitation. In their absence, therefore, a Three-Power Naval Conference, attended by the United States, Britain, and Japan, opened in Geneva in June 1927. Hugh Gibson, American ambassador to Belgium, was the chief American delegate; Bridgeman, First Lord of the Admiralty, and Lord Cecil represented Britain; Viscount Saito and Viscount Ishii represented Japan. After the first plenary session, the work of the Conference devolved upon a Technical Committee, where the divergencies between the British and American draft submissions gradually and surprisingly widened into a serious disagreement.

The British had been unwise enough to reopen the question of capital ships, which the American and Japanese delegations had come to Geneva unprepared to discuss and considered to have been finally settled at Washington in 1922. The issue was outside the Conference's terms of reference and was finally shelved, but only after it had created the impression in the minds of the American delegates that Britain was maneuvering to evade her Washington commitments. The Technical Committee was already in an irritated, suspicious mood when it turned to consider the question of cruisers. The United States wanted a small number of large cruisers; Britain wanted a large number of small cruisers. Both Powers were manifestly consulting their strategic requirements. Clearly the United States with two concentrated fleets in two oceans, was differently situated from Britain, whose fleets had to patrol 80,000 miles of imperial communications in five. Admiral Lord Jellicoe, who was attending the Conference as the special delegate of New Zealand, explained that the 114 cruisers possessed by Britain in 1914 had been insufficient for the security of her sea lanes, and he fixed the absolute minimum of Britain's cruiser requirements at 70 ships. His rejection of cruiser parity between America and Britain was strongly supported by Winston Churchill and the "Big Navy" wing of the British Cabinet in the fear that such cruiser parity would force Britain to abandon her blockade tactics of 1914–17 — tactics which, of course, the United States considered it had very good reasons for hoping, on a future occasion, to be able to defy. Japan, ironically enough, having forsaken the role of the "bad boy" which she had played with such damaging effect before 1922, was now acting as the anxious and indefatigable mediator between the other two exasperated Powers.

It was common knowledge that in the course of the discussions Gibson and Bridgeman had had "passages," that tempers had been short and voices raised. The Conference as a whole had labored under considerable misrepresentation in the press, especially in the American press. References to 1812 were all too common at American public meetings at the time and were extremely ill-conceived. The British, for their part, believed that the "Big Navy" interests and the armament firms in the United States were lobbying to wreck a reasonable agreement. Indeed, it was revealed two years later that American armament manufacturers had employed a certain William B. Shearer as a lobbyist to that end. On August 4, 1927, a significant anniversary, the Conference held its final plenary session; the delegates recapitulated their several points of view, and separated. Lord Cecil, that great advocate of peace, resigned his post in the British Cabinent a few days later.

The Conference, it may be said, had suffered shipwreck through lack of diplomatic preparation. A preliminary, informal exchange of views would have revealed the areas of disagreement beforehand. The worst part of the failure was the injury to Anglo-American relations. On both sides of the Atlantic, die-hard reactionaries were confirmed in their views. The Conservative press in Britain was freely discussing the renewal of the Anglo-Japanese Alliance. A body of opinion in the United States could only conclude that American naval construction ought to be speeded up to a point where other Powers would be compelled to accept limitation in sheer self-defense. In February 1929, President Coolidge approved a naval appropriation totaling $274,000,000 for the construction of an aircraft carrier and 15 cruisers of the very type Gibson had asked for and had been refused at Geneva.

In a competitive system of national states the effort to combine security with disarmament seemed perilously like an attempt to square the circle. The total expenditure on armament tells its own unambiguous story.

ARMAMENT EXPENDITURES OF THE GREAT POWERS

	1913	1930
United States	$245,000,000	$728,000,000
Britain	375,000,000	535,000,000
France	349,000,000	455,000,000

"Every up-to-date dictionary," wrote William James in 1910, "should say that 'peace' and 'war' mean the same thing. . . . It may even reasonably be said that the intensely sharp competitive preparation for war by the nations is the real war, permanent, unceasing; and that the battles are only a sort of public verification of the mastery gained during the 'peace' interval."

THE PACT OF PARIS

The failure of the Three-Power Naval Conference gave considerable impetus to one trend of opinion in the United States: that the root-and-branch abolition of war by specific engagement, rather than by the piecemeal limitation of armaments, would be the only enduring basis of peace. This rigorously logical view was conveyed informally to Briand, the French Foreign Minister, by Professor J. T. Shotwell of Columbia University. Briand, thus prompted, addressed a message to the American people in a newspaper announcement on April 6, 1927, the tenth anniversary of the American declaration of war, proposing a Franco-American agreement "outlawing" war as an instrument of national policy (see pp. 141–42) .

The State Department, perhaps a little taken aback by this unorthodox procedure, at first was unresponsive. Could it be that France was maneuvering to lure the United States into a policy of "parallel action" with the League of Nations in order to ensure American participation in collective action against aggressors? But public interest, roused by a brisk interchange of views in the daily press, disregarded these subtleties and began to seize upon the important slogan, "the outlawry of war." Secretary of State Kellogg, snowed under by a growing avalanche of petitions, at last adopted the Briand proposal, on condition that the agreement should be extended to include the other Powers. A generalized pact dovetailed much more neatly with the basic principles of American foreign policy than an explicit two-Power agreement, which might entangle the United States politically in European affairs. Senate debate on the pact afterward ran the gamut of opinion from a "friendly gesture" (Senator Swanson) to a "stupendous fact" (Senator Borah). But the Senate Committee on Foreign Relations was careful to add that the agreement would not commit the nation to punitive measures against the violators thereof. The pact would therefore be but a silken halter to hold the dogs of war.

The Pact of Paris, often called the Kellogg-Briand Pact, was signed by Briand, Kellogg, and the representatives of thirteen other nations on August 27, 1928. By the end of 1931, forty-five other nations had adhered, including the Soviet Union.[3] The two principal articles, the renunciation of war as an instrument of national policy, and the settlement of all disputes between nations by pacific means, were declarations of good intentions to which virtually any nation could extend verbal endorsement. But the almost universal acceptance of the pact could hardly offset its complete lack of coercive machinery. Its fragility in practice was clearly displayed only a year later at the time of the Sino-Soviet dispute over the Chinese Eastern Railway in Manchuria. Forty-two signatories reminded the disputants of their obligations under the pact. The rejoinder of Moscow was illuminating: "The Soviet Government states further that the Paris Pact does not give any single state or group of states the function of protector of this Pact. The Soviet, at any rate, never expressed consent that any states themselves, or by mutual consent, should take upon themselves such a right."

The importance of the Pact of Paris consisted least of all in its practical efficacy. For war cannot be abolished by resolution. Yet the pact seemed to signify a trend in American public opinion away from the "sullen and selfish isolationism," once condemned by President Wilson, toward an enthusiastic fellowship with other nations. It was still revealing that public opinion had pressed hard for the conclusion of the pact, while hesitating to provide it with teeth. The time now seemed more than ever remote when Secretary Hughes, aware of the strength of popular sentiment, had refused to open all letters postmarked Geneva.

THE WORLD COURT CONTROVERSY

The oscillation of American opinion between aloofness and international co-operation was excellently illustrated by the involved disputes over adherence to the World Court. The Permanent Court of International Justice, as it was formally known, was established under Article 14 of the Covenant of the League of Nations, "to hear and determine any dispute of an international character which the parties thereto shall submit to it." Elihu Root, former Secretary of State, had played a prominent part in drafting the Court's constitution, and he may well have hoped that the traditional willingness of the United States to settle international disputes by judicial arbitration would ensure its membership (see pp. 135–36).

In February 1923, when President Harding submitted to the Senate his proposal for American adherence to the World Court, he was at pains to point out that no obligations under the League Covenant would be assumed. But the "bitter-enders" who had defeated the ratification of the Treaty of Versailles were still powerfully entrenched. They condemned the World Court as a "League Court," and affirmed that membership would soon be opening a backdoor entry into the League itself. However, in spite of senatorial reluctance, both party platforms in the presidential election of 1924 favored adherence. President Coolidge himself had always been strongly predisposed thereto. The House of Representatives voted overwhelmingly for adherence in March 1925. The Senate then followed suit, but with five reservations, the last of which precluded the World Court from giving an advisory opinion on any matter affecting American interests without the prior consent of the United States. Since the proviso was not immediately accepted by the constituent nations of the World Court, President Coolidge took the stand that the question of American membership had lapsed.

Two years later, in 1928, the enthusiastic public reception of the Pact of Paris encouraged Secretary Kellogg to reopen the issue. A compromise formula, submitted by Elihu Root in 1929, was permitted to slumber in the pigeonholes of the Senate Committee on Foreign Relations until 1935. The public press, though at that time much disillusioned by the nonpayment of Allied war debts, and again swinging powerfully toward isolation, still favored membership. The rejection of the "Root formula" by 52 votes to 36 — 7 votes short of the necessary two-thirds majority — was achieved only by an intensive last-minute campaign by the isolationists, led by the Hearst press and Father Coughlin. The Senate, jealous of its own prerogatives in the field of foreign policy, had fought a skillful and pertinacious delaying action until the course of world events appeared to justify its resistance. Incidentally, it gave a good object lesson in the traditional function of the second chamber — that of delay.

THE FIVE–POWER NAVAL CONFERENCE AT LONDON

When Herbert Clark Hoover became President of the United States in March 1929, Anglo-American relations were still suffering from the after-effects of the unsuccessful Three-Power Naval Conference. The Pact of Paris, widely regarded as a counterstroke to the League of Nations, had never made a deep impression on British opinion. British Conservatives construed the American loan policy in Europe and the investment boom in New York as a phase of commercial imperialism especially directed at their own interests. The struggle for the oil and rubber of the Near and Far East and the fierce rivalry in Canada and Latin America had even provoked the London *Times* to exclaim editorially: "The resources of the whole United States are now being employed in an endeavour to crush the enterprise of British owners."

Into this strained atmosphere President Hoover brought the traditions of a Quaker and a long record of distinction in philanthropy. His feeding of Europe's hungry millions (see p. 55) and his successful tenure of the Department of Commerce under the Harding and Coolidge administrations had inspired the highest confidence in his ability to promote peace "by the limitation of arms and by the creation of the instrumentalities for the peaceful settlement of controversies." Then the advent of a Labor government in Britain under Ramsay MacDonald in 1929 opened the prospect of an offensive against heavy armaments from that quarter. London was fully aware of the uneasiness created in the Dominions, particularly in Canada, by the deterioration of Anglo-American relations. Both Washington and London appreciated the contradiction between their resounding protestations of peaceful intentions in the Pact of Paris and their steady accumulation of naval armaments. MacDonald himself visited the United States in October 1929 and helped to make straight the way for a new naval disarmament conference. The New York stock-market crash of the same month had its compensations and doubtless created that more chastened mood in which the United States was now to approach the international problems of the hour.

The Five-Power Naval Conference met in London between January and April 1930 and was attended by delegates from the United States, Britain, Japan, France, and Italy. Like the former Three-Power Conference, it began well enough. The principle of Anglo-American parity for all categories of ships was recognized from the start. The principle for the moment was only of theoretical importance, since the attainment of actual parity would have involved the United States in the expenditure of a billion dollars over the next five years, but it was an all-important diplomatic concession nevertheless. Moreover France and Italy were now in attendance. But no sooner had her delegates arrived in London than France proved the stumbling block. It was not in her nature to miss any opportunity for extending her security system. She now desired a revision of Article 16 of the League Covenant so as to render mandatory an economic boycott against a declared aggressor. A British blockade in pursuance of such a boycott might have led to a head-on collision with the United States, jealous as always of its rights upon the seas. Britain, inquiring what the attitude of the United States would be in that contingency, was given to understand by the American delegates that no commitment could be made. Accordingly France — and Italy *per consequens* — refused to become party to any naval agreement that might emerge from the Conference. The American policy of no entanglements and the French policy of total entanglements were in open conflict.

The remaining three powers, the United States, Britain, and Japan, came to an agreement among themselves in all their classes of ships on the main lines of the old Washington ratios. But, at the behest of Britain, an "Escalator Clause" was inserted in the agreement permitting construction above the maximum tonnages if any signatory considered itself to be threatened by the construction of a nonsignatory Power — notably by France or Italy. Undeniably the results of the Conference were meager. The high cost of building up to parity with Britain and the loophole afforded by the Escala-tor Clause alike disappointed the American taxpayer. It was a disgruntled Senate which ratified the agreement that summer, adding a resolution for good measure to the effect that the United States would not be bound by any "secret understandings" which the President was suspected of having reached with the British Government.

THE HOOVER MORATORIUM

The stock-market crash of 1929 will be discussed later in its general economic context (pp. 402–404) . But we should note here that the crash, when it occurred, gave the American people one more object lesson in the close interdependence of their economy with Europe's. From 1929, Germany could obtain no more American loans with which to pay reparations, and the Allies could obtain no more German reparations with which to pay their American debts. After a short and deceptive time lag the European financial structure began to crumble at its weakest points, Austria and Germany, and it was discovered with some surprise to what extent European prosperity during the later twenties had been supported by American funds. Financial chaos threatened to wipe out investments in Central Europe, and it seemed that the German Republic, staggering under its burdens, might revert to a dictatorship pledged to repudiate the country's obligations.

In 1931, President Hoover met the situation with a proposal for a moratorium of one year on all intergovernmental debts. Congress was only persuaded to support him when he linked the proposal with a stand against reduction or cancellation, and it would not agree to his further suggestion to recreate the World War Foreign Debt Commission in order to re-examine and, if necessary, revise the entire war-debt complex. But the Depression, like a creeping disease, continued to eat into the European economy, undeterred by Congressional resolutions. In December 1932, after the expiry of the Hoover Moratorium, six debtor nations, including France, failed to resume their debt payments, and others, including Britain, subsequently paid only token sums. In April 1934, in a mood of intense irritation, Congress passed the Johnson Act, which forbade American loans in the future to defaulting governments. The legislation was vindictive, but understandable. The American people had not yet fully realized that "prosperity in our time" was only temporarily possible if the rest of the world lay stricken by economic paralysis.

THE UNITED STATES AND THE SOVIET UNION

The collapse of the Tsarist regime in Russia under the strain of war, corruption, and inefficiency was enthusiastically but erroneously hailed in the United States as a triumphant assertion of the principle of "government by the consent of the governed." The shaky ministries of Prince Lvov and Kerensky between March and November 1917, on which the Allies relied to keep Russia in the war against Germany, were aided by American credits totaling $325,000,000. A mission under Elihu Root in June 1917 insisted that only a defeat of Germany could guarantee the survival of democracy in Russia, at a time when thousands of Russian deserters were "voting for peace with their feet." An American railroad commission undertook the enormous task of reorganizing the Trans-Siberian Railway. This substantial aid to Russia was naturally terminated when, in March 1918, the lately installed Bolshevik regime concluded peace with Germany. That regime, apart from its unwelcome economic doctrines, was generally regarded in the United States as the creation of a conspiratorial minority, which might soon be hurled from power by a reassertion of the popular will. The Bolsheviks, for their part, loudly complained that the occupation of eastern Siberia by American-British-Japanese forces in 1918 was a breach of the political ideals enunciated by President Wilson himself.

The withdrawal of American troops from Siberia two years later effected no improvement in relations, for by this time a "Red Scare" had gripped the United States. Ringing calls from Petrograd for a world-wide uprising of the proletariat, the formation of an American Communist party in September 1919, and a wave of industrial unrest all contributed to excite public alarm over a subversive ideology which ignored national frontiers. In 1920, when the Red Army was advancing on Warsaw, the State Department hastened to approve of a loan of $50,000,000 to Poland. Nor was Russia invited to the Washington Naval Conference. Trade relations were virtually disrupted; and the Sinclair oil interests, which had acquired an option to exploit the petroleum deposits of northern Sakhalin, dropped the concession when the State Department shook an admonishing finger. Yet, at the same time, it is pleasant to record that the American Relief Administration extended its operations to Russia in 1921 and saved innumerable lives in a country scourged by civil war and famine (see p. 270).

Soviet-American trade began a tardy and timid revival in the early twenties on a rather hand-to-mouth basis of short-term credits. Russian demands for industrial and agricultural equipment were well sustained, the average two-way trade exceeding $36,000,000 yearly during 1921–25. Although Soviet dumping on the American market after 1929 was met by embargoes on certain products, the balance of trade was so favorable to the United States that the business community was not averse to a resumption of normal diplomatic relations. The successive Secretaries of State — Colby, Hughes, Kellogg — were unanimous in opposing recognition, even though recognition would have facilitated the grant of long-term credits to Russia and ensured the acceptance of Soviet gold for the liquidation of ordinary commercial debts.

The State Department pointed warningly to the Soviet repudiation of American loans advanced to the former Tsarist and Kerensky governments and to the confiscation of American property in Russia during the initial period of War Communism. But the business community refused to be haunted by these ancient ghosts. Other Great Powers without exception had recognized the Soviet Union by the late twenties and were seeking to extend their markets there. Finally, in 1931, the growing campaign for recognition was powerfully, if accidentally, reinforced by the Japanese, whose invasion of Manchuria encouraged Washington and Moscow to draw together against the common threat to their Pacific interests. The United States recognized the Soviet Union in 1933, in President Roosevelt's first year in office (see pp. 596–97). Evidently the Russian question was one more battle in the long-drawn war between economic and political exigencies in the United States.

THE UNITED STATES AND LATIN AMERICA

The safety of the Canal Zone and a growing economic investment had, by 1914, greatly intensified American interest in the vast areas south of the Rio Grande. The dollar diplomacy of President Taft and Secretary of State Knox, however, yielded to President Wilson's loftier doctrine of "constitutionalism." Responsible government based on fair elections presupposed respect for law and a degree of popular education, neither of which flourished in the republics of the South. Elections, during which the authorities scrupulously followed the admonition to allow the people to vote but to count the votes themselves, too often resulted simply in a meaningless rotation of office among the members or clients of the various ruling cliques. Endemic revolutions tended to erect dictators instead of representative assemblies. Since irresponsible authority was repugnant to President Wilson's theories of government, he intervened in South American politics no less frequently than had his predecessors, though doubtless from more altruistic motives.

Mexico, which had relapsed into confusion since the popular rising against the dictator Porfirio Diaz in 1910, proved a stern testing ground for the Wilsonian ideals. General Huerta, stigmatized by Wilson himself as a "desperate brute," had disposed of his rival by assassination in 1913, and had installed himself as ruler *de facto* in Mexico City. President Wilson, disregarding the Jeffersonian policy of recognizing established governments, refused to extend him diplomatic recognition or to sell arms to his supporters. When a German merchantman put in at Veracruz with a cargo of arms in April 1914, President Wilson authorized the bombardment and occupation of the city.

The subsequent exile of Huerta, and the election of a Mexican President acceptable to Wilson, did not close the episode. The colorful bandit Francisco Villa, heading a force of peasant irregulars dissatisfied with the slow pace of land reform, began a series of bloody raids on the properties of the large landowners. A border affray in New Mexico, deliberately provocative, was designed to incite armed intervention and to carry him into the presidency in Mexico on a wave of nationalist hatred of the "gringo." President Wilson promptly ordered General Pershing, with a force of cavalry, into Mexico. But Villa proved elusive, and the Mexicans resented the presence of foreign troops on their soil. President Wilson, foreseeing American involvement in Europe, recalled the expedition in February 1917.

The entry of the United States into the First World War met with a mixed reception in Latin America. Mexico, Argentina, and Chile, together with four other republics, remained neutral. Five, including Bolivia, severed diplomatic relations with Germany. Eight, including Brazil, ultimately declared war (see p. 95). The actual contribution by the belligerent states to the Allied war effort in terms of front-line personnel, except in the case of Brazil, was little enough. Vast supplies of grain and meat were shipped to Europe, and a war boom of considerable proportions supervened. The consequent accumulation of capital, and the difficulty of obtaining manufactured goods from embattled Europe, gave some impetus to industrialization.

The restoration of peace in 1918 did not augur favorably for inter-American relations. The "Colossus of the North" had emerged from the conflict more powerful and self-confident than ever. The failure of the United States to join the League of Nations was regarded by Latin Americans as proof that American imperialism was resolved to accept no external control, and that the southward economic penetration of the United States, which had assumed such threatening proportions since the outbreak of war, would continue in new strength. In 1914 there was not a single United States bank in South America; by 1921 there were fifty-four. Bolivian tin, Chilean nitrate, Brazilian coffee flowed northward in profusion, in return for automobiles from Detroit and machinery from Pittsburgh. By 1931, American investments in South America reached a total of over $5,000,000,000, an increase of 1,700 per cent since 1914. The impoverished politicos and opportunist generals who rose to the surface of Latin-American politics accepted the largesse readily. Their armies and police had to be paid, and their supporters rewarded. The problem of liquidating the loans could be bequeathed to succeeding administrations.

The Pan-American movement, it was hoped, would mollify the growing fear of "*el peligro Yanqui* (the Yankee peril) ," promote closer political and cultural relations between the republics of the Western Hemisphere, and form a complement to the Monroe Doctrine. The first International Conference of American States had been held at Washington in 1889, but the ambitious projects for a customs union, a common silver currency, and an arbitral system for inter-American disputes which had there been presented were all voted down with scant ceremony. The Latin-American delegates suspected that the chief motive in calling the Conference had been to woo South Americans from their liking for British sewing machines and textiles. The same unsleeping distrust had severely limited the usefulness of the three subsequent conferences held before 1914 and, as we have seen, the distrust increased rather than diminished after the restoration of peace in 1918. A most unfortunate impression was created, for example, at the Santiago Conference in 1923, when the United States delegation blocked a Uruguayan proposal for an American League of Nations based on the absolute equality of its members. It was concluded therefore that the United States still regarded the Monroe Doctrine as a right of protectorship over the southern republics and not as a guiding principle of policy freely accepted by equals.

Renewed intervention by the United States in the mid-twenties brought the whole problem of inter-American relations to a head. The firm grip on the economic life of Nicaragua, guaranteed since 1912 by the presence of American marines, had seemingly been relaxed by 1925, and the marines were withdrawn. But within a year there were fresh revolutionary commotions, and the marines were back again. The Democratic opposition in Congress kept up a steady drumfire of criticism, especially as the military operations in Nicaragua lacked Congressional sanction. President Coolidge, stressing the "moral responsibility" of the United States toward the governments north of Panama, sent Henry L. Stimson to Nicaragua in 1927 to mediate between the rebels and the regime in power. Stimson was able to arrange a fair election under United States auspices, the results of which were accepted by both parties. Clearly, as an alternative to military intervention and resulting ill will, mediation was full of interesting possibilities.

The role of "honest broker" was put to a more severe test in Mexico. The celebrated Article 27 of the Mexican constitution of 1917 had declared all lands, waters, and mineral deposits to be the property of the nation, which could expropriate them in the public interest. Oil lands were to be controlled by the government, which was empowered to lease them to private individuals for a period not exceeding fifty years. Foreign concessionaires were required not to invoke the protection of their government in the event of dispute. In 1925, President Calles of Mexico began not only to apply the law to foreign-held oil concessions, but to make it retroactive. The agent of United States mediation in this delicate situation was Dwight Morrow, the newly appointed ambassador to Mexico and a member of the firm of J. P. Morgan. By laying the "big stick" on the shelf, by displaying a maximum of good will, and by granting the Calles regime the American loan of which it was in dire need, Morrow was able to arrange a temporary settlement. He also recognized the competence of the Mexican Supreme Court to pronounce on the rights of the oil companies held by United States interests. In return, oil concessions granted before 1917 were confirmed, and the fifty-year limitation on foreign-held concessions was dropped.

In spite of this progress, a powerful undercurrent of resentment against the United States persisted in the debates of the Sixth Pan-American Conference at Havana in January 1928. Indeed, the future President Roosevelt wrote that feeling was "so bitter against the United States that it threatened to bring out not only hostile speeches, but definitely hostile action towards the United States." The high tariffs of the United States — a familiar topic — and the interventionist policy in Nicaragua were assailed in turn. A provocative resolution to the effect that no American state should intervene in the internal affairs of another received thirteen votes, and the eloquence of Charles Evans Hughes, at the head of the United States delegation, barely blocked its adoption. Hughes developed the familiar argument that if there was a breakdown of government, if "sovereignty faltered" in a Latin-American state, intervention to protect the lives and property of citizens of the United States was justified.

Hoover brought with him, as he brought to Anglo-American relations, a new expectation of peace. His good-will tour of Latin America at the end of 1928, while he was President-elect, suggested that his administration would persevere in the policy of mediation and nonintervention. It was not to be long before his conciliatory gifts were exercised to the full. The stock-market crash of 1929 reacted on South America as it had reacted on Germany, short-term loans were called in, unsold surpluses of South American grain, meat, cotton, and coffee accumulated, exports sank, by 1933, to one-third of their value in 1929 and, as must always happen in Latin America, economic distress gave rise to a new wave of revolutions.

But, this time, the subversive mutterings in Haiti — occupied by United States marines since 1915 — were stilled, not by the intrusion of more marines, but by the appointment of the Forbes Commission, which recommended withdrawal. Guggenheim, the American ambassador in Cuba, took an early opportunity to condemn the Platt Amendment,[4] and added: "Our relationship with Cuba, insofar as the special protection of American citizens is concerned, is, and should be clearly understood to be, suicidal to our relations with other American republics under international law." When, in October 1931, the Dominican Republic and Brazil announced the suspension of interest payments on their foreign debts, Washington made no move to put in the receivers, and it was slowly borne in upon the defaulting states that their insolvency would not be used as an excuse for intervention in their national affairs. The new regimes thrown up by revolution in Argentina, Brazil, Chile, Bolivia, and Peru were unhesitatingly recognized by the United States. In the words of the Clark Memorandum,[5] the Monroe Doctrine was no longer to be regarded as "an instrument of violence and oppression" against Latin America, but was what President Monroe had doubtless originally intended it to be, a guarantee of freedom and territorial integrity. Manifestly, as European markets shriveled and shrank under the freezing blast of the Depression, Latin-American good will became an increasingly valuable asset to the United States.

RETROSPECT

The foreign policy of the United States in the twenties was that of a nation struggling to avoid the ineluctable consequences of having become a World Power. Presidents from Wilson onward wrestled mightily with the double problem of ensuring America's immunity from world conflict and the desire of the nation to enjoy in peace the material benefits which flowed from its unique economic position.

The policy of political isolation, coupled with commercial and financial intercourse with the rest of the world, was the contradictory inheritance taken up by President Wilson's Republican successors. In spite of the most earnest and resolute efforts, the two aspects of the policy, especially as applied to Europe, became increasingly incompatible. Trade follows the flag, and the flag, it may be added, follows trade. Both are parts of a single complex, between which in the modern world there is scant practical distinction. "What the United States lacks most," Theodore Roosevelt once observed to André Tardieu, "is an understanding of the fact that we have interests all over the world. I wish every American felt that American policy is a world policy, and that we are and shall be identified in the future with the great questions. Some of us are aware of this. But the American people as a whole must be accustomed to the idea. They must learn to understand the meaning of our world interests." Tardieu, repeating these words to Senator Lodge two days later, received the following comment: "Let us understand each other. Our policy is a world policy insofar as commerce is concerned. But I hold that we should not intervene in purely political questions outside of America. It is neither our interest nor our tradition. My policy and, I think I may say, the policy of our Senate is the policy of George Washington." We could hardly have had the two alternatives more perfectly expressed.[6]

24 THE BREAKDOWN OF THE SETTLEMENT

THE LOCARNO ERA

The interwar period lasted twenty years — from the Peace Conference of Paris in 1919 to the outbreak of the Second World War in 1939. It fell into two phases, the first of which this book has called the Period of Settlement, and the second the Period of Crisis. Though there is no easy dividing line in time between the two periods, the main watershed of events, so to speak, was provided by the stock-market crash in the United States in 1929 and the Depression which followed thereafter.

To its own contemporaries the Period of Settlement gave a convincing impression of mankind in convalescence, progressively achieving peace. A stability was returning to the world such as had not been known since 1914. The nations of Europe in particular were growing conscious of an intense weariness, and felt perhaps that a pause in their overmastering anxieties was no more than their due. The Locarno Pact in 1925 expressed and emblemized a universal desire. It is curious, curious to the point of tedium, how it has been possible in this book to write of each nation, with very few exceptions, as it entered these relatively passive years of the later twenties, as having achieved its peace, tranquilized its frontiers, established an apparently stable constitution, and recovered something of its "normal" prosperity and well-being. The difficult transition from wartime to peacetime economy seemed to have been made; reconstruction was going forward; the immediate monetary chaos had passed; the gold standard was generally restored; the vexatious problems of reparations and international debts appeared settled; production indexes everywhere were healthily rising. Even so realistic an observer as Winston Churchill described the year 1928 as "The End of the World Crisis." [1] Not often does history, in its relentless continuity, so decelerate the onrush of events and provide so positive an interregnum.

France, for example, in the Locarno era, under Poincaré, was making her way from financial weakness to financial strength. The franc was stabilized, industries were humming, and Paris was full of tourists. Britain, under a safe Conservative government, was trying to forget her General Strike and her million unemployed. A strange quiet had descended upon her, and in all her recent history it is doubtful that she had gone through — we had almost said enjoyed — three years quite so uneventful as 1927, 1928, and 1929. Germany, under Stresemann, was on the highroad to recovery. Foreign loans were flowing, industry was being rationalized, the Dawes Plan no longer seemed so humiliating or so burdensome. Poland, under Pilsudski, looked as if she too had learned the lessons of stability. The Middle Danube — Austria perhaps excepted — was generally content and confident. Even Hungary, unhappy, truncated Hungary, could almost be said to have prospered for a time. Italy was busy building up her Corporative State. The Soviet Union was in the initial stages of its first Five-Year Plan.

In the Balkans and the Near East the story of these years was not so uniformly optimistic, but a slackening of the political tempo, a feeling of "trust and wait" was very noticeable. Yugoslavia had achieved a royal dictatorship. Albania had found a king in the person of Zog I. Greece had made her choice, a republican constitution — and Venizelos. Turkey had re-elected Mustapha Kemal to the presidency and thereby given the seal of approval to his program of domestic reforms. Syria was recovering from the Druze Rebellion and was perhaps hoping for a better administration of her mandate. Palestine seemed to be on the way to solving her many problems. Iraq was fast attaining independent nationhood. Arabia was firmly in the hands of Ibn Saud. Even Egypt for the moment had become less fractious and restive. Across the Atlantic, the Americas in general, and the United States in particular, were in the midst of an unprecedented boom. Across the Pacific, China was still full of discords, but Chiang Kai-shek had established his government at Nanking, and for the first time in years the country showed some promise of a unified and public-spirited administration. Only Japan was uneasy and was, in fact, approaching the end of her period of watchful waiting.

But the peace, we know, was not to be. The freedom from want and fear, however much it had become an established reality, however passionately it was desired by the people of all nations, lasted less than a decade. Yet here was a world which could have ranked beside the great Trajanic phases of history, when a sense of assured well-being had settled upon its citizens and was beginning to allow them once more the luxuries of security and permanence. It was a world of highly diffused science, democracy, and humanitarianism. It was still hitched to the star of Progress. Its defects were admittedly many, but they could be regarded as defects of detail, each full of remedial possibilities, each a challenge to enterprise. To the contemporaries of the Locarno era there seemed to be nothing that normal intelligence, good will, and the lapse of time would not somehow heal. Yet in the space of a few years this world dissolved into depression, terror, disbelief, and war.

THE FAILURE OF THE VERSAILLES SYSTEM

Of the immediate and superficial "causes" of the breakdown the first is commonly taken to be the errors of statesmanship in 1919. It was then, arguably, at the Peace Conference of Paris that the festering germs of decomposition were injected into the world's body politic, germs which, however long and deceptive the delay, would ultimately show their symptoms. The one fact that stands out at Paris is that few national statesmen — perhaps not one — who signed the peace treaties wholeheartedly subscribed to the avowed principles thereof, and that they committed a perjury which, in the fullness of time, would surely exact its retribution. The basic ideology of the treaties, for good or ill, derived from President Wilson. But the victor states, forgathering in Paris, were already in process of "psychological retreat." France paid the Wilsonian code no more than an expedient lip service. She had other plans for securing her place in the world. The United States and the British Dominions, and to some extent Britain herself, were withdrawing into isolationism. Japan, Italy, Poland, and the host of lesser Powers came, negotiated, and signed with mental reservations of one kind or another. As one statesman at Paris put it, "President Wilson is the only Wilsonian here, and sometimes not even he!" There has perhaps never been a peace in the long history of war and peace which wholly adhered to its principles and, on the strict literal view, Versailles interpreted its original terms of reference with remarkable accuracy. But the basic spiritual contradiction was undeniable.

Nor has there ever been a treaty of comparable importance that was a finished and perfect document. But Paris, in 1919, was obsessed with finality. So unique an opportunity to legislate for the millennium was unlikely to recur, and the most had to be made of it. The British plea for a frankly temporary treaty was overridden. The Americans with their eighteenth-century Constitution at the back of their minds, thought traditionally in terms of inflexible written documents. Despite its vagueness and despite Article 19, there was, for instance, an extraordinary rigidity in the League Covenant. President Wilson himself regarded the Covenant as the culmination of all democratic history, a sacred and inviolable testament. The treaties of Trianon and Neuilly, if anything, were more rigid than Versailles. We do not need great sagacity to anticipate the fortunes of a series of treaties in whose principles the signatories had so little faith and which contained so little provision for peaceful, legal change.

The settlement left Europe with a string of "danger spots," not quantitatively considerable in themselves, but likely to demand revision and, as it afterward turned out, likely to provide aggressor Powers with a handle for troublemaking in the future. Danzig in itself, for example, was no more of a danger spot than Tangier, nor the Sudetenland than many a canton in Switzerland; but Danzig and the Sudetenland were very gifts for diplomatic exploitation at an inconvenient time. The new smaller nationalities would also doubtless demand revision, and would demand it periodically. Europe, it was said, had been "Balkanized"; exaggerated nationalism had reached its *reductio ad absurdum*. An Empire such as Austria-Hungary had been broken into fragments. In "Intermediate Europe," in that band of territories running from Finland to Greece, there were no less than fifteen minor independent states. They had been created on the assumption of the permanent weakness or the political good faith of the two Powers, Germany and Russia, which stood on either side of them, an assumption which needed only a few years to falsify. The Versailles system, in its pretended finality, expected an unalterable territorial configuration in Europe. The Locarno Pact, the French alliances, the League of Nations itself, all were custodians of a new *status quo*. It has been said that a league of nations in 1850 would have opposed the unification of Italy or Germany or the westward expansion of the United States, and the League of 1920 likewise became a bastion of conservatism, resistive of changes which consequently could only be effected in defiance of it.

The smaller nations needed time if they were to achieve more than a superficial and passing stability. Belgium, created in 1831, enjoyed eighty years of peace before her first major international crisis; Czechoslovakia enjoyed just twenty, and ten of those years were spent in fear and economic depression. In particular, many of these states, at the behest of the Wilsonian code, had adopted democratic constitutions. The war itself was regarded as the triumph of democracy and as the triumph of the rights of smaller nations. But democracy was a form of government for which these states neither by their education nor by temperament were always fitted, and it was a form of government, moreover, which they should best have attempted under conditions of assured peace. The bewildering, crisis-packed thirties did not provide the most favorable atmosphere for their difficult experiment, and except for an occasional financial dole in extremity, no Great Power ever extended them a helping hand.

Then the breakdown has been blamed to a great extent on the isolationism of the United States. But that is only another way of saying that the United States, like its fellows at Paris, repudiated the Wilsonian code and looked shortsightedly to its own interest first. The United States — again like its fellows — cast aside the whole psychosis of the war as quickly as possible and tried to re-create the familiar conditions of its former peace and domesticity. But the seriousness of its defection was not merely that the United States was so powerful and could have enforced, if it had wished, a greater practical observance of the Wilsonian code, but rather that, in repudiating that code, it repudiated the entire Allied cause. By its participation in the war in 1917 the United States had given the Allies the assurance of victory, it had inspired their last year of fighting, it had received the enemy's surrender, it had been in a position to dominate the Peace Conference, it had provided the only responsible ideology that the Allies had ever really had; and, after all this hope and promise, it had lamely withdrawn, leaving nothing to fill the dreadful vacuum.

Britain's isolationism was never so complete, and from the ideological point of view was never so serious. But the result of the combined isolationism of the United States and Britain was to leave France with the hegemony of Europe, and France, as we have said, was not a strong protector. France always regarded the international scene with military eyes, and unhappily, as time was to show, she no longer had the moral power to make her military power effective. The First World War had been won for her with British, American — and Russian — help, and the peace, as she conceived the peace to be, could only be secured with a continuance of that help. Yet she pursued a foreign policy out of all proportion to her own unaided strength. She tried to create a Europe which could be instantly quelled at her discretion by the mere threat of a preventive war, and when, in 1936, the last chance for that war arose, she failed to act. She multiplied alliances with states whom she was to forsake or who were to forsake her. Admittedly, she was not altogether to blame. She was the victim of her inheritance. But hers was a tragic story nonetheless.

British and French policies in the postwar years were constantly at variance. In general, British policy aimed at removing the causes of unsettlement in Europe; the French policy aimed at holding them rigidly in check. In general, the British took a more universal view; the French localized their attention on their hereditary enemy, Germany. It is arguable that either policy might have succeeded if it had been followed to the exclusion of the other. But the simultaneous and vacillating prosecution of both was disastrous. If nothing else, France should surely have been counseled by military expedience. She needed Britain as a powerful friend; yet time and again she prevented the necessary friendship from forming. In every international conference, from the Peace Conference onward, she seemed to stand in determined opposition to her former ally. After 1936 she and Britain did reach an understanding. At that time, it could be said, she had proved her case, and her implacable attitude toward Germany had been more than justified. But at that time, it could also be said, a Franco-British understanding was already too late to be effective.

Germany's state of mind was an integral part of the postwar complex. Doubtless she greeted the coming of peace in 1918 with the same hysterical relief as her enemies; doubtless large sections of her people experienced the same reaction to pacifism; doubtless she had suffered, and doubtless she felt humiliated and abased. But it is difficult to believe that Germany, in her heart of hearts, ever accepted military defeat in the sense that Russia accepted military defeat in 1917 or France in 1940. She ascribed her collapse in November 1918 to the Allied blockade, to Allied propaganda, and to her own political disunity at home — in other words, to causes that were temporary and reparable. She always denied that she had ever met decisive defeat in the field. She felt not the least contrition over her share in the events that had led to the outbreak of the war. The Allies stopped their propaganda at the Armistice and made no attempt to create in Germany a mood receptive to the peace conditions they intended to impose, conditions to which Germany therefore reacted in anger and, above all, in sheer astonishment. In after years, German military theorists and historians became more and more exercised in mind over the real concatenation of trickery and blundering to which an uninvaded country and an "undefeated" army and navy had so unbelievably surrendered. The background for the revolt against the "stab in the back" which Hitler was to use was prepared indeed before Versailles was signed.

To this extent, therefore, Versailles fell between two stools. It was both too harsh and not harsh enough. Either it should have been harsh enough to induce that conviction of defeat Germany was so far from feeling, or it should have been lenient enough to remove the sense of deception and injured innocence which were the main emotions of the German mass consciousness throughout the Weimar period. It has been said that the Allies in Paris in 1919 were obsessed with finality. Germany, on the contrary, was obsessed with the idea that the situation was a passing misfortune. Here too, then, was a disparity of views loaded with danger.

Then it has been argued that the First World War had not really effected a solution of the disequilibrium which had originally precipitated it. Many of the problems of 1914, far from being solved, had since been intensified. The interwar world was like a man who had just undergone a serious operation, an operation which had preserved his life, but not properly restored his health. It was still the same man with the same pathology deep in his system. Moreover he had afterward committed the crowning folly of thinking he was his old self again and could pick up the threads of his former ways just where he had dropped them. With the exception of Russia, and perhaps Turkey and China, the nations of the world did everything in their power to go back to the conditions they had enjoyed in 1914. The vanquished were often more forward-looking than the victors; but the victors tried to recreate for themselves a peace as nearly as possible like the familiar peace they had once known. They treated the war, not as a painful process of transformation, but as an unfortunate, mistaken lapse, itself to be forgotten and its results to be reversed. We might well believe that the Great Peace of 1914 in retrospect bade fair to become a sort of golden age, much as the memory of Imperial Rome was to the Middle Ages, a legendary norm which subsequent generations would always envy and futilely aspire to restore.

In Chapter 1 we drew a rough picture of the world of 1914. In 1929, at the point of the second collapse, the picture was not very different, except for the sharpening of some of its outlines. Science and industry were still producing their peculiar social and economic maladjustments. The struggle for markets continued; capitalist enterprise was oversaturated; poverty was still the lot of the many. Peoples were more closely knit together, but civilized life was everywhere becoming more complicated and expensive. Breakdowns in the system, if and when they occurred, were correspondingly more dangerous and irreparable; weapons, war, and the consequences of war were becoming incomparably more frightful. Mass politics was a phenomenon of tremendous, scarcely comprehended potentiality. Nationality was still a powerful force, both for culture and anarchy. The eight "problem" nations which we singled out in Chapter 1 (see pp. 4–5) were still in the forefront of international crisis, and none could say in what combination they might clash once more. The wheel of causation which set the First World War in motion was still grinding itself out to a finish.

Nationality, it is now the fashion to point out, is not an inevitable part of the natural order of things. Modern nationalism was a post-Napoleonic movement with a clear-cut, traceable history, and not necessarily a permanent and eternal institution. Conceivably it could enjoy its crowded hour and disappear. As we write, we do not know if the nation-states of Europe, Asia, and America will have become anachronisms before our time is past. The Second World War, in many ways, was already less nationalistic than the First — as witness the prevalence of sincere ideological quislingism — though the fervent patriotic defense of Britain, Russia, and China, and the resistance and partisan movements in Nazi Europe and Japanese Asia showed equally that nationalism was still no mean force in human affairs. Yet the Peace Conference of 1919 was a conference of nations and gave birth to a League of Nations. President Wilson celebrated the marriage of self-determination and nationalism, oblivious of the fact that the two parties to the contract were both mortal and might disappoint his hope of a compatible and fecund union. And it was not long before economists began to decry the egotistic nationalism of the interwar years with its shortsighted and mutually ruinous competition and to advocate the formation of larger economic blocs. Catholics fondly looked back to the nationless "one world" of the Middle Ages. Communists looked forward to a Communist state embracing the globe. Our immediate future would seem to belong less to the old national units than to supranational aggregations like the United States, the British Commonwealth, or the Soviet Union.

THE CRISIS OF DEMOCRACY

It is easy to be wise after the event. It is easy to say that the historian's business is to see mistakes and blunders, even while he tries to appreciate the intolerable difficulties under which great decisions have usually to be made. Yet, after all, the Peace Conference of Paris could only legislate against the ills it knew. So much of what we have been discussing in this chapter is blamable on no one, nor can we from the shallow depths of our professorial chairs carp and quibble over historical transactions whose ultimate motivations, even in the detachment of afterthought, we still hardly understand ourselves. Not the least tragic part of the situation in 1919 was the incapacity of victor statesmanship, through no fault of its own, to rise above its own limitations. There was always an element of human ignorance and helplessness at the Conference which it is terrible to contemplate. While the Conference was absorbed in the familiar idiom of frontiers, minorities, armaments, and reparations, the real crisis was being prepared at quite other levels. Versailles was rooted in a mentality that was passing, if not already past. Economics, for instance, except for reparations and certain minor tariff provisions, hardly figured in the peace treaties at all. But, in the event, this was the field in which the Locarno era first began to show its cracks and the world at large to slip avalanche-like toward the dread thirties.

The economic system which then broke down was part of the sociocultural complex which had flourished in Europe since the Reformation. It had been built on a frame of expanding populations, expanding territories, expanding wealth, and expanding material knowledge and technical skills. In many countries it had become integrally linked to a way of life which we call democracy. The British, American, and French Revolutions, the development of the British Empire, and the wars of liberation of the nineteenth century were all part of an economic-democratic movement which was confidently expected to spread throughout the world. This was the vision of 1914 — and of 1919.

Thus, to many of its participants, the First World War was interpretable as the conquest of the last remaining strongholds of feudal and aristocratic tyranny. The whole course of history, from the Anglo-Saxon moot to the League of Nations, could be written as the progressive liberation of man, culminating in a glorious, cataclysmic "war to end wars." By 1918 all the great autocracies had gone down to defeat — Tsarist Russia, Ottoman Turkey, Imperial Austria, Prussian Germany — not to forget Manchu China. Their oppressed peoples were set free; other oppressed peoples, from Ireland to the Philippines, were on their way to freedom; new groups were admitted to the family of independent nations. By 1919, it seemed, the world had at last been made safe for democracy.

Yet, in twenty years, the gains of centuries of blood, toil, and tears were lost. Democracy at the moment of its greatest triumph seemed to be a spent and sinking force. The Russian Revolution, it seemed to many, had fallen from its once high ideals and issued in a political system no less tyrannous than the one it had overthrown. Dictatorships of one form or another appeared in Turkey, Italy, and the Balkans. National Socialism was shortly to appear in Germany. Even France, the classic home of revolution, was soon to be at grips with her Fascist "Leagues." And all this happened, not only in so short a time, but often — and herein was the most frightening feature — as a voluntary renunciation. It happened not from reasoned argument, but in obedience to some blind upsurge of primitive passions. Men sold themselves to new masters not in horror and detestation, but of their free and almost fanatic choice, and exulted in their slavery.

The new dictators had confidence, adventurousness, and extraordinary dynamism. They had, in fact, everything that current democracy lacked. Far from holding its accustomed place in the van of progress, democracy seemed to have become the victim of its own complacency and felt itself to be conservative, nostalgic, and outdated. Surviving democratic states, which had known a vigorous parliamentary life and vigorous liberal institutions, stood on the defensive, jealously hugging the remnants of their riches, and encumbering themselves with bureaucratism and petty party corruption. Moreover, as events were to show so painfully, democracy also lost its accustomed tactical advantage in the great struggle of international politics. By a curious quirk of fate, its old strength was now its weakness. The liberal methods of open debate, free speech, tolerance of opposition, and frank and honest dealing even with enemies — however much they might still withstand a long-term trial of strength — were at an initial loss against totalitarian regimentation, propaganda, secrecy, deception, and surprise decisions. If it was to be a matter of the survival of the fittest, the prospects for democracy were problematical indeed.

We have said on an earlier page of this book that the real inwardness of this Age of Conflict is still largely hidden from us. But our ignorance, however pardonable, does not allay the urgency of speculation. We find about us today a goading, agonized thinking over the state into which the world has fallen, as if all civilization was engaged in a mass searching of conscience and confession. A large and growing literature descants upon the contemporary day of wrath. The real question seems to be, not only to try to explain a convulsion like Nazism, for example, in terms of Versailles, or American isolationism, or British complacency, or French vindictiveness, or even the Depression with its train of misfortunes, but to ask what sort of catalepsy had smitten the democratic peoples that so incredible a disorder should ever have been allowed to come to birth in the first place. The devilish works we have lately witnessed could not have begun to happen in Lincoln's day, or Theodore Roosevelt's, or Palmerston's, or Gladstone's. Why then in ours?

The deeper conflict of this Age of Conflict is not only political and economic, and modern history, in the last analysis, like the history of every time and clime, is governed by those imponderables which for want of a better name we call spiritual values. Politics is not enough, and more than a string of danger spots woven into a quarrelsome continent must be adduced to show how the peace of 1919 so utterly failed, how the victory on the Western front grew into the defeat of Munich, how step by step, the initiative in world affairs came to be transferred from the forces of law and order and progress, as we conceive them to be, to the forces of destruction. A future generation may well look back on this Age of Conflict of ours, as we look back on the French Revolution or the Reformation or the Fall of Rome, and see in it not so much the bankruptcy of a political and economic order, such as was doubtless more apparent to their respective contemporaries, but the bankruptcy of another order altogether.

The civilization, the whole sociocultural complex of today, in whatever detail or direction it may be expressed, reveals a deep-seated malaise. We have only to consider our chaotic arts and music, our styleless architecture, our literary aberrations, our empty churches, our overvocationalized and careerist education, our extravagant, unnatural urban life, our hectic pleasures, our declining birth rate, our uprooted homes and sundered families, our humorless cynicism, our falling standards of duty and collective obligation; and it is against such a background that we can best see the why and wherefore of our political and economic trends, our nationalisms and minorities, our frontiers and armaments, our regimes and constitutions, our Versailles and Locarnos, and all the other materials of this history.

As we write, a Second World War has come to an end, and once more a political settlement is proceeding. The readers of this book will probably belong to those peoples who won the second military victory, a victory greater than the first, and who can decisively influence that settlement. For these peoples there is strength and hope and great responsibility. That we shall have peace, that liberal ways of life will continue to flourish in our homelands, for this we work and watch. But whatever may happen or however it may happen, the essential values of our civilization must be made new, and that renewal must take precedence over whatever secular settlement there may be. We do not have to be philosophers or theologians to be able to say that the only victory and peace worth having are the victory and peace of the spirit, and that we would go gratefully and joyfully through any hell on earth if it meant a further step toward the redemption of our human race.

It is our misfortune, but also our privilege, to be the witnesses and participants in one of the epochal transformations of history. The future is full of difficulty. But civilization is not set in motion, nor its achievements won, except in the face of difficult things.

PART THREE

THE PERIOD OF CRISIS

25 THE DEPRESSION

THE CRISIS OF CAPITALISM

The "free" economic system of 1914 was well tried and old. It had been born some four centuries before in an age of revolt and reformation. It had become an integral part of "Western" civilization and of the "Western" way of life. It implied the freedom of the individual to certain "rights," the freedom to own and bequeath property, and to buy and sell for profit in competition with other individuals. In particular, it implied the abandonment of the former, medieval strictures against usury, and it permitted — nay honored and sanctified — the whole principle of lending and investing at interest.[1]

The system became linked with the prevailing mechanistic views of nature. The old classical "political economy" was a quantitative science. Wealth, industry, and trade were forces obeying laws as regular as gravitation. Economic incentives, such as profits and power, competition and war, were "natural" incentives. Certainly, in the early days of the system, supply and demand, prices and wages, deflation and inflation, booms and slumps could be almost mathematically equated. Credit, foreign exchange, purchasing power, the flow of goods, the vagaries of markets, the rise and fall of stocks, all seemed to regulate themselves with machine-like precision. The basic element in the system was money, and money, like an element in chemistry, had measurable, invariable properties. And money was conceived of as so much gold or the equivalent of so much gold. Foreign exchange operated in relation to a universal "gold standard."

In such a system the function of the state was negative. The state passed laws against obvious professional malpractices, but otherwise its noninterference with private enterprise was a principle as sacrosanct as a commandment. The state satisfied its own modest requirements — for example, its military and naval supplies — like any other buyer in the open market. It issued loans and banked its revenues like any individual capitalist. Nothing was ever heard in these halcyon days about full employment or social security. Appropriately the system was called *laissez-faire*.

The system was delicately adjusted and extraordinarily intricate. But, on the whole, it worked — for a time. It was responsible for the vast European expansion from the sixteenth to the twentieth centuries. Its harshness and egotism were often tempered in practice by the contemporary Christian conscience. Its very efficiency required that certain decencies should be voluntarily observed. Commercial probity developed its own checks and counterchecks. Honesty was usually found to be the best policy. Early business was often as paternalistic and benevolent as the feudalism it had replaced. But a time came when gradually the system worked no longer. The codes of the gentleman and the trader were fundamentally incompatible. The contemporary Christian conscience by itself could not control or succor the squalor and hideousness which unrestricted private enterprise left in its train. And then certain economists began to point out that, quite apart from its social consequences, the system was ultimately self-destructive. The logical conclusion of competition was the trust or corporation; the "small" man was undercut out of existence; the means of production, in Marxian parlance, became concentrated in fewer and fewer hands; new managerial techniques favored the creation of large combines. At the same time the commercial and colonial rivalry between nations increased. Especially after 1900, too many nations had industrialized themselves and were in a state of open or tacit warfare in fields which had formerly been mainly the preserve and monopoly of England. Mammon, like Cronus, was devouring his own children.

During the nineteenth century the state had perforce to legislate against the growing social evils of the system. The workers organized themselves to demand a fairer share in the plenty which their labor was producing. But in some ways more significant even than this, the state itself forsook its negative role and began actively to interfere in business. Napoleon III and Bismarck, each at the head of a "bourgeois empire," were very well aware of the political potentialities of trade. In the British colonial Empire, military power and commercial power were so interdependent as to be indistinguishable and were openly acknowledged and encouraged to be so. The new Japan founded its statehood upon a deliberate economic reconstruction. Foreign commercial treaties and foreign lending interlocked with foreign policy. Then the state tried its hand at management and ownership. In most countries the state ran the postal and telegraph services; in many it ran the railroads, and in a few a central bank. Finally, in the First World War, the state found itself compelled sooner or later to take over the entire national economy. It controlled raw materials, prices, wages, distribution, foreign exchange, and often labor; it made bulk purchases; it pared down excess profits by unprecedented taxation — all to the consequent overthrow of hitherto accepted economic principles.

After the First World War, the nations tended to revert to "orthodoxy." Even revolutionary Russia introduced her NEP. The ideals of the time were "security" in politics and "normalcy" in business, and in the twenties both seemed in fair way of attainment. Appearances were deceptive. Many nations, in the immediate postwar years, enjoyed a sudden boom, followed, after short relapse, by the steadier, almost world-wide recovery of the Locarno era. But the disruptive forces were only quiescent, awaiting an opportunity to reveal themselves. The Depression which supervened, as we now believe, was not just a more than usually severe business recession, but the veritable crisis of capitalism. Thereafter, step by step, we observe the total reversal of the older attitudes. Individual rights, once sacrosanct, except in time of war, were called into question in a time of peace; private enterprise gave way to various experiments in collectivism; economists theorized in terms, not of profits and prices, but of full employment, levels of expenditure, maximum output, and "freedom from want"; state interference assumed the proportions of "planning." Money ceased to be a tangible quantity convertible into gold and became more and more a statistical and bookkeeping algebra. The gold standard was generally abandoned.

But into the high metaphysics of these questions we do not intend to enter here. There is literature enough and to spare on the Depression easily accessible to the interested student. In the last chapter we hinted at our views as to the real sickness of this generation. Let us be content to say that the Depression of the early thirties developed from a number of causes, some arising directly out of the destruction and dislocation of the First World War, some arising out of a whole concentration of causes over four centuries of economic history, but all coming simultaneously into operation as if guided by some diabolical fate; let us also say that the Depression was assuredly the turning point of the twenty years' truce, that it destroyed the illusion of the postwar settlement, and that it created conditions which led directly to those monstrous shapes of things to be in our unhappy era — Japanese Manchukuo, Nazi Germany, Fascist Ethiopia, Fascist Spain, and the Second World War; and let us confine ourselves in this chapter, without theoretical argument, to a general historical review of the world's economic condition between 1919 and 1933.

THE POSTWAR BOOM

We have said that, in the immediate postwar years, many nations — notably the victor nations and former neutrals — enjoyed a sudden boom. Peace brought new demands, reopened old trade connections, and abolished a great part of the restrictions and rationings which wartime needs had imposed. Tired and self-denying populations celebrated their victory and their release in a feast of spending. Enterprises which the war had postponed or interrupted were put in hand; new companies started up like dry springs after rain. Reconstruction created all kinds of new markets. Demobilized armies were absorbed back into civilian occupations and brought new buying power with them. Fortunes were made by trades and industries which were in a position to take advantage of the situation.

But the postwar boom of 1919–20 was a boom rather of prices than of production. When the last war contract had been completed or canceled, when the last demobilized soldier had been refitted with civilian clothes, when the last bit of wartime savings or deferred pay had been spent, the nations were faced with the irreducible tasks of rebuilding their economies on a proper peacetime basis. The inevitable relapse was already under way in March 1919 when, reputedly at the behest of London, the Allies unpegged the currencies which they had so carefully stabilized each in terms

of the other during the war. The relapse started about a year later in Japan
and the United States, the two nations where the war had overstimulated
industry and where the public was especially prone to speculation. By the
end of 1920 the postwar boom was at an end; prices in every part of the
trading world had begun to decline. The nations of Europe, victors and
vanquished, were soon floundering in a sea of unbalanced budgets, chaotic
exchanges, and unemployment, a sea as full of monsters as any medieval
chart, but one fated to become all too familiar.

WAR DEBTS

The nations after the First World War were all enmeshed in a network
of indebtedness. The greater part of the costs of the war had been met by
loans; the new succession states were often established on loans; the huge
fabric of reconstruction and relief was erected on loans; new minor wars in
Central and Eastern Europe were fought on loans. Most of the obligations
had been contracted under conditions of haste and emergency, the terms
varied from one obligation to another and were often still to be negotiated,
and generally no interest had yet been paid. Britain, to take one example,
had collected by means of increased taxation one-third of her war cost of
£10,000,000,000 at the time that cost was being incurred. In this regard her
effort had been quite exceptional, for few countries had made substantial
wartime increases in their taxation. Her government expenditure in the
four years of war had exceeded her total government expenditure during
the preceding two centuries. Her national debt rose from £711,000,000 in
August 1914 to £8,078,000,000 at the end of 1919. The national debts of
forty of the world's Powers rose from $30,000,000,000 to $220,000,000,000
over the same period.

In August 1922, over the name of Balfour, the British Government boldly
advocated the cancellation of all wartime indebtedness. From a purely bookkeeping point of view Britain herself stood to lose thereby. But she had
adopted the policy of general cancellation after the Napoleonic Wars, and
on that occasion, on the long-term view, she had had no cause for regrets.
"His Majesty's Government," so ran the Balfour note of 1922, "content
themselves with saying once again that so deeply are they convinced of the
economic injury inflicted on the world by the existing state of things that
this country would be prepared (subject to the just claims of other parts of
the Empire) to abandon all further rights to German Reparation and all
claims to repayment by Allies, provided that this renunciation formed part
of a general plan by which this great problem could be dealt with as a
whole and find a satisfactory solution."

But the biggest of the creditor nations was the United States, and there
Balfour's pleas fell upon deaf ears. On the contrary, the United States resented the triangular connection between debts and debts, and reparations
and debts, which European statesmanship was always trying to establish,
and insisted that there must be no confusing of obligations separately contracted. As President Coolidge tartly asked, "They hired the money, didn't

they?" and presumably, so long as the incorrigible peoples that inhabited the European Continent wanted to fight wars, they must not be released from the consequences thereof (see p. 368).

Creditor nations were therefore constrained to invite their debtors "with the most perfect courtesy, and in the exercise of their undoubted rights" — in the words of the Balfour note — to conclude funding agreements with them. The first of Britain's funding agreements was with Rumania in October 1925, and those with Italy, France, Portugal, Greece, and Yugoslavia followed in 1926 and 1927. Rates of interest were charged proportionately to the presumed paying capacity of the debtors and averaged 1½ per cent; at these rates, only about a third of the original obligations would ever have been paid off. Meanwhile American funding agreements with thirteen debtor states were negotiated between 1922 and 1926 (pp. 367–68). If reparations are included in the general international debt complex, the following totals result: Germany had eleven creditors; the United States had sixteen debtors, Britain seventeen, and France ten. Twenty-eight states in all were involved as either creditors or debtors or both. In the year of the Hoover Moratorium, 1931–32, the transfers totaled $750,000,000.[2]

ECONOMIC NATIONALISM

The nations always gave the best reasons for their respective tariff policies of the interwar years, but the result was an anarchy of economic egotism. Even among former Allies tariffs were little changed, or were changed in an upward direction. Financial stringencies were always demanding new sources of revenue. A nation's trade needed to be defended against depreciated currencies abroad. Tariffs made a good bargaining point in negotiations between one government and another. The new succession states particularly, now building up their national economies de novo, often from shattered foundations, were overvulnerable to competition. But more than all these things, a sort of perfervid nationalism, partly idealistic, partly military, required that a nation protect itself against imports which could endanger its own "key" industries. National self-sufficiency appeared to confer strength and immunity; for the smaller nations it was almost a part of the very regalia of sovereignty.

France and Italy made energetic tariff increases. Germany followed suit from 1925 onward, as soon as she was released from commercial restrictions under Versailles. The succession states of the Middle Danube walled themselves about with tariffs and dismembered an area which the elementary facts of history and geography had marked out as one for close economic union. Even Britain forsook her traditional free-trade principles (see p. 563). The United States introduced the Fordney-McCumber tariff of 1922 and the Smoot-Hawley tariff of 1929–30, which represented perhaps the two most exaggerated and indefensible tariff increases in the history of any nation (see p. 368).

President Wilson had once proclaimed the need for "the removal, so far as possible, of all economic barriers and the establishment of an equality of trade conditions among the nations consenting to the peace and associating themselves for its maintenance." But, in practice, economic disarmament, like military disarmament, was beyond the will of the nations to achieve.

THE PROBLEM OF GOLD

One item in the program of normalcy was stabilization. International trade could make no headway with fluctuating currencies. Exchanges had to find their levels, and between 1919 and 1925 we find one group of nations resorting to deflation, if they could, and another group allowing inflation to take its own sweet way with the value of their money. Britain was the foremost example of the deflationary group. At the end of the war the pound was still pegged at 98 per cent of its dollar parity. But it fell as soon as the peg was withdrawn, it fell after the collapse of the postwar boom of 1919–20, and it fell again during the first Labor government in 1924, each time being painfully forced back to higher and supposedly healthier levels. In 1925, when Churchill was Chancellor of the Exchequer, Britain restored the gold standard at the full prewar value of the pound.

Doubtless there was something inviolable about the old sterling parity. It typified the strength and stability of the greatest of trading nations. It was at least an honest acknowledgment of debts and contractual obligations at their original values. Britain herself hoped that she might be setting an example, and that other nations might follow her back to parity, with beneficial results to all concerned. But the restoration of the gold standard put Britain at an "unfair" disadvantage with less generous rivals. Every debased currency could undersell her in foreign markets or even at home. Nor could she, on account of her intricate and menacing labor situation, reduce wages, extend hours, or take other orthodox means to meet the competition. Old-fashioned methods of ownership and operation, notably in the coal industry, prevented her from undertaking any very rapid or revolutionary schemes of rationalization. As we have seen, Britain patiently bore her burden of unemployment all through the recovery years of the Locarno era rather than break with her financial traditions and prestige. Perhaps she found some consolation in the fact that other members of the deflationary group, notably Australia and Japan, went through much the same distressing experiences as herself.

The inflationary group, provided the inflation was not allowed to get out of control and provided it was not accompanied by speculation, appeared at first to have the best of the bargain. For example, the French franc after many vagaries was stabilized in 1927 at about 25 to the dollar, a fifth of its prewar value. France was evidently content to accept a scaling-down of the value of domestic savings and capital, and a scaling-up of the cost in francs of her foreign obligations. Inflation enabled her to write off a goodly slice of her internal debt, to compete on favorable terms in foreign markets, to encourage the repatriation of capital which had escaped abroad, and eventually to buy gold in enormous quantities to replenish her gold reserve.[3]

Meanwhile her unemployment was negligible. To what extent France was motivated in all this, as in all her postwar policies, by ulterior political ends is not easy to determine. Perhaps it is fairest to give French statesmen and bankers the benefit of the doubt and to say that, in the beginning at least, they, like all the other experts of the day, were only imperfectly aware of the distant and indirect consequences of their acts.

Germany, another inflationary country, went too far and suffered the collapse of 1923 at the time of the Ruhr crisis. She subsequently restored her currency in the form of the new gold unit, the Reichsmark and, backed by foreign loans, she shared the prosperity of the Locarno era (see p. 167). The case of Soviet Russia was perhaps different; for there inflation was part of a deliberate policy to exterminate capital and pauperize the capitalist.

Yet however desirable stabilization might be, it was mechanically impossible if the point of reference was unsteady or shifting. The maldistribution of gold — or, more correctly, the change in the "normal" distribution of gold as it had been in 1914 — was perhaps the one "technical" cause of the failure to stabilize postwar exchanges and keep them stable. The maldistribution had already begun in the first year of the war, when so many currencies had gone off gold and when belligerents resorted more and more to gold as the most acceptable way of meeting the huge war bills abroad which they could not meet with loans. By 1919 the Scandinavian countries, the Netherlands, Switzerland, Argentina, Brazil, Japan, and above all the United States measured their wartime profits in their enormously increased gold reserves. After 1919 reparation payments and debts continued in much the same way to fleece certain Powers for the apparent benefit of others.

In the network of international indebtedness the principal creditor country, as we have said, was the United States, and the United States was entrenched behind a dollar value of forbidding height. But the great problem of transfer, in respect of both reparations and debts, was at first hardly understood. Before 1914 the transfer of funds had been a commonplace of international banking, and in 1919, though the sums were enormously greater, the creditor countries vaguely expected that the same processes of transfer would continue to operate. It was not easy for the creditor countries to realize that the only way a debtor could now support the burden of his payments was by maintaining an export surplus, which in turn prejudiced the creditor countries' employment situation at home. When, moreover, the creditor countries, and in particular the United States, began of set purpose to "protect" themselves against a too inconvenient influx of foreign goods — the Fordney-McCumber tariff of 1922 is a case in point — the export surplus became correspondingly more difficult to dispose of. The net result could only be a flow of gold to the creditor countries and ultimately to the United States. And the net result of the flow of gold was a fall of prices in Europe, the further reduction of purchasing power, and the further reduction of the capacity of the debtors to find more gold with which to make their payments.

The United States tried to disembarrass itself of the unwelcome pile of treasure and lent generously — too generously, as it proved — to Germany and Central Europe. But an irreducible residue of gold became sterilized. The situation was aggravated by France's policy of using her devalued franc for the purpose of buying gold, which she immediately consigned to a "war chest" and so sterilized also.[3] Gold-hoarding, whether in ancient Persia, sixteenth-century Spain, or eighteenth-century India, or in any other of the classic examples, never yet redounded to the benefit of the hoarder. But by 1929 half the world's gold supply lay in two countries, the United States and France, and the rest were going dangerously short. Meanwhile countries, deflationary or inflationary, were seeking to return to a gold standard and defeating their very object by thus creating an abnormal demand for gold. Visiting American financial experts, invited to reorganize some derelict national currency, invariably laid down three absolute desiderata: stability, a new central bank, and a gold reserve.

In the twenties every struggling country wanted gold. Mining centers, such as South Africa or Canada, stimulated their gold production but could not satisfy the universal hunger. Several countries, notably Germany, Austria, Czechoslovakia, Yugoslavia, Rumania, Italy, and Finland, adopted the practice of backing their currencies with *Devisen;* that is, with paper funds payable in foreign currencies which were themselves convertible into gold. The practice economized gold, and it may have been unavoidable, but it made a number of "poorer" currencies dependent on the "richer," with disastrous results if the "richer" should ever prove unstable.

Ill-advised international lending in the interwar years was a contributing cause of the economic unsettlement. In the old days before 1914, London had been the main provider of Continental loans, and London had long experience and was traditionally wary. But after 1919, Holland, Sweden, Switzerland, the United States, and other "profiteers" of the war began to interest themselves in the business and almost competed with one another in the dangerous sport of international finance. France also became a keen operator; but, as usual, France's lending was colored with political motives, and her loans were mainly military loans to her allies in Central and Eastern Europe.

However, when a situation arises where some countries have too much money and some too little, abnormal lending is bound to ensue. As soon as stabilization created the illusion of security, money on easy terms was to be had for the asking. Banks and investment corporations in the United States, supported by the aggressive salesmanship of those days, almost forced their idle funds on Berlin, Vienna, Budapest, Warsaw, Rome, and other capitals — not forgetting Latin America — and it would have been more than human if indigent governments and municipalities had not succumbed to so pressing a temptation. Borrowed funds paid Germany's reparations under the Dawes Plan, and foreign investments were sunk in municipal expenditures in Germany — parks, sports grounds, swimming pools, planetaria, huge public buildings in the "Germanic" style of architecture — which were often unproductive or only tardily yielded a proper interest. No doubt Germany found it an easy and stimulating game to pay her obligations with loans, and the loans with more loans, ad infinitum. An interesting cycle was set up;

American money poured into Germany; Germany paid reparations; the recipients of reparations, mainly Britain and France, paid their war debts to America. The situation might seem ridiculous if, by the standards of the day, it had not been perfectly in order. But it was certainly very dangerous. American speculators, despite the extent to which they had been playing the international market, still traditionally regarded foreign lending as a sideline to be exploited for a time and then dropped if and when more attractive opportunities arose at home. By 1928 those opportunities were present, and idle funds found better use in Wall Street than in Central Europe. Money for Germany was becoming tight; the old loans were harder to come by. Then, in 1929, Wall Street collapsed. Germany, and indeed all the nations of Central Europe, which had been refloating their ships of state on the assumption that the American tidewater would flow indefinitely, suddenly found the precious stream drying up from under them.[4]

A related and particularly vicious phenomenon of the twenties was the nervousness of short-term capital. At a time of uncertainty it was only to be expected that capital should fight shy of the usual opportunities for investment and prefer to remain in a liquid state. An atmosphere of bankruptcy and default was not conducive to the sale of stocks and bonds, however tempting the prospectus or however persuasive the salesman might be. Thus whenever rumor had it that this or that exchange was to be devalued, or that this or that country was to go off gold, vast amounts of capital took fright and disappeared to safer bourns. Heavy floating balances might be piled up in London, New York, Amsterdam, or in other reputedly stable centers — current account balances, time deposits, treasury bills, government securities — balances liable to withdrawal at short notice, useless, parasitic money, an embarrassing burden wherever it chose to alight. Finance companies were established in Switzerland, Luxembourg, and Liechtenstein especially to handle these deposits of "funk money."

There was a certain amount of professional gambling in foreign exchanges. Francs or marks or pesetas offered more excitement and a quicker turnover than any stock market. But there was also considerable precautionary investing in foreign funds. Wealthy Continental magnates would keep a secret account across some accessible frontier. Investment companies and even insurance companies built up several foreign balances, hoping perhaps that somewhere they had struck security. The *Devisen,* with which some governments backed their currencies, were entirely analogous. The French Treasury and the Bank of France, probably the worst examples of the practice, for years held sterling and dollar balances of over $1,000,000,000, a sum which constituted a kind of political blackmail, and which they were not averse to using as such.

THE LOCARNO ERA AND PARTIAL RECOVERY

Debts and reparations, unstable currencies and restricted tariffs notwithstanding, the later twenties did give the impression of a world being rapidly restored. The political benignities were reflected in a few flourishing years. The recovery was not uniform. Britain suffered the General Strike of 1926, and Japan the financial panic of 1927. But the European continent and the Americas enjoyed a productiveness and well-being that recalled — and sometimes surpassed — the good old days before 1914. The standardization of manufactured goods, new and original advertising and salesmanship, new capital construction, housing and commercial building, the development of the automobile, motion picture, radio, civilian flying, domestic laborsaving devices, all represented a solid body of achievement. A World Economic Conference met in Geneva in May 1927 with the express idea of consolidating the evident progress. The Conference discussed the further standardization of manufactured goods and the possible all-round reduction of tariffs. It listened to speeches, and it passed resolutions, of restrained optimism. In the words of its president, the Conference did seem "to mark the beginning of a new era, during which international commerce will successively overcome all obstacles in its path that unduly hamper it and resume that general upward movement which is at once a sign of the world's economic health and the necessary condition for the development of civilization." The Geneva Conference of 1927 remains today almost a curiosity among international conferences. Within a few years, far from resuming a general upward movement, international commerce was to lose one-quarter of its physical volume and two-thirds of its monetary value!

But while it lasted, it was in the United States that the recovery of the Locarno era was most spectacularly illustrated. Between 1925 and 1929 the American people enjoyed an unprecedented boom. New York was its center, and Wall Street was the very symbol of easy money. Technically, the boom had resulted from a deliberate policy of credit inflation on the part of the Federal Reserve Bank, and it presented all the usual phenomena of an ascending "business cycle." But, even more than this, it was a psychological reaction to the successful part the United States had played in the war and in the reconstruction of Europe. The United States had become on a greatly magnified scale what England had become after 1815. It was a young, expanding country whose resources had contributed decisively to a great military victory. Broken empires had adopted its democracy and begged for its largesse. It seemed to hold a lien on the wealth of all the world. European debts and reparations in a vast flood, by whatever circuit they flowed, found their eventual destination in its capacious lap. These were the grand, robust "roaring twenties." They were the days of one automobile to every four persons, and one telephone and one frigidaire to every other home. While other nations might expiate their follies and misfortunes in poverty, the United States gathered up the riches of its own vast continent and the tributes of a stricken Europe in the proud assumption that it was receiving no more than the just rewards of its peculiar virtues and energy. Only a few lonely Cassandras half-hesitatingly complained that the great boom was not being paced by a corresponding increase in production, that the prosperity of towns and industries was not being matched in agriculture, and that the fantastic speculation on the stock market bore no real relation to the intrinsic values thereof.

THE YOUNG PLAN

The Young Plan makes a convenient point at which to start the history of the Depression. It was a contradictory transaction, and its mood, so to speak, showed both the confidence and the anxiety of the time. It was clearly predicated on the continuance of the progressive conditions lately obtaining in Germany and in Europe, and yet at the same time it somehow contrived to insinuate more than one doubt as to the ultimate permanence of those conditions. It was negotiated in the noonday glow of the twenties; it was finally signed in January 1930, when the United States had already passed into the stock-market crash, and Germany was beginning to feel the first chills of the "economic blizzard."

The Dawes Plan was described in an earlier chapter (pp. 166–67). Since its signature in 1924 it had functioned fairly smoothly. Germany's annuities under the Plan had been paid on the nail and in full, albeit, as everyone knew, they had been paid with the help of foreign loans. But the Dawes Plan had never been intended as much more than a temporary settlement to tide over a crisis and, in particular, it had still left undetermined the total sum of Germany's reparations. The Germans themselves were not averse to reopening the whole reparations question once more, if the evacuation of the Rhineland could be expedited thereby and if a new settlement could be reached before the "standard" annuity of 2,500,000,000 gold marks ($595,-000,000) for 1928–29 seemed to put their liability at an unalterable high level. Accordingly, in September 1928, at the time of the Ninth Assembly of the League, representatives of the interested Powers, meeting privately at Geneva, decided to call "a committee of financial experts" with a view to reaching "a complete and final settlement of the reparations problem." The committee, under the chairmanship of the American Owen D. Young, sat in Paris in the earlier months of 1929 and formulated a series of recommendations which came to be known as the Young Plan.

The Young Plan was adopted after stormy sessions at a conference of the Powers — France, Italy, Japan, Britain, the British Dominions, and Germany — at The Hague in August 1929. Philip Snowden, the British delegate, Chancellor of the Exchequer of the Labor government of that year, roundly accused France of repudiating her debts — "bilking" as he picturesquely put it — and he took very serious exception to a proposed new apportionment of the reparations receipts far less favorable to Britain than were the former Spa percentages of 1920 (pp. 161–62). For a few delicious days a surprised and delighted Britain watched her Socialist Chancellor of the Exchequer doing doughty battle with French intransigence and egotism, and winning all but a complete victory. Most of the international conferences of this time seemed to hover on the brink of deadlock or collapse, but this one, for once, ended in a compromise greatly to the credit of Britain. The Young Plan was signed at last at a second conference at The Hague on January 20, 1930.

The Young Plan abolished the old Dawes Transfer Committee and thus placed squarely on Germany herself the burden not only of collecting the reparations payments but of transferring them to the recipients. Germany's exchange was to be protected by dividing the reparations into unconditional and conditional payments, the conditional being postponable whenever, in the opinion of a Special Advisory Committee, "Germany's economic life may be seriously endangered." The reparations figure was fixed at fifty-nine graduated annuities, derived from the Reich budget and railroads, and totaling 150,000,000,000 marks ($29,000,000,000 or £5,750,000,000). At the behest of France a new "sanction clause" was written into the agreements, providing for "full liberty of action" on the part of any creditor Power if the World Court should find Germany in voluntary default. Finally, there was created a new institution, the Bank for International Settlements, which was to act as trustee for the creditor Powers, as distributor of the reparations payments, as a link between the national central banks, and generally as "an organization, not simply concerned with the handling of reparations, but also with furnishing the world of international commerce and finance with important facilities hitherto lacking."

The Young Plan was well received everywhere but in Germany. The referendum upon it, instigated by the growing Nazi party, will be described in a later chapter (see p. 449). The fixing of the total reparations made little impression — there would have been protest in Germany however big or little the sum — and, in any case, high finance at this scale never meant much to the ordinary man. But the grim prospect of the payments continuing for fifty-nine years to 1988 was more readily appreciable and, war guilt or no war guilt, the transaction was an intolerable visitation of the iniquities of Versailles on guiltless generations yet unborn.

However, the Young Plan was ratified in Germany, and the necessary laws to give it effect were duly promulgated in March 1930. The Bank for International Settlements was declared open at offices in Basel. The final stages of the evacuation of the Rhineland were begun. For a moment all was quiet on the European front.

THE STOCK–MARKET CRASH IN THE UNITED STATES

"In the larger view," said President Hoover on March 4, 1929, on the occasion of his Inaugural Address, "we have reached a higher degree of comfort and security than has ever existed before in the history of the world. Through liberation from widespread poverty we have reached a higher degree of individual freedom than ever before. The devotion to, and concern for, our institutions are deep and sincere. We are steadily building up a new race, a new civilization, great in its own attainments. . . . Ours is a land rich with resources, stimulating in its glorious beauty, filled with millions of happy homes, blessed with comfort and opportunity. . . . I have no fears for the future of our country. It is bright with hope."

But, for the few that had eyes to see, the United States had been suffering a general retardation of business for some time before the critical year 1929 was reached. The usual economic indexes — industrial production, capital construction, carloadings, export surpluses, employment, and so forth — if they were still increasing, were increasing by relatively small fractions. Commodity prices rose to their peak in 1925 and, with some variations, then began to run into a decline. Most noticeable of all was the fall in agricultural prices throughout the North American continent. The great increase in crops, required throughout the war years, was no longer needed now that European harvests were returning to their old figure but, while the American farmer strove to adjust himself to a reduced economic level, he bought less and less from industry.

Yet the speculative boom in Wall Street continued meanwhile in full career. Prices of stocks were out of all relation to possible dividends or future expansion. The entire population, it seemed, had become amateurs in an art formerly confined to a small class of professional operators. Even well-known financiers and economists apostrophized the millennium of quick and easy profits for everybody. New investment trusts were floated almost daily. In midsummer of 1929, some $11,000,000,000 was being carried by brokers' loans and bank loans to uphold a nation-wide structure of borrowing on margin, to uphold in turn a pyramiding speculation of apparently illimitable altitudes.[5] Call money — a significant index — at one time went as high as 20 per cent.[5] The Federal Reserve Board, whose easy-money policy had originally contributed so much to the boom, tried belatedly to apply the brakes. In July 1928 it had raised the discount rate to 5 per cent, and in August 1929, raised it to 6 per cent. During 1929 it continually sounded its warnings, though perhaps never very loudly or very forcibly. Plainly no one wanted to play the unpopular role of kill-joy and spoilsport. The government gave no help, and the private banks, which might have encouraged a little remedial liquidation before it was too late, had generally entered recklessly into the national revel themselves.

The first indisputable declines in the stock market began in the second week of September 1929, and the general lowering trend was then stimulated by events abroad. On September 20, 1929, in London, occurred the failure of Clarence Hatry and his bogus companies, a failure not unlike those of Oustric, Stavisky, Kreuger, and other famous "bubbles" of these years. Withdrawals of gold from the Bank of England at the same time were causing some anxiety. On September 26 the bank rate in England, already at 5½ per cent, was raised to 6½ per cent. For the first three weeks of October, Wall Street was in a very nervous mood, but even experienced operators declared that the sharp twinges that the market had been feeling were no more than passing "indigestion." But once the selling had begun and had become general, it was accelerated by the huge margin calls which it automatically developed.[5] On October 23, almost in the last hour of the day's trading, the market suddenly collapsed. On October 24, "Black Thursday," the record number of 12,800,000 shares were sold, and 6,300,000 shares, another record, were sold on the curb market. Key stocks declined 50 to 75 points. The losses to American investors during October were put at $40,-000,000,000. Early in November, under a general conspiracy of "returning confidence," the market seemed to recover, but selling developed again on November 6 and, with some fluctuations, prices continued to fall thereafter.

The refusal of leading bankers, of the public — and of the government — to believe the evidence of their senses acted momentarily as a "psychological brake." A conference of bankers, meeting at the offices of J. P. Morgan and Co., as early as October 24 had mobilized $240,000,000 to support the market and had tried in particular to rally despondent newspapermen to their own cheerful views of the crisis. On October 30, John D. Rockefeller announced that he and his son were steadily buying large blocks of common stock. Government spokesmen at Washington, including President Hoover himself, sent out almost routine messages emphasizing their belief in the soundness of American business. Professors and economists, branching out into popular journalism, learnedly recalled other crashes in the country's checkered past — and, by inference, other recoveries.

But a mere artificial optimism could not dissipate the obdurate facts. The American investor felt like a man in boastful good health who has been suddenly laid low by a mysterious ailment, and whose doctor persists in assuring him that there is nothing really the matter. Throughout 1930 the contagion kept spreading. Markets, profits, wages, production, and prices steadily and inexorably continued to drop. Business seemed to be seized with a sort of catalepsy. To give one good index of the situation, General Motors turned out 5,500,000 automobiles in 1929 and 2,500,000 in 1931. In 1931 the Treasury reported the first deficit in recent American budgetary history. By 1933 wholesale prices had fallen by almost one-third, industrial production by more than one-half, the national income by more than one-half, and the value of merchandise trade by more than two-thirds. That most fearful and intractable of all economic indexes, unemployment, had become a major factor in American social life. In March 1933 the total number of unemployed was conservatively estimated at over 14,000,000.

Many social scientists in the United States are of the belief that, certainly in so far as the American people are concerned, the Depression was a far more shattering national experience than the two World Wars themselves, because of the mystery of its origin and the bleakness of its prospects, and also because of its uncontrollable, almost fatalistic operation among a people traditionally accustomed to commanding their own destinies of their own free will. For the first time in the history of the Western Hemisphere, man in all his rugged individuality seemed not the master of his fate.

THE PROPOSED AUSTRO–GERMAN CUSTOMS UNION AND THE FAILURE OF THE CREDIT–ANSTALT

The European stock exchanges sagged in sympathy with Wall Street, and a tendency to liquidate set in everywhere. But there was no immediate crash on the same quantitative scale or of the same dramatic intensity. The European "retreat from Locarno" was a far more gradual and drawn-out process. American lending in Europe, of course, came to an abrupt stop, and American loans were called in, to the special disadvantage of those states in Central Europe which, like Germany, had been financing themselves for so long on foreign loans and on the anticipation of more foreign loans to come. Throughout 1929 and 1930 the international trade of Europe had been declining, and all the indexes — prices, production, and employment — had been falling in unison. But it was not till March and May 1931 that the European recession produced, first in the proposed Austro-German Customs Union and then in the failure of the Austrian Credit-Anstalt, crises on a par with the American stock-market crash of a year and a half previously.

The vexed question of the Austrian *Anschluss* with Germany has been discussed elsewhere, and it is a question which we must meet again in a much aggravated form (pp. 191 and 614). But an Austro-German Customs Union might have been regarded as a more innocent transaction, especially in view of the fact that other bilateral trade pacts at this time between Germany and her neighbors had raised no suspicions or alarms. Certainly Austria by herself was too small a unit to resist the economic tensions of 1930 and 1931. She had owed her very preservation as a state to foreign financial intervention, and it was obvious that some such help must be forthcoming a second time if she was to continue in independent existence. But the announcement in March 1931 by Dr. Curtius, the German Foreign Minister, that an Austro-German "technical customs union" was under discussion was immediately met with storms of protest from Italy, from the Little Entente, and of course from France. Britain was noncommittal, but characteristically she evinced some interest in the legalities of the case.

France was already profoundly agitated over the alleged rearmament of Germany and the rise of the Nazi party. The new commercial *Anschluss* merely added fuel to her fears. The kaleidoscopic fortunes of the year had thrown enormous financial power into her hands, a power which she was now beginning to use to impose her own terms on European suppliants for aid. Since Poincaré's stabilization of the franc, she had found herself able to make increasing purchases of gold abroad and, in the present state of Europe, gold was as effective a weapon as powder and steel.[3] After months of bickering, which exacerbated all the old antagonisms between herself and Germany, France forced Austria and Germany to withdraw the proposals for their Customs Union. Dr. Curtius did not survive the defeat of his cherished scheme, and resigned. The legalities of the case meanwhile had been referred to the World Court at The Hague, and a judgment delivered in general support of the French objections. Austria was left to struggle with her difficulties, for a time, alone.

How serious those difficulties were had become apparent in May 1931, when the largest and most reputable banking concern in Vienna was discovered to be insolvent. The Credit-Anstalt für Handel und Gewerbe had been founded by the Rothschilds in the fifties of the last century, and its many interests had since become woven into the financial fabric, not only of Austria, but of the whole Middle Danube. Since 1919 it had continued to share a somewhat precarious life with the reduced city and state it principally served. Possibly there had been extravagances in its management; probably the long arm of French finance, at the time of the recently projected Customs Union, had been exercised against it.

The House of Rothschild, the Austrian National Bank, the Austrian Government, the Bank of England came forward with funds and guarantees. The Austrian Government announced that the Credit-Anstalt would be entirely reorganized. But the saving of one ship did not abate the storm, and other ships with sprung sides and leaky bottoms were now heaving to their destruction. At the end of May 1931, Germany hoisted distress signals. There was considerable talk of a complete default on reparations. Several German business and insurance houses declared bankruptcies. Brüning, the German Chancellor, went to confer with MacDonald, the British Prime Minister, and tried to impress upon him the extreme gravity of Germany's — and Europe's — condition, but MacDonald could give him small comfort. President von Hindenburg issued emergency decrees imposing drastic new taxation and cuts in public salaries and relief. Meanwhile German Nazis, Nationalists, and Communists were busy beating up trouble each in their own way.

Finally Hindenburg telegraphed President Hoover an appeal for his good offices on behalf of the desperately foundering Reich.

THE HOOVER MORATORIUM

On June 20, 1931, President Hoover made his proposal for "the postponement during one year of all payments on intergovernmental debts." The proposal, added the President, "represents our willingness to make a contribution to the early restoration of world prosperity, in which our own people have so deep an interest" (see p. 375).

The proposal not only carried the signature of the President of the United States, and therewith the evident endorsement of American opinion but, as everyone knew, it had also had the prior concurrence of London. It was received by the whole world — or almost the whole world — with sighs of relief. France alone raised objections. France had not yet felt the full impact of the Depression. She had suffered a slight rise in unemployment, but the figures had not been alarming. Her budget deficits had been no worse than usual. Gold poured steadily into her coffers, to the extreme puzzlement and concern of both London and New York.[3] The French Government and people deeply resented the fact that, though President Hoover had seen fit to consult London before publishing his moratorium, he had not extended the same courtesy to Paris. They resented the seeming world-wide conspiracy of condolence for a Germany who they firmly believed could pay reparations under the Young Plan or the Dawes Plan or any other plan if she really wanted and who was already climbing surreptitiously out of her military impotence. They regarded the entire Hoover transaction as a panic attempt to salvage American commercial debts to Germany. They knew well enough that a moratorium would be no temporary measure but the first step in cancellation of all reparations payments. Telegrams shuttled back and forth between Paris and Washington and, in the upshot, the moratorium was agreed, but only after it had lost its "full tonic value." Meanwhile the spate of bankruptcies in Germany continued. On July 13 the Darmstädter und Nationalbank, the Danatbank as it was called, one of the four big German joint-stock banks, declared itself insolvent. All the circumstances of the Credit-Anstalt episode were repeated on a magnified scale. For the next two days all German banks were decreed a holiday. The Berlin Stock Exchange, the Boerse, closed for two months.

A feature of these critical weeks was the constant traveling of ministers and experts from conference to conference and from capital to capital. Stimson, American Secretary of State, and Mellon, American Secretary of the Treasury, were then in Europe and took part in the same migratory process. Dr. Luther, President of the Reichsbank, lived for days on end in airplanes and railroad coaches. In July ministers and experts alighted in London to hold one of the most impressive international conferences of the interwar period. Seven Powers were represented in the persons of three premiers, six foreign ministers, and four finance ministers,[6] but they did little more than recommend that nothing should be done to aggravate the situation, a recommendation which meant, in practice, that existing foreign credits to Germany should not be withdrawn. One writer of the time has compared the London Seven-Power Conference of 1931 to a consultation of fashionable doctors, anxious to protect their professional reputations, at the bedside of a patient whose case they know to be hopeless but with whose relatives they know they will have to condole. In August a further meeting of bankers at Basel, convened by the Bank for International Settlements, initialed a "Standstill Agreement" on similar lines. In October, Laval, then French Premier, crossed over to Washington for conversations with President Hoover and drew up what was tantamount to yet another standstill agreement. Laval undertook to halt French gold withdrawals from the United States, and Hoover to spring no more moratoriums on the world without first consulting France. Evidently the policy of the moment was for a breathing spell.

THE FALL OF THE POUND

But while governments and banks might agree to "stand still," European John Citizen, nervous and grasping, did not. Any financial center which appeared to be vulnerable became subject to his panic withdrawals, and between July and September 1931 it was London's turn to be vulnerable. A good proportion of the credits to Germany, frozen under the Basel Standstill Agreement, had been granted by London. But, in addition to this, three important committees lately appointed by the British Government to inquire into public finance, one being the Royal Commission on Unemployment Insurance, reported during the summer of 1931, and their findings were both candid and disquieting. The Unemployment Insurance Fund was found to be running into debt at the rate of £1,000,000 a week; Britain's national expenditure was exceeding her national income; the next budget would show a deficit; in short, the island kingdom was living far beyond its means. Small blame on John Citizen for bethinking himself that London, for two hundred years the money market of the world, was irrevocably shaken, and for wondering perhaps whether the predatory public finance of the new Labor government was not corrupting the once sound and blameless economy of the country. At the end of July the Bank of England was losing gold at the rate of £2,500,000 a day, and restrictive measures were not appreciably stemming the outflow.

On August 24, 1931, Ramsay MacDonald and his Labor government resigned, and he at once formed an all-party National government expressly to deal with the economic crisis. A supplementary budget was passed on September 15, and generally created a good impression. But the same day the Admiralty reported that the announcement of pay cuts had led to "unrest" among the lower naval ratings at Invergordon. The British press played the incident down, but Continental papers magnified it into a serious mutiny. London's finance might well be shaky, but mutiny in the British Navy seemed to hint at new and unsuspected ramifications of the universal disorder. There were renewed losses of gold, and on one day, September 18, £18,000,000 was withdrawn from London.

On September 21, 1931 the British Government suspended the gold standard. The pound at once dropped in value and, after some fluctuations, settled at about 30 per cent below parity.

On receipt of the news from London, the European stock exchanges, with one or two exceptions, closed, and when they began to reopen a few days later, all their lists had substantially depreciated. Bank rates everywhere were protectively raised. Norway, Sweden, Denmark, Finland, all the nations and dependencies of the British Commonwealth — except South Africa, but including Ireland, India, Iraq, and Egypt — and a number of South American republics, all in quick succession went off gold. Japan went off gold three months later. Those countries with sterling reserves, the Devisen of which we have spoken, which did not follow suit suffered heavily. By April 1932 the only important financial Powers to remain on the gold standard were France, Italy, Belgium, the Netherlands, Poland, Rumania, Switzerland, and the United States. Germany kept up the fiction of a gold standard, but she was already trying out complicated experiments in exchange control.

France, so far freakishly immune, began to feel the pinch of the crisis. A week after the fall of the pound, the Banque Nationale de Credit was found to be in difficulties and was saved only by government action. In October, the Comptoir Lyon-Allemand failed. Returns for the year showed sharp decreases in the nation's exports and imports, and in December the Minister of Labor at last made an official admission of the fact that France had an unemployment problem.

No one had escaped it, not even France.

THE END OF REPARATIONS AND DEBTS

The Young Plan, by general consent, was already defunct. The German press was not only talking openly of repudiating reparations, but assumed the tone that repudiation was now only a matter of course. President von Hindenburg issued his emergency decrees, which had almost become a routine, and each time Germany was declared to be at the nether end of her resources. Just before Christmas 1931 the Advisory Committee, for whose meetings in special emergencies the Young Plan had provided, reported pessimistically both upon Germany's capacity to pay the conditional annuity in 1932 and upon the economic prospects for that year throughout the world. On January 9, 1932, Brüning, the German Chancellor, issued a categorical statement: "The situation in Germany makes the continuation of political payments impossible, and any attempt to uphold the political debt system would lead Germany and the world to disaster."

But a conference to legalize the inevitable was slow in meeting. Weeks and months went by while Britain and France approached "a common point of view." Mussolini lent the weight of his very considerable influence in favor of wiping the slate clean. "Only a stroke of the sponge will end the tragic bookkeeping of the war." Yet Laval in France, it seemed, was of set purpose continually postponing the date of the conference, no doubt hoping that the suspense would cause a further deterioration of Germany's position. But the conference met at last, at Lausanne, in June 1932. Herriot had now succeeded Laval as French Premier and represented France; Franz von Papen was German Chancellor and represented Germany; MacDonald represented Britain. Under the Lausanne Convention, signed on July 9, the long and tortuous story of reparations ended in their complete abolition. Certain compensatory bonds, amounting to 3 per cent of the Young Plan total, were to be deposited by Germany with the Bank for International Settlements, but they were hedged about with so many protective conditions that it was morally certain not a pfennig of them would ever reach their creditors.[7]

Lausanne had a sting in its tail of quite another kind. The "Allies" at the conference separately concluded among themselves a "gentlemen's agreement" not to ratify the Lausanne Convention "until a satisfactory settlement had been reached between them and their own creditors." In other words, the Allies intended to make quite sure that, if they granted Germany concessions with respect to reparations, their generosity would not go unrewarded with equivalent concessions made them by the United States in respect of their liabilities also. The Hoover Moratorium was drawing inexorably to its end and, unless some action were taken, the next installments on their American debts from the European debtors would fall due in December 1932. But the American Congress was in an unyielding mood. By no pleas or arguments would it admit the European thesis that reparations and debts were all a part of the same indissoluble complex. In American eyes, reparations were reparations, and debts were debts, and never the twain should meet; and Europe was Europe, the same old, incurable, quarrelsome, militaristic Europe, which could always find money for its armaments but none for its solemnly contracted obligations. The Lausanne "gentlemen's agreement" seemed to be barefaced blackmail, typical of all European diplomacy. In the event, when December came round, Britain paid her American debt installment in full and in gold, but under formal protest; Italy, Czechoslovakia, Lithuania, and Finland also paid; France, Belgium, Hungary, Poland, Estonia, and Yugoslavia defaulted.

Meanwhile more positive efforts than cancellation were being made. In the general spirit of *sauve qui peut* of the moment, self-protective measures by individual nations usually took the form of still higher tariffs and more rigid import quotas. At the same time there was a good crop of bilateral trade agreements and clearing agreements. Then groups of nations met to discuss the mutual removal of trade barriers, for instance, the "Oslo" group of Scandinavian countries or the agrarian group of Eastern Europe. In July 1932, at Ottawa, the nations of the British Commonwealth met in an attempt to negotiate a sort of customs union. But generally these efforts were parochial and far too tied to orthodoxy; and they were not notably successful. Something more comprehensive was clearly indicated.

Accordingly in 1933 the World Economic Conference was held in London. It was called mainly on the initiative of the British Government and, more particularly, on the initiative of the British Prime Minister, Ramsay MacDonald. That man of sublime faith, perhaps out of his Socialist inheritance, was unconquerable in his belief that the conference system was the norm of international relations, and that men of good will of whatever creed or color, freely assembled together, had it in them to melt the stoniest of problems. The Conference was to be a very considerable affair, bigger and better than the recent Seven-Power Conference in London. The need could hardly be exaggerated, the good will was there, and perhaps this time something would be accomplished.

The participation of the United States was an essential condition of any success the Conference might have. But, early in March 1933, Roosevelt took office as President of the United States in the midst of an acute banking crisis when every banking institution in the country was either closed or doing business under emergency restrictions. On March 9, the United States went off the gold standard. The new President, no less than the people he represented, was clearly averse to being drawn into an international discussion while the domestic situation was so confused. As he said, "I favor as a practical policy the putting of first things first." MacDonald visited Washington for exploratory conversations, but he failed to secure Roosevelt's interest in the debt question. It would be like playing *Hamlet* without the Prince of Denmark, but at all events the participation of the United States in the projected Conference was made contingent on the assurance that the debt question, the most vital of all questions, would be rigidly excluded from the agenda.

The World Economic Conference met in London in mid-June of 1933 under MacDonald's presidency. All the well-worn resources of staging and publicity were exhausted to magnify the supreme gravity of the occasion. King George welcomed the delegates of sixty-six states and commended them to their labors. If the Conference was prevented from discussing debts, it could at least discuss currency stabilization. Raymond Moley, an American economist, whom President Roosevelt had sent over as an observer at the conference, went beyond his instructions and proceeded to negotiate a regular currency agreement. President Roosevelt replied by repudiating his overzealous subordinate and, in a somewhat hasty, hectoring statement, he berated the Conference on "the specious fallacy of achieving a temporary and probably an artificial stability in foreign exchanges on the part of a few large countries only. The sound internal economic system of a nation is a greater factor in its well-being than the price of its currency in changing terms of other nations. . . ."

The President's statement may have been a frank exposition of isolationist economics, but it finished the prospects of the Conference. One or two groups of delegates made use of their attendance to come to special agreements among themselves, but these minor and incidental successes hardly redeemed the major failure. The World Economic Conference "adjourned" at last at the end of July 1933.

The epilogue of the World Economic Conference was a general debt default. In June 1933, Britain made a "token" payment of $10,000,000 in silver toward her current debt installment to the United States. Italy, Czechoslovakia, Rumania, Lithuania, and Latvia made similar "token" payments. Finland paid in full, in silver. France and the remaining debtor states defaulted. In December 1933 the same proceeding was repeated. In April 1934, Congress passed the Johnson Act closing American security markets to any foreign government which had defaulted on its debts. In June 1934 all the debtor states, except Finland, defaulted.

WORLD DEPRESSION

In his Inaugural Address in March 1933, President Roosevelt had delivered himself as follows: "Values have sunk to fantastic levels; our factories are without orders; taxes have risen; our ability to pay has fallen; government of all kinds is faced by a serious curtailment of income; the means of exchange are frozen; the withered leaves of our industrial enterprise lie on every side; farmers find no markets for their produce; and the savings of many years in thousands of families are gone. More important, a host of unemployed citizens face the grim problem of existence, and an equally great number toil with little return." The picture he drew of America at that moment was the same for all the world. Some figures are striking. In 1933, in terms of gold, world commodity prices, as compared with 1928, had declined by a third, and raw-material prices by a half. Production indexes had declined proportionately. The steel industry in the United States was operating at 10 per cent of capacity; the price of wheat at Winnipeg stood at the lowest level recorded in any primary market since the time of Queen Elizabeth. Huge stocks of goods remained unsold, and the world made discovery of that queerest of all paradoxes, "poverty in the midst of plenty." National incomes in many countries had dropped by over 40 per cent. Government revenues had declined, but government expenditures, especially for social services and relief, were higher than ever. Thirty million workers all over the world were estimated to be unemployed.

The immediate reactions of the Depression, however, were not alone on the home fronts. In 1931 the Japanese invaded Manchuria, and the crisis passed onto the international plane. It is to this phase that we must now turn.

26 THE FAR EAST: THE CHINESE REVOLUTION

AND THE RISE OF MODERN JAPAN

THE CHINESE REVOLUTION

Theodore Roosevelt used always to predict that the Pacific Ocean would belie its name and become the main storm center of world politics in the twentieth century. His prophecy advanced a long step toward fulfillment when in 1911 the reforming Manchu dynasty, conducting a policy of railroad nationalization highly offensive to provincial bondholders, was unseated by riots which crackled briskly through central and southern China. Out of the resulting turmoil, two dominant figures emerged. In the north, General Yuan Shih-kai, who accepted a mandate from the retiring Manchu regime to carry on the government, wielded a naked military power with the support of a formidable army of 80,000 men. In the south, where Western influences were stronger, the veteran revolutionary, Dr. Sun Yat-sen, headed a Nationalist party, the Kuomintang, professing republican ideals.[1] Efforts to link the two regimes failed in 1913. General Yuan, fascinated by the spectacle of the empty Dragon Throne in Peking, dismissed the constitutional assembly convened there, extinguished the resulting insurrection in the south, and drafted his own "constitutional compact," vesting absolute authority in himself.

General Yuan was notoriously anti-Japanese, and Tokyo entertained the deepest apprehensions lest he should consolidate and unify China under his ironfisted rule. The outbreak of the First World War gave Japan an unexpected opportunity for intervention. As Britain's ally, she declared war on Germany on August 23, 1914, and at once set her forces in motion against Germany's leased territories in Shantung (see p. 22). She retorted to General Yuan's protests against her action by confronting him with the celebrated Twenty-one Demands of January 1915, a virtual ultimatum which would have reduced China to the status of a Japanese protectorate.[2] If the General accepted the Demands, it was hinted from Tokyo that he could count on Japanese support for his designs on the imperial throne recently vacated by the Manchus. General Yuan considered however that he was being asked to pay an exorbitant price in order to become little more than a Japanese puppet. Nevertheless, in May 1915, two treaties were signed which granted the Japanese the fulfillment of all but Group 5, the most obnoxious of the Demands. When Yuan permitted the Demands to leak out, the Chinese Nationalists, once the reluctant admirers of their progressive neighbor from across the Yellow Sea, began to regard that neighbor as the first and foremost of their enemies.

General Yuan's death in 1916 removed the "strong man" on whom the Western Powers had reposed their hopes of stable government in China. His mantle proved too weighty for any other single pair of shoulders to bear, and its pieces were divided among local war lords whose bitter provincial rivalries held no prospect of salvation for China. A "legitimate" government under General Yuan's nominal successors continued to exist in Peking. It was this government which, seeking to enlist the support of the Allies, declared war on Germany in August 1917 on behalf of all China. Meanwhile, Dr. Sun and his Kuomintang exercised a shadowy sway over seven southern provinces from headquarters in Canton. Both the northern and the southern factions received generous loans and credits from Japan, which was anxious to perpetuate division and discord in China. Clearly, the "phantom republic" was scarcely capable of guiding its own destinies, and must appeal to the Western Powers for counsel and aid.

Unfortunately, China could make little claim on the gratitude of the victorious Powers at the Peace Conference. She had remained neutral until 1917, and her chief contribution to the Allied war effort thereafter had taken the form of labor battalions for service behind the lines on the Western front. Furthermore, Britain and the Allies were bound by prior secret agreements by which, in return for the use of a Japanese destroyer flotilla in the critical year 1917, they had undertaken to support Japanese ambitions in Shantung and in the North Pacific (see p. 120). Chinese envoys came to the Peace Conference at Paris, representing both Peking and Canton, but their united voice failed to block the transfer of the territories in question to Japan. They expressed their resentment by refusing to sign the Treaty of Versailles (see p. 120). Chinese students in the cities of the Yangtze Valley and the south endorsed the stand taken by the Chinese delegates at Paris by angry demonstrations. The Chinese envoys afterward signed the Treaty of St. Germain, which from their point of view contained no objectionable clauses, and thereby China became one of the original members of the League of Nations. But the formation of the Chinese Communist party in 1920–21 was an indication of China's rankling disillusionment over the peacemaking in Paris and of her corresponding inclination to turn elsewhere for the aid and inspiration she needed.

Dr. Sun, a close student of this incipient upheaval of Chinese opinion, was not slow in reaping party advantage from it. Spreading the wings of his eloquence to the favoring breeze, he made his famous speech of March 1921, setting forth the basic Three Principles of his program for China. His first principle — nationalism — signified the abolition of foreign spheres of influence, of treaty ports and concessions, and of all other such blots on Chinese sovereignty. The second principle — democracy — demanded a popularly elected legislature, to be assembled after a period of "political tutelage" during which the Kuomintang would instruct and train the people in democratic processes. The third principle — social justice — promised a gradual redistribution of the wealth of the nation and a minimum standard of living for every Chinese family. The three-point program involved an ultimate break with the traditions of three thousand years of Chinese history. Exclusive loyalty to the family was to be supplemented by allegiance to a demo-

CHINA AND JAPAN

Occupied by Japan, October 1938.
C.E.R. Chinese Eastern Railway.
S.M.R. South Manchuria Railway.

Scale of Miles
0   400   800

cratic government. A population 95 per cent illiterate, accustomed to the benevolent tyranny of the village elders and to the malevolent tyranny of provincial governors, was to be given eventually a measure of political responsibility. The wooden plow, the bamboo rake, and the water wheel were to be replaced by modern machinery and scientific agriculture. The iron grip of the landlord and the usurer on the peasantry was to be broken. Dr. Sun realized that these gigantic tasks could be accomplished, if at all, only by a major influx of foreign loans and foreign technicians. But to what extent could foreign loans and foreign technicians be reconciled in practice with a program of "China for the Chinese"? Could a China, skirting the very edge of chaos, find the resolution and self-discipline with which her neighbor, Japan, had Westernized herself? The attitude of the Western Powers toward these momentous questions was given indirect but unmistakable expression at the Washington Conference in 1921–22.

CHINA AND THE WASHINGTON CONFERENCE

The Washington Conference (pp. 363–66), convened by President Harding in November 1921, was conceived originally as a forum in which the leading Powers could debate on measures of naval disarmament. The incipient naval race between the United States and Japan, however, could be effectually checked only within the framework of a general settlement of Pacific problems. The quickening tempo of Japanese penetration of the Asiatic mainland, in Shantung no less than in Siberia, was viewed with disapproval in Washington. If the mounting strength of Japan, powerfully reinforced by her profitable participation in the First World War, was not to be applied to further adventures in the Pacific, she must be detached from her alliance of 1902 with Britain and included in an over-all agreement designed to safeguard the prewar *status quo* in the Far East. Nine interested Powers attended the Washington Conference — the United States, Britain, Japan, France, Italy, Belgium, the Netherlands, Portugal, and China. The ninth, China, was the more or less passive body politic around which Pacific issues were debated. Soviet Russia was a conspicuous absentee.

The Peking government was represented at Washington by a delegation headed by its Foreign Minister, Dr. Sze. The Canton regime of Dr. Sun, denied separate representation, refused to participate. Dr. Sze was permitted to present to the Conference's Committee on Pacific and Far Eastern Questions a ten-point declaration of principles which included a request that "immediately, or as soon as circumstances will permit, existing limitations upon China's political, jurisdictional, and administrative freedom of action are to be removed." The Committee, unimpressed, took its stand on familiar ground. It avowed the intention of the Powers to respect the independence and integrity of China, and it reaffirmed the doctrine of equality for the commerce and industry of all nations in Chinese territory. The principle of the "Open Door" having been thus reasserted,[3] the Powers showed little further interest in the Chinese demands on Japan to restore the former German possessions in Shantung. It was only when an influential group of United States Senators, distrustful of Japan's ulterior intentions in China, took up the cudgels on behalf of Dr. Sze that the Japanese delegation finally agreed to relinquish the disputed territory and leases in return for a solatium of $20,000,000. Baron Kato also consented to withdraw the more onerous clauses of the two treaties of 1915, thus providing verbal assurances — for what they were worth — that Japan had abandoned her broader ambitions of the Asiatic mainland.[4]

CHINA UNDER SOVIET INFLUENCE

Dr. Sun meanwhile, in 1921, had been elevated to the presidency of the "Chinese Republic" by a rump parliament in Canton. He observed with considerable chagrin that even the scanty successes at Washington had been gained by representatives of the rival regime at Peking. Simultaneously, he was urgently pressed from Peking to resign his presidency and thus restore the "unity" of China. The southern war lords, who did not relish Dr. Sun's efforts to curtail their semi-independent authority in the provinces, withdrew their allegiance and in 1922 drove him from Canton. Smarting under these successive rebuffs, Dr. Sun turned in desperation to Soviet Russia to repair his shattered fortunes. Early in 1923, in his place of exile in Shanghai, he received the Soviet emissary, Adolf Joffe. The resulting Sino-Soviet convention was little more than a marriage of convenience and bore all the character of a compromise. The contracting parties agreed that China was far from ripe for Communism, but at least Soviet support for the unification and subsequent independence of China was assured. The Kuomintang, too fragile as yet to serve as the basis of a broad national movement, was to reorientate its policy. It had not been a mass party in the past; in its checkered career it had attracted support mainly from students and, with reservations, from the merchant class. The remedy, obvious to Moscow but strong medicine indeed to Dr. Sun, was to open its ranks to the peasants and industrial workers.

Michael Borodin, former teacher in a commercial college in Chicago and Communist agitator in Scotland, was selected by Moscow as its chief political agent in China. His massive and unromantic exterior masked considerable abilities, though he lacked the experience and patience to pierce the Oriental obscurantism of his Chinese allies. His first task was to provide for the foundation in 1924 of a military college at Whampoa near Canton. The instructors, forty in number, were headed by the Russian General Bluccher, who had played a leading part in curbing Japanese expansion in Siberia in 1920–21. The principal of the college was a young and ardent supporter of Dr. Sun, Chiang Kai-shek, who had recently returned from a three months' tour in Russia.

The renewed vigor drawn by the Kuomintang from the Soviet connection was soon demonstrated. The conservative merchants of Canton, alarmed by the proximity of the Red specter, attempted to expel Dr. Sun from the city. But the forces of the Kuomintang, now ably led by the graduates of Whampoa, emerged victorious, and the private soldiery maintained by the merchants was scattered to the four winds. Dr. Sun's next objective was to win over the independent war lords of the north and thus to secure the collaboration of the Peking government in the unification of all China. The adroit Adolf Joffe had already begun to smooth the way for such collaboration under Soviet auspices by inducing Peking to extend diplomatic recognition to the Soviet Union. In the grip of a mortal illness, Dr. Sun proceeded northward by slow stages and reached Peking in December 1924. But, in March 1925, in the midst of his negotiations with the government leaders there, he died, seemingly on the very threshold of achieving his life's ambition.

Dr. Sun's death made him the saint and martyr of the Chinese Nationalist movement. His long and romantic career, not unlike that of Lenin in Russia, had seemed a very embodiment of revolution. His bell-shaped mausoleum of multicolored marble on the slopes of the Purple Mountain at Nanking, near the tombs of the early Ming emperors, became a center of pious pilgrimage. His political testament was read at the opening of every official ceremony.

Despite, and perhaps because of, his ardent nationalism, Dr. Sun had never wavered in his conviction that the regeneration of his country was practicable only with foreign aid. The policy of fighting fire with fire, however, was not without its dangers. By turning to the Soviet Union he solved immediate problems at the cost of creating greater ones for his successors.

CHIANG KAI–SHEK AND THE RUPTURE WITH THE SOVIET UNION

The diversified character of Dr. Sun's political legacy to Nationalist China was soon in evidence. His anti-foreign propaganda touched off a destructive chain of strikes and demonstrations among the textile workers and students of Shanghai in May 1925. International Settlement police under the command of a British inspector fired on the mob, and nine Chinese were killed. The inflamed Nationalists retaliated by declaring a boycott of British goods.

On the other hand, the advantages conferred by the Soviet alliance were tested and proved in the offensive of the newly trained Nationalist armies, planned by General Bluecher and led by the graduates of Whampoa. The northward sweep of the Nationalist forces was but feebly resisted by the scholarly Marshal Wu Pei-fu, the war lord controlling the middle Yangtze Valley. His troops, their discipline undermined by Communist propaganda, melted away at the first impact. Marshal Wu's capital of Hankow, the Chicago of China, fell in September 1926. There the Nationalist armies pivoted, and swept down the Yangtze to Nanking, which they took in March 1927, sacked, and looted, and which Chiang Kai-shek ultimately made the seat of the Nationalist government. Foreign residents in Nanking were evacuated under cover of fire from British and American gunboats. Chiang Kai-shek brought his victorious campaign to a fitting close with the occupation of the native quarters of Shanghai.

The Nationalist sack of Nanking, widely held to be Communist-inspired, raised in an acute form the problem of Chiang Kai-shek's future relations with the Soviet Union and with the Western Powers. The cleavage of opinion inside and outside the Kuomintang cut so deep that a continued compromise with the Communist wing in the Nationalist party was not feasible. The wealthy merchants and foreign residents of Canton, Shanghai, and the Yangtze Valley desired in the main a stable, orderly government under which trade could be peaceably conducted. Chiang Kai-shek himself, while welcoming Soviet aid, regarded Dr. Sun's half turn in the direction of the Soviet as a purely opportunist maneuver. The Nanking disturbances moreover had impaired Chiang Kai-shek's standing in the eyes of the conservative wing of the Kuomintang, and imperiled his prospects of securing financial aid from the Shanghai bankers. He therefore abruptly turned his troops against Borodin and the Communist element in the Kuomintang. Borodin, together with General Bluecher, fled to Moscow. They were joined there temporarily by Madame Sun, who upbraided Chiang for having "betrayed the revolution." A systematic liquidation of Borodin's supporters in Nationalist China followed, culminating in the extinction, after three days' bloody street fighting, of a Red "Commune" in Canton. But several Chinese

Communist groups took refuge in the mountains of southern Kiangsi province.

The emancipation of the Nationalist movement in China from Soviet leading strings was neatly symbolized in December 1927 by the marriage of Chiang Kai-shek and Soong Mei-ling (Wellesley '17), a marriage which bound Chiang closely to the important financial interests founded in the preceding half century by "Charlie" Soong. No difficulty was met in financing a renewed northward offensive, which culminated in the capture of Peking in June 1928. The city was renamed Peiping, or "Northern Peace," and the pro-Nationalist administration installed there extended the sphere of Chiang's nominal authority to the provinces immediately south of the Great Wall. Chiang did not venture north of the Great Wall into Manchuria, but he came to terms with the "Young Marshal," Chang Hsueh-liang, lately heir to his father, Chang Tso-lin, the Manchurian war lord, and gave him a seat in the council of the Nationalist government at Nanking.

Although Chiang Kai-shek seemed to be firmly seated in the saddle by 1929, the Chinese dragon was not yet effectively bitted and bridled, nor was its vast bulk responsive to his commands. The Nationalist government at Nanking wielded direct authority only in the provinces adjoining the lower Yangtze Valley. In the reaches of the upper Yangtze and in the north, the government's power was conditioned and limited by its relations, always delicately poised, with the provincial war lords nominally subject to Nanking. In the south, the radicals of Canton, disliking the concentration of power at Nanking, organized an upheaval which tore loose the city from central government control. Compared with these dominating groups, the leaders of the Chinese Communists, Mao Tse-tung and Chu Teh, were as yet flitting, evasive figures, developing an intense propaganda, but melting into the vast landscape of China when menaced by superior forces.

CHINA'S PROBLEMS, FOREIGN AND DOMESTIC

The Great Powers, fearful of the welding of a Sino-Soviet bloc which would radiate disturbing influences throughout Asia, had watched the flirtation of the Kuomintang with the Soviet Union in rising dismay. The riots of 1925 in Shanghai and the subsequent boycott of British goods had increased their apprehensions. Late in 1926 the British Foreign Office submitted a note to the Powers which had interests in China, outlining a revised policy based on the widest practical concessions to Chinese national feeling. By the end of 1927, Chiang Kai-shek was firmly ensconced in the lower valley of the Yangtze, which contained the hard core of British economic interests in China. The Powers, led by the United States and Britain, hastened therefore to extend diplomatic recognition to the new Nationalist government, in return for a satisfactory financial settlement of the property damage inflicted on their nationals during the Nanking disturbances. Tariff autonomy in China, conceded by the Powers in 1928, enlarged the revenues and improved the credit standing of the newly established regime. The abolition of extraterritorial rights was granted "in principle" by the United

States in August 1929 and by Britain in December 1930, but in practice both Powers envisaged a gradual and unhurried reduction of such rights over an unspecified period. The Nationalist government, unimpressed by this policy of cautious retreat, announced that China would assume jurisdiction over all foreign concessions and settlements by January 1, 1932, with or without the consent of the Powers concerned. Notwithstanding this, Chiang Kai-shek, anxious to expand the industrial and military potential of China, made heavy calls on Western experts and matériel. British exports of machinery to China trebled between 1928 and 1930. The city of Nanking, devastated in the sack of 1927, was restored with the aid of American architects. German military experts, headed by Colonel Bauer and later by General von Falkenhausen, replaced General Bluecher and his Soviet colleagues.

One of the main tasks of the new military experts was to direct operations against the headquarters of the Chinese Communists in southern Kiangsi. After 1928 these Communists had united with their party comrades of the neighboring Fukien province to form the beginnings of the Chinese Red Army. The Kiangsi contingent, mainly former soldiers of the Nationalist armies, were led by the irrepressible Chu Teh, formerly principal of the military training school of Nanchang. The Fukién contingent, a miscellany of miners, peasants, and insurrectionary soldiers, were organized into guerrilla groups by Mao Tse-tung, an intellectual educated at the University of Peking and in France and engaged thereafter in trying to build up trade-unions among the coal miners at Hanyang. The two contingents at first numbered some 4,000, but they were shortly swelled by discontented peasants and deserters from the Nationalist armies. The Communist policy of seizing and redistributing the large estates proved decidedly attractive to the poor cultivators of the soil, so long the victims of the rack-renter and usurer. The absence of large-scale collective farms was in marked contrast to the Soviet system; but the necessity of gaining mass support by encouraging peasant proprietorship was paramount. This adroit opportunism ensured the expansion of Communism into the provinces adjacent to Kiangsi, mainly through the progressive sovietization of the village councils. The loose and far-flung network of local soviets was formally provided with a nucleus in November 1931, when the Chinese Soviet Republic, headed by Mao Tse-tung, was proclaimed in Kiangsi. Its military forces were indifferently equipped, but could rely on the support of a well-disposed rural population. Consequently, when a punitive expedition, directed by Chiang Kai-shek in person, groped into Kiangsi province in 1931, the Communist forces were able to turn it back by slashing at its communications and denying it supplies.

Within the Kuomintang many of the old-line party members, followers of Dr. Sun, continued to gaze longingly toward Moscow, and deeply resented the intrusion of a military tyranny in so promising a Communist field as Kiangsi. The versatile but unprincipled Wang Ching-wei, once a close associate of Dr. Sun, sought to exploit the subterranean discontent in order to supplant Chiang Kai-shek in the leadership of the Kuomintang. For military support he relied on General Feng and the provincial war lords north of the Yangtze, who had been disturbed over a recent announcement by Chiang Kai-shek that they would probably have to consent to a reduction of the local armies in China. Wang set up a "Reorganizationist Government" at Peiping, which tottered to its fall when Chang Hsueh-liang of Manchuria renewed his allegiance to the Nationalist government at Nanking. Wang returned to the south and obstinately declared his intention of establishing yet another rival government, this time in the long-suffering city of Canton. General Feng concurrently retired into the remote fastnesses of Shansi "for philosophical meditation and the practice of calligraphy."

Chiang Kai-shek, it must be said, was not unaware of the forces of popular discontent which nourished and sustained the cause of Communism. In his speech of October 1930, for instance, he had taken his party severely to task. "The Manchus were overthrown," he said, "because they constituted a privileged caste. But now we, who staged the Revolution for the overthrow of the Manchus, have ourselves come to be regarded by the people as a privileged caste. They are now cherishing toward us the same hatred and repugnance with which they looked upon the Manchus." Yet the very magnitude of the country's difficulties prohibited swift or easy solutions. China, assailed simultaneously by all the problems of public disorder, regionalism, an unruly military, industrial immaturity, extremist ideologies — which in the West had been comfortably distributed at intervals over four centuries — required decades, not years, for a settlement. Nor was it easy for China to work out her own destiny so long as her internal weaknesses remained a standing invitation to foreign intervention. The persistent Communist dissension within the Kuomintang itself and the sullen resentment of dissatisfied war lords constituted the backdrop against which Japan's assault on Manchuria in 1931 must be viewed. Yet, paradoxically, Japanese penetration of the Asiatic mainland ultimately brought to China an installment of the priceless boon for which she had fought and agonized since 1911 — a degree of national unity.

THE RISE OF MODERN JAPAN

In 1868, fifteen years after the smoke-vomiting "black ships" of Commodore Perry had entered Yedo Bay and impressed the awe-stricken onlookers with the superiority of Western science, Japan had embarked upon a feverish program of modernization. Manifestly the seventeenth-century decrees which had expelled Europeans from the islands and forbidden native Japanese to travel abroad had been invalidated by the hard logic of events. The hermit kingdom must open its doors to Western efficiency, if not to Western intruders, if it wished to survive as an independent nation. Japanese statesmen, glancing across the narrow seas to China, could point to the late Opium War and the late Treaty of Nanking as convincing object lessons of the fate which Western imperialism meted out to the weak and defenseless.

The sealing of the kingdom had not immunized it against economic changes within itself. The traditional "rice economy" of Japan, based upon the payment of rent in produce by the peasant to his landlord, was retreating slowly and painfully before an emerging money economy. The increasingly luxurious habits of the landed warrior aristocracy had stimulated domestic demand to the advantage of a prosperous and self-confident merchant class. The former group, converting its rice revenues into cash at terms dictated by the merchants, began to slide into an economic abyss. The descent was slowed but not stopped by a multiplicity of desperate measures. The offspring of merchant families were admitted by marriage or adoption; a reckless currency inflation was set in train; and governmental cancellation of the debts of the landed class was demanded. The successive shoguns of the time were no more able to repair the growing crisis than to resist the commercial penetration of the country by foreign Powers. In 1867–68, the powerful clans of the west and south, raising the popular cry of "Expel the foreigner," overthrew the Shogun and restored the Emperor to his titular authority. Having accomplished a political revolution under the pretext of restoring the old order, these more progressive elements turned to the tremendous task of modernizing Japan's economy and of renovating her institutions.

In the event, the partial emancipation of Japan from the past was achieved with unexpected ease and dispatch. The modernization program, represented as a means of armoring Japan against foreign intervention, was popularized without difficulty. The warrior aristocracy, schooled to respect armed might, were quick to grasp the necessity of appropriating Western weapons and Western military techniques. But this required in turn the establishment of a powerful central government with effective authority over the human and material resources of the nation. The warrior aristocracy therefore consented to administer their formerly independent principalities as governors controlled from Tokyo. They relinquished their taxation rights to the central administration and received government pensions in return. Stripped and tautened for a headlong race toward Westernization, Japan thereafter meticulously sought out, studied, and imported the best Western models. Prussia, supreme since Sedan, was the obvious model for the new Japanese Army, even as Britain was the obvious model for the new Japanese Navy. The Criminal Code was patterned on that of France.

The Japanese constitution of 1889, like the Prussian constitution of December 1848, was imposed from above. As the gift of the Emperor, the Son of Heaven, to his people it was virtually sacrosanct. Under its provisions the Emperor, by reason of his divine descent, stood beyond politics and above criticism. His ministers, though they could be attacked in the Diet, were responsible ultimately to him alone. The Ministers of State for War and the Navy enjoyed the right of direct access to the Throne, thus bypassing the other ministers, who enjoyed only the right of indirect access through the Premier. A subsequent ordinance of 1895 decreed that these two ministers must always be active generals or admirals. By refusing to make appointments to these key posts the militarists could obstruct at will the formation of cabinets obnoxious to them. The power to grant taxes, nominally vested in the Diet, was limited by a provision automatically renewing the budget of the previous year should the current estimates fail to pass. Thus the Diet was little more than a sounding board of public opinion.

A vigorous oratory was practiced, and indeed criticism of the government was sometimes heard, but the effect on current policy was usually negligible. The militarists, the allied business interests, and the Elder Statesmen close to the Throne enjoyed a monopoly of power relatively undisturbed by parliamentary declamation. The moral cement of this rigidly authoritarian structure was provided by the deliberate revival of state Shinto, "the way of the Gods." Rooted in the ancient practice of ancestor worship, state Shinto inculcated a fiery patriotism based on the allegedly divine origin of the nation and of the imperial house. It was designed to harden the nation against the impact of liberal democracy, which would inevitably come to Japan in the wake of Western technology.

JAPAN AND THE ASIATIC MAINLAND

The militarists or the Camp, as they were called, the business interests or Zaibatsu, and the Elder Statesmen or Genro may have had a common end, but the means which they respectively advocated were not precisely identical. The militarists wanted a "positive" attitude in Asia and in the Pacific. Territorial acquisitions, they urged, would solve the pressing problems of a multiplying population and of a chronic deficiency in raw materials. Furthermore, a frequent rattling of the saber — though this point was not stressed in the Camp's public pronouncements — justified generous armament appropriations. The business interests, for example the powerful Mitsui and Mitsubishi corporations, affirmed on the contrary that commercial expansion and a careful cultivation of overseas markets would ensure Japanese prosperity without the risk of war. The Elder Statesmen often acted as mediators between the two schools of thought, but unhappily their collective influence slowly declined as death claimed them one by one, and by the thirties only the revered Prince Saionji survived.

The possibility of a complete economic partition of China among the Western Powers encouraged the Japanese in a policy of military occupation of vital areas on the Asiatic mainland rather than of a gradual economic penetration. The fear of a Russian descent on Korea, a wedge of territory under Chinese suzerainty lying between the islands of Japan and the mainland, precipitated the Sino-Japanese War of 1894. A further Russian penetration into the Liaotung Peninsula, at the southern tip of Manchuria, was countered even more decisively. In 1902 the Anglo-Japanese Treaty was signed, whereby Britain agreed to aid Japan in the event of the participation of France, Russia's ally since 1894, in a Russo-Japanese conflict. Having thus isolated Russia diplomatically, Japan declared war in 1904. The Tsarist Army and Navy, handicapped by long lines of communication and astoundingly inefficient leadership, suffered a series of disastrous defeats. Japan rose almost overnight to the status of a Great Power. Her triumph strengthened the prestige of the Camp, which could point to the effectiveness with which the sword of the Samurai had cut the tangled knot of Japan's continental problems.

Japan's policy during the First World War further illustrated her adroitness in extracting profit from the rivalries of the European Powers. A declaration of war against Germany on August 23, 1914 enabled her to seize the German territories in Shantung and the German islands in the North Pacific. She would doubtless have gone on to seize the Bismarck Archipelago and German New Guinea had not Australasian forces beaten her in the race. In 1915, when hostilities in Europe had settled into the exhausting deadlock of trench warfare, she confronted China with the Twenty-one Demands, and the veiled protectorate thus declared over China would have become a gruesome reality had the fortunes of the Allies in Europe suffered a further decline (see p. 412).

The restraining influence of the United States at this juncture was of the greatest importance. Washington considered that the principle of the "Open Door"[3] had been jeopardized by the Twenty-one Demands. Japan, seeking to win American recognition of her gains in China since 1914, initiated negotiations through Viscount Ishii with Secretary of State Lansing. The ensuing Lansing-Ishii Agreement of November 1917 was based upon a compromise. Japan reaffirmed her acceptance of the doctrine of the "Open Door," while the United States recognized Japan's "special" (not "paramount") interests in China. Elsewhere, Japan snatched eagerly at the skirts of opportunity. The dispatch of Japanese destroyers to the Mediterranean in 1917, at the height of the German submarine campaign, was paid for by a secret, postdated check on the German islands in the North Pacific, to be honored at the subsequent peace conference (pp. 76 and 120). Finally, the lengthy occupation of eastern Siberia by Japanese forces in 1918–22 reflected Japan's anxiety to exploit the weakness of the newly installed Soviet regime in Russia (see p. 262). Pressure from Washington and a growing realization in Tokyo that the collapse of the Soviet was not imminent induced Japan to withdraw her forces in November 1922.[5] It was perceived with profoundest regrets that the division of the carcass of the Russian bear must be indefinitely postponed, since the brute was not yet dead.

It was manifest by 1922 that the policy of military intervention on the Asiatic mainland was paying decreasing dividends. Civilian statesmen with business affiliations, such as Baron Shidehara, began to urge that a policy of peaceful commercial expansion would serve the ends of Japan equally well. Proximity to the Chinese market and low production costs gave Japan self-evident advantages over her competitors. The defeat of the Central Powers in 1918, furthermore, had instilled a wholesome respect for the military potency of the democratic Powers, and the solid front which those Powers had displayed against Japan at the Washington Conference suggested that further freebooting in the Pacific must await a more opportune season.

Japanese statesmen, aware that their country could not win a naval race with the United States, had come to the Washington Conference, in November 1921, prepared to make concessions, but determined to exact the maximum in return (pp. 363–66). They were compelled to agree to the evacuation of Japanese forces from Shantung and from eastern Siberia. They were obliged to accept the 5:5:3 ratio between the capital ships of the United States, Britain, and Japan. All these were humiliating military and diplomatic reverses. But the 5:5:3 ratio at least assured Japan of an incontestable superiority in her home waters in the West Pacific. The Conference moreover imposed no restrictions on her right to construct aircraft and submarines, nor on the size of her land forces. Dominating the narrow seas which divided her from China, Japan could consequently pour troops into the mainland at will, should an aggressive policy be resumed. In return for her acceptance of the 5:5:3 ratio, she insisted that the United States and Britain should forego the construction of forward naval bases from which their superior naval strength could be brought to bear against her home islands. The United States consequently renounced the right to construct naval bases or fueling stations west of Pearl Harbor. Britain undertook not to construct or extend fortifications in Hong Kong and in her insular possessions in the Pacific east of meridian 110°. This stipulation left Britain free to develop the new naval base at Singapore to accommodate a British Pacific Fleet of capital ships, which existed as yet only on paper. In sum, these arrangements left the Philippines, Guam, and the Aleutians dangerously exposed in the event of a Pacific conflict. Power for their defense would have to be projected from Singapore and Pearl Harbor, each three thousand miles from Japan and six thousand miles from each other. Reinforced by these vital strategic advantages, Japan could regard with equanimity the supersession of the old Anglo-Japanese Alliance of 1902 by the new, but entirely harmless, Four-Power Treaty between the United States, Britain, France, and herself (see p. 365).

THE PERIOD OF WATCHFUL WAITING

The immediate result of the Washington Conference and the withdrawals from Shantung and eastern Siberia was temporarily to curb the influence of the Japanese militarists. Yet they clung grimly to the vantage points of power assured to them by the constitution and waited for the moment when some new opportunity might put the initiative once more in their hands. In the middle twenties, Japan's political stage was monopolized by her domestic affairs. Here the continuing cause of tension, only partially held in check by a powerful social discipline, was the parlous condition of agriculture. The modernization of the country after 1868 had been carried out with an eye chiefly to military and industrial requirements. The role of agriculture was to supply cheap food to the factory workers, and to afford minimum subsistence to a large reservoir of peasant man power which could be readily diverted into the armed forces and into industry. Tax differentials were so adjusted that the landowner paid almost four times the amount due from the industrialist. The large landowner tended to pass along the burden to his tenants in the shape of increased rent.

The small peasant proprietor, meanwhile, was fighting a losing battle. The picturesque garden landscape of Japan betrays at once the hopeless splintering of the land into small, uneconomic units of an average of less than three acres per family. The indifferent soil, the erosive effects of heavy rain in the mountainous areas, and the expenditure of labor in terracing diminished the slender margin of profit even in the good years. The cultivation of silk, by which that profit had once been meagerly supplemented, was now adversely affected by the competition of the new rayon. Thus the small peasant proprietors amounted to no more than 34 per cent of the 5,500,000 farming families in Japan by 1918, and their numbers were being constantly reduced by migration to the industrial cities and by their involuntary acceptance of tenant status on lands once their own.

At the base of Japanese industry lay the small family concern of five workers or less, employing about 60 per cent of all industrial labor. But at the apex the government-sponsored growth of industry and banking after 1868 ensured an extraordinary concentration of economic power. The four great family trusts known collectively as the Zaibatsu — namely, the houses of Mitsui, Mitsubishi, Sumitomo, and Yasuda — had been selected originally by the government to preside over the rapid and orderly industrialization of Japan. The modernization of the army and navy and the wars of 1894, 1904, and 1914 had guaranteed a spectacular expansion. By the familiar device of the holding company, the four trusts had obtained commanding positions in the fields of industry, commerce, and banking. Nor was their economic predominance threatened by the competition of foreign capital, for government credits had been readily furnished them in order to reduce their borrowings abroad to the minimum. This concentration of power, coupled with low wages and ruthless rationalization, was a priceless asset to Japan in the world market. It was purchased, however, at a high cost in human suffering, and it did not entirely offset the deficiency of basic raw materials such as coal and iron.

A low standard of living, a high proportion of female labor, and a semi-feudal tradition of obedience to established authority combined to stifle industrial unrest in Japan. Trade-unions, formerly illegal, existed in the inter-war years only on sufferance. They included only 7 per cent of the workers, and they were kept under close surveillance by the authorities. Strikes during the depression of 1920–21 were usually brief and spasmodic, if only because low wages prevented the accumulation of adequate strike funds. A Communist party had existed underground since 1922, but vigorous police action and a powerful social discipline prevented its ideology from pervading the masses. The passage of a Manhood Suffrage Bill in March 1925 was only in appearance a step toward practical democracy. By conferring the vote on all self-supporting males of twenty-five years and over, it widened the electorate from 2,800,000 to 12,500,000. But the Diet which represented this increased electorate enjoyed, as we have seen, only limited powers. Further, imperial consent to the bill was delayed until the Diet consented to pass a Peace Preservation Act which made it a criminal offense to attempt to overthrow the constitution or to change the system of private property.

Social discipline was put to the supreme test when the great earthquake of September 1, 1923 reduced some of Japan's greatest cities to fire-blackened ruins. Her volcanic islands have always been aquiver; seismologists register a steady tally of some 1,500 minor quakes a year. But these were little more than the trembling of a leaf compared with the convulsions of that Saturday noontide in 1923. As the land heaved under the first shock, fires raced through the flimsy, inflammable timber buildings of Tokyo, Yokohama, and Nagoya. The broken mains, from which gouts of water spurted uselessly, prevented the fire services from bringing the flames under control. Three-quarters of Tokyo and a large part of Yokosuka, the most important Japanese naval base, were destroyed. The total loss of life was put at 160,000 and of property at $2,000,000,000.

In face of a calamity of such proportions, political rivalries shrank into insignificance. Twenty-two warships of the United States Pacific Fleet were immediately ordered to proceed under forced draft to Tokyo with clothing and food. Within a few weeks the people of the United States had contributed $5,000,000 for relief of the victims. The American press, headlining the catastrophe as "the greatest disaster in history," ransacked its libraries for details of the destruction of Pompeii and of the great Lisbon earthquake of 1755, which had taken a mere 50,000 lives. Observers prophesied, not altogether without foundation, that the expense and effort of reconstruction might abate the ardor of Japanese militarism for some time to come.

But behind the increasingly democratic frontage of Japan the old hatreds and ambitions still burned fiercely. The sense of diplomatic isolation which the Japanese delegates had carried away from the Washington Conference was strengthened by the United States Immigration Act of 1924, which prohibited the entry of Japanese nationals save for temporary residence. The Japanese ambassador in Washington hastened to lodge a formal protest. It was alleged that, not only had Japanese self-respect been needlessly and wantonly insulted, but that the old "Gentleman's Agreement" of 1907–08, whereby the Japanese Government had voluntarily undertaken to limit the immigration of its nationals to the United States, had been violated. The Japanese press frothed and fumed. But no one could deny that the new act was a normal exercise of sovereign rights (see p. 367).

The wrath prevailing in Tokyo did not pass unnoticed by Moscow. Formal diplomatic relations had not yet been established between the two capitals. Japanese occupation forces still remained in the Russian northern half of the island of Sakhalin, where they had installed themselves in 1918. It was possible that Japan, nursing a growing animosity against her associates of the First World War, would be willing to meet the overtures of her former foe. By the Soviet-Japanese treaty of January 1925, Japan consented to extend formal recognition to the Soviet Union. It was agreed that discussion of the liquidation of the debts of the Tsarist Government due to Japan should be postponed. Japanese troops were to be withdrawn from northern Sakhalin by May 1925. In return, Japan was permitted to exploit one-half of the area of the oil fields in the northern half of the island for a minimum period of forty years. Moscow was thus able to proceed, unhampered by Japan, to the fomentation of the virulent antiforeign campaign carried on by the Chinese Nationalists during 1925–27. The campaign was viewed complacently at first in Tokyo, since Japan's main interests, in Manchuria and North China, lay well out of its range; moreover, it served to divert Chinese hostility from Japan toward the United States and Britain.

General Chiang Kai-shek's emancipation of the Kuomintang from Communist control and the fiery northward sweep of the Nationalist armies in

1927 upset these nicely balanced calculations. The Nationalist tide surged closer to Manchuria and the maritime areas of North China, within the Japanese zone of influence. Baron Tanaka, the fire-eating soldier Premier of Japan in 1927–29, began to speak ominously of the necessity of pursuing "improved policies for the protection of her [Japan's] interests and prestige." As the Chinese armies approached Shantung, he dispatched substantial forces to that much-disputed province. In May 1928, 4,000 Japanese regulars ejected a newly installed Chinese garrison from Tsinan, the capital city of the province. A retaliatory boycott of Japanese goods at once swept through China. Merchants convicted of dealing with Japan were suspended in bamboo cages twenty feet above street level and bombarded with filth and opprobrious epithets by the passers-by. Under pressure of the boycott, Japanese industrialists urged moderation. Tanaka at last consented, in May 1929, to withdraw the Japanese forces from Tsinan, provided that the safety of Japanese residents was guaranteed.

The militarists, ever fearful of the "canker of a long peace," suffered a further rebuff at the Five-Power Naval Conference in London in 1930 (see p. 374). Admiral Kato, Chief of Naval Staff, refused point-blank to accept a proposed limitation in the number of auxiliary craft to be constructed by Japan. The British Prime Minister, Ramsay MacDonald, appealed direct to Premier Hamaguchi, "the Lion," in Tokyo, who unhesitatingly ratified the limitation. Within two weeks of this courageous defiance of precedent, Hamaguchi was shot and mortally wounded by a disgruntled "patriot." Clearly the pace was quickening. The militarists would not permit their powers to be defied without a struggle. The reduction in naval expenditure made possible by the London agreement might soon lead to similar slashes in the army budget. In their conflict with the civil authority, the militarists were soon to be aided by a redoubtable ally — the Depression.

DESIGN FOR CONQUEST

The Wall Street crash of October 1929 reacted swiftly and disastrously on the ill-balanced economy of Japan. Silk accounted for two-fifths of the total value of Japanese exports; and 90 per cent of this silk was absorbed by the American market. Further, as we have said, silk cultivation was a supplementary item in the meager income of the Japanese peasant. Rice prices had fallen steadily since 1921, in sympathy with a world-wide decline in raw-commodity values. The sternly deflationist policy of the big banks discouraged industrial activity. The Chinese boycott, operative since the Tsinan incident of 1928, had not been entirely raised. Consequently, Japanese foreign trade declined by approximately 30 per cent between 1929 and 1930. Unemployment figures in Japan rose by official admission to 360,000; but the readiness of the Japanese family to support its unemployed members masked the actual total, variously estimated at from 1,000,000 to 3,000,000. Retrenchment in naval and military expenditures, which accounted for over 28 per cent of the budget, seemed imminent if orthodox means for combating the crisis were to be used.

The situation was only too favorable for an act of aggression which would end the policy of conciliating China and at the same time prevent budget economies at the expense of the armed forces. The Nationalist government in China, also hard-hit by the Depression, faced a deficit of $280,000,000 for the fiscal year of 1931. At the same time, Tokyo was pressing for a satisfactory settlement of loans previously advanced to China, amounting in the aggregate to 500,000,000 yen ($250,000,000). Chiang Kai-shek's financial experts were pressing him to reduce his armies, and hence his military expenditures, which amounted to 85 per cent of his entire budget. Chiang, further distracted by the obstinate resistance of the Communists, was therefore completely absorbed with his own problems in the area south of the Great Wall.

North of the Great Wall, in Manchuria, the situation provided Japanese militarists with further arguments for aggression. In June 1928 the veteran Manchurian war lord, Chang Tso-lin, had been killed in a violent dynamite explosion which wrecked his special train. Responsibility for the incident was generally laid at the door of the Japanese, who notoriously resented the mounting independence of Chang in this special zone of Japanese influence. Chang's son and successor, the "Young Marshal" Chang Hsueh-liang, unwaveringly persevered in an anti-Japanese policy. He repudiated the considerable loans obtained by his father from Tokyo. He engineered "bandit" raids on the 220,000 Japanese settled in Manchuria. He pushed forward the provocative policy of constructing parallel tracks to the Japanese-controlled South Manchuria Railway. The Japanese interests imperiled by this hot blast of competition were not inconsiderable. The South Manchuria Railway Company, in which the Japanese Government held 50 per cent of the shares, had attracted a total Japanese investment of $500,000,000. Its terminal port of Dairen was exporting 60 per cent of the world crop of soybeans. Coal and iron deposits, exploited by cheap Chinese labor, helped to remedy the weaknesses of Japan's economic structure. It was intolerable, contended the militarists — shaping their argument to appeal to the industrialists — that interests of such magnitude should be jeopardized. Had not the time for "preventive action" arrived? The necessary provocation was not lacking. Captain Nakamura, a Japanese military intelligence officer, posing as an agricultural expert, had been detained by the Chinese authorities in a remote quarter of Manchuria pending investigation of his credentials. He was shot subsequently while trying to escape, a proceeding which "showed arrogant disrespect for the Japanese army and nation." None of the regular ingredients of a major conflagration was wanting.

One problem remained. What would be the attitude of the Soviet Union toward an eventual Japanese occupation of Manchuria? Such a move would flank eastern Siberia, and give Japan and the Soviet Union contiguous land frontiers. But there were good grounds for assuming that the Soviet reaction would not be unduly vigorous. The special Far Eastern Army of the Soviet Union, organized as recently as 1929, was a relatively untried force. Its supply problems were complex, since the first Five-Year Plan had envisaged industrial bases in western Siberia only. Soviet-Manchurian relations were far from amicable. The Chinese Eastern Railway, which served northern

Manchuria under joint Soviet-Manchurian control, had become a bone of contention between Moscow and Chang Hsueh-liang. A recent adherent to the cause of Nationalist China, Chang found himself in cordial agreement with the anti-Soviet policy of Chiang Kai-shek. In July 1929, with the full support of the latter, he seized the telegraph system of the railroad and interned Soviet officials and employees, on the ground that they were spreading Communist propaganda. Moscow retaliated by breaking off diplomatic relations with the Chinese Government. During the fall of 1929, undeclared Sino-Russian hostilities broke out in northern Manchuria. The conflict developed in favor of the Soviet forces. Chang Hsueh-liang therefore agreed to the restoration of the *status quo* on the Chinese Eastern Railway, pending a conference in Moscow to settle all outstanding disputes. The Chinese delegate was still cooling his heels there in 1931, his mission unaccomplished. In the circumstances, it seemed probable that the Soviet Union would simply hold a watching brief in the event of a Japanese attack on Manchuria.

Meanwhile the more distant international horizons seemed clear and favorable. The United States in 1931 was sliding steadily into the depths of the Depression. A financial crisis in Britain had swept the Labor ministry of Ramsay MacDonald from office, and a new coalition government had imposed drastic economies on the country. On September 15 naval ratings at Invergordon protested against a threatened pay cut, and for the first time in more than a hundred years that ancient arm of the sea, the British Navy, was reported to have mutinied. Four days later, on September 19, 1931, Japanese troops invaded Manchuria.

Japan's predatory leap brought to realization those remarkably prophetic words of P. S. Reinsch in 1922, when he was American minister in Peking: "Only the refusal to accept the results . . . of the last four years can avert making China either a dependence of a reckless and boundlessly ambitious military caste which would destroy the peace of the entire world, or bringing on a military struggle inevitable from the establishment of rival spheres of interest and local privilege in China. . . . If China should be disappointed in her confidence at the present time, the consequences of such disillusionment on her moral and political development would be disastrous; and we [in America], instead of looking across the Pacific toward a peaceable, industrial nation, sympathetic with our ideals, would be confronted with a vast materialistic military organization under ruthless control. . . . There will come a sinister situation dominated by the unscrupulous methods of the reactionary military regime centered in Tokyo, absolutist in tendency, cynical of the principles of free government and human progress. If this force, with all the methods it is accustomed to apply, remains unopposed, there will be created in the Far East the greatest engine of military oppression and domination that the world has yet seen. Nor can we avoid the conclusion that the brunt of evil results will fall on the United States. . . . In ten years there may be a very different situation. Then also our people, having grown wise, will be sure to shout: 'Why was not this stopped while there was yet time?' " [6]

THE MANCHURIAN CRISIS

On the night of September 18–19, 1931, a minor bomb explosion destroyed a short stretch — some purists estimated it at thirty-one inches — of the track of the South Manchuria Railway a few miles north of Mukden. Patrols of the Japanese Kwantung Army, a large garrison force responsible for the protection of the railroad, appeared promptly on the scene and were allegedly fired upon from ambush. Japanese reinforcements from Mukden cleared the adjacent barracks of Chinese troops. Almost simultaneously, Japanese troops occupied the old walled city in the center of Mukden, and installed themselves in Chang Hsueh-liang's great arsenal there. Within three days the Japanese forces, expanding rapidly from their customary positions inside the railroad zone, had occupied the chief strategic points in southern Manchuria. The headquarters of the Japanese Kwantung Army, formerly at Port Arthur, were transferred to Mukden as an indication of the permanent character of the occupation. Manifestly the commanders of the Kwantung Army had taken the bit between their teeth. Nor did they lack support from Tokyo, where the civilian members of the Cabinet, declaring the incident to be susceptible of peaceful adjustment, were ignored by the Minister of War.

The Chinese Nationalist government at Nanking, perceiving that the army of its adherent, Chang Hsueh-liang, was in no condition to resist this lightning onslaught, appealed to the League of Nations under Article 11 of the Covenant and to the United States under the Pact of Paris. The League Council requested both parties to withdraw their armed forces to their original positions as a preliminary to peaceful adjudication. Stimson, the American Secretary of State, appeared at this stage to be temporizing in the hope that the entire incident might blow itself out, and he avoided any precipitate action that might involve the United States in "complications." [1] In view of the state of opinion in the United States he could hardly have adopted any other attitude (pp. 593–94). The Kwantung Army, shielded from civilian interference from Tokyo by its military supporters in the Japanese Cabinet, did not allow the diplomatic shadowboxing at Geneva and Washington to interfere with its military operations. It pushed forward rapidly against the motley host of Chang Hsueh-liang, prefacing its advance with clouds of leaflets, dropped from airplanes, regretting that "Chang Hsueh-liang, that most rapacious, wanton, and stinking youth, is still failing to realize his odiousness." By the beginning of 1932, all organized resistance in Manchuria had been extinguished, and Chang was in full flight to the south. In March 1932, the victors renamed their conquest Manchukuo, "the

State of Manchu," and they picked out of his comfortable retirement Henry Pu Yi, the surviving head of the old Manchu dynasty which had foundered in 1911, and solemnly installed him as regent. Two years later, in order to give an air of legitimacy to the new "independent" state, they crowned him Emperor. The power behind the throne was, of course, the Kwantung Army, under whose auspices a ruthless and intensive exploitation of the country's resources was begun.

The penalty of Japanese aggression in Manchukuo was an intensification of anti-Japanese sentiment throughout China. A general boycott in 1932 reduced imports from Japan by 94 per cent. In January 1932, a Shanghai mob attacked five Japanese Buddhist monks, one of whom was killed, and the incident developed into a minor military campaign. A Japanese flotilla appeared off Shanghai, and its commander summarily demanded of Mayor Wu the punishment of the culprits and the dissolution of the boycott organization. Japanese marines were landed to enforce the demand and were thrown against the Chinese Nineteenth Route Army in the native quarter of the city. The Chinese retired after a five-week defense of great heroism and unexpected tenacity, having shown that they had military qualities quite equal to those of their antagonists. A truce was patched up in May 1932, and the bulk of the Japanese forces was withdrawn. Japan, fully occupied in digesting her Manchurian acquisitions, was not yet ready to extend hostilities so far south as Shanghai, where a "gunboat policy" might easily give rise to international complications.

Meanwhile the deliberations in the Council of the League of Nations had proceeded in an atmosphere of growing frustration. Prentiss Gilbert, the American consul in Geneva, was authorized by his government to sit in at the Council's meetings in October 1931, but his instructions were restricted, and the promise of active American support in the Council was therefore not realized. On November 21, 1931, a proposal on the part of the Japanese delegates to send out a commission of inquiry on the spot was adopted by the Council. It was a hollow enough gesture as, by then, the greater part of Manchuria had been occupied by the Kwantung Army. In the first week of 1932, the city of Chinchow was taken, and Chang Hsueh-liang retired to the south of the Great Wall. A few days later, as if to make up for his earlier cautiousness, Stimson issued a declaration to the effect that the United States would not recognize "any situation, treaty, or agreement which may be brought about by means contrary to . . . the Pact of Paris." But whatever practical effect this belated declaration could possibly have had on the Manchurian situation was gauchely offset by a subsequent announcement from London that, since Japan had given assurances in regard to a continued "Open Door" in Manchuria, the British Government found it unnecessary to make any similar declaration. In March 1932, however, the League Assembly adopted a resolution, introduced by the British Foreign Secretary, Simon, urging its members to follow the Stimson doctrine of nonrecognition.[1]

The League Council's commission of inquiry was eventually formed under the chairmanship of Lord Lytton, onetime Viceroy of India, and it traveled extensively in China and Japan. Its report, submitted in October 1932, denied that the Manchurian campaign could be justified as a defensive measure on the part of Japan, described the new regime in Manchukuo as a puppet creation, and proposed its replacement by an autonomous regime under nominal Chinese suzerainty. In September 1932, on the eve of the publication of the report, Japan made a defiant gesture and formally recognized Manchukuo. In March 1933, Japan gave notice of her withdrawal from League membership.

Amid the dust and flurry of diplomatic maneuvering the indisputable fact emerged that Japan's resumption of an aggressive policy in Asia had brought her tangible dividends. Further, the absorption of Manchuria fortified the prestige and resolution of those who had instigated her action. Early in 1932, young army officers in Japan committed a series of political assassinations, which counted Baron Dan, head of the Mitsui interests, and Premier Inukai himself among its victims. It was thereby conveyed unmistakably to surviving civilian statesmen that any effort to check the army's progress in Manchuria would be equivalent to signing their own death warrants. Trifling jail sentences were meted out to the assassins, who were represented as persons who had yielded to a regrettable but entirely patriotic impulse. General Sadao Araki, the apostle of antiforeignism at home and of imperialism abroad, gave vent to the prevailing militant temper in innumerable radio addresses: "Frivolous thinking is due to foreign thought. . . . Japan must no longer let the impudence of the white peoples go unpunished. It is the duty of Japan . . . to cause China to respect the Japanese, to expel Chinese influence from Manchuria, and to follow the way of imperial destiny."

THE JAPANESE PENETRATION OF NORTH CHINA

Every ineffective step which the League of Nations took against Japan could be represented as "Western meddling" to be answered by new and deeper thrusts into China. In February 1933 the League at last adopted the Lytton Report, and Japanese forces at once opened a full-dress invasion of Jehol province to the southwest of Manchukuo. Within a few days the feeble resistance of Chinese irregular forces had been brushed aside, and the province occupied almost without opposition. Japan now stood at the Great Wall, on the very threshold of China proper.

Chiang Kai-shek, hastening to mend his political fences in the north, was confronted by unpleasant alternatives. He was well aware of the military inferiority of his armies, a large proportion of which, moreover, was still engaged in battling the Communist forces in Kiangsi. North China furthermore was of secondary importance compared with the Yangtze Valley, which constituted the economic and territorial core of Nationalist China. The southward march of the aggressor must be impeded therefore by measures short of war. Chiang resorted to a policy of temporization and delay in North China by consenting to the establishment of a buffer regime, known as the Peiping Political Council. In May 1933 the new body concluded a precarious truce by virtue of which the Japanese forces withdrew to the north of the Great Wall. A demilitarized zone was defined south of the Wall, to be policed by a Japanese-approved "Peace Preservation Corps." Banditry, of course, reigned supreme in this political no man's land, which was a breeding ground of any such "incidents" as Japanese military convenience might prescribe.

The penetration of the area lying between the Great Wall and the Yellow River (Hwang Ho) was begun by the celebrated Colonel Doihara, the "Japanese Lawrence," who professed to have unearthed a powerful "autonomy" movement among the Chinese of Hopeh province. In November 1935, under this pretext, the Kwantung Army ordered the withdrawal of Chinese forces from the area, dissolved the local branches of the Kuomintang, and drove anti-Japanese activities underground. In December 1935, Doihara repeated the same technique in the more northerly province of Chahar, which was linked administratively with Hopeh under the puppet Hopeh-Chahar Political Council. Through the breaches thus driven in the Chinese customs system, great floods of cheap Japanese goods poured into North China. Korean drug peddlers, protected by their Japanese citizenship, spread their nefarious wares far and wide. Europe meanwhile was fully preoccupied by the tremendous spectacle of German rearmament. The Ethiopian crisis mounted to its denouement. Chiang Kai-shek made some show of diplomatic resistance to Japan, and referred meaningly, in a public address to the Kuomintang, to the necessity of making sacrifices for national honor and integrity. Nevertheless, the Chinese Nationalist government duly recognized Doihara's hybrid creations in Hopeh and Chahar.

THE RESURGENCE OF CHINESE NATIONALISM

The politically conscious elements among the Chinese people naturally reacted in fear and anger as Japan devoured their northern territories, "leaf by leaf, like an artichoke." Monster student demonstrations in favor of armed resistance were held in the university cities of North and central China, demonstrations which generous sluicings of ice-cold water, and even assaults by big-sword men, could not dampen or disperse. This "National Salvation Movement" impressed, but did not convince, Chiang Kai-shek and the shrewd politicians of Nanking. A motion at a Kuomintang assembly in May 1936 for the immediate dispatch of an expeditionary force against the Japanese in North China failed of adoption. Yet, in the view of the patriots, Chiang's policy of appeasement — like every policy of appeasement that was to be tried in these years — only sharpened the aggressor's appetite for more aggression. A Japanese "Economic Monroe Doctrine," in contravention of the "Open Door," went into operation in Manchukuo to the deliberate exclusion of American and British firms in the country. Discriminatory measures against foreign interests were successively applied to every Chinese province that the Japanese forces occupied. "As long as Chiang Kai-shek and his clique continue to dominate China," affirmed General Toyada, the Japanese commander of the North China garrison, "there can be no hope of the adoption of a friendly policy towards Japan. . . . Therefore the Japanese

Empire should act independently by starting to create a paradise of co-existence and mutual prosperity between the two countries. Co-operation among Japan, China, and Manchukuo, with the Empire as the center of gravity, can warrant peace in East Asia."

In the past, Chiang Kai-shek had always parried arguments for a more resolute policy against Japan by pointing out that national unity was impossible while Communism still existed in China. But, late in 1934, the Chinese Red Army had been forced out of Kiangsi province by the methodical advance of Nationalist forces, now under the direction of Chiang Kai-shek's newly arrived military adviser, General von Seeckt, former chief of the German Reichswehr. In an epic "Long March," a mass migration of five thousand miles over mountain and gorge, fighting all the way, the Chinese Red Army traversed the central provinces of China and established itself at last around Yenan in Shensi province, where it stood within easy reach of the Soviet supply routes traversing Mongolia and where, moreover, it could menace the right flank of the Japanese advance in North China. The "Long March," an extraordinary military feat, was intended to serve notice of the determination of Chinese Communism to bring the civil war in China to an end and to concert a joint effort against Japan.

During 1935–36, the Red Army leaders at Yenan pressed consistently for a united front in China. These exhortations, if not inspired by Moscow, nevertheless fell sweetly on Soviet ears. Soviet-Japanese clashes along the river Amur had become chronic at this time, and a covert *rapprochement* between the Soviet and the Chinese Nationalist governments might well have been expected. From the Soviet point of view, the unification of China on a basis of common resistance to Japan would doubtless deflect Japanese aggression toward China and relieve the pressure on the Soviet borderlands.

Chiang Kai-shek had once declared that "the Japanese are a disease of the skin, the Communists are a disease of the heart." He was not one to relax his former anti-Communist policy in a hurry. Indeed, he directed Chang Hsueh-liang — the same Chang whom the Japanese had so unceremoniously bundled out of Manchuria in 1931 — to attack and exterminate the elusive Red Army in Shensi. But intensive Communist propaganda and fraternization between the Nationalist and Communist forces dissipated Chang's warlike purposes. Chang himself was soon inclining a willing ear to a fiery group of his own staff officers, who insisted that "all Chinese guns should be turned outward against the common enemy." Chiang Kai-shek, scenting these intrigues, hastened by air to Chang's headquarters in the city of Sian and ordered the removal of Chang, his staff, and his army to the less infected south. Chang's counterstroke was prompt and dramatic.

Shortly before dawn on December 12, 1936, one of Chang's colonels, with a picked force, surrounded the temple near Sian in which Chiang Kai-shek had established his temporary headquarters, and overpowered the body-guard. Bursting into the temple itself, the assailants found that Chiang Kai-shek had already flown. A close search of the mountainside in the rear of the temple at length disclosed their quarry, injured by a fall while trying to escape in the darkness. But this "submission of advice by military force" involved nothing more drastic than a two weeks' detention of Chiang Kai-shek at Sian. The Nationalist government was informed meanwhile that the hospitality extended to Chiang Kai-shek was simply an effort to provide him with leisure for calm reflection on the subject of a united front against Japan. His personal safety was guaranteed. On Christmas Day he was released and, accompanied by his erstwhile captor, Chang Hsueh-liang, he returned to Nanking, where he received a frantic ovation from the relieved populace.

Chiang Kai-shek had refused to make specific concessions during his detention. Any surrender to his military subordinates under threat of force would have undermined his prestige, which his captors themselves were anxious to preserve intact. Chang Hsueh-liang had demonstrated his disinterested patriotism by accompanying his superior back to Nanking, and by submitting to a sentence of ten years' imprisonment — which he did not serve — he assisted his chief to "keep face." However, negotiations between Communists and Nationalists for a united front were protracted for several months and only reached a formal conclusion in September 1937. The Communists declared their acceptance of Dr. Sun's Three Principles (pp. 413–14), their abandonment of their policy of land confiscation, the discontinuance of their Soviet form of government, and their readiness to place their Red Army under Nationalist control. For his part, Chiang Kai-shek welcomed the Communists' declaration, but with a certain reserve: "If a citizen believes in the Three Principles and works actively for the salvation of the State, the government should not concern itself with his past, but shall give him opportunity to prove his loyalty in service to the Republic. Likewise, the government will gladly accept the services of any political organization provided . . . it is willing, under the banner of our national revolution, to join with us in our struggle against aggression."

"THE CHINA INCIDENT"

To keenly watching eyes in Tokyo the National Salvation Movement and the united anti-Japanese front in China had been highly unwelcome developments, clearly calling for preventive counteraction. A survey of the international scene indicated, moreover, that such counteraction had best be prompt and vigorous. Not only did Japan's withdrawal from the League of Nations in March 1933 show the world that she proposed to follow a "lone wolf" policy in China, but it was almost a challenge to foreign Powers with interests in China to combine against her. In the Chinese territories she had already engulfed, Japan was showing scant hospitality to foreign economic interests. A Japanese Oil Monopoly Bureau in Manchuria, for instance, assumed the exclusive control of the sale and distribution of petroleum, to the disastrous contraction of the operations of Standard Oil and other foreign firms. The meticulous crippling of non-Japanese enterprises would doubtless follow wherever the lengthening shadow of Japan should fall. A "Stop Japan" movement on the part of foreign Powers was therefore a matter of enlightened self-interest, if nothing else. It would complement China's own anti-Japanese front, and it might take practical form in financial and other material aids. Even if their other preoccupations, in these years of the Depression, prevented the Powers from risking themselves in outright acts of retaliation against Japan, they could at least lend China valuable economic reinforcements.

The United States and Britain therefore moved to underpin the shaky finances of the Chinese Nationalist government, whose revenues had been cut away by the Depression and by the loss in customs consequent upon Japanese smuggling. A British credit of £1,500,000 to the Chinese Nationalist government in April 1934 elicited a strong protest from Tokyo against "political loans." The United States provided $50,000,000 through its Reconstruction Finance Corporation. Unfortunately, the American policy of silver buying, instituted in 1934, encouraged the outflow of the metal from China, accentuated the downward trend of prices there, and enriched Japanese speculators in Manchukuo and North China, who exported every ounce of silver procurable. The impending collapse of the Chinese currency was averted by Sir Frederick Leith-Ross, a British Treasury expert. Chinese currency was placed on a managed paper basis, the note issue was centralized in a few of the leading banks, and existing silver stocks were nationalized and impounded by the government. The United States Treasury in 1936, by initiating direct buying of silver from the Chinese Government, provided it with the necessary dollar exchange for purchases in the American market. All this financial aid was highly distasteful to Tokyo, which had counted on the subtly paralyzing onset of the Depression to weaken Chinese resistance. Japanese militarists could bring forward once more the familiar arguments for a "positive" policy in China before their intended victim should grow too strong.

The balance of the world's naval armaments also contributed to the political complex in the Far East in these years. In December 1934, Japan formally announced her intention to abrogate the Washington naval ratios of 1922. At the London Naval Conference a year later, she demanded absolute naval parity with the United States and Britain (see p. 495). When her proposals for "a common upper limit" failed of acceptance, she withdrew from the Conference. In view of the relatively inferior shipbuilding capacity of Japan, a protracted race in battleship construction with the United States could never have ended in her favor. Here was a further argument for a quick, "positive" policy in China.

Finally, in every Japanese calculation, there was always the great unknown, the darkly lowering enigma of Russia. A Japanese war in China would be immensely complicated by the presence of an aggressively disposed neighbor on the flank and rear. The Far Eastern Army of the Soviet, commanded by the redoubtable General Bluecher and numbering 250,000 effectives, was in a state of permanent mobilization. The rapid colonization and industrialization of Siberia under the second Five-Year Plan had carried that territory far toward military self-sufficiency and freed it from dependence on Ukrainian munitions and Caucasian oil. The double-tracking of the Trans-Siberian Railway, taken vigorously in hand after 1933, had been completed to the Manchurian frontier.

Japan's "Economic Monroe Doctrine" in Manchukuo had borne as hardly and as provocatively on Soviet interests as on the interests of the other Powers. In 1935 the Soviet Union had been constrained to yield its last economic foothold thereby selling its rights in the Chinese Eastern Railway to Japan for 140,000,000 yen ($40,000,000). Then, seeking to test the extent of Soviet aggressiveness, Japan precipitated a series of border clashes along the Manchukuoan-Mongolian and Manchukuoan-Siberian frontiers. Although the Soviet's reaction on these occasions was vigorous to a degree, its forces showed no inclination to pass to the offensive. Tokyo drew the conclusion that the Soviet Far Eastern Army would remain a passive spectator of any Sino-Japanese hostilities that might now break out. However, an additional precaution was taken in the field of diplomacy by the signature of a German-Japanese Anti-Comintern Pact in November 1936. The signatories agreed to keep each other informed concerning the activities of the Comintern and to consult each other on necessary measures of defense. The Pact, of course, made no mention of the Soviet Government as such, but somewhat disingenuously singled out for special objuration the Comintern, the Soviet's conspirative instrument in the international sphere, and it was clearly designed to hamper the Soviet's freedom of action in Asia by multiplying its difficulties in Europe.

The internal situation in Japan had worsened by the middle thirties. The outburst of political assassinations during 1932 had been followed by a period of uneasy calm, and the nation had bent its efforts to beating the Depression by an "export offensive" of imposing dimensions. By the close of 1935, Japanese exports had regained the 1929 level. The decline in silk exports was more than offset by the great quantities of cheap Japanese cotton goods which inundated the markets of British India, the Netherlands East Indies, the Philippines, Latin America and, of course, Manchukuo and North China. But by 1936, quota barriers and tariff walls had risen everywhere, save in the territories under Japanese control, and the short-lived trade boom faltered. Even the leaders of Japanese light industry, the main sufferers from Chinese boycotts and hence the traditional opponents of military aggression in China, conceded at last that Japan must find compensation in wider fields in East Asia.

The junior army officers in Japan were an even more disturbing element. They were a class of hot-blooded young men, many of them born of rural families and, as they were promoted through the ranks, they looked askance at the wealthy industrialists who flourished while the farmers fought a perpetual crisis. They disapproved heartily of the termination of full-scale hostilities in China after 1933, since this termination had prejudiced their prospects of early and rapid advancement. On February 26, 1936, the accumulated discontent exploded in an incident popularly known, from its date, as "the Two Twenty-six." It was not unlike the contemporaneous Nazi purges in Germany and Austria, which indeed may have inspired it. Fourteen hundred men of the Imperial Guard and of the First Division, under the guidance of their captains and lieutenants, embarked on a systematic round of assassinations of public figures of "moderate" sympathies. Old Viscount Saito was disposed of at dawn in his own house. Finance Minister Takahashi, who had scrutinized defense estimates so carefully and pruned them so rigorously, was shot as he lay in bed. Admiral Okada, the Premier, warned in the nick of time by a system of alarm bells recently installed, took refuge in the large steel vault in his home which served as an earthquake shelter. The mutineers shot his brother-in-law, who markedly resembled him, and withdrew, under the impression that their work was satisfactorily completed. The next day, the Admiral experienced the indignity of being smuggled out of the house by his faithful servants, disguised as a mourner at his own funeral. The main body of the mutineers meanwhile occupied key points in central Tokyo. The summoning of the fleet into Tokyo Bay and a formal injunction from the Emperor were necessary before the mutineers consented to lay down their arms on the fourth day of the revolt. The rank and file were pardoned on the ground that they had acted under orders from their immediate military superiors, but fifteen of the ringleaders were tried by secret court-martial and shot. The city remained deathly silent throughout the crisis, the civil population contemplating the sanguinary drama with a calm expressive of their stunted political instincts.

The brief reaction against the militarists prevented them from securing the cabinet they desired until June 1937. The "National" ministry of Prince Konoye of that date was a link between the business interests and the militarists. Konoye was a protégé of the Elder Statesman, Prince Saionji, and was therefore acceptable to all parties. His vociferous Pan-Asianism commended him to the militarists. Thus the political preparations at home for a fresh onslaught on China were successfully completed. On July 7, 1937, a little more than a month after the installation of the Konoye ministry, the first shots in the renewed Sino-Japanese War were fired at the Marco Polo Bridge near Peiping.

The Marco Polo Bridge stood near the Peiping-Hankow railroad, the sole remaining connection between Peiping and Nationalist China. The "accidental" clash in that area therefore served Japanese strategic requirements most admirably. On the night of July 7, 1937, a small detachment of Japanese soldiery on "night maneuvers" advanced into the neighborhood of the bridge, then held by troops of the Chinese Twenty-ninth Army. A challenge from the bridge guard having produced no answer, a wild exchange of shots occurred in the darkness. Neither side incurred casualties. Next day, on the excuse that one of their number had disappeared, the Japanese began a painfully thorough house-to-house search of a near-by town. The missing soldier subsequently rejoined his unit. A Sino-Japanese committee of five army officers was nominated at the suggestion of the Japanese to affix responsibility for the shooting. While the committee was conducting its investigations on the spot, an outbreak of gunfire outside the town resulted in casualties among both the Chinese and Japanese forces concentrated there. The Nationalist government at Nanking expressed the view that the incident could be peacefully adjusted. But the three weeks during which negotiations were conducted were used by the Japanese to pour heavy reinforcements into North China. When all military preparations were completed, Japan dropped the hollow pretense of reaching a negotiated settlement. On July 26,

Peiping was occupied. No formal declaration of war was issued by either side. The Japanese always referred to the hostilities which now developed as the "China incident." It was nevertheless one of the preliminary opening bouts of the Second World War.

Compared with the loosely articulated provincial forces of the twenties, the Chinese Army of 1937 was at least politically integrated, and it acknowledged the central command of the Generalissimo, Chiang Kai-shek. The Chinese Red Army in Shensi had been incorporated into it as the Eighth Route Army. At the core of the Chinese Army were the German-trained divisions, "the Generalissimo's Own," numbering 300,000 men. But even these elite troops were woefully inferior, judged by modern European — and Japanese — standards. They were apparently well provided with rifles, machine guns, and grenades, mainly home-manufactured, but they lacked heavy equipment, notably tanks and artillery; their air force consisted of 200 serviceable planes; their transportation system, save in areas served directly by railroads, was primitive and inefficient. Even psychological disabilities had not been entirely overcome. Twenty years of sporadic civil war had not eradicated the inherent Chinese contempt for the soldier and for the military life, and it was with some surprise that the Japanese were to learn that the Chinese fighting man could rise to the most stubborn heroism and show a considerable tactical skill and adaptability.

Altogether the Chinese Army of 1937 is believed to have contained 200 divisions of 10,000 men each. But it was almost exclusively committed to the defense of the lower Yangtze Valley, the heart of Nationalist China. Consequently, little of it could be spared for the five provinces north of the Yellow River still unoccupied by the Japanese, and with the exception of rugged Shensi province, under the control of the Communist Eighth Route Army, all these five were overrun and lost by December 1937.

But Chiang Kai-shek decided upon a more resolute defense of Shanghai, the scene of the Nineteenth Route Army's successful stand in 1932, and he contributed to the operation the best troops under his command. The Japanese effected their first landing at Shanghai on August 13, 1937, and there developed a three months' battle involving 30 Chinese divisions and costing the Japanese 40,000 casualties. The tenacity which the Chinese for the second time displayed at Shanghai persuaded the Japanese to abandon the simple strategy of territorial expansion from the north and to concentrate upon an offensive against the heart of the Chinese resistance in the Yangtze Valley. The capture of the capital at Nanking, they hoped, might cause the collapse of the Chinese Nationalist government and bring the entire "China incident" to an early and satisfactory conclusion. Nanking was taken in December 1937 and was given over to the most shocking treatment at the hands of the Japanese soldiery. But, far from collapsing, the Chinese Government moved to Hankow and thence to Chungking, well protected by the difficult gorges of the upper Yangtze and by the broken mountainous terrain that flanked them, and from there Chiang Kai-shek, in a national manifesto, declared that he would continue the struggle till the ultimate victory of China.

The conduct of two simultaneous campaigns on the part of Japan — in the northern provinces and in the Yangtze Valley — though defensible on political grounds, was strategically weakening, and the first six months of 1938 were used by the Japanese command to effect a junction between their northern and southern forces. Chiang Kai-shek personally directed the defense of southern Shantung, and he drew heavily upon German advice and upon the recent experiences at Shanghai. The fighting was costly to both sides. The Chinese inflicted a sharp reverse on the Japanese at Taierchwang. They cut the dikes of the Yellow River in an effort to save the city of Chenchow. But one stubborn operation after another amounted to little more than a succession of delaying actions. Süchow fell on May 19. By midsummer the province of Kiangsu and a great part of Honan and Anhwei had been occupied by the Japanese. In the six months the Chinese are said to have suffered 200,000 casualties.

The Japanese immediately resumed their advance up the Yangtze. A considerable fleet of cruisers and gunboats co-operated with their land forces. Chinese forts and river booms were destroyed one after another. A secondary Japanese column advanced on Sinyang down the Peiping-Hankow railroad. Cholera and malaria added to the hardships of both armies. Hankow fell during October, and simultaneously a considerable Japanese expedition seized the city of Canton.

The fall of Canton concluded the first phase of the Sino-Japanese War. Since the shooting affray at the Marco Polo Bridge in July 1937, the Chinese had suffered 2,000,000 military casualties, killed and wounded, and the loss of their main seaports and all their most important centers of commerce, industry, and culture. Civilian sufferers to the number of 60,000,000 had been driven from their homes. Many of them had fled before the advancing Japanese into Szechwan province, thus immensely complicating Chiang Kai-shek's supply problems. Vast areas of the country had been flooded or "scorched." Japanese casualties were estimated optimistically at 500,000.

By all orthodox military standards the balance sheet of death and devastation might well have added up to a lost war. In all its technical aspects the struggle had been hopelessly one-sided. The Chinese had little with which to oppose the tactical training, the heavy equipment, the airplanes — and the ruthless conduct — of their enemy, except their numbers, their courage, and their growing experience in the art of modern warfare. But there was another side of the picture. Chiang Kai-shek had taken every advantage of terrain and geography, and he appears to have calculated to a nicety the maximum depth which the Japanese penetration could effect without obtaining the voluntary political conversion of the country. Useful materials, such as factory machinery in Hankow, were evacuated to Chungking whenever possible, under incredible difficulties, inadequate though those materials were for Chiang's military and civilian needs. A "scorched-earth" policy robbed the invader of much of what was left. Then sixty divisions were sent to operate within the Japanese lines and wage guerrilla war on the tenuous Japanese communications. At the end of 1938, though the area under nominal Japanese occupation was writ large on the map of China, the area under effective military control was confined to the coasts, the railroads, and the main northern and central cities.

Of late years, observers have tried ever more curiously to pierce the smiling, unruffled mask of Chiang Kai-shek and measure the real dimensions of the man behind it. Of his innate social conservatism there could be no shadow of doubt. His entry by marriage into the complex economic interests of the Soong family merely furthered and emphasized this conservatism. The pre-eminent value of order, of self-reliance and responsibility, of social discipline was infused into him from an ineradicable Confucianism, confirmed and reinforced by the austerities and exactions of a military career. The enormous prestige which he acquired at home and abroad in the triumphant twenties bore him well forward into the failing thirties before doubting voices became audible; and it was not till the Stilwell controversy of 1944, in the middle of the Second World War, that the great national hero of Free China in the remoteness of his capital at Chungking came to be represented to the world at large as the dictator of a military and political establishment eroded by inefficiency, treachery, and corruption. Then later, as the American campaign of 1944–45 in the Pacific broadened in scope, further insinuations were heard that Chiang was deliberately waging a waiting war till the general Allied victory should bring him a total solution of his problems, that his chief concern was the containment of the Chinese Red Army, and that the arms he was receiving from abroad were being held for the day when the Japanese capitulation would enable him to turn and destroy his Communist enemies in China.

The insinuations were severe. But recently they seem to have found independent confirmation in Chiang's own book, *China's Destiny,* a personal confession of faith which, completed in 1943, appeared in English translation two years later. In the book, Chiang condemns the Western imperialists and native war lords of the past and calls for the abrogation of all the unequal treaties which have destroyed "our nationhood and our sense of shame and honour." He refers in profound admiration to Sun Yat-sen, "the Father of our Country," and to Sun's Three Principles, "the basis of the Nationalist Revolution." All this is good and acceptable. But the tone certainly changes when he describes "the psychology of revolutionary reconstruction" and stresses the importance of the individual, not as an individual, but as a part of the state and nation. "Mass purpose and mass force are needed to implement the principles of the Kuomintang." The grand theme of the book is that of a strong, disciplined, and expanding China drawing her cultural virtues from her own ancient Confucianism and spreading those virtues among neighboring peoples which once acknowledged her sway. Thus China was to recover her former status as the political and cultural leader of Asia, a status from which she had been ousted only temporarily by a militant and brutalized Japan. It was not unlikely that Western democratic critics, reading the book, should be troubled by these affirmations of a *mission civilisatrice* in Nationalist China; for the West had fought and bled in two mighty wars in less than a generation to prevent one of its member nations from imposing its *Kultur* on the rest. Nor did these critics fail to notice the enormous discrepancy between the vision of a powerful, unified, and expanding China on the one hand and the existing parochial and demoralized Chungking regime on the other.

THE SINO–JAPANESE WAR AND THE POWERS

However, Chiang Kai-shek's literary self-revelations still belonged to the future. At the moment he and the Sino-Japanese War had been having other repercussions abroad. The reaction of the League of Nations toward the new outbreak of fighting in China in 1937 followed, with an ironical if depressing fidelity, the pattern of the Manchurian crisis of six years before. China appealed to Articles 10, 11, and 16 of the Covenant. In October 1937 the League duly declared that Japanese operations by land, sea, and air against China were not legitimate measures of self-defense, and that "such action cannot possibly facilitate or promote the friendly co-operation between the two nations that Japanese statesmen have affirmed to be the aim of their policy." But verbal admonitions made no impression on the offender, who in any case was no longer a member of the League. The Far Eastern Advisory Committee of the League further proposed a conference of the signatories of the Nine-Power Treaty (see p. 365) in the hope that Japan would accept friendly mediation of the conflict outside the framework of the League. The ensuing conference met in Brussels in November 1937. But Japan declined point-blank to attend, alleging that measures taken in self-defense fell outside the scope of the treaty in question. The conference drafted a resolution condemning Japan's attempt "to change by armed force the policy of China," and dissolved. The issue was thrown back into the lap of the League.

The machinery at Geneva ground laboriously along for another year. In accordance with Article 16 of the Covenant, the question for applying economic sanctions against Japan came up for consideration in September 1938. But the Czechoslovak crisis was then at its height and, on British initiative, the Council of the League merely urged individual members to consider what aid, if any, they felt capable of extending to China. Japan in return hastened to inform the League that, if any constituent nation applied sanctions, she would be compelled to take "appropriate measures."

The well-tested Japanese technique of timing aggression in the East to coincide with crisis in the West seemed to be returning good profits. Bonnet, the archappeaser in charge of French foreign policy, was resolved to give Japan no excuse for an attack on French Indo-China while he wrestled with the German problem in Europe and, in October 1937, the supply of munitions to Chungking, flowing along the Hanoi-Kunming railroad, was cut to harmless proportions. Britain continued to furnish aid to China through the ports of Shanghai and Hong Kong. But the Japanese blocked the Yangtze River route, which linked Shanghai with the interior, by declaring that war conditions had rendered it unsafe for traffic. The fall of Canton, in October 1938, choked off the inflow of supplies by way of Hong Kong.

The economic noose was tightening around Free China and, if the pressure was to be relaxed, alternative supply routes must be found. A partial answer to the problem was provided by the far-famed Burma Road. From Rangoon a railroad threaded its way northward through the endless Burmese paddy fields, past Mandalay with its gigantic walled fort, across the Gokteik Gorge — where American engineers in 1900 had constructed a "temporary" viaduct

— and reached its terminus at Lashio at the foot of mountainous Yunnan province. From Lashio a soft-surface road mounted through rugged country to Kunming. It was completed in 1937–38 at considerable cost in lives by a force of 100,000 coolies working under American-trained engineers. The third section of the route, from Kunming to Chungking, had already been constructed in 1935. Bad surfacing and landslides caused casualties and delays. In the rainy season, from July to September, traffic was brought to a complete standstill. Nevertheless the Burma Road circumvented the areas held by Japan and opened a back door into the Chinese hinterland. In December 1938, Britain announced a credit of $2,000,000 to Free China for the purchase of trucks.

In retaliation, during February and March 1939, Japan occupied Hainan and the Spratly Islands, thus establishing strategic positions athwart maritime communications between Hong Kong and Singapore. Further pressure, designed to remind Britain that her far-flung concessions in China were so many hostages to Japan, took the form of a blockade by Japanese soldiery of the British concession at Tientsin. In particular the Japanese demanded the surrender of four Chinese held in the concession on suspicion of assassinating the pro-Japanese Commissioner of Customs, and the surrender also of $48,-000,000 deposited there by the Chinese Nationalist government. The passage of food into the concession was restricted, British nationals were searched and subjected to indignities at the barriers, and Chinese farmers who tried to bring vegetables into the beleaguered settlement were shot.

The Chamberlain government in London was entangled in too many problems in Europe to make a strong diplomatic stand, and it prepared reluctantly to pay the price of appeasement. In July 1939, Sir Robert Craigie, the newly appointed British ambassador to Tokyo, opened discussions with the Foreign Minister, Arita. The Craigie-Arita Agreement recognized that "the Japanese forces in China have special requirements for the purpose of safeguarding their own security and maintaining public order in regions under their control. His Majesty's Government have no intention of countenancing any act prejudicial to the attainment of the aforesaid objects by the Japanese forces." The four suspect Chinese in Tientsin were surrendered to an inevitable fate two weeks later. Bitter editorials appeared in the Chinese Nationalist press, suggesting that an Oriental Munich had occurred. But the Nationalist deposit of $48,000,000 remained safely in the bank vaults of Tientsin. The policy of diplomatic appeasement was, however, an undeniable fact, and it did not contribute to the prestige of the white man in the East.

Washington for a time had made no greater show of strength than London. Public opinion in the United States was decidedly averse to any policy which might expose the nation to the risk of war. It was possible for President Roosevelt to refrain from using the neutrality legislation of 1935–37 to apply an arms embargo against the belligerents, on the ostensible ground that no formal declaration of war had been made by either China or Japan. An embargo, arguably, would have penalized the Chinese Nationalist government, which was in far more desperate need of armaments from abroad than Japan. But the continued sale of American gasoline, oil, scrap metal, and machinery to Japan was judged in Tokyo to be some assurance that the United States intended no drastic action. The bombing by Japanese aircraft of the United States gunboat *Panay* on the Yangtze, in December 1937, was settled by an indemnity of $2,214,000. The Japanese Government, mindful of its dependence on American supplies, and fearful of Anglo-American co-operation in China, paid the indemnity promptly and in full.

But, as Japanese armies swept from triumph to triumph in China during 1938, the antiforeign objectives in her program for a "New Order in East Asia" received increasingly aggressive definition. It was made abundantly manifest that in the "Co-prosperity Sphere" of Japan — Manchukuo and occupied China — foreign interests and holdings would be slowly eroded away. The doctrine of the "Open Door" was relegated to the category of "inapplicable ideas and principles of the past." The North China Development Company and the Central China Development Company were founded to facilitate the exploitation of occupied China (see p. 730). Under the weight of these huge monopolistic concerns the "Open Door" began slowly, remorselessly, to close. Washington's countermoves were diplomatic and economic in character. Secretary of State Hull, in the spirit of his predecessor, Stimson, stressed American nonrecognition of the exclusivist "New Order in East Asia" in a series of increasingly acid notes of protest. In December 1938 the Export-Import Bank announced a credit of $25,000,000 to Free China. Chiang Kai-shek, fortified by this token of American sympathy, rejected a Japanese peace offer on December 26. Six months later, in July 1939, Washington denounced the American-Japanese Commercial Treaty of 1911. Japanese jubilation over the Craigie-Arita Agreement, signed two days earlier, was thus sensibly modified. The way was cleared for a thoroughgoing embargo on trade with Japan.

The Japanese Government, with this weighty economic bludgeon hanging over its head, began to make conciliatory gestures. The Tokyo press discussed the possibility of a new commercial treaty with the United States, hinting that, in return, the Yangtze might be reopened to international traffic. Lest these proposals be construed as a confession of weakness, it was announced that negotiations were actively proceeding for the transformation of the German-Japanese Anti-Comintern Pact of 1936 into a full-fledged military alliance. But the exchanges with Berlin, inspired by the Japanese Army, were arrested in mid-air by the announcement of the Soviet-German Moscow Pact of August 1939. Japan, supping so familiarly with the Devil, had neglected to provide herself with the proverbially necessary long spoon.

The dynamism of Japan during these years had thrust Soviet policy perforce into the same pattern as the American and the British. It was designed to help China, to embarrass Japan, and above all to avoid war, but it followed the more unconventional, unscrupulous Soviet pattern. A month after the Marco Polo Bridge incident, a Sino-Soviet nonaggression pact was concluded at Nanking, coincident with the informal agreement between Chiang Kai-shek and the Chinese Communists. A thin but increasing trickle of Soviet military supplies began to flow into China by way of Sinkiang and Mongolia. But their quantity was shown, by the irrefutable logic of the

Chinese defeats, to be inadequate. In June 1939, Moscow extended a credit of 75,000,000 rubles to Free China, accepting tungsten, antimony, and tea in return for shipments of aircraft and other military supplies. The agreement stipulated further that the Nationalist forces should not encroach on the territory in Northwest China held by the Chinese Red Army, and that the Communist elements incorporated in the Nationalist armies should enjoy full right of assembly and of debate.

Japanese resentment at the increasing scale of Soviet aid to Free China was reflected in vicious and almost incessant patrol clashes on the Siberian borders. One of these, in July 1938, blazed up into a midget Soviet-Japanese war. The scene on this occasion was Changkufeng, a height of some strategic importance at the junction of the Siberian, Manchukuoan, and Korean frontiers, dominating the neighboring Korean port of Rashin and situated only some fifty miles from Vladivostok. Uncertainty about the exact frontier in the area gave some reason to the fighting. Early in August, Soviet aircraft heavily bombed the local railroad, causing a temporary suspension of traffic. Tokyo, seriously alarmed, ordered blackout practice for the cities in central and eastern Japan. An armistice was signed on August 10, 1938, and the usual mixed commission — subsequently ignored by both parties — was appointed to delimit the disputed frontier.

Soviet-Japanese hostilities stopped during the winter. But in the following summer of 1939, large-scale fighting broke out anew in the cattle country round Lake Buir on the Manchukuoan-Mongolian borderland. The Japanese threw some of their best troops into the battle and met with early successes. But mechanized units of the Soviet Far Eastern Army reinforced the frontier guards in the area, and by mid-September 1939, a Soviet offensive of considerable dimensions was in full career. Tokyo hastened to conclude an armistice which paved the way for frontier demarcation by another mixed commission. However, the scale and bitterness of the fighting had shown very clearly that the Soviet Union, for all its desire to avoid embroilment in a Far Eastern war, was not disposed to allow Japan to persevere undisturbed in her prodigious attempt to swallow the Chinese dragon.

The Soviet-German Moscow Pact of August 1939 and the outbreak of the war in Europe for the moment had cooled anti-Soviet ardor in Japan. It was evident that Germany was not yet prepared to play hammer to Japan's anvil by participating in a simultaneous onslaught on the Soviet Union. Further, Japan, having once acquired a broad continental bridgehead in Manchuria in 1931, had followed the line of least resistance southward — away from Soviet territory. If the southward trend continued, it would inevitably impinge on British, French, and Dutch colonial possessions in the Pacific. The defense of these areas by the Powers concerned would be enormously complicated if their resources were entangled and consumed in a distant European war. As in 1914, the generals and statesmen in Tokyo complacently calculated that the conflicts of the Western nations would provide Japan with golden opportunities for expansion in the Far East. Once again, in September 1939, Japan stood poised, prepared to snatch any advantage which the white man's civil war in Europe might offer.

28 GERMANY: THE RISE AND ESTABLISHMENT OF NAZISM

THE RISE OF HITLER AND NAZISM

Adolf Hitler, Führer of National Socialism, and Chancellor of the Third Reich, was born on April 20, 1889, at Braunau, across from Bavaria, on the Austrian side of the river Inn. He was the son of a village cobbler who had become a minor customs official. He was a morose, unsociable boy, always in sullen rebellion against his father and his schoolmasters. His one strong affection was for his mother, who probably pampered him to excess.

His early life was drab and aimless. He wanted to be a painter and, to judge by some of his surviving water colors, he was not without a conventional talent. But success smiled not upon his fitful efforts, and he appears to have spent his twentieth to his twenty-seventh years in utter poverty, wandering through Vienna and Munich, despising and avoiding manual work, but plying his uncertain craft and generally learning the hard lesson of existence. He picked up some skill as an architectural draftsman, and he colored post cards which a friend peddled in the streets. Incidentally he interested himself in politics and developed a rabid hatred of the proletariat and the Jews.

The First World War was his road to Damascus. "To myself that hour brought redemption from all the vexations of my youth," he wrote. "I am not ashamed to say that, in a transport of rapture, I sank down on my knees, and I thanked Heaven from an overflowing heart for having given me the good fortune to be alive at such a time." He served as a volunteer in a Bavarian infantry regiment and, though this part of his history is also indefinite and since corrupted by legend, there is no reason to doubt that he made a brave and efficient soldier. He won the Iron Cross and was promoted to the rank of lance corporal. At the time of the Armistice, in November 1918, he was lying in hospital, gassed and almost blinded.

The next five years he spent in Munich, living the life of a political waif in that fermenting, disillusioned world that was postwar Germany. He became a member of the so-called German Workers' party, one of the dozens of organizations or quasi organizations which were then trying to eke out a little dignity and fellowship and a little vicarious revenge for their country's humiliation. The Reichswehr used him as a spy at Communist meetings, and this somewhat casual employment brought him into touch with Roehm, a stalwart of the Bavarian Reichswehr.

The five years were years of development for both himself and his movement. He discovered a talent for oratory; he spoke tirelessly at public meetings; he wrangled with all comers at cafés and beer cellars. In 1920 the German Workers' party changed its name to the National Socialist German Workers' party (*National-Sozialistische Deutsche Arbeiterpartei*, N.S.D.A.P.), drafted a program of twenty-five points, acquired a newspaper of its own, the *Völkischer Beobachter*, and established its permanent headquarters in Munich. It boasted some 3,000 members and it grew rapidly. The first units of the Brown Shirts, the SA (*Sturmabteilung*), were formed in 1921 as a sort of Free Corps which provided ushers and "bouncers" at party meetings and terrorized the meetings of the left-wing parties. The Fascist salute with the outstretched right arm, the "*Heil Hitler!*," the swastika, the popular abbreviation "Nazi," and the entire technique of the public meeting with its flags and placards, marching and songs and mass effects were all in use at this time.

The party gained an important accession of power and notoriety during the Ruhr crisis, and especially after the Hitler-Ludendorff Putsch of November 1923, mentioned in an earlier chapter (see p. 166). For his part in the putsch Hitler was condemned to five years in the fortress of Landsberg-on-the-Lech. It was a reflection on the administration of justice in Germany at the time that the court violated the clear letter of the law in dealing with him so lightly that he, a foreigner, was not deported, and that finally he was released on probation after serving eight and a half months of his sentence. And he made good use of those months. Friends and helpers were allowed to visit him; he had time to study, to think, and to plan; and he dictated the greater part of *Mein Kampf*, the text and canon-to-be of National Socialism.

The years from 1923 to 1929 were the lean years of the Nazi movement, a hard, unrelenting interim occupied with underground politics and individual trials of strength not always of the most savory kind. The party organization was consolidated and developed, and its bigger personalities emerged. The SS (*Schutzstaffel*), or Black Shirts, the *corps d'élite* of the party and the personal entourage of the Führer, were formed in 1925. The struggle for power in the party, nerve-racking and soul-destroying as it was, had its educative value and was doubtless an excellent preparation for the larger struggle for power in the Reich which was to come. Advancement fell as much to ruthlessness and craft as to ability, and ruthlessness and craft were to be very useful qualifications in Nazi Germany.

Thus there was Ernst Roehm, already mentioned, a professional soldier, a Free Corps fighter and brawler at Communist demonstrations, an early member of the German Workers' party. He held a command in the SA, and planned to organize it as a secret army, an adjunct of the Reichswehr. There was Gottfried Feder, an economic theorist, and one of the authors of the original twenty-five point program. There was Hermann Göring, ace airman of the war, a leading participant in the putsch of 1923, and one of the first group of Nazis in the Reichstag. He survived the ravages of a vicious private life to become the mighty man of valor, "Iron Hermann" as he liked to be called, an immensely popular, swashbuckling hero, loud, genial, and obese, fond of his decorations, medals, and uniforms, a voracious collector of works of art, but credited with fiendish cruelties, first organizer of the Gestapo and the concentration camps, the future Minister of Air, Minister President of Prussia, Chief Forester and Huntsman, Plenipotentiary of the Four-Year

Plan, and *Reichsmarschall*. There was Dr. Joseph Goebbels, product of seven universities, a journalist, also one of the first Nazis in the Reichstag, of silvern but venomous tongue, lame in body and halt in mind, the future Minister of Propaganda, unpopular even with his colleagues but indispensable to the movement for his peculiar arts. There was Rudolf Hess, deputy and heir apparent of the Führer, general organizer at party headquarters, a mediocre, unbalanced, far from glittering personality, though at first a patient, faithful, industrious lieutenant. There was Wilhelm Frick, police official, jurist, lawyer, and zealous administrator. There was Alfred Rosenberg, a German Balt, formerly a student in Russia, then editor of the *Völkischer Beobachter*, at one time the principal theorist and philosopher of the movement. There was Robert Ley, gross, debauched, but able organizer of the Labor Front. There was Baldur von Schirach, poet, youth leader, and educator. There was Hans Frank, Nazi lawmaker and future Governor General of Poland. There was Julius Streicher, Jew-baiter and editor of *Der Stürmer*, the notorious anti-Semitic weekly. There was Heinrich Himmler, Chief of the SS and later of the Gestapo, meticulous investigator of crime, perhaps the most sinister man of them all. There were the Strasser brothers, Gregor and Otto, Catholics and Socialists, and at one time storm centers of an anti-Hitlerite heresy in northern Germany. At a later date there was Walter Funk, journalist and one of Hitler's economists; there was Joachim von Ribbentrop, former wine salesman, Hitler's adviser on foreign affairs, future ambassador to Britain and Foreign Minister; there was Albert Speer, architect and future Minister of Armaments; there was Hans Fritzsche, news editor and broadcaster; there was Artur von Seyss-Inquart, of Austrian (Sudeten German) extraction, future Chancellor of Austria and Commissioner of the Occupied Netherlands; there was Martin Bormann, the Führer's private secretary and chief of the party chancellery. Strange and abnormal men they all were, riven by jealousies and self-seeking, but assuredly in their several ways as extraordinary a company as ever bid for a place in history.

The Nazi party continued to grow, but it cannot be said that it flourished. Its membership was 27,000 in 1925 and 178,000 in 1929. But its representation in the Reichstag consistently fell. In three elections between 1924 and 1928, it returned 32, 14, and 12 Deputies successively. The years from 1924 to 1929 covered the single interval of stability enjoyed by the interwar Reich, and they were years marked by a recession, certainly a slackening in the popularity of all the "parties of discontent." The argument that Nazism, like the kindred cult of Fascism, derived the greater part of its strength from economic rather than from moral forces seems to be borne out by the facts of the case and, but for the grim resolution of the Führer and his aides, the movement might well have withered and disappeared under the benign fortunes of the Locarno era.

The financing of the party, the endless, heartless, heartbreaking scrounging for dues, subscriptions, gifts, and loans, makes no small part of the secret history of Nazism at this time. The *Völkischer Beobachter* paid well, but the party's other literature was an always expanding item, voracious of funds. Meetings, as ever, were extravagantly advertised and staged. Numberless rentals, stipends, pensions, and perquisites had to be met. It is hardly surprising that Hitler, like Mussolini in 1921, turned for help more and more to the big industrial magnates and to the Junkers, who were inclined to support an anti-Communist, nationalist movement. Fritz Thyssen and Hugo Stinnes, Schacht and Hugenberg, the magnates of the Farben Industries, Junker landowners, and princes of the blood were all subscribers to the cause. Old radicals in the party, like the Strasser brothers, were deeply apprehensive of the capitalist-monarchist influences which thence seeped into the movement and adulterated its pure and pristine socialism, but they were to learn, as the world was to learn, that Hitler never hesitated to sacrifice a principle if the needs of the moment were better served thereby.

THE CHANCELLORSHIPS OF MÜLLER AND BRÜNING

In 1929, National Socialism was still a sect of unruly fanatics, a curiosity among political parties, the product of abnormal conditions, and expected soon to become a forgotten freak of German history. Its membership still seemed to be drawn from the disgruntled and the unbalanced. Men of responsibility and common sense, men of education and property, might perhaps play politics with it — as a Thyssen or a Stinnes, for example, had done — but they would hardly fall victim to its power or influence themselves. The brutalities, the jealousies, and the known viciousness of the SA, the SS, and many of the party leaders were surely repellent to "decent-thinking" Germans. Abroad, Nazism was regarded as a reaction to the dislocations of the war, a painful stage which a people must go through in the quest for true democracy.

But 1929 was Germany's last year of economic stability. Hermann Müller, then Chancellor, found himself and his government in increasing difficulties. The fifth reparation annuity under the Dawes Plan had been paid punctually and in full (see p. 167), but the Reich budget, despite admitted manipulation of the figures, remained unbalanced. Some 15,000 businesses went bankrupt during the year. Fierce outbreaks of party squadrism were sure signs of deteriorating conditions. The May Day celebrations of 1929 cost over 200 casualties. The Young Plan was negotiated in December of that year (see p. 402). Nationalists and Nazis drummed up the four million signatures legally required to petition the government for a referendum against the Plan and, a few days before Christmas 1929, the German voters flocked excitedly to the polls to register their views on whether or not "further financial burdens based on the war-guilt acknowledgment shall be assumed." The referendum failed to repudiate the Plan, which was eventually ratified by the Reichstag by just 226 votes to 224, but it was a disturbing pointer of the Nazi growth. On October 3, 1929 had occurred the death of Gustav Stresemann, six years Minister of Foreign Affairs, the very symbol of the peace and progress of the Locarno era.

In March 1930, Müller, the Chancellor, requested President von Hindenburg for emergency powers under Article 48 of the Constitution (see p. 151). Hindenburg refused, on the advice of the Reichswehr, notably on the advice of the Reichswehr's political mentor, General Kurt von Schleicher; whereupon Müller resigned. A new, supposedly nonparty government, which was frankly a government of crisis, was formed under the Center leader, Dr. Heinrich Brüning, and it was clear, before he took office, that Brüning might have to rule by virtue of Article 48. Brüning did his best against six months' consistent obstructionism from parties of the extreme Left and Right in the Reichstag, and then called for new elections. If, however, he expected a popular reaction against extremism, he fatally miscalculated. Hitler and his Nazi troopers threw themselves into a whirlwind campaign of meetings and parades, oratory and terrorism in every town and hamlet of the Reich. The election took place on September 14, 1930, and the result was a Nazi landslide. Hitler won one sixth of the total vote and 107 seats. The new Reichstag was little more than a drop screen for Nazi demonstrations. The 107 marched into the chamber in uniform and in military formation and at once turned the sessions into a bedlam.

Brüning tried to combat the Nazis by stealing their thunder. He was *plus royaliste que le roi*. He never allowed it to be forgotten that his cabinet was composed of veterans of the First World War; he stood for the "active revision" of Versailles; he condoned a violent new phase of agitation against the Polish Corridor; in the matter of disarmament, he went to Geneva demanding the pledged disarmament of other nations (see p. 473); he supported his Foreign Minister, Curtius, in the matter of the Austro-German Customs Union, with what results have already been described (see p. 405). But, for all his efforts, Nazi influence was in the ascendant. Brüning could have been saved only by some striking economic concession from the Versailles Powers, but this he was never able to obtain. Hitler was now working hand in glove with Dr. Alfred Hugenberg, leader of the Nationalist party, a man who used his powerful newspaper interests for the promotion of extreme chauvinist and reactionary politics. On October 10, 1931, Hitler was received for the first time by President von Hindenburg. The confrontation of the two men was inconclusive, though the fact that it took place was significant of Hitler's rising prestige.

The presidential election fell due in March and April 1932. It was preceded by weeks of political jockeying, and it brought to a head the deep struggle of the German electorate between its loyalty to Hindenburg, and all he stood for, and the new idols of Nazism. After much weighing of the chances, Hitler put himself forward as the Nazi candidate. Ernst Thälmann, Communist party chairman, was the Communist candidate. Hindenburg was supported by Brüning and by all surviving moderate elements. The campaign was hard-fought and tumultuous. On the second ballot Hindenburg won 19,300,000 votes, Hitler 13,400,000, and Thälmann 3,500,000. Field Marshal Paul von Hindenburg, now aged eighty-four and almost senile, thus entered upon his second term as President of the Reich.

A few days after the election, Hindenburg signed a decree dissolving the Nazi SA and SS. The action was probably inspired by Schleicher, resolved as always to assert the power of the Reichswehr, but it appeared as a gallant, if belated and desperate attempt on the part of Brüning to assert the reality of constitutional law and order. During his last month of office, Brüning was ruling virtually by decree, appealing without compunction to Article 48 of

the Constitution. The economic recession was at its depths. The indexes
showed that, since 1929, industrial production had fallen by nearly a half,
and prices by nearly a quarter. Unemployment had risen from 2,000,000 to
6,000,000. Probably Brüning would not have lasted much longer in any event,
but he hastened his end by introducing a scheme for settling batches of unemployed ex-soldiers on derelict Junker estates in East Prussia — much to the
alarm of his own Junker President, Hindenburg, and of Hindenburg's Junker friends and advisers. On May 30, 1932, Brüning was dismissed.

Meanwhile, during April, elections for several of the State Diets had given
another reflection of the growing extremism. In the Prussian Landtag the
Nazis won 162 seats and the Communists 56, and the two parties were soon
brawling on the floor of the Chamber. Weimar and the Weimar era were
dead, and Nazism everywhere was set and girded to profit by their going. A
movement recruited hitherto from idealists, reactionaries, political wire pull-
ers, placemen, and adventurers was now swelled by the broad masses of the
lower middle class, "the uprooted and disinherited," the chief sufferers of the
Depression. Organized labor and Communism continued to cling to the Left;
industry and agriculture to the Right. Poverty and wealth, at the two ends of
the scale, thus remained relatively immune. But the midmost strata of the
population, the vast social "no man's land" which remembered the inflation
of 1923 and were sickened at the thought of a new pauperization, which were
frustrated and misused and hopeless of a future except under the *ultima
ratio* of violent leadership, all these were fatally predisposed to Nazi allure-
ments. In January 1930 the Nazi party membership was 200,000; in January
1931 it was 400,000; in January 1933 it was 900,000.

The Left offered no comparable attraction. The Communists could still
point to a slowly growing suffrage; every Reichstag election had increased
their votes; they had earnest, able leaders like Thälmann, or Torgler — the
only man in the Reichstag, it was said, who could stand up to Goebbels in
debate. They were regarded by the Nazis, to judge by Nazi propaganda and
conduct, as Germany's real enemy and peril. But their organizations were
scattered, mainly in the urban centers and over widely separated localities;
their leaders were usually at odds over fine points of doctrine and party
tactics; and Moscow, less internationally aggressive than of yore, had been
stinting on its former assistance. The Social Democrats, once the largest of
the parties numerically, had been long since too much identified with Weimar. They were fundamentally moderate at a time when extremism was the
order of the day. Their pacifist tradition put them at a disadvantage in a
contest where rubber truncheons were more effective than votes. As for the
extreme Right, the monarchists, the veterans' organization or Stahlhelm,
and the Reichswehr, though they had many of Hitler's aims and envied him
his successes, they lacked his perfervid demagogy, they had none of his mass
following, and they still had enough of the decencies to be incapable of stooping to his methods.

THE CHANCELLORSHIPS OF PAPEN AND SCHLEICHER

The struggle for power consumed eight confused and complicated months. President von Hindenburg's intimate circle at this time consisted of his secretary, Dr. Otto Meissner, and Meissner's friend, General von Schleicher; his own son, Colonel Oskar von Hindenburg, and Oskar's friend, Franz von Papen. Schleicher and Oskar in their young days had been officers of the Third Foot Guards, and Schleicher and Papen had been attached to the General Staff. Former comradeships and the pressure of present interests welded the circle into a virtual cabinet. The upshot was Hindenburg's appointment of Papen on June 1, 1932, to succeed Brüning as Chancellor, with Schleicher as Reichswehr Minister, Baron Konstantin von Neurath, a career official and former ambassador in London, as Foreign Minister, and Schwerin von Krosigk, another career official, as Finance Minister. Hitler promised Papen the Nazi party's support — for the time being.

Franz von Papen had been an officer in the crack cavalry regiment, the Fifth Uhlans. He was an elegant child of fortune with a flair for adventure and intrigue. By extraction he was not Prussian, but Rhinelander and Catholic, and through his wife he had contacts with big industry in the Saar. He was remembered by Americans as the German military attaché in Washington in 1915 who was expelled for espionage (see p. 28). Exactly what policy he now meant to follow — other than his own advancement — has never been very clear. At heart he was probably a monarchist. Contrary to expectation, he found little support from the Reichstag. His cabinet was so replete with Junker aristocracy that it was often called the "Barons' Cabinet." Toward the Nazis he was conciliatory, since they had promised to support him. He rescinded Brüning's late ban on the SA and SS and once more permitted them their activities, their meetings, their parades, their broadcasts, and their terrorism. At the Lausanne Conference, mentioned elsewhere (see p. 409), he was able to negotiate the virtual abolition of reparations. He liquidated the deadlock in the Prussian Landtag by arbitrarily dismissing the Prussian Premier, the Social Democrat, Otto Braun, who had held office since 1920, and assumed the authority himself. The Communists proclaimed a general strike in protest, but the workers, largely Social Democrat in sympathy and decimated by unemployment, made no response. The day was past when a general strike could break a putsch (see p. 155).

Two Reichstag elections were held during Papen's term, in the second of which, in November 1932 — incredible to relate — the Nazis lost 34 seats. The sudden recession in their strength led many a wishful observer to believe that the Nazis were at last reaping the consequences of their tactics and that their power had passed its peak. An incident at Potempa in Upper Silesia, not many nights before, when five drunken Nazi troopers had dragged a Communist worker out of bed and kicked him to death in the presence of his mother, had not smelled too sweetly in the nostrils of the German voter — and Hitler had since sent the five troopers, upon their conviction for murder, a telegram of "loyalty and consolation." For a short, fleeting moment it seemed as if the Nazi party was on the point of dissolution. Party comrades wavered in their allegiance; Gregor Strasser quarreled with Hitler and threw in his lot with Schleicher. Worse still, the elections had emptied the Nazi coffers, and the party was desperately in need of funds. Disconsolate storm troopers could be seen at street corners tinkling their collecting boxes in the faces of indifferent passers-by. Hitler, who had expected to ride to power on the late elections, was crazed with surprise and dejection.

Even now it is hard to thread a way through the morass of intrigue that followed. The struggle, at the last, seems to have lain between the "Nazi-energized masses" and the "Barons," that is, between Hitler and Hindenburg. Papen doubtless considered he could balance himself between both sides and thus continue as a sort of chief of staff in a virtual presidential dictatorship. He introduced public-relief works on a large scale — like Brüning he also anticipated later Nazi policy — and then he tried to score off Hitler's recent discomfiture at the polls. Hitler, with his usual sure instinct, appealed straight to the masses; all his speeches at this juncture had a strong proletarian ring. Schleicher meanwhile desired a restoration of orthodox parliamentary rule, and the old President, perhaps tired of the strain of decree government, was persuaded to support him.

In December 1932, Schleicher replaced Papen in the chancellorship. Schleicher regarded himself as the "man of decision," the "power behind the throne," and evidently thought he could make and unmake Papens at will. But Schleicher's problem was the same as that of the man he had ousted. The Nazis in the Reichstag pressed for an investigation into the *Osthilfe,* a fund for agrarian relief, originally instituted under Brüning, and since allegedly misappropriated in the interests of the big East Prussian Junkers. The Junkers naturally turned against Schleicher, and with them turned President von Hindenburg. Hindenburg took the attitude that Schleicher had "lost control" over refractory elements in the Reichstag. Schleicher, in effect, like Papen, had to make his choice between Hitler and Hindenburg.

Papen was now bargaining with Hitler — their intermediary was Ribbentrop, the first appearance of that gentleman — and Hitler, still floundering in uncertainty, was glad to clutch even at the straws which Papen threw out to him. Cleverly, all too cleverly, Papen resolved the fears and doubts of the Junker clique and built up a formidable anti-Schleicher coalition. He also succeeded in persuading Hindenburg that the new coalition, even under the nominal headship of the upstart "Bohemian corporal," would be safe and trustworthy. Thus, on January 30, 1933, Hindenburg appointed Adolf Hitler Chancellor of the Reich.

The affair of January 30 was nothing better than a deal, an insolent, disingenuous, Machiavellian deal. Every party to it got something and believed he would soon get more. The cabinet again was a "Barons' Cabinet." Papen became Vice-Chancellor and was deliciously revenged on Schleicher. Of the Nazis, Göring became Minister without portfolio, and Frick Minister of the Interior. The other offices were equitably distributed among potentates of the Nationalist party, Stahlhelm, Reichswehr, and Herrenklub. General von Blomberg, who had already fallen under Hitler's spell, was Reichswehr Minister. Neurath remained Foreign Minister and Krosigk remained Finance Minister. Three Nazis — Hitler, Göring, and Frick — in a cabinet of twelve did not seem a very serious proportion. Papen and his Junker aides might be pardoned for thinking they could hold the Nazis in check or for hoping that Hitler, for once in a position of high responsibility, might blunder himself into a spectacular fall. Yet Papen should also have remembered that Mussolini in 1922 had made three Fascist appointments in a cabinet of twelve!

But Hitler had the chancellorship. His triumph put new heart into his declining cause. The Nazi rank and file gave themselves over to an orgy of celebration. Göring, on the radio, proclaimed the rebirth of the Reich, the obliteration of fourteen years of shame, and the founding of a new German state in freedom and honor. On the night of January 30 a gigantic torchlight procession of 250,000 marched past the Führer, while President von Hindenburg, woodenly expressionless in another window of the Chancellery, stood watching the phenomenon to which he had now given his official consecration. And the people of Germany watched too, some in fear, some in hope, and all in amazement.

THE CHANCELLORSHIP OF HITLER

Hitler immediately put into effect his *Gleichschaltung*, a "leveling," "equalizing," or "co-ordinating" of the German body politic. Communism, the Nazi party's particular foe and scapegoat, was the first to feel the destructive wrath of the process. Communist meetings and papers were prohibited, and Communist leaders arrested. On the night of February 27, 1933 the Reichstag building caught fire, and a great part of the interior was gutted. Göring, "by a flash of intuition," recognized the outrage as "Communist arson," the first incident in a nefarious counterrevolutionary campaign directed at government property throughout Germany. A certain Marinus van der Lubbe, a Dutchman and reputedly a Communist, was arrested in the burning building. Also arrested were Torgler, chairman of the Communist fraction in the Reichstag, who had chanced to be in the building shortly before the fire broke out, and three Bulgarian Communist exiles, alleged to have been seen earlier in Lubbe's company, one of whom was Dimitrov, a veteran worker for the Comintern and in after years to become the Communist Premier of Bulgaria.

Göring promised to substantiate his flash of intuition with incontrovertible proofs. Lubbe and the other arrested persons were afterward given a flamboyant trial at Leipzig. Lubbe appeared to be mentally subnormal and was quite useless under examination. He was eventually executed, and the others were released. Meanwhile the Nazis made welcome use of the Reichstag fire as an electioneering cry and as their warrant for the extermination of Communism in Germany. On March 5, 1933, in a frenzy of hatred and fear of the "Red peril," the German electorate once more went to the polls. The Nazis turned on their terrorist machine; the SA were given "the freedom of the streets" to assault, torture, and kill as they pleased. Hitler wrung his hands over the reported atrocities, and did nothing to stop them. But, for all their efforts, the Nazis did not yet secure a clear majority. It is of interest to remember that in this last "constitutional" election in Germany, when it may be presumed that all the advantages of coercion and publicity lay with Hitler, the Nazi party commanded no more than 44 per cent of the German vote.

The new Reichstag held its sessions for the time being in the Kroll Opera in Berlin. On March 24, under the very pistols of the SA and SS and in the absence of all the Communist Deputies and most of the Social Democrats, who were under arrest, this Reichstag passed an Enabling Act — the Center party voting with the Nazis — and thereby vested Hitler and his government with dictatorial powers for four years. The Cabinet was "co-ordinated," Goebbels became Minister of Propaganda, and Hess Minister without portfolio. Göring, in addition to his cabinet office, was Prussian Premier and Prussian Minister of the Interior. Papen and his Junkers, a sorry crew, departed.[1] The Reichstag was reduced to a mere rostrum for the Führer's pronouncements.

From this moment onward the program of co-ordination reached into every part of the nation's life. Heiden, Hitler's biographer, has called it a "coup d'état by installments." The Nazi party was established as the one and only party permitted. All the national symbols received the Nazi imprint; the black-red-gold flag of the Weimar Republic was replaced by the monarchist black-white-red, with the Nazi swastika in its center. In the civil services, all politically unreliable officials were dismissed. The separate State constitutions were superseded, and the States, or Länder, were put under the authority of regents (Statthalter), who often enough were also the local Nazi district leaders (Gauleiter). In Bavaria, where some resistance was expected, the ministers were intimidated into compliance, but not before two of them had been beaten to death.

The police and legal system were co-ordinated. The SA was tantamount to a state police, with no inconvenient restrictions. Göring, as Prussian Minister of the Interior, had more real power than an Oriental satrap. By degrees the law became a pragmatic means to an end, arbitrary and changeable, wielding retribution for a great number of newly defined political crimes. The Führer, of course, was the supreme law lord of absolute powers. The fundamental rights and liberties of the individual citizen disappeared. Several new courts were set up, such as the People's Courts for trying cases of "high treason and treason against the state," and their judgments were wholly political. In the criminal courts, the judge or public prosecutor was empowered to hear or reject evidence, lodge an appeal, or order a retrial at his discretion. A Secret State Police or Gestapo (Geheime Staatspolizei) was created, originally under Göring's control, to be reorganized and greatly extended at a later date by Heinrich Himmler. Concentration camps were established, the first of a system which in due time was to number three hundred centers.[2] The SD (Sicherheitsdienst), an SS within the SS, virtually a private espionage force, was set up in June 1934 under Himmler's favorite lieutenant, Heydrich.

Trade, industry, and labor were co-ordinated. Dr. Schacht was appointed president of the Reichsbank and Minister of Economics, and embarked on his ingenious career as financier of the Nazi economy. Nazi supervisors sat on boards of directors. The trade-unions were destroyed and expropriated, and a new Labor Front under Ley provided for the workers' welfare, insurance, savings, and a certain amount of occupational training. Even the workers' leisure was co-ordinated in recreational organizations which bore the euphemistic name of "Strength through Joy (*Kraft durch Freude*)." The basic problem of the unemployed was attacked with vigor. Firms were required to increase their personnel; Jews, Communists, and women were replaced by the hundreds; road-building projects, notably the *Autobahnen*, and, above all, a huge rearmament program were initiated. Labor Service for young men and women was made compulsory and militarized.

Schools and universities were co-ordinated. Education, from the cradle to the grave, subserved the New Order. Teaching staffs and student bodies were purged of non-Aryan elements; it is said that between 1933 and 1938 one-third of the official university posts changed hands. Textbooks were rewritten. New courses were introduced, such as "defense science" and geopolitics; history and biology took a "racial" slant. Special Nazi schools were founded, like the Adolf Hitler Schools, somewhat on the lines of the Prussian cadet schools, to train selected boys for party leadership. The whole of the country's youth in all its extraschool activities was regimented in semimilitary organizations known as the Hitler Youth, nominally under the leadership of that "perfect Nordic," the poet, Baldur von Schirach, and into them were forcibly absorbed the old German Youth Movement, the various German adaptations of the Boy Scouts and Y.M.C.A., and the Catholic and other confessional youth societies. The *Bund Deutscher Mädel* was the corresponding organization for girls.

Culture and the arts were co-ordinated. A Reich Culture Chamber controlled the seven fields of literature, journalism, radio, film, drama, music, and painting and sculpture, and over this far-flung province Goebbels was ruler. The results, judged by aesthetic standards, might not always have been of the highest, but a vast productive activity was brought into the service of the Nazi state, and a hungry army of mediocre talent but of acceptable political leanings — novelists, journalists, dramatists — were enabled to enjoy the sweets of success and popularity. Architecture, characteristically colossal and "Germanized," yet often classical and traditional in style, was the personal monopoly of the Führer and his chosen master builders.

One year sufficed for Hitler to accomplish his revolution and transform the face of Germany. The German people may have been politically immature, and their social structure less surely laid than those of other Western lands. Yet their institutions one and all were overthrown with astonishing ease by a party whose beginnings were none too reputable and whose following in the electorate had at all times been doubtful. No other party or power in the field, it seemed, except the Nazi, was willing to face a fight for what it wanted or believed. One anti-Nazi group of left-wing parties and trade-unions organized itself as a "*Reichsbanner*." It was the only group of its kind, but its high-sounding militancy, when the test came, was confined to words and the usual recriminations between its leaders. At the last, Communists, Social Democrats, trade-unions, Center, Junkers, Stahlhelm, Reichswehr, Länder, civil service, Supreme Court, and universities, all shrank from action, defeatist and defeated before a force which had become clothed in the very armor of historic necessity. "It was no victory," said Spengler, "for the enemies were lacking."

The churches alone offered some resistance, mainly through the courageous action of individuals, a resistance that was therefore ill-concerted and was of declining effectiveness. And once, and once only, was it necessary to quell an important opposition within the party itself. For, in the midst of outward joys and celebrations, there had been grumbling. The long-standing rivalry between the two corps of troopers, the SA and the SS, broke out afresh, especially after Himmler's appointment to the SS leadership. The "old fighters" of the SA in many ways represented the left wing of the Nazi party, and they were disappointed that their revolution had not always realized the Socialist pretensions of the party in its earlier times. Nor had their revolution brought them the expected personal rewards. Party organizations had swelled beyond all reason, official posts and commissions had been scattered broadcast, yet the choicer plums had gone to the Nazi elite, the SS, and the thousands of zealous wearers of the Brown Shirt had been left unsatisfied. Even the hope that they might be incorporated into the Reichswehr on privileged terms, as Roehm, their leader, had urged so often, was disappointed. The Reichswehr was determined to pick and train its own recruits and looked askance at the rowdy, inchoate mass of near on 3,000,000 men which the SA had become. In sober truth Nazism had outgrown the SA. Power had made the party respectable and more exclusive. The earlier dynamism of the movement, of which the SA had been the vehicle, was clearly running down. As has happened in the history of revolutions before, the group of men which started the revolution was not always the group of men best fitted to carry it on. Recent speeches of SA leaders had sometimes struck a deprecatory, remonstrative, almost apologetic note. As for the Führer, he now liked to consort with aristocrats and magnates, and perhaps was a little embarrassed by the plebeian horde which clamored for donatives and reminded him too forcibly of the base degrees of his ascent.

On June 15, 1934, Hitler sent the entire SA on furlough. It was gesture enough to belie disturbing rumors, but it also effectively demobilized the SA at the very moment that its future was being decided. That some deviltry was afoot was plain enough when, two days later, that veteran troublemaker, Franz von Papen, speaking to students at the University of Marburg, chose to deliver himself of certain very pointed criticisms of the Nazi regime. Conceivably he was trying to anticipate some fancied anti-Nazi swing of public opinion. Meanwhile there was much dangerous talk of a "second revolution" and more dangerous talk of party purges. Roehm, it was said, was plotting treason against his Führer. There followed a couple of weeks of unendurable tension. The press was full of elliptical threats and recriminations. Goebbels and Hess, in a series of speeches and articles, made it their business to excoriate the "reactionaries."

On June 30, Hitler's blow fell. In a short, savage week end, during which he acted, in his own words, as "the Supreme Tribunal of the German people," he, Göring, Goebbels, Himmler, and the SS "destroyed without mercy the undisciplined and disobedient, the unsocial and sickly elements" of the party.

The official accounts afterward admitted to 77 deaths, but the real number is likely to have been nearer 1,000. Among the victims were Roehm, Gregor Strasser, and Schleicher and his wife. Several old scores were settled; the long arm of Hitler's vengeance even picked off the former Munich trio, Kahr, Lossow, and Seisser (pp. 165–66). Papen was only saved at the last minute, it was said, because of his personal relationship with Hindenburg.

"The Führer accomplished great deeds," said Göring afterward, "out of the greatness of his heart, the passion of his will, and the goodness of his soul. Faith in him is alone the basis of our life. Who dares touch that faith has ceased to be a German and must be destroyed."

The massacre of June 30, 1934, "the night of the long knives," has been interpreted as a sop to the Reichswehr, and certainly the Reichswehr must have been grateful for this highly demonstrative disciplining and purging of the "rival army." No doubt Blomberg had known of, and perhaps secretly encouraged, Hitler's plans for the removal of Roehm. But the Reichswehr all unawares played into Hitler's hands, and Hitler at this juncture was assisted by one of those lucky accidents which so often favored his career. On August 2, 1934, Hindenburg conveniently died. Hindenburg had been ailing for months, and it is a pertinent question whether, since 1932, he had been in full possession of his faculties. He was buried with impressive military pomp in the great war memorial at Tannenberg. Hitler declined to succeed to the title of President, a title which he declared the late Field Marshal had invested with "unique and nonrecurrent significance," and intimated that he would continue to be called Führer and Chancellor. But he succeeded none the less to the actualities of presidential authority. His position was submitted to one of the many national referendums at this time, and 90 per cent of the electorate voted "*Ja.*"

One of the consequences of Hindenburg's death was to relegate to Hitler the supreme command of the armed forces, hitherto a prerogative of the President, and Hitler was able to arrange matters so that every German soldier immediately took the oath of allegiance "unto death" to him personally. This was tantamount to a recognition of Nazism by the Reichswehr and one of the decisive events of the history of the Third Reich. Thus did Hitler achieve the pinnacle of autocratic power.

THE CHURCHES AND JEWRY

The churches, we have said, offered some resistance to Nazism, though it was of declining effectiveness. The Nazis tried to found a German "National" Church with an Aryan clergy and an "Aryan ethics." Nazi propaganda represented Christ as a Nordic martyr done to death by Jews. The movement had some success in the excitement of the first year of Nazi rule, and many Protestant pastors and their congregations were swept into it. But individual opposition by men like Pastor Niemöller made it clear to the Nazi leaders that severer, subtler methods of repression would have to be adopted. In 1935, Hans Kerrl was appointed Minister for Church Affairs and, under his direction, the co-ordination of the Protestant churches in Germany became a long-drawn, relentless persecution in the form of dismissals from churches, detentions in concentration camps, confiscations of stipends and properties, suppression of periodicals, and closing of schools and seminaries.

In their dealings with the Roman Catholic Church the Nazis appeared again to meet at first with some success. Hitler himself was a Catholic born — though an ostentatiously nonpracticing one — and the reigning Pope, Pius XI, was believed by some to be inclined to Fascism. All Hitler's earliest pronouncements on religious questions had been studiedly conciliatory. In July 1933 a concordat was signed with the Vatican regulating Catholic affairs in Germany. It granted freedom of faith and of worship, recognized the secrecy of the confessional, guaranteed the maintenance and inviolability of Catholic organizations, orders, charities, and schools, and gave bishops the right to publish pastoral letters. But thereafter Catholics were subject to the same kind of persecution as Protestants, the same kind of *"coup d'état* by installments," and the terms of the concordat, one by one, were violated. Catholic priests had to face trumped-up charges in the Nazi courts, such as charges of evading the currency regulations or of committing sexual offences. In March 1937 the papal encyclical, *Mit brennender Sorge,* was read from all Catholic pulpits in Germany, condemning the Nazi doctrines of the state and race. But, by the outbreak of the Second World War, the German churches, Catholic and Protestant, were in a sorry plight.

Toward the Jews the Nazis had no formal policy at first, though lootings, boycotts, expropriations, and the excesses of the prison and the concentration camp were their normal anti-Semitic ritual from the moment they came to power. Attempts to systematize and legalize the persecution followed in due course. Jews were debarred from the civil service, professions, universities, learned societies, armed forces, and from membership in the Labor Front, without which it was almost impossible to conduct a business. More and more disabilities and humiliations were heaped on the unhappy community. In 1935, by the so-called Nuremberg "Racial Laws," Jews were deprived of German citizenship, prohibited from contracting marriages with "citizens of German or kindred blood," and prohibited also from employing as domestic servants "female citizens of German or kindred blood under 45 years of age." After the pogrom of November 1938 there was a general "Aryanization" of Jewish property, destruction of synagogues, and a collective "fine" of a billion marks. As a distinguishing sign, Jews were forced to wear the yellow Star of David.

During the Second World War the Nazis proceeded to the "final solution" of the Jewish problem. Extermination became the official state policy, and it is believed that, out of a total European Jewish population of 9,600,000, some 5,700,000 were "missing from the countries in which they formerly lived," of whom at least 4,000,000 perished at extermination camps.[3] Well might Hans Frank, during his trial at Nuremberg, blurt out, "A thousand years will pass, and this guilt of Germany will still not be erased!" (See pp. 716–18.)

FULL EMPLOYMENT, AUTARCHY, AND REARMAMENT

Economically, the Nazis inherited both liabilities and assets. In 1932, Germany had 6,000,000 unemployed — some authorities have put the figure at 8,000,000 — and, by all standards of the day, she was bankrupt. But she still had her basic natural resources, and her people their high technical skills. The losses and deterioration of the First World War had long since been made good. The inflation of 1923 had wiped out the internal debt, and in 1932 Germany was free from reparations. In the chemical and optical industries she once more led the world, and she was making strides in shipbuilding and civil aviation. The "rationalization" and foreign loans of the Stresemann era had modernized her manufacturing equipment. Intensive cartelization was preparing her for a regimented national economy. Existing trusts, like Krupps and the Farben Industries, were all too ready to collaborate in the promised expansionist developments. Brüning and Papen had anticipated something of the new regime's methods with their price controls and relief works and, in Papen's time, business indexes were already showing unmistakable signs of a "normal" upswing.

It is interesting to note, in passing, that few of the Nazi economists were economists by training, and that Hitler and Göring never had to listen to "experts" who advised against their projects as "impossible." Funk was a journalist; Joseph Wagner a schoolteacher; Göring's aides, when he became a director of the Four-Year Plan, were army generals. Schacht, a banker, was almost a stranger in this company; but then no one could have described Schacht as orthodox. But the Nazis, for all their methods, clung obstinately to old forms. There was no outright nationalization, and confiscation only touched the properties of Jews and of other political undesirables. The illusion of private ownership was maintained and even encouraged. If the Nazis needed a new commodity, they created a company, not a government department, to produce it. The DEA (*Deutsche Erdöl A.G.*), to which was entrusted the production of oil and petroleum from home sources, was such a company, and so also was the prodigious Hermann Göring works, originally founded for the mining of iron ore. The parallel with the "war companies" of 1914 is obvious (see p. 49).

Nor was Nazi economics comprehensively "planned" in the way that Soviet economics was planned. In April 1933 Hitler created a Reich Defense Council (*Ministerrat für die Reichsverteidigung*), an inner circle of the highest ranking Nazis, which might have become a central planning office corresponding to the Soviet Gosplan. But its membership appears to have been very fluid, and Hitler doubtless invited to such meetings as it held whomsoever he desired at any particular moment. Göring's famous Four-Year Plan was a plan only in name. In general, Nazi controls were *ad hoc* transactions, typical mixtures of propaganda and coercion, with immediate returns as the standard of success. Co-ordination of effort derived rather from the men than the organizations in which they worked. The chain of command through the various government and party levels was tangled in the extreme. The ultimate decisions rested with the Führer, but his power of attorney, so to speak, was distributed over every lesser Führer in the hierarchy. There were few of these lesser Führers who did not hold office in more than one department, and the multiplication of their offices, like the multiplication of commercial directorships, enabled them to exercise authority, or at least to hold a watching brief, over several fields of activity at once. Thus Schacht, and after him Funk, was President of the Reichsbank as well as Minister of Economics; Göring was Prussian Premier, president of the Reichstag, Plenipotentiary of the Four-Year Plan, and Commander in Chief of the Luftwaffe. But at no point does it appear that jurisdictions were ever precisely defined. On the contrary, jurisdictions tended to grow and overlap in response to personal rivalries. Often indeed it seemed as if confusion and inefficiency were regarded by the Nazis themselves as desirable qualities befitting the spirit of their rule. And, moreover, many an indigent party man found a job at some dead end of the bureaucratic labyrinth who, in a different system, might have been redundant.

Yet, however indirect and capricious the authority might be, in total effect every stage of the economic process was under the most rigid control. Businesses could not be conducted without licences; firms were forcibly created or closed according to the policy of the moment. The import and distribution of materials were controlled. Contracts were graded according to priorities. Distribution to the consumer was rationed. Wage rates were stabilized at their 1933 levels — which were usually minimum levels — and thereby the entire price structure was also stabilized. The old free mobility of labor was gradually destroyed; workers were allocated to jobs like materials or capital. Profits were controlled by special taxes and levies. Businesses paid each other subsidies as appeared to be necessary. Dividends and interest rates were limited, and any excess was plowed back into the business or invested in government bonds. A huge flow of funds was thus diverted, by one channel or another, into the Reich Treasury. The result was a "closed" economy resembling at many points the total wartime economy of 1914–18.

Within the citadel of such an economy Germany could order her life at will. She could develop in isolation any "uneconomic" process. She could make up her shortages of raw materials with substitutes. She could plunder Jews and occupied countries. The public debt might rise; but — here was the real secret of totalitarian bookkeeping — the public debt could rise to any ceiling so long as the interest was a "safe" percentage of the national income.[4] Foreign trade alone was beyond Germany's absolute control, but foreign trade could be reduced to the unavoidable minimum. Foreign trade became organized barter, sometimes the crude interchange of goods for goods by individual contracts, sometimes a sort of deferred barter by means of clearing agreements.[4] Under cover of a nominal gold standard, rates of exchange might be made to vary almost *ad hoc* so as to squeeze the most out of every transaction. Money owed to foreign creditors was put into blocked accounts which could be bought by the government at a heavy discount or else paid off with goods which the anxious creditor did not really want.[4] Foreign balances could be used to purchase raw materials for armaments or to further economic penetration in politically desirable directions. Southeastern Europe was the classic example of the use of these techniques in all their variety to bring about an economic vassalage in the interests of Nazi *Grossraumwirtschaft*. And the manipulator-in-chief was Hitler's "wizard," Schacht.

The human costs of such a system were prodigious. Wages and prices might remain stable, but the purchasing power of those wages was reduced. The workers' pay envelope was continually whittled away by various compulsory dues, savings, and other incidental levies — such as Winter Relief and "Strength through Joy." Mere money indeed lost its traditional meaning. The economic unit of measurement was not the mark but the amount of work a man could do. Yet evaluated in cold statistics it seems that the standard of living of the mass of the German people under Nazism, that is from 1933 to 1939, markedly improved.[4] Unemployment, once so terrible a scourge, by 1936 was passing into a labor shortage. In addition, Germany succeeded in making herself, if not absolutely autarchic — Hitler himself always recognized that Germany could never be wholly independent of foreign trade — at least sufficiently self-contained to be free of the fear of another blockade like that of 1914–18. And she built herself the most powerful military machine in the world. In short, the balance sheet of the Nazi economics, from the Nazi point of view, could be acclaimed a formidable success. A well-knit, hard-working population of 70,000,000 stood ideologically inspired, physically trained, and materially equipped for the supreme business of making war.

THE NAZI FÜHRER AND THE NAZI IDEOLOGY

The man, Adolf Hitler, in appearance was unimpressive and unprepossessing. Short, spare, slightly mustached, with a strand of dark, lank hair across one brow, he had at first sight none of the lineaments of a world-shaking dictator. He was certainly not normal. His fantasies and hysterical storms, his claustrophobia, his persecution mania, his infinite capacity for hatred, his sudden alternations of mystic exaltation and suicidal dejection, were all symptoms familiar to the psychiatrist. His habits of life were simple and ascetic. He was a total abstainer and vegetarian. He played no games and took no recreation beyond an occasional Wagnerian opera, an occasional motion picture and, of course, an occasional retreat to his mountain haunt in Bavaria — though some biographers have hinted at other, less reputable amusements.

Yet there was a demoniac power in him. His followers have sworn to the extraordinary effect which his very look or word produced upon them, and even men unsympathetically disposed toward him would come away from his presence curiously shaken. His voice was rasping, but could throb with power. In action, in the heat of declamation, upon his rostrum, surrounded by his aides, facing a rapt and responding multitude, he was a being transfigured, "an unknown soldier uttering the thoughts of millions." At his greatest moments — and such moments no one can deny he had — he became the very symbol and embodiment of the Germany which worshiped him.

His mental caliber was not of a high order. He showed no trace of that seasoned moderation which is the mark of the philosopher and the intellectual. He had no use for learning. He disliked "experts." He never understood figures. He is supposed to have read extensively, not for education, but to provide materials for convictions already formed. He never quoted a classic author, ancient or modern. He swept away impatiently all the toilsome apparatus which had formerly made Germany so famous in scholarship and research. The only argument he ever knew was reiteration. Action, emotion, and will ruled his life, intelligence per se never. Yet he passes as an example of the wisdom of the unwise. He had that species of revelation "that often madness hits on, which reason and sanity could not so prosperously be believed of." His decisions seemed to be protected by a "sleepwalker's immunity." He had a way of cutting through the most complicated problems to solutions of extreme simplicity. Above all, he possessed the gift of prophetic self-assurance. His own *Mein Kampf,* with its vulgar but pseudoapocalyptic style, conveys throughout that compelling, infectious force of one that taught as having authority, and the same impression is given by reports we have of his intimate conversations. Incredible it is that such powers should have been lodged in a man whose beginnings had been so unpromising and mean, and who had failed in all the normal pursuits of life. Heiden has described him as "an overpowering nonentity . . . as a human figure lamentable, as a political mind one of the tremendous phenomena of history . . . in a world of normalcy a Nothing, in chaos a Titan." [5]

He had no scruples whatever. His political principles, like those of his spiritual kinsman Mussolini, were extemporized as the occasion arose and were afterward dropped with as little compunction as they had been taken up. He could slough off into forgetfulness promises and assertions made only a moment before. In so far as he was himself conscious of his deceptions, he could be disarmingly candid about them. Yet he deceived everyone continually and consistently and with amazing success. "I am willing to sign anything," he said on one occasion. "I will do anything to facilitate the success of my policy. I am prepared to guarantee all frontiers and to make non-aggression pacts and friendly alliances with anybody. It would be sheer stupidity to refuse to make use of such measures merely because one might possibly be driven into a position where a solemn promise would have to be broken. . . . Why should I not make an agreement in good faith today and unhesitatingly break it tomorrow if the future of the German people demands it?" [6]

He was a supreme artist of mass rule. He knew the German masses as a conductor knows his orchestra. He despised them and reviled them in private. But he had been one of them himself; he had never ceased to study them; he had plumbed the depths of their weakness and emotionalism. Whenever the author of *Mein Kampf* writes of "the psyche of the broad masses" he writes at once with the unmistakable touch of an artist describing his art. The curious reader may still ponder in his pages the canons of Nazi propaganda and the craft of the "big lie."

Nazism always gave the appearance of pursuing long-range purposes. It was famous for its "blueprints," prepared months and years in advance, for every stage of its progress. *Mein Kampf* is supposed to have laid down the

Führer's objectives, all of which he subsequently achieved one after another with clockwork precision.[7] Yet it is also true that the Nazi doctrine was changeable, opportunist, and contradictory. Its programs were hit-and-miss, hand-to-mouth affairs; its leaders fickle and unprincipled. If anything, it was like its cognate Fascism, a philosophy without a philosophy. Through its confusion of purpose and purposelessness, of ultimate and provisional, it is not easy to find a way.

The first and only Nazi manifesto was the twenty-five point program written in Munich in 1920 (see p. 447). It contained several articles of maturer Nazi ring, such as the union of all German-speaking peoples in a Greater Germany, the repudiation of Versailles, the disfranchisement of Jews and aliens, the submergence of the individual in the state, the control of the press, and social and agrarian reforms. But it was the only document of its kind in Nazi history. It cannot be regarded as important; the experiment of an explicit creed was not tried again.

Nazism began as a movement of revolt against the defeat of 1918 and against the national miseries which were alleged to stem therefrom. Its own propagandized aims during its early "period of struggle" included the restoration of national pride and dignity, the repair of the bankrupt economic order, the replacement of the weak democratic Republic by a strong authoritarian leadership, and the punishment of Jews and Communists and other "aliens" whose special vices and disloyalty were supposed to have led to the military collapse. But Nazism, like Fascism, soon found that it wanted something more positive to feed on than disillusion and revenge, and it found it in the doctrines of racism and the supremacy of the state and also in the so-called Führer principle.

Racism certainly defied the observable facts. It was the exaggeration of contemporary nationalism to the point of absurdity. The Celestials, the Chosen People, the Children of the Sun, the Heraclidae, and their numerous brethren belonged to a world of fable which no one with a smattering of modern science could be expected to take seriously. The pure race, like the pure language, never existed in any recorded time, and the Nazi leaders themselves, for that matter, made an oddly assorted anthropological gallery. The perfect Aryan, as the German humor of the day had it, was "as blond as Hitler, slim as Göring, and as manly as Goebbels." Yet this did not prevent the Nazis, ascientific as they essentially were, from believing in a sort of archetypal "Germanity" to which all the Aryan inhabitants of the Third Reich might rightfully claim kinship.

The Nazi version of racism was elaborated by the party philosopher, Rosenberg. Race, so ran the official argument, is the primordial force of human society. Politics, law, government, history are without meaning except in relation to the race that vitalizes them. Race generates all beauty, progress, and grandeur. The sovereign race of races is the Aryan or Nordic, a race born to rule, even as other races — the Latin, the Slav, the Semite, the Negro — are born to be ruled. The Nazi revolution must secure to this sovereign race its primacy and its deserts in the world, encourage its expansion, and above all preserve its purity. Accidents of the past, as in 1914, which caused the Jewish Slavs and the Jewish-Negro French to obtain a temporary advantage, must never be allowed to recur. Particularly the Jewish race, because unassimilable and parasitic, because a corruption and an adulteration of the pure strain, must be destroyed. Internationalism, whether it be found in the Roman Catholic Church, Jewry, Freemasonry, the League of Nations, or Communism, to mention but a few of its most dangerous expressions, are all antithetic to this supreme "folk myth."

The soil that nurtures the race is sacred to it. Blood and soil are the twin ingredients of the world's elect. The great, sprawling, amorphous cities of the modern age, however necessary to industrialism, are centers of deracialization, dung heaps of cosmopolitan Jewry, which depopulate the land and contaminate the sound health of the nation. The myth of a master race, a caste of supermen, living upon the ancient soil of its fathers, conquerors of a world of lesser breeds — this is the very apotheosis of nationalism, an ideal fit to fire the true Nordic heart, an object worthy to be won by true Nordic valor.

The race must increase and multiply. Its quantity and quality must be nurtured by organized eugenics, by a high birth rate, and by unlimited provision for physical education and public health. The highest morality is biological morality. The race must draw to itself its scattered colonies throughout the world. The race must also be in process of steady geographical expansion. It must have its living space (*Lebensraum*). Imperialism is the proper mark of its health and vitality. Thus the Third Reich was a "rising Power" doing battle with a host of "declining Powers" such as France and England. The hegemony of Europe belonged to it by right, and the leadership of the rest of the world would also fall to it in proportion as the declining Powers let go their weakening grip on their swollen possessions. "Today we count only 80,000,000 Germans in Europe," wrote Hitler in *Mein Kampf*. "We can only consider our foreign policy a success if, in less than 100 years, 250,000,000 Germans come to live on this continent. . . ."

The state is the race in being. It is much more than a political or geographical expression. The individual is part of the state, happiest in his complete integration with the state. Freedom, as understood by liberal democracy, is an effete and outworn code. The race, the folk, the state, is weakened by the nonconformity of its elements. The whole Nazi domestic program is contained in the word *Gleichschaltung*, conformity, leveling, equalization, co-ordination. Independence is hostility to one's fellows, treason to the state, and insubordination to the Führer. There should be no such thing as private life. The citizen's privilege is to live and work for the state. All his institutions, his politics, economics, law, science, religion, his house and family, even his leisure and recreation, have no other function than to serve the state. What benefits the state is right; what injures the state is wrong.

The Führer principle (*Führerprinzip*) was the official philosophical sanction of the Führer's own office and person. The Führer is much more than a democratic representative, and the popular "consent," which has elevated him to the supreme responsibility, is not to be measured by so crude a method as counting votes. The Führer is the very symbol of the race as is a king of his kingdom or a chieftain of his tribe. The Führer embodies his people in himself and expresses their collective will. He is the administrative head of the government, chief legislator and executive, supreme judge, party boss, and commander of the armed forces. His authority is unlimited; his decisions are infallible; obedience to him is an unquestioned and sacred duty.

The Führer governs through a hierarchy of lesser Führers, radiating downward from himself. And the same Führer principle operates at all levels. Every lesser Führer, be he Gauleiter or Blockwart, is the Führer of all he surveys. The Führers in the aggregate constitute the Leadership Corps, the new aristocracy, "the class of politically creative personalities," the concentration of all that is best in the race. It is not so much that the Führer and his Führers rule and command, as that they give organic form to the otherwise formless state. They are the elite of Germany, even as the Germans are the elite of the world.

Thus did Nazism interpret itself. We who, in its time, stood outside it — and against it — saw it very differently. For us, doctrines of race and state and Führer, however elaborately reiterated, were hardly to be considered as a "cause" of Nazism. They only skimmed the frothy crests of a whole sea of causes, constantly changing, powerfully flowing, disturbingly deep, full of strange and monstrous shapes.

Several of our contemporary writers have tried to trace the sources of the movement through the political and literary history of Germany to Fichte, Hegel, and Schopenhauer, to Treitschke, Nietzsche, and Richard Wagner, to the English expatriate, Houston Stewart Chamberlain, and since 1918 to Spengler, Moeller van den Bruck, and Count Keyserling. Some have searched back to the post-Jena Prussians, to Frederick the Great, to that favorite storm center of modern historians, Martin Luther, and even to the pagan Arminius. From such names as these they have constructed a ramifying pedigree wherein the features of Nazism, like prepotent characteristics — to use the language of genetics — have recurred again and again. The Germans, on this interpretation, become a people that in all ages has been given to violence and treachery, glorifying their race, sentimental but cruel, uncertain of themselves but outwardly arrogant, self-pitying but incapable of sympathy with another's point of view, politically immature and irresponsible, hating freedom and craving compulsion, a people whose history was one long *Black Record.*[8] Hitler was thus no sudden and wayward freak but a more than usually repellent example of a constant type.

There is not a people in Europe whose history has not been drenched with war; but war seemed to have entered into the German soul to a degree beyond all others. The country stood in the center of the Continent, had no natural frontiers east or west, and suffered repeated invasion. Everything it ever had it had had to fight for. The sense of insecurity was never absent. National unity and maturity developed painfully stage by stage, in the teeth of foreign opposition, and each stage was marked by war — 1813, 1864, 1866, 1870, 1914. Others might sometimes forget or minimize their wars. The Frenchman might look back to a revolution; the Englishman to a parliamentary enactment; but the German always looked back to a battle, and exulted in the fact. In such an atmosphere, the political luxuries permitted to more fortunately placed peoples, the free institutions, free speech, and free education, had had to be relatively denied to an ever struggling, once disunited Reich.

Unhappily for the world these trends and proclivities were once more translated into action at an epochal moment of German development. The Germans of 1914 were a people possessed, possessed by that spirit which, from century to century, has roused nations out of their static levels and given them their great periods of creativity and expansion. What starry horoscope or configuration of historic forces produces these moments we do not know; but Greeks, Romans, Goths, Franks, Arabs, Spaniards, French, English, Dutch, in their grand procession through history have all felt the influence and, in our day, the Germans certainly manifested all the usual signs of it. Especially since 1871, their national growth had been stupendous. No other nation — the United States perhaps excepted — so brilliantly exhibited the prizes of progress or made such formidable acquisitions of wealth and power. German historians and philosophers never wearied of marveling at their country's achievements and of predicting illimitable futures for it.

The defeat of 1918 checked the country's career, but did not halt it. "Yet in the sphere of force," wrote Winston Churchill of the First World War, "human records contain no manifestation like the eruption of the German volcano. For four years Germany fought and defied the five continents of the world by land and sea and air. The German Armies upheld her tottering confederates, intervened in every theatre with success, stood everywhere on conquered territory, and inflicted on their enemies twice the bloodshed they suffered themselves. To break their strength and science and curb their fury it was necessary to bring all the greatest nations of mankind into the field against them. Overwhelming populations, unlimited resources, measureless sacrifice, the Sea Blockade, could not prevail for fifty months. Small states were trampled down in the struggle; a mighty Empire was battered into unrecognizable fragments; and nearly twenty million men perished or shed their blood before the sword was wrested from that terrible hand. Surely, Germans, for history it is enough!" [9]

Yet surely for history it was not enough. Germany was far from exhaustion point. Some residue of energy still remained to be drawn upon and, in 1939, she was once more ready to challenge the world. German "dynamism" of the thirties, so often regarded as a wicked, cunning invention of the Nazis, was much more than the mere dynamism of revolution, and it was intensified many times over by the sense of frustration and injustice which any "rising Power" would feel if robbed of its deserts and thwarted in its destiny. The resumption of the interrupted expansionist career in 1933 was more exaggerated and convulsive than if it had been allowed to run a "natural," victorious course in 1914.

Another school of writers has taken the psychological approach. Time was when press and periodicals were full of articles on the defeat complex and the inferiority complex of the German people and on the mental reaction of the German middle classes to the miseries of the war, the blockade, the inflation, and the Depression. We used to read earnest, learned disquisitions on that morbid, gesticulating little man from Upper Austria, who symbolized the nation's revolt against its degradation. On this showing, Nazism became a technique for the restoration of national self-respect. The very race theory was an overcompensation for a race that had lost faith in itself. Nazi lust and violence were the natural reactions of a people which had not only borne intolerable suffering but believed that suffering to have been undeserved. Any ordinary man who has failed in the struggle for life may bear a grudge against the world, discredit the values he once accepted, give up the decencies of his breeding and education, and feel himself driven to antisocial courses. "The Germans," wrote one who knew them well, "have the peculiarity of believing, under all circumstances, that they have been wronged." [10] There was always something of the frustrate and habitual criminal in the Nazi state of mind.

Other writers — notably the French — have attributed the failings of the German character to its lack of classical culture. Germany missed the two great historical waves of classicism which have swept across Europe. Rome never conquered her — Caesar's legions only set foot across the Rhine on punitive forays — and the Renaissance in Germany took uncouth, barbaric forms and then ran to waste in the Thirty Years' War. And by classicism is to be understood, not merely a conventional devotion to a few Greek and Latin idols, but the whole tradition of intellectual self-discipline, sweet reasonableness, and good taste, with which the centuries of Greek and Latin learning have indoctrinated our Western civilization. In the nineteenth century Europe was shaken to its depths by the Romantic Movement. Literature and the arts assumed new emotional forms, highly intense and individualistic. The Western nations, like France and England, safely grounded in their classicism — almost to the extent of no longer being conscious of the fact — survived the ordeal, and indeed were enriched and stimulated by it. Germany, never so grounded and "notoriously addicted to intoxicants," seemed to fall back into a half-forgotten but always lurking primitiveness. Nazism in many ways was the final *reductio* of the Romantic Movement in Germany. Its apostles were all romantics. Its literature was excitable, lawless, catastrophic, distraught with a sort of ecstatic pseudo profundity. It was almost comically the reverse of classic moderation.[11]

All these various "explanations" of Nazism were put out at the time, though none were wholly exhaustive or wholly convincing — it could never be for any generation to diagnose its own pathology completely. But perhaps this last school of writers which we have mentioned, in our view, begins to reach the crux of the problem. Nazism, like Fascism, of which it was a close variant, came among us as a force subversive of the hitherto acknowledged values of our civilization. The German writer, Rauschning, described it as the "Revolution of Nihilism" and also warned the world that it was no isolated German phenomenon, but an assault on European culture and a part of a Western-wide phase of history. We live at a time of violent change and transformation. That a destructive agent, like Nazism, should have appeared at such a time belongs to the logic of the situation. Nazism was always hung about with the odor of decomposition.

To be sure, Nazism used civilization. But it used it not as an ethos but as a technique. It used all the arts and values of civilization and used them with consummate German thoroughness. For instance, it used the forms of law. Even Hitler himself was "Legality Adolf," as his more impatient henchmen nicknamed him. But the letter of the law was the instrument for corrupting its spirit. "Nazism was a combination of terrorism made legal and legality made terrible." It was perfectly in keeping that even the concentration-camp commandant was covered by "law," his powers defined, and his every foulness regularized on paper. Nazism used the forms of religion. Many have described it *as* a religion. It had its fanaticism, its crusading zeal, its craving for self-sacrifice and redemption. It lent itself to curious ceremonies. It was not so much an atheism as a paratheism, a Black Mass in borrowed vestments. "[It] emptied religious ideas of their content and transformed them into a profane meaning . . . [It] enriched the vocabulary of unbelief with the heritage of Christian ideas." [12]

By its inversion of all the accepted values, Nazism developed a technique of deception which gave it — temporarily — all the tactical and diplomatic advantages. It exploited specious grievances for quite other ends. It put forward high-sounding slogans without respect for their literal meaning. It appealed skillfully to the favorite arguments of its opponents and blackmailed their integrity. The "injustices" of Versailles became a screen for unlimited ambitions. Aggressions were launched amid fervent protestations of non-aggressiveness. Austria and Czechoslovakia were both victims of "self-determination"; Denmark and Norway were conquered for their "protection." German organizations abroad, under the pretense of cultural activities, "bored into" the land of their adoption. Commercial agents and tourists formed the advance guard of invasion.

All these things, then, Nazism used — law, religion, and the civilized values. But it used them "as a syncopated orchestra used the harmony and counterpoint of Bach or Mozart to produce a music on the cultural plane of the Voodoo." In the midst of a civilized world Nazism, in essence, was a harking back to a state of precivilization. Its Führer was a magnified tribal chieftain. Its swastika, like the Fascist fasces, was a sort of totem. It sacrificed a scapegoat to cleanse the tribe of its misfortunes. Its blood rites and initiations, its nocturnal festivals, its Wagnerian mysticism recalled a pagan ancestry. Its party rallies resembled nothing so much as a gathering of the clans to drum up the warlike passions. "I know now what Gibbon meant," said an English visitor to a Nuremberg *Parteitag*, "when he wrote of 'the licentious clamors of the barbarians.'"

Beneath all the diatribes against Versailles, beneath the theories of blood and soil, beneath the racism and the Führer principle, beneath all the forms and guises Nazism took, there existed a crude, irreducible atavism. Nazism was like a psychoanalysis exploring the "nightside of the soul." It was surrealism in politics and demagogy. It had a sure instinct for discovering, *dis*-covering, and playing upon the aboriginal, the elemental, and the degenerate in the German masses. In the words of Stephen Roberts, it was "a reversion to the oldest state of affairs of which our anthropologists have

any knowledge . . . it reconstructed the taboo system, the system in which
every part of the social structure depends on the unquestioning acceptance
of the edicts of the priests. . . . The Nazis in Germany probed back into
the subconscious and removed the obscurities — some people outside Germany call them advances — of centuries. They resurrected tribal instincts in
the mystical sanctions of a savage society." [13]

29 NAZI FOREIGN POLITICS: THE REACTIONS

IN CENTRAL AND EASTERN EUROPE

DISARMAMENT AND REARMAMENT

"I had to reorganize everything," said Hitler at conferences in 1939, "beginning with the mass of the people and extending to the armed forces. First, internal reorganization, eradication of appearances of decay and of defeatist ideas, education for heroism. While reorganizing internally, I undertook the second task — to release Germany from her international ties . . . secession from the League of Nations and denunciation of the Disarmament Conference. . . . After that, the order for rearmament; after that, the introduction of conscription; after that, the militarization of the Rhineland." [1] "For more than six years now I have been engaged in building up the German armed forces. During this period more than ninety billion Reichsmarks have been spent. . . . Today, ours are the best-equipped armed forces in the world, and they are superior to those of 1914. . . ." [2]

In 1933, the German Army consisted of 7 infantry divisions and 3 cavalry divisions; in 1939, 39 divisions, of which 5 were armored and 4 fully motorized. In 1933, the German Navy consisted of 1 cruiser and 6 light cruisers; in 1939, 4 battleships, 1 aircraft carrier, 6 cruisers, 22 destroyers, and 54 submarines. In 1933, Germany had no air force; in 1939, she had 2,400 first-line planes, not including trainers and transports. The industrial foundation developed concurrently. Out of the few factories permitted by the Treaty of Versailles there arose "the mightiest armament industry in the world. . . . Germany's crude steel production was the largest after America's. Her aluminum production very considerably exceeded that of America and of other countries. The output of her rifle, machine gun, and artillery factories was larger than that of any other state." [3]

These results were only obtainable by making the preparation for war the supreme object of the nation's economy. First moves followed immediately upon Hitler's assumption of power. On February 20, 1933, Schacht was host to Hitler and Göring at a meeting of some twenty industrial magnates, including Krupp von Bohlen of the Krupp armament works, and we are given to understand that the assembled company enthusiastically greeted "the great intentions of the Führer in the rearmament period of 1933–39." Krupp was then already boasting of his success in keeping Germany's war industries in being and in readiness in spite of the disarmament clauses of Versailles. Rearmament thereafter was a continuous and accelerating process limited only by the need for secrecy. In May 1935, a couple of months after Hitler's conscription decree, a Law for the Defense of the Reich was enacted, and

Schacht, then President of the Reichsbank, was appointed Plenipotentiary for War Economy. The law, originally kept secret, was only published at the outbreak of war in 1939. It was a general sanction of total economic mobilization of the country and was described by one of the Reichswehr generals as "the cornerstone of our preparations for war." The very name Reichswehr was changed to Wehrmacht, "the armed force and school of military education of the German people." In October 1936, Göring became Plenipotentiary of the Four-Year Plan with the main objective of putting the country on a war footing in four years. By 1937, Germany's armament program was sufficiently advanced for Hitler to ponder and plan military action against Austria and Czechoslovakia.

One of the most remarkable and revealing of Nazi documents to have survived is the record of a conference held in Hitler's Chancellery on November 5, 1937 between Hitler, Blomberg, Fritsch, Raeder, Göring, and Neurath.[4] Hitler asked that his statements on this occasion "should be looked upon, in the case of his death, as his last will and testament." Germany could never be absolutely autarchic in raw materials and food, argued Hitler, nor could she adequately participate in world economy overseas. The question for Germany, therefore, was the securing of greater living space, "an endeavour which at all times has been the cause of the formation of states and of the movements of nations." The question for Germany was "the greatest possible conquest at the least possible cost," and it was a question which could only be solved by way of force, whatever the risks thereof. Germany's rearmament was now virtually complete, her equipment was new, and further delay would incur the danger of obsolescence. "The ageing of the Nazi movement and of its leaders," said Hitler, "the prospect of a lowering of the standard of living and a drop in the birth rate, leaves us no choice but to act. If the Führer is still living, then it will be his irrevocable decision to solve the German space problem not later than 1943-45." All considerations, argued Hitler further, pointed to the desirability of an early conquest of Czechoslovakia and Austria. The aggravation of recent tensions in the Mediterranean and the continuance of the Civil War in Spain would sufficiently distract Britain and France from intervention, and the intervention of the Soviet Union would be forestalled by the rapidity of operations — for the attack on Czechoslovakia would take place "with lightning speed (*blitzartig schnell*)." The prospects of the conquest of food for Germany, added Hitler, would be improved "if a compulsory emigration of two millions from Czechoslovakia and of one million from Austria could be carried out."

But we anticipate.

The preparatory discussions on disarmament initiated by the League of Nations have been described in a previous chapter (see p. 145). The Disarmament Conference assembled at last in Geneva on February 2, 1932, twelve months before Hitler's assumption of power. Of the sixty-four states invited, fifty-nine had sent delegates, including the United States and the Soviet Union. The omens had not been good. Arthur Henderson, the British Labor leader and former British Foreign Secretary, already elected president of the Conference, had lately lost his place in the British government and his seat in the House of Commons. He continued to preside over the Conference, however, but he presided as a private individual and without the powerful position a more official status would have conferred upon him. Then, on that very February 2, Japanese were reported to be landing in Shanghai (see p. 431). On February 18, Dr. Brüning, the German Chancellor, uttered his demand for "equality," and reminded the Conference that German disarmament, under Versailles, was originally intended to be "a first step" toward general world-wide disarmament. "This is Germany's legal and moral right," he said, "which no one can contest. The German people are counting on the present conference to find a solution of the problem of general disarmament on the basis of equal rights and equal security for all peoples."

The life of the Disarmament Conference was as painful and protracted as its preparation, and the reader may be spared any too detailed discussion of it. The French delegate, Paul-Boncour, came with a proposal for the setting-up of an international force, a proposal which revived in a different form Léon Bourgeois's militarized League of 1919 (see p. 130). When this proposal failed of acceptance, he produced another, which amounted to a series of concentric Locarno Pacts embracing the world. The British delegate, Sir John Simon, came with a proposal for "qualitative disarmament"; namely, for the prohibition of all types of offensive weapons. This proposal was more sympathetically received, but the military experts, to whom it was eventually referred, could discover no distinguishing criterion between offensive and defensive weapons. The British and American experts, for instance, regarded the submarine as offensive and the battleship as defensive; the French experts thought precisely the opposite. The Germans had already a clear-cut test: offensive weapons were those which had been forbidden them by the Treaty of Versailles.

The Lausanne Conference on reparations, in June 1932, created a diversion of interest (see p. 409), and when the Disarmament Conference was resumed, a fourth proposal was laid before it, this time from President Hoover, a proposal for a general slicing of all existing armaments by one-third — though with necessary allowance for "Powers having colonial possessions." But none of the European delegates could be persuaded that armament was merely a problem of ratios. The German Government continued to demand that its claim to "equality" be recognized and implemented. From the French point of view, of course, the admission of such an "equality" would instantly grant an effective preponderance to the potentially stronger Power, Germany. Between July and September 1932, the German delegates withdrew from the Conference and only returned after the French had been induced to agree to a formula which accorded the Reich "an equality of rights in a system of security for all nations."

The Disarmament Conference again resumed its sessions in February 1933. Its progress to date had been negligible, and the prospects for its future were gloomy enough. Hitler was now Chancellor of the Reich, and Japan was about to announce her withdrawal from the League. The famous Draft Convention (see p. 145), so carefully drawn during the earlier preparatory discussions, had hardly figured in the present Conference's discussions at all, and it was evidence of the prevailing desperation that Ramsay MacDonald should now have come to Geneva with a proposal which somewhat resembled that neglected document. The so-called MacDonald Plan was, in fact, the text of a disarmament treaty containing precise figures of men and matériel.

During the summer months of 1933, the Disarmament Conference adjourned, and the World Economic Conference was held in the interim (see p. 410). But on October 14, a couple of days before it was due to reconvene, Germany announced her final and irrevocable withdrawal. "The Conference," ran Neurath's statement of the day, "will not fulfill its object, namely, a general disarmament. Its failure is due solely to the unwillingness on the part of highly armed states to carry out their contractual obligations to disarm [pp. 143 and 145], . . . and their attitude has made impossible the satisfaction of Germany's claim to equality of rights." On October 21, Germany also gave notice of her withdrawal from the League of Nations.

October 1933 was the virtual end of the Disarmament Conference, but it was permitted to keep up the fiction of existence for two more years. On October 20, 1935 came the death of the president of the Conference, Arthur Henderson, after four years' labor in vain.

THE REACTIONS OF THE LITTLE ENTENTE AND HUNGARY

As might be expected, the first states in Europe to react to these events were those nearest the center of disturbance, notably Czechoslovakia and her allies of the Little Entente. Of all the succession states of the Middle Danube, Czechoslovakia stood to lose most and most quickly by the revival of a militant Germany bent on reversing the provisions of Versailles. At one end of her territory lived 3,000,000 Sudeten Germans — a full 20 per cent of her population — not in themselves a normally discontented community, but perhaps liable to become so, and presumably to be counted into Hitler's dream of a Greater Reich; while at the other end of her territory lived 2,000,000 Slovaks who had never acquiesced in their unequal partnership in the Czech Republic (see p. 197). Czechoslovakia's perilous strategic position in the event of an Austro-German *Anschluss* need hardly be mentioned.

The German minorities in the two other states of the Little Entente, Yugoslavia and Rumania, were of negligible numbers, and both Yugoslavia and Rumania were further removed from the Nazi menace. But neither state could fail to take account of the changes wrought in the Middle Danube by Hitler's seizure of power. As early as February 16, 1933, while yet Hitler had not shown himself in his harshest colors, the Foreign Ministers of Czechoslovakia, Yugoslavia, and Rumania, respectively Beneš, Jevtich, and Titulescu, then attending the Disarmament Conference in Geneva, concluded a "Pact of Organization" of the Little Entente. The three contracting parties agreed upon "the complete unification of their general policy," renewed the Little Entente in perpetuity, and set up a permanent council of their Foreign Ministers to meet for consultation at regular intervals.

At first the position of Hungary, that perpetual waif of Europe, was not at all clear. No nation could expect to gain from Germany's recovery, and Hungary was not likely to be an exception to the rule. But Hungary and Germany had at least one common ground between them, a hatred of the peace treaties, and Hungary's enemies, like Germany's, were those Powers which had once made, and now maintained, "the Versailles system." Hungarians had the deepest contempt for the states of the Little Entente, some of whose peoples had once borne the Magyar yoke, and they were none too well disposed toward the ally of the Little Entente, France. Under the circumstances it was perhaps not very surprising that Hungary and Germany should be drawn together in a hesitating and tentative *détente*.

The Depression and the growth of Fascism in Hungary, during the early thirties, injected another factor into the situation. The Depression had shaken the long-enjoyed security of Bethlen's government and, in August 1931, in the face of a failure of the harvest and a run on the banks, Bethlen had at last resigned (see p. 201). Julius Gömbös, who succeeded him after a short interval, was one of the few commoners to achieve prominence in Hungarian politics. He was known for his Fascism and anti-Semitism, a bit of a fire-eater, who well understood the Fascist technology of the mass meeting.

There was no formal German-Hungarian pact, but the interchange of state visits was not without significance. Thus Gömbös visited Berlin in June 1933, at the height of Nazi disturbances then taking place in Austria. Göring and Papen visited Budapest at different times in 1934. Gömbös visited Warsaw in October 1934, an occasion of some importance in view of the German-Polish Nonaggression Pact signed earlier in that year. Thereafter it may be said that Hungary tended to revolve, though always uncomfortably, in the German orbit. In 1936, Gömbös retired on grounds of ill-health, and the Hungarian premiership passed to the more moderate, but still faintly Nazi-inclined Darányi.

The Middle Danube was a microcosm which played out in little the whole diplomacy of these years and foreshadowed the analogous alignments of the larger European world.

THE REACTION OF POLAND

Poland's domestic affairs tossed and plunged along the stormy course we described in Chapter 12, but her foreign policy had managed for a time to keep a surprisingly even keel and, in more than a decade, made only one important change of direction. Polish premiers came and went, but two men conducted the country's relations abroad. August Zaleski was appointed Foreign Minister after Pilsudski's coup of May 1926, and he resigned in November 1932. Joseph Beck, one of Pilsudski's "Colonels," a former fighter in his Legion, and subsequently his private secretary, succeeded Zaleski and showed an equally tenacious longevity in office. Altogether Beck survived six changes of ministry and fell at last only with the fall of Poland in 1939. We may roughly designate Zaleski's term by calling it "the French period," and the earlier part of Beck's term by calling it "the German period," of Polish foreign policy.

One of the primary assumptions of the Treaty of Versailles and of the Franco-Polish alliance of 1921 had been the permanent antagonism of the new Poland and Germany, and throughout "the French period," Polish-German relations were under a continual strain. Incidents on either side of the Polish-German frontier, incidents often puerile to anyone who did not share the passions of the participants, were constantly magnified by mutual provocation into serious crises. Patriotic associations had a way of holding demonstrations in border districts; prominent public men would make inflammatory speeches in border towns; "atrocities" would be mutually charged against German minorities in Poland or against Polish minorities in Germany, atrocities always liable to exaggeration and fertile material for propaganda. Schools which taught children of minority groups could always be depended on to provide excuses for disturbance. Zaleski and Stresemann in their meetings at Geneva were invariably at loggerheads. On every international problem Poland and Germany, as if in obedience to some blind mechanical law, would always be ranged on opposite sides. The Locarno Conference, the Allied evacuation of the Rhineland, Germany's admission to the League, the Austrian *Anschluss*, the launching of Germany's first "pocket battleship" — these and every other imaginable question raised a stir of suspicion and animus along the bristling frontiers of the two nations. Meanwhile the essential contention between Poland and Germany in the Corridor, in Danzig, and in Upper Silesia remained unsolved and insoluble, and meanwhile the Franco-Polish alliance of 1921 formed the basis of Polish military security and the only support of Poland's unstable equilibrium.

Poland's position was certainly not enviable. She lay between Germany and Russia, who were now becoming first-class Powers, and any prospective war in which they might be engaged — whether they fought against each other or as allies against a third party — must inevitably result in suffering, if not extinction, for the unhappy Polish fatherland. She had German and Russian minorities in great numbers within her territory. In the early thirties the Soviet Union was beginning to re-enter European diplomacy and to adopt an anti-German stand. If indeed Poland were forced to make a choice between Germany and the Soviet Union, many Poles thought she might do worse than choose Germany. At all events, Poland had a long history of Russian aggression and Russian oppression. Pilsudski, and presumably Beck, were typical and bitter Russophobes.

Danzig was always the barometer of Polish-German relations. Throughout "the French period" peace and security in the Free City seemed to hang by a thread. Yet, if we consider the involved constitution of Danzig, the division of authority, the opportunities for obstruction, and the ever-present clash of national and economic interests, we may be surprised that so much business was done by the port and that so much prosperity was enjoyed by the Danzigers.[5]

In the early thirties conditions were the worst possible. The Depression had reduced the trade of the city, and the competition with Gdynia, the new all-Polish seaport, had become infinitely sharper. The Nazis won their first converts in Danzig, and began to build up within it one of the most aggressive of their branches. In November 1930, in the elections to the Volkstag, the Danzig Assembly, the Nazis won 13 seats out of 72, and the 13 were just enough to give them a controlling vote over any possible combination in the multiparty chamber. Three years of chronic altercation followed.

A serious incident occurred in March 1933 at the Polish munitions plant at Westerplatte in Danzig Harbor. The Danzig authorities had withdrawn the harbor police in the area and thus left the munitions plant without protection. In March the Polish Government, allegedly as a precautionary measure, increased its own Polish guards at the plant from the legally constituted force of 88 to 200 men. The High Commissioner for Danzig at once appealed to the League. The incident might have been no better or no worse than many another such incident in ordinary times. But Hitler was now in power in Germany, and the Danzig Nazis were keyed up to explosion point. Rumors were flying round the city that both Nazis and Poles were preparing military coups. The Poles had once seized Vilna, and the Lithuanians had once seized Memel; and the seizure of Baltic cities had precedents of very vivid and uncomfortable memory. In April 1933, at new Volkstag elections, the Danzig Nazis won 38 seats out of the 72, a figure which gave them an absolute majority, but not yet the two-thirds majority required for a change in the city's constitution.

But surprise was always the essence of Nazism. Instead of further deterioration, as might well have been expected, the situation in Danzig now suddenly improved, and Danzigers and Poles astonished the world by establishing the most amicable relations.

Hitler's assumption of power in Germany in 1933 was expected to create new stresses and strains in all the "danger spots" of Europe, and especially in Danzig, the Corridor, and Upper Silesia. The Nazis' past fulminations against Versailles and their much-advertised ambition to gather into the Greater Reich the outlying colonies of the German race, no less than the actual record of German-Polish relations since the First World War — all this was a fearful accumulation of fact which the blindest optimism could not minimize. It was true that political agitators had often been sobered by responsibility, and Hitler in power might not be the same Hitler as Hitler "in the wilderness." But that Hitler in power would reverse the entire policy of Germany toward Poland was a prodigy beyond belief. Yet reverse it he did. In 1933, after a decade of strife, Poland and Germany not only accommodated their differences, but almost regarded one another with cordiality.

Early in 1933, so the story goes, the fiery Marshal Pilsudski had invited his ally, France, to join him in a preventive war against Hitler. Pilsudski had taken the measure of his man. The incident at Westerplatte, just described, it is now believed, had been engineered by him as a deliberate provocation and challenge to his German neighbor. But Daladier, who was then French Premier, not only declined Pilsudski's proposals, but he went over Poland's head and enrolled France with Britain, Italy, and Germany in the Four-

Power Pact of June 1933, a pact originated by Mussolini with the ostensible object of effecting a peaceful revision of the more unjust Versailles frontiers. This pact must be mentioned in the next chapter (see p. 486). It is enough to note here that it was little more than a diplomatic gesture on the part of Mussolini in the interests of his own prestige. Its eventual text was about as vague and harmless as could be. But it was highly disturbing nevertheless to all those states in Europe, notably Poland, who owed their very existence to the Versailles settlement. To Pilsudski the offense was unpardonable. He therefore consulted his independent interests and resolved to agree with his German adversary as quickly as possible.

Hitler was willing to postpone a final Polish settlement while he concentrated on the Middle Danube. In May 1933, he received the Polish minister in Berlin, and Beck simultaneously received the German minister in Warsaw, and both meetings were followed by pointedly pacific announcements. The improvement in German-Polish relations was immediate. Conversations between Berlin and Warsaw proceeded during the remainder of the year and were brought to a successful conclusion under Lipski, appointed Polish minister in Berlin in November 1933. A German-Polish ten-year nonaggression pact was finally signed on January 26, 1934.

The pact, when it was announced, made as much of a sensation as the Treaty of Rapallo in 1922 or the Moscow Pact of 1939. Nonaggression pacts were not uncommon, but this one represented Germany's first breach in "the Versailles Front," and it was a demonstrative revolt on the part of Poland against her military and economic "vassalage" to France. Poland, seemingly, was running with the hare and hunting with the hounds, and if Poland, a near-Great Power, was thus consulting her security, the weaker members of the French alliance system might find it necessary to do likewise.

On January 30, 1934, the first anniversary of his chancellorship, Hitler spoke to the Reichstag in Berlin. He discussed the Nazi race theory and the structure of the new German state. He claimed a reduction of the unemployed in the country by 2,000,000. He declared his fundamental desire for peace and friendship with all peoples. He hoped for reconciliation with Austria and France. He congratulated Britain on her contribution to the Disarmament Conference. He also greeted the better relationship with Poland. When he had come to power, he said, there was every prospect that Polish-German hostility would harden into a menacing political heritage, and it was his happiness to be able to show that two nations so disposed could always settle their differences. But the obedient Reichstag, it was observed, applauded these references to Poland rather less vociferously than other parts of the Führer's speech.

THE REACTION OF THE SOVIET UNION

We shall describe more fully in Chapter 34 the foreign policy of the Soviet Union at this time, but certain aspects of it should be mentioned in passing. During the early thirties the Soviet Union also readjusted itself to the situation created by the threat of Nazi aggression. Its attitude toward other nations changed; the attitude of other nations toward itself changed equally. It ceased, or appeared to cease, its own aggressive ways, which in the twenties had so alarmed the "capitalist" nations. It became less of an abnormality and less of a source of disruption. The Comintern dropped from its high estate as the headquarters of a militant crusade. By the early thirties the Soviet Union was considered worthy to rank as a "respectable" state; it was quickly casting off the role of the Great Inscrutable; it was eagerly sought after by, and was itself as eagerly seeking, those other nations which also felt their security endangered by the new aggressor Powers on their frontiers. Litvinov had succeeded Chicherin as Soviet Foreign Commissar in 1929. He had been prime mover of the Litvinov Protocol of that year (see p. 142), and he had since come to identify his name, more and more, with the Western democratic ideal of collective security.

The Soviet *rapprochement* with France was typical and interesting. In the summer of 1931 the Soviet Union and France were negotiating a trade agreement, and a political *rapprochement* grew out of meetings which that negotiation made possible. Opposing ideologies were no longer allowed to obstruct the happy process. If Francis I had found an ally in the Grand Turk, and Richelieu in the German Protestants, it was not for modern France to be too fastidious in her friendships. So argued the French chambers and the French press at the time, and no doubt the Russians were consoling any prick of conscience they may have had in the matter with similar reasonings. In November 1932 the Soviet Union and France signed a nonaggression pact.

Meanwhile the Soviet Union pursued its favorite policy of making bilateral nonaggression pacts with its neighbors. During 1932 it had already signed such pacts with Finland, Poland, Latvia, and Estonia. In 1933 it signed pacts with Lithuania and with Italy. In July 1933 it entered into a comprehensive convention, defining aggression, with Afghanistan, Estonia, Latvia, Persia, Poland, Rumania, and Turkey (see p. 542). Recognitions were exchanged with the United States in October of the same year (pp. 596–97). Further pacts and renewals of old pacts followed in 1934 and 1935.

At the same time the Soviet Union was changing its attitude toward the League of Nations. In the days of Lenin and Chicherin, Russians had always represented the League to be a counterrevolutionary conspiracy of capitalist states. Only reluctantly did the Soviet Union take part in the Preparatory Commission for the Disarmament Conference in 1927, and even then its delegate, Litvinov, had used the occasion for propaganda and criticism. Both Locarno and the Pact of Paris had been suspect in its eyes. But in the early thirties high Soviet spokesmen were bridling their tongues and curbing their usual tone of raillery toward Western institutions, and the prospective resignation from the League of Nations of the Soviet's two potential enemies, Japan and Germany, gave better reason and urgency to the Soviet Union's membership therein.

Barthou, French Foreign Minister, and Litvinov negotiated the Soviet Union's admission to the League in the early months of 1934. Powers great and small, beginning with Spain, the Little Entente, and Britain, one by one withdrew their objections to, or intimated their support of, Soviet membership. On September 15, 1934 a letter of invitation bearing thirty signatures was sent to Litvinov and was formally accepted by him. Three days later the Fifteenth Assembly of the League admitted the Soviet Union to membership and to a permanent seat on the Council.

THE REACTION OF AUSTRIA

After the settlement of her earlier revolutionary and financial troubles, Austria, it had been hoped, would settle down to a decent obscurity. Her *Anschluss* with Germany, like the Hapsburg succession, would remain only a distant possibility, unlikely ever to be realized. She would cease to be counted among the "danger spots" and "powder kegs" so beloved of scaremongering correspondents. She would even become a popular tourist resort and a center for medical and psychological research. Granted normal prosperity and normal good will she would enjoy a status as safe and as honorable as that of Belgium and Switzerland or any other of the old-established smaller nations of Europe.

But beneath the surface, Austria's moral and economic exhaustion had never been repaired, and her political stability only waited for each passing strain upon it to show its basic weakness. The condition of Austria in the twenties has been mentioned before (see p. 189). She was a small country by any standard. Yet she indulged herself in the luxury of nine provincial Diets and at least four political parties, and she was gradually relapsing into the factional obstructionism which had made havoc of her parliamentary experiment before 1914. In particular the Social Democratic Schutzbund and the reactionary Heimwehr (see p. 193), at on time no better than irregular bands of squadrists of the Italian pattern, had grown into veritable private armies and were dividing the country into opposing camps. Their parades — sometimes held provocatively on the same days and in the same towns — numbered as many as 15,000 to 20,000 demonstrators, and ended often enough in bloodshed. Prince von Starhemberg, that handsome gallant, was leader of the Heimwehr, converting his castles into secret armories and running arms with complete immunity from police interference.

Seipel resigned from the Austrian chancellorship in April 1929, and was followed by a succession of chancellors, all of whom, rather by force of circumstances than personal inclination, supported the Heimwehr and gave an unmistakable Fascist tinge to Austrian politics. The Depression broke on Austria in the early thirties. Curtius, the German Foreign Minister, proposed his ill-starred Austro-German Customs Union in 1931, with its revived *Anschluss* implications. The bankruptcy of the Credit-Anstalt followed shortly afterward (see p. 405). In 1931, in fact, not only did Austria sink into her former needy estate, but she enjoyed the doubtful distinction of being the precipitating cause of the general economic crisis in Europe. In May 1932, Dr. Engelbert Dollfuss, a Christian Socialist, became Chancellor at the head of a cabinet strongly representative of the Heimwehr. Dr. Kurt von Schuschnigg was his Minister of Justice, a man who was to be his constant associate and companion in his short term of office. Seipel, in retirement, died in August of the same year.

All in all, Austria was in no condition to resist the uncompromising and subversive forces of Nazism now in full development across her border. She already had her own Nazi party and, as in Germany, it had flourished almost barometrically in accordance with the country's economic distress. In 1928 the Austrian Nazis numbered a modest 7,000; in 1930 they were already 100,000. They maintained the closest connection with their spiritual brethren in Germany. They used German propaganda, German funds, and German tactics. Hitler himself regarded them as a branch of his own party, natives of his own native land, destined eventually to return to the Greater Reich. In July 1931, Hitler appointed a loyal henchman, Theo Habicht, special "Inspector of Austria."

In the Austrian municipal elections of April and May 1932 the Nazis began to win seats, and to win them in alarming numbers. German leaders of the eminence of Göring, Goebbels, and Gregor Strasser visited Austria to address meetings. An armed clash in these days between the Schutzbund and the Heimwehr was no novelty but, during and after the elections, Austrian towns and cities were treated to types of street demonstrations, accompanied by outrages on Social Democrats and Jews more savage and uncontrollable than anything that had been known before. In October 1932 a particularly provocative affray occurred in a working-class quarter of Vienna when a policeman and two Nazis were shot dead. Dollfuss at once appointed Major Emil Fey Minister for Public Security; he was one of the original founders of the Heimwehr and a man who had good reasons of his own for being well acquainted with terrorist methods.

In January 1933, Hitler assumed power in Germany. Nazism in Austria at once acquired the stature of a grave international issue, and the admitted liaison between the German and Austrian Nazi parties was now tantamount to the interference by one sovereign state in the domestic affairs of another. The German press began at once to publish evidence purporting to prove the "oppression" of their party comrades in Austria. Insulting anti-Austrian broadcasts were given, notably from Munich and notably from the mouth of Theo Habicht, Nazi Inspector of Austria, and there were even propagandist leaflet raids by German aircraft over the Austrian frontier. The German Government imposed a tax of 1,000 marks on all exit permits issued to its nationals for Austrian travel, and at a stroke destroyed the very lucrative German tourist trade in Austria. Dollfuss's protests to Berlin were entirely ineffectual.

In March 1933 the president of the Austrian National Assembly resigned. A constitutional technicality regarding the election of a successor automatically brought the sessions of the Assembly to an end. Miklas, then the Austrian President, refused Dollfuss's offer of resignation, but he allowed Dollfuss to take advantage of the absence of the Assembly to govern by means of emergency decrees. As a counterblast to the Nazis, an Austrian patriotic association, the Fatherland Front, mainly recruited from the Heimwehr, was now formed and given the tacit blessings of the Austrian Government. Public meetings and street demonstrations by any party but the new association were forbidden. The Social Democratic Schutzbund was dissolved. The Austrian Army was raised to the full strength permitted under the peace treaty. In June 1933, Major Fey ordered the dissolution of the Nazi party in Austria and began to eject Nazi Deputies from the provincial Diets.

In that June, Dollfuss had been in London for the World Economic Conference and had there scored a great personal triumph. The English newspapers had featured this diminutive little man — he was only four feet, eleven inches in height — as a modern St. George battling the Nazi dragon. But it cannot be said that Dollfuss's program on his return home, even under the plea of necessity, would have won him the same sympathy. Dollfuss determined to fight dictatorship with dictatorship, to cast out one devil by invoking another, and the role of Fascist and tyrant sat upon him far better than the role of St. George. He was already ruling without a parliament, and he now proceeded to destroy the last vestiges of democracy in the Austrian Republic. In August 1933 he issued a series of decrees depriving of their citizenship and property Austrians who supported any action from abroad against the Austrian Government and empowering the government to confiscate the property of political parties which had been banned.

In September 1933 a great Catholic Congress met in Vienna, and the Fatherland Front held an impressive rally simultaneously. It was a gala month, packed with historic centenaries. From the Austrian provinces 200,000 people came to attend the festivities. Dollfuss spoke in favor of a new constitution for a "German Christian Austria" on corporative lines. A few days later he reconstituted his cabinet and, Mussolini-like, he took most of the portfolios himself. Major Fey became his Vice-Chancellor. The Heimwehr under its leader, Prince von Starhemberg, joined the Fatherland Front en masse. Dollfuss tried to avoid the appearance of dependence on any one faction or party, but the ascendancy of the Heimwehr and of these new mayors of the palace, Fey and Starhemberg, was evident to anyone who had eyes to see.

Dollfuss was strong in diplomatic support from abroad. All the major Powers of Europe and the Little Entente had good reasons for fearing the spread of the Nazi contagion in the Middle Danube. With the Vatican, Dollfuss, a good Catholic and a Christian Socialist, preserved the most filial relations. In particular, Dollfuss and the Heimwehr had always been cordially disposed toward Italy, in spite of Mussolini's supposed partiality for Nazism at this time. Dollfuss's visits to Rome in 1933 and his somewhat ostentatious consultations with the Duce had become a regular feature of the diplomatic scene. Prince von Starhemberg frankly modeled his squads on the Fascist Militia and was a grateful and regular recipient of Fascist funds. Mussolini, for his part, never missed an opportunity to exert a protectorate over as much of the Middle Danube as would accept his advances. A tripartite pact in March 1934, between Italy, Austria, and Hungary, was the formal recognition of his Danubian interests.

Dollfuss probably overestimated his domestic and diplomatic position. In

February 1934 he felt himself strong enough to try conclusions with his old enemies of the Schutzbund and the Social Democratic party. Fey and Starhemberg talked threateningly of "cleaning up" Austria, and dispatched their squads to hunt for caches of Schutzbund arms. The Heimwehr quietly, but efficiently, "suppressed" unsympathetic local governments in the provinces and climaxed its campaign by hauling off into custody the Social Democratic Burgomaster of Vienna. Toward mid-February 1934 sniping and skirmishing between the Heimwehr and Schutzbund broke out in provincial capitals and towns. A veritable civil war raged in the working-class districts of Vienna. In four days' fighting casualties amounted to some 300 dead. A great block of workers' tenements, the Karl Marx-Hof, a fine piece of modern architecture which the Social Democrats were supposed to have converted into a "fortress," was mercilessly shelled by government artillery and left in a badly damaged condition. The Social Democratic leader, Otto Bauer, Dollfuss's particular bête noire, afterward escaped into Czechoslovakia.

The penalty for unsuccessful resistance to oppression is always more oppression. President Miklas and Dollfuss both promised clemency to the rebel Social Democrats, but the Fascistization of Austria under the strong arm of the Heimwehr and the Fatherland Front proceeded apace. On April 30, 1934 the new corporative constitution of Austria was promulgated, and the old National Assembly met for the last time to vote itself out of existence. In May, Starhemberg became Vice-Chancellor, and Fey resumed his former post as Minister for Public Security. Dollfuss's dictatorship was complete. But in destroying Social Democracy, as he and his successor were soon to learn, Dollfuss had destroyed the one popular force in Austria which might have helped him to put up an effective defense against the Nazi invasion.

In July 1934 the Nazis plotted to dispose of Dollfuss and to set up a government in Vienna under their own leaders, Rintelen and Habicht. An "Austrian Legion," mostly of Austrian Nazis who had escaped into Germany — their numbers were said to be between 30,000 and 50,000 — was mobilized behind the German frontier, ready to march into Austria. The Austrian Cabinet and police had some information of the coming putsch, but precautions in Vienna were not taken at once. The fact is that the Vienna police were much infected with Nazism, several ranking police officers were privy to the putsch, and even in Dollfuss's own entourage it had become impossible to say who were friends or foes, partisans or traitors.

On the morning of July 25, Dollfuss and his Minister, Fey, had remained in the Chancellery. Some time after midday a party of Nazis, wearing the uniforms of the Austrian police and of the regular Austrian Army, drove up in trucks, entered the building, overpowered the guard, forced their way into the Chancellor's room, and shot and wounded him. Fey was "arrested," but was afterward released unhurt. Perhaps from fear of establishing communications outside the building, perhaps from outright cruelty, the Nazis refused to send for either doctor or priest to attend the stricken Dollfuss, but they allowed a couple of police superintendents to give him first aid. Dollfuss died at last from loss of blood, after three hours of agony. Simultaneously another party of Nazis seized the Vienna radio station and broadcast the resignation of the government in favor of Rintelen.

Neustädter-Stürmer, the Austrian Minister for Public Welfare, went to the Chancellery and from the steps of the building tried to treat with the Nazis inside. He promised them safe conduct to the German border, provided that no loss of life had been incurred as a result of their action. But the Nazis were taken into custody as soon as the full extent of the tragedy in the Chancellery was discovered. Martial law was proclaimed in Vienna, and a series of arrests followed. Simultaneous Nazi uprisings in the provinces were sporadic and ill-concerted, and were quickly suppressed. Rintelen tried to commit suicide, but he afterward recovered from his self-inflicted wounds, and was sentenced to life imprisonment. Otto Planetta, the Nazi who had fired the actual shots at Dollfuss, was tried and condemned to death, and eventually went to the scaffold shouting *"Heil Hitler!"*

On the evening of July 25, Kurt von Schuschnigg succeeded to the Austrian chancellorship. At three o'clock the next morning Hitler called Papen out of bed and instructed him to go immediately to Vienna as minister to bring about "an easing of the general situation." Theo Habicht disappeared into well-deserved obscurity.

The Nazis had fully expected the putsch of July 1934 in Vienna to be one of their bloodless victories. But blood had been shed, and the putsch had not been a victory. Mussolini telegraphed the Austrian Government his condolences upon the death of a man to whom he was bound "by ties of personal friendship and common political views. . . . The independence of Austria, for which the Chancellor died, is a principle which Italy also will strenuously defend in these times of exceptional difficulty." At the end of July the Italian Northern Army, some 200,000 men, was mobilized at the Brenner frontier, ready to meet an attempted German invasion of Austria.

World-wide repugnance of Nazi tactics in Austria and the resolute military demonstration on the part of Italy had their effect. The Austrian Nazi movement suffered a sharp setback, and it was three full years before Hitler openly resumed his offensive against the land of his birth. In May 1935, in a speech in the Reichstag, Hitler denied that he had ever intended to interfere in Austria's internal affairs, or to bring about an annexation or *Anschluss*. In July 1936, after lengthy negotiations in which Papen was the intermediary, Austria and Germany concluded an agreement in "permanent settlement" of their mutual problems. Under the published terms of the agreement, Germany recognized the full sovereignty of Austria; Austria and Germany acknowledged their respective Nazi movements as the private affair of each state, an affair which neither would seek to influence, directly or indirectly; and Austria agreed to conduct her general policy, especially vis-à-vis Germany, in accordance with her "German character." Under the secret terms, Nazi organizations were to be started in Austria for German nationals, who were to be permitted the use of the swastika badge and other Nazi symbols; all Nazis in Austria were to be amnestied except those convicted of grave crimes; each country agreed to a mutual abstention from aggressive propaganda; and the Austrian Chancellor, "at a suitable moment

. . . in the near future," would summon leaders of "the national opposition in Austria," that is to say Nazi-minded Austrians, "to cooperate in assuming political responsibility."

Hitler, Schuschnigg, Mussolini, and Gömbös simultaneously, in a flutter of telegraphic communiqués, advertised their full recognition of Austria's independence and the continuance of their traditional, peaceful relations in the Middle Danube.

THE REACTION OF ITALY

Italy's first reaction to Nazism in Germany had been one of pronounced sympathy. Anything that embarrassed France, of course, suited her excellently well. Moreover, she could not but patronize a movement which appeared to have so decided an affinity with Fascism, and she was very ready to exploit the "spiritual" support which Nazism lent her to expand her self-importance in the world.

The Four-Power Pact of 1933 is almost forgotten now. In its day it was one of the many instruments intended to find a new basis of stability in a Europe that was thus suddenly thrown into flux and ferment. The pact was initiated by Italy. In its beginnings it was a characteristically Mussolinian maneuver to assert Italian prestige, and it was also a good example of that mildly avuncular relationship which the Duce of Fascism at this time bore toward the Chancellor of the Third Reich. Mussolini had often expressed his belief that if only the Great Powers of Europe — France, Italy, Germany, and Britain — could be induced to "collaborate," their peace would be secure. These Powers acting together could effect with safety all those treaty revisions and those frontier and colonial rectifications which justice and common sense demanded. So stated and so aimed, a Four-Power Pact would have been a simple and commendable transaction. It granted Italy a very cherished status within the Big Four of her world, and it recognized the "equality" of Germany. But correspondingly it offered a covert challenge to France's hegemony in Europe and to the status of France's allies. Poland and the Little Entente were very quick to realize that the new Concert of Mussolini would exclude them from the Four-Power pale and that they would probably be the first victims of those treaty revisions which the pact meditated. Under pressure from France, therefore, the pact's terms were so diluted that in the end the whole affair amounted to little more than a pious diplomatic gesture. But the original offense to France's allies still rankled nevertheless. Pilsudski, in high dudgeon, as we saw in the last chapter (pp. 477–78), went so far as to compound his nonaggression pact of January 1934 with Germany. For Ramsay MacDonald, the British Prime Minister, the Four-Power Pact was clearly an attempt to relieve some of the acknowledged harshness of Versailles and, as such, the pact might be interpreted as the first act in Britain's long program of "appeasement" in Europe. On June 7, 1933, the Four-Power Pact between France, Italy, Germany, and Britain was at last initialed in Rome.

One of the principles of Mussolini's foreign policy had always been rivalry with France and Yugoslavia in the Mediterranean and the Middle Danube, and it was to be expected that, in proportion as France's influence in the Middle Danube might decline, Italy's influence there would rise. The new restlessness in Germany and Pilsudski's recent nonaggression pact were all grist to Mussolini's mill. The situation was crystallized in March 1934 when Dollfuss, the Austrian Chancellor, and Gömbös, the Hungarian Premier, met with Mussolini in Rome and signed a tripartite pact pledging Austria, Hungary, and Italy "to concert together on all the problems which particularly interested them" and expanding their existing economic relations (see p. 482).

Meanwhile Mussolini continued to cultivate his German friendship. Almost a year to a day after the signing of the Four-Power Pact, between June 14 and 16, 1934, in carnival atmosphere in Venice, he and Hitler met for the first time. "In these hours which we spent together," Mussolini announced afterward, "our spirits were in intimate communion. . . . The personal relations thus initiated between the heads of the Italian and German governments will be maintained in the future." But the Venetian idyl had not been quite as idyllic as had been made out, and it was the end of the first phase of Mussolini's pro-Nazi policy. June 30, 1934 was "the night of the long knives" in Germany, and on July 25 Dollfuss was done to death in Vienna by Nazi troopers. These events were violent enough to cure any hope or wish Mussolini might till then have cherished that Nazism would develop in filial imitation of Italian Fascism. At the end of July he mobilized his divisions on the upper Adige, and the world was treated to the spectacle of militant, filibustering Italy belatedly facing up to the new Germanic menace from the North and joining in the common scramble to make over old enmities into new friendships. Mussolini now unashamedly revised his anti-Gallic and anti-Slavic policies of fifteen years' standing and offered the hand of peace to both his neighbors and former foemen, France and Yugoslavia. One result was the Franco-Italian Agreement of January 1935 — of which more anon.

On December 5, 1934, at Walwal, an obscure native settlement of the frontiers of Ethiopia, a body of native Italian troops exchanged shots with Ethiopian warriors. The incident might have been of little importance, but Mussolini seized upon it as an excuse for settling long-standing differences between Italy and Ethiopia. The result was Italy's invasion and conquest of Ethiopia, her consequent quarrel with the League of Nations, and her formation of an "Axis" with Nazi Germany, a series of events which, though simultaneous with those we are here about to describe in Europe, we had best relegate to a separate chapter.

THE REACTION OF FRANCE

In February 1934, Doumergue took office in France at the head of a government pledged to "truce, appeasement, and justice," and chose for his Foreign Minister Barthou, the Barthou who had formerly been president of the

Reparation Commission, one of the authors of the Ruhr invasion, and the close associate of Poincaré in the long struggle for the absolute and literal fulfillment of the Treaty of Versailles (see p. 163). Barthou was soon to make clear what he himself understood by "truce, appeasement, and justice." He arrived at the Quai d'Orsay to find negotiations in train to induce Germany to return to the Disarmament Conference, and these negotiations he categorically broke off. German rearmament was now a fact well known to the chancelleries of Europe, a fact over which he was resolved to shed no more tears. Instead he set about with consuming energy to overhaul France's alliance system, to furbish up old links, to forge new ones and, in short, to build a prison house so formidable that its German inmate, however powerful he grew, would not dare to try his strength against it. Short of a preventive war against Hitler, an alternative which France had already declined (see p. 477), there was no other policy open to her.

Barthou began by trying to mend the unfortunate effects of the recent German-Polish Nonaggression Pact and Poland's virtual desertion from "the Versailles Front," and toward the end of April 1934 he visited Warsaw for conversations with Marshal Pilsudski and Colonel Beck. It cannot be said that Barthou succeeded too well in thawing the chill which then characterized official Polish sentiments toward his country. But Barthou's visits to Prague a few days later, and then to Bucharest and Belgrade, were in the nature of a triumphal progress. If Poland was now determined to follow her own devices, the Little Entente at least remained in stanch association with France. The Balkan Pact had been concluded in the previous February (see p. 529), and Barthou might be excused a brief ecstasy of optimism over the "zone of peace" which, in his words, "stretched from Prague to Ankara."

But Barthou was weaving wider schemes than this. He had already been instrumental in drawing the Soviet Union into the League of Nations, and he now conceived a Grand Alliance in complete encirclement of Germany. In pursuance of this lofty purpose he proposed an East European Pact of Mutual Assistance, which would put the Soviet Union on guard upon the eastern frontiers of Germany, much as the Locarno Pact of 1925 had put France on guard on the western frontiers.

How Barthou's ambitious diplomacy would have ended we cannot tell. Conceivably he might have permanently attached the Soviet Union to a European peace system, a system strong enough to have forestalled and withstood that "one-by-one" strategy whereby Germany eventually destroyed her foes. Some commentators incline toward the view that Polish Russophobia would have prevented Poland's participation in the system and that indeed the villain in the piece, working against Barthou, was really the sinister Colonel Beck. At all events, on October 9, 1934, when Barthou was at Marseille to welcome King Alexander of Yugoslavia on a state visit to France, he and the monarch were struck down by the bullets of a Croat assassin.[1]

The prophets and the pessimists of Europe compared Marseille with that other assassination at Sarajevo which had once had such dire results. Some of the more prophetic and pessimistic ones thought they could detect the hand of Germany in the crime. Certainly a drama of blood and treachery, such as this, would have been in keeping with the Nazi character, and nothing could have been so diabolically well calculated to disrupt the entire anti-German coalition which Barthou had been so industriously constructing. It could have antagonized France and Yugoslavia, and thence disorganized the entire Little Entente. Furthermore, the assassin of Marseille was evidently one of a band of Croat revolutionaries who, exiled from Yugoslavia, had established themselves in Italy and Hungary and planned their lawless forays from their refuges abroad. The assassination, in addition, therefore involved Italy and Hungary, and indirectly jeopardized the *rapprochement,* now fast maturing, of Italy with Yugoslavia and with France.

The French Government exerted itself in every possible way to express its sorrow and concern over the assassination of Alexander and to compensate for its lack of proper precautions at Marseille. Several police officials were dismissed. The French Minister of the Interior resigned. Some days later, at Belgrade, a distinguished cortege followed in the dead monarch's funeral procession — President Lebrun and Marshal Pétain, King Carol, the Duke of Kent, Göring, Beneš, Titulescu, and other international notables — and perhaps the Yugoslavs were a little surprised and mollified by this evidence of the importance their king and country had suddenly assumed in the estimation of an anxious Europe.

The failure of Barthou's East European Pact, however, was not all loss. The logic of it was too convincing to be altogether denied, and even while his own busy negotiations were in train, smaller alliances on the same lines were already in formation. The Balkan States, Yugoslavia, Greece, Rumania, and Turkey, as we have mentioned elsewhere, had come together in a Balkan Pact in February 1934 (see p. 529). The Baltic States, Estonia, Latvia, and Lithuania, had likewise come together in a Baltic Pact in September 1934. Mutual assistance pacts between France and the Soviet Union, and between Czechoslovakia and the Soviet Union, shortly to be described, followed in 1935 (see p. 492).

Barthou's death brought the strange figure of Pierre Laval into prominence in France, and with him came a new pro-Italian phase of French foreign policy reciprocating the pro-Gallic advances which, as we have said above, Mussolini was now making. Laval succeeded Barthou as Foreign Minister in the then-existing government of Doumergue and continued as Foreign Minister under Flandin, whom he succeeded as Premier in June 1935. Presumably Laval's purpose was to detach Italy from her old diplomatic allegiances and draw her positively into France's anti-Nazi peace front. He was one of the most artistic negotiators of his day, a man of infinite resource — and surprisingly, of very real charm — and, it must be said, he enjoyed from the first a strong personal affinity for the Italian dictator.

In the early days of 1935, Laval visited Mussolini in Rome and there negotiated a thoroughgoing Franco-Italian Agreement. The whole field of French and Italian relations was covered, and covered, it would seem, greatly to the advantage of France. Italy's territorial acquisitions, under which she renounced all further claims on France in respect of African colonies, comprised large slices of about as arid a stretch of sand and rock as is to be found in North Africa, plus some thirteen miles of strategically useful coastline along the Strait of Bab el Mandeb, opposite the British base at Aden. In addition, Italy undertook progressively to liquidate her interests in Tunisia — in Tunisia, be it remembered, which she had eyed so jealously and so long, and which contained from 80,000 to 90,000 of her citizens.

The Franco-Italian Agreement, as far as we know, contained no secret clauses. But Mussolini's preparations for his war in Ethiopia were then well advanced; the Walwal incident had already occurred on December 5, 1934 (see p. 504); and there must surely have been some tacit understanding between Mussolini and Laval to the effect that if and when the war in Ethiopia should break out France would remain a docile and disinterested spectator. In no other way can we account for Italy's satisfaction over the barren gains which the agreement accorded her or for the extreme complaisance which Laval afterward showed toward Mussolini's imperial adventures.

"THE LAST YEAR OF PEACE"

The year 1935 began with the Saar plebiscite and ended with the outbreak of the Italo-Ethiopian War. In between were crowded events as significant for the future of Europe as any which took place in these years of storm and stress. These events were the German conscription decree in March 1935, the formation of the Stresa Front in April, the French and Czechoslovak mutual assistance pacts with the Soviet Union in May, the Anglo-German Naval Agreement in June, and the London Naval Conference in December. The series concluded with Germany's Rhineland coup in March 1936 and the outbreak of the Spanish Civil War in July 1936. Well might the "democracies" look back on 1935 as their "last year of peace."

The Saar plebiscite was a corollary of the Treaty of Versailles, under whose terms the inhabitants of the territory were now due to voice their own destiny (see p. 122). The Saar had felt the usual repercussions of the Nazi revolution, but it had been spared the extreme war of nerves of Danzig or the Corridor. No doubt Hitler expected the eventual plebiscite to result in a clear German victory, and he was not one to force a cheap success in a cause which mere legalities would inevitably win for him. The Saar was primarily Catholic and Social Democrat in affiliation, and Nazi proselytism had not made much headway there, but French hopes of the emergence of a decisive anti-Nazi bloc never materialized. Despite mounting excitement as the date approached and despite the Nazi campaign of open propaganda and underground terrorism, the plebiscite took place on January 13, 1935 in an orderly manner and according to plan.

The League Council delegated the arrangements for the plebiscite to a special committee, which in turn appointed executive organs in the territory itself. The local police were reinforced with some 3,300 troops — British, Italian, Dutch, and Swedish — under the command of a British general. The result of the plebiscite was an overwhelming majority for reunion with Germany. On March 1, 1935, amid hysterical rejoicing, the Saar returned to the Fatherland. Hitler paid a surprise visit the same day and toured the length of the territory. He declared afterward that he could now give his solemn pledge that Germany would make no further territorial claims on France; the frontier which had fluctuated for a thousand years at last had come to rest.

In all the events so far described in this chapter, the participation of Britain had been halting and distant. Britain, at first mainly in the persons of Ramsay MacDonald and Arthur Henderson, had made her contribution to the Disarmament Conference and the Four-Power Pact. Sir John Simon, Foreign Secretary under MacDonald, had been persuaded to confer a cautious benediction on Barthou's projected Grand Alliance. The truth is that Britain was still in an isolationist, almost anti-French mood and was neither yet so fearful of Germany nor yet so anxious for French friendship as was Italy at this time. British liberal opinion was profoundly smitten with a "guilt complex" over the Treaty of Versailles and was moving toward a policy of appeasing Germany — and Italy, and incidentally Japan — with what she considered were justifiable concessions.

Official Britain nevertheless was much exercised over reports of Germany's rearmament and, in particular, was awakening to the dangers and horrors of modern aerial warfare. Early in March 1935, over MacDonald's initials, the British Government issued a *Statement Relating to Defense,* which reviewed the whole position of British armaments. The paper made mention of Germany by name and of her rearmament in contravention of Versailles. Hitler affected to be deeply offended, contracted a "diplomatic" cold, and for some days absented himself from active business. In consequence, Simon postponed a prospective visit to Berlin. It was to have been a visit of some importance, and he was to have been accompanied by Anthony Eden, then in the Cabinet as Lord Privy Seal and now coming to the fore in British foreign politics. Yet the paper gave some point and excuse a few days later to Germany's public admission that she had an air force already in existence and that, in fact, it had been "officially" in existence since March 1, 1935. Göring himself gave an interview to that effect to a correspondent of the *Daily Mail.*

As the result of the reduced birth rate in France during the years of the First World War, the classes currently due to be called for service in the French Army were much under strength. On March 15, 1935, after a lengthy debate, the French Chamber approved a measure for prolonging the period of military service. Germany at once seized upon the measure as her cue. The following day, the German Government decreed universal compulsory military service in Germany and defined the peace footing of the German Army at twelve corps and thirty-six divisions or, as Hitler subsequently estimated it, at about 550,000 men. Germany, so said the accompanying proclamation of the German Government, had once disarmed herself in fulfillment of the Treaty of Versailles, but the victor nations had defaulted in their complementary obligations, and she could no longer endure a situation by which she remained a military vacuum in the midst of other heavily armed states, open to every threat and menace.

The German conscription decree lacked not drama and positiveness and, like so many of Hitler's acts, it came at a moment which exploited to the full the disunity and preoccupation of its possible opponents. A new Franco-Soviet pact was under discussion; Italy was engaged in her Ethiopian preparations; Britain, still in an anti-French mood, almost derived satisfaction from Germany's revolt against fifteen years of French egotism and obstructionism in Europe. Nevertheless, on April 11–14, representatives of the three Powers, France, Italy, and Britain — respectively Flandin and Laval, Mussolini, and MacDonald and Simon — met at the Piedmontese village of Stresa to concert some sort of protest against the German decree. They discussed Austria, they discussed an air pact, they reaffirmed their loyalty to Locarno and the League, and they "regretfully recognized that the method of unilateral repudiation adopted by the German Government had undermined public confidence in the security of a peaceful order." But what was not mentioned, though it was well known to all, was the fact that one of the parties at the Stresa Conference at that very moment was meditating in Ethiopia further unilateral breaches of the peace. The Stresa Front, as it came to be called, like Barthou's Grand Alliance, was soon to be relegated to the limbo of many other attempts to build up a united resistance to Nazi Germany.

Hitler's conscription decree, however, hastened the formation of two new alliances. Barthou's earlier proposal for an East European Pact of Mutual Assistance came within an ace of realization. On May 2, 1935, France and the Soviet Union entered into a Mutual Assistance Pact, providing for common consultation and immediate and automatic assistance in the event of unprovoked aggression against one of themselves on the part of a third Power. A fortnight later the pact was followed by a complementary and similarly claused Czech-Soviet Mutual Assistance Pact. But this time, the pact was to go into force only if France had already gone to the help of the attacked country in accordance with the existing Franco-Czech and present Franco-Soviet treaties.

THE REACTION OF BRITAIN

Naval armaments since 1931, throughout the world, had been reflecting the general political deterioration. The Japanese invasion of Manchuria had been the immediate cause of President Roosevelt's decision in 1933 to build the American Navy up to the full limits allowed under the Washington Treaty of 1922, and this in turn had been the immediate cause of the Japanese "replenishment program" of the same year. In December 1934 the Japanese Government availed itself of the privilege to denounce the Washington Treaty.

In Europe, Germany's new fleet of "pocket battleships" had been the object of the greatest curiosity and uneasiness. The *Deutschland* had been launched in March 1931, and two similar ships had been laid down in the two following years. All three were armored cruisers of 10,000 tons each and conformed to the stipulations of the Treaty of Versailles, but they were faster and more heavily armed than any other ship of the same class in the world. The British Admiralty feared that these ingenuities of naval architecture were intended as commerce raiders. The Soviet Union meanwhile was said to be engaged on a vast submarine program. France and Italy were in the incipient stages of a battleship-building race between themselves.

Such were the antecedents of the new naval conversations which were shortly to become due, and preliminary talks à deux were already taking place in London between representatives of the naval Powers in the latter part of 1934 and early 1935. But little appeared to be transpiring beyond the ventilation of irreconcilable points of view. The Japanese wanted parity; the Americans wanted the old ratios; the British wanted more cruisers; Italy wanted to outclass France; and France wanted to outclass Italy and Germany together. In April 1935 the Germans suddenly assembled twelve submarines from parts which they had been secretly manufacturing, and in July they announced that they had already under way a naval building program which included two battle cruisers, afterward named the *Scharnhorst* and *Gneisenau*, of 26,000 tons each. Both the submarines and the battle cruisers were in flagrant violation of Versailles. It was in the midst of these talks and preparations that the Anglo-German Naval Agreement of June 1935 was ineptly sprung upon the world.

Today that transaction has a noisome odor. But, before we condemn it, we should in justice think ourselves back into the attitudes of mind of the time. British statesmanship in 1935 was already chasing the will-o'-the-wisp of appeasement. Hitler was Chancellor of the German Reich, but he had not yet shown himself for what he was. Political courtesies, if nothing else, demanded that his professions should be taken at their face value, especially when, by repeated assurances, he had given out that he wanted nothing so much as the trust and friendship of England and that he would never allow Germany to repeat the former naval follies of Kaiser William II. In the British view it was impossible to expect a proud and vigorous nation like Germany to remain in a state of perpetual inferiority, and it was better to meet her inferiority halfway — or, in this case, one-third of the way — than to goad her, as France had always done, by exasperating and ineffective opposition. There also seemed to be good reasons at this time for expecting some kind of Western air pact. Of all the Powers, a Germany in the very midst of Europe stood to lose most from the depredations of modern bomber warfare and could surely be counted upon to show an even greater interest in air limitation than a Britain situated in the comparative immunity of her island. In 1935 the British and German peoples were enjoying better relations than at any other time during the Nazi regime. British tourists to Germany in that year and especially in 1936, the year of the Olympic Games in Berlin, were returning home with appreciative stories of the kindness and hospitality they had met. Organizations of veterans and students, youth groups, and football teams in the two countries were exchanging visits, and even the Germans must sometimes have been deceived by the signs.

Ribbentrop had come to England in midsummer of 1935. He was then German Minister Plenipotentiary-at-Large and perhaps one of the least attractive members of Hitler's entourage. He had been a wine merchant, enjoyed good social connections in his own country, and was well traveled abroad, notably in Canada. He had entered Nazi politics as an intermediary between Papen and Hitler in the critical days of 1932, and he had subsequently gained Hitler's confidence as an international expert and interpreter of the British point of view. In this last capacity he had built up in Berlin a virtual foreign ministry of his own. As a man pretending to gentlemanly attainments and displaying a veneer of cosmopolitanism, Ribbentrop, for all the rudeness incumbent on him as a good Nazi, scored a great personal success in the London of 1935. He was lavishly entertained, and entertained lavishly in return. He moved freely in certain rather "pro-German" and extreme Tory circles in England, and quite misunderstood their mood. Finally he persuaded the British Government to conclude a naval agreement permitting Germany a surface tonnage of 35 per cent of the British and a submarine tonnage of 100 per cent.

The Anglo-German Naval Agreement, as we now know, merely legalized Germany's naval program as already projected at the time, and doubtless she only intended to observe it until, and no longer than, that program was completed. But far worse was the effect of the agreement on the Continent. France, if anything, was more shocked by the publication of its terms than by the German conscription decree itself. Perfidious Albion, it would appear, was condoning Germany's rearmament and aiding and abetting her in new breaches of Versailles. The Stresa Front, which France, Italy, and Britain had only just established, was shattered utterly. How indeed was the concert of security to be built up, how indeed was the harmony of Locarno and the League to be preserved, if Britain, one of the chief supporters thereof, went behind the backs of her companions to negotiate treaties with the common enemy?

Even this was not the end. In the design of any of her new battleships under the agreement, Germany would have the further advantage of not being bound by the former 35,000-ton limit of the Washington Conference, to which, of course, she had never been a party. The two battleships, the *Bismarck* and the *Tirpitz,* which she now proceeded to lay down, were designed with a displacement of over 45,000 tons and, when completed, they would outclass any other vessel afloat. In other words, Germany, by the innocent ruse of building up to a third of the British tonnage, would set the entire naval world by the ears and start off a new armament race in super-battleships.

In the resulting outcry, the proposed Western air pact, on which Britain had so much set her heart, failed. Conversations upon such a pact were largely kept from the public ear, but there appears to have been no want of pressure or persistence about them. Chancelleries and embassies in London, Paris, and Berlin fairly hummed with proposals. Baldwin and Simon, then British Prime Minister and Foreign Secretary, were deeply engaged in the conversations. But Germany and France as usual were at odds. Germany claimed that the new Franco-Soviet Mutual Assistance Pact forced her to take into account the eventuality of an aerial war on two fronts. France claimed that no air pact would be of the slightest military value unless it could be reinforced by a new automatic assistance pact between herself and Britain.

The prospects of the aerial terror were perhaps much exaggerated beyond what did actually happen in 1940. Aerial warfare, as then imagined, could burst open in the hour, and Göring's Luftwaffe could lay all Paris in ashes, while France's own delegates at Geneva sat round a table "defining" the aggressor. But Britain claimed that France had pacts enough — that she was veritably buried in pacts — and that she still seemed neither satisfied nor grateful.

So rolled the old arguments back and forth. Today we know that the realities of the situation were not in the instructions of ambassadors or even in the yearnings of peoples, but in the wretched discords and hatreds of international human nature and in the cold, grim statistics of German rearmament. All through these latter months of 1935, as we shall describe in the next chapter, the Italo-Ethiopian crisis was mounting to breaking point; discussions were proceeding at the League Assembly in Geneva; the Italo-Ethiopian War began in October 1935; fifty nations declared sanctions against Italy.

The London Naval Conference met at last in December 1935, in an atmosphere of gathering gloom. It was to be the last of the series of interwar naval conferences that had begun so hopefully at Washington in 1921. It was attended by delegates of the United States, Britain, Japan, France, and Italy. But the United States and Britain refused to accept the Japanese proposals for "a common upper limit," and the Japanese delegates withdrew from the Conference. At the end of February 1936 the Conference was still sitting, but the Italian delegates, citing the Mediterranean repercussions of the Italo-Ethiopian War, now also withdrew. The United States, Britain, and France were therefore left to salvage what they could from the wreckage of the discussions. On March 25, 1936, they signed a Three-Power Naval Treaty which, having defined certain qualitative limitations, permitted any signatory to exceed these limitations if it felt itself being outclassed or outbuilt by a nonsignatory Power.

THE MARCH INTO THE RHINELAND

At the beginning of 1936, rumors were circulating that Germany would soon seek to alter by force of arms the demilitarized status which Versailles and Locarno had imposed upon the Rhineland, and the rumors were persistent enough to call for emphatic denials from the Führer himself.

The Franco-Soviet Mutual Assistance Pact, as we noted above, had been signed the previous May but, curiously enough, Laval, now French Premier, had shown no great anxiety to complete its ratification. Laval may have been delaying final action in deference to anti-Communist opinion in France, or perhaps he was already showing signs of his subsequent pro-Nazi predilections. He was apt at this time to keep Litvinov fretting in his antechambers while he dallied with Mussolini and Hitler. In January 1936, however, Sarraut succeeded Laval, and Flandin, the new Foreign Minister, laid the much-abused treaty before the Chamber. On February 27, after an unhurried and not too acrimonious debate, it was duly passed by the Chamber by a large majority and passed to the Senate.

But Germany did not wait for the outcome of this leisurely legislation. If it was the part of a parliament to deliberate, it was the part of a dictatorship to act. In the German view the entire Franco-Soviet *rapprochement* violated the Locarno Pact and introduced into Europe a new balance of power, against which her elementary rights demanded that Germany protect herself. On March 7, 1936, Hitler announced in the Reichstag that he had restored "the full and unrestricted sovereignty of Germany in the demilitarized zone of the Rhineland." He also announced new Reichstag elections in order that the German people might confirm "all that he and his colleagues had done." Simultaneously, the German Foreign Minister, Neurath, summoned a meeting in Berlin of the ambassadors of the Locarno Powers — France, Belgium, Italy, and Britain — announced the "symbolic" occupation of the Rhineland, proposed twenty-five-year nonaggression pacts both in the West and in the East, proposed an air pact, and even expressed Germany's willingness to re-enter the League of Nations.

The same morning, at dawn, contingents of the German Army to a supposed strength of 50,000 men had begun their march into the Rhineland and to the French borders beyond. Everywhere they were received by the populace with flags, flowers, and jubilation. The new election campaign in Germany, in accordance with Hitler's announcement, opened at once. On March 29, with prayers, songs, and the pealing of bells, the German electorate went to the polls. Ninety-nine per cent voted, and of that number nearly all voted for the Nazi party list.

The French Government spent these weeks of the Rhineland crisis in an agony of impotence and humiliation. The Sarraut ministry was not a strong one. It was admittedly a stopgap to mark time till impending elections. Sarraut's first impulse nevertheless had been to order partial mobilization, and some specialized units of the French Army were moved up to the Maginot Line. The general staffs of the French Army, Navy, and Air Force waited expectantly for their orders. Representatives of the Soviet Union, Czechoslovakia, and Yugoslavia assured Flandin of their fullest support under the terms of their several treaties. On March 8 the French Government dispatched to Geneva a veritable catalogue of breaches of her obligations which Germany by her action in the Rhineland had committed and called for an early meeting of the League Council. Sarraut broadcast to the French nation in bitter condemnation of Hitler's *"coup brutal."*

It is now known that German officers in the Rhineland operation carried sealed orders to retire at once if they encountered French resistance and that the whole venture would have collapsed ingloriously — with catastrophic results for Hitler — if France had shown the slightest resolution. But neither did the other Locarno Powers, Italy or Britain, evince any inclination to act upon their obligations. Italy was triumphantly winding up her Ethiopian campaign and was glad of a crisis which embarrassed the other Powers that recently had dared to pass sanctions upon her. The British attitude was no more than "correct." Eden, who had recently become British Foreign Secretary, made it plain to the German ambassador in London that the effect of Germany's repudiation of the Locarno Pact, a treaty "freely negotiated and freely signed," must inevitably be "deplorable." But the British people as a whole lost no sleep and shed no tears over the Rhineland. They felt that Hitler had some "right" on his side — after all, he was only going "into his own back-garden" — and they still failed to recognize the beast out of the bottomless pit that in due time would make war against them. Loungers in the clubs and bars of London talked with evident relish at the discomfiture of France and at the retribution she was now reaping for her shortsighted and egotistical policies in Europe.

The four Locarno Powers, France, Belgium, Italy, and Britain, met in Paris on March 12, 1936. Flandin demanded the withdrawal of the German troops from the Rhine, he demanded sanctions, he demanded reparations, he demanded guarantees, he demanded that the question of the compatibility of the Franco-Soviet Mutual Assistance Pact with Locarno should be submitted to the World Court. He threatened France's resignation from the League. He hinted at an entire reorientation of French foreign policy — presumably toward an accommodation with Germany. Yet it seems that, at this critical moment, Flandin was not sufficiently certain of France's legal case against Germany under the League Covenant and under the Locarno Pact. The meeting of the Locarno Powers was resumed in London. There too the League Council assembled and passed a resolution declaring Germany to be guilty of breaches of Versailles and Locarno. Under Eden's insistence, consultations were initiated between the French, Belgian, and British general staffs. But there still ensued no overt action against the culprit. Hitler, at a stroke, had transformed the entire military situation in Western Europe. The new fortifications which he doubtless intended to build along the French and Belgian frontiers — the West Wall, as it came to be called — would cut France off from all strategic connection with her allies in Central and Eastern Europe — and, in all this, not a hand had been raised against him.

Mussolini, from his balcony in Rome, announced his triumphant termination of the Italo-Ethiopian War on May 9, 1936, the League's sanctions against Italy were liquidated in July, and in the same month the Spanish Civil War broke out. And these things soon relegated the Rhineland crisis to a secondary place in the interest of European public opinion. In November 1936, Hitler announced the resumption of German sovereignty over the Kiel Canal and over the German rivers internationalized under the Treaty of Versailles (see p. 124).

One significant consequence of the Rhineland crisis was the isolationism of Belgium. King Leopold had already been moving tentatively in that direction. In October 1936 he made a formal statement to his cabinet, pointed to the rearmament of the Great Powers and to the deterioration of international good faith, and argued that no defensive agreement would save Belgium in a modern blitzkrieg and that therefore she must follow an exclusively "Belgian policy." Leopold visited London in March 1937, when it was announced that the British and French Governments had released Belgium from her commitments under the Locarno Pact (see p. 139).

31

ITALY: FASCIST IMPERIALISM

AND THE ITALO–ETHIOPIAN WAR

ETHIOPIA

Ethiopia, or Abyssinia, was an inland empire of northeastern Africa consisting of some 350,000 square miles of mountainous plateau, riven by deep gorges and gullies, generally covered with thick and scrubby forest, and relieved here and there by sparse grasslands. Its inhabitants were an ancient people, numbering perhaps 6,000,000, of Semitic and Negroid extraction. A few were Moslems, but most of them were Christians of the Coptic Church, and they supported themselves by agriculture and stock raising. Their political structure was primitively feudal. Their territory was divided among a number of provincial chiefs, or rases, who enjoyed varying degrees of independence of, or dependence on, whatever central government claimed the hegemony at the moment, and such political history as Ethiopia may be said to have had consisted of the almost perpetual warfare of these rases with one another.

The extreme inaccessibility of the country had long preserved it, like another Tibet, in isolation from the outside world, an isolation only disturbed by an occasional explorer, trader, or missionary. The main currents of Mohammedan conquest and European imperialism alike had passed it by, and until the Italian campaign of 1935 and the British campaign of 1940–41, it had generally been regarded as impracticable terrain for large-scale military operations. The construction of the Suez Canal in 1869, however, began indirectly to draw the country into the vortex of contending foreign Powers. In 1889, Italian aid enabled Menelik, Negus of Shoa, to usurp the Ethiopian throne, and Ethiopia virtually passed into Italy's "sphere of influence." In 1896, on the famous field of Adua, the same Menelik decisively repulsed an attempted invasion of his territories by an Italian army from Eritrea. During the first decade of the new century, the French built a railroad from their Red Sea colony at Jibuti and opened up the central areas of the country to commercial enterprise. Thereafter, French, British, Italians, Germans, Dutch, and Americans – and even Japanese – began to creep in. Foreign consulates and business houses were established. But it may still be said that, till 1918, Ethiopia largely continued to be a mysterious semimedieval fastness, a rugged, rocky highland beyond the usual swirl and eddy of world events.

Revolutionary changes in Ethiopia's ancient isolation were introduced by a new monarch, Ras Tafari Makonnen, son of a nephew of Menelik, and a protégé of France and Britain. He became regent in 1916 and soon proved to be a model "Westernizing" ruler. He was crowned Emperor Haile Selassie I in 1930. He styled himself the Lion of Judah and the King of the Kings, and he claimed descent from Solomon and the Queen of Sheba. In a series of sanguinary struggles he disciplined the feudal rases and established an unchallenged authority throughout his Empire. He built roads and schools and hospitals. He sent promising Ethiopian youths to complete their education in Europe and America. He granted concessions likely to promote trade and intercourse. He invited foreign advisers, experts, and technicians to his court. He gave his capital at Addis Ababa more and more the aspect of a modern civilized city. He introduced new laws for the abolition of Ethiopia's national vice, the slave trade. He even called together a parliament. The Powers of Europe at an early date recognized him for what he was when, in 1923, Ethiopia became a member state of the League of Nations. In 1928, Ethiopia and Italy signed a Treaty of Friendship and Arbitration.

In the military sphere alone the Emperor's revolutionary enterprises lagged. The Ethiopian was good fighting material, could he have been given modern weapons and training. But the imperial finances discouraged any too thoroughgoing military program, and various international treaties — though they were not always observed — restricted the importation of arms. More serious still, the old feudal constitution of the Empire put insuperable obstacles in the way of a unified command. When therefore, in 1935, the test of war came, there existed an "Imperial Guard," armed with Mausers, some machine guns, and some pieces of light artillery, but the vast mass of the Emperor's dusky warriors were still led by semi-independent rases, were arrayed in white cotton *shammas,* were armed with little better than matchlock rifles, and employed tactics little more advanced than that of Dervishes.

FASCIST IMPERIALISM

Italy regarded herself as an expanding Power. Her seizures and penetrations in Eritrea, Somaliland, and Libya between 1885 and 1912 had given her the beginnings of a colonial empire overseas. The First World War had been for her another step, a mightier effort, a severer trial — and a painful setback — in the same process. The Peace Conference in 1919 had mulcted her perfidiously — so she believed, and so later Fascist propaganda claimed — of the acquisitions in Africa which her Allies had given her to expect. But, under the guise of Fascism, she had resumed the old imperial drive thereafter. She had put behind her the shoddy, sordid relapse of her postwar socialism. The Corfu episode in 1923 had represented, in her eyes, the restless striving and straining of a people impatiently anticipating an era of conquest (see pp. 299–300).

There were indications that the middle thirties might be the time for new adventures. The Manchurian crisis of 1931 had demonstrated the weakness of the League. Italy began preparations for an Ethiopian war in 1932. Then the Depression, the advent of Hitler, and the rearmament of Germany turned her away from her former expansionist field in the Middle Danube and the Balkans toward less dangerous colonial regions which would be free from the risk of possible German rivalry. But these same events would also serve to distract those Powers, like France and Britain, which otherwise might be tempted to interfere in Italy's plans. France in the middle thirties moreover would be entering upon her "lean years" and must at all costs avoid serious military hazards (see p. 557). But France and Britain, it was all too evident, though victors in 1918, were now forsaking the heroic ideology of war, and they were acquiescing in acts of aggression as flagrant as that which Italy now meditated. Conquering Fascism indeed could well afford to despise such "decadent" nations, which under the cloak of a self-righteous pacifism disguised their weakness and rationalized the abdication of their historic pretensions in the world; and it could well afford to despise the pacifism of that "archhypocrite," England, who, having gorged herself with the goodly portions of the earth, now begrudged latecomers in the imperial race those very prizes she herself possessed to satiety.

So ran the favorite imperialistic argument in Italy. The economic situation and the pressure of population presented further arguments no less specious and urgent. Italy's population had passed the 40,000,000 mark and was increasing at the rate of 400,000 a year, and these numbers were supported on an area of less than 120,000 square miles, only two-thirds of which were fit for cultivation. Since 1921, immigration into the United States had been drastically restricted, and an important relief had been stopped up (see p. 367). In a land of few mineral resources, manufacturing and industries offered little counterpoise. Mussolini had many domestic triumphs to his credit, but they had not saved Italy from the Depression. The lira had been stabilized at too high a level in 1927, and Mussolini — unfortunately as it afterward turned out — had not only sworn to defend its value to the last drop of Italian blood, but had had his awful oath engraved on stone for all the world to see. In the early thirties the Italian budget showed a habitual deficit (and even then it had not included extraordinary expenditures for Ethiopia); the gold reserve was steadily dwindling; the trade balance was growing more adverse; the tourist trade, Peter's pence, and remittances from emigrants to the Americas had all been falling off. Latterly new taxes and controls over foreign exchange and over securities held abroad had all been pointing to an early economic collapse unless some extraneous cure or distraction could be found.

Ethiopia therefore promised the fulfillment of a high ambition and the solution of many present difficulties. It lay between Eritrea and Somaliland, territories already in Italian possession, territories which its conquest could link into a single, worthy imperium. Moreover, war against Ethiopia would not be a war against a brother European state — albeit Ethiopia was a member of the League. It would be a war against a primitive country which had given ample proofs of its barbarism and its incompetence in self-government. Italian propaganda at this time was always ready with gruesome statistics of the slave trade in Ethiopia or of the bloody repressions of the rases. Italy, it was argued, was manifestly entitled to carry the lights of civilization, even by force of arms, into this last stronghold of African darkness, to wipe out those standing insults to the dominance of the white man, insults of which the

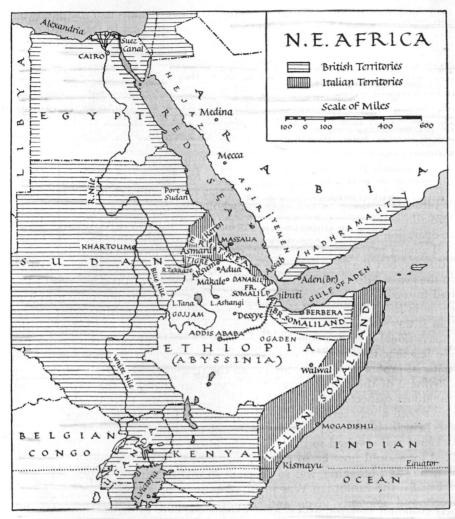

N.E. AFRICA

British Territories
Italian Territories

Scale of Miles
100   0   100   400   600

Battle of Adua in 1896 still remained a painful memory, and to extend in any way possible the blessings of the new Fascist order.

REACTIONS OF THE POWERS

But for the Western Powers, especially Britain, the issues were not so clear-cut or so convincing. It may be said that there were two views in Britain, the official view and the popular view, and to that duality may be attributed the tragic contradictions of British policy when the crisis developed. Official Britain — that is to say the Foreign Office, the Colonial Office, and the Conservative government — were fully aware of Mussolini's intentions in Ethiopia and apparently condoned them. Britain had scattered commercial stakes in Ethiopia. Lake Tana, for example, set in the midst of the Ethiopian plateau, was the source of the Blue Nile and therefore of the irrigation system of Egypt. And it was perhaps not pleasant to contemplate forcible changes of the *status quo* in the Red Sea and the growth of a potentially hostile Power athwart the British Empire's lines of communication with the East. But, even so, it might be necessary, if regrettable, to overlook a relatively unimportant incident in Ethiopia when far more dangerous developments were in the offing in other parts of the world, notably in Germany.

This may have been the official view in Britain. But, in the popular view, the war that was now impending was no incident; it was not just a local adventure in territorial brigandage; it was not even a "colonial" campaign. It thrust into naked prominence the whole ideology of the interwar era. Before all mankind it made trial of the great question whether the new law of co-operation and equity or the old anarchy of egoism and greed was to prevail among nations. Britain might, or might not, have material interests in Ethiopia, but the British people as a whole were far more deeply absorbed in the general doctrine which the four terrible years of the First World War had burned into their souls, the doctrine that war was not only a hideous thing in itself, and was likely to become even more so as time went on, but that it was also a disastrously expensive and impractical method of settling international disputes. As one of the victor nations of 1918, the British people felt that they were in a position to take stock of the poor moral and material profits they had gained from the struggle and, if Italy was still unconvinced of the folly of war, it only went to prove, as the British people sometimes suspected, that Italy's participation in the First World War had never been a very serious national experience. Like all "Northern" peoples, the British entertained a secret contempt for military Italy, and they were sickened and revolted to think that the ideals of peace they had fought and bled for should now be so crudely menaced by a nation which, for all its strutting and bragging, was so deficient in real fighting quality.

Finally, the Ethiopian War involved Italy in breaches of pledges she had freely and solemnly given and, however unimportant relatively the war might seem, the repudiation of principle was of ecumenical significance. As one writer of the time put it, "Whether I kill one man or two, I have still broken the Sixth Commandment." Thus between 1935 and 1936, Italy broke the Gas Protocol of 1925, the Italo-Ethiopian Treaty of Friendship of 1928, the Pact of Paris of 1928, to say nothing of the Covenant of the League of Nations — an impressive catalogue of derelictions, however big or little, or near or far, the occasion thereof.

The British Dominions, Canada, Australia, and New Zealand, could hardly feel themselves deeply involved, but they were loyal to their obligations as soon as the crisis came before the League of Nations. The attitude of South Africa, with her proximity to the theater of conflict, however, was clear and forthright from the start. General Smuts, who if he was not one of the fathers of the League, was at least one of its godfathers, was among the first to advocate extreme measures against Italy. Far from sympathizing with their fellow whites in a war against barbarian blacks, the Afrikanders sympathized with their fellow Africans battling for their independence against a new upsurge of European imperialism. The Irish Free State fell into line, despite her historic opposition to English politics and despite the fact that she was then engaged in her own economic war with the British Government.

France, for her part, was distracted by the return of the German terror. She was at that confused juncture of her affairs in which the death of Barthou had left her. Her system of alliances across Europe, once built on the presupposition of her military superiority, was in a state of flux, and none could say what front, if any, was the most possible or desirable one to concert against the new resurgent Germany. Britain, tired of French intransigence, had lately been striking out upon a policy of her own, a policy which had reached its most deplorable expression in the recent Anglo-German Naval Agreement, and France and Britain were more deeply estranged than at any time since the Ruhr crisis of 1923. The growth of the Fascist "Leagues" in France helped to tie the hands of any French government which wanted to pursue a "strong" policy toward Italy. An important human factor had also entered the situation in the person of Pierre Laval, Barthou's successor, whose unorthodox pro-Italian, anti-Russian, and anti-British predilections were already notorious and whose agreements with Mussolini in January 1935 had included a tacit condonation in advance of Mussolini's Ethiopian adventure (see p. 490). Certainly France's newly won friendship with Italy and all that that friendship signified was not now to be frivolously sacrificed on the altar of the British pacifist conscience.

Realistically minded Frenchmen found the rigidly moral and legalistic attitude of British spokesmen at Geneva incomprehensible to them. League or no League, Italy or no Italy, it was the German question which should have claimed the first attention of all good Europeans. Hitherto, so it seemed to French opinion, the British people had been complacently lukewarm in their support of collective security. The teeth had been taken out of the League Covenant and out of the Locarno Pact in deference to their squeamishness to Continental commitments; the Manchurian crisis and Germany's conscription decree had both been allowed to pass by; and the British Government's decision in 1935 to pick on Italy in order to demonstrate a very sudden and belated championship of the collective principle was a more than usually scandalous example of Albion's proverbial perfidy.

For the United States the Ethiopian crisis was the first real acid test of the practicableness of isolationism. We have spoken in an earlier chapter of American abhorrence of entanglements in wars in general and in wars of European origin in particular (see p. 361), but the American administration was perhaps better informed than the American people as to the limits to which, in the world of hard realities, that abhorrence might be pressed. The German conscription decree of 1935 and the seepage of information into the press during that year regarding the Italian military preparations against Ethiopia had already intensified the antiwar sentiment throughout the United States and, in August 1935, Congress passed a Neutrality Act prohibiting the export of American arms and munitions to any belligerent after the President had recognized a state of war. Evidently Congress had not appreciated at this stage that blanket legislation of this sort, however well intentioned, might have in application an effect opposite to that which it so passionately desired. The Neutrality Act, as was so soon to be shown, by cutting off the unhappy Ethiopians from an arsenal which might otherwise have been available to them, discriminated in favor of the aggressor and against the injured party in the dispute (see p. 598).

Nonetheless the actual outbreak of the Italo-Ethiopian War hardened rather than softened the isolationist heart, and the subsequent incidents, the Hoare-Laval Plan and the patent failure of the League's sanctions against Italy, seemed entirely to justify American opinion in its attitude. Secretary Hull exerted what diplomatic pressure he could and periodically berated the Italian ambassador in Washington, but that gentleman apparently was not impressed by purely moral strictures. It was common knowledge that, despite the official and public repugnance in the United States toward Italy's aggression, increasing amounts of American oil, scrap iron and steel, and other warlike commodities were being shipped to Italian ports.

THE WALWAL INCIDENT AND THE LEAGUE OF NATIONS

Almost from the moment, in 1928, when Italy and Ethiopia had signed their Treaty of Friendship, Italo-Ethiopian relations had begun to deteriorate, and to deteriorate, it seemed, as of set purpose. Italy was soon able to pile up a formidable list of grievances. She complained of discrimination against Italian agents in Ethiopia and of "affronts" to Italian consular officials. She complained of the increasing number of foreign experts and technicians in Ethiopia, among whom Italians were conspicuous by their absence. Warlike preparations on the part of Italy against Ethiopia were already begun by 1932 when Mussolini sent General De Bono on a confidential mission to Eritrea, and these preparations included political activities which extended deep into Ethiopian territory. Disaffected rases were generously plied with money and promises; disaffected communities were secretly armed and instructed for the great day of their deliverance. Mussolini was evidently trying to provoke a rebellion as a pretext for armed intervention.

In the event Mussolini used the time-honored technique of the border incident. On December 5, 1934, at Walwal, 1,500 Ethiopian warriors clashed with 500 native Italian troops with some loss of life to both sides.

Certainly Walwal might seem a poor enough excuse for a war. It lay within a no man's land of dreary, barren "camel-scrub desert" at a point where the border between Ethiopia and Italian Somaliland had never been properly demarcated. But the incident led to a brisk exchange of notes between the Italian and Ethiopian governments which discovered considerable indignation and obstinacy on both sides, and when, at the turn of the year, the two governments reported their respective versions to the League, the chances of a peaceful settlement were already gravely compromised.

The League Council at first postponed action on the case while Italy and Ethiopia went through the form of negotiations "out of court." But Mussolini, far from meditating a pacific settlement of the Ethiopian crisis, was busy reviewing his troops, speeding them on their departure for East Africa, and assuring them that they were embarking on a war of conquest for the greater glory of Italy. The crisis was discussed at last in the League Council in September 1935. Baron Aloisi, for Italy, presented a voluminous memorandum arraigning the backwardness and barbarity of the Ethiopian Empire and justifying Italy in anticipation for any measures which she might deem it necessary to take "to defend her own security, rights, and dignity." He also argued with considerable skill that the dispute lay outside the League's competence altogether. Meanwhile efforts at appeasement, offers of economic concessions and of "exchanges of territory" in Ethiopia, were roundly characterized by Mussolini as "not only unacceptable, but derisory." "Italy's need for expansion in East Africa," he said to an interviewer afterward, "is not to be satisfied by the cession of a couple of deserts, one of salt and one of stone . . . The League Council seems to think I am a collector of deserts."

Then on September 11, 1935, in the League Assembly, came the famous speech of Sir Samuel Hoare, the British Foreign Secretary. The British people, he said, "are deeply and genuinely moved by a great ideal . . . In spite of the grim experiences of the past, in spite of the worship of force in the present, the British people have clung to that ideal, and they are not prepared to abandon it. . . . The ideals enshrined in the Covenant and in particular the aspiration to establish the rule of law in international affairs, have appealed with growing force to the strain of idealism which has its place in our national character, and have become a part of our national conscience."

Hoare's speech, as a delegate who had heard it said afterward, was "one of the great electrifying moments in the history of the League." The Assembly and the world at large — and the British electorate, to whom, as we believe, it was mainly addressed — were not to know that it was other than an open and passionate avowal of the British Government's attitude. Negotiations were already in train which afterward betrayed and falsified every hope that the speech inspired. But, for the moment, the powerful stand, the apparently powerful stand, that the League now assumed toward Italy was in no small degree the consequence of it.

Meanwhile, much concerned over the possible Near Eastern repercussions of an Italo-Ethiopian war, the British Government had already ordered the Mediterranean Fleet to Alexandria and reinforced it with units from the Home Fleet and even from the China Squadron. The garrisons at Malta and Aden were brought up to strength. The British Government also sought to enlist the support of those Mediterranean states which it had reason to hope were sincere and responsible members of the League. In December 1935, Yugoslavia, Greece, and Turkey gave positive assurances of assistance in the event of an Italian attack on the British fleet, and they were promptly seconded by Czechoslovakia and Rumania. France, under Laval, bargained and evaded, but eventually promised support "fully and in advance" within her obligations under the Covenant. Yet, for all these verbal protestations by the Mediterranean Powers, it was clear enough to the British Government that Britain herself would have to bear the brunt of any extension of Italy's war in the Near East. As Hoare afterward declared, except for the dispositions of the British fleet, "not a ship, not a machine, not a man" was moved by any other member of the League.

SANCTIONS AND THE HOARE–LAVAL PLAN

On October 3, 1935 the Italian forces in Eritrea began the invasion of Ethiopia. "A solemn hour strikes!" cried Mussolini from his balcony in Rome. "Not only is an army marching on its objective, but forty million Italians are marching with that army."

At Geneva, between October 9 and 11, fifty out of fifty-four nations in the League Assembly concurred in the findings of the Council that the Italian Government had resorted to war in disregard of its covenants. The four dissenting states were Italy herself and Italy's "clients," Austria, Hungary, and Albania. Germany was about to withdraw from the League. A Co-ordination Committee was at once set up to examine the ways and means of imposing economic sanctions against the aggressor.

Article 16 of the Covenant obliged the states of the League to sever "all trade or financial relations" and "all intercourse" between themselves and the Covenant-breaking member. Mussolini threatened to meet the application of this article with dire reprisals, not excluding war. But even without these defiant thunders from the Duce, the League's problem was not a simple one and, perhaps not surprisingly, the Co-ordination Committee finally recommended a rather more restricted program of sanctions than honest opinion wished or than strict legality should have required. No doubt cowardice and cupidity played their part, but it is also a fact that the thoroughgoing economic boycott of a first-class Power, except by blockade and war, was soon found to be an almost insuperable task. However, a formidable array of nations accepted the proposals of the Co-ordination Committee, and on November 18, 1935 the League's first experiment in international sanctions went into force. Italy was deprived of arms, loans, and certain raw materials, and her own exports were denied by the signatory Powers.

It is not easy to assess the "leakages" in the scheme. The nonsignatory Powers were few and small, and the rift in the sanctionist front which they caused was unlikely to be vital. Germany was more important, but she had joined in the arms embargo, she had not yet developed her pro-Italian policies and, in her present economic condition, large increases in her Italian trade were not to be expected. The most serious potential leakage was the United States. Recent neutrality legislation did not cover oil, copper, trucks, tractors, scrap iron, steel, and the like, which were essential war materials. President Roosevelt pleaded with American traders not to increase their business with Italy above the normal figures, and no doubt greater support for the League could have been mobilized had not American opinion been revolted by the Hoare-Laval Plan (see pp. 598–99).

It speaks volumes for the rapid development of military science that between 1918 and 1935, a short interval of seventeen years, a single commodity should have become so essential. In 1918 oil was important to warfare — important, but no more; in 1935 warfare was impossible without it. We can as well imagine the Cossacks without horses, or the Elizabethan seamen without oak, as the Fascist armies in Ethiopia without oil. When therefore the League Co-ordination Committee began to discuss the extension of its list of embargoes to "petroleum and the derivatives, by-products and residues of petroleum," it lighted at once upon what was fated to be the supreme test of its purpose and authority. For a few short months in the winter of 1935, oil became the symbol of all the League's highest aims and aspirations.

France, in the person of her Premier, Pierre Laval, considered that she had already baited Italy more than was safe for their mutual friendship, and she was resolved that oil sanctions should not go into force. She pleaded with Britain to make one last effort at peace by negotiation before allowing the League to proceed too far along its present drastic course. Thus it was to happen that the discussion on oil sanctions and the final intrigue on the part of Laval to jettison the sanctionist front against Italy became the obverse and reverse, so to speak, the open and the hidden side, of the same melancholy episode.

Sir Samuel Hoare, the British Foreign Secretary, was a man of broad attainments and ripe experience, as sincere in purpose and straight in action as any good servant of the Crown. He had been Secretary for Air and Secretary for India. In every field his record had been unexceptionable. We may at least say, in extenuation of his diplomacy at the present juncture, that he took the "realistic" view. He probably believed — his information probably led him to believe — that Ethiopia's military position was desperate, and that any serious defense by her against an Italian attack was out of the question. He was fearful that Britain might be induced to make Ethiopia promises of support which, even if forthcoming, would not appreciably alter the course of her inevitable fate. Perhaps he had in mind Palmerston's onetime attitude on Denmark, which had ended only in the quicker defeat of that country and had left a nasty blot on the good name of England. Mussolini, on more than one occasion, had said that oil sanctions would lead to war, and he appeared to mean what he said. Hoare doubted whether the other Powers who so clamorously demanded strong action by the League would render Britain effective military assistance in an extremity, and he was sure, for one thing, that France would do so only with the greatest reluctance. Hoare did not doubt that Britain would be victorious in a conflict with Italy. But he considered that the losses the conflict might entail were not legitimate losses at a time when other potential enemies of Britain, of far greater strength than Italy, were engaged on heavy naval construction programs. The loss of half a dozen battleships, which was the British Admiralty's estimate of the probable cost of a naval war in the Mediterranean, would have resulted in a decisive unbalancing of British naval tonnage vis-à-vis Japan. British ships in 1935 were not yet provided with the antiaircraft devices they afterward had, and the Italian Air Force of that date, even discounting the exaggerations of Fascist propaganda, was believed to have superior first-line planes for Mediterranean warfare. In other words, Hoare's view in all essentials was Laval's view: Italy might be in the wrong, but Ethiopia was not worth a major war. And to that view he now committed his government and his country.

Laval's political strategy was one of procrastination. The Co-ordination Committee had intended to open its discussions on oil sanctions at the end of November 1935, but Laval obtained the postponement of its meetings upon one pretext or another, and employed the time so gained to obtain his British colleague's agreement to a new solution of the entire crisis. The Hoare-Laval Plan, as it was called, was drawn up during the first days of December 1935.

The details of the plan are now of little moment. We have already mentioned earlier similar appeasement efforts. Extensive Ethiopian territories were to be ceded to Italy outright, and other Ethiopian territories were to be assigned to Italy as "a zone of economic expansion and settlement." In exchange, the Italian port of Assab in Eritrea was to be ceded to Ethiopia. The two negotiators, Hoare and Laval, pledged one another to secrecy until the plan should have been submitted to the interested parties: Italy, Ethiopia, and the League. But Laval gave the plan immediate publicity in the French press. The British Government was placed in a terrible position. Baldwin, the Prime Minister, took refuge in denials and evasions. "My lips are not yet unsealed," he said in the House of Commons. "Were these troubles over I would make a case, and I guarantee that not a man would go into the lobby against me."

The British Parliament, press, and people, after a day or two of dumb astonishment, broke out into a chorus of expostulation. The aggressor in Africa, it seemed, had been virtually handed the spoils of a victory which he had not yet won, by a man who not long since, in the League Assembly, had categorically denounced his crime. Hoare returned from Switzerland, whither he had gone on vacation and where he had further impaired his somewhat exhausted health by injuring himself in a skating accident. At first he gave out that he would give the country a full account of himself, but he bowed to the storm and resigned. He was succeeded as Foreign Secretary by Anthony Eden. Laval in France meanwhile was given a drubbing at the hands of the Chamber but survived in office for another few weeks.

Mussolini, for his part, preserved a discreet silence and then, when the furor was safely abating, declared his rejection of the plan. For the League there was nothing left to do but perform the obsequies on oil sanctions as decently as possible, and it was decided to defer further consideration of the matter sine die. But the League, indirectly, had suffered a setback from which it was never to recover.

THE COURSE OF THE WAR

"Colonial" wars have usually been fought by small numbers of well-armed, well-disciplined Europeans against great numbers of poorly armed, poorly disciplined natives. But in Ethiopia, Mussolini took no chances. Arms and discipline as well as numbers were on his side. The complicated political situation in Europe and the problematic effect of sanctions demanded speed and decision, and plans which had been originally made for a three-year struggle were scrapped in favor of a campaign of a single season. Before the end of the war the Italian command disposed of ten divisions, or 250,000 white combatants, a number which, together with natives and labor battalions, amounted in all to 400,000 men; and this force was supported by a formidable array of tanks, motorized units, and aircraft. By contrast, the probable Ethiopian total was less than 300,000. Well might Mussolini say he preferred "to err by excess than by deficiency."

The Italian technical preparation was commensurate. Barracks, hospitals, airdromes and, above all, roads were constructed on the most ambitious scale. Within a few months, in 1935, the Red Sea port of Massaua and the Etritrean city of Asmara were virtually rebuilt. The conditions of climate and topography in Eritrea were as difficult as it is possible to imagine, but the huge masses of men and material moved with extraordinary smoothness, to the great chagrin of critics who had always derided the Italian ability for organization. If we may trust the Italian casualty lists, Mussolini's calculations were eminently justified. In seven months of war Italy lost only 3,000 men.

Against the huge armament which Italy thus brought into the field, the Ethiopians could oppose only their primitive man power. They had no heavy artillery, no tanks, and no air force. They are reported to have had 200 pieces of light artillery of antique pattern, 1,000 machine guns, and a scattering of antiaircraft guns. Their rifle ration for the campaign worked out at about 150 rounds per man. It was well said that the majority of the Emperor's army were more poorly armed than Italian noncombatants. Nor did tactics and leadership compensate for material deficiencies. Each one of the Ethiopian contingents was independently led by its own ras, and any sort of unified action was lost in personal and tribal jealousies. European officers in the Emperor's train were treated with traditional suspicion, and such advice as they gave was wasted on the desert air. The obvious type of fighting should have been guerrilla fighting. Wazir and Riffian tactics could have made the country impregnable. Yet the rases disdained to behave like "bandits" and, in their suicidal pride and ignorance, they persisted in maneuvering and fighting in compact masses.

In the course of the war both sides charged one another with barbarities in contravention of international treaties and, in 1936, Geneva fairly rang with mutual accusations. Both sides were believed to have used dumdum bullets. In particular, the Italians paid little respect to the Red Cross. On one memorable occasion an Italian airman, forced down behind the Ethiopian lines, was beheaded. But the gravest of all such accusations was in regard to chemical warfare on the part of Italy. De Bono was guiltless in this respect, but Badoglio afterward used gas as part of his more aggressive tactics. At the height of the campaign, especially in March 1936, the Ethiopian forces in retreat were constantly sprayed with mustard gas from the air, and whole areas which were likely to be used for the concentration of reserves were sometimes saturated with it. The Ethiopians had the means neither of protection nor of retaliation, and their appeals to the League brought them no redress. Italy's action was a clear breach of the Gas Protocol of 1925, to which both she and Ethiopia were adherents (see p. 145).

The Italian campaign lasted seven months, from October 3, 1935 to May 9, 1936, and occupied the interval between one rainy season and the next. The campaign fell into two main phases, the first under the leadership of General De Bono up to the end of November 1935, and the second thereafter under the leadership of Marshal Badoglio. The main blow was struck from the north, that is, from the Eritrean front, and here the Italian command concentrated nine out of the total ten divisions of the expeditionary force. A secondary blow was struck from the south, that is, from the Somaliland front, by the tenth division, under General Graziani.

The only practicable route for an army invading Ethiopia from the north was by way of the huge continuous escarpment, through Adua and Dessye, avoiding on the one side the deep ravines of the river Takkaze and its tributaries, and on the other side the burning wastelands of Danakil. The escarpment rises to a mean height of from seven to eight thousand feet, and the rarefied air at that altitude imposes some hardship on a man not accustomed to it. But the temperature is mild, and during the dry season the ground is tolerably well adapted to the type of mechanized warfare which the Italian Army now essayed.

The forces of General De Bono began their advance along this escarpment on October 3, 1935, and quickly occupied Adua and Aksum. Nowhere did the invaders meet with serious opposition, but the fall of Adua nonetheless was celebrated in Italy as a great victory, a revenge long overdue for the shameful defeat of 1896. Italian political preparations in Ethiopia bore their fruit, and the inhabitants of the invaded areas submitted to the advancing Italians with suspicious readiness. The priests of the Holy City of Aksum surrendered without resistance or protest. Haile Selassie Gugsa, the drunken and dissolute Governor of Tigré, a son-in-law of the Emperor, went over to the Italians with 10,000 of his men.

The next stage of the advance to Makale was hampered by unexpected rains, but the town was reached at last on November 8. Thereafter De Bono appears to have rested on his successes while his engineers and labor battalions worked on his lines of communication. Perhaps he was waiting for other rases to follow Gugsa's treacherous example and save the Italian forces from the necessity of fighting. General Graziani, operating from the south, penetrated the Ogaden, but also moved with remarkable cautiousness. Mussolini, in Rome, prodded his commanders with telegrams urging a more expeditious campaign, and then, losing patience, dismissed De Bono from his post.

Evidently De Bono was a better Fascist than a soldier. But he was an able organizer, and he had laid the groundwork for the subsequent Italian operations. His successor, Marshal Pietro Badoglio, was a better soldier than a Fascist — in fact, his party leanings had always been highly suspect. His appointment signified a bolder phase of the Ethiopian War. The greater battles of the campaign were fought under him in January, February, and

March 1936, all along the great escarpment, and ended everywhere in decisive victories for the Italians. The Emperor Haile Selassie himself was defeated at Lake Ashangi at the beginning of April. Thereafter the important strongholds fell quickly and easily into Italian hands. The final Italian spurt from Dessye to Addis Ababa was a triumphal promenade conducted by two of the longest columns of mechanized vehicles ever yet assembled in a modern war. On May 2, 1936 the Emperor left his stricken realm from Jibuti aboard a British warship. The Italian forces entered Addis Ababa three days later. Graziani's columns moving up from the south made contact with the northern columns. The campaign was at an end.

On May 9, 1936, Mussolini proclaimed the annexation of Ethiopia to Italy and the King of Italy's assumption of the title of Emperor.

THE LIQUIDATION OF SANCTIONS

In Britain the news of the Italian victory produced the profoundest depression. Enthusiasts of the League, the Labor party to a man, and several public figures continued to demand effective action against the aggressor. A throng of sympathizers welcomed the fugitive Emperor Haile Selassie to London, and the police had some difficulty in preventing the Ethiopian Legation from becoming a place of pilgrimage. But the British Government and the growing mass of "realists" in the country, once they had digested the shock and humiliation, were secretly relieved that the Italo-Ethiopian War had ended so soon and without more serious complications. Neville Chamberlain, Chancellor of the Exchequer, speaking presumably in a private capacity at a dinner of the Nineteen Hundred Club, averred that the continuation or intensification of sanctions would be "the very midsummer of madness." The government was grateful for his lead and, one after another, members of the Cabinet expressed themselves with increasing emphasis in favor of the liquidation of sanctions and the return to normal relations with Italy. "It cannot be expected by anyone," said Eden in the House of Commons, "that the continuance of existing sanctions will restore in Abyssinia the position which has been destroyed. That position can only be restored by military action. So far as I am aware no other government, certainly not this government, is prepared to take such military action."

In France, on June 4, 1936, Blum entered office at the head of the Popular Front, and it seemed as if France, at the very moment that Britain was bethinking herself of liquidating sanctions, was to suffer a prick of conscience in favor of a strong League policy. However Blum, for all his Socialist principles, acted realistically and gave out that he would acquiesce in whatever decision the League might make, and he hinted that practical considerations pointed to an end of sanctions. The British Dominions and the remaining states of Europe signified the same views. On June 20, President Roosevelt raised the American arms embargo on Italy and Ethiopia. The League Assembly met at the end of the same month. The Emperor Haile Selassie, a pathetic but dignified figure, came to Geneva to plead his cause in person. He spoke eloquently, but it was clear that he could expect nothing. A single lonely voice in favor of maintaining sanctions in full vigor was raised by the South African delegate. Sanctions against Italy ceased as from July 15, 1936.

THE ROME–BERLIN AXIS

In the early part of the Italo-Ethiopian conflict, Germany had maintained a scrupulously "correct" attitude. The result of the conflict was uncertain, and the result of the correlative sanctionist struggle was uncertain. But Germany was in a position to wait, and to gain some advantage whatever the end might be. In March 1936, Hitler made use of the preoccupation of the various Powers concerned to achieve his coup in the Rhineland, and the first signs of the subsequent Italo-German collaboration in Europe were evident in Italy's skillful exploitation of that crisis which so conveniently discomfited the League and the sanctionist Powers. The Rhineland, in short, was the end of the Stresa Front of 1935 and the beginning of the Rome-Berlin Axis.

Thereafter the *rapprochement* of Italy and Germany developed very rapidly, and by July 1936, when the Spanish Civil War broke out, it was sufficiently advanced to enable the two Powers to act in all but open concert in their joint affairs in Spain. Throughout 1936 a series of grandly staged state visits betokened the fast-maturing political realities. The Countess Ciano, Mussolini's daughter, enjoyed a month of social festivities in Berlin. The Prince of Piedmont attended the Olympic Games in Berlin. Goebbels visited Venice. Himmler visited Rome. Military missions, air missions, economic missions, youth missions exchanged visits. The series culminated at the end of October, when Count Ciano, Mussolini's son-in-law and lately appointed Italian Foreign Minister, spent some days in Berlin and Berchtesgaden "to co-ordinate the policies of the Italian and German Governments" and concluded with his German hosts the so-called October or Berchtesgaden Protocols, a secret agreement which was tantamount to an integration of German and Italian foreign policies. At the same time, Hitler recognized the Italian Empire of Ethiopia.

"The meetings at Berlin have resulted in an agreement between our two countries on certain questions, some of which are particularly interesting in these days," said Mussolini in a speech at Milan on November 1, 1936. "But these agreements that have been included in special statements and duly signed, this vertical line between Rome and Berlin, is not a partition (*diaframma*) but rather an axis (*asse*) round which all European states animated by the will to collaboration and peace can also collaborate."

In 1936 a new balance of the European Powers began to emerge. Italy and Germany in virtual alliance confronted the somewhat vague alignment of Britain, France, the Soviet Union, and a battered, shaken League of Nations.

32

SPAIN: THE REPUBLIC AND THE CIVIL WAR

SPANISH PARTIES AND POLITICS

Spain, a country which flared up into a civil war in 1936 and all but drew the rest of Europe into its fires, had lain for generations at a distance from the fiercer conflagrations of international politics. She had known civil wars before; hers was a people of passionate and recurrent violence, but of a violence which usually bred and spent itself within her own parochial limits. She had sometimes been the indirect occasion of international war — France and Prussia had clashed over "the Spanish succession" in 1870 — and she had herself fought a sordid and undistinguished war with the United States in 1898. But none of these wars within or wars without compared in significance with the Civil War of 1936. In that vicious, fratricidal year Spain became in miniature the battlefield of all the wider rivalries of Europe.

The map of Spain is square and blocky. But her social geography was as diverse and incoherent as that of medieval France or Italy. In a long history, Iberians, Basques, Celts, Phoenicians, Greeks, Carthaginians, Romans, Goths, Arabs, and French had left their seed and culture to fructify into an extraordinarily variegated nation. Four languages were spoken in the peninsula. Mountainous territory made for surprising alternations of climate and produce, and intensified the divisions and particularisms of the people. The Spaniard had always been proud and egotistical, fiercely independent, owing his first allegiance to his town or village, and in many ways he had never outgrown his ancient tribalism. Ortega y Gasset, in a well-known book, called the country "invertebrate." Time was when the Catholic Church and the Crown imposed their bond of unity, but of recent years the authority of both had been grievously declining.

Economically the country showed the same contrasts and contrariness. In some parts there existed a system of large landed estates — notably in Andalusia and Estremadura; in some parts there existed a system of small agricultural holdings; in the Basque country and in Catalonia was a most advanced industrialism. Generally peasants and workers were very poor. But poverty was never a disgrace in Spain. It was in the nature of the people to show an almost Irish contempt for economic betterment. Two of the twenty-two millions of the population lived in the two great cities, Madrid and Barcelona. Political partisanship lay between a feudal, clerical conservatism and the extremest forms of Communism and anarchism.

The Basques and the Catalans formed two separate nationalist groups in Spain, each with a distinctive history, language, and economic life. The Basque people were one of the great anthropological puzzles of Europe. They inhabited the three provinces, "the Three-One" of Vizcaya, Guipúzcoa, and Álava. Throughout their history they had preserved certain regional rights, and their land was deservedly known as a "land apart." Their iron mines near Bilbao had been worked since prehistoric times. Latterly the Basque people had adopted modern industries, and the great hydroelectric potentialities of their mountainous districts had been developed. They were devout Catholics and, like so many industrialized peoples, were often Socialists. Apparently their religious and political creeds were each faithfully observed without prejudice to the other.

Catalonia could almost be described as another "land apart." Ever since Charlemagne had established it as a frontier march, it had been more closely linked with trans-Pyrenean Europe than with the rest of Spain. Barcelona, its capital city and chief port, shared the life of Mediterranean France and Italy. Catalonia had fallen under the dominion of Aragon, but it had never lost its original centrifugalism, and it was among the first "submerged nationalities" in more recent times to heed the call of independence and self-rule. Barcelona meanwhile had grown into a great commercial center, like another Belfast, separated both in political sentiment and in economic interest from a more slowly moving agricultural hinterland.

Finally, Spain is not to be understood if we forget that she once ruled the greatest empire in the world. Spain in our day always had the air of a man down on his luck, too proud to complain, too proud even to trouble to hide his impoverishment, but incapable of putting off the onetime habit of gentility. So many Spanish institutions were old and corrupt. Church, Crown, army, and aristocracy were like an ornate façade concealing an advanced structural decay. It was typical that the army, for instance, absorbed half the peacetime revenues of the state and yet could show no modern equipment; but it had one officer to every eight men — and nearly 700 generals (in 1931) ! — and paid those officers so badly that most of them were forced to live by peculation. The wonder always was that the average Spaniard retained his vivid, individual vitality. But, in the words of Canovas, "Everything decays in Spain, but the race."

THE DIRECTORATE OF PRIMO DE RIVERA AND THE REPUBLICAN REVOLUTION

Alfonso XIII ascended the throne of his fathers in 1902, on his sixteenth birthday, in mind and heart a Bourbon, devoted to family and Church, fond of authority, proud of his kingly office, enjoying excitement and intrigue, yet shrewd beyond the ordinary, and willing perhaps to give constitutionalism an honest trial. But the best intentions could not mold events in Spain. Ministers and ministries were constant in nothing but change. Between 1902 and 1923 there were thirty-three different governments. Not a year passed but had its strikes and mutinies. The First World War brought a lull, and trade with the Allies greatly benefited the Spanish exchequer; but it was only a lull. The Spanish Army meanwhile carried on exhausting operations against Abd el-Krim and the Riff tribesmen in Morocco, and on one dreadful occasion it seemed that foolhardy orders from the King himself had involved the

SPAIN, 1936~1939

☰ Occupied by the Nationalists·
by the end of 1936

Spaniards in a major defeat. In September 1923 the Captain General of Catalonia, Don Miguel Primo de Rivera, the Marqués de Estella, headed a monarchist-military revolt against the government. In a long proclamation the General accused the professional politicians of bringing ruin on the country and declared that he and the army were acting only in honest indignation and with real support of public opinion.

It was not the first time a general had ruled in Spain, but the directorate of Primo de Rivera was significant by reason of the existence of other autocratic figures in the contemporary European scene. Mussolini had enjoyed power for a year; Mustapha Kemal was about to become the first President of the Turkish Republic. Indeed, on a visit to Italy in November 1923, Alfonso XIII and his General were indiscreet enough to express public approval of Fascist ways and works and, once returned to Spain, Primo de Rivera proceeded Fascist-like to destroy the remnants of constitutional rule, to suppress hostile political parties, to censor the press, to control public assembly and the universities, and to reorganize the country's economy upon what has since come to be called totalitarian lines. In 1926 the war against the rebel

Riffs in Morocco was at last brought to a favorable conclusion, albeit with essential assistance from France, and Primo de Rivera — again Fascist-like — was able to reinforce his position and popularity at home with the help of a military success abroad. Meanwhile new arterial roads, new irrigation schemes, and international exhibitions at Barcelona and Seville were among the directorate's more meritorious domestic monuments. A great deal of what Spain had afterward to show in the way of modern "European" life dated from this time.

Primo de Rivera was a man of high, if limited, principles, but he had all the quixotry of the legendary Spaniard, and he was certainly not of the stuff of which modern Caesars are made. He was the mayor of a palace revolution rather than the leader of a popular national revival, and his dictatorship wanted the rationale of those of his spiritual brothers, Mussolini and Kemal. He was garrulous, gallant, and sometimes slightly foolish, a habitué of cafés, fond of his pleasures. He governed for six and a half years, but brought no interval of real peace or real pacification. If anything, the Right became more violently rightist, and the Left more violently leftiest, and the moderate groups which might have kept the balance became steadily weaker. Primo de Rivera's worst mistake was his repressive policy in Catalonia. He finally lost even the support of the army. In January 1930 he resigned in favor of a "bridge government" under General Berenguer, pledged to a restoration of constitutional rule.

It was clear that events were moving toward one of those political upheavals which have so often punctuated the history of Spain. In midsummer of 1930, leading Republicans openly formed themselves into a Revolutionary Committee, and they were shortly joined by leading Catalans. A premature Republican outbreak at Jaca in the province of Huesca was suppressed by the government and was followed by capricious arrests, trials, executions, and reprieves. In April 1931, mainly to test public opinion, municipal elections were held and showed overwhelming Republican sympathies in the towns. A calamitous decline of the peseta heralded a change of regime. General Sanjurjo, commander of the Civil Guard,[1] declined to be responsible for the loyalty of his force, and King Alfonso, without actually abdicating, deemed it the better part of valor to flee the country. The Revolutionary Committee proclaimed a Provisional Government in Madrid, and the Catalans proclaimed an autonomous "state" in Barcelona. Elections, in May and June 1931, for a Constituent Cortes resulted in a decisive victory for the parties of the Left.

So signal a mandate from the people should have given promise of a stable popular government. With its majority the Cortes ought to have been able to shatter the sorry scheme of things and remold it nearer to its heart's desire. Certainly great hopes were entertained of the new Republic, both in Spain and abroad. By December 1931 the Cortes had voted a constitution. Alcalá Zamora had become President, and Azaña Premier, both honest but neither of them a particularly strong or distinguished man.

The new Republican legislators then addressed themselves to legislation. Their first concerns, as always in Spain, were the Church, the Catalan question, and the land. The Jesuit Order was dissolved, and its possessions were confiscated. Church schools were suppressed; and a start was made on nationalizing Church lands and properties; the state support of the clergy was abolished. A Catalan autonomy bill was passed. An agrarian law sought to amend the unequal and necessitous condition of the peasants; but it was slow in operation, and the peasants were soon resorting to the seizure of land by the quicker and more intelligible method of force. The result was sanguinary rioting in many parts of the country, the burning of churches and convents, and the murder of Civil Guards.[1] Meanwhile the Depression laid its wasting hand on Spain's industry and trade, and the attendant hardships of course were blamed upon the new government. General Sanjurjo, in a mood of reactionary despair, attempted unsuccessfully to set up a military directorate at Seville. On the whole the years 1932–33 brought no foretaste of the promised Republican utopia.

Perhaps Azaña had tried to placate too many irreconcilable viewpoints and personalities. He had pushed his revolutionary policy far enough to antagonize the grandees and the Church, but not far enough to satisfy his own partisans. In order to retain the support of extremist elements, he had tolerated outrages against churches and alienated moderate Republicans. A revulsion was inevitable, and in the elections of November 1933 the Left lost everywhere. The monarchists emerged from their hiding places to agitate openly for the restoration of King Alfonso. A Spanish Fascist party under the name of the Falangists, led by a son of Primo de Rivera, made its appearance. A weak, reactionary government took office under the Catalan Republican Lerroux in halfhearted coalition with the Catholic Popular Action party of Gil Robles.

It is not necessary to guide the reader through all the ups and downs of modern Spanish politics. The story would be tedious if it were not so tragic. Perhaps enough has been said to convey the impression that Spain was no country of sunny orange groves, colorful religious festivals, and laughing, dancing señoritas, but a country of blood and tears and of frightful extremes. The etchings of Goya are more illustrative of the real Spain than the music of Bizet and Rossini.

Two and a half years elapsed between the elections of 1933 and the outbreak of the Civil War in 1936. A certain amount of exhaustion induced a slackening in the tempo of events, but generally the interval developed along familiar lines. These were four strikes which can be designated as "general," as well as lesser strikes, military coups, and scattered outrages of one kind or another, too numerous to be mentioned. A rebellion broke out among the miners of Asturias in October 1934. It was a very considerable affair, and used afterward to be called "the rehearsal of the Civil War." It devastated the city of Oviedo, caused over 3,000 deaths, and was accompanied by more than usually savage mutilations and torturings. The government used Moorish troops against the rebels.

The elections of February 1936 oscillated back to the Left once more, and a combination of parties of the Left, led by Azaña and Casares Quiroga, was elected to office. The combination took the name of the Popular Front (*Frente Popular*) after the similar and contemporary improvisation in

France. The new government at once released political prisoners jailed under the former governments and set about filling the cells thus emptied
with as many of the prominent representatives of the Right as it could lay
its hands on. The vindictive swing of opinion even fastened itself on Alcalá
Zamora, the President of the Republic, and the Cortes suddenly voted his
impeachment, dangerously stretching a point of the constitution to do so.
Azaña was then elected President. Meanwhile, the revolutionary program of
1932 — especially the land seizures — was resumed.

The situation in 1936 had certainly worsened since 1931. The government,
despite its name, had far less popular backing than the Republic had originally had. The electoral system, in fact, had secured the Popular Front a
majority of seats in the Cortes upon a minority of votes in the country. Nonetheless, the domestic affairs of Spain might have continued to boil and
bubble, as for years they had already done, without spilling over into civil
war. Strikes, robberies, murders, the raiding of political clubs and newspaper
offices, the burning of churches and convents, the assaults on priests and
nuns — all these things had happened in Spain before. There was the usual
military plot. General Francisco Franco, Chief of the General Staff, who had
engineered it, was safely degraded to the governorship of the Canaries, and
several "politically active" army officers were retired on pension. The mildness of these punishments was significant of the government's weakness. But
it was not the first time in Spain, in these early months of 1936, that men had
sat nervously in the cafés of Madrid and Barcelona with the air about them
thick with potential calamity, and nothing had happened beyond what was
already normal to the restless disposition of Spain.

There was, however, one further factor in the situation in 1936 which was
unusual and dangerous. The moderate Center parties of the electorate had
fallen in strength to the point of ineffectiveness, and at the same time, at
either end of the scale, extremes of the Left and Right had become more
sharply defined and united — the Popular Front itself was a case in point.
And, if now these extremes are dubbed Fascist and Communist, or Nationalist and Republican, the situation becomes very much simplified, and a new
and very formidable hostility emerges. The words "Fascist" and "Communist" as applied to Spanish affairs may be inaccurate and misleading, and for
that reason "Nationalist" and "Republican" are less objectionable, but the
words do signify what was indeed the important fact of the moment, that in
1936 the chaos of the Spanish political parties was beginning to crystallize
into two rival coalitions and that each was forming a connection with powerful sympathizers outside the country.

On July 12–13, 1936, the prologue to the final tragedy was enacted in the
form of two murders, the first of a certain Castillo, and the second of Calvo
Sotelo. Castillo was a lieutenant of the Assault Guards [2] and a partisan of the
Left; perhaps he was not a particularly important personage. Calvo Sotelo,
however, was a former Finance Minister of Primo de Rivera, a Conservative
and monarchist; he had been deeply engaged in Fascist intrigue for years,
and many regarded him as the next in Spain's long history of dictators. His
was a very grave and symbolic assassination. It was the cue for the army's
revolt against the government.

THE OUTBREAK OF THE CIVIL WAR

The simultaneity of the army risings throughout Spain showed that the new revolt was no sudden coup, but a long and ably planned affair. The army in Morocco revolted on July 17, 1936, and during the following days the areas round Córdoba and Cádiz in the south and round Saragossa, Burgos, Valladolid, and Galicia in the north went over to the insurgent side. General Sanjurjo is credited with being the real organizer of the revolt, but he was killed in an air crash on his way to Seville to assume command of the insurgent forces. His place was eventually taken by General Franco, who had reached Morocco from the Canaries by plane.

The insurgents, or Nationalists, as they were now to be called, counted among their number most of the officers of the regular army, the Moorish Regulares, the Tercio (Foreign Legion), the Civil Guard,[1] and privately recruited bodies such as the Carlists[3] and the Falangists — at the beginning, a total of some 27,000 men. A good proportion of them had seen active service in Morocco, and some of them in Cuba, and they had also had experience in quelling civil disturbances in Spain. By the end of 1936 the Nationalists controlled about three-fifths of Spain. A Nationalist government had been set up at Burgos, and General Franco installed as "Chief of the Spanish State."

The fate of the Spanish Navy in these months was very mixed. The officers, almost to a man, were Nationalist; the men were Republican. Of the navy's two battleships, one was seized by the Nationalists and the other by the Republicans, and the lesser ships were more or less evenly divided. But the Spanish Navy was an even more corrupt and inefficient force than the Spanish Army, and though the Nationalists — with Italian and German help — for a time secured a tolerably effective command of Spanish waters, naval units on either side played a far smaller part in the Spanish Civil War than their original paper strength, their strategic opportunities, or their national maritime traditions gave reason to expect.

On the Republican side were ranged large sections of the peasantry, the urban workers, whole regiments of unofficered conscripts of the regular army, a few isolated army officers — notably Generals Miaja and Rojo — and the greater part of the Catalans and the Basques. The 6,500 Assault Guards[2] were about the only body of men with a corporate identity and a professional leadership. The trade-unions recruited many thousands of "militiamen" and armed them by the simple expedient of throwing open available military stores and armories. Such troops were adepts at tearing noisily up and down the streets of the bigger cities in motor trucks, which appears to have been their favorite occupation at first; they might have been well suited for guerrilla fighting in the mountainous country, especially in defense of their own localities. But they had high courage and revolutionary zeal, they had more than one spiritual link with other historic eruptions of the Spanish people, and time and experience would show what they were worth in sustained and regular warfare.

The Republicans commanded important economic resources which, given a chance, should have put them in a very favorable position. They had seized the gold reserves of the Bank of Spain. Their territories included the industrial districts of Madrid, Barcelona, and Bilbao and the Asturias coal mines. They held some of Spain's richest agricultural areas. Their most serious deficiencies were organization and leadership. The war from the Republican side — at least in the beginning — was conducted by "committees of defense," half juntas, half soviets, hastily improvised and usually taking the character of their respective political affiliation or locality. The Civil War, as some said at the time, was the triumphant assertion of regionalism. It was the heyday of the trade-unions and of those peculiar political groups, especially in Catalonia, the Anarcho-Syndicalists, the P.O.U.M., and the United Socialists.[4] The Communists, who had felt the influence of Moscow, would consult political commissars or hold meetings before acting on their orders. Certainly the traditions of these groups did not predispose them toward military discipline, and the political history of the war, behind the scenes, on the Republican side, largely consists of their constant feuds. Then, as a further complicating factor, there were wholesale experiments in the collectivization of industries and farms, experiments which were more successful perhaps than similar experiments of the Italian Socialists in 1920, but the methods of expropriation varied with the political views of the expropriators, and the results were not exactly uniform. The Republican government, eventually established at Valencia, under Largo Caballero, leader of the extreme Socialist wing, was fated to go through some very rough passages.

To the world at large, the outbreak of the Spanish Civil War came as a shock. Normally Spain had had a poor press. She was one of the "faraway" countries; since 1898 she had hardly figured as front-page news anywhere; she had been neutral in the First World War. Alfonso XIII was known as a man of shrewd and picturesque character; with his English Queen, he was always much photographed in society magazines; but Spain herself had never shared the familiarity with which her monarch was regarded abroad. Like the "turbulent Balkans," or like her own neighbor, Portugal, Spain's internal troubles and crises belonged to a normal, unchanging condition, to which the world had formerly paid but little heed. But this time it was clear that she had become the theater of a conflict bigger than herself and supremely important to the entire European family.

But even while at first the objects and alignments of the Civil War were still obscure, newspaper readers abroad were startled and appalled by reports of the savagery with which it was being conducted. Granted that civil wars reputedly are the bitterest of all wars, granted that the Spaniard is passionate and cruel, granted that the war had released overcharged and pent-up hatreds, granted too, as was soon quite obvious, that the reports of atrocities were exaggerated in one way or another by propaganda, granted many reasons and extenuations, the grim facts were shocking beyond the credence of contemporaries who, in 1936, had only begun their modern education in insensitiveness to horror.

Presumably the Nationalists had the greater opportunity for terrorism. Their forces made their biggest advances between August and October 1936, at a time when the taking of prisoners alive was accounted an uncommon clemency and when there were hostile towns and territories to pacify. But among the Republicans were men indoctrinated in political crime, and it was these who most indulged in class murders, in murders of priests, grandees, capitalists, factory managers, landlords, and army officers. The Anarcho-Syndicalists, who were strong in Barcelona, regarded class murder, "killing without hatred," as an ethical principle. Both Nationalists and Republicans seem to have been equally guilty of executing suspects on the flimsiest evidence or on no evidence at all. Courts and investigating committees were a farce. Murders from private grudges were common; murders of hostages were common.

REACTIONS OF THE POWERS

It is hard to establish the exact time when the Soviet Union, Italy, and Germany first began to utilize Spanish feuds and factions for their own ends. Certainly all three had fingers in the pie before 1936. The Soviet Union had maintained a loose affiliation with the Spanish Communists for years, and it had supplied funds and "ideological assistance" to interested groups. The Communist revolution had failed lamentably in Central Europe during the twenties, and perhaps the strategists of the Moscow Comintern found some consolation in a prospective, if belated, success in the Iberian Peninsula during the thirties. Spain, in fact, exhibited all those characteristics — a pauperized and embittered peasantry and proletariat, a privileged and oppressive aristocracy and Church — which should have made her ripe material for just such another social subversion as had occurred in Russia in 1917.

The Civil War in Spain, however, had broken out at one of those difficult transitional moments in Soviet affairs. Stalin had withdrawn from the old Trotskyist crusade for "permanent world revolution," though the Comintern continued in active being. The recent setbacks of the League, just when the Soviet Union had become a member of it, had thrown another element of uncertainty into the picture. The Soviet's verbal pronouncements were categorical enough, the Civil War was officially welcomed in Russia, and the usual greetings were showered, as only totalitarians know how, on the comrades fighting for the Republican cause in Spain. During August 1936 there were pro-Republican demonstrations and pageants all over the Soviet Union. The Soviet's political and ideological aid to the Republican government was considerable. The Soviet, through its Spanish embassy and consular officials, gave advice, direction, and eventually dictation. It largely inspired the International Brigades. But the Soviet's material aid to the Republican government, however liberal, was of a kind which could be easily discontinued and never amounted, as did the Italian, to an irrevocable commitment. It consisted of arms, machinery, and food, and much of these were bought by Soviet agents in Western Europe nearer the scene of action. Soviet personnel in Spain was limited to technicians, none of whom saw active service in the line. The Soviet's maritime disability, if nothing else, would have effectively prevented a direct military participation in the war.

Italy's intervention on the Nationalist side in Spain was more direct, more extensive, and more brazen. She was sincerely alarmed at the spread of Communism in Mediterranean Europe, and she was wholeheartedly at one with the ideological professions of General Franco and his partisans. She was also in an expansionist mood and hankering after military glory. An extension of her power in the Mediterranean would automatically weaken that of Britain and France. A Fascist Majorca, a Fascist Ceuta, even a Fascist Gibraltar were possibilities most pleasant to contemplate, possibilities which a good war in Spain might well convert into realities. Mussolini was ambitious to secure and eventually to annex Algeria. Then in May 1936, just two months before the outbreak of the Civil War in Spain, the fighting in Ethiopia had come to an end and, during the less attractive aftermath of that war, Mussolini might well have need of another heroic diversion for his Fascist veterans.[5]

Germany, like Italy, had her ideological stake in the Spanish Civil War. The Nazi press played up the wicked machinations of the Soviet Union and described unhappy Spain as the arena where the destructiveness and anarchy of Bolshevism was being pitted against the law and order of authoritarianism. Then Germany had need of Spanish raw materials, and any military assistance she lent Franco would put him under an obligation which he could later discharge by deliveries of those materials. The erection of a Fascist-minded state on the southwestern border of France, coincident with the recent German march into the Rhineland, had its evident strategic and diplomatic value. El Ferrol, Vigo, and Cádiz would make desirable U-boat bases.[5]

It is well attested that the Nazis used the Civil War to try out their newly forged weapons. In 1914, apart from an occasional military attaché sent to Manchuria or the Balkans, there was hardly a German soldier who had seen active service, and an entire generation of the German officer corps was wanting in experience in the field. In a war of the future, thanks to the Spanish laboratory, that deficiency could be remedied. Weapons would be available that had been tried, and instructors would be available that had used them. For example, the ferocious attack that German aircraft made on the Basque city of Guernica on April 26, 1937, if it was not useless brutality, was only explainable as "a vivisectional experiment" in modern bombing tactics. Combined operations of tanks and planes were tried constantly and at no time more successfully than in the final Nationalist drive down the Ebro in 1938.

The British and French attitudes to the Spanish Civil War reflected all the "weakness" to which the democracies in these years were so painfully subject. Neither country was united in opinion or in will. As in the Italo-Ethiopian War, official Britain — that is, the Foreign Office and the Conservative government — in the interests of caution and "peace," seemed to condone the Fascist aggression. It ignored Fascist threats to British imperial life lines and Fascist expropriations of British properties and investments. If anything, it gave its sympathy, though not a very hearty or convinced sympathy, to the Nationalists. English Catholicism was believed to be pro-Nationalist or, at any rate, anti-Republican. British Labor gave its sympathy to the Republicans and often clamored for action which British morale and British armaments were then in no position to undertake.

The British people generally were indifferent and could find little to choose between "the gangsters of Valencia" and "the gangsters of Burgos." They were discouraged by the recent outcome in Ethiopia, and they made no such outbursts of enthusiasm as had attended Sir Samuel Hoare's famous speech in the League Assembly in September 1935 (see p. 505). Appeasement was then their new watchword, and neither Italian troublemaking in the Mediterranean nor German troublemaking in Central Europe could rouse them from the pacifist lethargy into which they had sunk. Perhaps they derived some consolation from the thought that intervention in the civil wars of the past — as witness the miserable episode in Russia in 1919 — had invariably defeated its objects in the end, and that, after the present Civil War, a people of the fierce pride of the Spaniards would be more likely to extend the hand of friendship to those nations which had had the good sense to leave them to fight their battles by themselves.

In 1936 and subsequently, as we shall describe more fully elsewhere (pp. 567–70), Neville Chamberlain became pre-eminently responsible for British foreign policy and for the appeasement phase associated with his name. He was particularly concerned with conciliating Italy and with trying to tempt her out of her newly formed Axis with Germany and back into the Western fold. In January 1937, while he was still Chancellor of the Exchequer, Britain and Italy signed a "Gentleman's Agreement," mutually recognizing the interests of the two Powers in the Mediterranean. He became Prime Minister in May 1937 and initiated further discussions which came to a conclusion in the Anglo-Italian Agreement of April 1938 (see p. 614). Meanwhile he was in constant friction with his anti-Italian Foreign Secretary, Eden. In July 1937 a further diversion appeared in the outbreak of the Japanese war in China.

In 1936, France was administered by Blum's Popular Front, a government which ought to have had an ideological affiliation with its Spanish namesake. Then, for centuries, a first dictum of French foreign policy had been to prevent the growth of an understanding between Spain and any Central European Power. The parties of the Left in France, that is to say the parties of Blum's Popular Front, clamored like British Labor for action on the Republican side. But France had extraordinary need for caution. One of her frontiers marched with Spain, and the danger of immediate proximity was added to her other anxieties. She obtained little encouragement from the appeasement statesmen of Britain. Her workers at home were in a state of semirevolution; her Right was more afraid of Communism than of Fascism. All in all, her social fabric, it must now be admitted, was far gone into that paralysis which was shortly to bring her down to the military defeat of 1940. France in 1936, even more than Britain, had the pathetic aspect of a great nation buying peace at the price of its vital interests.

Toward the Spanish Civil War the United States observed throughout the strictest isolationism and repeated in all respects its attitude in the recent Ethiopian crisis, albeit, on the whole, American public opinion was pro-Republican and grew more so as the war continued. From the start the administration exerted itself to prevent the export of American war material to Spain. In August 1936, President Roosevelt delivered an address at Lake

Chautauqua, with an evident eye on Spain, on the theme: "I have seen war
. . . I hate war." "We shun political commitments which might entangle us
in foreign wars," he said. ". . . We are not isolationists except in so far as
we seek to isolate ourselves completely from war." In January 1937, by joint
Congressional resolution, the existing Neutrality Act and its embargo on the
export of arms and munitions were extended to both sides indifferently in
Spain.

THE NONINTERVENTION COMMITTEE

On July 30, 1936 three Italian military planes made a forced landing in
Algeria. Their crews were Italian but were wearing Spanish uniforms, and
they were presumed to be bound for General Franco's headquarters in
Morocco. Evidently they were the first installment of a heavy program of
Italian aid. On August 1 the French Government submitted a proposal to the
Italian and British Governments to the effect that all three Powers should refrain from sending supplies of war matériel to either belligerent in the Spanish war. The British Government suggested the extension of the proposal
to all interested Powers and, by the end of August, France, Italy, Britain,
Germany, the Soviet Union, and Portugal had adhered to a Nonintervention Agreement. In September a Nonintervention Committee, representing these and fifteen other states, began to hold regular meetings in London.

At no time during the entire Spanish Civil War did Europe seem to stand
so close to involvement as during the first few months of it. The conduct of
Italy in the matter of the planes, mentioned above, could easily have led to a
crescendo of repetitions, and the materials, machines, and men of the European Powers must soon have clashed in irrevocable conflict in Spain. The
Second World War was very narrowly prevented in 1936, and the Nonintervention Committee in London, farce though it so often was, must be credited
with the doubtful honors of that prevention.

The Nonintervention Committee had much the same effect as the Neutrality Acts of the United States. Theoretically well intentioned, it nonetheless gave the advantage to the aggressor Power, who had ready-made arms at
his disposal and who was not averse to breaking his word to obtain more. It
correspondingly penalized the nonaggressor Power. The strict letter of the
law was powerless against the "virtual acts of aggression," which, as the Spanish delegate reported to the League of Nations, Italy and Germany — and he
might have added the Soviet Union — were then committing in his country.

The problem of the volunteers was typical. In the early months of the war,
international volunteers arrived in great numbers in Spain. In particular
they had joined the Republican forces, and the so-called International Brigades saw action for the first time in the Battle of Madrid in November 1936.
These men were genuine volunteers, moved by their own initiative, in
response to the call of sentiment and propaganda. But the organized units of
Italian troops — and of German troops to a less extent — complete with their
uniforms, arms, and equipment, under their own officers, which fought on
the Nationalist side, belonged to another category altogether. They were

"Expeditionary Forces," and so indeed they were often described at the time in official Italian reports. The Nonintervention Committee spent weary weeks discussing the withdrawal of all non-Spanish nationals who were known already to have arrived and to be serving in one or the other of the contending Spanish armies. But the task was an idle one, especially while the Italian press was exulting in the deeds of valor performed by the Fascist youth in Franco's army, and while Mussolini continued to entangle his prestige ever more irretrievably in the prospects of a Nationalist triumph.

The problem of the naval patrol was also typical. Obviously, in order to prevent the arrival of foreign men and munitions in Spain, the country would have to be circled by some kind of inspection system. Thus, in the face of continuous Fascist obstruction, the Nonintervention Committee drew up a plan for the patrol of Spanish waters, divided the coast into zones, and assigned the zones to naval units of France, Britain, Germany, and Italy. A separate agreement was reached for the supervision of the land frontiers of Spain by a corps of neutral observers. The plan went into force at the end of April 1937. But the Republicans meanwhile had begun to retaliate against Franco's attempt to establish an independent naval blockade, and in May 1937, Republican aircraft bombed a battleship which was afterward discovered to be the German *Deutschland*. A German squadron replied by bombarding the undefended Republican seaside resort of Almería. In June, Germany and Italy withdrew from the patrol plan, and the entire Nonintervention Committee reached a virtual breakdown.

In the late summer of 1937 there was a mysterious outbreak of submarine piracy against French, British, and Soviet shipping in the Western Mediterranean. Italian submarines were suspected. This new development was considered at a conference at Nyon in September, attended by France, Britain, and the Soviet Union, in the persons of Delbos, Eden, and Litvinov, and by other affected Mediterranean countries. Germany and Italy declined to be represented in consequence of a Soviet imputation that Italy herself had been responsible for certain of the acts of piracy in question. The conference was one of the few occasions in the thirties when the Western Powers made a resolute stand against totalitarian lawlessness and aggression, and it showed what a righteous resolution could still accomplish. It was a personal triumph for the British Foreign Secretary, Eden. The conference agreed that submarines attacking any non-Spanish merchant ships would be counterattacked and destroyed and that the British and French fleets would give "practical effect" to that agreement. Italy was afterward persuaded to adhere. No further acts of submarine piracy were reported.

THE COURSE OF THE WAR

The first month of the war had been very confused. The fighting had broken out in several places at once, and it consisted for the most part of mutual mopping-up operations, the consolidation of sympathetic areas, and the strengthening of communications. There were neither pitched battles nor established fronts. The Republicans, with that strategic instinct which revolutionaries always seem to have, could more than offset the immediate tactical superiority of the Nationalist forces. The important engagements of these days, if engagements they can be called, were the seizures of Madrid and Barcelona by the Republicans and the seizures of Teruel, Saragossa, the Alcazar at Toledo, and the Balearic islands of Majorca and Iviza by the Nationalists.

Thereafter the war entered upon its campaigning phase. The two groups of Nationalist forces in the north and south of Spain converged upon the Tagus, relieved the beleaguered Nationalist garrison in the Alcazar at Toledo, and by early November 1936 were investing the suburbs of Madrid. The Basque Provinces and Asturias were cut off from the main Republican areas to the south and east. Simultaneously the Nationalists took Irún and San Sebastián, thus cutting off the Republicans from an important road link with France. The Nationalists — and their German and Italian allies — clearly expected the entire war would be successfully ended in a matter of weeks. On November 18, 1936, Germany and Italy recognized the Nationalist government. But at this point the Nationalists were stopped in their tracks. The Republican government retired to Valencia. General Miaja, a professional soldier, organized the Republican defense of Madrid, and he was reinforced by strong contingents, notably the first of the International Brigades. Foreign munitions were beginning to have their effect. Snub-nosed Russian fighter planes were being pitted against Junkers, Heinkels, and Capronis. Madrid held fast, and the Spanish Civil War developed into a long, tedious, and expensive struggle.

General Franco again tried to take Madrid in the early spring of 1937. He attacked in March. Strong Italian forces operated on his left wing toward Guadalajara. The stage was set for one of those spectacular triumphs dear to the Fascist heart. Mussolini, then on a visit to Libya, gave out that he was personally following, hour by hour, the glorious fortunes of his legionaries in Spain. But at Guadalajara, Mussolini's legionaires were put to rout by a detachment of the International Brigades. The Battle of Guadalajara was added to the sorry tradition of Adua and Caporetto. Madrid held fast for the second time.

For the remainder of 1937, General Franco turned his main attention to the Basque Provinces and Asturias. His slow, bitterly contested advance ended in his capture of Bilbao in midsummer, but organized resistance in the north persisted far into the autumn months. Meanwhile the Republican armies in the south could send no direct aid to their hard-pressed Basque comrades. But they could fight diversionary actions and, through the latter half of 1937, they launched repeated attacks along the Madrid and Aragon fronts. More important, they used the time to reorganize themselves and their government. In May 1937, Don Juan Negrin, a right-wing Socialist, had succeeded Largo Caballero as Premier at the head of a leftist, largely Communist-dominated coalition. Conscription was introduced throughout the Republican territories, and it is said that, by the end of 1937, the Republicans had an army of 800,000 men in the field. In October 1937 the Republican government moved to Barcelona. The brilliantly executed assault and capture of Teruel by Republican forces in December 1937 were the first fruits of the military and political reorganization that had been effected.

The debate for the withdrawal of foreign volunteers from Spain continued in London meanwhile round the table of the Nonintervention Committee. The Republicans constantly demanded that the cruel farce of nonintervention be ended and that the legal government of Spain be given the right to buy arms in its own defense. In April 1938 a thoroughgoing Anglo-Italian Agreement was signed in Rome, and one of the items of that instrument was a plan for the "proportional" evacuation of foreign volunteers from Spain, a plan which the Nonintervention Committee formally accepted and undertook to put into effect (see p. 614).

But Mussolini and Hitler were now too deeply committed, and even though, as there is reason to believe, the arrival of new Italian and German troops in Nationalist Spain was curtailed during 1938, the shipment of arms and supplies, on the contrary, was such as to give Franco decisive material superiority. As a measure of his confidence and impunity, Franco resorted to the bombing of civilians as part of a regular policy, and Barcelona in particular was subjected to some rather ineffectual raids — ineffectual, that is, by later standards of destructiveness. Appeals from Britain, France, and the Vatican against his tactics led to no result. Franco strengthened his position politically at this time by assuming the title of Captain General of Spain. An accompanying propaganda campaign was evidently intended to build him up as El Caudillo, a Duce on Fascist lines.

So long as Franco possessed the military power to bring the war to an end on his own terms he was unlikely to pay serious attention to the diplomatic exertions of the Nonintervention Committee. In February 1938 he started a series of actions designed to gain him his long-deferred victory. In that February the Nationalists recaptured Teruel and thereafter developed a steady, irresistible offensive down the Ebro to the sea. In April they captured Vinaroz, and Franco felt himself justified in broadcasting the termination of the war. But the Republicans, with sheer Iberian tenacity, continued to fight back. Barcelona resisted till January 26, and Madrid till March 28, 1939.

On April 20, 1939, three weeks after the fall of Madrid, the Nonintervention Committee in London wound up its work and dissolved. But the final departure of the volunteers in the Nationalist army was postponed till after they had had a chance to appear in Franco's victory parade in Madrid. The date was altered for one reason or another, and the parade did not take place till May 19, actually in pouring rain and in an atmosphere of intense depression. On May 20 complementary religious ceremonies were held in the Iglesia de las Salesas.

The Spanish Civil War had lasted nearly three years and had cost the country a million in deaths and exiles. The country had peace at last, but it was the peace of a desert.

THE BALKAN PACT

The tendency toward dictatorship exhibited by the Balkan States has been described elsewhere (see p. 206). But the Balkan States were far from favorably disposed toward the greater dictatorships of Germany and Italy. The stronger and more menacing Hitler and Mussolini grew the more closely the Balkan States combined for mutual support. The failure of the World Economic Conference in London in 1933 and the even more calamitous failure of the Disarmament Conference in Geneva gave shape and substance to the worst of Balkan fears. The Balkan Conferences had already made straight the way for an outright political agreement (pp. 214–15). Obvious precedents and examples were to be found in the Pact of Organization of February 1933, which had converted the Little Entente into a permanent diplomatic concert (see p. 174), and also in the string of nonaggression pacts which the Soviet Union at this time was making around its borders. The Soviet Union's implied withdrawal of its old claim on Bessarabia enormously relieved all the Balkan States of their ever-present dread of their powerful eastern neighbor (see p. 541).

Greece and Turkey had already been coming together — in the beginning, oddly enough, as it now appears, under the good offices of Italy (see p. 214). They signed a ten-year nonaggression pact on September 14, 1933 — though this time without the good offices of Italy — and their close accord was confirmed in a unique clause of the pact to the effect that, in future international conferences having a limited representation, Greece and Turkey should have a common delegate! This was truly a signal advance in Balkan *rapprochement*. The Greco-Turkish pact was shortly followed by a pact of friendship between Turkey and Yugoslavia which provided for judicial settlement, arbitration, and conciliation, as well as for nonaggression. Further Balkan *rapprochement* was symbolized in a series of ceremonial visits. King Alexander of Yugoslavia and his Queen, during 1933, the year before his tragic death, visited Bulgaria, Turkey, Greece, and Rumania, most of whose rulers shortly returned the compliment. King Boris of Bulgaria visited Belgrade in December 1933, thus effecting the reconciliation, long overdue, between Bulgaria and Yugoslavia.

A general Balkan Entente was therefore very much a possibility by the end of 1933. It was hastened at the last by the rapid rise of the Fascist Iron Guard in Rumania. This virulently anti-Semitic, pro-Nazi organization contrived the assassination of Rumania's Liberal Premier, Ion Duca, in December 1933.

Nicholas Titulescu, the Rumanian Foreign Minister, realized that no time must be lost in bringing a Balkan Pact to fruition. Bulgaria, still unwilling to accept the territorial limitations of the peace settlement of 1919 and to renounce her revisionist ambitions, stood aloof. Moreover, Bulgaria shied away from a clause in the proposed pact which defined an "aggressor" state as one which, *inter alia,* supported irregular armed bands, fearing thereby that she would be compelled to take effective steps to suppress the Macedonian Revolutionary Organization, the notorious IMRO, on her territory (see pp. 205 and 211).

A Balkan Pact which confined itself to a mutual guarantee of frontiers was viewed with great satisfaction by all nontotalitarian European Powers. Britain, it is true, regretted that the pact could not have been drafted in such a way as to obtain the adhesion of Bulgaria, but France and the Soviet Union, more especially the latter, were strongly in favor of it, with or without Bulgaria. Beneš of Czechoslovakia expressed his belief that the pact would at long last result in securing the Balkans for the Balkan peoples. Thus alone might the Balkans, that old storm center of Europe, find peace, immune from the rivalries of the Great Powers.

It was feared, especially among the Balkan States, that the pact might permanently alienate Bulgaria and Albania. Papanastasiou, the former Premier of Greece, who had been one of the inspirers of the earlier Balkan Conferences, tried in vain to persuade the Balkan foreign ministers to adopt instead the principles of the Draft Balkan Pact which had already been worked out at the Balkan Conferences or at least to "be content" with a pact providing for nonaggression and for the pacific solution of disputes, a pact to which all six of the Balkan States could subscribe (see p. 215). A pact which confined itself to the safeguarding of frontiers only, he warned, would render "more difficult the general entente of the Balkan peoples," and subsequent events proved him to have been right. But the objections of Papanastasiou and of those who thought as he did, in Yugoslavia as well as in Greece, were overruled. Greece, Rumania, Turkey, and Yugoslavia finally signed the Balkan Pact at Athens on February 9, 1934. Bulgaria refused her signature. Albania, on account of her close relations with Italy, was not invited to sign, but the pact was left open for her and Bulgaria's future adherence.

The four signatories of the pact declared that they wished "to contribute to the consolidation of peace in the Balkans" in the spirit of the Pact of Paris; they mutually guaranteed "the security of each and all their Balkan frontiers"; and they undertook to consult with one another on measures to be taken "in contingencies liable to affect their interests," as defined by "the Pact of Balkan Entente." In a secret Protocol-Annex, the signatories clarified more specifically the nature of their "understandings." Many described the pact as a defensive instrument "not directed against any Power". . . "Its object is to guarantee the security of the several Balkan frontiers against any aggression on the part of any Balkan State" and, in Article 1, they accepted a careful definition of an aggressor.[1] Other articles of the Protocol-Annex concerning aggression on the part of any non-Balkan Power — "if a Balkan State should associate itself with such an aggression" — were subsequently nullified by the declared reservations of Greece and Turkey that they could not be involved in war against a Great Power.

It is clear therefore that the Balkan Pact was premature, and that by setting aside the Draft Balkan Pact, it dealt the Balkan Conference and Balkan union movement, together with the general idea of inclusive Balkan co-operation, a mortal blow. This was explicitly acknowledged by several Balkan statesmen who had themselves supported the Balkan Pact and who had hoped for the eventual support of Bulgaria and Albania.

The Balkan Pact therefore interrupted the series of the Balkan Conferences. The Fifth Balkan Conference, which had been scheduled, never met, although Papanastasiou urged that there was now more reason than ever for continuing the steady constructive development of Balkan solidarity. The Yugoslav national delegation took the position that the Balkan Pact had "completed" the work of the Conferences; the Bulgarians believed that the Balkan States must accept either the Conferences or the pact, but not both, as they held the two to be incompatible; and the Albanians, even more offended by the pact than the Bulgarians, refused point-blank to attend any further Balkan Conferences. But Papanastasiou and the Greek delegation prepared a formal charter against the day of the Conferences' resurrection, the charter of an organization which they hoped would be a "Balkan Parliamentary and Social Union" permanently established at Istanbul. To an impartial observer it would appear that the pressure of world affairs had turned the Balkan States away from the path of their best interests. Their governments seemed to have been stampeded by the general trend toward regional security. Barthou's Grand Alliance and the projected East European Pact of Mutual Assistance were all aspects of the same picture and, to some extent, largely justified the hasty action of the Balkan governments. Bulgaria eventually joined the Balkan Pact in 1938 — albeit with definite reservations — when the need for her joining had become even more obvious and pressing. The events of 1941, however, confirmed certain fears expressed in 1934 that Bulgaria, left both isolated and encircled by a Balkan bloc, would respond once again to the advances of an outside Power.

So far as the Balkans were concerned, the new Balkan Pact seemed to have ushered in a new era. But scarcely a year passed before alarming European developments disturbed the new-found equanimity. Once again each Balkan government was forced to ponder whether its freedom of action was to be seriously threatened by one or more of the Great Powers. The Great Powers themselves were vacillating and unpredictable. At first France and Italy appeared to be determined to bury their mutual antagonisms, and they were joined by Britain in an active effort to keep Austria alive and preserve her political integrity. But plans and good intentions were disturbed by Germany's conscription decree and by Italy's invasion of Ethiopia. Politics in Southeastern Europe was thereafter dominated by the growing rivalry between the Soviet Union and Germany. In Balkan eyes, the Soviet Union seemed the less dangerous of the two colossi; but Czechoslovakia was the only member of either the Little Entente or Balkan Pact to go the length of making an alliance with the Soviet Union and, by this action, Czechoslovakia automatically withdrew herself from any close association with the Balkan nations. Yugoslavia, Rumania, Greece, and Turkey were all inclining toward isolationism, and all four of them recoiled from the possibility of being embroiled in any Central European conflict.

Before 1936 was over, Balkan faith in the efficacy of regional security agreements was badly shaken. In that year both Germany and Italy defied the League of Nations, sanctions failed against Italy, and Germany reforti-fied the Rhineland. Most significant of all in the eyes of Southeastern Europe was Italy's about-face in the formation of the Rome-Berlin Axis. Italian pressure toward the southeast dated from 1926; after 1933, that pressure had been duplicated by Germany. What hope was there for the Balkan countries, once Italy and Germany had united? Before 1937, the Axis made a deter-mined effort to weaken the Balkan Pact, and its next step was in the direction of breaking up the Little Entente. The geographical separation of Bulgaria from Italy and the continued support of the members of the Bal-kan Pact, who still desired and persistently worked for Bulgaria's adhesion, had given Bulgaria the strength to reject Italy's proffered clientage. Con-sequently German diplomacy concentrated upon uniting Yugoslavia with Bulgaria and detaching them both from Greece and Turkey — such, at least, seems to have been the most logical explanation of Germany's sudden desire to foster a strong South Slav bloc under German influence. Sofia did turn to Belgrade, instead of to Rome, and Belgrade was quick to respond.

In January 1937 a Bulgaro-Yugoslav pact of "inviolable peace and sincere and perpetual friendship" was signed. Thus ended a thousand-year-long feud in a political pact that was intended, in the words of the Yugoslav Premier, to "liquidate" and bury an "unhappy" Balkan past. It is note-worthy that the signatories had been careful to secure the previous approval of Rumania, Greece, Turkey, and Czechoslovakia. The next, and a less felicitous, event of Balkan importance was a sudden change in Yugoslavia's policy of "balance" — when in March 1937 the Yugoslav Government was enticed into signing a five-year nonaggression and arbitration pact with Italy.

AXIS PENETRATION OF THE BALKANS

We have already referred to Germany's economic penetration of the Bal-kans as part of the larger picture of Nazi economics (pp. 461–62). Dr. Schacht visited all but one of the Balkan capitals during 1936, and initiated his famous barter agreements.[2] He contracted to buy Balkan goods at rela-tively high prices, and gave long-term credits for the purchase of German machinery and armaments. Payment for Balkan goods was to be made in blocked marks, a seemingly innocent arrangement — until it was seen how enormous was the power Germany could shortly exercise over the creditor country. By the end of 1936, Germany had cornered over one-quarter of the trade of Southeastern Europe, chiefly at Italy's expense. The basic difficulty of the Balkan countries was that their choice of markets was so limited. Schacht was therefore able to persuade Balkan statesmen — often against their better judgment — to sign his proposed barter agreements for the simple reason that Britain was the only non-Axis country that could continue to buy Balkan exports. Britain indeed almost held her own in the Balkans till 1937, but she could never alone have absorbed all that the Balkans could produce.

It was not true, as so many German economists claimed, that Southeastern Europe could supply "almost all" Germany's needs. But it was true that many Balkan products complemented Germany's own and that, to this extent, a sound basis for an interlocking and mutually profitable trade existed.[3] And clearly it was to Germany's interest to stimulate a thorough-going economic exchange with an area which would always be free from possible naval blockade by an enemy power and which, under necessity, could be militarily dominated by her. There was also a sound basis for the Nazi policy of trying to check the industrialization of the Balkans. Under different methods and for different ends a solution of Balkania's major economic problems, including the fundamental one of overpopulation, in collaboration with an industrial Central Europe might well have been forthcoming. Possibly a switch-over from cereals to products, such as fruit and vegetables, poultry and cattle, that demanded more intensive labor could have been successfully effected. But, for the nonce, Balkan economics had perforce to follow other courses.

Meanwhile Italy's penetration of Albania proceeded at a rapid rate. From the Treaty of Tirana in 1927 to 1939, Albania was virtually an Italian protectorate (see p. 209). King Zog made a short-lived attempt in 1932 to hold off Italy's growing influence, and he even went so far as to decline a proffered customs union. After an Italian naval demonstration off Durazzo in 1934, King Zog relaxed his efforts in this direction, and during 1936 the Italo-Albanian bond was drawn more tightly than ever. Three years later, a month after Hitler's final extinction of Czechoslovakia, Mussolini sent an Italian army into Albania. King Zog and his Queen fled to Greece, and on April 14, 1939, Albania became united to Italy in a personal union, under Victor Emmanuel III, King of Italy and Albania and Emperor of Ethiopia.

THE BALKAN DICTATORSHIPS

By the thirties, at the time of which we are now writing, every one of the Balkan States had become a dictatorship. Usually the dictatorship took the "Latin" form, as was the case in Italy and as had once been the case in Spain, that is to say the dictatorship was a combination of rule by the legitimate monarch and a favorite premier. Since 1934 a regency, headed by Prince Paul, had ruled Yugoslavia with Stoyadinovich (after 1935) as Premier. Since 1935, King Boris III had ruled Bulgaria with Kiosseivanov as Premier. Since 1935 also, after tentative and unsuccessful efforts to govern constitutionally, King George II had ruled Greece dictatorially, first with General Kondylis and then, after 1936, with General Metaxas as Premier. In Rumania the dictatorial process matured more slowly but, by 1938, King Carol II found it necessary to govern his country, along Fascist lines, through a single party and an attendant squadrist militia. Albania had been ruled by King Zog I since 1928. The neighboring Turkish scene meanwhile was comparatively uneventful, but the Kemalist dictatorship, though presidential in form, continued strong and, in 1938, after Kemal's death, passed intact into the able hands of his successor, Inonu.

In Yugoslavia, after the assassination of King Alexander in October 1934, a Serbo-Croat regency, headed by Prince Paul, was set up to rule in the name of the young King Peter. For six months or so, there was a lull in the chronic Croat campaign for autonomy. Between May 1935 and February 1938 a parliamentary dictatorship governed the country, through the so-called Yugoslov Radical Union, under the premiership of Dr. Milan Stoyadinovich. The Union was composed of Orthodox Serb Radicals, Catholic Slovenes, and Bosnian Moslems. The Opposition, which steadily gathered strength, was centered in the Croat Peasant party, led by Dr. Vlasko Machek, who had the support of other democratic groups and also at first of the Croat nationalists. In 1937 this Opposition took the name of the Agrarian Democratic party. Its program was far-reaching and called for autonomy for Croatia, wider education, the improvement of conditions among the peasantry, and unrestricted freedom of speech and of the press. It mobilized all the anti-German, anti-Italian sentiment in the country, and flourished upon every *rapprochement* Stoyadinovich made with the Axis Powers. The barter agreements with Germany and the Italo-Yugoslav nonaggression pact of 1937 were unpopular in the country and were good grist to the Opposition mill.

Stoyadinovich's pro-Italian policy involved him in a bitter religious controversy. A concordat, signed in July 1937 with the Holy See, ostensibly to "regularize" the position of the Catholic Church in Yugoslavia, would have granted wider privileges to Catholic Yugoslavs. It was thus in effect an indirect bid for Croat support and an attempt to thin the ranks of Machek's party. Stoyadinovich's fruitless effort to force through a ratification of the concordat brought down upon him the wrath of the Orthodox Church without winning any appreciable Croat support in compensation.

Stoyadinovich's only popular move was the treaty of "inviolable peace and sincere and perpetual friendship" with Bulgaria in January 1937. The treaty was the fulfillment of the late King Alexander's earnest wish and it contributed to the formation of a strong South Slav bloc — though here too, as we have said already, Yugoslavia appeared to be playing a game which might be turned to German advantage. Eventually the Opposition proved too strong for Stoyadinovich, and he was forced to resign in February 1939, after Machek's Peasant party won a spectacular victory in the Croatian elections, and his demands could no longer be put off. The crisis in Czechoslovakia and, later, the Italian invasion of Albania were sufficiently convincing proof that particularism in Yugoslavia would soon be just another name for national extinction. The German-Polish crisis provided the final argument for domestic unity. In August 1939, after complicated negotiations, an agreement was reached by which the Croats obtained autonomy in all cultural and some economic fields, a new "Croatia" under its own governor was created, and the Yugoslav nation was reorganized on a federal basis. Machek, the Croat leader, became Vice-Premier, and five Croats joined the Yugoslav Cabinet. Yugoslavia faced the outbreak of the Second World War with a semblance of that unity she had sought for during the twenty years of her existence.

In Bulgaria, the most isolated of the Balkan nations, personal politics and a revitalized Agrarian party had dictated the policies of a succession of coalitions. The Depression, however, increasingly antagonized the peasantry. The inability of Bulgarian politicians to cope with economic problems or to suppress the terrorism of the Macedonian Revolutionary Organization, the IMRO (see p. 529), hopelessly discredited their governments. The Balkan Pact of 1934 seemed to make Bulgaria's isolation more pronounced and intolerable than ever, and a group of army officers planned and executed a *coup d'état* in collaboration with some political reformers. The army and its civilian collaborators (the "Zveno"), however, proved successful only in suppressing and disbanding the Macedonian Revolutionary Organization and made no better success than its predecessors in dealing with the country's economic problems. Disillusioned by its limitations, the army voluntarily abandoned politics and retired from the scene. In 1935, accordingly, a royal dictatorship painlessly supplanted the military dictatorship, and King Boris, together with his Premier and close friend, George Kiosseivanov, ruled Bulgaria without parliament till 1939.

King Boris had shown himself a dexterous statesman in these successive crises, and he had weathered the military *coup d'état* without losing face. He was sufficiently responsive to public opinion to promise a new constitution and eventually, in 1938, to allow the establishment of a consultative parliament. The Opposition in this new Sobranje, formed by a coalition of former Agrarian, Liberal, Radical Socialist, and Democratic elements, was called the Bloc of Five; but its influence was not comparable to that of the National and Social movement, under the leadership of Professor Tsankov, the original instigator of the revolt against Stambulisky and the Agrarian party in 1923 (see p. 211). This movement, though not officially National Socialist, undoubtedly worked in close touch with the German Nazis; and it maintained its strength at home by championing active revisionist policies, especially in the southern Dobruja. Yet the alignment of Bulgaria with Hitler's Greater Germany in 1941 surprised many close observers. For one thing, there was practically no anti-Semitism in Bulgaria, nor was there any German minority group, as in Rumania. More important, however, was the strong traditional and sentimental attachment of the Bulgarians to the Russians. This was no Communist sympathy, but rather a link — a very strong historic link in Bulgaria's case — between Russian Slav and Balkan Slav. It is to be questioned whether Nazi Germany ever had any other than a purely governmental alliance with Bulgaria and whether indeed King Boris's people were behind him in his pro-German policy. The only acceptable offering that Germany could make — aside from economic ties that were often more resented than otherwise — was the satisfaction of Bulgarian territorial revisionism, an empty and, as it proved, a somewhat anticlimactic gift.

In Greece, King George II, upon his restoration to the throne in 1935, proclaimed a general amnesty and began ruling constitutionally. But he was far from fortunate. The "brain trust," or government of experts, which he had caused to be formed, was not popular in the country, and his efforts were further jeopardized by the sudden deaths of several public men in Greece on whose help and counsel he had counted, including General Kondylis and the veteran Venizelos, then in Paris. Amid an epidemic of strikes and risings it was natural that he should look for the usual contemporary remedy — a strong man. In August 1936, General Metaxas, his Premier, alleging the danger of a Communist revolution, carried out a *coup d'état* and established a personal dictatorship. Metaxas was a distinguished staff officer and strategist who had received his military education in Germany. He now proceeded to organize Greece as a totalitarian, corporative state. He suppressed public liberties but embarked upon an extensive program of public works and social legislation, relying upon the army to support his every measure. He made an effort to retain the good will of Britain, France, and Turkey, but his growing economic and psychological dependence on Germany was soon too obvious to be denied.

In Rumania, we have said, the dictatorial process matured more slowly. The exiled Crown Prince Carol had been recalled in 1930 and had ascended the throne as King Carol II. Julius Maniu, the great Peasant leader, was then Premier, and he had made Carol's return possible in the hope that the King would rule constitutionally. Maniu, however, had been overoptimistic, and he soon found himself fighting a losing battle, not only with the King's absolutist tendencies, but with the increasing influence of the King's mistress, Madame Lupescu, and the court circles. A coalition cabinet of "the King's Friends" displaced his government for a year. But Maniu's Peasant party, though weakened by a split in its own ranks, returned to power again in time to meet the full impact of the Depression in Rumania. Under the circumstances, it never got a long chance to prove its genuine strength in the country or to vindicate the reforming zeal of its leader. The Liberals were reinstated at the end of 1933 together with their commercial and financial oligarchy, their program of industrialization at the expense of agrarian interests, and their extreme economic nationalism. Their foreign policy was more fruitful than their domestic and economic policies largely by reason of their distinguished Foreign Minister Titulescu, one of the chief negotiators of the Balkan Pact of 1934.

Meanwhile ominous currents were traceable in Rumania. The Iron Guard was Rumania's version of Fascist squadrism, and it claimed its first important victim when, in December 1933, the Liberal Premier, Ion Duca, was assassinated. It was shortly identified with all the forces of reaction in Rumania. The two anti-Semitic groups, Cuza's Christian League and Goga's National Christian party, were not very different from it. All these groups borrowed fresh strength and prestige from the Nazi seizure of power in Germany.

At the end of 1937 the King unexpectedly appointed Goga Premier, and Goga in a forty-five-day orgy of anti-Semitic legislation completely discredited himself and his party, both at home and abroad. Perhaps Goga's workmanship had been anticipated by the King, and his resulting unpopularity gave the King his chance. In spite of violent opposition from the Iron

Guard and Maniu's Peasant party, King Carol dissolved parliament, suspended the constitution, suppressed all political parties, and then, on February 10, 1938, proclaimed a royal dictatorship. He created a single party, the Front of National Rebirth, effectively supported by a National Guard.

It would be taking a charitable view of Carol's totalitarian revolution to interpret it as his attempted defense of Rumania against the Nazi menace. But, even if that was his intention, it did not succeed for long. With all his efforts and with all his bids for the support of the Rumanian minorities, he was powerless to protect a realm of such unique strategic position and of such unique agricultural and mineral wealth. Rumania's oil was vital to the Third Reich, and Rumania opened her doors to German control by signing a comprehensive commercial agreement with Germany in the late spring of 1939.

TURKEY

Turkey had turned instinctively to Britain as soon as she began to feel the European pressures of the early thirties. She joined the League of Nations in 1932, and early in 1934 began to slip unobtrusively out of her accord with Italy, which had dated from 1927–28. Italy's one golden deed in the Eastern Mediterranean had been the inauguration of Greco-Turkish *rapprochement* in 1930; but Greece and Turkey completed this good work on their own initiative, and the famous treaty of 1933 had been negotiated without Italy's good offices (see p. 528). When Turkey "requested" the signatories of the Treaty of Lausanne to consider a revision of the status of the Dardanelles, both Britain and France responded favorably (see p. 227). The Montreux Convention of July 1936 readjusted the situation, and Turkey became once again "Guardian of the Straits," and was allowed to refortify them. Thereafter British influence increased rapidly at Ankara, and the new *rapprochement* bore fruit in the "Gentlemen's Agreement" of January 1937 between Great Britain and Turkey. On May 12, 1939 the "Gentlemen's Agreement" was supplemented by an Anglo-Turkish Mutual Assistance Pact against possible aggression or in case of war in the Eastern Mediterranean, and this pact was itself supplemented a month later by a Franco-Turkish Mutual Assistance Pact (see pp. 639 and 640).

Turkey was the keystone of the arch between the Christian Balkans and the Moslem Near East. At the World's Fair in New York in 1939, Western sight-seers were impressed by the modern well-ordered Turkish Pavilion dominated by the statue of a man symbolizing the new Turkey. The man stood with one foot on the shore of Turkey-in-Europe and the other on that of Turkey-in-Asia, and underneath him were the words, "Turkey Unites Europe and Asia in Peace." That claim indeed Turkey made good. Her role in the Balkan Conferences and as one of the signatories of the Balkan Pact of 1934 has been described. To the east, she pursued the same policy, in the same pacific spirit. In July 1937 the Saadabad or Middle Eastern Pact of Nonaggression was signed between Turkey, Iraq, Iran, and Afghanistan, making Turkey the link between two interlocking alliances, the Balkan and Middle Eastern Pacts (see p. 236).

The Turkey of the thirties had great national prestige. She was strong at home and self-dependent. Her revolution was bearing good fruit and, because of its success, was a source of inspiration to the Arab peoples. Since the founding of the Republic, she had officially renounced all imperialist ambitions. It was generally believed that she was nonrevisionist and had no designs on any of her neighbors.

Only in one region could it be said that Turkey nourished revisionist ambitions, namely in Alexandretta on the Syrian border. At the end of the First World War, the Alexandretta zone, otherwise known as the Sanjak of Antioch and Alexandretta, had been occupied by French troops. In October 1921, by a special Franco-Turkish Accord, in deference to the considerable Turkish population there, the French had detached the zone administratively from their Syrian mandate and established in it a special, local regime with autonomous features. For a time Turkey had accepted the arrangement with good grace, but never really renounced her claim to the full and complete possession of the region (see p. 226).

After negotiating the Franco-Syrian Treaty of 1936, which contemplated the eventual independence of Syria and the inclusion of this sanjak in a special position within the Syrian state (see p. 244), Turkey revived the issue and initiated an agitation for the annexation of the region. During 1937 and 1938, at the time of the mobilization of the non-Axis Powers of the Mediterranean, Turkey and France entered into consultation for the removal of this potential Alsace-Lorraine of the Near East. By successive steps, the Sanjak of Antioch and Alexandretta became first the autonomous Republic of Hatay (under French mandate), and then, in July 1939, it was finally annexed by Turkey and shortly thereafter metamorphosed into the sixty-third vilayet of the Turkish Republic. On June 23, 1939 the conclusion of the process had already been anticipated by the signature of a special Franco-Turkish agreement, and the Hatay agreement was supplemented by specific Turkish guarantees to Syria and by a general Franco-Turkish Non-aggression Pact (see p. 640).

Unfortunately, however, Syria was bitterly resentful of this alienation of territory, and Syrians charged the French with the betrayal of their mandatory trust — for the sake of "making a deal with the Turks" — specifically with the violation of an article of the mandate which stipulated that no part of Syria or the Lebanon should be ceded or leased or in any way placed under the control of a foreign power.[4] A diplomatic problem was thus created between Turkey and Syria which was still unsolved when the latter ultimately achieved independence at the end of the Second World War.

SOVIET FOREIGN POLICY

The English-speaking peoples, in their long freedom from invasion — and even from the fear of it — have been spared the characteristic psychosis of those less fortunate nations of the world for whom invasion has been a repeated historical experience. Since the dawn of history the Russian steppe has been swept by great migrations. Vikings, Mongols, Lithuanians, Poles, and Swedes have beset it with raid and conquest. Latterly the Russian people fought the Napoleonic War of 1812, the Crimean War of 1854–56, the Japanese War of 1904–05, the Austro-German War of 1914–18, and the Civil War of 1918–20, every one of which followed the ancient pattern of "defense against aggression." All these things bit deep into the Russian soul.

The Russian people have also profoundly felt their technological inferiority. Invasion after invasion has taken advantage of their "backwardness." From Ivan the Terrible to Peter the Great, from Catherine the Great to Lenin, the Russian people have been laggard students of the arts and sciences of more "advanced" nations. The tensions between their temperamental isolationism and their periodically enforced need of foreign education have often been extraordinarily acute. "Those who fall behind are beaten," said Stalin in an address of 1931. "Old Russia was beaten by the Mongol khans; she was beaten by the Turkish beys; she was beaten by the Swedish feudal lords; she was beaten by the Polish and Lithuanian gentry; she was beaten by the British and French capitalists; she was beaten by the Japanese barons. All beat her — for her backwardness, for her military, cultural, political, industrial, and agricultural backwardness. She was beaten because it was profitable to beat her and because she could be beaten with impunity. Do you remember the words of the poet, 'Thou art poor and abundant, mighty and impotent, Mother Russia'? That is why we must no longer lag behind; that is why we must build up the socialist system of economy in the shortest possible time. There is no other way. Either we do so, or we shall be crushed."

Russia's basic problem through the centuries has been the founding of a unitary state in the midst of the Euro-Asiatic plain. Hers has always been an amorphous people in an amorphous land with a strong streak of nomadism and centrifugalism in their heart's blood, given as much to destructive revolts and upsurges from within as to invasion from without. Granted the social and geopolitical circumstances, a strong central authority was the prior need for the survival of any polity other than the tribal. The Russian is possessed of two fears of almost pathological intensity, the fear of external aggression and the fear of internal disruption. Modern Soviet totalitarianism, ensconced behind its iron curtain, is no new thing, but belongs to the age-old Russian pattern.

We do not excuse. We seek to explain. The Soviet attitude may appear to the universalist West as a wicked, dangerous perversity. The Russian state, in the view of many of us, is like the village eccentric who incarcerates himself in his cottage and will have dealings with no one but the tradesman. In One World his behavior is insane and intolerable and, for sanitary reasons, if none other, the police must break into his self-made confinement and let in the fresh air and sunlight. Yet it can be argued also, not unreasonably, that the Stalinist despotism of today, like other despotisms in Russia's past, may be a necessary discipline imposed on a people of multiple social groups and nationalities, inhabiting a vast, frontierless territory, and weakened by years of revolution and foreign war. It is an ironic and tragic fact that the man who himself once revolted against a cruel tyranny should now be wielding a tyranny no less cruel. Yet, but for his rigoristic rule, the area now covered by the Soviet Union might dissolve into its ancient elements, and Russia might once more become a roving tribal expanse preyed upon by every neighboring state.

Traditional fears were aggravated by the Marxian doctrine, and by the warnings of Lenin, that the capitalist Powers would surely assault the young Communist state in its moments of weakness. The Civil War and its long tale of "intervention" eventually came to an end in 1920 but, in Russian eyes, the basic conflict had not been resolved. The basic conflict had been renewed with other weapons in the subsequent campaign of misunderstanding and misrepresentation in the capitalist press abroad. Soviet Russia had been pointedly excluded from the Washington Conference at the end of 1921, though an interested Pacific Power, and her reception at the Genoa Conference in 1922 had been far from reassuring to her (pp. 162–63). Throughout the interwar years, the Soviet Union remained almost paranoically apprehensive of her neighbors, and the seeming reversals of principle, the seeming absence of principle in all Soviet diplomacy are arguably attributable to a sort of frenzied defense complex against capitalist-imperialist aggression. This attitude of mind, we might add, came all too easily to the average Communist leader, a man of revolutionary background — whether he were an old Bolshevik brought up in the lurking shadows of Tsarist conspiracy or a young son of the Soviet Union brought up in the lurking shadows of the party purge — a man whose normal emotions, from very childhood, were compounded of suspicion and betrayal.

It would be hard to imagine governments less desirous of war than Britain's and France's in the Locarno era. Yet the Soviet Union passed these halcyon years in a state of mortal panic over their fell designs against itself. Soviet opinion, for instance, regarded the League of Nations as a capitalist junta for the maintenance of the imperialist Versailles order. Locarno itself, because it excluded the Soviet Union and because it was concerned only with the Western European frontiers, could be read by inference as an acknowledgment that the Eastern European frontiers might still fluctuate, and perhaps be encouraged to fluctuate, at the expense of the Soviet Union under the impact of new wars. The carefree citizen of Britain or France would have been much surprised to learn that 1927 — of all years — was one in which the Soviet Union expected a treacherous military assault. Conservative governments had been established at that time in Britain and France; Poland and Lithuania had passed under reactionary dictatorships; Chiang Kai-shek had triumphed in China; Baron Tanaka had become Premier in Japan; within the Soviet Union, the struggle between Stalinists and Trotskyists was at its height; and all these events, in Soviet eyes, had a sinister concurrence. The London police raid on Arcos and the Soviet Trade Agency, in May 1927, a raid regarded by the British press with half-amused and cynical indifference, was interpreted in Russia as the climax of a long campaign all pointing in one direction (see p. 330). "Be on your guard!" cried Voroshilov, Commissar for War, in his speech to the Congress of Soviets in 1927. "You are surrounded by enemies." Chicherin even dubbed the Pact of Paris of 1928 as "an instrument for the isolation of, and the struggle with, the Soviet Union."

There is no simple formula for the interpretation of a foreign policy. "Defense" is one element in a complex situation. Defense does not always account for the indisputable facts of Russian expansionism now and in the past or for the aggressive activities of revolutionary Communism. The heirs of medieval Muscovy today would not be occupying one-sixth of the surface of the world if defense had been the sole and only motive of their statecraft.

Nonetheless the persistent theme of defense runs through, explains, and unifies many of the phases of Soviet diplomacy in the interwar years. To allay the omnipresent fear, Soviet diplomacy sought to enter into bilateral nonaggression pacts with the Soviet Union's territorial neighbors and near neighbors. It was the standard policy of the Soviet Union to entrench itself behind nonaggression pacts, much as France entrenched herself behind alliances. The first of the pacts, and the model for the rest, was the Treaty of Paris signed by the Soviet Union and Turkey in December 1925. The Soviet Union and Turkey agreed to remain neutral in any war involving the other, never to attack each other, nor to enter into blocs or coalitions hostile to each other. During 1926 and 1927, the Soviet Union signed similar pacts with Afghanistan, Persia, the Baltic States — and, as shall be mentioned again, with Germany. At the same time, no doubt under Soviet influence, a series of analogous, interlocking bilateral pacts were signed by Turkey, Afghanistan, and Persia.

Maxim Litvinov succeeded Chicherin as Soviet Foreign Commissar early in 1929 to become for the next ten years a familiar figure at Geneva and at every international conference of importance, a persistent advocate of peace by collective security. He had already made a dramatic appearance in 1927 at the Preparatory Commission for the Disarmament Conference and had appealed there for universal and total disarmament (see p. 145). In August 1928 the Soviet Union had adhered to the Pact of Paris and had thus signalized her inclusion in the prevailing pacific mentality of the Western world. Litvinov's first act in his new office was to set about constructing a similar pact applicable more particularly to the states within the Soviet orbit. Between February and July 1929, accordingly, the Litvinov Protocol, as it was called, was signed by nine states — the Soviet Union, Poland, Latvia, Estonia, Rumania, Lithuania, Turkey, Danzig, and Persia — and all solemnly affirmed the Pact of Paris as binding on themselves (see p. 142).

The Soviet Union's relations with Germany are of particular interest, especially in view of the events of 1939. There was little in the way of common ideological ground between the two countries, even in the Weimar period. The German Communist party had met with defeat in the early twenties, and the Comintern in Moscow had since evinced no great interest in it. But, for a time, the two countries had a diplomatic and an economic need of each other. It had been so in Bismarck's day; it was so in Stresemann's. To quote Stalin: "A rapprochement is necessary between the countries defeated in the World War, the countries which have been most hurt and robbed, and which, consequently, are in opposition to the dominating concert of the Great Powers." The Soviet Union was a field for unlimited economic development, and Germany could contribute the necessary machinery and technical skills therefor. Germany herself, afflicted with the claustrophobia of Versailles, was hungry to take a share in the exploitation of any *Lebensraum* as vastly unrestricted as the plains of Russia. The Reichswehr chiefs and the Red Army chiefs enjoyed intimate relations. Thus, whenever Germany felt weak, she turned eastward and invariably found there some solace from the pressure of the Western Powers. Throughout the Peace Conference of Paris in 1919 and the Ruhr episode in 1923, a Soviet-German *rapprochement* had been a very real threat. In 1922, at Rapallo, that *rapprochement* had become a fact (see p. 162). In 1926, just after Locarno, when the League of Nations had failed immediately to implement the Powers' promises of Germany's membership, Germany once more had turned eastward and signed with the Soviet Union a nonaggression pact, the Treaty of Berlin of April 1926 (see p. 140). The pact was extended by a Protocol signed in Moscow in June 1931. The Moscow Pact of 1939, which so astonished the world, had had its precedents indeed.

Early in the thirties, the Soviet Union was quick to revise its attitude to Germany. Its policy of general insurance against all external menace was being directed more specifically toward the rising German — and Japanese — challenge. In patent anticipation of developments West and East, the Soviet Union put in train a new series of nonaggression pacts in 1931 with Afghanistan, Turkey, and Lithuania, and these were extended in 1932 by similar pacts with Finland, Latvia, Estonia, and Poland. All these agreements signified by implication the renunciation of Russia's former historic expansionism in the Baltic, the Balkans, and the Near East. The Soviet Union signed no pact with Rumania, but it formally reaffirmed the Pact of Paris and the Litvinov Protocol with respect to Rumania, and thus assured the Rumanian Government that it had no designs on Bessarabia.[1] The Soviet security structure was crowned in November 1932 by the nonaggression pact with France, which we have noted elsewhere (see p. 479), and in 1933 by a similar convention with Italy. In 1933, at the World Economic Conference in London, Litvinov, who never missed an opportunity to press his policy of peace, proposed to the delegates from the signatory countries of the Litvinov Protocol that they should sign a multilateral convention defining aggression.[1] The proposal was accepted, and during July 1933 conventions to that effect were signed by the Soviet Union, Afghanistan, Estonia, Latvia, Persia, Poland, Rumania, Turkey, Lithuania, Czechoslovakia, Yugoslavia, and Finland. In November 1933, Litvinov was in Washington to exchange recognitions with President Roosevelt.

At the beginning of 1933 the United States was the only Great Power which had not established diplomatic relations with the Soviet Union. The United States had no need, economic or political, for such relations. An impenetrable official antagonism had dated from the time of the Bolshevik Revolution. The Communist "witch-hunting" of 1920 indicated the general attitude of the American administration and people, and the attitude had not relented through the prosperous twenties, despite the slowly growing commercial intercourse between the two countries, despite the many visits of American tourists and correspondents to Russia, despite the employment of American engineers and other technicians in Russia, or despite the forceful pleas of sympathetic American intellectuals.

But in the early thirties the situation had entirely changed. The continued nonrecognition of the Soviet Union was now a luxury which the United States could no longer afford. The Depression, the Japanese aggression in Manchuria, and to a less extent the establishment of Nazi power in Germany operated toward a reversal of the older policy. Moreover the Soviet Union itself was now a Power which it was unrealistic to ignore. The Soviet Government had long desired, and unmistakably hinted at, the desirability of a Soviet-American *rapprochement*. When Roosevelt was elected President, he set about translating the more favorable opinion in the United States into diplomatic action. First contacts were made between William C. Bullitt and Litvinov in London in July 1933 at the time of the World Economic Conference. In October, President Roosevelt by letter personally invited the Soviet President Kalinin to send representatives to explore "questions outstanding between our two countries," and in November, Litvinov arrived in Washington as special Soviet envoy. Formal Soviet-American relations were established by an exchange of letters between Roosevelt and Litvinov. Bullitt was appointed American ambassador in Moscow (see p. 597).

In 1934 the Soviet Union became a member state of the League of Nations. Here too was a reversal of attitude unthinkable a year or two before. Litvinov was now the champion of collective security and of co-operation with the "peace-loving" Powers of the world. Japan and Germany, potential enemies of the Soviet Union, were both on the point of withdrawing from the League. In the early part of 1934, Barthou had become Foreign Minister of France. He had roughly broken off negotiations for inducing Germany to return to the Disarmament Conference and had turned to the construction of a Grand Alliance, including the Soviet Union, for the containment of the Nazi Reich. Litvinov, once advocate of universal disarmament, now shared Barthou's vigorous realism and, at the resumed session of the Disarmament Conference in May 1932, he spoke of using the Conference not for its ostensible purpose of disarmament, but for the safeguarding of security and peace "by every possible means." On the same occasion he referred to the League of Nations in terms surprisingly and significantly different from the usual Soviet aspersions on that body. During the ensuing months, under Barthou's driving guidance, the ways were prepared for the Soviet's admission to the League. Soundings of individual member states showed, in fact, a remarkable unanimity in favor of admission. The only serious objector was Poland, who, since her nonaggression pact of January 1934 with Germany, had already seemed to have deserted "to the other side." Eventually, in September 1934, at the Fifteenth Assembly of the League, the Soviet Union was admitted to membership and to a permanent seat on the League Council.

Thereafter, till 1939, the Soviet Union acted as a loyal and enthusiastic member. Litvinov bore himself as the perfect League statesman. Barthou was assassinated in October 1934, as we have elsewhere described, and his Grand Alliance, in the form in which he had envisaged it, fell to the ground (pp. 488–89). But a reduced version of it came into being as the two mutual assistance pacts in May 1935 between the Soviet Union and France, and the Soviet Union and Czechoslovakia (see p. 492).

The Soviet Union had sought to repeat in the Far East the policy it had pursued in the Near East and West, though without the same success. The Japanese aggression in Manchuria in 1931 momentarily solved the perennial Soviet-Japanese rivalry in that area, but it provoked no strong Soviet countermeasures. In China, Chiang Kai-shek was anti-Soviet, his military advisers were German and, except for the regime of the Chinese Red Army in Kiangsi, Soviet influence in the Far East in these years was at a minimum. Litvinov strove manfully for a Soviet-Japanese nonaggression pact of the usual Soviet pattern, only to meet with nothing but rebuff. In March 1935, after protracted negotiations, the Soviet Union sold its interest in the Chinese Eastern Railway in Manchuria (or Manchukuo, as it then was) to Japan.

Rapprochements in the Far East had to wait for the full weight of events to develop. Further Japanese aggressions during 1933–35 in Jehol, Hopeh, and Chahar read their own object lessons both to the Soviet Union and to China. In March 1936 the Soviet Union signed a Protocol, virtually a nonaggression pact, with the Mongolian People's Republic. In November of the same year, Japan and Germany concluded their Anti-Comintern Pact. In August 1937, the month after the outbreak of "the China incident," the Soviet Union and China at long last signed a nonaggression pact.

PURGES AND TRIALS

In Chapter 18 we described the sabotage trials in the Soviet Union during the years 1928–33 (see pp. 286–88). The treason trials took place in the middle thirties. The two series of trials are not to be confused. The forensic techniques in both may have been similar; the occasions and purposes were widely different. But once more, it could be said, the theme was defense.

If English-speaking peoples have been free from invasion from without, they have also been free from invasions from within; their historic traitors have been rare, abnormal types, and they do not understand the empoisoned, dagger-thrust atmosphere in which some other peoples have habitually lived. The First World War was remarkable among wars for its almost total absence of treason and treachery in any of the belligerent camps. The treason trials in France in 1917 stand out as unique incidents for their time. But the Second World War told a different story. The lowering of moral standards as well as the rise of ideological loyalties at the expense of national loyalties were often in painful evidence. The Trojan Horse and the Fifth Column were well-known similes describing well-known phenomena. Quisling of Norway gave his name to his spiritual brothers in other lands. "Internal aggression," in Litvinov's phrase, was a recognized technique.

Revolutionary Russia was never free from some such internal aggression and, in view of the fears and phobias to which she was subject, its incidence and extent were easy to exaggerate. Interestingly enough, in the middle thirties, the Soviet Union was feeling its way to a more liberal regime. The first Five-Year Plan had drawn to an end and was officially acclaimed a triumphant success, and the second Five-Year Plan was well started on its way. Russian intellectuals and scientific workers were receiving back some of their old freedoms and privileges. Schools throughout the Soviet Union adopted less Russocentric curricula, especially in the teaching of history. There were rumors of an impending amnesty for many thousands of Social Democrats and other "deviators" then in exile in Siberia. The Ogpu became part of a specially created Commissariat of the Interior and thereafter was often called by the initials of this Commissariat, the N.K.V.D. Several kinds of political crime were removed from Ogpu jurisdiction — though, as once before in the reorganization of the political police in Russia, improvements in policy, personnel, and procedure were not immediately apparent. Younger folk began to borrow some of the trappings of Western culture; many of the men shaved and wore white collars; the women took to lipstick.

But then suddenly this happy process stopped. In 1933, Hitler came to power in Germany with his ferocious philippics against Communism and the "subhuman monsters" in the Kremlin. The late sabotage trials seemed to prove that the dark forces were still at work in Russia. On December 1, 1934, Sergei Kirov, one of Stalin's junior intimates and latterly party chief in Leningrad — and incidentally one of the supporters of the recent liberal trend — was assassinated. Since the murder of Uritsky in 1918, also the party chief of his day in Leningrad, no political crime of equal magnitude had been committed in Russia. One or two other assassinations had lately rent the peace of Europe — namely, of Ion Duca in Rumania, Dollfuss in Austria, and King Alexander of Yugoslavia and Barthou in France. All this was quite enough to stir up the old psychosis in Russia. Stalin and the inner Kremlin circle resolved on a veritable era of trials and purges.[2]

During December 1934, secret trials took place of dozens of "counter-revolutionary conspirators," many of foreign nationality, illegal entrants into Russia, and the greater number of them were summarily executed. In January 1935, Zinoviev and Kamenev, whose names had been mentioned in the diary of Kirov's assassin, were arrested and accused of having planned the murder of Kirov and of planning to murder Stalin with the aid, not only of Trotsky, but of the Nazi Gestapo. A plot was said to have been unearthed to detach the Ukraine from the Soviet Union; it was reported that the Nazis were holding Skoropadsky in Berlin, the Skoropadsky who had been puppet ruler of the Ukraine under the Austro-German occupation in 1918 and who was now allegedly being groomed as the Nazi governor of a future Ukrainian "Manchukuo" (see p. 262). Zinoviev was sentenced to ten years' imprisonment, and Kamenev to five.

For more than three years, in an atmosphere of mounting hysteria, the sanguinary inquisition continued. In August 1936, Zinoviev and Kamenev, together with other "Trotskyite" survivors, stood for retrial before the Supreme Military Tribunal, with Vyshinsky, Commissar for Justice, as state prosecutor. The defendants bore eloquent witness against each other, made fluent and highly dramatic confessions of their sins, and in general produced that picture of exaggerated self-immolation which we have since come to associate with Soviet trials. In the end all the defendants were sentenced to be shot, and their personal property was confiscated.

The trials did not interrupt the discussions that attended the drafting of the new Soviet constitution, eventually adopted in December 1936 — namely, the Stalin Constitution, which we described in Chapter 18 (pp. 290–91). On the contrary it has been argued that the blinding revelation of such widespread treachery in the Soviet Union was an additional reason, in Stalin's eyes, for the further solidification of his system in unassailable written form. December 1936 found the pogrom in Russia more ruthless and extensive than before. The Anti-Comintern Pact between Germany and Japan had just been signed with all its sinister implications for the Soviet state. Radek, once a leading light in the Comintern, was now under arrest, together with Sokolnikov, former Soviet ambassador in London, and Pyatakov, Vice-Commissar for Heavy Industry. Tomsky, President of the Trade-Union Council, committed suicide. Rykov, Lenin's successor as President of the Council of Commissars, was able for the moment to absolve himself from all charges. In January 1937, Radek, Sokolnikov, and Pyatakov were brought to trial for organizing a conspiracy "to expedite an armed attack on the Soviet Union, and to assist foreign aggressors to seize its territory." Radek and Sokolnikov were sentenced to ten years' imprisonment, and Pyatakov was shot. In April 1937, Yagoda, chief of the N.K.V.D., and self-styled "Swordbearer of the Revolution," was himself arrested for crimes committed during his term of office.

During 1937 tens of thousands were taken into custody, tried for alleged sabotage or conspiracy, and executed or exiled to remote parts of the Soviet Union. Separatist movements among the national minorities, notably in the Ukraine, suffered special persecution. There were wholesale administrative changes in the individual republics. Ten government heads, fifty commissars, and seven ranking party secretaries were removed from their offices. Priests, both Orthodox and Catholic, and even Moslem mullahs, were charged with espionage on behalf of Fascist Powers. Soviet ambassadors and diplomatic officials abroad were ordered home "to report." Karakhan, Vice-

Commissar for Foreign Affairs and former ambassador to China, was exe-cuted. Krylenko, Borodin, and other famous Bolsheviks in one way or another vanished from the scenes. Krivitsky escaped abroad. Even foreign residents, many of them Communist refugees in Russia — Béla Kun of Hun-gary was one — were imprisoned or deported.

In May 1937, Gamarnik, Chief of the Red Army Political Department, Vice-Commissar for War, and alleged associate of the late Pyatakov, commit-ted suicide. In June, a Supreme Military Tribunal, composed of Voroshilov, Budënny, and Bluecher, sentenced to death Marshal Tukhachevsky and seven other ranking generals of the Red Army, all former heroes of the Civil War, on charges of military conspiracy "with an unfriendly state."

Informed observers abroad gave several ingenious explanations of the trial of the generals. It was suggested that friction between the Red Army and the Soviet Government had already had a long history. Certainly the antagonism of soldiers and politicians has been a common phenomenon and one not exclusive to Russia. The Reichswehr and the Nazi party in Germany had occasionally been a recent example of that antagonism. Possibly the advent of Hitler had decided the Soviet Government to tighten up its control over the Red Army, a proceeding which the Soviet General Staff naturally re-sented. The Soviet and German general staffs, ever since the Treaty of Ra-pallo in 1922, had enjoyed a considerable intimacy, but whether that inti-macy now amounted to a conspirative deal against the Soviet Government we do not know. The generals were tried in camera by their own peers, in the presence of a hundred or more Red Army officers summoned from all over the Union; they confessed their guilt, and they were shot within twenty-four hours of receiving sentence. It is significant of the extraordinary condi-tion of the Soviet Union at this time that of the eight military judges at the trial, six were disgraced, degraded, or otherwise removed by the end of 1938, and only Marshals Voroshilov and Budënny remained in possession of their rank and position.

The last of the trials, in many ways the most important and most theatri-cal of them all, took place in March 1938. There were twenty-one defend-ants, among whom were Rykov, President of the Council of Commissars; Bukharin, editor of *Pravda* and one of the philosophers of Communism; Grinko, Commissar of Finance; Krestinsky, former ambassador in Berlin; Rakovsky, former ambassador in London and Paris; Rosengolz, head of the trade delegation in London; and Yagoda, former chief of the N.K.V.D. They were charged with conspiring with Trotsky and with the intelligence serv-ices of Germany and Japan to overthrow the Soviet Government. All con-fessed their guilt. Rykov, Bukharin, Grinko, Krestinsky, Rosengolz, and Yagoda were sentenced to death, and Rakovsky — then an old man in his seventieth year — to penal servitude for twenty years. At the end of 1938, two decades after the Revolution, of Bolsheviks prominent in Lenin's day there remained only Trotsky, in exile in Mexico, and Stalin and Molotov in Moscow.

The effect of these trials abroad was a mixture of mystification and horror. The year 1938 was the year of Hitler's Austrian coup and the year of Munich, the year of all years for a nation to appear sure, strong, and well-respected. But when, in 1938, the indefatigable Litvinov reaffirmed Soviet pledges to Czechoslovakia and France, and preached his jeremiads against the saboteurs of collective security, not a general staff in Europe believed for a moment that the Red Army, beheaded of scores of its ranking officers, shaken and demoralized, was in any position to support so bold a policy. The French in particular again and again avoided staff talks with the Red Army chiefs, any one of whom, it seemed, might suddenly be moved to confess to the most heinous treacheries and divulge vital military secrets. When Colonel Lindbergh, for instance, reported unfavorably upon the Soviet Air Force, his words fell upon already well-seeded soil; and when the Soviet forces in 1940 took so long to crack the defenses of the little republic of Finland, military authorities throughout the world merely felt that they had been confirmed in their low estimate of Soviet military prowess. Yet it now seems undeniable that the Great Purge strengthened the Soviet home front. The Soviet Union fought the Second World War free from Trojan Horses and Fifth Columns. "We shot our traitors," said a Soviet diplomat to a French interlocutor. "You made Cabinet ministers of yours!"

RETROSPECT AND PROSPECT

The historian or commentator of contemporary affairs, trying to be impartial, must find the appraisal of the Soviet experiment in Russia the most difficult of all the tasks with which this Age of Conflict confronts him. He may read every book and article, he may hear every lecture and broadcast, he may take part in every discussion on Russia that comes his way; he may even go to Russia himself. Yet, as he increaseth knowledge, he increaseth confusion, and his confusion will be aggravated by the feeling of the paramount importance of his subject and the paramount need for coming to final conclusions with it. In the question of Russia, as he well knows, he is not only being asked to judge the past but to see into the future, for Russia is the great hope or the great fear of every man.

The Russia of our day is for most of us a ferment of contradictory and emotionally overcharged associations. On the one hand, we have the known and well-attested barbarities of the Soviet regime, the party tyranny, the arrests and tortures, the liquidations and the labor camps, the malicious falsifications of Soviet propaganda, and latterly the exasperating methods of Soviet statesmanship in conference. On the other hand, we have a sense of the bigness and vision of the whole Soviet experiment, of an avid optimism and confidence that sometimes puts to shame our older civilization of the West. We have recollections of the Russian story in the Second World War and of the heroism on the part of the common Russian soldier before which the Verduns and Ypres of the earlier war seem almost like pale and faded legends. We have powerful intimations of great futures in gestation. How are we to integrate all this, and read rhyme and reason into it? How are we to reduce it to what interests us most in our present study — to a positive interpretation of Russian behavior on the international plane?

Soviet foreign policy can be explained in part — as we have already tried to explain it, and as Soviet propaganda explains it — as defensive pure and simple. Yet the explanation hardly squares with the long tradition of Russian pressure toward the Baltic, the Balkans, the Near and Far East. Constantinople and the Dardanelles, Northern Persia, and Manchuria have been the persistent objectives both of the Tsarist and the Soviet empires. Soviet territory shrank in the period of the Civil War in 1918–20 only to expand once more at the expense of separatist movements of border nationalities. In 1920 the Red Army carried the revolutionary advance to Warsaw. Today, after the parallel contraction and expansion of the Second World War, the Soviet Union incorporates territories in Europe beyond its frontiers in 1939 and indeed beyond the Russian frontiers of 1914. And meanwhile Comintern and Cominform have waged an unlimited aggressive ideological crusade.

It may be that we should not always look for too simplified interpretations of historical facts and processes. Simplification is the academic fault par excellence. The Russian people, it has been said, have always been "a compound of incompatibles," defying the neat detachment of the lecture room and textbook. Their history has been one of unexampled suffering and complexity, and is reflected in their national character. Tolstoy and Dostoevsky, Lenin and Stalin have a place in that character. The deep religiousness that was once the mark of "the Russian soul" and the strident atheism of the modern Communist have a place in that character. The Russian people appear to us to be at once inconstant and tenacious, servile and rebellious, loyal and anarchic, orthodox and schismatic, licentious and ascetic. They contain the dualism of East and West; they oscillate between extremes. They have many of the traits both of a primitive and sophisticated people. In themselves, they can be kindly, sociable, zestful, full of humor, frank, and sincere. They are curious and suspicious of the stranger, yet instinctively hospitable to him. Generally — though unhappily not always — they are free of that moral deformity which has marred the modern European revolutionary, notably the Nazi German. But so often all the more sympathetic and likable traits of the Russian people have been hidden behind a curtain of artificially created and protective xenophobia or otherwise denied by the way of life which, from time to time, political circumstances have forced them to lead and by the kind of government which, from time to time, they have permitted to rule over them.

There is not — and never was, and never will be — a short answer to the question, "What do the Russians want?" Foreign policies, like the national characters they express, are often changeable and inconsistent. Peoples, like individuals, have many moods and motives, and they can entertain quite happily within their collective consciousness, and even unware that they are doing so, the most surprising contradictions. And the Russians are not only separated from our Western understandings by their peculiar temperamental gulf, but they have been passing through a phase of their history which has produced in them more than their usual psychic conflicts.

Happily — or perhaps unhappily — Communist doctrinal writing provides us with one insight into our problem. For Communism is nothing without doctrine. We suggested elsewhere that the mark of Fascism and Nazism was their absence of philosophy (pp. 307–08 and 464–70). We might now suggest that the mark of Communism is too much philosophy. Marxist Communism is almost alone among the great historic ideologies and cults that have stirred mankind in that it sprang into being fully armed with a definite, intellectually argued, officially promulgated doctrine. Something of the doctrine we discussed in Chapter 17, but mainly in so far as it was embodied in the Soviet governmental structure. It remains to discuss now, not so much the doctrine itself, but the effects and implications of the very *existence* of a doctrine of such extraordinary rigidity, sufficiency, and finality.

Many a student of modern politics has remarked how elusive, in the superficial view, are the differences between democracy and Communism. Democracy and Communism, as seen today in practice, may seem to be poles apart. The free institutions of the one have little in common with the totalitarian institutions of the other. The popular assemblies of a democracy, even with their party "machines" and occasional corruptions, are hardly comparable with a one-party dictatorship of any kind. But, beyond this, the deeper sources of the antagonism of democracy and Communism are not so easy to discover. Historically, both have grown out of popular revolts against tyranny and want. Both seek to order this earthly scheme of things for the betterment of "the underprivileged and disinherited." Both ostensibly are kinds of "welfare politics." And if democracy sets high values on the individual human creature and regards the state as his servant, Communism predicts the eventual and total disappearance of the state so as to leave the individual to enjoy his rights and freedoms unmolested.

But democracy has never been a theoretic "system." Its doctrinal basis, ultimately and historically, is Christianity. Freedom of speech and of assembly, representative government and majority decisions are its means, not its ends. They are the technical, administrative, empirically tested means of securing a way of life — in the last analysis, Christian. If the Rights of Man or the Four Freedoms could have been better secured under absolute monarchy, then doubtless under absolute monarchy would Western democratic man have continued to grow and flourish. But it was the experience of our fathers that absolutism, however "benevolent," corrupts the monarch and destroys those things that are most desired in life. Democracy believes in no utopia. It is not perfectionist. It only seeks to give as practical an approximation to the basic human rights and freedoms as may reasonably be expected in an imperfect world. It does not look forward to a day when man will cease to be evil and when all crime and correction shall be done away. It only knows what is better, not what is best. Christian-like, it puts its heaven in a problematic future, not entirely within man's control. Democracy has never committed the offense of the builders of the Tower of Babel.

Democracy is a practical, pragmatic, evolutionary process that never ends. Its history is the history of experiment, a series of "New Deals," judged by their limited success. Communism, by contrast, is a theoretic system, a rigid, unalterable creed, once enunciated by a prophet, thence sacrosanct and applicable in its totality to any historic situation. It is a revolutionary, cata-strophic process, a sort of secular apocalypse. Its series of "Five-Year Plans" is to be forced through to completion irrespective, and even contemptuous, of "success." The Communist says, "This and this is the shape of things to come; it can be no other." The democrat says, "Perhaps, but first let's see it work." The Communist does not proceed by trial and error. He makes no final allowance for human frailty. He has no counterpart in his creed for original sin. Dialectical materialism and historic necessity are working on his side, and all he needs is the right tactic for the moment to hasten the inevitable, inexorable process. Success or failure neither proves nor disproves his thesis. Communism is true, not because it *works,* but because it is *the* doctrine. The Communist in his extreme *Theoristerei* is reminiscent of the German professor who proclaimed that Germany could not have lost the war in 1918 because that would not have conformed with "the German idea."

In the West our criterion of scientific truth is verifiability, and has been so since the Renaissance. The Russian, who stood on the periphery of the Renaissance and never wholly participated in it, equates truth quasi-scholas-tically with conformity to dogma. Democratic "truth" operates through com-promise, toleration, and the cross-fertilization of opposing views. Communist "truth" is vested in an uncompromising, intolerant, oracular, literal ortho-doxy. We must entirely miss the rationale of Communist propaganda, for instance, if we judge it by democratic or Western scientific standards. Com-munism will distort mere fact, it will rewrite mere history, it will even re-write biology that does not suit it — and this, not out of malice but out of high sincerity and righteous purpose.

The devotion of Communist writers to what seems to us to be no more than dialectical subtleties is strange and alien to our Western habits of mind. Stalin himself, as his writings show, was infinitely painstaking with the minu-tiae of doctrine. And this was not an amiable eccentricity, a pedantic weak-ness permitted to an otherwise busy and hardheaded man, but fundamental to his faith and training as a Communist. "The Party must be armed with revolutionary theory, with a knowledge of the laws of the movement, with a knowledge of the laws of revolution," he writes. "Without this it will be incapable of directing the struggle of the proletariat. . . ." In Leninist-Marxism Stalin clearly believed he possessed a view of human society and history, an exact science, a detailed and infallible instrument with which to orient himself to any political situation, with which "to grasp the internal connection of surrounding events, to foresee the course of events and to discern not only how and when these events are developing in the present but also how and when they must develop in the future." It is enough to notice, in this connection, the extent to which, in the Soviet Union, the writ-ten text has become endowed with irrefutable sanctity. The works of Marx, Lenin, and now of Stalin are pored over and revered in a way that recalls the Nazi fanatic's attitude to *Mein Kampf.* Publishing statistics are indicative and striking. *The Problems of Leninism,* Stalin's basic work, which bids fair to become Russian Communism's fundamentalist scripture, had up to 1947 run into eleven editions and 4,000,000 copies, and Stalin's *History of the All-Union Communist Party* into more than 30,000,000 copies.[3]

Our democratic ideology goes back to John Locke and other empiricists. Burke, in a famous passage, in the full democratic tradition, deplored "geometry and metaphysics in politics." Communist ideology goes back to Marx and through Marx to that "systematizer of system," Hegel. The two streams of ideas could never mix. It is not just that they disagree, but that their premises, their temperament, their entire thought and language find no common meeting point. There is no reconciliation between the state of mind that wrote *An Essay concerning Human Understanding* and the state of mind that wrote *The Phenomenology of the Spirit*. More distantly still, democratic ideology goes back to the deep sources of our Christian culture. And, if sometimes we forget that culture, we cannot deny that we in the West live in a climate of values derived from two millennia of Christianity and more particularly from the half millennium of Christianity since the Renaissance and Reformation. But, if we do forget that culture, then even more so are we at a disadvantage in dealing with another ideology which so positively knows, and exults in, its origins.

The opportunism of Communist politics is no derogation of the ultimate theoretical objective. The party "line" is tactical, a stratagem permitted and encouraged when it is felt to be necessary. "To carry on a war for the overthrow of the international bourgeoisie," writes Stalin, again quoting Lenin, "a war which is a hundred times more difficult, protracted and complicated than the most stubborn of ordinary wars between states, and to refuse beforehand to manoeuvre, to utilize the conflict of interests (even though temporary) among one's enemies, to refuse to temporize and compromise with possible (even though transient, unstable, vacillating and conditional) allies — is not this ridiculous in the extreme? Is it not the same as though, when making a difficult ascent of an unexplored and heretofore inaccessible mountain, we were to refuse beforehand ever to move in zigzags, ever to retrace our steps, ever to abandon the course once selected and to try others?" [4] But, be it noted, in these zigzags and maneuverings the mountain bedrock does not shift or change. Thus Brest Litovsk, the NEP, "Socialism in one country," the Moscow Pact, the dissolution of the Comintern, all the varying *rapprochements* with Western diplomacy, the pliant methods of Communist parties abroad, the occasional participation in parliamentary socialism, the very Soviet system itself, all these are temporary accommodations to be used only so long as they are tactically advantageous.

It is of interest to recall that the resolution of the Fourteenth Party Congress in 1925, adopting Stalin's thesis of "Socialism in one country," justified itself with quotations from Lenin's writings on the ultimate necessity of world revolution: "There is not the slightest doubt that a final victory of our revolution, if it remained isolated, if there were no revolutionary movements in other countries, would be hopeless . . . The existence of the Soviet republic side by side with imperialist states for a prolonged period is unthinkable. In the end either one or the other will conquer. . . . In order to achieve a solid victory, we must achieve the victory of the proletarian revolution in all, or at any rate in several, of the chief capitalist countries." [5] And it is of interest also to read, in the context of these passages, Stalin's own still valid and accepted affirmation:

"The dictatorship of the proletariat, the transition from capitalism to Communism, must not be regarded as a fleeting period of 'super-revolutionary' acts and decrees, but as an entire historical era, replete with civil wars and external conflicts, with persistent organizational work and economic construction, with advances and retreats, victories and defeats." [4]

"The law of violent proletarian revolution, the law of the smashing of the bourgeois state machine as a preliminary condition for such a revolution, is an inevitable law of the revolutionary movement in the imperialist countries of the world." [4]

"Without [a stubborn, continuous and determined struggle against the imperialist chauvinism of the Socialists of the ruling nations — Britain, France, the United States, Italy, Japan, etc.] — without such a struggle the education of the working class of the ruling nations in the spirit of true internationalism, in the spirit of *rapprochement* with the toiling masses of the dependent countries and colonies, in the spirit of real preparation for the proletarian revolution, is inconceivable. . . . Without this it would have been impossible to consolidate the Soviet power, to implant true internationalism and to create that remarkable organization for the collaboration of nations which is called the Union of Soviet Socialist Republics — the living prototype of the future union of nations in a single world economic system." [4]

"The victorious proletariat [of one country] having expropriated the capitalists and organized its own Socialist production, would stand up against the rest of the capitalist world, attracting to its cause the oppressed classes of other countries, raising revolt among them against the capitalists, and, in the event of necessity, come out even with armed force against the exploiting classes and their states." [4]

If this is the authentic voice of the Soviet Union, the former question we have discussed as to the defensiveness or aggressiveness of Soviet foreign policy takes on an almost irrelevant, unreal, and outmoded air. The quotations would seem to represent not a democratic debater's modest statement of a point of view, but a philosophy, a dogma, a declaration of faith of absolute certitude. They reveal a sort of eschatological world picture, a social and historical *reality*, in which the faithful Communist believes as a literal necessity. All other world pictures are heresy or fraud. What credence then, we may now ask, is to be put on Soviet professions of peace, however often or in whatever form repeated, so long as the official Soviet doctrine, uttered at the highest levels of infallibility, uncompromising, predetermined, and unalterable, is a doctrine of universal war?

35 FRANCE: TURMOIL AND SCANDAL

THE END OF PROSPERITY

France had withstood the first onset of the Depression with extraordinary resilience, and she was for a time an almost freakish oasis of prosperity and financial power in the midst of a desolate world. During 1930 the gold reserve of the Bank of France rose from 40,000,000,000 to 80,000,000,000 francs, the budget showed a surplus, and on one occasion the Premier, Tardieu, was so guilty of misjudgment — and of bad taste — as to declare his belief that France would continue to escape the economic ills which were then afflicting every other nation in the world. France's position was in strange contrast to her unhappy state of five years before (see p. 398).

In January 1931, Pierre Laval became Premier of France. He was a comparative newcomer. He was provincial born — his father had kept a café and butcher shop at Châteldon in Auvergne. He was always proud to call himself "a man of the people." He spent his early life in Paris as "a poor man's lawyer" and legal adviser to trade-unions. At that time he was regarded as a dangerous Socialist and revolutionary, and he was certainly one of the defeatists of the First World War. But he gradually matured into an exponent of thrifty conservative administration, a successful negotiator of workers' strikes, and he entered high politics, appropriately, as Minister of Labor, first under Poincaré in 1926 and then under Tardieu in 1930. He was Premier throughout 1931 at the heyday of France's financial supremacy, and he rode roughshod over all Europe. He may be said to have been responsible for those triumphs of French policy in that year, namely, the failure of the Austro-German Customs Union and the comparative failure of the Hoover Moratorium. Brüning, the German Chancellor, came to Paris like a humble suppliant at the table of the international Dives. In October 1931, Laval visited Washington and all but dictated to President Hoover of the United States (see pp. 405, 406, and 407).

But France's financial supremacy was not to last. Laval resigned in February 1932. The budget of that year was very different from the surplus budget of 1930. France too had now become a resentful, bewildered, and very frightened victim of the universal Depression. The Lausanne reparations settlement was a catastrophe, and so also — but in a different way — was the repudiation of the French war debt to the United States (see pp. 409 and 411). General elections swung back to the Left, and through 1932 and 1933 there was a succession of Radical Socialist premiers, such as Herriot, Daladier, Sarraut, and Chautemps. The slaughter of governments was a sure sign of the resumption of France's chronic Battle of the Budget. Extreme rightist interests were already launching an antiparliamentary campaign, and the Fascist "Leagues" began to appear in France in evident imitation of Italian and German prototypes. During the elections of May 1932, President Doumer was assassinated by a Russian *émigré* in Paris. The crime had no political implications, though, at the time, the Right tried to exploit it much as the British Conservatives had tried to exploit the "Red Letter" of evil memory (see p. 329). Albert Lebrun, then president of the Senate, was unanimously elected President of the Republic in succession to Doumer. In January 1934 the Stavisky affair burst upon the country.

THE STAVISKY AFFAIR AND THE SIXTH OF FEBRUARY

Serge Alexandre Stavisky was an unsavory scoundrel. Born in Kiev in the eighties, the son of a Jewish dentist, he emigrated with his parents to Paris. He was given a good education, and at one time was intended for medicine. But he drifted into petty crime, blackmail, forgery, and the drug traffic, and became a confirmed hanger-on of the Parisian underworld. He essayed the first of his bigger frauds in 1926, when he swindled 7,500,000 francs out of a stockbroker. He was arrested, but then "provisionally" released, and his trial was postponed. The transaction, however, whetted his appetite, and he now went on from strength to strength. He posed as a great financier, frequented fashionable vacation resorts, and cultivated an extraordinary variety of political friendships. He promoted bogus companies, backed a vaudeville theater, and bought up one or two boulevard journals. In December 1933 the authorities began to make inconvenient inquiries into his management of the Bayonne municipal pawnshop.[1] On January 8, 1934, at a villa near Chamonix, he was found by the police with a bullet through his head, apparently a suicide. It was suggested that the police themselves had shot him to prevent his revealing damaging information.

At any other time the Stavisky affair would have stirred no more than a muddy ripple. France had had other financial scandals before, and mass hysteria was something of a periodical phenomenon. But in 1934, France was more than ordinarily depressed, and the affair seemed to point unanswerably to the incompetence and corruption not only of recent governments in France, but of the entire principle of liberal democracy. Chautemps, now Premier, drew considerable suspicion on himself by refusing to appoint a parliamentary committee of inquiry into Stavisky's past immunity from arrest, presumably because Chautemps' brother-in-law was head of the Paris parquet, a body which initiated official prosecutions. It was easy enough for the Royalist paper, *L'Action Française,* to link Stavisky with Chautemps and with the Radical Socialist party, and hint, with great parade of circumstantial evidence, that the archswindler in the course of his career had enjoyed considerable protection from persons highly placed. At the end of January 1934, Chautemps resigned office.

Daladier returned to the premiership determined to form "an above-party government of strong men." He dismissed Chiappe, the Prefect of Police, who had been showing too much indulgence toward recent rightist demonstrations in the streets of Paris. But, however justified Chiappe's dismissal might have been, it weakened and demoralized the police force at a critical moment, the more so as Chiappe's second-in-command was then in the hospital undergoing an operation. On the afternoon of February 6, 1934, Daladier and his new government confronted the Chamber, and he was virtually howled down in the middle of his Ministerial Declaration. Meanwhile, across the Seine from the Chamber of Deputies, in the Place de la Concorde, various patriotic and League organizations had begun to assemble and were shortly battling the police. By nightfall, outright fighting had developed. In so far as they had any objective at all, the rioters tried to force the police cordon on the Pont de la Concorde and, had they succeeded, they would probably have made fire and havoc of the Chamber of Deputies. They tore up the street paving for ammunition and made very effective use of pieces of iron railing from the near-by Tuileries Gardens. They slashed at the horses of the mounted police with razors tied onto the ends of walking sticks. Automobiles and busses were overturned and set on fire. In the end 20 rioters and a policeman were killed, and well over 1,000 rioters, police, and spectators were more or less seriously injured. Nothing like it had been seen in Paris since the Commune. Nevertheless, despite riots without and hubbub within, the Chamber passed a vote of confidence in Daladier by a fair majority. But the next day, faced with the prospect of more disorders and bloodshed, Daladier resigned. It was particularly ominous that a government which had just won the confidence of the Chamber should be frightened out of office by "the blackmail of the street."

On February 8, 1934, Gaston Doumergue, onetime President of the Republic, came out of his retirement, like Poincaré in 1926, to form an emergency cabinet of all parties but the Socialists and Communists, and like Poincaré's cabinet in 1926, Doumergue's seemed to be a veritable galaxy of former premiers. Barthou was his Foreign Minister and Marshal Pétain his Minister of War. He appointed two committees, one to investigate the Stavisky affair and another to investigate the riots of "the Sixth of February." But the streets were still in ferment. Socialist and Communist trade-unions, on February 12, combined to organize a general strike — the germ, as it afterward proved, of the Popular Front — in protest against Fascism. On February 21 the truncated body of Albert Prince, a magistrate who might have been one of the principal witnesses in Doumergue's investigating committees, was found on the railroad tracks near Dijon in circumstances which pointed to an elaborate and particularly horrible suicide. Other suicides and attempted suicides followed. For weeks Paris lived in a daze of arrests, grillings, confessions, and deepening suspicion. Prominent names were recklessly bandied about. The press made jubilee, and with that unscrupulous license which French journalism enjoyed, and supported no doubt by that underground political bribery which French journalism also enjoyed, it revealed — or invented — the most intricate ramifications of public corruption.

Distracted though she might be at home, France followed a vigorous foreign policy in 1934. She bestirred herself to make a last effort to stop the rot in the international situation. Barthou, Doumergue's Foreign Minister, was a former chairman of the Reparation Commission and Poincaré's old colleague in the invasion of the Ruhr. He toured Europe, putting new strength into France's bemused and wavering allies. He obtained the Soviet

Union's admission to the League of Nations and prepared the way for the Franco-Soviet Mutual Assistance Pact. The full account of Barthou's diplomacy and his tragic end has been given elsewhere (see p. 488).

The Fascist "Leagues" in France had a flashy dangerousness, which in retrospect seems rather to recede in importance. But they were a symptom of the time, and they showed that Fascist ways and works could be attractive even to men of the independent fiber of the normal Frenchman. There were several kinds of these "Leagues," such as the Royalist *Camelots du Roi*, who were the storm troopers of the *Action Française;* the chauvinistic *Jeunesse Patriote;* and the pseudo-Bonapartist *Solidarité Française*, founded by the perfumer, François Coty. Of them all, the *Croix de Feu* was the best known and most influential. It had been founded in 1927 as an exclusive veterans' organization and had originally admitted to membership only first-line men who had been decorated for bravery. But it had gradually become involved in politics and identified its interests with the upper middle class. Its program, Fascist-like, was opportunist but always fiercely patriotic, antiparliamentarian and, of course, anti-Communist. By 1933-34, it had over 30,000 members and various affiliated youth groups. It was highly organized, possessed a certain quantity of firearms and even one or two airplanes, and specialized in sudden and ubiquitous mobilizations. Its members always wore a characteristic beret. Its leader was a Colonel de la Rocque, a professional soldier, not a scintillating personality, but able to create a *mystique* of his own. He maintained an unofficial connection with the army — herein lay the real menace of his movement — and any revolutionary action he might have essayed would probably have taken the form of a military coup in the regular Napoleonic tradition.

De la Rocque described Doumergue's government as "a poultice on a gangrenous leg," but his actual relations with Doumergue were closer than he allowed to be known. Doumergue, it was said, was trying to use de la Rocque much as Papen had once tried to use Hitler. But Doumergue was already digging his own political grave. A vain, pompous old man, at the head of an emergency cabinet, he had come to regard himself as indispensable, and took to giving patronizing broadcasts to the nation almost in the style of royalty. He revived Millerand's former attempted reforms of the presidential office, and was at once accused by the Left of brazenly maneuvering to smuggle dictatorship into France (see p. 317). On October 9, 1934, his Foreign Minister, Barthou, and King Alexander of Yugoslavia were assassinated at Marseille. But even without this blow, Doumergue's popularity was very shaken. In November 1934 he and his emergency cabinet resigned. At the last he allowed himself to be seen in public, in company with de la Rocque, a decrepit, half-senile figure, crowned with the Rocquian beret. Doumergue, after all, was far from indispensable, and his departure did not result in a revival of the street riots which had originally brought him into office.

THE POPULAR FRONT

Flandin, who had been appearing in ministerial posts since Laval's government in 1931, succeeded Doumergue in the premiership, and brought back to office with him most of Doumergue's outgoing cabinet. Laval, his former patron, was his Foreign Minister. The events of Flandin's term in the international field, the Franco-Italian Agreement, the Saar plebiscite, the German conscription decree, the Stresa Front Conference, the Franco-Soviet Pact, and the beginning of the Italo-Ethiopian crisis, have already been described. They were events disturbing enough to take the minds of most Frenchmen off their domestic affairs. Doumergue's controversy over the presidential prerogatives lapsed, and even the ardor of the "Leagues" was chilled for a time. In February 1935, Flandin introduced a bill to prolong the military service of certain classes in order to tide over "the lean years" when, as the result of the lowered birth rate during the First World War, there would now be a heavy decrease in France's young man power. It was this bill which Germany used as a pretext for her conscription decree (see p. 491).

Domestically Flandin's term of office was taken up with finance. The Depression was becoming unendurably heavy. The old familiar specters of an unbalanced budget and an endlessly growing public debt haunted the peace of France. The gold standard, however, was obstinately retained, and in the Chamber, in the intervals between the current international crises, the deflationists and the inflationists disputed the merits of their respective philosophies. In the spring months of 1935 there was a run on the franc of almost panic proportions. Bouisson followed Flandin in May 1935, in a government that lasted one day; Laval followed Bouisson till he was ousted in January 1936, shortly after the collapse of the Hoare-Laval Plan; Sarraut was in office at the time of Hitler's Rhineland coup of March 1936.

Meanwhile a new oscillation to the Left was in preparation. It was partly the inevitable reaction to the series of rightist governments which had begun with Doumergue. But it had novel and interesting features. It was to be a more ambitious and spectacular Cartel than the Cartel of 1924, and more than a mere accommodation for election purposes. This time it was to be a Popular Front which combined all three parties of the Left — Radical Socialists, Socialists, and Communists. Doubtless "the Sixth of February," the general strike of February 12, 1934, and the subsequent provocations of the Fascist "Leagues" had contributed to its formation. More particularly, France and the Soviet Union were enjoying a moment of *rapprochement;* the Franco-Soviet Mutual Assistance Pact was signed in May 1935 (see p. 492), and the Comintern in Moscow had lately been instructing the French Communists to act collaboratively. On Bastille Day, July 14, 1935, Radical Socialists, Socialists, and Communists held a monster demonstration in Paris, and Daladier the Radical Socialist, Blum the Socialist, and Thorez the Communist were seen marching arm in arm at the head of one of the processions. At the general election in the spring of 1936, the Popular Front won a convincing victory.

ᴊt government on
ᴊ ministerial list, but
ᴊy to the Popular Front
Yvon Delbos was Foreign
ᴊvernment were women — a

ᴊrance had tried a fresh political
Herriot's Cartel, Poincaré's National
Government, and now Blum's Popular
ᴊay as the definitive cure of the country's
had a new "savior"; five time it was pre-
ᴊnd of fluctuating governments and stabi-
ᴊme of enduring beneficence; five times great
ᴊnd bathos. In 1936, Blum came to office with
ᴊze of expectancy. Contemporary historians com-
ᴊ; the foreign press glowed with sympathetic an-

ᴊping reforms. He dissolved the "Leagues." He "de-
ᴊf France, that stronghold of reaction, and gave its
ᴊst shareholders a vote apiece along with its 40,000
with the result that a majority of the Bank's Board of
ᴊnceforth be appointed by the government. He took steps
ᴊe armament and aircraft industries. For the workers he
ᴊng-cherished program, a forty-hour week, vacations with
labor contracts, and a scale of minimum wages.
ᴊever had a chance. If he had come, as Herriot had come, in the
peace of 1924, he might have fulfilled his mission, and France
ᴊld would have been the better and happier for it. Clearly he
ᴊe France a New Deal, but circumstances over which he had no
ᴊarried him like an evil genius. The famous sit-down strikes were
in full swing when his government was formed and, according to one
ᴊ, a million workers were "in occupation" of their factories in mid-
ᴊr of 1936. The flight of capital, which had begun under Flandin, con-
ᴊ. In September 1936 the franc was devalued 30 per cent, and a tripar-
ᴊgreement was entered into with Britain and the United States for the
ᴊol of the three exchanges. But the devaluation of the franc, while bene-
ᴊ to foreign exchange, had the effect of raising prices in France and more
ᴊ offset the wage increases which the workers had been gaining. The
ᴊist "Leagues" had been officially dissolved, but that did not prevent their
ᴊppearing under altered names. Nor did it prevent the emergence of other
ᴊolitical eccentricities like the Popular party of the former Communist,
ᴊacques Doriot or the grotesque Fascist secret society, the Cagoulards, or
Hooded Men. A new "European Order" was being preached by the Neo-
Socialist, Marcel Déat, and closer Franco-German "cultural understanding"
by Ferdinand de Brinon. Meanwhile civil war had broken out in Spain,
where a legitimate Republican government, also bearing the name of a
Popular Front, was battling for its existence against Fascist reaction and

against the intervention of Germany and Italy, the potential enemies of France. Blum, in short, was continually distracted by matters extraneous but indirectly damaging to his program. He was like a man trying to preach a sermon in an air raid. It might have been a good sermon, but somehow it was beside the point, and the congregation, through no fault of the preacher, was not very attentive.

Superficially the year 1937 was not one of striking events. It was the year in which Hitler promised no "surprises," and France reflected the uneasy calm of her eastern neighbor (see p. 613). It was also the year of the Paris Exposition with its eccentric architecture along the banks of the Seine and deceptive display of returning prosperity and universal brotherhood. Blum meanwhile made less and less headway against his difficulties. He appealed for "a pause, so that we may consolidate the ground we have conquered," which meant that his government was to be absolved from initiating further reforms, especially if they involved increased expenditure. In June 1937, Blum resigned. Chautemps formed a cabinet, ostensibly a continuation of Blum's, and several of the outgoing ministers reappeared in his "Republican Combination," as he called it. But he relied increasingly on Radical Socialist support, and the Communists were no longer being instructed to act collaboratively. Blum remained Vice-President; Yvon Delbos remained Foreign Minister; Georges Bonnet was specially brought over from his ambassadorship in Washington to be Finance Minister and the new wizard that was to save the franc.

In December 1937, Yvon Delbos made his grand tour of France's allied capitals — Warsaw, Bucharest, Belgrade, and Prague. It was not the triumphal progress of Barthou's similar tour of three years before. At Warsaw, Colonel Beck declared that the time was ripe for demonstrating "the vitality, strength, and permanence" of the Franco-Polish alliance. At Bucharest, Tatarescu and Antonescu were still in power and anxious to be cordial. At Prague, Beneš responded with enthusiasm when he described his country as "a very extension (un prolongement) of France." Only in Belgrade did Stoyadinovich — then flirting with the Axis — give him an unmistakably chilly reception; but, as if in compensation, the pro-French demonstrations which greeted him in the streets of Belgrade were spontaneous and convincing.

But there was something, something not quite satisfying. In 1936, France had failed to prevent Hitler's remilitarization of the Rhineland, and France's entire strategic situation vis-à-vis her Eastern and Central European allies had been fundamentally changed. The Spanish Civil War, it is true, caused less agony of conscience in France than might have been expected. Public opinion in France, as in Britain, was refusing to face up to the facts in Spain. But France's pusillanimous Spanish policy was also torturing to her European allies. While the Popular Front in France had been trying to pursue its social revolution in its own artificial vacuum — and that none too successfully — its Spanish namesake and spiritual affiliate was being denied legitimate and desperately needed assistance, and the Fascist Powers were driving forward to yet another of their undeserved victories. Delbos, in fact, had returned from his grand tour far from sure of himself. Somehow, somehow the glory was departed from France.

In April 1938, Daladier again became Premier. He was Premier during the Munich crisis and at the outbreak of the Second World War.

RETROSPECT

Judgments on France, such as were common in 1940, often had the tone of funeral orations. It is pitiable to have witnessed the collapse of a great nation and a great civilizing Power. But the historical method gives a very limited view. We can describe wartime casualties and expenditures, the changes of governments and parties, the ups and downs of the franc, the behavior of labor and industry, the reaction to events abroad. All this is statistical stuff. The imponderables which really matter, the spirit and the morale of the people, cannot be more than hinted at. The history of France in the thirties is best told perhaps not in straightforward historical narrative, but in a play or novel, or even in a string of anecdotes.[2]

Many of the causes to which the great catastrophe have been attributed are only partial explanations. For instance, France lost over a million men in the First World War, a loss from which she never properly recovered. But Germany lost proportionately, and Russia more than proportionately, yet both afterward showed an unimpaired capacity for self-preservation. The defensive mentality, the Maginot complex, the *avare du sang*, the lack of a sense of adventure and experiment certainly derived from the deteriorating demography of France. The population was stationary, if not at the point of decline, and the depleted country could not afford the human expenditures of another war. In 1939, even with the return of Alsace-Lorraine, the French-born population of France did not exceed the figure in 1913. The basic, haunting, irremediable fact was always that France, a stationary nation of forty millions, could not fight on even terms with a rearmed Germany, a still-expanding nation of seventy millions, whose industrial output was three times as great as her own.

Under the circumstances French foreign policy could not be otherwise than weak. The old Right, the heirs of Poincaré and Barthou, hitherto the stanchest supporters of a strong foreign policy, by 1939 had become even more pacifist than the traditionally pacifist Left. The normal ideology of the Right was complicated by the fear of Communism. "Better Hitler than the Popular Front" was the common slogan. And the Left, by contrast, was often aggressively bellicose. Many Frenchmen could see no end to the routine repetition of Continental wars except in the absorption of the nations of Western Europe into a New Order, a sort of twentieth century Carolingian Empire — whether under German hegemony or not, whether under a totalitarian Führer or not, mattered little if peace were to be assured.

But wartime losses and demography did not account for the perversions and treacheries to which France was subject in these years. French political life was undoubtedly very corrupt. The constitution and the financial and party systems were undoubtedly out of date. The press was often suborned by vested interests and by foreign Powers. Recurrent "affairs" uncovered scandals which surprised even the cynics. Public servants had long since forsaken the tradition of responsibility. It was not that crosscurrents of propaganda were, say, Fascist or Communist, but that they were deliberately, satanically subversive, and the subversion had become an end in itself. And what was even more destructive than this was the presence of "sincere traitors," fired with missionary zeal, men of intellectual ability, like Déat, Doriot, de Brinon, who genuinely believed in their particular brand of perversion. In the complication of motives and in the turmoil of ideas, simple integrity was extraordinarily difficult. The normal, honest, self-respecting citizen no longer knew where his loyalties really belonged.

The extensive "scandal literature" which we now have on the Fall of France has familiarized us with the personal failings of many of the French political and military leaders. This one had been defeatist, even in 1918; or this one kept a mistress, an ambitious political hostess; or this one was in receipt of Nazi funds; or all of them were amoral, only understanding the politics of their own advancement; and so on. We do not need to mention names. But these things, the perversions, the treacheries, and the failings were not so much the causes as symptoms. France, it is impossible for us now not to admit, was deeply afflicted with the contemporary sickness, the more deeply perhaps because of her onetime premier role in the leadership of European culture. "It is true," writes Antoine de Saint-Exupéry, "that we can explain defeat by pointing to the incapacity of specific individuals. But a civilization is a thing that kneads and moulds men. If the civilization to which I belong was brought low by the incapacity of individuals, then my question must be, why did my civilization not create a different type of individual? A civilization, like a religion, accuses itself when it complains of the tepid faith of its members. Its duty is to indue them with fervour. It accuses itself when it complains of the hatred of other men, not its members. Its duty is to convert those other men. Yet there was a time when my civilization proved its worth — when it inflamed its apostles, cast down the cruel, freed peoples enslaved — though today it can neither exalt nor convert. If what I seek is to dig down to the root of the many causes of my defeat, if my ambition is to be born anew, I must begin by recovering the animating power of my civilization, which has become lost."[3]

BRITAIN: DEPRESSION, RECOVERY,

AND APPEASEMENT

THE NATIONAL GOVERNMENTS

Britain consumed the early thirties in a grim struggle with the Depression. MacDonald and his Labor government resigned in August 1931, but returned with an all-party National government expressly to deal with the crisis (see p. 408). It was not the first time in British history that a moment of emergency seemed to call for a coalition. Both the Liberal and Labor parties split over the issue, and the orthodox remnant in each carefully distinguished itself from the "National Liberals" and "National Labor" who now "deserted" them to support the new government. On September 21, 1931, Britain abandoned the gold standard.

The position of the National government was uncomfortable and anomalous. It had been more or less self-constituted and, beyond the solution of the financial crisis, it had neither object nor policy. The Conservatives revived all their old protectionist cries, with which of course Snowden, the Chancellor of the Exchequer, a Labor man and an austere free trader, would have nothing to do. In the end MacDonald advised the King to dissolve Parliament. Elections were held at the end of October 1931. Conservative, National Liberal and National Labor members of the government appealed to the country for a "doctor's mandate" — such was their not very imaginative slogan — to carry on the good work of financial recovery they claimed to have begun. The election was fought without much excitement, and experienced campaigners averred afterward that there was far less rowdyism than they had expected. The result was a general Conservative victory. The nation, in the way that is peculiar to the Anglo-Saxon democracy, had made up its collective mind that, for the moment, orthodox Conservatism would probably serve its interests best. The Communists and a new "Fascist party," led by Sir Oswald Mosley, both failed to win a single seat.

The government still called itself the National government and regarded itself as a continuation of its predecessor, but it was essentially Conservative in composition. MacDonald remained Prime Minister, though he was increasingly out of sympathy with his new colleagues. Neville Chamberlain, a leading Conservative and avowed protectionist, was Chancellor of the Exchequer. Snowden was afterward translated to the House of Lords, but for the time being retained a minor Cabinet post. Parliament at once joined battle over protectionism. Debates on a general tariff were opened by Neville Chamberlain early in February 1932, and were continued throughout the month. Chamberlain adduced all the classic arguments. Protection would rectify the balance of trade, stabilize the currency, produce revenue, encourage home industries and imperial reciprocity, and furnish a useful bargaining point in trade negotiations with other countries. An Import Duties Bill became law in February 29, 1932, and provided for a duty of 10 per cent ad valorem on a long list of goods. Thus did Britain, more than eighty years after the repeal of the Corn Laws, again become a protectionist country.

The fall of the pound, and the psychological reaction thereto, had given an indirect stimulus to trade, and it was undeniable that the country was showing the first faint gleams of economic recovery. Neville Chamberlain presented a balanced budget, the first of five which he was now to present in successive years. He sliced expenditures by a tenth, and he made full use of the new tariffs. An Exchange Equalization Fund of £150,000,000 was established to offset sudden withdrawals of gold and to absorb exceptional speculative movements. In July 1932 the Lausanne Conference made an end of German reparations, and later in the same month the Imperial Economic Conference met in Ottawa. The year 1933 was the year of the World Economic Conference in London and its attendant disappointments, but Britain's slow recovery seemed to continue. Trade agreements were signed with Denmark, Germany, and Argentina and, in spite of the current "sabotage trials" in Moscow, trade negotiations were even reopened with the Soviet Union. Britain defaulted on her debt installments to the United States in circumstances described elsewhere (see p. 411), and the relief therefrom contributed to Chamberlain's budget surpluses. The unemployed still cried out for succor, but there were now fewer of them. At the end of 1934 the figure stood at 2,000,000, and by the end of 1936, at 1,600,000. Trade indexes at home and abroad were rather more encouraging. The building trades, for instance, and armaments were showing a strong spurt of activity.

The National government, essentially a Conservative government, was doctrinally opposed to economic planning. It paid little attention to the somewhat boisterous revivals of Lloyd George's slogan, "We can conquer unemployment," or to Labor proposals for public works involving lavish expenditure. In a debate in the House of Commons at the end of 1934, Chamberlain explained that if the government had not embarked on public works and similar enterprises, the reason was that it believed its function to be not to spend money, but to create the conditions in which money could be spent. And on one occasion in 1935, Baldwin, when challenged in the House, admitted, in much the same vein, that the government had had no "plan" under consideration, but vigorously denied that unemployment was any the worse for that. The government's policy, he said, was to improve economic conditions by means of tariffs, subsidies, and similar devices.

Early in June 1935 the government was reconstructed. Ramsay MacDonald had been Prime Minister since June 1929 and Prime Minister of the National governments since August 1931. Six years of heavy responsibility had told upon his health, and his colleagues were said to be finding him increasingly short of temper and difficult to approach. His oratory wandered and lost itself in outworn grandiloquence. His foreign policy in previous years, to judge by the present state of Europe, had not been a success, and his long "titular" leadership of an all but Conservative cabinet, years after the crisis was past which had once justified it, was becoming faintly ridiculous. He was succeeded by his old rival, Stanley Baldwin, who thus became Prime Minister for the third time. Sir Samuel Hoare, formerly Secretary for India, became Secretary for Foreign Affairs. Anthony Eden, one of the younger Conservatives of growing prestige, especially as a supporter of the League and of collective security, was appointed to a new office, Minister for League of Nations Affairs. All this however was preparatory. Baldwin, hoping to remedy some of the anomalies of the National government, had already decided on an appeal to the country. Elections were fought in November 1935 in the electric atmosphere of the Italo-Ethiopian crisis. Hoare had just made his crusading speech in the League Assembly in condemnation of Italy's attitude (see p. 504), and it seemed as if the National government was asking for the support of the British people to deal sternly with the Roman aggressor. Baldwin himself, in his guise of a bluff, comfortable, yeomanly type of Englishman — always with his pipe — was well liked and well trusted, and to the great majority of voters his continuance as Prime Minister seemed as inevitable as it was satisfactory. The election figures showed a slight recession in the strength of the National government, but the overriding Conservative majority was safely retained. Labor trebled its representation, and the number of votes cast in its favor was far more formidable than the proportion of seats in the House it was actually able to secure. MacDonald, in a "tremendously keen, but filthy" contest, was heavily defeated in his old constituency at Seaham. Harbour, Durham, though another constituency was afterward found for him.

The government still called itself the National government. Baldwin remained Prime Minister. He was Prime Minister during the London Naval Conference, the Italo-Ethiopian War, Hitler's march into the Rhineland, the outbreak of the Spanish Civil War — and during the reign and abdication of Edward VIII. But the real force in the government, it was coming to be recognized, was the Chancellor of the Exchequer, Neville Chamberlain. Baldwin resigned from office in May 1937, after the coronation of George VI, and Neville Chamberlain was his logical successor.

THE OTTAWA CONFERENCE

When Neville Chamberlain introduced his Import Duties Bill in 1932, he claimed that the new legislation would offer advantages "to the countries of the Empire in return for advantages they now give or in the near future may be disposed to give us." The conference which was to implement that claim was convened in Ottawa in July 1932 at the invitation of the Canadian Government. At the time, it was publicized as the British Commonwealth's own answer to the Depression. Representatives of all the Dominions, Ireland, and India attended the conference.

Whatever its results and however sordid its sessions of bargaining seemed to be, the Ottawa Conference was at least a school of imperial economics, and it instilled in the delegates some none too pleasant educational surprises. The British Dominions had latterly developed considerable industries — Canada, for instance, had become a highly industrialized country — and they were no longer the producers of food and raw materials for the British market which they had been before 1914. Like Britain, moreover, they had developed substantial trade with non-Empire customers. "Empire free trade" and even "complementary production" were excellent slogans in theory, but they had long since been outdated by the march of facts.

The delegates at Ottawa discovered, therefore, as soon as they descended from their rhetorical clouds to the firm earth of statistics, that the existing commerce of their respective countries often cut across, and indeed was often antagonistic to, the imperial connection. The British delegates were made sharply aware of the fact that, from the crude economic point of view, Argentina or Brazil was more closely knit to the Commonwealth than Canada. Australia wanted to eat her Japanese cake and have her English cake as well. Canada declared she was selling less lumber in the British home market than was the Soviet Union. All the Dominions were highly protectionist, and though they were quite willing to co-operate in the raising of tariffs against non-Empire goods, they were all averse to lowering a single existing duty to their mutual advantage.

The Ottawa Agreement was eventually signed in August 1932. In essence it was just another *ad hoc* palliative in the style of orthodox Conservative economics. The Depression had plowed its wake through Dominion and Colony alike. Australia and New Zealand afterward, both under Labor governments, conducted extremely interesting and instructive experiments in recovery. But economic planning on a Commonwealth-wide scale was not yet a solution within the compass of practical politics. Under the Ottawa Agreement the Dominions did no more than undertake to keep their protective duties at a level that would give British producers "full opportunity of reasonable competition." Britain agreed to impose higher duties and quotas on primary products from non-Empire sources which competed with Dominion products, notably dairy and other agricultural products. It is possible that, on the whole, Britain sacrificed a good deal for the benefit of the Commonwealth but, more serious perhaps, the Ottawa Agreement caused severe losses to the old customers of Britain, losses only partially retrieved by subsequent separate trade agreements with Denmark, Germany, and Argentina. Continental economists argued that Ottawa aggravated the economic strains in Europe and gave a sharp fillip to the Nazi movement.

THE SILVER JUBILEE AND THE DEATH OF GEORGE V; THE REIGN AND ABDICATION OF EDWARD VIII

King George V had ascended the throne on May 6, 1910, to reign over a people during a generation of violent changes — and of changes, not least, in the ancient institution of monarchy. But he and Queen Mary had performed their many duties with unfailing devotion. Everywhere he identified himself with the life of Britain and the Empire. Everywhere he appeared as the necessary symbol of tradition and authority. Whether at an investiture at the Palace, a state welcome to a foreign potentate, an opening of Parliament, the launching of a battleship, a thanksgiving service at St. Paul's, or the unveiling of a national monument, the ceremonial perforce centered about the person of the monarch. When in many other countries thrones were toppling into dust and ignominy, Britain's never stood higher in the esteem and affection of her people.

At the end of 1928, King George was stricken with an attack of pleurisy. Immense crowds gathered daily to wait for the medical bulletins posted outside Buckingham Palace, and many Britons were surprised, and rather awed, by the demonstrations of anxiety which the King's illness aroused. In May 1935, with Queen Mary, he celebrated the Silver Jubilee of his accession. He died on January 20, 1936, at the age of seventy, in the twenty-sixth year of his reign.

The new King came to the throne as Edward VIII. As Prince of Wales he had been widely traveled, widely known, and widely adulated. He was youthful, almost immature, in appearance — though he was forty years of age at the time of his accession. The persistent bachelorhood of this most eligible of all Prince Charmings had always evoked much intriguing speculation. He was a man of independence of mind, not an uncommon quality in his family, but a quality which in his case he was quite prepared to assert.

The new reign began uneventfully. The King supported the government's drive to reduce expenditure by waiving a substantial portion of his income. He unveiled the Canadian War Memorial at Vimy Ridge. During the late summer of 1936 he went on a cruise in the Eastern Mediterranean aboard the luxury yacht *Nahlin,* touching at points in Dalmatia, Greece, and Turkey and, but for the unhappy sequel, the tour would have had considerable diplomatic value. In November, after his return home, he visited some of the distressed areas in South Wales; [1] he showed a decided disinclination to follow routes prescribed for him, and much to the embarrassment of the ministers in attendance, he sometimes expressed very outspoken views on the conditions he found.

It was at this juncture that the first rumblings of the Constitutional Crisis began to be heard. For some months past the yellow press in the United States — and not always the yellow press — had been reveling in accounts of the King's familiarity with a certain Mrs. Simpson, an American who had been divorced from her first husband ten years before and who was about to obtain a divorce from her second. The British press, by tacit agreement, had been preserving a discreet silence in regard to the affair. But on December 1, 1936 the Bishop of Bradford, in the course of an address to the Bradford Diocesan Conference, had let fall some general remarks which appeared to be directed at His Majesty's friendships and behavior. Whereupon the British press broke its self-denying ordinance and published the entire story. The biography of the unfortunate lady was exposed to the British public's gaze, together, of course, with photographs of the King's party on the recent *Nahlin* cruise, of which, it was now revealed, she had been a member. The

Spanish Civil War, Egypt and Palestine, the unemployed, and the new re-armament program were all dropped from the daily headlines to give place to this new sensation.

Once the initial shock and confusion had passed, sentiment in the country and in the Dominions, to an overwhelming extent, was profoundly outraged at the course of action the King was evidently proposing to take, and the British people discovered anew the strength which the old traditions and conventions still exerted over them. The churches, in particular, proved to be a very powerful influence. It was not that the lady in question was the citizen of a nonmonarchical state or that in marrying her the King would contract a morganatic union. An American marriage of the right kind would have been immensely popular in Britain. But neither homeland nor Dominions would have countenanced a double divorcee as Queen.

Baldwin, the Prime Minister, meanwhile gave a full account in Parliament of his pleadings with the King. Mrs. Simpson, to do her justice, offered to part from the King if he so decided. But, on December 10, he formally abdicated the throne. "I will not enter now into My private feelings," ran the wording of the abdication. "But I would beg that it should be remembered that the burden which constantly rests upon the shoulders of a Sovereign is so heavy that it can only be borne in circumstances different from those in which I now find Myself."

On December 12, 1936, Prince Albert, Duke of York, succeeded to the throne as George VI. One of his first acts was to create his brother, the former King, Duke of Windsor. His coronation took place with all its historic color and ceremony in Westminster Abbey on May 12, 1937.

THE APPEASEMENT POLICY

Baldwin, we have said, resigned from office shortly after the coronation of George VI and was succeeded by Neville Chamberlain. Baldwin had handled the Constitutional Crisis, as it was called, with consummate tact and skill, and he retired from his long period of public service in an aura of public esteem, with an earldom and the supreme honor of the Garter. "He laid down the wide authority he had gathered and carefully maintained," writes Churchill, "but had used as little as possible . . . " He had been "a profoundly astute party manager, thinking in majorities and aiming at a quiet life between elections." [2] He belonged perhaps to that school of Conservative statesmen — Sir Robert Walpole was his spiritual ancestor — who wait upon events, leave well alone, and seem to believe that all things work out for the best in the end. His successor was a different type of man.

Neville Chamberlain, like Baldwin, also belonged to the propertied class, inheriting a family business. He was insular and narrow, almost common-place, likely to be misled in questions outside his own technical purview and often "behind the times." He was of unexceptionable directness and honesty, of unassuming piety, sometimes chill and precise, overconfident in his own righteousness. But, whereas Baldwin had been passive, he was active. Whereas Baldwin was essentially lazy, Chamberlain, for all his years, was a man of passionate driving force who faced and fought his difficulties. His opinions and decisions, unfortunate though they often were, were positive and masterful. He took great pride in being "practical" and "sensible." One can well imagine him, conscious of his own capacities, watching with growing concern a Europe in process of deterioration, as a business might deteriorate, pleading for a candid re-examination and redress of the evils which were admitted to exist, and then urging himself at last to take a position of public responsibility such as would entitle him to demand, "Can't we practical, sensible men get together and settle this thing in a practical, sensible way?"

"War," said Chamberlain once, "wins nothing, cures nothing, ends nothing . . . In war there are no winners, but all are losers." "An ancient historian once wrote of the Greeks that they had made gentle the life of the world. I can imagine no nobler ambition for an English statesman than to win the same tribute for his own country." [3] Chamberlain became Prime Minister in May 1937, humbly, but with grim determination, to try to realize that ambition.

"The peace of Europe must depend on the attitude of the four major Powers — Germany, Italy, France, and ourselves," he said in a speech in the early part of 1938. "For ourselves, we are linked to France by common ideals of democracy, of liberty, and of parliamentary government . . . On the other side we find Germany and Italy are also linked by affinities of outlook and in the form of their government. The question that we have to think of is this. Are we to allow these two pairs of nations to go on glowering at one another across their frontiers, allowing the feeling between the two sides to become more and more embittered, until at last the barriers are broken down and the conflict begins which many think would mark the end of civilization? Or can we bring them to an understanding of one another's aims and objects and to such discussion as may lead to a final settlement? If we can do that, if we can bring these four nations into friendly discussion, into a settling of their differences, we shall have saved the peace of Europe for a generation." These were not the words of an idealist or a trained diplomat. They were the words of a company director recommending a merger to fend off a mutually ruinous competition. They were also the words of a man of perfect sincerity and enlightened self-interest.

Chamberlain well realized that such friendly discussions must be entered into from strength and not from weakness, and that, to use his own words, "the effort to remove the causes which are delaying the return of confidence in Europe" must be combined with "our programme for the re-establishment of our defence forces." But he seemed to believe that the sheer weight of rearmament might of itself act as a deterrent to aggressor Powers, and that designing enemies could be frightened into submission by huge budget figures. His was a typical financial rendering of the French colonial maxim — "Make a show of force, but do not use it," a maxim which proved effective enough against the tribesmen of Morocco, but was not to prove so effective against the tribesmen of Europe. Chamberlain's faith in physical wealth was tragically characteristic. "The richer country *must* win in the end," he used to say, and by inference the poverty of Germany, if strained beyond a certain point, must eventually encompass her destruction. He entered into the great

European rearmament race as if it were some fantastic auction in which victory went to the highest bidder and defeat to the struggling bankrupt. Unfortunately, in the present case, the richer country's expenditure on armaments per annum was one-third that of the poorer aggressor, and it also had a time lag of at least three years to make up.[4]

The fundamental error of appeasement, as we see it now, was the disparity of codes. The other pair of nations of which Chamberlain had spoken was not motivated by the same conventions as he was. There may be honor among businessmen, as there is honor among thieves. Businessmen can deal with businessmen, and thieves with thieves. But businessmen and thieves cannot deal one with another. Democracy and Nazism each obeyed a mutually contradictory scale of values which gave them no common ground for discussion or compromise. To bring them together into an agreement on the basis of contract was impossible. To Chamberlain contract was the very fabric of the life he knew. Contract was not only a matter of high sanctity but a matter of course which he never thought to question. To Hitler contract was a *ruse de guerre*. The *Ehre* of the German had never become associated, as "honor" in Chamberlain's bourgeois mind had become associated, with scraps of paper. Appeasement therefore was not so much a forlorn hope, tried too late. Appeasement subsumed a technique and a code — conference, discussion, compromise, concession, agreement, contract — which were as natural to Chamberlain as the very English he spoke, but wholly beyond the custom or comprehension of his opposite. Throughout the Chamberlain-Hitler episode, as it afterward developed, the impression is borne in upon us again and again that neither understood the other — and that Chamberlain only half realized the fact.

Yet while appeasement derived in part from Chamberlain, it also derived from the British people as a whole, who passionately desired that the great experiment should be tried, and they were themselves culpable, if ever a people were culpable, for the kind of leadership that Chamberlain gave them. What faults he had and what mistakes he made were their faults and their mistakes.[5] The minority, largely a Labor minority, which opposed Chamberlain in his day and clamored for a "strong" foreign policy was often made of those elements who were once most pacific and most belligerently insistent on their country's unilateral disarmament. To the very end, in 1939, when the country was on the brink of war, Labor Members in the House of Commons were still steadily opposing the government's rearmament and conscription measures. Churchill's lone warnings on the growing strength of Germany, notably her growing strength in the air, were regarded as the dangerous scaremongering of an incorrigible and irresponsible troublemaker.

Moreover, as is too often forgotten by adverse commentators, Chamberlain had continually to consider the British Dominions. Never at any time had the hands of British statesmen been so tied as now by the affairs of the Commonwealth. New liberties, however desirable, had converted the far-flung British family into a group of independent nations, each with an internal and external policy of its own. Canada was as isolationist as the United States and had to accommodate her attitude to a strong French-Canadian

minority which was largely indifferent to the British connection (see p. 341).
South Africa was absorbed in the triangular contest between Smuts, Hertzog,
and Malan and had to accommodate her attitude to a strong Boer minority
which was largely hostile to the British connection (343–44). Australia and
New Zealand were more concerned over the Japanese menace than the German (see p. 585). India had her own particular distractions. The possibility
therefore that the Commonwealth, like the Empire of 1914, would once
more participate wholeheartedly and collectively in the mother country's
war clearly had to wait upon the event and, in any case, was not a matter of
self-evident calculation in advance.

From time to time we have spoken of the extreme pacifism which consumed the British people during the interwar years, even to the willing
sacrifice of their historic position in the world. An example of the same
mood, nearer the Chamberlain era, is surely given by that remarkable
incident, the National Peace Ballot at the end of 1934. This ambitious
referendum of British public opinion, a sort of magnified Gallup Poll, was
organized by a committee representing the League of Nations Union [6] and a
number of other political and religious bodies. The voter was invited to
answer "Yes" or "No" to a series of questions: "Should Great Britain remain
a member of the League of Nations? Are you in favor of an all-round reduction in armaments by international agreement? . . . Do you consider that,
if one nation insists on attacking another, the other nations should combine
to compel it to stop by (a) economic sanctions, (b) if necessary, military
measures?" And so forth. *The Times* complained that the Peace Ballot was
"a deplorable waste of time and effort," and Sir John Simon pointed out in
the House of Commons that its questions were hardly fair. Chamberlain
himself dubbed it "terribly mischievous." But the Ballot evoked an extraordinary response, and the 11,559,165 votes which were cast represented nearly
40 per cent of the British electorate. The result, announced at a monster
meeting in the Albert Hall on June 27, 1935, was taken to be an overwhelming endorsement of the principle of collective security and peace.

The general election of November 1935, which returned Baldwin's National government to power, was fought in the shadow of the Italo-Ethiopian
crisis and under the afterglow of the National Peace Ballot. Baldwin was
severely censured for having admitted subsequently, in a speech of "appalling frankness" that, if at that time he had divulged what he knew of the
progress of Germany's rearmament, his party might have lost the election.
But Baldwin's "appalling frankness" cut two ways, and his censure surely
was also to be shared by the British electorate, which in its obstinate pacifism
was in no fit state to be told the truth.[7]

If this then was the precedent, appeasement was not so blameworthy.
Never did a statesman give a more democratic and more accurate interpretation of a people's will than did Chamberlain in 1937 and 1938. But the day
of disillusion, both for statesman and people, was at hand.

37 SOUTHEAST ASIA, THE EAST INDIES, AND AUSTRALASIA

THE NETHERLANDS EAST INDIES

The Dutch, overtaken by the British three centuries before in the race for points of commercial vantage in India, succeeded in retaining a most valuable consolation prize. It was a chain of some 2,000 islands spread over a distance of more than 3,000 miles, some of which contemporaries knew as the Spice Islands. In 1940 the Netherlands East Indies still supplied about 85 per cent of the world's pepper and, in addition, 90 per cent of its quinine, 49 per cent of its rubber, nearly 25 per cent of its tin, and 10 per cent of its petroleum.

Dutch rule in these islands was cast in the mold of a stern and efficient paternalism. On the eve of the First World War, the destinies of 50,000,000 native Indonesians, varying from the relatively cultured Eurasians to the head-hunters of New Guinea, were governed by a mere handful of 25,000 pure-blooded Dutch. But strange and disturbing winds of freedom were beginning to blow. The defeat of Russia by Japan in 1905 cast the first faint shadow of doubt on the doctrine of "white superiority" and inspired a group of Western-educated Javanese in 1908 to establish a nationalist society under the flamboyant title of Boedi Oetomo (Glorious Endeavor). The enhanced national self-consciousness of the Chinese minority in Java after the foundation of the Chinese Republic in 1911–12 encouraged the Moslem majority on the island to develop another nationalist society (Sarikat Islam). It was a more inflammatory organization than the relatively moderate Boedi Oetomo, and it drew upon the deep wells of economic discontent among the natives, whom it could always picture as the victims of exploitation by the Chinese minority.

The Dutch authorities attempted to calm the ferment by a mixture of concessions and force. In 1915 a law of 1854 banning political meetings was revoked. In 1918 a Volksraad, or People's Council, with advisory functions, was set up. Of its 39 members, a substantial minority were native delegates elected by local councils on the basis of an extremely restricted franchise. But the majority were Dutch, appointed directly by the Dutch Governor General. The number of delegates grew from 39 to 60 by 1925, but the proportion of natives to Europeans did not change.

This tardy progress toward native participation in the government provided an amplitude of inflammable material for the native demagogues. In 1920 the extremist wing of Sarikat Islam broke away from the parent body, formed the Indonesian Communist party, and intensified its agitatory activities among the workers in the processing industries. In the rural areas, where overpopulation had caused an excessive splintering and subdivision of the soil into farms uneconomically small, support was attracted by promises of freedom from taxes and from forced labor. During 1926–27 a sputtering train of strikes exploded into a full-scale revolt in Java and western Sumatra. Many of the slogans of the insurgents had been minted by the Third International. But the main dynamism of the revolt was drawn from a resurgent nationalism reinforced by economic discontent. In the end the revolt was suppressed with a heavy hand. Three of the ringleaders were executed. Some hundreds of their more dangerous adherents were relegated to a prison camp in the wild interior of New Guinea, whence escape was interdicted by the presence of Papuan head-hunters.

The sternly repressive policy of the Dutch administration after 1927 was balanced by a series of concessions which nationalists stigmatized as more apparent than real. The Volksraad was conceded a concurrent right of introducing bills and of amending legislation submitted to it by the Governor General. If, however, the Governor General and the Volksraad reached a deadlock in legislative or financial matters, the question was to be referred to the States-General at The Hague. The Volksraad was expanded to 60 delegates, of which 30 were natives. But nationalists hastened to point out that one-third of the natives were still nominated by the Governor General.

In 1927 the National Indonesian party was founded by Dr. Achmed Soekarno, a schoolteacher who presided over a nucleus of Javanese intellectuals mostly educated, like himself, in Holland. Unremitting agitatorial activities among the masses earned Soekarno a jail sentence in 1929 and banishment from Java in 1934. Cracks and fissures appeared which ran deep into the foundations of the party structure. The extremists bitterly assailed a large body of moderates who desired to co-operate with the Dutch in a cautious advance toward self-government. The Moslem element in the party was infuriated by the sharp criticism leveled by their non-Moslem colleagues against two of their cherished institutions, polygamy and the pilgrimage to Mecca. The successive cleavages, coalitions, and reincarnations of these splinter parties within the framework of the nationalist movement proceeded unchecked until 1938. In that year the seven factions into which the nationalists by then had split were federated into the Gapi, with an estimated membership of 500,000. This "Indonesian Unity Movement" was largely the work of the wealthy and astute Mohammed Hoseni Thamrin, a member of the Volksraad and former Acting Mayor of Batavia. The new coalition advocated a wider native participation in government leading ultimately to dominion status under the Dutch Crown.

If there was anything that could have persuaded the native leaders to plaster over the cracks in the nationalist movement it was the Depression of the early thirties. The disastrous drop in the prices of staple commodities cut the value of exports to a third. The crisis was reflected in unbalanced budgets and mass unemployment. Heavy salary slashes fell with particular severity on the Eurasians, who manned the lower grades of the civil service. This key group, previously highly favored by the Dutch, began resentfully to

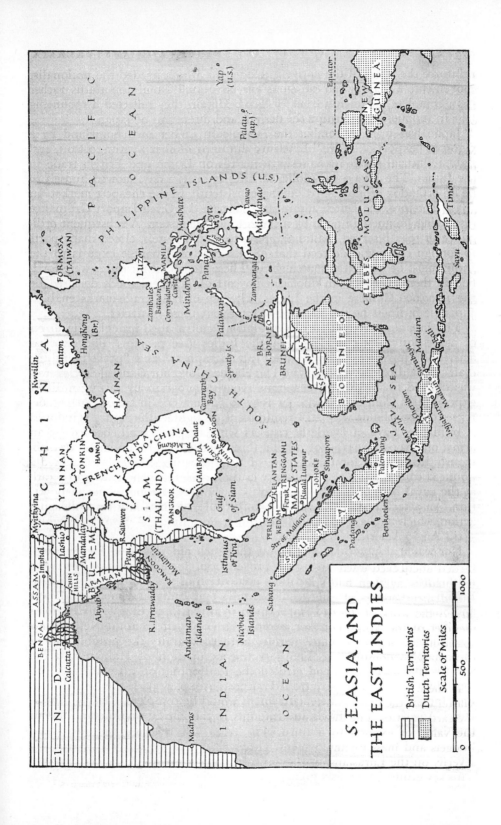

S.E. ASIA AND
THE EAST INDIES

British Territories

Dutch Territories

scale of miles

0   500   1000

reinforce the ranks of the native intelligentsia which headed the nationalist movement. The majority of Eurasians advocated Dominion status rather than complete separation from Holland. Herein they reflected a mounting fear in Indonesia concerning the designs and intentions of Japan.

Japan had tried to combat the Depression in her own homeland by a vigorous "export offensive." Extensive dumping of cheap rayon, cotton, and light industrial goods made serious inroads on Dutch and British trade in the Indies. The Java sugar coolie, earning 27 cents a day, showed himself to be an orthodox economist by buying consistently in the cheapest market. In 1933, therefore, the Dutch administration passed a Crisis Import Ordinance restricting Japanese imports by means of a quota system. A subsequent ordinance in 1935 reserved coastal shipping to Dutch vessels, closed many ports to foreign craft, and decreed that 38 per cent of Japanese exports to the Indies must be carried in Dutch ships. These trenchant measures were fortified in their effects by an unofficial boycott of Japanese goods declared by the 1,200,000 Chinese in the Indies. The use of false trade-marks enabled Japanese business houses partly to circumvent these obstacles.

The Japanese occupation of Canton in October 1938 brought the forces of aggression a long stride nearer the Indies (see p. 440). The ceaseless activity of Japanese "barbers" and "photographers" and "peaceful fishing craft" excited official comment at The Hague. Governor General Stachouwer was obliged to imperil his economic recovery program by raising military expenditures from $25,000,000 in 1937 to $60,000,000 in 1940. But the defenses of the islands were still reminiscent of eighteenth-century standards. A miniature navy of five light cruisers with auxiliary craft, backed by an army of 50,000 (1941) — of whom three-quarters were natives — was obviously inadequate for the defense of the sprawling archipelago. The announced construction of three heavy cruisers and a 40,000-ton floating dock at the naval base of Surabaya in Java clearly needed time for implementation. An attack on the islands therefore could be met only by a delaying action, which might at least hold the "Inner Possessions" — Java and Madura — till Anglo-American aid arrived.

Nor was it doubted for an instant that such aid would be forthcoming, even though, in order to avoid provocation, formal undertakings were neither asked nor given. A Japanese occupation of the Indies would disrupt British communications between Australia and India and menace Malaya and Singapore. The United States up to 1940 was importing virtually all its quinine, one-third of its rubber, and one-fifth of its tin from the Netherlands East Indies, and could hardly regard with equanimity the possible loss of these important supplies. The Japanese occupation of Hainan and the Spratly Islands in 1939 had girdled the Philippines on all sides save the south by a ring of enemy-controlled outposts (see p. 443). If the Netherlands East Indies fell, the hostile encirclement would be complete. Clearly, Anglo-Dutch-American possessions and interests in the Pacific would stand or fall together.

FRENCH INDO–CHINA

The French conquest of Indo-China in 1859–85 had not been completed without bitter and protracted resistance. But, for twenty years thereafter, so thoroughly was that resistance broken that the native peoples lay passive under the heavy hand of the conqueror. Japan's victory over Russia in 1905, however, touched off a series of local conspiracies and upheavals, notably in Annam. But the moderate majority of Annamese intellectuals, chiefly inspired by the writings of Rousseau, limited their activities to academic criticism of the French colonial administration. The forcible rounding up of 100,000 Annamese for labor and military service in France during the First World War stimulated both latent native discontent and native receptiveness to more subversive Western ideologies. In the twenties the nationalist movement fell into the hands of a new generation of fiery young intellectuals whose main preoccupations were terrorism and an intensive propaganda among native troops in the army. A series of attempts to assassinate Governor General Pasquier began in 1929. Native troops broke into open mutiny in Yenbay in February 1930 and shot down their French officers and noncommissioned officers. The mutiny crumbled under vigorous countermeasures, but not before violent outbreaks had spread elsewhere. Large numbers of insurgents were executed or deported to the penal settlement of Cayenne. Inevitably, the vicious circle of revolt and repression left the usual legacy of bitterness to both sides.

The economic distress of the early thirties sharpened the native unrest and threatened to provide the conspiratorial societies of the nationalists with a mass following. French Indo-China, with Siam and Burma, formed one of the great rice bowls of the Orient. Between 1928 and 1932, rice exports from Indo-China increased by nearly 250,000 tons, but the collapse in world prices reduced their value by one-half. Rural indebtedness reached alarming proportions. The government, in the face of a budget deficit of $2,000,000, appropriated $4,000,000 in order to guarantee bank loans to native farmers. Recovery was further assisted by the foundation of the Crédit Foncier Indo-Chinois, which advanced loans at moderate interest and so strove to rescue the farmer from the paralyzing grip of the usurer. But Indo-China remained immovably clamped to the French tariff system, which reduced the inflow of cheap foreign products in order to preserve the market for higher-priced French goods.

The tradition of high protectionism encouraged prompt countermeasures against Japanese commercial penetration after 1931. Import quotas on Japanese goods were introduced. An exchange compensation surtax of 25 per cent balanced the advantage afforded to Japan by the depreciated yen. But the specter of a Japanese military invasion could not be so easily exorcised.

The defense of French Indo-China became a matter of increasing concern to the French Government as the long battle front in China swung inexorably southward from the comfortable remoteness of Manchukuo. Further, the retirement of the government of Nationalist China to Chungking in 1938 made the communications system of French Indo-China one of the main channels of supply for the embattled capital. The Hanoi-Kunming railroad, linking the French possessions with southern China, straightway sprang into an importance second only to the Burma Road (pp. 442–43). The Japanese policy of slashing Chungking's life lines led at once to diplomatic pressure on the French government. Finally, late in 1938, Paris agreed to ban the passage of all war material through French territory.

Militarily, Indo-China was a most vulnerable hostage to fortune. Of 22,000,000 inhabitants, only 30,000 were French. The army consisted of 14,000 French regulars and 40,000 natives. The Annamese, who were the best military material in the colony, were politically the least reliable. They rebuffed an offer from Georges Mandel, Minister of Colonies in the Blum government, to throw open French military academies to them, and demanded military training schools on their own soil. The demand, in view of its explosive potentialities, was not conceded. A last-minute decision, in September 1939, to enlist a further 50,000 natives for service in the army was dangerous in the extreme, even though the proportion of French noncommissioned officers to native privates was as high as one to ten. In 1939, Indo-China's 1,800 miles of seacoast were protected by a fleet of three cruisers and two destroyers. The naval and air base at Camranh Bay, "France's Singapore," was still uncompleted when the Second World War broke out. The air force consisted of six squadrons of planes, mostly obsolete. All in all, the colony, left stranded by the fall of France in 1940, was in a pathetic defensive state.

SIAM (THAILAND)

The British penetration of Burma in 1824 and the Opium War with China in 1840–42 brought Europan imperialism almost to the borders of independent Siam. The relatively enlightened rulers of the Chakkri dynasty, heeding the warning, began laboriously to reorganize the Siamese Army, Navy, and administration along Western lines. But the diversions of the harem, the resistance of princes and nobles, and the inertia of the people caused the reform program to lurch forward by very intermittent fits and starts. Happily, the value of Siam as a territorial buffer zone between British Burma and French Indo-China ensured her political independence. Economically, however, she became firmly enmeshed in the commercial empire of Britain. British capital dominated the lucrative teak industry and a substantial proportion of the tin and rubber production. About 90 per cent of the Siamese public debt was held in London. Numbers of Chinese middlemen, seeking asylum in Siam from the civil agitations in their native land, came to control the rice and fishing industries.

The disturbing influences of the Chinese Revolution of 1911–12 and of the First World War did not spare Siam. A military clique, largely German trained, engineered two unsuccessful conspiracies in 1912 and 1917 against the able but spendthrift Rama VI. The King, well aware that his territory was completely encircled by Anglo-French possessions, declared war against the Central Powers in 1917. His reward, flattering to national self-esteem, was the abrogation of Germany's extraterritorial rights in Siam by the Treaty of Versailles. Between 1919 and 1925 the United States, Japan, France, and Britain also agreed in principle to the entire surrender of their special privileges at some future date.

The progress achieved by Siam did not, unfortunately, extend to the public finances which, under King Prajadhipok, successor to Rama VI in 1925, continued to be rife with corruption and inefficiency. The absence of an equitable land and income tax exaggerated the financial strain entailed by a top-heavy bureaucracy and by lavish pensions to the princes of the blood. The Depression of 1931 compelled stringent economies. The promotion of 92 high army officers was annulled in the interests of retrenchment. Civil service salaries suffered a graduated reduction of from 5 to 10 per cent. The military and civilian malcontents thereupon combined in a relatively peaceful revolt in June 1932 which placed the so-called People's party in control. The revolt, which numbered but two victims, was temporarily accepted by the King with truly royal urbanity. The convocation of a National Assembly virtually abolished an autocracy almost six centuries old. An attempt at counterrevolution by the displaced aristocratic groups, in which the King was implicated, failed in October 1933. Henceforward the military clique and the civilian bureaucrats, to whom the People's party had provided a convenient frontage, were firmly established in the seats of power.

The transformation of the old regime was not without its broader implications. British interests, with the indulgent connivance of the dynasty, had long since become entrenched in Siamese banking and foreign trade. The Chinese, constituting one-sixth of the population, flourished mightily, mainly through retail trade and usury. The revolution assumed from the first an anti-imperialist complexion, and aimed gradually to dispossess all foreign groups of their influence and property in Siam.

The Japanese alone retained a position of exceptional favor. Rumor had it that Colonel Luang Pibul Songgram, the strong man of the new administration, had drawn heavily on Japanese finances and Japanese advice while planning the revolt of 1932. The Colonel, as Minister of Defense, embarked upon a rapid expansion of the army, which by 1937 was accounting for 25 per cent of all budget expenses. The corresponding increase in the officer corps, mostly trained henceforward in the Military Academy at Tokyo, accentuated the militaristic and pro-Japanese trend in Siam. Lastly, the embarrassing problem of disposing of the pro-British King Prajadhipok was solved with some adroitness. Early in 1935 a would-be assassin lodged two bullets in the Colonel's body, but failed to inflict a mortal wound. The well-disciplined Assembly hastened to demand the consent of the King to a legislative measure empowering it to impose sentences of death without royal sanction. The King, unwilling to abandon his supporters to legalized persecution, refused. The Assembly retaliated by overriding his veto. The King, who had withdrawn to London, thereupon announced his abdication in a registered letter addressed to the Siamese people. His nephew and heir, the nine-year-old Prince Ananda, remained at school in Switzerland.

The policy of cultivating Japan as a counterpoise to Anglo-French influence proceeded apace. By 1932, Siam was supplying 85 per cent of Japan's rice imports. Japanese exports to Siam, stimulated by the depreciated yen, more than tripled between 1931 and 1933. The Siamese delegation to the League of Nations in 1933 therefore had solid economic reasons for its refusal to concur in the vote of censure of Japan's proceedings in Manchuria. The rapid success of Japan in the South China campaign of 1937–38 confirmed Colonel Luang Pibul's confidence in the wisdom of his pro-Japanese policy. Much as he may have wished to prevent the future incorporation of Siam in the Japanese Co-prosperity Sphere, the inescapable fact remained that the revolution of 1932 had expelled a strongly Anglophile dynasty, whose supporters made persistent efforts to remove the Colonel by assassination. Two further attempts to cut short his career, by bullet and poison respectively in November and December 1938, impelled him to assume the premiership himself. A military conspiracy to restore the monarchy was detected and crushed in the following month, no less than 50 of Siam's numerous generals being cashiered. The Siamese Legation in London announced shortly afterward that henceforth Siam would be known as Thailand, "Land of Free Men."

To the unprejudiced observer, it seemed that Siam was merely exchanging the white man's whips for the yellow man's scorpions. But it was at once soothing and profitable to the Siamese Government to adopt a policy of stern antiforeignism of the Tokyo brand. British teak concessions in the north were renewed, but on distinctly more onerous terms. Stringent legislation against foreign middlemen in April 1939 was designed to drive Siam's 1,500,000 Chinese from their strongly entrenched positions in the rice, rubber, and tobacco industries. The tin, oil, and shipping industries were assailed by discriminatory measures clearly indicative of the government's resolve ultimately to assume an undivided control over them. The immediate result was a formidable dislocation of the national economy. But, in 1941, Siam passed bodily under Japanese control.

MALAYA

Curving gently southeast from Siam is a long, slim tentacle of British-controlled territory, Malaya. At its southern tip lay the extensive fortifications of the island of Singapore, controlling the narrow straits which link the South China Sea with the Indian Ocean. Singapore, with the more northerly areas of Malacca and Penang, constituted collectively a Crown Colony known as the Straits Settlements. It was administered by a British Governor aided by an advisory council representative of the various nationalities of the colony. The four Federated Malay States, in the heart of the Peninsula, were brought together under British protection in 1896, chiefly in order to ensure the tranquillity necessary for their economic development. The native rulers, schooled in war and piracy, leaned heavily on their British resident advisers when the rapid expansion of the rubber and tin industries raised new and complex problems. The Unfederated Malay States included Johore in the extreme south of the Peninsula and a group of four sultanates in the far north. Here the native rulers retained a greater degree of authority than their peers in the Federated States. Their British advisers, for example, had purely consultative functions.

This cumbrous division of ten small political units was less the outcome of a "divide and rule" policy by the British than of the piecemeal character of their absorption. Administrative symmetry was of secondary importance to speedy exploitation. Malaya was a territory of only 50,000 square miles, but it produced nearly half the world's rubber and tin, and its total exports were valued at $300,000,000 yearly. It was therefore a prize of considerable magnitude. It had had no rubber till 1870, when the plants were first culti- vated from seeds smuggled out of Brazil in a British diplomatic pouch. With the advent of the automobile, the demand for rubber shot up enormously, and the rubber plantations in the Federated States of Negri Sembilan and Pahang began to expand in proportion, far outstripping Brazilian produc- tion. The collapse of rubber prices after the First World War inspired the well-known Stevenson Plan in 1922, which aimed at stabilizing the world price at a profitable level by restricting output. The plan proved defective, largely because the price was fixed at so high a level that it became possible for Dutch planters in Java, outside the ring, to expand production at a profit. An international agreement was finally reached in 1936, on the basis of export quotas which limited the heavy buying of Japan.

The production of tin, mined in primitive fashion by Chinese from very remote times, had attained only 2,000 tons yearly by 1870. The great open pits of whitish clay in the Federated State of Perak returned an increasing yield as the market expanded and Western capital and technique were introduced. Labor, chiefly Chinese, was cheap, wages rarely exceeding 50 cents per day. The high tempo of production, far exceeding that of Bolivia, did not slacken appreciably until the Depression of 1931. In August 1931 an international syndicate was formed to control production, and hence to raise prices to a remunerative level. Efforts to keep the price steady in the neigh- borhood of 60 cents per pound broke down in 1937, when a sudden collapse was followed by a steady rise to $1.28. The increased demand originated partly in the United States, where the policy of "stock-piling," introduced in 1939, revealed anticipations of a southward drive by Japan. Japan, who had leased some of the more productive mines in the Trengganu area, was pre- vented from purchasing in excess of normal requirements, though it was difficult to stop Japanese interests from acting through intermediaries. Man- ganese and bauxite, vital for the production of high-grade steel and alumi- num, could be purchased freely in Malaya. Japan imported 66,700 tons of bauxite from there in 1939.

The Japanese trade offensive of the early thirties was no less intensive in Malaya than elsewhere. Exports of Japanese textiles to the Peninsula rock- eted from an average of 46,000,000 yards in the years of 1927–31 to 127,000,- 000 yards in 1933. Quota restrictions, together with an import tax of 20 per cent on all foreign cottons and rayons, were applied in 1934, and within the next three years Japanese exports were thereby reduced by one-half.

The Japanese threat served to alleviate temporarily one of the chief sources of disturbance in Malaya. The Chinese, comprising 1,700,000 of

Malaya's population of over 4,000,000 (1931), maintained the closest political affiliations with their native land. The industry and thrift of these former immigrants guaranteed them rapid economic advancement. Thus they were able to subscribe generously to Chinese Nationalist finances. Chinese schools in Malaya multiplied rapidly, and their curriculum became decidedly "political." The Chinese vernacular press exhaled a glowing patriotism. The British administration, true to its policy of protecting Malay interests against encroachments by the immigrant races, reacted vigorously. The police were given power to close schools suspected of disseminating political propaganda and to exercise a wide censorship over the Chinese vernacular press. The establishment of branches of the Kuomintang in Malaya was prohibited in 1931. An Aliens Ordinance empowered the authorities to deport political undesirables. The Sino-Japanese clash in Manchuria, however, brought the ferment to a sudden and dramatic stop.

The Malays themselves, almost submerged by the inflow of Chinese and Indian immigrants into the tin and rubber industries, counted less than 45 per cent of the population in 1931. They remained obstinately attached to farming and fishing, and were in consequence elbowed economically into the background by the more enterprising newcomers. Poverty-stricken and debt-ridden, the prey of the Chinese or Indian middleman and usurer, they were slow in developing a sense of corporate identity. Their allegiance remained largely local and religious, not national. The scanty Malayan intelligentsia formed a Westernizing party (Kaum Muda) in the early twenties, but they made little headway either against their fellow "traditionalist" Moslems or against the mass apathy of the peasant population.

SINGAPORE

Singapore stood sentinel over the narrow sea lanes between the Indian Ocean and the Pacific. Its strategic and commercial value had been appreciated by the keen eye of its first Governor, Sir Stamford Raffles, who had purchased it for a song in 1819 from the Sultan of Johore on behalf of the East India Company. It was then a tiny fishing village. A century later, trade to the value of $750,000,000 passed through its harbor yearly.

The need for providing sufficient protection for this pearl of the Orient was felt only after the First World War — so slowly did the balance of naval power in the Far East begin to incline against Britain. In 1919, Admiral Lord Jellicoe returned from a tour of the maritime defenses of the British Empire seriously perturbed over the preponderance of naval power enjoyed by Japan in the Pacific, and convinced that a powerful British fleet, based on Singapore, was imperative. His views were given added weight by the heavy fire opened on the Anglo-Japanese Alliance at the London Imperial Conference two years later. The British Parliament almost simultaneously voted an appropriation of more than $50,000,000 to convert Singapore into the greatest naval dockyard of the Orient, capable of accommodating the heaviest battleships of a projected British Pacific Fleet. In view of this potential reinforcement of her position, it was possible for Britain to terminate her alliance with Japan at the Washington Conference of 1921–22 (see p. 365).

Subsequently the Singapore base became something of a football of party politics in Britain. Construction was begun in 1923, but the MacDonald Labor government in 1924 characterized the project as "wild and wanton folly" and ordered the suspension of operations. The Conservative Baldwin cabinet resumed construction with considerable vigor and, by the fall of 1928, the tremendous floating dock, towed out from the Tyneside shipyards, was safely moored at its destination after a four months' journey. In November 1929, however, Alexander, First Lord of the Admiralty in the second Labor government, announced that work on the base was to be slowed down, pending the forthcoming London Naval Conference (see p. 495). Construction was resumed once more after the substantial failure of that conference, and after Japan's Asiatic ambitions had been partly uncovered by her assault on Manchuria. A dry dock sufficient for the repair of the heaviest battleships was inaugurated at the formal opening of the base on February 14, 1938. The participation of three United States cruisers in the ceremonies was widely interpreted as foreshadowing the joint use of the base by the two nations, if the need arose.

The Japanese occupation of the Spratly Islands, 250 miles northeast of Singapore, scarcely a year after the formal opening, lent color to the contention that the base had been completed barely in time (see p. 443). Critics nevertheless hastened to point out the obvious fact that Singapore was thronged with all kinds of ships except capital ships, since, after the conclusion of the alliance with Japan in 1902, Britain had withdrawn the six capital ships normally stationed in Pacific waters. By 1938 the Pacific Squadron, based on Hong Kong, counted nothing more formidable than 4 heavy and 2 light cruisers, with auxiliaries. Japan could outmatch this pygmy force with 9 battleships, 12 heavy and 22 light cruisers, and 6 aircraft carriers. The creation of a screen of naval forces for the long-distance defense of Singapore awaited the creation of a British Pacific Fleet which, designed to comprise 5 capital ships and 70 cruisers, was timed for completion by 1942–43. The inexorable advance of the Japanese forces into South China and the Tokyo-inspired ferment in Indo-China and Siam created meanwhile a serious situation on the landward side of the base. Singapore, viewed from the Asiatic continent, was undoubtedly "out on a limb." While the tangled jungle of the Malayan interior might be regarded by certain tacticians as an important obstacle to invaders, it provided excellent cover for ground troops, and was practicable terrain for infantry infiltration of the type developed by the German High Command in 1918 and thence, presumably, instilled into the Japanese Army.

THE PHILIPPINES

The Philippines, "the orphan of the Pacific," taken over from Spain by the United States in 1898, lay at a distance of over 6,000 miles from the North

American continent. The indentations of the numerous islands actually gave them a longer coastline than the United States itself. They stood within easy striking distance of the Japanese island of Formosa, and they were situated squarely in the path of a Japanese drive toward the South Pacific.

The doctrine of American "trusteeship" had been proclaimed over the Philippines in 1898 and, in principle, was never subsequently abandoned. The preamble of the Jones Law in 1916 announced: "It is, as it always has been, the purpose of the United States to withdraw their sovereignty over the Philippine Islands, and to recognize their independence, as soon as a stable government can be established therein." By the end of the First World War, enlightened governors, such as Francis B. Harrison, had been able to effect considerable progress toward self-government and, by 1920, the moment seemed ripe for President Wilson to remind Congress that "it is now our liberty and our duty to keep our promise to the people of these islands by granting them the independence which they so honorably covet."

But American opinion on the Philippine question had undergone considerable changes during and immediately after the First World War. Suspicion of Japanese designs in the Pacific, coupled with a solicitude for the "Open Door" in China, strengthened the demand for retention and adequate defense of the islands. Further, American business had come to realize the economic possibilities of the Philippines, an important source of sugar, copra, and manila hemp. The question of independence, therefore, was temporarily shelved when the Republican administration of President Harding entered office in 1921. In place of the rather easygoing Harrison, General Leonard Wood was appointed Governor. The progressive admission of the Filipinos to administrative posts was checked. A semimilitary efficiency became the order of the day.

There was something to be said in favor of the new policy. Many of the Filipinos who had swamped the government service in Harrison's day were incorrigibly corrupt. The dominating moneyed element, the caciques, formed a tight caste whose first interest was usury, and whose last concern was the well-being of the miserable peasantry. The majority of the caciques were Roman Catholic — an evidence of the long Spanish occupation — and they entertained not the slightest sympathy for the Moslems of the southern islands. In all probability both peasants and Moslems preferred a strong and efficient administration to the grinding cacique tyranny.

Yet the politically conscious Filipinos, having tasted the forbidden fruit of liberty, could not resign themselves to its loss. An uprising took place in 1926 which was easily suppressed. The new American policy was expounded with soldierly bluntness by General Wood a few months later: "Philippine problems are part of America's Pacific problem. Their solution can never be achieved by the chatter of agitators. When the task is done, America will say so. Until America says so, her task is unfinished."

The Depression reacted contradictorily on the Philippine problem. American beet and dairy farmers and banks interested in Cuban sugar cried out against the keen competition of duty-free products from the Islands, and the American Federation of Labor agitated for restrictions on the importation of cheap Filipino labor. But it was realized that the Philippines had become so dependent on the American market that, if their political independence placed them outside the American tariff wall, it would involve too many painful economic adjustments. At the same time the strategic position of the Islands in the midst of an unsettled Pacific gave much food for anxious thought. As Japan pushed inexorably southward from her land bases in Manchuria, even the noisiest of Filipino nationalists became a little hesitant. The Filipino politico might still clamor for *independencia* at election time. His slogan netted votes from the peasantry, who only too often interpreted it as freedom from taxes. But privately he was willing perhaps to admit that the cry for independence was for domestic consumption only. In the United States were two schools of strategy. One school contended that the Japanese danger increased American military responsibilities and that Filipinos could not be left to face a probable Japanese conquest with their own unaided resources. The other contended that the defense of the Islands in any case would be so hazardous and expensive that withdrawal, while there was yet time to withdraw, voluntarily and with dignity, was the only policy consistent with long-term expedience.

In 1933, Congress, buffeted by these varied opinions, passed a bill granting Philippine independence over the presidential veto. The Philippine Legislature, condemning the naval and military reservations in the act as a violation of national sovereignty, rejected it. In 1934 the Tydings-McDuffie Act, with the objectionable features of the previous legislation removed, passed Congress, and this the Philippine Legislature accepted. The act provided for a transition period of ten years, during which the United States was to supervise and control the Islands' foreign relations, loans contracted abroad, and defense. Thereafter, complete political independence was conceded, the United States reserving only the right to maintain naval stations on the Islands. But the price of independence, it would seem, would be economic chaos, since 80 per cent of Philippine exports went to the United States. Furthermore, the 8,000 members of the Philippine Constabulary were obviously inadequate as a defense force against Japan. In 1937, Manuel Quezon, the Philippine President, enlisted the services of General MacArthur on his retirement as Chief of Staff of the United States Army in order to build up the Constabulary into a Philippine Commonwealth Army. MacArthur originally projected an expansion of 40,000 men a year, but lack of staff personnel reduced his program by 50 per cent.

In March 1938, in view of the multiple problems of defense and the approach of the Japanese armies in South China, President Quezon tried to dissuade Washington from laying down the white man's burden too hastily. After an exchange of telegrams, President Roosevelt agreed that the question of full independence should be postponed till 1960. Notice was served on Japan thereby that American determination to enlarge the political responsibilities of the Philippines by installments was not to be confused with a policy of scuttle and retreat from existing military commitments.

AUSTRALIA

Japan's southward surge in the later thirties did not come to Australians as a new threat, but as the militant intensification of an old one. The "yellow peril" had shown its face as early as 1851, when numbers of Chinese had entered Victoria as part of the coolie traffic of that time. Chinese freedom of entry was checked, first by the colonies, then by the federal government. The unexpected victory of Japan over China in 1895 and the acquisition of Samoa by Germany in 1899 inspired further anxiety among Australians, and were factors contributing to the federation of the individual colonies into the Commonwealth of Australia in 1901. Japanese immigration meanwhile grew to sufficient volume to become the subject of a "Gentleman's Agreement" in 1905. Japanese students, merchants, and tourists were to be admitted, but permanent settlement by Japanese nationals was banned. The further revelation of Japan's strength during her war with Russia in 1905 and persistent rumors of Japanese espionage along the Australian coast and the Great Barrier Reef determined Australia to put her defenses in order. Conscription for home defense was adopted in 1909, and the nucleus of a separate Australian Navy was formed in the same year.

During the First World War, Australia and Japan found themselves allies, but their alliance was always an uneasy one. Japan's seizure of the German islands in the North Pacific, and the patrolling of southern waters by her warships excited intense resentment in Australia. The British Government in London was at pains to explain that it had sanctioned the Japanese action and that Britain and Japan were allies under the treaty of 1902. The odd compound of apprehension and conciliation which characterized Australia's attitude toward Japan was given forceful expression at Versailles by her outspoken Premier Hughes. He took the lead in securing the rejection of a Japanese demand for racial equality, fearing that it was a veiled manifesto against immigration barriers (see p. 120). He disapproved of Japan's mandate over the former German islands in the North Pacific, control of which halved the distance between Japanese-held territories and Australia, and he as vehemently approved of Australia's and New Zealand's mandates over the former German islands in the South Pacific. Nevertheless, when the termination of the Anglo-Japanese Alliance was canvassed at the Imperial Conference of 1921, Hughes held out tenaciously for its continuance on the ground that Japan's faithful observance of her treaty commitments during the First World War had amply demonstrated her reliability as an ally. When the Anglo-Japanese Alliance was permitted to lapse in favor of the very nebulous Four-Power Treaty (see p. 365), a considerable body of opinion followed Hughes in asserting that one of the main props of Australian security in the Pacific had been swept away. The safe passage of the Singapore Bill through the British Parliament in 1923 helped to conciliate all sections of Australian opinion, which regarded the construction of the base as a *quid pro quo* for the relaxing of imperial ties with Japan.

The temporary abandonment of Japanese expansionist plans after 1922 and the growth of commerce between the two nations helped to dull the keen edge of Australian apprehension. Australian wool found a ready market in Japan. A high protective tariff in Australia acted as a dam against the mass inflow of Japanese goods, and created a favorable trade balance which Australia was anxious to preserve. The Depression further reduced imports from Japan in 1931 to 42 per cent of their 1929 value. The Ottawa Agreement of 1932 also seemed likely to make inroads on Japanese exports in the interests of inter-Commonwealth trade (pp. 564–65). Shrill threats of a trade war were raised in Tokyo. Tariff rates on Japanese textiles therefore were sharply reduced by the Lyons ministry in 1932.

The Japanese trade offensive of the early thirties poured increasing quantities of rayon and textiles over the top of the lowered tariff wall. Rumors of increased protection were heard in Canberra, the Australian capital, and at once aroused all the old tensions. Militarists in Japan, led by the Anglophobe General Terauchi, even called for a boycott of Australian products. But Britain spent nearly four times as much in Australia as Japan, an elementary fact which was driven home by Sir Ernest Thompson's mission to Australia in 1936 on behalf of the drooping Lancashire textile trade. At the end of 1936, a provisional Japanese-Australian trade agreement was reached, on a quota basis.

The signs and portents of relentlessly approaching conflict in the Pacific shifted Australia's attention from purely economic relations to the infinitely complex problem of defense. Australians in the grip of the Depression had not reacted violently to the Manchurian episode of 1931. It was generally calculated that the absorption and digestion of Manchuria would divert Japan's energies for a long time to come. But in 1934, Japan resumed her full freedom of action in naval construction, and in 1938 the Sino-Japanese War spread to South China. The Munich crisis of the same year, with its connotations of British military unpreparedness, suggested that the naval and military resources of the mother country would be mortgaged to the full in Europe in the event of war with Germany. The rapid approach to completion of the Singapore base was not completely reassuring; for in the absence of a major British Pacific Fleet it might well be by-passed by an invader pushing south. The United States, withdrawn behind its neutrality legislation, seemed inclined to cultivate its garden regardless of the acts of highway robbery perpetrated outside the legislative ring fence.

The problem of defense was aggravated by Canberra's venerable policy of a white but empty Australia. The British and Australian governments had twice combined their efforts, in 1922 and 1925, to provide assisted passages and farm land respectively in order to encourage the mass immigration of white settlers. But the lukewarmness of the powerful Australian labor unions and the onset of the Depression proved to be serious deterrents. Australia's population of 7,000,000 was largely left to thrive upon its own natural growth of some 52,000 births yearly. This scanty human crop was most unevenly distributed over the vast expanse of Australia's 3,000,000 square miles. Concentration was greatest in the southeastern belt stretching from Brisbane to Adelaide, where most of the industries and seaports lay. It ·

was thinnest on the threatened northern coasts, where the semidesert Northern Territory, with an area of 500,000 square miles, contained a population of 9,000. Port Darwin was the only defensive center in northern Australia which possessed direct land communications, via Birdum and Alice Springs (Stuart), with the sources of supply in the southeast, some 1,500 miles distant. Alternatively, the possibility of an amphibious operation directed against the vital southeastern coastal area was a contingency not to be lightly dismissed.

Preparations for defense, unhappily, became bound up with party differences and rival strategic doctrines. Lyons, the Conservative Premier, urged the building up of the Australian Navy, which, in co-operation with British forces, would intercept the foe far out to sea. Curtin, the leader of the Labor Opposition, contended that Japan would not move against Australia until Britain was deeply involved in a major European conflict and that little external aid could be expected therefore, if Britain's main naval forces were pinned down elsewhere. Curtin advocated consequently the construction of a powerful air force which could bomb enemy flotillas on the sea approaches to Australia. The superior fluidity of air power would guarantee its rapid concentration at any threatened point. The former conscription enactment of 1909 had been repealed in 1929, mainly as a pacifist gesture, by the Labor government of the time. But it was evident enough that a volunteer army — numbering 34,000 in 1937 — would be inadequate even for home defense. The urban and industrial areas on the outer rim of the country might thus be lost at the first onset, leaving only the grim prospect of withdrawal into the desert wastes of central Australia, the "dead heart" of the continent. Nevertheless, the present government had no wish to revive the past cleavages in Australian opinion over conscription for overseas service, and the Australian Army continued to be recruited on a voluntary basis. The Australian public naturally favored a policy of long-range defense, and advocated expansion of both the naval and air arm. Military expenditures, which doubled between 1933 and 1936, were devoted chiefly to these two services in roughly equal proportions. But in 1939 the main strength of the Australian Navy lay in its seven cruisers and seven destroyers, and that of the Australian Air Force in its 150 first-line planes.

The low industrial potential of the Dominion was a major obstacle to rearmament. Wool, grain, and meat had long been the staple products. Ores, however, were extensively mined; and the great Broken Hill Proprietary Company of New South Wales had turned to the production of steel under pressure of war needs in 1915. Indeed, the Iron Knob and Yampi Sound quarries, leased to Japanese concessionaires, had exported much iron ore and manganese to Japan until the government intervened in June 1938 to impose a total export ban on iron and manganese except to Britain and the Commonwealth. But oil, rubber, aluminum, nickel, and mercury were grievously lacking. Machine tools hardly existed, and the reservoir of skilled mechanics had dwindled with the fall in immigration. In the production of the more deadly implements of modern war, therefore, Australia started from scratch. The construction of the first aircraft factory was begun at Fishermen's Bend, Port Melbourne, in 1936. The all-important decision to employ American designs in aircraft production was taken in 1937. The first Bren-gun carriers rolled off the assembly lines in the same year.

It was not surprising, therefore, that Australia began to scan the northern horizon for allies. Geographically she was the southern terminus of the long, curving chain of islands which, from Sakhalin and Hokkaido in the north to the Netherlands East Indies in the south, formed a series of immense stepping-stones, a veritable Giant's Causeway, leading to the Dominion's northern littoral. British, American, and Dutch possessions were all involved in the task of setting a limit to Japan's drive to the south. But their defenses, as we have seen, were flimsy, none too well manned, and enclosed millions of natives whose attitude might be passive or dubious in the event of an attack. These considerations lent a dynamic and rather independent quality to Australian policy in the later thirties. On the one hand, apprehension led to efforts to conciliate Japan, such as the sweeping nonaggression pact proposed to all the Pacific Powers by Premier Lyons in 1937. On the other, it produced a strong demand by the Labor party that the armed forces should be kept at home, or at least in the Pacific area, in the event of a European conflict involving Britain.

With the United States, Australia's economic and cultural relations were very weak. Although some American automobiles, tobacco, and oil penetrated into the Australian market, in neither country was popular knowledge or appreciation of the other at all extensive. Australians, perhaps attaching too much importance to the similarity of language, were puzzled and disappointed at the American approach to international affairs, especially during the isolationist period. Americans, on the other hand, responded to the idea of remoteness implied in the phrase "down under" by dismissing Australia as a faraway country of which little was known, or needed to be known. Yet the curiously aloof trend sometimes noticeable in the Australian Government, the impression conveyed of being in the Pacific but not of it, could not long survive the appearance of the threatening clouds on the horizon of the "Near North."

In 1937, Australia appointed her first permanent diplomatic representative abroad — a Counselor in the British Embassy at Washington. Timid as the move was, it signalized a departure from the deep preoccupation with internal affairs and with the imperial connection between which the pendulum of party politics had swung since the First World War. Finally, early in 1939, the Australian Government announced that legations were to be established in Washington and Tokyo. Australia was no longer inclined to be drawn complacently along in the diplomatic wake of Britain. Yet there was no suicidal inclination "to cut the painter" or to contract out of the British Commonwealth. Australia was intent upon supplementing the protection she enjoyed under the crumbling *Pax Britannica* by forming links with the major powers of the Pacific. If Australia was to remain a stronghold of white exclusiveness, the laws of diplomatic attraction would swing American-Australian policy into the same direction. Out of the north, then, could come either aid and comfort or desolation and ruin. Political weather prophets might well speculate which would first appear there, the friendly faces of a kindred race or the spreading brownish-yellow tide.

NEW ZEALAND

Twelve hundred miles from Australia, across the Tasman Sea, lie the two major islands "capped by snow-clad peaks and protected by the thundering surf" which the Dutch explorers, in Abel Tasman's wake, loyally christened New Zealand. The ubiquitous Captain Cook declared the territory annexed to the British Crown in 1770; but the action was hastily disavowed by his government, which already had a plenitude of colonial problems in North America and had no inclination to add to them. Fear of French intervention finally led to the establishment of British sovereignty by the Treaty of Waitangi in 1840, which, however, confirmed the native Maoris in inalienable possession of their tribal and family land. The land provisions of the treaty were ill-observed; but the intermittent Maori wars that ensued from 1846 to 1870 did not discourage the inflow of settlers brought by the gold discoveries of 1853 and 1861. Thus the numbers of white colonists — only 27,000 at mid-century — rose appreciably; and many who had failed to strike it rich in the gold rush settled down to the less romantic but steadier occupation of sheep farming. Between 1851 and 1871 the sheep on the lush, rolling pastures of South Island rose from 250,000 to 10,000,000. The advent of refrigerator ships in the seventies opened up distant markets for meat exports.

The tide of immigration into New Zealand, in the second half of the nineteenth century, was almost exclusively British, and it had been drawn in particular from those classes in the mother country which had most felt the contemporary social and industrial changes. There had been no simultaneous influx of cheap foreign labor and, in course of time, terms of mutual respect were established with the fine Maori aborigines. By a series of happy accidents, therefore, New Zealand was able to build up a state of extraordinary unity, free from minority problems, left-wing in political outlook and, in a well-favored land of equable and friendly climate, she had developed a social system, British in its best elements, and without the social oppressiveness of its late-Victorian origins.

Legislative reform, especially during the depressed conditions of the late eighties and early nineties, had been highly radical. Universal manhood suffrage came in 1889, and women's suffrage in 1894. In the same year, the *annus mirabilis* of New Zealand labor, labor unions were fully legalized, an Arbitration Court was established to mediate industrial disputes, and the tottering Bank of New Zealand was reorganized under a majority of government-nominated directors. Four years later an Old Age Pension Act became law after bitter debate. John Ballance and "King Dick" Seddon, who initiated this legislative program, were not doctrinaire socialists but empiricists, seeking to establish by rule of thumb the delicate balance between the rights of the individual and the economic welfare of the young community.

Absorbed in their domestic issues, New Zealanders scarcely noticed the radical alteration in the balance of naval power in the Pacific during the early years of the twentieth century. The disconcerting growth of German naval power after 1898 had impelled Britain to concentrate much of her strength in home waters. The Anglo-Japanese Treaty of 1902 revealed that

Britain was casting Japan for the role of watchdog in the Far East and, in 1906, all major British naval units were withdrawn from Pacific waters. The situation manifestly demanded a policy of increased self-help on the part of New Zealand. Raised to the status of a Dominion in 1907, she introduced compulsory military training three years later. The Naval Defense Act of 1913 provided for the establishment of a New Zealand Naval Squadron, to be placed under the orders of the British Admiralty in time of war.

Thus girded and prepared, the new Dominion was able to put forth a maximum naval and military effort in the First World War. The scanty population yielded 124,000 men for active service, of whom 19,000 were killed in action. A hectic prosperity came with the war years, for Britain, New Zealand's best customer, purchased her meat, wool, and dairy products in bulk at guaranteed prices. The workers shared in the general well-being, though the continued militant temper of the New Zealand Federation of Labor was reflected in the widespread coal strike of 1917, at the very height of the war.

The postwar economic crisis of the early twenties was surmounted with only a moderate rise in unemployment. But the national economy, dependent largely on the export of a narrow range of foodstuffs and of primary commodities, was shaken to its base by the more prolonged Depression of the early thirties. Between 1929 and 1932 the national income fell away by nearly a half, and the value of exports by nearly a third. In this emergency the Coates cabinet, in September 1931, opened its ranks and formed a coalition government. The falling index of prices on the world market suggested a policy of cost reduction, especially in relation to wages. In April 1932 an Amendment Act was introduced, which threatened the standards of wages and hours which had been gradually built up by the Arbitration Court of 1894. In the same month, a demonstration by the unemployed in Auckland ended in some window smashing in Queen Street, and the government was obliged to take strong action against the dissemination of seditious literature, chiefly by a small Communist party. The financial structure was underpinned by the establishment of a Reserve Bank under government auspices in 1933. By 1935, exports had climbed painfully back to 90 per cent of their former value.

The bitter and searching physic prescribed by the Coates cabinet as a remedy for the Depression was not relished by the electorate, which returned a Labor majority in November 1935 and held 53 out of 76 seats in the House of Representatives. A spate of legislation followed which was to make New Zealand one of the most interesting "socialist" experiments in the world. Dairy farmers were accorded a guaranteed price, especially for their butter and cheese, and those struggling with debts contracted during the Depression were protected against eviction. A State Advances Corporation provided cheap long-term loans in the shape of first mortgages on property. A Finance Act restored all cuts in wages and salaries made during the Depression to the rates prevailing on March 31, 1931. An Agricultural Workers' Act established minimum-wage rates for workers on dairy farms. A Social Security Act consolidated and extended previous welfare legislation, providing insurance against sickness and unemployment, family allowances, a comprehensive national health service, and superannuation benefits. The cost of the act was defrayed by a tax of 5 per cent on all salaries, wages, and other income. If a deficit occurred, it was met out of general revenue. Compulsory arbitration of labor disputes was reintroduced. The closed shop was given legal sanction.

As the thirties wore on, the search for social security in New Zealand was increasingly jeopardized by the growing military insecurity in the Pacific. The Manchurian crisis in 1931 stirred opinion in New Zealand to an awareness of the inability of the League of Nations to check aggression, and of the weakness of the British imperial defenses in the Far East. The Coates government therefore pressed hard for effective League support of China, and applauded the resumption of construction work on the projected naval base at Singapore. Confidence in the League, however, could scarcely survive the Ethiopian fiasco, which inspired a striking memorandum from New Zealand to Geneva in 1936, pointing out that there had been a failure of will and a reluctance to accept the necessity of enforcing not only economic but military sanctions against disturbers of the peace. In the same year, New Zealand gave a lead to the other Powers with interests in the Pacific by banning the export of scrap iron to Japan.

New Zealand's basic strategic problem was the same as Australia's — though with the added isolation of her distance from Australia. Her own rugged territorial coastline was 4,000 miles in length, and her military man power, for all purposes, had to be drawn from a population of little more than 1,500,000. The expansion of her armed forces, the construction of airdromes and training schools, the purchase of planes, and the development of the naval base at Auckland increased defense expenditure fivefold between 1935 and 1940. In April 1939, New Zealand succeeded in arranging a Pacific Defense Conference at Wellington between staff representatives of Britain, Australia, and herself. One of the preoccupations of the Conference was the defense of the protective screen of islands to the north of Australia and New Zealand, which might serve the Japanese as steppingstones across the South Pacific. Following the recommendations of the Conference, strategic points in these outlying islands were garrisoned before September 1939. As Japanese designs became increasingly clear, New Zealand troops established themselves in the British colonial dependencies of the Fiji Islands and Samoa.

38 THE AMERICAS: NEW DEAL AND HEMISPHERE DEFENSE

ECONOMIC PLANNING

If the foundations of American isolationism were laid at Versailles, it is undeniable that they were widened and deepened by the Depression of the early thirties. The American people, as the familiar economic landmarks began to sway and totter about them, could devote little immediate attention to disturbances elsewhere. By 1932 unemployment reached an estimated 14,000,000, more than one-quarter of the country's working population. Factory pay rolls sank to one-third of the 1929 aggregate. No fewer than 1,400 banks failed in the course of 1932 (see p. 404).

The urgent task of buttressing the financial structure was first taken in hand by the Hoover administration, in spite of a professed belief that the economic blizzard would ultimately blow itself out. The Reconstruction Finance Corporation (RFC) was established by an act of Congress in January 1932. Provided with an initial grant of $2,000,000,000, its function was to furnish credit for underpinning banks, railroads, and industrial corporations. Under conservative direction, the RFC advanced more than $1,000,000,000 by midsummer. But this infusion of government-created credit was clearly a palliative rather than a panacea. Nor was it of much direct assistance to the small businessman. The struggling farmer received cold comfort from a Federal Farm Board, created in 1929, which sternly bade him grow less wheat and cotton lest the downward trend of agricultural prices should continue. By 1932 cotton had fallen from 16 cents a pound in 1929 to less than 6 cents, and wheat from $1.11 a bushel to 32 cents. The Treasury deficit for the calendar year was $2,885,000,000.

The presidential election of November 1932 was a landslide for the Democratic party. Hoover received a popular vote of 15,759,286 and carried 6 states with 59 votes in the Electoral College. Roosevelt received 22,813,786 and carried 42 states with 472 votes in the Electoral College. "In their need [the people of the United States]," said Roosevelt in his Inaugural Address, "have registered a mandate that they want vigorous action. . . . Our people have asked for discipline and direction in leadership. They have made me the present instrument of their wishes." The entire cycle of enactments which followed came to be known as the "New Deal," a slogan perhaps inspired by lingering recollections of Theodore Roosevelt's "Square Deal."

At the moment of the new President's inauguration the country was in the throes of a fresh wave of bank failures. Early in 1933, Congress had ordered publication of the advances made to financial concerns by the RFC. It appeared that over $16,000,000 had been loaned to the Union Guardian Trust Company of Detroit, of which nearly $9,500,000 was still outstanding in January 1933. There was an immediate run on the Trust Company; and the panic spread thereafter in ever widening circles. Governor Comstock of Michigan proclaimed an eight-day "bank holiday" early in February. Within a month, every state had imposed some kind of restriction on bank withdrawals.

Emergency banking legislation, in March 1933, permitted the reopening of banks under government license, if their condition was sound. By prohibiting the export of gold, the government strove to encourage a mild inflation, designed to raise the internal price level. The legislative attack on unemployment began with a Civilian Conservation Corps bill which placed 250,000 men at work immediately on forest conservation and flood control. The depressed prices of agricultural products, a persistent factor even in the "prosperous twenties," were combated by the Agricultural Adjustment Administration (AAA) under an Agricultural Adjustment Act which reduced the acreage under wheat, corn, rice, and other crops by voluntary agreement between the farmer and the Department of Agriculture. The farmer was compensated from the proceeds of a "processing tax" levied upon the manufacturer or middleman who first received the raw material. The same act empowered the administration to issue bonds to a maximum of $2,000,000,000 with which to refinance farm mortgages and thus prevent foreclosures.

The creeping paralysis which had overtaken industry was attacked by the National Industrial Recovery Act (NIRA) of June 1933. The legislation was based frankly on the assumption that the Depression, by encouraging cutthroat competition and wage-cutting by employers, had seriously weakened the purchasing power of the American public even at the current low price levels. Each industry was urged to draw up a code for "fair competition." The code had to give to the employee the right of collective barganing through a union of his own choosing. It had to prescribe maximum hours and minimum wages. It would become effective after presidential approval and would remain in force, in the first instance, for two years. If the producers in any industry failed to agree, the President was empowered to impose an appropriate code. Industries which conformed to the code and co-operated with the government were entitled to display a "Blue Eagle." At the same time, in furtherance of the presidential policy of "priming the pump," the expenditure of $3,300,000,000 on public works was authorized. The initial direction of NIRA — as befitted a governmental campaign against poverty and unemployment — was vested in a National Recovery Administration (NRA), headed by an army general of marked vituperative powers, Hugh S. Johnson.

New Deal legislation, in one respect, was frankly experimental, a series of empirical measures designed to meet an abnormal economic situation. Yet, in its underlying assumption, it was something more than a mere collection of ad hoc regulations. It premised the full co-operation of capital and labor inside an elastic framework of government controls. The future of the New Deal depended on the degree of cohesion attained by this triple alliance.

By implication it was opposed to the American tradition of rugged individuality. But its early, short-term effects were decidedly encouraging. Unhappily, the fundamental assumptions on which it was based were menaced by the emerging clash between capital and labor, and between capital and the government. The right of unionization and collective bargaining conceded by Section 7A of the NIRA precipitated a series of strikes in the automobile and textile industries. The newly established National Labor Relations Board (NLRB) was besieged with disputes. The alleged bias of the Board in favor of the employee did nothing to bridge the widening gulf between businessmen and the administration.

The President's social security program, introduced to Congress in January 1935, proved still more disconcerting to the orthodox. The Social Security Act embodied a comprehensive scheme for old-age and unemployment insurance, operated under state auspices and partly financed by joint contributions from employer and employee. A $5,000,000,000 Work Relief Program (WRP) proposed to put 3,500,000 unemployed to work. It was the forerunner of the much broader Works Progress Administration (WPA) under that curious, devoted man, Harry L. Hopkins, afterward to be Roosevelt's constant aide. Meanwhile the attack on the powerful utility holding companies and the creation of the Tennessee Valley Authority (TVA) brought redoubtable opponents into the field as the immediate crisis showed signs of receding.

The counterstroke was delivered by way of the Supreme Court. By returning a verdict for plaintiff in the famous Schechter case, in May 1935, the Court declared the major provisions of the NIRA to be unconstitutional. In January 1936 the Agricultural Adjustment Act was similarly invalidated as an invasion of states' rights. The President tried to rescue some parts of the NRA and AAA from the debris created by these shattering decisions and, reinforced by an overwhelming victory at the polls in November 1936, proceeded to submit a bill for the reform of the judiciary. His proposal to appoint a new Justice to the Supreme Court whenever any present member reached the age of seventy without retiring or resigning led to bitter controversy in an increasingly restless Congress. The cry "The Constitution is in danger!" proved particularly effective. The Supreme Court bill failed of passage before Congress adjourned in August 1937.

Meanwhile, organized labor proceeded on its tempestuous way. Rubber, steel, automobile, and airplane workers were unionized at great speed by the Committee for Industrial Organization (CIO), which split with the more conservative American Federation of Labor (A.F. of L.) and reorganized in 1938 as the Congress of Industrial Organizations. John L. Lewis provided militant leadership for this new organization of industrial workers, which at once plunged into bitter jurisdictional disputes with the A.F. of L.

Early in 1938 the President recommended to a highly apprehensive Congress an appropriation of $4,100,000,000 for relief and public works during the coming year. The Reconstruction Finance Corporation was empowered to loan private business a maximum of $1,500,000,000. Generous pump-priming, however, became decreasingly necessary as American business felt the stimulus of rearmament. The total of unemployed, estimated at 11,000,000 in 1937, began to shrink with unexampled speed. Ironically, the catastrophe of a general war seemed likely to bring an interim solution to the economic problems with which the government had wrestled for half a decade.

The Depression had also brought home to the American people the important, if minor, role of foreign trade in their national economy. Few Americans desired to adopt a Russian withdrawal into the recesses of a closed, self-sufficient autarchy. Consequently Secretary of State Hull chipped persistently at the towering tariff walls which held back American exports. Congress supported his efforts by the Trade Agreements Act of June 1934, which invested the government with power for three years to negotiate trade agreements with foreign Powers, and to raise or lower tariffs by a maximum of 50 per cent. Reciprocal trade pacts, covering a multitude of specific goods and commodities, were signed with fourteen nations by the middle of 1936. The effort to clear the choked channels of world trade was not without its international implications, since nations engaging in discriminatory practices against American commerce — Germany in particular — naturally found a shrinking market in the New World. Republican critics contended that the Hull policy permitted an inflow of competitive products to the domestic markets; but the government appeared confident that, on the whole, substantial advances had been made.

In retrospect, the New Deal emerges as a compromise. The crisis of 1933 affected such a broad sector of the electorate that the demand for prompt and decisive action by the government was politically irresistible. Yet a swift move in the direction of a fully controlled and regimented economy was repugnant to the American tradition and to its strong bent for personal independence and for empirical solutions. Consequently, while expanded governmental control of business was accepted in America as elsewhere as a weapon to combat the Depression, that control was not generally regarded as a panacea to be swallowed whole. After this middle-of-the-road policy had been chosen, the opposite pull and tug of conflicting interests ensured that the New Deal should not veer too far to the right or to the left. The election of 1938, which gave the Republicans 80 additional seats in the House and 8 in the Senate, was a warning signal to the more forthright New Dealers. In its labor and social welfare legislation, the Roosevelt administration conferred upon the United States within a few years the gains achieved in Britain, for example, over a period of half a century. Doubtless the speed of such legislation implied the need for subsequent modification in some respects. But the general trend was unmistakable. The United States was seeking a median point between unrestricted competition and a regimented economy.

THE MANCHURIAN CRISIS

The profound preoccupation of American opinion with the Depression at home and the corresponding tendency to relegate foreign affairs to second place were well exemplified in the Manchurian crisis (pp. 430–32). In

October 1931, a month after Sino-Japanese hostilities began, Secretary of State Henry L. Stimson reminded the parties of their obligations under the Pact of Paris (Kellogg-Briand Pact) to settle their differences peaceably. He also appeared to be making ready to give his independent diplomatic support to the League of Nations, to which China had appealed, and he authorized Prentiss Gilbert, the American consul in Geneva — though he gave him very limited instructions — to sit in at the League Council's October meetings. Unimpressed by this somewhat hesitant attitude, the Japanese forces pushed on remorselessly into southern Manchuria, paralyzing the activities of American concerns by a multitude of discriminatory measures imposed on the plea of "military necessity." The last flicker of Chinese resistance died with the fall of Chinchow in the first week of 1932. On January 7, 1932, in identical notes to Japan and China, Stimson enunciated his famous doctrine of nonrecognition of "any treaty or agreement . . . which may impair the treaty rights of the United States in China [notably the Open Door policy], . . . and any situation, treaty, or agreement which may be brought about by means contrary to . . . the Pact of Paris."

The simultaneous spread of hostilities to Shanghai excited proposals for an unofficial boycott of Japanese goods in the United States. But neither the American people nor their administration was disposed to impose economic sanctions on Japan by formal government action if, behind sanctions, there lurked the possibility of war. And Stimson was to be disappointed if, at this stage, he expected to find support in Britain, who herself had extensive economic interests in Shanghai. Indeed, "he sustained one of the coldest public rebuffs it has ever been the lot of an American Secretary of State to receive at the hands of a friendly power." [1] On January 11, it was curtly announced from London that, since Japan had given assurances in regard to a continued "Open Door" in Manchuria, the British Government did not consider it necessary to make any declaration on the lines of the Stimson doctrine of nonrecognition.

In view of the controversy that has been aroused by this incident, we may say that the British announcement was gauche in the extreme — we are told now that it was worded and issued by permanent officials of the Foreign Office without appreciating the effect it was going to produce. But Sir John Simon, the British Foreign Secretary, must have felt that there was little to be gained in trying to defend an "administrative integrity" which, in a revolutionary country like China, was still far from realization. The Stimson doctrine had been announced to the world after the fall of Chinchow, when to all intents and purposes the Japanese campaign in Manchuria had reached its objectives, and was a poor, wordy compensation for Stimson's hesitancy toward the League of Nations in the previous October. Britain, like the United States, was wrestling with economic crisis at home, and her naval and military resources in the Far East were a long way from justifying a stand against Japan. Threats without effective action, as Simon clearly implied, would further embitter relations without accomplishing any useful purpose.

In March 1932, Simon was to make some amends when the League Assembly unanimously adopted a resolution, introduced by himself, urging

League members to follow the Stimson doctrine. Nevertheless, the hard fact remained that Japan's aggression — the first of a series — had proceeded defiantly and that no Power, inside or outside the League, had been prepared to take the risk of war to stop her. Secretary Stimson, hampered by the apathy of public opinion and by pressure from isolationist Senators, found his field of action rigorously limited. But the Manchurian crisis, whatever its other lessons, at least destroyed the comfortable belief, so widely held by the British and American peoples in the easy twenties, that there was some magic influence in world opinion which could of itself force the sword from the nerveless grasp of an aggressor.

THE RECOGNITION OF THE SOVIET UNION

The recognition of the Soviet Union by the United States in 1933 was perhaps the most important diplomatic event of the first year of Roosevelt's presidency. It was a part of general policy of amelioration at home and abroad to which the new administration was expressly committed. In the gray days of the Depression any opportunity for increasing foreign trade could not be lightly passed by, and Russia was no longer, in Secretary Hughes's classic phrase, "a gigantic economic vacuum." The inauguration of the first Five-Year Plan in 1928 had caused a great expansion of Soviet demands for American locomotives, agricultural machinery, and electrical equipment. The ensuing Depression, coupled with the Soviet's difficulties in obtaining adequate credits and foreign exchange, by 1932 had reduced American exports to the Soviet Union to a mere $13,000,000. At the World Economic Conference in London in 1933, the Soviet delegate, Maxim Litvinov, shrewdly baiting the hook, had expressed the readiness of his government to place orders abroad totaling $1,000,000,000.

Nonetheless the recognition would be a complete reversal of policy from the Coolidge and Hoover days, when both the official and popular attitude of the United States toward the Soviet Union had been one of uncompromising abhorrence. American property to the estimated value of $440,000,000 had been confiscated in the turmoil of the Bolshevik Revolution. An American loan of $332,000,000 to the Kerensky government had not been honored by the Soviets, which had preferred counterclaims of their own for damages inflicted by American forces during the Siberian expedition. These were no small obstacles to be overcome before normal diplomatic relations between the United States and the Soviet Union could be restored. But perhaps the threatened debt defaults on the part of the European nations in 1933 showed that the Soviet Union was not the only black sheep in the flock of America's debtors, and made its shortcomings, if not less reprehensible, at least less exceptional.

But the recognition was dictated no less by the developing situation in the Far East, which was as alarming to the United States as to the Soviet Union. In October 1933, President Roosevelt sent a personal note to President Kalinin regretting past differences and adding that he would gladly receive any representatives that the Soviet Union might designate "to explore with me personally all questions outstanding between our two countries." Kalinin replied in equally cordial terms. During November, Litvinov arrived in Washington as special Soviet envoy. Between his hours of business at the White House and the State Department, he was dined and feted, and he used every occasion to declare his belief in the enduring peace and co-operation that must henceforth distinguish Soviet-American relations. Eight days of discussion sufficed for an agreement, and formal diplomatic relations were established by an exchange of notes between Roosevelt and Litvinov. Litvinov dropped all claims for damages against the United States on account of the American expedition in Siberia and pledged his government to give protection to American citizens in the Soviet Union and to abstain from revolutionary propaganda in the United States.

Further financial negotiations were deferred until the arrival of William C. Bullitt, the new American ambassador, in Moscow. The Soviet Union was reluctant to conclude an agreement in regard to existing debts without assurances of further loans from the United States. But the Johnson Act of 1934 prohibited the granting of loans to any government in default. Negotiations consequently collapsed early in 1935. However, a commercial treaty was concluded in July 1935 whereby the Soviet Union agreed to spend $30,000,000 in the United States in the following year. This scanty dribble of trade did little to fructify confidence on either side. Nor was the State Department entirely convinced that the Comintern was dead in the United States. The two giants of the Eastern and Western Hemispheres continued to eye each other warily across the chasm of mutual distrust bridged so precariously by the diplomatic understanding of 1933.

THE NEUTRALITY ACTS

The remoter origins of the United States' neutrality legislation in the thirties reached back to the First World War. The invigorating watchwords by which President Wilson had striven to elevate the conflict into something loftier than a punitive expedition — "the war for democracy" and "the war to end war" — had already begun to sound hollow by the early twenties. Sharp commercial and naval rivalry with Britain engendered a dull animosity which the outbreak of ill will over the war-debt question carried over into the thirties. A heavily armed France, grimly holding watch and ward over a rearming Continent, appeared to Americans as the stubborn defender of a chaotic *status quo* in the Old World. She, too, had repudiated her financial obligations to the United States, after contributing to a general financial collapse by hesitating to accept the Hoover Moratorium (see p. 406). Viewed against this background, the emergence of Hitler as the apostle of a German war of revenge seemed just such a warning tremor as had preceded the catastrophe of 1914.

Americans, as they watched the familiar storm signals flying in Europe, hardened their determination to "stay in the cyclone cellar" — all the more because they themselves were already involved in an exacting, if bloodless war on poverty and depression. In retrospect, popular opinion, so prone to seek scapegoats, ascribed the Depression in part to the irresponsible egotism of bankers and financiers. Big business lay temporarily under a cloud. It was a sign of the times, therefore, when a Senate resolution in April 1934 appointed a committee of seven, headed by Senator Nye, to investigate the activities of armament manufacturers and their financial associates during the First World War. Some of the disclosures were startling, and they were widely publicized. Public opinion straightway demanded clamorously that the "merchants of death" should be prevented from prodding the nation into another war. Obviously, it was argued, the price of peace was the sacrifice of war profits and a perfect impartiality toward all belligerents.

We need not submit these views to detailed analysis. It is sufficient to observe that they were widely held and deeply felt.[2] Consequently, the open announcement of German rearmament in March 1935, and Italian mobilization against Ethiopia in the summer of 1935, produced a tremendous upsurge of antiwar sentiment in the United States. Under the threat of a filibuster, the strong neutrality bloc in Congress rushed through a hastily devised resolution prohibiting the sale and transport of "arms, ammunition, or implements of war" to belligerents after the President had recognized, by proclamation, a state of war in any area. This Neutrality Act, as it was called, received the presidential signature in August 1935. Under its provisions the President could decide at his own discretion what articles were to be embargoed. He could similarly prohibit travel by American citizens on the vessels of belligerents, save at their own risk. He could exclude the submarines of the warring Powers from American ports. Manifestly the framers of the resolution had sought to avoid repetition of the struggle over neutral rights on the high seas and over neutral trade with belligerents which they believed had been one cause of American involvement in the First World War (pp. 25 and 26–27). But the legislation limited the embargoes to munitions, and in a major naval conflict it would probably have run afoul of the same kind of contraband controversy as had once raged in 1914–17. The State Department, better foreseeing the technical difficulties, would doubtless have appreciated a more flexible act empowering the President to restrict the transfer of arms to aggressors.

Shortly after receiving the presidential sanction, the Neutrality Act, with all its imperfections on its head, was applied to the Italo-Ethiopian War. Secretary Hull strove to stop one loophole by imposing a "moral embargo" on the export of oil, copper, scrap iron, and similar articles. But his unofficial pressure produced little effect. Exports from the United States to Italy rocketed from a monthly average of $25,000 in 1934 to $583,000 in November 1935. It is possible that, had the League of Nations imposed oil sanctions against Italy, the administration might have asked Congress for permission to follow suit (see p. 506). There is no doubt that Secretary Hull was deeply disturbed by Mussolini's forthright application of military force to gain Italian ends in Ethiopia. In an interview with the Italian ambassador, Rosso, in Washington in November 1935, Hull inquired "why his government had not taken $100,000,000 to Ethiopia and brought back a key to the entire Empire instead of expending several hundred million dollars in its military conquest with all the worry and threat of danger to the balance of the world." [3] He urged further that "the ambassador must realize the awful re-percussions that make their immediate appearance in far and remote parts of the world, and which are calculated to give this nation and perhaps others, including Italy, unimaginable troubles for a generation." [3] Secretary Hull was manifestly aware of the truth of the doctrine being preached even then by the queer, hoarse voice of Litvinov at Geneva, "Security is indivisible." But the steady flow of American supplies to Italy continued, and furnished an additional reason for the failure of the League Powers to pass from partial to full sanctions against the aggressor. Americans for their part regarded the unfortunate Hoare-Laval Plan for the partition of Ethiopia with intense distaste (see p. 506) . Any degree of American co-operation with the League, it was pointed out, might be stultified at any time by a sudden reversion to secret diplomacy of the old type.

The decision of the League in July 1936 to drop sanctions against Italy was an important turning point for the United States no less than for Europe. It was an open secret at Geneva that the application of economic sanctions against Italy was something in the nature of a rehearsal designed to test the effectiveness of such measures for future use against Germany, if ever that contingency should arise. Congress, more isolationist than ever, went on to build the Chinese Wall of neutrality still higher. When the embargo provisions of the Neutrality Act became due to expire, the act was prolonged till May 1937. A number of amendments were written into it, prohibiting, among other things, the granting of government loans and credits to belligerents. In January 1937, by joint Congressional resolution, the embargo was extended to both sides indifferently in the Spanish Civil War.

But foreign policy could not be conducted within the literal rigidity of a legislative enactment. American neutrality in practice encountered unforeseen technical difficulties just as much as the League's sanctions had done. The embargo denied arms to the legitimate Spanish Republican government at a time when Germany and Italy were sending aid to the rebel Nationalists. The net effect of the renewed Neutrality Act was to discriminate against the victim of aggression and the democratic party in the conflict. A further Neutrality Act accordingly was drafted and passed by Congress in May 1937. The ban on the export of munitions, on the transportation of arms to belligerents in American ships, on travel by American citizens on the vessels of belligerents, and on the granting of loans to warring Powers was retained. Furthermore, no American ship engaged in routine commerce with belligerents was to be armed. But the President was now accorded authority to permit the export of goods (other than arms and ammunition) to a belligerent if such goods were paid for on delivery, and if they were shipped from the United States by the purchaser.

The new "cash-and-carry" clause obviously favored any Power which controlled the seas and which possessed the necessary investments and credits in the United States. It need hardly be said that, in the event of a war in Europe, the act would operate in favor of the democracies and against the Axis. It was no less obvious that the United States, still struggling with the Depression, could not forego the possible war boom which would result from a new European conflict.

ISOLATION AND REARMAMENT

The United States, in the later thirties, bore more than one point of resemblance to Britain during the same period. A peace-hungry people, disillusioned over the course of events which they had sought in vain to mold to their own ways of thinking, were gradually made aware of the perils in which they lived and moved. There was one difference. Whereas the administration in Britain seemed to be aiding and abetting the people in their ostrichlike pacifism, the administration of the United States — and notably the President himself — was in advance of the people in its appreciation of the dangerous drift of events. The time lag between the administration and the people was perhaps in some respects unavoidable. It was manifestly impossible to publicize, for example, the highly confidential memorandum of Colonel Wuest, the American military attaché in Berlin, who reported to the State Department, as early as May 1934, the existence of "unusually close and friendly relations between Germany and Japan even to the extent of a possible secret alliance." [4]

In the end, the conversion of the American people to a more realistic and combative frame of mind had to be achieved by the incontrovertible facts, as they were now to develop in Europe and the Far East, rather than by the prodding speeches of President Roosevelt and his colleagues or by their notes and warnings to Axis dictators. The internal peculiarities of Nazi Germany evoked sporadic demonstrations and boycotts. Thus, on one occasion, the swastika flag was torn down from the *Bremen* in New York Harbor. But these incidents were mere ripples on the surface of a general national apathy. Popular radio commentators kept their listeners well informed — remarkably well informed — but their exciting and melodramatic manner of delivery bred a sort of immunity to news of crises from abroad. President Roosevelt provoked more criticism than approval by a speech in Chicago, in October 1937, when he sought to test public reaction to a policy of "quarantining" aggressor Powers. Isolationism at this time tended to crystallize readily round such well-known figures as Charles Lindbergh and Henry Ford. Under their leadership, it would adduce the comfortable thesis that Nazi energies were fully taken up by internal problems in Germany, or that Japan was too weak economically to engage in a major Pacific war, or that the simple facts of geography refuted so fantastic an idea as an Axis assault on the Western Hemisphere. These contentions met ready acceptance at a time when the state of affairs nearer home, pump-priming and the Supreme Court and unemployment — always unemployment — filled the mind of "the forgotten man."

Nevertheless, President Roosevelt persisted tirelessly in his quest for peace. The formation of the Rome-Berlin Axis in 1936 and Japan's renewed penetration of China in 1937 suggested only too clearly that the forces of aggression in Europe and Asia were reinforcing each other and synchronizing their efforts. In January 1938, President Roosevelt sent a personal letter to Neville Chamberlain, the British Prime Minister, to invite his co-operation in a conference at Washington for the discussion of outstanding international issues. If the Axis Powers and Japan stood aloof from the project, they would brand themselves plainly as unrepentant aggressors. If they participated, the onward rush toward global conflict might be checked. But Chamberlain, in a chilling reply, suggested a postponement of the conference. A general Anglo-Italian agreement was then pending, and President Roosevelt's proposals, it seemed to Chamberlain, might cut across that agreement and jeopardize its successful outcome (see p. 614). Needless to say, the conference in Washington was never held.

The Czechoslovak crisis of 1938, culminating in the Munich Agreement, will be described in the next chapter. It is only necessary here to mention the American reaction. The partial mobilization of the Czechoslovak Army in May of that year, in response to rumors of an impending Nazi coup (see p. 622), had encouraged the belief that the period of temporizing with Germany was past, and it seemed likely therefore that the renewed German threats against Czechoslovakia, later in September, would be met with firmness. President Roosevelt's note of September 26, urging all the parties concerned to continue negotiations for a peaceful settlement, was favorably received by the American people, since many believed that it was in essence directed to Hitler alone, the principal disturber of the peace. Hitler's reply, on September 26, was not without a smart diplomatic expertness. The Czechs, it ran, after a campaign of terrorization against the German minority, were in receipt of Germany's terms for a "rapid and peaceful solution" of the dispute. "It now lies not in the hands of the German Government, but in the hands of the Czechoslovak Government, to decide whether there shall be peace or war." The President's counterreply on September 27 placed the responsibility for a possible war squarely on Hitler's shoulders: "The present negotiations still stand open. They can be continued, if you give the word." But, in deference to isolationist opinion at home, the President concluded: "The Government of the United States has no political involvement in Europe, and will assume no obligations in the conduct of the present negotiations." [5]

The Munich Agreement between Germany, Britain, France, and Italy for the transfer to Germany of the Czechoslovak territories in dispute was signed on September 30, 1938 (see p. 628). The Czechoslovak crisis was resolved, as the President had urged, by peaceful means. The immediate reaction of the American people was one of heartfelt relief that war had been avoided. But only a few days were to pass before the damaging items on the balance sheet of Munich were fully understood, and a storm of criticism gathered against this "peace that passeth understanding." Czechoslovakia had enjoyed a high place in American esteem ever since Masaryk, during his visit to the United States in 1918, had himself wrought its foundations. It was a nation whose free institutions and healthy prosperity had distinguished it as the most successful of the interwar experiments in liberal democracy. It was suspected that the quasi-Fascist elements in Britain and France — "the Cliveden set" and "the two hundred families" — had allowed Hitler to blackmail them into preparing its destruction, and had struck a bargain in the interests of their own self-preservation over the heads of their respective peoples.

An "isolation of disgust" was very strong in the United States after Munich. But the shock of the Munich Agreement sharpened the sense of impending danger in the United States and so directed increasing public attention to the problems of defense. The possibility of a diplomatic "squeeze play" against the United States by the world-embracing coalition of Germany, Italy, and Japan could not be lightly discounted. Huge appro priations for armaments, from this moment, came before Congress in a per petual stream. Combined appropriations for the armed services amounted to $909,000,000 in 1936–37, and to $1,156,000,000 for the navy alone in 1938–39. Blueprints for industrial mobilization were drawn up in 1937, when the War Department earmarked 12,000 factories which would be converted straightway to war production when "M-Day" (Mobilization Day) dawned. In October 1938, Secretary Hull submitted to the President a comprehensive program of "stock-piling," involving vast purchases of strategic raw materials which might prove difficult of access in the event of a general war. Congressional isolationists, still suspicious, hinted darkly that these vast new armaments might be used to pull Britain's chestnuts out of the fire. Few, however, could logically object to a policy of rearmament presented not as a means of implementing collective action against aggressors, but solely as a guarantee of national security.

But the "isolation of disgust" did hinder President Roosevelt and Secretary Hull from extracting full diplomatic value from the new rearmament program. The administration could only hammer at the education of public opinion, meanwhile reinforcing the position of the democracies so far as that opinion permitted. Roosevelt's declaration in a speech at Queen's University, Kingston, Ontario, in August 1938, gave assurance that the United States would "not stand idly by if domination of Canadian soil is threatened by any other empire." In this instance, public reaction on the whole was favorable, since "hemisphere defense" was one of the accepted policies of the day. The President released another trial balloon in his report on the state of the nation in January 1939, affirming: "There are many methods short of war, but stronger and more effective than mere words, of bringing home to aggressor governments the aggregate sentiments of our own people." To this, Congress made no response. Indeed, the accidental revelation that the administration had permitted a French military observer to fly in one of the latest Douglas bombers aroused such outspoken criticism that the President was obliged to reaffirm, in his press conference of February 1939, the policy of "no commitments." A Congressional motion to strengthen the Pacific outpost of Guam was blocked.

The President, straining at the Congressional leash, cautiously instituted a policy of "parallel action" with the democracies. On April 14, 1939, the day after Britain and France had pledged support to Greece and Rumania, in the event of a threat to their independence (see p. 639), the President made a pointed and dramatic appeal to the German Führer. "You have repeatedly asserted," the note declared, "that you and the German people have no desire for war. If this is true, there need be no war." The note proceeded to request an undertaking from the Führer to refrain from attacking the territories of thirty specified nations, including Greece and Rumania. If such an assurance should be forthcoming, the note concluded, the relaxation of tension would permit general participation in a conference for promoting disarmament and reopening the choked channels of world trade.[6] Hitler vouchsafed no direct reply to this unconventional appeal. But in a subsequent speech to the Reichstag, he made mock of the President's concern for the world at large and countercharged that moralizing statesman with many of the iniquities of which he himself had been accused.

This effort of the President to test and to demonstrate Hitler's belligerent intentions made little impression in the United States, where the neutrality legislation was once more before Congress. The cash-and-carry clause of the Neutrality Act of 1937 expired on May 1, 1939. Secretary Hull desired a renewal and extension of the clause so as to permit the purchase of arms in the United States on the cash-and-carry principle, but he failed to convince the resolute isolationist bloc in the Senate. The Secretary contended that, if American arms were not available to nations acting in self-defense, the path of the aggressor was thereby made smoother. The isolationists, led by Senators Nye, Clark, and Bone, retorted that the neutrality legislation was framed, not in order to influence the outcome of distant conflicts, but in order to curb the activities of individuals who, for reasons of private profit, might precipitate the nation into war.

Such was still the position when, in the early hours of September 1, 1939, Hitler unleashed his impatient legions on Poland. President Roosevelt, in a radio speech to the nation, issued a warning — and a conditional promise. The warning to the effect that "when peace has been broken anywhere, peace of all countries everywhere is in danger," received less attention than the promise: "As long as it remains within my power, there will be no blackout of peace in the United States." The qualification, though indirect, was unmistakable. The will to peace was not sufficient to guarantee peace when aggression stalked the world.

"THE NEW ORDER IN EAST ASIA"

The successful onslaught of Japan upon Manchuria in 1931 had convincingly revealed that neither the League Powers nor the United States were prepared in the name of collective security to halt aggression in China. The steady infiltration of Japanese influence into North China during 1933–37 made it all too clear that the Manchurian episode was only the first step in the reduction of the entire Chinese Republic to the status of a Japanese protectorate. Washington was fully aware of the grandiose schemes of empire which obsessed the minds of the Japanese militarists. "Their aim," reported Ambassador Grew from Tokyo in a confidential report to Secretary Hull in December 1934, "is to obtain trade control and eventually predominant political influence in China, the Philippines, the Straits Settlements, Siam, and the Dutch East Indies, the Maritime Provinces and Vladivostok, one step at a time, as in Korea and Manchuria, pausing intermittently to consolidate and then continuing as soon as the intervening obstacles can be overcome by diplomacy or force . . . We would be reprehensibly somnolent if we were to trust to the security of treaty restraints or international comity to safeguard our interests or, indeed, our own property." [7] A year later, Saburo Kurusu of the Japanese Foreign Office was frank enough to outline the Japanese blueprint of the future distribution of global power in informal exchanges with a member of the American Embassy in Tokyo: "He said that Japan was destined to be the leader of the Oriental civilization and would in course of time be the 'boss' of a group comprising China, India, the Netherlands East Indies, etc. . . . He proceeded to say that the United States will lead the Americas both North and South. Great Britain is leading the European countries, but Great Britain is degenerating, while the rest of Europe is decadent. Therefore it will end by the United States leading the Occidental civilization, while Japan leads the Oriental civilization." [8]

The Roosevelt administration proceeded with utmost caution to take unostentatious countermeasures in the Pacific. A $50,000,000 credit was extended to the Chinese Government through the Reconstruction Finance Corporation in May 1934. Sales of American airplanes to China doubled between 1933 and 1934, though the total was still inconsiderable. The recognition of the Soviet Union by the United States in November 1933 was regarded in Tokyo as a preliminary move by Washington to establish counterpoises to Japan in the Pacific. A year later, Japan denounced the Washington naval agreement of 1922. Thereafter the steadily expanding naval appropriations of both Powers revealed that the race for supremacy in the Pacific was well under way.

The continuing deterioration of international relations in the Far East formed a gloomy and unpromising background for the London Naval Conference of December 1935–March 1936. Japan stood immovably on the principle of full naval parity with the United States and Britain. The American delegation was equally firm, since it was felt that substantial concessions would imply toleration, if not tacit approval, of Japanese expansionism. Japan thereupon withdrew from the Conference. From that moment onward, wherever she looked in the Pacific — toward the Soviet Union, toward China, toward the United States — she saw only enemies, actual or potential. Tokyo therefore sought an avenue of escape out of this unwelcome but well-merited isolation by concluding an Anti-Comintern Pact with Germany. By an irresistible logic, the aggressor in the East became linked with the aggressor in the West. The Japanese Foreign Office denied that the pact contained secret clauses envisaging German-Japanese military co-operation in the event of war. But the American, British, and Soviet embassies in Tokyo strongly suspected that the German and Japanese general staffs had reached a military understanding independently of their respective foreign offices.

The renewal of large-scale fighting in North China after the Marco Polo Bridge incident in July 1937 did not at first make a deep impression on public opinion in the United States. War in China was not precisely a novelty. The administration, aware that the cash-and-carry principle operated to the advantage of the Power holding command of the seas — in this case, Japan — did not invoke the Neutrality Act, on the ostensible ground that neither belligerent had formally declared war. The sale of munitions by American firms to both China and Japan was therefore perfectly permissible.

When Japan declared a naval blockade against Chinese shipping, the President informed American firms that the transport of their munitions must be carried out entirely at their own risk.

The sinking by Japanese aircraft of the United States gunboat *Panay* on December 12, 1937, together with three oil tankers which it was escorting up the Yangtze River, again showed the depth of popular aversion to involvement in war. Even a motion picture of the episode, which a resourceful American journalist had been able to smuggle out of China, failed to arouse any serious demand for retaliation. The Japanese made a prompt apology for their carelessness, paid an indemnity, and the affair was closed. The general conviction was that American material stakes in China were not sufficient to justify strong action. Extreme isolationists urged early withdrawal from the Far East lest another such incident might start the landslide toward war. Cautious strategists pointed out that American bases and naval strength in the Pacific were still far from adequate. The negative results of the Stimson doctrine of 1932 were still fresh in the public memory. On the other hand, the *Panay* incident, and accumulating reports of ruthless Japanese bombings of civilians in China, roused demands for an embargo on the sale of war materials to Japan. In July 1938 the government responded to the extent of imposing a moral embargo on the export of aircraft to Japan. In a letter addressed to 148 aircraft manufacturers, the Department of State affirmed that licenses would be issued only "with great regret" to any firm exporting aircraft or aircraft parts to countries the armed forces of which bombed civilian populations from the air.

Germany's triumph at Munich in September 1938 immensely increased the self-confidence of her partner in the Far East. The term "New Order in East Asia" attained a new force and clarity as it crept into official enunciations of policy emanating from Tokyo. A manifesto of the Japanese Government, in November 1938, defined the new dispensation as "a tripartite relationship of mutual aid and co-ordination between Japan, Manchukuo, and China." "It must be admitted," added Foreign Minister Arita in a burst of frankness, "that the economic activities of the countries which lie outside the limits of East Asia will have to be restricted." A State Department note of December 1938, refusing to recognize any New Order which infringed the "Open Door" principle, made little impression on Tokyo. Secretary Hull plainly indicated the shakiness of the foundations of the New Order in a conversation with the Japanese ambassador in Washington:

"The big consideration relates to the question whether all of China and the Pacific islands skirting it is to be Manchuria-ized by Japan, with international law destroyed and treaty observation abolished and all other nations not allowed into that one-half of the world — the door shut and locked by Japan, except over preferences for her own citizens. I added that if some one nation is to do this in one-half of the world, some other nation in the other half of the world might undertake to follow the same example, and nothing would be more absurdly impossible for the future progress of the population of the world, including the countries assuming this species of dominion, than such attempted course . . . I said that such efforts at domination, with no facilities for financing and progressive development, and the going forward on such a huge scale, could only result in disaster for all concerned. . . . The Ambassador," added Secretary Hull, "made no particular comment." [9] The diplomatic deadlock was complete.

In 1938 it was estimated that Japan obtained nine-tenths of her scrap iron and steel, two-thirds of her oil, and two-thirds of her metalworking machinery from the United States. A prolonged economic embargo would certainly have seriously embarrassed her capacity to wage a major war. Almost on the eve of the Second World War in Europe the United States did at last act as if some such measure was in serious contemplation. On July 26, 1939, two weeks after his admonition to the Japanese ambassador, Secretary Hull served notice of his government's intention to abrogate the old American-Japanese commercial treaty of 1911, which had bound each signatory not to engage in trade discrimination against the other. A clause of the treaty empowered either party to cancel it at six months' notice. At the end of that period commercial relations could be broken off entirely, or placed on a day-to-day basis.

The Japanese Government, with this economic sword hanging over its head, began to offer fragmentary concessions — the reopening of the Yangtze River to foreign shipping, and the release of American merchandise detained on the congested wharves of Shanghai. Washington was unmoved by these minor offerings, and was awaiting further advances when it received the startling news of the conclusion of the German-Soviet Moscow Pact. Japanese militarists, who had pressed persistently hitherto for the conversion of the Anti-Comintern Pact with Germany into a full-fledged and openly avowed alliance, were reduced to an embarrassed silence. Shortly afterward, Japan proclaimed her neutrality with respect to the imminent war in Europe.

In the circumstances, further American pressure on Japan would have been impolitic and would merely have driven her further into the arms of her German partner. The careful diplomatic handling of Japan, the State Department hoped, might restrain her from exploiting the war in Europe to make a last reckless plunge into the South Pacific. Expert opinion, especially in naval circles, subscribed to this policy. Manifestly, if the United States should become involved in hostilities both in the Atlantic and the Pacific, an enormous strain would be imposed upon her at a time when rearmament was still far from complete.

THE GOOD NEIGHBOR POLICY AND THE DEFENSE OF LATIN AMERICA

The Depression and the threat of war sharply spurred the Good Neighbor Policy toward Latin America. The exports of the United States to the southern republics had shrunk from over $900,000,000 in 1929 to less than $200,-000,000 in 1932. In these distressing circumstances, there was little point in bemoaning the epidemic of debt default which had swept over Latin America in the lean years of 1930–33. If the Good Neighbor Policy was to be maintained, if the powerful batteries of economic nationalism — quotas, exchange controls, and the like — were not to be brought to bear on the United States, it was essential to reassure the republics that the new Roosevelt administration was categorically opposed to a policy of intervention in their affairs such as had been practiced by certain earlier American administrations. Mexico had become a member of the League of Nations in 1931, meanwhile condemning the Monroe Doctrine as "an infantile theory, to cloak a tutelage on the part of the United States over Latin America." Argentina rejoined the League in the following year, justifying the action on the ground that the Monroe Doctrine was "a unilateral political declaration," not "a regional agreement."

The Seventh Pan-American Conference at Montevideo, in December 1933, gave Secretary Hull, head of the United States delegation, an opportunity to affirm that "no [Latin American] government need fear any intervention on the part of the United States under the Roosevelt administration." The delegates from Cuba, where the United States enjoyed a right of intervention under the Platt Amendment,[10] were openly skeptical. Within a year of the Conference the Platt Amendment had been abrogated, and a trade agreement concluded. Marines were withdrawn from Nicaragua in 1932 and from Haiti in 1933. The right of intervention in Panama in the event of disorder was renounced by treaty in 1936.

Having demonstrated that the Good Neighbor Policy was more than a slogan, Washington proceeded, on the basis of the better feeling thus created, to draw closer the bonds of political co-operation between the Americas. The Gran Chaco War between Bolivia and Paraguay in 1932–35,[11] which the League of Nations had proved powerless to arrest, in conjunction with the Ethiopian fiasco, had severely shaken Latin-American confidence in Geneva. The Civil War in Spain, a country with strong ties of history and culture with Latin America, was painful and disturbing. Generally the Latin-American masses sympathized with the Spanish Republicans, and the aristocracy and Church with Franco and the Nationalists. Finally, the formation of the Rome-Berlin Axis pointed to the danger of economic and ideological penetration of Latin America by the totalitarian states through the medium of the large German and Italian minorities in Brazil, Argentina, and Chile. President Roosevelt hastened therefore to call a conference at Buenos Aires in December 1936 to consider ways and means of safeguarding the peace of the Western Hemisphere. He attended the conference in person and, in his speech at the opening session, he pointed challengingly to the need for common consultation against "others, who, driven by war madness or land hunger, might seek to commit acts of aggression against us." The delegates were sufficiently impressed to accept a noncommittal resolution pledging mutual consultation in the event of a threat to the peace of the Americas, but they fought shy of creating any machinery or other obligatory procedure to implement the resolution. They also rejected a motion to extend the recent neutrality legislation of the United States to Latin America. On the other hand, they accepted with enthusiasm a protocol which reaffirmed the doctrine of nonintervention. Throughout the discussions Argentina, an aspirant herself for leadership among the southern republics, was the main stumbling block.

In 1938, the path of the Good Neighbor was beset with a new outgrowth of thorns, this time in Mexico. General Cárdenas had become President of Mexico in 1934, and under his guidance the slowly evolving Mexican Revolution seemed to gather not only greater speed but a more definite sense of direction. His extensive program of "co-operative socialism," including the construction of 2,000 rural schools and 1,200 libraries, exerted an increase of his government's pressure on foreign holdings and concessions in Mexico. The Mexican railroads were nationalized in 1937, with only vague promises of compensation to foreign bondholders. In the same year 17,000 oil workers struck, with the support and sympathy of the Cárdenas administration. After a contentious exchange with the oil companies over their rate of profit, President Cárdenas signed an expropriation decree in March 1938. Thirteen American and four British companies were affected, involving an estimated capital of $400,000,000. The oil companies, doubting that compensation from the Mexican Government would be adequate, exerted pressure by instigating a partial boycott of Mexican oil abroad. President Cárdenas thereupon turned to Germany and Italy, who had the necessary tankers for transshipping the oil. But trade with the Axis was largely on a barter basis, and did not greatly improve the Mexican Government's financial position. Great pressure from American oil interests did not seriously deflect the State Department from its policy of studied moderation toward Mexico. Secretary Hull took the stand that the Mexican Government had the right and the power to expropriate, but only in return for adequate compensation. After long and delicate negotiations, an interim settlement based on this principle was reached in 1942.

Hitler's triumph at Munich revealed the abyss before the democratic nations. But his mounting prestige, the internal rivalries among the Latin-American republics, and the dependence of some of them on Axis markets continued to prevent the formation of any clear-cut Pan-American defense pact. At the Eighth Pan-American Conference in Lima in December 1938, Foreign Minister Cantilo of Argentina took the lead in opposing "foreign entanglements," which might align Latin America with one or the other of the hostile coalitions in Europe. His appeal to isolationism was a little difficult to assail, since it was based on a traditional principle of United States foreign policy. The final Declaration of Lima, therefore, simply provided for consultation by the respective foreign ministers of the twenty-one American republics in the event of a threat to the peace and security of an American nation. Any such threat was declared to be a common concern, and was to be met by the measures which each government deemed appropriate. Thus, while the Declaration paid verbal homage to the United States thesis of "continental solidarity," none of the Latin-American republics sacrificed one iota of its ultimate freedom of action.

One persistent hindrance to better Pan-American relations was economic — and, connected therewith, was the growing interest of Germany in South America. The republics all actively resented the Smoot-Hawley tariff of 1930. Argentina especially, groaning under huge surpluses of meat and wheat, regarded sourly the towering tariff walls to the north. The concurrent decline in the prices of raw commodities further complicated Argentina's problems. Her wool, for example, which had sold in the United States at 57 cents per pound in 1920, brought only 27 cents in 1930. Argentina was compelled in consequence to cultivate her traditional European markets more carefully than ever. The Roca-Runciman treaty in May 1933 bound Britain not to reduce her purchases of Argentinian meat by more than 10 per cent. In return, Argentina agreed to use all money so obtained to buy British goods, after deducting sufficient funds for service on sterling loans and for dividends on British investments. Germany's bids for Argentinian meat and grain, and for Mexican oil and Brazilian cotton and coffee, could not be ignored. Admittedly, Germany paid by barter or in blocked marks. Admittedly the delivery of German goods, from locomotives to aspirin, was capricious and subject to arbitrary price adjustments. Nevertheless, Berlin's bilateral arrangements did keep the wheels of commerce in motion — even though only jerkily, and by methods which would have scandalized Adam Smith and the Manchester school of economic theory.

Axis economic penetration of South America was regarded in Washington as a counterblow to the Hull program of reciprocal trade agreements, though in fact it was British trade which suffered most severely. Actually the progress of Secretary Hull's commercial policy was not notably impeded. Between 1934 and 1940 a round dozen commercial treaties were concluded with Latin-American countries. The most significant agreements were those with Brazil, Cuba, and Venezuela, covering such varied items as sugar, manganese, and coffee. A powerful stimulus was imparted to the Hull program when the United States embarked upon the policy of "stock-piling" strategic raw materials in 1938. Production of Brazilian rubber and Bolivian tin shot up, in spite of competition from more abundant sources of supply in Malaya and the Netherlands East Indies. In 1939, Brazil with its abundant high-grade iron ore was accorded a loan by the Export-Import Bank of $20,000,-000 to initiate steel production.

A spearhead of ideological penetration of Latin America was provided by 200,000 Japanese, 1,300,000 Germans, and 6,000,000 Italians, mostly settled in Brazil and Argentina. The diplomatic and consular services of Germany, Japan, and to a lesser extent, Italy, directed agents who assiduously organized and indoctrinated these large minorities. Axis successes in Europe, the nervousness of wealthy individuals in face of a growing popular radicalism, the tendency of Latin Americans to envisage political activity in terms of allegiance to an individual leader, all seemed to provide fertile soil for the seeds of totalitarianism. But the foreign minorities did not always prove successful sowers of totalitarianism. The Japanese immigrants, with their willingness to work longer hours for lower pay, were far from popular with the masses. The Italian settlers had preserved a love of Italy, but none for the Duce. Further, the "strong men" and political-minded generals who rose so readily to the surface of South American affairs were indigenous products who were equally ready to defend their authority from assaults from the Right or from the Left. President Vargas of Brazil suppressed a revolt of the green-shirted Fascist *Integralistas* in 1938 with the same decisiveness that he had displayed against the Communist uprising of 1935.

As American policy crystallized round the slogan of "hemisphere defense,"

Washington opened an increasingly vigorous counterdrive against Axis penetration. In 1938 a Division of Cultural Relations, which was most active in the southern republics, was created in the State Department. United States military missions were sent to Mexico, Colombia, and Peru. The Latin-American public, and particularly military circles, were kept well informed concerning the progress of the United States rearmament program. Experience showed the disadvantages of the German barter system, especially as the preoccupation of the Axis with rearmament diminished the range and quantity of goods available for export. Lastly, it was obvious that in the event of a European conflict the British Navy could immediately prohibit commercial intercourse between Latin America and the Axis countries and that, in a troubled peace, Latin-American trade with nations hostile to the Anglo-Saxon Powers would never amount to more than a temporary expedient, liable to stoppage at any time.

RETROSPECT

The American people, bending their full energies to the defeat of the Depression, discovered resentfully that the earth-shaking march of the aggressors abroad was beginning to present them with equally crucial problems in foreign policy. Their debates on domestic and foreign issues were sharpened by the difficulty of resolving them within the framework of traditional ideas and practices. Old familiar economic landmarks were submerged, party lines were blurred, the traditional slogans "no entangling alliances," "no commitments abroad," "the Open Door in China" — offered doubtful guidance in a stormy, swiftly changing, and shrinking world. Problems of foreign relations, which at one time could have been solved in leisurely fashion by the dignified exchanges of the old diplomacy, could suddenly loom large and menacing and, blitzkrieg-fashion, could threaten instant war for the whole nation or economic loss for some section of it. Public opinion, whose customary premises had been cut away, might sometimes speak loudly, but at all times spoke confusedly and indecisively. The intermittent gusts of public opinion, blowing from all points of the political compass, lent an unsettled and faltering air to the government's conduct of foreign relations.

Washington, following the activist policy of the firewarden who rushes to extinguish the incendiary bomb whenever and wherever it falls, incurred suspicion because of that very activity. There was therefore — and the statement is broadly true of all the democracies — no uniform agreement as to where the national interest lay in the realm of foreign policy. The instinctive aversion to war among the people at large seemed to counsel a resolute isolationism. Yet isolationism, binding the hands of the government, hindered the United States from exerting an influence in world affairs proportionate to its strength. The economic problems which clamored for solution at home seemed often enough to relegate foreign policy to second place. Yet the government could logically contend that those very problems drew much of their virulence from maladjustments in the world at large. "Isolationism," urged Secretary Hull in 1935, "has been tried and found wanting. It has destroyed 22 billion dollars' worth of international trade. It leaves every nation struggling as best it can to save for itself whatever it can from the general wreckage. . . . The explosives packed in the current nationalistic tendencies may result, as they have resulted, in the further disorganization of social and economic fabrics." [12]

These conflicting influences help to explain the cycle of strong verbal protests against aggression by the State Department which, followed by a minimum of action, disconcerted the contemporary observer of the American scene. The United States, of course, was not alone in hesitating to bridge the fatal gulf between words and action. No democratic government might outstrip the often straggling and hesitant march of public opinion with impunity, though it might seek to educate the opinion. The problem, in truth, was an acute one. How could the ebb and flow of mass opinion, often affected by sentimentality, prejudice, and moral indignation, be harmonized with a consistently effective foreign policy based on the special information and knowledge available in part only to the State Department? The problem could have been acutely felt only in a democracy. It was for democracy to supply the solution.

We cannot leave this chapter without a glance at the man who dominated the period it describes. Franklin Delano Roosevelt was born in 1882 of a distinguished family of partial New York Dutch extraction. He was a distant cousin of Theodore Roosevelt, a predecessor in the presidency. He was educated at Groton and Harvard, and then practiced law in New York. In 1910 he began his political career as Democratic state senator from that Republican stronghold, Dutchess County, and at once opened his long fight against Tammany Hall and the corrupt political machine of that day. During the First World War he was Assistant Secretary of the Navy. Shortly after his return to civil life he was struck down by infantile paralysis. He had once been a man of fine physique, fond of athletics. The illness left him crippled, but it did not break his spirit or put an end to his public life. His was one of those rare characters whom physical affliction makes stronger and greater.

He was Governor of New York for two terms. He was nominated as presidential candidate by the Democratic Convention of 1932, and he defeated the Republican candidate, Hoover, in the ensuing election. He was re-elected President of the United States in 1936, 1940, and 1944 for the unprecedented period of four terms. He died during the fourth term, on April 12, 1945, as the Second World War was approaching its finale, still in his early sixties, exhausted by work and responsibility.

Roosevelt was that combination, far too uncommon in modern democracy, of keen political acumen and long-term idealism. His maneuvering was unmatched, though it always served a larger purpose. Naturally he made many enemies, but even the bitterest of them seldom questioned his essential integrity. He had infinite charm and the true leader's gift of inspiring confidence in desperate situations. He was master of an informal, but impressive oratory; his voice of slightly minor timbre was peculiarly adapted to his favorite medium of the radio. He often saw further and more clearly than his closest advisers, especially in foreign affairs. It used to be said that he was always one move ahead of public opinion; but no one now would deny the consistent accuracy of his vision. To a stricken Europe he gave a hope as great as President Wilson had ever given, a hope, moreover, that was far more realistic and substantial. His death, at the moment of his greatest triumph and indispensability, was one of the crushing tragedies of his era.

39 THE APPROACH OF WAR

DESIGN FOR CONQUEST

A preventive blow could have been struck at Germany in 1936 at the time of the Rhineland coup. It would have been justified by Germany's treaty violations alone. Thereafter, the "danger period" which had cost the Nazis so much anxiety, the period during which Germany's rearmament was still so undeveloped that a resolute Power, say France or the Soviet Union, could have attacked her without risk of serious war, passed rapidly beyond recall. For Germany, 1937 was a year of intensive, concentrated preparation. The blueprints were now factories; the assembly lines were rolling out their fantastic progeny; the whole country was filling with uniformed, marching men. During 1937, Germany is believed to have spent $4,500,000,000 on armaments; [1] by contrast, Britain and France together spent less than $2,000,-000,000; and the two pairs of figures, though steadily increasing up to 1939, continued to bear much the same ratio to each other. Hitler himself estimated Germany's total expenditure on armaments up to the Second World War as 90,000,000,000 marks ($37,500,000,000).[1] Even without the additional contributions of Italy and Japan against them, the Western democracies were being decisively outclassed and outrun in the great race.

"I have for a long time past made what I consider grave and startling statements about Germany's expenditure on warlike preparations," said Churchill in a speech shortly after the Rhineland coup — a lonely voice in a general conspiracy of silence. "Europe is approaching a climax. Either there will be a melting of hearts and a joining of hands between great nations which will set out upon realizing the glorious age of prosperity and freedom which is now within the grasp of the millions of toiling people, or there will be an explosion and a catastrophe the course of which no imagination can measure, and beyond which no human eye can see." But the absence of spectacular crises during 1937 was everywhere taken to be very reassuring. The Civil War continued in Spain; Japan's undeclared war broke out in China; the military purges occupied Russia. But the rest of the world seemed to lie under a hypnosis of uneventfulness. Had not Hitler himself, in his anniversary speech of January 30, 1937, declared that "the period of so-called surprises is at an end"? And, to be sure, for a whole year nothing came out of Germany but some mild propaganda for the return of the German colonies and some rather unpleasant legal prosecutions of monastic orders for alleged sexual offenses. Pastor Niemöller was confined to a concentration camp and, a few days before Christmas, Ludendorff, Germany's commander in the First World War, was borne to his last resting place amid the solemn pomp of a military funeral.

British statesmanship was then enjoying its last holiday of pacifism and, in particular, was exerting itself on behalf of an understanding with Italy. In January 1937 the so-called Gentleman's Agreement between Britain and Italy was signed in Rome, mutually recognizing the two Powers' interests in the Mediterranean area. At the end of April 1937, Sir Nevile Henderson arrived in Berlin as British ambassador with instructions to work for Anglo-German conciliation, and he so far interpreted his instructions as to form friendships with several of the Nazi leaders and publicly express his admiration for certain features of the Nazi order.

In May 1937, Neville Chamberlain became Prime Minister in Britain and inaugurated the final and classic phase of his country's appeasement policy. Anthony Eden was then Foreign Secretary, the stalwart representative of that wing of the Conservative party which still upheld the ideals of the League of Nations and of collective security. But it was already clear that the real direction of British foreign affairs had been assumed by Chamberlain himself and by his pacific colleague, Lord Halifax.[2] Whatever may have been his private feelings, in public Chamberlain showed no dismay over Italy's and Germany's continued intervention in the Spanish Civil War, nor over Italy's adherence in November 1937 to the German-Japanese Anti-Comintern Pact and the consequent extension of the Axis into a formidable combination triangularly embracing the globe. In January 1938, Chamberlain received a personal letter from President Roosevelt suggesting a conference in Washington between interested Powers to discuss the international situation (see p. 600) . "Here," writes Churchill, "was a formidable and measureless step."[3] But Chamberlain returned a chilling answer. He was then engaged upon his chosen mission of an Italian *rapprochement* and was preparing to accord Britain's recognition of Mussolini's Ethiopian Empire. Doubtless the President's intervention would have cut across his efforts. Eden, the Foreign Secretary, it is worth mentioning, was away on vacation at the time and was not consulted in the matter.

On April 16, 1938 the pending Anglo-Italian Agreement was signed in Rome by the British ambassador, Lord Perth, and the Italian Foreign Minister, Count Ciano (see p. 527) . It was intended to be a general settlement of the whole field of Anglo-Italian affairs in the Mediterranean and a permanent reconciliation of the two Powers after their recent unhappy differences over Ethiopia and Spain. Clearly it was Chamberlain's definitive attempt to detach Italy from her German connection and once more to bind her to the community of "peace-loving" nations. It mutually disallowed injurious propaganda, it provided for the exchange of information regarding armed forces of the two Powers in the Mediterranean and East Africa, and it reaffirmed the existing status of the Suez Canal. In particular, Italy agreed to the British formula for the proportional evacuation of foreign volunteers from Spain, and she disclaimed any territorial or political aims in regard to Spain or the Spanish possessions overseas. Britain agreed to take steps at Geneva to remove "such obstacles as may at present be held to impede the freedom of member states as regards recognition of Italian sovereignty over Ethiopia."

But this *rapprochement* with one of the major interventionist Powers in Spain, at the moment that that intervention was still continuing, and following so soon upon Chamberlain's rebuff of President Roosevelt's offer of diplomatic aid in Europe, had been more than Eden could stomach. He had already resigned in February, while the agreement was still under negotiation, and had been succeeded as British Foreign Secretary by Lord Halifax.

THE AUSTRIAN CRISIS

The Austrian *Anschluss* had always been a primary Nazi aim. It was mentioned on the first page of *Mein Kampf,* and no knowledgeable person, in or out of Germany, doubted that Hitler was committed to its fulfillment. Nazi leaders — including Papen himself on his arrival in Vienna in 1934 as the envoy of his Führer, though he was ostensibly upon a mission of peace — were often surprisingly unguarded when they spoke of it. Austria, they said, belonged to the great German Motherland, it was a part of the *Grossdeutsch-tum* and a first step in the renewal of the age-old Teutonic Drive to the East, the *Drang nach Osten.*

Yet, for nearly four years after the assassination of Dollfuss, the Nazis in Austria seemed to have forsworn their past. The Austro-German Agreement of 1936 gave a formal recognition to the tranquillity that now outwardly mantled the country. Hitler almost overreached himself in protestations of good will. The Nazi organizations in Austria meanwhile were subject to police interference, but they succeeded in keeping themselves in being and in secretly maintaining their old connection with their fellows in the Reich. Profiting from the improved situation, the Chancellor, Schuschnigg — the modest, scholarly, self-effacing, and pious Schuschnigg — gradually built up a personal autocracy in Austria such as even Dollfuss would not have dared to aspire to. He shed himself both of Dollfuss's earlier dependence on Italian Fascism and on the Heimwehr at home, and himself inclined rather toward a nostalgic affection for the exiled Hapsburgs. The powerful Major Fey was quietly dropped, and the handsome, fire-eating Prince von Starhemberg was ironically relegated to a minor post as head of the Mothers' Aid Section of the Fatherland Front. Miklas was still Austrian President, apparently sympathetic to the trend of affairs. Diplomatic Europe was complacently looking forward to continuation of the Schuschnigg regime, despite its dictatorial and monarchical eccentricities, when early in 1938 it was painfully surprised by news of new Nazi machinations in Austria.

In January 1938 the Austrian Government narrowly averted a Nazi putsch, a repetition in another form of the Habicht-Rintelen incident of four years before (see p. 483). Under the Austro-German Agreement of 1936 (see p. 484), a Committee of Seven had been permitted to set up offices in Vienna with the ostensible object of bringing about a reconciliation between German Nazism and the Austrian Fatherland Front. But it was common knowledge that the Committee was no more and no less than the headquarters staff of the illegal Austrian Nazi party and the center of Nazi propaganda in Austria. One of the Committee was Dr. Seyss-Inquart, an Austrian lawyer and an associate — though not yet a full member — of the Nazi party since 1931, afterward to become a man of some notoriety in his country's politics.

On January 26, 1938 a certain Dr. Tavs, the secretary of the Committee, was arrested, the offices of the Committee were raided and searched by the Viennese police, and evidence was uncovered of a considerable plot against the Austrian Government. One suspicious document found bore the initials "R.H." (Rudolf Hess?). Presumably the Nazi "liberation" of Austria was to be timed so as to be completed by January 30 and announced by Hitler himself in his anniversary oration on that day. Consequently there was widespread uneasiness when the expected anniversary oration was postponed some three weeks to February 20. The Führer used the interval to prepare a more overt assault on Austria than that devised by the Committee of Seven which had just been frustrated and, incidentally, to turn to his own advantage a tangled scandal in the Reichswehr.

On January 11, 1938 the Reichswehr Minister, Field Marshal von Blomberg, had quietly married a certain Erna Gruhn. The date was Göring's birthday, and Hitler and Göring had themselves graced the wedding ceremony with their presence. But Erna Gruhn, even without the unsavory police record which she was discovered to have, was far from qualifying as socially eligible by the standards of the German officer caste. Obviously Blomberg could no longer be permitted to remain as Reichswehr Minister. Hitler was incensed beyond measure to have to learn too late the real character of the lady in the case and deeply shaken in his faith in his trusted and beloved soldiers at the deception which he firmly believed Blomberg had put over on him. He forbade Blomberg to set foot in the Chancellery or even to wear uniform.

Blomberg's logical successor as Reichswehr Minister was Colonel General von Fritsch, Commander in Chief of the Army. But Göring had long had designs on the post for himself. According to one story, as credible as any at the time, Göring — with Himmler's help — deliberately set out to remove his rival, Fritsch, and ruin his character on a trumped-up charge of homosexuality. The indignant Fritsch, of course, denied the accusation in no uncertain terms and demanded an inquiry by a competent military tribunal. On February 3, after some days of wildest rumors, Hitler decided matters in his own fashion. He himself took over the Reichswehr Ministry and the supreme command of the army. Fritsch and other ranking officers were retired. Göring was consoled for the loss of the Reichswehr Ministry by being promoted Field Marshal. A new body, the High Command of the Defense Forces (O.K.W., Oberkommando der Wehrmacht), made its appearance as the chief military authority in Germany with new names — Keitel (popularly known as "Lakaitel" for his subservience to Hitler), Jodl, and Brauchitsch — in its highest offices. A Secret Cabinet Council (Geheimer Kabinetsrat) was created to advise the Führer on questions of foreign policy. Of this Secret Cabinet Council, which probably never held a single meeting, Neurath was appointed president. Ribbentrop, recently ambassador in London, succeeded Neurath as Foreign Minister. Meanwhile Blomberg had departed on his honeymoon to Capri. Fritsch was afterward exonerated by a military tribunal, but he was not reinstated. He died in mysterious circumstances in the Polish campaign of 1939.

At a stroke Hitler had rid himself of a number of contumacious generals,

he had fought and won another round in his long struggle for control of the
Reichswehr, he had rewarded loyal aides, and he had called together a cabal
of sympathetic coadjutors to assist him in his adventurous and insatiable
ambitions. The year of preparation, 1937, was passed, and the scene was set
for aggression — in Austria, and in Europe.

Papen, Hitler's envoy in Vienna, visited Berchtesgaden on February 6,
1938, a couple of days after the purge of the Reichswehr generals, and discussed the Austrian situation with his Führer. He returned to Vienna on the
8th, bearing an invitation to Schuschnigg to attend a meeting at Berchtesgaden. On the face of it Papen's was not an unusual proposal. The heads of
European states had met constantly during the past twenty years. Schuschnigg himself had been in favor of a meeting with Hitler for some time,
provided that it should be secret and that the discussions should be designed
to remove "such misunderstandings and frictions as have persisted in spite of
the agreement of 1936." All unsuspecting, he proceeded to Berchtesgaden, by
rail and road, on the early morning of February 12. He was accompanied
by the Austrian Under Secretary for Foreign Affairs, Dr. Guido Schmidt, and
by Papen.

The details of that agonizing interview in Hitler's mountain eyrie are now
known to us. Hitler received his guest significantly in the presence of Generals Keitel and Reichenau. In his private talks with Schuschnigg he delivered himself of a long harangue, a usual mixture of Hitlerian piety and
menace, on the theme of his achievements for Germany. "I am telling you
once more that things cannot go on in this way," he said. "I have a historic
mission; and this mission I will fulfill because Providence has destined me to
do so. I believe in this mission; it is my life. And I believe in God; I am a
religious man. . . . I have achieved everything that I set out to do and have
become perhaps the greatest German of history . . . If my advice were followed, peace would be possible. I would gladly spare the world another
world war, but I don't know whether it can be avoided if no one believes
me. . . ." [4]

Meanwhile Ribbentrop, Papen, the generals, and Guido Schmidt conferred in an adjoining room. Hitler closed the meeting at last with an
ultimatum: Any Austrian might profess the National Socialist creed; Austrian Nazis were to be allowed to engage in "legal activity" within the
framework of the Fatherland Front, and all imprisoned members of the
party, including the participants in the assassination of Dollfuss, were to be
amnestied; Seyss-Inquart was to be appointed Minister for Public Security,
a key post which carried with it control over the police; a hundred officers
of the German Army were to be immediately detailed for duty with the
Austrian Army. In default of immediate acceptance, Schuschnigg faced a
German military invasion of his country. Toward evening he signed. As a
concession, Hitler gave him three days to put the ultimatum into effect. The
newspapers afterward released the story that the two chancellors had met
"informally" at Berchtesgaden to discuss questions concerning Austro-German relations.

Schuschnigg spent the three days of grace in conferences with President

Miklas, with his cabinet, with leaders of the Fatherland Front, and even with the long-ostracized and persecuted Social Democrats. Mussolini at first gave out that Italy's position in regard to the Austrian question was "unchanged" and then, eventually, that he could give "no advice in the circumstances." The probabilities are that Mussolini was in the dark as to Hitler's intentions and certainly did not appreciate their seriousness. London and Paris likewise gave Schuschnigg little word of comfort. At the moment, Chautemps' "Republican Combination" was rocking to its fall, and France was without a government. As usual, the fates everywhere seemed to be conspiring in the Führer's favor. Schuschnigg bowed to the inevitable. The Nazi amnesty was decreed; the Austrian Cabinet was reconstructed with Hitler's nominee, Seyss-Inquart, as Minister for Public Security; Guido Schmidt was promoted from Under Secretary to Minister of Foreign Affairs.

On February 20, Hitler delivered his postponed anniversary speech. He regaled the Reichstag with three hours of sustained truculence, denouncing in particular the League of Nations, Britain's colonial empire, and the unsympathetic democratic press. He made a couple of derogatory references to Eden, the British Foreign Secretary — who just then happened to be on the point of resigning office. He paid compliments to Japan and announced his recognition of Manchukuo. He disclaimed all territorial interests in the Far East and in Spain. He referred with special significance to the 10,000,000 Germans outside the Reich. "Just as England upholds her interests all over the globe," he said, "so will present-day Germany know how to guard her own more restricted interests. And among those interests are the German people beyond our frontiers who are not in a position to secure their human, political, and philosophical freedom by their own unaided efforts."

Hitler's immediate plans in Austria were still obscure. Perhaps he hoped that Austria, under the efficient manipulation of Seyss-Inquart or under a renewed outbreak of squadrism on the part of the amnestied Austrian Nazis, would now fall effortlessly into his hands. But that he was now determined to achieve the realities of political control in Austria, whatever the means thereto might be, there can be no possible doubt. Contingents of the German Army were drawn up along the Austrian frontier "shamming military action." But Schuschnigg himself probably precipitated the more violent course. On March 9 he announced that he would hold a national plebiscite the following Sunday (March 13) on the question of Austrian independence. "I will know, I must know," came his voice over the Vienna radio, "whether the people of Austria want a free, German, independent, social, Christian, and united Fatherland." It was estimated that the plebiscite would have resulted in 60 to 80 per cent "*Ja.*" There were many afterward, even sympathizers, who criticized Schuschnigg's action as foolhardy and inept and who criticized in particular the rhetorical form the plebiscite was to take. But history would surely have judged him more severely if he had bowed to the inevitable without any gesture of protest or self-defense.

Hitler was in a fury to have his favorite device for appealing to public opinion being thus used against him. Under pressure of his further ultima-

tum, Schuschnigg called off the plebiscite. But the government in Vienna by
now had virtually collapsed. "The President has asked me to tell the people
of Austria that he has yielded only to force," said Schuschnigg in his final
radio address. "Because we did not wish to spill German blood, we have
ordered the Austrian Army to offer no resistance — and to retire . . . And so
I take leave of the Austrian people with a German farewell and a greeting:
God protect Austria."

At midnight, March 11, Miklas appointed Seyss-Inquart Chancellor. The
first units of the German Army by then had already crossed the Austrian
frontier. By midday March 12, Vienna was in occupation. Himmler, Heydrich, and the Gestapo took up prepared quarters. German and Italian troops
exchanged formal greetings at the summit of the Brenner Pass. Hitler himself drove into Braunau, his Austrian birthplace, the same afternoon and
was officially welcomed by Seyss-Inquart at Linz. On the morning of March
13 he visited his parents' graves at the near-by village of Leonding. He
reached Vienna during the evening. Throughout his route, buildings were
hung with swastikas, and the streets were thronged with masses of heiling,
hysterical partisans. Cardinal Innitzer, Archbishop of Vienna, ordered the
church bells to be rung. The swastika was flown from the spire of St.
Stephen's Cathedral.

Reactions among the European Powers were sharp and painful, but
entirely negative. Under a joint declaration, dating from the time of Dollfuss in February 1934, Britain, France, and Italy were pledged to consultation in the event of any action taking place which endangered Austrian
independence. Consultation indeed took place, but no action followed.
"Horrible, horrible!" cried Halifax afterward. "I never thought they would
do it!" In general, British Conservatives, as at the time of the Rhineland
coup in 1936, could not find it in their hearts to condemn an Austro-German *Anschluss,* however unpleasant the means thereof, so long as they
believed it was desired by a majority of both parties concerned. France was
still in the midst of a ministerial crisis, and incapable of affirming a definite
policy. Chautemps resigned on March 10, to be followed by Blum at the
head of a weak reconstruction of the old Popular Front. Italy was bound
to her German ally and accepted the invasion with professions of satisfaction. "Mussolini, I shall never forget you for this!" Hitler had telegraphed
from Linz on March 12, and Mussolini had made answer: "My attitude is
determined by the friendship between our two countries, which is conse-
crated in the Axis."

Hitler's "co-ordination" of his Austrian conquest was rapid and thorough.
President Miklas resigned. Austria was declared to be a *Land* of the Reich
and named the Ostmark. Hitler referred to Seyss-Inquart as his "Regent."
The Austrian National Bank was taken over by the Reichsbank, together
with its gold reserve of $100,000,000. The Austrian Army was incorporated
into the Reichswehr. Bürckel, former Nazi Governor of the Saar, reorganized
the Austrian Nazi party and was later created Commissioner for the Ostmark.
The "Austrian Legion," 14,000 strong, returned from its exile in Germany

to take its revenge upon its old enemies. Himmler and Hess laid wreaths on the grave of Dollfuss's assassin, Otto Planetta (see pp. 483–84).

In Vienna and in the country at large the usual Nazi *Gleichschaltung* went into force, and the leaders of the Fatherland Front, the Hapsburg legitimists, Freemasons, Social Democrats, and Jews bore the main brunt of its violence. Brutalities of which we have little ken and less understanding were loosed upon the defenseless country. Storm troopers systematically plundered houses, shops, and public premises. A common sight in Vienna in these days were "cleansing squads" of Jews, men and women, on their knees scrubbing off the sidewalks the propaganda signs which had been painted at the time of Schuschnigg's abortive plebiscite. Jews were dismissed from public offices, universities, and schools, and from professional appointments. Thousands fled to Czechoslovakia or Switzerland, but the frontiers were soon closed, and thousands more were stopped. Some writers have put the number of arrests of all types of citizens at between 30,000 and 40,000, many of whom eventually found their way to the concentration camps at Dachau and Buchenwald. Suicides numbered a hundred a day. Major Fey, his family — and even his dog — were found shot. Dollfuss's family escaped. Prince von Starhemberg was already in Switzerland. Sigmund Freud, the psychologist, was allowed to accept an invitation from England. Cardinal Innitzer and the Catholic hierarchy in Austria, having once greeted the Nazi invasion with joy and blessings — for which they earned the remonstrances of the Vatican and indirectly of Cardinal Faulhaber of Munich — soon repented their impulsive loyalty. The Catholic Church in Austria was "co-ordinated" with more than the usual Nazi ruthlessness. Catholic organizations were dissolved, Catholic properties confiscated, Catholic monasteries and convents closed. Later in the year the Cardinal's palace in Vienna was raided and sacked by Nazi mobs, and the Cardinal himself only escaped their fury by being put under protective arrest. Schuschnigg was confined in a room of the Hotel Metropole, the Gestapo headquarters in Vienna, for seventeen months, subject to the gross indignities since described in his book, and afterward in Gestapo prisons and concentration camps.

Hitler's material accessions in Austria were impressive. He added nearly 7,000,000 new citizens to the Greater Reich. He gained considerable resources in iron and timber, and he linked Austria's industry with Germany's. Vienna provided him with important controls over the road, river, and rail communications of the Middle Danube and therewith over the Danubian trade of Italy, Hungary, Yugoslavia, and Rumania. Strategically his accessions were no less impressive. He made direct territorial contact with Italy, Hungary, and Yugoslavia, and he encompassed Czechoslovakia, "the Bohemian Bastion," on three sides. As was his way, however, he hastened to belittle these gains abroad, and he was lavish of his pledges for the future. Göring, on his "word of honor," assured the Czechoslovak minister in Berlin that Germany had no hostile intentions toward his country. Göring repeated the same assurances to Sir Nevile Henderson, the British ambassador, and authorized him to convey them to His Majesty's Government in London. "It was the old refrain," remarked Sir Nevile afterward, "and carried ever diminishing conviction."

THE CZECHOSLOVAK CRISIS

Czechoslovakia and her dangerous minority problems have been described in an earlier chapter. The Republic was always considered by the Versailles Powers as one of the happier creations of their new order in Europe, and the success of its first years of statehood, the political maturity of its Czech population, the wealth of its resources and industries — and the skill of its propaganda abroad — had sometimes caused to be forgotten the heterogeneous and centrifugal elements in its composition. The Republic moreover occupied a position of the highest strategic importance in the heart of Central Europe. It lay behind mountain barriers whose natural strength had been improved by modern fortifications, and the output of its Skoda munition works was that of a first-class Power. It had become the keystone of the French and the Franco-Soviet alliance systems and the main bulwark against German expansion into the Middle Danube. Well might it be said in 1938, as in Bismarck's day, "He who controls Bohemia controls Europe."

The Depression had tested Czechoslovakia as it had tested every other country in the world. In 1931, for the first time since 1923, the Czech budget had showed a deficit, and the harvest had been the worst in years. The Czech government was in the hands of moderate coalitions which seemed incapable of initiative. Any sort of "plan" was difficult to devise without upsetting some party or interest essential to the government's support. The situation was ready-made for the provocation of latent racial and ideological discontents.

Of the Republic's 15,000,000 inhabitants, the Sudeten Germans numbered 3,000,000 (see p. 197), and the question of their political destiny had been revived in an acute form since the rise of the Nazi party in Germany. In the early thirties Sudeten extremists were already modeling themselves on Nazi prototypes. "Sports" organizations inculcated a distinctive German political mysticism, and their members wore semi-SA uniforms and drilled themselves on German lines. In October 1933, Sudeten Nazis anticipated an impending government ban by voluntarily dissolving themselves, but within a year they were flocking to the standard of Konrad Henlein, leader of the so-called Heimatfront. In December 1935, Masaryk resigned from the presidency of the Republic and was succeeded by the faithful Beneš. The continuity of foreign policy and the attitude toward Germany was maintained. Masaryk died almost two years later, aged eighty-seven, mercifully spared from seeing the destruction of the state he had done so much to build.

Konrad Henlein, who now appears as one of the protagonists of the Czechoslovak crisis, was a bank clerk and teacher of gymnastics. He was disarmingly mild of manner, not a scintillating character, though personable enough, and a persuasive pleader of his cause. He enjoyed reputable connections with non-German circles abroad, especially in Britain where, of course, he was careful to show himself as anything but the typical Nazi storm trooper. In 1935 his Heimatfront took the name of the Sudeten German party and won 44 seats in the Czech Chamber. He vehemently denied that it then had any Nazi or Pan-German aims or was otherwise than loyal to the existing democratic Czech state. However, Henlein met Hitler at the Olympic Games in Berlin in 1936, and it is clear that his party thereafter became secretly assimilated to Nazism and that the Sudetenland was regarded in Germany as a surreptitious Nazi *Gau*. After the Austrian *Anschluss*, Henlein intensified his activities. He founded a special terroristic Free Corps, known as the FS (*Freiwilliger Selbstschutz*), modeled and trained after the Nazi SS. Then suddenly, on April 24, 1938, speaking at a congress of his party at Karlsbad, Henlein threw off the mask and enunciated his Karlsbad Program, as it was called, demanding autonomy for the Sudeten areas, reparation for "injustices" inflicted on Sudeten Germans since 1918, and full liberty for Sudeten Germans to profess German political philosophy.

In that same April, on the 21st, Hitler and General Keitel, in conference, were discussing the incidents — "for example, the assassination of the German minister [in Prague] in connection with an anti-German demonstration" — which the German Army might use to unleash a lightning attack on Czechoslovakia.[6] "Case Green," as the plan for the attack was called, was then in an advanced stage of readiness. Meetings, consultations, and the issue of revised secret directives followed during the summer months. There were interchanges of views with Italy, of whose benevolent neutrality it was necessary to make sure, and with Hungary, who might even be invited to participate in the coming military action. Ribbentrop promised the Italian ambassador in Berlin that Mussolini would be the first to be informed of final decisions. Hitler gave repeated orders for speeding up the construction of the West Wall. Soviet air attack was expected and allowed for.

Tension nearly overpassed its factor of safety in May 1938. Hitler and Mussolini had just celebrated in Rome a more than usually flamboyant meeting. As a preliminary feint, Henlein was sent on a flying visit to London, where he impressed all his interviewers with his "moderation" and industriously minimized any adverse effects that might have been produced among his English friends by his recent Karlsbad Program. But German troop movements along the Czech frontier, over and above what could be explained away as "routine," were being reported. Sir Nevile Henderson, the British ambassador, ordered a special train for the evacuation of the women and children of the British colony in Berlin. On May 21 the Czech Government, believing that it had information of another of Hitler's "Rhineland marches," ordered partial mobilization. The "Little Maginot" on the Czech frontier was fully manned. Half a million Czechoslovaks were under arms. The British and French Governments added the weight of their solemn and repeated representations in Berlin.

But the crisis of May 1938 passed. Czech municipal elections were held on May 22 — Henlein's party secured 80 per cent of the Sudeten votes — and no untoward event took place. It is very probable that Hitler might have attempted an invasion of Czechoslovakia at that time, and certainly he was ready to exploit any advantage that might befall. The democratic press in Europe was jubilant and made out that Czechoslovakia, by her timely mobilization, had won a great victory. Every newspaper outside Germany — and Italy — proclaimed that the courageous action of a small but determined people had at last called the bully's bluff and turned him from his fell purpose. The principle of collective security had been brilliantly and bloodlessly vindicated. But whatever Hitler's actual intention may have been, the effect upon him of this premature rejoicing is not difficult to imagine. Hitler, writes Henderson, suffered "the worst brain-storm of the year" and "made up his vindictive mind to avenge himself upon Beneš and the Czechs."

But at this time it was the Great Power, France, which was giving more reason for anxiety than the little Power, Czechoslovakia. The Blum government, which had been formed at the time of Hitler's Austrian coup in March, had lasted exactly twenty-eight days. In April 1938, Daladier took office with a predominantly Radical Socialist and Socialist cabinet. Chautemps was Vice-Premier and Bonnet Foreign Minister. Paul Reynaud and Georges Mandel, comparative newcomers, were Ministers of Justice and of the Colonies respectively. Daladier indeed was to remain in office till March 1940, a commendably long period, but at no time during it could he have been described as the leader of a "strong" administration. Even in his original Ministerial Declaration his references to foreign affairs, the most important affairs of the hour, had been lamentably and ominously evasive.

Bonnet was a confirmed proponent of appeasement. He made a pathetic attempt to come to terms with Italy on the lines of the recent Anglo-Italian Agreement, and earned nothing but insult and scorn for his pains. On May 14, 1938, at Genoa, Mussolini made one of his most bellicose speeches and singled out France for a particularly venomous attack. "In one sphere which is much to the fore," he said — "I refer to the war in Spain — we [the French and ourselves] are on opposite sides of the barricade. They want the victory of Barcelona; we want the victory of Franco . . . In a tumultuous period, while Italy was engaged in a gigantic and bloody effort, sanctions were applied to her, and we have not yet forgotten them. Meanwhile everything diplomatic and political, which once passed under the name of Stresa, is dead and buried, and, as far as we are concerned, will never be resuscitated." Yet in that May, at the League Council in Geneva, France had helped to read the obsequies over the dead body of Ethiopia; in June, France closed the Catalan frontier to further shipment of arms to the Spanish Republican government; and in July the Paris Court of Appeal rejected the Spanish Republican government's claim to the Spanish gold reserve which had been held by the Bank of France since 1931. Appeasement could hardly have stooped lower.

Between July 19 and 22, King George VI and Queen Elizabeth made a state visit to France. The weather was perfect; Paris was superbly decorated for the occasion. The program was a lavish round of receptions, speeches, parades, reviews, music, and banquets. The Quai d'Orsay, the Elysée, the Tomb of the Unknown Soldier, the Hôtel de Ville, the British Embassy, and Versailles passed like scenes in a pageant. The King unveiled the Australian War Memorial at Villers-Bretonneux. All politics and statesmanship apart, the royal visit was a masterpiece of the French artistic genius. For a short, gorgeous, unforgettable week France was almost her own true self again.

The possibility of direct mediation of the Sudeten problem in Czecho-slovakia had been discussed during the spring of 1938 between the British and French Governments, and the appointment of Lord Runciman as "investigator and mediator" was discussed and confirmed at the time of the royal visit to France. Britain had no alliance or commitment in regard to Czechoslovakia as had France, and she was therefore in a position to propose an "independent" settlement of the Czech Government's difficulties. Chamberlain afterward gave out that the Czechs had themselves desired and asked for a British mediator, but it seems that Runciman was "wished" on them at the instance of the British Government. Runciman himself was a curious choice for so delicate and complicated a mission. He was a businessman and a shipowner, reputed to be wealthy, and he had been President of the Board of Trade. But he had no qualifications which suggested capacity or experience in Central European affairs. Lord and Lady Runciman arrived in Prague, however, on August 3, 1938. Behind the scenes British and French ministers were now urging the "stubborn" Czechs to yield the "maximum" concessions to their Sudeten subjects. Gedye, then correspondent for the *Daily Express*, writes how he spent "the sad summer of 1938 . . . absorbed in watching the superhuman efforts of the last stronghold of democracy in Central Europe to hold out against the devilish ingenuity of those who never ceased day or night to plot its destruction and seemed untiring in finding some new point of attack. And the real danger came never from the open enemy, but from the false friend, for that was the attack to which no resistance could be offered, since it came always in the subtle guise of warnings and of good counsel." [7]

Runciman's inquiries opened, however, with much appearance of good will on all sides. He duly met the Czech leaders, but he spent the best part of his time with Henlein and the Sudeten German party. Beneš and the Czech Premier, Hodza, with indefatigable resource, produced one plan after another, only to see each rejected by the inflexible Sudetens. The so-called Fourth Plan offered the Sudetens complete regional autonomy on a cantonal basis, a plan which, in Runciman's view, could have been made to cover the Karlsbad Program. But it was evident that the marionette Henlein was being worked from Germany, and that the firm purpose of himself and his party was not to allow any negotiations to succeed. Runciman did not consider it within his terms of reference "to mediate between Czechoslovakia and Germany." Meanwhile the war of nerves on the Czech frontiers continued. The Nazi press, in a campaign of incredible vulgarity, magnified almost daily incidents — many of them provoked by Henlein's Free Corps, the FS — into the most frightful atrocities. To judge by Goebbels's headlines in those days, the Sudetenland, at the hands of its sadistic Czech overlords, had degenerated into an inferno of robbery, torture, murder, and Bolshevism.

On September 6, Hitler opened the Nazi *Parteitag* in Nuremberg. On all hands it was expected that he would use the occasion to bring the Sudeten crisis to explosion point. Göring, rising to an almost apoplectic rhetorical effort, boasted that Germany now had impregnable fortifications on the Rhine, foodstuffs and raw materials for an indefinite blockade, an invincible army, a great navy, and the mightiest air force in the world. On September 12, Hitler spoke. "Three and a half million Germans are being oppressed in the Czech state," he said. "They too are the creatures of God. The Almighty did not create them that they should be surrendered by Versailles to a foreign Power which is hateful to them . . . I say that if these tortured souls cannot obtain rights and help by themselves, they can obtain them from us!"

Hitler's speech was hailed with riots — apparently organized riots — in the Sudetenland. The Czech Government proclaimed martial law in several districts. Henlein broke off relations with the Czechs and with Runciman, declaring that Hitler's speech had now superseded the Karlsbad Program. He then fled to Germany and thence broadcast his determination to lead the Sudetens "home to the Reich." Runciman returned to London.

BERCHTESGADEN, GODESBERG, MUNICH

Throughout September 1938 Hitler was in conference with his army chiefs. He was certainly not "bluffing," as some British and American newspapers of the time tried to make out. He was fully prepared for the alternative of war — and for war, if necessary, on a global scale. Göring's Luftwaffe was ready for all eventualities. Officials of the Ministry of Propaganda were called in to prepare in detail "refutations of our own violations of international law and exploitation of its violations by the enemy." [8] Five German armies were deployed against Czechoslovakia, ostensibly on autumn maneuvers. Brauchitsch was personally in command. The partially completed West Wall was manned — though only to the strength of five divisions. Göring is reported to have remarked: "A great war can hardly be avoided any longer. It may last seven years, and we shall win it."

But Hitler could still grant a respite for a bloodless settlement if the chance were forthcoming. On September 13 the British Prime Minister, Chamberlain, telegraphed him an offer, in almost abject terms, to meet him in personal conversation — "Please indicate earliest time at which you can see me and suggest place for meeting." Hitler accepted at once. Perhaps also, in his curious vanity, Hitler could not resist the prospect of entertaining the head of the British Government in suppliant mood at his own hearth at Berchtesgaden.

We have tried to appraise Chamberlain's motives at this time (pp. 567–70). It is only necessary to add here that the idea of holding a meeting with Hitler was entirely Chamberlain's, "an unconventional and daring" expedient which he had already been conning over for some days. He may indeed have hoped to gain time, but the more ulterior Machiavellianisms with which he has since been accused were no part of his character. He knew Hitler was "half mad"; he knew, as he afterward said, he was like a man, with no cards in his hand, called on to play poker with a gangster. "Even if it should fail," he was heard to repeat to himself, "I should still say that it was right to attempt it. For the only alternative was war." Certainly questions of dignity or prestige were not to be considered when millions of lives were at stake.[9]

Chamberlain arrived in Munich by plane, on the morning of September 15, and proceeded thence to Berchtesgaden by rail and automobile. He conversed alone with Hitler — except for an interpreter — and he conversed for three hours. Hitler, as was his wont, began by being receptive and moderate, and made the apparently innocent demand that the Sudeten question should be solved by means of "self-determination." Chamberlain accepted that solution for himself and undertook to submit it to his cabinet and to the French and Czech Governments. He returned to London the next morning, September 16. Cabinet meetings in London were attended by Runciman. Daladier and Bonnet crossed over from France. The result was the so-called Anglo-French Plan, urging the Czech Government to transfer to the Reich the Sudeten areas whose population was known to be more than 50 per cent German, and to accept an Anglo-French guarantee for the new Czech frontier. It was subsequently explained to the Czech Government that the transfer would be effected, where necessary, by plebiscite or would otherwise be regulated by "an international commission."

Chamberlain flew to his second meeting with Hitler at the picturesque Rhineland town of Godesberg on September 22, in the full belief that only the technical details for the transfer of the Sudeten areas remained to be settled. But self-determination now no longer satisfied the Führer. He wanted neither plebiscites nor commissions, but surrender, and surrender at once. In addition, since the meeting at Berchtesgaden, Hungary and Poland, both friends of Germany, had preferred claims to Czechoslovak territories inhabited by their respective nationals, claims which Hitler now took it upon himself to support. Chamberlain, shocked and reproachful, declared that he could not keep returning to London with fresh proposals only to discover as soon as he had secured their acceptance from the interested parties that they had been outdistanced by new events. The conference was resumed the following evening after an interchange of letters. Hitler then presented his "last word" in the form of a memorandum categorically demanding the evacuation of the Sudeten areas, as defined by him on an attached map, and their occupation by German forces between September 26–28. A moment of frank and angry talk from Chamberlain persuaded the Führer to change the operative date to October 1, and Chamberlain returned to London with the memorandum thus amended. The British press reported that the negotiations had failed.

The Czechs had acceded to the original Anglo-French Plan under virtual threat and blackmail. The British minister at Prague, on behalf of his government, had clearly intimated to Beneš that if Czechoslovakia rejected the plan she would be responsible for the ensuing war and the cause of her own destruction. The French minister, for his part, was under the painful necessity of adding that in that event, despite the Franco-Czech alliance and despite her repeated assurances, France would not fulfill her treaty obligations.[10] Beneš was also warned that a German invasion of Czechoslovakia would certainly be followed by invasions from Hungary and Poland. Hodza, the Czech Premier, resigned on September 22, and a government of "national concentration" was immediately set up under General Syrovy. On September 24, two days after Godesberg, the new Czech Government ordered general mobilization in Czechoslovakia.

The post-Godesberg negotiations were carried on in Berlin by Sir Nevile Henderson. There was a noticeable hardening of hearts since the first amiable exchange of views at Berchtesgaden. The Syrovy government, with a return of courage and confidence, characterized the new Godesberg Memorandum as "absolutely and unconditionally inacceptable." Meanwhile Litvinov stated in the League Assembly at Geneva that the Soviet commitments to Czechoslovakia still held good. The Soviet Government warned the Polish Government that it would denounce the Polish-Soviet Nonaggression Pact if Poland joined in an attack on Czechoslovakia. On September 24 the French Government ordered the mobilization of two categories, representing a partial mobilization of about 600,000 reservists. Meetings between the French and British general staffs began. General Gamelin and Lord Gort were in continuous consultation in London. Mussolini meanwhile was adding his appropriate contribution to the crisis in a series of belligerent speeches in the north of Italy — almost one speech a day for more than a week — demanding a "totalitarian" solution of the Sudeten problem on the lines of the Godesberg Memorandum. "If a United Front comes into being, for or against Prague, let it be known that Italy's place is already chosen."

On September 26, Hitler spoke to his battle-crazed myrmidons in the Sportpalast in Berlin. The speech was punctuated with jeering, offensive references to Beneš and renewed the demand for the cession of the Sudetenland by October 1. "This is the last territorial claim I shall make in Europe, but it is a claim from which I shall not recede and which I shall fulfil, God willing . . . Once the Czechs come to an understanding with their other minorities, I shall have no further interest in the Czech state; in fact I am prepared to guarantee it. We do not want Czechs any more. But so far as the Sudeten problem is concerned, I declare my patience at an end . . . We are resolved. Let Herr Beneš decide."

The stage was set for "Case Green," the German invasion of Czechoslovakia, to go into immediate effect. On September 28 the British Government acceded to the pressure of its First Lord of the Admiralty, that energetic rebel against appeasement, Duff Cooper, and ordered the mobilization of the navy. The same evening, Chamberlain broadcast to the British people. The voice which came over the air was that of an aged, weary, and broken man. "How horrible, fantastic, incredible it is that we should be digging trenches and trying on gas masks here because of a quarrel in a faraway country between people of whom we know nothing."

But it was Benito Mussolini, the Italian Duce, who dragged Germany, Czechoslovakia, and Europe back from the sheer abyss of war. About midday on September 28, urged by Chamberlain and Daladier to use his influence, he appealed to Hitler to postpone the march of the German Army for twenty-four hours.[11] The last-minute intervention of his warrior ally perhaps enabled Hitler to climb down without loss of face though, even now, in view of the military preparations, and the lengths to which the crisis had developed, Hitler's change of front is hard to explain. On that day the Italian

THE PARTITION OF CZECHOSLOVAKIA, 1938–1939.

▦ Ceded to Germany under the Munich Agreement, September 30th, 1938.

▧ Ceded to Hungary under the Vienna Award, November 2nd, 1938.

▩ Seized by Poland, October 2nd, 1938.

▨ Seized by Hungary, March 15th, 1939.

ambassador paid Hitler four visits in three hours and was twenty times in telephonic contact with Rome. The result was the Four-Power Conference at Munich.

The meeting of the four statesmen — Hitler, Chamberlain, Daladier, and Mussolini — began on the afternoon of September 29 at the Brown House in Munich, and the final Munich Agreement was drafted and signed in the early hours of the next day. The terms incorporated the essentials of the Godesberg Memorandum, but without its more peremptory details. The Czechs were given from October 1 to October 10 to complete their evacuation of the Sudeten areas, "without any existing installations having been destroyed." The German occupation would take place in four stages, and the final frontiers would be fixed not by Hitler's map, but by an international commission consisting of representatives of the four Powers and Czechoslovakia. Plebiscites were stipulated for the questionable districts, and the right of option into and out of the transferred territory was secured to any of its inhabitants. At the same time Hitler and Chamberlain signed an Anglo-German declaration renouncing war in the settlement of their national differences. Britain and France declared a guarantee of the new Czechoslovak frontiers against unprovoked aggression, a guarantee in which Germany and Italy undertook to participate once the revisionist claims of Hungary and Poland had been met. Britain afterward granted Czechoslovakia a loan of £10,000,000, ostensibly to tide over the temporary disruptive effects of the Munich Agreement on her economic life.

REACTIONS OF THE POWERS

The immediate reaction to Munich everywhere — except in Czechoslovakia — was one of joy and thankfulness. "No conqueror returning from a victory on the battlefield," said the London *Times* on October 1, "has come home adorned with nobler laurels than Mr. Chamberlain from Munich yesterday," and it would be hard to find an English paper of the date which did not express the same feelings. As Sir Nevile Henderson wrote to Chamberlain: "Millions of mothers will be blessing your name tonight for having saved their sons from the horrors of war. Oceans of ink will flow hereafter in criticism of your action."

The oceans of ink began to flow as soon as the immediate reaction had spent itself. It is true that Britain had no legal stake in or alliance with Czechoslovakia, and it is impossible to accuse her of evading obligations which she had never contracted. But Britain indirectly and undeniably breathed the atmosphere of dictation at Munich — and of dictation from a Power which she had once defeated and whose present form of government she despised. At the same time, no one realized better than the British people themselves that they were morally and materially unready for war. The idea of war in itself was "unpopular"; the idea of war over Czechoslovakia, "a faraway country . . . of which we know nothing," would have been much more so. The British rearmament program was only half-begun. The military authorities in Germany were perfectly well acquainted with the unpreparedness of the British air defenses, and they were perfectly well acquainted with the fact that in September 1938 the German air force was numerically superior to those of Britain, France, and Czechoslovakia combined. There were four antiaircraft guns in London on the day that the Munich Agreement was signed. For Britain to have said "No" to Hitler in 1938 would have been very different from saying "No" to Mussolini in 1935. The one meant a sedentary warfare of protests and sanctions; the other meant aerial warfare on an unimaginable scale.

France woke from the nightmare of Munich with feelings less of humiliation and shame than of utter confusion, and her mood thereafter can only be described as one of inertia, a refusal to think and a wish to forget. In her case the legal stake, the Franco-Czechoslovak alliance, had been clear, and it had been so often reiterated in the past as to make any casuistic dispute or evasion of it impossible. Yet France, like Britain, was unready for war — morally rather than materially unready. General Gamelin, Chief of the French General Staff, had asserted again and again his belief that the weak foreign policy which France had been pursuing did not reflect her real military strength, and he had complete faith in the Maginot Line. As we have said, the West Wall was manned with only five German divisions in September 1938. Yet the fact remained that France had pursued that weak policy and had pursued it ever since the outbreak of the Spanish Civil War — if not from the death of Barthou in 1934. Prominent and influential men, such as Bonnet, Daladier's Foreign Minister, had latterly been doctrinaire appeasers of the most pernicious kind.

The course of French foreign policy received its final seal and confirmation two months later, on December 6, when Ribbentrop visited Paris in ceremony and signed with Bonnet a Franco-German Declaration of Friendship.

For Czechoslovakia, Munich was a cruel defeat and a crueler betrayal. "It was not cowardice which brought us to this decision," broadcast the Czech Minister of Propaganda. "Even the bravest may find his courage, honor, and sentiment retreat before forces of blind pressure. God knows that sometimes a man needs more strength to live than to commit suicide . . . We have sacrificed ourselves for the salvation of Europe, as, ages ago, the Son of God sacrificed himself for humanity. Dear brothers, sisters, fathers, mothers, children, we shall not today reproach those who left us in the lurch. History will give judgment on the events of these days."

Czechoslovakia had remained loyal to the ideals of her founders; she had been unwavering in her democratic faith; she had not allowed herself to be suborned to Nazism as Poland, Yugoslavia, Rumania, and Hungary had sometimes been. She had always been assiduously flattered by the high regard of Western democracy, and she had made herself worthy of that regard. But now she had been condemned without a hearing. She had not been invited to Godesberg or to Munich, and she, a democratic country, had afterward been forced to accept the decisions of others respecting her very existence as a nation, without even being permitted to consult her own parliament. In terms of acres and cents, she lost to Germany her entire system of fortifications in Bohemia, three-quarters of her heavy industries, and essential roads and railroads; in terms of morale, her losses were incalculable.

Munich was the surrender of democracy's once strongest and last surviving outpost in the Middle Danube. It transformed the entire political and strategic situation on the Continent of Europe. It amounted in principle to the final subversion of Versailles. It broke the French alliance system beyond hope of repair. It loosened all the old allegiances and alignments. It destroyed the Little Entente. It left the Middle Danube prostrate before the advance of triumphant Nazism.

"We have suffered a total and unmitigated defeat," said Churchill in the House of Commons. "All is over. Silent, mournful, abandoned, broken Czechoslovakia recedes into the darkness . . . I think you will find that in a period of time, which may be measured by years but may be measured by months, Czechoslovakia will be engulfed in the Nazi regime . . . We have passed an awful milestone in our history, when the whole equilibrium of Europe has been deranged, and the terrible words have for the time being been pronounced against the Western democracies: Thou art weighed in the balance and found wanting!"

The German press did not minimize the significance of Munich. A dangerous enemy had been neutralized, the monstrosity of Versailles had been removed, the power of the Third Reich had been demonstrated, important new resources of men and material had been added to the German military establishment, *Mitteleuropa* had once more been made a realizable dream, and all had been accomplished bloodlessly and with the maximum of drama by the divine genius of Adolf Hitler.

But one incident should be mentioned at this point, an incident which must have dissipated any last lingering illusions that might still have existed abroad regarding the true nature of the Third Reich and the emollient effects of Munich upon the Nazi heart. On November 7, Herschel Grynszpan, a seventeen-year-old Jewish refugee, thinking to avenge the mistreatment of his parents in Germany, forced his way into the German Embassy in Paris and shot the first German he could find. His victim, an official of the Embassy, vom Rath, died of his injuries some days later. Hardly six weeks after Munich, on November 10, the anniversary of Hitler's Munich putsch of 1923, the Nazis opened their worst Jewish pogrom to date. Wrecking squads of troopers tore through the streets of Berlin and other cities, and even of Vienna, setting fire to Jewish shops, houses, and synagogues, ejecting whole families into the streets, making indiscriminate arrests, and sometimes picking on a defenseless individual for the more exquisite forms of torment. It seemed as if half the population of Berlin had gone berserk. The police made no attempt to interfere. Mothers perched children on their shoulders to let them see the sport.

Clearly the pogrom had been organized and was no capricious outburst, and the probabilities point to Göring as its organizer. At the time he was acutely worried over the stresses and strains which the Four-Year Plan was imposing on the German economy, and he was clutching at any relief that was ready to hand. Jewry offered him a goodly haul of wealth and labor. "I'm going to make barbaric use of the plenipotentiary powers given to me by the Führer," he said. On November 13, in a special decree, he ordered the Jews to make good at their own expense the damage which had been done during the pogrom, and in addition imposed a fine of 1,000,000,000 marks on the Jewish community for the murder of vom Rath.

The Soviet Union's reactions to Munich were not simple, and they are more difficult to describe. Munich fell at the precise moment when Moscow was bethinking itself of withdrawing into isolation and was turning to that policy which reached its logical conclusion in the Moscow Pact of August 1939. The Spanish Civil War and the trials and purges, meanwhile, had greatly complicated the process. Both before and after Munich, however, Litvinov gave repeated and categorical assurances that the Soviet Government would stand by its treaty obligations to Czechoslovakia. On September 21, before the League Assembly, he proposed a conference of the Powers to put a check upon further aggression in Europe. But all his pleas were ignored.

The Soviet Government had keenly resented being omitted from the Munich Conference. Certainly it would have been difficult to conceive of any Soviet delegate at that time attending a conference at which Hitler and Mussolini were also present. But the omission was construed by the Soviet Government not only as a slight, but as an indication that Britain and France were seeking to divert Hitler's expansionist energies away from themselves toward the East. German intrigue in the Ukraine, shortly after Munich, and Hitler's supposed meetings with the Grand Duke Vladimir, whom he allegedly designated as the future ruler of a Nazi-dominated Ukraine, gave some support to that view. Stalin at least was privately convinced that Britain and France intended to use the Soviet as the cat's-paw of their fears and ambitions. The Soviet Government subsequently denounced the Czech-Soviet Mutual Assistance Pact of 1935.

In the United States, as has been mentioned elsewhere (see p. 601), the first reaction to Munich was of profound relief that the peace had been preserved, and it was some days before the mood changed to one of undisguised disgust, not unmixed, for the first time in these critical years, with fear. Seven months previously the isolationists, however shocked, could still speak of the Austrian crisis, in the words of Senator Borah, as "a thing which is not of the slightest moment to the Government, as a Government, of the United States." At that time the administration made some effort to alleviate the distress of individuals in Austria, notably Catholics and Jews, and the issue of immigration visas from Austria was speeded up. Secretary Hull, in a speech which presumably reflected the views of the State Department, appealed for a "co-operative effort" among nations for the sake of peace and argued emphatically that "aloofness" encouraged and virtually invited other lawlessly inclined nations.

But Munich was a decisive turning point of American public opinion. As the crisis had mounted, news commentators deplored the degeneration of European affairs to a state comparable to "the manners of a top sergeant, the veracity of a paid propagandist, and the methods of a college cheer leader." President Roosevelt's notes of September 26 and 27 to the parties in the dispute were brave but inadequate (see p. 601). The ensuing "betrayal" of Czechoslovakia, a democratic country, which had always enjoyed the high regard and affection of the American people, found hardly even an isolationist voice to rise and excuse it. "Czechoslovakia has been sold down the river, but no man yet knows at what cost of blood and tears."

The Jewish pogrom in Germany in November which followed the assassination of vom Rath evoked the utmost horror in the United States. Not since the sinking of the *Lusitania* in 1915 had the general community of indignation in the American people, over a matter touching their foreign relations, been so intense and united. "I myself could scarcely believe," said the President at a press conference, "that such things could occur in a twentieth-century civilization." As a mark of protest the American ambassador, Hugh Wilson, left Berlin for home to give the President "a firsthand picture." Thus rebuked, the German Government recalled its own ambassador in Washington to explain "the singular attitude" of the United States.

THE FINAL EXTINCTION OF CZECHOSLOVAKIA

The international commission established under the Munich Agreement to devise the new Czechoslovak frontiers held its first meeting on October 1.

In the event, there were no plebiscites, and all important decisions were made by the German military members of the Commission, Keitel and Brauchitsch. Britain and France evinced no further interest in the guarantees of the new frontiers which at Munich they had solemnly pledged themselves to give. The isolation of the Czech Republic was about as complete as it was possible to be. The Poles seized the Teschen area and coal fields on October 2. By the so-called Vienna Award on November 2, the "Second Munich," Germany and Italy, in the capacity of mediators, assigned a generous strip of Slovakia and Ruthenia to Hungary. On November 21, Czechoslovakia ceded to Germany a corridor through the very heart of the country to be used for a new automobile highway connecting Vienna and Breslau, and to be regarded to all intents and purposes as German territory.

The "co-ordination" of the occupied Sudeten territory was quickly effected. Henlein reappeared in his old homeland as its Gauleiter. The remainder of the mutilated state, far from emerging a "sounder" Czechoslovakia, fast broke into its elements. All its former centrifugal and disruptive forces, now abetted by German agency, were given full play. The Slovak People's party demanded autonomy and showed unmistakable Nazi tendencies. On October 7 the first autonomous government of Slovakia was founded under Dr. Tiso, successor to Hlinka in the leadership of the Slovak People's party (see p. 197), and took up its quarters in Bratislava. An autonomous government was formed in Ruthenia a few days afterward. A sort of loose confederation was later recognized by Prague. The very name "Czechoslovakia" was changed to "Czecho-Slovakia." Ruthenia took the name of "Carpatho-Ukraine."

On October 5, Beneš resigned the presidency and went into voluntary exile. He was eventually succeeded by Dr. Emil Hácha, former Chief Justice of the Czechoslovak Supreme Court. Dr. František Chvalkovsky, a professional diplomat, was the new Foreign Minister, and the Hácha-Chvalkovsky combination at once reversed the former foreign policy of the state in favor of "permanently good relations with Germany." Far from disinteresting himself in the unhappy country, Hitler consulted Keitel in regard to its final military subjugation within a week of the Munich Conference. Hitler's directive for "the liquidation of the rest of Czecho-Slovakia" was in Keitel's hands on December 17. Meanwhile Slovakia was being bedecked with the usual trappings of a Nazi state. Czech officials, judges, and teachers were expelled from Slovak areas; all opposition parties were dissolved; laws were passed against Jews.

In Bohemia and Moravia, the 350,000 Germans who still remained within the revised Czech frontiers, under their efficient leaders Kundt and Karl Hermann Frank, demanded all manner of special privileges and were, in fact, encouraged to regard themselves as "citizens of the Greater German Reich with a special mission." In January 1939, Chvalkovsky was summoned to Berlin, much as Schuschnigg had once been summoned to Berchtesgaden. Hitler arraigned him on a long list of charges and presented him with a long list of demands, notably for the reduction of the Czech Army, the denunciation of the Czech-Soviet Pact of 1935, and the elimination of Jewish influence. Chvalkovsky returned to Prague to fulfill his German master's instructions and to destroy the last vestige of Czech independence and dignity.

Chvalkovsky, obedient though he might try to be in Prague, could not keep up the tragicomedy of amicable relations with his opposites in Slovakia. Hitler had already established his usual liaison with Tiso and the Slovak autonomist leaders. A new crisis came to a head in the second week of March 1939. The Czech Government at last broke off relations with the Slovak Government, and within twenty-four hours Hitler seized upon its action as an excuse for intervention. On March 11, Seyss-Inquart, Bürckel, and five German generals interrupted a Slovak Cabinet meeting in Bratislava and told the assembled Slovak ministers to proclaim the independence of Slovakia. On March 13, Hitler received Tiso in Berlin. The independence of Slovakia, he said, was not now "a question of days, but of hours. . . . If [Slovakia] hesitated or did not dissolve the connection with Prague, he [Hitler] would leave the destiny of Slovakia to the mercy of events, for which he would no longer be responsible." Before Tiso's departure home, Ribbentrop very solicitously handed him a copy, already drafted in the Slovak language, of a law proclaiming the independence of Slovakia. The next day the law was promulgated in Bratislava.

On the same day, March 14, 1939, the Czech President, Hácha, accompanied Chvalkovsky to Berlin. The meeting with Hitler took place at midnight in the Chancellery in the presence of Göring, Ribbentrop, Keitel, and other high-ranking Nazis. Hitler treated Hácha to one of his characteristic harangues, accused him of having broken the Munich Agreement, and announced that he had already given the order to the German forces to march into Czech territory and incorporate it into the Reich. During the conference, Hácha, an ailing man in his seventies, was in so exhausted a state that he had to receive medical aid. At one point Ribbentrop was chasing him round the conference table brandishing the text of an agreement for him to sign. But Hácha appears to have resisted the Nazi demands until Göring was removed to boast that "if German lives were lost, his [Göring's] Luftwaffe would blast half of Prague into ruins in two hours, and that would only be the beginning." In the early morning of March 15, Hácha signed the agreement. "In order to serve the end [of order and peace] and to reach a final pacification he confidently placed the fate of the Czech people and of their country in the hands of the Führer of the German Reich."

Several German units had already crossed the Czech border. By midday of March 15, Prague was in occupation. The Skoda armament works at Pilsen with "its vast store of munitions" fell intact into German hands. Hitler entered his new territory and from the Hradschin, the palace of the old Bohemian kings, he proclaimed Bohemia and Moravia a Protectorate of the Reich. Neurath was appointed Protector with Henlein and Karl Hermann Frank as his aides in office. The Hungarians simultaneously invaded Carpatho-Ukraine and annexed it to Hungary.

So ended the First Republic of Czechoslovakia.

Simultaneously Memel returned to the Reich. The transaction was prefaced by the usual press campaign in Germany and the usual efforts at appeasement on the part of the Lithuanian Government. The Lithuanian Foreign Minister, visiting Berlin, was bluntly told by Ribbentrop that the port and territory of Memel must be surrendered without more ado, and the Lithuanian Government had no alternative but acquiescence. In return Germany promised Lithuania a free harbor in Memel, and gave her the inevitable guarantee of nonaggression. On March 23, 1939, Hitler and the German Baltic Fleet visited the surrendered port.

THE POLISH CRISIS

Marshal Pilsudski had died in May 1935 but, in respect of her domestic affairs, his death had made little difference to Poland. Almost his last act had been to appoint General Śmigly-Rydz Inspector General of the Polish Army and the virtual executor of his political legacy. The Pilsudskian dictatorship, therefore, continued under a new master. Economic difficulties, an excitable if browbeaten electorate, and general political regimentation complete the picture of the Poland of the later thirties.

In respect of her foreign affairs, however, Poland was of greater interest. Certainly her position had never been enviable. She lay precariously between two great neighbors, Germany and the Soviet Union, which had risen again to the rank of first-class military Powers and with which she had long traditions of hostility. She had German and Russian minorities in great numbers living within her frontiers, and both of them were discontented. Since 1933 the Soviet Union had been re-entering European diplomacy and had seemed to be adopting an anti-German alignment. As we have seen, Poland made her choice in 1934, when she concluded the German-Polish Nonaggression Pact and effected the first breach in "the Versailles Front" (see p. 478). Poland badly needed friends; but her incontinent policy in the early days of her liberation, especially her irresponsible baiting of Lithuania and Czechoslovakia, was now bringing home its appropriate reward. Her Foreign Minister was Beck, as bitter a Russophobe as his former chief, Pilsudski.

But Poland was never happy in her German *rapprochement*. The situation was highly artificial and was all but acknowledged to be so. The Polish Socialist and Peasant parties were strongly opposed to the entire pro-German attitude which Beck and his "Colonels" represented. Poland felt all the shocks and repercussions of the Ethiopian crisis of 1935 and the Rhineland crisis of 1936. A painful hesitancy began to govern her foreign policy, a hesitancy common to many another smaller — and bigger — Power in the Europe of the day, trying frantically to predict the future. An attempt to thaw the recent frigid relations with France was a feature of the year 1936. General Gamelin, Chief of the French General Staff, visited Warsaw, and General Śmigly-Ridz visited Paris. The respective receptions of both soldiers were significantly cordial, and technical staff talks appear to have taken place on the second occasion.

As might be expected, affairs in Danzig provided an infallible index of German-Polish relations. The comparative peace which had reigned in the city in 1934, at the time the German-Polish Nonaggression Pact was signed, was already disturbed in February 1935, when elections were held returning a Nazi majority to the Danzig Volkstag. In January 1934, Sean Lester had been appointed the League of Nations High Commissioner for Danzig.[12] Rauschning had resigned the presidency of the Danzig Senate in November 1934, shortly to go into exile and write his classic exposures of Nazism, and Rauschning had been succeeded by Greiser. Greiser overrode the city's constitution in various ways and went out of his way to insult the High Commissioner. The Nazi majority in the Volkstag was soon reducing the sessions to a farce. Opposition papers in the city were arbitrarily suspended, and civil servants were made to declare their allegiance to the Nazi party or resign. Forster, the Nazi Gauleiter in Danzig, publicly announced that he did not regard himself as responsible to the authorities in Danzig, but to his Führer in Germany. Forster had not the slightest legal status in Danzig. He was a German national and a Deputy of the German Reichstag, one of Hitler's intimate circle and a regular visitor at Berchtesgaden. But he conducted himself as if he were of higher rank — as in the Nazi hierarchy he was — than Greiser, the president of the Danzig Senate.

At the end of July 1936, Sean Lester was in Geneva to make his report on the situation in Danzig to the League, and thither Greiser was invited to come. Greiser behaved as offensively as he could. He gave the Nazi salute in the Council chamber, and thumbed his nose and stuck out his tongue at journalists in the press gallery who laughed at him. He was making a display — as he thought — of Nazi temerity; he was making a display — as the League Council thought — of the kind of statesmanship which Nazism was now raising up to power and prominence in the world. In September 1936, Lester resigned.

In January 1937 the League Council adopted a report, drawn up by the Polish Government, amounting to a virtual renunciation of the League's control over Danzig. In May, at another election, the Nazis at last obtained their two-thirds majority in the Volkstag, and were entitled to make such constitutional changes in Danzig as they desired.[12]

Such was the background in Poland and Danzig at the time Hitler was encompassing the elimination of Austria and Czechoslovakia. At the end of 1938 the heat was being turned on Poland herself. In October of that year, at a luncheon at a Berchtesgaden hotel, Ribbentrop had demanded of Lipski, the Polish ambassador to Germany, the return of Danzig to the Reich and the construction of an all-German automobile highway and railroad, extraterritorially controlled, across the Corridor. The demands were formally renewed in January 1939, when Ribbentrop visited Warsaw, and again in March 1939, the day after the incorporation of Memel. On each occasion the demands were firmly rejected by Poland. Meanwhile the German press suddenly discovered evidences of Polish terrorism against German minorities in Poland and let loose the usual campaign of vituperation. Yet on January 30, 1939, during his anniversary speech, Hitler had celebrated the fifth anniversary of the German-Polish Nonaggression Pact in reassuring and friendly words. The Hitlerian technique was following its regular pattern.

Chamberlain in Britain at first made little reference to the German occupation of Prague and the final liquidation of Czechoslovakia. Questions were answered in the House of Commons with more than the usual equivocation. But the British press was agitated and accusing and, on March 17, at Birmingham, Chamberlain, though still exercising his "freezing gift for understatement," at last gave a speech which more fairly responded to the rising temper of the British people: "If it is easy to discover good reasons for ignoring assurances so solemnly and repeatedly given," he said, "what reliance can be placed upon any other assurances that come from the same source? . . . Germany has sprung a series of unpleasant surprises on the world, the Rhineland, the Austrian Anschluss, the severance of the Sudetenland. All these things shocked and affronted public opinion throughout the world. Yet however much we might take exception to the methods that were adopted in each case, there was something to be said . . . for the necessity of a change in the existing situation. But the events which have taken place this week [in Prague], in complete disregard of the principles laid down by the German Government itself, seem to fall in a different category, and they must cause us all to be asking ourselves: Is this the end of an old adventure, or is it the beginning of a new? Is this the last attack upon a small state, or is it to be followed by others? Is this, in fact, a step in the direction of an attempt to dominate the world by force?"

But the situation called for something more palpable than speeches and condemnations. Hitler's new demand for Danzig was indication enough of the way the wind would next be blowing. On March 31 the British Government extended a guarantee to Poland and, in Chamberlain's words, committed itself, "in the event of any action which clearly threatened Polish independence, and which the Polish Government accordingly considered it vital to resist with their national forces . . . to lend the Polish Government all the support in their power." The guarantee was so worded that the Poles themselves would be the judges of the right cause and the right moment for resistance. It was an epochal departure for British foreign policy, which traditionally shrank from entanglements in Europe east of the Rhine. Poland's conduct of her foreign relations since 1934 had not always been above suspicion, and her recent assault on the Czechs at Teschen was hard to forgive, but present emergencies were more exacting than the memory of past mistakes. France at once associated herself with the British action. On April 6, the guarantee was verbally confirmed in conversations with Colonel Beck in London.

"Case White," Germany's code name for her operation against Poland, was ready in April 1939. On May 23, Hitler held one of his briefing conferences with his high-ranking officers, including Göring, Brauchitsch, Keitel, and Raeder.[18] The entire political and military situation was surveyed. Germany, Hitler argued, had re-emerged as a Great Power, but all her demands for the necessities of life were regarded abroad as "encroachments." The problems of ideology and national unity had been solved; the problem of living space remained. "Danzig is not the subject of the dispute at all. It is a question of expanding our living space in the East and of securing our food supplies. The Polish problem is inseparable from conflict with the

West . . . [We must] *attack Poland at the first suitable opportunity* [under-scored in the original German text]. We cannot expect a repetition of the Czech affair. There will be fighting. Our task is to isolate Poland. The success of the isolation will be decisive. . . . Economic relations with Russia are possible only if political relations have improved." War with Britain and France might result, but a two-front war was to be avoided if possible. "If England intends to intervene in the Polish war, we must occupy Holland with lightning speed. . . . The war with England and France will be a life-and-death struggle. . . . The government must be prepared for a war of ten to fifteen years' duration . . ." And so forth. But the isolation of Poland was conditional upon the disinterest of the Soviet Union and, at this conference, Hitler vouchsafed for the first time his view that it might be necessary for him to come to a temporary *rapprochement* with the Soviet Union. A Soviet-German pact would have to be the preliminary of a Polish-German war.

SPAIN, ITALY, ALBANIA

It had been hoped in Britain that the end of the Spanish Civil War would at least rid the world of one source of perpetual tension, that the late Anglo-Italian Agreement might become infused with some of the reality it had always seemed to lack, and that there might even be a corresponding improvement in French and Italian relations. But the year 1938 had closed in Rome with violent anti-French demonstrations. François-Poncet, the new French ambassador in Rome, from his diplomatic seat in the Italian Chamber had himself been a witness of an offensive outcry — doubtless prearranged for his benefit — on the part of the Italian Deputies for "Corsica, Tunis, Savoy, Jibuti!" Some days later, on December 17, 1938, Mussolini had denounced the Franco-Italian Agreement of 1935.

On March 26, 1939, speaking in Rome at a giant rally of his squadrists on the twentieth anniversary of the Fascist party, Mussolini made it very clear that the recent successes of his German ally in Central Europe had only hardened his heart the more against France. The French Government, he said, "must not complain if the furrow which now separates our two countries, becomes so wide that it cannot be filled. We do not want to hear any more about brotherly, sisterly, cousinly, or any other sort of bastard relationship, because relations between states depend on a balance of forces between them . . . The word 'peace' has been rather overworked and has a nasty ring like bad memory. . . . The order of the day is more guns, more ships, more planes, even at the cost of dispensing with what is called civilian life. . . . As history teaches us, woe to them who cannot defend themselves!"

Early in April, Italian troop concentrations at Bari and Brindisi had been reaching suspicious proportions. Inquiries from Lord Perth, the British ambassador in Rome, elicited nothing beyond reassurances and evasions. But on April 7, Good Friday, Italian transports steamed across the Strait of Otranto and landed an Italian invading force in Albania. Evidently Mussolini in recent months had been feeling the need of some military demonstration on his part to parallel the success of his Axis partner in Central Europe.

Albania had always belonged to the Italian sphere of influence; it had been evacuated in disgraceful circumstances the year before the Fascist rise to power; but, of more recent years, it had been subject to increasing economic penetration on the part of Italy. The present Italian action plainly contravened a number of treaties, notably the Treaty of Tirana of 1927, and even the recent Anglo-Italian Agreement. But that particular difficulty could always be swept aside with a little ingenious dialectic and a little self-righteous arrogance. King Zog of Albania, Queen Geraldine, and their infant son fled to Greece, and the crown of Albania was assumed by King Victor Emmanuel III.

On April 13 the British and French Governments replied to this new Axis incursion into the Balkans by extending guarantees, on the lines of the recent Polish guarantee, to Greece and Rumania. A month later the British Government announced an Anglo-Turkish Mutual Assistance Pact, to go into immediate effect "in the event of aggression leading to war in the Mediterranean area." At the same time it became known that France and Turkey, preparatory to a similar pact, had nearly completed their negotiations for the transfer to Turkish possession of their old bone of contention in Syria, the Sanjak of Antioch and Alexandretta (see p. 537).

At this moment the United States Government entered the lists. On April 14, 1939, in his Pan American Day address in Washington, President Roosevelt used the following words: "The issue is really whether our civilization is to be dragged into the vortex of unending militarism, punctuated by periodic wars, or whether we shall be able to maintain the ideal of peace, individuality, and civilization as the fabric of our lives. We have the right to say that there shall not be an organization of world affairs which permits us no choice but to turn our countries into barracks, unless we be the vassals of some conquering empire." Two days later, President Roosevelt sent his famous message to the two European dictators asking them, as "an immediate measure of relief," to give assurances that their armed forces would not attack or invade, for a period of ten years, thirty states whose names he listed. The message was hailed everywhere but in Germany and Italy, where the press denounced it as "an infamous trick," "a tactical maneuver," "a shabby propaganda pamphlet." For a moment America took the place of England as the favored object of totalitarian scorn and execration.

Mussolini answered President Roosevelt's message in a public speech on April 20. He reprobated "the unjust attempt to put the two Axis nations in the dock," and asked how Italy could be accused of trying to set the world on fire at the moment when the whole of her energies were concentrated on the preparations for the great Fascist Exhibition to be held in Rome in 1942. The speech was not one of the Duce's best efforts, but it was more conciliatory than his recent belligerent utterances. Hitler made his answer in a speech of two and a half hours in the Reichstag on April 28. It was a considerable, well-prepared and — for Hitler — closely reasoned review of the Nazi movement, running the whole gamut from the *"Diktat"* of Versailles to the Czech crisis. As usual he labored the villainies of the Jews, the impostures of the League of Nations, the pacific purposes of the Third Reich, and the favors of Providence. His mood switched deftly from declamation to pleading, from menace to injured innocence, from arrogance to defensiveness. He denounced the Anglo-German Naval Agreement of 1935 and the German-Polish Pact of 1934, both of which, he claimed, had been superseded and destroyed by infringements of the other parties to them. To President Roosevelt he referred in terms of contempt and irony, suggesting a Monroe Doctrine for Europe, and hinting that the President would have rendered a nobler service to peace if he had redeemed the promises of Woodrow Wilson.

THE MOSCOW PACT

The summer of 1939 wore on in an atmosphere oppressive with gathering storm. In Britain, against strenuous Labor and pacifist opposition, Parliament passed a Military Training Act, conscripting men of twenty to twenty-one years of age, a measure which was as revolutionary an innovation in Britain's traditional domestic policy in peacetime as the recent Polish guarantee had been in her traditional foreign policy. The British armament drive was at last producing results; 2,000 first-line planes were expected by July 1939. Germany and Italy converted their Axis into a formal military alliance, a "Pact of Steel," as Mussolini called it. Germany and Denmark signed a non-aggression pact. France and Turkey, having settled the matter of Alexandretta to their satisfaction, entered into a mutual assistance pact in the Mediterranean. Several thousand Germans in the Tirol, at the behest of Mussolini, were uprooted from their ancient homeland and transferred to the Reich. The British sovereigns, King George and Queen Elizabeth, went on their tour of Canada and visited the United States, a felicitous and heartening, if somewhat transparent, piece of diplomacy. Meanwhile Hitler, edging toward Danzig and Poland, was putting into motion all those tactical thrusts and feints which the world had now come to regard as the usual preliminaries of a Nazi coup. The German press flogged the issues of encirclement and *Lebensraum* and berated the degenerate, imperialistic democracies which, in their pride and folly, still sought to obstruct the inevitable solution of Germany's national problem. All the atrocities which the Czechs were once supposed to have committed in the Sudetenland were trumped up again, often in the same words and with the same illustrations, and attributed to the Poles in the Corridor.

But the great question of the hour was Russia. The Peace Front which Britain and France had been constructing against Germany and which now included Poland, Greece, Rumania, and Turkey, was essentially unreal and incomplete without the adherence of the Great Power in the East. Since the German occupation of Prague in March, the British Government had been tactfully interrogating the Russian sphinx and trying to probe the riddle of the Soviet Union's future alignment in Europe. Sir William Seeds, the British ambassador in Moscow, and Litvinov, Ivan Maisky, the Soviet ambassador in London, and Lord Halifax, had engaged in continual, cordial, but apparently fruitless conferences. The Soviet press had ceased to upbraid Chamberlain for his nefarious tactics over Czechoslovakia, and the British Conservative press had ceased to upbraid the Soviet Union. Early in June the British Government sent William Strang, Chamberlain's aide at Berchtesgaden, a high official of the Foreign Office and an expert in Russian affairs, as a special emissary to Moscow to initiate discussions for an Anglo-Soviet pact. As a high German functionary is supposed to have said to Hitler: "You will know that Britain is in earnest on the day that the British working class accepts conscription and the Conservative party agrees to an alliance with Russia."

But, for those who had eyes to see, Joseph Stalin had not been satisfied with these mere contacts with Western democracy. As he himself said, he was not willing to pull Britain's chestnuts out of the fire. It was significant, moreover, that Hitler's speech on April 28 had omitted the usual references to "Jewish Marxism" and to the subhuman monsters who inhabited the Kremlin. On May 3, Litvinov, once the indefatigable supporter of the League of Nations, was suddenly relieved of his post as Soviet Foreign Commissar to be succeeded by the colorless, provincial, but grimly impassive party official and President of the Council of People's Commissars, Vyacheslav Mikhailovich Molotov. Some days later, a new Soviet ambassador arrived in Berlin and was received with marks of quite exceptional courtesy. On May 20, in conversation with the German ambassador in Moscow, Molotov on his own initiative asked for better German-Soviet "political bases" prior to a renewal of economic negotiations between the German and Soviet Governments. On May 23, as we have said, Hitler had divulged to his army chiefs that he was prepared for a temporary *rapprochement* in the East. But, though a sudden superficial cordiality distinguished German-Soviet ambassadorial meetings, the diplomatic process was slow and cautious, presumably to permit Molotov to overcome his intense distrust of his German opposites. At one moment Hitler ordered negotiations to be stopped. Then, on August 15, the German ambassador was instructed to inform Moscow that, in the belief of his government, ideological contradictions should not prohibit reasonable co-operation "of a new and friendly type," that there were no questions "between the Baltic and the Black Seas" which were not amenable to satisfactory settlement, and that Ribbentrop, the German Foreign Minister himself, would be prepared to make a short visit to Moscow "to set forth the Führer's views to Herr Stalin."

Meanwhile British and French officers, sent to Moscow early that August to open staff talks, though they were treated at first with every courtesy, soon found themselves working against mysterious delays and obstructions. It was reported at one time that the Russians were demanding that Britain and France extend their guarantees to cover the Baltic States; it was reported at another time that the Russians were laying claim to the military control of the Baltic area themselves and demanding rights of transit through Poland and Rumania. Negotiations were interminably protracted over the definition of "indirect aggression." The Baltic States themselves were averse to being drawn into discussions which appeared to be compromising their neutrality, and they preferred to negotiate separate nonaggression pacts with Germany. Poland was still clinging to her traditional Russophobia and regarded with very mixed feelings the prospects of Soviet adhesion to the democratic Grand Alliance against Hitler.

On August 21, the imminent conclusion of a German-Soviet nonaggression pact was announced in Berlin, and Ribbentrop proceeded by air to Moscow two days later for the ceremonial signing of it.

Three great military Powers were in the field in the summer of 1939, Germany, the Soviet Union, and the Western democracies, Britain and France. The certain element in the situation was the belligerency of Germany; the uncertain element was the alignment of the other two Powers, the Soviet Union and the Western democracies, each of which was exerting itself to avoid embroilment in the coming war. In Soviet eyes, the policy of collective security had died at Munich. Its great Soviet proponent, Litvinov, had just been retired. Stalin and his advisers believed and feared that, at Munich, the Western democracies had abandoned the East to German conquest and hoped to emerge unscathed and dominant from a Soviet-German war of annihilation. The Western democracies believed as firmly that the Soviet Union was playing the same game with themselves. The democracies knew well enough that another surrender to Germany would result in the final and irremediable recession of their power, and they were resolved at all costs to support Poland. But the democracies were handicapped by their own professed ethical scruples against making a "deal"; they could not traffic in the independence of small states and openly condone the Soviet Union's military ambitions in the Baltic. Germany, for her part, was interested only in securing the neutrality — or better still, the benevolence and complicity — of the Soviet Union and thereby in removing her overmastering fear of a war on two fronts.

The published text of the Moscow Pact was short and simple. The two contracting parties undertook to desist from any act of violence against each other, to give no support to any third Power which should make either of them "an object of belligerent action," to consult on questions of common interest, and to settle any future disputes "through friendly exchange of opinion." The Pact contained no "escape clause." It was to be valid for ten years. But in addition there was appended to the Pact a Secret Protocol to the effect: first, that, in the event of "a territorial or political rearrangement" in the Baltic States, the northern boundary of Lithuania should represent the boundary between the German and Soviet spheres of influence, while both parties recognized Lithuania's interest in Vilna — that is to say, Finland, Estonia, and Latvia should be relegated to the Soviet sphere of influence, and Lithuania to the German; second that, in the event of a similar rearrangement in Poland, the German and Soviet spheres of influence should be delimited approximately along the line of the Narew, Vistula, and San, and that the question of maintaining an independent Poland would be decided only "in the course of further political developments" and would, "in any case," be solved "by means of a friendly agreement"; and third, that the Soviet's interest — and Germany's disinterest — in Bessarabia was affirmed.

Even a world whose values were awry and whose experience of Hitler's blitz diplomacy was already long and bitter, could hardly credit so astonishing and so seemingly cynical an end to the war of ideologies between Nazism and Communism. The German and Soviet peoples themselves, no less than their respective sympathizers abroad, were profoundly shaken in their faiths. Opinion in Britain and France was revolted at what was considered the duplicity of the Soviet Government in negotiating the pact in secret at the very moment that an Anglo-French mission was in Moscow. But there was no time now for regrets or recriminations. On August 25, as if to show that she was not to be intimidated by the new development, Britain confirmed her Polish guarantee in a formal Anglo-Polish Alliance. Appeals to Hitler from Roosevelt and Chamberlain, a papal broadcast for peace, offers of mediation from Queen Wilhelmina of the Netherlands and King Leopold of Belgium, an eleventh-hour proposal for a second Munich from Mussolini, all these made no impression on the frenzied, infatuated Führer.

On August 22, 1939, the day before the signing of the Moscow Pact and a week before the attack on Poland, Hitler was conferring with his high-ranking officers at Berchtesgaden. "Everything depends on me, on my existence" he said. . . . "No one will ever again have the confidence of the whole German people as I have. There will probably never again be a man in the future with more authority. My existence is, therefore, a factor of great value . . . For us it is easy to make decisions. We have nothing to lose. . . . Our enemies have men who are below average, no personalities, no masters, no men of action . . . All these fortunate circumstances will no longer prevail in two or three years. . . . Therefore conflict is better now. I am only afraid that at the last minute some *Schweinhund* will make a proposal for mediation. . . . I shall give a propagandist cause for starting the war, never mind whether it be plausible or not. The victor will not be asked, later on, whether we told the truth or not. In starting and making a war, it is not the Right that matters, but Victory." [14]

On August 29, Hitler demanded the dispatch to Berlin of a Polish emissary with full powers to negotiate the cession of Danzig and the Corridor to Germany. The demand was unmistakably redolent of the recent Schuschnigg, Tiso, and Hácha incidents, but this time no emissary was sent. Final German proposals for a Polish settlement were prepared and, at midnight on August 30, Ribbentrop received Sir Nevile Henderson, the British ambassador, and read the text to him in German, at high speed, but refused to hand him a copy. Nor did copies of the proposals ever reach — no doubt they were never intended to reach — either the Polish ambassador in Berlin or the Polish Government in Warsaw, and the Poles remained in ignorance of this last gracious and magnanimous offer of the Nazi Führer. Early in the morning of September 1, 1939, without declaration of war, German troops and planes crossed the Polish border. The Second World War had begun.

PART FOUR

THE SECOND WORLD WAR

40 THE OPENING CAMPAIGNS

THE CONQUEST AND PARTITION OF POLAND

The first waves of the German Luftwaffe crossed the Polish frontiers at dawn on September 1, 1939. The German invasion forces were disposed in two army groups, a northern group of two armies commanded by Bock, and a southern group of three armies commanded by Rundstedt. The subordinate army commanders were Kuechler, Kluge, Blaskowitz, Reichenau, and List, all to become well-known names in the next six years of war. The forces numbered in the aggregate 56 divisions and 9 armored divisions, with a first-line air strength of 1,500 planes — some 1,000,000 men in all. Brauchitsch was in supreme command of all operations of the German Army, with Halder as his Chief of Staff.

The Polish Army, numbering 2,000,000 men on paper, was paralyzed by the bombing of its roads and railroads and was never fully mobilized. It met the impact of the German invasion with 30 divisions, a single armored brigade — and, incredible to relate, 12 cavalry brigades, fully horsed, booted, and spurred. In numbers concentrated for action, in position, armament, and means of transport, the Polish Army was hopelessly outmatched. The campaign was virtually decided in a week; organized Polish resistance collapsed in three weeks; Warsaw surrendered on September 27; a few isolated Polish units held out heroically and uselessly till the beginning of October. A Power of 30,000,000 population had gone down to overwhelming defeat. President Moscicki, Marshal Smigly-Rydz, and Colonel Beck fled to Rumania.

On September 17, without warning but in accordance with the secret protocol of the recent Moscow Pact (see p. 642), Soviet troops crossed the eastern frontiers of Poland and, meeting no resistance, proceeded to occupy the eastern Polish provinces. Under a new Frontier and Friendship Agreement on September 28, the Soviet and German Governments revised the terms of their original pact so that the greater part of Lithuania fell within the Soviet sphere of influence and Polish territories west of the river Bug fell within the German sphere of influence. In effect, the Soviet Union and Germany partitioned the conquered country along a line roughly coincident with the once famous Curzon Line (see p. 175). Germany reannexed to herself the pre-Versailles German territories in Poland; she also annexed the area around Lódź. The remaining core of German-occupied Poland was then organized as a Government General with Cracow as its capital and Hans Frank as its Nazi administrator. The persecution of the Jews and of the Polish intelligentsia and the economic exploitation of the country were put in hand with all dispatch.

The German conquest of Poland had been a perfect, textbook demonstration of the new blitzkrieg tactics. The German Army attacked a selected and isolated enemy. The first phase of its assault was made by the Luftwaffe. The Polish air force of perhaps 400 first-line planes was destroyed in 48 hours by the concentrated bombing of its airfields. "Artillery preparation" was provided simultaneously by the dive bomber, or Stuka, designed to spread terror as much as to demolish field obstacles and rearward communications. The centers of population, Warsaw in particular, were raided without mercy or respite. The second phase of the assault was made by the armored divisions, consisting for the most part of tanks, with motorcycles, light armored cars, and some motorized infantry in conjunction. An efficient spy system, or "fifth column," deep in the Polish rear, aided and abetted the terror and disorganization.

In this new warfare the old conception of a "front" ceased to have any meaning. A battle consisted, not of two continuous opposing fronts, but of deep and sudden infiltrations. All the advantages went to the side that seized and held the initiative in attack. The tank was conceived of as an independent arm, not as in 1918 as a mere protective weapon for advancing infantry. Often enough armored units raced ahead of the main body of infantry, from which they might become separated by several days' marching distance. They pressed home their attacks at weak points and by-passed strong points. Their primary objectives were the enemy's nerve centers, his road and railroad junctions, bridges, airfields, telegraph stations, and headquarters. Infantry "mopped up" afterward with air and artillery support. Once a deep armored penetration had been effected and exploited to the full, the defense could only have been restored by an armored counterattack of equal strength, and this was exactly the type of counterattack that the enemies of Germany in the first two years of the war had not the material to deliver. The new warfare developed an extraordinary fluidity. Contact between armored units could be maintained by wireless, and the whole battlefield, from the defender's point of view, became a ubiquitous, amorphous permeation, "like a plague of vermin in a garden."

INACTION IN THE WEST

Despite his "Pact of Steel" with Germany and despite his own hankering after warlike glory, Mussolini had resolved for the time being on nonbelligerency. Hitler was pleased to inform him that he could most usefully confine himself to military demonstrations. Actually, Italian unpreparedness could have counseled no other course. On September 1, 1939 the Fascist Grand

Council "declared and announced to the people that Italy would take no initiative in military operations." Repeating his Munich tactics of twelve months before, Mussolini had put forward last-minute proposals for a conference of the Powers "to review those clauses in the Treaty of Versailles which still disturbed the peace of Europe." But the realities now were not in the conference chamber. On September 3, 1939, Britain and — after some further hesitations — France were at war with Germany.

Australia and New Zealand at once declared war on Germany. The Viceroy declared war on behalf of India. In South Africa, Hertzog resigned, and General Smuts formed a government which at once declared war. In Canada, the declaration of war was delayed till September 10. Eire remained neutral.

The British Expeditionary Force of 158,000 men was dispatched to France under Lord Gort. The French General Gamelin was appointed Commander in Chief of the Allied Armies in France. In the Near East an Anglo-French army of 250,000 was gradually massed. The Anzacs were once more in Egypt on the banks of the Suez Canal.[1] But all these preparations did not immediately result in action. For all that the German invasion of Poland had automatically invoked the British and French guarantees, it was realized by all parties that the original treaties could only have acted as deterrents to Germany (see p. 637). There was no question of sending direct military aid to Poland, and the rapid destruction of the Polish airfields eliminated even the possibility of two-way aerial operations against Germany. The French launched a local diversionary offensive in the Saar, and within a few days occupied some hundred square miles of German territory. But the collapse of Poland robbed the offensive of its usefulness, the Germans began to counterattack and, during October, the French forces voluntarily retired to their original positions.

Hitler celebrated the Nazi conquest of Poland in a speech to the Reichstag on October 6, and hinted somewhat deviously at peace with Britain and France. He made no claims upon France, he said and, except for colonies, none on Britain. "Why therefore should there be war in the West? For the restoration of Poland? The Poland of Versailles will never rise again . . . It would be senseless to destroy millions of human lives in order to recreate a system which only the Poles themselves did not regard as an abortion." But Hitler's protestations after every crisis had a familiar ring. "We have taken up arms against aggression," said Daladier some days later. "We shall not lay them down until we have certain guarantees of security, a security which will not be called into question every six months." "The truth is," said Chamberlain, "that after our past experience it is no longer possible to rely upon the unsupported word of the present German Government."

And so the war in the West went on. But for the next six months it was a war of strangely little fighting. The winter of 1939–40 was one of the worst in living memory, and its severities doubtless contributed to the general military inaction. The French were ensconced in their Maginot Line, and the Germans in their Siegfried Line, the so-called West Wall. Two huge defensive systems confronted one another, and it seemed as if scientific position warfare in 1939 had become even more stationary and sterile than it had been in 1914–18. The shattering experience in Poland, in the view of its observers in France, became more and more unreal as it receded in time.

Even the war in the air failed to materialize. Britons for whom, for months past, Air Raid Precautions (A.R.P.) had become the uppermost preoccupation, found to their surprise that the sky above was not instantly filled with myriads of bombers nor the earth beneath rent with myriads of explosive fires. The densely populated centers of Britain and France — and Germany — did not share the fate of Warsaw. London poetizers claimed that the long weird silences and the impenetrable blackout — and no doubt the taut alertness of their own senses — revealed a world of beauty to them wholly new and unsuspected. The rival air forces engaged in reconnaissance flights over the Maginot Line and the West Wall and made photographic surveys of one another's territories which were important when the bomber war began in earnest, and they doubtless gained considerable incidental flying experience. The British made some leaflet raids over Germany which mainly served to alarm the German authorities over the ineffectiveness of their defenses. The British also carried out raids on Kiel, Helgoland, and Sylt, and the Germans on Scapa Flow. But it was clear that responsibility for first opening the aerial havoc in the West would not be taken by Germany until she was ready and not by Britain and France except in retaliation for German initiative. In the six months of the "phony war," as American correspondents called it, neither side lost much more than a single week's plane production.

It was the war at sea which was of greater interest in these first months than the war in the air or the war on land. Both sides at once resorted to the blockade strategy of 1914 and set about the destruction of one another's seaway commerce. The Cunard liner *Athenia* was sunk by a German submarine on the first day of the war. She was hardly a test case either navally or diplomatically — doubtless British precautionary measures at sea had not yet been undertaken — and the incident was useful mainly to serve warning on the world at large that the pirates of the *Lusitania* were ranging the seas again. But the German submarine continued to be active thereafter, and its depredations were more serious than had been expected. The *Courageous,* an aircraft carrier, was sunk on September 17, 1939, and the *Royal Oak,* a battleship, was sunk by a most daring action in Scapa Flow on October 14. About 750,000 tons of Allied merchant shipping were lost at sea by the end of the year (see p. 677).

It was the German surface raider which the British Admiralty in 1939 considered the prior problem at sea. Memories of the *Emden* in 1914 died hard, and the new German pocket battleships were far more efficient weapons than the *Emden* had ever been. In December 1939 the *Admiral Graf Spee* was intercepted off the Uruguayan coast, skillfully outmaneuvered, and severely damaged by three British cruisers of shorter range and lighter gun caliber. She eventually found a temporary neutral haven in Montevideo, and there, rather than renew the action, she was scuttled on orders from Berlin. Her captain afterward committed suicide. The *Admiral Graf Spee's* attendant supply ship, the *Altmark,* escaped, made her way back across the Atlantic, and two months later was at last seized in Norwegian territorial waters by the British destroyer *Cossack*. Three hundred British seamen, crews of British ships sunk by the *Admiral Graf Spee*, were found imprisoned in the *Altmark's* hold and rescued.

For Britain and France, the "phony war" was an economic war, and the war at sea was an essential part of it. It seemed to be the near realization of that ideal war of sanctions, once so beloved of League enthusiasts, an immobile war, a war without bloodshed and almost without discomfort. The Allied blockade of 1914–18 was renewed with all the efficiency that past experience and recent invention could devise. Measures which had once taken years to develop — the definition of contraband, the rationing of neutrals, the diversion of neutral ships to control ports for purposes of search — were applied in full rigor from the start of hostilities. In December 1939 were introduced the first navicerts, certificates granted by British consuls at ports of loading, testifying to the innocent character of the ship's cargo. The navicert system had the effect of transferring the holding up of contraband from the high seas to the ports of loading and thus relieved the shippers of delay and the British Navy of time wasted in visit and search. By the end of 1940 nearly 80 per cent of the world's merchant shipping was sailing under navicerts. Further pressure was applied to recalcitrant shippers by refusing repair, victualing, and bunkering facilities at British ports.

Unfortunately the conditions which had made the Allied blockade decisive in 1914–18 were not now repeated. We recall the spate of books which issued from the press in 1939, proving with infallible statistics that Germany could not win the war. But, except for oil, the German arsenals were amply stocked, and the German war plan specifically allowed for the prodigal consumption of oil only over short and sharply limited periods. The capacity of Germany's heavy industry was second only to that of the United States. Göring's Four-Year Plan had accumulated for Germany reserves of essential raw materials, and her production of ersatz goods had become a major industry. She had assiduously cultivated trade and barter relations with states not liable to blockade, notably in the Balkans and the Scandinavian countries. She had entered into a commercial agreement with the Soviet Union under the terms of the Moscow Pact.

The resources of Britain and France were impressive enough. We also recall that other spate of books in 1939 which regaled its readers with pictures of their limitless mineral and industrial wealth. They had loyal empires and most of the neutral world to draw upon. Their naval supremacy, while not wholly denying their enemy, at least assured them of a steady flow of supplies. "Cash and carry" tapped the resources of the United States and, by an act of Congress in November 1939, it was extended to include arms and ammunition. The two Allies, as between themselves, entered at once into the closest economic co-operation, and again set up all the well-tried machinery of the Inter-Allied Councils of 1917–18 (see p. 97). In a series of agreements they pooled their raw materials, food, shipping, and foreign credits. They organized competitive buying against Germany, especially in the Balkans. In March 1940, at a conference in London, their economic co-operation was reinforced by a comprehensive political treaty, by which they agreed first, not to conclude a separate armistice or peace and second, to maintain their "community of action" for a sufficient period after the war to ensure the settlement and reconstruction of Europe.

On the home front, Britain and France reorganized and expanded their administrative machinery. In Britain, Parliament passed a series of emergency enactments in September 1939, and in France, the chambers passed similar legislation in November. Chamberlain, the British Prime Minister, created an inner War Cabinet consisting of himself and nine other ministers. Winston Churchill was First Lord of the Admiralty, the post he had held in 1914. In France, Daladier reconstituted his cabinet, relegating Bonnet, the old champion of appeasement, to the Ministry of Justice. His attempt to include Socialists was not successful. The French Communist party was proscribed, and its leaders, including most of its representatives in the Chamber, were put under arrest. Daladier's compulsory unification of the government and the chambers was a far cry from the perfervid spontaneity of the *Union Sacrée* of 1914 (see p. 36). On March 20, 1940, after a stormy secret debate in a Chamber which was already dissatisfied with the lethargic prosecution of the war, Daladier resigned, to be followed by Paul Reynaud, former Minister of Finance.

RUSSIA, THE BALTIC, AND FINLAND

Soviet foreign policy at this time was dominated by the Moscow Pact of 1939. Official Soviet pronouncements, the speeches of Molotov and articles in *Izvestia*, harped on Anglo-French efforts to embroil the Soviet Union in a mutually destructive war with Germany and interpreted the ideological crusade of the Western democracies against Nazism as the cynical propaganda of the capitalistic classes to strengthen their power in the world. British and French Communists, in evident liaison with Moscow, used what influence they had to obstruct the war effort of their respective countries.

But diplomatic loyalty did not prevent the Soviet Union from taking full advantage of Germany's preoccupation in the West to strengthen its own territorial and strategic position. The secret protocol of the Moscow Pact and the subsequent Frontier and Friendship Agreement had designated the Baltic States as a Soviet sphere of influence. In September and October 1939, Soviet treaties with Estonia, Latvia, and Lithuania entitled the Soviet Government to establish military, naval, and air bases in these territories, and the treaties, no one doubted, were only preliminary to outright political annexation. Lithuania, by way of compensation, received the long-desired district and city of Vilna. Finally, under a further Soviet-German agreement, Germans resident in the area, the old German landowning "Baltic Barons," were evacuated to Germany. Evidently the Soviet Union had no relish for a "Sudeten" problem in the Baltic. Anti-Communist elements were deported.

It has been claimed that the peasants of the Baltic States were already ripe for Communism and were benefited by the removal of their reactionary German squires, and that Soviet expropriation of this area therefore had some justification. But the acute situation which now arose in the Soviet's relations with Finland was not so conveniently explainable. Late in October 1939, the Soviet Government formally demanded of Finland territorial concessions on the Karelian Isthmus and in the Petsamo area and a naval base at Hangö. It offered substantial territorial compensation elsewhere. But the concessions in the Karelian Isthmus would have deprived the Finns of the Mannerheim Line, so called after their Commander in Chief, Field Marshal von Mannerheim, a belt of fortifications which they had constructed there at a great expense. Certainly it was not likely that the Soviet Union would always tolerate the existence of such formidable military installations almost within artillery range of Leningrad. As one commentator remarked, one might as well have asked New York to rest contentedly beneath the fortifications of a foreign power on Staten Island. Negotiations between the Soviet and Finnish Governments continued through November 1939 and seemed at one time to be nearing a successful conclusion. But on November 28 the Soviet Union denounced its nonaggression pact with Finland, and two days later sent forward its troops to attack.

Finland appealed to the League of Nations and, on December 14, 1939, that body, with exceptional dispatch, declared the Soviet Union the aggressor Power and expelled it from League membership — the only state, we may remark in passing, ever to have been so expelled. The Soviet invasion of Finland roused world-wide indignation. The Finns had a long history of Russian oppression behind them, they had always been hostile to the Communist experiment in Russia, and the new Soviet-Finnish War seemed like the resumption of an age-old struggle. They defended themselves with the greatest tenacity, and proved themselves to be master tacticians in that type of winter warfare which now developed on their borders.

The Allies, Britain and France, seemed at this time to be making up for their inactivity in the West by planning campaigns elsewhere. It is believed, for example, that their commands in the Near East were contemplating diversions in the Balkans or the Caucasus as yet not very clearly defined, and Finland came to them at this juncture as a heaven-sent opportunity. They shipped an impressive list of supplies to the courageous little country. Even Italy sent planes, but these were held up in transit through Germany, and later she sent some technical personnel. Swedish volunteers came forward in considerable strength. Early in February 1940, Britain and France resolved to send an expeditionary force of 100,000 men to Finland and approached the Norwegian and Swedish Governments on the question of its passage. But the Norwegian and Swedish Governments refused their assent. Britain and France, it is interesting to remember, were within an ace of war with the Soviet Union in 1940.

But, in that February, the Soviet Government had reorganized its command on the Finnish front, had brought up considerable reinforcements especially of heavy artillery, and had launched a major offensive against the Mannerheim Line. A fortnight's bombardment and piecemeal advances — tactics reminiscent of Verdun in 1916 — gradually wore away the Finnish positions. By March 1, 1940, the Soviet forces were investing the port of Viipuri. The Finnish capital, Helsinki, and Hangö were bombed constantly. On March 12, in the midst of renewed Allied negotiations with Sweden for the passage of an expeditionary force, news arrived that Finnish representatives in Moscow had agreed to peace.

The Soviet-Finnish Treaty of Moscow was severer than the original Soviet demands of October 1939, but not so severe as might have been expected. Finland ceded the Karelian Isthmus, the port of Viipuri, several islands in the Gulf of Finland, some territory north and west of Lake Ladoga, a tract of land near Salla, a tract of land near Petsamo, and granted the Soviet Government a thirty-year lease on the port of Hangö. The Soviet Government reorganized its Karelian acquisition as a new Soviet republic.

THE GERMAN BLITZKRIEG IN THE WEST AND THE BATTLE OF FRANCE

Italy, technically a German ally, was preserving a correct and chill neutrality, reminiscent of her attitude in 1914. The Vatican, the King of Italy, several prominent Fascists such as Ciano, and the more responsible army and navy commanders were all opposed to intervention, and so also, so far as could be judged, was the great majority of the Italian people. Mussolini vacillated from day to day between moods of raging bellicosity and a sullen if grateful acceptance of the prosaic blessings of peace. Yet he was disturbed by Germany's recent pro-Soviet policy and by Germany's penetration of the Balkans, and he had permitted Italian aid to be sent to Finland. Early in 1940, Italy entered into a trade agreement with France for the delivery of Italian war material. Italy subsequently entered into a similar agreement with Britain, even though the British blockade had recently interfered with indispensable shipments to herself of German coal. On March 10, 1940, Ribbentrop visited Rome bearing a personal letter from Hitler to Mussolini on the general theme that "the destinies of our two states, of our two peoples, of our two revolutions, and of our two regimes are indissolubly linked." But, except from Mussolini himself, Ribbentrop met with a very indifferent reception. The Vatican, at the moment, was burning with indignation over Germany's treatment of Poland, and it is believed that, during his audience with the Pope, the German visitor was made to listen to some very plain speaking.

On March 18, Mussolini and Hitler met "in cordial colloquy" at the Brenner Pass, but the conference seems not to have altered substantially Italy's position. Mussolini was dazzled by Hitler's triumphs and convinced that sooner or later he must take his part in them, like a good ally, or sink forever into inglorious, irrevocable isolation. "It is humiliating to remain with our hands folded," he said later, "while others write history." At the same time he had no wish to have taken from him the freedom to make his great decision at the moment that suited him best.

The Nazi plans for the invasion of Denmark and Norway were drawn up in the winter of 1939 by Rosenberg and Admiral Raeder. Secret contacts were made with Major Quisling, leader of the Norwegian Nazi party, who, on one occasion in December 1939, came to Berlin to confer with Hitler in person. Admiral Doenitz, in command of the U-boat fleet, pressed for the use of a Norwegian port, preferably Narvik. German naval strategy was clearly aiming at an extension of "geographical range" and seeking to compensate for inferior strength vis-à-vis Britain by throwing out new operational bases. The invasion of Denmark and Norway, of course, would violate Nazi assurances, often from the mouth of Hitler himself, to respect the neutrality of the Scandinavian countries, and it would violate in particular the German-Danish nonaggression pact of May 1939. It was finally launched on April 9, 1940, and was indeed the first of the lightning Nazi thrusts which were now to embroil the Western world in open war. On that day, in the words of the German communiqué, "German armed forces assumed the protection of Denmark and Norway." The whole of Denmark was in effective occupation in less than twenty-four hours. King Christian issued a proclamation bidding the Danish people to accept the accomplished fact and maintain "a correct attitude."

The German invasion of Norway called for a more considerable campaign. It was perfectly prepared and timed. British naval units were already laying mines in Norwegian territorial waters, partly to force the German ore ships from Narvik into the open sea, where they might be intercepted, and partly in answer to reports of suspicious German naval activity; but the British Government and its Intelligence had certainly not calculated on an operation of the suddenness and magnitude that actually developed. By early morning of April 9, 1940, German warships were in action from Narvik to Oslo, and German transports were discharging their cargoes of men and machines. It is possible that some 100,000 Norwegian troops were in the field. The fighting was resolute, if confused, but all the main objectives appeared to have been taken by the enemy, as if by schedule, in the first days of the campaign. British and Norwegian destroyers and submarines struck at the German forces in the Skagerrak and wrought very heavy damage. But the main German communications were not sufficiently interrupted, and the German invaders were found to be willing to pay a calculated price for their success. The invasion was a first and convincing demonstration of the effectiveness of air power in amphibious operations. German fighter planes, from bases in Denmark, gained an immediate mastery over the narrow seas between Germany and Norway. The area was beyond British fighter range; British bombers had to fly a full 500 miles from bases in Scotland. The British Home Fleet could not be risked in action against such odds.

British advance detachments were landed on the coast of Norway at Namsos and Andalsnes as early as April 14, and were shortly followed by a sizable expeditionary force. Troops and supplies once designated for Finland were used in Norway. But again the course of the fighting was decided neither on land nor on the sea, but in the air. All the advantages went to the side with the nearest fighter bases. The British landing points in Norway and the seaward approaches thereto were mercilessly bombed. On May 1–2, the British expeditionary force was withdrawn. A British force afterward took, and for some weeks occupied, Narvik in the far north, and interrupted the shipment of Swedish iron ore to Germany which normally went through that port but, on June 8, in view of developments in France, this force too had to be withdrawn. Heavy German naval units attacked the British ships sent to cover the final evacuation and, in the confused action that followed, the British carrier *Glorious*, two cruisers, and nine destroyers were sunk and several other ships damaged. It was a serious British naval defeat, but the Germans themselves sustained such losses that, as Churchill writes, "at the end of June 1940, a momentous date, the effective German Fleet consisted of no more than one eight-inch cruiser, two light cruisers, and four destroyers."[2]

Meanwhile King Haakon and the Norwegian Government had escaped to London. The Germans set up their own administration in Norway under their collaborator, Major Quisling.

The Norwegian campaign had galvanized the British people and government. Complacence, like appeasement, had had its day, and Britain wanted — and needed — a more realistic and pugnacious leadership. Chamberlain resigned, and on May 10, 1940, Churchill became Prime Minister. Churchill's inner War Cabinet consisted of himself, Halifax, Chamberlain, and two Labor men, Attlee and Greenwood. Lord Beaverbrook, the newspaper baron, became Minister of Aircraft Production. Churchill's statement of policy in the House of Commons had little of the usual Chamberlainian tone of aggrievement and self-righteousness. "I have nothing to offer but blood, toil, tears, and sweat. We have before us an ordeal of the most grievous kind. We have before us many, many long months of struggle and of suffering. You ask, what is our policy? I will say: it is to wage war, by sea, by land, and air, with all our might and with all the strength that God can give us: to wage war against a monstrous tyranny, never surpassed in the dark, lamentable catalogue of human crime."

Germany's invasion of Holland and Belgium, prepared under the code name "Case Yellow" as early as October 1939, and originally intended for execution that November, was postponed until the spring probably in deference to strong opposition from more cautious elements in the German High Command. As it finally developed, the invasion was in essence a resuscitation of the Schlieffen Plan of 1914, a plan to turn the French flank across the more open and maneuverable territory to the northwest (see pp. 17–18); but this time it would involve three neutrals, Holland as well as Belgium and Luxembourg. It was prefaced with the usual diplomatic protestations on the part of Germany, that she was anticipating an insidious Allied attack, and that her only object was to extend the benefits of her protection to innocent peoples malignly threatened. The invasion was launched at last on May 10, 1940.

The German battle order consisted of three army groups under Bock, Rundstedt, and Leeb. The main concentration was in the center under Rundstedt between Aachen and the Moselle and consisted of four armies, of which one was the all-important armored corps under Kleist. Brauchitsch was in supreme command and Halder was his Chief of Staff. The Dutch and Belgian armies between them mustered 1,000,000 men. Parts of the complicated low-lying Dutch terrain had been flooded, and the Belgians were entrenched in modern fortifications along the Albert Canal and in the great strongholds at Eben Emael and Liége. But considerations of neutrality hitherto had always prevented joint defense talks between Dutch and

Belgian staffs. Since the inauguration of its "Belgian policy" in 1936 (see p. 497), the Belgian Government had also been meticulous in avoiding the least suspicion of a military understanding with France. But, during the winter of 1939–40, Gamelin had made secret contacts with his Belgian opposites and had agreed that, at the signal, four French armies would advance into Belgium and take up a line roughly between Antwerp and Namur.

Military critics have argued that the French High Command committed a grave blunder in thus belatedly preparing support for Belgium and have pointed to other famous battles in history where an army was enticed out of a favorable defensive position to meet with defeat in the open field. The fact is that the French plan of defense, ever since 1927 when Pétain had been French Commander in Chief, had always calculated on a mobile campaign in Belgium and, in accordance with the plan, the Maginot Line as it approached the Ardennes dwindled into a series of isolated strong points (pp. 322–23). The Ardennes itself, hilly and forested, and protected by the natural "tank ditch" of the river Meuse, was regarded as a sufficient obstacle to a mechanized force debouching from the East, and General Corap's Ninth Army in that sector was not only the weakest of the four French armies which Gamelin had now drawn up along the Belgian front, but also stood exactly opposite Kleist's armored corps. The dispositions of the French High Command, from the German point of view, could hardly have been better.

The Dutch defense collapsed in five days. German parachute troops seized the Dutch airfields. Strategic bridges fell intact to troops who wore false uniforms and had evidently been trained in detail for their tasks. The central area of the city of Rotterdam, after concentrated air attack, was left in flames. The Dutch army in the field suffered 100,000 casualties, a quarter of its strength. On May 14, 1940, the Dutch Commander in Chief capitulated. Queen Wilhelmina, the Dutch Government, and the greater part of the Dutch Navy escaped to England.

On May 11 the Belgians, under German onslaught, were already evacuating their positions along the Albert Canal. Eben Emael and Liége were taken in twenty-four hours. The Belgian Army retired to the Antwerp-Namur line, where it was met by Gamelin's armies coming up from France. But Kleist's armored corps dislocated the entire French plan by crashing through the allegedly impassable Ardennes, and then, on May 13, by crossing the Meuse. A fifty-mile breach was driven into the French lines between Sedan and Namur. Thereafter the invasion followed the pattern of the Nazi blitzkrieg. In a single, cataclysmic week, Arras, Amiens, Abbeville, and Boulogne fell to the invader. The greater part of three French armies and the ten divisions of the British Expeditionary Force were cut off from the rest of France. On May 28, 1940, King Leopold of the Belgians surrendered himself to the enemy and capitulated.

Reynaud, the French Premier, might well castigate the "incredible mistakes" of the French defense and promise condign punishment, but it is more than likely that the "hitherto unknown formula" of the German blitzkrieg would have overcome whatever dispositions the French High Command could then have made. The combination of dive bomber, tank, parachutist, and fifth column, the total disregard of risks and casualties by the attacking force, the terror bombing of towns, the deliberately induced exodus of the civil population, the chaos of the roads and rearward services, all this was beyond the conception of warfare obtaining in France. On May 18, Reynaud reconstituted his cabinet. He took the Ministry of Defense himself and appointed Marshal Pétain Vice-Premier. The next day he removed Gamelin from the supreme command and appointed General Weygand, former Chief of Staff to Marshal Foch. The resurrection of two heroes of the First World War, Pétain and Weygand, one now aged eighty-five and the other seventy-two, was a measure of the crisis, but public opinion in France was momentarily heartened.

Weygand's obvious plan on paper was to cut the ribbonlike salient which the German tank divisions were rolling out across the north of France. For some days the newspapers carried headlines on the "Battle of the Bulge," and indeed the salient at one point was driven into a waist some twelve miles wide. But, in the chaos that prevailed on both sides of the salient, co-ordination of operations was out of the question. The Germans were already fanning out along the Channel coast. Weygand himself had no longer any confidence that he could materially restore the situation. One French corps made a stand round Lille; a British brigade held out at Calais for three days; and behind this screen the British Expeditionary Force and the remnants of the French First Army retired on Dunkirk, the only port still free of the enemy.

The Germans conspicuously failed to press home their overwhelming advantage at Dunkirk. The probabilities are that Rundstedt considered the British were already broken and defeated, and preferred to conserve armor for the further operations against France. The Narvik involvement at this moment sufficiently accounts for the absence of an attempted interference on the part of German naval forces. Meanwhile, from every port and pier in the southeast coast of England, the British Admiralty was assembling a motley, impromptu fleet of over 850 vessels for the evacuation of the stranded Allied forces. Destroyers backed into the Dunkirk beaches and packed their decks with hundreds of men a trip. Seaside paddle steamers, river tugs, lifeboats, motor launches, fishing craft shuttled back and forth across the Channel. The R.A.F., the Royal Air Force, covering the evacuation, won its first victory over the Luftwaffe. Some 338,000 British, French, and Belgians were brought off to safety—but with the total loss of their equipment.

Weygand hurriedly organized new defenses along the southern banks of the Somme and Aisne. On June 5, 1940, the Germans resumed their attack. In two days' fighting the "Weygand Line" was pierced at either extremity, above Beauvais and above Reims. In an order of the day Weygand announced that the "Battle of France" had begun. The French Government retired to Tours and then to Bordeaux. Paris was declared an "open city" and on June 14 was surrendered without resistance. On June 15 the Germans entered Verdun, thus outflanking the main mass of the Maginot Line. Reynaud sent his final appeal to President Roosevelt: "The only chance of saving the French nation . . . is to throw into the balance, this very day, the weight of American power." But the President could commit himself to nothing beyond an increase of those supplies which the United States was already providing.

The Fall of France will test the breadth and impartiality of writers for years to come. "The greatest mistake a historian could make," writes Langer of this time, "would be to try to construct a neat, logical pattern when in actual fact everything was confusion and contradiction." [3] Even Reynaud's part is difficult to assess. The usual version represents him as the champion of a fight to the finish, if need be in a redoubt in Brittany or from the French colonies in North Africa. He pleaded for France to remain faithful to her treaty of March 1940 with Britain. On June 6, as an indication of his spirit, he had taken into his cabinet, as Under-Secretary for Defense, General de Gaulle, the soldier and military critic who had long since vainly advocated the proper mechanization of the French Army (pp. 322–23). But Reynaud, from the moment of his arrival at Bordeaux, was being dunned by the defeatists of his immediate circle. Mme de Portes, his mistress, besought him to surrender. Pétain and Weygand both regarded the situation as beyond hope. The city of Bordeaux, panic-stricken and overcrowded, was being intermittently bombed by German aircraft. On June 16, his nerve broken, Reynaud resigned. Pétain formed a new government with Chautemps as Vice-Premier, Weygand as Minister of Defense, and Admiral Darlan as Minister of Marine. Laval, though not a member of this ministry, had been active in its formation and had already made himself the center of a group of politicians at Bordeaux anxious for understanding and collaboration with Germany.

Pétain at once sued the enemy for an armistice and "a soldier's peace." On June 22, 1940, at Compiègne, in the same railroad coach in which in 1918 Foch had received the German Armistice Commission, the French delegates accepted Nazi Germany's terms.

Since the conference at the Brenner Pass on March 18, Italy's official anti-Allied attitude had become more and more pronounced, and an intensive press and radio campaign gradually prepared the Italian people for the inevitability of war. Mussolini rejected Reynaud's last-minute offer of concessions in respect of Italian claims in Tunis, Jibuti, and the Suez Canal. In a personal letter to Churchill he intimated his firm loyalty to his Pact of Steel with Germany. On May 29, 1940, he imparted to his military chiefs his decision to go to war but he did not make an open declaration till June 10, the day the Germans crossed the Seine. Even then the Italian Army delayed its offensive against French positions along the Alpine frontier till June 21, when the French delegates were already on their way to Compiègne.

Mussolini's action was as derisory as any in his career, but it roused the neutral world to a fine contempt and indignation and to a new awareness of the gravity of the war. "On this tenth day of June 1940," said President Roosevelt in his address to the University of Virginia at Charlottesville, "the hand that held the dagger has struck it into the back of its neighbor. On this tenth day of June 1940, from this university, founded by the great American teacher of democracy, we send forward our prayers and our hopes to those beyond the seas who are maintaining with magnificent valor their battle for freedom."

The Franco-German armistice confirmed Germany in the occupation of two-thirds of France, including the chief industrial areas — except Lyon — and the whole of the Channel and French Atlantic coast. The French armed forces were to be demobilized; all fortifications and military stores were to be surrendered; French merchant shipping was to be called home; French prisoners of war were to remain in German hands until the conclusion of peace. The French Government was to surrender on demand — presumably to the Gestapo — German political refugees in France. The French Navy was to be collected, demobilized, and laid up in ports, afterward to be designated, under German and Italian control. The German Government "solemnly declared that it does not intend to use the French Fleet for its purpose in war."

The Franco-Italian armistice was modeled on the German. But beyond the demilitarization of certain ports, the demilitarization of certain zones in Savoy, Tunis, and French Somaliland, and the surrender of military stores, the Italians gained only the strip of frontier territory they had taken in their belated Alpine offensive and the Red Sea port of Jibuti. Nice, Savoy, Corsica, and Tunis, for which they had so often clamored, remained in French possession. It almost seemed as if Hitler was inflicting on his ally the humiliation of denying him the benefit of the German victory.

The shock — and relief — of Dunkirk had prepared the British people mentally for the collapse of France, and the final armistice was only the least terrible of the succession of terrors which the Nazi blitzkrieg had brought in its train. Up to six days of the armistice, Churchill had still refused to release the French Government from its obligations, especially in respect of the treaty signed all too recently in the previous March. He made France an offer of complete union with Britain — a common citizenship, administration, possessions, and resources. It was a fine, if despairing gesture; but he was compelled by events to acquiesce at last in a separate French capitulation. He insisted, however, and he received assurances in return, that the French Navy would be handed over to Britain, or at least interned in ports where it would be useless to the enemy. His insistence was independently supported by the American ambassador in France, whose government was also profoundly disturbed at the prospect of the entire subversion of the hitherto existing relative naval strengths of the Atlantic Powers. "It was therefore with grief and amazement," said Churchill in the Commons afterward, "that I read the armistice terms . . . From this text it was clear that the French war vessels would pass into German and Italian control while fully armed."

Units of the French Navy which then happened to be in British ports — for instance in Portsmouth or Alexandria — could be, and were, forcibly interned. But powerful units also lay in French ports, especially at Oran in Algeria and at Dakar on the West African coast. Early on the morning of July 3, a British squadron stood off Oran, and the French commander, by ultimatum, was invited either to continue the fight against Germany and Italy, to permit internment at a British port, to permit internment at a neutral port, to scuttle his ships, or to face destruction at the hands of his own ally. He was offered indeed every possible choice consistent with military honor and with the ultimate interest of the Allied cause. But every choice he rejected. In the action that followed the British squadron sank the battleship *Brétagne* and set the battleship *Provence* on fire, the battleship *Dunkerque* was beached, and only the battleship *Strasbourg*, in a damaged condition, together with some smaller ships, escaped. On July 8, the battleship *Richelieu* was attacked and seriously damaged at Dakar.

It was a hard and sad necessity that turned one ally against another. But the British Government could not risk leaving the disposal of so formidable a weapon as the French Navy to the caprice of a group of defeated and potentially hostile men. The Pétain government afterward broke off relations with Britain. The British blockade was applied to the whole of France; the Royal Air Force bombed French ports and bases in German occupation. From a comradeship of arms Britain and France seemed to be drifting inexorably toward antagonism and open war.

Germany's acquisitions in the seventy days of her blitzkrieg in the West were impressive indeed. The coasts of Europe from the Arctic to the Bay of Biscay were in her hands. From a chain of bases she closely invested the seas surrounding the British Isles. She possessed the farms and pastures of Denmark and Holland, the fisheries and forests of Norway, the mines and industries of Belgium, and at least three-fourths of the wealth of France. She controlled the iron of Sweden. A "slave population" of 2,000,000 prisoners of war was at her absolute disposal. The leak in the Maginot Line indeed had loosed a flood which had engulfed 500,000 square miles and 150,000,000 human beings, and the flood was still in spate.

The French Government of Marshal Pétain established itself at Vichy in unoccupied territory, a virtual client of Hitler's expanding empire. The Fall of France and the intervention of Italy had upset the entire balance of forces in North Africa, the Balkans, and the Near East. The whole of British naval strategy in the Mediterranean had been based on the use of the French ports. Up to March 1940, the Anglo-French combination had dominated the scene; from July 1940, Britain was everywhere left suspended in dangerous isolation. The French commanders in Dakar, Madagascar, and Syria threw in their lot with Pétain. Greece and Turkey, once favored and eager partners in Allied alliances and guarantees, looked as if they would be lamely abandoned to their own devices. Hungary, Rumania, Yugoslavia, and Bulgaria were once more firmly knit to the Nazi system.

For a moment it seemed that Spain would enter the conflict, that Gibraltar would be besieged, and that the German occupation would be extended even to the Canary Islands and the Azores. On June 12, 1940, two days after Mussolini's intervention, the Spanish dictator, Franco, suddenly renounced his former declared neutrality for the equivocal and ominous status of non-belligerency. Spanish forces occupied the international territory of Tangier. In October, Serrano Suñer, the Spanish Foreign Minister, Franco's brother-in-law, a leader in the Falange, and advocate of Spain's immediate intervention in the war, visited Rome and Berlin. He made an appropriate opposite to Ribbentrop. One result of his mission was the meeting of Hitler and

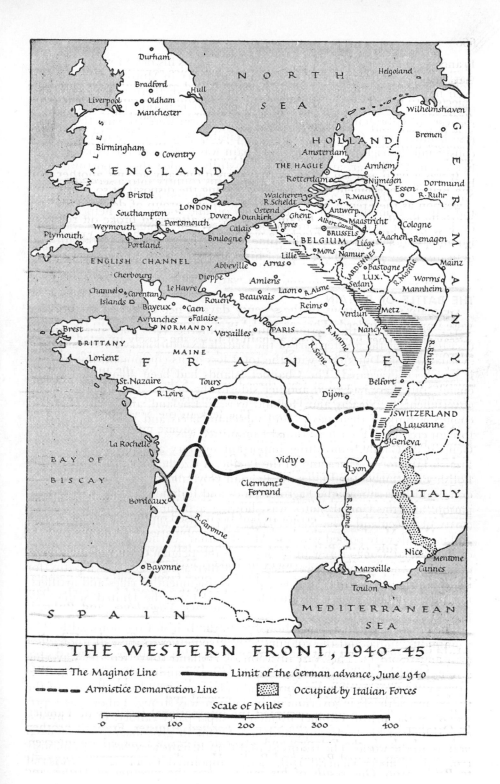

THE WESTERN FRONT, 1940–45

≡≡≡ The Maginot Line	▬▬▬ Limit of the German advance, June 1940
▬ ▬ ▬ Armistice Demarcation Line	░░░ Occupied by Italian Forces

Scale of Miles

0   100   200   300   400

Franco at Hendaye on October 23, when Franco, as his price for entering the war, made exorbitant demands for French territory in Morocco, Algeria, and even north of the Pyrenees. As was to be expected, there was a sharp and officially encouraged revival of the old popular agitation in Spain for the recovery of Gibraltar. German soldiers in uniform were crossing the Navarrese frontier from Occupied France, ostensibly "on leave," and receiving a conspicuously friendly welcome. But Spain was feeling all the exhaustion of her recent Civil War, and Franco successfully evaded the importunities of his brother dictator in Germany to plunge his country into a second ordeal. No doubt the threat of a British naval blockade and of a stoppage of essential imports from the Americas, especially oil and cotton, also helped him to decide against "a change in his foreign policy." Sir Samuel Hoare was British ambassador in Madrid at this time, conducting a mission as difficult and delicate as any in the whole field of his country's harassed diplomacy.

THE BATTLE OF BRITAIN

Yet, for Britain, the German blitzkrieg in the West had not been all disaster. By far the greater part of the British Expeditionary Force had been evacuated from Dunkirk — with the total loss of its equipment, but at least it had been evacuated. The Channel Islands had been abandoned to the enemy. But there had been another side to the defeat. The sovereigns and governments of Norway and Holland were in England, and with them had come the bulk of their navies and merchant fleets and their command of foreign credits. A French National Committee was set up in London under General de Gaulle, controlling important military and naval resources in French Equatorial Africa and in the Pacific. A Czechoslovak Committee, the Polish Government, and later the Belgian Government were set up in London. Danish territories, the Faeroe Islands and Iceland, were in British occupation, and the United States was showing a pointed concern for the security of Greenland. The Netherlands East Indies with their wealth in oil and minerals were pooled with the Allied military exchequer. The Governor of the Belgian Congo threw in his lot with the Belgian Government in London. The Americas were awakened to an increasingly active sympathy for the cause against Nazism. During July, a consignment of rifles and artillery, not new but nevertheless invaluable, arrived from the United States (see p. 698).

The defeat wrought a new fellowship in the British Commonwealth. The Dominions, India, and the colonies were responding to the call upon their men and resources. The Nazi invasion of Holland converted the wavering sympathies of Boer South Africa. An Air-Force training scheme was getting under way in Canada for Air-Force and radar personnel from all parts of the Commonwealth. The government in Britain was strong. Labor was represented in the British Cabinet by men of super-party caliber. Churchill was established in his leadership, and had begun to give magnificent martial oratory to the world. The troops available in Britain were being strenuously reorganized under General Dill, newly appointed Chief of the Imperial

General Staff (see Glossary), and General Brooke, newly appointed Commander in Chief Home Forces. Concrete strong points and earthworks were hurriedly constructed in the southeastern coastal areas. The Local Defense Volunteers — later renamed the Home Guard — absorbed a good deal of the nation's otherwise undirected man power and fighting spirit — but its units at this time often had to arm themselves with old rifles, shotguns, and even pikes. Yet the British people everywhere felt almost an exhilaration in knowing the worst, and knowing also that the worst was not without its compensations. There might be blood, toil, tears, and sweat, but there were also in Britain, in her Empire, and in her Allies reserves of men, material, and morale which might yet redress the German triumph over Europe.

Hitler issued his operational directive, "Sea Lion," for the invasion of Britain on July 16, 1940; the invasion date was originally fixed for August 15. The last British ship left the Dunkirk beaches on June 4, and the French armistice was signed on June 22. In view of Hitler's usual anticipation of his moves, the delay in the issue of "Sea Lion" is not easily explained. It is suggested that the Battle of France had surpassed the calculations of friend and foe alike and that Hitler was far from prepared for so sudden a switch of interest from France to Britain. Or it is suggested that Hitler expected a British capitulation without his having to exert further military pressure. The surprising mildness of several articles of the French armistice might have been designed to encourage that capitulation. Finally, in his curious tenderness for things British, Hitler might have hoped for a deal with Britain and with the British Commonwealth such as would have "guaranteed" their continued existence as organized political entities while assuring him of his own actual military supremacy. But the delay was invaluable to Britain. By a heroic industrial and organizational effort the Dunkirk army was entirely refitted. Hitler eventually postponed his invasion date to September 15, by which time there were sixteen British divisions of high quality available for action on the south coast of England, and of these three were armored. Also in that September, the United States handed over to Britain fifty destroyers in exchange for the lease of naval bases in Newfoundland, Bermuda, and the British West Indies (see p. 698). The destroyers were "over age," but they were adequate for reinforcing the British Navy's antisubmarine effectives in the Atlantic Ocean.

The German invasion of England was to have been carried out by two army groups, under the supreme command of Rundstedt. The first, consisting of two armies, was to land between Dover and Portsmouth; the second, consisting of one army, was to land, possibly some days later, in the Portland-Weymouth area. Barges for thirteen assault divisions, and for an equal number in reserve, were assembled in the harbors, estuaries, and canals in the Low Countries and northern France and were slowly moved into the sally points. Landing exercises were practiced on the Flemish and French beaches.

On the German side, behind the scenes, the precious weeks were being spent in acrimonious discussions between the German service chiefs over the tactical problems of the Channel crossing. Landing craft, such as the Anglo-American forces afterward possessed, were entirely lacking, and the mass of towed barges which it was proposed to use would run extraordinary risks in a late September in a stretch of water notoriously stormy. All records show that Admiral Raeder would give no guarantees in this respect. Recent German naval damage off Narvik had materially reduced the escort fleet available. But all were unanimous on one fundamental point. "Operation Sea Lion" would be an imaginary dream without air mastery sufficient to neutralize the British aerial and naval defense. An essential preliminary would therefore be an assault by Göring's Luftwaffe, the assault which indeed developed into what we now know as the Battle of Britain.

In August 1940, the Luftwaffe's strength is believed to have been about 3,600 first-line planes, of which 2,670 were assigned to the coming operation. The R.A.F. had some 1,475 first-line planes at home and some 500 overseas. But the British had the use of radar to compensate for the disparity of numbers, a new invention almost exclusively developed by British physicists and engineers, which enabled enemy aircraft to be "sighted" fifty, and often a hundred, miles before they approached their targets. German enticement and reconnaissance sorties were being intensified during the latter part of July. The main attack was ordered by Göring at a briefing conference of his Luftwaffe chiefs at his country house, Karin Hall, on August 6, and was launched two days later.

The battle allowed the British the all-out employment of R.A.F. Fighter Command, the one arm in which they enjoyed a high technical superiority and which — wisely, as it now appeared — they had declined to squander in the Battle of France. It was fought, in the words of the Air Ministry's account, "three, four, five and sometimes more than six miles above the surface of the earth by some hundreds of aircraft flying at speeds often in excess of three hundred miles an hour . . . [It] was not shrouded in the majestic and terrible smoke of a land bombardment with its roar of guns, its flash of shells, its fountains of erupting earth. There was no sound of fury — only a pattern of white vapour trails, leisurely changing form and shape, traced by a number of tiny specks, scintillating like diamonds in the splendid sunlight." The Fates in these months of 1940 were stern and terrible, but they were at least merciful in that, at this desperate moment, they gave the British the chance to fight a battle supremely suited to their national character, a battle of individual self-reliance and courage on the part of the fighting man and of stubbornness and comradeship on the part of every man, woman, and child in the island.

Göring's first targets were the south-coast harbors and Channel convoys. On August 12, he turned to the R.A.F. fighter airfields and fighter factories. He ordered a supreme effort to be made on "Eagle Day," August 13, but the heaviest action — and the heaviest German casualties of the entire battle — occurred on August 15, when the Germans lost 76 aircraft to the British 34. Radar, with miraculous precision, enabled R.A.F. fighter interception to concentrate at points often far out over the Channel and to scatter the German bomber formations before they came within striking distance of the coast. German directional radio beams were deflected or jammed by various counterdevices. Between August 19 and 23, aerial activity was somewhat reduced by bad weather. On August 24, fighting was resumed with German attacks mainly on the inner airfields and on R.A.F. Fighter Sector Stations around London. This was the crucial period of the entire battle. But, on September 7, Göring turned on London. The change of target was decisive. It was uncomfortable for London, but it was also Göring's admission that he had failed to destroy the R.A.F. fighter strength. Today we know that the Battle of Britain was then as good as won. London was bombed daily for a month — from September 7 to October 5. Heavy German losses continued, despite increased fighter protection. Sometimes German bombers were accompanied by as many as five fighters apiece. On September 15, the culminating date of this phase of the battle, the Germans lost 56 planes.

The Battle of Britain was a truly Elizabethan victory. A few hundred young British and Dominion fighter pilots, many of them not yet twenty years of age — and a few score Poles, Czechs, French, and Belgians — engaged and repulsed Germany's armada of bombers. "Never in the field of human conflict," said Churchill at the height of battle, "was so much owed by so many to so few." On September 17, Hitler gave orders that "Operation Sea Lion" should be postponed indefinitely. German aerial attacks after October 5 were made mainly at night. By the end of October, the battle was dying away. German interest had then switched to Midland arms towns, such as Coventry, which was "terror-raided" on the night of November 14 by 500 German bombers.

While R.A.F. Fighter Command had thus been defending Britain, R.A.F. Bomber Command had opened its counterattack on the invasion bases and on Germany herself, though its effort was slight enough by later standards. It had raided the concentrations of the German invasion barges, railroads and canals, oil refineries and synthetic-oil plants, and German war factories of all kinds. It had raided the Ruhr and Rhineland, it had raided as far as the Skoda works at Pilsen and the "industrial triangle" in northern Italy. On August 25, 1940, for the first time, it had raided Berlin.

One of the grateful surprises of the Battle of Britain was the small civilian loss of life. Industrial production, mainly concentrated in the Midlands and North, was not too seriously affected, and the flow of overseas shipping, though temporarily diverted from London and the Channel, was maintained. The material damage to buildings in the bombed areas was enormous, especially in the East End boroughs and docks of London. It was difficult to believe, in the nightly furnace, that the number of casualties was not greater. But Air Raid Precautions (A.R.P.), reorganized as the Civil Defense Service, had withstood the test of experience; "fire watching" for incendiary bombs was now a compulsory routine imposed on all civilians; repair and demolition squads went about their work with the greatest efficiency; the mass hospitalization which had been so carefully prepared was found to be much in excess of need; the medical authorities afterward reported highly on the good health of the population. Essential services — water, electricity, gas, sewerage, railroads, telephones — if interrupted, were interrupted for only short periods. Public morale, far from being broken, was infinitely fortified by the ordeal.

41 THE EXTENSION OF THE WAR

THE BALKANS, THE NEAR EAST, AND EAST AFRICA

It has always been the part of Britain, a maritime Power with interests and responsibilities all over the globe, whenever she has been engaged in a general war, to have to fight in many widely separated theaters. In particular she has tried to hold the great "strategic arc" represented by Gibraltar-Malta-Suez-Aden. Her position in the Mediterranean, after the Fall of France in 1940, was precarious in the extreme. The use of the French naval bases was denied her; Syria was taken over by Vichy; Malta was constantly bombed and almost isolated. Italian planes raided as far afield as Alexandria, Port Said, Suez, and Aden. In the Red Sea, Italian forces took over the French port of Jibuti under the terms of the armistice with France. In August 1940 they invaded and occupied British Somaliland. They seized trading posts on the borders of Sudan and Kenya. Considering the sparse forces opposed to them, it is a marvel that they did not do more. In September 1940 the Italian army in Cyrenaica, under Marshal Graziani, crossed the Egyptian frontier on the first stage, as it then seemed, of an attempted conquest of Egypt.

Admiral Cunningham, commanding the Alexandria Squadron, outnumbered at every point, could only maintain himself by superb bluff. "We started very weak at sea and even more so in the air," he said. "However, because of the very fact of our weakness, our policy had obviously to be one of aggressiveness, and it paid handsome dividends." The Mediterranean was closed to British merchant shipping, but one or two military convoys, carefully co-ordinated with Cunningham's offensive sallies, got through to Malta and Alexandria. During all the critical autumn of 1940, when even her friends were expecting her to capitulate in her own homeland, Britain was depleting and dividing her overstrained resources and running the Mediterranean gauntlet to build up her Army of the Nile, as it was then called, and repair as best she might the breaches in the Near East caused by the Fall of France. Churchill made the bold decision to send out to Egypt an armored division, complete with "Matildas," then one of the most formidable tank types in the world, badly though it was needed in England. To Egypt also came strong reinforcements from India, Australia, and New Zealand, and to Kenya from South Africa. By the winter of 1940, under General Wavell, Commander in Chief Middle East, there was a tolerably well equipped but widely dispersed British army of 80,000–90,000 men.

To Mussolini, the Italian Duce, as he surveyed the field at this time, the alternatives for diplomatic and military action must have looked numerous and enticing. He toyed for a while with the idea of creating a separate state of Croatia which he could carve out of Yugoslavia and take under Italian protection. He finally resolved on an attack on Greece, a country against which, ever since the Corfu incident of 1923, he had nourished a grievance. On October 28, 1940, without precisely notifying his German ally and in spite of the warnings of his most responsible generals, who better knew the poor moral condition and ill equipment of the Italian forces, his army in Albania began the invasion of the Greek Epirus.

But from this auspicious moment Mussolini's fortunes began to decline. In five months, for all his apparent relative strength, first in Greece, then in Cyrenaica, then in East Africa, his legions suffered one reverse after another. The Italian invasion of Greece in 1940 resembled the Austrian invasion of Serbia in 1914. The invader was met by defending forces of inferior material equipment and inferior numbers, but knowing their own terrain and choosing their own tactics, and inspired with a righteous courage. The British could implement their treaty guarantee to Greece only with naval and aerial aid, but that aid was quickly dispatched (see p. 639). The Greeks were commanded by General Metaxas, one of the brilliant strategists of his day. In November the Greeks themselves were advancing into Albania. From air bases in Greece the British were raiding Albanian and Adriatic ports. On November 11, 1940, Cunninghamian bluff achieved its most audacious triumph. A squadron of British torpedo planes of obsolete pattern and, by any reasonable standard, of insufficient numbers for the operation, taking off from the carrier *Illustrious*, raided the Italian naval base at Taranto, sank one battleship and seriously damaged two others, and by this single stroke put out of action half the capital strength of the Italian Navy.

By normal military standards the British offensive against Graziani's army on the Egyptian frontier, the First Libyan Campaign as it is called, again had little to justify it but audacity. Wavell has described it as a raid in force. But if the first stages were successful, he was prepared to develop the offensive into one of unlimited objectives. He was himself a campaigner of long experience in desert warfare under Allenby in the First World War, and he was an imaginative tactician of the modern mechanized school. His lieutenant and commander on the spot was General O'Connor, and the British forces immediately engaged numbered about 30,000 men. The offensive was launched, with complete surprise, on December 9, 1940. In two months' fighting of the greatest skill and precision and of perfect co-operation between all arms, the Army of the Nile swept across the Italian province of Cyrenaica deep into Libya, defeated an enemy of greatly superior numbers, and took 113,000 prisoners — all at a cost to itself of 1,774 casualties, of whom only 438 were killed.

The British campaign in East Africa began more slowly. It was confined at first to raiding operations. The Emperor of Ethiopia, Haile Selassie, appeared on the scene and, before the end of 1940, guerrilla revolts, with his collaboration and with British arms, were being stirred up against the Italian garrisons of Eritrea. In February, South Africans, moving up from Kenya, began the invasion of Italian Somaliland. In March the two forces were converging on Ethiopia. British Somaliland was reoccupied. On the northern approaches the Italian strong point of Keren alone offered any prolonged resistance. Early in April 1941 the combined British forces entered Addis Ababa. Mussolini's East African empire was at an end.

The British Navy meanwhile was making a further contribution to the general Italian rout. On February 9, 1941, in broad daylight, a heavy force bombarded Genoa, destroying power stations, railroad yards, and oil stores in the harbor. On the night of March 28, in a running engagement off Cape Matapan, two Italian fleets on the prowl for convoys bearing British aid to Greece suffered the loss of three cruisers and serious damage to one battleship. The British ships, using radar to direct their gunnery in the darkness, emerged from the action unscathed. Enemy merchant losses at this time were such that about 30 per cent of the ships proceeding from European ports to Africa were being sunk.

In the larger view, the Italo-Greek and Italo-British wars of 1940–41 were incidental to the greater war between Germany and the Soviet Union shortly to break out. The Moscow Pact of 1939 had served its two signatories well. Germany had secured herself against the complications of a second front while she overwhelmed the West; the Soviet Union had improved its frontiers in the Baltic and in Finland. The subsequent Soviet-German economic interchange had been mutually beneficial. The Soviet Union received war material and machinery, and Germany received wheat, oil, cotton, soya beans, chemicals, and rubber. But old fears and frictions had not been quieted. The Kremlin, which had counted on Germany's long and exhausting preoccupation with the Western Powers, was profoundly alarmed at the ease and decisiveness of her victories over them. The Moscow Pact had conceded the Soviet interest in the Baltic and Bessarabia, but Germany nonetheless resented the arbitrary manner in which the Soviet Government interpreted that concession. The Soviet occupation of the Baltic bases, the eviction of the German Balts, and the Soviet-Finnish War had all been highly disquieting to the Nazi Government (see p. 649). In mid-June 1940, while yet the Battle of France was at its height, the Soviet Union had unobtrusively completed its occupation of Lithuania, Latvia, and Estonia. Then, on June 26, just after the French armistice, the Soviet Union had delivered an ultimatum to Rumania categorically demanding the cession of Bessarabia and northern Bucovina, and in four days the territory was given up and occupied by Soviet forces. From this moment it may be said that, except for a certain ceremonial value, the Moscow Pact was dead, and its two signatories were engaging in an all but overt trial of strength and, of course, choosing for their purpose that old tiltyard of power politics, the Balkans.

During June 1940, King Carol's government in Rumania purged itself of pro-Ally elements, denounced the Anglo-French guarantee of 1939, and openly declared in favor of "a fundamental integration with the Axis system." But Carol's sycophancy had not protected him from the loss of Bessarabia to the Soviet Union, nor now from further losses of his precious provinces to Bulgaria and Hungary. On August 19, 1940, Rumanian and Bulgarian delegates met to arrange the transfer of the southern Dobruja to Bulgaria. On August 30, 1940, at a conference at Vienna, at the dictation

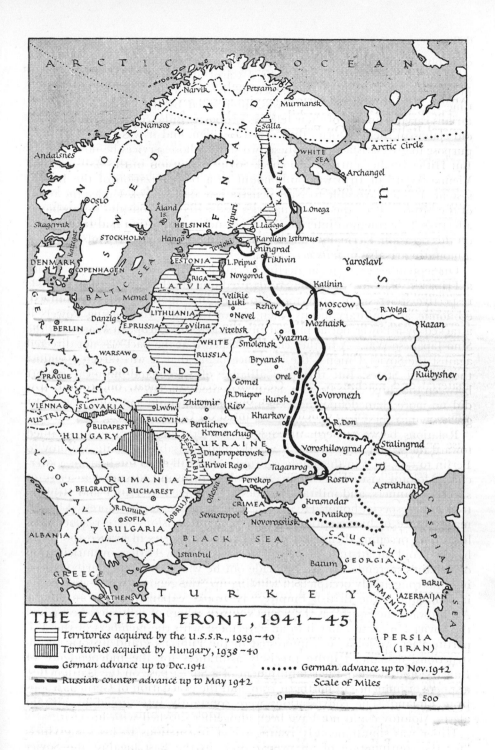

THE EASTERN FRONT, 1941—45

	Territories acquired by the U.S.S.R., 1939—40
	Territories acquired by Hungary, 1938—40
——	German advance up to Dec. 1941
– –	Russian counter advance up to May 1942
•••••	German advance up to Nov. 1942

Scale of Miles

0   500

of Ribbentrop and Ciano, Rumania was forced to yield about half of Transylvania to Hungary. The discredited Carol abdicated in favor of his son Michael, leaving General Antonescu as the real ruler of Rumania. For a time the nontotalitarian world was entertained by the spectacle of totalitarians carving up one of their fellow's property. Bulgaria and Hungary had old claims in the territories thus ceded to them, and it was part of Hitler's purpose to give satisfaction to these two states whose services he now desired. But Hitler further purposed to check Soviet expansion in the Balkans. The Vienna Award of 1940 was tantamount to a reorganization of the Balkan system on lines favorable to Nazi penetration and control. Under the terms of the Moscow Pact, the two signatories had agreed to consult "on problems affecting their common interests," but no such consultation had taken place on this occasion. Germany and the Soviet Union were clearly embarking on a mounting rivalry in *faits accomplis*.

On September 27, 1940, at Berlin, Germany, Italy, and Japan entered into a Tripartite Pact by which they recognized one another's leadership in their respective spheres and undertook "to assist one another with all political, economic, and military means when one of the three contracting Powers is attacked by a Power not at present involved in the European War or in the Sino-Japanese War." A further clause affirmed that the pact was not directed against the Soviet Union — the inference being that it was directed against the United States. But this new alliance of vague and inimical import between the three Axis Powers, again presented as a *fait accompli,* even if it did no more than define the existing situation, could not but arouse the greatest uneasiness in Moscow.

Relations between Germany and the Soviet Union became so strained toward the winter of 1940 that it was deemed advisable to invite Molotov to Berlin to take part in the gaudy courtesies of a full-dress totalitarian conference. Molotov visited Berlin in November 1940 and attended a series of speeches, dinners, and military parades all arranged by Hitler and Ribbentrop in his especial honor. He may have been momentarily impressed by the magnificence of his reception, but no positive decisions were reached. His hosts were preening themselves on their recent victories in France and could hardly avoid an attitude of patronage toward him. Hitler, in anticipation of Britain's surrender, which he made out he was then momentarily expecting, was congenially occupied in winding up "the gigantic world-wide estate in bankruptcy, the British Empire." He spoke expansively of "an Asiatic Area toward the South" as the Soviet's future sphere of influence; he invited the Soviet Union to enter into an agreement with the members of the Tripartite Pact. Molotov, less interested in the Führer's grand historic reconstructions, demanded quite precisely assurances for the independence of Bulgaria and Sweden, the establishment of a Soviet base on the Dardanelles, a sphere of influence in northern Iran, and the evacuation of German troops from Finland. The conversations were constantly interrupted by air-raid alerts. Molotov could not have been altogether satisfied with his visit.

Hitler was simultaneously issuing secret instructions to his army chiefs "for the continuation of all preparations in the East [against the Soviet Union]." Within ten days of Molotov's return to Moscow, Hungary, Rumania, and Slovakia joined the Tripartite Pact. Evidently the pact was to become a sort of "United Nations in reverse," as it has somewhat anachronistically been called, for the adhesion of all the Axis satellites. Hitler's basic operational directive, "Case Barbarossa," "for crushing Russia in a quick campaign," was ready on December 18, 1940. Nazi penetration of the Balkans meanwhile had reached a stage when it could no longer be disguised. In Rumania, in a three-day civil war, General Antonescu with Himmler's help purged the truculent opposition of the Iron Guard, once the favored agent of German-provoked disturbance. Rumania, by then, was full of German soldiers; the Rumanian oil fields were taken under German management; the country was virtually a German base. Early in 1941 it was evident that Bulgaria was submitting to the same fate. Hitler and the Tsar Boris had already met in conference. On March 1, 1941, Bulgaria adhered to the Tripartite Pact.

Yugoslavia under the regency of Prince Paul had been drawing Axisward for years. In October 1940 a trade treaty between herself and Germany seemed to signify her assimilation — in the economic sense if nothing else — into Hitler's New Order in Europe. But, while the Yugoslav Government might thus lean toward Nazism, it commanded little support from the main masses of the people. Yugoslav patriots were determined that the kind of political tribute which Rumania and Bulgaria were being forced to pay should not be levied on their country. In February 1941 a Yugoslav Government delegation, headed by the Premier, Cvetkovich, conferred with Hitler at Berchtesgaden. Ciano, the Italian Foreign Minister, was plying his own independent oar and negotiating directly with the Croat leader Pavelich with a view to setting up a separate Croat state under Italian protection. On March 25, 1941 the Yugoslav Government formally adhered to the Tripartite Pact.

But at this point Yugoslav patriots and army revolted. In a bloodless coup, General Simovich occupied Belgrade, installed the young King Peter on the throne, and himself assumed the premiership of an anti-Axis government. Prince Paul fled. Machek, the loyal Croat leader, consented to serve as Vice-Premier and thereby to demonstrate the solidarity of the Serb and Croat peoples. The Soviet Government threw off the last pretense of collaboration with Germany. It sent its warning to the several Balkan governments. On April 6, 1941 it solemnly reaffirmed the ancient Russian comradeship with the South Slavs and concluded with the new government of Yugoslavia a pact of friendship and nonaggression. Commentators of the time were quick to recall that the war in 1914 had been precipitated by Russia's decision to come to the aid of a Serbia threatened, then as now, by Teutonic aggression.

An interlude was provided, at this time, by the visit of Matsuoka, the Japanese Foreign Minister, to Berlin, Rome, and Moscow. The Japanese Government was sufficiently concerned over European developments to send a ranking Cabinet minister on a tour of investigation on the spot. Hitler and Ribbentrop were even more condescending to their Oriental visitor than they had been to Molotov. The conversations were entirely unreal, and we cannot help asking who among these undoubtedly informed and disingenuous men thought he was pulling the wool over whose eyes. Hitler regarded a Japanese war with the United States as undesirable but, should it occur, he said, Germany would promptly honor the Tripartite Pact and take her stand beside her Japanese ally. Matsuoka was confident that the Japanese Navy could destroy the American Navy "without trouble," and his only fear in this respect was that the American Navy would avoid giving battle. Hitler, for his part however, would have preferred a Japanese attack on Singapore and, Ribbentrop added, "the Führer, who certainly must be considered the greatest military expert of modern times," would advise Japan as to the best method for that attack. Ribbentrop, in confidence, hinted to Matsuoka that Germany could not much longer tolerate the growing unfriendliness of the Soviet Union and that she had at her disposal 240 "unemployed divisions," with which, if need be, she could totally crush the Soviet Army and the Soviet state.

Matsuoka, however, returned to Moscow and there, on April 13, 1941, he signed a Soviet-Japanese Neutrality Pact. He had acted apparently on his own initiative without consultation with Tokyo. His pact had much the same effect in the East as the Moscow Pact had once had in the West, and it was burst upon the world under similar circumstances of drama and surprise. Two old and declared antagonists, it seemed, had suddenly composed their differences. Both stood to make a temporary gain from mutual peace; both wanted a free hand in their respective spheres; both wanted an assurance meanwhile of the other's neutrality; both seized the opportunity of making an unmistakable assertion of resistance to dictation from Berlin. The importance of the pact had been underscored by unusual ceremonies in the Kremlin, and Stalin himself had afterward paid his Japanese guest the unprecedented compliment of attending his departure in person at the Moscow Railroad Station.

Since the late summer of 1940, Hitler had had under consideration a campaign against Greece by way of Bulgaria, but he had been anticipated by Mussolini's invasion of Greece. He had paid small attention to Mussolini's subsequent difficulties in Greece and North Africa. But records of his conferences about this time betray his declining confidence in the military prowess of his Italian ally and his increasing anxiety lest Balkan complications might prejudice his preparations for the approaching campaign in Russia. In particular, he was determined to eliminate British influence in Greece and in the Mediterranean. Early in 1941, German pilots and German planes began to appear and to attack British convoys passing the Sicilian Channel. In one famous engagement they damaged and all but sank the British aircraft carrier *Illustrious*. A German elite force, the so-called Afrika Korps, trained for desert warfare, was built up in Libya under General Rommel, one of Kleist's intrepid subordinates in the Battle of France.

Britain had already sent some aerial aid to Greece. The possible German invasion of Greece, however, would invoke the British guarantee of 1939 and involve a far heavier British military commitment. At the end of February 1941, Eden, then British Secretary for War, and General Dill, Chief of the Imperial General Staff, conferred with Wavell in Cairo, and it was decided to transfer a number of British troops from Cyrenaica and Egypt to Greece. The decision was afterward much criticized. Evidently political and military viewpoints were at odds. On the one hand it seemed imperative that, in a world of crashing alliances, one Power at least should still show respect for its plighted word. On the other hand Wavell's campaign in Libya was not completed, and to withdraw troops from a campaign which they might otherwise have won, to take part in a campaign which they were pretty certain to lose was hardly in the highest flight of military judgment. The Greek Government was averse to British aid unless it should be of such strength as to make the successful defense of Greece a reasonable possibility. During the month of March, 1941, 57,000 men — British, Anzacs, and Poles — under Wavell's subordinate, General Wilson, were duly put ashore in Greece.

German preparations for the invasion of Greece were already far advanced when the Yugoslav revolt in that same March confronted Hitler with an unexpected and urgent situation. On April 6, 1941, the day that the Soviet-Yugoslav pact of nonaggression had been signed, a German army under List simultaneously invaded both Yugoslavia and Greece. The Yugoslav leader Simovich and his Greek and British allies had had no time to concert a joint defense, and Hitler's legions found themselves as usual fighting against ill-prepared and ill-co-ordinated adversaries. They made their main thrust through Bulgaria toward Skoplje, thus isolating Yugoslavia from possible support from the south. For the rest, the operation was just another example of a Nazi blitzkrieg in all its usual virtuosity. Belgrade was bombed, as Warsaw, Rotterdam, and London had been bombed. Yugoslavia was eliminated as a fighting entity in five days.

The defense of Greece was as stubborn as inadequate numbers and inadequate equipment could make it. All the reputedly impregnable points in the classic mountainous terrain — the Monastir Gap, Olympus, Thermopylae — fell to the Germans one after another. Ports and railroads were heavily bombed by the Luftwaffe. The Greeks retired from their gains in Albania. The Greek Premier, Korizis, committed suicide. On April 23, 1941, the Greek Army laid down its arms. Out of Wilson's original force of 57,000 men, 43,000 were evacuated to the island of Crete. The Germans entered Athens on the 27th and hoisted the swastika on the Acropolis.

At the end of March 1941 a combined German and Italian force attacked the British in Libya, now much depleted by the transfer of their effectives to the Greek campaign and with their communications extended to the limit. The new Afrika Korps under General Rommel formed the spearhead of the attack, and it fought a campaign resembling Wavell's own offensive of the previous December — in reverse. In three weeks the British had retired once more to the Egyptian frontier, leaving behind them a single isolated garrison at the fortress of Tobruk.

At this moment disaster crowded in from all parts of the world. On May 2 a pro-Axis military coup flared up in Iraq in anticipation of further German successes in the Near East. Rashid Ali, a secret member of the local Iraqi

Fascist group, "the Golden Square," seized control and attached Royal Air Force bases in the country. On May 20, German air-borne forces invaded Crete and, in ten days of heavy fighting, compelled the British forces to withdraw. On May 24, away in the North Atlantic, the British battle cruiser *Hood,* the biggest warship in the world, was operating as part of a naval force concentrated to round up the new German battleship *Bismarck,* which was "loose" at sea and hunting for convoys, and she was sunk in action with her quarry. A few days later, as if in partial compensation for this chapter of calamities, the *Bismarck* herself went down to a combination of aerial attack, destroyer attack, and a terrific pounding from the battleships *Rodney* and *King George V.*

On June 18, at Ankara, Germany and Turkey entered into a treaty of friendship. Armed Axis ships were permitted to pass the Dardanelles. In the course of the summer, Germany carved up her conquests in Yugoslavia and Greece, even as she had carved up Poland and Rumania. The Balkans were wholly incorporated into the Nazi New Order.

THE GERMAN INVASION OF RUSSIA

In its origins, Nazism had been a narrow nationalist movement, a local German revolt. It was, as Mussolini once said of Fascism, "not an article for export." Yet Nazism, like all revolutions, had the seeds of universalism in it and, like all revolutions, its appetite grew with eating. Hitler's obvious parallel is Napoleon. Here too was a man born into a revolutionary time, who assumed a dictatorship, and then, by insensible degrees, found himself driven by the "logic of events" to lay hold of more and more of his neighbors' possessions. "Europe should never be other than one people" — thus Napoleon had rationalized the situation — "My desire was to create a European order, a European code, a European court of appeal." The significance of 1941 was that Hitler, like Napoleon in 1811, passed from the stage of a parochial tyrant to that of a universal man of destiny and that, in the same moment, his individual will ceased to control his individual actions, and we see him, as the final denouement approaches, ensconced in his Fortress of Europe, fighting by intuition, the sport of historical forces which he had himself conjured up but which had since grown too strong for him.

The parallel with Napoleon, as Gafencu has pointed out, goes further and holds true even in details.[1] Napoleon at Tilsit in 1807 concluded with the Russian dictator of his day a pact for the subdivision of Europe much on the lines of the Moscow Pact of 1939. The signatories granted one another a free hand on their respective sides of an arbitrary frontier. Yet they never ceased to hold one another in suspicion, in spite of periodic and ceremonial protestations of trust. Both looked upon the pact as a temporary accommodation, the one as a strategic device, the other as a purchase of time. Both continued in a tacit rivalry, notably in the Balkans and Near East. Moscow, like Tilsit, began to break down when Russia tried to extricate herself from her fellow signatory's economic demands. Moscow, like Tilsit, issued at last in open war when that fellow signatory's campaign against England was admitted to have failed. Finally, Hitler's campaign in Russia in 1941–45, vaster though it was, followed the ultimate course of Napoleon's — even to an accompanying Waterloo in the West.

Detailed preparations for war had begun on both sides in the autumn of 1940. The Russians constructed a deep belt of strong points, the so-called Stalin Line, along their frontiers, thus converting their new territorial acquisitions in the Baltic, Poland, and Rumania into a great "glacis" facing Germany. Hitler's directive, "Case Barbarossa," was ready, as we have said, in December. All dispositions were to be completed by May 15, 1941. That date was postponed while the campaign in Yugoslavia and Greece was brought to an end and "the German right shoulder" was freed. It is tempting to believe, therefore, that the British intervention in Greece delayed the invasion of Russia by five weeks, a margin of time which, in the event, was of decisive importance. Meanwhile, alternative German plans, operations in Spain and for the capture of Gibraltar, for instance, were all laid aside. Even air raids over England, from this moment onward, were reduced to a minimum. Every device was used to camouflage the massing of men and material on the Soviet borders, but by April 1941 — and probably much earlier — Moscow, London, and Washington were all aware of the German plan. Cripps, then British ambassador in Moscow, predicted June 22 as the date of invasion.

In that April 1941, Rosenberg, the philosopher of Nazism and "expert" on Russian affairs, was secretly appointed by Hitler as Reich Minister for the Eastern Occupied Territories with a view to his assuming responsibility for the civil administration of the German Army's conquests. The final spur to action was President Roosevelt's address of May 27, 1941, and his proclamation of "an unlimited national emergency" in the United States. The rising temper of the American people left Hitler with no alternative but to rush his New Order to completion. In another year the trans-Atlantic "arsenal of the democracies" might well become too strong for him, unless he could counterbalance it with Russian acquisitions on a Continental scale. On May 6 it was announced from Moscow that Stalin had personally assumed the presidency of the Council of People's Commissars. In anticipation of the approaching war he had thus embodied in himself, actually and symbolically, the supreme executive power in the Soviet Union.

On May 10, Rudolf Hess, the Nazi leader, then regarded as Hitler's deputy and successor designate, made a solo flight to Scotland and parachuted to earth near Glasgow. Many interpretations of this astonishing adventure were put out at the time; but it seems that Hess expected to contact influential persons in Britain who he imagined were in favor of a negotiated peace. With the air so thick with nonaggression pacts, the German attack on Russia might conceivably be prefaced with one between Germany and Britain. But there were no such peace advocates in Britain, and the deluded aviator was safely interned as a prisoner of war. On June 22, 1941, without ultimatum or declaration of war, the German attack began along the entire Soviet frontier.

Germany deployed against the Soviet Union 160 divisions, of which 20 were armored, and four-fifths of her Luftwaffe. This huge concentration was divided into three army groups, the northern commanded by Leeb, the central by Bock, and the southern by Rundstedt. The names of Kuechler, Kluge, Guderian, Reichenau, Stuelpnagel,[2] and Kleist appear among the army commanders. On the extreme left wing, in the far north, a Finnish contingent under the Finnish Marshal von Mannerheim "resumed the Soviet-Finnish War"; Hungarian and Slovak contingents were incorporated in the southern army group; a Rumanian contingent under Antonescu marched on the extreme right wing, clamoring to repossess the lost province of Bessarabia. The Red Army opposed with some 160 divisions and 55 tank brigades, divided into three army groups, the northern commanded by Voroshilov, the central by Timoshenko, and the southern by Budënny. In all 9,000,000 fighting men, Germans, Rumanians, Hungarians, Finns, and Russians, joined battle along a thousand-mile front. The so-called Battle of the Frontier lasted some three to four weeks, the "glacis" from the Black Sea to the Baltic was overrun, and the Stalin Line was breached throughout its length.

For the first time in the Second World War, Germany was at grips with a foe on land, not only more evenly matched, but fully appreciating her tactics. The fighting was swift moving. Fronts lost themselves in vast areas whose limits were often unknown to the very commanders on the spot. Pincers became pockets, and pockets pincers. Tank offensives were cut off from their supporting infantry; Russian guerrillas were left far behind in the rear. The geography of the campaign had hardly more significance than the surface of the sea at Jutland or Midway. Railroads, rather than places, were the strategic objectives. Peasant and civilian populations were indiscriminately swallowed up in the flood of battle. The resources of the land were put to the torch by the retreating Russians before they passed into German hands. In five months there followed the battles of Smolensk, Kiev, Odessa, Leningrad, Dnepropetrovsk, the Crimea, and Moscow. It is as easy to contemplate the clash of worlds in cosmic space as this stupendous warfare.

Yet if we are at a loss to itemize the welter of incident, we believe we can detect one broad military policy on the part of the Soviet High Command. It was, in a word, to buy cheaply and sell dearly. It was to admit the initial superiority of the German armament and warcraft, and thence the necessity of retirement, but always to exact the maximum price in German life. Generally the Soviet High Command did not concentrate its main masses in forward areas, it sacrificed the Stalin Line and, wherever and whenever it made the decision to stand and fight, as it did for instance at Smolensk, it fought so that it could still extricate the greater part of its effectives at the penultimate moment. Soviet strategy in 1940 was the exact opposite of the Grand Duke's strategy in 1914 which had met its quietus at Tannenberg (see p. 20). It was the adaptation to mechanized warfare of Foch's "elastic defense" of 1918 (see p. 99). The war, in effect, was not a war of gaining or giving ground, or of capturing or holding cities, or even of winning or losing battles, but of permanently destroying the aggressor nation's human resources. Russia so conducted her resistance that even if in the military sense she lost the war, in the demographic sense the Teutonic race would never recover from its victory. German military theorists had often expatiated on the war of annihilation. Thanks to Adolf Hitler, they were seeing their theories realized.

By the beginning of December 1941, the German armies and their allies had advanced 600 miles on their total front. They had taken Tikhvin, Novgorod, Kalinin, Orel, Kursk, Kharkov, and Rostov. In the north they closely invested Leningrad; in the south they closely invested Sevastopol, but both cities remained in Russian hands; in the center they stood within sight of Moscow. The whole of western European Russia and the Ukraine had been substantially devastated in the course of the campaign, and now lay under German occupation. The Soviet Government had retired to Kuibyshev, though Stalin himself had stayed in Moscow. On October 3, 1941, Hitler had openly claimed that "the enemy is already broken and will never rise again." A few days later the press chief, Dietrich, had given tongue to the sweeping assurance, "For all military purposes the Soviet Union is finished." On December 8, 1941, German operations for the year were officially declared to be at an end. The worst winter in living memory held Russia in its grip.

Almost immediately the Red Army opened its counteroffensive, clearly aiming to relieve the pressure on Moscow and Leningrad and to recapture Rostov and Kharkov. Russian guerrillas operated in the rear, harrying German lines of communication, destroying isolated garrisons. For six months, newspapers and radio gave out almost routine communiqués of a slow, plodding, and presumably expensive Russian advance over lost ground. The final gains were small compared with the areas under German occupation. Except for Mozhaisk near Moscow and Rostov, no important German strong points were liberated. But the watching world was infinitely surprised and heartened to see that the Red Army, in its first campaigning year of the war, had won the main "battle of calculation," that, for all its cruel losses and for all the hysterical announcements of its extermination which regularly proceeded from Nazi press headquarters, it was still a force in being, capable of major offensive operations. German troops, short of winter clothing, which Hitler in his overconfidence had never expected to be needed, suffered appalling hardships. Early in 1942, Brauchitsch, the German Commander in Chief in Berlin, Halder, his Chief of Staff, Leeb, and Rundstedt were all dismissed. Hitler himself assumed the supreme command of the Wehrmacht.

THE BATTLE OF THE ATLANTIC

Across the Atlantic Ocean another battle was now being fought, less spectacular and bloody than that in Russia, but as decisive in its element. On its outcome hung the life of Britain. And on its outcome also hung the possibility of an eventual assault on Germany from the West. The revised "cash and carry" of November 1939 and Lend-Lease of March 1941 were all a part of it. In terms of grand strategy the British Isles were being made the outpost, and the North American continent the base, of a great global effort against Nazi-dominated Europe. Between outpost and base lay the all-pervasive war at sea and, in particular, the Battle of the Atlantic.

The battle had begun within twelve hours of Britain's declaration of war on September 3, 1939 with the sinking of the *Athenia*. It ended at last with the German surrender on May 7, 1945. Tactically, the battle was a protracted competition of scientific ingenuities. Detecting devices, "asdic," radar, and "degaussing," the use of aircraft for spotting and depth charging, bombing attacks on U-boat pens and assembly plants, and on factories inland manufacturing U-boat parts, the whole parade of convoy and escort, all this was pitted against an offensive resourcefulness and invention that never flagged or tired.

The success of the convoy system in 1917–18 gave good reasons for hoping at first that the submarine in the Second World War would not be the all-important weapon that it had been in the First, and that Germany's main effort at sea would now be made by her surface ships. The fact that the German pocket battleships had been specifically designed as commerce raiders gave additional color to the notion. We described in the last chapter, for instance, the episode of the *Admiral Graf Spee*. But the U-boats of 1939–45 had a far greater operational range, speed, and destructive power than the U-boats of twenty-five years before, and they hunted now, not singly, but in "wolf packs," with a fleet of supply ships in attendance for refueling and minor repairs at sea. Furthermore, the situation in regard to bases was entirely changed. In 1914–18, Britain blockaded Germany along a narrow North Sea frontage and, in addition to her own bases, including those in Southern Ireland, she had the use of the French bases in the Mediterranean and North Africa. In 1940, after the Fall of France, she faced a Germany which occupied bases from Norway to Spain and round to the Black Sea, and she fought moreover without the use of the French bases and without her own former bases in Southern Ireland (see p. 336). In partial compensation, she had occupied Iceland and the Faeroe Islands, and she set about the naval development of Londonderry in Northern Ireland. At the same time, escort craft and patrol ships were in woefully short supply. Trawlers and other auxiliary ships could be improvised to some extent, but the extra cruisers, destroyers, and corvettes had to be built, and built in shipyards that were already overworked. Merchantmen could be armed both against submarine and aerial attack and, in three months of war, the Admiralty was able to announce that a thousand ships had been fitted with guns of some kind. Early in September 1940 came the grateful news of the transfer of the fifty American destroyers (see pp. 661 and 698).

The center of gravity of the Battle of the Atlantic moved constantly. No sooner had countermeasures been developed in one locality than the enemy withdrew and probed for another "soft spot" elsewhere. Official maps, since published, of the "phases" of the battle show graphically the shifting of the main area of the sinkings, now toward Britain and France, then north toward Iceland, then south toward Dakar, and so forth. After Pearl Harbor, when the United States transferred almost its entire Atlantic Fleet to the Pacific, the area shifted to the Caribbean and the North American coast. At the turning point, in the early summer of 1943, the maps become suddenly clear of sinkings and remain relatively clear to the final triumph in 1945.

Even so, U-boats in 1939–45 were able to sink merchant ships at only about half the monthly rate achieved in 1914–18; but the individual ships were heavier, and the aggregate tonnage sunk was rather more than doubled. The total Allied and neutral losses (including American) of merchant and fishing ships by U-boat and by enemy action of all kinds in the six years of the Second World War are shown in the accompanying table.

TOTAL ALLIED LOSSES OF MERCHANT AND FISHING SHIPS BY ENEMY ACTION, 1939–1945

(in thousands of tons gross)

	By U-boat	By mines, surface ships, aircraft, etc.	Totals by enemy action of all kinds
1939	421	325	746
1940	2,125	1,787	3,912
1941	2,126	2,061	4,187
1942	6,250	1,456	7,706
1943	2,579	624	3,203
1944	773	271	1,044
1945	263	133	396
Totals	**14,537**	**6,657**	**21,194**

Of this total loss of over 20,000,000 tons, the loss by U-boat represents 70 per cent, and losses by mines, surface ships, and aircraft 30 per cent. Three-quarters occurred in the Atlantic Ocean, and more than half were British.

PEARL HARBOR

The outbreak of war in Europe in September 1939 seemed to offer Japan a golden opportunity for winding up the "China incident" in complete freedom from "Western meddling." Chiang Kai-shek, however, was no more disposed to consider a Japanese peace in 1939 than he had been in 1937. Early in 1940, Japan installed the ingenious and pliant Wang Ching-wei, an ambitious renegade who had deserted the Chinese Nationalist government in 1938, as President of a "National Government of China" in Nanking. Wang pledged collaboration with "the Co-prosperity Sphere in East Asia," and the Japanese Government went through the motions of recognizing this miserable creation.

Meanwhile Japan's economic war with the United States had been mounting in tempo and irritation. Protests to Tokyo from the State Department had been acquiring an almost routine and familiar sequence. The sale of American aircraft to Japan had already been virtually stopped at the end of 1938 as the result of the State Department's tactful pressure on the manufacturers. In July 1939 the abrogation of the old American-Japanese commercial treaty of 1911 did not paralyze trade, but placed it on a day-to-day basis (see p. 444). In July 1940 an Export Control Act authorized the President to regulate or interdict the export of commodities essential for defense. Successive presidential proclamations defined a lengthening list of articles requiring licenses for export — machine tools, chemicals, and strategic metals.

At the same time the "moral embargo" on the sale of aviation gasoline was written into a definite enactment. Tokyo retorted menacingly that, if such measures continued, "future relations between Japan and the United States will be unpredictable." In September, as has been mentioned already, came the Tripartite Pact between Japan, Germany, and Italy with its implied menace to the United States, and in April 1941, the Soviet-Japanese Neutrality Pact. President Roosevelt at once ordered Japanese assets in the United States to be frozen. The British Government took similar measures.

The Fall of France in June 1940 had left French Indo-China wide open to aggression. Already in that June the French Government had agreed to suspend the transit of war materials to Free China by way of Indo-Chinese ports and railroads. On July 18, as a gesture to Japan, the British Government closed the Burma Road for a period of three months. Siam was then being incited to press claims for the restoration of portions of Laos and Cambodia, annexed to French Indo-China some forty years before. Clashes occurred along the Siamese frontiers, and Siamese forces ultimately occupied a portion of the disputed territory. The French Governor General of Indo-China, Decoux, found himself being compelled to permit Japanese air bases to be built in the colony, ostensibly to facilitate the Japanese bombing of Chiang Kai-shek's new defenses at Chungking.

Throughout 1941 the Japanese homeland devoted itself to a feverish acceleration of its preparations for war. Political parties were merged into a single, monolithic "Imperial Rule Assistance Association." Government control of industry, bitterly contested by the Zaibatsu, was slowly broadened by the progressive application of the National Mobilization Law, which had been passed in anticipation in 1938. Meanwhile, the militarists were regarding with growing restiveness the efforts of the Premier, Prince Konoye, to arrive at a settlement with the United States by diplomatic negotiations. In September 1941, Konoye sought to draw President Roosevelt into a "leaders' conference," in which outstanding differences could be settled by a direct exchange of views. President Roosevelt pointed out that substantial preliminary agreement was essential to the success of such a conference, and Konoye dropped the plan. But by that time Japanese military intelligence was obtaining from its agents in Hawaii detailed reports on the topography of Pearl Harbor and on the naval units lying there. The Minister of War, General Hideki Tojo, meaningly reminded Konoye that "to carry on negotiations, for which there is no possibility of fruition, and in the end to let slip the time for fighting would be a matter of the greatest consequence." In mid-October, Konoye at last gave up his struggle for moderation and resigned. He was succeeded by Tojo himself, "the Razor Brain" as he was called, at the head of a cabinet of army and naval officers.

The new cabinet, it was well said, "smelled of gunpowder." But there still appears to have been a last-minute division of opinion in Tokyo as to whether eastern Siberia or Indo-China and the Netherlands East Indies should be the next objective of Japanese imperialism. The navy chiefs were always more cautious than the army, and they were anxious in particular over the availability of oil for a long war. Admiral Yamamato, with candor and prescience, promised "a good show," but only for six months or, at the most, a year. Meanwhile the diplomatic negotiations with the United States could be continued as a blind, whatever the final strategic decisions might be. On November 15, 1941, Tojo's special envoy, Saburo Kurusu, arrived in Washington to assist the Japanese ambassador, Admiral Nomura, in the current negotiations and to convey his government's definitive proposals. He demanded for Japan full access to the resources of the Netherlands East Indies, the raising of the American financial and economic embargo, and the cessation of American aid to Chiang Kai-shek. On November 26, in a strongly worded note, Secretary Hull made counterdemands for a nonaggression pact between the Pacific Powers, the withdrawal of Japanese forces from China and from Indo-China, a joint guarantee of the territorial integrity of China, and Japanese recognition of the Chinese Nationalist government of Chiang Kai-shek.

At this time "Magic," the United States Army and Navy cryptanalytic divisions, had been deciphering the Japanese radio messages, and its interceptions indicated that the Japanese Government was putting little further confidence in the peaceful outcome of the Washington negotiations. Indeed, by November 1, Combined Fleet Operational Order No. 1 for the attack on Pearl Harbor, Malaya, and the East Indies had already been issued in Tokyo. On November 24 a first "alert" was sent to Pearl Harbor from Washington. The next day, in great secrecy, the Japanese task force for Pearl Harbor set sail, though the Japanese Foreign Minister simultaneously instructed Nomura to avoid giving the impression that Japan desired the negotiations to be broken off. On November 27, Secretary of War Stimson warned General MacArthur, commander of the United States armed forces in the Far East, stationed in the Philippines, that the negotiations appeared to be terminated "to all practical purposes." But United States Army and Naval Intelligence generally believed that Japan's first move would be directed against the East Indies or possibly Singapore. Army commanders on Oahu at the moment were more concerned about local sabotage; the Navy commanders were more concerned about their expeditions to Wake and Midway—expeditions which, however, had the fortunate result that two carriers and seven heavy cruisers were then in the relative safety of the open sea. No special air reconnaissance, therefore, was put up from Pearl Harbor; there was no change in week-end routines. The personnel manning the newly installed radar apparatus was still in the early stages of training. On the fateful morning the battleships, moored in pairs along Ford Island, were in "Condition 3," with about a quarter of their antiaircraft batteries manned and one-third to one-half of their officers ashore. In Japan, the formal decision to strike was made at an Imperial Conference on December 1.

The arrival of a sizable Japanese fleet of warships and transports in the Gulf of Siam, with obvious designs on Siam or Malaya, evoked a pointed inquiry from Washington concerning Japanese intentions. On December 6, as Japanese troops were pouring into Indo-China, President Roosevelt sent a personal appeal to Emperor Hirohito "to give thought in this definite emergency to ways of dispelling the dark clouds." Almost simultaneously "Magic" had begun to intercept Tokyo's reply to Secretary Hull's counterdemands of November 26. The reply amounted to an uncompromising and truculent rejection. As soon as its tenor and timing could be fully appreciated, General Marshall, Chief of Staff, prepared a hurried "alert" to Pearl Harbor. Static difficulties prevented the use of the Army radio, and the message was ultimately sent by commercial channels. "The Honolulu office . . . confided the telegram to a messenger boy who set off on his bicycle. He was pedaling on his way when the first bombs fell, and not unnaturally spent the next couple of hours in a roadside ditch." [2]

At 6:45 A.M. on December 7, 1941, the American destroyer *Ward*, on routine patrol off Pearl Harbor, detected and sank a Japanese midget submarine. Two privates spotted approaching planes at a distance of 137 miles from their radar station but the lieutenant to whom they reported judged the planes to be a flight of B-17's expected from the mainland and took no action. Thirty minutes later the first wave of 189 Japanese bombers appeared out of the morning haze, sweeping in low from the sea. Their marksmanship on a relatively concentrated target was devastatingly accurate. The battleship *Arizona*, struck in the forward magazine by an armor-piercing bomb, was almost completely destroyed. The *Oklahoma* received repeated torpedo hits, and capsized in shallow water. Six other battleships, three cruisers, and three destroyers were damaged more or less seriously and put out of commission. Heavy destruction was wrought among grounded aircraft, which were prevented from raising an adequate defensive umbrella over the harbor. Total American casualties for both services amounted to 3,435. The attackers lost 29 aircraft, 5 midget submarines, and 1 fleet submarine.

The Japanese attack on Pearl Harbor completed the alignment of the major forces in the spreading global conflict. The United States and Britain declared war on Japan on December 8, 1941. The British Dominions, the Netherlands Government in exile, and Chiang Kai-shek's Nationalist government followed suit. Three days later, in accordance with their Tripartite Pact, Germany and Italy proclaimed a state of war with the United States.

"THE YEAR OF AGONY," 1942

The British had watched the war of giants in Russia with mingled apprehension and amazement — and indeed with gratitude for the relief it brought, not only to their own homeland, but to the entire Near Eastern theater. The Nazi assault on Crete in May 1941, just before the invasion of Russia, though that assault led to a costly British withdrawal, had been the massacre of the German air-borne forces and of several German transport convoys, and it was in fact the last of this type of operation to be attempted by the German High Command. The expected attack on Cyprus, the next step in the Nazi advance to the East, consequently had not materialized. At the end of May 1941, British forces had succeeded in suppressing the pro-Axis coup in Iraq and in occupying all principal strategic points and airfields in the country (see p. 671). Syria, which had remained faithful to Vichy and whose authorities had lately established a suspicious liaison with Iraq, was occupied by British and Free French forces after a short but unexpectedly stiff resistance. During August and September 1941, British and Soviet forces occupied Iran, compelled the abdication of Riza Shah, and began the construction of a new "Burma Road" from the Persian Gulf to the Caspian Sea to be used for the transit of Lend-Lease aid to Russia.

In June 1941, British commands in Egypt had been reshuffled. General Auchinleck, then Commander in Chief in India, had succeeded Wavell, and Wavell had taken Auchinleck's place in India. A Middle East Supply Center (M.E.S.C.), lately set up in Cairo under the auspices of the British Ministry of Shipping, was allocating shipping space, organizing transport services, and encouraging local industries of wartime usefulness. A new force, known as the Eighth Army, was formed in the Western Desert, and in November this force launched an offensive against the combined German-Italian army in Cyrenaica. The Second Libyan Campaign, as it is sometimes called, was a harder fought operation than the first of a year before when O'Connor's fast-moving desert tactics had gained so brilliant a success. The British Eighth Army defeated Rommel's Afrika Korps in fluctuating, erratic battles, relieved Tobruk — which since April 1941 had remained under siege — and drove forward, point by point, to El Agheila on the Gulf of Sidra, the old high-water mark of February 1941.

The entry of the United States into active belligerency in December 1941 had righted the anomalous diplomatic position it had occupied for some time. American potential had been openly mobilized in the cause against Nazism ever since earlier visits of Harry Hopkins to London and Moscow, and of Beaverbrook to Washington. American ideological potential was mobilized as openly by the Roosevelt-Churchill meeting "at sea" on August 14, 1941, and by the subsequent publication of the Atlantic Charter (see Appendix G). Pearl Harbor, for all its shock and surprise, was the climax of a maturing process.

The immediate result of American belligerency was intensive political and military organization. Churchill, accompanied by the British Chiefs of Staff, spent Christmas week of 1941 in Washington, in a series of conferences with President Roosevelt and the American Chiefs of Staff. The visit was without precedent, and it was paramount for the future of Anglo-American co-operation. The total unification of military effort was planned. The Combined Chiefs of Staff, acting under their respective governments, were set up to direct the higher strategy of the war. The all-important decision was made to regard Germany as the prior enemy. Commands in the different theaters of the war were defined and allocated. A legion of co-ordinating boards and committees was set up. During the course of his stay, Churchill addressed a joint meeting of Congress, and he afterward visited Ottawa.

On January 1, 1942, at Washington, representatives of 26 "United Nations" signed a joint Declaration, subscribed to the principles of the Atlantic Charter, and agreed to apply their resources to the common struggle.[3]

All this was on the credit side. A survey of the war's fronts at the beginning of 1942 gave cause for sober optimism. The British Eighth Army was on the offensive in North Africa; Pearl Harbor, though a catastrophic loss, had galvanized the American people into action as no other argument would have done. The United Nations had come into being. Hopes ran high, so much so that a good deal of loose talk about a Second Front in Europe in 1942 — or at least a cross-Channel diversionary assault to relieve the pressure on the Red Army — appeared in the American and British press and more-over — most unfortunately as it afterward turned out — in the Soviet press as well. In actuality, 1942 was a year of almost unrelieved disaster, the veri-table "Year of Agony" of the Second World War. Axis offensives developed in North Africa, in the Pacific, and in Russia like a huge three-taloned claw closing upon the Eurasian hemisphere.

In January and February 1942, Rommel struck at the British Eighth Army at El Agheila in North Africa, advanced precipitately into Cyrenaica, re-captured Derna and Benghazi, and was brought temporarily to a halt forty miles west of Tobruk. The German and Italian forces in North Africa at this time had an evident superiority in numbers and material. Australian units were being withdrawn to the Pacific. Rommel visited Berlin in Febru-ary to luxuriate in the hero worship of his compatriots, and made lavish promises of victory to the Nazi press. Hitler acceded to his request for rein-forcements and, thus strengthened, Rommel prepared to launch the conquest of Egypt. The Luftwaffe intensively raided Malta and, though failing to subdue the heroic little island, temporarily reduced its effectiveness as an aerial and naval base. At the beginning of May it was reported that not more than a dozen serviceable fighter planes were left in Malta, and Allied con-voys proceeding to its relief through the Sicilian Channel were losing half their strength. The German naval command in Italy was pressing energeti-cally for an air-borne assault on Malta. In May, Rommel resumed the offen-sive; in June he took Tobruk, and thence advanced to El Alamein, a scant fifty miles from Alexandria. A grateful Führer created him Field Marshal in anticipation of his entry into Cairo and his subjugation of the Middle East.

Japan's offensive in the Pacific had begun, like an explosive discharge, in all directions. Within four days, from December 7 to 10, 1941, her air forces attacked Pearl Harbor, Singapore, Manila, Midway, Wake, and Guam, and her land forces seized footholds in northeast Malaya, Burma, Hong Kong, and Luzon. On December 10, in the absence of proper fighter pro-tection, Japanese shore-based aircraft sank the British battleship *Prince of Wales* and the battle cruiser *Repulse*, both operating against Japanese transports in the Gulf of Siam. The heavy double defeat which Japan had thus inflicted on the United States at Pearl Harbor and Britain in the Gulf of Siam eliminated naval interference and gave her a clear field in the Pacific. Resistance in Wake, Guam, and Hong Kong was extinguished by Christmas. Midway remained in American possession.

Less than a couple of months sufficed for Japanese land forces, under the command of General Yamashita, to infiltrate through the dense and sup-posedly impenetrable jungles of the Malay Peninsula. At the beginning of February 1942, they stood at the Strait of Johore, a thread of water some five hundred yards wide separating the mainland from the island of Singapore. Under cover of a heavy bombardment by land and air the Strait was crossed.

The defenders were pressed back to southern points on the island, while shattering air raids demoralized the population of the city of Singapore. The great naval base was blown up; stores and equipment were fired. On the evening of February 15, 1942, a weary, disorganized, and dispirited British garrison of 70,000 capitulated to 30,000 Japanese.

The inundation of Burma was no less humiliating and rapid. On December 9, 1941, two days after Pearl Harbor, advanced Japanese units crossed the Burmese frontier at the Isthmus of Kra. In January 1942 one Japanese force seized the town of Moulmein and thence advanced on Rangoon. A second Japanese force debouched into northern Burma from the Shan States and advanced on Lashio at the terminus of the Burma Road. In a disastrous campaign two divisions of British and Indian troops under General Alexander, preceded by a flood of refugees, withdrew by obscure jungle trails into Bengal. A Chinese force under General Stilwell, Chiang Kai-shek's newly appointed American Chief of Staff, struggled into Assam. By mid-May 1942, Burma was substantially a Japanese conquest.

The Japanese assault on the Philippines began on the day of Pearl Harbor. Destructive Japanese air raids on Clark Field near Manila and on the naval base at Cavite deprived General MacArthur, commanding the American-Filipino forces, of the bulk of his air and naval support at the very outset of the campaign. The Japanese expeditionary force under General Homma was thus able to select its points of landing on Luzon and, by the end of December 1941, several columns of invaders were converging on Manila. A skeleton Japanese force entered the city on January 2, 1942, while the main Japanese force pursued the defenders in the direction of the mountainous and well-wooded Bataan Peninsula.

Prepared positions, extending across the narrow neck of the Bataan Peninsula and protected from sea attack by the heavy guns of Corregidor at the entrance to Manila Bay, offered a prospect of holding the Japanese advance. For three months, the American-Filipino lines under General MacArthur stood firm against every tactical operation Japanese military ingenuity could devise — frontal attack, flank attack, sea-borne attack, and infiltration. Unrelenting bombardment, combined with the ravages of malaria, sapped the physical strength, if not the morale, of the garrison. Efforts to send reinforcements from Australia were initiated in January, but only one vessel in three reached its destination. On March 17, MacArthur relinquished his command in Bataan, on instructions from President Roosevelt, to assume command of new American concentrations to be built up in Australia, and left General Wainright to conduct the closing phases of the gallant defense. General Yamashita, fresh from his victory at Singapore, succeeding the now somewhat discomfited Homma, took Bataan at last on April 9 and Corregidor on May 6, 1942. Resistance continued mainly from Philippine guerrillas, at scattered points on the mainland, and provided the Japanese with opportunities for demonstrating their methods of "pacification."

The islands of the Netherlands East Indies fell to enemy offensives of a type that were now becoming so tragically familiar. Between January and March 1942, Sumatra, Borneo, the Celebes, Java, Bali, Timor, and the northern parts of New Guinea were overrun in rapid succession. On February 27, in the Java Sea, an attempt by a combined British, Australian, Dutch, and American fleet to intercept a superior Japanese force escorting a convoy was repulsed with the loss of five cruisers and seven destroyers. Japanese losses in the engagement and in the course of this part of the campaign are not known, but were probably considerable. A systematic "scorched-earth" policy and the destruction of oil fields robbed the conqueror of immediate material gain from his conquests, but the consolation was negative and mortifying. General ter Poorten, the Dutch Commander in Chief, capitulated with his army at Bandung on March 8.

The fall of Malaya, Burma, the Philippines, and the Netherlands East Indies brought the all-conquering Japanese armies into perilous proximity to Australia and India. The Andaman Islands in the Indian Ocean were already in Japanese hands. Northern Australia and Ceylon felt the spite of Japanese air raids. Far across the Pacific, in the Aleutian Islands, Attu and Kiska were occupied by small Japanese forces. An Anglo–South African seizure of Madagascar from Vichy forces — in the first sea-borne "invasion" of the war to be attempted on the Allied side — only barely anticipated a Japanese drive across the southern chord of the Indian Ocean. No one could yet say whether this phenomenal expansion of Japanese power had reached its limit or was still in the full momentum of its rage and energy.

In Britain, meanwhile, the mood was dismayed and critical. Yet public opinion, in its illogic, seemed far less galled by the series of disasters in the East than by an incident nearer home. On the night of February 11, 1942, the German battleships *Scharnhorst* and *Gneisenau*, lying for weeks at Brest under constant R.A.F. attack, slipped out of harbor, up the Channel and through the Strait of Dover, under attack from shore-based torpedo-carrying aircraft on the way and, though damaged by mines, succeeded in escaping to home ports in Germany.

In March 1942 the British Government, deeply concerned over the worsening political situation in India, sent Sir Stafford Cripps to Delhi as bearer of an "offer" to the Indian leaders. Since the start of the war the Indian Army and Indian industry had been taking their full part, but the old internal divisions and the old mistrust of British intentions in India had been intensified rather than quieted by the imminence of the Japanese invasion. Cripps was authorized to offer the creation, as soon as possible after the war, of a self-governing "Indian Union" with Dominion status and with a constitution of its own making — and with the acknowledged right, if it so desired, to secede from the British Commonwealth. Meanwhile, however, the defense of India must remain the responsibility of the existing British Government. After exhaustive discussions, the offer was rejected by Nehru and the Indian National Congress, mainly on the ground that its solicitude for the Indian minorities would involve some sort of political partition in India; but it was, for the same reason, more favorably received at first by Jinnah and the Moslem League. The Congress categorically demanded the independence of India, not after the war, but "here and now." The offer therefore signally failed to unite and mobilize Indian political opinion against Japan. Undeniably it failed because it did not meet the defeatism and disillusion of the

Indian leaders. The offer was, as Gandhi is reported to have said, a "post-dated check on a bank that was obviously crashing."

The over-all war situation was so serious that, on April 23, 1942, Churchill called for a secret session of the House of Commons. "No one will accuse me," he said, "of glozing over the ugly realities . . ." He spoke of the fall of Singapore and of the fighting then in progress in Burma and the Bay of Bengal, in Libya, and round Malta. He spoke of the possible Japanese invasions of India and Australia. He spoke of naval losses, including the *Prince of Wales* and *Repulse*, losses totaling a third of the British strength in capital ships at a time when Pearl Harbor had crippled the United States Pacific Fleet. He spoke of the destruction of merchant shipping in the Atlantic. And against all this he could show little but the shipbuilding and aircraft-building programs in Britain and the United States, the augmentation of British bomber attacks on German centers of production — and "the firmness of spirit, sense of proportion, steadfastness of purpose which will now once again carry great peoples and a greater cause to a victorious deliverance."

In May and June 1942, American naval victories in the Pacific, the two battles of the Coral Sea and of Midway, indicated a strong and welcome recovery in one theater of the war at least (see p. 745). In that June a Roosevelt-Churchill meeting took place in Washington and was shortly followed by a Chiefs of Staff meeting in London. It was decided that a Second Front in Europe could not be put into effect "before late 1943 at the earliest. . . . and might be postponed until the spring of 1944" and that the most likely area for Anglo-American operations in the near future would be North Africa. In August, a Churchill-Stalin meeting took place in Moscow, and it fell to Churchill to break the news to his Russian ally that the Second Front in Europe, so urgently pleaded, was not yet to be.

Early in May 1942, as a preface to the German summer operations in Russia, an army under Manstein attacked the Soviet naval base and fortress of Sevastopol and took it after a tremendous siege of seven weeks. In June, Bock, in command of an army group of eight armies in the Ukraine, launched a general offensive. The rapid and sustained German advance of 1941 was momentarily resumed. Once more the Nazi press and radio announced the imminent destruction of the Red Army and the collapse of the Soviet Union. Voroshilovgrad, Rostov, Bataisk, Maikop, and Novorossiisk had all fallen by September; the German Sixth Army had reached the Volga and was threatening Stalingrad; the First Panzer Army, under the veteran tank general, Kleist, was deep in the open country north of the Caucasus. Vital supply routes from Iran by way of Baku and Astrakhan were cut. The German High Command was credited with planning a vast wheeling maneuver up the Volga toward Kuibyshev and Kazan, a maneuver worthy of Schlieffen, which would have enveloped the central Moscow area and rolled up the entire Eastern front.

But the German maneuver was brought to a standstill at Stalingrad. The fortunes of that great battle we defer to a later chapter.

42 THE HOME FRONT

GERMANY

It is proper to begin this chapter with Germany, as German belligerency was, so to speak, the archetype and example of all the others. Germany saw the ultimate evolution of that total war once predicted by Clausewitz, brought into being by Ludendorff, and elevated into a positive doctrine by Hitler. Germany went to war in 1939 with the highest degree of technical preparation. Her leaders knew exactly the kind of war they wanted to fight, and they had forged exactly the kind of weapons with which to fight it. If nothing else, the German war plan of 1939 represents a gigantic intellectual achievement.

Years of propaganda and coercion had welded the German people into a unanimous, cohesive instrument. All likely classes and parties of dissent had been eliminated. This time there would be no "stab in the back." Nonetheless, it was a serious shock to the Nazi leaders that the war, when it came, the great day for which they had labored so incessantly, was so indifferently received by the German people at large. Most of the potential rejoicers, it is true, had already been called to the colors, and only a small professionally exuberant minority of party members was left. But, at the crucial test of war, Nazi mysticism conspicuously failed to inspire the spontaneous single-minded ecstasy of 1914. The popular mood in 1939 was rather of a sullen, nameless dread of the actualities of war. It was as if the German people, for the first time, had awakened to the full realization of the consequences of the regime they had hitherto so heedlessly and so vociferously supported.

The victories in Poland and France brought, so far as we can judge, reactions of relief, pride, hopes of an early peace, but no wild elation, no public rejoicing. Casualties in the fighting had been extraordinarily light. Living conditions in Germany meanwhile had not deteriorated. The dreaded bomber war had taken shape at first only in the very scattered and rather comical Allied leaflet raids. The initial bombing by the Royal Air Force — notably the bombing of Berlin on August 25, 1940 — had been a nasty shock and had cast some reflection on Göring's boastful utterances regarding the inviolable defenses of the Reich, but in honesty it must be said that it had not been very effective. The failure of the Battle of Britain had been easy for propaganda to minimize. The legend of the Führer's infallibility emerged unscathed. They might not rejoice; but the German people in 1940 could still give grateful credit for their many triumphs to the farseeing and invincible genius of Adolf Hitler.

During the early months of 1941, the constant theme of Nazi propaganda was Germany's indissoluble friendship with the Soviet Union. The very force and reiteration of these protestations should perhaps have been their own warning. The invasion of Russia therefore took the German people by surprise. The Moscow Pact in 1939 had been one *volte-face;* and this was another, for all that it meant a resumption of the former familiar anti-Communist attitude. However, it was not doubted that the Russian campaign would repeat the pattern of the French, if indeed on a wider scale, with heavier casualties, and over a longer period of time. Every military authority in Europe in fact had underestimated the Soviet Union. The British and French Allies had lightheartedly run the risk of involvement in war with the Soviet Union over Finland, and there are signs that Hitler did not originally deploy his full resources on the Eastern front, but was already directing that several of his war factories should be converted to the production of consumer goods for the benefit of a brave and deserving civilian population. "The brittle state edifice" in Russia, if attacked, would surely fall sooner than the Third Republic of France, that once-reputed first-class Power and custodian in chief of the military art. The individual German soldier went into battle in 1941 long nourished on the belief that the Red Army, lately purged of its top-ranking officers, was riddled with treachery and that its rank and file were a mob of subhuman monsters incapable of discipline and ignorant of modern arms.

Triumphant communiqués from the Eastern front reported, as if by routine, "the mightiest victories in the history of the world." "The enemy is already broken," cried Hitler in a speech in October 3, 1941, "and will never rise again." All that remained for the German Army to do in Russia, it seemed, was a police operation against disorganized enemy units which, in their perversity, refused to surrender. Yet, instead of victory and peace before Christmas, the German people found themselves committed to a total war of indefinite duration and unlimited sacrifice, a war for which they were psychologically unprepared and for which their leadership and military dispositions were entirely inadequate. At the end of 1941, the German Army in Russia was strewn out across vast, amorphous territories, which had been deliberately "scorched," with its communications stretched to the limit, harried by guerrillas, and digging in for a winter which happened to be the worst in living memory.

German casualties in Russia, it was believed in Germany, were far higher than the High Command's communiqués or Hitler's speeches vouchsafed. An average check of any family or neighborhood showed that often as much as 20 per cent of the men who were known to be on the Eastern front had fallen. The hasty levy of warm clothing, made throughout Germany shortly after Christmas 1941 — "Goebbels' jumble-sale" as the British newspapers called it — indicated that all was not well. The German home front that winter was full of harrowing rumors, and it was commonly whispered that more German soldiers in Russia were dying from exposure and frostbite than from enemy action.

The upshot was intensified preparation for 1942. There occurred in Germany a production crisis on a par with that of 1916 (see p. 53) . For the first time in the war, despite her conquests, Germany began to feel the pinch of shortage. Supplies of coal and oil, it was found, had been allowed to decline. The German coal mines in 1941 produced 15 per cent, and some even 25 per cent, less than in 1940. But the demand for coal had risen steeply, notably on account of the lengthened railroad distances on the Eastern front. The railroads were unequal to the emergency calls now made upon them. For some years past, the new motor roads, the *Autobahnen,* and the new commercial airlines had been an attractive diversion of public interest, and the railroads were discovered to be suffering from serious neglect. There was less rolling stock in Germany in 1942 than in 1914. All the privations inflicted by the Nazis on the German people since 1933 had had a cumulative effect which, by some diabolic fate, suddenly reached a peak in the winter of 1941–42, and it was a winter whose exceptional severities we have already mentioned. Plant and machinery had deteriorated from the wear and tear of eight years of intensive use. Maintenance and replacements had always been shelved in the supreme calculation on a successful blitzkrieg.

In January 1942, a national emergency program, somewhat recalling the Hindenburg Program of 1916, was initiated (see p. 53). Ley threw in the support of the Nazi Labor Front with the slogan, "Two must do the work of three." Industries not considered important for war purposes were "silenced"; civilian passenger traffic was drastically cut; automobiles began to appear ingeniously propelled by charcoal gas. But it was soon evident that exceptional methods would be in order, and the driving power would have to be provided by the Nazi party itself. In February 1942, Fritz Todt, then Minister of Armaments, was killed in an air crash, and he was succeeded by Hitler's architect, Albert Speer.

Speer's appointment in the field of home economy had much the same effect as Ludendorff's in 1916 (see p. 53). Speer realized at once that the crisis at bottom was a labor crisis, and his first step was to demand of Hitler, and obtain, unconditional priority for himself over all sources of civilian labor, German and non-German. His aide was the then relatively unknown Fritz Sauckel, former Gauleiter of Thuringia, whom Hitler now appointed Plenipotentiary for Labor Allocation (*Arbeitseinsatz*). A series of almost panic labor decrees followed and, as we shall describe in the next chapter, forced deportation of foreign workers was started in the occupied territories. The Speer-Sauckel combination formed an absolute economic dictatorship over all Nazi Europe.

The food situation took a sudden change for the worse in the winter of 1941–42. That ever ominous phenomenon, the food line, appeared in the streets. We need not particularize the story of shortages, rising prices, secret hoarding, ersatz and adulteration, and ever widening controls. It is a familiar story, and it was soon being repeated for other commodities besides food — clothing, footwear, and household articles. But the controls were largely party-managed, and the average gauleiter was never the most efficient or the most honest of administrators. To the absolute shortages therefore was now added an element from which the Germany of 1914–18 had been entirely free — a corrupt officialdom. And all this occurred at the moment when fresh batches of workers, including agricultural workers, were being called to the colors and when Germany's allies in the Mediterranean and Balkans were crying out for additional supplies. The German conquests, however much they might add to the mineral and man-power resources of Greater Germany, in the matter of food were largely a liability. Slovakia, Rumania, Denmark, and Normandy, for example, yielded their quota of produce, but they were minor items in the balance sheet. Nothing was available from that promised El Dorado of plenty, the Ukraine, systematically "scorched" by the retreating Red Army.

During 1942, the Nazi authorities tried a variety of experiments to coax higher production out of the German workers, "those faithful and honest comrades on the home front." Medals were given "for outstanding achievements." Existing wage controls prevented any general interference with the basic pay envelope, but piecework rates, overtime rates, and Sunday work were generously introduced. Often extra pay took the far more acceptable form of food. Meanwhile the Gestapo hung about the wings and contributed its own form of encouragement in the arrest and incarceration of grumblers, loafers, and other "promoters of disturbance." Hitler, in a speech in April 1942, intimated clearly enough that terrorism would be an incentive and that he would not hesitate, however reluctantly, to have recourse to it. "One thing I expect," he said, "is that the nation gives me the power to intervene immediately and to act on my own initiative as circumstances demand, when the fate of the nation is at stake." During the summer of 1942 the press constantly featured court proceedings and heavy sentences against workers.

Meanwhile the general tone of Nazi propaganda was changing. Hitler, of course, had promised that the summer campaign of 1942 in Russia would bring the victory denied in 1941. The winter of 1941–42 had been "a hard test, a bitter trial." "Worse things cannot and will not happen again. . . . That we overcame that winter is proof that Providence is well pleased with the German people." But gone was the old exultant assurance. Ultimate peace would now be reached by no quick and simple road. The categoric alternative was no longer between war and peace, but between survival and annihilation. Despite "monster successes" in Russia, the global war was still spreading, and events seemed to have passed beyond human control. "We are being destroyed by our victories (*Wir siegen uns zu Tode*)." By 1942 the United States, the decisive victor of 1918, had once again been added to the foes of the Fatherland. Japan, by compensation, was a distant and incalculable ally. Germany herself had become one element in a widening conflict, in which she no longer held the initiative or was even the only focal point.

Then, at the end of 1942, came the Battle of Stalingrad. An irresistible whispering campaign, by a sort of mass telepathy, had already prepared the German people for the great tragedy before the German High Command published its official admission. The fateful communiqué was broadcast at last to the accompaniment of solemn strains from Wagner's *Götterdämmerung*. A three-day public mourning was proclaimed for the 350,000 heroes of the Sixth Army who, "obedient to the Führer's command," had defended themselves to the last man. The Führer himself, who had normally used every major occasion of the war to deliver a public exposition, was strangely silent. Goebbels was his chief spokesman, and Goebbels, from this moment onward, comes forward undeniably as the most courageous and resourceful of the Nazi leaders. Rumor had it that the Führer had suffered a nervous breakdown. When at last he did appear, on March 21, 1943, his speech lasted only a few minutes, and his voice sounded tired and monotonous. And, by that March, Stalingrad was not the only defeat to be explained away. The fighting in North Africa could hardly be dismissed as "an insignificant reverse" at "the periphery of events."

On January 27, 1943, after the Battle of Stalingrad, Sauckel decreed the total mobilization of the home front. Compulsory labor was instituted for men from 16 to 65 years and for women from 17 to 45. Small shops and industries were merged, and employees thereby released were drafted into the army or into munition work. Some 6,000,000 children were mobilized for industry and agriculture. Prisons and concentration camps were converted into "production workshops."

We have no comprehensive or unbiased figures of German production, and we cannot say how successful in fact all these measures were. And, by 1942, what Germany was gaining by her successive mobilizations she was beginning to lose to Allied air attack. Probably Sauckel's mobilization of January 1943 had raised another 2,500,000 native German workers. But we have the impression that thereafter German labor reached the point of diminishing returns. Every new decree, every new rationalization or reorganization seemed to result in an indirect, and often quite unforeseen, curtailment of net performance. The incessant extension of regulations multiplied administrative personnel and thus aggravated the very shortage it was intended to mitigate. Factories were infested with efficiency experts and demonstrators, controllers and informers, who might have been put to better use at the benches themselves. It was difficult for an industry to "digest" unskilled or reluctant workers and, even after time and expense had been given to their training, their efficiency was limited. Long hours offered no solution. Modern industrial medicine and psychology have their doubts as to the value of a man compelled to work sometimes 80 and even 90 hours a week. Living conditions meanwhile were not exactly improving. The housing shortage, which had been already serious in 1939, was now intensified by bomb damage. The German people as a whole in 1942–43 had long since reached the limit of regimentation and, in their intense weariness, could respond no more to the tempting or threatening exhortations made to them.

Of organized resistance in Germany in the war years there was little or none. Articles and books, lately published, have sought to portray a strong and widely ramifying underground anti-Nazi movement. But, if any such "Other Germany" existed, it was powerless and ineffective. The concentration camp had long since taken care of opposition leaders and suspects. What resistance there was arose from sudden fits of desperation and was therefore unorganized and confined to individuals — here and there a surviving Social Democrat or Communist, a student or professor, a priest or pastor. Resistance of this sort was a cruel story of courage wasted. Politically, it was less than useless. From time to time there was an epidemic of chain letters or of chalking up of anti-Nazi signs and slogans, and there was a certain amount of deliberate popular grumbling, "going slow," spreading the latest obscene anecdote or rhyme about the Nazi leaders, listening to foreign broadcasts, and helping Allied prisoners of war or Gestapo victims. These manifestations increased with the reverses in Russia and the mass importation of foreign workers.

There was more than one attempt on Hitler's life. But assassination by itself would have left the political consequences unconsidered. An organized putsch, with a planned change of government, alone could have made the necessary impression on the course of events. From time to time it seemed that a group of generals might lead such a putsch. Hitler had conducted a long struggle with the General Staff ever since his rise to power. Pliant tools, like Keitel and Jodl, were in command. It was only in 1942 that serious disaffection once more appeared at high army levels. There was then a busy, conspiratorial group in the *Abwehr*, the Counterespionage Service. After Stalingrad, Field Marshal von Paulus, commander of the Sixth Army, broadcast to Germany from his captivity in Russia instigating revolt. During the retirement on the Eastern front in 1943, there were cases of officers refusing to execute suicidal orders "to hold on to the last man." The fall of Mussolini in Italy in 1943 and the installation of a government under Marshal Badoglio made the obvious model for a like-minded incident in Germany. But likely generals, such as there were, tended to wait upon events. They could hardly strike at times when Hitler was riding upon success, and to strike when his fortunes were in reverse looked like treachery to the Reich. The war would not stand still in order to provide a conspiratorial group with just the most suitable interval for taking action. Moreover, every German had sworn a personal oath to his Führer, and revolt involved a wrench to conscience which apparently the German mind could not take without flinching. Many essential recruits to a military putsch were lost from this single obstacle. The almost insuperable sanctity of the soldier's oath was indeed curious among a people for whom other forms of good faith were so lightly held.

In the end, the one and only attempted military putsch which had an authentic political organization behind it was a failure and, in any case, it came too late.[1] After January 1943, the Allies were committed to their formula of "unconditional surrender" and would hardly have consented to negotiate with any German government of whatever political coloration which had made itself successor to the Nazi rule. On July 20, 1944, after elaborate preparations extending over a year, a member of this adventurous band planted a bomb at Hitler's headquarters on the Eastern front. The bomb exploded, but Hitler only sustained minor wounds and burns. The same night he was fit enough to broadcast to the German people assuring them of his miraculous escape from a plot laid by "an extremely small clique of ambitious, conscienceless, criminal and stupid officers, who are now being mercilessly exterminated." Subsequently Goerdeler, former Mayor of Leipzig, Field Marshal von Witzleben, two generals, and four other officers were tried for their part in the putsch and hanged. Probably there were over three hundred executions in all, and many others variously implicated, such as Generals Beck, Stuelpnagel,[2] and Rommel, committed suicide or were quietly put to death (see p. 770).

But a putsch in 1944 was too late. By that date it was already a sign of defeat. The once invincible German Army was retreating on all fronts, and the Allies were forming their own views as to the best ways and means of ending the war. Allied bombing, day and night, was reducing the cities of Germany to smoking rubble. Nazi leadership itself was undergoing change. Hitler was apt to disappear into long silences. Göring was sunk in dissipation and obscurity. More and more actual power was passing into the hands of Himmler, Goebbels, and the party secretary, Bormann. Never indeed were the criminal cynicism and irresponsibility of Nazi leadership so manifest as with the growing imminence of military collapse. Nazi propaganda, at the last — so far had the situation deteriorated — was trying to whip up the German people to the extremity of despair by warning them that, if they lost the war, they would themselves be called to account by a revengeful enemy for the barbarities that Nazism had committed in their name.

"I am a profoundly religious man," said Hitler in a speech in 1943. "I believe that Providence, having designed a man for great purposes, does not break that man before he has achieved them. But, if the German people should fail under the present test, I would not shed a single tear for them; for then they would deserve their fate."

BRITAIN

Already before the outbreak of the war preparations for the mobilization of man power in Britain were well advanced. A voluntary National Service campaign for the recruitment of men and women for the forces, civil defense, and industry had been launched in November 1938 shortly after the Munich crisis. The Military Training Act followed in May 1939. Under further enactments men eligible for military service were distinguished from men in "reserved" occupations whom it was expected that a highly mechanized war would require to be kept at their benches and desks. Strong Labor elements in the country and in Parliament fought against conscription and the direction of labor, but the government, it was evident, preferred the policy of compulsion to the policy of voluntary enlistment and, generally speaking, the great mass of the people took the view of the government. Compulsion was better for efficiency and better for morale. Compulsion abbreviated the long, tortuous, and wasteful experimentation of the First World War and ensured from the start that the burdens and sacrifices would be equitably spread over the whole community and not borne primarily by its more public-spirited and patriotic citizens.

Enactments on September 3, 1939 and subsequently, recalling "DORA" of 1914 (see p. 38), put the country on a war footing. On May 22, 1940, at the height of the fighting in France, an Emergency Powers Bill was introduced to enable the government to issue regulations "requiring persons to place themselves, their services, and their property at the disposal of His Majesty,

as may appear to him to be necessary . . . for the defense of the Realm . . ."
The bill was presented to Parliament by Chamberlain and Attlee and was
passed unanimously by the Commons and Lords through all its stages in a
single afternoon. "Such was the tempo of the hour." One regulation, issued
under the authority of the act and simultaneously with it, was the famous
Regulation 58A, which empowered the Ministry of Labor to "direct" any
person to perform any service, "which that person is, in the opinion of the
Minister, capable of performing." In December 1941, an act was passed
conscripting women. At the end of 1943, young men were compulsorily
directed to coal mining after an intensive publicity campaign, including
broadcasts to schools, had failed to produce the recruitment required. The
result of this legislative series was the effective levy of a population of un-
military traditions, normally abhorrent of dictatorial methods.

The broad outlines of the allocation of man power were determined by
the War Cabinet. Man-power surveys and budgets were prepared periodically by the Ministry of Labor in collaboration with other government departments concerned. In September 1943, at the peak of the national mobilization, of 15,920,000 men of working age in Britain, 15,000,000 were in the
forces, civil defense, or industry, the balance being mainly students, invalids,
or men otherwise unfit; and of 16,020,000 women of working age, 7,250,000
were in the forces, civil defense, or industry. Of these figures, 5,000,000 men
and 600,000 women were in the forces or in full-time civil defense. Each of
the three fighting services had its auxiliary women's service — the Women's
Royal Naval Service (WRNS), the Auxiliary Territorial Service (ATS),
and the Women's Auxiliary Air Force (WAAF). Further enactments extended conscription to British subjects, men and women, residing in foreign
countries and to Allied nationals in Britain. Friendly aliens and refugees
were employed to the fullest advantage. Finally some 250,000 German and
Italian prisoners of war were put mainly to heavy unskilled work in agriculture and forestry.

All the controls of the First World War went into force — control of prices,
foreign exchange, shipping. New business could not be registered without
special permit. Gasoline for private cars was repeatedly cut, till it was only
available for doctors, district nurses, and other essential users. Rationing of
meat and butter was introduced in December 1939 and was gradually extended to other foods. Bread was not rationed but was mixed with "rough-
age," and white flour was prohibited. The amount and nutritive value of the
nation's larder declined in the course of the war, but public health was good,
despite additional nervous strains, and actual cases of malnutrition were far
fewer than in the bad old days of unemployment in the thirties. There was a
marked rise in the production of milk — itself a tribute to British wartime
dairying — the increase being mainly allocated to children and nursing
mothers. Subsequently rationing of soap, clothing, and footwear was introduced. Manufacturers produced standardized "utility" clothing, footwear,
and household articles, government-controlled and government-subsidized.
Luxuries in general disappeared. Building, except for bomb-damage repair
and wartime construction, stopped altogether. But, despite all these short-

ages and restrictions, it can be said that Britain's wartime consumer market worked with fair efficiency and sufficiency and with an almost total absence of public discontent or of black marketing.

The Battle of the Land represented one of the greatest British civilian triumphs of the war and the greatest single permanent contribution to the country's long-term economy. The land, neglected after a century of industrial and commercial expansion, was suddenly restored to a place of honor, and it was perhaps a matter of grateful surprise for the average Briton to learn that his agriculture, even in 1939, still employed more labor than any other of his occupations and to learn also that, in the midst of a world which was steadily exhausting its soil fertility, the arable acreage of his little island was more productive than that of any other country.[3] During the war years land brought under the plow increased from 12,900,000 to 19,400,000 acres, and principal crops harvested were sometimes doubled. By the end of the war two-thirds of the food consumed was being produced in the country. And these quantities were achieved at a time when 100,000 regular male agricultural workers were serving with the forces and were only partially, if proudly, replaced by the Women's Land Army. Visitors who remembered "the green desert" that was rural England in 1939 hardly recognized the landscape "turned brown-side up," burgeoning with new life and comeliness, which they saw three and four years afterward. As in the First World War urban open spaces and even bombed sites between buildings were converted into vegetable gardens and, at the height of the "Dig for Victory" campaign, some million and a half city and suburban allotments were being tended by private gardeners in their off hours from daily work.

The full story of British industry in the Second World War cannot yet be told. The information necessary, both for the wartime years and for the antecedent peacetime rearmament, has not been published.[4] However, the following partial figures of production, from September 1939 up to the invasion of France in June 1944, give some indication of the magnitude of the industrial effort: nearly 2,000,000 tons of naval vessels and 4,700,000 tons of merchant vessels, not including repair work on vessels damaged by enemy action; 35,000 pieces of field artillery and antiaircraft artillery; 3,700,000 machine guns and submachine guns; 2,000,000 rifles; 25,000 tanks; nearly 1,000,000 wheeled vehicles; and over 100,000 aircraft of all types. And this program was being carried out under conditions of blackout, constant air-raid interruption, difficult transportation, damaged and crowded housing, and other wartime discomforts and impediments.

Official and voluntary organizations made great exertions to sustain civilian welfare and morale. Nothing was forgotten which could in any way relieve the dangers, anxieties, and indescribable drabness of the war. Canteens, clubs, and hostels were opened for munition workers and civil-defense workers. Maternity homes, rest centers, nurseries, and day nurseries were provided for the women and children. The Red Cross, the Y.M.C.A., the Y.W.C.A., the Society of Friends, the Salvation Army, and other bodies labored devotedly in their several fields. The C.E.M.A. (Council for the Encouragement of Music and the Arts), initiated by the Pilgrim Trust and partly financed by American well-wishers, mobilized theatrical and artistic talent for concerts, plays, ballet, lectures, and art exhibitions throughout the country. In all sorts of unexpected and lesser directions Britain's "psychological war" was being carried on. Public authorities kept open their parks and gardens with grass trimmed and flower beds in bloom. Women's cosmetics and hairdressing, far from disappearing with other dispensable luxuries, were officially encouraged. The promoters of this great campaign were largely unadvertised and unacknowledged, but their efforts were no small part of the war on the home front.

The total monetary costs of the war for Britain have been estimated at $120,000,000,000. Taxation of all kinds was unprecedentedly heavy. Income tax was sharply graduated and rose to 50 per cent on incomes above $10,000 and to 75 per cent on incomes above $50,000 per annum. A purchase tax was imposed on a wide range of consumer goods often up to a third or more of their wholesale value. The excess-profits tax was 100 per cent. The national debt rose to £22,000,000,000 ($90,000,000,000), or nearly $2,000 per capita.

Winston Churchill became Prime Minister and Minister of Defense at the head of an all-party National Coalition on May 10, 1940, the day of the German invasion of Holland and Belgium. He instantly stepped into a position of exceptional personal power. "I felt as if I were walking with Destiny," he writes, "and that all my past life had been but a preparation for this hour and for this trial. Eleven years in the political wilderness had freed me from ordinary party antagonisms. My warnings over the last six years had been so numerous, so detailed, and were now so terribly vindicated, that no one could gainsay me. I could not be reproached either for making the war or with a want of preparation for it. I thought I knew a good deal about it all, and I was sure I should not fail." [5]

Coalition governments have their own peculiar difficulties, not least because they are usually formed in moments of extreme emergency. There are more candidates than offices, and good men of national or party eminence have to be satisfied with lesser posts or left out altogether. The more ardent and censorious opinion in the country had hoped for a "purge" of "the guilty men," notably the appeasers of the Munich era. But Churchill was adamant against disruptive proscriptions at a time when the country's prior need was unity and comradeship. "If the present tries to sit in judgment on the past," he said, "it will lose the future." Churchill created a War Cabinet consisting of himself, Halifax, Chamberlain, and two Labor men, Attlee and Greenwood. It was remodeled from time to time. Chamberlain resigned in October 1940, on grounds of ill-health, and died a month later; he was succeeded by Anderson, the Home Secretary. Halifax went to the United States as British ambassador in December 1940 and was succeeded, both in the War Cabinet and as Foreign Secretary, by Eden. Beaverbrook, Kingsley Wood, Bevin, Oliver Lyttelton, Cripps, Casey, and Woolton served for different periods in different capacities. Sir Edward Bridges was Secretary to the War Cabinet and General Ismay Deputy-Secretary (Military).

The Chiefs of Staff Committee consisted of the three service chiefs: Admiral Sir Dudley Pound was First Sea Lord till his death in October 1943, when he was succeeded by Admiral Sir Andrew Cunningham; General Sir

John Dill was C.I.G.S. (Chief of the Imperial General Staff) till his transfer to the United States in December 1941 to become British representative on the Anglo-American Combined Chiefs of Staff, when he was succeeded by General Sir Alan Brooke; Air Marshal Sir Cyril Newall was Chief of Air Staff till his appointment as Governor General of New Zealand in September 1940, when he was succeeded by Air Marshal Sir Charles Portal (see Glossary).

Upon the War Cabinet and the Chiefs of Staff Committee — two small bands of men, seldom numbering more than ten all told, meeting together periodically, at first daily — devolved every major political and strategic decision during five tremendous years. Churchill, as Prime Minister and Minister of Defense, stood as liaison between them. There was none of the friction between statesmen and soldiers, between the "Frocks" and the "Brass Hats," of the First World War. "In spite of the turbulence of events and the many disasters we had to endure," writes Churchill, "the machinery worked almost automatically, and one lived in a stream of coherent thought capable of being translated with great rapidity into executive action." [6]

Churchill's National Coalition did not survive the defeat of Germany in 1945. However much the British people might idolize him as a war leader, they still reserved their doubts of his qualities as the possible Prime Minister of their first peacetime government and, as the war neared its end, it was becoming clear that, in all the problems of reconstruction, the two major political parties would take up very divergent attitudes. The Conservatives looked to a return to private enterprise, and Labor to nationalization and "planning," and any preparations therefore, for postwar decontrols, reconversion of industry, and housing for example, were unrealistic till the nation's basic political choice could be settled. Already early in 1944, before the Normandy landing, the government had been defeated in Parliament over an item in the Education Bill then being debated.

By 1945 the life of the existing Parliament had long exceeded its statutory limit. Churchill himself was said to be in favor of an early resumption of party politics. A rash electioneering broadcast which he gave created the most unfortunate impression that he was trying to capitalize on his wartime record. Rumor had it that Lord Beaverbrook, the newspaper baron, was now one of his closest advisers and, in the opinion of many, a Churchill-Beaverbrook alliance would have been an even more monstrous incubus than the Lloyd George-Northcliffe alliance of evil memory in 1918–19. The Labor Party Conference, meeting in Blackpool in May, just after the German surrender, pledged its full support in the war against Japan but was almost unanimous against a continuance of the Coalition. On May 23, 1945, Churchill and his government resigned.

Churchill formed an all-party "Caretaker Government" to tide over the interval till the general election. That election was fought in July, while the Potsdam Conference was in session. The rival party manifestoes all stressed domestic issues. To give time for the men in the forces to poll their votes, the results of the election were not announced till July 26. Churchill and the Conservative party were heavily defeated. The forces' vote, it was commonly believed, was even more left-wing than the civilian. On July 27, 1945, Attlee formed an all-Labor government. Churchill has since observed, in irony but without rancor, that he exercised the chief power in the state for five years and three months of world war, "at the end of which time, all our enemies having surrendered unconditionally or being about to do so, I was immediately dismissed by the British electorate from all further conduct of their affairs." [5]

THE UNITED STATES

On the evening of September 3, 1939, President Roosevelt gave a radio address "to the whole of America." The nation, he said, would remain a neutral nation, but he did not ask, as President Wilson had asked on a similar occasion twenty-five years before, that every American would remain neutral in thought as well. "Even a neutral cannot be asked to close his mind or his conscience." "I hope the United States will keep out of this war. . . . As long as it remains within my power to prevent it, there will be no blackout of peace in the United States." On September 5, he formally proclaimed the neutrality of the United States and invoked the Neutrality Act of 1937 with its embargo on the shipment of arms to belligerents (see p. 599).

But on September 21, 1939, at a special session of Congress, the President called for a repeal of the embargo. The engulfment of Poland by Germany and the Soviet Union had exerted its effect on Congressional and public opinion alike. However anxious the nation in general might be to avoid involvement in the war, the majority was almost equally intent on providing an indeterminate degree of assistance to the European democracies. In November 1939, Congress accordingly passed a revised Neutrality Act, prohibiting loans to belligerents, travel on belligerent vessels, and the arming of American merchantmen, and prohibiting American citizens, ships, and planes from entering a combat zone covering the North Sea and eastern Atlantic. In return for these considerable reaffirmations of neutrality, the isolationist bloc in Congress agreed to the reincorporation of the "cash-and-carry" principle in the new act and to the raising of the arms embargo so that belligerents might now purchase arms in the United States on the same principle (see p. 648).

It was to be expected that public interest and anxiety should subside during the months of the "phony war." Early in 1940, Sumner Welles, Under Secretary of State, went on a tour of Europe reminiscent of Colonel House's tour in 1915 (see p. 73), with a general commission to study the prospects of peace. The uselessness of his excursion was shortly to be seen in April, when Germany invaded Denmark and Norway. President Roosevelt denounced this latest "unlawful exercise of force." He exerted himself, in personal appeals to Mussolini, to keep Italy out of the war. On June 10, he responded to Italy's intervention with his address at the University of Virginia at Charlottesville (see p. 656). He took into his cabinet two Republicans, both firm advocates of increased aid to Britain, Henry L. Stimson, whom he made Secretary of War, and Frank Knox, whom he made Secretary of the Navy. Some 500,000 Enfield rifles, 80,000 machine guns, and 900 .75-mm. guns from old stocks of the First World War were sold and shipped to Britain in time to meet the threatened German invasion. In July 1940, Congress hurried through an additional armament appropriation of $5,000,-000,000 to be devoted in large part to a 70 per cent increase in naval tonnage. In September, Congress passed the Selective Service Act. In the same month, by means of the "Destroyers for Bases Deal," the United States placed 50 of its overage destroyers at the disposal of Britain in return for the gift or lease of a string of bases stretching from Newfoundland to British Guiana.

The American people were clearly girding themselves, physically and psychologically, to meet the situation created by Hitler's blitzkrieg in the West, the Fall of France, and the possible fall of Britain, and they were startled into a realization of the tacit, unacknowledged protection which had hitherto been afforded them by the existence of British power in the Atlantic. The ease with which the French Navy might have fallen as spoils to the aggressor was particularly alarming to them. Move and countermove were now piling up against each other. In September 1940, Germany, Italy, and Japan concluded their Tripartite Pact, binding themselves to act jointly against any Power, not yet a belligerent, which might make war on any one of them. The signatories specifically denied that the pact was directed against the Soviet Union. By implication, the pact was therefore directed against the United States and faced the United States with the menace of a two-front war in the Atlantic and Pacific. The presidential election was then being fought, and isolationism was already an obsolescent issue. The American people, if unconvinced by speeches and suspicious of "propaganda," could not but respond to the force of events.[7] Wendell Willkie, the Republican candidate, began, in the early stages of the election campaign, by cautiously balancing himself astride the fence on the isolationist issue, but he finally came down on the same side as his Democratic opponent: "All aid to the democracies short of war." On November 5, 1940, Roosevelt was elected President of the United States for a third term.

Strengthened by his victory, the President created an Office of Production Management with the declared objective of a two-ocean navy, 50,000 planes a year, and a modernized army of 1,000,000 men. Almost daily, it seemed, reports appeared in the press of new billions for war services, while the national debt soared to further record heights. In his "fireside chat" of December 29, 1940, the President voiced another of his many warnings against present and growing dangers: "In a military sense, Great Britain and the British Empire are today the spearhead of resistance to world conquest. . . . We are planning our own defense with the utmost urgency, and in its vast scale we must integrate the war needs of Britain and the other free nations which are resisting aggression. . . . We must be the great arsenal of democracy . . ." In his address to Congress on January 6, 1941, the President described the "Four Freedoms" — freedom of speech, freedom of worship, freedom from want, and freedom from fear — "no vision of a distant millennium," but "a definite basis for a kind of world attainable in our own time and generation . . . the very antithesis of the so-called new order of tyranny which the dictators seek to create with the crash of a bomb."

Early in January 1941, Congress began discussions of a bill for greatly extended aid, mainly to Britain. In public hearings it was pointed out that Britain had already exhausted her available assets of $4,500,000,000 in the United States and could no longer resort to "cash and carry" for the sustenance of her war effort. Lawyers of the Treasury Department unearthed a partial solution in a statute of 1892 authorizing the Secretary of War to lease army property "not required for public use" for a period of five years. This germinal idea was elaborated in consultations between the President and his advisers and was introduced into Congress as H.R. 1776, otherwise known as Lend-Lease. The bill was speeded through the Senate by 60 votes to 31, and through the House by 317 votes to 17, and it received the presidential signature on March 11, 1941. In the most sweeping terms it enjoined that "any defense article" could be sold, transferred, exchanged, leased, or lent to any country "whose defense the President deems vital to the defense of the United States," and that in order to avoid the old tangle of the Allied debts of the First World War repayment was to be made "in kind or property, or any other direct or indirect benefit which the President deems satisfactory." An initial appropriation of $7,000,000,000 gave some indication of the extent of the aid envisaged. In the beginning the chief responsibility for this huge scheme was put in the hands of that frail, many-sided, devoted man, former Works Progress Administrator and President Roosevelt's constant companion and adviser, Harry L. Hopkins. Edward R. Stettinius was appointed administrator in August 1941. Meanwhile the Canadian Government had moved in the same general direction by making Britain its first billion-dollar gift. Henceforth the economics of Britain and North America were completely integrated in a common war effort.

The American people were manifestly in that indeterminate zone between active and passive belligerency. In successive addresses the President, Secretary Hull, and other departmental chiefs drew the appropriate lessons from each aggressor's sally and carefully anticipated the corresponding repercussions on the nation's temper. The enormous industrial weight of the United States, so greatly developed since the First World War, was now to be thrown without reserve behind the democracies. But, again as in the First World War, the aid would not be fully effective unless the implements of war were safely delivered. Hitler's submarine wolf packs were ranging the Atlantic and inflicting losses so severe that the British Admiralty shortly suspended publication of sinkings. In April 1941, by agreement with the Danish minister in Washington, the United States established air bases in Greenland, a possession of Denmark, and shortly took over a second Danish territory, Iceland, then in British occupation. Thus the American "neutrality patrol" was extended to a point within 700 miles of Scotland. On May 21 the *Robin Moor*, an American merchantman, was sunk in mid-Atlantic. On May 27 the President proclaimed "an unlimited national emergency." But the submarine incidents — the *Greer*, the *Kearney*, the *Reuben James* — continued. The old story of 1915–17, it seemed, was being repeated. The long retreat from isolation was all but complete, and the American people well prepared for the final rupture by the end of 1941 when the Japanese attacked Pearl Harbor.

The shift to a full war basis in the United States had to be not only comprehensive, but rapid. The smooth operation of the Selective Service Act had already increased the army to 1,500,000 at the time of Pearl Harbor. The War Manpower Commission in 1942 planned to raise the enrollment to 10,800,000 by the close of 1943. The Navy was to absorb 2,000,000 — a number roughly equal to the sum total of American troops who saw active service in the First World War. The Army Air Forces were to be expanded to 2,000,000 to man and service the 50,000 planes a year which President Roosevelt had demanded. Women's auxiliary services were created in 1942 — the Women's Army Corps (WAC) with an eventual enrollment of 100,000, and the Women's Reserve of the Navy (Waves) [8] with an eventual enrollment of 86,000.

The withdrawal of these millions into the forces raised complicated labor and social problems. In December 1941 the representatives of 11,000,000 labor-union workers gave a "no-strike pledge" on the understanding that prices should not be permitted to outstrip wages. A National War Labor Board was established in January 1942 to co-operate with an Office of Price Administration (OPA) in stabilizing prices and wages. Although no strikes were authorized by the A.F. of L. or the CIO, the continued rise of prices provoked a strike call in 1943 by John L. Lewis to the 400,000 members of the United Mine Workers. An even more continuous and serious problem was the high rate of labor turnover and absenteeism. However, a backlog of 7,000,000 unemployed (1940) cushioned the impact of labor shortages. Four million women were added to the ranks of industrial labor during 1942–43.

The shipping problem appeared almost at once in a most acute form. The German submarine offensive accounted for over 9,000,000 tons of Allied shipping in the first twenty months of the war. Under the relentless driving force of Henry J. Kaiser, the builder of Boulder Dam, the slogan of "a ship a day" was realized in 1943. During the first nine months of 1943, American shipyards delivered over 15,000,000 tons of merchant shipping. In the entire course of the war, they delivered 5,425 ships with a total of 53,000,000 tons. In the last analysis, America's war was a sea war, and her "bridge of ships" across the oceans of the world to the far-flung fighting fronts was the decisive logistic achievement.

The allocation of American production under Lend-Lease proved to be a strategic and political problem of great delicacy. Britain, the Near East, China, and later India, Australia, and New Zealand, all had high priority claims. But perhaps no claims were so pressing, yet of such problematic benefit, as those of the Soviet Union. The early German successes in Russia seemed to indicate a general Soviet military collapse, and Lend-Lease in the circumstances promised to be little more than the delivery of welcome booty to the enemy. Harry Hopkins, as the President's special emissary, returned from a visit to Moscow with a profound conviction that Soviet resistance would be ultimately effective. In October 1941, when Moscow was threatened, Leningrad encircled, and the Ukraine lost, President Roosevelt placed $1,000,000,000 of Lend-Lease material at the disposal of the Soviet Union. But the material could only reach its Russian destination in the face of tremendous obstacles. After Pearl Harbor, the Pacific route to Vladivostok was used only by Soviet merchantmen. The British-operated North Atlantic convoy route to Murmansk, "Hell's Alley" as it was called, was beset by German submarines and aircraft based on Norway. Ultimately the Persian Gulf provided the most useful backdoor entrance to the Soviet Union, though the harbor facilities were poor and the single-track Trans-Iranian Railway lacked rolling stock, and its traffic was often stopped by landslides (see p. 681). By mid-1943, nevertheless, 100,000 tons of supplies monthly were moving along the railroad, by which time Lend-Lease administrators were noting with satisfaction a significant decline in the Soviet demands for barbed wire. Evidently it was the Germans, thrown so decisively on the defensive, who then required that commodity. During 1942–43, Lend-Lease began to comprise a variety of new items. A greater proportion of foodstuffs was furnished as the British and Soviet larders ran low. American cartoonists delighted to depict the puzzled, if gratified, expressions of Red Army soldiers as they investigated the piles of Spam, Snax, Mazola, and Post Toasties discharged on their quays.

Lend-Lease to 38 nations, from March 1941 to September 1946, amounted to $50,690,000,000. Of this total, the British Commonwealth received 65 per cent, and the Soviet Union 23 per cent. In goods, services, and miscellaneous payments under reverse Lend-Lease, the United States received approximately $10,000,000,000, over 80 per cent of which came from Britain.

The organization of this military and industrial effort entailed an enormous administrative expansion in Washington. We have already mentioned the War Manpower Commission, the National War Labor Board, and the Office of Price Administration (OPA). In January 1942, the Office of Production Management was merged into the newly created War Production Board under Donald M. Nelson. At the apex of the system stood the Joint Chiefs of Staff, under the direction of the President, bearing the primary responsibility for the strategic conduct of the war and for the broad program of war requirements, munitions, and transport. A single team — Admiral William D. Leahy, Chief of Staff to the President; General George C. Marshall, Chief of Staff to the Army; Admiral E. J. King, Commander in Chief of the Fleet and Chief of Naval Operations; and General Henry II. Arnold, Commanding General of the Army Air Force — served on this body throughout the war. An Office of Strategic Services was placed under the jurisdiction of the Joint Chiefs of Staff for the collection and analysis of military information and for the planning of "special services." The Combined Chiefs of Staff, created "to ensure complete coordination of the war effort of Great Britain and the United States," consisted of the Joint Chiefs of Staff and British members, notably Field Marshal Sir John Dill.

Perhaps the total effort of the United States in the Second World War can best be given in short statistical form. In the six years, the American arsenal produced 17,000,000 rifles and sidearms, 315,000 pieces of artillery and mortars, 87,000 tanks, 2,434,000 trucks, 80,000 landing craft, 296,000 planes, and 53,000,000 tons of shipping. The total monetary costs of the war have been estimated at $317,000,000,000. The national debt rose to $263,000,000,-000 or about $1,750 per capita.

President Roosevelt's personal ascendancy grew with the progress of the war and the evident fulfillment of his long-advocated foreign policy. Yet on the home front he met a persistent, fractious, almost irresponsible opposition. The Congressional elections of November 1942 resulted in a continuance of the nominal Democratic majorities in both Houses, but many of the Democrats were anti-Roosevelt. Thus the administration failed in its attempts to fix prices, to put a ceiling on salaries, and otherwise to control the rocketing upswing of the cost of living. In 1943, when the National Resources Planning Board produced its scheme for social insurance, Congress abolished the Board and ordered its files and records to be handed over to the National Archives. It almost seemed as if the nation and its elected representatives wanted to show that, despite the war — even because of the war — they were abnormally sensitive of any encroachment on their basic "American" rights, and indeed that involvement in a war against totalitarianism was all the more reason for resisting totalitarianism at home, however mild or however helpful to the national effort.

However, in November 1944, when it came to the point, after weeks of hard campaigning during which the bogy of the fourth term was exploited to the full, Roosevelt was re-elected President of the United States over the Republican candidate, Thomas E. Dewey. The new Vice-President was Harry Truman. Subsequently Cordell Hull resigned his office as Secretary of State, after a twelve-year tenure, and was succeeded by Stettinius.

As the United States braced itself for global war, Washington strove more ardently than ever to realize the "hemisphere solidarity" which had guided the policy toward Latin America in the thirties. Within three weeks of the outbreak of war in Europe, in accordance with the consultative machinery devised at the Pan-American Conference at Lima in 1938 (see p. 608), the foreign ministers of the twenty-one American republics met at Panama and thence issued a Declaration establishing a "neutrality zone" of coastal waters extending 300 miles offshore as far north as Canada, in which hostile acts by non-American belligerents would not be tolerated. The running fight between the German pocket battleship *Admiral Graf Spee* and three British cruisers off Uruguay in December 1939 revealed the brittleness of this paper prohibition. The foreign ministers met again at Havana in July 1940 and issued the so-called Act of Havana providing for a collective trusteeship by the American republics, notably over the French and Dutch islands in the West Indies, left orphaned by events in Europe. The ministers also adopted a resolution that aggression by a non-American state against any one of the American republics should be considered as aggression against all.

In December 1941 the six Central American republics and the three island republics declared war on Japan, Germany, and Italy; Mexico, Colombia, and Venezuela severed relations. The twenty-one foreign ministers met for the third time at Rio de Janeiro in January 1942. They set up an Inter-American Defense Board to study measures for the defense of the hemisphere, devised comprehensive arrangements for economic collaboration, and recommended that the republics which had not already done so should sever diplomatic relations with the Axis Powers. At the end of January, only Argentina and Chile were still standing out against the pressure of their hemispheric colleagues and had not severed diplomatic relations. During 1942, Mexico and Brazil went the length of declaring war on the Axis Powers. During 1943, Bolivia declared war on the Axis Powers, and Colombia on Germany.

Washington had a number of strong cards in its hands. A broadening stream of loans and credits from the Export-Import Bank for the establishment or expansion of defense industries in the more well-disposed republics appealed to the military regimes in Latin America. A diversion of Lend-Lease supplies in the same direction helped to prepare the ground for standardization of arms and equipment on the United States pattern. Wartime purchases compensated for normal markets now closed by the Nazi conquests in Europe. The loss of merchant shipping, particularly crippling in view of Latin America's dependence on coastwise trade, was made good from United States shipyards. Lastly, as the fortunes of war turned against the Axis, even the most hesitant republics began to adjust their foreign policies to the course of ineluctable events. Chile eventually severed relations with the Axis in January 1943, and Argentina in January 1944. But, by then, the relations between the United States and a still recalcitrant and Fascist-minded Argentina were unprecedentedly bitter.

The foreign ministers met for a fourth time at Mexico City in February 1945 to put the cornerstone on the Pan-American regional system, but Argentina was not represented. The United Nations was then a fact, and declaration of war was a precondition of membership therein. The ministers adopted the Act of Chapultepec which, much in the words of the Havana resolution, declared that aggression against any one of the American republics would be considered as aggression against all. But the act also made it clear that such aggression now signified aggression by one American republic against another, and it provided for consultation on sanctions against the aggressor including, ultimately, the use of armed force. In that February, Paraguay, Chile, Peru, Venezuela, and Uruguay hastened to declare war on the Axis, and Argentina restored the unanimity by declaring war, if reluctantly, in March.

CHINA

The withdrawal in 1938 of the Chinese Nationalist government under Chiang Kai-shek to Chungking, in the far recesses of undeveloped Szechwan province, exposed it at once to a host of intractable problems. The industrial backwardness of the area caused a veritable famine in war materials and consumer goods. The province was but scantily served by railroads. After the Japanese occupation of French Indo-China and Burma in 1940–41, territorial contact with the outer world was severed save for tenuous highway links with the Soviet Union across Sinkiang (Chinese Turkestan). The extensive gaps in the war economy of Free China were partly filled by smuggling operations in the Japanese-occupied territories. In addition, small but increasing quantities of air-borne supplies were carried by American airmen from India at heavy cost in lives over the fabulous "Hump," the southern spurs of the

Himalayas. Cargoes consisted largely of gasoline and military supplies, and did not alleviate the critical shortage of consumer goods.

The Chinese Nationalist government, in the face of mounting expenses, had recourse to the printing press. By 1944 the total note issue had risen to well over 100,000,000,000 Chinese dollars, and prices had mounted 500-fold since 1937. Credits of £50,000,000 from Britain and $500,000,000 from the United States in February 1942 did little to check this runaway inflation. The government, toiling hopelessly up the dizzy spiral of currency inflation, finally decreed that the land tax should be rendered in produce instead of in money. Hoarding of foodstuffs by landlords and middlemen was combated by decrees enforcing the sale of grain to the government at rates officially fixed. The equitable application of these measures, however, faltered when it reached the level of local administration, where graft and "squeeze" abounded.

These serious economic dislocations inevitably relaxed the springs of the Chinese war effort. Chiang Kai-shek constantly remonstrated with his supporters "on the bad old habits of insincerity, display, indolence, and procrastination." Man power was abundant, but morale was low, and heavy equipment was lacking. Chinese spokesmen took exception to the Allies' decision to concentrate so much of their resources against Germany, and declared that, by 1944, China had received only half of one per cent of American Lend-Lease supplies. The transport bottleneck into China was, however, a manifest obstacle. Nor could it be gainsaid that the Chinese armies would require lengthy training in the handling of modern weapons of war. The Chinese GI no longer carried, in addition to more lethal weapons, the umbrella and the teapot which had amazed Western observers a generation before; but, with his threadbare yellow and brown uniform, his antiquated rifle, his ration of dry rice kernels suspended in a long blue stocking about his neck, his straw sandals, he fell only too often far short of Western military standards in all save courage — the resigned but tenacious courage of his peasant origin.

But these more obvious problems of shortage and suffering, however magnified in the case of China, were not untypical of a "backward" nation in a total war. The great problem of China's home front, the problem of continuing historical importance, was the antagonism between the Nationalist government and the Chinese Red Army (see p. 434). Since 1937 the two parties had unitedly fought the Japanese invader, though not always without occasional clashes with one another. In January 1941, a more serious "incident" had occurred when a body of Nationalist troops — probably without the knowledge of Chiang Kai-shek — had attacked and decimated 5,000 men of the Communist "New Fourth Army" while they were withdrawing across the Yangtze. From that moment the war in China lapsed for three years into a wasting and sporadic triangular struggle between Nationalist, Communist, and Jap. Organized Japanese operations were limited in scope. Territorial advances, if any, were secondary to the destruction or capture of rice and grain crops, especially in the "rice bowl" round Changsha.

But the decision of the "Quadrant" Conference in Quebec in 1943 to intensify the war in the Pacific induced a greater dynamism into Japanese strategy in China (pp. 760–61). Early in 1944, the Japanese launched a major offensive along the Hankow-Canton railroad against the forward bases of the United States Fourteenth Air Force, established there for aerial assault on the Japanese mainland and incidentally on Japanese shipping in the China Sea. In six months the Japanese were approaching Kweilin and Chihkiang and were about to effect a junction with a contingent of their comrades pushing north from Indo-China. The operation threatened to cut Free China in halves. Chinese troops to the number of 600,000 melted away in confusion. The disaster evoked demands from General Stilwell, Chiang Kai-shek's American Chief of Staff, for a radical revision of policy on China's home front. He proposed that the military blockade of the Chinese Red Army by the Nationalists should be lifted, and that both forces should unite in a single striking force against the Japanese. He pressed Washington to dispatch arms and equipment directly to the Chinese Red Army. In return, the Reds would be asked to permit the establishment of American air bases in their territories within bombing range of Japan. The American ambassador in Chungking, Clarence Gauss, urged simultaneously the need of a fully representative "War Council" to which all Chinese parties, including the Communists, would be admitted. As a result of these agreements, twenty-five elite Chinese divisions would be made available for a campaign for the reopening of the Burma Road.

The mutual and invincible suspicion between the Nationalist government and the Chinese Red Army was not overcome. In despair Stilwell abandoned all hope of military unification and proposed that he should assume direct command of the Nationalist forces himself. Chiang Kai-shek resented the proposal intensely. It imperiled his own authority, which was based upon the co-operation of the provincial generals loosely subject to his command, and it was badly received by the provincial generals themselves, who feared that a high centralization of command in the hands of a foreigner would conduce to a ruthless disregard of local interests. "The cure for China's trouble is the elimination of Chiang Kai-shek," wrote Stilwell in July 1944. "The only thing that keeps the country split is his fear of losing control. He hates the Reds and will not take any chances on giving them a toehold in the government. The result is that each side watches the other and neither gives a damn about the war against Japan. If this condition persists, China will have a civil war immediately after Japan is out." The clash of views and of personalities, publicized in the American press under the caption, "Vinegar Joe and the Reluctant Dragon," was terminated by the recall of General Stilwell at the request of Chiang Kai-shek himself in October 1944.

Stilwell's successor in China, General Wedemeyer, tried to keep aloof from political entanglements. But politics and strategy could not be divorced entirely. A land offensive against Japanese forces in China would be a helpful complement to the final American assault on the home islands of Japan. But Chiang Kai-shek had lost all access to the coastal areas of China, where the only Chinese forces operating were guerrilla and partisan units under Communist leadership. Meanwhile the American press was showing a rising concern over the internal cleavages which were crippling China's war effort.

Chiang Kai-shek, fully aware of the importance of continued American aid, hastened to affirm that "the Chinese Communist problem is a purely political problem, and should be solved by political means," and in May 1945 negotiations were at last opened between the two estranged parties. But the distrust remained. The Communists demanded full recognition of their party, the speedy convocation of a popular assembly based on universal suffrage, the release of political prisoners, the abolition of secret police, the lifting of the military blockade of the Red Army, and equitable allotment of military supplies. These terms suggested to Chiang Kai-shek that the Communist tail was trying to wag the Chinese dog. He offered the Communists minority representation in Chungking, provided that the Red Army was scaled down to ten divisions and incorporated into the Chinese Army. In spite of keen chaffering spread over many months, an air of unreality hung over the negotiations. As the American Pacific campaign by-passed China, and Japan sank slowly to her knees, both Nationalists and Communists prepared to seize the fullest advantage from the approaching peace.

JAPAN

Pearl Harbor did not signify to the Japanese people the beginning of a new conflict, but rather the intensification of an old one, originating in 1931. Indeed, the Japanese press, which had raged furiously against the economic embargo imposed by the United States, contended that Pearl Harbor was simply the transition from economic to military warfare. The intoxication induced by early victories ensured enthusiastic acceptance of official propaganda to the effect that Japan had finally thrown off the discriminations and disabilities which she had suffered for so long at the hands of Western Powers. The subsequent sweep of Japanese forces to the northern confines of Australia fortified public confidence in the ability of the armed forces to retain the territories gained with such apparent ease. It was conjectured that, at worst, the relinquishment of the nonessential portions of these conquests would readily purchase a negotiated peace from the Allies. Consequently, plant and equipment expenditures actually declined in Japan during 1942; and the output of tankers, merchant shipping, and aircraft in particular remained far from adequate to cope with the American counteroffensive which was being slowly forged in distant Australia.

Some anticipation of coming stringencies was signified by the full application of the National Mobilization Law (see p. 678) and the Major Industries Association Ordinance of 1941. This latter ordinance placed the supply of raw material, labor, and capital for each key industry in the hands of control associations headed by a president with comprehensive powers. These associations were ardently sponsored by the Zaibatsu and manned almost exclusively by its representatives. Throughout 1942, under pretext of enhancing war production, they mercilessly eliminated or absorbed small concerns.

Economic manipulation of this kind could be winked at by the government so long as Japan was riding the floodtide of success. But, by the end of 1942, there were dismaying indications — notably at Guadalcanal (see p. 745)

— that the tide was beginning to recede. The easy optimism in Tokyo began to waver at the dreary prospect of a long war. In January 1943, Tojo, the Premier, informed the nation elliptically that, since Japan was no longer a "have-not" nation, she possessed all the necessary resources for a prolonged struggle. In March 1943, after bitter exchanges with the Zaibatsu representatives in the Diet, he was conceded semidictatorial powers over key industries. To placate the Zaibatsu he accepted a Cabinet Advisory Board of seven leading industrialists who, in theory, supervised war production in joint session with the Cabinet, but who, in actual fact, only "expressed opinions in their own specialized field."

In August 1943, following the decisions of the "Quadrant" Conference at Quebec to intensify the war against Japan, Tojo announced a new program of "economic mobilization." (See p. 760.) In November he established a Munitions Ministry with himself as Minister, to absorb related government departments, allocate raw materials, fix prices, enforce priorities, and generally step up production in war industries. The new ministry was instructed to devote special attention to light aircraft metals and to centralize aircraft production hitherto split between separate Army and Navy controls.

The ministry only partially achieved its objects. The Army and Navy, in the matter of aircraft production, continued to work in rivalry, and the control associations were often able to circumvent the priorities regulations. Aircraft production nevertheless reached a peak in 1944. Thereafter all industries began to feel the effects of the heavy losses of merchant shipping and the advance of American forces into territories supplying oil, bauxite, and metals. With such dwindling resources, however well she ordered her economy, Japan could hardly have hoped to match the immense resources now being brought up against her. By mid-1944, American forces stood in the Marianas, and the economic base of Japan's defenses was, in effect, confined to the so-called Inner Zone of her Co-prosperity Sphere. On July 18, 1944, nine days after the fall of Saipan, Tojo resigned. He was succeeded by General Kuniaki Koiso.

In January 1945, American bombers from their newly established base in Guam began methodically to smash the industrial centers of Japan. On the night of March 9, 15 square miles of Tokyo were destroyed in a single raid. Nearly half of Yokohama was destroyed in a raid of one hour. By midsummer 1945, bombs were being dropped at the rate of 50,000 tons a month. One after another of Japan's crowded, flimsily built, inflammable cities was being reduced to ashes. Under the fiery deluge the government somewhat tardily announced a policy of "industrial decentralization." But the attempt to establish factories outside the devastated urban areas involved problems of dismantling, transport, and rebuilding which even added to the existing economic disarray.

The bombing touched off a seemingly endless chain of disturbance and confusion. Roughly 5,000,000, or a sixth of the urban population, were homeless; 8,000,000, or a quarter, had fled to the rural areas. All schools were closed for a year. Family solidarity was strong enough to assure a welcome from relatives for the great mass of the fugitives, most of whom were women and children, but the congested transportation system was hardly able to cope with the traffic, and the stories of horror and destruction which the fugitives took with them did nothing to improve the morale of the countryside. But often enough war workers also were in flight, and their displacement increased the gnawing problem of industrial absenteeism. The problem grew to major proportions as the rice ration was reduced, and beans and potatoes were offered as substitutes. Workers spent several days per week scouring the countryside for food. Farmers jealously hoarded their precious stocks of rice or released it at fancy prices through the black market. The police were ordered to search the baggage of city-bound passengers for food, but moderate amounts were always being permitted to slip through with their connivance.

In many ways, the devastations and evacuations were less demoralizing than the incredible ineptitude of Japanese "victory" propaganda and the almost mechanical lying of the war communiqués. Yet, with all the fearful stresses imposed upon it, there were still no major fissures on the home front. Postwar interrogation by the United States Bombing Survey has revealed that, while only 10 per cent of the civil population had expected defeat before December 1944, the proportion had grown to over 50 per cent by June 1945. But the decline of confidence did not express itself in active popular resentment or in an upsurge of politically dissident forces. It found expression, if anything, in a great and terrifying apathy among civilians, save in the all-absorbing search for food.

As the year 1945 advanced, blow after blow fell on the Japanese home front. Iwo Jima was lost in March. In April, the Soviet Union denounced the neutrality pact signed with Japan four years previously. The Koiso cabinet resigned to make way for a cabinet headed by the elderly Baron Kantaro Suzuki, a naval hero of the Russo-Japanese War of 1904–05. The new cabinet created a Civilian Volunteer Corps, a sort of home guard armed with a strange miscellany of weapons from bows and arrows to homemade bazookas. Each member was urged to display "the Kamikaze spirit" (see p. 783), and was furnished with a *Handbook on How to Build Fortifications* to acquaint him with the technicalities of last-ditch defense. In June 1945, assurances were given to the Zaibatsu, who were pressing for "nationalization" of industry in order to pass on the expense of repairing their bomb-shattered factories to the government, that all war loss and damage would be met by the Treasury. In the same month, the Cabinet was voted emergency powers by the Diet. The home islands, divided into eight "self-sufficient" regions in anticipation of the coming invasion, were to be defended yard by yard.

The end of the war in Europe released overwhelming Allied strength for service in the Pacific; and the Japanese people were reminded continuously of that fact by half a million leaflets dropped from the air. Equally nerve-racking was the prior warning given by United States Bomber Command of its intention to raid individual cities. The civilian population was thus given an opportunity to evacuate the area, where production was paralyzed in consequence, and the punctual execution of the raid at the time and day announced emphasized the completeness of American control of the air. By July 1945 the destruction of the rail ferries linking the home islands virtually suspended the movement of raw materials to the factories and of food to the bigger cities. An Anglo-American task force of 122 warships, including 9 battleships and 20 aircraft carriers, was ranging at will in Japanese coastal waters, pouring an enormous weight of metal on industrial plants and communications.

On August 6, 1945 the first atomic bomb was dropped on Hiroshima, destroying over half the city and causing 70,000–80,000 deaths. On the 8th, the Soviet Union declared war, invaded Manchukuo, and thereby shattered the last remaining hope, once so sedulously nursed by Japanese propaganda, that Moscow would be too preoccupied with domestic reconstruction to participate in a Far Eastern war. On August 9 the second atomic bomb was dropped on Nagasaki. Military extremists were prepared to continue a suicidal resistance in order to extract tolerable peace terms. But the Zaibatsu was now using its influence to prevent the reduction of its surviving properties to heaps of rubble reminiscent of Germany. An important peace faction, which included three admirals, Suzuki among them, and three former premiers, Konoye among them, was deviously exerting itself to bring the conflict to an end. On August 14, at the intervention of the Emperor, the Suzuki cabinet accepted the Allied terms and resigned the following day. A small group of army officers tried, but failed, to block the reading of the Emperor's surrender message by seizing the radio station in Tokyo, from which it was broadcast by Hirohito in person.

Although Japan's ground forces of 6,000,000 men were virtually intact at the end of the war, her strength at sea and in the air and her economic resources were almost entirely shattered. She had lost 12 battleships, including her two superbattleships of 64,000 tons, 19 aircraft carriers, 34 cruisers, 126 destroyers, and 125 submarines. On "V-J Day" she had afloat, more or less severely damaged, only 1 battleship, 4 aircraft carriers, and 3 cruisers. Of 65,500 aircraft constructed since 1941, over 50,000 had been destroyed. Of an original fleet of merchant ships of some 6,000,000 tons, increased in the course of the war by new building and by capture to 10,000,000 tons, almost 9,000,000 tons had been sunk or disabled. Allied naval blockade and air raids had reduced industrial production to 25 per cent of the prewar figure, and had cut the carrying capacity of the railroads by one-half. Civilian casualties amounted to over 800,000, including 330,000 dead. Oil supplies had fallen so low during and after 1944 that the tactical movements of the Japanese Navy had been severely curtailed in the interest of conservation. Total coal supplies were about halved, and imports of coal, notably from Korea, were halted altogether.

These statistics afford a ready and obvious clue to the causes of the Japanese defeat. But there were other, more deep-seated causes. The economic structure of Japan was clearly undeveloped for the defense of a newly won, widely-scattered maritime empire. The 4,000-mile outer perimeter of the empire, stretching from the Aleutians to New Guinea, was highly vulnerable to a foe who, steadily increasing in strength, could select his point of attack. Nor, as we shall describe in Chapter 44, did the "beneficent imperialism" of Japan sufficiently engage the gratitude and co-operation of her "younger brothers" in that empire. Japan's military and industrial leaders, dazzled by their own and by Germany's initial victories, failed to foresee the ability of the Allies to wage simultaneous wars in Europe, the Near East, and the Pacific, and they were entirely mistaken in their conviction that the un-military, comfort-loving Americans, as they pictured them, would never wage a total war of unlimited objectives. There were, furthermore, the insolence and arbitrariness of the Japanese militarists and the insensate professional rivalry between the two armed services which was at the bottom of so much of Japan's seeming administrative ineptitude in the conduct of the war. Finally there was the megalomania, bred by the nation's self-admiration at its meteoric rise to power and by its long immunity from defeat, a megalomania which bore little relation to realities.

THE AXIS–OCCUPIED TERRITORIES IN EUROPE

THE NEW ORDER IN EUROPE

The ideological sanctions of the New Order in Europe went back to the earliest pronouncements of the Nazi movement. But it was not till the Nazis began to organize and "co-ordinate" their conquests that the full extent, the extraordinary thoroughness — and indeed the vision — of their policy was appreciated abroad. Concepts which belonged to the demented dreamworld of Hitler's *Mein Kampf* or Rosenberg's *Mythus,* incredible on paper, were translated into fact. The Reich of a Thousand Years, ruled by and for a master race, a Power to which all the world should be tributary, has been tagged by its enemies with every derogatory adjective in the dictionary, but it has never been accused of poverty of imagination.

As was usual in Nazism there was considerable conflict of doctrine. The detail of Nazi politics, as we have had occasion to notice before, was always very hand-to-mouth. The map of Europe developed under the expanding occupation showed all the accidents of its history. Short-term objectives conflicted with long-term; the immediate needs of strategy and economics conflicted with the more permanent requirements of the New Order; deliberately incited national feuds and factions conflicted with the larger ideal of a united, integrated Europe. Some of the new frontiers seemed to have been drawn to no reason or principle except in so far as they were a demonstrative and vindictive reversal of Versailles. The propaganda of the occupation meanwhile, in so far as it was addressed both to Germans and to their vassals, varied with the varying fortunes of the war.

Nazism was always haunted by a sort of historical romanticism. The Third Reich, by its very name, implied a successorship to two other Reichs of ascendant Germandom in former times. There was an alleged coincidence between Nazi Europe and the Europe of the early Middle Ages when once before Aryans lorded their might over inferior breeds of men — Normans and Burgundinary in France, Visigoths in Spain, Lombards in Italy, Scandinavians in the Baltic, and Teutonic Knights in Poland. The armistice of 1940 in France was not only a strategic instrument but a delimitation between "Frankish" and "Latin" France. The occupied territories often looked like medieval fiefs organized for the benefit of their new Teutonic barons. Italy was suitably relegated to her medieval role of leadership in the Mediterranean under the superior direction of a Transalpine Teutonic Empire.

The treatment meted out to individual occupied territories varied according to race and, to a less extent, according to the degree of opposition they had offered to their conquerors. Thus Danes and Luxembourgers, who ranked as "Aryans" and had succumbed without resistance, were offered virtual German citizenship. The Danes were so favored indeed as to be obliged to join the Anti-Comintern Pact. The French — the Latinized, Negroidized, Hebraicized French — were only fit to fall into deserved decay. The worst treatment of all was reserved for peoples like the Poles, who were not only inferior in the "hierarchy of blood" but who had also dared defend themselves against their rightful masters. A policy of divide and rule revived the latent nationalistic differences between Flemings and Walloons, French and Bretons, Czechs and Slovaks, Serbs and Croats, Bulgars and Greeks.

These many principles took form in the frontiers and administrations that were Nazi Europe, so much so that the entire system — if system it can be called — gave the impression of expediency and experiment to be revised at some convenient opportunity in the postwar era. For normally the German had a thorough mind, fond of neat, architectonic patterns, and could hardly have remained content with so fortuitous a creation.

Roughly, there were five categories of administrations in Nazi Europe. First, there were the territories annexed or wholly incorporated into Germany — Austria, the Sudetenland, Memel, Danzig, Teschen, Eupen-Malmédy, Luxembourg, Alsace-Lorraine, part of Slovenia, "Warteland," Bialystok, and the extensions of East and West Prussia. Second, there were the two territories not incorporated into Germany, but regarded as parts of "Greater Germany" and designated for future German "colonization" — the Protectorate of Bohemia-Moravia, administered by a Reich Protector, at first Baron von Neurath; and the Government General of Poland, administered by the Governor General, Hans Frank. Third, there were the territories of immediate strategic importance administered by German military governors — Belgium and a part of northern France, under General von Falkenhausen;[1] Occupied France, Brittany, and the British Channel Islands, successively under the two Generals von Stuelpnagel;[2] a reduced Serbia; Macedonia; the Aegean Islands and Crete, and the Russian "Operational Base," including the Crimea. Fourth, there were the territories under semicivilian, "autonomous" rule — Denmark, for a time under her own king and parliament; Norway under a Reich Commissioner, Joseph Terboven, assisted by the pro-Nazi Norwegian cabinet of Vidkun Quisling; Holland under another Reich Commissioner, Seyss-Inquart of Austrian fame, assisted by a cabinet of Dutch secretaries of state; and Unoccupied France with its government at Vichy. Fifth, there were the two "Commissariats," Ostland and the Ukraine, ruled by German Commissioners responsible to a special Reich Minister for Eastern Occupied Territories in the person of that prophet of German expansion in the East, Alfred Rosenberg.

Similarly, in the Italian part of the New Order, there were the annexed territories — a much enlarged Albania, part of Slovenia, and Dalmatia; there were the territories under Italian military governors — Mentone and the French Alpine frontier, Corsica, and Greece; and the territories under semi-civilian, "autonomous" rule — a newly created "Croatia" (see p. 665) and a re-created Montenegro. Finally, there were the satellite or "legionnaire" states — Slovenia; Hungary, including half of Transylvania and part of the

Banat; Rumania, including Bessarabia and "Transnistria"; Bulgaria, including Thrace and parts of Serbia and the Dobruja; and Finland.

These administrations entailed a redrawing of the map of Europe. France, Belgium, and Yugoslavia were divided against themselves; Poland and Czechoslovakia were liquidated; the satellites were variously enlarged. But the common denominator in this strange patchwork is not far to seek. Whatever the name and style, the realities of military, political, and economic control were not in doubt. The Nazis exerted an absolute mastery. The wealth of some twenty nations and populations totaling 250,000,000 were impressed into their service. From their fortress heartland they might well hope to dominate Eurasia and thence the world.

Generally two lines of economic policy were observable. The first was the obvious, short-term policy of spoliation. Raw materials, armaments, finished products, industrial machinery, rolling stock, foodstuffs, anything in short which could be described as having an immediate military value, were seized, sent to Germany, or otherwise held at the disposal of the conqueror's war machine. The second was the less obvious, long-term policy of constructing a united, integrated Europe. In this Europe, in Hitler's own words, Greater Germany would be "the steely core. . . . a block of one hundred millions, indestructible, without flaw, without an alien element, the firm foundation of our power." Thence would radiate outer rings of vassal states. Europe would fulfill her destiny and become, for the first time since the Roman Empire, a political and economic entity. She would be like a "biological organism," each part whereof would serve its appropriate purpose and yield its appropriate products. Of this New Order, Berlin would be the administrative and financial center; Germany herself would be the main industrial area; the vassal states — except as producers of raw materials and certain unfinished goods natural to them — would be the agricultural areas. Even England, when conquered, would be largely pastoralized.

Financial controls were imposed in all the occupied territories, and the imposition was made easier by the fact that, in most of the countries concerned, lately sufferers and participants themselves in the critical state of world economics, controls of one kind or another existed already. These controls permitted the extension into the occupied territories of those industrial and financial techniques, especially in respect of foreign exchange, which the Nazis had perfected in the years between 1933 and 1939. Sometimes the whole of the banking business of a country or region would be taken over, especially in the cases where, as the result of military operations, the local bank premises had been destroyed or the personnel had disappeared. Of course, gold reserves were seized when and where they could be found. Occupation costs were charged to every "hostile" territory. In France, for example, the annual German occupation costs exactly equaled France's war budget of 1940. Clearly the Germans were guided by France's "capacity to pay" and probably relished the poetic justice of using France's war budget against herself. The Germans were consequently able to accumulate sizable credit balances in each country with which to pay for their requisitions or to acquire controlling interests in the country's commercial enterprises.

The Germans were legatees of a whole variety of "windfall gains" as they called them — arising from the confiscation of Jewish, anti-Nazi, and Allied properties, from collective fines imposed on municipalities and townships for acts of "hostility" or sabotage, and from the reimbursement of German reparations paid between 1920 and 1932. We have the authority of Thomas Reveille for saying that all these seizures, occupation costs, and "windfall gains" in one year probably aggregated 90,000,000,000 marks ($36,000,000,-000) — or the figure which Hitler estimated to be the cost of Germany's re-armament between 1933 and 1939 [3] (see p. 471).

The shortage of labor, a phenomenon which developed on all home fronts in the First World War, had already reappeared in Germany in 1937 and, by 1939, was her basic economic problem. At the same time the immediate effect of the war and the occupation was to create unemployment in all the invaded countries. It was a similar situation in 1916 which had induced the German High Command of that day to resort to the Belgian deportations (pp. 55–56). As was so often the case, the First World War provided the prece-dent and education for the Second, but in the Second World War the whole-sale deportations in occupied Europe were used not only as an economic, but also as a political weapon. Germany's conquests in 1940–42 delivered millions of native levies and prisoners of war into her hands. Nazi racial doctrines went into practice, and all Europe was soon a laboratory in which *Herren-volk* and *Hilfsvolk*, the master race and its modern helotry, worked out their appropriate relations to one another. The result was a forcible displacement of populations unprecedented since the time of ancient Assyria and Babylon.

The Government General of Poland was significantly termed an *Arbeits-reich*. Plans for the exploitation of Polish labor had been prepared several months in advance of the invasion and were put into force by the Governor General, Hans Frank. In normal times there had always been a certain amount of seasonable Polish migration. Voluntary recruitment on similar lines was tried at first, but then abandoned, and the Poles were rounded up by SS raiding squads — in the streets, in their homes, in railroad stations, even in churches. If any tried to escape deportation by flight, their homes were burned down and their families held as hostages against their return. These unfortunates in the thousands were herded together at assembly points resembling concentration camps, crowded onto trains, and transported to Germany often in open trucks without the elements of decency or sanitation and often during zero and sub-zero weathers. A high percentage, sometimes as much as a quarter, arrived at their destinations so incapacitated by their treatment that they often had to be sent back — under the same inhuman con-ditions as they had already suffered. Once in Germany, they were housed and fed on the general principle of "exploitation to the highest possible extent at the lowest conceivable degree of expenditure." Terror was the incentive of production; starvation, lack of medical care, excessive work, as well as the more positive forms of physical torture were the ordinary incidentals of existence. Violations of discipline, malingering, attempts to escape were punishable by transfer to a concentration camp or, "in especially severe cases," by "special treatment" — special treatment being the euphemism for

AXIS – OCCUPIED TERRITORIES IN EUROPE

Territories incorporated into Germany: Austria, Sudetenland (1), Memel, Danzig, Teschen, Eupen-et-Malmédy (2), Luxembourg (LUX.), Alsace (3), Lorraine (4), part of Slovenia (SLOV.), Wartheland (5), and Bialystok (6). West Prussia (7) and East Prussia (8) were enlarged. Alpenvorland (9) and Adriatrisches Küstenland (10) were formed in 1943 after the collapse of Italy.

Territories not incorporated into Germany, but regarded as part of "Greater Germany." The Protectorate of Bohemia-Moravia (PROT.), and the Government General of Poland.

Territories under German military administration: Belgium and a part of northern France, Occupied France and Brittany, Serbia, Macedonia (11), the Aegean Islands, Crete, and the Russian Operational Base including the Crimea.

Territories under Italian military administration: Mentone and the French Alpine frontier territories, Corsica and Greece.

German-controlled territories under semicivilian administration: Denmark, Norway, Holland, Unoccupied France, Reich Commissariat Ostland, and Reich Commissariat Ukraine.

Italian-controlled territories: Albania, Dalmatia, Croatia, and Montenegro (12).

Satellite States: Slovakia, Hungary including Transylvania (13), Rumania including Bessarabia (14) and Transnistria (15), Bulgaria including Thrace (16) and part of the Dobruja (17), and Finland.

hanging — possibly the most merciful of the possible sentences. In the words of Greiser, Gauleiter of Warteland, "For us Polish nationality is only labor power and nothing more."

The policy begun in Poland was extended in the wake of military operations to the West and then to the Russian East. The deportees were put to all kinds of work — agriculture, road and railroad repair, coal mining, industries including armaments, and fortifications. Western deportees on the whole, as a tribute to their higher "civilization" and technical skills, usually received better treatment, but the general condition of slavery, especially in 1942 and afterward, applied to all races without discrimination. We have already mentioned the Speer-Sauckel controllership of labor and the labor mobilization decree of January 1943 in Germany (see p. 690). Collateral measures were simultaneously introduced in all occupied territories. Puppet administrations lent their aid, and many a collaborator owed his job to his resourcefulness as procurer of the demanded human commodity. In Holland, appropriately, the deportations went by the name of "Operation Sauckel." Even the concentration camps were combed for labor. "The custody of prisoners for sole reasons of security, education, or prevention is no longer the main consideration." On March 23, 1943, it was announced that the two-thousandth train carrying the millionth Polish worker had left the Government General. In September 1943, at the end of his first year as Plenipotentiary for Labor Allocation, Sauckel reported to his Führer that 3,638,056 foreign workers had been fed into Germany's war economy. The total figure of this huge displacement of peoples has been put at 4,795,000, of which in Sauckel's own admission, "not even 200,000 came voluntarily."

"Germanization" was defined at Nuremberg as "the obliteration of the former national character of the conquered territories and the extermination of all elements which could not be reconciled with the Nazi ideology." The policy went hand in hand with the economic and demographic spoliation we have been describing. Its character and method is sufficiently indicated from the fact that it was put in charge of Himmler whom Hitler, in October 1939, appointed Reich Commissioner for the Consolidation of Germandom (*Reichskommissar für die Festigung des deutschen Volkstums*). The peripheral areas of "Greater Germany" were designated for his operations. The ultimate objective was the creation of that "steely [German] core . . . without an alien element, the firm foundation of our power."

Indigenous Germans or *Volksdeutsche,* already inhabitants in these peripheral areas, were usually former members of local Nazi parties. During preinvasion days, they had constituted a fifth column and, after the invasion, they had, of course, received their reward in special positions and privileges. But the fate of non-Germans in these areas was deportation, enslavement to the Nazi war machine, or eventual "extermination through work." Lemkin has coined the word *genocide* for "the destruction of a nation or of an ethnic group." [4] Particularly must the intelligentsia be removed — for example, "the Polish intelligentsia and clergy, who have been politically active in the past" and who had provided the political, patriotic, and religious leadership of the state. "For us, the end of this war," said Himmler, "will mean an open road to the East, the creation of the Germanic Reich. . . . We shall bring home 30,000,000 human beings of our blood; we shall be the sole decisive power in Europe; we shall take twenty years to rebuild and spread out our villages and towns; we shall push the borders of our German race 500 kilometers further to the East." "Thanks to the heroic courage of our soldiers," wrote Hans Frank in his diary, "[Poland] has become German, and the time will come when the valley of the Vistula, from its source to its mouth at the sea, will be as German as the valley of the Rhine."

Germanization was applied in varying degrees in the South and West. The Slovenes were marked out for the same destructive treatment as the Poles. Alsace-Lorraine was entrusted to Bürckel, of Austrian fame. His task was somewhat helped by the fact that a third of the population had already been evacuated to France before the German invasion, though considerable numbers probably returned after 1940. In September 1941 he instituted mass expulsion of "racially alien elements" at first to France, and then, after the labor crisis of 1942, to Germany and Poland. A small French minority which opted for German citizenship was sent to "re-education" camps. Probably some 500,000 Alsatians and Lorrainers were deported in all, and their properties confiscated for the benefit of "loyal elements" or German settlers. In Brittany, the Germans encouraged a Breton separatist movement, and detached the province from the rest of France for purposes of military administration. Breton prisoners of war were treated as "non-French." The partly Flemish-speaking departments, Nord and Pas-de-Calais, were administered jointly with Belgium.

Jews in the occupied territories suffered the fate of their brethren in the Reich. All the satellite countries introduced anti-Semitic legislation, notably Hungary and Rumania, where the Jews had always been so important an element in the population. The actual detail and chronology of the Jewish liquidation in Europe may have varied from place to place and from time to time, but there is no doubt of its thoroughness and deliberation. Generally "usable" Jews would be screened from the "unusable," the "usable" being earmarked for deportation to factories or labor camps and the "unusable" being segregated into ghettos or other reservations for extermination. It was calculated that a contingent of Jews would normally yield a usable quota of 25–30 per cent.

The mass slaughter of human beings raises considerable mechanical, sanitary, and aesthetic problems. Some of the ghettos were reduced by starvation, some by military action, some by a combination of both. The ghetto in Warsaw, for example, with its remnant of 56,065 Jews, was systematically destroyed by SS and Wehrmacht units in an operation which lasted several days, and "the pluck, courage, and devotion to duty" displayed by these forces against a desperate and destitute people was afterward recorded in an ornate memorial volume, signed by the SS general who commanded the operation and presented by him to the Governor General, Frank. But the principal machinery of extermination was the murder plant, such as at Auschwitz (Oswiecim) or Mauthausen, with its gas chambers and crematoria. At Auschwitz during 1944, we are informed, Jews were being dispatched at the rate of 12,000 a day. A certain Rudolf Hoess, former commandant at

Auschwitz, was eventually tried and hanged at Warsaw for his part in the taking of 4,000,000 human lives, the greater proportion of which were Jews.

RESISTANCE

The story of the resistance is not suited to a chronicle. The mythology which, thanks to Hollywood, has grown up around it, however well deserved, has only dramatized certain of its exceptional incidents. Generally it was a story of day-to-day routines by unknown individuals, the story of a kind of valor that, in the nature of the case, had to be anonymous and unrecorded.

The resistance took many forms, from simple boycott to guerrilla warfare. It was not given to every patriot to kill an SS man, but the more peaceful ways of non-co-operation were as various as human ingenuity. In the long, dreary, nerve-racking siege it was something even to keep oneself and one's hopes alive. For the more active spirits there was the spreading of information, usually obtained from the B.B.C. (the British Broadcasting Corporation) ; there was an underground journalism of over a hundred regular resistance papers; there was the secret "grapevine" to assist the escape of Allied airmen and prisoners of war; there was unlimited incidental espionage. Workers in the factories, especially in the factories producing war material, would "go slow" and depress output even in cases where the working week was extended to 100 hours. It was impossible to supervise every worker and every manual operation. The most precise and ruthless inspection could not prevent "dud" shells and bombs from being delivered to the depots. Workers removed essential parts of machines; they put powdered glass into lubricating oil and sugar into gasoline; they started fires and explosions. In the country at large, peasants and agricultural laborers hid or spoiled their crops. Saboteurs blew up roads, railroads, and bridges and wrecked telephone, telegraph, and electric power lines. Sabotage was gradually organized; special personnel were trained in England and parachuted into occupied territories with radio sets, arms, and explosives. Toward the second half of the war, and especially just before the Allied invasion of Normandy, the resistance was being directed like a regular military operation.

The resistance in its more organized phases usually showed certain common features. It was invariably linked with political parties. Industrial workers had a tradition of resistance behind them and a conscious class solidarity, and they had special opportunities for sabotage. The first cells of the resistance often grew out of the trade-unions. The Communists were already acquainted with the cell system and with all the technique of underground activity. The churches, with their memories of persecution and martyrdom, provided another ready-made organization. Catholics found apt use for their doctrines of sanctuary, secrecy of the confessional, and inviolability of the priesthood. But political and ecclesiastical partisanship reflected too often the complexities of the former peacetime state. The situation varied from Denmark, Norway, or the Protectorate with their unified resistance to Yugoslavia or Greece, where the factions in the resistance movement fought one another as well as their common enemy and where, in addition, they became embroiled in the power politics of their greater allies. In addition, it often happened that the resistance movement in a country took a revolutionary form, while that country's official government in exile was reactionary. The consequences were later in painful evidence if the resistance movement afterward arrogated to itself the functions of the first liberation government.

The Protectorate of Bohemia-Moravia was marked out from the first for special mistreatment, and the resistance in it was roused or cowed accordingly. In March 1939, Hitler had appointed Baron von Neurath Protector, directly responsible to himself. Neurath's Secretary of State and the real driving force in the earlier history of the occupation was the Sudeten German and former supporter of Henlein, Karl Hermann Frank (pp. 633 and 634) — not to be confused with Hans Frank, the Governor General of Poland. Hacha remained "President" of a "Committee of National Trusteeship" of fifty subservient Czech colleagues with entirely phantom prerogatives, and made periodic and ineffectual appeals to the Czech people "to realise their changed condition and to accept the advantages of their incorporation into Greater Germany." Henlein extended his party network over the territory, and all other parties ceased to exist. The Nuremberg anti-Semitic laws were introduced. Local Germans were granted special privileges and were regarded as the aristocracy of the Protectorate.

Hitler evidently purposed the total strategic and cultural destruction of the "Bohemian Bastion," and his campaign was made the more barbarous by his insane hatred of a people whom he had once injured. But the Czechs with their long history of revolt were not ready to submit without a struggle. There were student demonstrations on October 28, 1939, the twenty-first anniversary of the Czechoslovak Republic, and again some days later at the funeral of a medical student, Jan Opletal, who had been arrested and beaten to death by the Gestapo during the earlier demonstration. The Gestapo characteristically replied with a ferocious raid on student hostels, mauled, tortured, and raped at will, and carried off 2,000 students for further treatment at Dachau and Buchenwald, of whom some 500 survivors, physically and morally broken, were eventually released.

A long-term program of Germanization was directed especially against the cultural life of the Czech people. Czech universities were closed to Czechs; Czech learned and historical societies, as well as the *Sokol,* the famous physical-culture institution, were dissolved; Czech libraries and art galleries were rifled of their treasures. Great numbers of Czech schools were closed and, in the few that remained open, the children were subjected to Nazi educational methods on the general theme that the "Masaryk-Beneš period" was a historical aberration which a benign Führer had now been sent to rectify. National holidays, national colors, national songs were prohibited; several national monuments and memorials were demolished. Former members of the Czech Legion were deprived of their pensions. Clergy were arrested, monastic orders dissolved, and ecclesiastical properties confiscated. Intellectuals in concentration camps in 1940 were estimated at 70,000.

The German invasion of Russia in 1941 was the signal for the first serious wave of sabotage on the part of Czech munition workers in the Skoda factories. In September 1941, Neurath, who did not seem to have the heart to deal with the situation, went on extended leave on grounds of "undermined health," and effective control passed into the hands of Reinhard Heydrich, one of the most intelligent and savage of Himmler's lieutenants, who at once initiated a new reign of terror. In 1942 Heydrich became the instrument of the labor deportations in the Protectorate and, on May 26 of that year, he announced the total conscription of Czech youth. But, on the 27th, a grenade was thrown at his car as he was driving through one of the less frequented suburbs of Prague, and he died of his wounds some days later. A state of emergency was declared; the Gestapo combed the country; a reward of 10,000,000 crowns ($250,000) was offered for information leading to the apprehension of his assailants. Executions took place daily of persons young and old, eminent and obscure, charged with complicity; the village of Lidice, where one of the assailants had allegedly hidden, was razed to the ground, and its inhabitants massacred. The Berlin radio afterward announced that the wanted men had been shot in a skirmish in an old disused church, but it is probable that the real culprits were never discovered. Heydrich was succeeded by a man of similar kidney, one Daluege, another of Himmler's lieutenants. In August 1943, Wilhelm Frick, former Reich Minister of the Interior, became Protector. The evergreen Karl Hermann Frank retained his office as Secretary of State throughout these changes.

The resistance in Yugoslavia reared its head from the first days of the occupation. Colonel Draja Mihailovich organized his "Chetniks" on the model of the Serb bands which, in times past, had risen up to fight the invader. But he was not a strong commander, despite the glamorizing which his exploits for a time were given in the Allied press. His movement was composed of independent and scattered guerrilla forces, largely drawn from regulars of the disbanded Yugoslav Army and waging war both on the enemy and on native nonconformists. He attempted no large-scale fighting but chose rather to husband his few resources for eventual harrying operations on the flank of the future Allied liberation. Indiscriminate massacre by the Germans, after his every raid, was its own validation of his limited strategy. Furthermore he was an ardent Serb nationalist and monarchist, an opponent of federalism in Yugoslavia — for the Croats, in his view, were a treacherous people — and, more important still, a bitter enemy of Communism.

The German invasion of Russia in 1941 was accompanied by a new terrorism and partisan activity in Yugoslavia, and there emerged therefrom the resistance movement of Josip Broz, afterward known as Tito. The new leader was a Croat by birth and a blacksmith by early occupation. He had deserted from the Austro-Hungarian Army in the First World War, had subsequently fought in the Russian Civil War, and had returned to his homeland a trained and disciplined agitator for the Communist cause. He had spent his term in prison and "underground." Once the war in 1941 had become meaningful to the Communists, his role was obvious, and he set out to capture the upsurging resistance in his country for his own purposes.

At a meeting in the early autumn of 1941, Tito and Mihailovich agreed on joint action against their mutual enemy, but not on the division of their commands. Divergent purposes engendered distrust and, before the end of the year, the two leaders were at open war with one another. Mihailovich's influence thereafter began to fall away and, at the end of 1943, Churchill, partly in vexation over his inactivity and partly in response to the reckless charges against him of complicity with the Nazis, took the initiative in transferring Anglo-American aid to his Soviet-supported rival. Likewise, the political prizes in Yugoslavia went to Tito. He organized an "Anti-Fascist Council for the National Liberation," and this Council, purportedly gathered from the whole country and representing all the democratic parties, spread its hierarchy of committees into such villages and districts as the fortunes of the day allowed it to control. In November 1943 the Council met under the effective dominance of Tito, now styling himself Marshal and Acting Minister of National Defense and, assuming the status of a government, it passed resolutions forbidding King Peter and the Yugoslav government in exile to return home till the people had decided for themselves their constitutional future.

The government in exile in London, meanwhile, was too torn by dissension to be able to offer constructive leadership to, or impose its authority on, the embittered factions in Yugoslavia. By making Mihailovich Minister of War in 1942, it had already shown its hand. In June 1944, however, under British pressure, King Peter at last agreed not to return home until a plebiscite had been held, and he sent his latest Premier, Ivan Subasich, to negotiate with Tito. In July, a coalition cabinet was formed representing the interests of both the King and Tito, and a joint subordinate body was charged with co-ordinating matters involving the war, foreign affairs, and reconstruction. In August 1944, pursuant to this policy of co-operation, King Peter designated Tito as sole leader of the Yugoslav forces of resistance. But the Red Army was now on the borders of Yugoslavia. Tito secretly flew to Moscow and made his own independent bargain with the prospective liberators of his country. In October 1944, Belgrade was free, and Tito was in control.

The Axis occupation of Greece brought untold hardships upon the Greek peoples. A succession of impotent puppet governments, continuous friction between the German and Italian occupation authorities, jackal operations by Bulgarians in Thrace and Macedonia, the depredations of the Gestapo, disease, food shortages, and the resulting starvation of thousands of the Greek people, all contributed to reduce the depleted country to misery and political chaos. Resistance groups were diverse and fiercely divided against each other. Chief among them were EAM (National Liberation Movement) with its military organization known as the ELAS (Greek Popular Liberation Army), and EDES (Greek Democratic Liberation Army). EAM, by far the best organized and tough-spirited of the groups, was an outgrowth of the prewar Greek Communists under the direction of Moscow. Fighting occurred during 1943–44 between EAM and EDES at the time of the Soviet military successes and the consequent increase of Communist pressure in Greece. The whole future character of the Greek Government was called into question, and the old conflict between monarchical and republican interests was reopened in sharpened form. The urgency of these problems was manifest as the advance of the British Eighth Army in North Africa brought within sight the possibilities of an Anglo-American liberation of Greece.

The British Government was committed to the restoration of King George in Greece, and it was also much concerned over the political complexion of some of the Greek resistance groups. As was becoming all too evident, EAM, the dominant resistance group, was more pro-Communist than anti-Nazi, or even pro-Greek, and it was entrenching itself firmly for the eventual seizure of power in Greece. Strategic interests in the Near East and the Turkish fear of Soviet encirclement forced the British Government into an attitude of uneasy and reluctant hostility to Communism in Greece.

There was continual friction between the Greek resistance leaders and the Greek government in exile, particularly after that government had refused to include within itself representatives of the resistance or to undertake that the Greek King should not return to his country until a plebiscite had been held. Mutinies broke out in Greek army and naval units in Egypt in April 1944 and were quelled with difficulty. King George afterward issued a statement from Cairo pledging to submit freely to the judgment of his people when Greece was liberated. In May 1944, Greek leaders, including resistance delegates, held a conference in the Lebanon, presided over by Papandreou, the Greek Social Democrat, who had been appointed by King George to form a government. A National Charter was formulated which included resolutions to suppress terrorism in Greece and to "unify" and "discipline" the Greek resistance forces.

The Germans withdrew from Greece in October 1944, and Papandreou and his government entered Athens to find EAM in virtual control. The ELAS, the military organization of EAM, was then 30,000 to 50,000 strong, materially and ideologically well armed, and naturally enough it did not yield to Papandreou's attempt to disarm and disband it with British support. On the last day of 1944, Archbishop Damaskinos became Regent and, on February 12, 1945, a truce was signed between ELAS and the British General Scobie. But the situation was still uncertain as Greece passed into the postwar era.

COLLABORATION

At the other end of the scale was collaboration. In most countries there were industrialists, bankers, and civil servants to be found who took kindly to their German satraps. There were also the leaders and members of local "Nazi" parties — Moravec in Czechoslovakia, Degrelle in Belgium, Mussert in Holland, Clausen in Denmark, Quisling in Norway — the last of whom gave his name to the entire tribe. The motivations of these men were mixed and complex. Some loved their earthly possessions; some seized the opportunity for power; some believed they could best protect the interests of their country by remaining at their posts; some were sincere converts to Nazism; most were ordinary, bewildered mortals swept into situations beyond their control. Generally it can be said that, whereas the resistance so often had a revolutionary flavor, genuine collaboration was invariably of the Right. But it can also be said that collaboration was mainly helpful to the Germans in the early period of the occupation. After the labor deportations and after the German military reverses, the inevitable doubts and desertions set in. In 1943, even the "Model Protectorate" of Denmark revolted and had to be subjected to military rule.

The classic home of collaboration was Vichy. On July 10, 1940, at Vichy in Unoccupied France, a National Assembly of the French Chamber and Senate, under the presidency of Herriot, overwhelmingly voted Marshal Pétain full powers to promulgate a new constitution for France. Two days later Pétain assumed the title of Chief of State, repealed the republican constitution of 1875, and indefinitely adjourned the Chamber and Senate. He appointed Pierre Laval Vice-President and later Foreign Minister. On October 24, 1940, at Montoire, on the initiative of Laval, Hitler and Pétain met in conference, and Pétain formally and irrevocably "entered upon the path of collaboration." Vichy had some analogies with the contemporary dictatorships. A totalitarian ideology seemed to be conveyed by Pétain's watchword, "Work, Family, Country," replacing the former revolutionary triad, "Liberty, Equality, Fraternity." "The French State (*l'État Français*)" was used in place of the word Republic. Familiar totalitarianisms were introduced, the usual censorships and controls, youth organizations, and anti-Semitic enactments.

Yet, whatever future historians may say about Pétain's character and motives, he did at least try at first to resist the harshest forms of Nazi pressure and intimidation. In December 1940, at the height of the expulsions of population from Alsace-Lorraine, he summarily dismissed Laval and sent a note to Hitler defining the extent of his willingness to collaborate. He took Flandin for his Foreign Minister and Admiral Darlan, Commander in Chief of the Navy, for his Minister of the Interior. He made his protest, though it cannot be said that much was gained by it. Flandin was almost Germanophile, and Darlan had been violently Anglophobe ever since the destruction of the French Fleet at Oran, and in their hands the path of collaboration could only become smoother, broader, and steeper. In February 1941, Darlan became Vice-President, Foreign Minister, and Minister of the Interior. Laval meanwhile intrigued in Paris for his own return and advancement.

The United States remained in diplomatic relations with Vichy till the North African landing — and so also did Canada, Australia, New Zealand, and the Latin-American republics. Vichy, after all, in the view of the State Department, was the legal successor of the Third Republic and nothing was to be gained by a rupture. Bullitt was American ambassador to France until the end of 1940, when Admiral Leahy succeeded him. The Admiral came to Vichy very much in the capacity of personal representative of President Roosevelt. He remained till April 1942, exerting himself to minimize the malign influence of Darlan and Laval and to prevent Pétain from granting the Germans concessions beyond the letter of the armistice, and sending his President a series of now classic reports on the ever shifting situation in France.

There is no need to follow the story of Vichy through all its detail. Generally it was a long, dull battle of wits between Laval, Darlan, and Pétain, the last named gradually failing in energy and influence. The Germans held all the realities of power and, though they began by using that power with discretion, the political deterioration in France was an inevitable process. The people, both of Occupied and Unoccupied France, suffered great privations. The social and economic barrier between the two zones was rigidly maintained. Worst of all, nearly 2,000,000 Frenchmen were prisoners of war in the hands of an enemy who did not scruple to use them as a kind of blackmail. The mere absence of these men from their homes for six years disastrously depressed the nation's birth rate — as, no doubt, the Germans intended it should do. Former "Leaguers," Déat and Doriot, tried to form political parties with totalitarian principles, collaborating with Germany, the main difference between them apparently being that Déat opposed, and Doriot supported Pétain's government. But they managed to recruit a contingent, the so-called Tricolor Legion, whose members wore a Nazi type of uniform, pledged fealty to Hitler, and served against the Soviet Union on the Eastern front.

The pace quickened during 1941. The French resistance movement, born at the time of the Battle of Britain, took increased encouragement from the great defense of the Soviet Union. Underground newspapers with appropriate titles, *Combat, Franc-Tireur, Libération, L'Humanité,* were circulated in the thousands. Attacks on German soldiers in Occupied France led the German Military Governor, General von Stuelpnagel,[2] to retaliate by shooting hostages — fifty Frenchmen for every German killed. Terror bred terror, and the Germans began to lose confidence in Darlan's ability to cope with the spreading unrest. Hitler's henchmen in Germany, Sauckel and Speer, meanwhile were casting avid eyes on the unemployed French masses.

In April 1942, a series of meetings between Pétain, Darlan, and Laval, under the watchful eyes of Abetz, Hitler's ambassador to France, and of Fernand de Brinon, Vichy's own representative in Paris, concluded with the formation of a new government at Vichy. Pétain entrusted Laval with "the effective direction of internal and foreign policy" and made him the virtual dictator of Unoccupied France. The discredited Darlan was not a member of the new government, but he remained Commander in Chief of the armed forces and successor designate of Pétain. Laval's term of office was punctuated with the derailing of trains, the blowing up of bridges, assassinations, and the inevitable executions of hostages. But he fulfilled to the best of his ability the object that the Germans had in mind when they supported his return to power. He opened an intensive propaganda campaign to induce French workers to volunteer for service in Germany, and he was promised a proportionate return of French prisoners of war in exchange. Even so, the campaign achieved so meager a success that, in September 1942, compulsory recruitment was instituted in both Occupied and Unoccupied France. Such was the situation in November 1942, when the Anglo-American landings took place in North Africa (see pp. 748–52).

GOVERNMENTS IN EXILE

Meanwhile, official governments of countries overrun by the Nazis were often able to establish themselves in exile. They were joined by as much of their combatant and merchant navies as could evade capture, and their territorial possessions and assets abroad were pooled with the Allied war chest. They built up fighting contingents. They engaged in propaganda, notably broadcast appeals and news services to their homelands. They kept in touch with their national resistance movements. They were beneficiaries of American Lend-Lease.

In 1940, King Haakon of Norway and Queen Wilhelmina of the Netherlands with their respective families and governments made good their escape. King Christian of Denmark and his government remained in Denmark, but a Danish Council was organized in London late in 1940 and rallied all Free Danes to itself. King Leopold of the Belgians remained a voluntary prisoner of war in German hands, but the Belgian Government eventually reached London. A Czechoslovak National Committee was set up in London with Beneš as President and Jan Masaryk, the son of the late Thomas Masaryk and lately Czech minister in London, as Foreign Minister and, in 1941, after the German invasion of Russia, it was recognized by Britain and the Soviet Union. During 1941, King Peter of Yugoslavia and his government were established in London, and King George of the Hellenes and his government were established in part in London and in part in Cairo.

After the Fall of France, General de Gaulle was recognized by the British Government as "the leader of all Free Frenchmen wherever they may be, who rally to him in support of the Allied cause." But his French National Committee in London was not granted the recognition of a government in exile. The United States cold-shouldered him even after December 1941, when it broke off relations with Vichy. Certainly de Gaulle was not a man of sympathetic personal appeal, and he was just the type of émigré reactionary who failed to understand the revolutionary character of the resistance in his homeland. Yet courage and dignity he did not lack, and he made himself the symbol of French patriotism in a dark hour. The greater part of French Equatorial Africa — with the unhappy exception of Dakar — came over to his side. Madagascar was overcome after a short but dangerous revolt in 1942. Free French forces took part in operations in Libya and the Near East and in many forays by sea and air.

The most tangled and tragic of all the stories of the governments in exile was that of Poland. On September 19, 1939, just before his flight from Poland, President Moscicki resigned in favor of Raczkiewicz, former Marshal of the Sejm, then in Paris, who appointed General Sikorski Premier and Commander in Chief. Marshal Śmigly-Rydz, in internment in Rumania, was "dismissed" from his offices and honors. Units of the Polish Navy, several Polish merchantmen, and the Polish gold reserve of $100,000,000 were safely withdrawn. Some 100,000 Poles fought in the Battle of France, and scores of Polish pilots in the Battle of Britain. The Polish Army in the Near East, organized under General Anders, eventually numbered 150,000 men. In 1940, after the Fall of France, the Polish Government was transferred to London.

In exile, the Polish affairs proceeded smoothly enough at first. In December 1941, Sikorski visited Moscow and resumed relations broken off at the time of the Soviet invasion of Poland in September 1939. He twice visited the United States to negotiate Lend-Lease aid and to rally the support of Americans of Polish descent. In London he was on the best of terms with Beneš and the Czechoslovak Committee. But Polish affairs deteriorated suddenly in 1943. The Soviet forces were then recovering their lost territories and, if they maintained their advance, must soon be crossing the former Polish frontier. Soviet-Polish relations, which were safely academic in 1940–42, were now of urgent and unavoidable practical importance. Old antipathies persisted even under the stress of war and vitiated a relationship which, from every point of view, ought to have been one of alliance and comradeship. The Polish Government in London was largely drawn from the old squirearchical element, the same set as Pilsudski's "Colonels," among whom a hatred of Russia and of Communism was a traditional article of belief. The Polish Government inconveniently recalled that, in spite of frequent inquiries, no proper information had been vouchsafed in regard to the whereabouts and welfare of the millions of Poles deported by the Russians in 1939, and it was plainly dissatisfied with Russian explanation that these Poles had now been granted Soviet citizenship. It reaffirmed its claims to the eastern Polish frontier of 1920. In April 1943, the Germans announced the discovery of the bodies of 8,000 Polish officers buried in a common grave at Katyn, a village near Smolensk, Polish prisoners of war allegedly massacred by the Red Army during the fighting in that area in 1941. Soviet-Polish diplomatic relations were once more broken off. Then, in July 1943, at the height of the Katyn crisis, General Sikorski was killed in an airplane accident. He was succeeded by Mikolajczyk of the Peasant party, hitherto Vice-Premier.

The Polish-Soviet rupture was a major embarrassment to the United Nations and indeed to the entire Allied cause. It was the first open sign of the rift between East and West. The Kremlin was clearly resolved to impose its own political pattern on Intermediate Europe (see p. 846) and to cure, by force or friendship, the historic anti-Russianism of its Western neighbors. And to every protest it could always return the unanswerable answer of its own military predominance, present or prospective, in the territories in question. The situation was unendurably aggravated by the fact that both parties could put forward records of loss and suffering at the hands of the same enemy, records which somehow they considered entitled them to a satisfaction of their most contradictory demands.

Independently of its Western allies, the Soviet Government had been giving support to groups of Polish partisans of Communist sympathies, out of whom arose in July 1943, in the very month that Mikolajczyk became Polish Premier, the so-called Lublin Administration. In November 1943, at the Teheran Conference, Stalin induced Roosevelt and Churchill to agree to the Soviet claim to an eastern Polish frontier corresponding to the old Curzon Line. The agreement was not explicitly revealed, but Churchill shortly afterward announced a virtual recognition of it in the House of Commons in the course of one of his periodic reviews of the war. Then, in July 1944, the Lublin Administration brought matters to a head by declaring that it was "the sole legal source of authority in Poland" and that "the *émigré* government in London is an illegal and self-styled authority based on the illegal Fascist Constitution of 1935." (See pp. 181–82.) And, if this was not enough, there occurred the attempted liberation of Warsaw by the Red Army in August 1944 and the German massacre of the insurgent partisan forces in the city (see p. 773).

Mikolajczyk, then visiting Moscow at Stalin's invitation, found himself being asked to accept the *fait accompli* of agreements regarding the future constitution of Poland already reached between Lublin and the Soviet Government. He was strongly pressed both by the Soviet and British Governments to enter into a coalition with Lublin. In November 1944 he at last resigned, and it was clear that the Polish Government in London would have little further influence with its former Anglo-American allies. Early in 1945, the Lublin Administration transformed itself into a Provisional Government of the Polish Republic and, at the Crimea Conference in that February, Allied diplomacy gave its formal seal of approval to the existing situation.

44 THE JAPANESE–OCCUPIED

TERRITORIES IN EAST ASIA

THE CO–PROSPERITY SPHERE IN EAST ASIA

By mid-1942, Japan presided over a widely flung maritime empire of impressive bulk and unlimited riches. In a short six months of warfare, the Co-prosperity Sphere had swollen to 3,000,000 square miles, with 450,000,000 inhabitants — almost one-fifth of the human race — and accounted for 95 per cent of the world's rubber, 70 per cent of its tin, 70 per cent of its rice, 85 per cent of its copra, and 90 per cent of its quinine. Raw materials were abundantly available such as would make Japan a self-sufficient, almost unchallengeable Power. The organization and government of these resources would doubtless be determined by the conflicting demands of a long-term beneficent imperialism and immediate military needs.

Japan's imperialism sprang, in the first place, from a profound belief in the divine origin, not only of her imperial family, but also of her people and her very islands, and in her manifest destiny to extend the benefits of her supernaturally ordained good fortune to nations still dwelling in outer darkness. If the beckoning vision was resisted by the white man, then his obstinacy was to be overcome by a vast pan-Asiatic campaign under Japanese leadership. Nor was this ideology conceived in an idle hour by some empty gazer standing on the lunatic fringe of Japanese politics. It bore the imprimatur of responsible statesmanship. Its main lines had already been forecast as early as 1858 in a memorial submitted to the Emperor by an intimate adviser, Baron Hotta. An interim program for an empire in East Asia, as a halfway house to world dominion, was described in the so-called Tanaka Memorial, which Baron General Giichi Tanaka was reported to have submitted to the Emperor in 1927. The authenticity of this document itself is not beyond question, but it reflected accurately enough the aspirations of the Japanese militarists: "Our first step was to conquer Formosa, and the second to annex Korea . . . The third step is yet to be taken, and it is the conquest of Manchuria, Mongolia, and China. When this is done, the rest of Asia, including the South Sea Islands, will be at our feet. . . . For the sake of self-preservation and of giving warning to China and the rest of the world, we must eventually fight America. . . ."

The Japanese Army was deemed to have substantially completed the third step of this program with its successful occupation of Hankow and Canton in 1938. Prince Konoye, the Japanese Premier, announced simultaneously the advent of a "New Order in East Asia," an era of abundance and stability ensured by the harmonious co-operation of Japan, China, and Manchukuo.

The Soviet Union was a matter deserving attention, and more aggressive military opinion in Tokyo would doubtless have considered a campaign in eastern Siberia as the next appropriate step — the more so as the Japanese Navy still appeared to be averse to an all-out Pacific adventure. But the fall of the Netherlands and France in May and June 1940, the consequent dereliction of their East Asia possessions, and the evident preoccupation and weakness of Britain, all presented an opportunity which it would have been folly to pass by. In September 1940, Admiral Sokichi Takahashi was writing: "The New Order in East Asia . . . means the inclusion of all the South Pacific region — the Netherlands East Indies, French Indo-China, the Philippines, etc. It means the drawing together of all the northern and southern peoples, saving them from the colonial exploitation of Europe and America in order to establish an Asia for the Asiatics. Its objective is the well-being of all races. . . ." By 1940, Premier Konoye was no longer referring to "the New Order in East Asia," but to "the New Order in Greater East Asia." The Nazi New Order in Europe and the North Atlantic was to be neatly matched by another in East Asia and the South Pacific, in which the native peoples, released from foreign yoke, would function as "younger brothers" of Japan.

How this fine vision was to be squared with Japan's immediate military needs only events would show. Even without the ever present facts of war, the incorporation of the new territories into a comprehensive, well-articulated Co-prosperity Sphere and the switch of their economies away from the United States and Europe would have taken many patient years to accomplish. Meanwhile the disruption of traditional channels of trade could not but depress the welfare of the new empire. "Autonomy" and "independence" would be perilous, two-edged gifts to be given, under pressure of war, to stricken, discontented, and largely ignorant peoples. In the end, Japan's policy of dispensing showy concessions with one hand while gathering tribute with the other deceived no one. The relatively brief experience of Japanese rule was enough to convince all but the most favored and flattered of native collaborators that yellow imperialism was infinitely more rapacious and oppressive than white.

However, it all began bravely enough. The Japanese advanced into their promised lands under the banner of liberation and brotherhood. Their occasionally brusque methods at first might be justified by their apologists on the score of military necessity. Their worst atrocities were committed against white prisoners of war, white civilians whom they interned, native supporters of white regimes, notably Indian and Filipino soldiers who retained their loyalties — and, of course, against the Chinese. The "Death March" after Bataan, for example, and the conditions under which the Siam-Burma railroad was afterward constructed, conformed to this pattern. But among friendly Asiatics they came as friendly Asiatics. Thus to the Siamese, whom the propagandists of Tokyo had always bracketed with themselves as one of the two Oriental peoples to have stood firm and unsubmerged amid the advancing tide of white imperialism, they came as allies and equals. They dispersed their troops thinly over Siam's strategic centers and made every effort to obscure the fact that the troops were there as an army of occupation.

They fostered Japanese-Siamese "cultural pacts" and sponsored a Japanese Cultural Institute in the Siamese capital, Bangkok. To the Burmese they came as fellow Buddhists. Their troops fraternized with the Burman villagers — though not, be it noted, with the Karens. They introduced educational reforms in Burma with the object of eliminating the alien British influence and restoring the purity of the original Burmese civilization.

With such aims openly avowed, the Japanese had little trouble in finding collaborators and, in so far as was practicable, they invariably installed or adopted a local potentate as their puppet ruler. Luang Pibul Songgram was their choice in Siam (pp. 577–78), Ba Maw in Burma, Emilio Aguinaldo and José Laurel in the Philippines, and later Soekarno and Mohammed Hatta in Indonesia — and, of course, the "Emperor" Pu Yi in Manchukuo (see p. 431), and Wang Ching-wei in Occupied China (see p. 677). In Malaya, they won over the native rulers with assurances that their lives, properties, and dignities would be respected.

But pleasing as these fictions might be, the Japanese showed no qualms about establishing for themselves the realities of military and economic control, and their administrations in the occupied territories, empirically various in form as those of the Nazi New Order in Europe, were nonetheless efficient instruments for their purpose. The "Empire" of Manchukuo, the creation of the Kwantung Army, was virtually administered by that army's commander in chief. Wang Ching-wei was President of the so-called "National Government of China" in Nanking, but the real ruler of Occupied China was the Japanese "ambassador," General Nobuyuki Abe. In Indo-China, no doubt in deference to Berlin, which did not want to embarrass the Vichy government unnecessarily, the Japanese retained and worked through the French Governor General, Decoux, and his civil service, but again the real ruler of the territory was the "ambassador," Yoshizawa. The Netherlands East Indies were entirely reorganized. Java, Madura, Sumatra, Celebes, and Borneo were divided into a series of districts, each headed by a military governor who was advised and assisted by an exclusively Japanese council, half-civil, half-military in constitution. The capital city, Batavia, which comprised a district in itself, received a Japanese mayor — an ex-director of the great business house of Mitsubishi. The mayoralties of other larger cities, with the exception of Surabaya and Serabang, were awarded to native collaborators. Overriding authority reposed in the hands of the commander in chief of the Japanese forces in Java. Dutch officials were interned; but their Eurasian subordinates, numerous in the middle and lower ranks of the administrative hierarchy, were retained. Malaya was similarly "centralized" under a series of Japanese military governors under the overriding authority of the commander in chief of the Japanse forces in Singapore.

The instruments of economic exploitations were also various. A favorite was the "national policy" company, similar to the great monopolistic companies already operating in Korea, such as the North China Development Company, the Central China Development Company, and the series of companies in Manchukuo. A Central Company for the Development of the East Indies had barely time to get started before the Japanese forces lost control of the territory it was intended to cover. Elsewhere the evidence points to the infiltration of the Zaibatsu-dominated control associations (see p. 706), invariably with the co-operation of the Japanese army commanders on the spot. The magnates and agents of home industry might not always be given an enthusiastic welcome in the occupied territories but, so long as they showed proper deference for the military authorities, they were accepted as a necessary part and complement of the imperial process.

In general, it may be said that the Japanese had little in the way of a preconceived, over-all economic "plan." There was considerable division of opinion between the Zaibatsu, who persisted in regarding the Co-prosperity Sphere as a producer of profits and dividends, and the militarists, who were more concerned over its potentialities as a source of war materials. The grand design of a centralized "workshop" in the Japanese home islands, at the handle of a spreading fan of agricultural and raw-material countries, was a later ideological importation from Nazi Europe. Thus no attempt was made to remove existing industries, and new industries, provided they did not compete with those of Japan, were not discouraged.

Manchukuo had been largely agricultural and pastoral at the time of the invasion of 1931; but, under the very independent and enterprising control of the Kwantung Army, it had become the laboratory of an ambitious Five-Year Plan and then, after 1941, of a projected Ten-Year Plan of industrial development, and the limiting condition in the process had not been "policy" but the crude limits set by the shortage of Chinese labor, especially in the coal fields. Production figures in Manchukuo could hardly have been high so long as the coal fields were operating at the excessively low rate of a fifth of a ton of coal per man per day. Borneo and the oil areas of the East Indies were marked out for future industrial centers. Later, in 1942–43, in an attempt to balance scarcity and surplus in the Co-prosperity Sphere, there were some changes effected in local products, changes sometimes forcibly effected. Thus rubber plantations were cleared for rice in Malaya; rubber, sugar, and coffee plantations were cleared for rice in Java; sugar plantations were cleared for cotton in the Philippines, and the sugar surpluses still obtaining were turned over to the manufacture of industrial alcohol; and so forth. But interference with traditional crops was not always understood by the native cultivator, and was understood by him even less when it was accompanied by military surveillance. All in all, it could be said that, perhaps with the exception of Manchukuo, Japanese economy in the Co-prosperity Sphere was a pretty *ad hoc* affair, and that, in any event, wartime pressures left little time or opportunity for the initiation of any "plan" that there might otherwise have been.

Currency alone appears to have been planned; but here the plan miscarried. The currency of each occupied territory was intended to have been based on the Japanese yen. The so-called Yen Bloc was thus created. Puppet central banks would then issue notes against reserves of yen notes, and their operations would be strictly supervised by the Bank of Japan. Tokyo would thus become the financial center of the Co-prosperity Sphere. Furthermore a "banker's bank" would be established under the name of the South Seas Development Bank, whose capital would be entirely government-subscribed, and only government-controlled banks, such as the Yokohama Specie Bank or the Bank of Taiwan, would be permitted to open branches in the occupied territories. Such was the intention, but only a beginning was made of it. The Yen Bloc came to include no more than Manchukuo and North China, and elsewhere the Co-prosperity Sphere was a chaos of currencies in which the Nanking yuan, the Hong Kong dollar, the Indo-Chinese piaster, the Siamese baht, the Burmese rupee, the Straits dollar, the Dutch guilder, the Philippine peso, and various Japanese military notes were all in circulation.

COLLABORATION AND "INDEPENDENCE"

But there was something almost unreal in these measures and administrations. The building of the new empire had to wait upon the war being fought around its periphery. The series of Japan's victories seemed to have been halted at the Battle of Midway in June 1942 (see p. 745). In the single month of November 1942 followed four setbacks which shattered the hope of an early peace — El Alamein, North Africa, Stalingrad, and Guadalcanal (see p. 745). The Allied "Hitler first" strategy, however, suggested that Japan might be permitted a breathing space before the full fury of the rising global counteroffensive broke in the Pacific theater. The ability of Japan to wage a long war of attrition and to preserve at least a part of her empire depended on her ability to make the best use of its resources. Beneficent imperialism must be quickly sacrificed in the paramount interests of defense.

In the same November 1942, the Japanese Government announced the formation of the Greater East Asia Ministry to absorb a number of former colonial departments, the Manchurian Affairs Board, the East Asiatic Affairs Board, and the South Seas Affairs Board. This major administrative upheaval, which required no less than two cabinet decrees and 78 ordinances for its implementation, placed the Army in the person of Premier Tojo in firmer economic command of the Co-prosperity Sphere. The new ministry controlled all matters pertaining to foreign trade, the supervision of commercial organizations, and the training of administrative personnel in the Sphere. "The building up of Greater East Asia," affirmed Kazuo Aoki, the chief of the new ministry, "is absolutely inseparable from the continuance of the war." And the new defensive strategy was given indirect expression by Admiral Nomura in a radio address: "The Axis Powers," he explained, "do not have to attack any more to win; they need only hold out in conquered positions."

In November 1943, as the American forces were closing in on Rabaul, Surabaya, and Tarawa, a Greater East Asia Conference assembled in Tokyo under the chairmanship of Foreign Minister Shigemitsu, flanked by ten major dignitaries of the Greater East Asia Ministry. Occupied China was represented by its puppet President, Wang Ching-wei, the "Republic" of the Philippines by its President-elect José Laurel, Burma by her collaborationist Head of the State, Ba Maw, and Manchukuo and Siam by her Premier and a prince of the blood respectively. The "Provisional Government of Free India," inaugurated under Japanese auspices in Singapore in the previous month, was represented by the brilliant renegade, Subhas Chandra Bose, a former president of the Indian National Congress. The deliberations of the delegates concluded with the issue of a "Greater East Asia Declaration," which reaffirmed the principle of "Asia for the Asiatics" and pledged all the signatories to joint defense of their countries against "European imperialism." Bose elaborated on the necessity for military co-operation and, in a brutally frank address, warned his fellow delegates that the roseate vision of the Co-prosperity Sphere in East Asia could be realized only through a conclusive victory in the war.

The full conflict between beneficent imperialism and military needs was therefore joined. The policy of prolonging hostilities in the all too distant hope of bringing the war-weary enemy to a negotiated peace would receive a powerful reinforcement if the resistance of the native peoples of the Co-prosperity Sphere could be effectively mobilized. But such a policy, however desirable for Japan herself, would make for increasing economic distress and disillusionment among those peoples, severed from their usual markets and pillaged by their nominal ally. Japanese strategic thinking differentiated between an Outer Zone and an Inner Zone of the Co-prosperity Sphere. The Outer Zone — Indo-China, Siam, Burma, the Netherlands East Indies, Borneo, and the Philippines — was to be held as long as possible while it was methodically stripped of any removable materials it contained that could contribute to the defense of the Inner Zone — North China, Manchukuo, Korea, and Formosa, and the Japanese home islands. But both the Outer Zone and the Inner Zone — the expendable Outer Zone even more than the more precious Inner Zone — were now to have thrust upon them the most flattering political concessions undisguisedly designed to engage their loyalty and co-operation.

The year 1943 was distinguished for the first tentative instances of this auspicious policy. In Occupied China, the Japanese renounced their extraterritorial rights and concessions, in return for which the Nanking government declared war on the United States and Britain. Prepared by this recognition of the "equality" of China, Tokyo and Nanking were joined, in October 1943, in a formal treaty of alliance which united the two governments in the majestic enterprise of liberating the East from white imperialism. Nanking was accorded majority representation on the board of directors of the Central China Development Company — though the power of ultimate decision still lay with Japanese "advisers." In Burma, following Ba Maw's visit to Tokyo, the Japanese made ostentatious preparations for creating "an independent Burmese State" as part of the Co-prosperity Sphere and, in due course, on August 1, 1943, a Burmese Declaration of Independence was issued in Rangoon. Ba Maw at this time was being entitled Head of the State, Supreme Commander of the Burmese Army, and *Adipadi,* a Pali word roughly equivalent to Führer. In the East Indies, in March 1943, the Japanese sponsored the merging of the political parties, labor organizations, and youth societies into a single *Poetera* (Centralization of People's Strength) under the leadership of two Indonesian nationalists, Achmed Soekarno and Mohammed Hatta, and then, in October, inaugurated a "Central Council" of Indonesian nationalists in Java. Even in the more backward and disunited Malaya, the Japanese instituted rudimentary forms of self-government in the form of native advisory councils, topped by a central Consultative Council in Singapore. And in the more hostile Philippines, they similarly sponsored organs of political independence. In September 1943 they appointed José Laurel President-elect of a forthcoming Philippine "Republic." The Franco government in Spain granted this republic its formal recognition. The Tokyo radio, seeking to impress the Roman Catholic majority of the Filipinos, affirmed that the Vatican had followed suit. A hasty denial issued by the Vatican was jammed by Japanese censorship.

In July 1943, Siam was exceptionally favored by "a visit of inspection" on the part of Premier Tojo himself, who was received with a pomp befitting one who bore priceless gifts. Luang Pibul's ministers were suitably rewarded, and his wife was given jewelry valued at $75,000. In October the Japanese transferred to Siamese sovereignty the four Unfederated Malay States (Kelantan, Trengganu, Kedah, and Perlis) ceded to Britain by Siam in 1909, and then, for good measure, threw in two of the smaller Shan States of western Burma (Kengtung and Mong Pan). Even so, Siamese irredentists were not entirely satisfied.

But by 1943 the war was not going so well, and the Co-prosperity Sphere was not fulfilling the promise of its name. A serious food shortage already existed even in Manchukuo, a shortage most unusual in that country of broad, rolling expanses of brownish-yellow soil, normally capable of an abundance of soybeans, millet, and corn. It was caused in part by the withdrawal of agricultural labor into the mines and industries and in part by the recalcitrance of the Manchukuoan farmer who, forced to sell his surplus to the government for export at low fixed prices, either curtailed production or funneled it into the black market.

In Occupied China, the deterioration in the main was political and military. Occupied China was conquered territory, and its people had hardly been encouraged to forget their original hostility. The Nanking government of Wang Ching-wei was without any effective powers. It collected a few taxes and kept up a nominal supervision of educational matters, but had not the least control over its own predatory and disorderly rabble of "National" soldiery. Its function was to hide the nakedness of Japanese military despotism and to accept responsibility for the unpopular measures dictated to it by its masters. Latterly the fidelity of its major officials, chiefly ex-members of the Kuomintang who had seceded with Wang Ching-wei, was ensured by various ingenious devices. Thus their sons were conscripted for training as cadets in Japanese military academies and kept there as virtual hostages.

Occupied China was infiltrated with partisan groups which, left much to their own devices by their remote and otherwise preoccupied chiefs in Chungking, were roaming at will and living like bandits. Mining operations, for instance in the important iron-ore areas of northern Shansi, were suspended on account of guerrilla activity. Nor did it appear that the Japanese themselves were overdisciplined or overscrupulous in their dealings even with their collaborator friends. Local producers resented the petty graft which accompanied the grant of business licenses and the resale of their merchandise by the authorities to greedy Japanese middlemen. The Japanese moneylender became no less familiar a figure than the Japanese carpetbagger, and was particularly obnoxious to the hapless Chinese farmer who, between low government-controlled prices for his produce and the inflated cost of industrial goods and implements, sank deeper into debt. And then, crime of crimes, the Japanese Government sponsored a revival of the demoralizing but lucrative opium traffic. The sale and use of the narcotic were carried on in government-controlled dens, euphemistically postered as "Centers for the Eradication of the Opium Habit." The once brilliant and supple Wang Ching-wei had long since become a figure of no account when he died in Tokyo late in 1944, after a long illness.

Meanwhile Anglo-American submarine and aerial operations were making devastating inroads on the 3,000,000 tons of the Japanese merchant navy assigned to Pacific routes. The Outer Zone of the Co-prosperity Sphere was rapidly becoming a maritime empire without ships, though the average native citizen thereof understood little of the great battle beyond the gradual emptying of his bazaars, the reduction of his living conditions to barter level, the requisitioning of his chattels, even his own impressment into forced labor — and the gradual transformation of his onetime Japanese ally and liberator into little better than a freebooter and slaver.

The worsening situation subjected the Sphere's administrative machinery to a test to which it proved quite unequal. Even without the extra stress of war, it is doubtful if Japanese officialdom would ever have been ready for the great imperial expansion. As it was, inexperience and corruption intensified all the effects of blockade and approaching military defeat. In August 1944 the Japanese Government revealed something of its plight in this respect by announcing that the number of officials in Japan would be henceforth reduced by 30 per cent in urban and by 20 per cent in rural areas in order to furnish an additional 100,000 administrators for the Co-prosperity Sphere, and these officials were prepared for their exacting new posts by no more than one month's preliminary instruction in the recently established "Training Institute for the Development of the South." Their graft and petty tyranny in office moved Premier Tojo himself to remonstrance: "Unless our people act very carefully in their daily contacts with other people, we may hurt their feelings. . . . Even if they are inferior to us, we must treat them with true love and understanding."

RESISTANCE

The resistance in Nazi-occupied Europe grew with the approach of the Nazi defeat. The resistance in Japanese-occupied East Asia grew similarly, but for somewhat different reasons. The Nazis founded their New Order on open force and terror, and its peoples, with insignificant exceptions, had no illusions and were hostile from the first day of the occupation to the last. The Japanese founded their Co-prosperity Sphere, at least in the beginning, on the ideal of a common Asiatic citizenship and the promise of a common benefit to all, and its peoples, in the Japanese view, had only themselves to blame if they failed to appreciate the immense favors being bestowed on them. Unfortunately for the Co-prosperity Sphere, the war destroyed its minimum economic precondition. The resistance, once a sort of Risorgimento directed against the mutually hated white man, was gradually turned against the new Japanese overlords. Grants of independence with which the Japanese tried to purchase support only encouraged native nationalism to more defiance. But the resistance in East Asia had this in common with its European counterpart. Its political flavor was invariably revolutionary, even as collaboration was invariably reactionary. Otherwise its political motivations were complex in the extreme and reflected all the localisms of its participants.

A spasmodic nationalist rising in Indo-China in 1940–41 had been ruthlessly suppressed by combined French and Japanese forces. The incident, not large in itself, had been played down at the time and had not been allowed to interfere with the establishment of Japanese control in the territory. But leaders of the rising who had escaped joined a group of Annamese exiles at Liuchow in China later in 1942 and there formed an Independence League. This League embraced all shades of opinion from moderate republican to Communist and included in its program a national constitution on a democratic basis, a national army to operate against the Japanese, the abrogation of all unequal treaties between Indo-China and foreign Powers, a national bank, and reforms such as an eight-hour day, social insurance, and popular education. The chief architect of the League was the veteran Annamese revolutionary, Ho Chi-minh, a former schoolteacher, Moscow-trained Communist, and onetime associate of Borodin in China, a man long familiar with the political underworld of the East. Despite a fondness for aliases which earned him the sobriquet of "the man with twenty names," he had been detected and detained on several occasions by the political police of the Kuomintang during intermittent periods of exile in China. By stressing the anti-Japanese aspect of his program, however, Ho Chi-minh contrived to open up negotiations with Chinese and American officials at Kunming in southern China. American equipment and officer personnel were shortly provided, and guerrilla warfare on a small but increasing scale was being waged as early as 1943 in the jungles of northern Tonkin. Such were the modest beginnings of what was to become the Democratic Republic of Viet Nam ("Land of the South").

In Malaya, the resistance reflected the country's racial composition and divisions. The Malays appear to have been generally content to accept the collaborationist policies of their native rulers, but the Chinese elements in the population, both Kuomintang and Communist, were decidedly less submissive. The conflict of Kuomintang and Communist in China excluded the possibility of close co-operation between their affiliates in Malaya. In the upshot, therefore, the effective leadership of the resistance in Malaya was assumed by the Chinese Communists, who formed the backbone of the Malayan Communist party. Numbers of these Communists, lately provided with British arms in order that they might participate in the defense of Singapore, had since taken to the jungle and had conducted thence a localized and spasmodic guerrilla warfare not unmixed with private thuggery and kidnaping.

Early in 1944, British liaison officers were parachuted into Malaya from aircraft operating from bases in India and Burma. They were agreeably surprised to find that the rank and file of the resistance, the Malayan People's Anti-Japanese Army (MPAJA), was by no means exclusively Communist. Many were rubber tappers, tin-mine coolies, and vegetable gardeners, who took to the jungle but returned to their villages between forays. Out of these, a full-time nucleus of 3,500 men was organized, with an equal number in reserve. Headquarters changed location frequently to avoid detection. Eventually some 300 British training personnel were attached to the MPAJA, and regular contacts were effected with British submarines in Emerald Bay. By May 1944, at the time of the British recapture of Rangoon, the MPAJA had become a respectable force with a corporate spirit of its own and an ebullient morale. But it was still difficult to maintain a strict discipline and prevent seasonable outbreaks of looting and dacoity (gang robbery). Politically, the MPAJA continued to the end to be a medley of local animosities, though, as a group, it was generally obedient to the Moscow "party line."

In Siam, the resistance was inspired by that remarkable man, Luang Pradit Manudharm, or Pridi, as he was generally called, lawyer, Socialist, former Minister of Finance, at one time the close political associate, and then the rival, of Luang Pibul. During 1943, Pridi's agents made contact with Allied officers in Chungking, and his pro-Allied movement began to win a certain amount of support in the Siamese National Assembly (see p. 577) and even in the Siamese Army and police. Tojo's "visit of inspection" in July 1943 put a check on the movement, as it was doubtless intended to do. But the National Assembly became more and more restive under the authoritarianism of Pibul as the chances of a Japanese victory receded. Tojo and his cabinet in Japan resigned in July 1944. His Siamese protégé, Pibul, under increasing attack in the National Assembly, resigned one week later, and he was succeeded by a civilian ministry largely composed of colleagues of Pridi, who himself assumed the title of Regent on behalf of the absent King.

In Siam, therefore, the resistance first arose, not with the emergence of an underground partisan force, but with the defection of the government. Pridi, while keeping up the pretense of collaboration with Japan, became by degrees the undeclared supporter of the Allies. But it was during his term of office and with his secret co-operation that Siamese nationals, usually university students, who had volunteered in Britain and the United States and had been trained for intelligence and sabotage, were parachuted into Siam, and some of them, before the war was over, were transmitting valuable military information by radio from the police station in Bangkok with the connivance of the city's chief of police. Clandestine airfields were constructed in northern Siam to facilitate the entry of Allied personnel and supplies. A partisan rising of some 60,000 fighting men, scheduled for November 1945 to coincide with landings on the Siamese seaboard by forces under Lord Louis Mountbatten, was only forestalled by the capitulation of Japan.

The resistance in the Philippines followed a different pattern again. The Philippines were American and therefore initially "hostile" and were clearly marked out for discriminatory mistreatment. Filipino auxiliaries, along with

American troops, had resisted the Japanese invasion. They had shared the honors at Bataan and also the spectacular cruelties and humiliations of the "Death March" from Bataan to Fort O'Donnell. The subsequent Japanese mopping up and "pacification" in the interior had been brutal in the extreme. The Philippines had long been stereotyped in Japanese thinking as "the green pastures," a land overflowing with a wealth that would enable its masters to live in luxury and ostentation. Japanese bureaucrats therefore competed briskly for appointments to Manila, which developed a hectic life oddly at variance with the industrious austerity of wartime Tokyo, and the resulting administration was openly more predatory and corrupt than in any other territory of the Outer Zone.

Cultural reforms were imposed with a severity indicating that the Japanese expected a long period of re-education before American influence could be eradicated. Military regulations demanded from the Filipinos outward marks of respect and deference. The vulgar American custom of shaking hands was declared abolished. Bowing schools were opened to give instruction in the exact depth of obeisance owed to the various grades of Japanese officialdom. An initial purification of schoolbooks was begun by an ordinance which insisted that brown paper be pasted over politically offensive passages, and eventually new schoolbooks were issued replete with Japanese propaganda. Languages other than Tagalog and Japanese were banned. As material privations increased under the stress of the war, the system of "thought control," familiar to the Japanese people, was applied to the Filipinos in order to steel them to further sacrifices. Instructors emphasized the virtues of order and discipline as the only sure foundations of the Co-prosperity Sphere.

In the circumstances the resistance in the Philippines started early, spread widely, and was uncommonly savage. Unhappily it was also disunited. Several movements sprang up — the Blue Eagles, the Free Panay Guerrillas, the Cavite Guerrillas. But the two principal movements grew out of the American-led United States Army Forces of the Far East (USAFFE) and the Hukbalahap (People's Army against Japan). The former, composed in the main of Philippine army personnel and members of the Nationalist party, was recognized by the United States Army, and it was therefore eligible for regular pay and allowances. It was on the worst possible terms with the Hukbalahap, and armed clashes were frequent. The "Huks" were largely drawn from the revolutionary peasantry of central Luzon, which had always been a disaffected area. The political basis of the movement was laid early in 1942, when the Filipino Communist party, Socialist party, and Civil Liberties Union merged with the Chinese Communist and Kuomintang adherents in the islands to form a United Resistance Front. Moderate and lukewarm elements rapidly deserted this coalition, but the solid Socialist and Communist core remained. The military arm of the movement was organized into flying bands of a hundred men each, usually led by a political commissar versed in Marxist theory. They were sufficiently well armed with weapons seized after the capitulation of Bataan to become a thorn in the side of the Japanese. A punitive expedition in March 1943 pushed them back into the swamps of Candaba; but they emerged and resumed operations when the immediate danger was past. On the revolutionary front, landlords were ambushed as "collaborators" and done to death with bamboo staves in order to save ammunition. Indeed, the "Huks" acted in many cases so independently and paid off their grudges so freely that their nonrecognition by the United States was not very surprising. For their part, the "Huks" bitterly resented the withholding of their pay and the extension of other discriminatory benefits to the less aggressive USAFFE.

Thus the Philippines were already in full ferment, with wide areas under martial law, in June 1944 when President Roosevelt, as part of the political preparation for the coming American counterinvasion, signed a resolution, passed by both houses of Congress, granting the independence of the territory immediately upon the expulsion of the Japanese. But it remained to be seen what relations the returning government in exile of Sergio Osmeña would succeed in establishing with the resistance movements, divided among themselves, but not divided in their antagonism to the old order.

RETROSPECT AND PROSPECT

In 1945 the Japanese made two final grants of independence — to Indo-China and to Indonesia. If they were to be driven from their empire, they could at least leave behind them a situation calculated to confuse and embarrass their enemies. Early in March 1945, in Indo-China, they accused the Governor General, Decoux, of "insincerity" and "a hostile attitude," placed him together with other senior French officers in "protective custody," disarmed and interned French troops, and declared their recognition of an autonomous state of Viet Nam, composed of Tonkin, Annam, and Cochin China, presided over by the Emperor Bao Dai of Annam. Some days later the French Colonial Minister, Giacobbi, announced from Paris that Indo-China, after the war, would be raised to the status of an autonomous federation with its own Council of State within the French Union. But it was the Japanese declaration which carried the immediate practical effect. On August 22, when Japan was at the point of capitulation, the Emperor Bao Dai conveniently abdicated, and Ho Chi-minh proclaimed Viet Nam a democratic republic.

On August 5, 1945, General Terauchi, Japanese Commander in Chief of the Southern Area, hastily summoned the Indonesian leaders, Soekarno and Hatta, by air to his headquarters in Saïgon to sign the instrument of independence drawn up in the name of the Japanese Emperor. Soekarno and Hatta themselves delayed the publication of this little ceremony until after the Japanese surrender, which took place less than a week after their own return to Batavia. On August 17, 1945, the two leaders proclaimed the independence of the Indonesian Republic — not in the name of the Japanese Emperor, but in that of the Indonesian people.

Time, which no man can purchase, passed an irrevocable verdict against Japan's dream of empire. The illimitable potentialities of both Inner and Outer Zones were not realizable under the existing economic dislocations, shipping losses, industrial removals, flight of population, scorched-earth policy, and the resistance. Nor could the Japanese themselves provide the necessary technical skills or a reasonably efficient and honest administration. Even without the distractions of war, the Co-prosperity Sphere would have needed years, nay decades, for its development. Politically, the consequences were far-reaching and long-continuing. The native peoples of the Co-prosperity Sphere had not just accepted Japanese aid against the white man in order once more to accept white man's aid against the Japanese. In five violent years they had seen both white man and Japanese in defeat, and the myth of two invincibilities exploded. Their resistance was shot through with revolutionism and the high inspiration of independence. Their fight had not been for any imperialism, however beneficent. Returning British, French, Dutch, and American Powers found them quite ready to take charge of their own national destinies.

45 THE TURNING POINT

THE TURNING POINT

The Second World War lasted nearly six years and fell into two clearly marked phases of roughly equal length. The story of the first phase has been told. It was a confused phase. Nations were involved, fronts were started up, and great battles were joined, in several parts of the world at once. There was little apparent connection in the welter of events except, on the Axis side, a general expanding offensive and, on the Allied side, a stubborn resolution to hold out. Chapter 41 ended on a gloomy note. In the late summer of 1942, except for the American naval victories of the Coral Sea and Midway and the American landing on Guadalcanal (see p. 745), the war in all its theaters had shown nothing but Allied reverses. The Battle of the Atlantic was in one of its most anxious phases; the German Sixth Army was nearing Stalingrad; the Afrika Korps was striking for Cairo; Japanese forces were readying for a spring on Australia and India.

We called 1942 the "Year of Agony" of the Second World War. But it was also, in Churchill's words, "the end of the beginning." For the three great Allies, Britain, the United States, and the Soviet Union, the year was the one which saw the final translation of their immense potential into actuality. It was the period during which, despite their initial losses and defeats, they were at last overhauling the technical advantage that lay with the Axis at the beginning of the war. From then onward, gradually, but irresistibly, they passed over to a general offensive, and the whole scattered global melee unified itself into what must surely be the grandest strategic plan in the history of warfare.

We have already described, especially in Chapter 42, something of the character of this total Second World War, which so absorbed a belligerent people's entire genius, wealth, and energy. It was a war of machines, it was itself a machine, and the machine could not be built in a day. It called for long-term planning and the scientific integration of mass detail. Its weapons and processes were extraordinarily complicated. A tank, for example, was made of 7,000 parts out of 40,000 pieces of material. A tank meant the thought and sweat of men working at painfully acquired disciplines and techniques. It meant elaborate discussion, experiment, "development," retooling of factories, then the training of the men who were to use it, and afterward repeated adjustments and improvements as the result of battle experience. Teams of designers and technical experts — "the back-room boys" and "boffins" as the British wartime slang had it — in office and laboratory pored over their instruments and apparatus, working against time, creating these intricate monsters. From the moment that an idea was born to the moment that the new weapon began to roll off the assembly line might be two years. Churchill ordered the "Mulberry" prefabricated harbors, used in the invasion of Normandy, in May 1942, and they were towed into position in June 1944. Often enough, some new tactical development outdated a weapon almost before the design of it was off the drawing board, and the entire process had to be started anew. But once a design was adopted, modern mass-production methods enabled it to be turned out in almost any quantity. At the height of its productive effort in 1943–44, the United States was producing one ship a day and one airplane every five minutes. The Second World War saw a great many new inventions or developments of old ones which long afterward will still be affecting our ways of life — radar, penicillin, jet propulsion, and nuclear fission — and all were the result of long, intensive collaboration, often between hundreds of workers.

When the weapons were produced and the men trained to use them, even then it was not the end of the story. Never was there a war so dependent on organization and co-operation among the several services, commands, and allies. The victories by land, sea, and air were not only feats of industrial production and feats of arms, but feats of staffwork. Every gun and shell used in the Eighth Army's opening barrage at El Alamein in October 1942 was brought by sea round the Cape to Egypt. The North African landing with its 850 ships, the Sicilian landing with its 2,000 ships, and the Normandy landing with its 4,000 ships were accomplished with the precision of clockwork. Days, weeks, months of anxious and secret planning with charts and timetables went into these operations. Boards and co-ordinating committees proliferated in London and Washington. Public opinion used to criticize the enormous office staffs buried beneath their piles of reports and forms. But without such organization, for all its incidental irritations, the war could never have been fought.

The Second World War was a total war, a scientific war, a mechanized war, a coalition war, a technocratic war, as well as a fighting war. The men who were most successful in the direction of it were men who were relatively young and of junior rank in the First World War, who had learned the lessons of that war, men of wide and pliant imaginations, trained to large-scale thinking, and possessing a flair for modern managerial techniques, men indeed who seldom appeared in the public eye, but stuck to their desks and the conference table. General Marshall was the outstanding example. Clearly the aggressor Power, whose war production and war organization at first was well advanced, had had an overwhelming advantage. In 1939 and 1940, Hitler's war machine was a reality; Britain's existed largely on paper; America's was not even on paper. There is a time lag in total war, and in 1940 the time lag nearly gave Hitler his victory. By the end of 1942, a year after Pearl Harbor and two years after Dunkirk, the United States and the British Commonwealth were at last outclassing the aggressor at his own game and fighting the total war on even terms.

Inter-Allied co-operation recalled the elaborate organizations of the First World War. The principal body now was the Combined Chiefs of Staff in

Washington, formed in February 1942 "to insure co-ordination of the war effort of Great Britain and the United States, including the production and distribution of war supplies, and to provide for full British and American collaboration with the United Nations now associated in prosecution of the war against the Axis powers." It included, on the American side, Admiral Leahy, General Marshall, Admiral King, and General Arnold; and, on the British side at different times, Field Marshals Dill, Brooke, and Wilson, Admirals Somerville, Pound, and Cunningham, and Air Marshal Portal. There were some dozen other joint boards and committees, all located in Washington, notably the British Joint Staff Mission, the Combined Production and Resources Board, the Combined Raw Materials Board, the Combined Shipping Adjustment Board, the Permanent Joint Board on Defense (for the United States and Canada), and the Pacific War Council. They covered every military and economic requirement and commitment of the United States, Britain, Canada, and the Latin-American republics.

The Second World War was also a "humanitarian" war — at least for the Anglo-American forces in it. The irresponsible slaughter of the Somme, the Chemin-des-Dames, Verdun, Passchendaele, and the Meuse-Argonne were not repeated. The Red Army still adhered to a policy of mass casualties and, to some extent, so also did the Wehrmacht. The Russian and German military deaths for the Second World War have been estimated at 6,000,000 and 3,000,000 respectively.[1] But to the British and American Chiefs of Staff economy of life was the prior condition of good generalship. British military deaths for the Second World War amounted to 303,240 for Great Britain and over 109,000 for the Dominions, India, and the colonies — a total of over 412,240. And to this figure should be added 30,000 deaths of merchant seamen and fishermen, and 60,500 deaths of civilians mainly by air raid. The United States Army, Air Force, Navy, Marine Corps, and Coast Guard lost 322,188.[2]

Medical and psychological services were developed far beyond what had been acceptable in the First World War. Penicillin, sulfa drugs, and blood plasma were among the new remedies available — though again, it is true, mainly for the Anglo-American forces. Gangrene was almost unknown. Fatalities to wounded were less than half the figure of the First World War. The dangerously wounded were often evacuated by air. Meanwhile infinite thought and care were expended on the comfort, physical and mental, of the serviceman. Special organizations attended to rehabilitation and resettlement. The Red Cross and USO (United Service Organizations) handled the recreational and entertainment activities in the American forces; the British counterpart was NAAFI (Navy, Army, and Air Forces Institutes).

The new Allied strength was already making itself felt in the Pacific theater toward the middle part of 1942. Admiral Nimitz was now Commander in Chief of the United States Pacific Fleet. General MacArthur had been recalled to Australia from his inspired stand at Bataan to become Supreme Commander of the Southwest Pacific Area. On April 18, Colonel Doolittle's bombers from the carrier *Hornet* had raided Tokyo. American troops, after convoyed voyages of over six to seven thousand miles, were arriv-

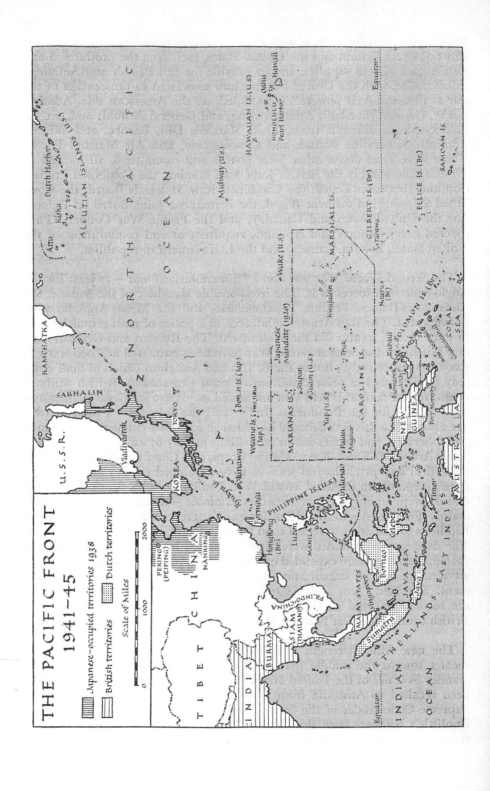

THE PACIFIC FRONT
1941–45

Japanese-occupied territories 1938
British territories
Dutch territories

Scale of Miles

0   1000   2000

U.S.S.R.

KAMCHATKA

SAKHALIN

TOKYO

Vladivostok

KOREA

TIBET

CHINA

PEKING
(PEIPING)

NANKING

Formosa

Hong Kong (Br.)

PHILIPPINE IS. (U.S.)

Luzon

MANILA

Mindanao

Okinawa

Ryukyu Is.

Volcano Is. (Jap.)

Iwojima

Bonin Is. (Jap.)

MARIANAS IS.

Saipan

Guam (U.S.)

Yap (U.S.)

Palau

Angaur

CAROLINE IS.

Truk

Japanese
Mandate (1920)

MARSHALL IS.

Kwajalein

N O R T H   P A C I F I C

O C E A N

ALEUTIAN ISLANDS (U.S.)

Attu

Kiska

Dutch Harbor

Midway (U.S.)

HAWAIIAN IS. (U.S.)

Oahu

HONOLULU

Pearl Harbor

Hawaii

Wake (U.S.)

GILBERT IS. (Br.)

Tarawa

Nauru (Br.)

ELLICE IS. (Br.)

SAMOAN IS.

Equator

INDIA

BURMA

SIAM
(THAILAND)

FR. INDOCHINA

MALAY STATES

Singapore

Sumatra

Java

JAVA SEA

Borneo

Celebes

Timor

N E T H E R L A N D S   E A S T   I N D I E S

NEW
GUINEA

Port Moresby

Rabaul

Bougainville

SOLOMON IS. (Br.)

Guadalcanal

New Georgia

CORAL
SEA

AUSTRALIA

INDIAN   OCEAN

Equator

ing in strength and were being quartered in camps along the fringes of the Australian continent, in New Zealand, Samoa, and other Pacific islands. By June 1942, 150,000 men of the American Navy, Marine Corps, and Army were in the area. The problem of transport and communications over immense distances in a difficult, sparsely settled country was being solved. Australian and New Zealand units were returning from the Near East.

A Japanese concentration of warships and transports in the Bismarck Archipelago, evidently in preparation for a descent upon Australia, had been sighted and dispersed by American and Australian shore-based aircraft as early as March 1942. A second, more powerful concentration in the Marshalls set sail during April and headed for the Coral Sea, with New Caledonia as its probable objective. Between May 7 and 11, the Japanese concentration was heavily engaged by aircraft from the American carriers *Lexington* and *Yorktown* and lost during the action the carriers *Ryukyu* and *Shokaku,* probably three cruisers, and several transports. The *Lexington,* hit by torpedoes and burning fiercely, was eventually abandoned and sunk. The entire action was over when the main United States Pacific Fleet arrived upon the scene.

A month later the Japanese gambled a fleet of some 80 warships and transports, their most powerful naval concentration to date, in an audacious attempt on Midway. The stakes were high. The possession of this operational base of the American Pacific defense system would have threatened the Australian supply line and given Japan a forward base for action against the very shores of the United States. The Japanese fleet, however, was anticipated with uncanny precision by American Intelligence. On June 3-5 it was attacked by bombing and torpedo planes and forced to turn back with the loss of four aircraft carriers and two cruisers. The carrier *Yorktown* was crippled during the engagement and was later sunk by an enemy submarine as she limped back to Pearl Harbor for repairs.

The Battles of the Coral Sea and Midway demonstrated that the United States had recovered strength enough to halt Japanese naval offensives. In particular the loss of Japanese aircraft carriers, six in all – not to mention others severely damaged – irretrievably depleted the enemy's aerial power. Yet, undeterred by their first major defeats at sea since their emergence as a Great Power, the Japanese continued to pour troops and supplies into northern New Guinea, preparatory to an overland drive across the difficult jungle-clad Owen-Stanley Mountains to Port Moresby. The seizure by American navy and marine forces of beachheads on Tulagi and Guadalcanal in the Solomons in August under General Vandegrift indicated, however, that the Japanese advance in the Pacific had at last reached its high-water mark. In New Guinea, the Japanese began to give ground under attacks by Australian, New Zealand, and later American forces and to retrace their steps across the Owen-Stanley Mountains. American air raids on Japanese bases at Lae and Salamaua paralyzed the Japanese supply system on the island. At the end of the year, Japanese remnants were making a desperate last stand at Buna and other coastal points, in complete isolation from one another.

On the night of August 8, off Savo Island, the Japanese inflicted a sharp reverse on American and Australian ships screening the operations on Guadalcanal, which became from this moment the focal point of a long-protracted struggle. Vandegrift's marines clung to their gains. Their spirited defense of Henderson Field indicated the whole future pattern of the Pacific war, which was to center so much around the progressive seizure of island airfields. Sporadic naval actions developed out of persisting Japanese attempts to land reinforcements. From October, the marines were relieved by army units, and the campaign in the Solomons was brought to an end under General Patch. Enemy survivors on Guadalcanal were mopped up in February 1943, fighting to the last man.

NORTH AFRICA

The first convoy of American troops arrived in Northern Ireland in January 1942. But commitments in the Pacific prevented a massive build-up of American strength in Britain till the summer of the same year. In June 1942 a European Theater of Operations was created with headquarters in London with Eisenhower as commanding general, Admiral Stark as naval commander, and General Spaatz commanding the United States Eighth Air Force. General Bedell Smith shortly arrived as Chief of Staff. On July 4, 1942, Independence Day, American bombers raided German airfields in Holland, their first targets in Europe.

In June and July 1942, as we have related (see p. 685), at a Roosevelt-Churchill meeting in Washington and an Anglo-American Chiefs of Staff meeting in London, the decision was taken to defer the Second Front in Europe and mount a North African campaign. There was no time to be lost. The situation in North Africa appeared to be deteriorating daily. Rommel and his Afrika Korps were on the offensive — the fortress of Tobruk, in fact, had fallen while the Washington meeting was in progress. The halt in El Alamein gave the all-important breathing space. But the supply and reinforcement of the British Eighth Army in North Africa involved maritime dispositions unprecedented even in the Pacific theater. An infantry division of this time required 3,000 motor vehicles and 400 tons of supplies a day; an armored division in action required 70,000 tons of gasoline, 350 tons of ammunition, and 50 tons of spare parts a day. Quantities of this magnitude had now to be transported to Egypt round the Cape and up the Red Sea. Yet, in the three months that followed the fall of Tobruk, the Eighth Army was virtually re-equipped and converted into a force ready to recover the initiative.

However, the Second Front found an echo in a cross-Channel "diversionary assault" on August 19, 1942, carried out at Dieppe by a largely Canadian contingent. The operation was far from a success, even if it provided valuable experience for future use. Thereafter, except for an occasional commando raid, no further cross-Channel operations were attempted till the invasion of 1944. In the same August 1942, Churchill went for his first conference with Stalin at Moscow. His main tasks were to enlist Stalin's strategic co-operation in the campaign which the Anglo-American Allies were now planning in North Africa and to disabuse his Russian ally of overconfident anticipations of a Second Front in Europe in the near future — or even of further diversionary assaults of any scale. Except for Lend-Lease, the Red Army must continue to fight alone in Europe during 1942 and probably during 1943 as well. Churchill returned to England via Egypt and made use of the occasion to reorganize the British command in the area. He appointed as Commander in Chief Middle East, General Alexander, formerly commander in Burma. General Gott, whom he appointed to command the Eighth Army, was killed in a plane crash, and the command eventually went to General Montgomery.

On the last day of August 1942, in an attempt to complete his long drive for Egypt, Rommel attacked the Eighth Army at El Alamein. But the Eighth Army was already strong enough to inflict upon him a heavy repulse. Late in the evening of October 23, Montgomery launched his own offensive, which we now know as the Battle of El Alamein, the opening round of what was to be the third and last of the British Libyan campaigns. Preliminary mine-lifting was done under moonlight by infantry. An artillery barrage from 1,000 guns, recalling in intensity the great bombardments on the Western front in the First World War, broke the crust of the enemy's resistance and opened up a way for the British armor. Twelve days' fighting ended in the total rout of the German and Italian armies. Rommel himself was not present at the beginning of the battle. General von Stumme, his deputy commander, was killed, and General von Thoma, commander of the Afrika Korps, was taken prisoner. The pursuit was pressed closely. The enemy forces were harried by air and by naval bombardment along the coast road as they streamed back to Libya, and only a downpour of rain, when they reached Mersa-Matruh, temporarily held up the British armor and saved them from complete destruction. Enemy losses in the battle were put at 60,000 men, 1,000 guns, and 500 tanks.

"The Battle of Alamein," said Churchill afterward, "was the turning point in British military fortunes during the world war. Up to Alamein we survived. After Alamein we conquered." On November 7–8, 1942, Anglo-American forces effected landings in Morocco and Algeria. On Sunday, November 15, church bells were rung in England for the first time since 1939.

The Anglo-American sea-borne invasion of North Africa had been decided, as we have said, at the conferences in Washington and London in June and July 1942. Political preparations had begun with earlier American conversations with anti-Vichy groups in Algeria, conversations which had been going on intermittently ever since the Fall of France in 1940, largely by Robert D. Murphy, the American consul general in North Africa. But any success these conversations might have had had always been stalled by the absence of a responsible French leader with a popular appeal able to rally, not only the Free French forces of de Gaulle in Britain, but the forces of French patriotism everywhere. Then, early in 1942, General Giraud escaped from his confinement in Germany and returned secretly to France. He had commanded a French army in Belgium in 1940, when he had been taken prisoner. His seniority and his irreproachable record of service — irreproachable both militarily and politically — marked him out as the man the Anglo-American Allies had been waiting for. Contacts were made with him at Marseille and with his agents at Algiers. During the night of October 22–23,

1942, just as the Battle of El Alamein was opening, a British submarine landed the American General Clark and a party of officers at a rendezvous at a house on the Algerian coast where details of the impending Allied invasion of North Africa and of possible French collaboration were discussed with local representatives. Yet, despite the thick blanket of security, some hint of the invasion must have leaked out, for Admiral Darlan, Commander in Chief of the armed forces of the Vichy government, chose that moment to make a somewhat ostentatious visit to North Africa and Dakar to inspect the French defenses. These tense preinvasion weeks give a fine flavor of Hollywoodlike intrigue — light signals from darkened windows, hide-and-seek in underground cellars, and sudden swoops by secret police.

Gallipoli in 1915 was the classic reminder of the extraordinary hazards of sea-borne invasions. But the Japanese had lately shown themselves masters of the operation; the British had effected landings in Madagascar and at Dieppe, and the Americans on Guadalcanal. There had also been regular amphibious exercises by British and American marines in peacetime years. But, even with these precedents, the invasion now contemplated had novel military and diplomatic features. The Anglo-American operations in North Africa were placed under the supreme command of General Eisenhower, and all naval operations under the command of Admiral Cunningham. On the night of November 7, 1942, some 850 ships — warships, transports, and landing craft — in three great convoys, one from the United States and two from England, arrived respectively at Casablanca, Oran, and Algiers. Fighter cover was provided from Gibraltar. There was the minimum of interference by enemy submarines and aircraft. The landings encountered some French resistance, but serious fighting occurred only at Casablanca. The German reaction was an immediate occupation of Vichy France. French naval units, lying at Toulon, were scuttled by their crews before the Germans arrived. German forces shortly occupied Bizerte and Tunis and set about preparing a stiff defense. Italians occupied Corsica and Nice.

The invasion of North Africa was not only tactically audacious. It was a prodigious strategic and political gamble. Its success and its bearing on subsequent operations in Europe have since endowed it with a logic and obviousness which, at the time, it could not have had. Certainly it did not amount to the Second Front for which the Soviet Government had been so desperately and insistently pleading, and it effected little relief to the enormous burden of fighting which the Red Army was then bearing. The Soviet Union appeared to be *in extremis*. Presumably it was learning the lesson of total war, even as were the Western Allies, but its subsequent astonishing recovery was not yet in sight. The great counteroffensive at Stalingrad had not yet been launched. The invasion of North Africa might itself have failed. But, even had it succeeded, the possible defeat of the Red Army would have released German divisions for operations in Spain and Turkey to the consequent isolation and collapse of the entire position which the Anglo-American Allies were establishing. Throughout the operation, the Franco government in Spain was an unknown, unpredictable quantity.

The Anglo-American troops met a very mixed reception from the civilian population in Algeria. The political situation was involved and delicate in the extreme. The local administrative officials were pro-Vichy, and French businessmen and landowners were inclined to Fascism. The Arabs were restive and were fearful that the newcomers would rescind the anti-Jewish legislation of the Vichy regime. De Gaulle and his British sponsors were generally unpopular, and de Gaulle in addition was disliked by the American Government. General Giraud arrived on the scene in the full expectation that he was to command the entire operation, and had to be gently disabused by Eisenhower. Admiral Darlan therefore appeared as a heaven-sent solution of many intricate difficulties. He had returned to France from his visit of inspection in North Africa a few days before the invasion, but he now flew back in haste, ostensibly to visit the sickbed of an ailing son. His record at Vichy had not been such as to commend him to the Allies, but he seemed momentarily the man who could best win over the pro-Vichy elements in North Africa and, if he could not swing them convincingly to the Allied cause, at least he could neutralize their most pernicious effects. As such he was eventually accepted by Giraud — and by Eisenhower, who, as a soldier, desired nothing so much as to be able to carry out his invasion with as little bloodshed as possible and would accept help from any quarter which contributed to that result.

Darlan at least showed his value by officially ordering the cessation of French resistance in North Africa forty-eight hours after the first landings and by securing the co-operation of the French governors of Morocco, Algeria, and Dakar. With Eisenhower's concurrence, he set himself up as French political chief in North Africa, with Giraud as military chief. Throughout he protested that he was faithful to Pétain, now helpless in German custody, and was carrying out Pétain's secret wishes. But, on Christmas Eve, Darlan was assassinated in his office in Algiers by a young French patriot. Giraud was designated his successor. Final judgments on Darlan are still best deferred. The installation of a collaborator and turncoat in high office under the victorious Allies, however much his accidental usefulness might be, seemed a sordid enough deal at a moment when an oppressed and stifled world was gasping for a breath of idealism. It was one of the pathetic problems of the liberation that the fervid simplicities of popular patriotism should so often have had to be complicated by political and military "expedience."

The Anglo-American landings in North Africa had been made with surprising ease — a convincing demonstration of the Allied command of the sea. In just three weeks, 185,000 men, 20,000 vehicles, and 200,000 tons of supplies were safely put ashore. Meanwhile the Eighth Army was chasing and bombing Rommel across Libya. It looked as if Axis power in North Africa would soon collapse and the campaign be quickly brought to an end. American parachute troops occupied Bône; commandos raided points five miles from the key port of Bizerte; British MTB's were raiding the port itself in full daylight; the leading units of the British First Army with American reinforcements reached Mejez-el-Bab on November 25, 1942.

But then the difficulties accumulated. The British First Army in Algeria, under the command of General Anderson, then amounted only to two divisions. Both the British and American troops were inexperienced. The supply problem was acute. Harbors, notably Algiers, needed to be cleared, the coastal railroad was in disrepair and, in any case, inadequate; the few roads were only metaled in irregular stretches. Around Christmas, heavy rains soaked the airfields and made fighter support of advanced troops impossible. The Germans had all the logistic advantages, and their reinforcements were being ferried over the short lap from Europe by transport plane at the rate of 1,500 men a night. By December 1 they were counterattacking strongly. Mejez-el-Bab became the focal point of an oscillating battle in which the honors ultimately rested with the Germans. At the turn of the year, the Axis strength in Tunisia amounted to 150,000 men, still being reinforced, strongly entrenched in rough, easily defensible, semimountainous terrain, backed by first-class ports, all-weather airfields, and by a relatively fertile, well-roaded country.

The Eighth Army under Montgomery had continued its career in Libya. It took Tripoli on January 23, 1943, and by the end of the month was approaching the southern borders of Tunisia and the fortified system known as the Mareth Line, where it seemed that Rommel might make a more determined stand. Since the Battle of El Alamein in October, the Eighth Army had covered 1,400 miles and, at the height of the pursuit, its pace had been as much as 40 miles a day. It had outfought at every point a wary and resourceful foe. It had left its last railhead 1,000 miles behind and maintained its supplies and communications with a fleet of 120,000 trucks. The British Navy had served it well, protecting its seaward flank and its attendant coastwise shipping; essential ports along its route had been put into use in a matter of days. This time the campaign would not be lost, as the previous Libyan campaigns had been lost, by an insufficiency of transport. The terrain and the climate in Libya improved with the advance. After Tripoli there were flowering gardens and green grass to greet men many of whom had seen nothing but the desert for three years. Meanwhile, a French column under General Leclerc traversed the Sahara from Lake Chad and joined the flank of the Eighth Army before the Mareth Line.

In January 1943, for ten days, Roosevelt, Churchill, and their Chiefs of Staff held one of their great conferences at Casablanca. "The entire field of the war was surveyed theatre by theatre throughout the world, and all resources were marshalled for the more intense prosecution of the war by sea, land and air." The North African campaign, as was now evident, was succeeding beyond expectation. The Soviet defense of Stalingrad, as was now also evident, was coming to an end in an even greater victory. The main decisions of the conference were to launch an attack on Sicily in the course of the summer, to resume the massing in Britain of the army necessary for the eventual invasion of Western Europe, to step up the strategic bomber attack on Germany in preparation for that invasion, and finally to intensify the antisubmarine war. Afterward, to the press, Roosevelt announced that the aim of the United Nations was the "unconditional surrender" of Germany, Italy, and Japan and that only on such a basis could he see assured the future peace of the world. Stalin had been invited to the conference but had excused himself from attending "on account of the great offensive [in Russia] which he himself, as Commander in Chief, was directing," but he subsequently adhered to the formula of "unconditional surrender." One by-product of the conference was the formal meeting and reconciliation of the French leaders, Giraud and de Gaulle.

On his arrival at the Mareth Line, Rommel's command was merged with that of the Axis forces in Tunisia under Field Marshal von Arnim. The Allied forces were reorganized for the final stages of the campaign with General Alexander as Eisenhower's deputy and commander of the joint Anglo-American-French army in North Africa. General Wilson succeeded Alexander as Commander in Chief Middle East. A Tactical Air Force was organized, consisting of fighters and light and medium bombers, for the closer support of the ground forces.

The Germans delivered the opening attack at the Kasserine Pass on February 14, 1943, and inflicted heavy American casualties including the loss of some 100 tanks. But it was the last German offensive in the Tunisian theater. The Mareth Line was broken by the Eighth Army in frontal battles during the last week of March and by a cross-desert flanking move round its southern end carried out in the main by the New Zealand Division. The first links between the Eighth Army and the Americans were made on April 7. The Anglo-American forces gradually took the initiative, and sporadic, local actions developed into a general offensive. Tactically, the battles were often experimental combats between new types of tanks. The Germans fought with their usual stubbornness and skill. At sea, their communications with the European mainland were now subject to incessant attack by submarines, motor torpedo boats, and aircraft. Apparently they were satisfied that their campaign, though it was now clear that no sort of success could come of it, was justified as a gigantic delaying action.

The end, when it came, came quickly. German supplies, especially of oil, were being exhausted under the Allied blockade by sea and air, and under the intensive bombing of Axis airfields in Tunisia and Sicily. The Italians, curiously enough, who had never greatly distinguished themselves in North Africa, in their capriciousness were now inspired by the hopelessness of their position to fight with conspicuous courage. Their commander, Field Marshal Messe, was the last general officer to surrender and, with a typical native gesture, insisted on giving his sword in person to Montgomery. The last Axis units were rounded up in their refuges on Cape Bon on May 13, 1943.

In the final count, 250,000 Germans and Italians were killed or captured in Tunisia. The naval benefits to the Allies were immediate. The Mediterranean Sea throughout its length was reopened for Allied shipping, and the long route round the Cape was obviated. Targets in Italy, Central Europe, and the Balkans were brought within bomber range. Important material resources in Algeria, Tunis, and Libya were made available. A base was provided for Allied attack upon "the soft under-belly of the Axis." A French army had been reborn. Above all, the Allies, after years of defeat, had the satisfaction of a great victory. Months of intricate preparation had been brilliantly vindicated. Anglo-American co-operation had been tested and tried in the field of action.

The postscript of these events in North Africa was further progress in the settlement of the French political situation. As we have said, the French leaders, de Gaulle and Giraud, had met at Casablanca in January 1943, at the time of the Churchill-Roosevelt conference, and were formally reconciled. A general unification and co-ordination of all French pro-Allied forces was in train. In May 1943, in Occupied France, an underground Council of Resistance was organized to include representatives from the main resistance groups and from de Gaulle's Free French in London. In June, in Algiers, a French Committee of National Liberation was set up, with de Gaulle and Giraud as joint Presidents, to reorganize the French Army, to receive the allegiance of all parts of the French Empire, except Indo-China which was under Japanese occupation, and to institute a purge of former collaborationists. The reconciliation of de Gaulle and Giraud had served its purpose, even if it did not last. Giraud afterward retired, evidently wearied of the unending personal rivalry, leaving de Gaulle the undisputed master of the scene. In November 1943, also in Algiers, a Consultative Assembly began to hold meetings. It was composed of some hundred members, largely self-nominated on the initiative of Félix Gouin, a Socialist, who acted as its chairman, and it purported to be a sort of parliament in exile and custodian of the French democratic tradition. Subsequently, in May 1944, this Assembly passed a resolution inviting the Committee of National Liberation to become "the Provisional Government of the French Republic." Thus, by the time of the Allied invasion of Normandy, de Gaulle was firmly established in his leadership, and French political organs and a French Army were in being, waiting to move into metropolitan France.

STALINGRAD

It may be that one day an authentic and credible account of the Eastern front in the Second World War will be available to English-speaking readers. The mere names of Dunkirk, Bataan, Guadalcanal, El Alamein, Arnhem, Okinawa, or of any of the other great battles fought by the Western Allies conjure up pictures even to those who did not participate in them. But the best informed and most imaginative of us cannot mentally reconstruct a battle like Stalingrad. Can we conceive, in the mind's eye, of two anonymous masses of men, locked in continuous month-long combat, woefully provided with roads and railroads, in ruined streets and shattered buildings, in sub-zero weather, with a vast snow-laden steppe on one side of them and a frozen river two miles wide on the other? Any attempt that we may make in this book to describe the Eastern front must be little more than a catalogue of names and dates, and the very baldness of our narrative, however excusable, cannot but misrepresent the character and magnitude of this theater of the war.

Stalingrad has been compared with Verdun, though the tactical and strategic circumstances were different in either case. More men were engaged at Verdun, more were killed and wounded, and the battle lasted longer, than at Stalingrad. In point of casualties and duration, Verdun remains the greatest battle of all time. But there was the same sense of ultimate decision in both, the same elemental ferocity, the same "death grapple between two fanaticisms," the same blind disregard of cost, the same feats of that almost automatic heroism which lies beyond exhaustion, the same triumph of spirit over despair.

The Battle of Stalingrad may be said to have begun at the end of August 1942, when armored units of the German Sixth Army crossed the great bend of the river Don less than fifty miles from Stalingrad. The time and season were already causing extreme anxiety to the German High Command, for hardly two months of campaigning weather were then left to complete the gigantic maneuvers across the Caucasus to Baku and up the Volga to Kazan which the German High Command was credited to be planning, maneuvers which would have effected the final envelopment of the Red Army and perhaps brought the war in Russia to an end. Soviet communiqués made no attempt to minimize the peril of the situation. For the first time in the entire Russian campaign, the Red Army could no longer rely on indefinite retirement to relieve its plight. The moral, material, and strategic stakes at Stalingrad were acknowledged by both sides to be paramount.

We may well ask whether the Germans, flushed as they were with uninterrupted victories, expected or wanted a decisive battle to develop at this point. We may ask why they chose to direct their armored spearheads at Stalingrad when they knew that armor was at a disadvantage in prolonged street fighting and when all their previous advances had been made by by-passing the great urban obstacles in their path, why indeed they permitted themselves to become entangled in a battle of attrition, above all at so critical a moment, when all their previous successes in Russia had been won in swift maneuver on open ground. Or we may ask, if the Germans had really intended to take Stalingrad by assault, why had they failed, when far stronger positions, from Eben Emael to Sevastopol, had all gone down before them. The Battle of Stalingrad continued through September and October into November 1942. The German Sixth Army was now under the command of General von Paulus, with Hitler's personal orders not to retire. Then, as had happened the year before, the Red Army opened its own general winter offensive. Rzhev on the upper Volga and Leningrad for some weeks had already been the theater of major Soviet actions. Late in November, similar Soviet actions began in the Caucasus.

On November 19, 1942, under the command of Marshal Zhukov, the Soviet forces in the Stalingrad sector went over to the offensive. One army under Rokossovsky attacked to the north of the city, and another army under Yeremenko attacked to the south, the two armies forming, as it were, the arms of a great pincers. At first the dimensions of the offensive were not realized by the outside world, and it was only gradually, as one terse Soviet communiqué followed another, that the immense resources, the strategic sweep and timing and, above all, the long and secret Soviet rearward reorganization could be appreciated. Within a week, the arms of the pincers had closed round the German Sixth Army. Manstein, now commanding the German army group in the theater, tried to relieve the encircled forces and lost half his armor in the attempt. He sent supplies by transport plane, but the supplies dwindled as the Russians progressively occupied the airfields remaining in the Stalingrad pocket. The final surrender of the German Sixth Army — 137,500 men out of an original 300,000 — together with its commander, Paulus, only recently created Field Marshal, and 15 general officers, was made on January 31, 1943. Simultaneous operations in the Caucasus and on the Don accounted for another 300,000 enemy casualties, largely Italian and Rumanian. Since September 1942 the Germans had lost a fifth of their total strength on the Eastern front. The entire German position in southern Russia was momentarily at the point of collapse.

The Battle of Stalingrad was soon merged into the general Soviet winter offensive. On January 1, 1943, the Soviet forces had taken Velikie Luki. Sorties round Leningrad rolled back the German investment lines and raised the siege of the city, a siege which had lasted sixteen months. Between January and March the headlines announced a succession of towns and cities liberated — Maikop, Krasnodar, Rostov, Voroshilovgrad, Kharkov, Rzhev, Vyazma. At the end of March, the Germans counterattacked and recaptured Kharkov. Operations came to an end with the spring thaw. Hitler's armies had lost, at enormous cost, all the ground they had gained in 1942.

From this moment the Red Army never looked back. Except for local halts and reverses, it maintained the initiative, and its progress westward, if expensive, was steady and continuous. The Western Allies, like their enemies who bore the weight of it, were slowly brought to a realization of the colossal military power that had at last come to birth in the Soviet Union. Months of doubt were changed to something akin to a new apprehension. Here was an elemental squandering of blood and national vitality beyond the imagination of the scientific warmakers of London and Washington — and even of Berlin.

THE COLLAPSE OF ITALY

The battles in North Africa were the beginning of the elimination of Italy, the destruction of Fascism in its original homeland, and a deep breach in the southern glacis of the Nazi Fortress of Europe. Thereafter every Mediterranean country was a fair field for military and political exploitation by the Allies. In May 1943, at the so-called "Trident" Conference in Washington, between Roosevelt, Churchill, and the Combined Chiefs of Staff, the decision was taken "to extend Allied influence in the Mediterranean to a point where Italy should be forced to withdraw from the war." A target date of May 1, 1944 was set for a cross-Channel attack, and plans for the operation were to be prepared by August 1943. The strategy in the Pacific was generally confirmed.

Early in June 1943, Sicily and Sardinia were already being subjected to softening-up raids. Italy's "Helgoland," the small fortress of Pantelleria, was reduced by concentrated aerial and naval bombardment, and its Italian commander raised the white flag before a single Allied soldier was put ashore. Lampedusa and other islands in the Sicilian Channel surrendered after briefer tastes of the same treatment. The Allied force, the Fifteenth Army

Group, under the command of Eisenhower's deputy, Alexander, made its first landings in Sicily on the early morning of July 10. Patton commanded the United States Seventh Army to the left, and Montgomery the British Eighth Army to the right. The enemy had expected the invasion, but tactical surprise as to exact date and position was as complete as in the invasion of North Africa. The Allied conquest of Sicily was completed in rather more than a month. The Seventh Army, after initial difficulties at Gela, swung across the center and west of the island, and took Palermo on July 22. The Eighth Army, now strongly reinforced by Canadians, made a more plodding progress in the east, against mainly German resistance, and took Catania on August 5. Crack Italian regiments laid down their arms after a token resistance. The civilian population greeted the invaders tumultuously. The Germans transported 60,000 men to the mainland, two-thirds of their total strength, including the famous Hermann Göring Division, in one of the most successful "Dunkirks" of the war. The first Allied units themselves crossed the Strait of Messina on August 17, to be followed by two divisions of the Eighth Army on September 3.

Mussolini's fall from power was announced on July 25, 1943, a fortnight after the Sicilian landings. Successive military disasters had produced their logical effect upon a man and regime that needed perpetual victories for their sustenance. A nation which had been taught to regard itself as the heir and reincarnation of the Roman Empire had seen its colonial possessions lost, its armed forces scattered, its economy bankrupted, and its very soil occupied by its own ally. The end had not been far to seek.

A forecast of approaching political crisis in Italy had been given in February 1943, two weeks after the Eighth Army had captured Tripoli, when Mussolini had "purged" his cabinet, dismissed Ciano from the Foreign Ministry, and then appointed him Italian envoy to the Holy See. In March there had been a serious workers' strike in Turin. Only July 19, Mussolini met Hitler at Feltre but nothing transpired from the meeting. Neither Mussolini nor Hitler was then in a position to offer the other material aid or moral consolation. On the same day, the 19th, Rome was bombed for the first time. A panic-stricken crowd surged into the neutral sanctuary of Vatican City and converted the Piazza of St. Peter's into a huge refugee encampment.

Mussolini summoned the Fascist Grand Council on July 24 — its first meeting since 1939 — to face a revolt of his onetime supporters, led by Ciano, Grandi, and the former Minister of Education, Bottai. Nineteen out of twenty-six members of the Grand Council, after debates lasting far into the night, passed a resolution demanding that he immediately relinquish command of the armed forces of Italy. The next day Mussolini reported to the King, hoping and expecting to enlist the King's support, and was bluntly told that he was no longer Premier. He was arrested as he left the palace and driven off in a waiting police car.

On that day, July 25, King Victor Emmanuel issued a proclamation announcing his own assumption of the command of the armed forces, the resignation of Mussolini, and the formation of a new government under Marshal Badoglio. Spontaneous popular demonstrations broke out all over

Italy. It was as if pent-up torrents had been suddenly released. Fascist symbols were torn down from buildings and street hoardings. The Fascist party, its functionaries, and police dissolved and disappeared. Forgotten leaders of Italian democracy emerged from hiding or incarceration to give impromptu gatherings of bemused listeners at street corners their first exhibition of free speech in more than twenty years.

Badoglio, it seemed, as head of the new government, was mainly interested in extricating his country from the dread verdict of "unconditional surrender" and more particularly from the possible vengeance of its former German ally. On August 13 a second air raid on Rome served to remind him that the Allies were still his enemies and that they were in no relenting mood. On September 2, the day before the Eighth Army's landings on the toe of Calabria, Badoglio through private envoys to Eisenhower at last signified his acceptance of "unconditional surrender." A week of secret parleys followed, and the eventual armistice was not made public until September 8. On September 16, Badoglio broadcast to the Italian people and called upon them "to fight the Germans in every way, everywhere, and all the time." It was a virtual Italian declaration of war on Germany.

The Allies had expected a convenient chaos in Italy, a chaos which would itself deliver the country to them without the need of further military effort on their part. But there was still one undefeated and resolute enemy in Italy, an enemy apt at taking rapid countermeasures. The Germans used to full advantage "the Forty-five Days" between July 25 and September 8. They gained complete control of the Po Valley, and they occupied Rome and Vatican City. They sent a parachute company to rescue Mussolini from his confinement in a hotel in the Abruzzi mountains and set him up as head of a "Republican Fascist State" in northern Italy, a rallying point for all such loyal Fascist elements as could still be found. Allied prisoners in Italian camps were handed over to German guards to be transported to the Reich. Rommel assumed the command of all the German forces in northern Italy. The United States Fifth Army, under General Clark, landed on the Salerno beaches on September 9 in an attempt to cut off the whole of southern Italy. But the military situation by then had deteriorated. The Americans found the Germans ready and waiting, and fought there one of the stiffest actions of the war.

The King of Italy, the Crown Prince Umberto, and Badoglio escaped to Bari, where they set up their government. The greater part of the Italian Navy, under broadcast instructions from Badoglio and Cunningham, sailed under its own steam for Malta and other ports under Allied control. Its surrender released considerable Allied naval strength for service in the Atlantic and Pacific. The Germans made a halfhearted and unsuccessful effort to hold Sardinia. Their effort to hold the more strategically important island of Corsica was frustrated by a rising of local partisans and the prompt landing of Free French forces. Some twenty-five Italian divisions in the Balkans were left "out on a limb." Partisans in Yugoslavia were stimulated into new activity, and regular Allied liaison was established with Tito by air and parachute. The Germans remained for the time being in effective occupation of the Istrian Peninsula and of Crete, Rhodes, and the Aegean area. On September 15 the Fifth Army at Salerno made contact with the Eighth Army racing up from Calabria, and the two armies, now deployed abreast, began their slow and painful progress northward. Naples was taken on October 1. Bad weather was an unexpected and serious obstacle and, for long months, sunny Italy was a land of torrential rains, flooded gorges, and mud-sodden roads. The campaign was becoming a succession of formidable river crossings — the Sangro, the Volturno, the Garigliano. At the end of January 1944, an American corps with a British division landed at Anzio, in an attempt once more, as at Salerno, to turn the flank of the German positions from the sea. But thereafter the diversion of landing craft to England in preparation for the invasion of France prevented a repetition of these leapfrog landings up the cost of Italy, and the campaign was perforce relegated to a secondary place in Allied strategy. The great natural fortress of Cassino, blocking the approaches to Rome, was bombed and stormed in a series of heavy actions between March and May. Rome eventually fell on June 4. Florence fell on August 12, 1944.

At the end of 1943, Allied forces and commands in Italy had been reorganized. Eisenhower returned to England, taking with him well-tried commanders of the North African and Italian campaigns, Montgomery, Tedder, Bradley, and Patton. Wilson was appointed Supreme Allied Commander in the Mediterranean area, with Devers as Deputy Commander. Doolittle, the bomber of Tokyo, was commander of the United States Fifteenth Air Force, but was shortly transferred to the command of the United States Eighth Air Force in Britain, and Spaatz became commander of the United States Strategic Air Force in Europe. Alexander remained Allied commander in Italy, with Clark as commander of the Fifth Army and Leese as the new commander of the Eighth. The Allied army in Italy had now as mixed a composition as any which fought the Axis in any part of the world — Americans, British, Canadians, New Zealanders, South Africans, Indians, French, Poles, Brazilians, Italians, Africans, and a special all-Jewish brigade. On the German side, Rommel was recalled to take his part in the battles in France, leaving Kesselring in command of the German forces in Italy.

KURSK AND OREL

The German army in Russia after 1942, it has been argued, was in "natural" decline. The further it penetrated the Russian plains the thinner did it have to spread its numbers. Its reserves of man power were not inexhaustible and could not be expended with the same irresponsible abandon as hitherto. In 1943 the strength of a high percentage of German divisions in Russia could only be maintained with foreign recruits. Even the newly formed *Waffen SS* divisions contained "ideological volunteers" from various parts of Nazi Europe. The German home front, as we have seen in Chapter 42, was unprepared and inadequate for the sudden strains which developed at this time. Yet Hitler, in supreme command, ordered suicidal operations rather than cut his losses and match his ambitions to his real resources.

In 1943 the Soviet Union, like its Western Allies, was at last converting its war potential into actuality, and the Red Army soldier, for the first time in his history, was going into battle with equipment equal to his enemy's. Siberian and Asiatic man power was being drawn upon. Lend Lease and the Anglo-American bombing of German munition centers were favorable weights in the scales. The arrival of 200,000 American trucks and jeeps revolutionized the Soviet transport situation.

The year 1943 on the Eastern front looked at first as if it might again repeat the course of 1941 and 1942. The closing operations of the winter of 1942–43 had left a Soviet salient round Kursk and a German salient round Orel. Both invited attack. On July 5, 1943 some forty German divisions under Kluge opened against the Soviet salient round Kursk what appeared to be the start of the regular German summer offensive. The maneuver was no surprise. Both sides had been concentrating for action; both sides, throughout that June, had been making local attacks in the same area for the testing of their enemy's defenses and for the capture of information. In the event, two well-prepared armies met "in the most violent battle of machines of war."

But the days of the Nazi blitzkrieg were over. In less than a fortnight the German offensive had exhausted itself. The Germans lost 70,000 officers and men and more than half the armor with which they had first attacked. On July 12, 1943 the Soviet forces opened their counteroffensive against the German salient round Orel. Reports of the battle indicate a Soviet use of artillery that recalls El Alamein; evidently the Red Army commanders had simultaneously made the same tactical discovery as Montgomery. On August 5, Orel was stormed and taken. The Soviet offensive spread along the entire Eastern front. Through September, October, and November came reports of the liberation of Kharkov, Taganrog, Novorossiisk, Bryansk, Smolensk, Kremenchug, Nevel, Dnepropetrovsk, Perekop, Kiev, Gomel, Zhitomir. The names of Red Army commanders were becoming well-known to the Anglo-American press — Sokolovsky, Rokossovsky, Vatutin, Koniev, Malinovsky, and Tolbukhin. On November 4, 1943, a special Soviet communiqué reviewed the results of four months' fighting since the start of the German offensive round Kursk. "The Red Army restored to the country 140,000 square miles of the greatest economic and strategic value, . . . one of the most fertile agricultural regions, liberated 38,000 inhabited localities . . . and inflicted 900,000 casualties." Of the Germans it could be said that they conducted their withdrawals in masterly fashion. They were retreating, but they were still retreating in good order and at their own pace. They held stubbornly to pivotal points, the fortified positions known as "hedgehogs," usually road and railroad junctions. Manstein's "retirement according to plan" was no euphemism.

Early in December 1943 the Germans attempted a counterattack somewhat recalling their counterattack at Kharkov in the previous March. They took Zhitomir, but they failed to stabilize the line. The Red Army retook Zhitomir on Christmas Eve. Berdichev fell on January 5. At that moment a new Soviet offensive under Sokolovsky was launched against the fortified railroad center of Vitebsk, the pivotal point of the German defense system in

White Russia. Great pincer drives under Vatutin and Koniev threatened Manstein's army group in the Ukraine with a second Stalingrad. Further south, Malinovsky and Tolbukhin were engaged in a similar action against Krivoi Rog. In the north, Soviet forces recovered Narva and reached Lake Peipus. When the fighting died down in the spring of 1944, the Red Army stood on the borders of Estonia and Latvia and had crossed into the former Poland and Rumania.

THE PACIFIC AND SOUTHEAST ASIA

By the end of 1943 the scales in the Pacific war were leaning heavily in favor of the United States. The difficult Buna campaign in New Guinea was completed by June 1943. The capture of New Georgia, with its important airfield at Munda, between June and August, was the logical outcome of the earlier American success at Guadalcanal. Salamaua in New Guinea fell to American and Australian forces in September. These operations definitely ensured the security of Australia and provided bases for the eventual offensive action northward.

It was then nearly two years since Pearl Harbor. The losses of that unhappy incident had been repaired, and the United States had steadily regained a decisive superiority by sea and air in the Pacific Ocean. The great battle of mobilization and production on the American home front had been won. The bulk of the United States Navy, including all its aircraft carriers, was now concentrated west of Hawaii under the command of Admiral Nimitz. Correspondingly, the Battle of the Atlantic was assigned almost wholly to the British Navy. At the same time, American submarines and aircraft had been methodically paring away the Japanese merchant fleet. The Japanese conquests, as we have seen, had not yet achieved that minimum of economic consolidation sufficient for their own defense, and the numerous islands under Japanese occupation were often heavy liabilities without regular supplies and naval protection. The Japanese Navy in 1943 was already conserving itself and avoiding open battle, and the Co-prosperity Sphere was becoming an atomized congeries of isolated and rather helpless units.

Three island chains, like three concentric crescents, lie between Asia and Australasia. The first comprises Malaya and the Netherlands East Indies. The second comprises the Philippines and New Guinea. Both these had been used by Japan in her blitz of 1942. The third comprises the Ryukyus, Bonins, Marianas, Carolines, Marshalls, and Gilberts, tiny volcanic or coral dots upon the immense astronomic surface of the Pacific Ocean, relatively undefended by the enemy and thus inviting to the type of maritime offensive which the American forces were now preparing. A "blitz in reverse" along this third island chain would by-pass the other two and would virtually outflank the entire Co-prosperity Sphere.

The American offensive in the Pacific was fought with consummate warcraft, with an unstinted use of material and an extreme economy of personnel.[3] True to their character the Americans relied on their native inventiveness and their machines to by-pass territory — and to save life. The success of their fighting methods was proved by the fact that, at the conclusion of hostilities, a Japanese army of more than 2,000,000 men was still in the field and was forced to lay down its arms without battle. Numerous Japanese detachments were left stranded throughout the theater of fighting. As MacArthur afterward reported: "These enemy garrisons represent no menace to current or future operations. Their capacity for organized offensive effort has passed. The various processes of attrition will eventually account for their final disposition. The actual time of their destruction is of little or no importance, and their influence as a contributing factor to the war is already negligible. The actual process of their immediate destruction by assault methods would unquestionably involve heavy loss of life without adequate compensating advantages." [4]

The American offensive was fought over immense areas. The Pacific Ocean covers half the surface of the globe. Panama and Singapore are at nearly antipodal points. From Manila to Honolulu measures 5,000 miles, the length of the Pacific coast from Skagway to Guatemala, or more than twice the length of the Mediterranean. The Solomons from tip to tip measure 1,000 miles, the distance from Baltimore to Miami, or twice the length of Great Britain. Only a highly specialized development of naval architecture and fleet organization could stretch the effective range of warships to meet these conditions. The basic operational unit was the aircraft carrier, the "movable airfield," which extended the navy's striking power and enabled an attack to be delivered on enemy ships and land bases far beyond the reach of normal gunfire. After the Battles of the Coral Sea and Midway, the American naval task force was always built around the aircraft carrier.

The immediate objectives of the offensive were airfields or places where airfields could be made. Naval or aerial bombardment, or both, prepared the way for a landing, a landing if possible at a point some distance from the main center of the enemy's resistance. As it was said in the First World War "Artillery conquers, infantry occupies (*L'artillerie conquiert, l'infanterie occupe*)." Infantry stormed ashore from landing craft; bulldozers followed almost at their heels; airstrips were being prepared, and planes were landing, while fighting at the periphery of the bridgehead was still continuing. Communications, throughout the action and afterward, were maintained by sea and air, and transport inland was maintained by the ubiquitous and never-failing jeep. The same process was carried on, from island to island, from airfield to airfield, ultimately from Guadalcanal to Okinawa. Incidental naval engagements often developed out of attempts by Japanese forces to relieve garrisons thus isolated and beleaguered.

The "Quadrant" Conference at Quebec in August 1943, attended by Roosevelt, Churchill, and their Chiefs of Staff, met in a mood of confidence. The mounting output of American shipyards justified an intensification of the offensive in the Pacific. General MacArthur and Admiral Nimitz were directed to pursue their operations so as to reach the Philippines by the end of 1944, and the Ryukyus by the beginning of 1945. Admiral King forecast that, somewhere during these operations, the Japanese Navy would be encountered and defeated.

Tarawa, a coral atoll in the Gilbert Islands, the first step along the third island chain, was brought under attack by Admiral Mitscher's task force in November 1943. Japanese pillboxes and blockhouses, constructed of steel, coconut logs, and sandbags, resisted the preliminary sea and air bombardment of 2,200 tons of shells and 700 tons of bombs. Heavy losses were incurred before the defenders were dislodged in a four-day battle of extreme ferocity. In February 1944, Kwajalein in the Marshalls was seized in the same way, though with fewer casualties. In June and July, Saipan and Guam in the Marianas were seized, less than 1,500 miles from Japan, a distance well within the range of the new B-29 Superfortresses which were now appearing over the Pacific. Four hundred Japanese aircraft were destroyed during the latter operation "in the Marianas turkey-shoot," and the air arm of the Japanese Navy was thereafter a negligible factor. Incidental raids were carried out on Truk, the Japanese naval base in the Carolines, and on Yap and Palau, the last being only 500 miles from the Philippines. In the North Pacific, in the Aleutian Islands, Attu was retaken by American and Canadian forces after a sharp struggle; in August a landing party on Kiska found it already evacuated by its Japanese garrison.

At this moment the front which had been causing the Allied leaders the gravest anxiety was the Chinese. The Chinese Foreign Minister, T. V. Soong, had attended the "Quadrant" Conference at Quebec in August 1943 and had painted the military situation in his country in the gloomiest colors. He no more than confirmed the despairing appeals that had been coming from Chungking for some time. China had been virtually at war with Japan since 1931, for twelve years. Like the Soviet's, her armies always seemed to have unlimited space for their successive retirements, and her allies took the comfortable view that, however heavily she was punished, she could always retire a little deeper into her hinterland and continue to hold out somehow. But it was becoming clear, in 1943, that China could retire no more and might even be forced to sue for a separate peace. Her economic position was catastrophic, and strong hints of her internal political difficulties were leaking out. The Burma Road had been cut when Burma had been lost, and supplies could only be sent her by air over the great mountain "Hump" above Assam. Yet 46,000 tons of supplies a month were eventually being dispatched to China by that hazardous route, a figure which represents one of the great logistic achievements of the war.

The "Quadrant" Conference at Quebec created the Southeast Asia Command (SEAC) under Admiral Lord Louis Mountbatten. General Stilwell, Chief of Staff to Chiang Kai-shek, was appointed his deputy. It was decided to expedite the construction of the new road to China from Ledo in Assam and to construct airfields in China whence the B-29 Superfortresses could bomb the Japanese mainland. It was also decided to mount an offensive in northern Burma in the winter of 1943–44. The further "Sextant" Conference, held in Cairo in November 1943, was attended by Chiang Kai-shek in person, and these decisions were worked out in greater detail. But it was all too evident that, in view of the immense Allied commitments, especially of shipping and landing craft, for the Pacific, for Italy, and eventually for Europe, little could be spared for China and Burma, and that Stilwell would remain, in Marshall's words, "at the end of the thinnest supply line of all."

Courage and ingenuity had therefore to make up for the paucity of resources. The British, Indian, African, American, and Chinese troops in this area fought through an almost impassable mountainous and jungle terrain, an intolerable climate, and widespread incidental disease, against a cruel and tenacious foe. Nor were they always highly honored for their exploits — the British Fourteenth Army in Burma under General Slim used to be called "the forgotten army," so little publicity did it receive. In addition, the political situation in Delhi, like the political situation in Chungking, was not altogether helping the vigorous prosecution of the war. Yet northern Burma was now the theater of a remarkable campaign led by some of the most brilliant personalities in any Allied army.

The British Brigadier Wingate, with his own specially trained force of British and Indian jungle fighters, carried on a guerrilla war deep behind the Japanese lines on the upper Irrawaddy River, harrying Japanese communications and outposts, destroying bridges and supply dumps. Stilwell's Chinese troops and the American "Galahad" force of jungle fighters under General Merrill operated in the hill country to the north and west of Myitkyina. All these forces were largely supplied by air, and there were at times as many as 25,000 to 100,000 men in the jungle dependent on air-borne food and ammunition. A further Chinese force from Yunnan advanced down the Salween River. The British Fourteenth Army pressed forward into Arakan toward Akyab. Mountbatten's naval forces raided Sabang at the northern tip of Sumatra. The enemy made counterthrusts at Imphal in Assam, intending to sever the Bengal Assam railroad, on which the Allied forces in northern Burma depended. A Japanese force actually crossed the Indian frontier at this point for the first and only time, heralding its advent with a proclamation that an "Indian Army" was marching with it to liberate India from British tyranny.

Myitkyina, the key town in northern Burma, was captured at last on August 3, 1944, some weeks after the monsoon had broken. The campaign had not yet been conclusive. Lashio and the Burma Road had not been freed from the enemy. Wingate did not live to see the full results of his tactics. He had died in an airplane crash in March. Stilwell was relieved of his command shortly after the capture of Myitkyina, in circumstances which we have elsewhere described (see p. 705). General Sultan succeeded to the command of the American forces in Burma, and General Wedemeyer became Chief of Staff to Chiang Kai-shek.

Meanwhile, in southern China, there had been a parallel flurry of military activity. A Japanese offensive had developed in December 1943 in the "rice bowl" in the region of Changsha, and it was resumed early in 1944, both from Changsha and Canton, and directed against American airfields recently established for the operation of the B-29's. Several of these airfields round Kweilin and Chihkiang were lost, and the planned American aerial assault on Japan from southern China, for the time being, was disrupted. In 1944 it could be said that, in a military sense, China was no longer an effective belligerent.

THE AERIAL ASSAULT ON GERMANY

On the night of May 30, 1942, R.A.F. Bomber Command made its first 1,000-plane raid, with Cologne as its target, and followed up, during that summer, with raids of equivalent weight on Essen and other industrial cities of the Ruhr. The United States Eighth Air Force was then being organized in Britain. The air war was developing into an extensive, many-faceted campaign — the bombing of the enemy's naval bases and U-boat pens, participation in the Battle of the Atlantic, mine laying, the transportation of troops and supplies, parachutage to partisan forces in Europe, as well as the bombing of German industry and communications. It required an enormous establishment in ground crews, construction squads, medical services, meteorological services, photographic services, intelligence, and research. It required the constant development of new types of planes and new technical devices — precision sights, radar and other "blind" navigational aids, "pathfinder" tactics. It required a massive industrial foundation. In the spring of 1942, the American output was already 3,000 planes a month, and the Canadian aluminum industry was producing 80 per cent of the R.A.F.'s aluminum supplies.

Unlike the German raids in the Battle of Britain, the raid was now a sudden mass attack. "Concentrated" attack was defined as attack at the rate of 800 bombers an hour; the subsequent "superconcentrated" or "saturation" attack was defined as attack at the rate of 1,800 bombers an hour, the attack itself lasting 15 to 20 minutes. The operation required the most accurate and detailed planning as to routing and timing. The defenses were often taken by surprise and overwhelmed. By 1943, when it was clear that the invasion of France was not yet to be attempted, the aerial assault represented the main part of the Anglo-American war effort in Europe, and "area" bombing for the obliteration of German industry was already the adopted policy. In March 1943 the Battle of the Ruhr began. In four months, over 7,000 tons of bombs were dropped on Essen in six raids, over 5,000 on Duisburg in five, 4,000 on Düsseldorf in two, and 3,500 on Wuppertal in one. At the end of July, over 7,000 tons were dropped on Hamburg in three of the most terrible raids to date. Hamburg was the greatest man-made inferno before Hiroshima.

In 1944, R.A.F. Bomber Command's main interest was concentrated on the invasion of France, which we shall describe in the next chapter. The United States Eighth Air Force in Britain was integrated with the United States Fifteenth Air Force in the Mediterranean to form the United States Strategic Air Force in Europe under General Spaatz. The Tactical Air Force, which, as we have seen, had originally been an innovation of the Tunisian campaign, was assigned to immediate invasion targets, and the support of the invasion forces. Strategic targets were fighter-production factories, synthetic rubber and ball-bearing factories, oil refineries, railroad rolling stock and switchyards, dams and dikes, coastal shipping, river and canal barges, research stations, and later the V-1 and V-2 depots and launching sites. This was also the year which saw so many missions by single fighter bombers, picking off, for example, a Gestapo headquarters in an occupied capital, planting a bomb at the mouth of a railroad tunnel, slicing the arches of a viaduct, or the lock gates of a canal. As the Red Army moved westward, an agreement was reached with the Soviet Government for the use of airfields behind the Soviet lines in Rumania and Poland, and Danubian and Balkan targets could then be bombed en route. But "shuttle bombing," as it was called, might have been more effective with greater Soviet cordiality and co-operation.

The Reich was encircled by Allied air power. The outstanding impression of the latter days of the war was the plenitude of resources. The 10-ton bomb was first used in March 1945, and the 11-ton bomb was then being developed. German cities could be subjected for an hour to an ordeal exceeding that which London had experienced in the whole of the Battle of Britain. Yet the total assessment of this campaign of devastation, both the physical extent and the military value, are still problematical. In the course of the war the R.A.F. attacked some 70 German cities according to a comprehensive and carefully ordered strategic and economic plan. In 23 of these a third or more of the built-up area was destroyed and, in 46, about half of the built-up area was destroyed. In Berlin, nearly 6,500 acres, or 10 square miles, were destroyed. Hamburg, Cologne, Dresden, Bremen, Frankfurt, Hanover, Munich, Nuremberg, Stuttgart, and the Ruhr cities were visited by proportionate destructions.[5] In London, we may note in passing, 600 acres were destroyed, in Plymouth 400, and in Coventry 100. But it is impossible to arrive at a reduction factor for the conversion of these figures into losses of industrial output. Bombing always had additional incidental effects. Some million German workers, allocated to clearance and repair, were diverted from other occupations. Traffic holdups on damaged roads, railroads, and canals, and the destruction of workers' housing were latterly very serious. Dispersion of industries was expensive and put an increased load on the country's transport services.

At the same time, loss of civilian life, surprisingly, as in the Battle of Britain, was far below expectation. In 1943, 8 civilians were killed for 10 tons of bombs; in 1944, 3 were killed per 10 tons. Total civilian deaths from air raid in Greater Germany throughout the war have been put at 305,000. The human organism indeed proved extraordinarily resilient, and it is arguable that the demoralization brought upon Germany by dictatorship and defeat was undoubtedly a great deal worse and more enduring than any immediate injuries to the people, physical or psychological, that could be charged to the actual aerial assault. The after-aspect of ruin indeed was often more terrible than the immediate cause of it.

46 THE CLOSING CAMPAIGNS

NORMANDY AND THE RHINE

The latter months of 1943 were months of conferences and ceremonies. In August 1943, Churchill and his Chiefs of Staff met their Canadian opposites at Quebec. Churchill visited Roosevelt at Hyde Park. Churchill, Roosevelt, their Chiefs of Staff, their Foreign Ministers, and the Chinese Foreign Minister, T. V. Soong, again met at the "Quadrant" Conference at Quebec.

The priority of the war against Japan on the agenda of the "Quadrant" Conference was doubtless intended to placate the large section of American opinion which had always regarded Japan as the chief enemy and which strongly suspected that Europe was monopolizing the resources of the Anglo-American partnership. As we noted in the last chapter, T. V. Soong had described the distressing military situation in his country and pleaded for more aid (see p. 761). The Conference considered that the increasing output of American shipbuilding justified an intensification of MacArthur's and Nimitz's offensive in the Pacific. It created the Southeast Asia Command (SEAC) under Admiral Lord Louis Mountbatten and decided to mount an offensive in northern Burma. Yet the Conference also adopted in principle "Operation Overlord" for the cross-Channel invasion of France.

In October 1943 the foreign ministers, Hull, Eden, and Molotov, met in Moscow. In November, Roosevelt, Churchill, and Chiang Kai-shek met at the "Sextant" Conference in Cairo for the further elaboration of plans in China and Burma. Later in November, Roosevelt, Churchill, and Stalin met in Teheran. In December, Roosevelt and Churchill met in Cairo. General Eisenhower was selected for the command of "Operation Overlord."

It is not necessary to particularize on published political decisions of these conferences — as distinct from their military decisions. The official bulletins were couched in the usual language: "There were frank and exhaustive discussions of the measures to be taken to shorten the war . . ." The destruction of Nazism and Fascism and the punishment of Germans guilty of atrocities were declared to be primary Allied war aims. The formula of "unconditional surrender" was reaffirmed. The political shape of the world to come was not defined; but the independence and integrity of Austria and of Iran were assured. Japan was to be stripped of all territories which she had taken "by violence and greed," including Manchuria, Formosa, and Korea. Poland was to secure East Prussia, but otherwise her problems and her present crucial situation in the forward area of the Red Army's advance were left unresolved. A European Advisory Commission was to be established in London for "the examination of European questions arising as the war develops." There were preliminary discussions on a future "system of international cooperation and security" to replace the League of Nations. No French representative was admitted to any of these conferences.

The rising power of the Allies and the success of their arms in the Pacific, the Mediterranean, and Russia produced the inevitable diplomatic perturbation among Axis satellites and neutrals. The signature in Moscow, in December 1943, of a new Czech-Soviet Mutual Assistance Pact was significant and appropriate. Early in 1944 the Allies made strong efforts to detach Finland from German control. Soviet and Finnish delegates met to discuss peace in Stockholm in February 1944, and a Finnish envoy proceeded to Moscow for further negotiations in March. The Soviet terms were enticingly moderate. But Finland either could not, or would not, withdraw from the war, and she elected to meet the coming Soviet assault upon her territory by force of arms. The possibility of a separate Finnish peace, nonetheless, had been sufficiently alarming to the German Government. Ribbentrop visited Helsinki in person to bring promises of further German aid. In March, German forces anticipated a possible defection of Hungary by a total occupation of the country. On May 12, 1944, in a joint declaration, the United States, Britain, and the Soviet Union solemnly warned the Axis satellites against further collaboration with Germany and against "their present hopeless and calamitous policy of opposing the inevitable Allied victory."

Strong efforts were also made to persuade Turkey to join the Allied front, and considerable Lend-Lease supplies, ostensibly to help her maintain her neutrality, were shipped to her. But in March 1944 it was announced that no more such shipments would be made. Turkey's usefulness as an ally dwindled with the Allied ascendancy in the Mediterranean and Black Sea areas. But Turkey consented to curtail her exports of chrome to Germany and to close the Dardanelles to German armed ships. An Anglo-American oil embargo on Spain forced that country to stop its exports of wolfram to Germany and to expel Nazi agents from Spanish soil. Sweden was persuaded to restrict considerably her exports of iron ore and steel products to Germany.

All these measures and transactions synchronized with the preparations for the supreme enterprise, the invasion of France. The year 1943 had seen the war's turning point well passed. It had brought the Allied victories in the Pacific, in North Africa, Sicily, and Italy; it had brought the fall of Mussolini; it had brought the aerial assault on Germany up to new levels of weight and power; it had brought the Red Army's advance beyond the Don and the Dnieper.

Not least, the year 1943 had brought a virtual end to the German submarine menace at sea. March 1943 had been the climax of the enemy's naval effort in the North Atlantic. In the words of the British Admiralty's official account, "the months of April and May 1943 will probably be chosen by future historians as the critical period when the offensive at sea finally passed into the hands of the Allies." Antisubmarine devices were now very formidable. Convoys of Allied merchant ships were being escorted by ever larger numbers of destroyers and corvettes, many of them built in Canada and manned by Canadian crews, and later by a new class of vessel for which the old name of frigate was revived. The air umbrella was widened till there were only some 300 miles of the Atlantic gap, "the Black Pit," as it was called, not regularly patrolled by land-based planes spotting and hunting their quarries and, over this 300 miles, the convoy was accompanied by escort aircraft carriers and merchant aircraft carriers. Independent flotillas of destroyers, known as Support Groups, went hunting on their own for U-boat packs in the most dangerously infested waters.

The statistics of sinkings which we quoted in Chapter 41 tell their own story of the results of all these measures (see p. 677). Convoy and escort commanders at this time were reporting signs of deteriorating morale on the part of the enemy. Probably there were still a hundred German submarines at sea in the early months of 1943, and German building yards were maintaining their output, but the submarine commanders "were failing to press home their attacks, even when favorably placed for doing so." The invasion of France was entirely conditional upon the preliminary victory in the Battle of the Atlantic.

The build-up for the invasion of France was a stupendous logistic undertaking. A million and a half men had to be trained and equipped, and transported and maintained in Britain. The Air Forces required 163 fields. By July 1943, the flow of men from the United States had reached 150,000 a month, and the flow of material had reached 750,000 tons a month. The most serious problem was that of landing craft, a problem which, in Marshall's words, "was to plague us to the final day of the war in Europe." Two artificial harbors, the famous "Mulberry" harbors, were built for emplacement along the invasion beaches.[1]

It is no reflection on the courage and magnificence of the Anglo-American undertaking in France that the quality of the German Army in 1944 was so far below its quality in 1940. Allied plans for the invasion of North Africa and of France had both originally been made at a time when the war on the Eastern front was still uncertain and when it seemed that the forces which Hitler could release for service in the West, by all reasonable calculation, would be immensely strong. In June 1944 there were some sixty German divisions in France, believed to be a quarter of the total German Army then in the field but, of this sixty, only the armored and parachute divisions could have been regarded as first-class fighting troops. Latterly France had been converted into a training center for the refitting and reorganization of mutilated divisions from the East. The practice of recruiting foreigners, which we noticed as early as 1943, had been extended. In particular, rearward German services had been generously diluted with non-German "volunteers," often from prisoner-of-war camps, and their value was very dubious. Russians served in antiaircraft batteries. Second-line German levies, the *Volksgrenadier,* were being used for garrison purposes.

For weeks before the invasion, Nazi propaganda had been magnifying the defensive preparations in the West. "The Fortress of Europe" and "the Atlantic Wall" had become slogans out of all relation to the reality. Certain sectors, notably the Pas-de-Calais, the coasts of Belgium and Holland, and all the principal seaports were fortified; the West Wall had been stripped of much of its armament for coastal defense; but points elsewhere had little more than earthen fieldworks hastily thrown up. The Allied forces which invaded Normandy encountered a belt of strong points, heavily concreted gun positions, mine fields both at sea and on land, underwater obstacles, wire entanglements, and tank traps. Poles and stakes had been driven into the ground on all possible aircraft landing areas. But more than one Allied commander afterward gratefully admitted how surprised he was that, with all the time and resources at hand, the Germans had not constructed more formidable defenseworks. The fact is that, in the Second World War, as was demonstrated in campaign after campaign, static positions were at a disadvantage, and the odds lay with the army that seized and held the initiative.

Hitler appointed Rundstedt to the supreme command in the West and placed under him two army groups of two armies each, a northern Army Group B under Rommel and a southern Army Group G under Blaskowitz. Rommel's army group defended the Channel and the Low Countries, the sectors considered to be of greatest danger and vulnerability, and it comprised a full two-thirds of Rundstedt's total strength. Unhappily Rommel and Rundstedt, from the beginning of their association, disagreed over the vital question of the placing of their reserves. Rommel wanted to fight his battle at the beaches and push the invaders back into the sea; Rundstedt wanted to let the invaders come ashore and then crush them in a pitched battle at a point chosen by himself some miles inland. Furthermore, of three crack armored divisions, totaling 600 tanks, manned by the most highly trained and fanatical Nazi troops in France, two were under direct orders from Berlin and were not to be moved until so ordered by Hitler himself. Rommel and Rundstedt apparently were in agreement in their forecast that the main Allied invasion attempt would be made upon the Pas-de-Calais. Hitler, as usual relying "on intuition," believed it would be made upon Normandy.

The problem of unified command on the Allied side, the problem which had caused so much frustration and jealousy in the First World War, never arose in the Second. The European theater was always dominated by that remarkable personality, the American General Eisenhower, perhaps as great a statesman as he was a soldier, a man of infinite tact, humor, and strength, the ideal coalition general. He had been Supreme Commander in North Africa, and he was now Supreme Commander of the Allied Expeditionary Forces, for "operations aimed at the heart of Germany and the destruction of her armed forces." His deputy commander was Air Chief Marshal Sir Arthur Tedder, an appointment significant of the part that air power was expected to play in the invasion. Admiral Sir Bertram Ramsay commanded the Allied Naval Expeditionary Force; Air Chief Marshal Sir Trafford Leigh-Mallory commanded the Allied Expeditionary Air Force. Field Marshal Sir Bernard Montgomery commanded the assault forces, composed of the British Second Army under General Dempsey and the United States First Army under General Bradley.

In England as invasion day, "D-day," approached, the southern counties were sealed off as a security measure by police cordon. To the civilian inhabitants in the area, the rumble of trucks and tanks on the roads, the roar of passing planes, and muffled spurts of firing from the artillery ranges were familiar sounds at all times of the day and night. Assault craft assembled at embarkation ports. Bombers attacked German airfields and communications. By the time the invasion was launched, the Allies had established an absolute aerial supremacy over the Channel. In the last few days before D-day, 1,000-bomber waves were dropping 5,000 tons on German coastal defenses and targets inland. All the Seine and Loire bridges, except one, were demolished. Commandos wrecked the German radar installations. French resistance groups, now organized as the F.F.I. (French Forces of the Interior) under their own leader, General Koenig, were regularly contacted, and sabotage materials were dropped to them. Meanwhile meteorologists studied the one unpredictable element, the weather. May would normally have been the ideal month for the great venture. But final decisions were postponed and, in spite of continued unpromising weather reports, Eisenhower gave orders to move on June 6.

On June 6, 1944, at 2 A.M., British and American air-borne divisions were dropped over points at the two ends of the Allied assault area, at Caen and Carentan. Aerial bombardment of coastal defenses began at 3 A.M. and naval bombardment shortly after sunrise. Mine sweepers preceded the convoys of landing craft. In all, a fleet of 4,000 ships of all kinds converged upon the beaches of Normandy and encountered no serious enemy resistance by sea or air. The British Second Army assault divisions landed to the left between Caen and Bayeux, the United States First Army to the right west of Bayeux. There was some loss at sea from rough weather; shore obstacles were fouled; amphibious tanks suffered particularly. But, on the first day, 130,000 men and 20,000 vehicles were landed; the "crust" of the German system was broken. By the sixth day, 326,000 men, 54,000 vehicles and over 100,000 tons of stores had been landed. The bridgehead was 50 miles wide and 8 to 12 miles deep. The "Mulberry" harbors had been towed into position. The most critical time came during the storm which raged throughout the four days from June 19 to 22 and virtually wrecked the "Mulberry" harbor in the American sector.

The initial surprise had been complete. The German commanders, we have said, expected the main invasion to be attempted on the Pas-de-Calais and, in any case, they did not believe that a Channel crossing would be risked in the then prevailing rough weather. An Allied "diversion" toward Flanders was carried out with dummy paratroops. The Allied air attacks had destroyed roads and bridges, almost immobilizing the German reserves and isolating the battlefield. German divisions took as many as five days to cover fifty miles, marching at night to evade air attack. The first German counterattacks were delivered piecemeal on the initiative of divisional commanders on the spot. British forces failed to take Caen. American forces, in costly fighting, gradually occupied the Cotentin Peninsula and, on June 26, entered Cherbourg.

By July 2, 1944 an Allied army of nearly 1,000,000 men had been landed in Normandy — at a cost of 61,000 casualties, of whom 8,975 were killed. The Allied plan of campaign, generally credited to Montgomery, was for the British forces to contain the main German strength, especially the German armor, at Caen, and for the American forces, trained and equipped for mobility, to effect a breakout into Brittany and Maine and thence to turn eastward in a wide enveloping movement to the Seine. All through July the Germans counterattacked round Caen, and were held there. The American break-out was launched on July 25. Heavy bombers to the number of 1,500 laid down a "carpet" of 3,390 tons of bombs on a narrow front. Bradley's forces, organized as the United States First Army under Hodges and later the United States Third Army under Patton, deployed rapidly through the penetration thus effected into the open country beyond Avranches. A German counterattack toward Avranches, ordered, it is said, by Hitler himself, was beaten off. The subsequent American enveloping movement trapped 100,000 of the enemy in the "Falaise pocket." On August 15 a new American army under General Patch, with strong French reinforcements, landed in southern France and began to advance inland up to the Rhone Valley. The Germans in northern France were now retiring under pressure to the Seine and making a general withdrawal toward their own frontiers. Since D-day, total German losses had mounted to 400,000 men killed, wounded, or missing, over 1,000 tanks, and 3,500 aircraft. Rundstedt, opposed to the continuation of the war, had been superseded by Kluge early in July; and Kluge was succeeded by Model, a "retreat specialist" from the Eastern front, at the end of August. Rommel, wounded in Normandy, and then allegedly implicated in the attempt on Hitler's life on July 20, died in mysterious circumstances [2] (see p. 692).

There was one lively interlude at this time. Shortly after D-day, the Germans, from launching sites in the Pas-de-Calais, began to fire over to England their V-1's, or flying bombs — "buzz bombs" or "doodlebugs" as they were soon nicknamed. These were among Hitler's "secret weapons," with which he hoped to redress the Allied successes. They were small pilotless planes, jet-propelled. With proper time and opportunity for development, they might have amounted to a very serious menace. As it was, they gave the London area a decidedly uncomfortable two months. A great balloon barrage and antiaircraft defense were prepared for them in Kent and Sussex, and thousands of them were destroyed in mid-passage. They were essentially terroristic and were directed indiscriminately against civilians. In the event, they made no difference to the course of Allied strategy. Later, in August, the Germans sent over their V-2's, or rocket bombs, flying at supersonic velocity, a much more terrible weapon, against which there was no defense and which wrought great devastation, especially in the East End of London, until the advancing Allies began to capture their launching sites. In the winter of 1944–45, the V-1's and V-2's were aimed at urban centers still within range, notably Brussels and Antwerp.

By the end of August 1944, the Allied strength in France amounted to 2,000,000 men. The Canadian First Army under Crerar and the British Second Army under Dempsey formed the Twenty-first Army Group under Montgomery and operated in the north. The United States First Army under Hodges and the United States Third Army under Patton formed the Twelfth

Army Group under Bradley and operated in the center. The United States Ninth Army under Simpson, temporarily a part of the Twelfth Army Group, operated against German garrisons holding Brest and other French ports in the west. The United States Seventh Army under Patch and the French First Army under de Lattre de Tassigny formed the Sixth Army Group under Devers and operated in the South. Eisenhower established the Supreme Headquarters of the Allied Expeditionary Force (SHAEF) in Normandy, then at Versailles, and ultimately at Reims. The F.F.I. were in full activity throughout the country.

On August 19, 1944, units of the F.F.I. and local partisans had risen in Paris. Six days later a French armored division under Leclerc, together with an American infantry division, completed the liberation of the city. Allied forces were rolling forward through northern France and Belgium. The destruction of the main German armies in the West seemed in sight. Optimistic newspaper reporters were predicting an end to the war before Christmas. The Germans made their stubbornest stands at the ports, Brest, St. Nazaire, Lorient, Le Havre, Boulogne, and Calais, in order to deny to the Allies harbor facilities indispensable for the supply of their great deployment and, when the ports were captured, one by one, they were often found to be in so damaged a condition that even the minimum clearance and repair to make them serviceable was a major engineering undertaking. The German occupation of Walcheren closed the Scheldt estuary and immobilized the port of Antwerp.

The Germans, however, made a remarkable recovery on their own frontier. The Siegfried Line or West Wall, the old West Wall, the onetime complement to the Maginot Line, was now to be Hitler's main defense of his Reich. But the West Wall was weak at its northern end in Holland, just as the Maginot Line had been weak at its northern end, and Montgomery believed he had good chances of turning the German position by an attack at that point and "bouncing" a crossing of the Rhine. Late in September 1944, an attack was carried out by a combined British, American, and Polish air-borne army of three divisions under General Brereton in the tangled canal and dike system round Arnhem and Nijmegen. Over 2,800 planes and 1,500 gliders were used in the first two days. The British Second Army was intended to drive forward, make junction with the air-borne army, and exploit the situation thus created. The operation was the most considerable of its kind to date.

The Battle of Arnhem was a heroic gamble to end the war quickly. It failed, and its failure meant another winter and more months of hard fighting before the final defeat of the enemy could be accomplished. The headlong Allied advance through France had evidently overreached itself. Time was needed for the resting and refitting of divisions, many of whom had been in continuous action for four months, and especially for the reconstruction of ports and communications. Roosevelt and Churchill met for their second conference at Quebec, the "Octagon" Conference, a few days before the Arnhem landings, for one of their periodic reviews of the military and political situation. Eisenhower reported a general stiffening of enemy resistance. Some of the hardest fighting of the campaign took place during that November and early December — the clearance of the Scheldt and the capture of

Walcheren by the Canadian First Army, the penetration of the flooded Roer area by the British Second Army and the United States Ninth Army, and the costly advance beyond Aachen through the Hürtgen Forest by the United States First Army. But the grinding attrition suffered by the enemy contributed toward his ultimate defeat.

The bomber offensive against German industry had been maintained meanwhile throughout 1944. Attacks were concentrated on so-called panacea targets, which were supposed to be so vital that their destruction would instantly paralyze the enemy's war economy. Among such targets were the molybdenum mine at Knaben in Norway, the ball-bearing factories at Schweinfurt in northern Bavaria, the oil refineries at Ploesti in Rumania, the Dortmund-Ems Canal, and certain railroad viaducts. Huge loads of bombs were dropped — 53,000 tons on Germany alone in the single month of November 1944.

Air Marshal Harris has claimed that, as a result of these raids, Krupps at Essen virtually ceased work in October. Yet he has also acknowledged that synthetic-oil plants were often restored to full production within a few weeks of a "highly successful" attack.[3] Probably, as we have suggested elsewhere (see p. 764), more injurious to German industry than the physical damage to plant and buildings were the indirect effects of the bomber offensive — notably the enforced dispersal of factories and the consequent extension of rail distances, or the diversion of man power to clearance and repair, or the destruction of workers' housing.

As a postscript to these events we should mention the final destruction of the German battle fleet. In April 1944, in a single raid on Kiel, the *Admiral Scheer* was capsized at the quayside and the *Admiral Hipper* was so badly damaged in dry dock as to be made entirely unseaworthy. The *Schlesien* and the *Elbe* had both to be beached. Later in the same month, the *Lutzow* was sunk in the canal at Swinemünde. In the autumn the *Tirpitz* was sunk as she lay in the protection of a Norwegian fiord, after two raids and three direct hits by 12,000-pound bombs.

WARSAW AND BUDAPEST

In April 1944, forces of Tolbukhin's army group broke through the Pere-kop Isthmus, joined hands with Yeremenko's Maritime Army from Kerch, and cleared the Crimea at a cost to the enemy of 100,000 casualties. Sevasto-pol fell on May 9, and with its capture was restored the Soviet command of the Black Sea. In June, in the Karelian area in the far north, the Russians breached the old Mannerheim Line which had proved so tough an obstacle in 1940. Viipuri fell on June 20.

The Red Army on the Eastern front now consisted of some 300 divisions of over 5,000,000 men. In the north, in the Finnish and Baltic areas, were five army groups; in the center, in the White Russian area, were three army groups; in the south, in the Ukrainian area, were four army groups — the greatest massing of them all — under Koniev, Malinovsky, Tolbukhin, and

Petrov. Against these stood 200 German divisions of perhaps 2,000,000 men, disposed in four army groups, from north to south under Kuechler, Busch, Model, and Kleist. The lack of German reserve power was indeed all too evident. All German units were woefully under establishment both in men and machines. The increasing enlistment of alien mercenaries recalled the polyglot hordes of the later stages of the Thirty Years' War.

During June 1944, in the center, the Russians resumed their assault on Vitebsk, and that stubborn stronghold, together with the German defensive system in White Russia, the Fatherland Line, which was anchored to it, was overrun. Through July the Soviet northern army groups invaded the Baltic States; the central army groups crossed the (Polish) Bug into the very heart of Poland; the southern army groups crossed the (Ukrainian) Bug into "Transnistria."

At the end of July 1944, Rokossovsky, in command of one of the central army groups, was fast approaching Warsaw. The protecting fortress of Siedlce fell on July 31. In six weeks the central army groups had advanced 400 miles. They were now much extended and needed to pause for reorganization. But Rokossovsky still hoped to cross the Vistula and seize Warsaw — much in the same way as Montgomery in the West was simultaneously preparing to "bounce" a crossing of the Rhine. In Warsaw itself, Polish partisans under "General Bor," responding to appeals from the Moscow radio, were in open insurrection and had taken possession of several districts in the city. But on August 1 the Germans before Warsaw counterattacked, brought Rokossovsky's forces to a sudden halt, and then turned savagely on the partisans. The Soviet High Command refused Anglo-American planes the use of airfields behind the Soviet lines so as to enable a shuttle service to be organized for dropping arms and supplies to the partisans. In extenuation of the Soviet action, it has been argued that the partisans had been precipitate and should have waited for the outcome of Rokossovsky's operations, and that, in the turmoil in Warsaw, arms and supplies might have as likely fallen into German hands. At all events, Warsaw for a second time was the scene of one of the ghastly incidents of the war, an incident not greatly helpful to the already strained relations between Moscow and the Polish Government in London.

Meanwhile the Soviet advance continued in the northern sectors. Tartu in Estonia was taken on August 25, Tallinn on September 22, and Riga in Latvia on October 10, 1944. Remnants of the German Baltic Army were left stranded in the tip of Courland. Further north, Finland was already taking steps to withdraw from the unequal conflict. During August, Marshal von Mannerheim became Finnish President and appointed a new government, which shortly broke off relations with Germany and requested the withdrawal of German troops from Finnish soil. Finnish delegates proceeded to Moscow and signed an armistice there on September 10.

In the south, the army groups of Malinovsky and Tolbukhin were heading into Rumania. Antonescu's regime was in dissolution. His opponents had already made secret contacts with the Allies. On August 22, Jassy fell to the Russians. The next day, the young King Michael caught Antonescu completely unprepared when he called him into his study, dismissed him from office, and locked him in a vault for safekeeping. Michael then announced the cessation of hostilities and appointed a pro-Soviet cabinet under General Sanatescu. The Germans replied with a savage bombing of Bucharest; whereupon the new cabinet declared war on Germany. By August 30, Soviet forces had occupied Bucharest and the oil fields at Ploesti. Rumanian delegates signed an armistice in Moscow on September 13, 1944.

Bulgaria, who had never been a full belligerent and had not even declared war on the Soviet Union, hastened to make her peace with the victors. Since the mysterious death of Tsar Boris in 1943, a series of regents for the young Simeon had kept up a show of collaboration with Germany. But changing of cabinets and arresting of ministers were now no longer expedients sufficient to keep Bulgaria in line. In August 1944, Bulgarian emissaries made secret contacts with the Allies in Cairo. On September 2, under Allied pressure, a new cabinet was installed, headed by pro-Allied and veteran democrats, which broke off relations with Germany. On the 5th, amid feverish, last-minute efforts to avoid open hostilities, the Soviet Union made a surprise declaration of war on Bulgaria, and Soviet forces were shortly pouring into the country. The cabinet sued for an armistice and declared war on Germany. But on September 9 a strong-arm gang broke in on the cabinet meeting, and a new government and Regency Council, both acceptable to the Soviet, were ostensibly put in charge of Bulgarian affairs. Bulgarian delegates signed an armistice in Moscow on October 28, 1944.

By October 1944, fighting had ended in the Baltic States, and in Rumania and Bulgaria. The Red Army crossed the borders of East Prussia and of Hungary. Malinovsky was driving toward Budapest. Tolbukhin took Nish on October 16 and Belgrade on October 20 and effected a junction with Tito's partisans. Transylvania and Ruthenia were cleared of German and Hungarian forces. In Greece, during October, British forces landed at Patras and had thence taken Corinth, Athens, and the Piraeus. Papandreou and his government returned to Athens.

Hungary was all but lost to the Germans. On October 15, 1944, in a broadcast, the Regent, Admiral Horthy, bitterly reproached the Nazis for their infringements of Hungarian sovereignty and announced that he would sue for an armistice. Horthy found himself promptly deposed, and a government was set up under the pro-Fascist Szalasi. In November and December, Malinovsky's and Tolbukhin's army groups advanced into the Hungarian plain. Hungarians greeted the Russians as allies and deserted to them in the thousands. The Hungarian General Miklos, at the head of the Hungarian First Army, went over to the Russians with offers to form a new government. In the latter part of December, elections for a provisional assembly were held in the liberated parts of Hungary; the assembly duly met at Debrecen on December 21 and set up a government under Miklos, which at once declared war on Germany. Hungarian delegates signed an armistice in Moscow on January 20, 1945. The Germans continued to hold out in the citadel of Buda even as they were still holding out in Warsaw.

THE COLLAPSE OF GERMANY

At the end of 1944, on every front, west, south, and east, Allied armies were swarming toward Germany. In the West, their advance had reached points roughly coincident with the Belgian and French frontiers. They stood on German soil near Düren and Trier and had crossed the Saar. The United States Ninth Army was in the line north of Aachen. On the German side, Rundstedt had been recalled to the supreme command in France, and Model was relegated to Rommel's former command, Army Group B. In the south, in Italy, the Allied advance had reached Ravenna and Forli. British forces were operating in Greece and Dalmatia. In the East, the Red Army stood on German soil in East Prussia; it had advanced just short of Warsaw and Budapest.

On December 16, 1944, in the Ardennes area, the Germans suddenly launched an offensive, a "spoiling offensive," somewhat recalling the Battle of Kursk on the Eastern front more than a year before. The offensive had been ordered by Hitler himself with the object of retaking Brussels and Antwerp, and perhaps disorganizing the entire Allied position in Belgium, and he had briefed his generals in person at a special conference four days previously. Rundstedt was directed to attack with 24 divisions, 10 of them armored, across his old Ardennes battlefield of 1940. Like all Hitler's projects, the offensive showed a flash of strategic insight. It caught the American Intelligence off guard. But it had to be fought with an insufficiency of material and with forces which were generously reinforced with raw recruits of the *Volksgrenadier*. Rundstedt had little faith in it, but was helpless in the face of the Führer's categorical commands. Foggy weather concealed the preparations and prevented Allied aerial counteroperations, though R.A.F. Bomber Command, with the use of radar, made several damaging sorties over the battlefield. In a week of hard fighting, the Germans almost reached the river Meuse at Dinant.

The "Battle of the Bulge," as it came to be called, was the Wehrmacht's last blow. Eisenhower halted all offensive operations along the front and hastened every reserve to the haunches of the German salient. As the weather cleared, 5,000 Allied aircraft were loosed upon the German supply lines. Patton and the United States Third Army counterattacked from the south; and Montgomery, temporarily placed in command of the greater part of the United States First and Ninth Armies, attacked from the north. By the end of January the Germans had been forced back to their original positions. The battle had cost them 120,000 men, killed, wounded, and prisoners, 600 tanks, and 1,600 planes, a loss they could ill afford.

Thereafter the German armies in the West, under the Allies' unrelenting pressure, on the ground and in the air, were steadily driven back to their final destruction in the heart of the Fatherland. On March 7 an American armored division crossed the Rhine at Remagen over a bridge which the enemy, by an extraordinary blunder, had failed to demolish. Two weeks later, on the night of March 23, behind the most successful air drop of the campaign, units of the British Twenty-first Army Group crossed the Rhine above Wesel. By the last week in March all territory on the west bank of the Rhine had been cleared of the enemy, and the bridgeheads on the east bank were rapidly expanding eastward.

In November 1944, Roosevelt had been re-elected President of the United States for a fourth term. The next formal Allied conference between himself, Churchill, and Stalin took place shortly after his inauguration, on February 4–11, 1945, at Yalta in the Crimea. The conferees agreed that the three Allied Powers should occupy separate zones in Germany and that France should be invited to take over a fourth zone. They agreed to establish a Control Commission with headquarters in Berlin. "The plans and policies for enforcing the unconditional surrender terms . . . will not be made known until the final defeat of Germany has been accomplished." The Conference reaffirmed "the inflexible purpose of the Allies" to destroy German militarism and Nazism, to disarm and disband all German forces, to break up the German General Staff, to destroy or remove German military potential, to bring all war criminals to justice, and to eliminate the Nazi party, its organizations and influence, and to exact reparation "in kind to the greatest extent possible." It agreed to call a conference at San Francisco in April 1945 to prepare the Charter of the United Nations. It reaffirmed the Atlantic Charter. It agreed that the states of liberated Europe must solve "by democratic means their pressing political and economic problems," and pledged "the earliest possible establishment, through free elections, of governments responsive to the will of the people." It agreed to the formation of a Polish Provisional Government of National Unity, which should include "democratic leaders from Poland itself and from Poles abroad," and which should hold "free and unfettered elections as soon as possible." It agreed that the eastern frontier of Poland should generally follow the Curzon Line, but that she must receive "substantial accessions of territory," presumably at the expense of Germany, to the north and west. It recognized the Tito-Subasich agreement regarding Yugoslavia (see p. 721). By a further secret convention, the Soviet Union agreed to enter the war against Japan "two or three months after the German surrender" on condition that the Soviet Union receive from Japan territories seized from the former Russian state in Sakhalin, Manchuria, and Port Arthur, and also the Kurile Islands.

On his way back from the Crimea Conference, at stopping points aboard American warships, President Roosevelt conferred with King Farouk of Egypt, Emperor Haile Selassie of Ethiopia, and King Ibn Saud of Arabia. He met Churchill again at Alexandria. General de Gaulle declined an invitation to a meeting at Algiers as a mark of protest against the exclusion of France from the Crimea Conference, thereby committing as grave a diplomatic discourtesy as any in his stubborn career. On March 1, at Washington, Roosevelt made a "personal report" to Congress on the Conference and broadcast to the American people. Rumors were then appearing in the press, and being denied, regarding the President's failing health. Such rumors had not been uncommon ever since his election to a fourth term. Those who knew him best had perhaps grown used to the evident marks of strain which twelve years as President had left on him. He had staged "comebacks" before, and his mental and physical resilience was extraordinary. His daily round and his public appearances continued as normally. But he died suddenly on April 12, 1945 — struck down on the very eve of the military victory and denied from making his contribution to the greater and more congenial task, the building up of a free and stable international order.

Roosevelt was succeeded by Vice-President Harry Truman. The conference to draw up the Charter of the United Nations was duly opened at San Francisco with an address by the new President, broadcast from Washington on April 25 — the day that American and Soviet forces made contact on the Elbe. The Charter was signed by the assembled delegates of fifty nations at San Francisco on June 26.

The Rhine proved to be the last serious obstacle in the West. The Allied advance beyond it was made against a demoralized and broken enemy. The aerial accompaniment was now virtually unopposed. The dread, proud Luftwaffe that had once consumed Warsaw, Rotterdam, Belgrade, and London in flame and terror had ceased to exist as an effective weapon. The main Allied thrust on land was made north and south of the Ruhr by the British Second Army and the United States Ninth Army. The United States Third and Seventh Armies struck toward Mainz and Frankfort. During March an average of 10,000 Germans a day were being taken prisoner on the Western front. In April the figure rose to 50,000. The Wehrmacht was clearly in the last agonies. There were several fantastic rumors of a desperate stand to be made by a new Nazi guerrilla force, the "Werewolves," in a "Southern Redoubt" in the Bavarian uplands.

Allied operations in Italy meanwhile had been somewhat curtailed by heavy withdrawals of effectives to France. But on April 9, 1945, Clark's forces launched their final offensive of the campaign, seized Bologna, and broke into the Po Valley. Mantua, Parma, and Verona fell in quick succession. Turin and Genoa were seized by Italian partisans, and Trieste by Yugoslavs. On April 28, Mussolini and twelve of his cabinet were recognized attempting to cross the frontier into Switzerland and "executed" by Italian partisans. On April 29, at Caserta, German officers, on behalf of the German armies in Italy, accepted unconditional surrender. Hostilities in Italy ceased at noon on May 2, 1945.

On the Eastern front, German counterattacks before Warsaw and Budapest had paralleled the Ardennes offensive. It took the whole of January 1945 for Malinovsky and Petrov to invest and reduce Warsaw. Isolated German units were still holding out in the citadel of Buda up to mid-February. What was still left of these two handsome and historic cities was largely destroyed in these obstinate operations.

Thereafter the Red Army swept irresistibly into Austria and Germany with Vienna and Berlin as its ultimate goals. The Polish winter had been exceptionally mild, and general fighting had continued along the entire front without the usual seasonal interruption. The central army groups were now advancing toward Königsberg, Poznań, and Breslau. As in the West, the Germans clung to the seaports. Memel fell on January 27, 1945, Gdynia and Danzig on March 30, and Königsberg on April 8, though in each case the main Soviet lines by the date had passed far beyond. Poznań and Breslau were taken during February and March. Further south, Bratislava was taken by Malinovsky's forces on April 4, and Vienna by a great concentration of Malinovsky's and Tolbukhin's forces on the 13th. At the moment, Zhukov, now commanding one of the central army groups, was already in the suburbs of Berlin.

The end of Hitler and his Reich now came quickly. He had spent some weeks on the Western front at the time of the Ardennes offensive and had returned to Berlin in mid-January 1945. The attempted assassination of July 1944 had left him partly deaf and had probably aggravated his former maladies. In the last phase, he is described as broken in health, a stooping, shambling figure, ashy pale, convulsed with stomach cramps, his hands in a perpetual tremor, with fits of depression alternating with his ever more frequent storms and rages. He took no exercise, worked round the clock, and slept three hours in the twenty-four. He suffered from the occupational disease of all tyrants, the phobia of treachery; betrayal and bad faith lurked in every shadow; every man's hand was raised against his sacred person. A quack physician is said to have been giving him constant drug injections. At this time, the Chancellery building in Berlin being badly damaged and burned, he and his immediate circle occupied somewhat restricted quarters in a concrete air-raid bunker in the Chancellery garden.

Hitler's fifty-sixth birthday, April 20, 1945, was a day of critical conferences. The Allied advance, east and west, was about to cut Germany in halves; Russian shells were already thudding round the bunker. The magnates of the regime, Göring, Goebbels, Himmler, Bormann, Ribbentrop, Speer, Doenitz, Keitel, Jodl — and Eva Braun — were all in attendance. The main problems before them were allocation of political authority under the fast deteriorating military situation, the successorship to the Führer in the now very probable event of his death, and diplomatic contact with the enemy for a cessation of hostilities. Yet in the bunker, in that "subterranean madhouse," in the midst of these understandable and legitimate problems, we still see the old party strifes and intrigues continuing, and the old personal hatreds, instead of being decently buried by the proximity of disaster, seeking out new opportunities for their gratification; we still see the fanatic rivalry of court favorites snatching at positions of command, however momentary, in a state and army both of which had largely ceased to exist.

In the upshot, Hitler appointed Admiral Doenitz to the command of the German forces in the northern half of Germany, and Doenitz shortly left for headquarters at Plön in Schleswig-Holstein. The remainder dispersed or stayed as their duties seemed to dictate — Keitel and Jodl to their headquarters at the front, Göring to Berchtesgaden, Himmler and Speer to their respective offices in Berlin. Göring attempted to open secret peace parleys with the enemy in the West. Himmler became immersed in similar parleys of great intricacy through Count Bernadotte of the Swedish Red Cross. Himmler appears to have believed that he could found a new political party and survive the wreck of Germany with himself securely at its head. For Hitler, the revelation of these peace intrigues was the unkindest cut of all. The oldest and most trusted of his lieutenants, it seemed, were meditating desertion. Speer, Himmler, and Ribbentrop eventually joined Doenitz at Plön. Meanwhile Goebbels and Bormann remained with Hitler in the bunker — and with them Eva Braun, Hitler's mistress, and the Goebbels family.

On the night of April 28, Hitler gave orders for a last-ditch defense of the Chancellery — the Russians were now only a few streets away — and to that end he summoned to Berlin General Ritter von Greim, a high-ranking officer of the Luftwaffe, appointed him Commander in Chief of the Luftwaffe in succession to the traitorous Göring, and then sent him to find and collect what German pilots and aircraft were still available for operations. Greim, in the last plane to leave Berlin, with Hitler's desperate and impossible instructions in his pocket, made off for Doenitz's headquarters at Plön. Next Hitler married Eva Braun, and wrote his will and his political testament, in which he reviewed his career, protested his desire for peace, expelled Göring and Himmler from the Nazi party, and appointed Doenitz Reich President, Minister of War, and Commander in Chief of the Wehrmacht. Copies of the document were entrusted to envoys, who left the Chancellery on foot to penetrate the Soviet lines as best they could, with orders to proceed to Plön. On April 30, in the afternoon, after elaborate farewells among those present, Hitler and Eva Braun committed suicide. Their bodies were burned in gasoline. No traces were ever found. Goebbels and his family committed suicide. Bormann escaped alive and was never heard of again.

Doenitz broadcast his assumption of authority to the German armed forces and people on May 1 and called on them for further efforts in the struggle against Bolshevism. He formed a new government with Count Schwerin von Krosigk as Foreign Minister, a career official who had been Finance Minister since Papen's day in 1932. Ribbentrop was ignored. Admiral von Friedeburg was appointed Commander in Chief of the German Navy. On May 2, Doenitz moved his headquarters from Plön to Flensburg, near the Danish border. The same day he sent Friedeburg to Montgomery with proposals to capitulate in the West but to continue fighting in the East. Montgomery rejected the offer and demanded unconditional surrender on all fronts.

The final German capitulation was patchy and piecemeal. There was neither the need nor the opportunity for theater. Eisenhower issued instructions that subordinate commanders could accept surrenders on their respective fronts. On May 4 the unconditional surrender of the German forces in Holland, northwest Germany, and Denmark was signed at Montgomery's headquarters on Lüneburg Heath. On May 7 the general instrument of surrender was signed by Jodl at Eisenhower's headquarters at Reims and ratified by Keitel on May 9, at Zhukov's headquarters at Berlin. Surrenders of isolated German units, in Norway, the Aegean, and Bohemia were announced severally in the course of the next few days.

The Potsdam Conference — or the Berlin Conference, to give it its official name — was held in the Cecilienhof in Potsdam between July 17 and August 2, 1945. The United States was represented by President Truman and Secretary of State Byrnes; the Soviet Union was represented by Stalin and Molotov. In Britain, Churchill's National Coalition had lately dissolved, and the results of the subsequent general elections were not announced till July 26, while the Potsdam Conference was actually in session (see p. 696). Churchill and the Conservative party were heavily defeated, and a Labor government took office under Attlee, with Bevin as Foreign Secretary. For the first half of the Potsdam Conference, therefore, Britain was represented by Churchill and Eden, with Attlee in attendance; and, for the second half, by Attlee and Bevin. There was no French representative.

The Crimea Conference had been the high point of Allied unity and comradeship in arms, but even there the Polish question had been acute.[4] Potsdam revealed further deep disagreements between the Soviet and the Anglo-American Allies, not only over the Polish question, but also over German reparations and over the political settlement in Eastern Europe and the Balkans. However, none of this was publicly divulged. An unexceptionable report of the agreements reached at the Conference, the lengthiest and most comprehensive of these inter-Allied pronouncements, was issued on August 2. It announced the formation of a Council of Foreign Ministers of the five Allies — the United States, Britain, the Soviet Union, France, and China — charged to undertake the preparation of the peace treaties for Italy, Bulgaria, Finland, Hungary, and Rumania. It enunciated the political and economic principles which should govern the treatment of Germany in the initial control period, effect her total disarmament and denazification, bring home to her people at large the absolute conviction of their military defeat, and prepare for the eventual reconstruction of her political life on a democratic basis. It indicated, in sufficiently specific terms, the industrial levels to be permitted to Germany and the reparations to be exacted. It recognized the transfer of Königsberg to the Soviet Union. It reaffirmed former Allied declarations to bring war criminals to justice. It reserved the final delimitation of the western frontier of Poland to the future peace settlement, but assigned an area of Polish "Administration" up to the Oder and Neisse rivers and including Danzig. It expressed satisfaction over the formation of the Polish Provisional Government of National Unity. It urged the orderly and humane transfer of German populations from Poland, Czechoslovakia, and Hungary.

During the Conference, Stalin had still temporized on the question of an immediate Soviet declaration of war on Japan, though he was informed by Truman of a "new" secret weapon in the hands of the United States. On July 26, from Potsdam, Truman, Attlee, Stalin, and Chiang Kai-shek, in the names of their governments, issued an ultimatum to Japan warning her of the immeasurable armed forces now at their disposal and demanding her instant and unconditional surrender. "The alternative for Japan is complete and utter destruction."

THE COLLAPSE OF JAPAN

We retrace our steps to consider the East in 1944. Burma was then becoming, like Italy, a relatively forlorn theater of the war, by-passed by greater happenings elsewhere. But the situation there had very considerably improved since the hard battle for Myitkyina. By the end of 1944, Japanese forces in Burma were cut off by the developing naval blockade from their supply centers in their distant homeland, and like the many isolated Japanese units in the Pacific, they were progressively suffering siege conditions. British submarines were roaming freely in the Strait of Malacca and the Java Sea, complementing the efforts of American submarines further east. British planes were raiding Rangoon, Bangkok, and Singapore without meeting serious opposition. Wingate's jungle fighters in the heart of Burma, whose tactics originally had only been made possible by the generous provision of aircraft, were now operating in freedom from Japanese aerial interference. Troops, equipment, guns, jeeps, even bullocks and mules were being set down on airstrips in the immediate battle area. By 1945 nearly 100,000 tons of supplies a month were being flown to Allied forces in the Burmese forests.

The monsoon of 1944 had restricted but not wholly stopped the fighting in Burma, and the Allied advance had continued beyond Myitkyina. Operations were intensified with the return of good weather. Three main Allied forces were then closing in on central Burma — the British Fourteenth Army under General Slim, pressing eastward from Imphal and Arakan, the American-Chinese force under General Sultan pressing southward from Myitkyina, and the Chinese force pressing westward from Yunnan. The immediate objective, the reopening of the Ledo and Burma roads, was declared to have been achieved on January 22, 1945. Mandalay was taken on March 20, and Pegu, fifty miles from Rangoon, in mid-April. Meanwhile British amphibious and air-borne forces were preparing for a descent on the extreme tip of Burma from the sea. They landed south of Rangoon on May 1, and the city fell, almost without loss, in the course of the next two days. Except for Japanese remnants still holding out in the northern and eastern jungles upcountry, the Burmese campaign had been completed.

Assault craft were now arriving from Europe, but the further operations for the reconquest of Malaya and Singapore, to which they were to be assigned, were anticipated by the main Japanese surrenders of August 1945.

Plans for the closing phases of the war against metropolitan Japan had been made earlier in September 1944 at the Roosevelt-Churchill "Octagon" Conference at Quebec. Reports at hand from MacArthur and Nimitz had been so favorable that Marshall, then at the Conference, had approved plans for an assault on Leyte in the very center of the Philippine archipelago. On September 17, the day after the Conference closed, American forces landed on Angaur in the Palau Islands, 550 miles from the nearest point in the Philippines. A month later, on October 19, 1944, a huge armada of 750 ships, stretching from horizon to horizon, bore the four divisions of the United States Sixth Army, numbering 250,000 men, under General Krueger, toward Leyte. The covering naval forces consisted of six battleships with their accompanying screen of cruisers and destroyers. A carrier task force, under Admiral Halsey, stood out at sea.

How seriously the Japanese High Command viewed this new American eruption was sufficiently indicated by the sudden appearance of the main elements of the Japanese Navy after months of hiding "in cold storage." The loss of the Philippines would sever Japan's last supply links with the Netherlands East Indies, the pride of her Pacific empire and her major source of oil. The Japanese High Command made the decision to commit its fleet in the greatest naval battle of the Second World War. A "suicide squadron" tried to lure away Halsey's task force, while two other squadrons, from the north and south of Leyte Gulf, would close in upon the American transports in the midst of landing operations. Meanwhile attacks would be made by a new force of Japanese "suicide planes." During October 23–26, in and around Leyte Gulf, there was fought a series of naval and aerial actions. The Japanese squadron from the north was on the verge of entering the Gulf when, perhaps suspecting a trap, its commander decided to withdraw. Evidently both sides were at a high pitch of nervousness for their big ships in the vulnerable conditions of narrow waters. The final result was a great American victory. The Japanese lost 3 battleships, 6 carriers, and 10 cruisers, and suffered severe damage to at least 4 battleships and 10 other cruisers. The Americans lost the light carrier *Princeton,* 2 escort carriers, 2 destroyers, and 1 destroyer escort.

MacArthur proceeded to the methodical conquest of Leyte. It was to be the first step in a Philippine campaign on which he had set his heart. "I have returned," he said on landing. There were then some 250,000 Japanese troops stationed at different points in the Philippines under the command of General Yamashita, "the Tiger of Malaya," the victor of Singapore and Bataan but, writes Marshall, "most of them might as well have been on the other side of the world so far as the enemy's ability to shift them to meet the American thrusts was concerned." [1] A long trail of wrecked and sunken transports and escort craft was all that was left of persistent Japanese attempts to succor these beleaguered forces. At the last, a few precarious loads of Japanese supplies were even being run through the American blockade by sailboat.

On December 15, American forces landed on Mindoro, and on January 9, 1945, on Luzon. In February, American forces took Cavite and Corregidor, and the enemy was making a last house-to-house stand in Intramuros, the ancient walled section of Manila. Field Marshal Count Hisaichi Terauchi, supreme Japanese commander in the Philippine and Malayan area, moved his headquarters from Manila to Saïgon in Indo-China. Manila itself was cleared and occupied on February 23. But the final wresting of the Philippines was still a protracted task and was not completed until the beginning of July. Meanwhile strong Australian forces, reinforced by a Dutch contingent, had landed in Borneo. In all these operations the Japanese fought with their usual fanatic tenacity. They allowed themselves to be burned in their concrete holes by flame throwers or buried alive in the shattered masonry rather than surrender. Their casualties were five times those of their attackers, but the haul of their prisoners after an engagement was a fraction of their dead.

On February 19, 1945, three divisions of the United States Marines fought their way ashore on Iwo Jima, only 750 miles from Tokyo. The island was a jungle of dwarf rocks, lava ledges, smoking sulphur pits, and deep caverns, and the Japanese had seamed it with a maze of blockhouses, pillboxes, and bunkers. Gains at first were counted in yards but, in eighteen days, the enemy's defenses had been split by a breakthrough across the waist of the island from sea to sea. Iwo Jima was taken at a cost of 20,196 American casualties, killed, wounded, and missing. In the first week of April, four divisions of the United States Tenth Army under General Buckner were landed on Okinawa in the Ryukyus, only 350 miles from the southern tip of the Japanese mainland. The Japanese were again elaborately entrenched; the terrain was "decidedly rugged and cut up with many cliffs, natural and man-made, limestone and coral caves"; the fighting was the fiercest and most costly of the entire Pacific campaign. The island was not cleaned up till the end of June, at a loss to the Japanese of 109,629 killed and 7,871 taken pris-oner, and to the Americans of 12,500 killed or missing. General Buckner was himself killed in the closing actions.

Japanese "suicide planes" had made their first appearance at Leyte, but had not been very effective. During and after the Okinawa operations, how-ever, they constituted a formidable threat. The Kamikaze ("divine wind") squadrons, so named after the providential typhoon which shattered the attempted Mongol invasion of Japan in 1281, were composed of two types of aircraft. The more refined variety was a twenty-foot plane with a massive charge of TNT in its nose, which was launched from a "mother" bomber and guided to its objective by a single suicide pilot. Much more numerous was the improvised type, a single-engined fighter, laden with a maximum weight of explosive, designed to explode on contact. Aircraft carriers, with their flat, unarmored flight decks, were ideal targets for these weapons of supreme desperation, especially if their gasoline-filled planes had not been flown off. The thin-skinned destroyer, too, was highly vulnerable. But even on the heavily armored battleships and cruisers the Kamikaze could inflict, if not mortal injury, at least very serious damage. In the course of the Okinawa campaign, the Kamikaze accounted for 36 American destroyers and smaller craft sunk and 368 other American vessels of all classes damaged. The protracted assault is believed to have cost the Japanese 7,800 planes.

On April 5, 1945, the Soviet Government gave notice that it would de-nounce the Soviet-Japanese Neutrality Pact of 1941. The Koiso ministry in Tokyo thereupon resigned and, with pointed defiance, was replaced by a new ministry under Baron Suzuki, one of the admirals of the Russo-Japanese War of 1904–05. But the merciless erosion of Japanese strength did not wait upon Cabinet changes. The American air forces in the Pacific were reorgan-ized under General Spaatz for the final assault. Since the taking of Saipan and Guam in the Marianas, Japan had been within range of the B-29 Super-fortresses. In the nine months from November 1944 to the surrender in Sep-tember 1945, B-29's made 32,000 sorties against Japan — more than a hundred a day — dropped 169,000 tons of bombs, and lost 437 aircraft and over 3,000 personnel. With the taking of Iwo Jima and Okinawa, the mainland island of Kyushu was within fighter range. Japan was methodically pounded with high explosive and fire bomb, paralyzing her interisland transportation system, her railroads and industries, and incinerating her inflammable and crowded cities. Her harbor mouths were thickly sown with mines dropped from the air and, outside this deadly barrier, American and British fleets ranged with impunity within very sight of her coasts. Her remaining battleships were bombarded as they lay heavily camouflaged in harbor berths of river estuaries. The surrender of Germany, releasing further massive Allied naval and military resources for the Pacific, presaged the descent of new torrents of fire and steel. The Suzuki cabinet in Tokyo, however, was still temeritous enough to reject the Potsdam ultimatum of July 26 "as unworthy of public notice." It sought to enlist the Soviet Union as mediator in a negotiated peace. But the Soviet Union had other intentions in the Far East. It had already denounced its neutrality pact with Japan, and it was patently preparing to implement its Crimea undertaking to enter the war.

The Potsdam ultimatum had not explicitly revealed the nature of that "complete and utter destruction" which was to befall Japan if she refused the alternative of surrender. But it was shortly common knowledge that, in the week before the Potsdam Conference, an experimental atom bomb had been successfully tested in the deserts of New Mexico. As human discoveries go, "splitting the atom" had had a short, but intensive history. Ever since the early experiments with radioactivity between 1904 and 1919, Western science had been haunted by the problem of releasing the vast stores of energy normally locked in the primary particles of the material universe. But it was not till the late thirties that experiments with the isotopes of uranium, then being carried out simultaneously in Italy, France, and Germany, had opened up the tremendous possibilities of nuclear fission. By 1939, international competition for the development of an atomic weapon was already started. The French Government, just before the Fall of France, purchased the largest available quantity of heavy water from the Norsk Hydro Company of Norway, and subsequently British commandos raided heavy-water plants in Norway to prevent the precious fluid from falling into the enemy's hands. In April 1940 the Thomson Committee was set up by the British Air Ministry and, rather more than a year later, reported that the manufacture of an atom bomb was a feasible proposition. The basic material required was uranium 235, and the great difficulty was its isolation in sufficient amounts from ordinary uranium. The British War Cabinet set up a "Directorate of Tube Alloys" to implement the work of the Thomson Committee.

At the same time, reports were exchanged with American scientists, who had been conducting independent investigations. In October 1941, Roosevelt proposed to Churchill that all British and American efforts in this direction be combined and all research be concentrated in the United States. The Canadian Government was brought into the scheme, in view of the fact that Canada was one of the world's richest known sources of uranium ores and that Canadian hydroelectric engineering was peculiarly fitted for the production of the essential heavy water. A British-Canadian laboratory was set up in Montreal, and a few British scientists were assigned to the larger American projects. Eventually the United States spent $2,000,000,000, over a period of four years, on experiments and production processes for the manufacture of the atom bomb. In the final count, the credit for the preliminary theoretical development fell to many scientific workers of many different nationalities — some, ironically, were political refugees from Fascism and Nazism — but thereafter almost the whole of the huge technological burden was carried by the United States. At this point of time, no other nation could have expended the necessary industrial effort nor recruited the necessary scientific personnel.

On August 6 the first atom bomb was dropped on Hiroshima from a solitary B-29 flying at high altitude. In the midst of this superhuman fire-spout, 78,000 persons were killed, 14,000 were missing, and 37,000 were injured, not counting thousands more who afterward developed curious disorders as the result of exposure to gamma rays. The American "divine wind" had blown, and there was no possible reply to it. On August 8 the Soviet Union declared war on Japan, and three army groups under Marshal Vasilevsky launched a converging offensive toward Harbin against the Japanese Kwantung Army in Manchuria. At any other time a Far Eastern war between the Soviet Union and Japan would have been a very considerable affair. The land forces of both Powers were composed of picked troops, independently organized of homeland supplies, and long prepared for just such a conflict. But the Soviet Union was now fighting an enemy that was already in process of abandoning further resistance. The 750,000 men of the Kwantung Army, after a few days of fighting, broke up into isolated units, most of which proceeded to surrender in detail. On August 9 a second atom bomb, of different type but even greater destructive power, was loosed on the naval base at Nagasaki. The configuration of the city somewhat limited the area affected but, within that area, obliteration was absolute.

Even now, extreme Japanese militarists opposed a general capitulation, and it seemed for a moment as if the war would deteriorate into a disorganized scramble of guerrilla actions by individual Japanese chieftains at the head of such forces as would still bear them obedience. But, on the night of August 8, the Emperor held a meeting of the Cabinet and of Elder Statesmen and was advised to sue for peace. On August 10 the Japanese Government offered to accept the Potsdam ultimatum of July 26 "with the understanding that the said declaration does not comprise any demand which prejudices the prerogatives of the Emperor as a sovereign ruler." The Allied reply, transmitted by the United States Secretary of State, at once required that "from the moment of surrender the authority of the Emperor and the Japanese Government to rule the State shall be subject to the Supreme Commander of the Allied Powers." On August 14 the Suzuki cabinet accepted the Allied terms and, on the following day, resigned. Prince Higashikuni formed a new government. On August 28 the first American troops went ashore unopposed on Japanese soil in Sagami Bay.

On September 2, 1945, in Tokyo Bay, aboard the battleship *Missouri*, in the presence of General MacArthur, Admiral Nimitz, and ranking Allied officers, Japanese delegates signed the instrument of unconditional surrender. During the next three weeks, Japanese commanders formally surrendered in their respective areas in Harbin, Rabaul, Borneo, the Netherlands East Indies, Nanking, Singapore, Hong Kong, and Rangoon.

PART FIVE

POST–1945

47 **THE ORGANIZATION OF PEACE**

THE ORIGINS OF THE UNITED NATIONS

The joint Declaration of the United Nations was signed at Washington on January 1, 1942, by representatives of the twenty-six Allies pledging their full resources, military and economic, to the common struggle.[1] The Declaration contained an explicit adherence to the "purposes and principles" of the Atlantic Charter. A permanent United Nations Organization to take the place of the League of Nations, "for the maintenance of world peace and security and the promotion of world economic and social advancement," was under serious discussion at high political levels during the ensuing year. The foreign ministers, in conference in Moscow in October 1943, formally recognized the necessity for establishing such an organization. Discussions were continued at the end of 1943 at the Cairo Conference between Roosevelt, Churchill, and Chiang Kai-shek, and at the Teheran Conference between Roosevelt, Churchill, and Stalin. Meanwhile the general plan, now fast maturing, was further prospered by the conference at Hot Springs, Virginia, in May and June 1943, which created the Food and Agriculture Organization (FAO), and the conference in Washington in November 1943, which created the United Nations Relief and Rehabilitation Administration (UNRRA), two organizations subsequently to become Specialized Agencies of the United Nations.

Representatives of the United States, Britain, the Soviet Union, and China — notably Stettinius, Cadogan and Halifax, Gromyko, and Wellington Koo — conferred at Dumbarton Oaks, near Washington, between August and October 1944, to make "tentative proposals" for the future organization. Soviet and Chinese representatives did not meet together, as the Soviet Union was not at war with Japan. A General Assembly and a Security Council were projected, somewhat on the lines of the similarly named bodies of the League of Nations, and in addition an International Court and an Economic and Social Council. But it was at Dumbarton Oaks that the first sharp differences arose over the voting procedure to be adopted in the Security Council. A working formula for that procedure was agreed upon at the Crimea Conference between Roosevelt, Churchill, and Stalin in February 1945 but, as we shall see, it remained thereafter a highly contentious issue. Thus primed and prepared, the representatives of fifty nations assembled at San Francisco on April 25, 1945, to draw up the Charter of the United Nations. At that time the Polish question was unsettled, and no Polish representative attended the San Francisco Conference, but under Article 3 of the Charter, as it was drawn up, Poland was afterward enabled to count herself an original member — the fifty-first.

The San Francisco Conference lasted two months in an atmosphere of high enthusiasm and hard work. The delegations were headed by a galaxy of political distinction and experience. Stettinius and Cordell Hull, and Senators Connally and Vandenberg represented the United States; Eden, Attlee, Cranborne, and Halifax represented Britain; Molotov and Gromyko represented the Soviet Union; Bidault represented France; T. V. Soong and Wellington Koo represented China; Spaak represented Belgium; Jan Masaryk, Czechoslovakia; Manuilsky, the Ukraine; Subasich, Yugoslavia; Mackenzie King represented Canada; Forde and Evatt, Australia; and Smuts, South Africa. The delegates had before them the Dumbarton Oaks proposals, and the Crimea agreement in regard to voting procedure in the Security Council, and the mass of their own amendments totaling some twelve thousand items. The work was divided among four commissions and their several subcommittees. The most lively discussions were over the trusteeship of non-self-governing territories, the registration and revision of treaties, regional arrangements and, of course, the voting procedure in the Security Council. All were questions which in one form or another had been controverted twenty-six years before when the League Covenant was drawn up. The final draft of the Charter was unanimously adopted at the Conference's ninth plenary session and signed by the delegates of the fifty nations on June 26, 1945.

The Charter came formally into force on October 24, 1945, when, under its Article 110, ratifications had been deposited by the United States, Britain, the Soviet Union, France, China, and twenty-four of the other signatory nations. The General Assembly and Security Council met for the first time in London in January 1946. Trygve Lie, the Norwegian Foreign Minister, was elected Secretary General. At the time of writing, fifty-nine nations have become members.[1]

THE CONSTITUTION OF THE UNITED NATIONS

The Preamble of the Charter recalls the lofty language and resolution of the League Covenant. Under Article 1 of the Charter, the purposes of the United Nations are stated to be the maintenance of international peace and security by means of effective collective measures, the development of friendly relations among nations, the achievement of international co-operation in economic, social, cultural, and humanitarian problems, and the promotion of human rights and fundamental freedoms. Under Article 2, the United Nations recognizes the sovereign equality of all its members and requires their good faith in the peaceful settlement of international disputes, their abandonment of the threat or use of force, and their assistance in any action which it shall deem necessary to take in accordance with the Charter.

Constitutionally the United Nations functions through a General Assembly, a Security Council, and a Secretariat. The General Assembly consists of representatives of all the member nations. The Security Council consists of the representatives of eleven member nations, of whom the five Great Powers — China, France, the Soviet Union, Britain, and the United States — are permanent members, and the other six are elected by the General Assembly for two-year terms, three retiring every year. The Secretariat is a permanent body consisting of a Secretary General and staff, and acts as the United Nations' permanent civil service. The headquarters of the United Nations is in New York, but an important European office is maintained in the old League of Nations buildings in Geneva.

The Charter provides for a Trusteeship Council for the trust territories. It creates an International Court of Justice as the principal judicial organ of the United Nations. It also provides for an Economic and Social Council and for a series of Specialized Agencies, which we shall briefly discuss later in this chapter.

THE GENERAL ASSEMBLY AND SECURITY COUNCIL

The articles in the Charter of the United Nations concerning membership and administration call for no explanation. The contentious material is contained in the articles concerning the Security Council and the "Great Power veto," the settlement of disputes, threats to peace and acts of aggression, regional arrangements, trusteeship, and the control of armaments. The Charter requires the registration and publication of international treaties entered into by its members, but it contains no article corresponding to Article 19 of the League Covenant, providing for the revision of treaties which have become inapplicable or obsolete.

The General Assembly consists of all members of the United Nations. Each member may have five representatives, but only one vote. Decisions of the General Assembly "on important questions" are reached by a two-thirds majority. But the General Assembly has few substantial powers. The Economic and Social Council and the Trusteeship Council are its subordinate organs, elected by it and responsible to it. But otherwise it can only "consider general principles of co-operation . . . including the principles governing disarmament," "call the attention of the Security Council to situations which are likely to endanger international peace," "receive and consider annual and special reports from the Security Council," and so forth. In effect, the General Assembly is the deliberative and consultative chamber and platform of the smaller states, even as the Security Council was intended to become the concert of the Great Powers.

The Security Council is the body of "primary responsibility" in the United Nations. It was designed to have the authority, the respect, and the "teeth" which, in the view of many critics, the old League of Nations had so often lacked. In addition to its eleven members, it is entitled to invite a nation, not one of its members, or not even a member of the United Nations, to participate, without vote, in its discussion of any question affecting the interests of that nation. Under Articles 33–51, any member of the United Nations may bring to the attention of the Security Council a dispute likely to endanger international peace. The Security Council has power to call upon the parties to settle the dispute by negotiation, arbitration, recourse to the International Court, or by other peaceful means. It has the power to investigate the dispute itself and recommend appropriate procedures for settlement. It also has power "to determine the existence of any threat to peace, breach of peace, or act of aggression," and to decide first upon provisional measures to prevent an aggravation of the situation and then upon measures, not involving the use of armed force, such as the severance of economic or diplomatic relations. Finally, "should the Security Council consider that measures [so provided] would be inadequate . . . it may take such action by air, sea or land forces as may be necessary to maintain or restore international peace and security." All members of the United Nations are under obligation to contribute to the maintenance of peace and to make available to the Security Council, "on its call and in accordance with special agreement," the necessary armed forces, assistance, and facilities, "including rights of passage." The Security Council is also to be responsible for establishing a system for the regulation of armaments. A Military Staff Committee, consisting of the chiefs of staff or other representatives of the five permanent members of the Security Council, is to advise the Security Council on its military requirements, on the employment of forces placed at its disposal, and on the regulation of armaments.

All these very considerable powers vested in the Security Council were intended not only to restore the peace already broken, but to anticipate the very threats to peace in the early stages, and to act quickly and decisively before that threat lapsed inevitably into hostilities. Yet the exercise of these powers — and here is the rub — depends upon the unanimity of the five permanent members of the Security Council, the five Great Powers. Under Article 27 of the Charter, decisions on "procedural matters" are to be made by an affirmative vote of seven members, but decisions "on all other matters" are to be made by an affirmative vote of seven members, "including the concurring votes of the permanent members." This voting procedure was in accordance with the agreement made at the Crimea Conference. But it results in practice in the so-called Great Power veto and is tantamount to granting any one of the five Great Powers the absolute right to annul the operation of the Charter at will. Yet it was a necessary concession to realism. For upon the five Great Powers would fall the main burdens of any future military action under the Charter, and none of them would have been induced to become members of the United Nations to the prejudice of political and military independence. Probably the statesmen at Crimea had never foreseen that the veto would be used otherwise than veto powers in most democratic constitutions are normally used — that is, only on rare occasions and with a proper sense of responsibility. The League of Nations had sometimes been obstructed by its unanimity clause; but here was a unanimity clause that might become even more insuperable and perverse.

It had been hoped by its creators that the League of Nations would have superseded all the alliances of the old diplomacy, and the League Covenant had given a very grudging recognition of "regional understandings like the

Monroe Doctrine." But the United Nations appeared to encourage the formation of "regional arrangements," and the Security Council was prepared to
make use of such arrangements for the pacific settlement of local disputes
and for the enforcement of action under its authority. The Act of Chapultepec, Western Union, and the North Atlantic Pact could be regarded by
their several sponsors as in no way repugnant to the ideals of the Charter.

THE TRUSTEESHIP SYSTEM

The trusteeship system of the United Nations is a virtual revival of the
mandates system of the League of Nations. Generally that mandates system
was acknowledged to have worked very well. The Mandatory Powers, most
of whom already had a long tradition of responsible colonial administration
behind them, had seldom abused their trust. But, in re-creating a body to
correspond, and to act as successor, to the League's Mandates Commission,
the opportunity was taken both for widening and for more closely defining
its functions.

The Charter recognizes that certain members of the United Nations
would have to assume responsibility for the administration of "non-self-
governing" territories, notably the former mandated territories, territories detached from enemy states as a result of the Second World War, and "territories voluntarily placed under the system by states responsible for their
administration." The members in question must accept "as a sacred trust"
the well-being and the political, economic, social, and educational advancement of the inhabitants of these territories. The administration of trust
territories, as they were now to be called, by their respective administering
authorities would then be in accordance with specific trusteeship agreements
and would be supervised by a Trusteeship Council operating under the
authority of the General Assembly.

The General Assembly at its first session, in February 1946, passed an
interim resolution on "non-self-governing peoples" acknowledging that the
trusteeship obligations of the Charter were already in force. The Trusteeship Council was established in December 1946 and met for its first session
at Lake Success on March 26, 1947. It then consisted of representatives of
the five administering authorities, namely, the former Mandatory Powers,
Britain, Australia, New Zealand, France, and Belgium; the three other
permanent members of the Security Council, namely, the United States, the
Soviet Union, and China; and two other members, Iraq and Mexico, elected
by the General Assembly. The Trusteeship Council meets twice annually,
and appoints a President, Vice-President, and committees. The Secretary
General of the United Nations and his staff act as its secretariat. It receives
the annual reports of the administering authorities and presents to the
General Assembly its own annual report on the discharge of its responsibilities. It accepts and examines petitions, presented orally or in writing, by
the inhabitants of the trust territories or by other interested parties, and it
sends representatives to inspect the trust territories.

To date, nine trusteeship agreements have been negotiated with the five administering authorities, namely, those for Tanganyika, and parts of Togoland and the Cameroons with Britain; for New Guinea with Australia; for Western Samoa with New Zealand; for Nauru jointly with Australia, New Zealand, and Britain; for parts of Togoland and the Cameroons with France; and for Ruanda-Urundi with Belgium. All these agreements were discussed in detail by the General Assembly prior to approval, and all define in each case the obligations of the administering authority and the rights and interests of the inhabitants of the territory in question. In addition the Security Council has accepted an agreement entitling the United States to administer the former Japanese mandated islands in the Pacific as a "strategic trusteeship."

The question of Palestine will be discussed in a later chapter (pp. 870–74).

THE INTERNATIONAL COURT OF JUSTICE

The International Court of Justice, "the principal judicial organ of the United Nations," was an integral part of the League of Nations. Its Statute was expressly based upon the Statute of the former World Court (pp. 135–36) almost without amendment and was annexed to the Charter. The Court's jurisdiction extends only to disputes of a specifically "legal" character voluntarily submitted to it by member nations. The former "Optional Clause" is retained and is still operative. Thirty-two nations are now subscribers to the clause. At the same time the Charter expressly states that "each member of the United Nations undertakes to comply with the decision of the Court . . . in any case to which it is a party."

All members of the United Nations are automatically parties to the Statute of the Court. Other nations, not members of the United Nations, may become parties "on conditions to be determined in each case by the General Assembly upon the recommendation of the Security Council." The General Assembly, the Security Council, and the Specialized Agencies may request the Court to give advisory opinions. The seat of the Court is still The Hague. In April 1946, the former World Court was wound up and the new Court met for the first time. The Court's first case was that of the Corfu Channel brought against Albania by Britain in 1947.[2]

THE ECONOMIC AND SOCIAL COUNCIL AND THE SPECIALIZED
AGENCIES

In 1939 the League of Nations had created a Special Committee for the Development of International Co-operation in Economic and Social Affairs, generally called the Bruce Committee after its chairman, the High Commissioner of Australia in London (later Lord Bruce of Melbourne). The Committee proposed an over-all integration of the League's economic and social work. Its further activities were prevented by the outbreak of war in that year, but the idea behind it was reborn in the Economic and Social Council of the United Nations, formulated in the Charter. That Council consists of eighteen members of the United Nations, elected by, and responsible to, the General Assembly, six elected each year for a term of three years. It may initiate studies, prepare draft conventions for submission to the General Assembly, call international conferences "on matters falling within its competence," and in particular it may make agreements with, and co-ordinate the activities of the Specialized Agencies.

Of these Specialized Agencies there are now thirteen — the International Labor Organization (ILO) ; the Food and Agriculture Organization (FAO) ; the United Nations Educational, Scientific, and Cultural Organization (UNESCO) ; the International Civil Aviation Organization (ICAO) ; the International Bank for Reconstruction and Development; the International Monetary Fund; the World Health Organization (WHO) ; Universal Postal Union (UPU) ; the International Telecommunication Union (ITU) ; the International Refugee Organization (IRO) ; the International Trade Organization (ITO) ; the Intergovernmental Maritime Consultative Organization (IMCO) ; and the World Meteorological Organization (WMO). The United Nations Relief and Rehabilitation Administration (UNRRA) was dissolved in 1947.

Certain of these agencies we shall now discuss.

THE INTERNATIONAL LABOR ORGANIZATION (ILO)

The International Labor Organization (ILO) is the one League institution which has survived under its old name. Its origin and functions have been described elsewhere (pp. 134–35). In 1940 it was moved to Montreal, and it continued its work there throughout the Second World War. It resumed the regular sessions of its General Conference at Philadelphia in 1944. It sent representatives to Bretton Woods, to UNRRA, to the FAO, and to San Francisco. In deference to Soviet reservations, it was not expressly mentioned by name in the Charter of the United Nations.

An agreement defining the relationship between the ILO and the Economic and Social Council was approved by the ILO and by the General Assembly at the end of 1946. The ILO has fifty-nine members. Its Director General, as he is now entitled, was Edward Phelan of Britain, lately succeeded by David Morse of the United States. Its headquarters is divided between Geneva and Montreal, and it maintains branch offices in Washington, London, Paris, and other cities. It continues its former good work, its research, information services, reports, and publications. Latterly it has been showing increasing concern with problems of man power, full employment, and migration.

THE UNITED NATIONS RELIEF AND REHABILITATION ADMINISTRATION (UNRRA) AND THE INTERNATIONAL REFUGEE ORGANIZATION (IRO)

As early as September 1941, under British initiative, an Allied conference was held in London to prepare estimates for the relief and rehabilitation of devastated Europe. The United States, then a neutral, was not represented, but the American ambassador in London gave the conference an assurance that American co-operation would be forthcoming. During 1942, plans for a vast economic reconstruction of Europe, partly financed and managed by Americans, was being freely discussed in the United States, and a somewhat premature start was made in the recruiting and training of American personnel for the task. In November 1943, at Washington, at a conference of the representatives of forty-four members of the United Nations, the United Nations Relief and Rehabilitation Administration (UNRRA) was created. Recent Allied military successes in Europe held out the prospect that the new organization would early be called into action in the territories newly liberated from the Axis. Meanwhile the Allied Military Government of Occupied Territory (AMGOT), the first of the Allied occupation regimes, was in being in Sicily and Italy.

UNRRA operated through a Council of its members, meeting annually in different cities, and a Director General. It had some ten thousand workers in the United States and in countries abroad. It was financed by thirty-one of the forty-eight nations eventually enrolled in its membership. It collaborated with the Combined Food Board, an intergovernmental body composed of American, Canadian, and British representatives, meeting in Washington and controlling large-scale transportation of foodstuffs. Its first Director General was Herbert H. Lehman, former Governor of New York State, and its second, from April to December 1946, Fiorello La Guardia, former Mayor of New York City.

UNRRA was a provisional organization for immediate needs. It worked in former Axis-occupied territories in Europe and Asia, among refugees and displaced persons and, on occasions, it supported entire populations. It provided food, clothing and footwear, medical stores, industrial and agricultural equipment, vehicles and rolling stock, and building materials. It provided livestock and feed for animals. It provided services in the form of hospitals and welfare centers, fully staffed and equipped. Its biggest recipients were the countries of Eastern Europe and the Balkans, including White Russia and the Ukraine, but it also sent supplies to China, Korea, and the Philippines. At one time it was feeding the entire population of Athens. It cared for two million Italian children. Five millions in Yugoslavia were wholly or partly dependent upon it.

There was sometimes a certain amount of friction. Usually UNRRA transferred its supplies in bulk to a receiving government at an agreed port or railhead. But it insisted on having observers with full freedom of movement in the country in question to check the distribution. It also insisted that no political discrimination should be exercised, and that all classes, parties, and creeds should share equally in its benefits. But often it seemed that the receiving government regarded the observers as the paid agents of "American imperialism," and there were several countries where UNRRA might have accomplished more but for local suspicion, obstruction, and dishonesty.

UNRRA brought its work to an end in June 1947, though a number of its contracts were allowed to run on to 1948. In its four years it had expended nearly $4,000,000,000, of which $2,668,000,000 was contributed by the United States. Its record is no mean one, and thousands all over the world at this day gratefully owe their health and their very lives to it.

An International Refugee Organization (IRO) was proposed and its constitution approved by the General Assembly in December 1946. It was to be concerned with the repatriation of refugees, their legal and political protection, and their transport to, and resettlement in, countries willing and able to take care of them. Like UNRRA, whose duties in this field of activity it has inherited, it is a provisional, temporary organization, and its work, it is expected, will be completed by mid-1951.

THE FOOD AND AGRICULTURE ORGANIZATION (FAO)

The decision to create a Food and Agriculture Organization (FAO) was made at a conference of forty-four nations at Hot Springs, Virginia, in May and June 1943. The constitution of the FAO was drawn up by an Interim Commission and signed by the representatives of thirty nations at a conference at Quebec in October 1945. It is an advisory and consultative body. It operates through a Conference of members meeting at least once a year, a World Food Council and other committees, and a Director General and staff of experts. It now has fifty-seven members. Its Director General from the conference at Quebec to May 1948 was Sir John Boyd Orr of Britain, lately succeeded by Norris E. Dodd of the United States.

The FAO collects and disseminates information "relating to nutrition, food and agriculture" — and "agriculture" includes fisheries and forestry; it promotes research and education in its field and improved methods of agricultural production and marketing; it furnishes technical assistance and organizes missions of investigation and advice. Its work is acknowledged to be urgent and world-wide. The prevailing malnutrition even in many "advanced" countries, the recent famines, notably in India, and the long-term problems of soil exhaustion and soil erosion are all of unusual pertinence in the welfare of nations today. The good life which our social philosophers dream of will not be a reality so long as half the world's population lives below subsistence level. The FAO is already one of the great forces in international affairs, an example of what may be accomplished by voluntary, "functional" co-operation.

Emergency feeding of some 5,000,000 starving children in twelve European countries and China has recently been undertaken by the United Nations International Children's Emergency Fund (UNICEF) . Funds contributed by governments have been supplemented by the results of the United Nations Appeal for Children in fifty countries.

THE UNITED NATIONS EDUCATIONAL, SCIENTIFIC, AND CULTURAL ORGANIZATION (UNESCO)

The United Nations Educational, Scientific, and Cultural Organization (UNESCO) reproduced in a much extended form the functions of the League's Committee on Intellectual Co-operation (see p. 134). Its first germ was conceived at a meeting of Allied ministers of education in London in 1942. Its constitution was signed by representatives of forty-four nations at a conference in London in November 1945. It derives from the declaration that, "since wars begin in the minds of men, it is in the minds of men that the defenses of peace must be constructed." It is an advisory and consultative body only. It operates through a General Conference of members meeting annually, an Executive Board, a Director General, and a Secretariat. It now has forty-five members, and its Director General was Julian Huxley of Britain, lately succeeded by Jaime Torres Bodet of Mexico. Its headquarters is UNESCO House, Paris. It aims to promote mutual knowledge and the understanding of peoples through all means of mass communication, to give fresh impulse to popular education and equality of educational opportunity, to suggest "educational methods best suited to prepare the children of the world for the responsibilities of freedom," to preserve the world's books and monuments, and to encourage the exchange of students and teachers.

THE INTERNATIONAL MONETARY FUND AND THE WORLD BANK

The long-term program for mending the chaotic monetary aftermath, not only of the war itself, but of the previous years of depression and totalitarianism, for financing industrial re-equipment, and for restoring international trade was put in the hands of various organizations largely created by American and British initiative. Thus a United Nations Monetary and Financial Conference, which was held in July 1944 at Bretton Woods in New Hampshire, created the International Monetary Fund, to which member nations should contribute according to adjustable quotas and which should be used to maintain exchange stability, avoid competitive exchange depreciation, cushion sudden fluctuations, and generally regulate a multilateral system of payments. Thus each national currency was to be assigned a value in terms of gold or of the American dollar, a value which the member in question was then obligated not to change without consultation with the Fund. Forty-five nations are now members of the Fund and thirty-six par values have so far been assigned. Unhappily, however, the basic obligation has already been disregarded, notably by France's devaluation of the franc in 1948 (see p. 822) — and, as some would argue, by Britain's devaluation of the pound in 1949 (see p. 832).

The same conference at Bretton Woods agreed to set up an International Bank for Reconstruction and Development, or World Bank, as it came to be called, a long-term credit institution for the purpose of financing projects which have been unable to obtain private capital, in particular "the most useful and urgent projects, large and small." To date the World Bank has furnished credits totaling over $170,000,000 to eleven countries. It is to be emphasized that the World Bank is a long-term institution, and its functions have not been invalidated by subsequent, additional, short-term measures, such as the European Recovery Program (ERP).

THE INTERNATIONAL TRADE ORGANIZATION (ITO)

In December 1945 the United States Department of State published a paper, *Proposals for Expansion of World Trade and Employment*. After intensive study and discussion at high official levels, the United States Government about a year later published a further *Suggested Charter for an International Trade Organization*. The Economic and Social Council set up a Preparatory Committee of representatives of nineteen states to prepare an agenda and draw up a charter for consideration at an International Conference on Trade and Employment. The Preparatory Committee held meetings in London in the winter of 1946 and further meetings at Geneva from April to October 1947, when it adopted a draft of an International Trade Charter, covering the flow of capital particularly to undeveloped countries, access to markets, reduction of tariff barriers, and the elimination of discriminatory and restrictive trade practices. A General Agreement on Tariffs and Trade was signed simultaneously by the representatives of twenty-three nations. The Agreement consisted of a schedule of tariff concessions applying to about two-thirds the import trade of the signatories and a half of total world imports, and it gave interim effect to certain principles of the Trade Charter until that Charter should come into operation.

In November 1947, at Havana, Cuba, sixty nations, virtually the entire trading world outside the Soviet Union, met to discuss the draft Trade Charter, and the document was eventually signed on March 24, 1948 by fifty-three nations. The ITO will come into being when this Charter has been ratified by the specified number of nations. It will be composed of a Conference, an Executive Board, a Director General, and staff. But, to date, the nations in question have not shown a pronounced alacrity to ratify and are clearly waiting for a lead from the United States.

THE WORLD HEALTH ORGANIZATION (WHO)

The constitution of the World Health Organization (WHO) was drawn up at a conference in Paris in March and April 1946, and was signed by the delegates of sixty-one nations, including the Soviet Union and the Ukrainian and White Russian Soviet Republics, at an International Health Conference in New York in the following July. It is to operate through a World

Health Assembly, an Executive Board, and a Director General and Secretariat. Its purpose is to act as the directing and co-ordinating authority in international health work, to help eradicate epidemic diseases, prevent accidental injuries, improve nutrition, housing, sanitation, and working conditions, promote maternal and child welfare, and promote mental health, especially "as affecting the harmony of human relations."

The WHO came formally into being in April 1948, and the first World Health Assembly was held in Geneva in the summer months of that year. The WHO has established itself as one of the influential bodies of the United Nations — in many ways a counterpart of the FAO — and it has published ambitious projects for combating tuberculosis, malaria, venereal diseases, and cholera. The WHO was one of the few Specialized Agencies of which the Soviet Union and the Ukrainian and White Russian Soviet Republics were members, but they withdrew early in 1949.[3]

THE MILITARY STAFF COMMITTEE

The Military Staff Committee, which was to advise the Security Council on its military requirements, met for the first time in London in February 1946, and thereafter continued its sessions in New York. It was instructed by the Security Council to prepare the special military agreements with the members of the United Nations in regard to the contributions to the proposed international force which, in accordance with the Charter, those members would be called upon to make. It submitted its report on this question to the Security Council in April 1947. Several articles in the report were not unanimously agreed by the delegates, the most contentious article being that on "over-all strength." The American, British, French, and Chinese representatives argued that the contributions which the five permanent members of the Security Council should be called upon to make should be "comparable" and logically apportioned to their respective technical and strategic situations; that, for example, one Power might contribute the major part of the land forces, another might contribute the major part of the naval forces, and so forth. The Soviet representatives argued, on the contrary, that such an arrangement would give one Power an undue advantage over another and would be inconsistent with the avowed equality of status of the Powers under the Charter and that therefore the contributions of the five permanent members of the Security Council should be "not only of equal over-all strength but also of the same composition, that is, of equal number of land, sea, and air forces." As the French delegate wryly remarked, the Soviet attitude could only be inspired "above all by mistrust applied in advance to the very institution of an armed international force." To date this fundamental divergence of views has not been reconciled.

Under the Charter, the Military Staff Committee was to advise the Security Council on "the regulation of armaments and possible disarmament." The General Assembly might also consider "the principles governing disarmament." In February 1947 the Security Council set up a Commission for Conventional Armaments consisting of representatives of its own members.

The control of atomic energy was expressly excluded from the Commission's terms of reference. But little transpired from the protracted deliberations of the Commission beyond one further exhibition of the East-West schism. In July 1948 the Commission adopted by 9 votes to 2 (the Soviet Union and the Ukraine) a resolution, submitted by the British representative and amended by the American and Canadian representatives, setting out principles for a practical plan for the regulation of armaments. In August the Commission virtually agreed to dissolve itself "until an atmosphere of international confidence and security has been created."

THE ATOMIC ENERGY COMMISSION

Pronouncements on the control of atomic energy had been made by several Allied statesmen in the winter of 1945, notably the joint pronouncement by President Truman, Prime Minister Attlee, and the Canadian Prime Minister MacKenzie King in Washington in that November. Discussion of the problem was taken up at the Conference of Foreign Ministers in Moscow in December 1945, and at the sessions of the General Assembly and Security Council in London in January 1946. The resulting Atomic Energy Commission of the United Nations held its first meeting in New York in June 1946. It was composed of representatives of the members of the Security Council and of Canada. The inclusion of Canada was in deference to the part which she had played in the early research and manufacture of atomic bombs, and to the fact that some of the richest uranium deposits known were to be found in the Dominion. Specifically the Commission was a creation of the Assembly, but it was in fact a subordinate organ of the Security Council. It was empowered "to deal with the problems raised by the discovery of atomic energy and other related matters."

At its first meeting the Commission had before it proposals, presented by the American representative, Bernard M. Baruch, for the establishment of an international Atomic Development Authority (ADA) for the managerial control or ownership of all atomic energy activities potentially dangerous to world security, for the inspection and licensing of all other atomic activities, for the promotion of the beneficial uses of atomic energy, and for "research and development responsibilities of an affirmative character intended to put the Authority in the forefront of atomic knowledge and thus enable it to comprehend, and therefore to detect, misuse of atomic energy." When an adequate system of control had been agreed and put into effective operation, the United States would voluntarily renounce its present technical advantage, halt its manufacture of atomic bombs, destroy existing bombs, and put the ADA in possession of information "as to the know-how for the production of atomic energy." "The subject," said the American representative, "goes straight to the veto power contained in the Charter of the United Nations. . . . There must be no veto to protect those who violate their solemn agreements not to develop or use atomic energy for destructive purposes."

The Soviet representative, Gromyko, proposed on the contrary as a prior step, the conclusion of a rigid international agreement to prohibit the use of atomic weapons and to destroy all existing atomic weapons within three months from the entry into force of the agreement. He further proposed an international control commission "within the framework of the Security Council," having its own inspectorial apparatus with the necessary rights of information and access. But clearly the Soviet representative's proposals were already running counter to the American. The other representatives could not see the virtues of an inspectorial apparatus however elaborately constituted, if in fact it were to be subject to the Security Council and thence to the veto provisions which the Soviet Union had so often abused. They had already had experience with the discourtesies and obstructions which the Security Council's commissions of investigation had met when working in territory under Soviet control.

The Scientific and Technical Committee set up by the Commission to examine the purely scientific and technical problems involved reported that effective control was "technologically feasible," and at once put the discussions upon a basis of practical realism. Inspection was then a political, not a scientific problem. But inspection as such was soon seen to be the whole issue between the Powers. The Soviet representative, Gromyko, evinced no appreciation or gratitude for the United States's original generous gesture to share its technical knowledge with the world once adequate safeguards had been provided. For its own political and military reasons, the Kremlin could not take kindly to the idea of Soviet territory being invaded by an army of inspectors with rights of free and unfettered travel, prying at will into every mine and factory it operated. Gromyko was entirely unimpressed by the argument that all states alike would have to submit to the same derogations of their hitherto jealously guarded privacies. But, at bottom, the Atomic Energy Commission was struggling with the same problem that had bedeviled all the relations of the Powers since their victory in 1945. Russia's ingrained tradition of suspicion of the West could not be reconciled with proposals which would have meant overriding the entire existing system of international relations based on the doctrine of national sovereignty.

In May 1948 the Atomic Energy Commission decided by 9 votes to 2 (the Soviet Union and the Ukraine) to suspend its work. "Agreement on international control is dependent . . . on co-operation in broader fields of policy, and failure to achieve it arises from a situation beyond the Commission's competence." On September 23, 1949, President Truman announced that an atomic explosion was known to have recently occurred in the Soviet Union and that this development, though always foreseen, called all the more urgently for an effective, enforceable system of international control.

48 THE PEACE TREATIES WITH ITALY, RUMANIA, BULGARIA, HUNGARY, AND FINLAND

THE FOREIGN MINISTERS COUNCIL

At the end of the war in 1945 the grandiose precedent of the Peace Conference of Paris of 1919 was in everyone's mind. But the conditions of that conference did not now obtain. There were no dominating figures, such as President Wilson, Clemenceau, and Lloyd George. President Roosevelt was dead, Churchill out of office, and Stalin reluctant to leave Russia. The peacemaking of 1945–47 was conducted in the main not by heads of states, but by their foreign ministers, at *ad hoc* conferences convened at intervals in different places. The full-dress conference which did assemble in Paris in July 1946 was in all essentials still a foreign ministers' conference.

Discussions in regard to peace had taken place, and certain prospective lines of policy had been laid down, at the conferences at Teheran, the Crimea, and Potsdam. At the Potsdam Conference in July 1945, the "Big Three" — the United States, Britain, and the Soviet Union — had agreed to delegate to a council of the foreign ministers of the United States, Britain, the Soviet Union, France, and China the task of preparing five peace treaties with the five Axis satellites — Italy, Rumania, Bulgaria, Hungary, and Finland. They had agreed furthermore that, for the discharge of that task, only those Powers should participate which had signed the armistices, except that, in the case of the treaty with Italy, France should be regarded as a signatory. Consequently, within the Foreign Ministers Council, four Powers would draft the treaty with Italy, three the treaties with Rumania, Bulgaria, and Hungary, and two the treaty with Finland. This apparently innocent, entirely correct, and conveniently flexible "four-three-two" formula, however, was soon to create the first serious difficulty of the peacemaking.

The opening meeting of the new Foreign Ministers Council — attended by Byrnes, Bevin, Molotov, Bidault (representing France), and Wang Shih-chieh, the Chinese Foreign Minister — was held in London in September 1945. The Council agreed readily enough that the five treaties should include a Bill of Rights or other appropriate affirmation of the fundamental human freedoms lately set forth in the Charter of the United Nations. But thereafter the delegates were treated to their first outright exhibition of the Soviet's tactical methods in conference. Procedural questions, arising out of the "four-three-two" formula, eventually broke up the meeting, and the discussions upon the substantive peace terms were left to be continued in subcommittees. It was tacitly accepted by all parties that the Big Three should have the overriding decision in all matters of importance. But the Soviet delegate had probably not previously appreciated that the support of France — and no doubt that of China also — would be invariably weighted against the Soviet Union and on the side of the United States and Britain, and he thence embarked on a somewhat ungenerous campaign to try to obtain the exclusion of France and China from future discussions.

The impasse was partially resolved at a meeting of the Foreign Ministers in Moscow in December 1945, held without French and Chinese representatives. Byrnes at length secured adoption of a proposal — but not before he had dangled the hint of a loan before the Soviet Union — to the effect that those Powers which had signed the armistices — including France, in the case of the treaty with Italy — should draw up the terms of peace and that these terms should then be considered at a general conference of all members of the United Nations which had "actively waged war with substantial military forces against European enemy states."

The second meeting of the Foreign Ministers Council — Byrnes, Bevin, Molotov, and Bidault — was held in Paris between April 25 and May 16, 1946. The atmosphere had grown still more tense. A crisis was mounting in Iran, where Soviet troops were in occupation. Several clamant problems were before the Council, namely Trieste, the Italian colonies and possessions overseas, reparations, the navigation of the Danube, the creation of democratic governments in the Balkans and in Eastern Europe, and the Franco regime in Spain. In all of these, the United States and Britain stood in sharp conflict with the Soviet Union, with France trying to steer a middle course. Molotov accused the Western Powers of seeking to form an "Anglo-Saxon bloc," and there were heated exchanges, notably between Molotov and Bevin. After nineteen days of inconclusive discussion, Byrnes asked for a recess "permitting each of us to give undivided attention to re-examination of our positions in the hope of finding means of reconciling them."

The Foreign Ministers Council reconvened in Paris between June 15 and July 12, 1946, for the continuation of its second meeting. The cleavages were manifest and undisguised. In the matter of Trieste, the Soviet Union demanded that the city and the surrounding area should be awarded to Yugoslavia; the Western Powers demanded that they and their predominantly Italian population should remain Italian. Clearly the Soviet Union was preferring the claims of its Slavic client; and clearly the Western Powers were seeking to deny an important Mediterranean base to a potentially unfriendly Power. The problem was aggravated by the memory of the treatment of the adjacent Yugoslav territory during the recent Italian occupation. It recalled the Fiume crisis which had so disturbed the Peace Conference of 1919 (see p. 119). A commission of investigation representing the Council was sent out to Trieste and drew up proposals for four different frontier demarcations, the American most favorable to Italy, the British rather less favorable to Italy, the Soviet most favorable to Yugoslavia, and the French again steering a middle course. In the end, the Council accepted the French proposal. Trieste, together with about 300 square miles of the surrounding area, was to become a Free Territory, whose independence "shall be assured by the Security Council of the United Nations." The remainder of Istria and the ports of Fiume and Pola would go to Yugoslavia. A governor for the Free Territory with full powers, who should not be "a citizen of either Italy, Yugoslavia, or the Free Territory," was to be nominated by the Security Council in consultation with the Italian and Yugoslav Governments. The compromise created "a second Danzig" and satisfied no party. When it was announced, the Yugoslavs declared that they would sign no such treaty with Italy nor withdraw Yugoslav troops from that part of Istria which was to be assigned to the Free Territory.

In the matter of the Italian colonies and possessions overseas, the Foreign Ministers Council decided that the Dodecanese Islands, in accordance with the wishes of the inhabitants, would be ceded to Greece and that Italy would renounce her sovereignty over her North African colonies, Libya (Tripolitania and Cyrenaica), Eritrea, and Italian Somaliland. But the problem of eventual disposal and trusteeship of these North African colonies was deferred. Molotov, perhaps not very seriously, claimed the trusteeship of Tripolitania for the Soviet Union. No decision was reached regarding the navigation of the Danube.

THE PEACE CONFERENCE OF PARIS

The Peace Conference of those members of the United Nations which had "actively waged war with substantial military forces against European enemy states," assembled in the Luxembourg· Palace in Paris between July 29 and October 15, 1946. The states numbered twenty-one in all — the United States, Britain, the Soviet Union, France, China, Australia, Belgium, Brazil, Canada, Czechoslovakia, Ethiopia, Greece, India, the Netherlands, New Zealand, Norway, Poland, South Africa, the Ukraine, White Russia, and Yugoslavia — and they were represented by over 1,500 delegates. Bidault represented France and was host and chairman of the Conference. Byrnes, the American Secretary of State, was accompanied by the American ambassadors to Britain and to the Soviet Union, respectively Averell Harriman and Bedell Smith, and by Senators Connally (Democrat) and Vandenberg (Republican). Attlee at first and then A. V. Alexander, First Lord of the Admiralty, represented Britain; Bevin, who was unwell, was present at the later stages of the Conference. Molotov, accompanied by Vyshinsky, represented the Soviet Union. As on the occasion twenty-seven years before, some of the most remarkable and picturesque personalities belonged to the "smaller" states — Spaak of Belgium, Jan Masaryk of Czechoslovakia, Kardelj of Yugoslavia, and Manuilsky of the Ukraine. Field Marshal Smuts, the only delegate who had also been at Paris in 1919, represented South Africa, Mackenzie King represented Canada, and Evatt represented Australia. Among the enemy delegates who were permitted hearings at the Conference were De Gasperi, Saragat, and Bonomi of Italy, and Tatarescu of Rumania.

But in spite of the array of talent and distinction and the attempt to capture the spirit of high decision, the total result of the Paris Peace Confer-

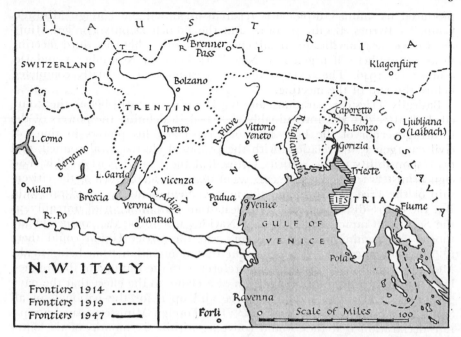

N.W. ITALY

Frontiers 1914 ......
Frontiers 1919 - - - - - -
Frontiers 1947 ▬▬▬

ence of 1946 was meager and anticlimactic. Procedural questions continued to vex and harass the discussions. The machinery of the Conference included a General Commission — which actually never met — a Military Commission, a Legal and Drafting Commission, five Political Commissions for each of the five treaties, and two Economic Commissions. Plenary sessions were to be held at intervals. The smaller states were all represented on these bodies, but they objected that a proposed two-thirds majority ruling would virtually deprive them of a voice in the important decisions. The smaller states at the Conference indeed constituted a problem which, as once before, had sometimes to be very arbitrarily solved (see p. 111).

The voting in the commissions repeatedly divided the "Soviet Six" — the Soviet Union, Czechoslovakia, Poland, the Ukraine, White Russia, and Yugoslavia — from the non-Soviet remainder. Some progress was made in regard to territorial adjustments (other than Trieste) and in regard to reparations. The Conference wound up its labors at a plenary session on October 15. The Yugoslav delegates, still disputing the Trieste settlement, absented themselves from the session.

THE FIVE TREATIES

Elections in the United States in November 1946 resulted in a Congress largely dominated by Republicans. But the change in political color at home, it was evident, would make no difference to the country's foreign policy. It is probable that this display of the temper of the American people produced its salutary diplomatic repercussions, and the Foreign Ministers Council — Byrnes, Bevin, Molotov, and the French Deputy Foreign Minister, Couve de Murville, in the absence of Bidault — held its third meeting in an atmosphere of urgency in New York between November 4 and December 12, 1946. The texts of the five treaties were virtually completed before the end of the meeting.

Basically Trieste, reparations, and the Danube were still before the Council. Day after day was interminably absorbed in defining the powers of the future governor of the Free Territory, especially his powers in times of civil emergency, his relations with the proposed elected local council, and his responsibility to the Security Council of the United Nations. The Foreign Ministers reached agreements upon items of detail, such as the citizenship of the Free Territory and the management of its port and railroads. But the entire discussion over Trieste had an inevitable air of unreality, as the Security Council of the United Nations was to be the competent authority for nominating the governor, and the Soviet Union could there resort to obstructive tactics to prevent that nomination from being made. Molotov argued strongly against any reference to the Danube in the treaties, but eventually agreed to the insertion of a clause to the effect that the navigation of the Danube should be "free and open for the nationals of all States . . . on a footing of equality." The Foreign Ministers issued a separate declaration that they would convene, within six months of the entry into force of the treaties, a further conference, at which they and the Danubian countries should be represented, to establish a Danube navigation authority.

The five treaties of peace with Italy, Rumania, Bulgaria, Hungary, and Finland were signed successively by Byrnes, Molotov, and Bevin in Washington, Moscow, and London, and then by Bidault and Allied and enemy delegates at a brief ceremony on February 10, 1947, at the Quai d'Orsay in Paris. Protests of one form or another against the treaties were lodged by Yugoslavia and Italy, and a campaign for revision was begun by all the enemy states except Finland. Upon his signature of the treaties, Byrnes resigned office and retired into private life.

Under the Italian treaty, Italy accepted the creation of the Free Territory of Trieste and the accompanying territorial and political readjustments which we have described. Certain small areas on the Franco-Italian frontier were ceded to France.[1] The Italo-Austrian frontier was left unchanged, and the southern Tirol and the Brenner Pass remained in Italian possession. As we have said, Italy renounced her sovereignty over her North African colonies, but their disposal was left to a future conference of the Powers to be held within the coming twelve months. Ethiopia had already reverted to her former independent status of 1935. The Italian Army was not to exceed 250,000 men, the Navy 25,000, and the Air Force 25,000. All naval vessels, except two battleships, four cruisers, and some smaller ships were surrendered to the Allies. Italy restored all looted Allied property. She was to pay reparations, over a period of seven years, to the victims of her aggression — $100,000,000 to the Soviet Union, $125,000,000

to Yugoslavia, $105,000,000 to Greece, $25,000,000 to Ethiopia, and $5,000,-
000 to Albania — the sources of such reparations being factory equipment,
war material and, after two years, current production. She was to assist in
the apprehension and surrender of war criminals for trial by Allied tribunals.

Except for the territorial losses in North Africa and the enforced demilitarization, the Italian treaty could hardly be described as harsh. But Italy
was a country of ancient civilization and of inexhaustible associations for
all cultured people and, for all her recent Fascist follies, she had never acquired the sinister record of her German partner. The Italian resistance
movement in the closing months of the war had materially contributed to
the Allied victory, and it deserved its appropriate recognition. And, no
doubt, the influence of Italian-born citizens of the United States helped
somewhat to alleviate the final verdict. We should add here that, at the time
of writing, the provisions in the treaty regarding Trieste are largely inoperative, and that the Security Council of the United Nations has so far failed
to agree upon the choice of a governor of the Free Territory. The Anglo-
American military occupation of Trieste continues. The disposal of the
colonies is still unsettled.

Under the Rumanian, Bulgarian, and Hungarian treaties, the whole of
Transylvania was returned to Rumania; a rectification of the Hungarian
frontier opposite Bratislava was made in favor of Czechoslovakia; and Rumania's cession of Bessarabia and northern Bucovina to the Soviet Union
was confirmed. Bulgaria retained the southern Dobruja, but she failed to
make good her claim to Western Thrace against Greece. Greece likewise
failed to secure northern Epirus. All Allied looted property was restored,
and reparations were to be paid to the Soviet Union, Czechoslovakia, and
Greece. There were clauses providing for the reduction of army, navy, and
air-force strengths and for the surrender of war criminals.

Under the Finnish treaty, the Finnish-Soviet frontiers of the treaty of
March 1940 were restored, with the exception that the Petsamo area was
now ceded to the Soviet Union. Porkkala was leased to the Soviet Union for
fifty years as a naval base, and all communications thereto from Soviet territory were put under Soviet control. The Finnish Army was not to exceed
34,400 men, which was roughly the strength of the Finnish standing army
of 1939, and Finnish naval and air-force units were to be proportionately
reduced. Finland restored looted Soviet property and agreed to pay reparations to the Soviet Union to the amount of $300,000,000 in commodities,
valued in American dollars, over eight years. Again there was a clause for
the surrender of war criminals. Certain political provisions forbade organizations of a "Fascist type" or organizations conducting anti-Soviet propaganda. They were provisions which clearly gave the Soviet Government considerable powers of interference in Finnish domestic affairs.

ALLIED CONTROL IN GERMANY

The capitulation of May 1945, signed by Jodl and ratified by Keitel, was the last official act of the Third Reich. Total war had ended in total defeat. Germany had temporarily ceased to be a political organism. German troops placed themselves obediently under the nearest Allied commanders. U-boats one by one returned to their bases. There was no scuttling of ships. No armed opposition was encountered as the Allied forces proceeded without hitch to occupy their appointed zones. The "Werewolves," the much advertised Nazi guerrilla force in the "Bavarian Bastion," failed to materialize. The Nazi party leaders went into hiding or surrendered themselves; some committed suicide; but none resisted. The German population as a whole was stunned and apathetic or, at least in the Western zones, made a pathetic show of greeting the Allies as liberators.

The country was a shambles. Whole cities were reduced to heaps of rubble and tangled iron. Roads were blocked by fallen buildings, and bridge after bridge had been demolished. A host of foreign slave workers and "displaced persons" to the number of 10,000,000, suddenly released from organized duress, were roaming at large levying a long deferred vengeance on their former oppressors. But the most awful symbols of the fallen regime were the concentration camps, discovered by the advancing Allies in the last incredible miseries of overcrowding, filth, starvation, and disease.

The European Advisory Commission, whose formation we noted elsewhere (see p. 765), had worked out the detailed administrative machinery of the future control commission. It had also roughly delimited, as early as November 1944, three Allied zones of occupation. The decision to invite France to take over a fourth zone — though largely at the expense of the zone already allocated to the United States — was reached at the Crimea Conference. Further revisions were made at the Potsdam Conference in July 1945, where it was also agreed that Königsberg (afterward renamed Kaliningrad) should be assigned to the Soviet Union for eventual annexation and that a Polish "Administration" should be established up to the Oder and Neisse rivers. In the eventual allocation, the American zone comprised Bavaria, parts of Württemberg and Baden, and the enclave of Bremen. The British zone comprised northwestern Germany, the Ruhr, the Lower Rhine, "Lower Saxony," and Schleswig-Holstein. The French zone comprised the Palatinate, the Saar, and the remaining parts of Württemberg and Baden. The Soviet zone comprised central Germany. Contrary to the line traced at Potsdam, the district and port of Stettin on the Baltic was arbitrarily handed over to the Poles for inclusion in the Polish "Administration." Greater Berlin, within the Soviet zone, was divided into four sectors, severally occupied by the four Allies, and was made the seat of the Allied Control Council, the supreme Allied authority in Germany. The area itself was administered by a four-Power body called the Kommandatura.

The Potsdam Conference furthermore had agreed upon "the political and economic principles to govern the treatment of Germany in the initial control period," namely the "five d's" of future Allied occupation policy — demilitarization, denazification, deindustrialization, decentralization, and democratization. The Conference laid down that "so far as practicable, there shall be uniformity of treatment of the German population throughout Germany"; that all armed forces or paramilitary organizations should be disbanded, all arms and munitions and the facilities for their production destroyed; that Nazism and all its institutions should be extirpated, war criminals brought to trial, and education and law democratized; that democratic principles should be introduced into the provincial States or *Länder;* that, during the period of occupation, Germany should be treated as a "single economic unit"; that controls imposed on German economy should be such as to assure a production sufficient "to maintain in Germany average living standards not exceeding the average of the standards of living of European countries"; that industrial capacity not so required should be demolished or removed; that reparations should be paid in part from capital equipment and in part from external assets — "current production," be it noted, was not mentioned in this context — and that such reparations "should leave enough resources to enable the German people to subsist without external assistance"; and, for the rest, that all industrial war potential should be eliminated, and cartels and syndicates broken up.

It is now a matter of history that many of these provisions failed. The East-West schism was not foreseen, but neither was the full depth of the German collapse realized. Not an organ of civilized society was left. No power on earth could have legislated in advance for conditions in Germany at that time. The Allied armies, the control commissions, and the faithful UNRRA at first had veritably to govern the country. Roads, railroads, canals, docks, telegraph lines had to be cleared and repaired, displaced persons cared for, and a start made on the "reactivation" of the most essential mines and industries. In these days it was the policy of Allied governments to recruit "technical" experts for their personnel in Germany, and numbers of these men and women, who had never done a desk job in their lives, found themselves in the midst of a ravaged, chaotic land in positions of authority which would have taxed experienced administrators. All of them were overworked and harassed by conflicting instructions, and the little German assistance then available, hesitantly and obsequiously rendered, was of very mixed usefulness. "In my *Kreis,* for the first months of the occupation," wrote a control commission officer, formerly a building contractor in an East End borough of London, "I was a sort of mayor, housing officer, harbor master, sanitary inspector, and fuel overseer combined. I ran everything from saw-mills to hospitals. I even repaired the heating system in the local concert hall and organized an orchestra to play there."

The Allied Control Council met regularly in Berlin and issued its orders, directions, laws, and proclamations on the surrender of arms, disposal of war material, demobilization of armed forces, employment registration, wages and working hours, food rationing, taxes, housing, census, police, repeal of Nazi laws and liquidation of Nazi organizations, and so forth. There was even a directive on the demilitarization of sport. But the tendency was inevitable for each one of the Allies to interpret these measures in its own way. The "five *d's*" meant different things in different zones. As the demarcation lines hardened, the zones jealously guarded such autonomy and resources as they had and began to lead a life reflecting the attitude of the occupying Power. "The Americans came to Germany as tourists," said a commentator, "the British as colonial governors, the Russians as freebooters, and the French as military police." By degrees an almost distinctive national character was subtly stamped upon the four quadrants of the country.

Demilitarization was relatively the least difficult part of the Allied program. The German army organization was already destroyed. Several ranking officers were held for trial as war criminals. Military installations, weapons and ammunition dumps, fortifications, air-raid bunkers, and self-evident industrial war plants which could not be allocated to reparations were dismantled or blown up. The process was lengthy and hampered by lack of Allied personnel, but at least the total occupation prevented the trickery and concealment which had formerly vitiated the Versailles settlement (pp. 154 and 156–57). It was hoped that the disarmament clause of the eventual German peace treaty would merely need to recognize the accomplished fact.

Denazification was again not difficult — relatively. Nazi organizations were dissolved, and all Nazi signs and emblems were prohibited. Here again the process was hampered by lack of Allied personnel. Hundreds of Nazi suspects were kept waiting in confinement for months while their cases were worked through by the few Allied officers that could be assigned to the task. Then the process had its political and economic repercussions. Generally the Americans took the rigidly doctrinaire view that there was some generic difference between proven active Nazis and Germans who were demonstratively passive or outright anti-Nazi; the British were more interested in the practicalities of restoring some kind of working economy and were nonplussed to find that few technically competent Germans were without taint and that even the removal of well-known and well-attested Nazis from key positions had often to be weighed against their industrial and administrative usefulness; the Russians were mainly intent on using denazification as a method for forwarding the social revolution; while finally the French were largely indifferent to the whole business on the theory that "a boche was a boche," an irretrievably fallen creature to whom relative degrees of iniquity could hardly apply.

Admittedly denazification was neither complete nor thorough in any of the zones. Whole classes of "culprits," notably the younger Nazi party members, were eventually exempted and discharged. In 1946, denazification courts were set up in the *Länder*, conducted by Germans but under Allied supervision. Denazification was generally considered to have been concluded by the end of 1947. War criminals and concentration-camp commandants were tried by Allied military courts in the zones or by courts in the particular country where the offenses had been committed.

Between November 1945 and October 1946, the trial of the German major war criminals took place before the International Military Tribunal at Nuremberg, the old medieval city and latterly the scene of Nazi party rallies. Arrangements had been elaborate. A mass of documentary evidence, itself a monument to German meticulousness and for all time a precious historical record, was garnered by Allied investigating teams throughout Germany and sifted and studied for months. A four-Power agreement in London in August 1945, with its annexed charter defining procedure and jurisdiction, was the formal constitution of the Tribunal. Nineteen further members of the United Nations adhered to the agreement. Three categories of crime were laid down: crimes against peace, war crimes, and crimes against humanity.[1] The Tribunal was conducted by four members, an American, a British, a French, and a Soviet, with four alternate members. The British member, Lord Justice Lawrence, was President. Every facility was given the accused to obtain counsel of their choice. In the courtroom itself, wired headphones enabled the proceedings to be followed in any one of four languages. A huge interpreting, secretarial, and photographic division was installed. Accommodation was provided for some 250 newspaper correspondents. The twenty-two accused [2] were the chief surviving political and military leaders of Nazi Germany, impressive living symbols of the defeated regime, facing trial to answer, not only for their individual guilt, but for their collective guilt against the laws and usages of the civilized world. Of the twenty-two, six were condemned on all counts.[1] Göring, Ribbentrop, Keitel, Jodl, Rosenberg, Frick, Seyss-Inquart, Sauckel, Bormann (in absentia), Kaltenbrunner, Frank, and Streicher were condemned to death by hanging; Raeder, Funk, and Hess to life imprisonment; Speer and Schirach to twenty years; Neurath to fifteen years; Doenitz to ten years; and Fritsche, Papen, and Schacht were acquitted. The Tribunal also condemned as "criminal organizations" the Nazi Leadership Corps, the Gestapo, the SS and SD.[3] The Soviet member of the Tribunal, we should note, strongly protested against the acquittals and against the failure to condemn the German General Staff as a criminal organization. Fritsche, Papen, and Schacht were afterward tried by German denazification courts and condemned to periods of imprisonment.

The Nuremberg trial has been criticized on many grounds. The authority and competence of an international criminal court without precedent in international law, it has been argued, cannot be made to rest upon a charter drawn up by a coalition of victors for the purpose of punishing defeated enemies. The technical difficulties, the mass of evidence, and the complexity of the issues involved could not help but drag out the proceedings to unexpected length; public interest flagged; and the drama and effectiveness of a quick trial and quick sentence had to be foregone. But the crimes themselves and the need for making an example of their chief perpetrators were not denied. Outraged peoples of many nations would not have allowed the repeated pledges of Allied leaders to bring their tormentors to justice to have been left unfulfilled. The insulting farce at Leipzig after the First World War could not be repeated (see p. 153). At Nuremberg, the proceedings were conducted with scrupulous fairness, dignity, and discipline. There was no presumption of guilt; defending counsel suffered not the least suspicion of obstruction or intimidation; the vicious atmosphere of certain recent political trials was debarred; the individual prosecutors acted up to the ecumenical spirit of the trial and did not merely press for a narrow retribution for atrocities committed against their own people or on their own soil; the evidence submitted was painstakingly objective, cumulative, and overwhelming — by far the greater part of it consisted of documents of the defendants' authorship — and not even German historical casuistry is ever likely to succeed in calling it into question.[4]

Demilitarization and denazification, we have said, were relatively easy. Deindustrialization, on the contrary, was difficult in the extreme. The Potsdam Conference had called for the treatment of Germany as "a single economic unit." But the joint administrations for communications, transport, finance, industry, and foreign trade, originally planned, were never set up. The French, who had not been signatories at Potsdam, objected to centralization of any sort, and the Russians soon showed that they had their own ideas in regard to currency, taxation, and banking. Eventually a Level of Industry Agreement was worked out, using steel as a yardstick and, in March 1946, the Allied Control Council announced that the steel level would be 5,800,000 tons per annum. It was intended that surplus equipment over and above that required for the permitted levels would be available for reparations. Here too were disagreement and misunderstanding, as the figure for steel actually achieved in 1946 was less than half the stipulated 5,800,000 tons.

The fact is that Allied planning at this time was largely being made in a bureaucratic vacuum in total misappreciation of the country's real moral and economic condition. The dislocation of organized life was more serious than the physical destruction left by the war. Food was scarce, and rations had constantly to be cut. The black market flourished, with the eternal cigarette as the accepted currency. Any house or building which had survived with roof and windows tolerably intact was overcrowded. Living space per head in the British zone, for example, was estimated at 65 square feet. The mass migration of displaced persons and of "exchanged populations" complicated the entire rationing and housing systems. During 1946 some 4,000,000 Germans, expelled from Poland, Czechoslovakia, and Hungary, arrived in the Western zones, and the greater part of the German prisoners of war held by the United States and Britain were being repatriated simultaneously. The net budgetary deficit in 1946 to the United States and British Governments for their two zones in Germany was $500,000,000.

German industry was a series of interlocking vicious circles based on one essential commodity — coal. For example, it was argued that coal production could be stepped up if the miners could be better housed. But housing required building materials, notably roofing tile and glass, which themselves required coal for their manufacture. However, by the end of 1946, partly as

CENTRAL EUROPE, POST-1945

1 Nordrhein-Westfalen	4 Bavaria	8 Saar	12 Mecklenburg
(North Rhine-Westphalia)	5 Württemberg-Baden	9 Rheinland-Pfalz	13 Brandenburg
2 Niedersachsen	6 Hessen	(Rhineland-Palatinate)	14 Sachsen-Anhalt
(Lower Saxony)	7 Bremen Enclave	10 Württemberg	15 Sachsen (Saxony)
3 Schleswig-Holstein		11 Baden	16 Thüringen (Thuringia)

British Zones   American Zones   French Zones   Soviet Zones

a result of better food rations for the miners, the output of the Ruhr coal pits rose to 200,000 tons a day, though this was still only half the output of 1939. At this time, about the only commodity in Germany not seriously reduced was electricity. It was curious, in the shattered cities, where so many public services were at a standstill, to see the streetcars and electric-lighting systems all operating normally. But here too coal was the basic, if indirect, agent of production. The electric power was brought in part from Switzerland, a former neutral undamaged by hostilities, but German coal was exported to Switzerland to pay for it.

Decentralization was both economic and political. Economic decentralization signified the breakup of the old cartels, notably the big combines of heavy industry, which had supported Germany's militarist regimes of 1914 and 1933. But, in this, the policies of the occupying Powers were soon found to be sharply at variance. The Americans with their "trust-busting" traditions were at odds with the British, who were indifferent to decartelization as such, whereas the Russians, with quite another economic philosophy,

were more interested in taking over German industries in their zone, ejecting their former owners and "reconcentrating" them on a communized
basis in their so-called Soviet AG's (*Aktiengesellschaften*). Eventually the
Americans and British made a start bi-zonally to break up big combines like
the Farben Industries, Henschel, Siemens, and others. They also broke up the
bigger banks, but they then linked the fragments to a sort of federal reserve
system. In view of the admitted economic paramountcy of the United States,
it was to be expected that American views would mostly prevail in all these
arrangements.

Political decentralization and democratization were aspects of the same
process. In the course of 1946, in accordance with the agreements at Potsdam, the occupying Powers set up in their zones new German States, or
Länder, as indicated on the map (see p. 811), each with some degree of autonomy, though still under Allied control and subject to the overriding veto of
their respective Allied commander, and each with a "democratic" constitution and popularly elected Diet (*Landtag*). It was then to be the avowed
policy of the occupying Powers to transfer the local civil administration to
these Diets, to induce in the German people a sense of responsibility for
their own government and for their own economic recovery, and concurrently to cut down the numbers of the Allied administrative personnel in
Germany. Meanwhile Greater Berlin formed a sort of separate *Land,* with
an elected City Council of its own. On February 25, 1947, the Allied Control
Council signed a law liquidating the state of Prussia. Henceforth the king
dom of Frederick the Great and the Hohenzollern Kaisers would cease to
figure on the map of Europe.

But each zone was soon an operational field for the distinctive political
philosophy of its occupying Power. In each zone, inevitably, every German
in office was *persona grata* with his Allied superiors. As no German political party could be formed in any zone without the authorization of the occupying Power, it was soon seen that the Russians would have ways and
means of encouraging, and the Western Powers would have ways and means
of discouraging, the German Communist party. In April 1946, in the Soviet
zone, the Communists fused with the Social Democrats to form a German
Socialist Unity party (*Sozialistische Einheitspartei Deutschlands* — SED) under Soviet sponsorship. Appropriately, Social Democrat plebiscites in the
American, British, and French zones decisively rejected a similar fusion.
Elections for the new Diets were held in all zones during 1946 and early
1947. The SED won handsomely in the Soviet zone, and the "liberal" parties,
mainly the Catholic "Christian Democrats" and the Social Democrats, won
handsomely in the American, British, and French zones.

"BIZONIA"

During 1946, just about the time that the Level of Industry Agreement
was reached, the Soviet industrial policy in Germany changed. From a policy of low-level production coupled with the extensive removal of capital
equipment the Soviet turned to a policy of high-level production coupled

with the leaving of capital equipment *in situ*. Evidently the Soviet Government had discovered that the dismantling and transport of heavy factory plant were expensive processes and that it would be easier and cheaper to derive reparations from "current production." When therefore the Control Council moved to set up the administrative arrangements to implement the Level of Industry Agreement, the Soviet authorities balked. Reparations from "current production" were nowhere explicitly banned in any of the Allied agreements but, in the Anglo-American view, they were incompatible with the agreed reparations plan or with the treatment of Germany as "a single economic unit." In May 1946, General Clay, the American commander, suspended reparations deliveries to the Soviet from the American zone.

General Clay's action was, however, only one incident in an already sadly deteriorating situation. Soviet policy in the Soviet zone, so it seemed to the Western Powers, had been un-co-operative in the extreme. The Soviet authorities made arrests at will and deported political undesirables, skilled workers, and even children. They broke up the big landed estates and introduced agrarian reforms on Soviet lines. Perhaps the Germans — and the Western Powers — could not have expected to see other than a pretty rough attitude from a people which had lately been used so ill themselves. But the Western Powers were less exasperated at Soviet notions of justice and political revolution in the Soviet zone than at the persistent refusal of the Soviet authorities to furnish the Control Council the information and even the elementary statistical returns required for reasonable quadripartite administration. During the early part of 1946, it was evident that American and British administrations were progressively drawing together to the exclusion of the Soviet — with the French standing aside from all three, though for other reasons. Western and Soviet commanders in Berlin were lodging constant complaints against each other for provocative articles in the German newspapers in their respective jurisdictions.

In September 1946, Byrnes, the American Secretary of State, speaking to a mixed audience of American and German officials at Stuttgart, made an important over-all statement of American policy in Germany, defended the efforts that had been made to achieve a unified and balanced economy in the country, called for a common currency reform to prevent "runaway inflation," and announced that the American and British Governments would shortly proceed to the economic fusion of their two zones. On December 2, 1946, with the ground thus prepared, an agreement for that fusion was signed by Byrnes and Bevin. The other two occupying Powers, France and the Soviet Union, were invited to join "on identical terms at any time." A revision of the permitted levels of industry for "Bizonia," thus created, put the steel level at 10,700,000 tons per annum, to be reached in three years.

ATTEMPTED PEACE SETTLEMENT

The Foreign Ministers Council, whose meetings we described in the previous chapter (pp. 800–801), had failed to reach agreement upon a German treaty at the time that the treaties with the five Axis satellites were drawn up. But it was realized at the Council's meeting in New York in December 1946 that the consideration of that treaty could be delayed no longer. Preliminary soundings by the Foreign Ministers' deputies were made in London in January 1947, and the Foreign Ministers themselves — Marshall (who had just succeeded Byrnes), Bevin, Bidault, and Molotov — met in Moscow in March.

The first few days of the Moscow Conference were taken up with replies to accusations from Molotov regarding the slow progress of demilitarization and denazification in the Western zones. There were lively and inconclusive skirmishes over China, Albania, and the return of prisoners of war and displaced persons. The Foreign Ministers discussed the control of the Ruhr, they discussed a constitution for a federalized Germany, they discussed the German-Polish frontier, and they discussed a four-Power treaty of guarantee to prevent the rearmament of Germany. But the crux of the discussions was reparations. Molotov brought up the story that the Soviet Union had been pledged $10,000,000,000 in German reparations in a secret protocol of the Crimea Conference,[5] though the figure, he said, was a tenth of the Soviet Union's material losses in the war. It should be paid in part, he claimed, from German current production. But, inasmuch as the American and British Governments were already financing German food imports in their two zones, so Marshall and Bevin were careful to point out, the payment of reparations out of current production would mean little more than the transference ultimately of American and British funds to the Soviet Union. Molotov claimed German assets in Austria for reparations, but again Marshall and Bevin would only concede the claim if an adequate definition and valuation of these assets could be arrived at.

The Foreign Ministers Council — Marshall, Bevin, Bidault, and Molotov — met again in London in November 1947. The conference lasted twenty-one days and, while there often seemed to be apparent agreement in matters of substance, disagreements arose over detail so impossible as to rule out further discussion. Molotov read out elaborate allegations against the nefarious practices of the Western Powers in Germany, allegations to which Marshall and Bevin made reply with increasing impatience. The main issues again were German assets in Austria and German reparations from current production. On December 15, 1947, the Foreign Ministers Council adjourned sine die.

GERMANY AND WESTERN UNION

The German settlement, it was clear, was now all of a piece with the political and economic developments in the wider European and North American world. As we shall describe elsewhere, the European Recovery Program had been announced in June 1947 (see p. 834), and Western Union was under serious discussion (see p. 836). In March 1948, Britain, France, and the "Benelux" countries (Belgium, the Netherlands, and Luxembourg) signed the fifty-year defensive Treaty of Brussels (see p. 835). In April 1948 the sixteen nations of the European Recovery Program, together with "Bizonia" and the French zone in Germany, both in the capacity of "contracting parties," created the Organization for European Economic Co-operation (OEEC). (See p. 836.) In the same April and May, a conference on Germany between the representatives of the United States, Britain, France, and the Benelux countries was held in London and, on June 2, it issued a series of recommendations, or "the London Decisions," as they were sometimes called, namely, to associate the Benelux states in all discussions regarding Germany affecting their interests, to establish an International Authority for the Ruhr, to convene a Constituent Assembly for Western Germany, and to co-ordinate the economic policies of "Bizonia" and the French zone. The significance of the new agreement was the final alignment of the United States, Britain, and France in Germany. "Bizonia" had become "Trizonia" and was linked with the European Recovery Program. On June 18, the much discussed and long heralded currency reform was put into operation in Trizonia. A new Deutschemark replaced the former Reichsmark. On June 23, after acrimonious and inconclusive discussion in the Control Council in Berlin, the Deutschemark was also put into operation in the American, British, and French sectors in Berlin. Sokolovsky, the Soviet commander, in a proclamation, banned the Deutschemark in the Soviet zone and also in the Soviet sector in Berlin.

The currency reform was certainly long overdue. Without it, German economic rehabilitation was a mirage. Its effects were beneficial and immediate. Production began to rise, absenteeism among the German workers declined, consumer goods appeared in greater quantity in the shops, the farmer brought his produce to town, the black market for the moment seemed to be crippled. For the first time since the war Germans had money that bought something and was worth working for. For the first time since the war food ceased to be an obsession. By midsummer of 1949, industrial production was back to three-quarters of its figure in 1936. British and French firms were becoming concerned over German competition.

But, even before the introduction of the new currency in the Western zones and in the Western sectors of Berlin, the Soviet authorities had resorted to measures of "defense." Berlin lay entirely within the Soviet zone, and toward the end of January 1948, American, British, and French traffic to and from Berlin passing through the Soviet zone was being stopped, delayed, searched, or otherwise obstructed. Protests of American, British, and French commanders in Berlin were all unavailing. By degrees a Soviet blockade of Berlin by road, railroad, and canal was established. The Western Powers began to supply their troops and the German population of their sectors in Berlin by the only means available to them — by air — and they gradually built up their famous "airlift," which eventually bore per day 3,000–4,000 tons of food, fuel, and other necessities of life to well over 2,000,000 persons.

It seemed that the Soviet authorities might even seek to interfere with the airlift. Soviet forces carried out parachute operations near the air corridors. In April 1948 a particularly ugly incident occurred, when a Soviet fighter collided in mid-air with a British transport plane over Gatow airfield in Berlin, killing the Soviet pilot and the British crew. In June, as the crisis mounted, sixty American superfortresses crossed the Atlantic and arrived at airfields in England, unmistakably advertising the intention of the United States to tolerate no further similar incidents.

Protests in Berlin were superseded by representations at diplomatic level. Beginning July 31, 1948, the American and French ambassadors and the British representative in Moscow were engaged in arduous discussions with Molotov and, on occasion, with Stalin himself. Throughout they made it plain that, while their governments would be willing to accept the Soviet mark as the sole currency in all four sectors of Berlin, they would not accept terms for the use of the currency which would place the financial and economic life of the city under exclusive Soviet direction. At the end of August, a draft directive was finally hammered out but, when the four commanders met in Berlin, Sokolovsky disregarded the directive. In September, the United States, Britain, and France referred the entire dispute to the United Nations. In February 1949 the United States and Britain established a counterblockade and halted all traffic across the eastern frontier of Bizonia. In May 1949, nearly a year and a half after its first imposition, the Soviet blockade of Berlin was raised.

THE BONN CONSTITUTION

On September 1, 1948, at the height of the Berlin crisis, a German Parliamentary Council or Constituent Assembly of sixty-five delegates, nominated by the Diets of the eleven *Länder* of the three Western zones in accordance with the London Decisions, met at Bonn to draw up a Basic Law or provisional German constitution. By May 1949, after eight months of debate which were often reminiscent of the old German party asperities, the Basic Law was adopted by the Parliamentary Council, ratified by the *Länder* Diets, and approved by the three Western occupying Powers, and, on May 23 at Bonn, the Federal Republic of Germany was proclaimed.

The Basic Law starts off with a declaration of fundamental human rights — freedom of conscience, freedom of speech and of "peaceful" assembly, equality before the law, respect for private property, and so forth — and then proceeds to describe the constitution of "a democratic and social Federal State." The Federal Parliament or Bundestag, elected for four years by universal, direct suffrage of the whole Federal Republic, forms the lower chamber. The Government consists of a Chancellor, elected by the Bundestag and responsible to it, and the Federal Ministers. The Federal Council or Bundesrat, consisting of members of the *Länder* Diets, forms the second chamber. The President of the Republic, with largely ceremonial duties, is elected by majority vote of the Federal Assembly or Bundesversammlung, consisting of members of the Bundestag and Bundesrat. There is no article corresponding to Article 48 of the Weimar Constitution (see pp. 151, 449, and 450). The respective jurisdictions of the Federation and the *Länder* are carefully defined — foreign affairs, currency, customs, certain taxes, trade agreements, and so forth being reserved to the Federation. A Federal Constitution Court decides upon disputes between the Federation and the *Länder* and also interprets the Basic Law.

Elections for the Bundestag were held throughout the three Western zones in August 1949 and returned the Christian Democrats with 139 seats, the Social Democrats with 131 seats, and nine other parties with an aggregate of 132 seats (Communists, 15 seats). In September, Professor Heuss was elected President of the Republic, and Dr. Adenauer (Christian Democrat) was appointed Chancellor.

An Occupation Statute regulating the relations between the three Western occupying Powers and the Federal Republic was announced in Washington on April 8, 1949. It reserved to the three occupying Powers the fields of disarmament, reparations, foreign affairs, and displaced persons; but, subject to such limitations, the Federal Republic was to enjoy "full legislative, executive, and judicial powers in accordance with the Basic Law." Civilian control in the three Western zones would be exercised respectively by three High Commissioners (an American, a British, and a French), and military control by three Commanders in Chief. On September 15, 1949 the Occupation Statute went into force, and military government as such in Western Germany was terminated. Simultaneously in April, the six Powers of the London Conference of June 1948 drew up a statute for the International Authority for the Ruhr, to be composed of representatives of the six Powers and of Germany. A new agreement was reached on the very vexed question of continued reparations deliveries and dismantling of industrial war plants.

The Soviet counterblast to all these measures was the establishment in Berlin in May 1949 of a "People's Congress" and a constitution "for the whole of Germany."

AUSTRIA

By the end of April 1945, Vienna and the greater part of Austria had fallen to the Red Army. The Soviet set up a provisional Austrian government under Dr. Karl Renner, the former Social Democratic leader and Chancellor in 1919 (see p. 188), and with a party composition of Social Democrats, Christian Socialists, and Communists in almost equal numbers. On May 14, 1945, a Soviet-sponsored declaration was broadcast from Vienna to the effect that the German *Anschluss* was dissolved and the Republic of Austria was re-established according to the constitution of 1920.

During June and July 1945, Austria was divided into four Allied zones of occupation. The American zone comprised Upper Austria and Salzburg; the British zone, Styria and Carinthia; the French zone, Vorarlberg and the Tirol; and the Soviet zone, Lower Austria and the Burgenland. Vienna and its environs, like Berlin, lay within the Soviet zone and was divided into four sectors of occupation under the joint administration of an Allied Control Council of four Allied commanders. Austria in many ways took on the aspect of an occupied Germany writ small, with the difference that she had a provisional government of her own, albeit a weak and sadly encumbered one. However, that government was formally recognized by the four Allied Powers in October 1945. Elections shortly took place which returned a National Assembly composed overwhelmingly of moderate parties, with four Communists. Renner was elected President of the Republic.

The Soviet authorities in the Soviet zone were already freely requisitioning factory plants, farm equipment, livestock, and even food and clothing. Denazification and the prosecution of war criminals proceeded in all four zones. But, in general, it seemed at this time that the Allied occupation of Austria would not be too onerous, that the lapses of 1938 would not be too heavily charged to the largely innocent and defenseless Austrian people, and that, in a word, the Moscow declaration of October 1943, regarding the liberation and restoration of the country (see p. 765), would be reasonably fulfilled. Currency reforms were passed by the National Assembly in November 1947, were approved by the Allied Control Council, and were introduced into all four zones, with much the same benefits as attended the similar currency reforms in Western Germany in 1948. But this early mood of temperate optimism passed all too quickly.

As in 1919, the most serious problems of the moment in Austria were not political, but economic and moral. The food situation was very bad. The diet of the great mass of the Austrian people was being supplemented by UNRRA; but that organization was wound up in 1947. The British Government made a grant of $50,000,000 toward the economic recovery of Austria, and Austria was one of the beneficiaries of American interim aid in December 1947. From time to time the Soviet authorities released foodstuffs from their zone. The FAO at this time gave Austria the melancholy distinction of being one of the worst-fed countries in Europe.

In the summer of 1946 the Soviet authorities set about the seizure of former German assets in Austria, notably oil refineries and river transport, on the ground that they were German and therefore available for reparations. The Austrian Government and the Western Allied commanders in Vienna protested against the Soviet's unilateral action and in vain demanded a proper designation and accounting of the seized properties. The question came before the Foreign Ministers Council at its ill-starred sessions in Moscow and London in 1947 and, as we have said, was left unsettled. The growing disagreement, here as elsewhere, between the Western and the Soviet authorities, the black market, the problem of the displaced persons to the number of 300,000, the shortages, the artificial division of the country into occupation zones, all were profoundly unsettling to the Austrian people and killed any initiative on their part to take an active interest in their own salvation. And while the Foreign Ministers Council, in successive conferences, failed to draft an Austrian peace treaty, the one point on which it did agree was the one point most keenly resented by the Austrian people — namely the decision to leave the southern Tirol in Italian possession (see p. 804).

50 WESTERN EUROPE, BRITAIN, AND THE BRITISH COMMONWEALTH

FRANCE

On August 25, 1944, General de Gaulle arrived in liberated Paris to receive the acclamations of the French people. On August 30 the Provisional Government and Consultative Assembly, whose formation we described in another place (see p. 752), were transferred from Algiers to Paris. De Gaulle assumed office as Premier, with Georges Bidault, former president of the Council of Resistance (see p. 752) and leader of the new Catholic party, the MRP, as Foreign Minister. France was proclaimed a republic, hereafter to be known as the "Fourth Republic," and the Vichy Government was declared to be abolished with all its laws and ordinances. On October 23 the Provisional Government was recognized by the United States, Britain, and the Soviet Union. Whatever might be the present or future disabilities of France, it could at least be said that she was almost unique among liberated European nations in having thus achieved without friction the union of her former government in exile and her resistance movement at home.

The situation was of peculiar difficulty. The war still continued; fighting was in progress in eastern frontier districts. The turmoil left by the enemy's occupation and retreat had to be liquidated. American and British armies were now "in occupation," commandeering important buildings and public services, using the roads, railroads, and seaports. Considerable sums of money put into circulation by them aided inflation while giving the impression of prosperity. The Provisional Government, strictly speaking, had no constitutional status; it could style itself the trustee, but not the legal successor, of the Third Republic. The surviving civil service was short of personnel, and much of the personnel it had was politically suspect. The press — always so important and characteristic in France — appeared almost at once and, though its circulation was hampered by the transport shortage, it would offer some reflection of the state of public feeling.

During the winter of 1944–45, political parties old and new, including the new left-wing Catholic progressives, the MRP (*Mouvement républicain populaire*), held party congresses and organized themselves for electoral action. Generally five political groups emerged: the Right; the former Radical Socialists in the center; and three left-wing parties — the MRP, the Socialists, and the Communists. The Right was too much identified with collaboration to exert any considerable influence; the Radical Socialists were too much identified with the fallen Third Republic. Consequently the real power resided in the three left-wing parties, the "tripartite coalition," which now constituted the main body of the Provisional Government.

After the first exhilaration of victory, the French people began more soberly to take stock of the physical and moral chaos of their country. Loss of life since 1939 from military operations, Allied bombing, and resistance was put at 500,000, far less than the loss of life in the First World War, but still a formidable figure to be subtracted from a declining population. Railroads, roads, bridges, rolling stock, canal and river shipping had been destroyed in the course of air attack and ground operations. The Atlantic seaports, where isolated forces of Germans had held out till well into 1945, were found on liberation to have been systematically demolished. The province of Normandy, as was to be expected, had suffered the worst damage, and here alone 500,000 persons were homeless. There were the usual shortages of food, clothing, fuel, and the other necessaries of life, especially in the towns. The long German servitude had left deep psychological scars. In particular it had bred a contempt for law and order. The heroes of the resistance, returning to civil life, had to learn the painful lesson that the qualities which had been virtues under the occupation now were almost antisocial. Young people who had grown up in a time of war in at atmosphere of fake identity cards, fake ration cards, black marketing, lying propaganda, betrayal, and terror could hardly be converted overnight into a citizenry fit for a new redeemed democracy in time of peace.

The dilatory punishment of the former collaborators, the failure to wipe clean the disgrace and degradation of the occupation, was perhaps most exasperating and mortifying to the French people at this time. But the purge was hampered by the lack of legal personnel and the mountainous tasks of investigation. Accusations numbered over 100,000. Yet to the man in the street, who little appreciated the technical difficulties, delay seemed to follow delay, and still not one traitor had been shot. Many Vichy ministers and prefects were still at liberty, often in the same posts they had filled during the occupation. However, late in 1944, trials of collaborators, notably journalists, artists, and actors, made a beginning. In July and August 1945, Pétain himself was at last brought to trial and sentenced to death, the sentence being afterward commuted to life imprisonment. Laval, along with 600 others, suffered the supreme penalty. But the purge in France was very reminiscent of the denazification of Germany. It was neither thorough nor complete, nor was it always conducted even with ordinary dignity.

French military participation in the closing stages of the war compensated somewhat for the misfortunes of 1940. But French pride was in an abnormally sensitive state, and de Gaulle made the most of any and every circumstance or incident which could be used for the enhancement of French prestige. In December 1944 he visited Moscow and with Stalin signed a pact of mutual assistance. He demonstrated his diplomatic annoyance at not being invited to the Crimea Conference by refusing subsequently to meet President Roosevelt. But in August 1945, in company with Bidault, he visited Washington for a series of meetings with President Truman and Secretary Byrnes, and a communiqué was afterward issued emphasizing "the perfect harmony of views" of France and the United States "for the construction of the post-war world." France took a permanent seat in the Security Council of the United Nations; she was assigned a zone of occupation in Germany; a French representative — usually Bidault — attended the Foreign Ministers Council. In March 1947, at Dunkirk, France and Britain signed a treaty of alliance. In a word, France enjoyed complete diplomatic reinstatement and recovery of her former international status.

It obviously behooved the Provisional Government to proceed to a reestablishment of the old constitution or to the establishment of a new one. On July 12, 1945, in a broadcast, de Gaulle announced a forthcoming referendum to test the French electorate's preference for a return to the constitution of the Third Republic (of 1875) or for the election of a Constituent Assembly. The referendum in October 1945 — in which women in France voted for the first time — returned a Constituent Assembly with 152 Communists, 150 MRP, 143 Socialists, 28 Radical Socialists, and 113 members of eight other parties. The MRP had been methodically organized and was believed to have been strongly supported by the new women's vote but, even so, its electoral success had been remarkable. No less remarkable, in the opposite sense, had been the collapse of the Radical Socialists, the old party of the Third Republic. Of the total 586 men and women who composed the Assembly, over 400 were products of the resistance. De Gaulle, after fierce bickering with the Communists, became President of the new Assembly.

The pattern of political rivalry in France was beginning to emerge. From its origins the former Third Republic had had a long history of controversy over the question of the presidential prerogatives (see p. 317). It had been founded as a reaction against dictatorship; all its old fears had lately been excited by the contemporary trend to dictatorship in Europe. The powers of the President in the Constituent Assembly had been a point at issue in the recent referendum. De Gaulle himself had shown an inclination for dictatorial methods, and was already at odds with the leftist parties. He was a soldier who presumably might inherit the Napoleonic traditions and, though often sympathetic to moderate socialist proposals, he seemed to be drawing to himself rightist elements who saw no way out of the country's distress except under strong authoritarian, military rule. He had personal force, not unmixed with vanity, and he seemed to be creating a one-man *mystique* of his own. The prevailing chaos — strikes, inflation, rising prices, black market — might easily play into his hands. At the other extreme were the Communists, who had their own philosophy of dictatorship. In between lay the moderate parties, eventually to organize themselves early in 1948 as "the Third Force."

On January 20, 1946, after an altercation with the leftist parties over military appropriations, de Gaulle suddenly resigned. He was succeeded by the Socialist Gouin, again at the head of a "tripartite coalition" of the three leftist parties. A constitution committee drafted a new constitution, which proposed a single-chamber legislature and a presidential office of virtually no powers. This constitution was approved by the Constituent Assembly with the MRP voting against, but was afterward rejected by a popular referendum. Elections for a second Constituent Assembly were held in June and resulted in a gain of 25 seats by the MRP. Bidault formed a new government. A second constitution was drawn up, this time proposing a bi-cameral chamber and a presidential office of distinct but still limited powers, and was approved by the new Constituent Assembly. De Gaulle came out of his restless retirement to make a series of speeches demanding the rejection of the constitution on the grounds of the presidential question. But the constitution was approved by a popular referendum in October 1946 — the third referendum in the course of the year — with considerable "protest abstentions."

The first elections under the new constitution were held in November 1946, the Communists gaining rather more than a quarter of the vote, mainly at the expense of the Socialists. The election marked the end of the "tripartite coalition" and the final severance of the Communists from their brothers of the other two leftist parties. Early in 1947, the Socialist Vincent Auriol was elected President of the Republic. But, from now onward, a succession of premiers — Blum (Socialist), Ramadier (Socialist), Schuman (MRP), Marie (Radical Socialist), Schuman, Queuille (Radical Socialist), Bidault (MRP) — recalling the old permutations of French politics, wrestled with the growing financial and industrial confusion in the country. France was evidently feeling the fully developed effects of the postwar economic aftermath. In January 1947 the Monnet Plan was published, so called after its principal author, Jean Monnet, a plan for the full utilization of France's resources and for the modernization of her equipment. In July 1947, France was one of the sixteen nations of the European Recovery Program (see p. 834). But despite evident improvements, she was compelled in January 1948 to devalue the franc. Native revolts in Indo-China and Madagascar and the withdrawal from Syria gave further tasks to her now very harassed governments. De Gaulle made characteristic broadcasts announcing that he would shortly return to active politics at the head of a "Rally of the French People" (Rassemblement du Peuple français — RPF), but indicated little of his political program beyond his usual repugnance for Communism. During 1947 and 1948 there were several workers' strikes which were not only for wage increases but which showed distinctive political objectives and showed also the extent of Communist infiltration into the trade-unions. The coal miners' strike in October 1948 was an avowed challenge to the government and to the European Recovery Program. The miners barricaded themselves in the mines and could only be ejected by regular troops.

While de Gaule at one extreme and the Communists at the other thus appeared to be mobilizing for revolutionary action, the moderate middle parties, girded together as "the Third Force (la troisième Force)," were with difficulty holding their own. By the end of 1948, despite the continuance of strikes, the beneficial effects of a good harvest, industrial reconstruction, and the European Recovery Program were to be observed in the evident slackening of tensions. Six months before, it was said, a change of government was a virtual crise de régime; at Christmas 1948 a change of government would have been no more than just another of the normal reshuffles of French party politics. Significantly, Queuille was Premier for over a year — from September 1948 to October 1949 — and meanwhile the militant threats both of de Gaulle and of the Communists seemed to be on the ebb. But it

still remained to be seen whether the old round of French political life —
unbalanced budgets, borrowing, inflation, party jobbery, unstable ministries,
with dictatorship hanging like a sword of Damocles — was going to be fundamentally very different.

ITALY

In Chapter 45 we described the formation of the Badoglio government
and the Italian surrender (pp. 755–56). Marshal Badoglio had declared
war on Germany, but he failed to mobilize morale for further fighting
among a people who had never had much heart for the war in any event
and who now wanted nothing so much as an end to privation, bombing,
and alien occupation. The Allied campaign against Germany was to continue in Italy till May 1945 but, except for the Italian partisans in the
north and some Italian recruited forces with the Allied armies, afterward
known as the Italian Corps of Liberation, the Italian people as a whole
took no willing part in it. Some twenty-five Italian divisions were left
stranded in the Balkans. Most of the men in them were disarmed by the
Germans and sent to Germany for forced labor; a few escaped, and some
joined the Yugoslav partisans under Tito.

On September 11, 1943, Mussolini was rescued by German paratroopers
from his place of confinement in the Abruzzi mountains. He was taken to
Verona, where he was installed as head of a "Republican Fascist State" with
Graziani as Minister of Defense. Early in 1944, under evident German inspiration, Ciano, De Bono, and other members of the Fascist Grand Council who had voted for Mussolini's deposition were tried for treason and
shot. By the end of 1944, as the Allies advanced, the neo-Fascist headquarters was moved from Verona to Milan. Mussolini set up his own headquarters on Lake Garda. Subsequently, a few days before the German surrender
of May 1945, he and twelve of his cabinet were discovered by Italian partisans, attempting to escape to Switzerland, and were summarily "executed."
His body was removed to Milan and hung in the Piazza Loretto, the scene
of recent neo-Fascist mass executions of hostages (see p. 777).

Meanwhile, in Allied occupied territory, political Italy began to return
to life after its long demise. Six underground political parties came out of
hiding — the Liberal, Labor Democrat, Christian Democrat, Action, Socialist, and Communist. Intellectuals, like the philosopher Benedetto Croce
and the lawyer Enrico De Nicola, emerged from semi-incarceration to take
an active part in their country's affairs. Exiles came back from abroad —
Count Sforza from the United States, and the Communist, Palmiro Togliatti, from the Soviet Union. In April 1944 the King retired from public life
— but did not abdicate — and was succeeded by Crown Prince Umberto as
"Lieutenant General." Badoglio formed the first government of liberation,
a coalition of the above-mentioned six parties, with Croce, Sforza, and
Togliatti as Ministers without portfolio.

In the north, under German occupation, Italian partisan forces were
gradually organized into a Committee of National Liberation (*Comitato*

della Liberazione Nazionale — CLN) in liaison with the Allies. As the Germans retired, and towns and villages were liberated, local units of the CLN took over administrative control till properly constituted authorities could be appointed. The assistance rendered the Allied cause by the CLN and the Corps of Liberation was far from contemptible, but unhappily it did not purchase the diplomatic respect of the Powers at the subsequent Peace Conference. Evidently there were deep psychological misconceptions on both sides. Italians generally were mortified at their treatment as "enemies" when they thought they should have qualified as Allied cobelligerents. The disappointed emotions of liberation, followed by the final retributive peace, inflicted perhaps a more lasting injury on Italian national morale than the physical devastation throughout the country left by the actual tide of hostilities.

Politically Italy at this time resembled other liberated nations of Europe. Popularity lay with the Left. Former partisans of the CLN, now participating in political life, lent in addition a decided air of revolution. Of the six parties mentioned, three dominated Italy in 1945. The first was the Christian Democrat party, a Catholic clerical party, successor to the *Popolari* of 1919 (see p. 294) and now led by Alcide De Gasperi. The second was the Socialist party, eventually to split into a right-wing faction under Saragat and a left-wing faction under Nenni. The third was the Communist party led by Togliatti. The three were "mass" parties and corresponded to the contemporary MRP, Socialist, and Communist parties in France. Of the other parties, the Liberal party, furthest to the Right, was the party of "liberal" property owners and entrepreneurs and claimed as members such men as Croce, Nitti, and Einaudi; the Labor Democrat party was Socialist of the so-called Reformist group and was led by Bonomi; and the Action party was mainly a party of anti-Fascist and Socialist intellectuals, many of whom had been refugees abroad. There were still a number of other parties, notably the Republican party, boasting a Risorgimento ideology, led by Pacciardi, former commander of a Republican brigade in the Spanish Civil War, and claiming as members such men as Sforza. Out of such materials was Italy to forge her new postwar democracy.

Unhappily that democracy was neither stable nor greatly commanding of respect. From Badoglio's government in April 1944 to May 1948 — in a space of four years — Italy had fifteen governments. As in contemporary France, the governments were mainly permutations of the moderate Left in growing opposition to the Communists. Elections for a Constituent Assembly, coupled with a referendum on the monarchy, were held in June 1946. Women voted for the first time. The three "mass" parties swept the board; the referendum returned a narrow majority in favor of a republic. Enrico De Nicola was elected Head of the State. De Gasperi formed a government — the fourteenth of the series — with Sforza as Foreign Minister, and later with Einaudi as Minister of Finance. In December 1947, after long debates, the Constituent Assembly passed the constitution of "a democratic Republic founded upon work," having a president and a central bicameral legislature and dividing the country locally into twenty-four semiautonomous regions each with its own elected authority. King Victor Emmanuel III died in exile in Egypt on December 28, 1947, the day after the promulgation of the new constitution.

Italy's affairs were now becoming inextricably entangled in the wider mesh of postwar power politics, and she reflected in herself the predominant East-West schism in Europe. In 1947 she was already a battlefield between Communism and Western democracy anxiously watched by the rest of the world. The Italian peace treaty and the circumstances of its preparation have already been described (pp. 801–802). It is only necessary to repeat here that, though the treaty was mild enough among dictated peace treaties of this day and age, the reaction to it in Italy was one of bitter humiliation and even of real surprise. The clauses creating the Free Territory of Trieste were perhaps more passionately resented than the loss of the overseas empire, and Trieste typically became a bone of contention between the moderate Left parties and the Communists. On the other side of the ledger was the substantial and continuous American aid which Italy received from 1943 onward in loans and grants of various kinds amounting to some $1,700,000,000. Italy was a beneficiary under the "interim" aid of December 1947, and she was invited to participate in the European Recovery Program (pp. 834, 835, and 922). Yet the two million unemployed in 1947 indicated the real economic condition of the country.

Political drifts and trends came to a head during the party jockeying that preceded the elections which were to be held under the new constitution. A wave of Communist-inspired strikes in the autumn months of 1947 appeared to be part of a regular campaign preliminary to a Communist seizure of power in Italy. Left-wing Socialists under Nenni were now acting in full collaboration with the Communist party. New rightist parties emerged, notably the "Party of the Common Man (*Uomo Qualunque*)," which was plainly a party of discontent with little in the way of a positive program, and there was a monarchist party, and even a neo-Fascist party parading under the title of the "Italian Social Movement (*Movimento Sociale Italiano*)." As election fever mounted, the Congress of the Italian Communist party, meeting in Milan in January 1948, declared that the party would seize power by force if it lost the election. Rumors were flying about concerning the formation of private militias and resistance brigades. Pacciardi, now Vice-President in De Gasperi's government, was made Minister of Public Order with the unenviable responsibility for the peaceful conduct of the elections. In February 1948 came the Communist seizure of power in Czechoslovakia, an incident which convulsed every neighbor and near-neighbor of that country (pp. 853–54). On March 20 the United States, Britain, and France issued a joint proposal that Trieste should once more be restored to Italian sovereignty. The three Powers cited the repeated failure of the Italian and Yugoslav Governments to agree upon a governor for the Free Territory; but, inasmuch as the Soviet Union supported Yugoslav claims in Trieste, the proposal was well calculated to cramp and confuse the Italian Communist party.

In the event the elections were held in April 1948 in relative calm. Over

90 per cent of the electorate voted. The result was a clear victory for De Gasperi exceeding all expectations.[1] His Christian Democrat party won more than half the seats; the Communists rather less than a third; the rightist parties — the Common Man, the Monarchists, and the Social Movement — made very small showings. In May, after the new parliament had assembled, Einaudi was elected first President of the Italian Republic. De Gasperi continued as Premier.

The elections had been watched from abroad with the keenest anxiety and excitement. It was felt that Italy — indeed all Western Europe — was undergoing a most crucial test. If Italy had fallen to Communism, France must surely have followed, and once more an isolated Britain might have been left to face a hostile Continent across the narrow protective waters of the Channel. But moderate Christian Democracy had not only won, but won decisively. The feeling of relief and settlement in Italy, nevertheless, was not immediate. An attempt on the life of the Communist leader, Togliatti, on July 14, 1948, was followed by a nation-wide general strike organized by the Communist-dominated Confederation of Labor and, though this was firmly suppressed by the government, lesser strikes and demonstrations continued into 1949. Unemployment still stood at about 2,000,000. However, industrial production indexes crept back to 1938 levels; land reform measures promised an alleviation of the chronic agrarian problem, especially in the south. Italy participated in the European Recovery Program, in the North Atlantic Pact (see p. 925), and in the Council of Europe (see p. 837). Perhaps it was a sign of the growing domestic peace that De Gasperi remained Premier and, at the time of writing, is still the Premier of Italy.

SPAIN

We return for a moment to 1939 (see p. 526). Since his victory, General Franco had built up in Spain a modern totalitarian regime. He tried to wrap his own person about with the vestments of a Fascist dictator. He was El Caudillo, the Spanish Duce. His ideology was, however, peculiarly Spanish and was compounded of a fervent Spanish nationalism and a fervent Spanish Catholicism. He enacted the usual controls, censorships, and restrictions upon private liberties. He obliterated all the signs of Catalan and Basque autonomy. He suppressed Communism and Freemasonry. Subsequent reports of his cruelties to his late enemies were doubtless much exaggerated; but he declared no amnesty, and his police continued to hound the "Red hordes" and "Marxist rabble." Yet he claimed to base his authority on popular support and insisted always that "we belong to the people."

Meanwhile Franco set about "the material and spiritual reconstruction" of Spain, the building of the devastated areas, the promotion of social services, housing, and schools. But there was little agricultural or agrarian reform. Church lands and revenues were restored. Traditional religious ceremonies and festivals were revived in all their splendor. During the Second World War, profitable trade relations were established with Britain, Germany, and Italy. There was the usual story of shortages, inflation, and black market. Generally the country's recovery was rapid beyond expectation. On July 18, 1942, on the anniversary of the "Glorious Rebellion," as a sort of definitive consolidation of his regime, Franco announced the creation of a new Cortes, a distinctly corporative body composed of government nominees who had rendered "eminent services to the state." But despite occasional threatening moves, despite his declaration of nonbelligerency, Franco did not enter the Second World War (see pp. 658–60).

The Allied victories in North Africa and thereafter in Western Europe soon posed Franco with several delicate questions, including that of his very continuance in power. All the Spanish parties were shortly maneuvering for position. In March 1945, perhaps somewhat prematurely, Don Juan, pretender to the Spanish throne, issued a proclamation from his exile in Italy calling for Franco's resignation and for a restoration of the monarchy. In October 1945, Franco adjusted himself to the altering political situation to the extent of withdrawing the Spanish troops which had occupied Tangier, and the international status of that territory was re-established (see p. 658). But he revealed his complete misunderstanding of the psychological situation at the moment when he wrote a personal letter to Churchill virtually offering an Anglo-Spanish alliance against the Soviet Union.

Considerable diplomatic pressure was being exerted to induce a change of government in Spain. Exiled political groups, Republican and monarchist, intrigued from the side lines. The conferences at San Francisco and Potsdam had pointedly debarred Spain from membership in the United Nations and, in February 1946, the General Assembly adopted a resolution that "they would not support the application for admission to the United Nations of the present Spanish Government, which, having been founded with the support of Axis Powers, does not possess by reason of its origins, its nature, its record, and its close association with aggressor states the qualifications necessary to justify its admission." In March 1946, the United States, Britain, and France, in a joint declaration, animadverted upon the past and present iniquities of Franco's regime and expressed the hope that "leading patriotic and liberal-minded Spaniards may soon find the means to bring about a peaceful withdrawal of Franco, the abolition of the Falange and the establishment of an interim or caretaker government under which the Spanish people may have an opportunity of freedom to determine the type of government they wish to have . . . ."

In June 1947 the Cortes passed an Act of Succession, providing for a Council of Regency which should propose a person of royal blood as King of Spain in the event of the present headship of the state becoming vacant. Evidently Franco was moving in the direction of monarchy and perhaps preparing for an orderly and face-saving abdication of power. Meanwhile, in the course of 1947, by the curious logic of power politics, the United States, Britain, and France began to look a little less censoriously at Spain. The conviction was growing that the likely alternative to Franco might not be monarchy but Communism, a conviction which Franco naturally was sedulous to propagate. It was belatedly realized that Spain might become a strategic strong point ready to the hand of Western Union, and that American Flying Fortresses might find convenient nesting grounds behind the Pyrenees. As we write, affairs in Spain have reached a somewhat hypocritical lull, which may be broken by sudden events at any time. Some indication of the future may have been given by Franco's ceremonial visit to Lisbon and his meeting with Don Juan there in October 1949.

BRITAIN

The general elections of July 1945 had resulted in a heavy defeat for Churchill and the Conservative party. It must be admitted that the British people, afterward, were a little pricked in conscience at having so served their great wartime leader; opinion abroad, especially in the United States, was stunned at the seeming ingratitude. But, as we have suggested elsewhere (see p. 696), there were several domestic factors in the situation, and the country's decisive swing to the Left at the first sign of peace was not wholly unexpected — nor wholly undesirable. The Labor majority in the election — 392 Labor seats to 189 Conservative — was certainly a very convincing demonstration of the electorate's hopes and desires.

On July 27, 1945, Attlee formed a Labor government, with Dalton as Chancellor of the Exchequer, Bevin as Foreign Secretary, and Sir Stafford Cripps as President of the Board of Trade. It was the first Labor government in Britain with a clear majority, and it came to power with an explicit socialist program of aims. Attlee himself had none of the color of his predecessor in office. He was the "safe" leader of his party, eminently moderate, personally well liked and respected, an experienced administrative head, and likely to be a good leader of a fractious, strong-willed cabinet. The country was left in no doubt as to his domestic policies. From the very opening of the new Parliament, in the speech from the throne, the King had made mention of measures for the public ownership of key industries and services. Britain, clearly enough, was to become a socialist state. "Planning" and "social justice" were the new watchwords. There was a curious, almost unreal optimism in the air. Dalton's supplementary budget in October 1945 cheerfully reduced the income tax and the Excess Profits Tax and restored personal allowances to prewar levels. These were the days when the bookshops blossomed out with masses of volumes — attractively produced despite the paper shortage — describing the cities and housing schemes which were to adorn the face of Britain. Reports, after the manner of the Beveridge Report,[2] delineated the country's future social and economic structure. Meanwhile, unlike 1919–20, wartime controls were not hastily abolished. Demobilization of man power and of industry was a deliberate, gradual process. Many supporters of the government indeed believed that the recent regimentation was not an unmixed evil and had prepared the country for an easy and painless translation into an era of planning. In the immense economic complexities of the modern world, it was argued, the old cutthroat chaos of private enterprise would never restore the nation's prosperity.

A first parliamentary session of nearly fifteen months saw the passage of eighty-four acts, a mass of legislation unprecedented in British parliamentary history. The Bank of England was brought under public ownership. After intensive debate, coal was the first great industry to be nationalized, and the long story which had begun with the strikes of the early twenties (pp. 326–27) thus came to an end. Henceforth, nearly 2,000 British coal mines would be operated by a National Coal Board, appointed by the Minister of Fuel and responsible to him. The coal owners received about $750,000,000 in indemnities. A Transport Bill was proposed for the nationalization of railroads, canals, and long-distance road transport, and there were debates, very bitter debates, on a bill for the nationalization of steel. Parliament repealed the Trades Disputes Act, passed shortly after the General Strike of 1926 (see p. 330), an act which Labor had always regarded with particular dislike as a piece of punitive legislation.

The legislative surfeit continued into the second parliamentary session. To speed up the pace the government had recourse to the "guillotine" to cut short lengthening debates on several important measures during committee stage. Labor spokesmen argued that the government's program of reforms was already long overdue, and sufficient discussion of it had gone on, both inside and outside Parliament, for years past. The House of Lords, heretofore somewhat fallen in prestige, was restored to some of its historic eminence to become a chamber where debates could be continued in relative freedom and leisure. During 1947, Parliament passed the Transport Act and an Electricity Act nationalizing the electricity supply industry. Early in 1948, Parliament passed an act nationalizing the gas industry and a National Health Service Act, "nationalizing the doctors" and extending free medical services to the entire population.[3]

But the original optimism was already subsiding. The very completeness of the military victory of 1945, as in 1918, had disguised the country's real fatigue and economic dislocation. The government had been living in its own doctrinaire vacuum and had perhaps recked too little of the gathering pressures outside. In April 1946, Dalton, the Chancellor of the Exchequer, introducing his budget, disclosed a deficit of £300,000,000 ($1,500,000,000). In July the Minister of Food was forced to introduce bread rationing for some months. It was hardly to the credit of the socialist government — with all its "planning" — that the one staple food of the people which had not been rationed during the war should have to be rationed upon the return of peace. During the summer and autumn of 1946 there were cuts in meat and fuels, the "basic" gasoline ration was abolished, a ban was imposed on vacation travel abroad, the import of foreign books and motion-picture films was restricted, and sharp shortages occurred in cigarettes and tobacco. The winter of 1946–47 was one of the coldest and most uncomfortable on record and placed exceptional burdens on fuel stocks. A "switch-off" of electricity supply due to fuel shortage in February 1947 was estimated to have cost the country £200,000,000 ($1,000,000,000) in lost exports.

Meanwhile something had gone very wrong with the great spurt in the building industry which was to have repaired the bomb-devastated towns and provided thousands of new homes for returning servicemen and their families. Building materials, it was said, were in short supply — almost every building material but brick and cement had to be imported from abroad — the building-trades employees were not working, the industry was clogged with bureaucratic controls, and so forth. In the daily press, at public meetings, in the Commons, the latest recurrent theme at this time was that of industrial "incentives" to supersede the more primitive economic incentives of the past which full employment had now removed. During 1947 the government intensively publicized the seriousness of the growing adverse balance of payments and called for a nation-wide drive to step up the export trade. The slogans "Export or die" or "You are living on tick" were posted on billboards and railroad stations. Exhibitions — such as "Britain Can Make It" and "the British Industries Fair" — were organized to bring British products to the notice of foreign buyers. Finally, a National Service Act, conscripting men between the ages of eighteen and twenty-six, was passed, a grim reminder to the British people that, in addition to their other cares, they were not yet finished with the business of preparing for war.

In September 1945, immediately after the Japanese surrender, the United States Government canceled all outstanding contracts for Lend-Lease. The decision was proper, as Lend-Lease had been a wartime measure. But it was made without warning and came as a shock to former Lend-Lease beneficiaries, notably Britain. Lord Keynes and Lord Halifax were sent over to Washington to negotiate with American Treasury representatives a financial arrangement which would tide over, in particular, the problems raised by the cessation of Lend-Lease and, in general, the longer-term problems of the reconversion from war to peace. Disagreement of experts over needs and principles was not serious. The main difficulty was to devise a plan acceptable to the legislatures and electorates of the two countries. Both sides, as we have already suggested, were far from realizing the extent of the dislocations of the war. American Congressional opinion was averse to reviving and perpetrating expenditures which were thought to have been brought to an end. British Parliamentary opinion was averse to contracting new obligations and hoped for an early return to national self-reliance. However, on December 7, 1945, the negotiators in Washington announced an agreement which would take the form of a loan of $3,750,000,000 from the United States to Britain at an interest of 2 per cent, the capital being repayable in fifty annual installments commencing December 31, 1951. In addition, the net liability of Britain with respect to Lend-Lease was reduced to $650,000,-000, to be repaid to the United States simultaneously and on the same terms. The agreement was approved by the House of Commons and House of Lords in the face of strong opposition, and was approved by Congress after protracted debates and close voting in July 1946. A Canadian loan of $1,250,-000,000 was provided under an agreement signed in Ottawa in March 1946.

The loans were drawn upon far faster than had been expected; and both were exhausted by the end of 1947. A credit which, it had been hoped, would have lasted over a transitional gap of four to five years, while the switchback to peacetime production could be made, lasted in fact rather less than two. There were various reasons suggested for this disastrous abbreviation. The rise of prices in the United States and the virtual inflation in that country sharply reduced the real value of the loans. The cost of the American commodities imported by Britain rose from 40 to 50 per cent in the two years, 1946–47, while complementary export prices in Britain had not risen to nearly the same extent. In general, throughout 1945–48, the prices of imported foods and raw materials rose faster than the prices of manufactured goods for export. Meanwhile the volume of Britain's exports had failed to maintain the promise of the initial postwar recovery, partly on account of the shortage of fuel required for manufacture. Inflationary pressure in Britain had tended to drive up production prices and had diverted goods intended for export to the home market, and too great a proportion of what had eventually been exported had gone to non-dollar destinations. In 1946, for example, 10 per cent of Britain's exports had gone to the United States, Canada, and Argentina, but she had derived 40 per cent of her imports from those three countries and, in that year, her trade deficit with the three countries was over £400,000,000 ($2,000,000,000).

In the absence of a universal convertible currency standard, the world's former system of "multilateral" trade was very severely restricted. A British buyer could not pay indirectly, say for a Canadian purchase, by selling goods to Italy, who would in turn sell Italian goods to Canada. International trade was now largely limited to "bilateral" transactions between pairs of buyers. Thus the British deficit of nearly £140,000,000 ($700,000,000) to the United States in the first half of 1947 could be balanced only by an equivalent increase of British exports to the United States.

The war had greatly reduced Britain's former "invisible" exports — returns on her overseas investments, shipping charges, banking, and insurance. In the aggregate, the $40,000,000,000 held in 1939 by British investors abroad, a sum which formerly yielded annual dividends of $1,000,000,000, had largely vanished. All but a small "unrealizable" portion of Britain's immense prewar investments in the United States, for example, had been liquidated in 1941 (see p. 699). Britain could no longer rely, as had been her habit in a more comfortable past, on "visible" deficits being offset by "invisible" surpluses. Her loans to wartime European allies and to governments in exile over the past years had amounted to $8,000,000,000, little of which would now be collectible. Finally, to complete the picture of her parlous economic condition, Britain had to discharge various relief services as well as exceptional commitments in Germany, Greece, and in other parts of the world. The national exchequer was being constantly tapped by unexpected expenditures of a humanitarian and political nature, none of which showed compensatory financial returns. At the end of 1947, the American and Canadian loans had been exhausted, almost the whole of the quota of dollars available to Britain from the International Monetary Fund had been drawn, and the adverse balance was running at the rate of $700,000,000 a year. In partial relief, the government suspended the convertibility of sterling into dollars and accepted a loan of £80,000,000 ($400,000,000) in gold from South Africa. "Sterling balances" exceeding £3,500,000,000 ($14,000,000,000), namely, debts incurred during the war for wartime supplies mainly from the Dominions, India, Egypt, Argentina, and Portugal, could only be "frozen" or repaid in small successive amounts in the shape of British products.[4] But for the European Recovery Program, the state of Britain would have been serious indeed (see pp. 834–35).

Sir Stafford Cripps succeeded Dalton as Chancellor of the Exchequer in November 1947, and the government's recovery measures thereafter were introduced under his name. New targets were set for industry; every effort was made to increase the output per man shift, especially in the coal mines, and to reduce workers' absenteeism; capital expenditure was discouraged. An Anglo-American Council of Industrial Productivity was established to advise British manufacturers on American production methods. In the course of 1948, the export drive reached 147 per cent of the volume of exports in 1938, a very remarkable achievement. Steel production reached the record level of 14,877,000 tons. Over 2,000,000 tons of merchant shipping was under construction. The country's slow but steady progress was reflected in the increase in consumer goods, especially household goods. The shops were better stocked, and the shopkeepers — a significant index — were more courteous and anxious to sell. Several commodities, such as shoes and certain other kinds of clothing, were derationed. A considerable release of paint materials enabled houses and buildings, long neglected during the war years, to be repainted, and the consequent architectural refreshment was immensely heartening.

The year 1948 in Britain closed on a more confident note. Thanks to the European Recovery Program, an over-all balance of payments was in sight. Exports in the first quarter of 1949 rose to 156 per cent of their volume in 1938. The situation suddenly and unexpectedly worsened in the early summer of 1949, partly because of the current business recession in the United States, and partly because of the general transition from a seller's to a buyer's market and the consequent difficulty of selling higher priced British goods in dollar areas.[5] All in all, British exports to the United States dropped by 30 per cent. The dollar deficit for the total sterling area jumped from $1,650,000,000 at the end of 1948 to $3,000,000,000 by mid-1949. On September 18, 1949, Britain devalued the pound from $4.03 to $2.80, and some weeks later the Prime Minister announced cuts in government expenditure amounting to £250,000,000. The critical days of 1931 seemed to have returned.

THE EUROPEAN RECOVERY PROGRAM AND WESTERN UNION

The economic dislocations of the war went far deeper than was generally realized in the immediate postwar months. The war, at any rate in the victor countries, had ended on a note of very excusable optimism. Two years had to pass for it to be understood that the superficial devastation — even in a devastated country like Germany — was less baleful and irremediable than the accompanying subversion of economic life. The words of the Atlantic Charter now had an air of almost pious unreality. In that document the signatories had declared their desire "to further the enjoyment by all states great or small, victor or vanquished, of access, on equal terms, to the trade and to the raw materials of the world which are needed for their economic prosperity" and "to bring about the fullest collaboration between all nations in the economic field, with the object of securing for all improved labor standards, economic adjustment, and social security," and these worthy principles had been recognized in the Declaration of the United Nations of 1942 and embodied in the Charter of 1945. But how woefully short they fell of actual needs was to appear in due course.

We have given some accounts of UNRRA, the FAO, and other Specialized Agencies concerned with postwar recovery. It is no derogation of those organizations to say that they were only partial helps each in its respective field. What they were constituted to do they did. But by 1947 it was being borne in upon responsible framers of national policies that the remaking of the world was not going to be just a matter of *ad hoc* largesse or of financial mechanics. Herein had been the deeper miscalculation of the American and Canadian loans to Britain in 1945. Even the massed experience of the past eventful era, with all its revolutions and slumps, could not provide the guide for the present situation. What was wanted, it was dimly realized, was leadership and a comprehensive political reorganization. And this was the meaning of the European Recovery Program — and its concomitant, Western Union.

The immediate and overwhelming political fact in 1946 was the East-West schism. There had been premonitory signs of it at the Crimea Conference; it was in full and admitted evidence at Potsdam. In Western countries, a dutifully blinkered press, keeping up the good spirit of wartime alliance, was profuse with pained surprise and friendly remonstrance. But its arguments were lost on the Russians; international conferences regularly foundered on the same old rock; the operative word in Molotov's vocabulary was always "No." On March 15, 1946, it was Churchill, then visiting the United States, who, in a speech at Fulton, Missouri, gave utterance at last to what many felt and had not dared to say. He spoke as a private citizen "with full liberty to give my true and faithful counsel in these anxious and baffling times," but the presence of President Truman as his chairman lent the occasion a peculiar significance. He delivered a frank homily on "war" and "tyranny." The United States, he said, was at the pinnacle of power, but "with primacy in power is also joined an awe-inspiring accountability to the future." "A shadow has fallen upon the scenes so lately lighted by the Allied victory," he continued. "Nobody knows what Soviet Russia and its Communist international organization intend to do in the immediate future or what are the limits, if any, to their expansive proselytizing tendencies," and he thence proceeded to dilate at length upon the "iron curtain" which had lately descended across the center of Europe.

Through 1946, wherever the forces of power politics met — in Iran, Greece, Korea, northern Italy, Yugoslavia, to say nothing of the United Nations — by a seemingly inexorable logic, the Western Powers stood in absolute opposition to the Soviet Union. The "cold war" was on. In December 1946 the United States and Britain merged their zones in Germany into a single "Bizonia" to the exclusion of the Soviet zone (see p. 813). Early in 1947 the five treaties of peace with the former Axis satellites — Italy, Rumania, Bulgaria, Hungary, and Finland — were concluded, as we have already described (pp. 804–805), in circumstances fully reflecting the selfsame conflict. In March 1947 the Foreign Ministers Council met in Moscow for their fruitless discussion of the German and Austrian settlements (see p. 814).

The popular mood in the United States was one of gnawing perplexity and even of aimless exasperation waiting for a new initiative, when Secretary of State Marshall, speaking at Harvard University on June 5, 1947, broached the idea of the European Recovery Program. "It has been obvious during recent months," said Marshall, "that visible destruction was probably less serious than the dislocation of the entire fabric of European economy. For the past ten years conditions have been highly abnormal . . . The demoralizing effect . . . the possibilities of disturbances . . . the desperation of the people concerned" must have consequences upon the economy of the United States that "should be apparent to all," and "it is logical that the United States should do whatever it is able to do to assist in the return of normal economic health in the world, without which there can be no political stability and no assured peace. Our policy is directed not against any country or doctrine, but against hunger, poverty, desperation, and chaos . . . Such assistance, I am convinced, must not be on a piecemeal basis as various crises develop." But, he continued, "there must be some agreement among the countries of Europe as to the requirements of the situation and the part those countries themselves will take in order to give proper effect to whatever action might be undertaken by [the United States] Government . . . The initiative, I think, must come from Europe . . ."

Under such auspices, Bevin, the British Foreign Secretary, called for an immediate conference of European nations, and for a moment it seemed as if the Marshall offer might succeed in breaking down the estrangement of the Soviet Union. A conference of twenty-five nations assembled in Paris. Molotov arrived with a numerous delegation giving every appearance of an intention to take part, but his opening speech, a compound of orthodox Marxism and undiluted economic nationalism, showed at once that Soviet co-operation was to be offered only on Soviet terms. He bluntly affirmed that the United States had reached the imperialist phase of its economic history, that it was extending credits in order to force its way into foreign markets, and that the mooted European Recovery Program was a desperate attempt to ward off the approaching crisis of American capitalism. Finally he withdrew not only the Soviet delegation, but the delegations of the Soviet's Eastern European satellites.

Britain and France therefore proceeded without Soviet participation and, on July 12, 1947, sixteen nations — Austria, Belgium, Britain, Denmark, Eire, France, Greece, Iceland, Italy, Luxembourg, the Netherlands, Norway, Portugal, Sweden, Switzerland, and Turkey — set up in Paris a Committee of European Economic Co-operation (CEEC). The Committee's report, the Paris Report as it was called, published in September, outlined a scheme for increasing the agricultural and industrial output of the sixteen nations and of Western Germany, controlling their exchanges and price structures, and reducing their tariff barriers — and for special dollar credits of $22,400,000,000. The scheme seemed already to be in process of implementation when, during July, the Benelux states (Belgium, the Netherlands, and Luxembourg) entered into a comprehensive customs agreement. A similar agreement was mooted between France and Italy.

The political counterpart of these agreements had already been prepared by the signature at Dunkirk in March 1947 of a treaty of alliance between Britain and France. Events, economic and political, took on the form of an inseverable causal chain. The European Recovery Program (ERP) was wholly merged into the project for Western Union. Countermeasures from the Soviet East were to be expected and were not long in coming. In September 1947 a Communist Information Bureau, or Cominform, was set up in Belgrade. The Soviet Union extended its influence in Eastern European countries by encouraging them to enter into a series of interlocking bilateral "treaties of friendship and mutual assistance" and complementary trade agreements. Under evident Soviet pressure, Communist parties consolidated their power in Hungary, Poland, and Rumania. The hanging of Petkov in Bulgaria and the imprisonment of Maniu in Rumania injected into the situation the political complications and acerbities of personal martyrdom. In December, in London, the Foreign Ministers Council, resuming its discussion of the German and Austrian settlements, once more failed to agree and came to an abrupt, ill-humored end. The United States Congress passed a bill, in anticipation of ERP, to extend interim aid to France, Italy, Austria, and China. In February 1948, the Communists seized power in Czechoslovakia. On March 17, Britain, France, and the Benelux states (Belgium, the Netherlands, and Luxembourg) signed a fifty-year defensive Treaty of Brussels against "armed attack in Europe," providing for economic, social, cultural, and military co-operation. A permanent Consultative Council of the five signatories of the new treaty and a Defense Committee would be set up.

An account of the passage of the Foreign Assistance Act through Congress and its complicated domestic motivations must be left to Chapter 54 (pp. 921–23). The act was signed by President Truman on April 3, 1948. Under its terms the United States would make grants totaling over $6,000,000,000 in the first year. It enjoined that its beneficiaries would take steps to stabilize currencies, balance budgets, reduce tariffs, remove restrictive trade practices, control inflation, furnish the United States with strategic materials and, if required, deny the same materials to nonparticipating nations. It was intended to effect the economic mobilization of Western Europe and generally promote by mid-1952 a self-reliant, self-sufficient, and politically and militarily self-defensive, wholly viable unit. It would operate through an Economic Co-operative Administration (ECA) in Washington with branch missions in each participating European nation. Ostensibly the act had no "strings" but it was an open secret that the ECA would discontinue aid to any nation in the event of "changed conditions," notably in the event of that nation going Communist. On April 16, in Paris, representatives of the original sixteen nations of the CEEC signed a convention creating an Organization for European Economic Co-operation (OEEC) to act as the European counterpart of the ECA. Under the so-called London Decisions of June, the three Western-occupied zones of Germany were drawn into the plan (see p. 815).

At the end of 1948, ERP represented an acknowledged success. In the nine months a total of $4,044,000,000 had been allocated. Productivity was rising; theoretical target figures had been adopted which would make a viable Western Europe by 1952. The easing of tensions, particularly in France and Italy, indicated that ERP's political objectives were being satisfied. On April 19, 1949, President Truman signed the authorization bill for $5,430,000,000 for the next fifteen months.

But ERP was soon to feel the worsening circumstances of 1949. European exports were flagging as the result of the continued high costs of production. Strong utterances of impatience were coming from Washington that the nineteen nations now in the Program,[6] while apt at distributing American aid, were not implementing their undertakings to free their trade and unify their economies. The first step to meet the situation was to be a general devaluation, notably that of Britain. In November 1949, OEEC met in an atmosphere of emergency to devise its further course of action.

The idea of Western Union, in one form or another, as we have already had occasion to note (see p. 215), had a long and respectable history behind it. The approach of the Second World War and the war itself might be expected to vitalize any doctrine which promised to avert some of the causes of a similar conflict in the future. Public interest was evidenced and stimulated by such bodies as Federal Union in Britain in 1938, such books as Clarence Streit's *Union Now* in 1939, such conferences as that of the European Union of Federalists at Montreux in 1947 and the Congress of Europe at The Hague in 1948 — the last named being notable for the active presence of Churchill. In a world of declining nationalisms, it was widely believed that "regional arrangements," in the words of the Charter of the United Nations, might form the pattern of the future international order. Western Europe, one such possible region, it was said, was going through the same sort of growing pains as the American colonies of 1787.

Western Union in 1948 had reached high official and ministerial levels. Meetings between the premiers, foreign ministers, and ministers of trade of Sweden, Norway, Denmark, and Iceland showed that the Scandinavian countries were alive to the project and were considering their participation in it. The British Cabinet and Foreign Office had adopted the idea and were now presumably concerned only with the necessary administrative machinery. "I would regard it as the crowning event of my life," said Bevin in a speech at this time, "to establish European unity on a sound, definite and progressive basis. What I want to avoid is a mere talking shop for the passing of resolutions. What I want is a practical organism in Europe, in which we shall cease to be English and French, cease to be English and Italian, cease to be English and Belgian, but will be European, an organism that can carry out European policy in the face of the new development of the world." In July 1948, at The Hague, the Consultative Council of the five nations of the Treaty of Brussels began discussions of a joint European assembly or parliament or, as it was shortly to be called, a Council of Europe. In January 1949, it was announced that Field Marshal Montgomery had been appointed Chief of a Western Union Defense Committee, consisting of 150 ranking service officers and American observers, with headquarters at Fontainebleau. The Statute of the Council of Europe was signed in London on May 5, 1949, by the foreign ministers of Belgium, Denmark, France, Ireland, Italy, Luxembourg, the Netherlands, Norway, Sweden, and Britain and the first meeting of the Assembly of the Council of Europe was held at Strasbourg in the following August and September.

The North Atlantic Pact, of which more anon, could be read as an extension of Western Union (see p. 923).

THE BRITISH COMMONWEALTH

The postwar years saw great changes in the British Commonwealth and Empire — or, perhaps it would be truer to say, they saw the further and faster development of old existing trends. The new Dominions of India, Pakistan, and Ceylon were formed; Burma became an independent republic; Newfoundland joined Canada; various events of the greatest importance took place in Eire, South Africa, Egypt and the Sudan, Malaya, Jamaica and the British West Indies, and the tropical African colonies; the Palestine mandate was brought to an end.

These changes and developments, at first sight, might seem to add up to a loosening of ties and an abdication of British power. But they are not open to quite so facile an interpretation. The British Commonwealth and Empire in the postwar years was still a vast field of experiment in human welfare. It was still served by some of the finest administrative talent that its many races could produce. In the world of postwar "planning," its future economic and social potentialities were a study worthy of all the care that accumulated knowledge and experience could offer. In the world of postwar power politics, it had enormous strength and many weaknesses. We cannot hope, in a short section, to review even a fraction of this interesting field. Sections on India, Burma, Malaya, Egypt, and Palestine in other chapters must suffice for a continuation of what we have written on these countries individually in earlier chapters of the book. But it might be appropriate, in the present context, to discuss some of the "international" aspects of post-1945 imperial politics, more especially the interrelations of Britain, the Commonwealth, and Western Union.

In Chapter 21 we described the growth of British imperial ideology. In 1939 the Dominions had severally entered the Second World War as sovereign Powers according to their several constitutional procedures. Eire had remained neutral. It is to be noted, for instance, that Canada's declaration of war on Germany in September 1939 followed that of Britain by some days and her declaration of war on Japan in December 1941 preceded that of Britain by some hours. Devoted as were their services to the Allied cause, the Dominions gave those services independently. They mobilized their own resources, recruited their own forces, appointed their own commanders, and participated as equals in high strategic discussions. Since 1945 the Dominions again advanced in international status. They were separately members of the United Nations and separately represented at the San Francisco Conference in 1945, at the Paris Peace Conference in 1947, and at other international conferences of that time, and at all of them they made distinctive and forceful contributions. They increasingly made diplomatic and consular appointments in foreign capitals.

Since 1945, while the technical problems of inter-imperial consultation arose in sharpened form, it would seem that a greater decentralization in the Commonwealth was in fact both sought and achieved. Mackenzie King, the Canadian Prime Minister, emphasized his desire for informality in Commonwealth relations and asked that every care should be taken, not only to leave each Dominion in unfettered control of its own affairs, but to avoid even the appearance of an explicit and unified Commonwealth point of view. St. Laurent, Canadian Minister of External Affairs and afterward Mackenzie King's successor as Prime Minister, argued more than once against reducing Commonwealth relations to formal terms or specific commitments. Evatt of Australia, in a broadcast in September 1948, spoke of "an entirely new principle, namely that within the Commonwealth the leadership and initiative need not always rest upon Britain herself. On the contrary, in certain areas and for certain purposes far greater, and perhaps the greatest, responsibility may have to be placed on one or more selected members of the Commonwealth group," and he went on to emphasize "the necessity for devising flexible machinery for high-level Commonwealth and international cooperation in the ever-changing world situation today." On such showing, anything in the nature of a permanent Imperial Secretariat could only be a consultative, not a policy-making, body and would never supersede multilateral consultation through existing official channels. The periodic Imperial Conferences of Dominion Prime Ministers would continue to be held.

Nor is it to be thought that this new principle was unwelcome to Britain herself. Two World Wars had left her with such diminished resources that she could hardly be expected to bear the same weight of responsibility as heretofore, and she was glad enough to relegate a greater share of the old imperial burden to her younger partners. The loans which she received from Canada and South Africa in 1946 and 1947 and the outright monetary gifts from Australia and New Zealand gave a clear indication of her changed position. Furthermore, over the same period of the two World Wars, the entire demographic basis of the British Empire had shifted. With her falling birth rate, Britain had ceased to be one of the world's great exporters of men, and the white Dominions would now have to rely more and more on their own human resources or on non-British immigration for the peopling of their territories.

Canada came out of the Second World War with an impressive military and economic record, an enormously enhanced international importance, and the promise of an even greater future. She had vast natural resources, and she had long been one of the principal food-exporting countries of the world. But the war had greatly expanded her industrial economy. After the United States, Britain, and the Soviet Union, she had been fourth largest producer of war materials for the United Nations. Her total war costs had exceeded $16,000,000,000 and, alone among the United Nations, she had received no Lend-Lease aid from the United States. Since 1945, it had become known that she possessed some of the richest uranium deposits in the world.

Canada's inclusion in the Security Council of the United Nations in 1947 was no more than a just acknowledgment of her new position. She was an Atlantic, Pacific, and Arctic Power, an American and British Power. She was a naval and air Power of no small consequence. Willy-nilly, she would have to play a part — a big part — in the wider theaters of Commonwealth and world relations. Two factors had always been prime in her international behavior, first her internal tensions, arising to a great extent out of her dual English and French nationalism, and second her contiguity to the United States. Big in area, she had less than one-tenth the population of her southern neighbor, and it was inevitable that, despite French Canadian dislike of American influence, the events of 1941–45 would draw her to that neighbor.

In August 1940 — before Pearl Harbor, be it noted — under the Ogdensburg Agreement, Canada and the United States had created a Permanent Joint Board of Defense at Washington. Though born of wartime emergency, the very title of the Board implied that military co-operation between the two Powers would be prolonged beyond the close of hostilities. The United States retained the bases in Newfoundland acquired in the "Destroyers for Bases Deal" in 1940. The continual exchange of service personnel, the standardization of arms, and the mutual availability of naval and air facilities were the premises of the joint defense policies. The Alaska Highway, hastily constructed during the war, at a cost of $115,000,000, as a supply route through British Columbia for American forces and outposts in the North Pacific, and the Northwest Staging Route, a chain of airfields strung between Edmonton and Alaska, over which quantities of Lend-Lease supplies had been flown to the Soviet Union, were both relegated to Canadian management in 1947, but no one doubted that the former joint American-Canadian controls over them could and would be reintroduced in the event of an emergency.

Canada's financial and commercial necessities also drew her to her southern neighbor. In the past, under the so-called Atlantic triangle, Canada had been able to level off her adverse dollar balance with the United States by means of a highly favorable balance of payments with Europe — and chiefly with Britain. But the easy, golden days of free dollar-sterling convertibility lay in the past. Alleviations arising from the European Recovery Program, which allotted European recipients some $700,000,000 for purchases in Canada, and from the huge demands for Canadian metals, entailed by Washington's rearmament and stock-piling program, merely tied the economy of Canada even more indissolubly with that of the United States. Canada was becoming a great treasure store of minerals for those consuming monsters, American industry and the American defense services.

Since 1945, with the growth of the East-West schism, Canada's Arctic territories assumed a sudden strategic importance. The Permanent Joint Board of Defense, aimed originally at Germany and Japan across the Atlantic and Pacific oceans, had now to reorientate itself to quite another direction. The Canada of the atomic age was no longer a "fire-proof house," lying on the safe periphery of world events, but rather a buffer state, the likely Belgium of a third world war. The shortest line from Moscow to New York lay right across the province of Quebec. In Alaska and British Columbia, moreover, was a still unforgotten tradition of Russian expansionism which the Soviet Union might at any time revive. Thus the United States planned a network of airfields from Alaska to Baffin Island and on to Greenland. Radar stations across the same area, to cost an estimated $160,000,000, would give warning of the approach of hostile aircraft across the polar wastes. American and Canadian military authorities carried out expeditions and maneuvers to study the paralyzing effects of the awful cold of these far latitudes on human and mechanical efficiency.

Isolationist Canadians, particularly the French Canadians, no doubt resented this unexpected inversion of their onetime geographical immunity and the resulting intrusion of Americans in their affairs, just at a time when they were congratulating themselves on the widening gulf between their country and Britain. But whatever the views of these Canadians, they could not deny that, for better or for worse, they were now part and parcel of the strategic interests and requirements of the United States, and the more realistic-minded Canadians of whatever race made a virtue of necessity and began to take the inevitable for granted. The postwar diplomatic behavior of the Soviet Union, the Soviet abuse of the veto in the Security Council, and the deadlock in the Atomic Energy Commission were galling and alarming. During 1946, investigations by a royal commission revealed the existence of a Soviet spy ring, emanating from the Soviet military attaché in Ottawa, which had been trying to obtain information on atomic energy and radar from Canadian government employees and research workers and from the Progressive-Labor (Communist) Member of the Canadian House of Commons. If there was one thing that united Canadians, whether French-speaking or English, whether Catholic or Protestant, whether isolationist on nonisolationist, that thing was the fear of Communism. As we write, the official foreign policy of Canada is co-operation with the United States and Britain, and Canadian opinion has come out strongly on the side of Western Union and the North Atlantic Pact.

Australia and New Zealand presented a wholly different set of circumstances and consequently a different attitude to Commonwealth relations. Their populations were predominantly of British origin, and neither had large minority or immigrant groups which could exercise a discordant influence on national policy. Consequently they were Dominions which, though more distant from Britain geographically, had closer ties of sentiment with her than any other territory of the Commonwealth. But the ties were not allowed to prejudice their independence. And their record gave them every claim to independence. Their contingents in the two World Wars had always won the highest military honors — it used to be said by the Germans that the appearance of an Anzac division in the line could always be taken as a sign that serious "business" was afoot. They were represented at international conferences by men both forceful and outspoken.

Australia's post-1945 policy seemed a contradiction of assertiveness and uncertainty. Released from the overwhelming fear of foreign conquest, she hardly knew where her future security lay; she both resented and welcomed the admitted American paramountcy in the Pacific. Thus, to give one example, she demanded in 1946 that American forces evacuate Manus Island in the Admiralty Islands north of New Guinea which, during the war, the United States Navy at a cost of $400,000,000 had constructed into a first-class base, even though she lacked the means to use it herself and even though, when she had re-established possession, she did not provide so much as a caretaker force for its minimum maintenance. Australian opinion, nonetheless, showed the keenest interest in American participation in future Pacific defense. In the early months of 1948, Menzies, leader of the Opposition in the Australian Parliament, was advocating a Pacific Pact, on the lines of the proposed North Atlantic Pact, to include Australia, New Zealand, India, Pakistan, Ceylon, and the United States, and arguing that, in essence, the menace in the East was the same as the menace in Europe — it was the same Communist menace on both sides of the world. Then, as if to make her influence felt in another direction, Australia participated in the Asian Conference at Delhi in January 1949, held to condemn "Dutch aggression in Indonesia."

South Africa was the one Dominion in the post-1945 years which still enjoyed a relative strategic isolation and could consequently indulge the luxury of restive internal politics undisturbed by external threats. She regarded all African affairs as her affairs, her cardinal policy was the security and *status quo* of the African continent, and she claimed to be as interested in the Mediterranean Sea as in the Indian or South Atlantic oceans. The decline of French and Italian, and the disappearance of the German, influence in Africa had left herself and Britain — and perhaps Egypt — as the only countries with the pretensions of a Power in her part of the world. But the growing divergence of view, as between her Boer and British citizens, regarding the treatment of her colored peoples and concerning the part that those colored peoples should be expected to play in their own future, infected her entire relationship with the British tropical African colonies, where far-reaching economic developments were in prospect and where a liberal racial policy was the order of the day. Her handling of her Indian minority was a matter of increasing resentment in India and of embarrassment to Britain.

In September 1939, Smuts had formed a coalition government and, in addition to the premiership, had taken the ministries of Defense and of External Affairs. For six years he had guided a loyal South African participation in the war. Smuts himself had played the role of a representative Allied statesman and cofounder of the United Nations. Nationalist parties under Hertzog and Malan had tried, but failed, to form a united Opposition. Hertzog, moreover, had fouled his own nest with his pro-Nazi utterances. In 1942 he had died, and the extreme Malan found himself alone as Nationalist leader. Meanwhile the German invasion and treatment of Holland had clinched the sympathies of the Boers with the Allied cause. South African forces fought in Kenya, Ethiopia, North Africa, and afterward in Europe. But 1945 brought back the old-time rifts. The Indian question in Natal and the Transvaal was already to the fore before the war was over. Serious droughts and more serious soil erosion gave great distress to farmers. A cabinet reshuffle left Smuts and his United party alone in the government. The United Nations General Assembly declined to approve South Africa's incorporation of South-West Africa and failed to obtain South Africa's consent to the transference of the territory to the new Trusteeship Council. In the spring of 1947, the King and the royal family made a state visit to South Africa, and the evident enthusiasm with which they were received perhaps concealed the approaching Nationalist swing of South African politics. At elections in May 1948, Smuts was unexpectedly defeated. Malan formed a government with strongly secessionist aims and a declared intention to rescind recent grants of parliamentary representation to Indian and native communities.

It is too early to say how permanent Malan's type of nationalism may be or how long South Africa's favored strategic isolation will last. It is our own view that Boer nationalism is a provincial anachronism out of touch with the present course of world affairs. A threat to the Mediterranean would at once redound to the importance of the Cape route and to the British naval base at Simonstown. The trans-African air routes of the future, the discovery of uranium in the Congo, and Britain's economic plans in the tropical colonies will all have far-reaching effects on South Africa. Nor will it be possible much longer to overlook the fact that Negro political consciousness in Africa, however primitive or embryonic it may now seem, may take a Communist form.

India's attitude to Commonwealth relations in the immediate postwar period was still uncertain. She was a new Dominion in 1947, beset by internal troubles and by the administrative chaos consequent on the withdrawal of British officials (pp. 911–12). She was living down old hatreds, conscious of her military weakness, and undecided whether she would even continue in the Commonwealth in allegiance to the King. Yet one of the happy surprises of India's first years of independence was the high level of statesmanship of her leaders in the international field.

India's co-operation with the United Nations was not in doubt. From the foundation of the organization she was an enthusiastic member, and her Prime Minister, Nehru, on more than one occasion, reiterated his adherence to it. There was more than a little of Gandhi's teaching in modern India's expressed belief in the ideals of peace and in the folly of war as a means of settling international disputes. But in India, as in other nations of the Commonwealth, the last word lay with interest and strategy. India stood on the brink of Soviet Asia within bomber range of Soviet Turkestan. She was dependent on Britain for the bulk of her military supplies and for technical instruction. Yet, her possible Allies in the event of war, Britain and the United States, lay at the two further ends of the world and might hardly be in a position to bring her aid. Her alignment in any definite defensive bloc might provoke the very attack which it was intended to prevent. All in all, India's obvious policy was neutrality. As Nehru, in a speech in 1948, put it: "It is not our business to enter into other people's quarrels . . . I have come to the conclusion that the less we interfere in international conflicts the better, unless our own interest is involved. . . . It is not in consonance with our dignity just to interfere without any effect being produced. Either we should be strong enough to produce some effect or we should not interfere at all."

While advocating neutrality, India nevertheless evinced a tendency to take the initiative — not the leadership, as Nehru was careful to say — in East Asian affairs. In March 1947, before the attainment of Dominion status, an Asian Relations Conference was held at Delhi "to focus attention on the social, economic and cultural problems of the different countries of Asia." It was attended by delegations from twenty-four countries, including Turkey, Burma, China, Korea, Malaya, Viet Nam (Indo-China), the Philippines, and the Soviet Asian Republics, but not from Moslem India or the Arab states. Both Gandhi and Nehru were active at its sessions. But, apart from some discussion of "imperialist domination," of immigration, and of an Asian neutrality pact or Asian "Monroe Doctrine," the Conference concerned itself with questions of welfare, agriculture, science, and education. Of far greater importance from the political point of view was the Asian Conference of January 1949, also at Delhi, which issued a joint protest condemning "Dutch aggression in Indonesia." It was attended by delegations from nineteen countries — including, as we have said, Australia.

One complicating factor in India's foreign and Commonwealth relations was Pakistan. While India herself had it in her to become a unit with a national and cultural viability of her own, Pakistan, divided in two pieces, leaned heavily upon her affiliation with the wider Moslem world; and, while India took her place naturally as a Far Eastern Asian state, Pakistan tended to think of herself as a Middle Eastern state closer to a possible Arab League. There was little prospect of a common policy between an India and a Pakistan so oppositely inclined.

Finally there was Ireland. There was always Ireland! Eire had declared herself neutral in September 1939, and remained so throughout the war. Her Prime Minister, De Valera, refrained from raising controversial issues and made only occasional passing references to Partition, "the unnatural dismemberment" of Northern Ireland from the South which was "the obstacle to unified defense." Eire suffered severe shipping shortages and consequent coal and gasoline shortages, and in general she was far from finding herself in the favored economic position she had enjoyed in the First World War. The use of her ports was strictly denied to the British Navy (see p. 336). The diplomatic representatives of the Axis remained in Dublin, converting the city, as the British said, into a second Lisbon, a veritable hive of enemy espionage and propaganda. In 1944 the government rejected requests from the United States and Britain for their expulsion. In May 1945, De Valera expressed his formal condolences to the German minister in Dublin on the death of

Hitler. Meanwhile, of course, Northern Ireland had entered the war as part of the United Kingdom and had played a full and loyal part in it. Londonderry somewhat compensated for the loss of the neutral Eire ports.

The end of the war in 1945 immediately revived an interest in Eire's international status. De Valera was at pains to develop his thesis of "external association." "We are an independent Republic," he said, "associated as a matter of external policy with the States of the British Commonwealth." In June 1947, in the Dail, he further defined his position in the words: "As a matter of external policy we are associated with the States of the British Commonwealth of Nations. We are not members of it. . . . If [those States] regard the existence of the King as a necessary link, if they consider that it is the bond they have, then we have not got that bond." Nonetheless, he reaffirmed his adherence to the External Relations Act of 1936, by which Eire had accepted the King "for the purposes of the appointment of diplomatic and consular representatives and the conclusion of international agreements" (see p. 335).

But generally, in the first postwar years, Eire was more concerned with reconstruction and with the usual contemporary problems of trade deficits and the dollar shortage. There were only intermittent references to Partition in the debates in the Dail. Eire applied for membership in the United Nations in 1946 and again in 1947, her application on each occasion being vetoed in the Security Council by the Soviet Union. However, Eire was included in the European Recovery Program and was one of the first countries to receive assistance. It seemed at this time that Eire had somewhat forsaken her fractious past and would lie quietly on the fringes of Commonwealth and international politics.

But, at elections in February 1948, De Valera and his Fianna Fail party lost their absolute majority in the Dail, and a coalition of former antigovernment parties was formed by Costello, leader of the Fine Gael party. The new government's platform was entirely one of domestic and industrial measures. It was therefore a matter of some surprise, in July 1948, when McBride, Costello's Minister for External Affairs, delivered himself, apropos of Western Union, as follows: "Our usefulness in this respect is largely nullified by the fact that we ourselves suffer from an injustice, in that our country is artificially divided against the overwhelming majority of the people. . . . The continuance of Partition precludes us from taking our rightful place in the affairs of Europe." Costello, visiting the United States and Canada shortly afterward, made statements to the effect that his government would shortly proceed to the repeal of the External Relations Act. And, sure enough, in December 1948, the Dail passed a Republic of Ireland Act, repealing the External Relations Act and incidentally renaming the country "the Republic of Ireland," thus breaking the last tenuous tie with the British Crown. The Republic was formally inaugurated in Dublin on Easter Monday, April 18, 1949.

Sir Basil Brooke, Prime Minister of Northern Ireland, stoutly reaffirmed Northern Ireland's loyalty to the Crown, to Britain, and to the Commonwealth. The British Government itself took the line that Partition was none of its business and was for Irishmen to settle, that it would not support any changes in Ireland to the prejudice of the constitutional position of Northern Ireland against the express wishes of the Northern Irish people, and that, finally, if Southern Ireland was now seceding from the Commonwealth, as the new act seemed to imply, then it was mainly interested in regularizing the status of Irish residents in Britain.

From what we have tried to say in this section, it would appear that the several British Dominions have their own special problems. Foreign policy is "a function of each rather than a function of all." The great question is not just that of "liquidating an empire" but of recognizing that here is a widely scattered group of sovereign states of diverse origins, races, economies, and strategies, but with an infinitely valuable historical and ideological link. The association of such a group of nations in peace or war cannot be other than a voluntary one. In their remarkable elasticity, they will come together or stand apart as seems best to them under ever changing circumstances. Whatever may happen, it is unlikely that these nations, unconsciously conforming to the practical empiricism of the British character, will ever agree to neat or literal political instruments binding them in advance to unknown and contingent situations. They may sympathize with, they may individually join, this or that regional arrangement, such as Western Union or the North Atlantic Pact; but they will hardly join it as a Commonwealth bloc.

At the Conference of Commonwealth Prime Ministers in London in April 1949, a formula was devised which would enable India to become "a sovereign independent Republic" while yet retaining her full membership in the Commonwealth under the King as "the Head" of that Commonwealth. "Accordingly the United Kingdom, Canada, Australia, New Zealand, South Africa, India, Pakistan, and Ceylon hereby declare that they remain united as free and equal members of the Commonwealth of Nations, freely cooperating in the pursuit of peace, liberty and progress."

51 EASTERN EUROPE AND THE SOVIET UNION

In Chapters 12 and 24 we gave the name of "Intermediate Europe" to the band of lesser states stretching from north to south — Finland, Estonia, Latvia, Lithuania, Poland, Czechoslovakia, Austria, Hungary, Rumania, Yugoslavia, Albania, Bulgaria, Greece — and we might add Ruthenia and the Ukraine (see pp. 175 and 384). Geography, economics, and population have made this a mixed and checkered territory. Unlike Western Europe, it never experienced a common cultural consciousness. It always lay at the fringes of great historic movements — Catholicism, Orthodoxy, the Renaissance, and the Reformation. It was the sport of greater Powers on either side of it. Before 1914, Austria, Germany, Russia, and Turkey disputed it, and its fluctuating frontiers responded to their diplomacy and warfare. After 1918, Pilsudskian Poland, the Little Entente, Balkan union, and variously mooted Danubian schemes formed, or attempted to form, regional combinations within it; France, with her alliance system, tried to exercise an anti-German hegemony over it; in 1938–41, Nazi Germany penetrated, conquered, and "co-ordinated" it; in 1945, almost the whole area, with the exception of Finland, Greece, and Austria, passed under Soviet control. As we write, Intermediate Europe, again with the exception of Finland, Greece, and Austria, signifies the "Iron Curtain" states. It is proper perhaps that we should consider the post-1945 affairs of these states, and of the Soviet Union, in a single chapter.

THE SOVIET UNION

The German invasion of 1941–42 cost the Soviet Union more than half of its output of coal, two-thirds of its iron ore, one-half of its steel, one-quarter of its engineering industries, and nearly half of its grain lands. In partial compensation for the disaster, the Soviet successfully effected a prodigious evacuation of industrial equipment, much of it to areas beyond the Urals and, in the second year of the war, Soviet industry claimed to be producing a larger quantity of arms and military equipment than in 1940. By the summer of 1943, Soviet production of tanks and aircraft may have surpassed the German production of the same date.

In the devastation of their retirement in 1943–45, the Germans acted with all their native thoroughness. "German destructiveness did not consist merely in blowing up factories and power stations and locomotives and tractors," writes Crankshaw, "but was carried down to the last detail — so that all the way from Mozhaisk to Smolensk, for example, every single telegraph pole along that interminable railway line had been chopped down to six inches from the ground, and wheelbarrows were destroyed or removed with as single-minded a passion as five-ton trucks and tractors . . . The present shortage of tractors, horses, and cows to pull the ploughs, which themselves no longer exist, is such that a most familiar sight in the sowing of this year (1947) was to see twenty or thirty peasant women turning the soil of a hundred acre field with spades and dibbing the potatoes in by hand." [1]

According to one Soviet spokesman the Germans inflicted $128,000,000,000 damage in a territory of a former population of 88,000,000. They left 25,000,000 persons homeless; tore up 40,000 miles of railroad; destroyed industrial equipment normally employing 4,000,000 workers, coal mines normally producing 100,000,000 tons of coal per annum, and iron mills normally smelting 11,000,000 tons of iron per annum. Loss of life to the Soviet Union, military and civilian, in the course of the war has been put at anything from 15,000,000–20,000,000. [2]

Some recoveries were effected in the wake of the Red Army, notably the restocking of farms. In the autumn of 1945 it was officially stated that three-quarters of the arable land in the Ukraine had been restored to cultivation. By New Year's Day 1946, 2,500,000 persons had been "transferred" from dugouts to dwellings. But long-term reconstruction was launched with the fourth Five-Year Plan in March 1946, the first of the three successive postwar Five-Year Plans, intended eventually to surpass the "bourgeois, capitalist countries" of Europe and America. Targets for 1950 were modestly put at 25,400,000 tons of steel, 250,000,000 tons of coal, and 35,400,000 tons of oil, [3] while the output of foodstuffs and consumer goods was to equal the prewar level, and industry as a whole to operate at 48 per cent above that level. Simultaneously the Soviet Government attacked the problem of postwar inflation with characteristic ruthlessness. A new ruble note was issued, exchangeable for the old at the rate of one to ten; bank deposits up to 3,000 rubles were exchangeable at par; and savings of co-operatives and collectives at the rate of four to five.

Political reconstruction was simultaneous. Elections to the two chambers of the Supreme Soviet were held in February 1946 (see p. 290). Several government changes were shortly announced. The aged President Kalinin resigned on grounds of ill-health, to be succeeded by the former trade-union leader, Shvernik. A Council of "Ministers" replaced the former Council of People's Commissars, of which Stalin remained Premier or Chairman, and Molotov remained Deputy Premier and Foreign Minister (see p. 291). The N.K.V.D. took the name "MVD" (see p. 544). The Politburo and other party organizations presumably were unaffected and remained as before (see p. 277). Stalin retained control over the Red Army by virtue of his offices as Marshal, Supreme Commander in Chief, and Minister of the Armed Forces. A modernization of the civil and criminal codes was projected; the death penalty was abolished. At the same time there was a shake-up of political orthodoxies allowed to lapse during the war, a rooting-out of "grave ideological shortcomings" and other "survivals of bourgeois, capitalist thought," all evidenced by a new wave of purges of party officials, factory and collective managers, writers, artists, and scientists. The controversies

over Varga, the economist, and Lysenko, the geneticist, were the more publicized counterparts of the process.

But there were betraying indications early in 1947 that the Soviet Union
was running into an economic crisis similar to that of Western Europe. Severe droughts in many areas had spoiled the first postwar harvest of 1946,
and the harvest of 1947 was not much better. Nevertheless, with a sort of aggressive flourish, food rationing was declared abolished in December 1947.
The shortage of man power, resulting from the losses of the war, was the
most serious debit item in the economic balance sheet. Concurrently the international situation had been deteriorating. The Truman Doctrine was
enunciated in March 1947, and the European Recovery Program in June.

Soviet needs had been imperative enough in 1945–46. Harsh reparations
clauses at Soviet behest had been written into the peace treaties with Italy,
Rumania, Bulgaria, Hungary, and Finland. The deadlock in the Foreign
Ministers Council over the German and Austrian settlements had been
largely caused by reparations difficulties (see p. 814). Soviet troops had
stripped occupation zones from Germany to Manchuria of movable goods.
But in 1947 an even greater importunity was manifest. The Communization
of the Eastern European states in 1945–46 had had in the main a political
and military objective — the same objective, in fact, as had inspired the Soviet security pacts of 1925–37 (pp. 540–41); in 1947 the Soviet Government
clearly purposed the total incorporation of these states into its current Five-
Year Plan and regarded their political reorganization as subsidiary thereto.
The end of UNRRA, which had so generously aided these states in the immediate postwar years, had the effect of turning their attention to new possible sources of supplies. The enforced withdrawal of Czechoslovakia from
the European Recovery Program in June 1947, and the Communist coup in
1948 signified that this rich, industrial land could not be allowed to desert
the Soviet economic system. But the same pattern of Soviet domination was
demonstrable, if in less dramatic form, in all the "Iron Curtain" states. The
Soviet Government encouraged among them the conclusion of a series of interlocking trade agreements and bilateral military alliances. From time to
time it eased up on its demands for reparations, notably from Hungary and
Rumania, in favor of compensatory commercial interchanges. Thus Intermediate Europe, whose main economic ties had formerly been with Germany, was assimilated to a new eastward clientship.

At the end of September 1947, at Warsaw, a conference was held of the
Communist parties of Yugoslavia, Bulgaria, Rumania, Hungary, Poland,
France, Czechoslovakia, Italy, and the Soviet Union. It passed "a resolution
on the interchange of experience and co-ordination of activities" and decided
to set up an information bureau, or Cominform as it came to be called, in
Belgrade. The conference was addressed by Zhdanov, Chairman of the Supreme Soviet and Secretary of the Central Committee of the Communist
party, in one of the weightiest expositions of Soviet foreign policy since
the war:

The Soviet's armed forces in the Patriotic War, said Zhdanov, had liberated the freedom-loving peoples of Central and Southeastern Europe from

the Fascist and Hitlerite invaders, removed the collaborators, permitted the workers, peasants, and progressive intellectuals to form People's Republics, and introduced measures of agrarian reform and nationalization. The war had eliminated the capitalist Powers, Germany, Italy, and Japan, reduced France to no significance, and indeed left only the two capitalist Powers, the United States and Britain, of which the second, much weakened, was wholly dependent on the first. The United States had entered the war at the concluding stage, when the issue was already decided, its territory had not been bombed or occupied, and its human casualties were relatively small. For the United States the war was "primarily a spur to extensive industrial growth and enrichment." Since the war the United States had been utilizing its military and economic might "in a new frankly predatory and expansionist course," designed to establish its imperialist world supremacy and reduce its capitalist partners, notably Britain, to subordination and dependence. The obstacle to these designs was the Soviet Union and its growing international influence in the new democracies and among the workers of all countries, including the workers of America, "who do not want a new war for the supremacy of their oppressors."

Meanwhile, continued Zhdanov, the more malignant warmongers, following Churchill's lead, were hatching plots for a preventive war upon the Soviet Union and for the use of America's temporary monopoly of the atomic weapon. A democratic, anti-imperialist camp, headed by the Soviet Union, was now aligned against an antidemocratic, imperialist camp, headed by the United States. The one pursued a policy of peace; the other had sabotaged all resolutions in the United Nations for the reduction of armaments and the prohibition of atomic energy for warlike purposes, maintained "the largest army in the capitalist world," was preparing bacteriological weapons, building a chain of naval and aerial bases, standardizing arms and equipment with its partners, and subsidizing warlike preparations with financial assistance. The Truman Doctrine and the Marshall Plan, though differing in form of presentation, were both expressions of the same policy. But there were also weighty reasons in the threatened economic crisis in the United States "for Marshall's official generosity." The Soviet Union had never objected to taking advantage of foreign credits, but such credits must be "free from enslaving conditions." A special mission therefore devolved on Communist parties today to resist capitalist expansion and aggression, to uphold their national honor and independence, and to prevent the enthrallment of Europe.

In July and August, 1948, at Belgrade, in pursuance of the Foreign Ministers' declaration in 1946 (see p. 804), a conference was held to discuss the navigation of the Danube. It was attended by representatives of the United States, Britain, France, and the Soviet Union, in their capacity as members of the Foreign Ministers Council, and by representatives of the Danubian countries, Czechoslovakia, Hungary, Yugoslavia, Bulgaria, Rumania, and the Ukraine. A representative from Austria attended in an advisory capacity. The contention of the Western Powers that the Danube Statute of 1922 (see p. 207) was still valid was voted out by the Soviet Union and its satellites.

A Draft Convention was adopted establishing a new Danube Commission, consisting of one member of each of the Danubian countries, thus excluding the former Western European members of the Danube Commission of 1922. The United States representatives at the conference voted against adoption of the Draft Convention; the British and French representatives abstained.

POLAND

The Polish question had been the first open point at issue between East and West in the new phase of power politics. In the closing months of the Second World War, the question had cast a heavy gloom over Allied unity and over the hopes and ideals of the United Nations. Poland had not attended the San Francisco Conference, and she had become a member of the United Nations after an admitted legal equivocation. At the Crimea Conference in February 1945, it had been decided that the Provisional Government, "now functioning in Poland," should be reorganized "on a broader democratic basis" as the Polish Provisional Government of National Unity, which should then be pledged "to the holding of free and unfettered elections [in Poland] as soon as possible." (See p. 776.) This government was eventually installed in Warsaw, with Beirut, Osóbka-Morawski, and Gomulka, all of the former Provisional Government, as President, Premier, and Vice-Premier respectively and with Mikolajczyk of the government in exile in London as another Vice-Premier. But the rump of the government in exile in London refused to dissolve itself, and numbers of men serving in Polish contingents in Britain, Italy, and the Middle East did not return home.

The country itself was in a pitiable condition. It had been bombed, fought over, and looted by two great armies. Under the Nazi occupation it had suffered the treatment which we described in Chapter 43 (pp. 715–16 and 717–18). Nazi extermination policies had fallen most heavily on those classes of education and technical skill which were now required for reconstruction. The Soviet Government had re-established the Polish eastern frontier of September 28, 1939 and had permitted Polish occupation of Eastern Germany up to the Oder-Neisse line under the guise of a Polish "Administration" which was to all intents and purposes an annexation. Native Germans in East Prussia and Silesia were expelled in the thousands, and the area thus vacated was opened to Polish colonization. In effect, the Poland of 1919–39 had been moved bodily a hundred miles westward. In September 1946 the government announced a Three-Year Plan for the reconstruction of large-scale industry as a state enterprise, and a beginning was made with the collectivization of the land.

The promised elections in Poland were not held till January 1947, and they were then neither free nor unfettered. Numbers of both the candidates and the election watchers of Mikolajczyk's Peasant party were in jail on polling day. The Polish Government, in reply to a note from the United States, declared that the elections would be conducted "in accordance with the traditions of Polish democracy." The official election results gave 383 seats to the Communist progovernment bloc, 27 to the Peasant party, and 34 to lesser parties. Mikolajczyk resigned and was succeeded as Deputy Premier by Gomulka, a Communist. In October 1947, just after the establishment of the Cominform, he fled to England.

The Polish Government proceeded with its double program of political consolidation and economic recovery. The Socialists were merged with the Communists. The Peasant party, weakened by the loss of its leader, Mikolajczyk, offered little resistance, Osóbka-Morawski and Gomulka were relieved of their offices for their lukewarm attitude to the Cominform and for other rightist deviations. There were even arrests of officers of the partisan army of the Warsaw rising of 1944. The youth of the country was enrolled in a nation-wide "Service of Poland" and subjected to a mixture of military training and ideological indoctrination. Only the Catholic Church opposed the universal process, and rumbles of future religious conflict were sounding when Cardinal Hlond, Primate of Poland, died in October 1948.

HUNGARY

At the end of 1944, in the wake of the Red Army, General Miklos had set up a liberation government at Debrecen under Soviet auspices (see p. 774). "People's courts" conducted a purge of former collaborators and "reactionaries." Sweeping agrarian reforms broke up the old estates and redistributed the land to peasants in lots of 5 to 20 acres. A Soviet-Hungarian commercial treaty, negotiated in great secrecy, signified the virtual economic subjugation of the country to the Soviet interest. However, elections for a Hungarian National Assembly, held in November 1945, resulted in a victory for the moderate agrarian Smallholders' party and a decisive Communist defeat. Hungary was declared a republic with a constitution that read "like the Bill of Rights and the Four Freedoms rolled into one." Tildy, a Smallholder, was elected first President, and Nagy, another Smallholder, formed a coalition government largely composed of his party.

But one of Nagy's Vice-Premiers was Rákosi, Secretary of the Hungarian Communist party, a former colleague of Béla Kun (see p. 199) ; and Nagy's Minister of the Interior was Rajk, a Communist who by virtue of his office controlled the police and exercised a wide jurisdiction defined in a "Law for the Defense of Hungarian Democracy." The Hungarian peace treaty was signed in Paris in February 1947, but the Soviet commander, General Sviridov, was still in Hungary with enough Soviet forces at hand when the new crisis developed. Early in 1947 the Minister of the Interior, claiming to have discovered a plot for the restoration of the former Regent, Horthy, instituted a wave of arrests directed particularly against the Smallholders' party. Kovacs, the Smallholders' secretary, was himself arrested by the Soviet authorities and was afterward reported to have made confessions while in prison, implicating other members of his party. In May the government was remodeled. Nagy, then in Switzerland, resigned and refused to return home. Dinnyes, a Smallholder but a more pliant one, became Premier and announced a Three-Year Plan, virtually a Communist program of national reconstruction. Elections were held in August 1947, under a revised electoral law disfranchising political undesirables, and resulted in general Communist gains. A new Communist-dominated government was formed, though still with Dinnyes as Premier. Throughout these events, strong notes were exchanged between the United States and British Governments and the Soviet Government, each side accusing the other of breaches of the Crimea agreements and of "flagrant interference" in Hungarian affairs.

In June 1948 the new government passed a bill secularizing education in Hungary. Cardinal Mindszenty, the Roman Catholic Primate, protested vigorously in pastoral letters and ordered the tolling of the church bells as a sign of mourning. The disagreement between government and cardinal developed into a regular state-church conflict which both sides, and indeed all Europe, were evidently regarding as a trial of strength. Two days after Christmas 1948, the Cardinal was arrested and brought to trial before a "people's court" for high treason and conspiracy against the state. The incident recalled the Stepinac case in Yugoslavia not long since (see p. 855). On the first day of the trial a letter was read, alleged to have been written by the Cardinal, in which he confessed his "essential guilt." In a cruel, anticlimactic atmosphere of puzzlement and dismay, the Cardinal was sentenced to life imprisonment.

Meanwhile, in July 1948, President Tildy had been forced to resign and was succeeded by the pro-Communist Szakasits; in December 1948 the Premier, Dinnyes, was likewise forced to resign and was succeeded by the pro-Communist Dobi. Rajk became Foreign Minister. Early in 1949 a new "People's Independence Front" was formed largely under Rákosi's influence and, in elections in May, this new organization received a vote of some 90 per cent. Rákosi announced forthcoming constitutional changes on Soviet lines. The steady political consolidation of Hungary was beginning to claim victims from its own former protagonists. Tito in Yugoslavia, as we shall shortly relate, had lately shown that even the most trusted might stray from correctitude, and any suspects of a similar deviationism in neighboring states must needs be brought to book. In September 1949, accordingly, Rajk was tried for being "a Fascist spy," "a Trotskyite saboteur," "an American imperialist agent," "a Tito renegade" — to mention but a few of the decorative epithets bandied about in courtroom and press on this occasion; he confessed his guilt on all charges, and was hanged.

CZECHOSLOVAKIA

Czechoslovakia's new phase of alignment with the Soviet Union had begun with a Czech-Soviet treaty of alliance signed in 1943 with the Czech government in exile. Recollections of Munich, the fear and hatred of Germany, sentiments of Slavic solidarity, and the recent victories of the Red Army all operated in the same direction. Beneš visited Moscow in March 1945 in order to dramatize his return to Czechoslovakia from the East and, while there, he agreed to form a liberation government including Communists and Slovaks. In the first week of May, Patton with the United States First Army could have occupied Prague but was restrained by Eisenhower, who did not wish to prejudice his good relations with the Soviet General Staff. Czech partisans, anticipating liberation, were in full revolt and the German surrender already signed at Reims, when on May 9, 1945 the first Red Army units drove into Prague.

On the whole, Czechoslovakia had escaped the worst ravages of the war. The Protectorate of the occupation years had been subject to the spoliation and persecutions we described in Chapter 43 (pp. 719–20), but physical damage was relatively light; and Slovakia had been one of Hitler's nursed and favored model provinces. Prague in 1945 was in happy contrast to devastated Warsaw and Budapest. The country therefore settled down to the tasks of peace with distinct advantages. The government, under the presidency of Beneš, took the form of a Provisional National Assembly until elections could be arranged for a Constituent Assembly to devise a new constitution. Presidential decrees required the breaking up of large landed estates and the nationalization of industries, banks, and insurance. A purge was instituted of all former collaborators. Hácha died in prison; Moravec committed suicide; Tiso was later shot. A beginning was made with the expulsion of 3,000,000 Germans from the Sudetenland and of 650,000 Magyars from southern Slovakia. Teschen was reoccupied by Czech forces. Ruthenia was ceded to the Soviet Union.

The political history of post-1945 Czechoslovakia really opens with the elections for the Constituent Assembly in May 1946. Of a heavy "compulsory" poll, 38 per cent of the votes went to the Communist party, and the remainder to seven other "National Front" left-wing and Catholic parties. The Assembly elected Beneš President of the Republic. On July 8, 1946, Gottwald, the Communist leader, took office as Premier with eight members of his party, in a cabinet of twenty-three. Jan Masaryk, of no party, was Foreign Minister; Nosek, a Communist, formerly trained in the methods of the Soviet N.K.V.D., was Minister of the Interior and by virtue of that office, Chief of Police.

The Communist pattern was not immediately imposed on the country. Nationalization halted at 75 per cent of industrial capacity; farms were not collectivized; the labor unions retained their political independence; religious conscience and practice were free. Beneš and Jan Masaryk were appropriately friendly to the Soviet Union while still cherishing their former attachments with Western countries and the United States. The first signs of trouble occurred on July 1, 1947, when the Czechoslovak Government decided to co-operate in the Marshall Plan. Gottwald was summoned to Moscow for reprimand, and Czechoslovakia was not represented among the sixteen nations of the European Recovery Program. A five-year Czech-Soviet trade agreement was signed by way of compensation.

The familiar campaign for "the second Revolution" was launched in February 1948. Nosek, the Minister of the Interior, began by replacing eight ranking officials with Communists. Twelve ministers of the cabinet demanded that the officials be reinstated and, when Nosek refused, they resigned "deeming it pointless to continue attending meetings of a government whose decisions were not carried out." The Czechoslovak Communist party at once issued a manifesto calling for the support of the workers; action committees began to "take over" the press and radio; the usual plots were unearthed against "reactionaries" and "foreign imperialists." On February 25, Beneš gave way and accepted the resignations of the twelve ministers. Two days later Gottwald was sworn in as Premier with twelve members of his party in a cabinet of twenty-four. Jan Masaryk remained Foreign Minister, the only non-Communist from the previous cabinet. To complete his triumph, Nosek instituted a purge of journalists, army officers, university professors, and other actual or potential critics of the new regime. Throughout these eventful days, there were virtually no popular opposition or counterdemonstrations. Beneš, said to be in ill-health, made no public appearances. On March 10, a couple of days after birthday celebrations in honor of his father, the first President of Czechoslovakia, Jan Masaryk was reported to have committed suicide by throwing himself from a window of the Foreign Ministry.

YUGOSLAVIA

The end of the war found Yugoslavia economically gutted and politically rent asunder by a many-edged civil war which had shed more of the nation's blood and energy than the war against the Nazi invader. Ostensibly the agreement of June 1944 between Marshal Tito and Subasich was still in force (see p. 721). Under its terms and under the promptings of the Crimea Conference, Tito's Council for the National Liberation was to be broadened to include as members Deputies of irreproachable record from the last pre-war Yugoslav National Assembly. And accordingly, in Belgrade in March 1945, a provisional government took office with Tito as Premier and Minister of National Defense, Subasich as Foreign Minister, and three other ministers hailing from the Yugoslav government in exile in London.

Meanwhile the once unitary kingdom was being reorganized into six constituent federal states. The former entities of Serbia, Croatia, and Slovenia reappeared, and along with them a new Montenegro and a new Bosnia-Herzegovina. The sixth state, a republic of Macedonia, was made out of Yugoslavia's ten thousand square miles of that ancient and much lacerated territory and was formally instituted, amid a fever of cultivated Macedonian national consciousness, with its own language and alphabet, and with its own native citizens at the head of its affairs. The new federalism doubtless brought great satisfaction to Yugoslavia's various centrifugal groups, whose old hostilities the war, the occupation, and the resistance had all so much intensified.

But, as was soon apparent, it was not these federal states, but Tito's central government in Belgrade — and the Communist party — which held the realities of power. That government clearly considered itself as something quite other than a neutral and interim custodian of authority until such time as elections could be held to ascertain more fairly the people's desired political form and color. During the resistance, the Communists had invariably dominated the regional committees of the Council for the National Liberation (see p. 721), and these same Communists now occupied the chief administrative posts in the federal states. Nor were the London exiles in the central government of sufficient numerical strength or ministerial rank to offer an effective barrier to well-organized Communism. As for the Marshal, he was now apostrophized by the journalists and poets of the land as "the greatest son of Mother Yugoslavia" and with other lyrical superlatives. The techniques of mass adulation of the leader followed an established pattern, and the chants which greeted his every appearance were disquietingly reminiscent of the salutations once practiced in Berlin and Rome.

The Communist party, however, did not come into the open. It published no membership figures nor the names of its Central Committee. It operated from behind a National Front, ostensibly embracing several political parties and pledged to republicanism, to private property, and to a full roster of civil rights. The leader of the Democratic party, who was one of the London exiles in the central government — and who had soon resigned from that government because he was never invited to its meetings — tried to organize an Opposition; the Catholic hierarchy in Croatia protested against cases of persecution and violations of civil rights; Subasich made his contribution in a letter of resignation couched in strong language; from London, King Peter denounced the Marshal's dictatorship. But the various political parties had soon to face the unpalatable alternatives of voluntarily merging themselves into the National Front or of dissolving under pressure. In November 1945, elections were held for a bicameral Constituent Assembly, and it was afterward officially announced that the National Front had won 85 per cent of the votes.

The Constituent Assembly met forthwith, abolished the monarchy, and proclaimed the Federal People's Republic of Yugoslavia. On January 31, 1946, after a labor of two months, it unanimously adopted an elaborate federal constitution very much after the pattern of the Soviet constitution of 1936. The provisional government resigned, and a new government succeeded with Tito at its head and all the major portfolios firmly in Communist hands.

It is impossible in these modern totalitarian states to measure the extent of the popular support behind them. Their method of rule, support or no support, is coercion first and eternal vigilance thereafter. Party and police, headed respectively by the party secretary and minister of the interior, exercise their powers without respect for persons, without respect even for the letter of a judicial process, and usually without respect for adverse effects abroad. Collaborators, rivals, suspects of opposition of whatever kind are hounded to their doom. In March 1946 the resistance leader Mihailovich was arraigned for war crimes and for collaboration with the enemy and, after a trial at which American and British officers were prevented from giving evidence, was sentenced to be shot. In October of the same year, Archbishop Stepinac, head of the Catholic hierarchy in Croatia, was sentenced to sixteen years' hard labor. These were men famous beyond their country's frontiers; but we can only guess at the untabulated thousands of lesser known who paid forfeit without the slender comfort of foreign diplomatic protests or of international news dispatches.

Meanwhile Tito had set about repairing the shattered economy of Yugoslavia. When the tide of hostilities had receded, more than half the livestock had gone, practically every truck and automobile, and almost half the peasant carts. The human population had been reduced by 10 per cent. UNRRA provided immediate relief to the extent of 14 per cent of its total expenditure, and millions of Yugoslavs survived the desperate winter of 1945–46 only through its devoted service (see p. 793).

The government's own organized efforts, partly out of necessity, partly out of doctrinaire policy, took the form of the nationalization of industries, sweeping agrarian reforms, and the creation of state corporations for foreign trade, all supervised by a Federal Planning Commission and a Federal Control Commission. Trade agreements were sought out, not only with neighboring regimes in Intermediate Europe, but with any foreign country which had machinery or raw materials to exchange or sell. In April 1947, Tito introduced a Five-Year Plan involving extensive land reclamation, irrigation, industrialization, electrification, and improvements in transport to a total investment of $6,000,000,000. Meanwhile, the people themselves showed a primitive hardihood and recuperative vitality regardless of, and indeed in spite of, their government's official political philosophy, and it remained to be seen how far and how quickly a "plan" could answer their two basic perennial problems, their technical backwardness and rural overpopulation.

The cardinal point of Yugoslavia's foreign policy, given the character of the regime, was the closest association with the Soviet Union. The relationship had been confirmed and typified by a Soviet-Yugoslav treaty of friendship, mutual assistance, and postwar co-operation and by a concurrent trade agreement, both signed in Moscow in April 1945. Yugoslavia identified herself with the Soviet interest in the United Nations; she assisted the Greek guerrillas; she rejected the European Recovery Program; she joined the Cominform. At the same time she cultivated the friendship and co-operation of her Communist neighbors. In August 1947, Dimitrov of Bulgaria was invited to Belgrade to sketch out the general lines of a defensive alliance and of an economic co-operation which was eventually to include a customs union and, in the November following, Dimitrov and Tito met again to sign a treaty of friendship and mutual assistance amid heady talk of Slavic unity in the Balkans.

But this shining fraternalism was not the whole story. Even in 1944–45, despite the fervors of the liberation and of Slavic sentiment, despite the community of doctrine, there were already indications that unshadowed agreement was going to be hard to maintain. Complaints were reaching Moscow regarding the conduct of the Red Army in Yugoslavia. In May 1945, Yugoslav forces had found the forces of the Western Allies blocking their way to Trieste, and subsequently, in the Foreign Ministers Council, Soviet diplomacy had failed to secure to Yugoslavia the possession of that much desired port (pp. 801–802). From time to time, the public pronouncements of Marshal Tito carried a tone of something less than humble subservience to Moscow. In 1946, on the ground of the heavy expense involved, the Yugoslav Government requested that the Soviet recall 60 per cent of the Red Army officers attached to the Yugoslav Army and, in 1948, began to restrict the movement of Soviet civilian technicians in Yugoslavia.

The break came on March 18, 1948, when the Soviet Government, alleging unfriendly treatment, recalled all its officers and technicians from Yugoslavia. An exchange of notes followed between Tito and the Communist party, the one side elaborately refuting the Soviet's charges and professing devotion to the Soviet Union and the other making long grievances of rising wrath. But nowhere did Tito exhibit the required penitence and contrition. On the contrary, Yugoslav Communism, in its pride of achievement and buoyant self-confidence, clearly asserted that it was pursuing a line of its own whensoever local conditions necessitated modifications in the strict application of doctrinal socialization. Each party to the dispute sought the support of the states of the Cominform, but that body, however, showed no wavering in its Soviet allegiance and duly handed down a verdict accusing its brother Yugoslavs of "a hateful policy" dictated by "exaggerated ambition, megalomania, and conceit."

On June 28, 1948 the Cominform expelled Yugoslavia from membership and shortly moved its headquarters to Bucharest. Gradually the Soviet Union and its satellites began to impose economic "sanctions" and to denounce their several treaties with the backslider state. The Five-Year Plan, launched so auspiciously a year before, was in danger of complete breakdown. But Yugoslavia signed compensatory trade agreements with Britain and Italy and negotiated loans from the International Bank and the Export-Import Bank. As we write, Tito appears to be firmly in power in Yugoslavia, while the unresolved Soviet-Yugoslav dispute rises to levels of vituperation altogether new to diplomatic intercourse. But only the future can show to what extent a Communist Yugoslavia can maintain her political and territorial integrity and a genuine economic recovery in isolation from the Great Power to the East to which she owes her very restoration as a state and which has so often proved its infinite resourcefulness in finding the means of enforcing compliance and exacting retribution.

ALBANIA

In December 1944, under President Enver Hoxha, a provisional government took control bearing all the now familiar forms. A Communist-dominated Movement of National Liberation implemented the customary united-front device. A domestic program proposed to end the "feudalism" of Albania's clan system, to redistribute the land to needy peasants, and to bring all mines and refineries under state management. Elections in December 1945 returned a Constituent Assembly composed almost entirely of members of the Movement of National Liberation. A People's Republic of Albania was proclaimed, and a constitution adopted largely modeled on the contemporary constitution of Yugoslavia. Hoxha emerged as Premier, Foreign Minister, and Defense Minister of a new government.

The postwar period had begun with an uneven competition between British and Soviet influence in Albania. British agents in Albania during the war had aroused Hoxha's suspicion by their manifest leaning toward the more conservative resistance groups, and they had patronized the Greeks who were agitating for the annexation of southern Albania. Finally, both the United States and Britain had deferred recognition of the new Albanian regime in default of assurances of fair conduct at the elections to the Constituent Assembly and in default of assurances of the continuing validity of treaties in force at the time of the Italian conquest of 1938. The Soviet Union, on the contrary, from the first had celebrated the new regime with a laudatory press campaign, accorded it unqualified diplomatic recognition, and welcomed it into the sovietized community of Intermediate Europe. Thus Albania gave her every possible support to her great protector, assisted the Greek guerrillas, refused to receive the United Nations' investigating mission from Greece, entered into the closest political and economic ties with Yugoslavia, and then, as obediently, despite her geographical and economic isolation, broke off these relations at the time of the Tito controversy.

Meanwhile the deterioration of Anglo-Albanian relations had ended in an open dispute. In May 1946, Albanian coastal batteries fired on two British warships passing through the Corfu channel. In October, while the Albanian Government was still evading settlement of the incident, two British destroyers struck mines in the same channel and suffered heavy injury and loss of life. The Albanian Government took the initiative in protesting to the United Nations against what it described as a flagrant violation of its territorial waters. In January 1947 the British Government, in turn, after more fruitless correspondence with the Albanian Government, brought the dispute before the Security Council. Two months later the Soviet delegate vetoed a resolution to assess Albania with indirect responsibility for laying the mine field, and the Security Council then resolved, with the Soviet Union and Poland abstaining, to refer the issue to the International Court of Justice.[4]

BULGARIA

Bulgarians dated the new era of their country from September 9, 1944, when, by the *coup d'état* which we described elsewhere (see p. 774), a Soviet-sponsored government and Regency Council had been installed in office. The new Premier, Georgiev, and a number of his colleagues belonged to the Zveno, not a political party but rather a pressure group of army officers and substantial businessmen; but the government as a whole was representative of the wartime alliance of political parties known as the Fatherland Front. The Bulgarian Communists played at first a tactful, half-concealed role in these arrangements, curiously at variance with the reputation which had made them the most resolute and persecuted members of the international movement. Theirs was one of the parties in the Fatherland Front, energetic but not over conspicuous. They held only four of the sixteen ministerial posts in the new government; but two of the posts were the ministries of the Interior and of Justice, which carried with them control over the police and the courts. The party giants, Georgi Dimitrov and Vasil Kolarov, were in the Soviet Union and remained there for another two years awaiting the best psychological moment for their return. Tsola Dragoicheva probably wielded more actual power than any other person in Bulgaria, but she was content to do so from a modest secretarial office.

On October 28, 1944, in Moscow, two months after the end of hostilities, a Bulgarian delegation signed a formal capitulation. Under its terms Bulgaria set about liquidating the errors of her wartime record. She disgorged her territorial gains at the expense of Greece and Yugoslavia, but not of Rumania, and committed herself to support a Soviet army of occupation and to bring war criminals to justice. In pursuance of this praiseworthy objective, the Fatherland Front set up 68 "people's courts," and, in the course of 1945, disposed of 3 regents, 22 ministers, 68 parliamentary deputies, 8 royal councillors, over a score of ranking army officers, and more than 1,500 other persons of varying degrees of eminence. In addition, perhaps ten times as many more of the lesser citizenry enjoyed even slighter judicial formalities as they were sent to their fate.

Economic policy included the usual Communist program, but it was effected cautiously and gradually. Little impression was made upon the way of life of the great mass of small peasant proprietors, constituting three-fourths of Bulgaria's population. But large landed holdings were broken up for redistribution or collectivization, and some progress was made in the absorption of the existing peasant co-operatives. Trade agreements were signed with the Soviet Union in 1945 and thereafter with other neighboring states. A Two-Year Plan of industrial development was issued in April 1947, shortly followed by a law nationalizing industries and mines.

Elections for a national parliament were announced for August 1945 and, as the auspicious date approached, political parties, the Social Democrats and even the powerful Agrarian party, were split, one faction merging with the Fatherland Front, and the other staying uncomfortably outside. As soon as it felt strong enough, the Fatherland Front resorted to the device of submitting to the electorate a single list of 276 candidates, containing the names of 95 Communists, 95 Agrarians, 46 Zveno, and 31 Social Democrats. The United States and British Governments protested against these strange maneuverings and momentarily secured a postponement of the elections and a relaxation of pressure on the Opposition. But the elections took place in mid-November 1945, and the Fatherland Front won the sweeping victory it had planned. Subsequent Anglo-American pressure failed to secure the inclusion of Opposition members in the new government, which was eventually formed in March 1946, under the peremptory personal intervention of Vyshinsky himself, the Soviet Deputy Foreign Minister. Georgiev remained Premier, but he now had an all-Communist roster of ministers.

On September 8, 1946 the government held a plebiscite to permit the Bulgarian people to choose between monarchy and republic. Out of 4,000,000 votes, fewer than 200,000, according to the official reckoning, were cast for the retention of the monarchy. Bulgaria accordingly was proclaimed a republic, and the six-year-old Tsar Simeon went to join his grandfather, Victor Emmanuel of Italy, in exile. Elections for a Constituent Assembly to draw up a republican constitution were held in the following October, and resulted in 366 seats for the Fatherland Front, of which 279 were Communist. Georgi Dimitrov and Vasil Kolarov returned home from the Soviet Union, the former to take office as Premier and the latter as President.

Communism had once more triumphed. All that was left to be done was the final liquidation of surviving resisting elements in the country, notably the national Church, the universities, and the Agrarian party. Petkov, leader of the Agrarian party, was selected as the victim of one of the highly dramatized trials of these times and, despite fresh Anglo-American protests, was duly convicted and hanged. On December 4, 1946, the Constituent Assembly adopted a constitution closely modeled upon that of Yugoslavia. Bulgaria, in effect, was attired in all the conventional vestments of a People's Republic.

The foreign policy of the Fatherland Front began with a strong Slavic orientation. Despite old grievances against Serbia and Yugoslavia, which were seemingly part and parcel of Bulgaria's national existence, despite Bulgaria's pariah-like status in the interwar years and in the days of the Balkan union, and despite the Bulgarian spoliation of Yugoslavia in 1941, there was now a strong current of desire for a reconciliation. The Yugoslavs were no less disposed toward a new start in neighborly relations. In January 1945 the Bulgarian Government issued a statement on its foreign policy covering a diversity of good intentions — toward the Soviet Union "eternal friendship," toward Yugoslavia "the closest possible alliance and fraternal collaberation," toward the rest of the world "friendly relations."

In 1947 a part of this policy was realized in a Bulgar-Yugoslav commercial agreement. In midsummer Dimitrov paid a ceremonial visit to Yugoslavia, and at the town of Bled he and Tito announced an extensive program of political alliance and economic co-operation. In November Tito visited Bulgaria and signed an alliance of friendship and mutual assistance, the basic provisions and language of which were now standard in agreements between the Communist-controlled states of Intermediate Europe. But in January 1948 it seems that Dimitrov, this man who was the very personification of Communism, in a moment of exuberance went beyond the bounds of discretion. He announced that, when the time was ripe, the countries of Eastern Europe and the Balkans intended to form a federation of states in alliance with the Soviet Union. A fortnight later Pravda struck down the fervid Dimitrov; the countries mentioned, it said, had no need for a "problematical and artificial federation or customs union"; their proper task was the protection of their independence and sovereignty through mobilizing their domestic democratic forces. A scramble of penitent denials issued from Sofia. Dimitrov himself, speaking before a Fatherland Front congress, admitted that the Pravda's critical comments were "a timely, valuable, and useful warning against possible inappropriate infatuation harmful to the people's democracies."

On March 18, 1948, Dimitrov took a delegation to Moscow where he signed the standard political alliance with the Soviet Union. It was on this same March 18, we should note parenthetically, that the Soviet Union recalled its officers from Yugoslavia and precipitated its rift with Tito. The Dimitrov incident presumably was closed, but it illustrated well enough the lurking dangers of a sudden, ill-considered access of independent thinking even in one of the more stalwart leaders of a satellite state. On July 2, 1949, it was reported that Dimitrov had died in a Moscow sanatorium.

RUMANIA

General Sanatescu's government of August 1944, under King Michael (see p. 774), was composed in the main of his fellow army officers; but it also included the leaders of four former political parties, now joined together as the Democratic Bloc and commanding overwhelming popular support, as well as the leader of the Rumanian Communist party. In co-operation with a somewhat moribund left-wing agrarian faction, the so-called Plowman's Front, and a group of bourgeois intellectuals, the Communist party resorted at once to the device of creating a united National Democratic Front.

Sanatescu's term of office was replete with accusations rising antiphonally from the Communists and Soviet occupation authorities to the effect that he was defaulting on reparations, harboring war criminals, or stirring up hatred against the Soviet Union. He obediently remodeled his government, then resigned to give place to a new government under General Radescu, each change inevitably increasing the number of Communists in office. Meanwhile the Crimea Conference was held in February 1945 and published its agreement that broadly democratic interim governments pledged to free elections should be formed in Eastern Europe. But on February 24, within a fortnight of the Conference, when American and British members, in the interest of implementing the agreement, asked for a meeting of the Allied Control Commission in Bucharest, the Soviet chairman refused. Their conversation took place as a Communist-led demonstration in the streets resulted in the death of eight persons. On February 27, Vyshinsky, the Soviet Deputy Foreign Commissar, arrived in Bucharest and presented King Michael with a two-hour ultimatum demanding the formation of a government based "on the truly democratic forces of the country." It is reported that, to give point to his demands, he slammed the door as he left the royal presence, while Russian troops paraded in front of the palace grounds. Finally Vyshinsky was good enough to inform the King that Petru Groza, leader of the Plowman's Front, must be appointed Premier with a chosen list of ministers, or he would not be responsible for the continuance of Rumania as an independent state.

Thus Groza became Premier on March 2, 1945. He was one of the wealthiest men in the country, a political opportunist of long experience, latterly working with the Communist party. His ministers included an ex-premier of evil record as a pogrom instigator and rigger of elections, a priest who had been a member of the Iron Guard, a general relegated home for black-market operations, and others of no less imposing repute. But the realities of power rested in the hands of the Communist Minister of the Interior, Georgescu, and three high Communists who kept in the background, namely Ana Pauker, Vasile Luca, and Emil Bodnaras. The installation of Groza was followed by the retrocession of Transylvania to Rumania (see p. 668) in a fanfare to make it appear as a special grace from the Soviet Union to the new Premier rather than as a provision of the armistice but, what was momentarily of far greater importance, there were no simultaneous economic concessions. The wholesale lifting of Rumanian goods and industrial equipment by the Soviet occupation authorities continued without compensation.

In the circumstances, the Western Powers could not but continue to take an anxious and exasperated interest in Rumania's domestic affairs. While the Soviet Government recognized its protégé, Groza, in August 1945, a week after the Potsdam Conference, the United States and British Governments declined to follow suit. On August 20, King Michael, drawing encouragement from the American and British attitude, summoned Groza to the palace and demanded his resignation. Groza, however, strong in the support of Moscow — which he visited that September as the honored guest of Stalin himself — continued to govern on his own account. Eventually, on the last day of December 1945, a three-Power commission, composed of the American and British ambassadors in Moscow, together with Vyshinsky, arrived in Bucharest and obtained from Groza a formal commitment to hold free and early elections. On February 5, 1946, the United States and Britain somewhat reluctantly recognized the Rumanian Government. They informed Bucharest, however, that they did so on the assumption that the elections would be held not later than the month of May. After various artificial delays, elections were indeed held — in October — and it was afterward announced that 89 per cent of the electorate had voted and 80 per cent had voted for parties of the National Democratic Front.

However well fortified and dignified by forms of law, the regime was not neglectful of its cruder physical consolidation. Groza's first concern in March 1945 had been a purge of the army and police. Undesirable officers were removed or demoted, and reliable Communists installed in their place. Antonescu was brought to trial before a people's court in May 1946 for many crimes of his dictatorship, found guilty, and shot. A more systematic persecution of opposition parties during 1947 culminated in the arrest of the aged and ailing leader of the Peasant party, Julius Maniu (see p. 212), on charges of conspiring to overthrow the government. His Peasant party was forcibly dissolved, and his trial took place to the accompaniment of a violent press and radio campaign throughout the country. He was finally condemned to a life sentence on the strength of confessions extorted from his imprisoned colleagues. One by-product of the trial, however, was the damaging information elicited in regard to Tatarescu, the Foreign Minister, one of the non-Communist members of the Government, who consequently resigned. He was succeeded by that remarkable woman revolutionary, former Soviet citizen, Comintern official, and general of the Red Army, Ana Pauker. At the same time, Vasile Luca became Minister of Finance, and Emil Bodnaras Minister of War. The secret inner Communist triumvirate thus assumed open control.

On December 30, 1947 the last vestige of the old order disappeared when, without previous intimation to the public, King Michael announced his abdication in phrases bearing the stamp of Communist composition. The government proceeded to the establishment of a Grand National Assembly on republican lines. Elections for this high-sounding body were held in March 1948, and the National Democratic Front, in the official returns, was accorded 90 per cent of the votes and 405 of the 414 seats. A constitution was adopted, evidently inspired by the Yugoslav constitution of 1946. In June 1948 the Grand National Assembly unanimously passed an act whose effect was to nationalize over a thousand business enterprises without compensation, including many of American, British, and other foreign ownership. Only the companies in which the Soviet Union had an interest were exempt.

Agrarian reform had been enacted with Groza's installation of 1945. But agrarian reform was an old story in Rumania. Eighty-five per cent of the land had already been redistributed in the time of Julius Maniu's government in 1918–21 (see p. 212), and there was little left for Groza and his Communist friends. The more serious agricultural problems of the moment had been the two years of parching drought, which had reduced the grain crop to half its normal figure, and the currency inflation, which had been particularly ruinous to the habitually money-hoarding peasants. Only a Soviet grain loan and an American gift of emergency rations staved off the threat of famine for half a million people. But a new agrarian reform was enacted in 1949 by the Grand National Assembly and took the very Russian form of the forcible dispossession of kulaks and other so-called capitalist elements in the villages. Report had it that some 17,000 peasant families were surprised in the middle of the night and hauled away in trucks to unknown destinations.

During 1949 the Grand National Assembly celebrated the ultimate consolidation of Communist power in Rumania with the dissolution of non-Communist elements even within the National Democratic Front and with the establishment of a rigid state control of all religious bodies and church schools. In May 1949, General Radescu, from his refuge in Switzerland, announced the foundation of a National Committee to seek to restore human rights and fundamental freedoms to his native land. But at home all causes but that of Communism appeared to be lost. Of the countries under Soviet influence in Intermediate Europe, Rumania seemed the most submerged.

GREECE

Papandreou had returned to Athens in October 1944, in the wake of the liberating British forces, pledged by the National Charter of the previous May to preside over a government widely representative of Greek political life (see p. 722). The state of Greece in that autumn might have discouraged any government, however strong or able. The country was in economic ruin; the national habits had been corrupted by the occupation; public administration had utterly collapsed; four years of starvation was in tragic evidence everywhere. But the one question that momentarily overshadowed every other was the peaceable disbandment of the rival resistance groups (see p. 721).

The powerful left-wing resistance group, EAM, and the more moderate EDES were both represented in Papandreou's government. Each naturally was intent on the prior disbandment of the other. Nondiscriminatory orders to disband from General Scobie of the Allied High Command in Greece were entirely ineffective. After scarcely two months of uneasy co-operation, EAM resigned from the government and, in December 1944, open fighting broke out between ELAS, the militant arm of EAM, and the British occupation forces. Churchill and his Foreign Secretary, Eden, arrived in Athens on Christmas Day, thereby advertising the enormous importance the British Government attached to Greek affairs, but neither Churchill's pleas nor scoldings made any impression on the unruly factions. The Left still resisted Scobie's order, and the Right, pleased to have the British smite its enemies, saw no virtue in compromise. On the last day of 1944, Archbishop Damaskinos accepted an invitation to become Regent on behalf of the still-exiled King George.

Early in 1945, in the face of a full-scale British offensive, ELAS capitulated under terms. The government promised an amnesty for political crimes and pledged itself to the maintenance of civil liberties. As an organization, ELAS faithfully disbanded and even delivered up more than its specified quota of arms. But some four thousand of its members took to the mountains or fled into Yugoslavia, whence they could doubtless hatch further trouble for their homeland. The net result of this tangled course of events was to raise the prestige of the Right, the heirs of the former Royalists, and to commit the British to the Right's support. Meanwhile EAM, discredited by the defeat of its militant arm, began to lose its wartime character as a union of left-wing national elements, leaving the always more powerful Communists dominant in its ranks.

In the circumstances the next step in Greece, the holding of popular elections, proved none too easy. Through 1945, Admiral Voulgaris with an ostensibly nonpolitical government of army and navy officers tried but failed to elicit the participation of the Left, which, in its discouragement, was clearly averse to facing the electoral test. A British official who went out to Greece in November had virtually to install the octogenarian Liberal, Sophoulis, as head of a new government, much to the wrath of the Regent, who felt his dignity affronted by such intervention. But Sophoulis, worried by the spread of disturbances, himself sought to postpone the elections. However, the great day was fixed for March 31, 1946 and, under the eyes of over a thousand foreign observers, the Greek people went to the polls. The Royalists, headed by the Popular party, won an overwhelming majority, gaining 231 of the 354 seats in the chamber, the republicans 51, and the other parties, not taking a stand on the burning constitutional issue, 67. The results might appear to have been a satisfactorily convincing expression of the people's will, the more so as they had been reasonably free from falsification and intimidation. But one loophole was left. It was afterward announced that only 49 per cent of the registered voters had cast their ballots, and this fortunate occurrence was enough for EAM to claim that the remaining 51 per cent were largely its own supporters who had deliberately boycotted the elections. Nevertheless Sophoulis gave place to Tsaldaris, head of the Royalist Popular party, and Tsaldaris, rejecting British advice and paying little attention either to economic problems or to the growth of guerrilla bands in the mountains, ordered a plebiscite on the monarchy. On September 1, 1946, the plebiscite was held; 69 per cent voted for the monarchy, and before the month was out King George ceremoniously returned to his kingdom.

The settlement of the constitutional issue meant no improvement in the basic economic plight of Greece. Relief from UNRRA and loans and gifts from the United States and Britain tided over the worst, but without lasting results. Guerrillas, supported by Greece's Communist-dominated neighbors, were growing in numbers and effectiveness and, as the keystone of danger, the British Government was preparing to terminate its aid and evacuate its troops. The four thousand ELAS members who had escaped in the early part of 1945 had now grown into an organized rebel body and were clearly taking their part in the great international contest for the expansion of Soviet Communism. The situation in Greece was therefore past desperation when, in March 1947, President Truman announced the policy called after him, the Truman Doctrine (see p. 920).

We shall describe in another place the passing of the Greek-Turkish Aid Act in the United States and the subsequent participation of Greece in the European Recovery Program (pp. 920–21). It was originally provided that Greece's portion should be distributed between her civilian and military needs, but it was soon apparent that more than half these millions were being poured into the war against the guerrillas. Meanwhile Greek affairs had come up before the United Nations. Early in 1947 a commission of inquiry was sent out to the Balkans by the Security Council and, on the basis of its majority recommendations, the United States submitted a resolution to the Security Council condemning the activities of the three northern neighbors of Greece and calling for a further commission of good offices to promote peace in the troubled region. In July 1947 the Soviet, supported by Poland, vetoed the resolution. In October the General Assembly, the larger forum where the veto was not operative, adopted a comparable resolution formally calling upon Yugoslavia, Albania, and Bulgaria to cease aiding the guerrillas. But the Special Committee which the Assembly now sent out to Greece did not include Soviet and Polish members. Just before Christmas 1947, there came the news of the establishment of a defiantly self-styled "First Provisional Democratic Government of Free Greece" under the Communist guerrilla leader "General Markos."

During 1948 the forces of the Greek Government mounted offensives which drove the guerrillas out from one area after another. Yet the campaign seemed to be as unending a labor as the diplomatic struggle in the United Nations. Rebel activity flared up in Macedonia and even in the Peloponnesus. The Greek General Staff announced repeated successes, but defeated guerrilla units invariably evaded capture across a friendly northern frontier. Then the quarrel between Yugoslavia and the Cominform spread its confusion to Greece; in July 1949, Tito closed the Yugoslav frontier, and in August, 51 American dive bombers were added to the Greek air forces. In October it appeared that guerrilla resistance was at last collapsing.

RETROSPECT

We have described "the pattern of Soviet domination" — to use the phraseology of a recent book by one of its victims.[5] And it was a pattern of extraordinary consistency. The Soviet Union first sponsored a "united front," usually a coalition of left-wing elements, which was controlled by the local Communist party or else formed a screen behind which the local Communist party operated. The victory of this united front was then secured at elections which, far from being free within the meaning of the Crimea agreement, were rigged with a shamelessness unprecedented even in this area of traditional political corruption. The emergent body was a People's Republic — or a constituent assembly whose function it was to draw up a constitution for a People's Republic — modeled ultimately on the Soviet constitution of 1936. The procedure was faithfully executed, often under the leadership of returned, Communist-trained exiles — Tito, Rajk, Nosek, Dimitrov, Ana Pauker — and, in specially difficult cases was supervised by a Soviet emissary on the spot — Sviridov, Vyshinsky. Details and nomenclature might vary in all these arrangements, but the essentials, as we have suggested, were regular in the extreme.

The key post, both in the early provisional liberation government and in the subsequent People's Republic, was the Ministry of the Interior, which carried with it the control of the police and which, of necessity, was always reserved to a ranking Communist. Purges were instituted by people's courts in insolent defiance of local public opinion or foreign censure. The trial and condemnation of prominent individuals — Petkov, Stepinac, Maniu, Mindszenty — who symbolized opposition parties and interests in their own persons, were deliberately dramatized for public edification and terrorization. Organized resistance was conspicuous by its absence. Even the national army bowed to the inevitable, and once-powerful political parties allowed themselves to be split or dissolved. Yet Soviet troops — except in Rumania, Bulgaria, and Hungary — were never in open evidence and appeared to exert no pressure. On occasion the regime would need to be consolidated by the further purge of deviationists, actual and potential, among its own supporters — Gomulka, Rajk.

The series of People's Republics was bound together by a network of bilateral military alliances and trade agreements. Economic policy included state control of industry, nationalization, agrarian reform, and occasionally collectivization, and was sometimes organized on the Soviet analogy as a Two-Year, Three-Year, or Five-Year Plan. There was, of course, no serious objection to trade with Western nations provided that such trade did not prejudice the collective independence, exclusiveness, and solidarity of the system. But it is to be noted that these alliances and agreements were bilateral. Lesser regional arrangements, such as any revival of Balkan union, within the greater regional arrangement were rigidly disallowed. The crowning ornament of the system was the Cominform. From this inexorable synthesis only Finland, Austria, Greece — and Yugoslavia — had escaped.

THE WAR AND ITS AFTERMATH

The Middle East — to use the term that has now acquired general accept-ance [1] — had not been a battlefield of the Second World War as it had been in the First. It had been threatened by invasion, and the threat had not entirely faded till after the Battle of El-Alamein in October 1942. Except for the revolt in Iraq and the forcible occupation of Syria and Lebanon in 1941 (see p. 680), there had been no actual hostilities in the area. There had been wartime currency crises, consumer's shortages, and an unprece-dented rise in the cost of living; but there had been neither famine nor en-slavement. The Middle East Supply Center (M.E.S.C.) had serviced the whole area; critical civilian needs had been met. But, psychologically speak-ing, the war had ended for the Middle Eastern peoples in 1943.

Yet, though neutral in deed, the Middle Eastern peoples were not always neutral in thought, though Turks, Persians, and Arabs all shared a fervent hope that, in this Second World War, their lands might not become a Great Power battlefield. They all watched the spectacle of the fall of France; they all noted the reluctance of the Soviet Union to turn against Germany before the Nazi invasion of 1941; and they also noted the isolationist arguments current in the United States before Pearl Harbor. Only one group, the tiny minority of European Jews in Palestine, was inescapably committed to the war for the destruction of Nazism. Many observers felt that Axis fifth col-umnists had succeeded in permanently alienating, or at least estranging, the Arab peoples from the cause of the United Nations. Axis propaganda had divided Syria-Lebanon against itself — an implacable Vichy regime had been imposed upon the mandate, and its youth organizations became actively pro-Nazi, though never pro-Italian. Some nationalist Arabs could not forget that their hopes of independence had been deferred, after the First World War, and some of their lands partitioned by the Allies. There were sufficient pro-Axis elements in Iraq to support the revolt of 1941. The Yemen had been in treaty relations with Italy since 1926. And Egypt, swayed by pro-Italian pressures, had allowed herself to be protected by British arms — against invading German-Italian armies — only with reluctance.

On the other hand, Saudi Arabia, through the influential person of its ruler, Ibn Saud, remained staunchly pro-British throughout the war, as did Transjordan and its Emir Abdullah. The flight from Palestine of the pro-Nazi Mufti Hajj Amin el-Husseini, left the field open to the more pro-British Arab factions who collaborated thenceforth with the British Ninth Army in Palestine and Syria (see p. 253). Many observers in the Middle East remained convinced that — if it had come to a showdown — a substantial majority of the Arabs would have thrown in their lot with the western democracies. Traditionally, in their daily lives as in their religion, the Arabs of Islam have more in common with democratic peoples and principles than with totalitarian states. They are strong individualists, antipathetic to regimentation and militaristic ideology. The more they had to do with Axis agents and Axis dictatorial methods, the more likely they were to react against Axis governments. In any case, once Rommel and his Italian colleagues had been defeated by the British Eighth Army, and the soldiers of the democratic West had demonstrated their valor and disproved the Axis myth of their decadence, the Arab countries re-established themselves as the natural allies of the United Nations.

The Second World War greatly increased what might be called the Middle Eastern regional self-consciousness. The Middle East Supply Center, at first a British and latterly an Anglo-American organization, imposed a measure of economic unity upon the area. Many countries of the Middle East and Africa, including all the Arab states and Iran, were thus temporarily drawn together for the war effort and operated with the "sterling bloc." More constructive than a mere control agency, the M.E.S.C. worked out a complex program for the entire area. It allocated supplies according to the needs of individual countries; regulated imports, exports, shipping, and overland transportation, according to the principle of the greatest good to the greatest number of needy civilian consumers; stimulated internal trade and intercommunication between the Arab countries; and developed their own natural resources as much as was practicable in a wartime economy. The necessity for considering Arab national problems on a regional basis made for a certain habit of thought and, even after wartime rigors had been relaxed, the advantages of economic planning and co-operation were not forgotten. In 1948 the Arab League supported the formation of a United Nations Middle East Economic Commission.

Furthermore the war again demonstrated the strategic importance of the Middle East. The Arab countries found themselves in a better bargaining position, internationally speaking, than ever before. Their almost unlimited petroleum reserves, their central position along the East-West air routes, and their exceptional natural facilities for the development of air bases and fields suited both to military and commercial purposes, all made the Middle East a very critical area in international politics. The arguments for solidarity, the advantages to be gained from collective action, were plain to Arab leaders.

But the relative poverty of the Middle East as a whole, the inadequacy of its natural resources — petroleum excepted — and its industrial underdevelopment, made for economic dependence on the West. The Middle East still needed Western technology and instruction for any financial, economic, or administrative reforms it might attempt. The Arab governments, having served their apprenticeship under Western tutelage, recognized the further need for education, for agrarian reforms and rural development, for public health and medical services, for improved methods of transportation and irrigation. They still wanted to learn from the West everything that the West could teach; but they wanted now more than ever to free themselves from dependence upon the West and to establish their independence, *de facto* as well as *de jure*, upon their own terms.

During and after the Second World War the vexed problems of Palestine's future became the catalyst of Arab unity. Palestine was the only Arab country freed from the Turks that had not obtained its independence; and Palestine was held by the Arabs to constitute the inalienable strategic core of their world. No foreign intrusive population could be suffered to drive a wedge, economically or culturally, between the organic parts of that world. A Jewish national state in Palestine would make, in Arab eyes, "a bridgehead for foreign imperialism"; it would inevitably expand beyond its frontiers, push further and further into their midst, and eventually destroy Arab unity. The fervor and determination of the Zionists to achieve their national objectives roused a corresponding fervor and determination in the Arabs to "defend" their "homelands" against Zionist encroachment "before it was too late."

The Arab League was the political form of the Arabs' answer to this total situation. It was an appropriate sequel to the long story which had begun with the Arab renaissance we have described above (pp. 220–23). It had received official British encouragement, as early as May 1941, in a speech by Foreign Secretary Eden. It had taken shape under the initiative and leadership of Nahas Pasha of Egypt and Nuri Pasha of Iraq. It had the active sponsorship of King Farouk and King Ibn Saud. A Preparatory Conference was held in September 1944 in Alexandria, and the Arab League came into being on March 23, 1945, at a further conference at Cairo, attended by the dignitaries of seven Arab states — Egypt, Saudi Arabia, Iraq, Syria, Lebanon, Transjordan, and the Yemen. King Farouk's Minister of Arab Affairs, Abd el-Rahman Azzam Bey (later Pasha) became the first Secretary General of the League.

The Arab League predated by one month the United Nations Conference at San Francisco. It was a demonstration of Arab unity at a critical time and an anticipation of the principle of "regional arrangements" which the United Nations was afterward at pains to recognize. As an international power bloc today — whether or not the Arab countries receive Anglo-American military and economic aid — its potentialities must be enormous. Nor is it intended to be a political organization alone. It has economic and cultural commissions ancillary to it which have outlined long-range plans for co-operation among its confederated peoples.

Although an Arab League was the logical answer to the growing movement for Arab unity, the League in its present form — a loose confederation — represents a moderate, compromise solution. A few Arab leaders believed that closer federation was desirable. Many others believed that either a close federation, or else a loose confederation, of all the Fertile Crescent states should form a nucleus to which Egypt, Saudi Arabia, and the Yemen might subsequently adhere. For geographic and economic reasons the re-creation of a "Greater Syria" — Syria, Lebanon, Palestine, and Transjordan — in close alliance with Iraq appeared to be a logical first step in the progressive unification of the independent Arab world. Such a plan was formally worked out by Nuri Pasha of Iraq, but he withdrew his Fertile Crescent proposal when Egypt urged an inclusive Arab League in 1944–45. Agitation for a "Greater Syria" has continued, however, within the framework of the Arab League. King Abdullah began an active campaign therefor in 1946, directly after Transjordan received its independence. But republican Syria and Lebanon distrusted monarchist leadership, particularly in the person of Abdullah and all the Arab states were fearful of Abdullah's ambitions. To date, only a closer union between the Hashemite kingdoms, Transjordan and Iraq, has resulted from Abdullah's scheming. And this dynastic Hashemite entente is frowned upon, for different reasons, by Saudi Arabia and Egypt. At the moment of writing there is talk of reviving the moribund Saadabad Pact between Turkey, Iraq, Iran, and Afghanistan (see p. 236), with the significant additions of Transjordan and Pakistan. Were this pact to become revitalized and its membership thus enlarged, the future of the Arab League would be shaped by its relations with this other regional organization. Effective co-operation between the two would require superior statesmanship.

Another potentially important postwar development was the Moslem Arab agitation for an Islamic revival, though care was taken to avoid alienating the Christian Arab communities. Islamic reforms were widely discussed. But after 1947 the narrower, more exclusive type of nationalist-Moslem revival group made headway at the expense of more constructive elements. The most powerful and dangerous of these groups is the Moslem Brotherhood, the Ikhwan el-Muslimin, which originated in Egypt, very obscurely, in 1929. This militant organization has today more than 150,000 members, operates largely underground, and has become violently reactionary and xenophobic. Most of the recent political assassinations in Egypt, including that of Prime Minister Nokrashy Pasha, have been perpetrated in the name of the Moslem Brotherhood.

PALESTINE

The proposals contained in the British Government's White Paper of 1939 had not been implemented when the Second World War broke out (see p. 254). They had been unfavorably received by the Mandates Commission but were not definitively rejected by the League of Nations. They remained therefore, particularly in their immigration and land provisions, the British Government's policy toward Palestine throughout the war period. But they were increasingly resisted by the Zionists, as the need of a haven for Europe's persecuted Jews became ever more acute.

In the first years of the war, Palestine was subjected to the heavy pressure of "illegal" immigration. Jews were encouraged to escape from European ports, in unseaworthy boats and without quota assignments, to force their way into the country, even after tragic disasters to two of their boatloads of refugees. But generally these first years of the war were sufficiently quiet in Palestine to encourage a fleeting hope that Jews and Arabs might at last be learning to co-operate in their own interests. The first signs of a new phase of trouble appeared in May 1942, when a conference of American Zionists at the Biltmore Hotel in New York adopted Ben Gurion's "Biltmore Program," as it was called, repudiating the White Paper of 1939 and demanding the establishment of a Jewish State or Commonwealth in Palestine and the creation of a Jewish Army. The Mandatory Power was urged to hand over control of immigration to the Jewish Agency and to abolish restrictions on the sale of land. Considered extreme in 1942, even by many Jews in Palestine, this program eventually furnished the minimum basis for Zionist post-1945 demands.

As the fear of war receded and Palestine seemed less and less likely to be a field of hostilities, underground activities of both parties increased. Both Jews and Arabs maintained illegal paramilitary organizations. The Haganah and the Irgun Zvai Leumi constituted the Jewish forces — the Irgun being a terrorist group of Fascist type. The Futuwa and the Najada were the Arab organizations — though, in contradistinction to their policy in 1938, Palestine Arabs now played a passive role in their own defense, in the hope thereby of obtaining a favorable postwar settlement. In 1943 a large-scale theft of military equipment from Allied stores in Palestine and Egypt was traced to Jewish organizations. Late in 1944, as a seeming overture for what was to follow, Lord Moyne, British Minister of State in the Middle East, was assassinated in Cairo by two young members of the notorious "Stern Gang," a Jewish terrorist group affiliated with the Irgun.

The Jewish Agency began to lay plans for bringing a million or more European Jews into Palestine immediately upon the end of the war in Europe. The Arab League, established in March 1945, was exerting its pressure on the United Nations. The San Francisco Conference ruled against the discussion of Palestine, despite appeals from Jewish organizations and from five Arab states. But momentarily frustrated at San Francisco, the Zionists redoubled their efforts to exert pressure on the governments of the United States and Britain. American and British representatives were then working in an Intergovernmental Committee on Refugees, and President Truman sent Earl G. Harrison to Germany to report on the plight of displaced persons, with particular reference to the problems and needs of Jews.

On August 31, 1945, in anticipation of the approaching end of authorized immigration under the provisions of the White Paper of 1939, President Truman wrote to the British Prime Minister, Attlee, requesting on the basis of the Harrison Report the admission into Palestine of 100,000 additional European Jews. The British Government in its reply, after explaining its inability to accede to the President's request "because of conditions in Palestine," suggested the establishment of a joint Anglo-American Committee of Inquiry to "examine" and "review" the Palestine question. A period of co-operation between the United States and British Governments was thus initiated, a co-operation marred by the insistence of President Truman upon the early admission of 100,000 Jews — even before a decision with respect to the future of Palestine could be reached. The British Government meanwhile permitted a temporary emergency quota of 1,500 a month. Strong and organized protests issued from the Arab camp. Azzam Pasha, on behalf of the Arab League, reminded the United States Government of President Roosevelt's written promise to Ibn Saud that no decision regarding the basic situation in Palestine would be taken without "full consultation with both Arabs and Jews." In October 1945, Egypt, Iraq, Syria, and Lebanon, in a joint note, warned the United States that war would follow any attempt to establish a Jewish state in Palestine. In Britain, Bevin, the Foreign Secretary, reminded the House of Commons that the Arabs had rights in Palestine and that they should not be called upon to bear the full weight of the results of European persecution of the Jews.

In November 1945, the Anglo-American Committee of Inquiry was set up, and it completed its report by April 1946. After conducting hearings in Washington, London, and the Middle East and making a survey of Jewry in Europe, it recommended against partition and expressed the conviction that Palestine should be neither a Jewish nor an Arab state. In the words of its report: "We regard it as essential that . . . Jew shall not dominate Arab and Arab shall not dominate Jew in Palestine; that Palestine shall be neither a Jewish state nor an Arab state; . . . that Palestine must ultimately become a state which guards the rights and interests of Moslems, Jews and Christians alike . . . We emphatically declare that Palestine is a Holy Land, sacred to Christian, to Jew and to Moslem alike; and because it is a Holy Land, Palestine is not, and can never become, a land which any race or religion can justly claim as its very own . . . The fact that it is the Holy Land, sets Palestine completely apart from other lands and dedicates it to the precepts and practices of the brotherhood of man, not those of narrow nationalism." The Committee went on to recommend a long enough preliminary period of trusteeship for the existing "hostility" between Jews and Arabs to "disappear." It also made eight other recommendations — ten in all — and one of these was for the immediate admission of 100,000 Jewish displaced persons, even though "receiving so large a number will be a heavy burden on Palestine."

Neither government accepted the report in its entirety. President Truman was only willing to act upon the admission of 100,000 Jews; the British took the position that a decision with respect to the future status of Palestine was prerequisite to such large-scale immigration. A subsequent Grady-Morrison Plan for provincial autonomy in Palestine was no better received. And two parallel conferences held by the British with the Arabs and the Jews — the Jews had refused to attend an official tripartite conference — ended in deadlock. Meanwhile, two developments nearer Palestine had caused further complications. In March 1946 the British Government recognized the independence of Transjordan, and the Emir Abdullah was shortly crowned King of "the Hashemite Kingdom of Transjordan"; and in June, that old troublemaker and former collaborator, the Mufti of Jerusalem, Hajj Amin el-Husseini, who had lately been living in France, appeared in Egypt.

In April 1947 the British Government referred the Palestine question to the United Nations and, in May, gave formal notice that it would terminate the mandate in a year's time and withdraw all its troops by August 1948.

In Palestine there had been a steady deterioration of internal security. Irregular Jewish attacks, on an increasing scale, were being directed against British personnel, military installations, communication centers, naval vessels, airfields, and oil pipe lines and refineries. The British were eventually forced to concentrate 100,000 troops in Palestine and had frequently to resort to local curfews and martial law. In spite of countermeasures, attempted illegal Jewish immigration continued on a large scale, and camps were established on Cyprus to take care of the intercepted immigrants.

In April 1947 the General Assembly of the United Nations met to consider the Palestine question and, in due course, appointed a Special Committee of Inquiry, consisting of the representatives of eleven nations, to recommend a solution. The Committee's eventual majority recommendation was for partition: its minority recommendation was for a united, federally organized Palestine. In November 1947, the General Assembly voted the partition of Palestine into Jewish and Arab states, stipulating an economic union between them and an internationalized Jerusalem enclave. But no administrative machinery was set up, and no provision was made to implement the partition by force. The Arab states and the majority of the population of Palestine rejected the scheme out of hand, despite the fact that both the United States and the Soviet Union were behind it. In the face of such opposition, it was abundantly clear that partition without military force to maintain it would scarcely be feasible. No Power was prepared to provide the force required. One thing was certain: Britain would not provide the force. British officials, who had weighed and balanced partition schemes between 1937 and 1946 and had found them wanting, were cool to such a recommendation. British public opinion, increasingly outraged by the terrorism of the Jewish armed gangs, which official Jewish organizations seemed to do nothing to restrain, and disappointed by the general lack of comprehension, outside of Britain, of the British Government's years of painstaking effort in Palestine, had received the decision to terminate the mandate with evident relief. It would never have tolerated a substantial reinforcement of British troops or any extension of the now rapidly approaching date of their departure. The United States Government, also unwilling to contemplate the use of force, proposed early in 1948 that a special meeting of the General Assembly should review the partition recommendation. A special meeting was accordingly convened and the United States delegation submitted a plan for temporary trusteeship over Palestine pending an exhaustive review of the recommendation.

On May 15, 1948 the British mandate came to an end, and on the same day a Jewish Provisional Government proclaimed the State of Israel. The recognition of the United States followed immediately — to the surprise of the United States delegation to the United Nations. The recognition of the Soviet Union came a couple of days later. Further review of the partition recommendation by the General Assembly was thereby rendered impracticable.

The result was war. The seven Arab states supported the Arabs in Palestine; the Arab League assumed direction of the Arab resistance; Arab armies and irregulars from Transjordan, Iraq, Syria, Egypt, and Lebanon launched invasions. Fighting was heaviest in and around Jerusalem, in the Negeb, and in Galilee. Jewish terrorists of the Irgun and Stern Gang broke loose, defying all authority, and their victims included many neutrals — one of the first being the American consul general. An uneasy truce was finally agreed to by the Jews and the Arabs, under the auspices of the United Nations. Count Folke Bernadotte of Sweden was sent to Palestine as official United Nations mediator to supervise the truce and to make recommendations for a negotiated peace. But his assassination by a splinter group of the Irgun, in September 1948, bade fair to sabotage the work for which he gave his life, and the ineffective truce in Palestine broke down. Early in October, fighting was renewed between Israeli and Egyptian troops in the Negeb; and before the end of the month an Israeli offensive in Galilee had swept across the frontier of Lebanon. The Provisional Government of Israel disregarded the United Nations' cease-fire orders. The Israeli Army — greatly strengthened by arms, ammunition, and fighter planes smuggled into Jewish Palestine by an airlift operated from Czechoslovakia — forged its way across the Sinai frontier, thirty miles into Egypt. The British sent troop reinforcements to Aqaba in fulfillment of treaty obligations with Transjordan and warned the Israelis against further penetration of Egypt. Meanwhile the Arabs of Palestine, it would seem, did not help their cause by their own divisions. In September 1948 they created a provisional government with temporary headquarters at Gaza. In December a Palestine Arab Congress, held at Jericho, acclaimed Abdullah of Transjordan as King of Palestine.

Early in 1949 an Israeli-Egyptian armistice, unmistakably reflecting the favorable military position of Israel, was negotiated at Rhodes under the auspices of a United Nations Commission headed by Dr. Ralph Bunche, who had been in Palestine as Count Bernadotte's assistant. But armistice was not peace. And peace would depend, not only upon Arab recognition of Israel's frontiers, but also upon the solution of other problems — notably an international agreement as to the status of the Holy Places and the disposition of 800,000 Arab refugees driven from their homes in Palestine.

SYRIA—LEBANON

The Franco-Syrian and Franco-Lebanese treaties of 1936 had never been implemented (see p. 244). At the outbreak of the war in 1939, the constitutions of Syria and Lebanon had been suspended by the Mandatory Power, and their legislatures dissolved. The territories had thence passed under a repressive Vichy administration and Axis aid for Rashid Ali's revolt in Iraq — combat planes, arms, and munitions — had been facilitated by the Vichy-controlled Mandatory Government. In the summer of 1941, Syria and Lebanon had been forcibly occupied, as we have elsewhere related, by British and Free French forces (see p. 680). The Free French commander, General Catroux, had announced that he had come to terminate the mandatory regime and to proclaim the peoples of Syria and Lebanon "free and independent."

General de Gaulle demurred in the implementation of Catroux's proclamation. He wanted to maintain "the pre-eminent and privileged position" of France in its ex-mandated territories, and he insisted that Syrian and Lebanese independence should be conditional upon the signing of treaties with France. In 1941, on September 27 and November 26 respectively, the French officially proclaimed the independence of the two republics — with reservations. But it was not until March 1943 that provisional governments were appointed in Syria and Lebanon for the purpose of organizing elections. During the interim there was much friction between the French and the local nationalists, irritated by France's delaying tactics; and there was also friction between the French and the British, who perforce, for security reasons, were in joint military occupation. In August 1943 the new Syrian Chamber met and elected Shukri el-Quwatli President; and shortly thereafter, in September, the new Lebanese Chamber elected Bishara el-Khoury President.

As it developed, however, the French had no intention of letting go until they had to. A typical crisis occurred in Lebanon some six weeks after the new Chamber had been installed. President el-Khoury, a Maronite Christian, and Premier Riyadh el-Solh, a Sunni Moslem, initiated a series of reforms. With strong Maronite-Moslem support, they amended the basic Lebanese law and therein deleted all reference to the rights of the Mandatory Power — now irrelevant in their eyes, since Lebanon had become a sovereign state. The Lebanese Chamber voted unanimously to amend the law, overriding vigorous protests from the French Committee of National Liberation in Algiers. Thereupon the French Delegate General, Helleu, arrested el-Khoury, most of his cabinet, and the Chamber and set up a puppet government. The United States and Britain immediately brought pressure to bear on the French Committee in Algiers, Helleu was recalled, el-Khoury and his colleagues were restored to office, and the incident was closed. But, as a result, French prestige suffered a sharp setback, and Lebanon emerged stronger and more united than ever before. Yet, even in 1944, when the French were beginning to transfer their authority to the Syrian and Lebanese Governments with respect to antiquities, postal services and telegraphs, customs, and other "common interests," they tried — unsuccessfully — to obtain an agreement on a "University Convention" which would have assured them cultural hegemony in these countries.

Between July and September 1944, the two republics of Syria and Lebanon were recognized by the Soviet Union, Britain, and the United States and, early in 1945, both became members of the United Nations. But then a new crisis developed. French troop "replacements" began to disembark at Beirut, some of them Senegalese, ostensibly for redeployment in the Far East. Mindful of the French attack against Damascus that was organized from Lebanon in 1920 (see p. 241), still resentful over French intervention in the recent Alawi "revolt" in Latakia, and fearful for their future independence, the Syrians indulged in sporadic and often violent anti-French demonstrations. The French themselves were creating incidents, apparently

in a deliberate attempt to stir up trouble. On May 27, 1945, in an atmosphere of increasing tension, and without any prior notice, the French
started an indiscriminate three-day bombardment of Damascus — just at
the time that the United Nations was being organized at San Francisco.
The Syrians retaliated by surrounding French garrisons in Homs and
Hama and by disarming the French officers in the Jebel Druze. Churchill
sent a vigorously worded message to de Gaulle and ordered British forces
to move in and restore order. The French eventually evacuated their civilians, under British escort, and withdrew most of their troops to Lebanon.
At the first meeting of the United Nations Security Council in January 1946,
both Syria and Lebanon registered complaints against the continued presence of foreign troops on their soil. Six months later the last French troops
were withdrawn, and the two republics were free at last to turn their undivided attention to the arduous tasks of economic and financial rehabilitation.

Both Syria and Lebanon became loyal supporters of the Arab League,
although, in the beginning, Lebanon had viewed it with certain reservations. As a state with a Christian majority of 51 per cent, there were elements in Lebanon that feared absorption into an Arab Moslem world.
When the Arab League was in process of formation, Lebanon vetoed a
proposal which would have given the Council of the Arab League a control
over the foreign policies of its member states and, in the Constitution of the
Arab League, largely in deference to Lebanese representations, individual
sovereignties were entirely unrestricted.

Syria and Lebanon had eighteen months of domestic peace. But in November 1947 they were agitated anew by the Palestine partition plan.
Strikes, mass meetings, and antiforeign demonstrations — notably against
nationals of the United States and the Soviet Union, both of whose governments had supported partition — took place in Syria and in Lebanon. Feeling against partition ran particularly high in Syria, where attacks were made
on the United States and French legations and on the headquarters of the
Syrian Communist party. Syria outlawed the Communist party forthwith,
and Lebanon somewhat later in 1948. But the Soviet-directed Communist
press continued to function in Beirut.

After May 15, 1948, with the official ending of the Palestine mandate,
some Lebanese and large numbers of Syrian irregulars joined the Palestine
Arabs in their war against the Israelis. Arab military reverses and inadequate staff co-ordination had chaotic repercussions in the republics. Military
elements began to wield undue influence in Syrian politics — foreshadowing
the military *coup d'état* that was to overturn the Syrian Government early
in 1949. In Lebanon the situation was complicated by the presence of
special divisive factions, notably a few Christian groups which still remained
pro-French and which, allegedly, were not unfriendly to the idea of an independent Israel. The majority of Lebanon's Christian Arabs, however,
were stanch supporters of Arab unity; they stood with all the Christian
Arab groups of Palestine who gave unwavering support to Arab Moslems
on the Palestine issue. Finally both Syria and Lebanon were flooded with

thousands of Arab refugees from Palestine, and their governments were heavily taxed with the problem of caring for these destitute displaced persons.

TRANSJORDAN

In March 1946 the British Government recognized the independence of Transjordan, hitherto technically a part of the Palestine mandate. The Emir Abdullah was shortly crowned King of Transjordan, thus becoming the fifth monarch in the Arab League. As a son of the late Sherif Hussein of Mecca, he was also the second independent representative of the Hashemite dynasty of the Hejaz, and he lost little time in cementing the family bond with his Hashemite relatives in Iraq. In June 1947, Transjordan and Iraq accordingly entered into a very close treaty of "brotherhood and alliance," virtually a military pact.

As long as Abdullah had been restrained by the British mandate, his neighbors — notably his ancient foeman, Ibn Saud — had had very little to fear. Abdullah had always had ambitions, and he now had the liberty to put them into effect. And moreover he also had the strength. An Anglo-Transjordan treaty in 1946, which replaced the mandatory relationship, had given him a relatively powerful army, British trained and equipped. Abdullah's first move was to resurrect the "Greater Syria" plan, of course under his leadership, a plan to which we have already referred. He even went the length of trying to seduce Druze tribesmen from their loyalty to Syria. The Council of the Arab League, realizing the necessity for a united front on the eve of the international showdown on Palestine, began by remonstrating with Abdullah and ended by ordering him to halt his schemes. And Abdullah was not then foolhardy enough to bid open defiance to the Arab League.

In 1947, after the General Assembly of the United Nations had voted the partition of Palestine, Abdullah threw himself into the defense of the Palestine Arabs. Transjordan was in a position of unusual freedom for taking military action, as she was the only one of the seven Arab states which, thanks to the Soviet veto, was not a member of the United Nations. In May 1948, Abdullah and his famous Arab Legion, which had stood by the British so loyally throughout the Second World War, invaded eastern Palestine, where they played an outstanding part in the defense of the Judean hills and the Old City of Jerusalem.

Abdullah would have none of the subsequent Arab government at Gaza and demanded its dissolution. He encouraged Arab factions in Palestine to dissociate themselves from it. Finally, as we have said, a Palestine Arab Congress was held at Jericho which acclaimed Abdullah as King of Palestine. The six other states of the Arab League denounced the Congress and its proposed unification of Arab Palestine and Transjordan. But Abdullah went ahead with his plans for unification, and he appointed a new Mufti of Jerusalem, Sheikh Hasan el-Din Jarallah to replace Hajj Amin el-Husseini, thus indirectly throwing down a challenge not only to the Husseini factions in Palestine, but to the entire Arab League. Thereafter he renamed Transjordan "the Hashemite Kingdom of Jordan."

In March 1948, just two months before the British termination of the Palestine mandate, another Anglo-Transjordan treaty replaced the earlier treaty of 1946 and provided for a permanent "Anglo-Transjordan Joint Defense Board" to co-ordinate defense in the common interest of both parties. During the Israeli offensive of December 1948 in the Negeb it seemed not impossible that an Israeli armored column might violate the Transjordan frontier, and Abdullah appealed for British aid under the terms of the new treaty. A British force was promptly sent to reinforce the Transjordan port of Aqaba, and its presence no doubt warded off Israeli aggression eastward and perhaps facilitated the Israeli-Arab armistice negotiations of 1949.

IRAQ

When King Ghazi was accidentally killed in an automobile accident in April 1939, four-year-old Feisal II succeeded to the throne of Iraq, and his uncle, the Emir Abdul Illah, was appointed Regent (see p. 258). Thereafter, increasing difficulties were created for the British in the country, who were victimized at every turn by intensive Axis propaganda instigated by the German and Italian ministers to Iraq. The pro-British Premier, Nuri Pasha el-Said, obtained a diplomatic break with Germany. But in April 1940, pro-Axis elements forced Abdul Illah to replace him with Rashid Ali el-Gailani, a secret member of the "Golden Square," the local Fascist group. In April and May 1941, Rashid Ali took courage from the British reverses in Libya and Greece, seized the government by a *coup d'état* and, in his desire to strike before British reinforcements could arrive, he attacked Royal Air Force bases in Iraq without waiting for adequate Axis assistance (see p. 680). The Royal Air Force, strengthened with lightning speed by units from Palestine and by Arab detachments from Transjordan, routed the Iraqi rebels in six weeks. The Regent was afterward reinstated, and Nuri Pasha again became Premier.

Thereafter Iraq's war was a quiet one. The only fighting in which she participated was a punitive expedition against the Barzani Kurds, who had been suffering acutely from wartime shortages and black-market operations. The Kurds came to terms temporarily with the Iraqi Government, but re-embarked upon their revolt in 1945, as soon as the war was over. Mulla Mustapha, leader of these Iraqi Kurds, eventually led a thousand of his followers across the border into Iran, where he joined Iranian Kurds who were trying to establish an autonomous government with Soviet aid.

In the postwar years, Iraq was preoccupied by a number of problems. Kurdish troublemaking was not suppressed till after the flight of Mulla Mustapha in 1947. Communist activities in the northern oil fields and among the Shi'a Moslems of southern Iraq were such that the Iraqi Government was moved to outlaw the Communist party. A new Anglo-Iraqi treaty, the so-called Treaty of Portsmouth, which was intended to supersede the basic treaty of 1930, but which still committed the British to equip and train an Iraqi army and to participate in the defense of the country, was unacceptable to ardent Iraqi nationalists. News of the signing of the treaty in January 1948 led to violent demonstrations in Baghdad and rioting by over 6,000 students, who were already bitter on the Palestine issue and inflamed by Communist propaganda. In the end the Regent, Abdul Illah, was reluctantly constrained to state that the treaty did not realize "the national aims of Iraq" and could not therefore be ratified.

Iraq became a loyal and faithful member of the Arab League. Nuri Pasha, at one time an advocate for "Greater Syria" and a confederation of the Fertile Crescent states, refrained from pushing his own plan for the sake of Arab unity within the larger organization. Iraq carefully rounded out her good relations with her Moslem neighbors. On June 10, 1947, she signed a close treaty of "brotherhood and alliance" with Transjordan. Two days later the Iraqi Senate ratified a comprehensive treaty of friendship with Turkey, providing for joint control of the upper waters of the Tigris and Euphrates, for the planned development of power and irrigation facilities, and for cultural co-operation. On the Palestine issue, Iraq was the most anti-Zionist of all the Arab states. Iraqis in 1948 gave considerable military assistance to Palestine Arabs; and the Jewish community of Iraq even offered its support to the Arabs in the Arab-Zionist conflict.

EGYPT

Egypt was an unquiet field. As the threat of invasion in 1942 had receded from her frontiers, she had revived all her old domestic conflicts. There was a split in the Wafd party between Nahas Pasha and his Coptic Minister of Finance, Makram Ebeid. In November 1944, Egypt became a lightning rod for Zionist agitation over Palestine when two Jewish terrorists of the Stern Gang in Cairo assassinated Lord Moyne, British Minister of State in the Middle East. King Farouk had recently dismissed the Wafdist government of Nahas Pasha and appointed the moderate Saadist leader, Ahmed Maher Pasha, to succeed. Elections in January 1945 confirmed an ample Saadist majority and, on February 24, in time to meet the deadline for the projected San Francisco Conference, Egypt declared war on Germany and Japan, and forthwith qualified as a member of the United Nations. But the same day, as he finished reading the King's war decree, the Prime Minister, Ahmed Maher Pasha, was assassinated by an Axis partisan. Fahmy Nokrashy Pasha, Vice-President of the Saadist party, immediately became Prime Minister, and later was succeeded by Sidky Pasha, a Liberal Constitutionalist and a former Prime Minister.

The Egyptian Government made various efforts to set its own house in order. In September 1945 it announced a five-year rehabilitation plan costing £25,000,000 (about $100,000,000) and covering an enlightened expansion of social, medical, educational, and agricultural services. It took drastic repressive measures against Communists, notably at the time of the strikes in the textile factories in the latter part of 1946. But nationalist agitation continued in a sharpened form and was directed specifically toward a revision of the Anglo-Egyptian Treaty of 1936, which could not be legally revised in less than twenty years without the consent of both parties. "The unity of the Nile Valley," that is to say, the unification of Egypt and the Sudan under the Egyptian Crown, was now an issue as important to Egyptian nationalism as the withdrawal of British troops. The British Government took the position that its primary aim in the administration of the Sudan since 1899 had been the welfare of the Sudanese people, who must themselves be consulted in the matter of their future government.

In October 1946, Sidky Pasha went to London in the hope of reaching an agreement with the British Foreign Secretary, Bevin, and returned to Cairo with the draft of a new treaty and a British pledge of complete withdrawal of troops from Egypt. But the hostility of Nahas Pasha to the government, conflicts within the Wafd party, and the usual intemperate opposition of Makram Ebeid Pasha and of extreme nationalists, notably members of the Moslem Brotherhood, ended in the rejection of the new treaty, the resignation of Sidky, and the breakdown of Anglo-Egyptian negotiations.

In December 1946, when Nokrashy Pasha formed a government, he would have preferred to turn his attention to internal reforms and the urgent problems of inflation, unemployment, housing, and public health, but Nahas and Ebeid, aided and abetted by the Moslem Brotherhood, forced him to continue to press for treaty revision. Nokrashy offered to grant the Sudan a degree of self-rule within the framework of Nilotic unity, but the British Government would not be moved from the principle that there must be "no impairment of the right of the Sudanese people ultimately to decide their own future." The problem was complicated by the situation in the Sudan itself, where the Umma, the strong Sudanese Independence party led by el-Mahdi, was implacably set against any recognition of Egyptian sovereignty; whereas the Ashigga party, fearful of Mahdist domination, desired independence through union with Egypt. In April 1947, Egypt took the Anglo-Egyptian treaty dispute to the United Nations. The Security Council had to hold the issue over until that August, because of the current Palestine crisis; but neither then nor at a later meeting was any decision reached. As we write, the Anglo-Egyptian Treaty of 1936 remains legally in force.

The failure to secure satisfaction from the United Nations, coupled no doubt with the Palestine partition plan of November 1947, had its reaction in a strong wave of xenophobia in Egypt, not mitigated by the fact that Britain, the United States, and the United Nations' World Health Organization (WHO) had been acting in concert to save the country from a severe cholera epidemic. In May 1948, as we have already related, fighting broke out between the Egyptian and Israeli armies in the Negeb area of Palestine. The Israeli offensive against Egypt in December, which penetrated some thirty miles into Egyptian territory, was only halted by a warning from the British that the latter would feel bound under the Anglo-Egyptian Treaty of 1936 to come to the aid of the Egyptians.

Internal security in Egypt deteriorated with the humiliations of military defeat. The Moslem Brotherhood continually stirred up student riots. Finally in December 1948, after the Cairo Chief of Police had lost his life in one of these riots, Nokrashy Pasha ordered the dissolution of the Brotherhood, only to be himself assassinated in retaliation. The year ended in deep gloom for the Egyptian people, aggrieved by domestic tragedy and routed by "the upstart army of an upstart state."

ARABIA

In 1945, at the end of the Second World War, the Kingdom of Saudi Arabia, ruled by King Ibn Saud, was by far the most important political entity in the Arabian peninsula. The only other independent state was the Kingdom of Yemen. British influence was paramount in the crown colony of Aden, and in the Aden Protectorates, including the historic Hadhramaut. The Gulf Sheikhs of Kuwait, Bahrein, Qatar, and the Trucial Coast, and the Sultan of Muscat and Oman, though formally independent, were all in close treaty relations with the British Government and were dependent on the British Government for the conduct of their foreign relations.

The other factor in the Arabian complex was the growth of American influence. Since 1933, two American companies, the Arabian-American Oil Company ("Aramco") and the British-registered Bahrein Petroleum Company, have exploited the oil fields in Saudi Arabia and Bahrein Island under exclusive concessions. But it was not until the war highlighted the enormous importance of these Arabian oil fields that the American people came to be aware of their value; and only since 1945 have the fields come to be regarded as a vital American interest. Other American oil interests divided equally with the British the vast oil resources of Kuwait and were represented in the subsidiary companies of the Iraq Petroleum Company, which had concessions along the eastern Arabian coasts.

A fundamental review and revision of the many oil agreements in the Persian Gulf area was brought about in 1947, resulting generally in the principle of closer co-operation between the three "giants" of Middle Eastern oil production, the Anglo-Iranian Oil Company, the Iraq Petroleum Company, and the Arabian-American Oil Company, but resulting also in the continuance of the effective Anglo-American oil monopoly in the region.

In Saudi Arabia, the development of these American oil interests brought other American business in its wake. American aviation and radio companies were granted contracts by the Saudi Arabian Government. The Bechtel International Company made a survey of possible harbor, transportation, and utility developments. An American agricultural mission initiated a model experiment in the oasis of El Kharj, fifty miles south of the Saudi capital of Riyadh.

Generally speaking, King Ibn Saud's wider objectives were two — one with respect to his own desert kingdom and the other with respect to the Arab world at large. For a long time these objectives seemed mutually complementary. In Saudi Arabia, Ibn Saud sought to develop and modernize the somewhat sparse natural resources and limited potentialities, all within the framework of fundamentalist Islam. Outside Saudi Arabia, he sought to promote the cause of Arab independence and unity. When rebellion first flared in Palestine, he mediated, urging moderation and patience on the Palestine Arabs in 1936 and again in 1938. He relied on fair treatment and justice at the hands of Britain and later of the United States. And, during the Second World War, he received material help from both countries. He made his first journey outside Saudi Arabia to intercede with President Roosevelt for the Arabs of Palestine. From the earliest days of the Arab League he was the strong supporter of moderate and constructive Arab policies.

After November 1947, however, when the General Assembly of the United Nations voted the partition of Palestine, Ibn Saud began to find his two objectives increasingly incompatible. The development of Saudi Arabia with American financial and technical aid proved somewhat embarrassing to the King in view of United States support for the partition of Palestine. Nevertheless, he gave every protection to American oil interests, and the Saudi "Minister of Development" continued to budget for the building of railroads, highways, and airfields, for electrification and water supply projects, for harbor facilities, schools, and hospitals. Aramco's transdesert pipe line and a railroad from Riyadh to Dhahran on the Persian Gulf, projected with Aramco aid, were both begun. But at the same time Ibn Saud gave the support of his immense prestige, as well as considerable financial and military aid, to the Palestine Arabs and to the Arab League.

Unlike Saudi Arabia, Yemen in these years was only just beginning to emerge from centuries of medieval isolation. The kingdom was granted American recognition in 1946, and a Yemeni mission visited the United States to explore the possibility of American aid for surveying and developing Yemen's presumably great natural resources. In September 1947, Yemen was admitted to membership in the United Nations. But the aged Imam Yahya could not adapt himself to the changing spirit of the times. His reactionary hand continued to lie heavily, too heavily, on his people. In February 1948, smouldering discontent blazed into a brief civil war. The Imam and three of his sons lost their lives, and a "Free Yemen party," recruited from middle-class and supposedly liberal elements in the country, set up an ephemeral "constitutional" government with the aid of one of the younger princes. But in the spring of 1948 the late Imam's eldest son and designated successor, Saif el-Islam Ahmad, succeeded in overthrowing the revolutionaries and in re-establishing Shi'a theocracy in Yemen.

IRAN (PERSIA) [2]

We have elsewhere described the Anglo-Soviet occupation of Iran in 1941 and the abdication of Riza Shah in favor of his son, the young Mohammed Riza (see p. 681). In January 1942 the Iranian Government entered into a treaty with Britain and the Soviet Union granting them all facilities for the prosecution of the war and receiving from them in return a guarantee to defend Iran, to respect her sovereignty and territorial integrity- and to withdraw their armed forces within six months of the termination of hostilities. With a view to developing a supply corridor to the U.S.S.R., advance units of the United States Army began to arrive in the summer of 1942 to prepare the ground for the American Persian Gulf Command, consisting of some 28,000 troops.

The occupation greatly improved the country's transportation system and should have been of economic benefit. But heavy droughts, wholesale Soviet "purchases," together with a Soviet-Iranian financial agreement and a munitions contract (both of them hard bargains from the Iranian point of view), and finally, the incompetence and corruption of Iranian officials contributed to a general financial and food crisis with which the Iranian Government was quite unable to cope. By the end of 1942, by request of the Iranian Government, the country was being largely administered through American military, financial, and agricultural advisers. The American financial mission under Dr. A. C. Millspaugh, though given extraordinary legal powers, was hampered at every turn by Iranian officials and by influential Iranian speculators, and its efforts to operate in the northern Soviet-occupied zone were completely frustrated by Soviet agents and the Soviet military. Late in 1943, after Iran had declared war on the Axis, Roosevelt, Churchill, and Stalin, meeting at Teheran, reaffirmed the guarantees given Iran in 1942. In 1944, would-be concessionaires, two American, one British, and one Soviet, were competing for oil concessions. The proposed Soviet concession included demands for all mineral and subsoil rights and communications throughout the 216,000 square miles of the Soviet-occupied zone. In December 1944 the Majlis, the Iranian National Assembly, came to the rescue and passed legislation prohibiting its ministers from conducting negotiations regarding oil with foreign interests. Meanwhile runaway inflation had driven up the cost of living by 1,000 per cent, and the ensuing distress provided an ideal culture for the germination of a radical party, the Tudeh (Masses), as it was called, which was Communist in all but name.

The peace of 1945 brought no peace to Iran. Late in 1945 a Soviet-sponsored revolt broke out in the northwestern province of Iranian Azerbaijan. A "Democratic" government was set up in Tabriz under ex-members of the Tudeh party. Iranian Kurds, assisted by Soviet agents, issued a declaration of autonomy and eventually were joined by a strong contingent of their brethren who had escaped across the Iraqi borders. In January 1946, Iran complained to the United Nations Security Council against Soviet interference in her domestic affairs. Vyshinsky, the Soviet delegate, admitted the charge, but insisted that Iran and the Soviet Union could settle their difficulties by bilateral negotiation. However, when the Soviet refused to evacuate "certain areas" of Iran on March 2, 1946, the date set for evacuation by the Anglo-Soviet treaty of 1942, Iran again complained to the Security Council. The strained situation was thus growing into a serious international issue. Indeed, it provided the first open sign of the East-West schism, as we have called it in this part of our book, a sign which could no longer be blinked at even by the most pacifically intentioned observer of world events; it provided the first great crisis in the United Nations; it provided the Security Council with the occasion for its first demonstration of strength; it provided the Soviet Union with its first major postwar diplomatic discomfiture. The United States and Britain insisted on the evacuation of the Soviet forces. On April 4, 1946, Gromyko, the Soviet delegate in the Security Council, who had lately been boycotting its sessions, at last announced that the Soviet forces were being evacuated from Iran. Simultaneously in Teheran, the Iranian Premier, Ahmad Qavam, felt himself obliged to accede to Soviet demands for the formation of a Joint Soviet-Iranian Oil Company. But the oil concession had to await the approval of the Majlis, which had just been dissolved pending an election; and this election of the new Majlis had to await the Soviet evacuation of Iran.

The Iranian Government therefore emerged very successfully from its contretemps with the Soviet Union. And, to Soviet surprise, it broke the revolt in Azerbaijan and re-established its authority in the province. Elections for the Majlis were held at the end of 1946 and returned a highly self-confident body of legislators. In October 1947, under public encouragement from the American ambassador in Teheran, the Majlis, by a vote of 102 to 2, declined to approve the Soviet demand for an oil concession. An angry Soviet Government retaliated by accusing the Iranian Government of "treacherously violating obligations and gross discriminations against the Soviet Union."

Fresh trouble in Azerbaijan followed, presumably Soviet inspired. Qavam resigned in December 1947, giving warning as he did so that revolution was brewing in the northern provinces. In January 1948 the Soviet Union made charges of fresh violations, this time of the old Soviet-Persian treaty of 1921 (see p. 236), and alleged that the United States was being permitted to establish strategic bases in Iran and to militarize the country. The charges were denied by the United States and Iranian Governments. In February, Iran turned the tables by accusing the Soviet Union itself of violation of the 1921 treaty. Shortly thereafter the Iranian Government took action against various separatist leaders in the northwest and against the Tudeh party.

Economic reconstruction and development of the country were thus bedeviled by its external affairs. During the summer of 1948, the Shah and the Majlis announced an ambitious Seven-Year Plan. Largely drafted by American consultants, it was to be implemented with the continued co-operation of American technical advisers. But no sooner was this project set in motion than in February 1949 an attempt was made on the life of the Shah, and the Tudeh party, allegedly implicated in the attempted assassination, was promptly outlawed. This, of course, was the signal for another crisis in Soviet-Iranian relations. Soviet military activity was rumored across the borders, and frontier incidents were reported in the northern provinces. As we write, the Soviet-Iranian war of nerves follows its fitful course, and Iranians live under the threat of a Soviet invasion of their country.

TURKEY

Turkey's neutrality in the Second World War had been more useful to the Allies than any ill-considered belligerency would have been. She had none of the material or military resources to withstand the attack of a modern mechanized army. Invaded and occupied, she would have been a heavy liability. But neutral, she was a welcome buffer against Axis penetration in the Middle East. And once the war was over, as an important key state, unweakened by loss, she was in a position to take an effective part in the postwar byplay of East-West power politics.

On February 23, 1945, Turkey declared war on Germany and Italy and, on the same day, signed a Lend-Lease agreement with the United States. Two months thereafter followed a trade agreement with Britain. Unfortunately, Turkish hopes for security received a sharp setback from another quarter. Unrelenting Soviet press and radio attacks upon her were already in full cry. In March the Soviet Union denounced the nonaggression pact of 1925, and in June made informal demands that Turkey should "retrocede" Kars and Ardahan to Soviet possession, permit Soviet bases in the Dardanelles and make provision for joint Soviet-Turkish defense of them, revise the Montreux Convention, and recognize various territorial changes in the Balkans. The Turkish Government rejected the Soviet demands as being inconsistent with the full maintenance of Turkish sovereignty.

In the spring of 1946, there were important developments on the home front which had far-reaching effects on Turkish political and social life. The People's party, hitherto the only party permitted in Turkey, consented to an Opposition. A new Democrat party was formed and soon gained substantial influence and, in midsummer of 1947, a third group, the Turkish Conservative party, came into existence. The two new parties brought sufficient pressure on the People's party to cause the Turkish Government to relax the stringent police regulations in effect since 1940 and to restore civil rights under the constitution. At the same time the two parties, desirous of building up their strength throughout the country, found it expedient to recognize the basic allegiance of the Turkish peasantry of Islam. A nationwide campaign was launched to restore Koranic instruction in the schools, and in May 1948, as a result of the campaign, the People's party voted a resolution which permitted religious teaching in the primary schools and provided for special theological schools for imams and a new Ulema under government supervision.

These developments were evidently a reaction against the harsh secularizing tendencies of the earlier Kemalist reformation. But they indirectly helped to clear the good name of Turkey from the frequent charge of totalitarianism and enabled her to take her place beside the democratic Powers. During 1947, when Greece was fighting for her national existence against Communist-supported guerrillas, the Turkish Government took the decision to accept an offer of assistance from the United States. In March 1947 in Washington, President Truman enunciated the policy called after him the Truman Doctrine, and in May Congress passed the Greek-Turkish Aid Act.

Turkey was allotted $100,000,000 as a buttress against cumulative Soviet pressure; she stipulated that the sum should be administered by herself and applied almost wholly to military expenditure. She was subsequently one of the sixteen nations of the European Recovery Program. Relations between Turkey and Britain became progressively closer. Turkish orders for fighter planes were placed in Britain and, in March 1948, the basic Anglo-Turkish alliance of 1939 was reaffirmed.

It is proper perhaps to consider the post-1945 affairs of the territories of the East in a single chapter. Their peoples have much in common. They share the same sort of economic problems, arising from their intensive peasant agriculture and, except in Japan, their undeveloped industries — and above all from their dense and multiplying numbers. Most of them have been subject to white man's "exploitation." Their great masses live at subsistence level, are largely illiterate and politically unsophisticated. Many of them are of ancient origins, sometimes dating back to civilizations older than the West, but now strong in the new resurgent nationalism and adjusting themselves, with the usual difficulties, to the science and technology that have overtaken them. The gradual withdrawal of Western imperialism has left them an open field of rivalry for the two prime ideological forces of the modern age, democracy and totalitarianism. All but India, Pakistan, and part of China had lately been united under the Japanese conquests of 1941–43 as partners of the Co-prosperity Sphere. Since 1945, political speculation has increasingly cast them for a self-conscious regional association.

CHINA

Chiang Kai-shek, in common with his allies, had counted on victory in the Pacific in 1946. The premature collapse of Japan in 1945 upset his military and political dispositions and opened up prospects which, though seeming fair, were yet charged with incalculable menace. The United States Air Forces in China were hastily diverted to the tremendous task of transporting 80,000 Chinese Nationalist troops and their equipment from the south to the key centers of Shanghai, Nanking, and Peiping in order to forestall a disastrous extension of Communist influence from the north into the sudden vacuum which the Japanese surrender had created. Many of the Japanese occupation forces had docilely laid down their arms before their own Chinese puppet auxiliaries, who unanimously transferred their allegiance to the Chinese Nationalist Government. Nevertheless the Chinese Red Army poured into the provinces of Chahar, Hopeh, Jehol, and Shantung, while the radio from the Communist capital at Yenan provocatively broadcast that "Chiang Kai-shek, whose policy has been to sit aside, watch others fight, and wait for victory, has no right to accept the Japanese surrender."

Meanwhile Dr. T. V. Soong, the Nationalist Foreign Minister, returning home from the San Francisco Conference via Moscow, had signed there, on August 14, 1945, a Sino-Soviet treaty of friendship and alliance. The two signatories agreed to render each other all possible aid during the postwar reconstruction period, to respect each other's sovereign rights, and not to interfere in each other's internal affairs. In a series of addenda to the treaty, the Soviet Union agreed to furnish, exclusively to the Chinese Nationalist Government, "as the Central Government of China," "moral support" and "military supplies and other material resources." For these very considerable benefits, the Chinese Nationalist Government conceded the independence of Outer Mongolia; it admitted the Soviet Union to joint ownership, for a period of thirty years, of the Chinese Eastern Railway and the South Manchuria Railway; it agreed to the conversion of Port Arthur into a naval base for the exclusive use of Chinese and Soviet ships and to the lease to the Soviet Union of one-half the installations and equipment of the free port of Dairen, again for a period of thirty years. Stalin gave a separate assurance that the Soviet forces would begin their withdrawal from Manchuria three weeks after the Japanese surrender.

The treaty was as important a landmark as Sun Yat-sen's agreement with the Soviet in 1923 (see p. 416). On the strength of it, Chiang Kai-shek invited the Communist leader, Mao Tse-tung, to Chungking to negotiate a settlement of the Nationalist and Communist differences. But Mao, far from accepting Chiang's hegemony, envisaged the future China as a loose federal union in which each province would retain a substantial independence and, on this basis, he demanded in particular the right to appoint governors in the provinces which the Communists had wholly or partly absorbed — Chahar, Hopeh, Jehol, and Shantung. He regarded with undisguised suspicion the proposal that the Chinese Red Army should be scaled down to twenty divisions prior to its integration with the Nationalist armies.

In October 1945, heavy fighting broke out between Nationalist and Communist forces south of the Great Wall. Both sides were evidently maneuvering with an eye to Manchuria, whence, by virtue of the recent Sino-Soviet treaty, Soviet occupation forces were shortly scheduled to withdraw.

In December 1945 the task of mediation was entrusted to General Marshall, the United States Chief of Staff, who was sent to China with ambassadorial status as President Truman's special envoy. He was initially successful in inducing the two parties to accept a truce. But the somewhat tardy withdrawal of the Soviet occupation forces from Manchuria in the spring of 1946 and the stripping of the province of its machinery and equipment by the retiring forces imposed an unbearable strain on the truce. The Chinese Red Army hastened to seize key cities in Manchuria. Nationalist forces moved to eject them, and the truce dissolved in a wild flurry of fighting round Changchun, Harbin, and Mukden. Generally Nationalist forces succeeded in occupying the chief centers north of the Great Wall, while the Communists occupied the adjacent countryside.

General Marshall, convinced after long and painful experience that no compromise was in sight, broke off his mediatory efforts in January 1947 on his appointment as American Secretary of State. In his final report he berated the extremists on both sides with vigor and impartiality. He affirmed that the dominant reactionaries in the Nationalist Government were rejecting a compromise in the smug assurance that they would receive American aid in any event. The extreme Communists, no less culpable, were prepared to wreck China's economy and to plunge her people into further untold suffering in order to achieve their ends. "The salvation of the situation," said Marshall, "would be the assumption of leadership by the liberals on both sides."

But, as 1947 wore on, Nationalist operations in Manchuria and Shantung seemed to be losing their momentum. Alarming rumors of corruption, political favoritism, and poor morale, reminiscent of the Stilwell days in Chungking, seeped back from the fighting fronts. Meaningless territorial gains could still be made. Yenan, the Communist capital, fell to the Nationalists in March 1947; but its modest administrative buildings and roughhewn caves were stripped and deserted when the victors entered. The Chinese Red Army, undeterred, continued to harry the Nationalist communications and to isolate Nationalist garrisons, which, one after another, began to surrender. By the end of 1948, the north was lost to the Nationalist Government, except for a few hard-pressed survivors in Kalgan, Peiping, and Tientsin. The considerable Communist forces thus released were launched on a direct drive upon the Yangtze Valley and Nanking. In November 1948 a great battle for Süchow had developed, involving over a million men.

The catastrophic decline of the Nationalist forces was manifest, and so also was its cause. Nationalist successes in 1945–46 had been won with Chinese elite divisions, largely American trained and equipped. But the rank and file of the other divisions was of poorer material, drawn from a conscripted peasantry, miserably paid in outrageously inflated currency. The civilian population was indifferent or hostile and, particularly in Manchuria, it had been further antagonized by the Kuomintang officials and carpetbaggers who had been swarming into the province. Provincial commanders in Nationalist China had always enjoyed great freedom of action, and their military philosophy, comparable to that prevailing in eighteenth-century Europe, discouraged them from last-ditch stands, if instead they could "make a deal."

The Nationalist Government had returned to Nanking in May 1946, but it had brought with it the Chungking habit of the reckless printing of money. Customs receipts, always an important item in the Chinese revenue, had never recovered from the Japanese blockade. By 1947–48 the Nationalist economy lay almost prostrate. The unofficial exchange rate of the Chinese dollar had sunk to 93,000 to the American dollar, compared with an official rate of 12,000. The budget of 1947–48 abounded in astronomical figures. Military expenditures amounted to 16,000,000,000 Chinese dollars or 80 per cent of the budget, and the total budget deficit, on paper, was 26,000,000,000.

The responsibility of the Kuomintang itself for this all-enveloping disaster could hardly be gainsaid. A constitution for Nationalist China, adopted at Nanking on Christmas Day, 1946, had not subjected the party to any real reforms. Nevertheless the constitution had been hailed by Chiang Kai-shek as the outward and visible sign of his country's emergence from an era of military rule and political tutelage into the era of democracy once so ardently desired by Sun Yat-sen. But the overriding authority of the Supreme National Defense Council, which was a close corporation of the Kuomintang and was presided over by Chiang Kai-shek in person, remained unaffected. Elections for the popular National Assembly under the new constitution — the first general elections in Chinese history — were held in November 1947. The Communist areas, of course, returned no delegates. In the areas under Nationalist control, the Kuomintang machine worked furiously and to such good effect that Kuomintang delegates outnumbered the other parties by six to one. In April-May 1948, before the Assembly met, the government took the additional precaution of placing some hundred suspect delegates under house arrest to discourage overt opposition. Even so, there was quite a clamor in the Assembly's opening sessions for a searching inquiry into the inefficient conduct of the war. In short, a narrowly representative, irresponsible government had been set up in Nationalist China, the very sort of government which was most unlikely to survive the military defeats then being suffered by its forces in the field.

By contrast, the Chinese Red Army was better equipped than ever before, chiefly with captured Japanese and American arms. Enormous quantities of Lend-Lease supplies passed with incredible speed into Communist hands by reason of mass surrenders of Nationalist troops and by secret sale. Moreover the Chinese Red Army was preceded by a potent propaganda well attuned to peasant ears. The sixteen-point basic program of the Chinese Communist party in October 1947 promised the cancellation of agricultural debts and the reparceling of the land. It tempted the allegiance of landowners, Kuomintang officials, and army officers by guaranteeing them land on an equal basis with the peasantry if they crossed into the Red camp. Merchants and manufacturers were assured that their plants and other property would be exempt from expropriation.

The Communists' governmental structure in northern China and Manchuria showed some interesting adaptations to experience. Chinese Communism since the early forties had been decrying "dogmatism" and dwelling rather on the need of modifying the strict tenets of Marxism to the special wants and indigenous traditions of a China that was still a semifeudal, semicolonial country. Mao Tse-tung's *New Democracy*, published in 1940, contended that there must be neither a dictatorship of the proletariat nor a tyranny of private capital, but a government which represented and blended all "revolutionary classes," defined as the Communists, Socialists, and the lesser bourgeoisie. Mao's views excited considerable opposition among the more orthodox of his adherents; but the division of opinion was not insuperable, since "the new democracy" could always be regarded as a typical Communist tactical compromise on the road to eventual Communist reorganization of Chinese society. The evidence suggests that Mao's principles were faithfully applied in the People's Councils in Shensi, Manchuria, and northern China. The large estates were not immediately cut up for redistribution unless the owners were proven enemies of the regime. Assurances that private capital in the industries of the "liberated" provinces would be immune from expropriation were certainly intended to diminish apprehensions in the heavily industrialized Yangtze Valley and did, in fact, prevent the wholesale flight of business interests as the Red Army approached this vital area.

Meanwhile the plight of the Chinese Nationalist Government had become a major issue of American foreign policy. Lend-Lease to China had been continued after the Japanese surrender and, by the close of 1948, it had reached a total of $1,700,000,000. Large quantities of surplus military equipment, including that stocked in Okinawa, were placed at the Nationalist Government's disposal. But after the failure of Marshall's attempt at mediation, this flow of arms and supplies was checked, and a credit of $500,000,000 at the Export-Import Bank was allowed temporarily to lapse. Meanwhile American hesitations were further excited by reports that the Chinese Red Army was receiving Soviet equipment via Dairen and Port Arthur, where, contrary to the Sino-Soviet treaty of 1945, the Soviet Government was maintaining an exclusively military administration.

When Marshall announced the principles of the European Recovery Program in his address at Harvard University in June 1947, a brisk controversy arose at once over its possible extension to China. On the one hand, it was argued that the United States had expended a total of $3,500,000,000 since 1937 in buttressing the Nationalist Government, and that, despite this aid, the Kuomintang had failed to liberalize itself, to clean up the manifest corruption in its ranks, or to check the advance of the Chinese Red Army. On the other hand, it was argued that, if Greece and Turkey were to be bolstered and reinforced against Communist pressure, logic demanded that a similar course be followed in China. If the Nationalist Government collapsed, the Chinese Red Army would reign supreme from Changchun to Canton, to the consequent subversion of the entire balance of forces in the Far East and Pacific. Congress thereafter voted $400,000,000 for aid to China, of which $275,000,000 was to be in the form of nonmilitary assistance to be devoted to rural rehabilitation and distribution under partial American supervision. There was an obvious wisdom in the decision to pour funds into agricultural improvement, to try to contribute a little to the solution of China's perennial economic problem, and perhaps thereby to influence the political allegiance and outlook of the peasant masses.

In December 1948, Madame Chiang Kai-shek made a dramatic flight to Washington to appeal for an outright declaration from President Truman that aid to the Nationalist Government would be resumed and that an American Commander in Chief, presumably General MacArthur, would be appointed in China. But the response in Washington was wholly unenthusiastic. The Truman administration had no desire to add to its already heavy expenditures under the European Recovery Program. Further, it was pointed out, with some pertinence, that the armies of the Nationalist Government did not lack the equipment, but the will to fight.

The decomposition of the Nationalist armies proceeded without abatement in 1949. On January 21, General Fu Tso-yi surrendered Peiping to the besieging Red forces under a separately negotiated agreement. It was manifest that Chiang Kai-shek could no longer control his field commanders, or bend them to his policy of "no surrender." On the same January 21 he closed his twenty-four years' leadership in China and resigned the presidency. Chiang's withdrawal was chiefly designed to facilitate peace negotiations with the Communists, who entertained an unsleeping distrust of their old enemy.

But he still retained active contact with the Nationalist Government in his "retirement"; and did not omit to take with him $150,000,000 in gold, 75 per cent of the Nationalist Government's gold reserves.

Peace talks with the Communist leaders were formally opened at Peiping, the new Red capital, in April 1949. The Communist delegation, fully aware of the desperate position of the opposition, presented an ultimatum early in the proceedings. It demanded unopposed crossing of the Yangtze for the Red armies; the absorption of Nationalist Government troops into the Communist forces; an interim coalition government headed by the Red leader, Mao Tse-tung; and the punishment of Chiang Kai-shek and his chief associates as war criminals. The negotiations foundered on these demands; and the Red armies, pushing forward with renewed speed, entered the Nationalist Government capital of Nanking unopposed on April 24. The Nationalists defiantly announced their intention to continue the struggle from their new capital of Canton. But the pillars of Nationalist power on the mainland were cracking and crumbling everywhere. Chiang therefore began to construct a last bastion of resistance on the island of Formosa, inaccessible to the Reds by reason of their lack of a naval force.

The defeat of Japan, the decline of the Chinese Nationalist Government, and the steady withdrawal of British power from the Far East created a semi-vacuum, into which the conflicting influences of the United States and the Soviet Union were drawn as if in obedience to a law of nature. The slow, glacierlike advance of Russia eastward and southward, begun long since in Tsarist times, brought her once more to her old objectives of Korea, Dairen, and Port Arthur. The American countermove to reinforce the Nationalist Government with money and arms seemed an admitted failure. Japan and the Philippines remained as strategic and political advance points of United States influence in the Pacific world.

JAPAN

The broad principles of policy to be pursued by the occupation authorities after the surrender of Japan had been officially proclaimed by Truman, Attlee, Stalin, and Chiang Kai-shek in the Potsdam ultimatum of July 26, 1945 (see p. 780). Japanese militarism was to be eliminated for all time; points in Japanese territory were to be occupied by the Allies; Japanese sovereignty was to be limited henceforth to the four main "home" islands; Japanese nonmilitary industries were to be maintained for the support of a peaceable economy, and access would be permitted to raw materials. Since the United States had borne the main burden of the war in the Pacific, President Truman insisted that the commander of the occupation forces should be designated by Washington, and that if any differences arose among the occupying Powers, the views of the United States should prevail. Thus the Far Eastern Commission, convoked in Washington in September 1945, representing the eleven Powers which had contributed to the defeat of Japan, was a purely consultative body.[1] On this ground the Soviet Union declined to participate in its deliberations. General MacArthur, as Supreme Commander of the Allied Powers (SCAP), directly responsible to President Truman, retained the chief initiative in forming and applying occupation policies. After September 1945 he was flanked by a four-Power Allied Council sitting in Tokyo; but this was again only a consultative body.

The destruction of Japanese militarism and war potential in their more obvious aspects proceeded with dispatch. By mid-October 1945, the Japanese Imperial General Headquarters and General Staff were dissolved, and shortly thereafter the War and Navy Ministries. The War Ministry was split into two demobilization ministries, which effected the rapid and orderly return of military and naval personnel to civilian life. Military and civilian aviation was prohibited. In November, SCAP decreed the dissolution of the four great business dynasties of the Zaibatsu — the Mitsui, Mitsubishi, Sumitomo, and Yasuda. Satellite concerns were restored to independence.

The cult of the Emperor was declared abolished. Hirohito issued an imperial rescript on New Year's Day 1946 to the effect that "the ties between us and our people are not predicated on the false conception that the Emperor is divine and that the Japanese people are superior to other races and fated to rule the world." The Emperor gave point to his announcement by "breaking seclusion," holding halting conversations with his embarrassed subjects during surprise visits to factories and bomb-shattered areas, and even calling upon General MacArthur at his headquarters. But the prestige of the Emperor was by no means weakened by these unprecedented acts of condescension. A noisy minority of extreme leftists clamored for the deposition of the Emperor and the inauguration of a republic. But the vast majority of Japanese, shaken and confused by a catastrophic war and its aftermath, seemed relieved to discover that at least the Throne had survived the mortal storm.

The liquidation of the old order in Japan created a political vacuum, which SCAP attempted to fill. A written constitution, drafted by American and Japanese experts, secured the overwhelming approval of both houses of the Japanese Diet by October 1946. The Throne remained hereditary, but sovereign power was transferred from the Emperor to the people at large and was to be exercised through a popular bicameral Diet. The executive body, the Cabinet, was to be selected by the Premier, himself formally appointed by the Emperor, but designated by the Diet and responsible to it. The Emperor, as a constitutional sovereign, could only act on the Cabinet's advice.

The doctrine of cabinet responsibility was drawn largely from the British tradition; but other aspects of the new constitution revealed American influence. The constitutionality of any law, for example, was determinable by a Supreme Court. All constitutional amendments were to be initiated by the Diet with the concurring vote of two-thirds of each house and submitted to popular referendum for ratification. The rights of the individual were safeguarded with meticulous care. Equality before the law, the right to choose and dismiss public officials, freedom of speech and freedom of assembly, a free press, the right to work and to organize labor unions, and the inviolability of property were guaranteed. A broad measure of local self-government was provided for, including the election of officials by popular vote. If democracy was to take real hold in Japan, it would have to be based on the solid, routine experience acquired in the unspectacular tasks of local government. There were many outside Japan who criticized this imposition of alien political forms on a conquered people by their conquerors and pointed to the discouraging precedent of the Weimar Republic in Germany. But it was undeniable that, if the old order was to go, something new and better must be devised to take its place. For the moment the Japanese people were acting with their usual docility and rendering General MacArthur an adulation second only to the Emperor himself. Only the future could show the extent of their sincerity and their willingness and competence to use the precious lore of democracy.

A sweeping program of land reform, pressed remorselessly by SCAP through a somewhat protesting Diet, became law in October 1946. Virtually one-half of Japan's 5,700,000 farming families cultivated their scanty patches of land as tenants, not as full proprietors. Their leases, usually concluded by verbal agreement, were revocable at will; and many hapless sharecroppers relinquished as much as 70 per cent of their annual produce to grasping and absentee landlords. The new reform obliged absentee landlords to surrender their lands to the government in exchange for 24-year annuity bonds. Owner cultivators were restricted to the maximum of $7\frac{1}{2}$ acres, save in the barren northern island of Hokkaido, where the upper limit was set at 30 acres. Of the 5,000,000 acres of land thus made available for distribution to the lesser tenantry, the Japanese Government had purchased 4,000,000 acres by March 1948. The sale of the land at an equitable price was conducted through local and prefectural land commissions, which permitted the purchaser to extend his payments over 30 annual installments.

The transfer of land proceeded with some briskness in 1946–47, but lost speed considerably in the course of 1948. Many tenants lacked the means to purchase their holdings even on the easy terms offered. Disgruntled landlords formed protective associations and began to exert a restraining influence on the land commissions. Further, it was suspected that a good deal of land was being purchased by intermediaries for subsequent transfer *sub rosa* to former owners. In short, land reform alleviated, but could not entirely cure the maladies of Japanese agriculture, still confronted by the basic problem of too large a population on too little cultivable land.

Japan's industrial recovery caused SCAP increasing concern as the occupation continued. She had been stripped of an empire from which she had drawn the greater part of her raw materials, strained by a procession of wars since 1931, and ravaged by the terrible bombings of 1944–45. A severe shortage of consumer goods had been coupled in the last year of the war with reckless overissue of currency. In 1945, tax revenues yielded only 15 per cent of the budget. Japanese industrial workers, caught in the vicious circle of irregular employment and high prices, began to stir resentfully. Their average wartime wage of 150 yen ($15) per month had been raised to 600 ($40) by the summer of 1946; but the price of rice had risen fifteen-fold since 1937.

The remedy for low wages seemed to lie in unionization and collective bargaining, which were legalized by the new constitution. A tidal wave of new entrants burst over the labor unions, which counted over 5,000,000 members by 1948, fifteen times the number in the late thirties. Of these, over 1,000,000 belonged to the Japanese Federation of Labor (JFL), a conservative organization particularly powerful in the textile and tobacco industries. Over 1,500,000 belonged to the Congress of Industrial Organizations (CIO), an industrial union of a more aggressive type, chiefly of white-collar workers and employees of the iron, steel, and chemical industries. An epidemic of strikes, beginning in the Bibai coal mines of Hokkaido, spread rapidly through the country during the second half of 1946. Alternatively, many disaffected workers stayed on the job, but impounded the product of their labor with the object of exchanging it directly for farm produce.

The demands of the embattled workers, though excessive in view of the current economic conditions in Japan, did not bear the stamp of extremism. They asked for wage increases, an eight-hour day, vacations with pay, and joint labor-management councils. But there was undoubtedly some Communist infiltration into the CIO; and the impounding of the product of their labor by some workers squared exactly with Marxist economic philosophy. Consequently, SCAP issued admonitory pamphlets in November 1946 warning workers to shun "political strikes." Unheeding, the JFL and CIO announced a nation-wide strike of 2,600,000 government employees for January 1947. Twenty-four hours before the strike call became effective, SCAP issued a general prohibition, on the ground that the national welfare was involved. The veto was accepted by the unions, and the strike order canceled.

Clearly these uncertain economic conditions were not calculated to inspire the common man in Japan with confidence in the sagacity of the victors or in the new democratic regime which the victors sponsored. There was also the danger that they might seriously delay recovery, and thus transform Japan into a long-term liability to the Allied Powers. The conservative press in Tokyo never wearied of pointing out that the manifest deterioration of Soviet-American relations enhanced the strategical importance of Japan. On this ground alone, the argument proceeded, it would be impolitic to permit the country to degenerate into an economic slum, weakened by poverty and rent by discord.

American policy more recently has moved increasingly in the direction of positive aid to Japan. In April 1947, the Far Eastern Commission declared that the Japanese people were entitled to the standard of living prevailing in the years of 1930–34. In May, Under Secretary of State Acheson affirmed that, in the interest of world recovery, it was necessary to promote the economic revival of Germany and Japan, "the workshops of Europe and Asia." An obvious field for American effort lay in the light industries of Japan, which could be safely encouraged without adding substantially to her war potential. Thus in April 1948, the United States Export-Import Bank granted a cotton credit of $60,000,000 to the textile industry, then operating at 15 per cent of its production in 1937. In the following August, SCAP announced the restoration of the control of port facilities in Tokyo, Yokohama, and Kobe to the Japanese Government. But all these and similar measures would have to wait upon discussions of higher strategic policy in Washington — whether indeed Japan was to be built up as an outer bastion of American Pacific defense or was to be regarded as an expendable liability.

KOREA

Korea, which has not hitherto figured in this book, acquired her post-1945 international importance largely by reason of her artificial division into Soviet and American occupation zones and her conversion thereby into one of the many fields of Soviet-American conflict. Korea's independence "in due course" had been resolved at the Cairo Conference in November 1943 and was implied in the Potsdam ultimatum of July 26, 1945. Her immediate future was settled without hope of appeal at the Crimea and Potsdam Conferences, where it was decided that, when the Soviet entered the war, its forces should occupy the northern half of her territory down to the 38th parallel and that American forces should occupy the remaining southern half. There was no simultaneous understanding with regard to the withdrawal of the two forces.

Nonetheless the Koreans hailed "V-J Day" as their liberation from thirty-five years of harsh police rule and economic exploitation at Japanese hands. Korean nationalist *émigrés* returned from China, where they had maintained a "government in exile" ever since the cruel Japanese repressions in Korea in 1919, and set up in Seoul, the Korean capital, a People's Republic of left-wing, popular front complexion. When General J. R. Hodge led his corps into the southern zone nearly a month after the Japanese surrender, he declined to recognize this republic, on the ground that it was a puppet creation. He installed instead a Korean Advisory Council of eleven members drawn from the ultraconservative and landlord class. Meanwhile the Soviets sponsored an affiliate of the People's Republic in their own northern zone under the title of the North Korean People's Interim Committee.

The fundamental geographical and political bisection of Korea thus effected was not healed. Soviet and American authorities continued to develop the organization of their own zones each after their own fashion. Korean affairs were discussed at the Moscow Conference in December 1945, and it was there agreed to establish "a provisional Korean democratic government" under a five-year trusteeship of the United States, the Soviet Union, Britain, and China, flanked meanwhile by a United States-Soviet Joint Commission. But Korean nationalists naturally protested against the trusteeship principle, and the Joint Commission adjourned after fruitless bickering.

In November 1946, the American Military Government announced that elections for an interim Legislative Assembly would be held in the American zone, half popularly elected, half nominated. General Hodge reserved the right to make "suggestions" to this Assembly as well as the right of veto and of dissolution. Pre-election riots and disturbances occurred on a considerable scale, despite a precautionary arrest of several members of the Korean Communist party, and were only quelled by the imposition of martial law.

The elections resulted in a strongly conservative and not very representative Assembly. But experimentation of this sort might well be endless and, in any case, it did nothing to bring the two zones nearer together. A further meeting of the Joint Commission was held in the summer of 1947, following a request by Secretary Marshall to Molotov, but was again adjourned with nothing achieved.

In September 1947 the United States pressed the thorny problem of Korea into the not entirely willing hands of the General Assembly of the United Nations. The Soviet Union responded to this move by proposing joint withdrawal from Korea by the end of 1948. It declined to participate in the dispatch of a temporary commission by the United Nations to preside over an impartial election in both occupied zones. When the temporary commission reached Korea in January 1948, the Soviet authorities forbade its members to cross the 38th parallel into the Soviet zone. The commission thereupon recommended elections in the American zone for a new National Assembly. The elections were duly held in May 1948 amid fresh disturbances, in which 589 persons were officially admitted to have lost their lives. Groups of the Right, however, won a working majority under the leadership of Dr. Syngman Rhee, formerly a student at Harvard and Princeton, an ardent admirer of President Wilson, and onetime president of the Korean government in exile in China. At the opening session, Rhee affirmed that the Assembly would speak for the whole country and had empty seats reserved in the chamber for the absent delegates from northern Korea. Soviet authorities greeted the outcome of the elections by depriving the American zone of electric power, furnished by the Yalu River plants in the north, on the plea that the American Military Government had failed to maintain agreed rice deliveries.

The new Assembly under Rhee's leadership proceeded to organize the Democratic Republic of Korea, which was formally proclaimed on August 15, 1948 — the third anniversary of the capitulation of Japan — with the diplomatic recognition of the United States and China. Rhee entered into an agreement with General Hodge for the training of Korean forces by American officers. The Korean police were increased from 26,000 to 60,000 men; and it was announced that recruiting would continue till "the quota" (unrevealed) had been reached.

These belligerent measures paralleled the situation in the Soviet zone. A People's Militia, armed with captured Japanese equipment, had existed there since the end of 1945. Sedulously trained by Soviet officers, it numbered perhaps 50,000 men by 1948. It constituted the fighting arm of the Soviet-sponsored People's Interim Committee. The moving spirit in that Committee was now the Secretary General of the North Korean Communist party, Kim Il-sung, who had become an almost legendary figure during thirty years of underground activity against the Japanese. At his prompting the People's Interim Committee proceeded without delay to inaugurate drastic agrarian reforms. Similarly, for the benefit of the industrial workers, a labor code introduced new scales of hours, wages, vacations, and social insurance. Labor unions were encouraged to expand their membership and were integrated into the North Korean Federation of Labor. Banks, industries, and transportation were socialized. Early in 1948 the Soviet commander, General Chistyakov, permitted a hand-picked assembly to draft a provisional working constitution for a "Democratic People's Republic" applicable to all Korea. Next, in April 1948, political leaders in the American zone were invited to attend a coalition conference in Pyengyang, the capital of the Soviet zone. The conference passed resolutions calling for the formation of a united Korean government, the abolition of dictatorship and of monopoly capitalism, and the immediate withdrawal of all foreign troops.

Manifestly the Soviet intention was "to beat the Americans to the draw." A subsequent Soviet offer in September 1948 to participate in a joint withdrawal, to be completed by the end of 1948, was regarded with suspicion and rejected by Washington. Nevertheless, Moscow announced that Soviet occupation forces would leave by January 1, 1949. But if indeed American troops left likewise, the Democratic Republic in the American zone would be protected only by semitrained native troops from the danger of a "spontaneous" invasion by the People's Militia. A revolt of army elements in the south in November 1948 revealed that the military establishment of the Democratic Republic was not completely reliable.

Economically, the zonal division in Korea was reminiscent of the unnatural situation in occupied Germany. Industries and hydroelectric plants were located mainly in the north, which in turn depended on the rice-bowl area in the south for its food supplies. The exchange of goods and services across the 38th parallel, never lively, dwindled and died as the political crisis deepened. The division was exacerbated by the maintenance of the landlord system in the south and by the heavy representation of the larger landowners in the National Assembly. Late in 1948 the new American Military Governor, General Dean, contrived to introduce into the Assembly a comprehensive land redistribution bill, which envisaged government purchase of landholdings in excess of $12\frac{1}{2}$ acres and the sale of the land thus acquired to the tenantry in return for easy installment payments. The creation of a large class of peasant proprietors would undoubtedly strengthen the social foundations of the Democratic Republic. But stiff resistance to the measure could be anticipated in the Assembly; and if it passed into law, many tenants would find even installment buying beyond their means. This dismaying possibility indicated the fundamental problem of all Asia, that of peasant poverty, the grinding, unimaginable poverty of the Orient. The poorer tenant, with the bony hand of famine ever at his throat, shackled by debt, could not accumulate the few surplus dollars by which he might redeem himself and his family from his age-old economic servitude.

FRENCH INDO-CHINA

In Indo-China, at the end of August 1945, as we have related elsewhere, the Annamese Emperor Bao Dai had abdicated (see p. 739). The Democratic Republic of Viet Nam, under the presidency of Ho Chi-minh, claiming sovereignty over Annam, Tonkin, and Cochin China, declared its independence and the annulment of all former treaties with France. Considerable quantities of arms and equipment were seized from the complacent Japanese occupation forces. General Gracey, landing at Saïgon in September at the head of a British-Indian contingent, neither rejected nor acknowledged this self-styled republic. His instructions were purely military; he was to disarm all Japanese in Indo-China south of the 16th parallel. Chinese Nationalist forces were charged with a similar task north of the parallel. Ho Chi-minh, explaining to the somewhat aloof General that he was pro-Ally but anti-French, accepted these arrangements. But he protested violently when 4,000 French troops, interned by the Japanese, were liberated and brought into Saïgon to act as civil guards to protect French property from the native nationalists.

The stiff fighting that ensued between French and native nationalists made an unpromising accompaniment to the negotiations opened in October 1945, between the Viet Nam Republican government and the French High Commissioner, Admiral Thierry d'Argenlieu. The Republican government stood firmly upon its recent declaration of independence. The French demanded that it should be incorporated into an Indo-Chinese Federation linked with the French Union and headed by the High Commissioner with authority over defense and foreign policy.

In the meantime, French reinforcements, including an armored division under General Leclerc, were pouring into Saïgon. The Republican government withdrew to Hanoi in the north and directed its resistance to the French from there. Nevertheless diplomatic exchanges continued, and a provisional cease-fire agreement was reached at Hanoi in March 1946. France recognized the Viet Nam Republic as "a free state within the Indo-Chinese Federation." French troops were to enter northern Indo-China to relieve the Chinese Nationalist forces, which had alienated the inhabitants by their merciless requisitions. French troops were to be gradually withdrawn from Republican territory over a period of five years, with the exception of garrisons stationed in naval and air bases. Viet Nam conceded that its permanent armed forces would not exceed 10,000 men. The future of Cochin China, to which Viet Nam had laid claim, was to be determined by a plebiscite of its inhabitants.

But further differences arose in the course of a conference convoked at Dalat in Tonkin to work out the details of the Hanoi agreement. The Republicans contended that the French High Commissioner, far from being the executive authority for the Indo-Chinese Federation in matters of defense and foreign policy, could not be regarded as more than the diplomatic representative of France accredited to themselves. Meanwhile the French were proceeding to their own settlement of the question of Cochin China. French troops were now in full occupation of that rich and productive colony, and d'Argenlieu was lending a ready ear to a group of wealthy Cochin Chinese landowners who approached him with proposals for "self-government." On June 1, 1946 the provisional "Free State" of Cochin China was inaugurated in Saïgon as a constituent member of the Indo-Chinese Federation. The inauguration ceremonies were performed in the square before the cathedral, which could easily be commanded by machine guns.

The Dalat conference was resumed at Fontainebleau in France. In these more tranquil surroundings, the delegates groped their way to a few points of agreement. The projected Indo-Chinese Federation was to have a single currency and a single customs union. But there was no solution forthcoming in regard to Cochin China. The precarious Hanoi cease-fire agreement was clearly at the mercy of local incidents. In December 1946, a dispute over the collection of customs at Haiphong broadened the general hostilities. Hanoi was occupied by French forces after heavy house-to-house fighting, and Ho Chi-minh and his ministers fled the city. By February 1947, some lingering embers of resistance in Hanoi were stamped out, and isolated French garrisons elsewhere were relieved. But with an army of 110,000 men the French could hold only the urban centers and vital strategic points. The rural areas remained the preserves of roving bands of Annamese partisans. Few of the conventions of civilized warfare were observed by either side. There was a high incidence of tropical diseases among the newly arrived troops, many of whom were German ex-prisoners of war enlisted in the French Foreign Legion.

These limited military successes encouraged d'Argenlieu to speed the reorganization of the parts of Indo-China which stood outside Viet Nam. In February 1947 the "Free State" of Cochin China was accorded official recognition. In the same month, the young King Sihanouk of Cambodia, prompted by d'Argenlieu, announced the termination of absolutist rule and the establishment of a limited monarchy under a constitution to be drafted by a forthcoming Cambodian National Assembly. The monarchy in Laos underwent a similar, if less drastic, transformation. The separate nationalist movements of Cambodia and Laos, both antimonarchic and anti-French, were driven underground.

The obstinate problem of Viet Nam remained. Official French policy, enunciated by the French Premier, Léon Blum, at the close of 1946, affirmed that negotiations could not be resumed until order had been restored. But the Republicans perceived the disadvantage of coming unarmed to the conference table; and their depredations, particularly their attacks on French convoys converging on Saïgon, continued unabated. The uneasy conditions resulted in serious economic dislocation. Plantation owners at the height of the terroristic campaign scarcely knew whether to welcome the absence or the presence of their coolies. In December 1947 the French opened tentative negotiations with a view to inducing the Annamese Emperor Bao Dai, in exile in Hong Kong, to return to his native realm. But the French were not then prepared to concede the Emperor's prior demand for the independence of Annam, and the negotiations were temporarily broken off. Undaunted by the Emperor's coyness, the French pushed forward vigorously with the establishment of a puppet regime. On May 23, 1948 a promonarchist provisional government was set up in Hanoi and was recognized by the High Commissioner as the legitimate authority in all the territories claimed by the Republic of Viet Nam. The head of the government was Nguyen Xuan, an Annamese who had become a French citizen and had risen to the rank of lieutenant general in the French army. The legislative branch of the government was established in October 1948, and was chosen by a handpicked electorate from which all popular elements were excluded.

Further agreements were signed in Paris in March 1949, providing for the unity and independence of Viet Nam within the French Union. In June the Emperor Bao Dai was invested as Head of the State of Viet Nam with Nguyen Xuan as Premier. But Ho Chi-minh and his confederates were still at large in a considerable part of the country.

The spirit of compromise has been notably lacking in Indo-Chinese politics. On the one hand stood a traditionally authoritarian colonial administration, unschooled in the art of tactful concession and habituated to the use of military force. On the other stood a newly resurgent Annamese nationalism, headlong and confident in the manner of youth, but old in the traditional resistance methods, the brigandage and assassination, of a submerged people. The explosive slogans of Liberty, Equality, and Fraternity had helped to plunge France and Europe into turmoil for a century. Applied in the Orient with a powerful admixture of racial hatred and Marxist absolutism, they offered little prospect that the travail of Indo-China would be speedily ended.

SIAM (THAILAND)

At the Japanese surrender in 1945, the Regent, Luang Pradit Manudharm, or Pridi, as he was familiarly called, and his civilian clique were in a dominant position in Siam (see p. 737). He had, as he thought, recommended himself to the victorious Allies first by his secret, and then by his increasingly open, support of the Allied cause. Two days after the Japanese surrender, the Bangkok radio announced that Siam's declaration of war against the United States and Britain in 1942 had been illegal and unpopular and that Burmese and Malayan territories, lately donated to Siam by Japan, should be immediately restored. This penitential announcement was made in the name of Prince Ananda Mahidol, who was completing his legal studies in Switzerland and whose return to Siam and assumption of authority under the constitution of 1932 were known to be favored by the British Government. But it remained to be seen whether the Allied Powers could be thus dissuaded from exacting a heavy penalty from the present Siamese Government for the sins of its pro-Japanese predecessor.

The American Department of State responded reassuringly that Siam, having acted under duress, was not regarded as an enemy Power. British interests in Siam, on the other hand, had suffered severely during the Japanese occupation. Hence the final Anglo-Siamese peace treaty in January 1946 did not err on the side of leniency. Siam agreed to abandon all acquisitions of British territory made during the war and to indemnify property holders there for all damages inflicted on them. She assumed responsibility for the protection of British interests throughout the country, permitted British banks and commercial houses to resume business, discharged the arrears of interest, restored trade with neighboring states under British control, gave full facilities to British Commonwealth civil air lines, and agreed to conclude a new treaty of commerce and navigation.

An ancient ghost was laid by a clause prohibiting the construction of a canal across the Isthmus of Kra linking the Indian Ocean with the Gulf of Siam.[2] In November 1946 a Franco-Siamese treaty was signed retroceding the Cambodian territories, lately occupied by Siam, to French Indo-China (see p. 678).

The internal situation of the country was difficult. When, in December 1945, Prince Ananda Mahidol returned to his native land — once again officially named Siam — he encountered a rising currency inflation, a corresponding discontent among low-salaried government employees, and a racking controversy over the restitution of government-controlled industries to private ownership. Thus it was under the gloomiest auspices that he promulgated a new democratic constitution in April 1946, replacing the unicameral National Assembly of 1932 with a Senate and House of Representatives in which all members were elective. The new constitution had been conceived by Pridi, who dominated the administration from behind a protective screen of his political familiars. But these auxiliaries were far from impeccable, and not even Pridi's immense prestige was enough to clean up the corruption which was traditional in Siamese politics.

As the government toiled and labored under its domestic and foreign burdens, it was smitten by a political thunderbolt. On June 9, 1946 the newly installed King Ananda Mahidol was found dead in the Barompinan Palace of Bangkok. The gunshot wound in his head was at first officially pronounced as accidental. The prevalence of doubt on this point led, however, to the appointment of a special commission of inquiry which reported, with eminent discretion, that the death had been due to suicide, accident, or assassination. The police favored the accident theory; and the Chief of Police in Bangkok, to demonstrate his case, went so far as to shoot a pig in the presence of the members of the Senate and House. But the majority of the commission subsequently reversed its findings, and affirmed that death was probably by assassination. The late King was succeeded by his Boston-born brother, eighteen-year-old Prince Phumiphon Aduldet. A Council of Regency was established in the absence of the Prince, who was then studying in Switzerland.

From the dense cloud of suspicion and supposition, one certainty emerged; the unsolved tragedy would provide invaluable political ammunition for the foes of the government. Luang Pibul Songgram, collaborator with the Japanese, had faded into retirement after his fall in 1944 and, since the Japanese surrender, had been placed under detention (see p. 737). But he was released in March 1946, by order of the High Court of Justice in Bangkok, together with other prisoners held on war crimes. The political pressure which he and his fellow militarists now exerted was demonstrable in the rapid rise and fall of ministries during the winter of 1946 and spring of 1947. In May 1947, Pibul publicly announced his re-entry into politics, declaring his intention, appropriately enough, in the course of one of the kite-flying contests so popular in Siam. In retrospect, his political strategy had been acute. He had withdrawn to the wings of the political stage in time to escape the odium of submitting to the heavy penalties exacted by the victorious Powers and then returned to the limelight in time to make the most of the country's economic discontents.

Late in October 1947 the government agreed to pay over $6,000,000 to British and Australian interests as compensation for tin ore diverted to Japan during the war. Less than two weeks later, Pibul seized power in Bangkok by a bloodless *coup d'état*. His aides scoured the city in twenty old Japanese tanks and armored cars, but encountered no resistance worth the name. The current Premier, forewarned, had already fled to a lamasery. Pibul assumed the title of Supreme Commander of the Defense Forces, and was carried shoulder-high into the Defense Ministry buildings by cheering soldiers. The Siamese people accepted the coup with resignation rather than enthusiasm. They recalled with distaste Pibul's military rigidity during his previous tenure of power and his clamorous insistence that they should wear hats and shoes, cease to sit on the streets, and reduce their consumption of betel nut. Pibul sought to give his regime a popular front complexion; but, in elections in January 1948, his party won only seven seats. In April 1948 he formed a ministry himself and, though pledged to observe the principles of constitutional government, embarked on a career of repression directed against "Reds and other subversive elements" and against the Chinese community in Siam. In the general doomsday, Pibul's old political opponents were not allowed to go unscathed. Criminal proceedings were ordered against Pridi and four others for King Ananda Mahidol's assassination. The action took place *in absentia,* since the accused were reported to be in hiding. It is superfluous to add that the official appellation of Siam was once more changed to Thailand, "the Land of Free Men." Early in 1949 the government suppressed disturbances in Bangkok alleged to have been inspired by Ho Chi-minh in Indo-China and by Chinese Communists.

Scarcely three years after the defeat of the Axis, therefore, Siam had emerged as a pseudo-Fascist dictatorship. But, even without Pibul's rigorous rule, Siam would appear to be an unlikely field for Communism. The coolie on the rubber plantation and in the tin mine, living at the rate of 40 cents a day, was perhaps a volatile, uncertain element. But 88 per cent of Siam's population were peasants treading stolidly in the deeply grooved paths of tradition and oblivious to their government's earnest appeals for the introduction of improved agricultural techniques. Rice, the staple product, was grown mainly in small holdings in sufficient quantities to make it an important exportable commodity. Large estates were few. Hence the phenomenon of a suppressed, debt-ridden tenantry, so general in East Asia was not apparent; nor was Siam affected by that potent source of discontent elsewhere, the inflationary rise in the price of rice.

Meanwhile the government derived its appropriate reward from the growing Anglo-American rivalry in Siam. By 1948 no less than fourteen air lines, including British and American corporations, were making Bangkok the very hub of East Asian aerial traffic. British and Australian interests had formerly controlled 70 per cent of Siam's output of tin. But American buyers competed for supplies from independent purchasers and prospected for new sources of ore. Washington's policy of stock-piling inspired a bid for a portion of the tin accumulated in Siam during the war, and one-half of the backlog went to American smelters. Tin and rubber, which used to go to Singapore for processing, were brought direct to the United States from Bangkok by four American shipping lines. In 1939 there was only one American firm in the whole of Siam. At the time of writing there are no less than thirty. The Soviet Union ran a poor third in the economic race, buying all the rubber and tin available from lesser Chinese producers. The Soviet embassy in Bangkok, however, was remarkably well-staffed — an indication perhaps of the growing importance ascribed by Moscow to this potentially rich and strategic country.

MALAYA

When the British returned to Malaya in September 1945, they found at first no outburst of resentment and revolt, as in French Indo-China. But the modicum of self-government conceded by the Japanese had immensely stimulated the political consciousness of the minority of educated Malays. Economically, the Japanese occupation had resulted in a stoppage of the normal channels of trade and had left behind it the usual inflation. In October 1945 the British installed a military government and devised hasty plans for anticipating possible political unrest. They proposed that a centralized Malayan Union should embrace the whole of the peninsula, except Singapore, with a common citizenship for all inhabitants, and be administered by a British governor, advised by partly native councils.

The formal announcement of these proposals in January 1946 evoked the first storm of protest. Demonstrations were led by the United Malay Nationalist Organization (UMNO), founded at Ipoh in November 1945, under Makhtarruddin, a native Malay and a Moslem. The membership of the UMNO grew rapidly to 60,000 and included Malays, Indians, and Chinese — much to the dismay of the British, accustomed in the past to the hostility of these three ethnic communities.[3] The UMNO demanded the right of self-determination, a free and united Malaya, co-operation between the various racial communities, lower taxes and financial aid for the peasantry, and better wages and working conditions for labor. The rulers of the nine native states were emboldened by the uproar to add their own note of protest. They resented the transfer of their crown lands and financial assets to the projected central government and demanded, in particular, control over the membership of their own native advisory councils, and an oath of allegiance to themselves, not to the Union. As a mark of disapproval, they absented themselves — with the exception of the Sultan of Johore — from the inauguration ceremony on April 1, 1946, when Sir Edward Gent was installed as the first Governor of the Malayan Union.

Consequently, within a year of her liberation, Malaya had joined the political ferment of her East Asian neighbors. The British made a further attempt to meet her problems, following a conference of British representatives, native rulers, and the UMNO in Kuala Lumpur at the end of 1946.

A constitution, this time in the form of a loose federation, was introduced in 1947. In January 1948 the nine native rulers severally signed treaties with Britain. The new federal government was installed a month later under Sir Edward Gent as High Commissioner. His jurisdiction did not extend to Singapore, which remained a crown colony under separate administration. Malcolm MacDonald, as Governor General of Malaya and Commissioner General for Southeast Asia, exercised authority over both areas.

It might appear, then, that the British Government was pursuing in Malaya the old, imperialist policy of "divide and rule." But its statesmanship was solidly based on the incontrovertible fact that Malaya was not a nation, but an uneasy assemblage of ethnic communities — Malay, Indian, and Chinese.[3] The diverse criticisms leveled by each of these against the new constitution revealed the difficulty of contriving a settlement acceptable to all. The Malays demanded that the Executive Council under the new constitution should be instantly transformed into an elective body. The Chinese were antagonized by the administrative severance of the federal government from Singapore, where they were chiefly concentrated and where they formed 80 per cent of the population. Both Chinese and Indian immigrants resented the provisions requiring fifteen years' residence as a qualification for citizenship. Furthermore, Singapore as the base of the British Pacific Fleet was of immense strategic importance, and Malaya's exports of rubber and tin made her a precious arsenal for the all too scarce American dollar. Finally, there was the universal problem of Communism.

Communism in Malaya sprouted out of the secret societies so prevalent among Chinese immigrants. The extension of the trade-union movement furnished the originally small Malayan Communist party and Communist Youth party with ample opportunity to broaden their activities. During the Japanese occupation they had formed the backbone of the resistance movement under the title of the Malayan People's Anti-Japanese Army (MPAJA) (see p. 737) but, at the conclusion of hostilities, the majority of them had evaded the unpleasant obligation of handing in their arms to the British military government. Thereafter they had applied themselves to the task of permeating the Pan-Malayan Federation of Trade-Unions, which controlled 60 per cent of trade-union membership in the peninsula. They were assisted by the current economic distress and were able to foment the usual strikes. They were also encouraged by the British withdrawal from India and Burma and by the advance of their fellow Communists in China.

By 1948 the veterans of the MPAJA had launched a regular campaign of terrorism in the chief centers of tin and rubber production. Larger groups carried out hit-and-run attacks on plantations and mining equipment. Smaller bands specialized in assassination — the skillfully devised ambush for the white man's automobile, or the rapid spatter of bullets from the shelter of rubber trees. During June and July 1948, more than fifty persons, chiefly European and Chinese, were assassinated. The government retaliated by outlawing the Pan-Malayan Federation of Trade-Unions, the MPAJA, and the Communist party with its subsidiary Communist Youth party. The death penalty was also invoked for the possession of unlicensed firearms. Land and air attacks were launched against the elusive guerrillas, chiefly in the tin-mining area of northern Perak. But the greater part of the Malayan terrain is jungle, the assassin of the morning may be an apparently law-abiding farmer or fisherman of the afternoon, and in the dim arboreous recesses his mobile bands could fight or flee, dissolve or re-form in primeval freedom. In September 1948 the Guards Brigade was ordered out from England to essay the unpleasant tactics of jungle fighting. But sporadic bandit warfare continued into 1949.

THE NETHERLANDS EAST INDIES

In August 1945 an Anglo-Dutch agreement was signed, under which the British were to disarm and repatriate the Japanese in the Netherlands East Indies but thereafter permit the return of the former Dutch administration. A scanty British-Indian contingent under General Christison arrived in Java early in October. During the fateful interval, Soekarno's Indonesian Republic (see p. 739) had furnished its forces of 100,000 men with weapons appropriated from the Japanese and had established rudimentary organs of central government. Soekarno assured General Christison of his co-operation in disarming the Japanese, but added that, if Dutch troops or officials landed, they would be resisted. General Christison's demand that the Republican "Peace Preservation Corps" should surrender its arms precipitated brisk fighting in Surabaya. Efforts to arrange a cease-fire agreement collapsed when the General's envoy, Brigadier Mallaby, was shot dead as he motored through the city to arrange final details.

The murderers of Mallaby were not handed over, and the ensuing punitive expedition broadened into full-scale hostilities both in Java and Sumatra. Resistance proved to be unexpectedly stubborn, and the outnumbered British found it necessary to rearm and deploy Japanese troops. Under heavy pressure, the Indonesian forces were pushed back step by step into central and eastern Java. Despite the hostilities, the Dutch Governor General, Van Mook, consented to open negotiations with the self-declared Republic. He preferred to treat, however, not with Soekarno, who was thoroughly compromised in Dutch eyes by his previous collaboration with Japan, but with the politically untainted Republican Premier, Sjahrir. In November 1946, as the British forces were making ready to leave, Van Mook and Sjahrir initiated a draft agreement at Cheribon. The Dutch recognized the Indonesian Republic as the *de facto* authority in Java, Sumatra, and Madura. A United States of Indonesia was to be constituted by January 1, 1949, to include the Indonesian Republic on the one hand, and the autonomous states of Borneo and the Great East (Celebes, Bali, the Moluccas, Timor, etc.) on the other, the whole to be linked with the Kingdom of the Netherlands in equal partnership under the Dutch Crown. The people of any island might hold aloof if they expressed a desire for nonparticipation by plebiscite.

The interpretation of the agreement gave rise to far-reaching differences almost at once. The strictly legalistic Dutch regarded it not as a formal treaty, but as a tentative convention subject to revision. The Republic viewed it as a recognition of Indonesian independence. In consequence, the Dutch demand that law and order should be preserved by a joint Dutch-Indonesian police force was rejected. The efforts of the Indonesians to ship plantation products abroad were checked by a Dutch naval blockade. Finally, the cease-fire agreement accepted at Cheribon was disregarded by both sides. Dutch troops, aided by a $100,000,000 loan from the United States for the purchase of war supplies, reconquered a considerable part of Java and Sumatra. Indonesian forces infiltrated constantly into the Dutch lines and terrorized the civilian population.

In the summer of 1947 the Dutch launched a long-prepared and well-mounted offensive in central and eastern Java. As they neared the Republican capital of Jogjakarta, the United States offered to mediate a settlement. The proposal was rebuffed by the Republicans. Shortly thereafter India and Australia called the situation in Indonesia to the attention of the Security Council of the United Nations, which unanimously voted a resolution calling on the parties to cease hostilities and reach a settlement by peaceful means. The Security Council's action at once brought up an issue of crucial importance, far transcending the immediate dispute. The Dutch argued that the hostilities constituted "police action of a strictly limited character" and that the United Nations was precluded from interference in the domestic affairs of its members.[4] In the upshot, both parties yielded with bad grace to a proposal to negotiate under the auspices of a Committee of Good Offices appointed by the Security Council.

The Committee of Good Offices contrived to bring the parties to the council table in December 1947. Mohammed Hatta, the most capable administrator and economist among the Indonesian Socialists, was now Premier and chief negotiator for the Republic. A cease-fire agreement was concluded, but neither side observed it to the full. Meanwhile Hatta was at odds with extremists in his own camp who were denouncing all attempts at a diplomatic settlement. In the late summer of 1948, an ominous figure arrived in Java in the person of Muso, a veteran Indonesian Communist, who had spent twenty-two years in exile in the Soviet Union. Under his guidance, the disgruntled Indonesian Communists seized Madiun in central Java and announced that the Republic had been "Sovietized."

Premier Hatta, rejecting a Dutch offer of assistance, cleared the Madiun area with his own forces, but the majority of the Communists took to the jungle and continued to resist. Simultaneously the Dutch decided to take drastic measures. In December 1948 they broke off the negotiations which the Committee of Good Offices had been falteringly conducting and reaffirmed their original plan of 1946 to establish a United States of Indonesia. In a week of fighting, between December 18 and 25, 1948, they captured all the major cities remaining in Republican hands in Java and Sumatra. Dutch paratroops seized the Republican leaders in the course of a surprise attack on Jogjakarta.

Under American initiative, the Security Council of the United Nations, then meeting in Paris, called on both sides to cease fire and withdraw their forces to their previous positions. Simultaneously Washington suspended Marshall aid to Indonesia. But, though Indonesian guerrilla outbreaks continued, it was clear that the Dutch had the situation under control, and the next long, tortuous phase of negotiations with the Republican leaders began. In the summer of 1949 the Dutch evacuated Jogjakarta, and the liberated Republican leaders returned to their capital to elaborate the basis of a federal government for Indonesia. On August 3 the Dutch and Republican Governments simultaneously proclaimed the termination of hostilities, and a few days later Premier Hatta at the head of a Republican delegation arrived at The Hague for a full-dress round-table conference upon a constitution for the United States of Indonesia.

THE PHILIPPINES

When organized Japanese resistance in the Philippines was finally broken in the summer of 1945, the Islands were littered with the debris of war and racked by deep-seated political conflict. Half of the city of Manila lay in ruins; Cebu and Zamboanga had been gutted almost completely. Sugar production, a significant index, was 100,000 tons for 1945–46, barely a tenth of the prewar average. The price of rice, another significant index, had risen eightfold. Gold-mining equipment in Paracale, Masbate, and elsewhere had been bombed, burned, looted, or commandeered for dispatch to Japan. It was estimated that two years' rehabilitation would be required before the copper mines of northern Luzon and chromite production in Zambales could show substantial recovery.

In June 1944, President Roosevelt had signed a resolution of both houses of Congress granting Philippine independence immediately upon the expulsion of the Japanese (see p. 739). But political restoration upon this or upon any other basis was hindered at first by the absence of a clearly marked national leader acceptable to Filipinos and Americans alike. During the occupation, members of the powerful Philippine Nationalist party had collaborated with the Japanese. The party's titular head, the reserved and scholarly Sergio Osmeña, evacuated before Bataan, had since been presiding over a Philippine government in exile in Washington. He returned to Manila with the stigma of many another repatriated émigré of these times who had lived in comfort and security while the battle raged through his homeland, and the strong line he now took against collaborators looked a little forced and hollow. Manuel Roxas, head of the opposing Liberal party, had worked with the resistance against the Japanese, had accepted office in the Japanese-sponsored Philippine "Republic," had continued to act as MacArthur's secret liaison with the resistance, had then been attached to MacArthur's headquarters with the rank of brigadier general, and finally emerged as presidential candidate. These surprising changes, despite MacArthur's subsequent vindication, might make Roxas for a time a suspicious political leader and colleague.[5]

Nor was the outlook for the lesser parties any more promising. The

Democratic Alliance was a hastily improvised, loosely jointed coalition of groups which had been active in the resistance. Its platform called for the instant and condign punishment of collaborators and for the redistribution of the land, and it thus drew upon itself the hostility of most professional politicians and of the landlords. Most fatal of all, it was widely regarded as the political arm of the Hukbalahaps, the revolutionary peasant party of central Luzon, whose activities against the Japanese and against the local landlords we have described (see p. 738). Since the liberation, the "Huks" had evaded the order to surrender their arms. During the occupation they had seized much land from absentee or fugitive estate owners, and a looted Japanese or American rifle was often the most that a new proprietor possessed by way of title deeds.

Current legislation pending in Washington added to purely domestic difficulties. The Bell Trade Act provided for a continuance of free trade between the two countries for a period of eight years after the Philippines should have obtained their independence, and thereafter for a graduated duty on Philippine products entering the United States. The act froze the import quotas on Philippine sugar, cordage, coconut oil, and tobacco at 1940 levels, and pegged the Philippine peso at the very high rate of 50 cents to the American dollar. The act was greeted with dismay in the Philippines, inasmuch as the American market had formerly absorbed 80 per cent of Philippine exports. Even if the hitherto open door was to be closed only gradually after an eight-year period of grace, the eventual impact on the economy of the islands would be considerable, and the high value of the peso would effectually prevent a future Philippine government from stimulating export trade by currency devaluation. The Tydings Rehabilitation Act, also pending in Washington, authorized an appropriation of $520,000,000 for the payment of private and public war-damage claims in the Philippines. But the act stipulated that no claims above $500 could be entertained till the Bell Trade Act had been accepted by the Philippine Government.

The two acts had passed both houses of Congress and were awaiting President Truman's signature when the presidential election was held in the Philippines in April 1946. Roxas, who stressed in his florid campaign oratory the absolute necessity of American aid in the task of reconstruction, defeated Osmeña by a little more than 200,000 votes in a total poll of 2,500,000. One week later the acts were signed by President Truman, and were subsequently approved by the Philippine Congress.

On July 4, 1946, the Republic of the Philippines was formally inaugurated in an impressive ceremony at Manila. The American flag was lowered, and in its stead was hoisted the red, white, and blue standard of the Republic, embellished with the golden sun of freedom and three stars. President Roxas proclaimed that the American flag "has been lowered from the flagstaffs of this land not in defeat, not in surrender, not by compulsion, but by the voluntary act of the United States." The United States, however, was permitted to retain 23 bases on the islands on a 99-year lease. In March 1947, the Philippine Government agreed to a reciprocal military-aid pact, valid for five years in the first instance, and to accept the services of an Advisory Military Mission of American officers.

The efforts of the Philippine Government to secure a substantial loan from the United States were only partially successful. President Truman set up a joint Philippine-United States Financial Commission to inquire into the real extent of the Philippine needs. The report of the Commission in June 1947 recommended a more intensive utilization of the existing resources of the islands in lieu of further loans. It estimated that half the foreign-exchange receipts for the period 1947–50 would be derived from nonrecurring American expenditures on war-damage claims and military installations. Thereafter the inflow of American dollars was expected to drop, and American import duties on Philippine products would begin to operate in 1954. The report condemned therefore the current lavish spending on consumer goods. It proposed the rapid extension of the iron, steel, and chemical industries to offset the existing overdependence of Philippine economy on raw material exports such as sugar, coconut oil, copra, and timber.

Roxas had already taken some tentative steps in the direction of economic diversification. A Rehabilitation Finance Corporation had been established late in 1946, patterned after the Reconstruction Finance Corporation of the United States, to grant loans to individuals or corporations for the rehabilitation and development of agricultural and industrial enterprises. Roxas also approached the H. E. Beyster Corporation of Detroit, a firm of consulting engineers, which drew up a ten-to-fifteen-year program of industrial expansion. But there were few signs of urgency in implementing this draft program. The current prosperity contributed to obscure the need for long-range economic planning.

Moreover, industrial expansion of any sort rested on an uncertain basis so long as the agrarian foundations of the Republic remained insecure. The steeply terraced rice fields of central Luzon had become once again an amphitheater of conflict. The dull animosity of the "Huks" against an unreformed and unreforming government had flamed into lively hostility when President Roxas ordered the exclusion from the legislature of seven elected Congressmen sympathetic to their cause. The "Huks" demanded the immediate implementation of a law of September 1946, which reduced the landlord's maximum share of the annual crop to 30 per cent of the total. As leaders of the resistance movement against the Japanese, the "Huks" also demanded the veterans' benefits granted to other partisans. Meanwhile, no government official dared to enter "Huklandia" without powerful escort; and bloody clashes occurred between the "Huks" and the constabulary.

Hostilities increased in scope late in 1946, when President Roxas threw in regular troops following the refusal of the "Huks" to lay down their arms as a preliminary to government consideration of their grievances. Roxas clung to the formula that this vicious little war in Luzon, virtually a continuation of the resistance of the occupation years, was no more than "police action." But in March 1948, when he formally outlawed the "Huks," it was still raging and spreading. In the following month, Roxas died suddenly of a heart attack. His successor, the former Vice-President Elpidio Quirino, reopened negotiations with the "Huks." He undertook to declare a general amnesty on condition that they surrender their arms by August 15. Simultaneously, the Philippine Congress voted in favor of restoring the "Huk" leader, Luis Taruc, to his seat in Congress. But Taruc, sent to central Luzon by the government to negotiate a settlement with the "Huks," identified himself with their cause. By August 15, only 200 rebels had relinquished their arms. The government declared ominously that negotiations would not be resumed.

As 1948 drew to a close, brisk local fighting was reported as government troops drove into Pampanga province in central Luzon, one of the chief centers of disaffection. The Philippines, evidently, were not to be spared the irrepressible conflict between established authority and a militant agrarian radicalism, a conflict which was shaking the pillars of East Asian society from China to the Netherlands East Indies.

INDIA AND PAKISTAN

India in her Commonwealth relations and international relations has been discussed in another context (pp. 842–43). It remains here to say something of her home affairs and, in particular, of her attainment of Dominion status.

Since the Cripps offer in the spring of 1942 (see p. 684), the political situation in India had become as serious as at any time in the period covered by this book. The Working Committee of the Indian National Congress had passed its famous "Quit India" resolution in July 1942; the government had replied by putting Gandhi and several Congress leaders under detention; an outbreak of violence and sabotage had followed, notably in Bihar along the army's lines of communication with the Assam front. The Moslem League under Jinnah was now fully committed to its plan for a separate Moslem state of Pakistan (pp. 355–56), while Hindu opinion was as adamant for "No Partition," and each side was trying to blackmail the government into acceptance of its particular thesis as the price of full cooperation in the war effort. Nevertheless an Indian army of over 2,000,000, participating in campaigns in the Near East, East and North Africa, Italy, Burma, and Malaya, at a total cost of 180,000 casualties, would seem to have represented a war effort of no mean magnitude. In October 1943, Field Marshal Lord Wavell became Viceroy. At that moment the worst famine in India for forty years was raging in Bengal.

Gandhi was released in 1944 on grounds of ill-health. His fellow Congress members were released in 1945, and the old fight was rejoined. The advent of the Labor Government in Britain resulted in no immediate change in British policy toward India. Government missions and leaders' conferences of the usual Indian pattern followed through 1945 and 1946 to the accompaniment of a new wave of disturbances in the country. Basic differences between the Congress and the Moslem League had now developed into an open struggle for the assumption of political power. In

October 1946, Wavell at last succeeded in expanding the Viceroy's Executive Council into an "interim government," composed of both Hindu and Moslem members, thus giving India her first wholly responsible cabinet. But by then both parties, Hindu and Moslem, were thoroughly alarmed at the current disturbances, which in Bihar and Bengal alone had cost over 10,000 lives. The British authorities in India were becoming increasingly concerned over their ability to maintain law and order by the traditional methods and were clearly averse to risking the lives of British personnel in a conflict which Indians themselves were provoking.

On February 1947, Attlee came out with the blunt pronouncement of a deadline — that coming June — for the transfer of power in India from British to Indian hands, and India's future constitution, whatever it might be, would have to be completed by that date. At the same time Admiral Lord Mountbatten, lately Allied Supreme Commander in Southeast Asia, succeeded Wavell as Viceroy. The British Government's shock tactics and the immense personal ascendancy which the new Viceroy was able to establish over the Indian leaders, no less than the continual spread of riot and massacre, all produced a new and sobering urgency. The Viceroy was in London in June for Cabinet conferences and came back to India with a "procedural plan" providing for the immediate partition of India into Hindu and Moslem states. Attlee introduced an Indian Independence Bill into Parliament, and the two Dominions of India and Pakistan were formally instituted on August 15, 1947. Mountbatten himself became the first Governor General of India, and Jinnah the first Governor General of Pakistan.

Disturbances continued, but they were now the responsibility of the two new Dominions. The Sikh community, betrayed by a partition which cut right through its homeland, set out to exterminate the Moslems in the new province of Eastern Punjab, assigned to the Indian side of the line. Revenge retaliated on revenge; minority millions fled from one Dominion to the other seeking their security among their fellows. Generally the Indian States, in one way or another, were obliged to accede to the appropriate Dominion, and they usually did so peacefully. But Kashmir became the theater of a minor civil war when its Moslem community made common cause with North-West Frontier tribesmen to overthrow the ruling Hindu maharajah. Eventually the question of Kashmir was referred to the Security Council of the United Nations. On January 30, 1948, Gandhi was assassinated in Delhi.

With such precedents, peace in India might seem a cruel hallucination. Informed and even sympathetic opinion fully expected the new Indian constitution to fail, and India to lapse into her eighteenth-century chaos. Yet, as we write, India and Pakistan are strangely calm. The Dominion of India has safely incorporated Hyderabad, but not Kashmir. Indian leaders like Nehru, the Prime Minister, Patel, Minister for the States and for Home Affairs, and Rajagopalachari, now Governor General, though long schooled in destructive criticism and revolt, have displayed the stature of statesmen. Jinnah died in September 1948, and was succeeded as Governor General of Pakistan by no less eminent a man, Khwaja Nazimuddin.

On May 15, 1946 a new constitution went into force in Ceylon, creating a Ceylonese Parliament with full powers, except in matters of defense and external affairs.

BURMA

In May 1945, a fortnight after the capture of Rangoon, the British Government issued a white paper emphasizing its firm intention to assist Burma "to attain a status equal to that of the Dominions and this country" and to associate Burmese with Britain in the process. The returning British Governor created an Executive Council of nine Burmans and of Karen and other minority representatives (see p. 358), which was shortly exercising the functions of a government. U Aung San, leader of the extreme secessionist and revolutionary Anti-Fascist People's Freedom League (AFPFL), as the former Thakin party now styled itself (see p. 359), at first refused and then consented to participate in the Executive Council. In January 1947 he headed a group of representative Burmese on a visit to London and discussed with members of the British Government the election of a Constituent Assembly in Burma. Evidently the concessions in the white paper had not gone far enough to satisfy Burmese opinion, which was now veering toward total independence and separation from the British Commonwealth.

The Constituent Assembly was elected in April 1947, and U Aung San and his AFPFL secured 173 out of 210 elective seats; in addition 44 seats were awarded to representatives of the frontier peoples, the Shans, Kachins, and Chins (see p. 358). But on July 17, 1947, during a session of the Executive Council, a posse of gunmen forced its way into the chamber and assassinated U Aung San and six other members of the Council. U Saw, who had been Burmese Prime Minister in 1940, and nine conspirators were tried and sentenced to death for the crime. Ba Maw, of occupation fame (pp. 732 and 733), was among those at first arrested but then released, and he appeared at the trial as a witness for the defense.

Thakin Nu, Vice-President of the AFPFL, succeeded U Aung San. A constitution, drawn up by the Constituent Assembly, somewhat recalling the Irish constitution of 1937, was approved by the Assembly in September 1947. A British-Burmese treaty, governing matters arising out of the transfer of power, was signed in London by Attlee and Thakin Nu. The Union of Burma, an independent, republican sovereign state, came into existence on January 4, 1948.

Unhappily, independent Burma has not shared the peace of her Indian neighbor. As we write, the Burmese Government finds itself beset by a mixture of disruptive forces, composed in the main of the two Communist wings of the AFPFL, the Karens, irregular gang robbery, and chaotic public finances. The outcome is not in sight.

54 THE AMERICAS

THE AFTERMATH OF THE WAR

Twice in one short generation had the United States been forced out of a traditional isolation to participate in great world wars; twice had it made a major contribution to the victory of the side it had espoused; twice had it acquired an all but decisive leadership among its fellow nations. But the second occasion left it in a position very different from the first. After the Second World War, its economic power was relatively greater; it had only one chief partner, or rival, in the policies it intended to pursue; and its people had reached a state of political sophistication which made another isolationist relapse impracticable and unlikely. The conviction was general that, with the Second World War, the old order was gone forever; that the growing range and deadliness of modern weapons made mock of any security that still relied on distance; that, in the One World of the future, no nation could again live to itself alone; and that, in short, the fortunes of mankind, in war or peace, were henceforth indissolubly interlocked.

From the middle thirties to the middle forties the American economy had been stimulated by the demands of approaching or actual war. The national income, which had been $74,000,000,000 in 1937, was $182,000,000,000 in 1944. Despite the transfer of 12,000,000 men and women to the forces, industrial production rose by 80 per cent, and agricultural production by 36 per cent. The strong upward surge of agricultural prices had raised the net farm income from $6,400,000,000 to $18,200,000,000. But, after 1945, whatever was to happen to these massive figures — whether they rose, stood stable, or declined — would greatly depend upon the wider state of world affairs. Prosperity was no longer a function of domestic supply and demand. The pent-up purchasing power of American consumers in 1945 might conceivably guarantee an absorptive home market for the immediate postwar years. But that purchasing power might be exhaustible; demands might not be unlimited. Even in the latter thirties full production had been increasingly dependent on the existence of foreign markets. By 1938, American exports had already exceeded those of every other country and constituted 14 per cent of the total value of the world's international trade. But further developments in this direction in an era of quotas, tariffs, and trade deficits were problematical. The American people in 1945 were acutely aware that another "boom and bust" might cost them their newly won international position, and that their economic system — their very democracy — stood as an example to all the world and especially to that part of it which wanted and expected them to fail.

In the sphere of strategy the long period of America's effortless and almost unconscious security had ended. In the nineteenth century, the main aggressive power centers of the world were to be found in Europe. The British Navy then dominated the Atlantic approaches to the New World. The United States and its hemispheric neighbors were safe from European encroachment, unless, as in 1812, the encroachment was made by Britain herself, or unless, as in 1861, it was made with her consent. Further, the European Powers were otherwise absorbed by the tasks of national unification, economic development, and imperialist expansion in Africa and the East. On the Pacific approaches, Japan, aroused from her hermit isolation, seemed more likely to become a counterpoise to Russian aggression than a threat to American tranquillity. In this isolationist elysium, the United States was left largely unmolested to solve its own tasks of national unification, its expansion into the West, and its modest imperialist ventures in the Philippines and Caribbean Sea.

But from 1914 onward, a new weapon, the submarine, demonstrated the insufficiency of the old British naval cordon; in 1941 the bomber and torpedo plane penetrated the very bases of the American fleet; and in 1945 the atom bomb and rocket projectile tipped the scales overwhelmingly in favor of the offensive and roughly took away the last lingering vestiges of geographical security. Meanwhile the international primacy of Europe had fallen away, leaving the United States and the Soviet Union, two Powers of profoundly different ways of life, whose peaceful or warlike relations would now be the main determinants in the future history of the world. The general situation as it faced the American people in 1945 was full of novelty, responsibility, and danger.

Yet, if this transformation we have described was acknowledged by the American people, they still seemed chary of facing up to its total implications. It is true of the American people, as of other peoples, that they needed time fully to realize even the short-term consequences of the great conflict in which they had been engaged. Co-operation, not isolation, was now to be the watchword of their post-1945 foreign policy. Thus the United States co-operated with, and often dominated, the new international organizations — the United Nations, the Specialized Agencies, the International Court, the Military Staff Committee, the Atomic Energy Commission, the control councils in Germany and Austria, and the Foreign Ministers Council. But, at home, the attitude was an odd compound of impatience and uncertainty. The American people in 1945–46 seemed to be racing back to the old free economy which was their tradition, but they were doing so more as a reaction from the irritations and restrictions of the war than from an absolute belief that that economy was now, in fact, continuable. Their armed forces were demobilized, ships laid up, and airfields junked, despite an underlying, half-confessed thought that, after all, they might not yet be done with war — or, at least, with preparedness for war. Controls were lifted, but the lifting was accompanied by the mental reservation that, with another business recession of the too familiar type, with another heavy drop in production or employment, with another threat of war, the controls might need to be restored. The American people in 1945–46 seemed almost as if they were trying to make the most of an interval of unchallengeable supremacy before the full burdens of the future descended on them. They alone held the grand secret of atomic energy, and they might possibly indulge in a last furlough of normalcy while the monopoly remained.

"The nation's release from the urgency of war," reported Eisenhower in January 1946, "started an emotional wave to get men out of the army . . . This is wholly understandable . . . But I am frank to say that I had never anticipated that this emotional wave would reach the proportions of near-hysteria." In that January, mutinous demonstrations by the men themselves against delays in their demobilization were taking place in theaters as far as Frankfurt and Manila. Yet statistics hardly corroborated the men's complaints. In round figures, 5,000,000 had been demobilized by the end of 1945, nearly 7,000,000 by April 1946, and nearly 9,000,000 by July 1946. The War Department was admittedly reluctant to release certain categories of men with special technical qualifications, however high their accumulation of discharge points. It contended that the annual draft under the existing Selective Service Act had steadily declined since 1945, and that Congress, with an election in prospect in 1946, might not extend the act for another year. It feared that the rapid, disorganized tempo of demobilization would reduce the army to a collection of semitrained units inadequate even for occupation duties in Europe and the East. The State Department might add that the stiffening of American policy toward the Soviet Union must be supported by effective military strength.

The decontrol of industry was equally unceremonious and precipitate. The United States had not suffered directly from bombing or invasion, and there was no need, as in some European countries, to invoke the aid of the government as over-all planner in the tasks of recovery. No special scarcities required the continuance of distributive controls. The increased capacity of industry and the construction of wartime equipment suggested that new potentials existed which were waiting, nay straining, for the signal to go into high production of peacetime consumer goods. Businessmen urged the lifting of raw-material and price controls so that they might take advantage of pent-up demands at home and of hungry foreign markets once served by Germany and Japan. Organized labor pressed no less insistently for the scrapping of wage controls. The general public, flushed by new earnings, demobilized men with gratuities, all demanded a carefree spending revel.

The War Production Board, which had regulated the production effort of the nation by a strict system of priorities and allocations, suffered drastic amputation of its powers within a few weeks of the Japanese surrender and died in December 1945. The Office of Price Administration (OPA) under its Administrator, Chester Bowles, fought a grim battle against price inflation in the teeth of an implacably hostile majority in Congress. In April 1946, price control was extended in principle to June 1947, but Congress tacked on so many crippling amendments in response to ardent lobbying by special interests that the principle was submerged under a flood of exceptions. OPA, suspended in June 1946, was virtually liquidated by the following October. Little except rent controls survived the wrecking activities of Congress. Food prices, which had crept upward by approximately 50 per cent since Pearl Harbor, rose a further 60 per cent between July and October 1946.

Organized labor, which by 1945 numbered a quarter of the nation's 50,000,000 wage earners, showed no disposition to stand idly by while the value of its take-home pay was lost in the inflation. The War Manpower Commission had relinquished most of its controls over workers in essential industries, and a strike was no longer a federal offense. The first blow fell in the automobile industry in November 1945, when 180,000 employees of General Motors struck on the issue of a 30 per cent increase in wages. Three-quarters of a million steel workers followed suit in January 1946. A threatened strike in the oil industry was only stopped by the seizure of refineries by the government. John L. Lewis's United Mine Workers were accorded an increase of 18.5 cents per hour after the government had temporarily taken over the strike-bound mines. Similar action by the government in May 1946, in the case of the railroads, did not deter the strike of a quarter of a million trainmen and engineers. Congress granted the President emergency powers by an overwhelming vote of 306 to 13, and the strike movement collapsed under threat of heavy penalties. Nonetheless, late in 1946, when Congressional elections were pending, John L. Lewis once more brought out his mine workers, and a test case which was ultimately carried to the Supreme Court was fought out on the legality of his action.

In November 1946, in the Congressional elections, the Republicans won substantial majorities — 57 in the House and 6 in the Senate. The result was taken to be a convincing vote of "no confidence" in the administration. The President could only pledge himself "to co-operate in every proper manner" with Congress and pleaded in particular that the nation's foreign policy should continue to be conducted "on a bipartisan basis." The Republicans, nothing loath, with the support of a number of Southern Democrats, proceeded to implement their victory. The Labor-Management Relations Act, more generally known as the Taft-Hartley Act, became law over the President's veto in June 1947. It allowed employers to sue unions for damages committed by their members in the course of industrial disputes, prohibited the use of union funds to support candidates for political offices, empowered the government to serve injunctions against strikes likely to disable the national economy, and outlawed the closed shop. Apart from its immediate punitive effects, the act taught an important lesson, a lesson which European trade-unionism had long since known, that organized labor must become politically conscious and unite for legislative action. In the sensitive, highly articulated structure of the modern state, there is no disjunction between economics and politics. They are the obverse and reverse of the same coin.

Demobilization and decontrol, even with the incidental industrial unrest and inflationary pressure which they seemed to have caused, nonetheless did not fulfill the gloomiest prognostications of the administration's more pessimistic economic advisers. Nothing therefore seemed less necessary and was less sympathetically received in Congress than hints or suggestions reminiscent of the New Deal. In September 1945, in his message to Congress, the President had uttered a warning against "a rapid decrease of wage incomes and of purchasing power," and he had gone on to make proposals for an extension of unemployment insurance, a minimum wage of 65 cents per hour, a housing program devoted to slum clearance, and public works. Further legislation on health, education, and medical care was to be considered at future sessions of Congress. The plain fact was that, by 1946, 9,000,000 more persons were in gainful civilian employment than in 1929 and the market at home and abroad was buoyant. Item after item of the President's legislative program was mangled in committee. In January 1946, so heavy was the mortality among bills, that the President was moved to bring the issue of Congressional obstruction before the nation in a radio address.

As the American people studied the bill for $317,000,000,000, which the Second World War had cost them, their old isolationist resentment against Europe as the breeding ground of wars and of distasteful ideologies might well struggle with their humanitarian and missionary desire to aid the shattered Continent. From their doubts and heart searchings emerged initially a sort of partial, *ad hoc* attempt to clear up the economic debris of the war. Thus UNRRA was continued into 1947, and piecemeal loans were made to individual European countries. Beyond this, it was hopefully expected that the new International Bank, the International Monetary Fund, and the other organizations of the United Nations would provide an adequate machinery for world recovery.

In September 1945, Lend-Lease was abruptly terminated. By that date a total of $48,500,000,000 had been expended, compared with $7,800,000,000 in reverse Lend-Lease. In original conception, Lend-Lease had been based on the debt experiences after the First World War, and it was well recognized that the United States would benefit little from imposing an impossible load of unpaid and unpayable liabilities on the weary shoulders of its wartime allies. A "master" Lend-Lease agreement with Britain therefore scaled down her liabilities from over $31,260,000,000 to $650,000,000 and set the pattern for a series of agreements with other recipient countries (see p. 830).

The settlement was generous, but its promptitude betrayed American optimism as to the economic resilience of Europe. Thus the administration's first impulse was to reject British requests for a loan made in that same September 1945. But, after three months of keen negotiation, a loan of $3,750,000,000 was announced from the United States to Britain at an interest of 2 per cent, the capital being repayable in fifty annual installments commencing December 31, 1951. Britain consented in return to abandon all exchange controls on transactions with the United States within one year of the effective date of the new agreement, and blocked sterling held in London amounting to $14,000,000,000 was to be freely convertible into dollars by any country holding sterling balances (pp. 829 and 830–31). After a discursive and occasionally acid debate in Congress, the agreement received a somewhat dubious assent in July 1946. By that date almost every European country, with the conspicuous exceptions of Yugoslavia and the Soviet Union, had become recipients of new American loans aggregating $1,830,000,000.

"THE COLD WAR"

By 1946, Soviet-American friction had already developed to such an extent that the new co-operativeness in foreign policy which we have been describing was becoming another name for opposition to the Soviet Union. By almost imperceptible stages the very work of world peace and recovery to which the United States was now being committed resolved itself into a species of warfare, the "cold war," as it was called, of unlimited extent and incidence.

Almost any example suffices for illustration. The United States had furnished 72 per cent of UNRRA's operating funds and 90 per cent of its supplies, and the very continuance of UNRRA therefore came to depend on an increasingly suspicious and economy-minded Congress. The crop failure of 1945 in Southeastern Europe and the concurrent disinclination of several Western European governments to accept too much of the proffered relief resulted in a concentration of UNRRA's activities among the Soviet satellite states. Several of these states had been giving offense to their benefactors by putting irritating obstructions in the way of UNRRA observers, whom they treated as agents of "American imperialism." Finally, in August 1946, the destruction of two American transport planes by Yugoslav fighters over Yugoslav territory went just a little too far in the exemplification of their ingratitude. The demise of UNRRA was decided in December 1946. But here was an emergency organization, originally inspired by the highest humanitarian motives, thus caught up and cut off in the newly emerging phase of world power politics. (See pp. 793–94.)

A policy of "containing" the Soviet Union, of applying "counterforce" wherever Soviet expansionist pressure became perceptible, logically gave those neighbors of the Soviet Union which had not yet been engulfed a prior claim to American assistance. Thus Greece, enfeebled by Axis invasion and occupation, had been kept in a state of uproar by Communist-led guerrillas constantly supplied from Bulgaria, Yugoslavia, and Albania, all members of the Soviet bloc (pp. 863–65). A small British occupying force was trying to maintain the peace and loyalty of the harassed country. Late in 1946 the Greek Government requested the United States for a considerable sum for postwar reconstruction. Meanwhile, during 1946, Turkey had been confronted by repeated Soviet demands for a share in the defense of the Dardanelles and for the return of Kars and Ardahan, ceded by Russia in 1918 under the Treaty of Brest Litovsk (see p. 95). The maintenance of a Turkish army of 650,000 men, mobilized in response to this persistent Soviet war of nerves, swallowed up half of Turkey's national budget. Then, during discussions in the Foreign Ministers Council on the Italian peace treaty, the Soviet Union had advanced claims for a trustee-ship of Tripolitania. All in all, the Soviet's determination to break out of its strategic prison house in the Black Sea was being very forcibly brought to the notice of its wartime allies. In January 1947 a mission of American economic experts was sent to Greece to study Greek requirements. The mission had not yet reported when the British Government informed the State Department that the economic and military aid which Britain had been giving Greece and Turkey since 1945 would have to be discontinued after March 31 and, if necessary, the two countries abandoned to Soviet control. The economic situation in Britain which had dictated this decision must have been serious indeed to have thus driven her to renounce her century-old policy of excluding Russian influence from the Straits and the Middle East.

In March 1947, in a message to Congress of exceptional urgency, Presi-dent Truman enunciated the policy called the Truman Doctrine. He opened with a somber reflection on the gravity of the world situation and, in exemplification, proceeded to make particular reference to Greece and Turkey. The very survival of Greece as a free nation, he said, was menaced by a militant, Communist-led minority which was exploiting human want and misery to create political chaos. Economic and military aid must be provided if the country was to evolve into "a self-supporting and self-respecting democracy." Further, "Turkey now needs our support. Since the war, Turkey has sought financial assistance from Britain and the United States for the purpose of effecting that modernization necessary for the maintenance of her national integrity. . . . If Greece should fall under the control of an armed minority, the effect upon her neighbor, Turkey, would be immediate and serious. Confusion and disorder might well spread throughout the entire Middle East." "I believe," the President averred, "that it must be the foreign policy of the United States to support free peoples who are resisting attempted subjugation by armed minorities or by outside pressure." He requested that $400,000,000 be applied to eco-nomic and military aid to Greece and Turkey and that American military missions be sent to reorganize and train the Greek and Turkish forces. "If we falter in our leadership," he concluded, "we may endanger the peace of the world — and we shall surely endanger the welfare of this nation. Great responsibilities have been placed upon us by the swift movement of events."

The Truman Doctrine fell with stunning force on a public opinion which had not been prepared by antecedent publicity for a departure of policy so bold and comprehensive. Congress and people were far from con-vinced that all nations threatened by totalitarian penetration should automatically qualify for American assistance. It was argued that the sums represented an initial step toward unprecedented and incalculable com-mitments abroad, that the United States was entangling itself in the bank-rupt traditions of Old World diplomacy, and that all aid to needy countries should be internationally sponsored and disbursed through the United Nations. Advocates of United Nations participation were somewhat quieted by Senator Vandenberg's amendment providing that American assistance should cease if ever the General Assembly or Security Council declared that action taken by the United Nations rendered its continuance unnecessary or undesirable. With this vote-catching modification, the Greek-Turkish Aid Act was eventually passed by Congress with respectable majorities and was signed by the President on May 22, 1947.

THE EUROPEAN RECOVERY PROGRAM

The Greek-Turkish Aid Act, as its opponents feared, was only an initial step. But the question before the American administration and Congress was not just of granting a sum to this or that country in distress but rather of co-ordinating into a single scheme all the various sums which were now to be so imperatively demanded. If every case for aid was to be presented singly and in succession the patience of the nation and of its legislators might wear very thin. Furthermore, a policy of plugging gaps as they arose in the world's defenses against Communism would hardly reduce the economic despair inside those defenses, a despair which might well bring Communism into power, notably in Italy and France, by the ordinary processes of democratic politics.

It was also becoming abundantly clear that the hoped-for automatic recovery of Europe was not taking place. The postwar mood of optimism was already sinking. The rise of prices in the United States was reducing the real purchasing power of dollar loans to European governments. Former "invisible" incomes had been largely liquidated during the war. The rapid depletion of the British loan indicated a predicament that was typical of most countries of Western Europe. Thus any heavy expenditure on food and tobacco left small surplus for capital equipment, and dollar-hungry countries, using their precious currency on their most pressing needs, were obliged to return again to the doorstep of a puzzled, protesting Congress. On May 8, 1947, the day before the House finally approved the Greek-Turkish Aid Act, Under Secretary of State Dean Acheson, in a speech at Cleveland, pointed to the yawning gap between current American exports of $16,000,000,000 and imports of $8,000,000,000, and affirmed that the imbalance must be remedied by increased imports, a removal of trade barriers, and further loans. "Until the various countries of the world get on their feet and become self-supporting," he said, "there can be no lasting peace or prosperity for any of us." The speech suggested that the new installment of aid to Europe which the administration envisaged was not to be presented in the controversial form of an anti-Communist bribe, but as a comprehensive program of economic stabilization advantageous to the giver and the receivers alike. Thus, on June 5, at Harvard University, Secretary Marshall laid down the principles which were shortly to be embodied in the European Recovery Program.

We have already described the European Recovery Program (ERP) as it appeared to its sixteen European beneficiaries (pp. 835–36). We have only to note here its implementation in the United States. On June 22, 1947,

President Truman announced that he had requested three committees to advise him on various aspects of the plan. An official committee under Secretary of the Interior Krug reported that the natural resources of the United States, agricultural land excepted, would not be inordinately depleted by the contemplated aid to Europe. The President's Council of Economic Advisers reported favorably on the capacity of the American economy to bear the burden of a further foreign aid program without creating hardships and restrictions at home. An unofficial committee under Secretary of Commerce Averell Harriman, with the CEEC's Paris Report before it (see p. 834), measured the availability of American resources against the estimated needs of the sixteen nations. It whittled down the figure of $22,400,000,000 mentioned in the Paris Report to an absolute maximum of $17,000,000,000. Meanwhile, two hundred Congressmen of both parties were touring Europe to inform themselves at first hand on current conditions. In December 1947, Congress passed the Interim Aid Act, providing a "stopgap" aid of $597,000,000 to France, Italy, Austria, and China, while the larger ERP was still under debate.

The American people, on the whole, appeared to give a qualified approval to ERP. The political left still demanded loudly but vainly a nondiscriminatory program under the auspices of the United Nations. The Middle West, where isolationism lingered most stubbornly, disliked the idea of bearing continued taxation for the benefit of an incorrigible, spendthrift Europe. The great majority, it must be admitted, found the project difficult to digest mentally in its multifarious detail, but appreciated it as an indirect shoring-up of sagging markets at home and abroad and therefore as a sort of insurance against the postwar slump, which many were still half-expecting "somewhere round the next corner" — and finally as a logical extension of the government's now established bipartisan anti-Soviet policy.

Even so, the progress of the new legislation would have been slow and minutely contested if events in Europe had not played into its sponsors' hands. In December 1947 the meeting of the Foreign Ministers Council in London was compelled by Soviet intransigence to abandon its discussion of the German and Austrian settlements. In February 1948 the Communists seized power in Czechoslovakia, a country which, ever since its birth in 1918, had always been a strong favorite for American sympathy. The American press was quick to point out the parallel with the events of 1938–39, when once before Czech democracy had been obliterated under the heavy weight of a totalitarian Power. In March 1948 the fifty-year Treaty of Brussels suggested that Western European countries were themselves taking the initiative toward a political and economic integration which it was in the interest of the United States to encourage. Finally an alarming situation was developing in Italy, where a Communist bloc was campaigning to take power at the next election. (See pp. 814, 853–54, 835, and 825–26.)

The administration eliminated from the draft bill a request for a four-year appropriation of $17,000,000,000 when it became clear that the present Congress did not desire to have taken from its successors the right of periodical examination of the plan. A much-amended bill was approved by the Senate on March 10, 1948, with only 17 dissenting votes. After a contentious amendment to include Spain had been dropped, the bill passed both houses by a voice vote on April 2, and was signed by the President on the following day. The Foreign Assistance Act, as it was called, provided for a single package of $5,300,000,000 for the first year of ERP, $465,000,000 for China, and a further $275,000,000 for Greece and Turkey. Conditions were stiff and elaborate. The beneficiaries were to take steps to stabilize currencies, balance budgets, reduce tariffs, remove restrictive trade practices, control inflation, furnish the United States with strategic materials and, if required, deny the same materials to nonparticipating nations. President Truman nominated Paul G. Hoffman, president of the Studebaker Corporation, as chief of the Economic Co-operation Administration (ECA), which was to be the agency of the program in Washington, and nominated Harriman as "roving ambassador" and observer for the program in Europe. On April 16, as we have described elsewhere, the sixteen European nations created their counterpart Organization of European Economic Co-operation (OEEC). (See p. 836.)

THE NORTH ATLANTIC PACT

Debates on ERP in Congress had inevitably raised the further question of supplementary military aid. If Western Europe was to serve as an effective outpost of the American hemisphere against the menace from the Soviet East, economic aid alone might not be enough. The Treaty of Brussels indicated that five Western European countries were themselves alive to the danger and to the remedy. But the treaty might involve those countries in a heavy rearmament program, lay a new burden on their already overstrained resources, and thus frustrate the very ends of ERP. In June 1948, after a perfunctory debate, the Senate passed, with only four dissenting votes, a resolution of Senator Vandenberg advocating the participation of the United States in a North Atlantic defensive system. The resolution indicated that the United States was turning away from the United Nations, veto-ridden and lacking effective force and, like the Brussels Powers, was openly consulting its security in a regional arrangement.

In November 1948 came the presidential election. In view of the general right-wing, anti-New Deal trend of the nation's politics and the seeming popularity of the current legislation of the Republican majority in Congress, all interpreters of public opinion were agreed in forecasting an over-whelming victory for the Republican candidate, Governor Thomas Dewey of New York. Nevertheless President Truman decisively won, and the concurrent Congressional elections resulted in Democratic majorities in both Houses. This "greatest upset in American history" was in part a personal tribute to Truman himself; it was in part a confirmation of the administration's foreign policy and showed perhaps a still-lingering fear of the Republican party's traditional isolationism. But it was, far more than this, a popular expression of view that the United States had reached a turning point in its post-1945 domestic affairs. The Taft-Hartley Act had been the climax of extreme Republican reactionism and had deeply stirred the growing "social democrat" elements — in the European sense of the term — in American labor. At the same time, the heavy defeat of the third presidential candidate, Henry Wallace, showed that the electorate, for all its new leftward oscillation, was far from any sympathy for a man tarred with pro-Soviet affiliations. The Truman vote, it would appear, was the vote of "the common people" — labor, farmers, foreign-born minorities, Negroes — who had had time to recover from their postwar impatience and were now far less afraid of a mild New Dealism than a reversion at Republican hands to the irresponsibilities of the pre-1929 era.

Exploratory conversations on a North Atlantic Pact were started in Washington in December 1948, immediately after the presidential election, between the United States, Canada, and the five Brussels Powers. It appeared that France would be expected to provide the main part of the ground forces, heavily armored and highly mobile, Britain the tactical air force, and the United States the strategic air force. There would be a joint command, joint use of bases, standardization of equipment, and a new "peacetime Lend-Lease." Early in 1949 the United States began to sound out the attitudes of Denmark and Norway. The adhesion of these countries would bring with it the control of strategic Arctic territories — Danish Greenland and Iceland, and Norwegian Spitsbergen (Svalbard) — and of the exit of the Baltic, where the Soviet Union maintained a large and growing submarine fleet. The missing links in the chain would then be Spain and Ireland (see p. 844). Sweden, it seemed, too uncomfortably near the Soviet Union, would cling to the policy of neutrality which had already served her well in the two World Wars.

The Soviet Union exerted itself against this fast-maturing alliance. Norway, in reply to a Soviet warning in January 1949, assured the Soviet Union that she would never take part "in a policy with aggressive aims" and would not join in any agreement "involving obligations . . . to open bases for foreign Powers' military forces on Norwegian territory, so long as Norway is not attacked or exposed to threats of attack." There was some talk of a "peace offensive" from the Kremlin. Stalin made use of an interview with an American journalist to suggest a personal meeting with President Truman in Poland or Czechoslovakia to discuss a world peace pact and the disarmament of Germany. President Truman countered with an invitation to Washington, which Stalin declined "on doctors' advice." Dean Acheson, who had just succeeded Marshall as Secretary of State, commented that the members of the United Nations were already pledged not to resort to war, that attempts to settle the further questions of disarmament and of Germany had always been stultified by the Soviet bloc, and that the United States would not discuss "with any nation any matter of interest to other nations without the participation of those other nations."

Meanwhile critics of the administration's foreign policy were pointing out that a war-torn Russia was unlikely to risk an act of aggression involving a major Power, that the Soviet Union itself might have some grounds for alarm at the extension of American military aid to so many of its peripheral countries, that the projected North Atlantic Pact might be the first of a series encircling the globe and interminably committing American resources and prestige. Direct military aid, they argued, was not fitted to meet the characteristic Communist methods of infiltration. Neither arms nor dollars had prevented the decomposition of Nationalist China or checked the onward march of the Communist idea in East Asia. But whatever the validity of these criticisms, they were chiefly negative. Those who favored a positive and dynamic American foreign policy pointed out that Soviet pressure had always increased at any sign of weakness or conciliation on the part of other nations and had correspondingly decreased at any demonstration of strength and unity. The United States had trodden the path of co-operation and appeasement in 1945–46, only to end in a blind alley. A well-armed United States at the head of a North American–Western European Grand Alliance might better succeed in bringing the power-conscious Russians to the council table and to an agreement. Doubtless the cost of the policy would be considerable; but the alternative — to leave non-Communist Europe to its fate — was not to be thought of.

The North Atlantic Pact was signed in Washington on April 4, 1949, by the foreign ministers of Belgium, Canada, Denmark, France, Iceland, Italy, Luxembourg, the Netherlands, Norway, Portugal, Britain, and the United States. In a carefully worded preamble, the signatories reaffirmed their faith in the purposes and principles of the Charter of the United Nations and "their desire to live in peace with all peoples and all governments," thus robbing the pact of the overtly aggressive designs ascribed to it by Moscow. The core of the pact was contained in its Article 5: "The Parties agree that an armed attack against one or more of them in Europe or North America shall be considered an attack against them all and consequently they agree that, if such an armed attack occurs, each of them, in exercise of the right of individual or collective self-defence recognized by Article 51 of the Charter of the United Nations, will assist the Party or Parties so attacked by taking forthwith, individually and in concert with the other Parties, such action as it deems necessary, including the use of armed force, to restore and maintain the security of the North Atlantic area." The signatories further agreed to establish a Council and a Defense Committee. After extensive hearings in the Senate Foreign Relations Committee and lively public controversy, the pact was ratified by the Senate on July 21, 1949, by 82 votes to 13.

The destruction of the Axis, the relative decline in the strength of Britain and France, the weakness of the so-called "Third Force" embodied in Western Europe, gave an air of inevitability to the emergence of rivalry between the two great power blocs, the United States and the Soviet Union. Europe no longer radiated its former measure of influence in the world. Indeed power was now injected into Europe from outside, from Washington and Moscow. But the decline of Europe induced a corresponding restlessness in her colonial possessions and indeed in all "backward" territories where her influence had been felt. East Asia, no less than Europe, was being swept by the same historical forces — Communism had already won a startling success, for instance, in China — and the inevitable question arose: Was the

United States to mobilize "counterforce" in every part of the globe where the incessant activities of it great rival made an appearance?

The answer was given in Point Four of President Truman's inaugural address in January 1949: "We must embark on a bold new program for making the benefits of our scientific advances and industrial progress available for the improvement and growth of under-developed areas. More than half the people of the world are living in conditions approaching misery. Their poverty is a handicap and threat both to them and to more prosperous areas. In co-operation with other nations, we should foster capital investment in areas needing development. In due time, as our stability becomes manifest, I believe that those countries which now oppose us will abandon their delusions and join with the free nations of the world in a just settlement of international differences." The address was the logical outcome of policies pursued over the past two years. American economy was increasingly involved in the long battle against the unholy alliance of poverty and Communism all over the world.

THE UNITED STATES AND LATIN AMERICA

We have noted from time to time in this book the development of the Pan-American system and its outcome in 1945 in the Act of Chapultepec (see p. 703) and in the almost simultaneous recognition of such "regional arrangements" in the Charter of the United Nations. The attractive slogan of "collective action against aggression," however, concealed endless possibilities of political manipulation. In November 1945, Uruguay officially requested the American republics to consider the possibility of collective action against Argentina, on the ground that Perón's policies there constituted a potential threat. Colonel Juan Perón, a colorful figure well versed in the latest refinements of demagogy, had held the substance of power in Argentina as the executive of a conservative-military clique since 1943. His ardent admiration for European Fascism had cooled toward the close of the war. His government had given assurances of future good behavior at the Chapultepec Conference of 1945 and had secured American support for the admission of Argentina into the United Nations. Perón persevered nonetheless in protecting Nazi agents and declined to expel or dissolve business concerns blacklisted by the Allies. The action of Uruguay, in part motivated by her standing apprehension of a powerful and ambitious neighbor, gained instant support from the State Department. But Latin-American opinion generally, fearing a dangerous precedent, displayed no enthusiasm for positive action.

A conference of American foreign ministers, scheduled to meet in October 1945 at Rio de Janeiro to lay the foundations of the permanent treaty of mutual assistance envisaged in the Act of Chapultepec, was pointedly postponed by the State Department, "in view of recent developments in Argentina." Perón, scenting an opportunity, responded to the implied challenge. He stepped out from the protective façade of political clients behind which he usually operated, and announced that he would run as candidate in the Argentinian presidential election. In February 1946, two weeks before the election, the State Department published its celebrated Blue Book, demonstrating with the aid of captured German documents the extent of the wartime collaboration between Argentina and the Axis. This injudicious attempt to sway the forthcoming election was easily construed by the adroit Perón as foreign intervention in Argentinian domestic affairs and turned to his own advantage, and the election, which was reasonably free from coercion, gave him the desired majority.

The Perón imbroglio, like everything else at this time, was soon found to have its Russian aspect. Cuba, Mexico, Colombia, Uruguay, Costa Rica, Chile, Nicaragua, Venezuela, Brazil, Guatemala, and Argentina had all extended diplomatic recognition to the Soviet Union between 1942 and 1946. The economic misery of the great mass of the Latin-American people provided fertile soil on which the seeds of Communism could be scattered. The powerful Confederation of Latin American Workers, headed by the Mexican labor tycoon, Vicente Lombardo Toledano, did not commit itself to an unreservedly Marxist program, but its spokesmen at every opportunity always thundered against "Yankee imperialism."

The Inter-American Conference on the Maintenance of Peace and Security assembled at Rio de Janeiro at last in mid-August 1947. The delegates were agreed that aid to a victim of unprovoked aggression should be a definite obligation decided by a two-thirds majority vote. The United States delegates, however, succeeded in carrying a qualifying amendment to the effect that "no state should be required to furnish armed forces without its consent." In common with the United Nations, therefore, the inter-American system was not to have an independent armed force at its disposal. Finally the Conference defined a defense zone embracing a vast area from Alaska and Greenland to Antarctica to which these collective measures should apply. The resulting treaty was signed in September.

Some of the complaisance of the Latin-American republics at the Rio Conference doubtless arose from the desire to qualify for American military equipment under the inter-American military co-operation bill, which was trailing its snail-like passage through Congress, and also for any possible extension of Marshall aid. Once the hectic flush of wartime prosperity had begun to fade, most of the republics were found to be laboring under conditions not dissimilar to those of Europe. The Allied blockade and preclusive American buying of raw materials had made the economy of the republics more dependent than ever on their powerful northern neighbor. The rise of prices in the United States had helped to dissipate their dollar credits, and from 1946 to 1947 their aggregate adverse trade balance had grown from $340,000,000 to $1,800,000,000. Inflation meanwhile had driven up living costs, estimated on a base of 100 in 1937, to 175 in Uruguay, 334 in Peru, 364 in Mexico, and 437 in Chile.

Recovery plans in the republics proliferated, ranging from Bolivia's modest $88,000,000 to Argentina's $1,500,000,000 Five-Year Plan. In Mexico, Brazil, and Chile there was a significant growth of government-controlled development corporations and "mixed" companies. Foreign economic interests were not spared. In 1947, for instance, the Perón government in

Argentina bought out 2,600 miles of British and French railroads at a cost
of over $600,000,000. Most of the republics resorted to higher tariffs or
some sort of licensing to curtail their dollar imports. But opinion in Washington was averse to granting direct financial aid until it appeared that
the republics were practicing a greater measure of self-help, such as tightening up their taxation systems and slashing their heavy military budgets.
Furthermore, Latin America was not in the territorial front line of the
"cold war" against the Soviet Union and, in the matter of aid therefore,
was fated to run a poor third to Western Europe and China.

The Ninth Pan-American Conference was held at Bogotá, the Colombian
capital, in March-April 1948. Economic questions were high on the agenda
but, after inconclusive discussion, were shelved in favor of a forthcoming
economic conference at Buenos Aires, scheduled early in 1949. The political work of the Conference culminated on April 30 with the signing of a
Charter creating an Organization of American States to conduct inter-
American affairs as a regional agency within the United Nations. The
Governing Board of the Pan American Union in Washington was to be
the permanent Consultative Council of the new Organization. General
policy was to be decided by the Inter-American Conferences, meeting at
intervals of five years. The Conference of Foreign Ministers was retained
"to consider problems of an urgent nature and of common interest to the
American States." Inter-American disputes were to be settled by conciliation
and arbitration. An Inter-American Defense Board would make recommendations in regard to collective action against aggression.

On April 9, while the Conference was in session, Dr. Jorge Gaitan,
Liberal candidate for the Colombian presidential election, was shot dead
as he was leaving his law office in Bogotá. In the preceding month, the
Liberals had withdrawn from the coalition cabinet, headed by the Conservative President, Mariano Pérez, in protest against the breaking of strikes
by government action. Gaitan was immensely popular with the masses, and
his murder was followed by violent demonstrations. The rioters caught the
assassin red-handed — though he was not identified — and promptly beat
him to death with shoeshine boxes. They then attacked the chief government buildings, which were set on fire and gutted almost without exception.
Carrying red banners, they invaded the Capitol, where the Conference was
in session, and attempted to seize Lauriano Gómez, the Colombian Foreign
Minister, Conservative leader, and head of the Colombian delegation at
the Conference. Liquor stores and churches were sacked as criminal elements joined in the disturbances.

President Pérez declared martial law in Bogotá, imposed a strict censorship of news, and condemned the disturbances as Communist inspired.
Troops and police were set in motion, and light artillery was used to blast
persistent snipers in church steeples. By April 11 the Colombian Government claimed that order was restored. Twelve Communist leaders were
arrested, and diplomatic relations with the Soviet Union were broken off.
But no proof of complicity was sustained against the twelve, who were
released after a few days.

The Bogotá disturbances were symptomatic of the broadening popular ferment in Latin America. Save in Mexico, the revolutionary cycle had usually changed the political heads of the republics, leaving basic economic and social problems largely untouched. Since the Second World War, the old inequalities of wealth, the weakness of the middle class, the tradition of violence in politics, and the growth of an aggressive and politically-minded labor movement had been tremendously complicated by the price inflation and the ever present menace of Communism. Recent events, elsewhere than Bogotá, had already been telling their own story. Thus in Brazil, in October 1945, the fifteen-year dictatorship of President Vargas had been overthrown by the conservative coalition of General Eurico Dutra who, despite his political designation, had thence set about economic and social reforms embodied in a special Bill of Rights for labor. In Venezuela, in the same month, the Socialist *Acción Democrática* of Rómulo Betancourt seized power with the aid of a radical group of young army and navy officers and eventually introduced a constitution with universal suffrage and "New Deal" measures for farmers and workers. In Bolivia, in July 1946, the blood-thirsty and reactionary regime of President Villaroel was overthrown by a popular uprising in La Paz, where the bodies of the President and his aides were suspended from lampposts, and a revolutionary committee of labor leaders and intellectuals announced the restoration of civil liberties and the introduction of a democratic constitution. In Chile, in September 1946, a Left bloc, including the Communists, elected Gabriel Videla to the presidency. In Peru, during 1946–47, the social democratic coalition known as the Apra party (American Popular Revolutionary Alliance) outnumbered any other single party in the Peruvian Congress and gained a brief foothold in the Cabinet.

Yet, in general, Latin America had her own revolutionary tradition, prior to Communism and opposed to it. During 1947–1948, Latin-American governments were stiffening their resistance to Communism, irrespective of their political coloration at the moment. The authoritarian regimes, drawing support from the military, the landowners, and the Church, could not afford to remain inactive. The democratic regimes could not accept as fellow travelers the exponents of total dictatorship. And both types of regimes, authoritarian and democratic, perhaps were also motivated by a desire to demonstrate their fitness for dollar aid from Washington. Early in 1947, President Perón of Argentina declared measures against Communists and broke off negotiations for a trade treaty with the Soviet Union. In May 1947, Brazil outlawed the Communist party. In October 1947, Chile instituted a roundup of Reds and severed diplomatic relations with the Soviet Union. In October 1948, following an uprising in Callao in which naval personnel were implicated, Peru dissolved the Apra party.

REARMAMENT

The Army, backed by its war-won prestige, had been pressing the administration since 1944 for universal military training (UMT) in the United

States. In October 1945, President Truman lent his support to the May-Gurney bill, which proposed a year's compulsory training on condition that the trainees should not go overseas during that period. Congress and the people showed little enthusiasm for the bill or for UMT in any form. Voluntary enlistment was traditional and appropriate to returning conditions of normalcy, and the push-button warfare of the future, so it was being argued in numerous articles in the press, had ended the era of the mass army. Congress was more sympathetic toward the Army's technical requirements and, in 1946, readily passed the Stock-piling Act, designed to ensure a sufficiency of strategic raw materials. Otherwise Congress tended to consult political expediency by favoring an enlarged Navy and Air Force, for which adequate volunteer recruits were always forthcoming, and then consoled the armed services as a whole with a record-breaking defense appropriation of $11,000,000,000 for the year 1947.

But with the widening of the East-West schism, American rearmament and its cognate problems could no longer be evaded. However understandably reluctant Congress might be, the startling developments in Europe and Asia — the Communization of Czechoslovakia, the Treaty of Brussels, Western Union, the Berlin blockade, the victorious career of the Chinese Red Army — forced upon Congress's attention the question of American military preparedness. On March 17, 1948, the day the Treaty of Brussels was signed, President Truman again requested Congress to adopt the principle of UMT. Triangular discussions between Secretary of Defense Forrestal, Air Secretary Symington, and the Joint Chiefs of Staff resulted in a compromise program for the expansion of the armed forces, and in June 1948, to meet the requirements of this program, Congress passed a bill compulsorily drafting men nineteen to twenty-five years of age for a service period of twenty-one months. A long schedule of exempt categories was intended to avoid undue interference with professional and technical education. The induction of nearly 10,000,000 youths began promptly in August 1948. Universal military training; the prospective expansion of the armed forces to 2,000,000 men; a 70-group air force; the world's most powerful navy, patrolling the Atlantic, Pacific, and Mediterranean; a defense appropriation of over $15,000,000,000 for 1949 — all seemed to indicate that the military burdens which had oppressed the nations of Europe from the French Revolution to the Second World War had been permanently extended to the United States.

The National Security Act of July 1947 provided the parallel administration reforms. It created a single Department of Defense, to which the three Secretaries of the Army, Navy, and Air Force would be responsible, all three enjoying access to the President but not holding Cabinet rank. It also created a National Security Council, which would occupy itself with the interrelation of military, political, and research policies, and a Central Intelligence Agency, which would gather military and political information from abroad and make it available to government agencies concerned. The perennial feud between the Air Force and the Navy over the respective merits of land-based and carrier-based planes for strategic bombing was decided in favor of the Air Force, but the Navy was given exclusive responsibility for antisubmarine operations, and funds were made available for a 65,000-ton supercarrier. The Joint Chiefs of Staff, created in 1942, remained the body responsible for strategy and the broad program of war requirements (see p. 701).

The National Security Act, however, did not bring about that happy co-ordination of the three services that had been its purpose. In February 1949, General Eisenhower, who had become president of Columbia University, was appointed "temporary" chairman of the Joint Chiefs of Staff; this move indicated that a new effort at conciliation was to be made. But Secretary of Defense Forrestal, tired of the months of bickering behind the scenes, resigned in March, and Eisenhower was shortly taken seriously ill. The services' dispute was now public property and was being aired in Congressional committees with typical American forthrightness. To the "man in the street" the dispute appeared to have been narrowed down to two main issues, the Navy's 65,000-ton supercarrier and the Air Force's B-36 bombers. Hardly had Forrestal's successor, Louis Johnson, assumed office than he stopped the construction of the carrier, the keel of which had been laid with much ceremony only a week before. In July 1949, President Truman submitted to Congress a new plan for the co-ordination of the three services, a plan which eventually passed Congress in the form of a Military Unification Act. General Bradley was appointed Chairman of the Joint Chiefs of Staff.

The services' dispute in the United States signified normal professional jealousies, but it also signified the extreme uncertainties of preparing for a future war. On September 23, 1949, President Truman announced the Soviet discovery of atomic fission; basic military conceptions had once more to be rethought. Since 1948 the policy of "containing" the Soviet Union had automatically extended the outer circle of American defenses to Canada and the Arctic, to Western Europe and the North Atlantic, to the Philippines and Japan — even to the Middle East. But the fortification of this far-flung strategic empire in the fast approaching atomic era was going to be the supreme challenge to America's technical and administrative genius.

RETROSPECT

And so we bring this book to an end. In point of time the period it covers is not very considerable — a generation at most. In the number of significant events, the period must surely be the most crowded of any of which we have record. These years we have described have seen two world wars, the fall of nine empires, the rise of as many new nations, one revolution — the Russian Revolution — surpassing several lesser revolutions, and a Depression that has confounded the economic thought and custom of three centuries. These years have seen two experiments in the organization of peace, the League of Nations and the United Nations; they have seen three experiments in totalitarian government, Soviet Communism, Fascism, and Nazism; they have seen the decline of nationalism and the trend toward "regional arrangements"; they have seen the decline of Europe as the primary power center of the world; they have seen the growth in importance, as yet potential rather than actual, of East Asia and Latin America. In particular, they have seen the emergence of two great opposing blocs, the United States and the Soviet Union, each preaching its own philosophy of peace and human welfare and each standing to the other in undisguised hostility for the defense and consolidation of that philosophy.

These years have also seen, outside the immediate field of politics but closely affecting it, the further extension of scientific techniques and their bifurcation into a still increasing control of nature and command of wealth and into a still increasing destructiveness and terror. They have seen the discovery and development of new resources as well as the thoughtless "mining out" of older resources that are often more precious and irreplaceable. They have seen the leveling and collectivization, so to speak, of society, the end of social privilege based on birth and culture, and correspondingly the final triumph of mass man, mass social techniques, mass politics, mass economics, mass communication, mass education, mass entertainment, and mass warfare.

In the course of this book we have restricted ourselves to war and politics, for this is the form into which so much of the contemporary tragedy has been cast. But this is not to say that war and politics exhaust our relevant interests. The thought is constantly breaking through that "something" is very wrong with the world over and above the particular conflict of men and peoples which has been the staple of our narrative. Civilization — and certainly Western civilization — is passing through one of the greatest transformations, if not the greatest, of its history. The core and content of our lives are now in extreme crisis.

Perhaps the crisis most forcibly appears to us in the seeming lack of a spiritual revolution to accompany and direct our technological and social revolution. Apart from Communism, our era has brought forth no vital political doctrine, and to a great extent we are kept sustained and energized by spiritual capital left us from past generations. Even the Soviet Union in its extremity in 1942 had virtually to revive the old mythology of Holy Russia. The thinkers who now wield the most considerable influence — let us say, Marx, Nietzsche, Kierkegaard, even Berdyaev — are destructive, or at least diagnostic, but in no sense creative. Yet the veriest amateur of historical studies must acknowledge that it is out of great spiritual movements that civilizations are made.

But, while we know that "something" is wrong with the world, we also know that there can be no going back. There are no more normalcies for this age to return to. The past is gone with all its pleasantries. Whatever comes now will be new, and will make all things new. It will be a transfiguration, not a revival. It will come perhaps today, perhaps tomorrow. For the wind bloweth where it listeth. And so will be the next long episode in the incredible human drama.

NOTES

CHAPTER 1

1. The Battle of Kossovo (Kosovo-Polje), 1389, when the Serbs were defeated by the Turks.

2. The Belgian guarantee dated from 1839 and that of Luxembourg from 1867, Prussia being a guarantor in either case.

CHAPTER 2

1. The Siege of Plevna, 1877, when the Turks held up the Russian army invading the Balkans.

2. See Note 2, Chapter 1, above.

3. There is a considerable literature on the Schlieffen Plan. See, for example, H. Holborn in E. M. Earle, ed., *Makers of Modern Strategy*, Princeton University Press, 1944.

4. The term "High Command" will be used in all our chapters on the First and Second World Wars. The correct form in the First World War was: German, O.H.L., *Die Oberste Heeresleitung;* Austro-Hungarian, A.O.K., *Das Armee-Ober-Kommando;* French, G.Q.G., *Le Grand Quartier Général;* and the Russian Stavka. The High Command in the field is not to be confused with the General Staff, the peacetime organization.

5. There is a considerable literature on the Tannenberg campaign. See, for example, B. H. Liddell Hart, *A History of the World War,* Little, Brown, 1934, Chap. IV, 2, and Winston S. Churchill, *The Unknown War,* Scribner, 1931, Chaps. XII–XIV.

6. Winston S. Churchill, *The Unknown War,* Scribner, 1931, Chap. XVI.

7. The name "Anzac" was coined from the initials of the Australia and New Zealand Army Corps.

CHAPTER 3

1. The Battle of Coruña, 1809, when a British army under Sir John Moore, after a disastrous retreat, repulsed the French under Marshal Soult and succeeded in withdrawing by sea.

CHAPTER 4

1. Generally, in this book, the head of a parliamentary government in Europe — for example, the French Président du Conseil or the Minister President of Prussia or Hungary — will be referred to as "Premier," and the head of the government in Britain and the British Dominions will be referred to as "Prime Minister."

2. See Note 4, Chapter 2 above.

3. The French parliamentary committees were very similar in principle to the committees of the United States Senate and House. The select committees in Britain perform much the same functions, but they are created from time to time for

special purposes and are not permanent inquisitors of the government's good behavior. See R. K. Gooch, *The French Parliamentary Committee System*, Appleton-Century, 1935.

4. It is interesting to compare these figures with the American — noting, however, that the American figures are *only for seventeen months*, from April 6, 1917, to November 11, 1918: rifles, 2,500,000; machine guns, 182,000; shells, 17,000,000; and 11,754 planes. B. Crowell and R. F. Wilson, *How America Went to War, The Armies of Industry*, Yale University Press, 1921, Vol. I, pp. 34–40, 332, and 342.

5. Frederick Edwin Smith, lawyer and Conservative statesman; knighted 1915; created Earl of Birkenhead 1922. He was Attorney General and Lord Chancellor, 1919–22, and Secretary of State for India, 1924–28.

6. Dorothy Macardle, *The Irish Republic*, London, 1937, Chap. XI, p. 126n. The figures are for Ireland only and do not include Irishmen resident outside Ireland.

7. The Irish Volunteers, founded by John MacNeill in 1913; the Citizen Army, founded in Dublin by James Larkin and James Connolly, also in 1913; and Sinn Fein, founded by Arthur Griffith in 1900. All supported uncompromising political seaparation from England, in contradistinction to the Irish Nationalist party, led by John Redmond, which, for the time being, supported Asquith's Home Rule Bill of 1912.

8. The Committees of Zemstvos and Towns were unofficial philanthropic provincial and urban organizations, managed by civilians largely on a volunteer basis. See T. I. Polner, *Russian Local Government during the War and the Union of Zemstvos*, Yale University Press, 1930.

9. There is no definitive record of Russian losses in the First World War. The figures we give here need analysis if they are to mean anything. See the chapters on "Man Power" and "Losses" in N. N. Golovine, *The Russian Army in the World War*, Yale University Press, 1931.

10. Field Marshal Colmar Baron von der Goltz was appointed German Governor General of Belgium in September 1914. He was succeeded in December 1914 by General Moritz Ferdinand Count von Bissing, who died in April 1917 and was succeeded by General Ludwig von Falkenhausen.

11. H. Pirenne, *La Belgique et la Guerre mondiale*, Paris, 1928, Chap. VII, p. 195.

CHAPTER 5

1. The writer acknowledges borrowing this very descriptive figure from B. H. Liddell Hart, *A History of the World War*, Little, Brown, 1935, Chap. VI.

2. The French casualties at Verdun were 535,000; the German were 427,000. See an analysis of these figures in the British official *History of the Great War, Military Operations, France and Belgium, 1916*, London, 1932, Vol. I, Note II, pp. 496–97.

3. The British casualties on the Somme were less than 419,654; the German were more than 445,322. See the British official *History*, Note II, pp. 496–97.

4. Sir Mark Sykes was a lieutenant colonel in the British Army, assigned to political duties with the French Foreign Ministry at the beginning of the First World War. François-Marie-Denis-Georges Picot was a representative of the French Foreign Ministry and onetime Consul General in Syria.

5. "Intensified," *verscharft*; "unrestricted," *uneingeschränkt*.

6. Winston S. Churchill, *The World Crisis, 1916–1918*, Scribner, 1929, Chap. V.

CHAPTER 6

1. The House vote was 373 to 50, the Senate 82 to 6.

2. The pertinent passages in Hankey's memorandum are quoted in the British official *History of the Great War: Naval Operations*, London, 1931, Vol. V, pp. 10–14.

3. In the American constitutional system members of the Cabinet are not, and must not be, members of Congress. But American readers should be reminded that

this "separation of powers" is the reverse of the usual democratic procedure in Europe. In Germany, before 1918, "democratization" meant the granting of ministerial appointments to Reichstag Deputies, so as to bring the German constitutional system into line with those of England and France.

4. J. W. Wheeler-Bennett, *The Forgotten Peace: Brest Litovsk*, Morrow, 1939.

CHAPTER 7

1. During the entire war period German submarines succeeded in torpedoing only five American transports. Three of the five sank, two returned damaged to port. All five were on return voyages to the United States when struck, and were therefore carrying no troops. B. Crowell and R. F. Wilson, *How America Went to War, The Road to France*, Yale University Press, 1921, Vol. II, Chap. XXIX, pp. 427–28.

2. Erich Ludendorff, *Meine Kriegserinnerungen, 1914–1918*, Berlin, 1919, p. 435.

3. American troops were put into a quiet section of the line near Nancy in October 1917 and suffered their first casualties on November 3, 1917. The first major action, however, took place in May 1918 at Cantigny in the Amiens salient. American divisions fought at Château-Thierry in June 1918. Fourteen American divisions were in the line in August 1918 at Ypres, Arras, Reims, Verdun, and St. Mihiel, and in Alsace. Three hundred thousand American troops fought in the Second Battle of the Marne, 550,000 in the action at St. Mihiel, and 1,200,000 in the Meuse-Argonne. About 1,200 participated in the Battle of Vittorio Veneto in Italy.

4. By "elastic" defense the front line was thinly held, and the main shock of the enemy's attack was taken by the more strongly defended second line.

5. Erich Ludendorff, *op. cit.*, p. 493.

6. Bulgaria had participated in the Balkan Wars of 1912–13.

7. The United States never declared war on Bulgaria and did not withdraw its usual diplomatic representation in that country.

8. The Kaiser signed his abdication from his place of exile on November 28, 1918.

9. W. L. Langer, *ed., An Encyclopedia of World History*, Houghton Mifflin, 1940, p. 960, gives the military casualties of the principal belligerent Powers as 7,940,000 dead and 19,536,000 wounded.

CHAPTER 8

1. "Mr. Hughes, am I to understand," asked Wilson on this occasion, "that if the whole civilized world asks Australia to agree to a mandate in respect of these islands, Australia is prepared to defy the appeal of the whole civilized world?" "That's about the size of it, President Wilson," replied Hughes. Paul Birdsall, *Versailles Twenty Years After*, Reynal and Hitchcock, 1941, Chap. III, p. 72.

2. Harold Nicolson, *Peacemaking*, 1919, Harcourt, Brace, 1939, Chap. III, pp. 58–59.

3. D. Lloyd George, *The Truth about the Peace Treaties*, London, 1938, Vol. I, Chap. IV, p. 237.

4. The Powers at the Peace Conference in plenary session were:

The United States	5 seats	
Britain	5	
Canada	2	
Australia	2	British Empire
South Africa	2	14 seats in all
New Zealand	1	
India	2	
France	5	
Italy	5	
Japan	5	

The following 3 seats each: Belgium, Brazil, Yugoslavia (Serbia).

The following 2 seats each: China, Czechoslovakia, Greece, Hejaz, Poland, Portugal, Rumania, Siam.

The following 1 seat each: Bolivia, Cuba, Ecuador, Guatemala, Haiti, Honduras, Liberia, Nicaragua, Panama, Peru, Uruguay.

The delegates of the five principal Powers included, in addition to those mentioned in our text: for France, Marshal Foch, André Tardieu, Jules Cambon, Léon Bourgeois; for Britain, Bonar Law, G. N. Barnes, Viscount Milner, Winston Churchill, Lord Robert Cecil, Lord Hardinge, Sir Maurice Hankey, J. M. Keynes, Philip Kerr; for Italy, Salandra and Scialoja, and later Nitti and Tittoni; for the United States, Colonel House, Henry White, General Tasker H. Bliss, Norman H. Davis, Thomas W. Lamont, Bernard M. Baruch, Vance McCormick, Herbert Hoover, George Louis Beer, Joseph Clark Grew, Samuel Gompers; and for Japan, Viscount Chinda. Also for India, the Maharajah of Bikaner and Lord Sinha.

5. The Commission on the League of Nations seemed to include the most illustrious names of the Conference: President Wilson, Colonel House, Lord Robert Cecil, General Smuts, Léon Bourgeois, Orlando, Hymans, Venizelos, Dmowski, Kramář, Vesnich, Makino, and Chinda.

6. But the Chinese delegates signed the Treaty of St. Germain which, from their point of view, contained no objectionable clauses, and thereby China qualified as one of the original members of the League of Nations.

7. G. P. Gooch, *Germany*, Scribner, 1925, Chap. X, pp. 214–15. But, on this question of the continuation of the blockade of Germany after the Armistice, see Note 1, Chapter 10, below.

CHAPTER 9

1. Paul Birdsall, *Versailles Twenty Years After*, Reynal and Hitchcock, 1941, Chap. 1, p. 9.

2. Owing to frequent cancellations and renewals, it is difficult to determine the status of the Optional Clause in any one year. The figures quoted are from M. O. Hudson, *The World Court, 1921–1938*, 5th ed., World Peace Foundation, 1938, pp. 14–15, 30–31.

3. The fifteen Powers which signed the Pact of Paris on August 27, 1928, were the United States, Australia, Belgium, Britain, Canada, Czechoslovakia, France, Germany, India, Irish Free State, Italy, Japan, New Zealand, Poland, and South Africa. By the end of 1931, forty-five more states had adhered.

4. The Litvinov Protocol was signed in Moscow on February 9, 1929, by the Soviet Union, Poland, Latvia, Estonia, and Rumania. Lithuania and Turkey adhered on April 1, Danzig on April 30, and Persia on July 4, 1929.

5. Sumner Welles, *The Time for Decision*, Harper, 1944, Chap. I, p. 3.

6. We might translate these words by using those of George Washington in his first annual address to both houses of Congress on January 8, 1790: "To be prepared for war is one of the most effectual means of preserving peace."

7. As the result of the assassination of the Soviet representative, Vorovsky, on May 10, 1923, at Lausanne, the Soviet Union had refused to send representatives to Geneva. The Soviet-Swiss feud was not ended till April 1927.

CHAPTER 10

1. The facts concerning the continuation of the blockade after the Armistice are given in: F. M. Surface and R. L. Bland, *American Food in the World War and Reconstruction Period*, Stanford University Press, 1931, pp. 189 ff; H. W. V. Temperley, *A History of the Peace Conference of Paris*, London, 1920, Vol. I, p. 313 ff; Lindley Fraser, *Germany between Two Wars*, Oxford University Press, 1944, pp. 30–36; J. H. Morgan, *Assize of Arms*, Vol. I, London, 1945, pp. 187–90.

2. It is to be remembered that Ebert was Provisional President. He was never elected President of the Reich.

3. "Direct action" was a term much used by the British trade-unions to describe a general strike for the purpose of exerting political pressure on the government. (See pp. 326 and 329.)

4. These figures are from *Verhandlungen der verfassunggebenden Deutschen Nationalversammlung*, Berlin, 1920; *Verhandlung des Reichstags*, Berlin, 1920–25; and *Verzeichnis der Mitglieder des Reichstags*, Berlin, 1925–33.

CHAPTER 11

1. J. M. Keynes, *The Economic Consequences of the Peace*, London, 1919, Chap. V, p. 124.

2. Rathenau's assassination was one of many at this time. We have already mentioned Erzberger's. One estimate gives 376 political assassinations in the first three years of the Weimar Republic. See E. J. Gumbel, *Vier Jahre Politischer Mord*, Berlin, 1922.

3. On November 15, 1923, the mark dropped to 4,200,000,000,000 to the United States dollar. Gustav Stolper, *German Economy*, London, 1940, Pt. IV, Chap. 2, p. 151.

4. General Charles G. Dawes served in France in 1917 on the Administrative Staff of the Commander in Chief of the A.E.F. Later he was appointed General Purchasing Agent, and in 1919 resigned from the Army and returned to the United States as Director of the Federal Budget Bureau. In 1929 he was appointed ambassador to Britain.

5. See Note 2, Chapter 10 above.

6. This point is well brought out by R. T. Clark, *The Fall of the German Republic*, London, 1935, Chap. IV, p. 124.

CHAPTER 12

1. In the latter part of the eighteenth century Poland was partitioned between her three powerful neighbors, Austria, Russia, and Prussia. The first Partition was in 1772, the second in 1793, and the third in 1795 and 1796.

2. The White Russians or Byelorussians, of course, are not to be confused with the anti-Soviet "White Russian" *émigrés*. White Russia is now the Byelorussian Soviet Socialist Republic.

3. A Uniat (Uniate) is a Christian of the Eastern rite who acknowledges the supremacy of the Pope, but retains his own liturgy.

CHAPTER 13

1. We are using the term "Christian Socialist," rather than "Christian Social." The full German name of the party is *Christlich-Soziale Partei Oesterreichs*.

2. The former Hungarian Prime Minister, Teleki, who was also a distinguished geographer, has told the following anecdote about this problem of Teschen: "I once asked a very prominent Czech politician how many Poles there were in the district of Teschen. He said, 'Perhaps 40,000, perhaps 100,000.' I said 'How does it happen that you give me such different figures just when the question seems to be of momentous importance?' He replied, 'Well, the figures change. The peoples of certain villages are changing their nationality every week, according to their economic interests and sometimes the economic interests of the mayor of the village.' " W. Kolarz, *Myths and Realities in Eastern Europe*, London, 1946, Chap. I, p. 30.

3. The convention of June 1921 between Rumania and Yugoslavia, who were both Balkan Powers, was an alliance against Hungary and also against Bulgaria. It was therefore interested in the maintenance of the Treaty of Neuilly as well as the Treaty of Trianon.

CHAPTER 14

1. "Macedonia" was comprised, roughly, within the three Turkish vilayets of Kossovo, Monastir, and Salonika. Modern Macedonian history may be summarized as follows:

In 1870 a firman, or edict of the Sultan, established an independent Bulgar Church, with a Bulgar Primate, or Exarch. This firman further conceded to the Christian residents of any other district inhabited by Bulgars the right to be transferred from the jurisdiction of the Greek Patriarch to the Bulgar Exarch, provided that a petition was made by two-thirds of the population of the Christian parish in question. Hence the propaganda. As Professor Schevill puts it so neatly, Macedonia became "the scene of a triangular struggle conducted chiefly with the tools of church and school for the conquest of the *mind* of the inhabitants; and if by the close of the nineteenth century the bulk of the Vardar Slavs had gone over to the Bulgar camp, the Serbs had at least managed to gain a foothold to the north of the Shar Dagh Mountains, while the Greeks solidly maintained their traditional grip on the southern district contiguous to Thessaly." Ferdinand Schevill, *History of the Balkan Peninsula*, Harcourt, Brace, 1933, p. 434.

In 1893, as we have said in our text, the Internal Macedonian Revolutionary Organization (IMRO) was founded by Macedonian patriots for the purpose of emancipating Macedonia from the Ottoman Turks. By 1903 Macedonia had so fallen into anarchy that the Sultan was forced to agree to its international policing. Five of the Great Powers undertook this job, and they likewise organized an international financial commission for the control of Macedonian finances.

After the Balkan War of 1913, Macedonia was divided between Greece and Serbia. During the First World War it was seized and occupied by Bulgaria. In the interwar period, 1919–39, most of it was absorbed into Yugoslavia. During the Nazi occupation in the Second World War it was separately administered by a German Military Commander.

2. David Mitrany, *The Effect of the War in Southeastern Europe*, Yale University Press, 1936; J. S. Roucek, *The Politics of the Balkans*, McGraw-Hill, 1939.

3. Friedrich Naumann, *Mitteleuropa*, Berlin, 1915; English translation, *Central Europe*, Knopf, 1917. A recent history of the Western European Union movement is given in Andrew and Frances Boyd, *Western Union*, London, 1948, Chap. II.

CHAPTER 15

1. The term "Near East" is used in the earlier Parts of this book. There is still no general agreement as to the proper demarcation of "Near East," "Middle East," and "Far East." Since the Second World War "Middle East" has come to displace "Near East." See Note 1, Chapter 52, below.

2. The Ottoman Sultan-Caliph played a dual role in the Islamic world. As Sultan, he was military and civil head of the Ottoman Empire. As Caliph, he was "Commander of the Faithful" and titular (theoretical) and spiritual head of all Moslems. The title Caliph was assumed by Selim, the Osmanli Sultan who conquered Egypt in 1517. Thereafter the Sultan was *de facto* (if not *de jure*) successor of the Arab Caliphs who had succeeded Mohammed. The Sultan-Caliph represented the indivisible union of the temporal and spiritual powers of Islam, vested in the person of a single supreme ruler.

3. Pan-Turanianism is a Turkish racist-nationalist philosophy. It is perhaps comparable to the Nazi Aryan myth, but has none of the Nazi extremism. The word "Turanian" is normally used of Asiatic languages that are neither Semitic or Indo-European, but Ural-Altaic.

4. The Capitulations were special treaties, some dating as far back as the sixteenth and seventeenth centuries, which granted extraterritorial rights and privileges to nationals of "Capitulatory" Powers.

5. The Dervishes were members of fanatical Moslem sects, who lived in communities withdrawn from the world, somewhat analogous to monastic orders.

6. The Shari'at is the sacred law of Islam, based primarily on the Koran.

7. Early in 1934, the Imam Yahya of Yemen finally entered into treaty relations with the British — though his only cordial foreign relations, then and afterward, were with Italy.

8. Ibn Saud, on his side, recognized the special position of Britain in the Gulf Principalities; and this in turn precipitated a diplomatic controversy between Persia and Britain concerning the status of the Bahrein Islands.

9. And we should include here the Bahrein Petroleum Company (BAPCO). See Chapter 52, p. 881.

10. It is noteworthy that this Soviet-Persian treaty of 1921 gave Soviet forces the right of access to northern Persia at their discretion — i.e., whenever they considered themselves to be "in danger" or considered the Soviet position in the Caucasus to be threatened by another Power. See Chapter 52, p. 884.

11. Fellaheen are the peasantry, and effendis are the clerical group and the minor officials.

CHAPTER 16

1. These three relatively small religious groups have been disproportionately influential, particularly in intellectual spheres. The English Quakers have long had an important secondary school in the mountains above Beirut. The American University of Beirut, which began life as a Protestant college in 1866, has had a traditionally fine medical school and has been famed throughout the area for the training it has given in character-building and citizenship. The French Jesuit University of St. Joseph, also in Beirut, has had an outstanding reputation for scholarship and for its archaeological and legal studies.

2. Records of the eighth session of the Permanent Mandates Commission of the League of Nations, February and March 1926 (extraordinary session in Rome); and tenth session of the Permanent Mandates Commission in November 1926. For a most illuminating discussion of the Permanent Mandates Commission with respect to France and the Syrian mandate, see Elizabeth P. MacCallum, *The Nationalist Crusade in Syria*, Foreign Policy Association, 1928, Chap. XI, pp. 226–51.

3. The text of the "Damascus Protocol" is translated and printed in George Antonius, *The Arab Awakening*, Lippincott, 1939, pp. 157–58.

4. The Diaspora, or Dispersion, refers to all Jewish communities that were settled *outside* Palestine after the Roman conquest, notably after the destruction of the Temple at Jerusalem by Titus in 70 A.D.

5. Royal Institute of International Affairs, *Information Papers* No. 20: *Great Britain and Palestine, 1915–1945*, p. 11. For the text of the Feisal-Weizmann Agreement of January 1919, see George Antonius, *op. cit.*, pp. 437–39; and for discussion of this agreement and Feisal's condition, or stipulation, see *ibid.*, pages 282–86, and Dr. Chaim Weizmann's autobiography, *Trial and Error*, Harper, 1949, p. 247.

6. The severe economic depression which occurred between 1925 and 1928 affected, almost exclusively, the members of the Jewish National Home.

7. According to Sir John Hope Simpson's estimate, only 6,544,000 dunums (one dunum equals about one-fourth acre) of cultivable land were available in Palestine, as against Zionist estimates of some 16,000,000 dunums. The official British estimate lay midway between the two. The important implication of these various estimates involved potential immigration quotas. If the Hope Simpson estimate was to be acted upon eventually, Jewish immigration would necessarily be curtailed in future quotas. Therefore the Zionists took fright as soon as Sir John's findings were endorsed by the Government's White Paper. The Hope Simpson Report also raised the "serious" issue of Arab unemployment. For the above estimates, see p. 71 of the *Palestine Report* of 1937 (see Bibliography).

8. Hajj Amin held simultaneously the two highest Moslem offices in Palestine. He was the Grand Mufti (or supreme religious official) of the Arab Moslems of Palestine, and he was the President of the Supreme Moslem Council (or principal civil and administrative position). He was therefore the leading representative of his

family, and his family (a branch of the Husseini) was one of the two most powerful in Palestine. They were extreme nationalists, as contrasted with their rivals, the Nashashibi, who were moderate nationalists.

9. Unabridged *Palestine Report* of 1937, *Cmd.* 5479, Col. 135, pp. 24 and 19, and pp. 306–07 and 396. Published by His Majesty's Stationery Office, London.

10. *Statement of Policy*, May 1939, *Cmd.* 6019. Quotations in this and the succeeding paragraph are from this White Paper.

11. It is significant, for the future relations of these two tribal kingdoms, to note that, in the boundary agreement of 1925, Ibn Saud reserved his position on the Aqaba-Ma'an frontier between Trans-Jordan and the Hejaz. He accepted the *status quo* only for the duration of the British Mandate.

12. Colonel G. E. Leachman was a British political officer whose activities in Mesopotamia, the eastern Syrian Desert, and northern Arabia were comparable to those of Colonel Lawrence in the west.

CHAPTER 17

1. "Great Russia" appears on the pre-1914 maps of Russia. It was the core, so to speak, of European Russia and included an area roughly within a 200-mile radius of Moscow, as distinct from West Russia, Little Russia, South Russia, and Kazan.

2. On December 23, 1917, Milner for Britain and Clemenceau for France signed a convention for dividing Russia into "zones of influence." See Louis Fischer, *The Soviets in World Affairs*, London, 1930, Vol. II, App., p. 836.

3. See Bruce Lockhart, *Memoirs of a British Agent*, London, 1932. (Published in the United States as *British Agent*, Putnam, 1933.)

4. A kulak was a peasant owning his land and employing labor. The inference is that he had become rich by exploitation and was an enemy of Communism.

5. W. H. Chamberlin, *The Russian Revolution*, London, 1935, Vol. II, Chap. XXIII, p. 75.

6. The requisitions under the system of War Communism took everything and then turned over a residue for the peasant's food and sowing. The grain tax was a levy, by which the peasant gave up a part of his produce to the authorities — much along the lines of the old-fashioned tithe — and kept the remainder to use as he pleased. See L. E. Hubbard, *The Economics of Soviet Agriculture*, London, 1939, pp. 79–82.

7. The State would "wither away." This famous phrase is from Engels and occurs in his *Anti-Dühring*. But Marx has something like it, almost on the last page of his *Misère de la Philosophie:* "There will then be no more political power properly speaking, since political power is precisely the official expression of (class) conflict in the social system."

8. Nicolas Berdyaev, *The Origin of Russian Communism*, London, 1937, Chap. I.

9. J. Stalin, "The Foundations of Leninism," Chap. VIII, in *Problems of Leninism*, Moscow, 1947, pp. 80–91.

10. Quoted by W. H. Chamberlain, *The Russian Revolution*, London, 1935, Vol. II, Chap. XXIII, p. 77.

11. This is disputed. It has been suggested that Lenin's mother belonged to a family of German Jews settled in Russia.

CHAPTER 18

1. N. A. Timasheff, *The Great Retreat*, Dutton, 1946.

2. Compare these figures with American production for the peak year, 1929: 550,000,000 tons of coal; 138,000,000 tons of oil (crude petroleum); 43,000,000 tons of pig iron; 57,000,000 tons of steel; 771,000 trucks, etc.; 4,587,000 automobiles. (The tons are metric tons.) *Statistical Year-Book of the League of Nations, 1938–39,* Geneva, 1939.

3. Eugene Lyons, *Stalin: Czar of all the Russias,* London, 1940, Chap. XXI, p. 181.

4. Allan Monkhouse, *Moscow, 1911–1933,* London, 1933, Chap. XXI, p. 296, and Chap. XXII, p. 316.

5. See Note 4, Chapter 17, above.

6. In this section I have been guided by the two books by J. F. Hecker, *Religion under the Soviets,* Vanguard, 1927, and *Religion and Communism,* London, 1933, and by R. P. Casey, *Religion in Russia,* Harper, 1946. There is not nearly enough up to-date, objective literature on the religious question in the Soviet Union.

CHAPTER 19

1. Italy proclaimed a protectorate over Albania in June 1917.

2. The *fasces* was the Latin name for a bundle of rods tied around the haft of an ax. It was an emblem of unity and authority, and was carried by the Roman lictors, who attended the magistrates.

3. The *Guardia Regia* was a special force, numbering 25,000, which had been created by Nitti during his premiership in 1919 to assist the police in maintaining order. The force was disbanded by Mussolini soon after he came to power.

4. The reference is to the withdrawal of the plebeians of the city of Rome to the Aventine Hill in 493 B.C.

5. Requoted from H. Finer, *Mussolini's Italy,* London, 1935, Chap. VI, p. 191.

6. B. Mussolini, article on "Fascismo" in the *Enciclopedia Italiana,* requoted from H. Finer, *op. cit.,* Chap. VI, pp. 173 and 174, and Chap. VII, p. 222.

7. Requoted from H. W. Schneider, *Making the Fascist State,* Oxford University Press, 1928, Chap. V, p. 253.

CHAPTER 20

1. It should be remembered that the French word, *réparation,* means repair or making good. In English, reparation also has the sense of the French *indemnité,* the payment of monetary compensation. Much misunderstanding has arisen from this verbal difficulty.

2. So says General de Gaulle, *France and Her Army,* London, 1945, the last page.

3. Léon Daudet was a Deputy in the Chamber and a member of the *Action Française*.

4. The presidential question in France has been keenly debated ever since the constitution of 1875 which, in anticipation of a possible restoration of the monarchy, had deliberately reduced the President to a figurehead. The question was still very much alive in the constitutional plebiscites of 1945–46.

CHAPTER 21

1. Sir Austin Chamberlain, Chancellor of the Exchequer (1903–06 and 1919–21) and Foreign Secretary (1924–29), was the younger half-brother of Neville Chamberlain, Chancellor of the Exchequer (1923–24 and 1931–37) and Prime Minister (1937–40). Their father was Joseph Chamberlain, the Victorian statesman and "Liberal Unionist."

2. Arcos Ltd. (from the initials of the Anglo-Russian Co-operative Society) was the trading company in London representing the Soviet Co-operative Societies.

3. Land purchase has had a long history in Ireland. In some ways it was analogous to the agrarian reforms in other European peasant countries, designed to buy out the landlords (often absentee landlords) for the benefit of landless and indigent tenants; but it was complicated by the peculiar nature of Irish landlordism. However, by a series of acts (the Land Act of 1923 being the last), provision was made for the issue of bonds, out of which compensation to the landlords would be made, and which were guaranteed by the British Government. The purchasers of

land paid off their debts in part by means of annuities and in part by government bonus. After the establishment of the Free State, Cosgrave agreed to collect and pay to the British Government the full amount of the annuities.

De Valera's argument always was: "The Land Purchase Annuities themselves arise from the repurchase of confiscated lands from the successors of English soldiers and adventurers to whom they were given as rewards for their services to the English Crown in the sixteenth and seventeenth centuries, and their restoration to the successors of the rightful owners. There is no moral code that would fasten the cost of this belated act of restitution upon the Irish people." Dorothy Macardle, *The Irish Republic,* London, 1937, App. II, 36, pp. 1026–28.

4. Sir James Craig, Premier of Northern Ireland, was created Viscount Craigavon of Stormont in 1927.

5. The relative birth rate of the two populations is of vital importance in this connection. In 1931 the English-speaking birth rate was 16 per 1,000, and the French-Canadian was 26 per 1,000. There are over 1,000,000 Americans of French-Canadian descent, mostly in New England. See F. R. Scott, *Canada Today,* Oxford University Press, 1938, p. 14.

6. A recent classic example was the plebiscite in Canada on April 27, 1942, for conscription for overseas service. Of the eight provinces in the Dominion, Quebec alone returned a vote of "No."

7. Readers of this book will recall the old controversy over the selection of Washington, D.C., as the capital of the United States.

CHAPTER 22

1. The Indian census is taken every ten years. The figures are: 1901, 294,000,000; 1911, 315,000,000; 1921, 320,000,000; 1931, 353,000,000; 1941, 388,000,000.

2. Purdah, by definition, is a screen or veil. It refers (a) to the secluded life of Moslem women, and (b) to the veil worn by Moslem women when in public. Some Hindu castes adopted purdah, for instance in Rajputana.

3. Hindus and Moslems are referred to as "communities," and their joint affairs and problems as "communal." In Indian parlance, therefore, a "communal" riot is always a riot between Hindus and Moslems.

4. The personal revenue per annum of the Nizam of Hyderabad, reputedly the wealthiest of the Indian princes, was $50,000,000. See John Gunther, *Inside Asia,* Harper, 1939, Chap. XXVII, p. 450.

5. The name "Congress" is misleading, especially to Americans. The Indian National Congress, it must be remembered, is a political party, membership in which is open to both Hindus and Moslems on payment of a small subscription.

6. "Hartal" is the word for a workers' strike. But, unlike a strike in the trade-union sense, a hartal is often without any specific organization.

7. The Government of India imposed an excise duty on the manufacture of salt, a duty which, though small, fell upon all, including the poorest of the poor. With his usual acumen, Gandhi picked on something which affected all castes, classes, and communities.

CHAPTER 23

1. See Note 3, Chapter 26, below.

2. According to Secretary of State Lansing, the scope of American war preparations was so huge that Japan refused to believe that American forces were to be sent to the European theater only, and suspected that some of them might be employed, possibly in concert with Britain, to restrain her in China. *War Memoirs of Robert Lansing,* Rich and Cowan, 1935, Chap. XX, pp. 285–86.

3. See Note 3, Chapter 9, above.

4. In February 1901, Orville Hitchcock Platt, chairman of the Committee on

Cuban Relations, introduced the amendment (to an army appropriations bill) which bears his name. It provided for American military intervention in Cuba in certain contingencies, and forbade Cuba to enter into any treaty with a foreign Power to the prejudice of her independence.

5. The Clark Memorandum was drafted by J. Reuben Clark, Assistant Secretary of State, in 1928, and made public in 1930. It repudiated unofficially the "Theodore Roosevelt Corollary" of 1904 to the Monroe Doctrine, which had asserted that "chronic wrongdoing" in a Latin-American state "may force the United States, however reluctantly, in flagrant cases of such wrongdoing . . . to the exercise of an international peace power."

6. André Tardieu, *The Truth about the Treaty*, Bobbs-Merrill, 1921, Chap. XIV, pp. 470–71.

CHAPTER 24

1. Winston S. Churchill, *The World Crisis: The Aftermath*, Scribner, 1929, Chap. XX.

CHAPTER 25

1. The reader will appreciate my indebtedness to W. H. Tawney's *Religion and the Rise of Capitalism.*

2. H. G. Moulton and Leo Pasvolsky, *War Debts and World Prosperity*, Brookings, 1932, pp. 5–6.

3. In 1929 France's gold reserve was over 40,000,000,000 francs; in 1930 it was over 80,000,000,000. Paul Einzig, *France's Crisis*, London, 1934, p. 130.

It is very difficult to say to what extent France herself was responsible for the extraordinary financial dominance which she enjoyed between 1928 and 1931. Foreign opinion is always apt to attribute to a country dark and sinister designs in national successes which have resulted only from the shrewd exploitation of opportunities as they arose. Certainly the violent fluctuation of the franc between 1920 and 1926 was hardly an indication of deep foresight of any kind, even though Poincaré's final stabilization of the franc at a fifth of its prewar value afterward proved to be of the greatest advantage to France.

But other circumstances made their contribution. The interwar taxation system in France was very lenient on excess profits and left relatively unscathed a large class of wealthy investors with funds which could be transferred abroad. The Spa percentages of 1920 had originally allotted 52 per cent of German reparations receipts to France. French debt-funding agreements with Britain and the United States were negotiated in 1926, when French finances were still in a parlous condition, and granted such favorable terms that the capital value of the debts was virtually halved. By 1928, when French finances had recovered, receipts from reparations exceeded the interests on debts.

In the early months of 1931 France attained the peak of her financial hegemony. A country which in 1926 had been on the brink of bankruptcy now hoarded a huge fortune of gold, and looked on complacently while the rest of the world floundered in the morass from which she had so successfully extricated herself. From the day the Austro-German Customs Union had been frustrated, Austria succumbed to French financial vassalage. Hungary and Bulgaria were weaned away from Italian influence and reduced to the same state. Even the old allies in the Little Entente, Czechoslovakia, Yugoslavia, and Rumania learned that political friendships entail a price. Britain was forced to borrow gold from France in the fight to save her pound, and Laval in Washington all but dictated terms to President Hoover.

4. In 1930, American private long-term investments in Europe were $3,500,000,-000, of which $1,210,000,000 were to Germany.

5. Brokers' loans may be made on a "time" basis or on a "call" or "demand" basis. Rate of interest on a "time" loan is usually agreed between the broker, who

borrows, and the bank, which lends, and it continues unchanged for the duration (30 days to 1 year) of the agreement. The "call" or "demand" loan, as its name implies, may be terminated "at call" by borrower or lender at any time, and the rate of interest is on a day-to-day basis. "Call money," or the call loan rate, depends on the state of the market and may change during the day as new loans are made.

Purchases of stock may be made by a broker on behalf of a client against a deposit of a percentage of the purchase price, the broker holding the stock as security. In effect, this is a loan from broker to client. Before 1929, the New York Stock Exchange informally required of its member firms that this percentage, or margin, should be at least 17 per cent of the market value of the stocks. In the spring of 1929, the percentage was increased to 20 per cent. The margin itself, of course, was usually more stock — and so also was the broker's collateral. And this is where the trouble began.

See Raymond Vernon, *The Regulation of Stock Exchange Members*, Columbia University Press, 1941.

6. Three premiers: MacDonald, Brüning, and Laval; six foreign ministers: Henderson, Curtius, Briand, Stimson, Grandi, and Hymans; four financial ministers: Snowden, Flandin, Mellon, and Mosconi. All of which was sufficient indication of the importance of the occasion.

7. It would be appropriate to note at this point the final balance sheet of German reparations. The whole question, however, is very complicated and, to my knowledge, no up-to-date publication exists which sets out the full facts. Etienne Mantoux, after long study, wrote: "A total of some 35 to 38 milliard marks had been received by Germany from abroad between 1920 and 1931, as against the 21 milliards she paid for reparation." Etienne Mantoux, *The Carthaginian Peace*, Oxford University Press, 1946, Chap. V, p. 155. See also "Reparations and War Debts," Supplement to *The Economist*, London, January 23, 1932; and C. R. S. Harris, *Germany's Foreign Indebtedness*, Oxford University Press, 1935.

CHAPTER 26

1. The Kuomintang began as the Association for the Regeneration of China, founded in 1894. In 1905 it was merged into the larger Revolutionary Alliance, out of which sprang the present Kuomintang. The Revolutionary Alliance was a network of secret societies, opposed to the Manchu dynasty and kept together mainly by the unremitting activity of Dr. Sun. Propaganda was spread chiefly by young Chinese educated in the United States, Europe, and Japan. Generous subscriptions were obtained from well-to-do Chinese scattered throughout the Pacific area. It was claimed that the alliance had a membership of 300,000 in 1912. It was reorganized as the Kuomintang (National People's party) in 1912.

2. The Twenty-one Demands were presented to the President of China, Yuan Shih-kai, by the Japanese on January 8, 1915, and would have given Japan virtual political and economic control in Shantung, Manchuria, eastern Mongolia, and Fukien. The Japanese strove to prevent the publication of the Demands, especially of the fifth group, the most obnoxious of them. But the Demands leaked out and were published in full in the Peking newspapers on January 25, 1915, and in the ensuing furor the Japanese took the stand that they had been submitted "for consideration" only. The Demands in the fifth group included the employment by China of Japanese "advisers" in political, military, and financial matters; joint Sino-Japanese control of police in important Chinese cities; the purchase from Japan of a minimum of 50 per cent of China's war equipment; and the establishment of arsenals in China under joint Sino-Japanese operation. In May 1915, China was virtually forced to sign two treaties accepting the Demands in a modified form. See T. E. Lafargue, *China and the World War*, Stanford University Press, 1937; and P. E. Eckel, *The Far East since 1500*, Harcourt, Brace, 1947, pp. 391–93.

3. The scramble for monopolistic concessions in China at the end of the nineteenth century prompted Britain and the United States to take the lead in formulating a doctrine designed to assure Western Powers equal trading opportunities

throughout China. The first of the "Open Door" proposals, embodying this doctrine, was made by John Hay, Secretary of State, in 1899, since when the "Open Door" in China has been a cardinal principle of United States foreign policy. See P. E. Eckel, *The Far East since 1500,* Harcourt, Brace, 1947, pp. 353–55.

4. Senator Lodge gave expression to American disapproval in somber prophetic vein in a speech delivered in 1919: "Japan is steeped in German ideas and regards war as an industry because from war she has secured all the extensions of her Empire. . . . She means to exploit China and build herself up until she becomes a power formidable to all the world. It is not merely that she will close the markets of China and obtain commercial and economic advantages. . . . Japan will be enabled to construct . . . a power which will threaten the safety of the world. . . . But the country that she would menace most would be our own, and unless we carefully maintain a very superior navy in the Pacific, the day will come when the United States will take the place of France in another great war to preserve civilization." Quoted in F. R. Dulles, *China and America,* Princeton University Press, 1946, Chap. X, pp. 148–49.

5. Japanese forces in Siberia numbered 72,000 men as compared with the maximum of 12,000 prescribed by her original agreement with the United States and Britain. The unwavering support which they gave to the terroristic regime of their puppet, Semënov, is explained by General Graves, the commander of the American forces in Siberia. W. S. Graves, *America's Siberian Adventure, 1918–20,* Cape, 1931, p. 108.

6. P. S. Reinsch, *An American Diplomat in China,* Garden City, 1922, Chap. XXVIII, p. 337–38, and Chap. XXXI, pp. 365–66.

CHAPTER 27

1. The whole of this very controversial incident has been recently re-examined in the light of available documents by Sara R. Smith in *The Manchurian Crisis, 1931–1932, A Tragedy in International Relations,* Columbia University Press, 1948.

CHAPTER 28

1. Papen remained Vice-Chancellor at least till June 30, 1934, and probably till August of the same year. Hugenberg resigned on June 29, 1933.

2. An authority, whom I am not at liberty to quote, estimates about 300 concentration camps in Greater Germany in 1940–44, not including the Government General of Poland or the Protectorate of Bohemia-Moravia. Probably there were another 300 in the occupied territories. The standing population of all these camps may have been 1,500,000, and the total number that passed through them since 1933, 10,000,000. The average expectation of life of a prisoner was two years.

3. These figures were mentioned several times during the Nuremberg Trial. See *Trial of the Major War Criminals,* Nuremberg, 1947, Vol. I, pp. 247–53.

4. Nazi economics is described in a number of books. See, for instance, C. W. Guillebaud, *The Economic Recovery of Germany,* London, 1939; Thomas Reveille, *The Spoil of Europe,* Norton, 1941, esp. Chap XVII; and L. Hamburger, *How Germany Has Controlled Business,* Brookings, 1943.

5. Konrad Heiden, *Der Führer,* London, 1945, Chap. VIII, p. 147.

6. H. Rauschning, *The Voice of Destruction,* Putnam, 1940, Chap. IX, pp. 109–10.

7. It is a common mistake to regard *Mein Kampf* as a "program." It is a confession of faith. And not all of it, by any means, was fulfilled as the Führer hoped, even up to 1941.

8. Lord Vansittart, *The Black Record,* London, 1941.

9. Winston S. Churchill, *The World Crisis,* Scribner, 1931, Bk. III, Chap. LV, p. 848.

10. Leopold Schwarzschild, *World in Trance,* London, 1943, Chap. VII, p. 190.

11. The romanticism of the Nazis is the theme of Peter Viereck, *Metapolitics, From the Romantics to Hitler*, Knopf, 1941.
12. Papal Encyclical, *Mit brennender Sorge*, 1937, Paras. 25 and 28.
13. S. H. Roberts, *The House That Hitler Built*, Harper, 1939, end of Part I, Chap. IV.

CHAPTER 29

1. *Trial of the Major War Criminals*, Nuremberg, 1947–49, Vol. XIX, p. 449, and Vol. XXVI, Doc. 789 — PS, p. 328.
2. *Ibid.*, Vol. II, p. 316, and Vol. XXX, Doc. 2322 — PS, p. 174.
3. *Ibid.*, Vol. II, pp. 218–19, and Vol. XXXVI, Doc. 028 — EC, pp. 112 ff. See also *Nazi Conspiracy and Aggression*, U. S. Government Printing Office, 1946, Vol. VII, pp. 250 ff.
4. *Trial of the Major War Criminals*, Nuremberg, 1947–49, Vol. II, pp. 262–73, and Vol. XXV, Doc. 386 — PS, pp. 402–13. See also *Nazi Conspiracy and Aggression*, U. S. Government Printing Office, 1946, Vol. III, pp. 295 ff.
5. Under its constitution, the Free City of Danzig had a High Commissioner appointed by the League of Nations who decided upon all differences between Danzig and Poland. But Danzig and Poland had the right to appeal his decisions to the League Council. The harbor was administered by a Commission of five nominees of Danzig and Poland under a neutral (usually Swiss) president. The legislative assembly consisted of a Volkstag of 72 members and a Senate of 20 members. The Free City was included in the Polish customs area, and a great part of it was included in the Polish postal service. The railroads were operated by the Polish railroads. Foreign policy was controlled by Poland.

CHAPTER 30

1. The actual assassin was a Macedonian and a member of the Macedonian Revolutionary Organization (the IMRO), but he was in Croat employ (Pavelich).

CHAPTER 32

1. The Civil Guard (*Guardia Civil*) corresponded to the French gendarmerie and were organized on semimilitary lines. The Republicans changed their name to *Guardia Nacional Republicana*.
2. The Assault Guards (*Guardias de Asalto*) were the shock brigades, a second semimilitary police, formed in the first year of the Republic in 1931.
3. The Carlists were extreme monarchists and took their name from the brother of Ferdinand VII, Don Carlos, whose claim to the throne was contested in the Carlist wars of the early nineteenth century.
4. These groups are discussed in A. J. Toynbee, *Survey of International Affairs*, for 1937, London, Vol. II, pp. 88 ff.
5. R. W. Seton-Watson, *From Munich to Danzig*, London, 1939, Chap. VI, pp. 262–63. But I know of no definitive account of the strength of foreign troops in Spain. The Foreign Policy Reports of the Foreign Policy Association, New York, occasionally refer to the question — see those of January 15, 1937, and April 1, 1938, by C. A. Thomson and J. C. de Wilde; and Ciano has occasional references — see G. Ciano, *Diplomatic Papers*, London, 1948, pp. 86 and 143–44.

CHAPTER 33

1. The definition of "aggression" in so far as it affected the Balkan States is discussed by T. I. Geshkoff, *Balkan Union*, Columbia University Press, 1940, pp. 206–08. See also Note 1, Chapter 34, below.
2. Schacht did not include Bucharest in his itinerary, but that was undoubtedly

because Titulescu was still in office. So long as Titulescu remained Rumanian Foreign Minister, which he did until August 1936, there would have been little point in visiting Bucharest, Titulescu being a stanch supporter of the League and a united front of all potential victims of aggression against their potential aggressors. Titulescu was also a supporter of both the Little Entente and the Balkan Entente, and of *rapprochement* with Russia. His dismissal by King Carol in August 1936, after two and a half years in office, was a blow to the solidarity of Southeastern Europe and a sign of the waning prestige of the League in that part of the world. See A. J. Toynbee, *Survey of International Affairs,* for 1936, London, pp. 517–18 and 529, Note 1.

3. Balkan agrarian produce, foodstuffs, livestock, grain, oil (only in Rumania), timber, and tobacco — especially the foodstuffs and the tobacco — are complementary to the industrial production of Germany, but they are not completely adequate. Furthermore, the Balkans could never supply enough butter, oil seeds, metals, or cotton for Germany's needs. Nor do the Balkans produce rubber, tin, jute, coffee, or cocoa; they do not export wool; and their supplies of copper, lead, zinc, and nickel are very small. See *Political and Economic Survey of Southeastern Europe* published by the Information Department of the Royal Institute of International Affairs; and also A. J. Toynbee, *Survey of International Affairs,* for 1936, London, pp. 526–33.

4. Article 4 of the French Mandate for Syria and Lebanon reads: "The Mandatory shall be responsible for seeing that no part of the territory of Syria and the Lebanon is ceded or leased or in any way placed under the control of a foreign Power." The article is identical with Article 5 of the British Mandate for Palestine and was written into all the mandate instruments.

CHAPTER 34

1. See A. J. Toynbee, *Survey of International Affairs,* London, for 1933, pp. 182–83 and 278–82; and for 1934, pp. 381–83. See Note 1, Chapter 33 above.

2. I do not attempt to analyze a story that has baffled well-known observers of Russia. For myself, I still find Duranty's account of these trials by far the most credible. See Walter Duranty, *The Kremlin and the People,* Reynal and Hitchcock, 1941.

3. Historicus, "Stalin on Revolution," in *Foreign Affairs,* New York, Vol. 27, No. 2, January 1949.

4. All these passages are quoted from J. Stalin, *Problems of Leninism,* Moscow, 1947, "The Foundations of Leninism," pp. 41, 45, 65–66, 78, and "The Problems of Leninism," p. 162.

5. Resolution of the Fourteenth Communist Party Congress, 1925. Quoted from a broadcast by E. H. Carr, "World Revolution and Soviet Foreign Policy," B.B.C., London, reprinted in *The Listener,* London, February 3, 1949.

CHAPTER 35

1. This is a matter which always puzzles students of this episode. The French municipal pawnshops are mentioned in the article on "Pawnbroking" in the *Encyclopaedia Britannica.* See also F. Astier, *Des Monts-de-Piété,* Paris, 1914.

2. Such as Ilya Ehrenburg's *Fall of Paris.*

3. Antoine de Saint-Exupéry, *Flight to Arras,* London, 1942, Chap. XXIII, pp. 140–41.

CHAPTER 36

1. The "distressed" or "special" areas in England at this time were those in the coal fields, or the shipbuilding or other industrial districts, whose recovery was never expected to take place. These areas were particularly bad in South Wales and Durham.

2. Winston S. Churchill, *The Gathering Storm*, Houghton Mifflin, 1948, Bk. I, Chap. XI, p. 201, and Chap. XII, p. 220.

3. Keith Feiling, *The Life of Neville Chamberlain*, London, 1946, Chap. XXIII, p. 321.

4. See Note 1, Chapter 39, below.

5. It has always seemed to me that one of the signs of real strength which the British people showed in their dark period in 1939–41 was that there was no popular literature of recrimination. "Cato's" *Guilty Men* remains the one despicable exception.

6. The League of Nations Union was founded in London in 1919 as a society whose aims were "to secure the whole-hearted acceptance by the British people of the League of Nations as the guardian of international right . . ." Lord Grey, Lord Robert Cecil, Gilbert Murray, and other distinguished men were active in it. Its successor today is the United Nations Association.

7. Baldwin's famous "appalling frankness" speech of November 12, 1936, still provokes discussion. See R. Bassett, "Telling the Truth to the People" in *The Cambridge Journal*, Cambridge, Vol. II, No. 2, November 1948.

CHAPTER 38

1. See Sara R. Smith, *The Manchurian Crisis*, Columbia University Press, 1948, Chap. VII, p. 235. See Note 1, Chapter 27, above.

2. We have already forgotten the fierce conviction with which these views were once held. See, for instance, H. L. Engelbrecht and F. Hanighen, *Merchants of Death*, Dodd, Mead, 1934, which was so widely read.

3. *Peace and War: United States Foreign Policy, 1931–1941*, U. S. Government Printing Office, 1943, pp. 298 and 300.

4. *Ibid.*, p. 222.

5. *Ibid.*, pp. 428–29.

6. *Ibid.*, pp. 455–58.

7. *Ibid.*, p. 239.

8. *Ibid.*, p. 303.

9. *Ibid.*, pp. 466–67.

10. See Note 4, Chapter 23, above.

11. The Gran Chaco War of 1932–35 originated in the effort of Bolivia to find an outlet through the jungle country (Chaco) which separated her from the river Paraguay. The same area was claimed by Paraguay. One of the most ferocious small-scale wars of modern times resulted.

12. *Peace and War, op. cit.*, p. 257.

CHAPTER 39

1. See Leopold Schwarzschild, *World in Trance*, London, 1943, Chap. IX, p. 259; Winston S. Churchill, *The Gathering Storm*, Houghton Mifflin, 1948, Bk. I, Chap. XIII, pp. 226–28; J. F. Kennedy, *Why England Slept*, Funk, 1940, p. 113; and Notes 1, 2, and 3, Chapter 29, above.

2. Lord Halifax, formerly Baron Irwin, Viceroy of India, (1926–31). Succeeded to the Viscountcy of Halifax in 1934. Foreign Secretary, 1938–41. British ambassador to the United States, 1941–45.

3. Winston S. Churchill, *The Gathering Storm*, Houghton Mifflin, 1948, Bk. I, Chap. XIV, pp. 251–55; and Sumner Welles, *The Time for Decision*, Harper, 1944, Chap. II.

4. Kurt von Schuschnigg, *Austrian Requiem*, Putnam, 1946, Chap. I, pp. 14–25.

5. *Ibid.*, Chaps. XII–XIV.

6. *Trial of the Major War Criminals*, Nuremberg, 1947–49, Vol. II, p. 275, and Vol. XXV, Doc. 388 — PS, pp. 415–16.

7. G. E. R. Gedye, *Betrayal in Central Europe*, Harper, 1939, Chap. XXXIII, p. 410 (*Fallen Bastions*, London, 1939, p. 421).

8. *Trial of the Major War Criminals,* Nuremberg, 1947–49, Vol. III, pp. 56–58.
9. Keith Feiling, *The Life of Neville Chamberlain,* London, 1946, Chap. XXV, p. 359.
10. John W. Wheeler-Bennett, *Munich, Prologue to Tragedy,* London, 1948, Pt. I, Chap. IV, pp. 120–23; Hubert Ripka, *Munich, Before and After,* London, 1939, Chap. III, pp. 78–79.
11. It is important to establish that the initiative at this juncture was Chamberlain's. There seems to be no doubt that he urged Daladier and Bonnet, and then Mussolini, to agree to a four-Power conference. See J. W. Wheeler-Bennett, *op. cit.,* Chap. IV, p. 164; and Keith Feiling, *op. cit.,* Chap. XXVIII, pp. 372–73.
12. See Note 5, Chapter 29, above.
13. This conference was mentioned several times at Nuremberg. *Trial of the Major War Criminals,* Nuremberg, 1947–49, Vol. II, pp. 278–84, and Vol. XXXVII, Doc. 079 — L, pp. 546–56. See also *Nazi Conspiracy and Aggression,* U. S. Government Printing Office, 1946, Vol. VII, p. 847 ff.
14. *Trial of the Major War Criminals,* Nuremberg, 1947–49, Vol. II, pp. 286–91, Vol. XXVI, Doc. 798 — PS, pp. 338–44, and Vol. XXVI, Doc. 1014 — PS, pp. 523–24. See also *Nazi Conspiracy and Aggression,* U. S. Government Printing Office, 1946, Vol. III, pp. 581 ff.

CHAPTER 40

1. "Anzacs." See Note 7, Chapter 2, above.
2. Winston S. Churchill, *The Gathering Storm,* Houghton Mifflin, 1948, Bk. II, Chap. XVI, p. 657.
3. W. L. Langer, *Our Vichy Gamble,* Knopf, 1947, Chap. I, p. 20.

CHAPTER 41

1. I am following Grigore Gafencu, *Prelude to the Russian Campaign,* London, 1945, Pt. I, Intro.
2. Walter Millis, *This is Pearl!,* Morrow, Chap. VII, p. 342n.
3. For the twenty-six United Nations which signed the Declaration of January 1, 1942, see Note 1, Chapter 47, below.

CHAPTER 42

1. We should not forget other attempts on Hitler's life. See Fabian von Schlabrendorff, *Offiziere gegen Hitler,* Zürich, 1946.
2. See Note 2, Chapter 43, below.
3. A statement of this sort should be supported by figures, which we have not the space to quote at any length. However, we give the following yields for wheat (in quintals per hectare) for the years 1934–38:
Belgium 27.3
Canada 7.1
Denmark 30.6
France 15.8
Germany 22.9
Netherlands 30.3
Soviet Union 9.3
United Kingdom 23.1
United States 8.7
Yearbook of Food and Agricultural Statistics, 1947, Washington, 1947, published for the Food and Agriculture Organization of the United Nations, which also gives figures for other agricultural products, all telling a similar story.

4. *Statistics Relating to the War Effort of the United Kingdom, Cmd.* 6564, H. M. Stationery Office, London, 1944. The first volume of the history of Britain's war effort has lately appeared: W. K. Hancock and M. M. Gowing, *British War Economy,* H. M. Stationery Office, London, 1949.

5. Winston S. Churchill, *The Gathering Storm,* Houghton Mifflin, 1948, Bk. II, Chap. XVII, p. 667, the last page.

6. Winston S. Churchill, *Their Finest Hour,* Houghton Mifflin, 1949, Bk. I, Chap. I, pp. 16–17.

7. It is interesting to note how little President Roosevelt's speeches appeared to influence public opinion in the United States — if we may judge by the public-opinion polls. See P. E. Jacob, "Influence of World Events on U. S. Neutrality Opinion," in *Public Opinion Quarterly,* Princeton University Press, March 1940.

8. Named after the expression, "Women's Appointed Volunteer Emergency Service."

CHAPTER 43

1. General Baron Alexander von Falkenhausen. He headed the German military mission to China in the late twenties. I have not been able to discover whether he had any family relationship to General Ludwig von Falkenhausen, Governor General of Belgium in 1917–18. See Note 10, Chapter 4, above.

2. General Otto von Stuelpnagel was Military Governor of Occupied France from October 1940 to February 1942, when he retired. He committed suicide in prison in Paris in 1948 while awaiting trial. In February 1942, he was succeeded as Military Governor by General Karl Heinrich von Stuelpnagel, who had commanded an army in the invasion of Russia in 1941 and was afterward implicated in the plot against Hitler in July 1944 (see p. 692). There was also a General Siegfried von Stuelpnagel, who does not appear in our history. I have not been able to discover any family relationship between these men.

3. Thomas Reveille, *The Spoil of Europe,* Norton, 1941, Chap. VIII, p. 114. See also Note 2, Chapter 29, above.

4. Raphael Lemkin, *Axis Rule in Occupied Europe,* Carnegie Endowment, 1944, Chap. IX, pp. 79 ff.

CHAPTER 45

1. In answer to a question in the House of Commons, on October 22, 1945, Attlee stated that casualties to the German armed forces in the Second World War were estimated at about 3,000,000 killed and 3,400,000 "permanently wounded." "No estimate is available for the number missing." *Parliamentary Debates (Hansard),* October 1945, p. 1815. The figure of 6,000,000 Russian killed is commonly mentioned, but I have never seen an authoritative statement.

2. Winston S. Churchill, *Their Finest Hour,* Houghton Mifflin, 1949, Bk. I, Chap. I, p. 6.

3. Our information regarding the strength of the American forces in the Mediterranean and European theaters is pretty complete. But I have seen no corresponding figures for the Pacific theater. A correspondent sends me the following for the total strengths of the American forces in the Pacific and East Asian theaters on V-J Day:

Army (excluding Hawaii)	1,129,840
Navy (including Hawaii)	1,997,000
Air Force (excluding Hawaii)	196,957
Marines (including Hawaii)	187,500
TOTAL	3,511,297

4. General of the Army George C. Marshall, etc., *War Reports,* Lippincott, 1947, pp. 220–21.

5. Sir Arthur Harris, *Bomber Offensive,* London, 1947, Chap. XII.

CHAPTER 46

1. General of the Army George C. Marshall, etc. *War Reports,* Lippincott, 1947. Quotations and figures in this chapter are mainly from General Marshall's Third Report, pp. 156, 157, 179, and 230.

2. It is generally accepted that Rommel was quietly "executed" on Hitler's orders. See an article by Peter De Mendelssohn, "Speidel's Story," in *The New Statesman,* London, October 29, 1949.

3. Sir Arthur Harris, *Bomber Offensive,* London, 1947, Chap. XI, p. 239.

4. Roosevelt had returned from the Crimea Conference in a state of "supreme exultation." Clearly the rift with the Soviet Union began afterward. See R. E. Sherwood, *Roosevelt and Hopkins,* Harper, 1948, Chap. XXXIII, pp. 869–70.

CHAPTER 47

1. The original fifty nations that attended the San Francisco Conference were:

Argentina	Egypt	*Nicaragua
*Australia	*El Salvador	*Norway
*Belgium	Ethiopia	*Panama
Bolivia	France	Paraguay
Brazil	*Greece	Peru
Byelorussian S.S.R.	*Guatemala	Philippine Republic
(White Russia)	*Haiti	Saudi Arabia
*Canada	*Honduras	Syria
Chile	*India	Turkey
*China	Iran	Ukrainian S.S.R.
Colombia	Iraq	*Union of South Africa
*Costa Rica	Lebanon	*U.S.S.R.
*Cuba	Liberia	*United Kingdom
*Czechoslovakia	*Luxembourg	*United States
Denmark	Mexico	Uruguay
*Dominican Republic	*Netherlands	Venezuela
Ecuador	*New Zealand	*Yugoslavia

* The United Nations that signed the Declaration of January 1, 1942. Poland also signed, making the twenty-sixth.

Poland was admitted on October 24, 1945, and was allowed to count as an original member.
The following were subsequently admitted:
Afghanistan on Nov. 19, 1946
Burma on Apr. 19, 1948
Iceland on Nov. 19, 1946
Israel on May 11, 1949
Pakistan on Sept. 30, 1947
Siam on Dec. 16, 1946
Sweden on Nov. 19, 1946
Yemen on Sept. 30, 1947

2. See Note 4, Chapter 51, below.

3. The Soviet Union, the Ukrainian Soviet Socialist Republic, and the White Russian Soviet Socialist Republic retain their membership in the Universal Postal Union (UPU) and the International Telecommunication Union (ITU).

CHAPTER 48

1. The areas ceded to France under the Italian Treaty were the Little St. Bernard Pass, the Mont Cenis Plateau, the Mont Thabor-Chaberton area, and the Tenda-Briga area.

CHAPTER 49

1. The Nuremberg Charter, as we have said, laid down three categories of crimes. There were four counts listed in the indictment: common plan or conspiracy; crimes against peace; war crimes; and crimes against humanity.

2. There were to have been twenty-four defendants, but Robert Ley committed suicide in prison on October 25, 1945, and the Tribunal decided not to proceed against Gustav Krupp von Bohlen und Halbach on account of his mental and physical condition.

3. The Tribunal decided not to condemn as "criminal organizations" the SA, the Reich Cabinet, and the German General Staff and High Command. The Soviet member afterward recorded a vigorous dissent from this decision. See *Trial of the Major War Criminals,* Nuremberg, 1947–49, Vol. I, pp. 342 ff.

4. On April 14, 1949, twenty-one German "minor war criminals" were sentenced by a United States Military Tribunal at Nuremberg. Of these we may mention: Ernst von Weizsaecker, head of the Foreign Office under Ribbentrop, sentenced to seven years; Ernst Wilhelm Bohle, Chief of the Foreign Department of the Nazi party, five years; Hans Heinrich Lammars, Chief of the Reich Chancellery, twenty years; Walther Darré, Minister of Agriculture, seven years; Otto Dietrich, Nazi Press Chief, seven years; and Schwerin von Krosigk, Ribbentrop's successor as Foreign Minister in 1945, ten years. Otto Meissner was acquitted.

5. *The New York Times,* March 25, 1947. Also *The World Today* (Chronology, etc.), London, 1947, Vol. III, No. 7, pp. 206–07.

CHAPTER 50

1. The Italian elections of April 1948 resulted as follows:

	Chamber seats	Senate seats
Christian Democrats	307	130
Communists and Left-Wing Socialists	182	74
Right-Wing Socialists	33	12
National Bloc (Common Man Party and Liberals)	18	9
Monarchists	14	4
Democrats	9	3
Italian Social Movement	6	2

2. Sir William Beveridge, *Social Insurance and Allied Services, Cmd.* 6404, H.M. Stationery Office, London, 1942.

3. It is not altogether correct to describe the new medical services in Britain as "free." About ⅔ the cost of the service is borne by the Exchequer, about ¼ by National Insurance to which all the beneficiaries contribute, and the remainder by local rates.

4. Sterling balances are Britain's "debts" to India, Egypt, Ireland, Australia, New Zealand, Argentina, Iraq, etc., on account of wartime purchases from those countries. The total was £3,500,000,000 in March 1946, India's share being over £1,200,000,000.

5. This is admittedly a very perfunctory account of the causes of Britain's devaluation in September 1949. Like the devaluation of September 1931, it may take a long time to reach a definitive analysis. There are the long-term causes, perhaps imperfectly understood. There is the evident end of the seller's market. There are the more immediate and specific causes, such as the slowing up of the American stockpiling program and the resultant decline of American purchases of raw materials, notably rubber. The reader does not have to be told that the situation is not a simple one.

6. The nineteen ERP countries were the sixteen mentioned on p. 834, and the three Western zones of Germany. With the creation of the Federal Republic of Germany the number becomes seventeen.

CHAPTER 51

1. E. Crankshaw, "The U.S.S.R. Revisited," in *International Affairs*, London, Vol. XXIII, No. 4, October 1947, p. 403.

2. These figures were published in a letter to *The* (London) *Times* from A. Sudachkov, April 7, 1947.

3. Compare these with the figures in Note 2, Chapter 18, above.

4. The International Court took up the case — its first — in February 1948 and rendered its verdict in April 1949. The Court overwhelmingly vindicated the British claim to the right of innocent passage through the Corfu Channel, but it found that the British mine-sweeping operations, undertaken after the explosions, had violated Albania's sovereignty. By a vote of eleven to five the judges held Albania responsible for the fact that the British destroyers ran into the mines.

5. Stanislaw Mikolajczyk, *The Pattern of Soviet Domination*, London, 1948.

CHAPTER 52

1. The term "Near East" is used throughout Parts I, II, and III of this book and is understood to comprise Turkey, the Eastern Mediterranean, and the Arab states. But the term is a vague one and is sometimes taken to include the Balkans and Persia. During the early years of the Second World War, the term "Middle East," in Anglo-American military terminology, came to be applied to Turkey, the Arab states, and Persia to distinguish these countries from the Axis-dominated countries of the Balkan Near East, and the term has now found its way into United Nations terminology. We use the term occasionally in Part IV and adopt it fully in the present Part V.

2. The name "Persia" was changed to "Iran" in 1932, as we noted in Chapter 15, p. 236. Iran has since been the official name and appears as such in the United Nations lists. But generally Anglo-American usage continues to be Persia — possibly because of the risk of typographical confusion between Iran and Iraq.

CHAPTER 53

1. The eleven Powers on the Far Eastern Commission were Australia, Britain, Canada, China, France, India, the Netherlands, New Zealand, the Philippines, the Soviet Union, and the United States.

2. There had been many rumors in the thirties of the construction under Japanese initiative of the Kra Canal, cutting the Isthmus of that name, thus linking the Indian Ocean and the Gulf of Siam and rendering Singapore entirely useless.

3. In 1941, 43 per cent of the population of Malaya was Chinese, 41 per cent Malay, 13 per cent Indian, chiefly Tamil, and 3 per cent British, Singhalese, etc. The term "Malay" is usually used of the indigenous population of Malaya; "Malayan" is usually used of the immigrant Chinese and Indian population and their descendants.

4. The Dutch argued that, under Article 2, Section 7 of the Charter, the United Nations was precluded from intervening in the domestic jurisdiction of its members. On the other hand, Article 37 permitted the Security Council to take action in a dispute which it deemed likely to endanger the maintenance of international peace and security.

5. Immediately after the Philippine presidential election in April 1946, General MacArthur issued a statement to the effect that Roxas had acted as his liaison agent with the resistance movement during the Japanese occupation.

GLOSSARY

The following words and terms of common diplomatic usage appear in the text:

Casus belli. An event or incident which may be a cause of, or justification for, war.

Démarche. "Faire une démarche" is to make representations, usually involving a revision or change of policy.

Détente. A relaxation of strained relations.

Fait accompli. An accomplished fact, action or event, presumably irrevocable.

Rapprochement. A drawing together of two nations or governments, especially after a period of strained relations.

Refroidissement. A cooling of relations between two nations or governments, formerly warmly disposed toward one another.

Status quo (ante bellum). The state or condition existing (before a war), used especially of the restoration of former existing frontiers.

See Chap. X on "Diplomatic Language" in Harold Nicolson, *Diplomacy,* Harcourt, Brace, 1939.

The following names of British Cabinet offices appear in the text:

The Chancellor of the Exchequer corresponds to the American Secretary of the Treasury. The First Lord of the Admiralty corresponds to the Secretary of the Navy; he is usually, but not always, a civilian. The senior officer of the Admiralty is the First Sea Lord. He is always a high naval officer, but is not a member of the Cabinet; he would correspond to the American Chief of Naval Operations.

The Lord President of the Council, the Lord Privy Seal, and the Chancellor of the Duchy of Lancaster are old, honorific titles. They provide a means of giving a man a cabinet post without departmental duties, very much on the lines of a Minister without Portfolio.

See W. Ivor Jennings, *Cabinet Government,* Cambridge University Press, 1936, Chaps. III and IX.

The Chief of the Imperial General Staff (C.I.G.S.) is the senior officer of the British Army and corresponds to the Chief of Staff of the United States Army.

APPENDICES

A. THE REICHSTAG PEACE RESOLUTION, JULY 19, 1917 — passed by the German Reichstag by 212 votes to 126.

As on the fourth of August so also now on the threshold of a fourth year of war, the words of the speech from the throne hold true: "We are not impelled by the lust of conquest." Germany has taken up arms in defense of her freedom, her independence, and the integrity of her soil.

The Reichstag strives for a peace of understanding and a lasting reconciliation among peoples. Violations of territory and political, economic, and financial persecutions are incompatible with such a peace. The Reichstag rejects every scheme which has for its purpose the imposition of economic barriers or the perpetuation of national hatreds after the war. The freedom of the seas must be secured. Economic peace alone will prepare the ground for the friendly association of peoples. The Reichstag will actively promote the creation of international organizations of justice.

But so long as the enemy governments dissociate themselves from such a peace, so long as they threaten Germany and her allies with conquest and domination, then so long will the German people stand united and unshaken, and fight till their right and the right of their allies to live and grow is made secure. United thus, the German people is unconquerable. The Reichstag knows that in that sentiment it is at one with the men who battle heroically to protect the Fatherland. The imperishable gratitude of our people goes out to them.

B. THE WILSONIAN CODE, as we have called it, consisted of a series of pronouncements made by President Wilson during 1918:
  The Fourteen Points, January 8, 1918,
  The Four Principles, February 11, 1918,
  The Four Ends, July 4, 1918,
  The Five Particulars, September 27, 1918.
Space prevents us from quoting these pronouncements in this Appendix, except the Fourteen Points. The full texts are, of course, available in the current press, and also in H. W. V. Temperley, *A History of the Peace Conference of Paris*, London, 1920, Vol. I, pp. 431–48, and Alma Luckau, *The German Delegation at the Paris Peace Conference*, Columbia University Press, 1941, pp. 137–39.
  The Fourteen Points are as follows:

1. Open covenants of peace, openly arrived at, after which there shall be no private international understandings of any kind, but diplomacy shall proceed always frankly and in the public view.

2. Absolute freedom of navigation upon the seas, outside territorial waters, alike in peace and in war, except as the seas may be closed in whole or in part by international action for the enforcement of international covenants.

3. The removal, so far as possible, of all economic barriers and the establishment of an equality of trade conditions among all the nations consenting to the peace and associating themselves for its maintenance.

4. Adequate guarantees given and taken that national armaments will be reduced to the lowest point consistent with domestic safety.

5. A free, open-minded, and absolutely impartial adjustment of all colonial claims, based upon a strict observance of the principle that in determining all such questions of sovereignty the interests of the populations concerned must have equal weight with the equitable claims of the government whose title is to be determined.

6. The evacuation of all Russian territory and such settlement of all questions affecting Russia as will secure the best and freest co-operation of the other nations of the world in obtaining for her an unhampered and unembarrassed opportunity for the independent determination of her own political development and national policy and assure her of a sincere welcome into the society of free nations under institutions of her own choosing; and, more than a welcome, assistance also of every kind that she may need and may herself desire. The treatment accorded Russia by her sister nations in the months to come will be the acid test of their good will, of their comprehension of her needs as distinguished from their own interests, and of their intelligent and unselfish sympathy.

7. Belgium, the whole world will agree, must be evacuated and restored without any attempt to limit the sovereignty which she enjoys in common with all other free nations. No other single act will serve as this will serve to restore confidence among the nations in the laws which they have themselves set and determined for the government of their relations with one another. Without this healing act the whole structure and validity of international law is forever impaired.

8. All French territory should be freed and the invaded portions restored, and the wrong done to France by Prussia in 1871 in the matter of Alsace-Lorraine, which has unsettled the peace of the world for nearly fifty years, should be righted, in order that peace may once more be made in the interest of all.

9. A readjustment of the frontiers of Italy should be effected along clearly recognizable lines of nationality.

10. The peoples of Austria-Hungary, whose place among the nations we wish to see safeguarded and assured, should be accorded the freest opportunity of autonomous development.

11. Rumania, Serbia, and Montenegro should be evacuated; occupied territories restored; Serbia accorded free and secure access to the sea; and the relations of the several Balkan states to one another determined by friendly counsel along historically established lines of allegiance and nationality; and international guarantees of the political and economic independence and territorial integrity of the several Balkan states should be entered into.

12. The Turkish portions of the present Ottoman Empire should be assured a secure sovereignty, but other nationalities which are now under Turkish rule should be assured an undoubted security of life and absolutely unmolested opportunity of autonomous development, and the Dardanelles should be permanently opened as a free passage to the ships and commerce of all nations under international guarantees.

13. An independent Polish state should be erected which should include the territories inhabited by indisputably Polish populations, which should be assured a free and secure access to the sea, and whose political and economic independence and territorial integrity should be guaranteed by international covenant.

14. A general association of nations must be formed under specific covenants for the purpose of affording mutual guarantees of political independence and territorial integrity to great and small states alike.

C. A MEMORANDUM OF OBSERVATIONS by the Allied Governments accompanying the American note to Germany on November 5, 1918.

The Allied Governments have given careful consideration to the correspondence which has passed between the President of the United States and the German Government. Subject to the qualifications which follow, they declare their willingness to make peace with the Government of Germany on the terms of peace laid down in the President's address to Congress of January 1918, and the principles of settlement enunciated in his subsequent addresses. They must point out, however, that Clause Two relating to what is usually described as the Freedom of the Seas, is open to various interpretations, some of which they could not accept. They must therefore reserve to themselves complete freedom on this subject when they enter the peace conference.

Further, in the conditions of peace laid down in his address to Congress of January 8, 1918, the President declared that invaded territories must be restored as well as evacuated and freed. The Allied Governments feel that no doubt ought to be allowed to exist as to what this provision implies. By it they understand that compensation will be made by Germany for all damage done to the civilian population of the Allies and their property by the aggression of Germany by land, by sea and from the air.

D. THE BALFOUR DECLARATION — conveyed in a letter from Balfour, then British Foreign Secretary, to Lord Rothschild.

Foreign Office
November 2nd, 1917

DEAR LORD ROTHSCHILD,

I have much pleasure in conveying to you, on behalf of His Majesty's Government, the following declaration of sympathy with Jewish Zionist aspirations which has been submitted to, and approved by, the Cabinet.

"His Majesty's Government view with favour the establishment in Palestine of a national home for the Jewish people, and will use their best endeavours to facilitate the achievement of this object, it being clearly understood that nothing shall be done which may prejudice the civil and religious rights of existing non-Jewish communities in Palestine, or the rights and political status enjoyed by Jews in any other country."

I shall be most grateful if you will bring this declaration to the knowledge of the Zionist Federation.

Yours sincerely

ARTHUR JAMES BALFOUR.

E. THE FIRST WORLD WAR AND THE ARABS OF ARABIA

The so-called era of imperial expansion, embarked upon by Ibn Saud in 1913, was inevitably interrupted by the First World War, when Arabian domestic politics were complicated by the intrusion of foreign politics. The Turks, allied with Germany, preserved the loyalty of Ibn Rashid — for a consideration. In general, they promised him support against his hereditary Saudi rival, plus a subsidy. The Turks also benefited by the loyal co-operation of the Imam Yahya of the Yemen, with whom they had been in close accord since the definitive settlement of their outstanding differences in 1911. From this *rapprochement* with the Central Powers sprang the later pro-Axis policy of the Imam, and the Italo-Yemeni treaty of 1926. As for Britain, a dual Arabian policy was initiated, owing to the separate needs of the Egyptian and Mesopotamian campaigns. On the west, Anglo-Egyptian policy was bound to support Sherif Hussein in the latter's desire to revolt against his Turkish suzerain.[1] Geographically, it was necessary for the Allies to secure the good will of the ruler of the Hejaz. But even more important to Britain was the fact that the Sherif of Mecca was the only Moslem ruler who could logically hope to obtain any widespread support in the Islamic world against the Caliph-Sultan of the Ottoman Empire — partly because he was the titular Protector of the Holy Cities, and partly because of the ancient connection of his own family with that of the Prophet Mohammed. On the other hand, the Government of India recognized the geographical necessity of securing the good will of Ibn Saud on the Mesopotamian–Persian Gulf side of Arabia; and his value as a potentially strong ally was not underestimated. Accordingly Sir Henry McMahon, in Cairo, entered upon the famous negotiations with Hussein that resulted in precipitating the Arab Revolt which commenced in June 1916; whereas Sir Percy Cox, Chief Political Officer of the Mesopotamian Ex-

[1] Apparently the Sherif had long planned revolt against the Turks — his earlier loyalty to them (in 1910) had been in the nature of a blind, and to obtain a freer hand in Arabia.

peditionary Force, obtained a treaty of friendship from Ibn Saud, for which the ground had been ably prepared by Captain W. H. I. Shakespear.[2] Thus on December 26, 1915, Ibn Saud actually signed a treaty with Britain which recognized his *de facto* independence and which gave in exchange a guarantee of Saudian neutrality for the duration of the war; and the Wahhabi ruler even agreed to British mediation in his dealings with other Arab chiefs, and made it possible for the Government of India to benefit from an informal political blockade of the Arabian coast of the Persian Gulf. In return for which, Ibn Saud received a monthly subsidy of £5000, which was paid to him by the India Office until April 1924.

Meanwhile, in the Egyptian-Sherifian camp, Sir Henry McMahon and Sherif Hussein eventually reached an understanding, through an exchange of letters, by November 1915 — although the Sherif failed to act thereon before Ibn Saud came to sign his treaty with the British in December.[3] This was a less decisive (one might also say more ambiguous) agreement than was come to with Ibn Saud; and it is noteworthy that Hussein, although even more used to the ways of European diplomacy than his Saudi rival, had neither the political acumen nor the foresight to negotiate a formal treaty with Britain. By the terms of the Hussein-McMahon correspondence (in which was included the "Pledge" of October 24, 1915), Britain agreed to "recognize and support the independence of the Arabs" in all portions of the Ottoman Empire south and east of, approximately, the 37° latitude, with four notable exceptions. Aden and the "vilayets of Bagdad and Basra" were to be reserved to Britain; the "district" of Alexandretta and "portions of Syria lying to the west of the districts of Damascus, Homs, Hama, and Aleppo" (because they "cannot be said to be purely Arab") were excluded from the territory promised to the Sherif. Furthermore, Britain made a point of specifying that any commitments made to Hussein were to be "without prejudice to our existing treaties with Arab chiefs," and warned him expressly that any territorial engagements made by Britain could only be taken to refer to "regions . . . wherein Britain is free to act without detriment to the interests of her ally, France." Lastly, Britain guaranteed the inviolability of the Moslem Holy Places. In return, once the revolt was consummated, Hussein agreed to look only to Britain for "advice and guidance." [4]

One of the most significant paragraphs in Sir Henry McMahon's letter from Cairo to the Sherif Hussein, dated October 24, 1915, is as follows: "The districts of Mersin and Alexandretta, and portions of Syria lying to the west of the districts of Damascus, Homs, Hama, and Aleppo, cannot be said to be purely Arab, and must on that account be excepted from the proposed delimitation." [5] By inference, the Palestinian "districts" were likewise thus excepted from the "proposed delimitation" for the same reason (that is, their inhabitants could not be said to be "purely Arab"). If, by the way, the "district of Damascus" could have been taken to refer to the whole Vilayet of *Syria*,[6] then the exclusion of all *southern* "portions

2 Captain W. H. I. Shakespear, British Political Agent at Kuwait, had visited Riyadh just before the war started, and had reached a comprehensive understanding with Ibn Saud which (it is said) even went the length of envisaging mutual assistance against the Turks. It is thought by some experts that had Captain Shakespear not been accidentally killed early in 1915 (in a desert action between the Arab followers of Ibn Saud and the pro-German Ibn Rashid), a more active, less passive Anglo-Saudi alliance might have been negotiated. But it is difficult to see how a more active Saudi alliance would have worked in with the obviously inescapable Hashemite partnership on the Anglo-Egyptian-Palestinian front.

3 In other words, before any of Britain's commitments to Hussein became operative, through the latter's intervention in the war, Ibn Saud was already in treaty relations with Britain. So the charge, occasionally made, that Britain's terms to these two Arabian rivals were mutually contradictory, cannot be substantiated. *Cf.* paragraph 4 of Letter No. 4 from McMahon to the Sherif, October 24, 1915. See note 4.

4 Texts of the letters are printed in: Information Department Papers of the Royal Institute of International Affairs, No. 20a, *Great Britain and Palestine, 1915–1939*, pp. 113–15; also, George Antonius, *The Arab Awakening*, London, 1938.

5 Published by George Antonius, *op. cit.*, p. 419. See also map of the Turkish Vilayets, p. 245.

6 See map, p. 245.

of Syria lying to the west" of that vilayet might have been taken to include Palestine. Actually, it seems likely that in 1915 there was an intentional ambiguity in the notes exchanged between McMahon and Hussein, if only because at that time it would have been unwise for either the British or the Arabs to make an explicit or binding statement with respect to the Palestinian part of Syria.

From June 5, 1916, when Hussein and the Arabs of the Hejaz entered the war as allies of Britain, the Sherif was paid a monthly subsidy of £200,000 — and throughout the war he received what has been alliteratively referred to as a constant stream of corn, cash, and cartridges. This subsidy was paid to Hussein in full, by the British Foreign Office, until February 1919; and during the year thereafter he received a somewhat smaller amount.

For the duration of the war, responsibility for Arab affairs was distributed among several British leaders and departments. Sir Henry McMahon, under the authority of the Foreign Office, continued to take charge of the Red Sea, from Cairo. The Arab Bureau, also housed in Cairo and organized under Dr. D. G. Hogarth, assumed direction of the Arab Revolt. Sir Reginald Wingate at Khartoum had charge of the development of Arab policy in the Sudan, and Saiyid Ali Marghani collaborated with him. Elsewhere, in Mesopotamia and in eastern and southern Arabia, Arab affairs were in the hands of the Anglo-Indian authorities. This included Yemen and the Asir; and in April 1915 the Government of India signed a treaty with the Idrisi ruler guaranteeing the independence and security of the Asir.

In October 1916, T. E. Lawrence, then a second lieutenant, made his first visit to the Hejaz in company with Ronald Storrs. While on that visit he met Sherif Hussein's sons — notably Feisal, with whom he subsequently organized the "Revolt in the Desert." That was after the Anglo-Hejazi understanding had been reached, and after the Revolt had actually been initiated. Contrary to popular belief, therefore, Lawrence had nothing (personally) to do with any "promises" made to the Arabs. But Lawrence did have everything to do with the successful desert campaign that followed, the strategy of which he directed, and the rigors of which he shared equally with his trusted Arab friends. And his brilliant guerrilla tactics gave General Allenby able and timely support in the British conquest of Palestine and Syria.

On November 7, 1918, a joint Anglo-French Declaration was issued simultaneously in Palestine, Syria, and Iraq — an official communiqué that was given prominence in the local press as soon as it was given out by G.H.Q. of the Egyptian Expeditionary Force. This (subjoined) Declaration was interpreted by the Arabs as an official French or allied endorsement of the McMahon Pledge, and as such it gave them legitimate ground for hope that their independence would be recognized and established according to the terms of the McMahon Pledge.

The text of the Anglo-French Declaration follows:

"The goal envisaged by France and Great Britain in prosecuting in the East the War set in train by German ambition is the complete and final liberation of the peoples who have for so long been oppressed by the Turks, and the setting up of national governments and administrations that shall derive their authority from the free exercise of the initiative and choice of the indigenous populations.

"In pursuance of those intentions, France and Great Britain agree to further and assist in the setting up of indigenous governments and administrations in Syria [that is, including Palestine] and Mesopotamia which have already been liberated by the Allies, as well as in those territories which they are endeavouring to liberate, and to recognize them as soon as they are actually set up.

"Far from wishing to impose this or that system upon the populations of those regions their [that is, France's and Great Britain's] only concern is to offer such support and efficacious help as will ensure the smooth working of the governments and administrations which those populations will have elected of their own free will to have (sic?) ; to secure impartial and equal justice for all; to facilitate the economic development of the country by promoting and encouraging local initiative; to foster the spread of education and to put an end to the dissensions which

Turkish policy has for so long exploited. Such is the task which the two Allied Powers wish to undertake in the liberated territories." [7]

F. THE COVENANT OF THE LEAGUE OF NATIONS

For the sake of saving space only those Articles are quoted which are discussed in this book. The full text of the Covenant is easily available, notably in the *Encyclopaedia Britannica.*

The Amendments in force in 1938 are printed in italics, with the date of their adoption in brackets.

ARTICLE 8.

1. The Members of the League recognise that the maintenance of peace requires the reduction of national armaments to the lowest point consistent with national safety, and the enforcement by common action of international obligations.

2. The Council, taking account of the geographical situation and circumstances of each State, shall formulate plans for such reduction for the consideration and action of the several Governments.

3. Such plans shall be subject to reconsideration and revision at least every ten years.

4. After these plans shall have been adopted by the several Governments, the limits of armaments therein fixed shall not be exceeded without the concurrence of the Council.

5. The Members of the League agree that the manufacture by private enterprise of munitions and implements of war is open to grave objections. The Council shall advise how the evil effects attendant upon such manufacture can be prevented, due regard being had to the necessities of those Members of the League which are not able to manufacture the munitions and implements of war necessary for their safety.

6. The Members of the League undertake to interchange full and frank information as to the scale of their armaments, their military, naval and air programmes and the condition of such of their industries as are adaptable to warlike purposes.

ARTICLE 10.

The Members of the League undertake to respect and preserve, as against external aggression, the territorial integrity and existing political independence of all Members of the League. In case of any such aggression, or in case of any threat or danger of such aggression, the Council shall advise upon the means by which this obligation shall be fulfilled.

ARTICLE 11.

1. Any war or threat of war, whether immediately affecting any of the Members of the League or not, is hereby declared a matter of concern to the whole League, and the League shall take any action that may be deemed wise and effectual to safeguard the peace of nations. In case any such emergency should arise, the Secretary-General shall, on the request of any Member of the League, forthwith summon a meeting of the Council.

2. It is also declared to be the friendly right of each Member of the League to bring to the attention of the Assembly or of the Council any circumstance whatever affecting international relations which threatens to disturb international peace or the good understanding between nations upon which peace depends.

ARTICLE 12.

1. The Members of the League agree that, if there should arise between them any dispute likely to lead to a rupture they will submit the matter either to arbi-

[7] George Antonius, *op. cit.*, pp. 435–36.

tration *or judicial settlement* or to enquiry by the Council, and they agree in no case to resort to war until three months after the award by the arbitrators *or the judicial decision,* or the report by the Council.

2. In any case, under this Article the award of the arbitrators *or the judicial decision* shall be made within a reasonable time, and the report of the Council shall be made within six months after the submission of the dispute. [September 26, 1924]

ARTICLE 13.

1. The Members of the League agree that, whenever any dispute shall arise between them which they recognise to be suitable for submission to arbitration *or judicial settlement,* and which cannot be satisfactorily settled by diplomacy, they will submit the whole subject-matter to arbitration *or judicial settlement.*

2. Disputes as to the interpretation of a Treaty, as to any question of international law, as to the existence of any fact which, if established, would constitute a breach of any international obligation, or as to the extent and nature of the reparation to be made for any such breach, are declared to be among those which are generally suitable for submission to arbitration *or judicial settlement.*

3. *For the consideration of any such dispute, the Court to which the case is referred shall be the Permanent Court of International Justice, established in accordance with Article 14, or any tribunal agreed on by the parties to the dispute or stipulated in any Convention existing between them.* [September 26, 1924]

4. The Members of the League agree that they will carry out in full good faith any award *or decision* that may be rendered, and that they will not resort to war against a Member of the League which complies therewith. In the event of any failure to carry out such an award *or decision,* the Council shall propose what steps should be taken to give effect thereto. [September 26, 1924]

ARTICLE 14.

The Council shall formulate and submit to the Members of the League for adoption plans for the establishment of a Permanent Court of International Justice. The Court shall be competent to hear and determine any dispute of an international character which the parties thereto submit to it. The Court may also give an advisory opinion upon any dispute or question referred to it by the Council or by the Assembly.

ARTICLE 15.

1. If there should arise between Members of the League any dispute likely to lead to a rupture, which is not submitted to arbitration *or judicial settlement* in accordance with Article 13, the Members of the League agree that they will submit the matter to the Council. Any party to the dispute may effect such submission by giving notice of the existence of the dispute to the Secretary-General, who will make all necessary arrangements for a full investigation and consideration thereof. [September 26, 1924]

2. For this purpose the parties to the dispute will communicate to the Secretary-General, as promptly as possible, statements of their case with all the relevant facts and papers, and the Council may forthwith direct the publication thereof.

3. The Council shall endeavour to effect a settlement of the dispute, and, if such efforts are successful, a statement shall be made public giving such facts and explanations regarding the dispute and the terms of settlement thereof as the Council may deem appropriate.

4. If the dispute is not thus settled, the Council, either unanimously or by a majority vote, shall make and publish a report containing a statement of the facts of the dispute and the recommendations which are deemed just and proper in regard thereto.

5. Any Member of the League represented on the Council may make a public statement of the facts of the dispute and of its conclusions regarding the same.

6. If a report by the Council is unanimously agreed to by the members thereof, other than the representatives of one or more of the parties to the dispute, the Members of the League agree that they will not go to war with any party to the dispute which complies with the recommendations of the report.

7. If the Council fails to reach a report which is unanimously agreed to by the members thereof, other than the representatives of one or more of the parties to the dispute, the Members of the League reserve to themselves the right to take such action as they shall consider necessary for the maintenance of right and justice.

8. If the dispute between the parties is claimed by one of them, and is found by the Council to arise out of a matter which by international law is solely within the domestic jurisdiction of that party, the Council shall so report, and shall make no recommendation as to its settlement.

9. The Council may in any case under this Article refer the dispute to the Assembly. The dispute shall be so referred at the request of either party to the dispute provided that such request be made within fourteen days after the submission of the dispute to the Council.

10. In any case referred to the Assembly, all the provisions of this Article and of Article 12, relating to the action and powers of the Council, shall apply to the action and powers of the Assembly, provided that a report made by the Assembly, if concurred in by the representatives of those Members of the League represented on the Council, and of a majority of the other Members of the League, exclusive in each case of the representatives of the parties to the dispute, shall have the same force as a report by the Council concurred in by all the members thereof other than the representatives of one or more of the parties to the dispute.

ARTICLE 16.

1. Should any Member of the League resort to war in disregard of its Covenants under Articles 12, 13 or 15, it shall *ipso facto* be deemed to have committed an act of war against all other Members of the League, which hereby undertake immediately to subject it to the severance of all trade or financial relations, the prohibition of all intercourse beween their nationals and the nationals of the Covenant-breaking State, and the prevention of all financial, commercial or personal intercourse between the nationals of the Covenant-breaking State and the nationals of any other State, whether a Member of the League or not.

2. It shall be the duty of the Council in such case to recommend to the several Governments concerned what effective military, naval or air force the Members of the League shall severally contribute to the armed forces to be used to protect the Covenants of the League.

3. The Members of the League agree, further, that they will mutually support one another in the financial and economic measures which are taken under this Article, in order to minimise the loss and inconvenience resulting from the above measures, and that they will mutually support one another in resisting any special measures aimed at one of their number by the Covenant-breaking State, and that they will take the necessary steps to afford passage through their territory to the forces of any of the Members of the League which are co-operating to protect the Covenants of the League.

4. Any Member of the League which has violated any Covenant of the League may be declared to be no longer a Member of the League by a vote of the Council concurred in by the representatives of all the other Members of the League represented thereon.

ARTICLE 17.

1. In the event of a dispute between a Member of the League and a State which is not a Member of the League, or between States not Members of the League, the State or States not Members of the League shall be invited to accept the obligations of membership in the League for the purposes of such dispute, upon such conditions as the Council may deem just. If such invitation is accepted, the pro-

visions of Articles 12 to 16 inclusive shall be applied with such modifications as may be deemed necessary by the Council.

2. Upon such invitation being given, the Council shall immediately institute an enquiry into the circumstances of the dispute and recommend such action as may seem best and most effectual in the circumstances.

3. If a State so invited shall refuse to accept the obligations of membership in the League for the purposes of such dispute, and shall resort to war against a Member of the League, the provisions of Article 16 shall be applicable as against the State taking such action.

4. If both parties to the dispute, when so invited, refuse to accept the obligations of membership in the League for the purposes of such dispute, the Council may take such measures and make such recommendations as will prevent hostilities and will result in the settlement of the dispute.

ARTICLE 18.

Every Treaty or international engagement entered into hereafter by any Member of the League shall be forthwith registered with the Secretariat, and shall, as soon as possible, be published by it. No such Treaty or international engagement shall be binding until so registered.

ARTICLE 19.

The Assembly may from time to time advise the reconsideration by Members of the League of Treaties which have become inapplicable, and the consideration of international conditions whose continuance might endanger the peace of the world.

ARTICLE 21.

Nothing in this Covenant shall be deemed to affect the validity of international engagements, such as Treaties of Arbitration, or regional understandings like the Monroe doctrine, for securing the maintenance of peace.

ARTICLE 22.

1. To those colonies and territories, which as a consequence of the late war have ceased to be under the sovereignty of the States which formerly governed them, and which are inhabited by peoples not yet able to stand by themselves under the strenuous conditions of the modern world, there should be applied the principle that the well-being and development of such peoples form a sacred trust of civilisation, and that securities for the performance of this trust should be embodied in this Covenant.

2. The best method of giving practical effect to this principle is that the tutelage of such peoples should be entrusted to advanced nations who, by reason of their resources, their experience, or their geographical position, can best undertake this responsibility, and who are willing to accept it, and that this tutelage should be exercised by them as Mandatories on behalf of the League.

3. The character of the Mandate must differ according to the stage of the development of the people, the geographical situation of the territory, its economic conditions and other similar circumstances.

4. Certain communities formerly belonging to the Turkish Empire have reached a stage of development where their existence as independent nations can be provisionally recognised subject to the rendering of administrative advice and assistance by a Mandatory until such time as they are able to stand alone. The wishes of these communities must be a principal consideration in the selection of the Mandatory.

5. Other peoples, especially those of Central Africa, are at such a stage that the Mandatory must be responsible for the administration of the territory under

conditions which will guarantee freedom of conscience and religion, subject only to the maintenance of public order and morals, the prohibition of abuses such as the slave trade, the arms traffic and the liquor traffic, and the prevention of the establishment of fortifications or military and naval bases, and of military training of the natives for other than police purposes and the defence of territory, and will also secure equal opportunities for the trade and commerce of other Members of the League.

6. There are territories, such as South-West Africa and certain of the South Pacific Islands, which, owing to the sparseness of their population, or their small size, or their remoteness from the centres of civilisation, or their geographical contiguity to the territory of the Mandatory, and other circumstances, can be best administered under the laws of the Mandatory as integral portions of its territory, subject to the safeguards above mentioned in the interests of the indigenous population.

7. In every case of Mandate, the Mandatory shall render to the Council an annual report in reference to the territory committed to its charge.

8. The degree of authority, control or administration to be exercised by the Mandatory shall, if not previously agreed upon by the Members of the League, be explicitly defined in each case by the Council.

9. A permanent Commission shall be constituted to receive and examine the annual reports of the Mandatories and to advise the Council on all matters relating to the observance of the Mandates.

ARTICLE 23.

Subject to and in accordance with the provisions of international Conventions existing or hereafter to be agreed upon, the Members of the League —

(a) Will endeavour to secure and maintain fair and humane conditions of labour for men, women and children, both in their own countries and in all countries to which their commercial and industrial relations extend, and for that purpose will establish and maintain the necessary international organisations.

(b) Undertake to secure just treatment of the native inhabitants of territories under their control.

(c) Will entrust the League with the general supervision over the execution of agreements with regard to the traffic in women and children, and the traffic in opium and other dangerous drugs.

(d) Will entrust the League with the general supervision of the trade in arms and ammunition with the countries in which the control of this traffic is necessary in the common interest.

(e) Will make provision to secure and maintain freedom of communications and of transit and equitable treatment for the commerce of all Members of the League. In this connection, the special necessities of the regions devastated during the war of 1914–18 shall be borne in mind.

(f) Will endeavour to take steps in matters of international concern for the prevention and control of disease.

G. THE ATLANTIC CHARTER — Statement issued by President Roosevelt and Prime Minister Churchill, after their meeting "at sea," on August 14, 1941.

The President of the United States and the Prime Minister Mr. Churchill, representing His Majesty's Government in the United Kingdom, being met together, deem it right to make known certain common principles in the national policies of their respective countries on which they base their hopes for a better future for the world.

First: Their countries seek no aggrandizement, territorial or otherwise;

Second: They desire to see no territorial changes that do not accord with the freely expressed wishes of the peoples concerned;

Third: They respect the right of all peoples to choose the form of government under which they will live; and they wish to see sovereign rights and self-government restored to those who have been forcibly deprived of them;

Fourth: They will endeavor, with due respect for their existing obligations, to further the enjoyment by all states, great or small, victor or vanquished, of access, on equal terms, to the trade and to the raw materials of the world which are needed for their economic prosperity;

Fifth: They desire to bring about the fullest collaboration between all nations in the economic field, with the object of securing for all improved labor standards, economic adjustment and social security;

Sixth: After the final destruction of the Nazi tyranny, they hope to see established a peace which will afford to all nations the means of dwelling in safety within their own boundaries, and which will afford assurance that all the men in all the lands may live out their lives in freedom from fear and want;

Seventh: Such a peace should enable all men to traverse the high seas and oceans without hindrance;

Eighth: They believe that all of the nations of the world, for realistic as well as spiritual reasons, must come to the abandonment of the use of force. Since no future peace can be maintained if land, sea or air armaments continue to be employed by nations which threaten, or may threaten, aggression outside of their frontiers, they believe, pending the establishment of a wider and permanent system of general security, that the disarmament of such nations is essential. They will likewise aid and encourage all other practicable measures which will lighten for peace-loving peoples the crushing burden of armaments.

BIBLIOGRAPHY

This bibliography is not intended to be a specialist's bibliography, nor is it a bibliography of sources used in this book. The authors have assumed that the specialist will find his own way into his field, and that this book is of too general a kind to need an elaborate bibliographical apparatus. The authors' object is to give a short "further-reading list" of accessible, useful material, well worn in the estimation of acknowledged authorities. Government publications and institutional literature are occasionally included, but periodicals not at all. The list for the Second World War must necessarily be very provisional.

GENERAL AND REFERENCE

Annual Register: A Review of Public Events at Home and Abroad, London, 1758–1949

Encyclopaedia Britannica, Chicago, London, Toronto, 1949. Articles on the World Wars and on recent events and persons. The more important articles have bibliographies appended to them.

Keesing's Contemporary Archives: Weekly Diary of Important World Events, London, 1931–50

William L. Langer, ed., *Foreign Affairs Bibliography, 1919–1932*, Harper, 1933, for Council on Foreign Relations

Walter Consuelo Langsam and J. M. Eagan, *Documents and Readings in the History of Europe since 1918*, Lippincott, 1939

Arnold J. Toynbee and others, *Survey of International Affairs*, Oxford University Press, 1921–38. Annual surveys published under the auspices of the Royal Institute of International Affairs.

J. W. Wheeler-Bennett, *Documents on International Affairs*, Oxford University Press, 1928–40. A companion to the Toynbee, above.

Robert Gale Woolbert, ed., *Foreign Affairs Bibliography, 1932–1942*, Harper, 1945, for the Council on Foreign Relations. A sequel to the Langer, above.

PRE–1914 AND THE FIRST WORLD WAR

S. Miles Bouton, *And the Kaiser Abdicates: The Story of the Death of the German Empire*, Yale University Press, 1920. An account of the collapse of Germany in 1918.

Frank P. Chambers, *The War behind the War, 1914–1918: A History of the Political and Civilian Fronts*, Harcourt, Brace, 1939

Winston S. Churchill, *The World Crisis*, 3 vols., Scribner, 1931

—— *The Aftermath* is Vol. 4 of *The World Crisis*.

—— *The Unknown War: The Eastern Front*, Scribner, 1931.

C. R. M. F. Cruttwell, *A History of the Great War, 1914–1918,* Oxford University Press, 1936. A general history.

Michael T. Florinsky, *The End of the Russian Empire: A Study in the Economic and Social History of the War,* Yale University Press, 1931. An account of the war and the latter days of Tsarist Russia.

Edmund von Glaise-Horstenau, *The Collapse of the Austro-Hungarian Empire,* Dutton, 1930. An account of the war and latter days of Hapsburg Austria-Hungary.

Basil Henry Liddell Hart, *A History of the World War,* Little, Brown, 1935. A military history.

Burton J. Hendrick, *The Life and Letters of Walter H. Page,* Garden City, 1927. The recognized biography of Walter Hines Page, American ambassador to Britain.

Harold D. Lasswell, *Propaganda Technique in the World War,* Knopf, 1927. An isolationist's view of wartime propaganda.

T. E. Lawrence, *Seven Pillars of Wisdom,* Doubleday, 1935. Colonel Lawrence's account of the Arab Revolt.

David Lloyd George, *War Memoirs,* 6 vols., Little, Brown, 1933–37. A record of the war years and of his wartime government.

Erich Ludendorff, *My War Memories: Ludendorff's Own Story,* Harper, 1919. By the commander of the German Army in the last two years of the war. Indispensable for an appreciation of the German position.

Nicholas Mansbergh, *The Coming of the First World War: A Study of the European Balance, 1878–1914,* Longmans, Green, 1949. A current reconsideration of the old material.

Sir Frederick Maurice, *The Armistices of 1918,* Oxford University Press, 1943. Commentary and documents.

Walter Millis, *Road to War: America 1914–1917,* Houghton Mifflin, 1935. An isolationist view of America's neutral period.

M. V. Rodzianko, *The Reign of Rasputin: An Empire's Collapse,* London, 1927. The end of Tsarist Russia as related by the president of the Duma.

Arthur Rosenberg, *The Birth of the German Republic, 1871–1918,* Oxford University Press, 1931. A political history of Germany during the war.

Harry R. Rudin, *Armistice, 1918,* Yale University Press, 1944. Commentary and documents.

J. W. Wheeler-Bennett, *The Forgotten Peace: Brest Litovsk, March, 1918,* Morrow, 1939

Brand Whitlock, *Belgium: A Personal Narrative,* Appleton, 1919. By the American minister to Belgium during the German occupation.

THE PEACE CONFERENCE OF PARIS AND THE PEACE TREATIES, 1919–1920

Paul Birdsall, *Versailles Twenty Years After,* Reynal and Hitchcock, 1941. Versailles rethought and redocumented. Favorable to Wilson.

David Lloyd George, *Memoirs of the Peace Conference,* 2 vols., Yale University Press, 1939. Published in England (1938) as *The Truth about the Peace Treaties.* Lloyd George's apologia for the Peace Conference.

Harold Nicolson, *Peacemaking, 1919,* Houghton Mifflin, 1933. A personal commentary and description.

Charles Seymour, *Intimate Papers of Colonel House,* 4 vols., Houghton Mifflin, 1926–28. Informative on President Wilson's diplomacy and the work of the American delegation at Paris.

Harold W. V. Temperley, *A History of the Peace Conference of Paris,* 6 vols., London, 1921–24. Ranks almost as the official history.

THE LEAGUE OF NATIONS AND THE QUEST FOR PEACE IN THE INTERWAR PERIOD

(For the mandates and related questions, see the section on The Near East, below.)

Raymond Leslie Buell, *The Washington Conference*, Appleton, 1922

Edward Hallett Carr, *The Twenty Years' Crisis, 1919–1939: An Introduction to the Study of International Relations*, London, 1939.

Viscount Cecil (Lord Robert Cecil), *A Great Experiment: An Autobiography*, Oxford University Press, 1941. An account of the League by one of its creators and protagonists.

C. Howard-Ellis, *The Origin, Structure, and Working of the League of Nations*, Houghton Mifflin, 1928

Manley O. Hudson, *The Permanent Court of International Justice*, Macmillan, 1934

Salvador de Madariaga, *Disarmament*, Coward-McCann, 1929. A personal exposition of the whole problem.

David Hunter Miller, *The Drafting of the Covenant*, Putnam, 1928. Complete historical record.

—— *The Peace Pact of Paris: A Study of the Briand-Kellogg Treaty*, Putnam, 1928

Denys P. Myers, *Handbook of the League of Nations: A Comprehensive Account of Its Structure, Operation, and Activities*, World Peace Foundation, 1935

—— *World Disarmament: Its Problems and Prospects*, World Peace Foundation, 1932

E. J. Phelan, *Yes and Albert Thomas*, London, 1936. A popular account of the International Labor Organization and of its first director.

William E. Rappard, *The Quest for Peace since the World War*, Harvard University Press, 1940

James T. Shotwell, *War as an Instrument of National Policy and Its Renunciation in the Pact of Paris*, Harcourt, Brace, 1929. The ideology and history of the Pact of Paris by one of its originators.

J. W. Wheeler-Bennett, *The Disarmament Deadlock*, London, 1934. A history of the Disarmament Conference at Geneva.

—— and Maurice Fanshawe, *Information on the World Court, 1918–1928*, London, 1929

—— and F. E. Langermann, *Information on the Problem of Security*, London, 1927

Arnold Wolfers, *Britain and France between Two Wars: Conflicting Strategies of Peace since Versailles*, Harcourt, Brace, 1940. A study of Anglo-French diplomacy in Europe, 1919–39.

Alfred Zimmern, *The League of Nations and the Rule of Law, 1918–1935*, Macmillan, 1939

REPARATIONS, DEBTS, AND THE DEPRESSION IN THE INTERWAR PERIOD

H. W. Arndt, *Economic Lessons of the Nineteen Thirties*, Oxford University Press, 1944

Karl Bergmann, *The History of Reparations*, Houghton Mifflin, 1927. A German view.

J. P. Day, *An Introduction to World Economic History since the Great War*, Macmillan, 1939

David Lloyd George, *The Truth about Reparations and Debts*, Doubleday, 1932. Lloyd George's defense of the Versailles reparations clauses.

H. V. Hodson, *Slump and Recovery, 1929–1937*, Oxford University Press, 1938

John Maynard Keynes, *The Economic Consequences of the Peace*, Harcourt, Brace, 1920. Keynes' prophetic condemnation of the Versailles reparations clauses.

Étienne Mantoux, *The Carthaginian Peace*, Oxford University Press, 1946. A French reply to Keynes, above.

Harold G. Moulton and Leo Pasvolsky, *War Debts and World Prosperity*, Brookings, Washington, D.C., 1932

J. W. Wheeler-Bennett, *The Wreck of Reparations: Being the Political Background of the Lausanne Agreement, 1932*, Morrow, 1933

THE APPROACH OF THE SECOND WORLD WAR AND THE SECOND WORLD WAR

(See also the sections on The Americas, France, Germany, etc., below. The present section covers general, diplomatic, and military works.)

P. M. S. Blackett, *Military and Political Consequences of Atomic Energy*, London, 1948

Gilbert Cant, *The Great Pacific Victory: From the Solomons to Tokyo*, Day, 1946

Winston S. Churchill, *Blood, Sweat, and Tears*, Putnam, 1941. Published in England (1941) as *Into Battle*.

—— *The Second World War*, Vol. I, *The Gathering Storm*, Vol. II, *Their Finest Hour*, Houghton Mifflin, 1948, 1949

Henry Steele Commager, *The Story of the Second World War*, Little, Brown, 1945

John R. Deane, *The Strange Alliance: The Story of Our Efforts at Wartime Economic Co-operation with Russia*, Viking, 1947

Dwight D. Eisenhower, *Crusade in Europe*, Doubleday, 1948

Cyril Falls, *The Second World War: A Short History*, London, 1948

Grigore Gafencu, *Prelude to the Russian Campaign: From the Moscow Pact to the Opening of Hostilities in Russia*, London, 1945

James W. Gantenbein, ed., *Documentary Background of World War II, 1931 to 1941*, Columbia University Press, 1949

Louise W. Holborn, ed., *War and Peace Aims of the United Nations*, World Peace Foundation, 1943, 1948

Walter Karig and others, *Battle Reports*, 5 vols., Rinehart, 1944–1949. Prepared from official sources.

Masuo Kato, *The Lost War: A Japanese Reporter's Inside Story*, Knopf, 1946

William L. Langer, *Our Vichy Gamble*, Knopf, 1947

Edgar McInnes, *The War*, 6 vols., Oxford University Press, 1940–1945

Alan Moorhead, *Montgomery: A Biography*, Coward-McCann, 1946

L. B. Namier, *Diplomatic Prelude, 1938–1939*, Macmillan, 1948

Nazi-Soviet Relations, 1939–1941: Documents from the Archives of the German Foreign Office, U. S. Department of State, 1948

Fletcher Pratt, *Fleet against Japan*, Harper, 1946

Roger W. Shugg and H. A. De Weerd, *World War II: a Concise History*, Infantry Journal, 1946

Milton Shulman, *Defeat in the West*, Dutton, 1948

Sara R. Smith, *The Manchurian Crisis, 1931–1932: A Tragedy in International Relations*, Columbia University Press, 1948

H. R. Trevor-Roper, *The Last Days of Hitler*, Macmillan, 1946

Voices of History series, 1941–42, 1942–43, 1943–44 ed. by Franklin Watts; 1944–45, 1945–46 ed. by Nathan Ausubel, Crown. Speeches and papers of national wartime leaders.

J. W. Wheeler-Bennett, *Munich: Prologue to Tragedy*, Duell, Sloan & Pearce, 1948

Elizabeth Wiskemann, *The Rome-Berlin Axis: A History of the Relations between Hitler and Mussolini*, Oxford University Press, 1949

THE AMERICAS

(See also the section on China and Japan, below.)

Thomas Andrew Bailey, *A Diplomatic History of the American People*, Crofts, 1946

—— *Woodrow Wilson and the Great Betrayal*, Macmillan, 1945. President Wilson and the rejection of the Treaty of Versailles in the United States.

Hanson W. Baldwin, *The Price of Power*, Harper, 1948. An appraisal of America's post-1945 strategic position.

Charles A. Beard, *American Foreign Policy in the Making, 1932–1940: A Study in Responsibilities*, Yale University Press, 1946. A polemic dissertation on presidential and party attitudes to European entanglements.

—— *President Roosevelt and the Coming of the War*, Yale University Press, 1948. Severe criticism of Roosevelt's foreign policy.

Samuel Flagg Bemis, *A Diplomatic History of the United States*, Holt, 1942

T. A. Bisson, *America's Far Eastern Policy*, Macmillan, 1945. Criticism of recent American policy in the Pacific.

Dorothy Borg, *American Policy and the Chinese Revolution, 1925–1928*, Macmillan, 1947. An inquiry into Secretary Kellogg's policy in the Far East.

Crane Brinton, *The United States and Britain*, Harvard University Press, 1945. By a proponent of Anglo-American amity.

James F. Byrnes, *Speaking Frankly*, Harper, 1947. By the former Secretary of State.

John C. Campbell, and others, *The United States in World Affairs, 1945–1947; 1947–1948*, Harper, 1947–48, for the Council on Foreign Relations. A comprehensive compilation.

Foster Rhea Dulles, *China and America: The Story of Their Relations since 1784*, Princeton University Press, 1946

—— *The Road to Teheran: The Story of Russia and America*, Princeton University Press, 1944

J. K. Fairbank, *The United States and China*, Harvard University Press, 1948

William S. Graves, *America's Siberian Adventure, 1918–1920*, Cape and Smith, 1931. By the officer commanding the American expeditionary force to Siberia.

A. Whitney Griswold, *The Far Eastern Policy of the United States*, Harcourt, Brace, 1938

Cordell Hull, *Memoirs*, Macmillan, 1948. By the former Secretary of State.

Robin A. Humphreys, *The Evolution of Modern Latin America*, Oxford University Press, 1946

Japan, 1931–1941, 2 vols., Government Printing Office, Washington, D.C., 1943. Documents bearing on American-Japanese relations up to Pearl Harbor.

Walter Johnson, *The Battle against Isolation*, University of Chicago Press, 1944. A popular account.

John Holladay Latané and David W. Wainhouse, *A History of American Foreign Policy, 1776–1940*, Odyssey, 1941

Kenneth Scott Latourette, *The United States Moves across the Pacific: The A. B. C.'s of the American Problem in the Western Pacific and Far East*, Harper, 1946

Walter Lippmann, *U. S. Foreign Policy: Shield of the Republic*, Little, Brown, 1943. Effective polemics by a leading American publicist.

Walter Millis, *This is Pearl! The United States and Japan, 1941*, Morrow, 1947. An account of the events immediately preceding Pearl Harbor.

William Starr Myers, *The Foreign Policies of Herbert Hoover, 1929–1933*, Scribner, 1940

Allan Nevins and Louis M. Hacker, *The United States and its Place in World Affairs*, Heath, 1943. A collection of essays on various aspects of American foreign policy.

Peace and War: United States Foreign Policy, 1931–1941, Government Printing Office, Washington, D.C., 1942. Introduction and selected documents.

Nathaniel Peffer, *America's Place in the World*, Viking, 1945. An inquiry into America's responsibilities in the post-1945 world.

Robert E. Sherwood, *Roosevelt and Hopkins: An Intimate History*, Harper, 1948. Published in England (1949) as *The White House Papers of Harry L. Hopkins*, 2 vols.

George Soule, David Efron, and Norman T. Ness, *Latin America in the Future World*, Farrar and Rinehart, 1945. Largely concerned with the economic prospects of Latin America.

Harold and Margaret Sprout, *Foundations of National Power: Readings on World*

Politics and American Security, Princeton University Press, 1945. A comprehensive source book by two specialists in American naval history.

Nicholas John Spykman, *America's Strategy in World Politics,* Harcourt, Brace, 1942. An excursion into geopolitics.

Edward R. Stettinius, Jr., *Lend-Lease: Weapon for Victory,* Macmillan, 1944. By the chief administrator of Lend-Lease, and former Secretary of State.

—— *Roosevelt and the Russians: The Yalta Conference,* ed. by Walter Johnson. Doubleday, 1949

Henry L. Stimson, *The Far Eastern Crisis: Recollections and Observations,* Harper, 1936. The Secretary of State describes the Manchurian crisis.

—— *On Active Service in Peace and War,* Harper, 1948. The latter part of the book covers the author's activities as Secretary of War during the Second World War.

Robert Strausz-Hupé, *The Balance of Tomorrow: Power and Foreign Policy in the United States,* Putnam, 1945. A tractate against isolationism.

Graham H. Stuart, *Latin America and the United States,* Appleton-Century, 1943

United States Relations with China, with Special Reference to the Period 1944–1949, U. S. Department of State, 1949

Sumner Welles, *The Time for Decision,* Harper, 1944

—— *Where Are We Heading?,* Harper, 1946. Criticisms of American foreign policy by the former Secretary of State.

BRITAIN AND THE BRITISH COMMONWEALTH
(INCLUDING IRELAND AND INDIA)

William Henry Chamberlin, *Canada, Today and Tomorrow,* Little, Brown, 1942

Winston S. Churchill, *The Aftermath,* Scribner, 1929. Account of the twenties from an English — and Churchillian — viewpoint.

R. Coupland, *The Indian Problem, 1833–1935; Indian Politics, 1936–1942; The Future of India,* Oxford University Press, 1942–43.

W. Y. Elliott, *The New British Empire,* McGraw-Hill, 1932. Imperial ideology and inter-imperial relations.

G. T. Garratt, *An Indian Commentary,* London, 1928

R. H. Gretton, *A Modern History of the English People,* London, 1930

Denis Gwynn, *The Irish Free State, 1922–1927,* London, 1928

W. K. Hancock, *Survey of British Commonwealth Affairs,* 2 vols., Oxford University Press, 1937–42

Lady (Mabel Hélène) Hartog, *India in Outline,* Cambridge University Press, 1944

Rita Hinden, *Empire and After: A Study of British Imperial Attitudes,* London, 1949. The history of imperial ideology.

John F. Kennedy, *Why England Slept,* W. Funk, 1940. An account of Britain during her appeasement and rearmament phase.

C. W. de Kiewiet, *A History of South Africa: Social and Economic,* Oxford University Press, 1941

John MacCormac, *Canada, America's Problem,* Viking, 1940

Nicholas Mansergh, *The Commonwealth and the Nations: Studies in British Commonwealth Relations,* London, 1948

Penderel Moon, *Strangers in India,* Reynal and Hitchcock, 1945. Indian problems and British policies.

Malcolm Muggeridge, *The Sun Never Sets: The Story of England in the Nineteen Thirties,* Random, 1940

Jawaharlal Nehru, *Toward Freedom,* Day, 1941. Published in England (1936) as *An Autobiography.*

G. Raleigh Parkin, *India Today: An Introduction to Indian Politics,* Day, 1946

W. Alison Phillips, *The Revolution in Ireland, 1906–1923,* Longmans, Green, 1923

F. R. Scott, *Canada Today: A Study of Her National Interests and National Policy,* Oxford University Press, 1938

Albert Viton, *Great Britain: An Empire in Transition,* Day, 1940

Mason Wade, *The French-Canadian Outlook: A Brief Account of the Unknown North Americans,* Viking, 1946

FRANCE

D. W. Brogan, *France under the Republic, 1870–1939,* Harper, 1940. Published in England (1940) as *The Development of Modern France.*

Shepard Bancroft Clough, *France: A History of National Economics, 1789–1939,* Scribner, 1939

Jacques Maritain, *France My Country: Through the Disaster,* Longmans, Green, 1941. Reflections on the Fall of France.

André Maurois, *Tragedy in France,* Harper, 1940. Published in England (1941) as *Why France Fell.*

Charles A. Micaud, *The French Right and Nazi Germany, 1933–1939: A Study of Public Opinion,* Duke University Press, 1943

Katharine Munro, *France, Yesterday and Today: A Short Survey,* London, 1945

Hon. George Peel, *The Economic Policy of France,* Macmillan, 1937. Expert study of French finance.

Dorothy M. Pickles, *The French Political Scene,* London, 1938. A handbook on interwar French politics.

—— *France between the Republics,* London, 1946. A sequel to the foregoing.

Raymond Poincaré, *How France is Governed,* McBride, 1919. A dissertation on the French republican system.

André Siegfried, *France: A Study in Nationality,* Yale University Press, 1930

Richard L. Stokes, *Léon Blum: Poet to Premier,* Coward-McCann, 1937. A biography.

Edmond Taylor, *The Strategy of Terror,* Houghton Mifflin, 1940. An account of "the war of nerves" in France between 1938 and 1940.

David Thomson, *Democracy in France: The Third Republic,* Oxford University Press, 1946

Alexander Werth, *The Twilight of France, 1933–1940,* Harper, 1942. Published in England (1942) as *A Journalist's Chronicle.* An all-round description of the state of France in the thirties.

GERMANY

(See also the section on The Approach of the Second World War, above.)

W. F. Bruck, *Social and Economic History of Germany from William II to Hitler, 1888–1938,* Oxford University Press, 1938

Peter De Mendelssohn, *Design for Aggression,* Harper, 1947. Published in England (1947) as *The Nuremberg Documents.* The Nuremberg evidence written into a connected narrative.

William E. Dodd, Jr. and Martha Dodd, eds., *Ambassador Dodd's Diary, 1933–1938,* Harcourt, Brace, 1941. Diary of the American ambassador to Germany.

Lindley Fraser, *Germany Between Two Wars: A Study of Propaganda and War Guilt,* Oxford University Press, 1944. The interwar mentality of Germany.

Hans Ernest Fried, *The Guilt of the German Army,* Macmillan, 1942. The responsibility of the German Army for the militarist tradition and armament policy in Germany.

G. P. Gooch, *Germany,* Scribner, 1925. A general history.

Konrad Heiden, *Der Führer: Hitler's Rise to Power,* Houghton Mifflin, 1944. Biography of Hitler and general history of the Nazi party.

Adolf Hitler, *Mein Kampf,* Reynal and Hitchcock, 1940

—— *My New Order,* Reynal and Hitchcock, 1941. A collection of Hitler's speeches, with a running commentary.

Nathaniel Micklem, *National Socialism and the Roman Catholic Church*, Oxford University Press, 1939

J. H. Morgan, *Assize of Arms: The Disarmament of Germany and Her Rearmament, 1919–1939*, Oxford University Press, 1945. A former Control Commission officer describes his experience of German evasion and duplicity.

Thomas Reveille, *The Spoil of Europe: The Nazi Technique in Political and Economic Conquest*, Norton, 1941

Stephen H. Roberts, *The House that Hitler Built*, Harper, 1937. History and analysis of the Nazi movement.

Arthur Rosenberg, *A History of the German Republic*, London, 1936. An account of the Weimar Republic.

Herbert Rosinski, *The German Army*, Harcourt, Brace, 1940. Historical and political background.

Godfrey Scheele, *The Weimar Republic: Overture to the Third Reich*, London, 1946

Frederick L. Schuman, *The Nazi Dictatorship: A Study in Social Pathology and the Politics of Fascism*, Knopf, 1936

Leopold Schwarzschild, *World in Trance: From Versailles to Pearl Harbor*, Wyn, 1942. A sustained indictment of Germany and the German people.

Gustav Stolper, *German Economy, 1870–1940*, Reynal and Hitchcock, 1940. By an economist and former Deputy of the Reichstag.

J. W. Wheeler-Bennett, *The Wooden Titan: Hindenburg in Twenty Years of German History, 1914–1934*, Morrow, 1936

The following are appended as a separate list. Our generation has been well served by its newspaper correspondents, and these books are all fine examples of their labors.

Wallace R. Deuel, *People under Hitler*, Harcourt, Brace, 1942

Douglas Miller, *You Can't Do Business with Hitler*, Little, Brown, 1941

Edgar Ansel Mowrer, *Germany Puts the Clock Back*, Morrow, 1939

Douglas Reed, *The Burning of the Reichstag*, London, 1934

William L. Shirer, *Berlin Diary*, Knopf, 1941

Howard K. Smith, *Last Train from Berlin*, Knopf, 1942

Otto Tolischus, *They Wanted War*, Reynal and Hitchcock, 1940

The following books are also appended as a separate list. There is now a considerable literature on the philosophy, ideology, and prehistory of Nazism, and these books represent a selection.

Rohan D'O. Butler, *The Roots of National Socialism, 1783–1933*, Dutton, 1942

Alfred Cobban, *Dictatorship: Its History and Theory*, Scribner, 1939

F. W. Foerster, *Europe and the German Question*, Sheed & Ward, 1940

Erich Meissner, *Confusion of Faces: The Struggle Between Religion and Secularism in Europe*, London, 1946

William Montgomery McGovern, *From Luther to Hitler: The History of Fascist-Nazi Political Philosophy*, Houghton Mifflin, 1941

Franz Neumann, *Behemoth: The Structure and Practice of National Socialism*, Oxford University Press, 1942

Michael Oakeshott, *Social and Political Doctrines of Contemporary Europe*, Cambridge University Press, 1939

Leslie Paul, *The Annihilation of Man: A Study of the Crisis in the West*, London, 1944

H. Rauschning, *The Revolution of Nihilism: Warning to the West*, Alliance, 1939. Published in England (1939) as *Germany's Revolution of Destruction*.

—— *The Voice of Destruction*, Putnam, 1940. Published in England (1939) as *Hitler Speaks*.

S. D. Stirk, *The Prussian Spirit: A Survey of German Literature and Politics, 1914–1940*, London, 1942

A. J. P. Taylor, *The Course of German History: A Survey of the Development of Germany since 1815*, Coward-McCann, 1945
Peter Viereck, *Metapolitics: From the Romantics to Hitler*, Knopf, 1941

THE MIDDLE DANUBE

(See also the section on The Approach of the Second World War, above.)

M. Margaret Ball, *Post-War German-Austrian Relations: The Anschluss Movement, 1918–36*, Stanford University Press, 1937
Franz Borkenau, *Austria and After*, London, 1936
Malcolm Bullock, *Austria, 1918–1938: A Study in Failure*, London, 1939
G. E. R. Gedye, *Betrayal in Central Europe: Austria and Czechoslovakia, the Fallen Bastions*, Harper, 1939. Published in England (1939) as *Fallen Bastions*. An eyewitness narrative of Nazi aggression in Austria and Czechoslovakia.
C. A. Macartney, *Hungary*, London, 1934
—— *Hungary and Her Successors*, Oxford University Press, 1937
—— *The Social Revolution in Austria*, Cambridge, 1926
Robert Machray, *The Struggle for the Danube and the Little Entente, 1929–1938*, London, 1938
Joseph S. Rouček, etc., *Central Eastern Europe: Crucible of World Wars*, Prentice-Hall, 1946. A historical and general compendium.
Hugh Seton-Watson, *Eastern Europe between the Wars, 1918–1941*, Macmillan, 1945
R. W. Seton-Watson, *A History of the Czechs and Slovaks*, London, 1943. The last chapter gives a review of interwar Czechoslovakia, Munich, and the Nazi occupation.
Elizabeth Wiskemann, *Czechs and Germans: A Study of the Struggle in the Historic Provinces of Bohemia and Moravia*, Oxford University Press, 1938. History and description of an ancient nationalist conflict.

ITALY

D. A. Binchy, *Church and State in Fascist Italy*, Oxford University Press, 1941
Margaret Boveri, *Mediterranean Cross-Currents*, Oxford University Press, 1938. History and strategy of the Mediterranean.
Herman Finer, *Mussolini's Italy*, London, 1935. History and description of Fascist Italy.
Muriel Grindrod, *The New Italy: Transition from War to Peace*, Oxford University Press, 1947. A short account of post-1945 Italy.
Denis Gwynn, *The Vatican and War in Europe*, London, 1940. A general history of the Papacy in its international relations since 1914.
Maxwell H. H. Macartney and Paul Cremona, *Italy's Foreign and Colonial Policy, 1914–1937*, Oxford University Press, 1938
Herbert L. Matthews, *The Fruits of Fascism*, Harcourt, Brace, 1943. A description of Italy, especially at the beginning of the Second World War.
Elizabeth Monroe, *The Mediterranean in Politics*, Oxford University Press, 1938
Benito Mussolini, *The Political and Social Doctrine of Fascism*, Carnegie Endowment, 1935. A translation of Mussolini's well-known article on Fascism in the *Enciclopedia Italiana*.
Herbert W. Schneider, *Making the Fascist State*, Oxford University Press, 1928. History and description of the Fascist movement.
Cecil J. S. Sprigge, *The Development of Modern Italy*, Yale University Press, 1943

SPAIN

Gerald Brenan, *The Spanish Labyrinth: An Account of the Social and Political Background of the Civil War,* Cambridge University Press, 1943

Salvador de Madariaga, *Spain,* Scribner, 1931. Introduction to modern Spanish history and politics.

E. Allison Peers, *The Spanish Tragedy 1930–1936: Dictatorship, Republic, Chaos,* Oxford University Press, 1936. An account of the Revolution and outbreak of the Civil War.

—— *Spain in Eclipse, 1937–1943,* London, 1943. A sequel to the foregoing.

Robert Sencourt, *Spain's Ordeal: A Documented History of the Civil War,* Longmans, Green, 1940. Generally Catholic and pro-Nationalist.

POLAND AND THE BALTIC

The Baltic States: Estonia, Latvia, and Lithuania, Oxford University Press, 1938. A survey of Baltic politics and economics by the Information Department, Royal Institute of International Affairs.

Raymond Leslie Buell, *Poland: Key to Europe,* Knopf, 1939

Henryk Frankel, *Poland: The Struggle for Power, 1772–1939,* London, 1946

J. Hampden Jackson, *Finland,* Macmillan, 1940

Robert Machray, *The Poland of Pilsudski,* London, 1936

William John Rose, *Poland Old and New,* London, 1948

THE SOVIET UNION

Alexander Baykov, *The Development of the Soviet Economic System: An Essay on the Experience of Planning in the U.S.S.R.,* Cambridge University Press, 1946

Max Beloff, *The Foreign Policy of Soviet Russia, 1929–1941,* 2 vols., Oxford University Press, 1948

Nicolas Berdyaev, *The Origin of Russian Communism,* London, 1937. The philosopher tries to show that the Soviet adaptation of Marx is in the Russian tradition.

—— *The Russian Idea,* Scribner, 1947. Contemporary Russian thought against its Christian background.

F. Borkenau, *The Communist International,* London, 1938. An account of the activities of the Communist International in different countries.

Edward Hallett Carr, *The Soviet Impact on the Western World,* Macmillan, 1947

William Henry Chamberlin, *The Russian Revolution, 1917–1921,* 2 vols., Macmillan, 1935

Edward Crankshaw, *Russia and the Russians,* Viking, 1947

D. J. Dallin, *The Real Soviet Russia,* Yale University Press, 1947. A critical commentary of the domestic scene.

I. Deutscher, *Stalin: A Political Biography,* Oxford University Press, 1949

Maurice Dobb, *Soviet Economic Development since 1917,* International Publishers, 1948

Walter Duranty, *USSR: The Story of Soviet Russia,* Lippincott, 1944

Louis Fischer, *The Soviets in World Affairs: A History of the Relations between the Soviet Union and the Rest of the World,* 2 vols., London, 1930

Michael T. Florinsky, *Toward an Understanding of the U.S.S.R.: A Study in Government, Politics, and Economic Planning,* Macmillan, 1939

Philip Grierson, *Books on Soviet Russia, 1917–1942: A Bibliography and a Guide to Reading,* London, 1943

Samuel N. Harper, *The Government of the Soviet Union,* Van Nostrand, 1937. More than its title indicates. A general review of the Soviet state.

Arthur Koestler, *The Yogi and the Commissar*, Macmillan, 1945. A personal account and condemnation of Soviet Communism.

Harold J. Laski, *Communism* (The Home University Library), Holt, 1927

Bernard Pares, *A History of Russia*, Knopf, 1944

N. Popov, *Outline History of the Communist Party of the Soviet Union*, 2 vols., International Publishers, 1934. The official orthodox history.

Arthur Rosenberg, *A History of Bolshevism from Marx to the First Five Years' Plan*, Oxford University Press, 1934

Rudolf Schlesinger, *The Spirit of Post-War Russia: Soviet Ideology, 1917–1946*, London, 1947

David Shubb, *Lenin: A Biography*, Doubleday, 1948

T. A. Taracouzio, *War and Peace in Soviet Diplomacy*, Macmillan, 1940. Soviet foreign policy through its many phases and changes up to 1939.

Nicholas S. Timasheff, *The Great Retreat: The Growth and Decline of Communism in Russia*, Dutton, 1946

—— *Religion in Soviet Russia, 1917–1942*, Sheed & Ward, 1942

Julian Towster, *Political Power in the U.S.S.R., 1917–1947: The Theory and Structure of Government in the Soviet State*, Oxford University Press, 1948

Leon Trotsky, *The History of the Russian Revolution*, 3 vols., Simon and Schuster, 1932

Sidney and Beatrice Webb, *Soviet Communism: A New Civilization*, Scribner, 1938

THE BALKANS

(See also the section on The Near East, below.)

Robert Bishop and E. S. Crayfield, *Russia Astride the Balkans*, McBride, 1948

Theodore I. Geshkoff, *Balkan Union: A Road to Peace in Southeastern Europe*, Columbia University Press, 1940. An account of the Balkan confederation movement, 1930–35.

Robert Joseph Kerner and Harry Nicholas Howard, *The Balkan Conferences and the Balkan Entente, 1930–1935*, University of California Press, 1936

Stephen P. Ladas, *Exchange of Minorities: Bulgaria, Greece, and Turkey*, Macmillan, 1932

Reuben Henry Markham, *Rumania under the Soviet Yoke*, Meador, 1949

—— *Tito's Imperial Communism*, University of North Carolina Press, 1947

William Hardy McNeill, *The Greek Dilemma: War and Aftermath*, Lippincott, 1947

David Mitrany, *The Effect of the War in Southeastern Europe*, Yale University Press, 1936. Balkan problems, especially economic, in the twenties.

Marion I. Newbigin, *Geographical Aspects of Balkan Problems in Their Relation to the Great European War*, Putnam, 1915

Stoyan Pribichevich, *World without End: The Saga of Southeastern Europe*, Reynal and Hitchcock, 1939. On the social life, agrarian problems, and the cooperative movement in the Balkans.

Joseph S. Rouček, *The Politics of the Balkans*, McGraw-Hill, 1939

—— *Balkan Politics: International Relations in No Man's Land*, Stanford University Press, 1948

Ferdinand Schevill, *The History of the Balkan Peninsula: From the Earliest Times to the Present Day*, Harcourt, Brace, 1933. The historical background of the Ottoman Empire and its dissolution.

Frank Smothers, William Hardy McNeill, and Elizabeth Darbishire McNeill, *Report on the Greeks*, Twentieth Century Fund, 1948. Findings of a Twentieth Century Fund team which surveyed conditions in Greece in 1947.

South-Eastern Europe: A Political and Economic Survey, Oxford University Press, 1939, for the Royal Institute of International Affairs.

THE NEAR AND MIDDLE EAST
(INCLUDING THE OTTOMAN EMPIRE AND TURKEY)

George Antonius, *The Arab Awakening: The Story of the Arab National Movement*, Lippincott, 1939. A documented history, beginning in the Napoleonic era.

Edward Atiyah, *An Arab tells His Story: A Study in Loyalties*, London, 1946. Autobiography of a contemporary Arab philosopher.

Gertrude L. Bell, *Letters, Selected and Edited by Lady Bell*, Boni and Liveright, 1928. By the first woman "political officer."

Norman Bentwich, *England in Palestine*, London, 1932

—— *Palestine*, London, 1940. By a former Attorney General for Palestine.

Eleanor Bisbee, *The New Turks*, University of Pennsylvania Press, to be published in 1950. How republicanism worked in the first generation.

Carl Brockelmann, *History of the Islamic Peoples*, Putnam, 1947

Sir Valentine Chirol, *The Egyptian Problem*, London, 1920

Charles M. Doughty, *Travels in Arabia Deserta*, 2 vols., Random, 1937. With an introduction by T. E. Lawrence. Describing northwestern Arabia and Beduin life and customs.

L. P. Elwell-Sutton, *Modern Iran*, London, 1941

The Encyclopedia of Islam: A Dictionary of the Geography, Ethnography, and Biography of the Muhammadan Peoples, 4 vols., Leyden, 1913–34; and *Supplement*, 1938

H. A. R. Gibb, *Whither Islam? A Survey of Modern Movements in the Moslem World*, London, 1932

Christina Phelps Grant, *The Syrian Desert: Caravans, Travel, and Exploration.* Macmillan, 1938. Including the post-1918 development of transport and communications over the land bridge.

Great Britain and Egypt, 1914–1936, Oxford University Press, 1936, by the Information Department, Royal Institute of International Affairs.

Great Britain and Palestine, 1915–1945, Oxford University Press, 1946, by the Information Department, Royal Institute of International Affairs.

James Heyworth-Dunne, *Introduction to the History of Education in Modern Egypt*, London, 1939

Philip K. Hitti, *History of the Arabs*, Macmillan, 1940

A. H. Hourani, *Minorities in the Arab World*, Oxford University Press, 1947

—— *Syria and Lebanon: a Political Essay*, Oxford University Press, 1946

Harry N. Howard, *The Partition of Turkey: A Diplomatic History, 1913–1923*, University of Oklahoma Press, 1931

Philip Willard Ireland, *Iraq: A Study in Political Development*, London, 1937

George E. Kirk, *A Short History of the Middle East, from the Rise of Islam to Modern Times*, London, 1948

T. E. Lawrence, *Seven Pillars of Wisdom: A Triumph*, Doubleday, 1936

—— *Revolt in the Desert*, Doran, 1927. An abridgment of *Seven Pillars.*

George Lenczowski, *Russia and the West in Iran, 1918–1948: A Study in Big-Power Rivalry*, Cornell University Press, 1949

J. de V. Loder, *The Truth about Mesopotamia, Palestine and Syria*, London, 1923. Account of Allied commitments to the Arabs and the establishment of the three mandates.

Elizabeth P. MacCallum, *The Nationalist Crusade in Syria*, Foreign Policy Association, 1928. For the Druze Rebellion, its antecedents, and its results.

J. A. R. Marriott, *The Eastern Question: An Historical Study in European Diplomacy*, Oxford University Press, 1940

Viscount Alfred Milner, *England in Egypt*, London, 1909

Elizabeth Monroe, *The Mediterranean in Politics*, Oxford University Press, 1938

Robert R. Nathan, Oscar Gass, and Daniel Creamer, *Palestine: Problem and Promise*, Public Affairs Press, 1946. An account of the contemporary economy of Palestine.

Palestine: Royal Commission Report, (Peel Report), Cmd. 5479, H. M. Stationery
    Office, London, 1937
Palestine: A Study of Jewish, Arab, and British Policies, 2 vols., Esco Foundation
    for Palestine, Yale University Press, 1947. Moderate Zionist survey.
H. St. J. B. Philby, *Arabia,* Scribner, 1930. Account of the Wahhabis, Ibn Saud, and
    the Ikhwan Movement, and of Anglo-Arab relations during and after the First
    World War.
*Report of the Anglo-American Committee of Enquiry regarding the Problems of
    European Jewry and Palestine,* Cmd. 6808, H. M. Stationery Office, London,
    1946
Freya Stark, *The Arab Island: The Middle East, 1939–1943,* Knopf, 1945
Sir Ronald Storrs, *Memoirs,* Putnam, 1937. Published in England (1937) as *Orien-
    tations.* The author was for nine years Governor of Jerusalem, first Military
    Governor, later Civil Governor.
Bertram Thomas, *The Arabs: The Life Story of a People Who Have Left Their
    Deep Impress on the World,* Doubleday, 1937
Arnold J. Toynbee, *The Islamic World since the Peace Settlement,* Oxford Univer-
    sity Press, 1927
—— and Kenneth P. Kirkwood, *Turkey,* Scribner, 1927
K. S. Twitchell, *Saudi Arabia,* Princeton University Press, 1947
Doreen Warriner, *Land and Poverty in the Middle East,* Oxford University Press,
    1948
Hilary Wayment, *Egypt Now,* London, 1948
Donald Everett Webster, *The Turkey of Atatürk: Social Process in the Turkish
    Reformation,* American Academy of Political and Social Science, 1939
Chaim Weizmann, *Trial and Error: The Autobiography of Chaim Weizmann,* Har-
    per, 1949
Donald N. Wilber, *Iran, Past and Present,* Princeton University Press, 1948
Sir Arnold T. Wilson, *Persia,* London, 1932. A historical survey.
Sir George Young, *Egypt,* London, 1927. A historical survey of modern Egypt by a
    British diplomat.

CHINA AND JAPAN

(See also the section on The Americas, above.)

Ruth Benedict, *Chrysanthemum and the Sword: Patterns of Japanese Culture,*
    Houghton Mifflin, 1946
Hugh Borton, *Japan since 1931: Its Political and Social Developments,* Institute of
    Pacific Relations, 1940
Chiang Kai-shek, *China's Destiny and Chinese Economic Theory,* ed. P. Jaffe, Roy,
    1947. Chiang's political creed and testament.
China Handbook, 1937–45, with Supplement for 1946, Macmillan, 1947. An official
    compilation.
Paul E. Eckel, *The Far East since 1500,* Harcourt, Brace, 1947
I. Epstein, *The Unfinished Revolution in China,* Little, Brown, 1947. A study of
    the widening scope of the Chinese Revolution under Communism.
George Stuart Gelder, *The Chinese Communists,* London, 1946
Randall Gould, *China in the Sun,* Doubleday, 1946. Reporting on China during
    and after the twenties.
O. M. Green, *The Story of China's Revolution,* London, 1945
Joseph C. Grew, *Ten Years in Japan: A Contemporary Record,* Simon and Schus-
    ter, 1944. By the former American ambassador to Tokyo.
D. C. Holtom, *Modern Japan and Shinto Nationalism: A Study of Present Day
    Trends in Japanese Religions,* University of Chicago Press, 1943
Stanley K. Hornbeck, *The United States and the Far East: Certain Fundamentals of
    Policy,* World Peace Foundation, 1942.
Harry Paxton Howard, *America's Role in Asia,* Howell, Soskin, 1943. One of the
    earlier criticisms of the policy of "putting China on the U. S. payroll."

Harold Isaacs, *No Peace for Asia,* Macmillan, 1947. A survey of the post-1945 nationalist movements in Asia.

Philip Jaffe, *New Frontiers in Asia: A Challenge to the West,* Knopf, 1945. A discussion of the economic opportunities available to the United States in the Far East.

F. C. Jones, *Manchuria since 1931,* Oxford University Press, 1949. A case-study of Japanese imperialism in action.

Kenneth Scott Latourette, *A Short History of the Far East,* Macmillan, 1946

Owen Lattimore, *Solution in Asia,* Little, Brown, 1945

Richard E. Lauterbach, *Danger from the East,* Harper, 1947. Reporting on the complex problems of occupation policy in Japan.

Mao Tse-tung, *China's New Democracy,* New Century, 1945. By the political chief of the Chinese Communist party.

Harriet L. Moore, *Soviet Far Eastern Policy, 1931–1945,* Princeton University Press, 1945. A factual introduction.

E. Herbert Norman, *Japan's Emergence as a Modern State,* Institute of Pacific Relations, 1940. The modernization of Japan described by a Canadian diplomat.

Harold S. Quigley, *Far Eastern War, 1937–1941,* World Peace Foundation, 1942. A factual summary.

Lawrence K. Rosinger, *China's Wartime Politics, 1937–1944,* Princeton University Press, 1945

—— *China's Crisis,* Knopf, 1945

David Nelson Rowe, *China among the Powers,* Harcourt, Brace, 1945. An assessment of China's international position at the close of the Second World War.

Sun Fo, *China Looks Forward,* Day, 1944. The hopes and fears of a moderate Chinese liberal.

Otto Tolischus, *Tokyo Record,* Reynal and Hitchcock, 1943. Experiences of the correspondent of the New York *Times* in Japan on the eve of hostilities.

Harold M. Vinacke, *A History of the Far East in Modern Times,* Crofts, 1941

Theodore H. White and Annalee Jacoby, *Thunder out of China,* Sloane, 1946. Criticism of the National Government of China by former *Time* correspondents.

SOUTHEAST ASIA AND THE EAST INDIES

Jan O. M. Broek, *The Economic Development of the Netherlands Indies,* Institute of Pacific Relations, 1942

John Leroy Christian, *Modern Burma: A Survey of Political and Economic Development,* University of California Press, 1942

Paul E. Eckel, *The Far East since 1500,* Harcourt, Brace, 1947

Rupert Emerson, Lennox A. Mills, and Virginia Thompson, *Government and Nationalism in Southeast Asia,* Institute of Pacific Relations, 1942

C. Hartley Grattan, *Introducing Australia,* Day, 1942. Australia described by an Australian for the American reader.

Roger Lévy, Guy Lacam, and Andrew Roth, *French Interests and Policies in the Far East,* Institute of Pacific Relations, 1941. An orthodox account of French colonial policy in the Pacific to 1940.

Lennox A. Mills, *British Rule in Eastern Asia: A Study of Contemporary Government and Economic Development in British Malaya and Hong Kong,* Institute of Pacific Relations, 1942

Catherine Porter, *Crisis in the Philippines,* Knopf, 1942. The Philippines on the eve of Pearl Harbor.

Charles Robequain, *The Economic Development of French Indo-China,* Oxford University Press, 1945

Virginia Thompson, *Thailand: The New Siam,* Institute of Pacific Relations, 1941

Amry Vandenbosch, *The Dutch East Indies: Its Government, Problems, and Politics,* University of California Press, 1942

INDEX